# SUPER-MINI
# THESAURUS

*Editor*
Martin Manser

*Assistant Editors*
Rosalind Fergusson
Jenny Roberts
Gloria Wren

# CHAMBERS

CHAMBERS
An imprint of Chambers Harrap Publishers Ltd
7 Hopetoun Crescent, Edinburgh EH7 4AY

This edition first published in PVC by Chambers 1997
Previously published as *Chambers Compact Thesaurus* 1994

ISBN 0-550-10041-5

Typeset by Chambers Harrap Publishers Ltd, Edinburgh
Printed and bound in Great Britain by
Omnia Books Ltd, Glasgow

# Introduction

A synonym is a word that means something similar to another word, and a thesaurus is a listing of such words. This thesaurus lists about 150,000 synonyms for common English words. *Chambers Super-Mini Thesaurus* is based on *Chambers Thesaurus*, which itself is drawn from the extensive *Chambers Dictionary* database.

This thesaurus has been compiled to help you find the most appropriate word for a particular occasion. You will be able to include a more exact term in an essay or a report, a livelier phrase in a speech or a simpler expression in a letter. We hope that not only will your skills in using English improve, but also that you will enjoy sampling more of the varied delights of the English language.

Suppose you want to find a synonym for the word *summarize*, either because you have used this word already, or because you want to vary the style of what you are writing or saying. If you look up the entry **summarize**, you will see a list of synonyms arranged according to shades of meaning, and in order from the most common to the least frequently used, or specialized, term: outline, précis, condense, abridge, abbreviate, shorten, sum up, encapsulate, review.

Many entries are divided into numbered sections, indicating that the word has several meanings. After each number comes either a key synonym in small capitals or an example to help you find precisely which meaning you want. For example:

**arrest** *v* **1** *arrest a criminal*: capture, catch, seize, nick (*infml*), run in, apprehend, detain. **2** STOP, stem, check, restrain, inhibit, halt, interrupt, stall, delay, slow, retard, block, obstruct, impede, hinder.

This means that for the sense shown by the example *arrest a criminal* the synonyms are capture, catch, seize, *etc*, and for the sense shown by the key synonym STOP, other possible synonyms are stress, check, restrain *etc*.

Note that no one word can be used in the place of another word in every context. So if you are not sure of the meaning or use of one of the words included as a synonym, look up the word in a general dictionary such as *The Chambers Dictionary*.

At the end of many entries, antonyms – words that mean the opposite of another word – are shown after the symbol ⇄ For example, at **boring**: interesting, exciting, stimulating, original.

Two hundred special entries are printed with a shaded background. These entries, *eg* at **animal**, **chemical elements**, **flower** and **sport**, are lists of related words which present examples of different flowers, sports, *etc*. A separate list of all these entries is given at the end of this introduction.

*eg* **sport**

> *Sports include*: badminton, fives,
> lacrosse, squash, table-tennis, ping-pong
> (*infml*), tennis; American football,
> baseball, basketball, billiards, boules,
> bowls, cricket, croquet, football, golf,
> handball, hockey, netball, pétanque,
> pitch and putt, polo, pool, putting,
> rounders, Rugby, snooker, soccer,
> tenpin bowling, volleyball;...

# Abbreviations

| | | | |
|---|---|---|---|
| *adj* | adjective | *prep* | preposition |
| *adv* | adverb | ® | trademark |
| *conj* | conjunction | *sl* | slang |
| *infml* | informal | *US* | American English |
| *interj* | interjection | *v* | verb |
| *fml* | formal | ⇄ | antonym(s) |
| *n* | noun | | |

# Special entries

Lists of related words appear in the main text under the following entries:

accommodation
agriculture
aircraft
alphabets and
  writing systems
amphibian
anatomical terms
anchor
angel
animal
anniversary
arch
architecture and
  building
armed services
art
art and craft
artist
atom
ballet
biological terms
bird
boats and ships
bones
book
brain
bridge
building
bulb
butterfly
camera
canonical hours
car
castle

cat
cattle
celebration
cheese
chemical
  elements
chemistry
Chinese calendar
church
circle
class
clocks and
  watches
clothes
cloud
coat
collective nouns
collectors and
  enthusiasts
colour
communication
computing
cook
cosmetics
crime
crockery
currency
cutlery
cutter
dance
dinosaur
doctor
dog
drink

drug
ear
education
educational terms
engine
entertainer
entertainment
eye
fabric
family
farm
female
fencing
fish
flag
flower
food
footwear
fruit
fuel
fungus
furniture
game[1]
game[2]
gem
government
grass
hairstyle
hat
heart
heraldry
herbs and spices
house
insect

invertebrate
jewellery
Jewish calendar
karate
knot
language
languages
legal
literature
luggage
male
mammal
mania
marsupial
mathematical
  terms
meal
measurement
meat
medical terms
medicine
minerals
mollusc
monkey
mouth
mushrooms and
  toadstools
music
musical
  instruments
musical terms
musician
mythology
nobility

| | | | |
|---|---|---|---|
| nut | politics | science | time |
| official | pottery | sexual | tool |
| paint | prosody | shape | tower |
| paper | punctuation | shop | travel |
| parliaments and political assemblies | race | shrub | tree |
| | rank[1] | singer | vegetable |
| party | recording | smell | vehicle |
| pasta | region | soldier | vein |
| pastry | religion | song | vitamin |
| performance | religious officer | sport | war |
| philosophy | reptile | star | weapon |
| phobia | rhetoric | storm | weather |
| photography | rock | story | wind |
| physics | rodent | study | wine |
| planet | room | sweets | wood |
| plant | ruler | symbol | writer |
| plastic | sacred writing | taste | zodiac |
| poem | sale | tax | |
| | say | theatrical | |

# Acknowledgements

The editor would like to thank Susan Rennie for her invaluable editorial advice and Peter Schwarz for his technical expertise in processing the text of this book.

# A

**abandon** v 1 DESERT, leave, forsake, jilt, ditch (*sl*), leave in the lurch (*infml*), maroon, strand, leave behind, scrap. 2 abandon ship: vacate, evacuate, withdraw from, quit. 3 RENOUNCE, resign, give up, forgo, relinquish, surrender, yield, waive, drop.

**E₃** 1 support, maintain, keep. 3 continue.

**abandoned** adj 1 DESERTED, unoccupied, derelict, neglected, forsaken, forlorn, desolate. 2 DISSOLUTE, wild, uninhibited, wanton, wicked.

**E₃** 1 kept, occupied. 2 restrained.

**abandonment** n 1 DESERTION, leaving, forsaking, jilting, neglect, scrapping. 2 RENUNCIATION, resignation, giving up, relinquishment, surrender, sacrifice, waiver, dropping, discontinuation.

**abashed** adj 1 ASHAMED, shamefaced, embarrassed, mortified, humiliated, humbled. 2 CONFUSED, bewildered, nonplussed, confounded, perturbed, discomposed, disconcerted, taken aback, dumbfounded, floored (*infml*), dismayed.

**E₃** 2 composed, at ease.

**abate** v 1 DECREASE, reduce, lessen, diminish, decline, sink, dwindle, taper off, fall off. 2 MODERATE, ease, relieve, alleviate, mitigate, remit, pacify, quell, subside, let up (*infml*), weaken, wane, slacken, slow, fade.

**E₃** 1 increase. 2 strengthen.

**abbey** n monastery, priory, friary, seminary, convent, nunnery, cloister.

**abbreviate** v shorten, cut, trim, clip, truncate, curtail, abridge, summarize,

précis, abstract, digest, condense, compress, reduce, lessen, shrink, contract.

**E₃** extend, lengthen, expand, amplify.

**abbreviation** n shortening, clipping, curtailment, abridgement, summarization, summary, synopsis, résumé, précis, abstract, digest, compression, reduction, contraction.

**E₃** extension, expansion, amplification.

**abdicate** v renounce, give up, relinquish, surrender, cede, yield, forgo, abandon, quit, vacate, retire, resign, step down (*infml*).

**abdomen** n belly, guts, stomach, tummy (*infml*), paunch, midriff.

**abdominal** adj ventral, intestinal, visceral, gastric.

**abduct** v carry off, run away with, run off with (*infml*), make off with, spirit away, seduce, kidnap, snatch, seize, appropriate.

**aberration** n deviation, straying, wandering, divergence, irregularity, nonconformity, anomaly, oddity, peculiarity, eccentricity, quirk, freak, lapse, defect.

**E₃** conformity.

**abhor** v hate, detest, loathe, abominate, shudder at, recoil from, shrink from, spurn, despise.

**E₃** love, adore.

**abhorrence** n hate, hatred, aversion, loathing, abomination, horror, repugnance, revulsion, disgust, distaste.

**E₃** love, adoration.

**abhorrent** adj detestable, loathsome, abominable, execrable, heinous, obnoxious, odious, hated, hateful, horrible, horrid, offensive,

repugnant, repellent, repulsive,
revolting, nauseating, disgusting,
distasteful.

**Ea** delightful, attractive.

**abide** v 1 BEAR, stand, endure,
tolerate, put up with, stomach,
accept. 2 REMAIN, last, endure,
continue, persist.

**abide by** 1 *abide by the rules*: obey,
observe, follow, comply with, adhere
to, conform to, submit to, go along
with, agree to. 2 FULFIL, discharge,
carry out, stand by, hold to, keep to.

**ability** n 1 CAPABILITY, capacity,
faculty, facility, potentiality, power.
2 SKILL, dexterity, deftness,
adeptness, competence, proficiency,
qualification, aptitude, talent, gift,
endowment, knack, flair, touch,
expertise, know-how (*infml*), genius,
forte, strength.

**Ea** 1 inability. 2 incompetence,
weakness.

**abject** adj 1 CONTEMPTIBLE,
worthless, low, mean, ignoble,
dishonourable, deplorable,
despicable, vile, sordid, debased,
degenerate, submissive, servile,
grovelling, slavish. 2 MISERABLE,
wretched, forlorn, hopeless, pitiable,
pathetic, outcast, degraded.

**Ea** proud, exalted.

**ablaze** adj 1 BLAZING, flaming,
burning, on fire, ignited, lighted,
alight, illuminated, luminous,
glowing, aglow, radiant, flashing,
gleaming, sparkling, brilliant.
2 IMPASSIONED, passionate, fervent,
ardent, fiery, enthusiastic, excited,
exhilarated, stimulated, aroused,
angry, furious, raging, incensed,
frenzied.

**able** adj capable, fit, fitted,
dexterous, adroit, deft, adept,
competent, proficient, qualified,
practised, experienced, skilled,
accomplished, clever, expert,
masterly, skilful, ingenious, talented,
gifted, strong, powerful, effective,

efficient, adequate.

**Ea** unable, incapable, incompetent,
ineffective.

**able-bodied** adj fit, healthy, sound,
strong, robust, hardy, tough,
vigorous, powerful, hale, hearty,
lusty, sturdy, strapping, stout,
stalwart, staunch.

**Ea** infirm, delicate.

**abnormal** adj odd, strange,
singular, peculiar, curious, queer,
weird, eccentric, paranormal,
unnatural, uncanny, extraordinary,
exceptional, unusual, uncommon,
unexpected, irregular, anomalous,
aberrant, erratic, wayward, deviant,
divergent, different.

**Ea** normal, regular, typical.

**abnormality** n oddity, peculiarity,
singularity, eccentricity, strangeness,
bizarreness, unnaturalness,
unusualness, irregularity, exception,
anomaly, deformity, flaw,
aberration, deviation, divergence,
difference.

**Ea** normality, regularity.

**abolish** v do away with, annul,
nullify, invalidate, quash, repeal,
rescind, revoke, cancel, obliterate,
blot out, suppress, destroy, eliminate,
eradicate, get rid of (*infml*), stamp
out, end, put an end to, terminate,
subvert, overthrow, overturn.

**Ea** create, retain, authorize, continue.

**abolition** n annulment, nullification,
invalidation, quashing, repeal,
abrogation, cancellation,
obliteration, suppression,
eradication, extinction, end, ending,
termination, subversion, overturning,
dissolution.

**Ea** creation, retention, continuance.

**abominable** adj loathsome,
detestable, hateful, horrid, horrible,
abhorrent, execrable, odious,
repugnant, repulsive, repellent,
disgusting, revolting, obnoxious,
nauseating, foul, vile, heinous,
atrocious, appalling, terrible,

reprehensible, contemptible, despicable, wretched.
**F3** delightful, pleasant, desirable.

**abominate** v hate, loathe, detest, abhor, execrate, despise, condemn.
**F3** love, adore.

**abomination** n hate, hatred, aversion, loathing, abhorrence, repugnance, revulsion, disgust, distaste, hostility, offence, outrage, disgrace, anathema, horror, evil, curse, plague, torment, bête noire.
**F3** adoration, delight.

**abort** v miscarry, terminate, end, stop, arrest, halt, check, frustrate, thwart, nullify, call off, fail.
**F3** continue.

**abortion** n miscarriage, termination, frustration, failure, misadventure.
**F3** continuation, success.

**abortive** adj failed, unsuccessful, fruitless, unproductive, barren, sterile, vain, idle, futile, useless, ineffective, unavailing.
**F3** successful, fruitful.

**abound** v be plentiful, proliferate, flourish, thrive, swell, increase, superabound, swarm, teem, run riot, overflow.

**about** prep **1** REGARDING, concerning, relating to, referring to, connected with, concerned with, as regards, with regard to, with respect to, with reference to. **2** CLOSE TO, near, nearby, beside, adjacent to. **3** ROUND, around, surrounding, encircling, encompassing, throughout, all over.
adv **1** about twenty: around, approximately, roughly, in the region of, more or less, almost, nearly, approaching, nearing. **2** run about: to and fro, here and there, from place to place.

**about to** on the point of, on the verge of, all but, ready to, intending to, preparing to.

**above** prep over, higher than, on top of, superior to, in excess of,

exceeding, surpassing, beyond, before, prior to.
**F3** below, under.
adv overhead, aloft, on high, earlier.
**F3** below, underneath.
adj above-mentioned, above-stated, foregoing, preceding, previous, earlier, prior.

**above-board** adj honest, legitimate, straight, on the level, fair, fair and square, square, true, open, frank, candid, guileless, straightforward, forthright, truthful, veracious, trustworthy, honourable, reputable, upright.
**F3** dishonest, shady (infml), underhand.

**abrasion** n graze, scratch, scratching, scraping, scrape, scouring, grating, grinding, abrading, chafing, chafe, friction, rubbing, erosion, wearing away, wearing down.

**abrasive** adj scratching, scraping, grating, rough, harsh, chafing, frictional, galling, irritating, annoying, sharp, biting, caustic, hurtful, nasty, unpleasant.
**F3** smooth, pleasant.

**abreast** adj acquainted, informed, knowledgeable, in the picture, au courant, up to date, in touch, au fait, conversant, familiar.
**F3** unaware, out of touch.

**abridge** v shorten, cut (down), prune, curtail, abbreviate, contract, reduce, decrease, lessen, summarize, précis, abstract, digest, condense, compress, concentrate.
**F3** expand, amplify, pad out.

**abridgement** n **1** SHORTENING, cutting, reduction, decrease, diminishing, concentration, contraction, restriction, limitation. **2** SUMMARY, synopsis, résumé, outline, précis, abstract, digest, epitome.
**F3** **1** expansion, padding.

**abroad** adv **1** OVERSEAS, in foreign

parts, out of the country, far and wide, widely, extensively. **2** AT LARGE, around, about, circulating, current.

**F3 1** at home.

**abrupt** *adj* 1 *abrupt departure*: sudden, unexpected, unforeseen, surprising, quick, rapid, swift, hasty, hurried, precipitate. **2** SHEER, precipitous, steep, sharp. **3** BRUSQUE, curt, terse, short, brisk, snappy, gruff, rude, uncivil, impolite, blunt, direct.

**F3 1** gradual, slow, leisurely. **3** expansive, ceremonious, polite.

**abscond** *v* run away, run off, make off, decamp, flee, fly, escape, bolt, quit, clear out (*infml*), disappear, take French leave.

**absence** *n* 1 NON-ATTENDANCE, non-appearance, truancy, absenteeism, non-existence. **2** LACK, need, want, deficiency, dearth, scarcity, unavailability, default, omission, vacancy.

**F3 1** presence, attendance, appearance. **2** existence.

**absent** *adj* 1 MISSING, not present, away, out, unavailable, gone, lacking, truant. **2** INATTENTIVE, daydreaming, dreamy, faraway, elsewhere, absent-minded, vacant, vague, distracted, preoccupied, unaware, oblivious, unheeding.

**F3 1** present. **2** alert, aware.

**absent-minded** *adj* forgetful, scatterbrained, absent, abstracted, withdrawn, faraway, distracted, preoccupied, absorbed, engrossed, pensive, musing, dreaming, dreamy, inattentive, unaware, oblivious, unconscious, heedless, unheeding, unthinking, impractical.

**F3** attentive, practical, matter-of-fact.

**absolute** *adj* 1 UTTER, total, complete, entire, full, thorough, exhaustive, supreme, consummate, definitive, conclusive, final, categorical, definite, unequivocal,

unquestionable, decided, decisive, positive, sure, certain, genuine, pure, perfect, sheer, unmixed, unqualified, downright, out-and-out, outright. **2** OMNIPOTENT, totalitarian, autocratic, tyrannical, despotic, dictatorial, sovereign, unlimited, unrestricted.

**absolutely** *adv* utterly, totally, dead, completely, entirely, fully, wholly, thoroughly, exhaustively, perfectly, supremely, unconditionally, conclusively, finally, categorically, definitely, positively, unequivocally, unambiguously, unquestionably, decidedly, decisively, surely, certainly, infallibly, genuinely, truly, purely, exactly, precisely.

**absorb** *v* 1 TAKE IN, ingest, drink in, imbibe, suck up, soak up, consume, devour, engulf, digest, assimilate, understand, receive, hold, retain. **2** ENGROSS, involve, fascinate, enthral, monopolize, preoccupy, occupy, fill (up).

**F3 1** exude.

**absorbing** *adj* interesting, amusing, entertaining, diverting, engrossing, preoccupying, intriguing, fascinating, captivating, enthralling, spellbinding, gripping, riveting, compulsive, unputdownable (*infml*).

**F3** boring, off-putting.

**abstain** *v* refrain, decline, refuse, reject, resist, forbear, shun, avoid, keep from, stop, cease, desist, give up, renounce, forgo, go without, deny oneself.

**F3** indulge.

**abstemious** *adj* abstinent, self-denying, self-disciplined, disciplined, sober, temperate, moderate, sparing, frugal, austere, ascetic, restrained.

**F3** intemperate, gluttonous, luxurious.

**abstinence** *n* abstaining, abstention, abstemiousness, self-denial, non-indulgence, avoidance, forbearance, refraining, refusal, restraint, self-restraint, self-control, self-discipline, sobriety, teetotalism, temperance, moderation, frugality, asceticism.

**F3** indulgence, self-indulgence.

**abstract** *adj* non-concrete, conceptual, intellectual, hypothetical, theoretical, unpractical, unrealistic, general, generalized, indefinite, metaphysical, philosophical, academic, complex, abstruse, deep, profound, subtle.

**F3** concrete, real, actual.

*n* synopsis, outline, summary, recapitulation, résumé, précis, epitome, digest, abridgement, compression.

*v* 1 SUMMARIZE, outline, précis, digest, condense, compress, abridge, abbreviate, shorten. 2 EXTRACT, remove, withdraw, isolate, detach, dissociate, separate.

**F3** 1 expand. 2 insert.

**abstraction** *n* 1 IDEA, notion, concept, thought, conception, theory, hypothesis, theorem, formula, generalization, generality. 2 INATTENTION, dream, dreaminess, absent-mindedness, distraction, pensiveness, preoccupation, absorption. 3 EXTRACTION, withdrawal, isolation, separation.

**absurd** *adj* ridiculous, ludicrous, preposterous, fantastic, incongruous, illogical, paradoxical, implausible, untenable, unreasonable, irrational, nonsensical, meaningless, senseless, foolish, silly, stupid, idiotic, crazy, daft (*infml*), farcical, comical, funny, humorous, laughable, risible, derisory.

**F3** logical, rational, sensible.

**abundant** *adj* plentiful, in plenty, full, filled, well-supplied, ample, generous, bountiful, rich, copious, profuse, lavish, exuberant, teeming, overflowing.

**F3** scarce, sparse.

**abuse** *v* 1 MISUSE, misapply, exploit, take advantage of, oppress, wrong, ill-treat, maltreat, hurt, injure, molest, damage, spoil, harm. 2 INSULT, swear at, defame, libel, slander, smear, disparage, malign, revile, scold, upbraid.

**F3** 1 cherish, care for. 2 compliment, praise.

*n* 1 MISUSE, misapplication, exploitation, imposition, oppression, wrong, ill-treatment, maltreatment, hurt, injury, molestation, damage, spoiling, harm. 2 INSULTS, swearing, cursing, offence, defamation, libel, slander, disparagement, reproach, scolding, upbraiding, tirade.

**F3** 1 care, attention. 2 compliment, praise.

**abusive** *adj* insulting, offensive, rude, scathing, hurtful, injurious, cruel, destructive, defamatory, libellous, slanderous, derogatory, disparaging, pejorative, vilifying, maligning, reviling, censorious, reproachful, scolding, upbraiding.

**F3** complimentary, polite.

**abyss** *n* gulf, chasm, crevasse, fissure, gorge, canyon, crater, pit, depth, void.

**academic** *adj* 1 SCHOLARLY, erudite, learned, well-read, studious, bookish, scholastic, pedagogical, educational, instructional, literary, highbrow. 2 THEORETICAL, hypothetical, conjectural, speculative, notional, abstract, impractical.

*n* professor, don, master, fellow, lecturer, tutor, student, scholar, man of letters, pedant.

**accelerate** *v* quicken, speed, speed up, pick up speed, step up, expedite, hurry, hasten, precipitate, stimulate, facilitate, advance, further, promote, forward.

**F3** decelerate, slow down, delay.

**accent** *n* pronunciation, enunciation, articulation, brogue, twang (*infml*), tone, pitch, intonation, inflection, accentuation, stress, emphasis, intensity, force, cadence, rhythm, beat, pulse, pulsation.

**accentuate** v accent, stress, emphasize, underline, highlight, intensify, strengthen, deepen.
Ea play down, weaken.

**accept** v 1 *accept a gift*: take, receive, obtain, acquire, gain, secure. 2 ACKNOWLEDGE, recognize, admit, allow, approve, agree to, consent to, take on, adopt. 3 TOLERATE, put up with, stand, bear, abide, face up to, yield to.
Ea 1 refuse, turn down. 2 reject.

**acceptable** adj satisfactory, tolerable, moderate, passable, adequate, all right, OK (*infml*), so-so (*infml*), unexceptional, admissible, suitable, conventional, correct, desirable, pleasant, gratifying, welcome.
Ea 1 unacceptable, unsatisfactory, unwelcome.

**acceptance** n 1 TAKING, accepting, receipt, obtaining, getting, acquiring, gaining, securing.
2 ACKNOWLEDGEMENT, recognition, admission, concession, affirmation, concurrence, agreement, assent, consent, permission, ratification, approval, stamp of approval, OK (*infml*), adoption, undertaking, belief, credence.
Ea 1 refusal. 2 rejection, dissent.

**accepted** adj authorized, approved, ratified, sanctioned, agreed, acknowledged, recognized, admitted, confirmed, acceptable, correct, conventional, unorthodox, traditional, customary, time-honoured, established, received, universal, regular, standard, normal, usual, common.
Ea unconventional, unorthodox, controversial.

**access** n admission, admittance, entry, entering, entrance, gateway, door, key, approach, passage, road,

path, course.
Ea exit, outlet.

**accessible** adj 1 REACHABLE, get-at-able (*infml*), attainable, achievable, possible, obtainable, available, on hand, ready, handy, convenient, near, nearby. 2 FRIENDLY, affable, approachable, sociable, informal.
Ea 1 inaccessible, remote.
2 unapproachable.

**accessory** n 1 EXTRA, supplement, addition, appendage, attachment, extension, component, fitting, accompaniment, decoration, adornment, frill, trimming.
2 ACCOMPLICE, partner, associate, colleague, confederate, assistant, helper, help, aid.

**accident** n 1 CHANCE, hazard, fortuity, luck, fortune, fate, serendipity, contingency, fluke.
2 MISFORTUNE, mischance, misadventure, mishap, casualty, blow, calamity, disaster. 3 *road accident*: collision, crash, shunt (*sl*), prang (*sl*), pile-up.

**accidental** adj unintentional, unintended, inadvertent, unplanned, uncalculated, unexpected, unforeseen, unlooked-for, chance, fortuitous, flukey, uncertain, haphazard, random, casual, incidental.
Ea intentional, deliberate, calculated, premeditated.

**acclaim** v praise, commend, extol, exalt, honour, hail, salute, welcome, applaud, clap, cheer, celebrate.
n acclamation, praise, commendation, homage, tribute, eulogy, exaltation, honour, welcome, approbation, approval, applause, ovation, clapping, cheers, cheering, shouting, celebration.
Ea criticism, disapproval.

**accommodate** v 1 LODGE, board, put up, house, shelter. 2 OBLIGE, help, assist, aid, serve, provide, supply, comply, conform. **3** ADAPT, accustom, acclimatize, adjust, modify, fit, harmonize, reconcile, settle, compose.

**accommodating** adj obliging, indulgent, helpful, co-operative, willing, kind, considerate, unselfish, sympathetic, friendly, hospitable. ◿ disobliging, selfish.

**accommodation**

> Types of accommodation include: flat, apartment, bedsit, bedsitter, digs (infml), lodgings, hostel, halls of residence, rooms, residence, dwelling, shelter, pad (infml), squat (infml); bed and breakfast, board, guest house, hotel, youth hostel, villa, timeshare, motel, inn, pension, boarding-house; barracks, billet, married quarters. see also **house**; **room**.

**accompany** v **1** ESCORT, attend, convoy, chaperon, usher, conduct, follow. **2** COEXIST, coincide, belong to, go with, complement, supplement.

**accomplice** n assistant, helper, abettor, mate, henchman, conspirator, collaborator, ally, confederate, partner, associate, colleague, participator, accessory.

**accomplish** v achieve, attain, do, perform, carry out, execute, fulfil, discharge, finish, complete, conclude, consummate, realize, effect, bring about, engineer, produce, obtain.

**accomplished** adj skilled, professional, practised, proficient, gifted, talented, skilful, adroit, adept, expert, masterly, consummate, polished, cultivated. ◿ unskilled, inexpert, incapable.

**accomplishment** n **1** the accomplishment of a task: achievement, attainment, doing, performance, carrying out, execution, fulfilment, discharge, finishing, completion, conclusion,

consummation, perfection, realisation, fruition, production. **2** SKILL, art, aptitude, faculty, ability, capability, proficiency, gift, talent, forte. **3** EXPLOIT, feat, deed, stroke, triumph.

**accord** v **1** AGREE, concur, harmonize, match, conform, correspond, suit. **2** GIVE, tender, grant, allow, bestow, endow, confer. ◿ **1** disagree. **2** deny. n accordance, agreement, assent, unanimity, concert, unity, correspondence, conformity, harmony, sympathy. ◿ conflict, discord, disharmony.

**according to** in accordance with, in keeping with, obedient to, in conformity with, in line with, consistent with, commensurate with, in proportion to, in relation to, after, in the light of, in the manner of, after the manner of.

**accordingly** adv in accordance, in accord with, correspondingly, so, as a result, consequently, in consequence, therefore, thus, hence, appropriately, properly, suitably.

**accost** v approach, confront, buttonhole, waylay, stop, halt, detain, importune, solicit.

**account** n **1** an account of what happened: narrative, story, tale, chronicle, history, memoir, record, statement, report, communiqué, write-up, version, portrayal, sketch, description, presentation, explanation. **2** LEDGER, book, books, register, inventory, statement, invoice, bill, tab, charge, reckoning, computation, tally, score, balance.

**account for** explain, elucidate, illuminate, clear up, rationalize, justify, vindicate, answer for, put paid to, destroy, kill.

**accountable** adj answerable, responsible, liable, amenable, obliged, bound.

**accumulate** v gather, assemble,

collect, amass, aggregate, cumulate,
accrue, grow, increase, multiply,
build up, pile up, hoard, stockpile,
stash (*infml*), store.
**F3** disseminate.

**accumulation** n gathering,
assembly, collection, growth,
increase, build-up, conglomeration,
mass, heap, pile, stack, stock, store,
reserve, hoard, stockpile.

**accuracy** n correctness, precision,
exactness, authenticity, truth,
veracity, closeness, faithfulness,
fidelity, carefulness.
**F3** inaccuracy.

**accurate** adj correct, right,
unerring, precise, exact, well-
directed, spot-on (*infml*), faultless,
perfect, word-perfect, sound,
authentic, factual, nice, true,
truthful, veracious, just, proper,
close, faithful, well-judged, careful,
rigorous, scrupulous, meticulous,
strict, minute.
**F3** inaccurate, wrong, imprecise,
inexact.

**accusation** n charge, allegation,
imputation, indictment,
denunciation, impeachment,
recrimination, complaint,
incrimination.

**accuse** v charge, indict, impugn,
denounce, arraign, impeach, cite,
allege, attribute, impute, blame,
censure, recriminate, incriminate,
criminate, inform against.

**accustomed** adj used, in the habit
of, given to, confirmed, seasoned,
hardened, inured, disciplined,
trained, adapted, acclimatized,
acquainted, familiar, wonted,
habitual, routine, regular, normal,
usual, ordinary, everyday,
conventional, customary, traditional,
established, fixed, prevailing, general.
**F3** unaccustomed, unusual.

**ache** v 1 HURT, be sore, pain, suffer,
agonize, throb, pound, twinge, smart,
sting. 2 YEARN, long, pine, hanker,

desire, crave, hunger, thirst, itch.
n 1 PAIN, hurt, soreness, suffering,
anguish, agony, throb, throbbing,
pounding, pang, twinge, smarting,
stinging. 2 YEARNING, longing,
craving, itch.

**achieve** v accomplish, attain, reach,
get, obtain, acquire, procure, gain,
earn, win, succeed, manage, do,
perform, carry out, execute, fulfil,
finish, complete, consummate, effect,
bring about, realize, produce.
**F3** miss, fail.

**achievement** n 1 *the achievement of
our aims*: accomplishment,
attainment, acquirement,
performance, execution, fulfilment,
completion, success, realization,
fruition. 2 ACT, deed, exploit, feat,
effort.

**acid** adj sour, bitter, tart, vinegary,
sharp, pungent, acerbic, caustic,
corrosive, stinging, biting, mordant,
cutting, incisive, trenchant, harsh,
hurtful.

**acknowledge** v 1 *acknowledge an
error*: admit, confess, own up to,
declare, recognize, accept, grant,
allow, concede. 2 GREET, address,
notice, recognize. 3 *acknowledge a
letter*: answer, reply to, respond to,
confirm.
**F3** 1 deny. 2 ignore.

**acknowledged** adj recognized,
accepted, approved, accredited,
declared, professed, attested,
avowed, confirmed.

**acknowledgement** n 1 ADMISSION,
confession, declaration, profession,
recognition, acceptance.
2 GREETING, salutation, notice,
recognition. 3 ANSWER, reply,
response, reaction, affirmation.
4 GRATITUDE, thanks, appreciation,
tribute.

**acquaint** v accustom, familiarize,
tell, notify, advise, inform, brief,
enlighten, divulge, disclose, reveal,
announce.

**acquaintance** n 1 AWARENESS, knowledge, understanding, experience, familiarity, intimacy, relationship, association, fellowship, companionship. 2 FRIEND, companion, colleague, associate, contact.

**acquire** v buy, purchase, procure, appropriate, obtain, get, cop (sl), receive, collect, pick up, gather, net, gain, secure, earn, win, achieve, attain, realize.
FB relinquish, forfeit.

**acquisition** n purchase, buy (infml), procurement, appropriation, gain, securing, achievement, attainment, accession, takeover, property, possession.

**acquit** v absolve, clear, reprieve, let off, exonerate, exculpate, excuse, vindicate, free, liberate, deliver, relieve, release, dismiss, discharge, settle, satisfy, repay.
FB convict.

**acquittal** n absolution, clearance, reprieve, exoneration, exculpation, excusing, vindication, freeing, liberation, deliverance, relief, release, dismissal, discharge.
FB conviction.

**acrid** adj pungent, sharp, stinging, acid, burning, caustic, acerbic, biting, cutting, incisive, trenchant, sarcastic, sardonic, bitter, acrimonious, virulent, harsh, vitriolic, nasty, malicious, venomous.

**acrimonious** adj bitter, biting, cutting, trenchant, sharp, virulent, severe, spiteful, censorious, abusive, ill-tempered.
FB peaceable, kindly.

**acrimony** n bitterness, rancour, resentment, ill-will, petulance, gall, ill temper, irascibility, trenchancy, sarcasm, astringency, acerbity, harshness, virulence.

**act** n 1 DEED, action, undertaking, enterprise, operation, manoeuvre, move, step, doing, execution, accomplishment, achievement, exploit, feat, stroke. 2 put on an act: pretence, make-believe, sham, fake, feigning, dissimulation, affectation, show, front. 3 LAW, statute, ordinance, edict, decree, resolution, measure, bill. 4 TURN, item, routine, sketch, performance, gig (sl).
v 1 BEHAVE, conduct, exert, make, work, function, operate, do, execute, carry out. 2 PRETEND, feign, put on, assume, simulate, mimic, imitate, impersonate, portray, represent, mime, play, perform, enact.

**act on** 1 act on orders: carry out, fulfil, comply with, conform to, obey, follow, heed, take. 2 AFFECT, influence, alter, modify, change, transform.

**acting** adj temporary, provisional, interim, stopgap, supply, stand-by, substitute, reserve.
n theatre, stagecraft, artistry, performing, performance, play-acting, melodrama, dramatics, theatricals, portrayal, characterization, impersonation, imitating.

**action** n 1 ACT, move, deed, exploit, feat, accomplishment, achievement, performance, effort, endeavour, enterprise, undertaking, proceeding, process, activity, liveliness, spirit, energy, vigour, power, force, exercise, exertion, work, functioning, operation, mechanism, movement, motion. 2 killed in action: warfare, battle, conflict, combat, fight, fray, engagement, skirmish, clash.
3 LITIGATION, lawsuit, suit, case, prosecution.

**activate** v start, initiate, trigger, set off, fire, switch on, set in motion, mobilize, propel, move, stir, rouse, arouse, stimulate, motivate, prompt, animate, energize, impel, excite, galvanize.
FB deactivate, stop, arrest.

**active** adj 1 BUSY, occupied, on the go (infml), industrious, diligent, hard-working, forceful, spirited, vital, forward, enterprising, enthusiastic, devoted, engaged, involved, committed, militant, activist. **2** AGILE, nimble, sprightly, light-footed, quick, alert, animated, lively, energetic, vigorous. **3** IN OPERATION, functioning, working, running.

**F₃** 1 passive. **2** inert, dormant. **3** inactive.

**activity** n **1** LIVELINESS, life, activeness, action, motion, movement, commotion, bustle, hustle, industry, labour, exertion, exercise. **2** OCCUPATION, job, work, act, deed, project, scheme, task, venture, enterprise, endeavour, undertaking, pursuit, hobby, pastime, interest.

**actor** n actress, play-actor, comedian, tragedian, ham, player, performer, artist, impersonator, mime.

**actual** adj **1** REAL, existent, substantial, tangible, material, physical, concrete, positive, definite, absolute, certain, unquestionable, indisputable, confirmed, verified, factual, truthful, true, genuine, legitimate, bona fide, authentic, realistic. **2** CURRENT, present, present-day, prevailing, live, living.

**F₃** 1 theoretical, apparent, imaginary.

**actually** adv in fact, as a matter of fact, as it happens, in truth, in reality, really, truly, indeed, absolutely.

**acumen** n astuteness, shrewdness, sharpness, keenness, quickness, penetration, insight, intuition, discrimination, discernment, judgement, perception, sense, wit, wisdom, intelligence, cleverness, ingenuity.

**acute** adj **1** SEVERE, intense, extreme, violent, dangerous, serious, grave, urgent, crucial, vital, decisive, sharp, cutting, poignant, distressing.

**2** an acute mind: sharp, keen, incisive, penetrating, astute, shrewd, judicious, discerning, observant, perceptive.

**F₃** mild, slight.

**adamant** adj hard, resolute, determined, set, firm, insistent, rigid, stiff, inflexible, unbending, unrelenting, intransigent, unyielding, stubborn, uncompromising, tough, fixed, immovable, unshakable.

**F₃** hesitant, flexible, yielding.

**adapt** v alter, change, qualify, modify, adjust, convert, remodel, customize, fit, tailor, fashion, shape, harmonize, match, suit, conform, comply, prepare, familiarize, acclimatize.

**adaptable** adj alterable, changeable, variable, modifiable, adjustable, convertible, conformable, versatile, plastic, malleable, flexible, compliant, amenable, easy-going.

**F₃** inflexible, refractory.

**adaptation** n alteration, change, shift, transformation, modification, adjustment, accommodation, conversion, remodelling, reworking, reshaping, refitting, revision, variation, version.

**add** v append, annex, affix, attach, tack on, join, combine, supplement, augment.

**F₃** take away, remove.

**add up** **1** ADD, sum up, tot up, total, tally, count (up), reckon, compute. **2** AMOUNT, come to, constitute, include. **3** it doesn't add up: be consistent, hang together, fit, be plausible, be reasonable, make sense, mean, signify, indicate.

**F₃** 1 subtract.

**addict** n **1** ENTHUSIAST, fan, buff (infml), fiend, freak, devotee, follower, adherent. **2** DRUG-ADDICT, user (infml), dope-fiend, junkie (infml), tripper (sl), mainliner (sl).

**addicted** adj dependent, hooked,

obsessed, absorbed, devoted, dedicated, fond, inclined, disposed, accustomed.

**addiction** n dependence, craving, habit, monkey (sl), obsession.

**addition** n 1 ADDING, annexation, accession, extension, enlargement, increasing, increase, gain. **2** ADJUNCT, supplement, additive, addendum, appendix, appendage, accessory, attachment, extra, increment. **3** SUMMING-UP, totting-up, totalling, counting, reckoning, inclusion.

**F₃** 1 removal. 3 subtraction.

**in addition** additionally, too, also, as well, besides, moreover, further, furthermore, over and above.

**additional** adj added, extra, supplementary, spare, more, further, increased, other, new, fresh.

**address** n 1 RESIDENCE, dwelling, abode, house, home, lodging, direction, inscription, whereabouts, location, situation, place. **2** SPEECH, talk, lecture, sermon, discourse, dissertation.

v lecture, speak to, talk to, greet, salute, hail, invoke, accost, approach, buttonhole.

**adept** adj skilled, accomplished, expert, masterly, experienced, versed, practised, polished, proficient, able, adroit, deft, nimble.

**adequate** adj enough, sufficient, commensurate, requisite, suitable, fit, able, competent, capable, serviceable, acceptable, satisfactory, passable, tolerable, fair, respectable, presentable.

**F₃** inadequate, insufficient.

**adhere** v 1 STICK, glue, paste, cement, fix, fasten, attach, join, link, combine, coalesce, cohere, hold, cling, cleave to. **2** adhere to the agreement: observe, follow, abide by, comply with, fulfil, obey, keep, heed, respect, stand by.

**adherent** n supporter, upholder,

advocate, partisan, follower, disciple, satellite, henchman, hanger-on, votary, devotee, admirer, fan, enthusiast, freak, nut.

**adhesion** n adherence, adhesiveness, bond, attachment, grip, cohesion.

**adhesive** adj sticky, tacky, self-adhesive, gummed, gummy, gluey, adherent, adhering, sticking, clinging, holding, attaching, cohesive.

n glue, gum, paste, cement.

**adjacent** adj adjoining, abutting, touching, contiguous, bordering, alongside, beside, juxtaposed, next-door, neighbouring, next, closest, nearest, close, near.

**F₃** remote, distant.

**adjoin** v abut, touch, meet, border, verge, neighbour, interconnect, link, connect, join, combine, unite, couple, attach, annex, add.

**adjourn** v interrupt, suspend, discontinue, break off, delay, stay, defer, postpone, put off, recess, retire.

**F₃** assemble, convene.

**adjournment** n interruption, suspension, discontinuation, break, pause, recess, delay, stay, deferment, deferral, postponement, putting off, dissolution.

**adjudicate** v judge, arbitrate, umpire, referee, settle, determine, decide, pronounce.

**adjust** v 1 MODIFY, change, adapt, alter, convert, dispose, shape, remodel, fit, accommodate, suit, measure, rectify, regulate, balance, temper, tune, fine-tune, fix, set, arrange, compose, settle, square. **2** ACCUSTOM, habituate, acclimatize, reconcile, harmonize, conform.

**F₃** 1 disarrange, upset.

**adjustment** n 1 MODIFICATION, change, adaptation, alteration, conversion, remodelling, shaping, fitting, accommodation, rectification, regulation, tuning, fixing, setting, arranging, arrangement, ordering, settlement. **2** HABITUATION, orientation, acclimatization, naturalization, reconciliation, harmonization, conforming.

**ad-lib** *v* improvise, extemporize, make up, invent.
*adj* impromptu, improvised, extempore, extemporaneous, off-the-cuff, unprepared, unpremeditated, unrehearsed, spontaneous, made up. ⊟ prepared.
*adv* impromptu, extempore, extemporaneously, off the cuff, off the top of one's head, spontaneously, impulsively.

**administer** *v* **1** *administer an organization*: govern, rule, lead, head, preside over, officiate, manage, run, organize, direct, conduct, control, regulate, superintend, supervise, oversee. **2** GIVE, provide, supply, distribute, dole out, dispense, measure out, mete out, execute, impose, apply.

**administration** *n* **1** ADMINISTERING, governing, ruling, leadership, management, execution, running, organization, direction, control, superintendence, supervision, overseeing. **2** GOVERNING BODY, regime, government, ministry, leadership, directorship, management, executive, term of office.

**administrative** *adj* governmental, legislative, authoritative, directorial, managerial, management, executive, organizational, regulatory, supervisory.

**admirable** *adj* praiseworthy, commendable, laudable, creditable, deserving, worthy, respected, fine, excellent, superior, wonderful, exquisite, choice, rare, valuable. ⊟ contemptible, despicable, deplorable.

**admiration** *n* esteem, regard, respect, reverence, veneration,

worship, idolism, adoration, affection, approval, praise, appreciation, pleasure, delight, wonder, astonishment, amazement, surprise. ⊟ contempt.

**admire** *v* esteem, respect, revere, venerate, worship, idolize, adore, approve, praise, laud, applaud, appreciate, value. ⊟ despise, censure.

**admirer** *n* follower, disciple, adherent, supporter, fan, enthusiast, devotee, worshipper, idolizer, suitor, boyfriend, girlfriend, sweetheart, lover. ⊟ critic, opponent.

**admissible** *adj* acceptable, tolerable, tolerated, passable, allowable, permissible, allowed, permitted, lawful, legitimate, justifiable. ⊟ inadmissible, illegitimate.

**admission** *n* confession, granting, acknowledgement, recognition, acceptance, allowance, concession, affirmation, declaration, profession, disclosure, divulgence, revelation, exposé. ⊟ denial.

**admit** *v* **1** CONFESS, own (up), grant, acknowledge, recognize, accept, allow, concede, agree, affirm, declare, profess, disclose, divulge, reveal. **2** LET IN, allow to enter, give access, accept, receive, take in, introduce, initiate. ⊟ **1** deny. **2** shut out, exclude.

**admittance** *n* admitting, admission, letting in, access, entrance, entry, acceptance, reception, introduction, initiation. ⊟ exclusion.

**adolescence** *n* teens, puberty, youth, minority, boyhood, girlhood, development, immaturity, youthfulness, boyishness, girlishness.

**adolescent** *adj* teenage, young, youthful, juvenile, puerile, boyish, girlish, immature, growing, developing.

*n* teenager, youth, juvenile, minor.

**adopt** *v* take on, accept, assume, take up, appropriate, embrace, follow, choose, select, take in, foster, support, maintain, back, endorse, ratify, approve.

**E3** repudiate, disown.

**adorable** *adj* lovable, dear, darling, precious, appealing, sweet, winsome, charming, enchanting, captivating, winning, delightful, pleasing, attractive, fetching.

**E3** hateful, abominable.

**adore** *v* love, cherish, dote on, admire, esteem, honour, revere, venerate, worship, idolize, exalt, glorify.

**E3** hate, abhor.

**adorn** *v* decorate, deck, bedeck, ornament, crown, trim, garnish, gild, enhance, embellish, doll up, enrich, grace.

**adult** *adj* grown-up, of age, full-grown, fully grown, developed, mature, ripe, ripened.

**E3** immature.

**adulterate** *v* contaminate, pollute, taint, corrupt, defile, debase, dilute, water down, weaken, devalue, deteriorate.

**E3** purify.

**advance** *v* **1** PROCEED, go forward, move on, go ahead, progress, prosper, flourish, thrive, improve. **2** ACCELERATE, speed, hasten, send forward. **3** FURTHER, promote, upgrade, foster, support, assist, benefit, facilitate, increase, grow. **4** *advance an idea*: present, submit, suggest, allege, cite, bring forward, offer, provide, supply, furnish. **5** *advance a sum of money*: lend, loan, pay beforehand, pay, give.

**E3 1** retreat. **2** retard. **3** impede.

*n* **1** PROGRESS, forward movement, onward movement, headway, step, advancement, furtherance,

breakthrough, development, growth, increase, improvement, amelioration. **2** DEPOSIT, down payment, prepayment, credit, loan.

**E3 1** retreat, recession.

**in advance** beforehand, previously, early, earlier, sooner, ahead, in front, in the lead, in the forefront.

**E3** later, behind.

**advanced** *adj* leading, foremost, ahead, forward, precocious, progressive, forward-looking, avant-garde, ultra-modern, sophisticated, complex, higher.

**E3** backward, retarded, elementary.

**advancement** *n* furtherance, promotion, preferment, betterment, improvement, development, growth, rise, gain, advance, progress, headway.

**E3** demotion, retardation.

**advantage** *n* **1** ASSET, blessing, benefit, good, welfare, interest, service, help, aid, assistance, use, avail, convenience, usefulness, utility, profit, gain, start. **2** LEAD, edge, upper hand, superiority, precedence, pre-eminence, sway.

**E3 1** disadvantage, drawback, hindrance.

**advantageous** *adj* beneficial, favourable, opportune, convenient, helpful, useful, worthwhile, valuable, profitable, gainful, remunerative, rewarding.

**E3** disadvantageous, adverse, damaging.

**adventure** *n* exploit, venture, undertaking, enterprise, risk, hazard, chance, speculation, experience, incident, occurrence.

**adventurous** *adj* daring, intrepid, bold, audacious, headstrong, impetuous, reckless, rash, risky, venturesome, enterprising.

**E3** cautious, chary, prudent.

**adverse** *adj* hostile, antagonistic, opposing, opposite, counter, contrary, conflicting, counter-

productive, negative,
disadvantageous, unfavourable,
inauspicious, unfortunate, unlucky,
inopportune, detrimental, harmful,
noxious, injurious, hurtful,
unfriendly, uncongenial.
**F3** advantageous, favourable.

**adversity** *n* misfortune, ill fortune,
bad luck, ill luck, reverse, hardship,
hard times, misery, wretchedness,
affliction, suffering, distress, sorrow,
woe, trouble, trial, tribulation,
calamity, disaster, catastrophe.
**F3** prosperity.

**advertise** *v* publicize, promote,
push, plug (*infml*), praise, hype (*sl*),
trumpet, blazon, herald, announce,
declare, proclaim, broadcast, publish,
display, make known, inform, notify.

**advertisement** *n* advert (*infml*), ad
(*infml*), commercial, publicity,
promotion, plug (*infml*), hype (*sl*),
display, blurb, announcement, notice,
poster, bill, placard, leaflet, handbill,
circular, handout, propaganda.

**advice** *n* **1** WARNING, caution, do's
and don'ts, injunction, instruction,
counsel, help, guidance, direction,
suggestion, recommendation,
opinion, view. **2** NOTIFICATION,
notice, memorandum,
communication, information,
intelligence.

**advisable** *adj* suggested,
recommended, sensible, wise,
prudent, judicious, sound, profitable,
beneficial, desirable, suitable,
appropriate, apt, fitting, fit, proper,
correct.
**F3** inadvisable, foolish.

**advise** *v* **1** COUNSEL, guide, warn,
forewarn, caution, instruct, teach,
tutor, suggest, recommend,
commend, urge. **2** NOTIFY, inform,
tell, acquaint, make known, report.

**adviser** *n* counsellor, consultant,
authority, guide, teacher, tutor,
instructor, coach, helper, aide, right-
hand man, mentor, confidant(e),

counsel, lawyer.

**advocate** *v* defend, champion,
campaign for, press for, argue for,
plead for, justify, urge, encourage,
advise, recommend, propose,
promote, endorse, support, uphold,
patronize, adopt, subscribe to,
favour, countenance.
**F3** impugn, disparage, deprecate.
*n* defender, supporter, upholder,
champion, campaigner, pleader,
vindicator, proponent, promoter,
speaker, spokesperson.
**F3** opponent, critic.

**affable** *adj* friendly, amiable,
approachable, open, expansive,
genial, good-humoured, good-
natured, mild, benevolent, kindly,
gracious, obliging, courteous,
amicable, congenial, cordial, warm,
sociable, pleasant, agreeable.
**F3** unfriendly, reserved, reticent, cool.

**affair** *n* **1** BUSINESS, transaction,
operation, proceeding, undertaking,
activity, project, responsibility,
interest, concern, matter, question,
issue, subject, topic, circumstance,
happening, occurrence, incident,
episode, event. **2** *have an affair*:
relationship, liaison, intrigue, love
affair, romance, amour.

**affect** *v* **1** CONCERN, regard,
involve, relate to, apply to, bear
upon, impinge upon, act on, change,
transform, alter, modify, influence,
sway, prevail over, attack, strike,
impress, interest, stir, move, touch,
upset, disturb, perturb, trouble,
overcome. **2** ADOPT, assume, put on,
feign, simulate, imitate, fake,
counterfeit, sham, pretend, profess,
aspire to.

**affectation** *n* airs, pretentiousness,
mannerism, pose, act, show,
appearance, façade, pretence, sham,
simulation, imitation, artificiality,
insincerity.
**F3** artlessness, ingenuousness.

**affected** *adj* assumed, put-on,

feigned, simulated, artificial, fake, counterfeit, sham, phoney (*infml*), contrived, studied, precious, mannered, pretentious, pompous, stiff, unnatural, insincere.

F3 genuine, natural.

**affection** *n* fondness, attachment, devotion, love, tenderness, care, warmth, feeling, kindness, friendliness, goodwill, favour, liking, partiality, inclination, penchant, passion, desire.

F3 dislike, antipathy.

**affectionate** *adj* fond, attached, devoted, doting, loving, tender, caring, warm, warm-hearted, kind, friendly, amiable, cordial.

F3 cold, undemonstrative.

**affirm** *v* confirm, corroborate, endorse, ratify, certify, witness, testify, swear, maintain, state, assert, declare, pronounce.

F3 refute, deny.

**affirmative** *adj* agreeing, concurring, approving, assenting, positive, confirming, corroborative, emphatic.

F3 negative, dissenting.

**afflict** *v* strike, visit, trouble, burden, oppress, distress, grieve, pain, hurt, wound, harm, try, harass, beset, plague, torment, torture.

F3 comfort, solace.

**affliction** *n* distress, grief, sorrow, misery, depression, suffering, pain, torment, disease, illness, sickness, plague, curse, cross, ordeal, trial, tribulation, trouble, hardship, adversity, misfortune, calamity, disaster.

F3 comfort, consolation, solace, blessing.

**affluence** *n* wealthiness, wealth, riches, fortune, substance, property, prosperity, opulence, abundance, profusion, plenty.

F3 poverty.

**affluent** *adj* wealthy, rich, moneyed, loaded (*sl*), flush (*infml*), well-off,

prosperous, well-to-do, opulent, comfortable.

F3 poor, impoverished.

**afford** *v* **1** HAVE ENOUGH FOR, spare, allow, manage, sustain, bear. **2** PROVIDE, supply, furnish, give, grant, offer, impart, produce, yield, generate.

**affront** *v* offend, insult, abuse, snub, slight, provoke, displease, irritate, annoy, anger, vex, incense, outrage.

F3 compliment, appease.

*n* offence, insult, slur, rudeness, discourtesy, disrespect, indignity, snub, slight, wrong, injury, abuse, provocation, vexation, outrage.

F3 compliment.

**afraid** *adj* frightened, scared, alarmed, terrified, fearful, timorous, daunted, intimidated, faint-hearted, cowardly, reluctant, apprehensive, anxious, nervous, timid, distrustful, suspicious.

F3 unafraid, brave, bold, confident.

**after** *prep* following, subsequent to, in consequence of, as a result of, behind, below.

F3 before.

**again** *adv* once more, once again, another time, over again, afresh, anew, encore.

**against** *prep* **1** *against the wall*: abutting, adjacent to, close up to, touching, in contact with, on. **2** OPPOSITE TO, facing, fronting, in the face of, confronting, opposing, versus, opposed to, in opposition to, hostile to, resisting, in defiance of, in contrast to.

F3 **2** for, pro.

**age** *n* **1** ERA, epoch, day, days, generation, date, time, period, duration, span, years, aeon. **2** OLD AGE, maturity, elderliness, seniority, dotage, senility, decline.

F3 **2** youth.

*v* grow old, mature, ripen, mellow, season, decline, deteriorate, degenerate.

**agency** n **1** *recruitment agency*: bureau, office, department, organization, business, work. **2** MEANS, medium, instrumentality, power, force, influence, effect, intervention, action, activity, operation, mechanism, workings.

**agent** n **1** SUBSTITUTE, deputy, delegate, envoy, emissary, representative, rep (*infml*), broker, middleman, go-between, intermediary, negotiator, mover, doer, performer, operator, operative, functionary, worker. **2** INSTRUMENT, vehicle, channel, means, agency, cause, force.

**aggravate** v **1** *aggravate a problem*: exacerbate, worsen, inflame, increase, intensify, heighten, magnify, exaggerate. **2** (*infml*) ANNOY, irritate, vex, irk, exasperate, incense, provoke, tease, pester, harass.
**F3** **1** improve, alleviate. **2** appease, mollify.

**aggregate** n total, sum, amount, whole, totality, entirety, generality, combination, collection, accumulation.
*adj* cumulative, accumulated, collected, combined, united, added, total, complete, composite, mixed, collective.
**F3** individual, particular.

**aggression** n **1** ANTAGONISM, provocation, offence, injury, attack, offensive, assault, onslaught, raid, incursion, invasion, intrusion. **2** AGGRESSIVENESS, militancy, belligerence, combativeness, hostility.
**F3** **1** peace, resistance. **2** passivity, gentleness.

**aggressive** *adj* argumentative, quarrelsome, contentious, belligerent, hostile, offensive, provocative, intrusive, invasive, bold, assertive, pushy, go-ahead, forceful, vigorous, zealous, ruthless, destructive.
**F3** peaceable, friendly, submissive,

timid.

**aggrieved** *adj* wronged, offended, hurt, injured, insulted, maltreated, ill-used, resentful, pained, distressed, saddened, unhappy, upset, annoyed.
**F3** pleased.

**aghast** *adj* shocked, appalled, horrified, horror-struck, thunderstruck, stunned, stupefied, amazed, astonished, astounded, startled, confounded, dismayed.

**agile** *adj* active, lively, nimble, spry, sprightly, mobile, flexible, limber, lithe, fleet, quick, swift, brisk, prompt, sharp, acute, alert, quick-witted, clever, adroit, deft.
**F3** clumsy, stiff.

**agitate** v **1** ROUSE, arouse, stir up, excite, stimulate, incite, inflame, ferment, work up, worry, trouble, upset, alarm, disturb, unsettle, disquiet, discompose, fluster, ruffle, flurry, unnerve, confuse, distract, disconcert. **2** SHAKE, rattle, rock, stir, beat, churn, toss, convulse.
**F3** **1** calm, tranquillize.

**agitator** n troublemaker, rabble-rouser, revolutionary, stirrer (*sl*), inciter, instigator.

**agony** n anguish, torment, torture, pain, spasm, throes, suffering, affliction, tribulation, distress, woe, misery, wretchedness.

**agree** v **1** CONCUR, see eye to eye, get on, settle, accord, match, suit, fit, tally, correspond, conform. **2** CONSENT, allow, permit, assent, accede, grant, admit, concede, yield, comply.
**F3** **1** disagree, differ, conflict. **2** refuse.

**agreeable** *adj* pleasant, congenial, likable, attractive, delightful, enjoyable, gratifying, satisfying, palatable, acceptable, proper, appropriate, suitable, fitting, in accord, consistent.
**F3** disagreeable, nasty, distasteful.

**agreement** n **1** SETTLEMENT, compact, covenant, treaty, pact,

contract, deal, bargain, arrangement, understanding. **2** *be in agreement*: concurrence, accord, concord, unanimity, union, harmony, sympathy, affinity, compatibility, similarity, correspondence, consistency, conformity, compliance, adherence, acceptance.
**E3 2** disagreement.

**agricultural** *adj* agronomic, agrarian, farming, farmed, cultivated, rural, pastoral, bucolic.

---

*Types of agricultural implement and machinery include:* axe, chainsaw, clover broadcaster, fertilizer distributor, field sprinkler, fork, hayfork, pitchfork, hoe, potato planter, rake, hayrake, reaping hook, saw, scythe, shovel, sickle, spade, wheelbarrow, whetstone; all-terrain vehicle (ATV), baler, bale wrapper, cultivator, drill, corn drill, seed drill, fertilizer spreader, fork-lift truck, front end loader, harrow, combination seed-harrow, disc harrow, harvester, combine harvester, hedgecutter, irrigator, milking machine, mower, flail mower, muckspreader, potato planter, plough, reversible plough, wheel plough, power lift, rotary hoe, Rotovator®, scarifier, slurry tanker, sprayer, tedder, tractor, trailer.

---

**agriculture** *n* agronomics, farming, husbandry, cultivation, culture, tillage.

**ahead** *adv* forward, onward, leading, at the head, in front, in the lead, winning, at an advantage, advanced, superior, to the fore, in the forefront, in advance, before, earlier on.

**aid** *v* help, assist, succour, rally round, relieve, support, subsidize, sustain, second, serve, oblige, accommodate, favour, promote, boost, encourage, expedite, facilitate,

ease.
**E3** hinder, impede, obstruct.
*n* help, assistance, prop, support, relief, benefit, subsidy, donation, contribution, funding, grant, sponsorship, patronage, favour, encouragement, service.
**E3** hindrance, impediment, obstruction.

**ailing** *adj* unwell, ill, sick, poorly, indisposed, out of sorts (*infml*), under the weather (*infml*), off-colour, suffering, languishing, sickly, diseased, invalid, infirm, unsound, frail, weak, feeble, failing.
**E3** healthy, thriving, flourishing.

**ailment** *n* illness, sickness, complaint, malady, disease, infection, disorder, affliction, infirmity, disability, weakness.

**aim** *v* **1** POINT, direct, take aim, level, train, sight, zero in on (*infml*), target. **2** *aim to achieve*: aspire, want, wish, seek, resolve, purpose, intend, propose, mean, plan, design, strive, try, attempt, endeavour.
*n* aspiration, ambition, hope, dream, desire, wish, plan, design, scheme, purpose, motive, end, intention, object, objective, target, mark, goal, direction, course.

**aimless** *adj* pointless, purposeless, unmotivated, irresolute, directionless, rambling, undirected, unguided, stray, chance, random, haphazard, erratic, unpredictable, wayward.
**E3** purposeful, positive, determined.

**air** *n* **1** ATMOSPHERE, oxygen, sky, heavens, breath, puff, waft, draught, breeze, wind, blast. **2** APPEARANCE, look, aspect, aura, bearing, demeanour, manner, character, effect, impression, feeling.
*v* **1** *air a room*: ventilate, aerate, freshen. **2** *air an opinion*: utter, voice, express, give vent to, make known, communicate, tell, declare, reveal, disclose, divulge, expose, make public, broadcast, publish, circulate,

disseminate, exhibit, display, parade, publicize.

**aircraft**

> *Types of aircraft include*: aeroplane, plane, jet, jumbo, Concorde, airbus, helicopter, monoplane, two-seater, air-ambulance, freighter, sea-plane, glider, hang-glider, microlight, hot-air balloon; fighter, spitfire, bomber, kite (*infml*), jump-jet, dive-bomber, chopper (*sl*), spy plane, delta-wing, swing-wing, troop-carrier, airship, turbojet, VTOL (vertical take-off and landing), warplane, zeppelin.

**airless** *adj* unventilated, stuffy, musty, stale, suffocating, stifling, sultry, muggy, close, heavy, oppressive.
🔁 airy, fresh.

**airy** *adj* **1** ROOMY, spacious, open, well-ventilated, draughty, breezy, blowy, windy, gusty. **2** CHEERFUL, happy, light-hearted, high-spirited, lively, nonchalant, offhand.
🔁 **1** airless, stuffy, close, heavy, oppressive.

**aisle** *n* gangway, corridor, passage, passageway, alleyway, walkway, path, lane.

**alarm** *v* frighten, scare, startle, put the wind up (*infml*), terrify, panic, unnerve, daunt, dismay, distress, agitate.
🔁 reassure, calm, soothe.
*n* **1** FRIGHT, scare, fear, terror, panic, horror, shock, consternation, dismay, distress, anxiety, nervousness, apprehension, trepidation, uneasiness. **2** DANGER SIGNAL, alert, warning, distress signal, siren, bell, alarm-bell.
🔁 **1** calmness, composure.

**alarming** *adj* frightening, scary, startling, terrifying, unnerving, daunting, ominous, threatening, dismaying, disturbing, distressing, shocking, dreadful.
🔁 reassuring.

**alcohol** *n* drink, booze (*sl*), liquor, spirits, hard stuff (*sl*), intoxicant.

**alcoholic** *adj* intoxicating, brewed, fermented, distilled, strong, hard.
*n* drunk, drunkard, inebriate, hard drinker, dipsomaniac, wino (*sl*), alkie (*sl*).

**alcove** *n* niche, nook, recess, bay, corner, cubby-hole, compartment, cubicle, booth, carrel.

**alert** *adj* attentive, wide-awake, watchful, vigilant, on the lookout, sharp-eyed, observant, perceptive, sharp-witted, on the ball (*infml*), active, lively, spirited, quick, brisk, agile, nimble, ready, prepared, careful, heedful, circumspect, wary.
🔁 slow, listless, unprepared.
*v* warn, forewarn, notify, inform, tip off, signal, alarm.

**alias** *n* pseudonym, false name, assumed name, nom de guerre, nom de plume, pen name, stage name, nickname, sobriquet.
*prep* also known as, also called, otherwise, formerly.

**alibi** *n* defence, justification, story, explanation, excuse, pretext, reason.

**alien** *adj* strange, unfamiliar, outlandish, incongruous, foreign, exotic, extraterrestial, extraneous, remote, estranged, separated, opposed, contrary, conflicting, antagonistic, incompatible.
🔁 akin.
*n* foreigner, immigrant, newcomer, stranger, outsider.
🔁 native.

**alight**[1] *v* descend, get down, dismount, get off, disembark, land, touch down, come down, come to rest, settle, light, perch.
🔁 ascend, board.

**alight**[2] *adj* lighted, lit, ignited, on fire, burning, blazing, ablaze, flaming, fiery, lit up, illuminated, bright, radiant, shining, brilliant.
🔁 dark.

**align** *v* **1** STRAIGHTEN, range, line

up, make parallel, even (up), adjust, regulate, regularize, order, co-ordinate. **2** ALLY, side, sympathize, associate, affiliate, join, co-operate, agree.

**alike** *adj* similar, resembling, comparable, akin, analogous, corresponding, equivalent, equal, the same, identical, duplicate, parallel, even, uniform.

**Ea** dissimilar, unlike, different.

*adv* similarly, analogously, correspondingly, equally, in common.

**alive** *adj* **1** LIVING, having life, live, animate, breathing, existent, in existence, real. **2** LIVELY, animated, spirited, awake, alert, active, brisk, energetic, vigorous, zestful, vivacious, vibrant, vital.

**Ea 1** dead, extinct. **2** lifeless, apathetic.

**all** *adj* **1** EACH, every, each and every, every single, every one of, the whole of, every bit of. **2** COMPLETE, entire, full, total, utter, outright, perfect, greatest.

**Ea 1** no, none.

*n* everything, sum, total, aggregate, total amount, whole amount, whole, entirety, utmost, comprehensiveness, universality.

**Ea** nothing, none.

*adv* completely, entirely, wholly, fully, totally, utterly, altogether, wholesale.

**all right** *adj* **1** SATISFACTORY, passable, unobjectionable, acceptable, allowable, adequate, fair, average, OK (*infml*). **2** *are you all right?*: well, healthy, unhurt, uninjured, unharmed, unimpaired, whole, sound, safe, secure.

**Ea 1** unacceptable, inadequate.

*adv* satisfactorily, well enough, passably, unobjectionably, acceptably, suitably, appropriately, adequately, reasonably, OK (*infml*).

**Ea** unsatisfactorily, unacceptably.

**allay** *v* alleviate, relieve, soothe, ease, smooth, calm, tranquillize, quiet, quell, pacify, mollify, soften,

blunt, lessen, reduce, diminish, check, moderate.

**Ea** exacerbate, intensify.

**allegation** *n* accusation, charge, claim, profession, assertion, affirmation, declaration, statement, testimony, plea.

**allege** *v* assert, affirm, declare, state, attest, maintain, insist, hold, contend, claim, profess, plead.

**alleged** *adj* supposed, reputed, putative, inferred, so-called, professed, declared, stated, claimed, described, designated, doubtful, dubious, suspect, suspicious.

**allegiance** *n* loyalty, fidelity, faithfulness, constancy, duty, obligation, obedience, devotion, support, adherence, friendship.

**Ea** disloyalty, enmity.

**allergic** *adj* sensitive, hypersensitive, susceptible, affected, incompatible, averse, disinclined, opposed, hostile, antagonistic.

**Ea** tolerant.

**alleviate** *v* relieve, soothe, ease, palliate, mitigate, soften, cushion, dull, deaden, allay, abate, lessen, reduce, diminish, check, moderate, temper, subdue.

**Ea** aggravate.

**alliance** *n* confederation, federation, association, affiliation, coalition, league, bloc, cartel, conglomerate, consortium, syndicate, guild, union, partnership, marriage, agreement, compact, bond, pact, treaty, combination, connection.

**Ea** separation, divorce, estrangement, enmity, hostility.

**allocate** *v* assign, designate, budget, allow, earmark, set aside, allot, apportion, share out, distribute, dispense, mete.

**allocation** *n* allotment, lot, apportionment, measure, share, portion, stint, ration, quota, budget, allowance, grant.

**allot** *v* divide, ration, apportion,

share out, distribute, dispense, mete, dole out, allocate, assign, designate, budget, allow, grant, earmark, set aside.

**allotment** n division, partition, allocation, apportionment, measure, percentage, lot, portion, share, stint, ration, quota, allowance, grant.

**all-out** adj complete, full, total, undivided, comprehensive, exhaustive, thorough, intensive, thoroughgoing, wholesale, vigorous, powerful, full-scale, no-holds-barred, maximum, utmost, unlimited, unrestrained, resolute, determined.
E3 perfunctory, half-hearted.

**allow** v 1 PERMIT, let, enable, authorize, sanction, approve, tolerate, put up with, endure, suffer. 2 ADMIT, confess, own, acknowledge, concede, grant. 3 *allow two hours for the journey*: allot, allocate, assign, apportion, afford, give, provide.
E3 1 forbid, prevent. 2 deny.

**allow for** take into account, make provision for, make allowances for, provide for, foresee, plan for, arrange for, bear in mind, keep in mind, consider, include.
E3 discount.

**allowance** n 1 ALLOTMENT, lot, amount, allocation, portion, share, ration, quota. 2 REBATE, reduction, deduction, discount, concession, subsidy, weighting. 3 PAYMENT, remittance, pocket money, grant, maintenance, stipend, pension, annuity.

**alloy** n blend, compound, composite, amalgam, combination, mixture, fusion, coalescence.

**allure** v lure, entice, seduce, lead on, tempt, coax, cajole, persuade, win over, disarm, charm, enchant, attract, interest, fascinate, captivate, entrance, beguile.
E3 repel.
n lure, enticement, seduction,

temptation, appeal, attraction, magnetism, fascination, glamour, captivation, charm, enchantment.

**allusion** n mention, reference, citation, quotation, remark, observation, suggestion, hint, intimation, implication, insinuation.

**ally** n confederate, associate, leaguer, consort, partner, sidekick, colleague, co-worker, collaborator, helper, helpmate, accomplice, accessory, friend.
E3 antagonist, enemy.
v confederate, affiliate, league, associate, collaborate, join forces, band together, team up, fraternize, side, join, connect, link, marry, unite, unify, amalgamate, combine.
E3 estrange, separate.

**almighty** adj 1 OMNIPOTENT, all-powerful, supreme, absolute, great, invincible. 2 ENORMOUS, severe, intense, overwhelming, overpowering, terrible, awful, desperate.
E3 1 impotent, weak.

**almost** adv nearly, well-nigh, practically, virtually, just about, as good as, all but, close to, not far from, approaching, nearing, not quite, about, approximately.

**alone** adj only, sole, single, unique, solitary, separate, detached, unconnected, isolated, apart, by oneself, by itself, on one's own, lonely, lonesome, deserted, abandoned, forsaken, forlorn, desolate, unaccompanied, unescorted, unattended, solo, single-handed, unaided, unassisted, mere.
E3 together, accompanied, escorted.

**aloof** adj distant, remote, offish, standoffish, haughty, supercilious, unapproachable, inaccessible, detached, forbidding, cool, chilly, cold, sympathetic, unresponsive, indifferent, uninterested, reserved, unforthcoming, unfriendly, unsociable, formal.

**sociable**, friendly, concerned.

**aloud** *adv* out loud, audibly, intelligibly, clearly, plainly, distinctly, loudly, resoundingly, sonorously, noisily, vociferously.
**F3** silently.

## alphabets and writing systems

*Alphabets and writing systems include:* Byzantine, Chalcidian alphabet, cuneiform, Cyrillic, devanagari, estrangelo, finger-alphabet, futhark, Glagol, Glossic, Greek, Gurmukhi, hieroglyphs, hiragana, ideograph, initial teaching alphabet (i.t.a.), International Phonetic Alphabet (IPA), kana, kanji, katakana, Kufic, linear A, linear B, logograph, nagari, naskhi, ogam, pictograph, romaji, Roman, runic, syllabary.

**also** *adv* too, as well, and, plus, along with, including, as well as, additionally, in addition, besides, further, furthermore, moreover.

**alter** *v* change, vary, diversify, modify, qualify, shift, transpose, adjust, adapt, convert, turn, transmute, transform, reform, reshape, remodel, recast, revise, amend, emend.
**F3** fix.

**alteration** *n* change, variation, variance, difference, diversification, shift, transposition, modification, adjustment, adaptation, conversion, transformation, transfiguration, metamorphosis, reformation, reshaping, remodelling, revision, amendment.
**F3** fixity.

**alternate** *v* interchange, reciprocate, rotate, take turns, follow one another, replace each other, substitute, change, alter, vary, oscillate, fluctuate, intersperse.
*adj* alternating, every other, every second, interchanging, reciprocal, rotating, alternative.

**alternative** *n* option, choice, selection, preference, other, recourse, substitute, back-up.
*adj* substitute, second, another, other, different, unorthodox, unconventional, fringe, alternate.

**altitude** *n* height, elevation, loftiness, tallness, stature.
**F3** depth.

**altogether** *adv* totally, completely, entirely, wholly, fully, utterly, absolutely, quite, perfectly, thoroughly, in all, all told, in toto, all in all, as a whole, on the whole, generally, in general.

**altruistic** *adj* unselfish, self-sacrificing, disinterested, public-spirited, philanthropic, charitable, humanitarian, benevolent, generous, considerate, humane.
**F3** selfish.

**always** *adv* every time, consistently, invariably, without exception, unfailingly, regularly, repeatedly, continually, constantly, perpetually, unceasingly, eternally, endlessly, evermore, forever, ever.
**F3** never.

**amalgamate** *v* merge, blend, mingle, commingle, intermix, homogenize, incorporate, alloy, integrate, compound, fuse, coalesce, synthesize, combine, unite, unify, ally.
**F3** separate.

**amateur** *n* non-professional, layman, ham (*infml*), dilettante, dabbler, enthusiast, fancier, buff (*infml*).
**F3** professional.
*adj* non-professional, lay, unpaid, unqualified, untrained, amateurish, inexpert, unprofessional.
**F3** professional.

**amaze** *v* surprise, startle, astonish, astound, stun, stupefy, daze, stagger, floor (*infml*), dumbfound, flabbergast (*infml*), shock, dismay, disconcert, confound, bewilder.

**amazement** n surprise, astonishment, shock, dismay, confusion, perplexity, bewilderment, admiration, wonderment, wonder, marvel.

**ambassador** n emissary, envoy, legate, diplomat, consul, plenipotentiary, deputy, representative, agent, minister, apostle.

**ambiguity** n double meaning, double entendre, equivocality, equivocation, enigma, puzzle, confusion, obscurity, unclearness, vagueness, woolliness, dubiousness, doubt, doubtfulness, uncertainty. **E3** clarity.

**ambiguous** adj double-meaning, equivocal, multivocal, double-edged, back-handed, cryptic, enigmatic, puzzling, confusing, obscure, unclear, vague, indefinite, woolly, confused, dubious, doubtful, uncertain, inconclusive, indeterminate. **E3** clear, definite.

**ambition** n 1 ASPIRATION, aim, goal, target, objective, intent, purpose, design, object, ideal, dream, hope, wish, desire, yearning, longing, hankering, craving, hunger. 2 a woman of ambition: enterprise, drive, push, thrust, striving, eagerness, commitment, zeal. **E3** 2 apathy, diffidence.

**ambitious** adj 1 ASPIRING, hopeful, desirous, intent, purposeful, pushy, bold, assertive, go-ahead, enterprising, driving, energetic, enthusiastic, eager, keen, striving, industrious, zealous. 2 FORMIDABLE, hard, difficult, arduous, strenuous, demanding, challenging, exacting, impressive, grandiose, elaborate. **E3** 1 lazy, unassuming. 2 modest, uninspiring.

**ambivalent** adj contradictory, conflicting, clashing, warring, opposed, inconsistent, mixed,

confused, fluctuating, vacillating, wavering, hesitant, irresolute, undecided, unresolved, unsettled, uncertain, unsure, doubtful, debatable, inconclusive.

**amble** v walk, saunter, toddle (infml), stroll, promenade, wander, drift, meander, ramble. **E3** stride, march.

**ambush** n waylaying, surprise attack, trap, snare, cover, hiding-place.
v lie in wait, waylay, surprise, trap, ensnare.

**amenable** adj accommodating, flexible, open, agreeable, persuadable, compliant, tractable, submissive, responsive, susceptible, liable, responsible. **E3** intractable.

**amend** v revise, correct, rectify, emend, fix, repair, mend, remedy, redress, reform, change, alter, adjust, modify, qualify, enhance, improve, ameliorate, better. **E3** impair, worsen.

**amendment** n revision, correction, corrigendum, rectification, emendation, repair, remedy, reform, change, alteration, adjustment, modification, qualification, clarification, addendum, addition, adjunct, improvement. **E3** impairment, deterioration.

**amends** n atonement, expiation, requital, satisfaction, recompense, compensation, indemnification, indemnity, reparation, redress, restoration, restitution.

**amiable** adj affable, friendly, approachable, genial, cheerful, good-tempered, good-natured, kind, obliging, charming, engaging, likable, pleasant, agreeable, congenial, companionable, sociable. **E3** unfriendly, curt, hostile.

**amid** prep amidst, midst, in the midst of, in the thick of, among, amongst, in the middle of, surrounded by.

**amnesty** n pardon, forgiveness, absolution, mercy, lenience, indulgence, reprieve, remission, dispensation, immunity, oblivion.

**among** prep amongst, between, in the middle of, surrounded by, amid, amidst, midst, in the midst of, in the thick of, with, together with.

**amount** n quantity, number, sum, total, sum total, whole, entirety, aggregate, lot, quota, supply, volume, mass, bulk, measure, magnitude, extent, expanse.

**amount to** add up to, total, aggregate, come to, make, equal, mean, be tantamount to, be equivalent to, approximate to, become, grow.

**amphibian**

> *Amphibians include*: frog, bullfrog, tree frog, toad, horned toad, midwife toad, natterjack, newt, eft, salamander, congo eel, axolotl.

**ample** adj large, big, extensive, expansive, broad, wide, full, voluminous, roomy, spacious, commodious, great, considerable, substantial, handsome, generous, bountiful, munificent, liberal, lavish, copious, abundant, plentiful, plenty, unrestricted, profuse, rich.
**E3** insufficient, inadequate, meagre.

**amplify** v enlarge, magnify, expand, dilate, fill out, bulk out, add to, supplement, augment, increase, extend, lengthen, widen, broaden, develop, elaborate, enhance, boost, intensify, strengthen, deepen, heighten, raise.
**E3** reduce, decrease, abridge.

**amputate** v cut off, remove, sever, dissever, separate, dock, lop, curtail, truncate.

**amuse** v entertain, divert, regale, make laugh, tickle (*infml*), crease (*infml*), slay (*infml*), cheer (up), gladden, enliven, please, charm,

delight, enthral, engross, absorb, interest, occupy, recreate, relax.
**E3** bore, displease.

**amusement** n entertainment, diversion, distraction, fun, enjoyment, pleasure, delight, merriment, mirth, hilarity, laughter, joke, prank, game, sport, recreation, hobby, pastime, interest.
**E3** boredom, monotony.

**amusing** adj funny, humorous, hilarious, comical, laughable, ludicrous, droll, witty, facetious, jocular, jolly, enjoyable, pleasant, charming, delightful, entertaining, interesting.
**E3** dull, boring.

**anaemic** adj bloodless, ashen, chalky, livid, pasty, pallid, sallow, whey-faced, pale, wan, colourless, insipid, weak, feeble, ineffectual, enervated, frail, infirm, sickly.
**E3** ruddy, sanguine, full-blooded.

**anaesthetize** v desensitize, numb, deaden, dull, drug, dope, stupefy.

**analogy** n comparison, simile, metaphor, likeness, resemblance, similarity, parallel, correspondence, equivalence, relation, correlation, agreement.

**analyse** v break down, separate, divide, take apart, dissect, anatomize, reduce, resolve, sift, investigate, study, examine, scrutinize, review, interpret, test, judge, evaluate, estimate, consider.

**analysis** n breakdown, separation, division, dissection, reduction, resolution, sifting, investigation, enquiry, study, examination, scrutiny, review, exposition, explication, explanation, interpretation, test, judgement, opinion, evaluation, estimation, reasoning.
**E3** synthesis.

**analytic** adj analytical, dissecting, detailed, in-depth, searching, critical, questioning, enquiring, inquisitive, investigative, diagnostic, systematic, methodical, logical, rational, interpretative, explanatory, expository, studious.

**anarchic** *adj* lawless, ungoverned, anarchistic, libertarian, nihilist, revolutionary, rebellious, mutinous, riotous, chaotic, disordered, confused, disorganized.
**F3** submissive, orderly.

**anarchist** *n* revolutionary, rebel, insurgent, libertarian, nihilist, terrorist.

**anarchy** *n* lawlessness, unrule, misrule, anarchism, revolution, rebellion, insurrection, mutiny, riot, pandemonium, chaos, disorder, confusion.
**F3** rule, control, order.

**anathema** *n* aversion, abhorrence, abomination, object of loathing, bête noire, bugbear, bane, curse, proscription, taboo.

**anatomical terms**

*Anatomical terms include*: aural, biceps, bone, cardiac, cartilage, cerebral, dental, diaphragm, dorsal, duodenal, elbow, epidermis, epiglottis, Fallopian tubes, foreskin, funny bone, gastric, genitalia, gingival, gristle, groin, gullet, hamstring, helix, hepatic, hock, intercostal, jugular, lachrymal, ligament, lumbar, mammary, membral, muscle, nasal, neural, ocular, oesophagus, optical, pectoral, pedal, pulmonary, renal, spine, tendon, triceps, umbilicus, uterus, uvula, voice-box, vulva, windpipe, wisdom tooth, womb. *see also* **bone**.

**ancestor** *n* forebear, forefather, progenitor, predecessor, forerunner, precursor, antecedent.
**F3** descendant.

**ancestral** *adj* familial, parental, genealogical, lineal, hereditary, genetic.

**ancestry** *n* ancestors, forebears, forefathers, progenitors, parentage, family, lineage, line, descent, blood, race, stock, roots, pedigree, genealogy, extraction, derivation, origin, heritage, heredity.

**anchor** *v* moor, berth, tie up, make fast, fasten, attach, affix, fix.

*Types of anchor include*: car, double fluked, grapnel, kedge, killick, mushroom, navy, sea, stocked, stockless, yachtsman.

**ancient** *adj* **1** OLD, aged, time-worn, age-old, antique, antediluvian, prehistoric, fossilized, primeval, immemorial. **2** OLD-FASHIONED, out-of-date, antiquated, archaic, obsolete, bygone, early, original.
**F3 1** recent, contemporary. **2** modern, up-to-date.

**anecdote** *n* story, tale, yarn, sketch, reminiscence.

**angel** *n* **1** *angel of God*: archangel, cherub, seraph, divine messenger, principality. **2** DARLING, treasure, saint, paragon, ideal.
**F3 1** devil, fiend.

*The nine orders of angels are*: seraph, cherub, throne, domination/dominion, virtue, power, principality, archangel, angel.

**angelic** *adj* cherubic, seraphic, celestial, heavenly, divine, holy, pious, saintly, pure, innocent, unworldly, virtuous, lovely, beautiful, adorable.
**F3** devilish, fiendish.

**anger** *n* annoyance, irritation, antagonism, displeasure, irritability, temper, pique, vexation, ire, rage, fury, wrath, exasperation, outrage, indignation, gall, bitterness, rancour, resentment.
**F3** forgiveness, forbearance.
*v* annoy, irritate, aggravate (*infml*),

wind up (*infml*), vex, irk, rile, miff (*infml*), needle, nettle, bother, ruffle, provoke, antagonize, offend, affront, gall, madden, enrage, incense, infuriate, exasperate, outrage.
**F3** please, appease, calm.

**angle** n 1 CORNER, nook, bend, flexure, hook, crook, elbow, knee, crotch, edge, point. 2 ASPECT, outlook, facet, side, approach, direction, position, standpoint, viewpoint, point of view, slant, perspective.

**angry** adj annoyed, cross, irritated, aggravated (*infml*), displeased, uptight (*infml*), irate, mad (*infml*), enraged, incensed, infuriated, furious, raging, passionate, heated, hot, exasperated, outraged, indignant, bitter, resentful.
**F3** content, happy, calm.

**animal** n creature, mammal, beast, brute, barbarian, savage, monster, cur, pig, swine.

---

*Animals include*: cat, dog, hamster, gerbil, mouse, rat, rabbit, hare, fox, badger, beaver, mole, otter, weasel, ferret, ermine, mink, hedgehog, squirrel, horse, pig, cow, bull, goat, sheep; monkey, lemur, gibbon, ape, chimpanzee, orang-utan, baboon, gorilla; seal, sea lion, dolphin, walrus, whale; lion, tiger, cheetah, puma, panther, cougar, jaguar, ocelot, leopard; aardvark, armadillo, wolf, wolverine, hyena, mongoose, skunk, racoon, wombat, platypus, koala, polecat; deer, antelope, gazelle, eland, impala, reindeer, elk, caribou, moose; wallaby, kangaroo, bison, buffalo, gnu, camel, zebra, llama, panda, giant panda, grizzly bear, polar bear, giraffe, hippopotamus, rhinoceros, elephant. *see also* **amphibian**; **bird**; **cattle**; **dog**; **fish**; **insect**; **reptile**.

---

*adj* bestial, brutish, inhuman, savage, wild, instinctive, bodily, physical,

carnal, fleshly, sensual.

**animate** adj alive, living, live, breathing, conscious.
**F3** inanimate.

**animated** adj lively, spirited, buoyant, vibrant, ebullient, vivacious, alive, vital, quick, brisk, vigorous, energetic, active, passionate, impassioned, vehement, ardent, fervent, glowing, radiant, excited, enthusiastic, eager.
**F3** lethargic, sluggish, inert.

**animosity** n ill feeling, ill-will, acrimony, bitterness, rancour, resentment, spite, malice, malignity, malevolence, hate, hatred, loathing, antagonism, hostility, enmity, feud.
**F3** goodwill.

**annex** v 1 ADD, append, affix, attach, fasten, adjoin, join, connect, unite, incorporate. 2 ACQUIRE, appropriate, seize, usurp, occupy, conquer, take over.

**annexe** n wing, extension, attachment, addition, supplement, expansion.

**annihilate** v eliminate, eradicate, obliterate, erase, wipe out, liquidate (*infml*), murder, assassinate, exterminate, extinguish, raze, destroy, abolish.

**anniversary**

---

*Names of wedding anniversary include*: 1st cotton, 2nd paper, 3rd leather, 4th flowers/fruit, 5th wood, 6th iron/sugar, 7th copper/wool, 8th bronze/pottery, 9th pottery/willow, 10th tin, 11th steel, 12th silk/linen, 13th lace, 14th ivory, 15th crystal, 20th china, 25th silver, 30th pearl, 35th coral, 40th ruby, 45th sapphire, 50th gold, 55th emerald, 60th diamond, 70th platinum.

---

**annotation** n note, footnote, gloss, comment, commentary, exegesis, explanation, elucidation.

**announce** v declare, proclaim,

report, state, reveal, disclose, divulge, make known, notify, intimate, promulgate, propound, publish, broadcast, advertise, publicize, blazon.
🖃 suppress.

**announcement** *n* declaration, proclamation, report, statement, communiqué, dispatch, bulletin, notification, intimation, revelation, disclosure, divulgence, publication, broadcast, advertisement.

**announcer** *n* broadcaster, newscaster, newsreader, commentator, compère, master of ceremonies, MC, town crier, herald, messenger.

**annoy** *v* irritate, rile, aggravate (*infml*), displease, anger, vex, irk, madden, exasperate, tease, provoke, ruffle, trouble, disturb, bother, pester, plague, harass, molest.
🖃 please, gratify, comfort.

**annoyance** *n* 1 NUISANCE, pest, disturbance, bother, trouble, bore, bind (*sl*), pain (*infml*), headache (*infml*), tease, provocation. 2 *express one's annoyance*: irritation, aggravation (*infml*), displeasure, anger, vexation, exasperation, harassment.
🖃 2 pleasure.

**annoyed** *adj* irritated, cross, displeased, angry, vexed, piqued, exasperated, provoked, harassed.
🖃 pleased.

**annoying** *adj* irritating, aggravating (*infml*), vexatious, irksome, troublesome, bothersome, tiresome, trying, maddening, exasperating, galling, offensive, teasing, provoking, harassing.
🖃 pleasing, welcome.

**annul** *v* nullify, invalidate, void, rescind, abrogate, suspend, cancel, abolish, quash, repeal, revoke, countermand, negate, retract, recall, reverse.
🖃 enact, restore.

**anoint** *v* 1 OIL, grease, lubricate, embrocate, rub, smear, daub.
2 BLESS, consecrate, sanctify, dedicate.

**anomalous** *adj* abnormal, atypical, exceptional, irregular, inconsistent, incongruous, deviant, freakish, eccentric, peculiar, odd, unusual, singular, rare.
🖃 normal, regular, ordinary.

**anomaly** *n* abnormality, exception, irregularity, inconsistency, incongruity, aberration, deviation, divergence, departure, freak, misfit, eccentricity, peculiarity, oddity, rarity.

**anonymous** *adj* unnamed, nameless, unsigned, unacknowledged, unspecified, unidentified, unknown, incognito, faceless, impersonal, nondescript, unexceptional.
🖃 named, signed, identifiable, distinctive.

**answer** *n* 1 REPLY, acknowledgement, response, reaction, rejoinder, retort, riposte, comeback, retaliation, rebuttal, vindication, defence, plea.
2 SOLUTION, explanation.
*v* 1 REPLY, acknowledge, respond, react, retort, retaliate, refute, solve.
2 *answer one's needs*: fulfil, fill, meet, satisfy, match up to, correspond, correlate, conform, agree, fit, suit, serve, pass.

**answer back** talk back, retort, riposte, retaliate, contradict, disagree, argue, dispute, rebut.

**answerable** *adj* liable, responsible, accountable, chargeable, blameworthy, to blame.

**antagonism** *n* hostility, opposition, rivalry, antipathy, ill feeling, ill-will, animosity, friction, discord, dissension, contention, conflict.
🖃 rapport, sympathy, agreement.

**antagonist** *n* opponent, adversary, enemy, foe, rival, competitor, contestant, contender.

**ally**, supporter.

**antagonistic** *adj* conflicting, opposed, adverse, at variance, incompatible, hostile, belligerent, contentious, unfriendly, ill-disposed, averse.
**Ⓔ** sympathetic, friendly.

**antagonize** *v* alienate, estrange, disaffect, repel, embitter, offend, insult, provoke, annoy, irritate, anger, incense.
**Ⓔ** disarm.

**anthem** *n* hymn, song, chorale, psalm, canticle, chant.

**anthology** *n* selection, collection, compilation, compendium, digest, treasury, miscellany.

**anticipate** *v* **1** FORESTALL, pre-empt, intercept, prevent, obviate, preclude. **2** EXPECT, foresee, predict, forecast, look for, await, look forward to, hope for, bank on, count upon.

**anticlimax** *n* bathos, comedown, let-down, disappointment, fiasco.

**antics** *n* foolery, tomfoolery, silliness, buffoonery, clowning, frolics, capers, skylarking, playfulness, mischief, tricks, monkey-tricks, pranks, stunts, doings.

**antidote** *n* remedy, cure, counter-agent, antitoxin, neutralizer, countermeasure, corrective.

**antipathy** *n* aversion, dislike, hate, hatred, loathing, abhorrence, distaste, disgust, repulsion, antagonism, animosity, ill-will, bad blood, enmity, hostility, opposition, incompatibility.
**Ⓔ** sympathy, affection, rapport.

**antique** *adj* antiquarian, ancient, old, veteran, vintage, quaint, antiquated, old-fashioned, outdated, archaic, obsolete.
*n* antiquity, relic, bygone, period piece, heirloom, curio, museum piece, curiosity, rarity.

**antiquity** *n* ancient times, time immemorial, distant past, olden days,

age, old age, oldness, agedness.
**Ⓔ** modernity, novelty.

**antiseptic** *adj* disinfectant, medicated, aseptic, germ-free, clean, pure, unpolluted, uncontaminated, sterile, sterilized, sanitized, sanitary, hygienic.
*n* disinfectant, germicide, bactericide, purifier, cleanser.

**antisocial** *adj* asocial, unacceptable, disruptive, disorderly, rebellious, belligerent, antagonistic, hostile, unfriendly, unsociable, uncommunicative, reserved, retiring, withdrawn, alienated, unapproachable.
**Ⓔ** sociable, gregarious.

**anxiety** *n* worry, concern, care, distress, nervousness, apprehension, dread, foreboding, misgiving, uneasiness, restlessness, fretfulness, impatience, suspense, tension, stress.
**Ⓔ** calm, composure, serenity.

**anxious** *adj* worried, concerned, nervous, apprehensive, afraid, fearful, uneasy, restless, fretful, impatient, in suspense, on tenterhooks, tense, taut, distressed, disturbed, troubled, tormented, tortured.
**Ⓔ** calm, composed.

**apart** *adv* **1** SEPARATELY, independently, individually, singly, alone, on one's own, by oneself, privately, aside, to one side, away, afar, distant, aloof, excluded, isolated, cut off, separated, divorced, separate, distinct. **2** *tear apart:* to pieces, to bits, into parts, in pieces, in bits, piecemeal.
**Ⓔ 1** connected. **2** together.

**apathetic** *adj* uninterested, uninvolved, indifferent, cool, unemotional, emotionless, impassive, unmoved, unconcerned, cold, unfeeling, numb, unresponsive, passive, listless, unambitious.
**Ⓔ** enthusiastic, involved, concerned, feeling, responsive.

**apathy** n uninterestedness, indifference, coolness, impassivity, unconcern, coldness, insensibility, passivity, listlessness, lethargy, sluggishness, torpor, inertia.
**Ea** enthusiasm, interest, concern.

**ape** v copy, imitate, echo, mirror, parrot, mimic, take off, caricature, parody, mock, counterfeit, affect.
n monkey, chimpanzee, gibbon, gorilla, baboon, orang-utan.

**aplomb** n composure, calmness, equanimity, poise, balance, coolness, confidence, assurance, self-assurance, audacity.
**Ea** discomposure.

**apocryphal** adj unauthenticated, unverified, unsubstantiated, unsupported, questionable, spurious, equivocal, doubtful, dubious, fabricated, concocted, fictitious, imaginary, legendary, mythical.
**Ea** authentic, true.

**apologetic** adj sorry, repentant, penitent, contrite, remorseful, conscience-stricken, regretful, rueful.
**Ea** unrepentant, impenitent, defiant.

**apology** n acknowledgement, confession, excuse, explanation, justification, vindication, defence, plea.
**Ea** defiance.

**appal** v horrify, shock, outrage, disgust, dismay, disconcert, daunt, intimidate, unnerve, alarm, scare, frighten, terrify.
**Ea** reassure, encourage.

**appalling** adj horrifying, horrific, harrowing, shocking, outrageous, atrocious, disgusting, awful, dreadful, frightful, terrible, dire, grim, hideous, ghastly, horrible, horrid, loathsome, daunting, intimidating, unnerving, alarming, frightening, terrifying.
**Ea** reassuring, encouraging.

**apparatus** n machine, appliance, gadget, device, contraption, equipment, gear, tackle, outfit, tools, implements, utensils, materials, machinery, system, mechanism, means.

**apparent** adj seeming, outward, visible, evident, noticeable, perceptible, plain, clear, distinct, marked, unmistakable, obvious, manifest, patent, open, declared.
**Ea** hidden, obscure.

**apparently** adv seemingly, ostensibly, outwardly, superficially, plainly, clearly, obviously, manifestly, patently.

**apparition** n ghost, spectre, phantom, spirit, chimera, vision, manifestation, materialization, presence.

**appeal** n 1 REQUEST, application, petition, suit, solicitation, plea, entreaty, supplication, prayer, invocation. 2 ATTRACTION, allure, interest, fascination, enchantment, charm, attractiveness, winsomeness, beauty, charisma, magnetism.
v 1 appeal for help: ask, request, call, apply, address, petition, sue, solicit, plead, beg, beseech, implore, entreat, supplicate, pray, invoke, call upon.
2 ATTRACT, draw, allure, lure, tempt, entice, invite, interest, engage, fascinate, charm, please.

**appear** v 1 ARRIVE, enter, turn up, attend, materialize, develop, show (up), come into sight, come into view, loom, rise, surface, arise, occur, crop up, come to light, come out, emerge, issue, be published. 2 SEEM, look, turn out. 3 appear in a show: act, perform, play, take part.
**Ea** 1 disappear, vanish.

**appearance** n 1 APPEARING, arrival, advent, coming, rise, emergence, début, introduction.
2 LOOK, expression, face, aspect, air, bearing, demeanour, manner, looks, figure, form, semblance, show, front, guise, illusion, impression, image.
**Ea** 1 disappearance.

**appendix** n addition, appendage,

adjunct, addendum, supplement, epilogue, codicil, postscript, rider.

**appetite** n hunger, stomach, relish, zest, taste, propensity, inclination, liking, desire, longing, yearning, craving, eagerness, passion, zeal.
**F3** distaste.

**appetizing** adj mouthwatering, tempting, inviting, appealing, palatable, tasty, delicious, scrumptious (infml), succulent, piquant, savoury.
**F3** disgusting, distasteful.

**applaud** v clap, cheer, acclaim, compliment, congratulate, approve, commend, praise, laud, eulogize, extol.
**F3** criticize, censure.

**applause** n ovation, clapping, cheering, cheers, acclaim, acclamation, accolade, congratulation, approval, commendation, praise.
**F3** criticism, censure.

**appliance** n machine, device, contrivance, contraption, gadget, tool, implement, instrument, apparatus, mechanism.

**applicable** adj relevant, pertinent, apposite, apt, appropriate, fitting, suited, useful, suitable, fit, proper, valid, legitimate.
**F3** inapplicable, inappropriate.

**applicant** n candidate, interviewee, contestant, competitor, aspirant, suitor, petitioner, inquirer.

**application** n 1 REQUEST, appeal, petition, suit, claim, inquiry.
2 RELEVANCE, pertinence, function, purpose, use, value. 3 DILIGENCE, industry, assiduity, effort, commitment, dedication, perseverance, keenness, attentiveness.

**apply** v 1 REQUEST, ask for, requisition, put in for, appeal, petition, solicit, sue, claim, inquire.
2 apply oneself to a task: address, buckle down, settle down, commit, devote, dedicate, give, direct,

concentrate, study, persevere. 3 USE, exercise, utilize, employ, bring into play, engage, harness, ply, wield, administer, execute, implement, assign, direct, bring to bear, practise, resort to. 4 REFER, relate, be relevant, pertain, fit, suit. 5 apply ointment: put on, spread on, lay on, cover with, paint, anoint, smear, rub.

**appoint** v 1 NAME, nominate, elect, install, choose, select, engage, employ, take on, commission, delegate, assign, allot, designate, command, direct, charge, detail.
2 DECIDE, determine, arrange, settle, fix, set, establish, ordain, decree, destine.
**F3** 1 reject, dismiss, discharge.

**appointment** n 1 ARRANGEMENT, engagement, date, meeting, rendezvous, interview, consultation.
2 JOB, position, situation, post, office, place. 3 NAMING, nomination, election, choosing, choice, selection, commissioning, delegation.

**appraisal** n valuation, rating, survey, inspection, review, examination, once-over (infml), evaluation, assessment, estimate, estimation, judgement, reckoning, opinion, appreciation.

**appreciate** v 1 ENJOY, relish, savour, prize, treasure, value, cherish, admire, respect, regard, esteem, like, welcome, take kindly to.
2 appreciate in value: grow, increase, rise, mount, inflate, gain, strengthen, improve, enhance. 3 UNDERSTAND, comprehend, perceive, realize, recognize, acknowledge, sympathize with, know.
**F3** 1 despise. 2 depreciate. 3 overlook.

**appreciation** n 1 ENJOYMENT, relish, admiration, respect, regard, esteem, gratitude, gratefulness, thankfulness, indebtedness, obligation, liking, sensitivity, responsiveness, valuation, assessment, estimation, judgement.

2 GROWTH, increase, rise, inflation, gain, improvement, enhancement.
3 UNDERSTANDING, comprehension, perception, awareness, realization, recognition, acknowledgement, sympathy, knowledge.
**Fa** 1 ingratitude. 2 depreciation.

**appreciative** *adj* 1 GRATEFUL, thankful, obliged, indebted, pleased.
2 ADMIRING, encouraging, enthusiastic, respectful, sensitive, responsive, perceptive, knowledgeable, conscious, mindful.
**Fa** 1 ungrateful.

**apprehension** *n* dread, foreboding, misgiving, qualm, uneasiness, anxiety, worry, concern, disquiet, alarm, fear, doubt, suspicion, mistrust.

**apprehensive** *adj* nervous, anxious, worried, concerned, uneasy, doubtful, suspicious, mistrustful, distrustful, alarmed, afraid.
**Fa** assured, confident.

**apprentice** *n* trainee, probationer, student, pupil, learner, novice, beginner, starter, recruit, newcomer.
**Fa** expert.

**approach** *v* 1 ADVANCE, move towards, draw near, near, gain on, catch up, reach, meet. 2 APPLY TO, appeal to, sound out. 3 BEGIN, commence, set about, undertake, introduce, mention. 4 RESEMBLE, be like, compare with, approximate, come close.
*n* 1 *the approach of winter*: advance, coming, advent, arrival. 2 ACCESS, road, avenue, way, passage, entrance, doorway, threshold. 3 APPLICATION, appeal, overture, proposition, proposal. 4 ATTITUDE, manner, style, technique, procedure, method, means.

**appropriate** *adj* applicable, relevant, pertinent, to the point, well-chosen, apt, fitting, meet (*fml*), suitable, fit, befitting, becoming, proper, right, correct, spot-on (*infml*), well-timed, timely,

seasonable, opportune.
**Fa** inappropriate, irrelevant, unsuitable.
*v* 1 SEIZE, take, expropriate, commandeer, requisition, confiscate, impound, assume, usurp. 2 STEAL, pocket, filch, pilfer, purloin, embezzle, misappropriate.

**approval** *n* 1 ADMIRATION, esteem, regard, respect, good opinion, liking, appreciation, approbation, favour, recommendation, praise, commendation, acclaim, acclamation, honour, applause.
2 AGREEMENT, concurrence, assent, consent, permission, leave, sanction, authorization, licence, mandate, go-ahead, green light (*infml*), blessing, OK (*infml*), certification, ratification, validation, confirmation, support.
**Fa** 1 disapproval, condemnation.

**approve** *v* 1 ADMIRE, esteem, regard, like, appreciate, favour, recommend, praise, commend, acclaim, applaud. 2 *approve a proposal*: agree to, assent to, consent to, accede to, allow, permit, pass, sanction, authorize, mandate, bless, countenance, OK (*infml*), ratify, rubber-stamp (*infml*), validate, endorse, support, uphold, second, back, accept, adopt, confirm.
**Fa** 1 disapprove, condemn.

**approximate** *adj* estimated, guessed, rough, inexact, loose, close, near, like, similar, relative.
**Fa** exact.
*v* approach, border on, verge on, be tantamount to, resemble.

**approximately** *n* roughly, around, about, circa, more or less, loosely, approaching, close to, nearly, just about.

**apt** *adj* 1 RELEVANT, applicable, apposite, appropriate, fitting, suitable, fit, seemly, proper, correct, accurate, spot-on (*infml*), timely, seasonable. 2 CLEVER, gifted, talented, skilful, expert, intelligent,

quick, sharp. **3** LIABLE, prone,
given, disposed, likely, ready.
**E3** 1 inapt. 2 stupid.

**aptitude** *n* ability, capability,
capacity, faculty, gift, talent, flair,
facility, proficiency, cleverness,
intelligence, quickness, bent,
inclination, leaning, disposition,
tendency.
**E3** inaptitude.

**arbitrary** *adj* **1** RANDOM, chance,
capricious, inconsistent,
discretionary, subjective, instinctive,
unreasoned, illogical, irrational,
unreasonable. **2** DESPOTIC,
tyrannical, dictatorial, autocratic,
absolute, imperious, magisterial,
domineering, overbearing, high-
handed, dogmatic.
**E3** 1 reasoned, rational, circumspect.

**arbitrate** *v* judge, adjudicate,
referee, umpire, mediate, settle,
decide, determine.

**arbitration** *n* judgement,
adjudication, intervention,
mediation, negotiation, settlement,
decision, determination.

**arbitrator** *n* judge, adjudicator,
arbiter, referee, umpire, moderator,
mediator, negotiator, intermediary,
go-between.

**arch** *n* archway, bridge, span, dome,
vault, concave, bend, curve,
curvature, bow, arc, semicircle.
*v* bend, curve, bow, arc, vault,
camber.

*Types of arch include*: basket
handle, convex, corbel, equilateral,
four-centre, Gothic, horseshoe, keel,
lancet, Norman, ogee, parabolic,
round, segmental, shouldered, skew,
stilted, tented, trefoil, Tudor.

**archaic** *adj* antiquated, old-
fashioned, outmoded, old hat (*infml*),
passé, outdated, out-of-date,
obsolete, old, ancient, antique,
quaint, primitive.

**E3** modern, recent.

**archetype** *n* pattern, model,
standard, form, type, prototype,
original, precursor, classic,
paradigm, ideal.

**architect** *n* designer, planner, master
builder, prime mover, originator,
founder, instigator, creator, author,
inventor, engineer, maker,
constructor, shaper.

**architecture and building**

*Architectural and building terms
include*: alcove, annexe, architrave,
baluster, barge-board, baroque, bas
relief, capstone, casement window,
classical, coping stone, Corinthian,
corner-stone, cornice, coving, dado,
decorated, dogtooth, dome, Doric,
dormer, double-glazing, drawbridge,
dry-stone, duplex, Early English,
eaves, Edwardian, elevation,
Elizabethan, façade, fanlight, fascia,
festoon, fillet, finial, flamboyant,
Flemish bond, fletton, fluting, French
window, frieze, frontispiece, gable,
gargoyle, gatehouse, Georgian,
Gothic, groin, groundplan, half-
timbered, Ionic, jamb, lintel, mullion,
Norman, pagoda, pantile, parapet,
pinnacle, plinth, Queen-Anne, rafters,
Regency, reveal, ridge, rococo,
Romanesque, roof, rotunda,
roughcast, sacristy, scroll, soffit,
stucco, terrazzo, Tudor, Tuscan,
wainscot, weathering.

**archives** *n* records, annals,
chronicles, memorials, papers,
documents, deeds, ledgers, registers,
roll.

**ardent** *adj* fervent, fiery, warm,
passionate, impassioned, fierce,
vehement, intense, spirited,
enthusiastic, eager, keen, dedicated,
devoted, zealous.
**E3** apathetic, unenthusiastic.

**arduous** *adj* hard, difficult, tough,
rigorous, severe, harsh, formidable,

strenuous, tiring, taxing, fatiguing,
exhausting, backbreaking, punishing,
gruelling, uphill, laborious, onerous.
**F3** easy.

**area** n locality, neighbourhood,
environment, environs, patch,
terrain, district, region, zone, sector,
department, province, domain,
realm, territory, sphere, field, range,
scope, compass, size, extent, expanse,
width, breadth, stretch, tract, part,
portion, section.

**argue** v 1 QUARREL, squabble,
bicker, row, wrangle, haggle,
remonstrate, join issue, fight, feud,
fall out, disagree, dispute, question,
debate, discuss. 2 REASON, assert,
contend, hold, maintain, claim,
plead, exhibit, display, show,
manifest, demonstrate, indicate,
denote, prove, evidence, suggest,
imply.

**argument** n 1 QUARREL, squabble,
row, wrangle, controversy, debate,
discussion, dispute, disagreement,
clash, conflict, fight, feud.
2 REASONING, reason, logic,
assertion, contention, claim,
demonstration, defence, case,
synopsis, summary, theme.

**argumentative** adj quarrelsome,
contentious, polemical, opinionated,
belligerent, perverse, contrary.
**F3** complaisant.

**arid** adj 1 arid landscape: dry,
parched, waterless, desiccated, torrid,
barren, infertile, unproductive,
desert, waste. 2 DULL, uninteresting,
boring, monotonous, tedious, dry,
sterile, dreary, colourless, lifeless,
spiritless, uninspired.
**F3** 1 fertile. 2 lively.

**arise** v 1 ORIGINATE, begin, start,
commence, derive, stem, spring,
proceed, flow, emerge, issue, appear,
come to light, crop up, occur,
happen, result, ensue, follow. 2 RISE,
get up, stand up, go up, ascend,
climb, mount, lift, soar, tower.

**aristocracy** n upper class, gentry,
nobility, peerage, ruling class,
gentility, élite.
**F3** common people.

**aristocrat** n noble, patrician,
nobleman, noblewoman, peer,
peeress, lord, lady.
**F3** commoner.

**aristocratic** adj upper-class,
highborn, well-born, noble, patrician,
blue-blooded, titled, lordly, courtly,
gentle, thoroughbred, élite.
**F3** plebeian, vulgar.

**arm**[1] n limb, upper limb, appendage,
bough, branch, projection, extension,
offshoot, section, division,
detachment, department.

**arm**[2] v provide, supply, furnish,
issue, equip, rig, outfit, ammunition,
prime, prepare, forearm, gird, steel,
brace, reinforce, strengthen, fortify,
protect.

**armed services**

> *Units in the armed services include:*
> task-force, militia, garrison; *air force:*
> wing, squadron, flight; *army:* patrol,
> troop, corps, platoon, squad, battery,
> company, brigade, battalion, regiment;
> *marines:* Royal Marines,
> commandos; *navy:* fleet, flotilla,
> squadron, convoy. *see also* rank.

**armoured** adj armour-plated, steel-
plated, iron-clad, reinforced,
protected, bullet-proof, bomb-proof.

**armoury** n arsenal, ordnance depot,
ammunition dump, magazine, depot,
repository, stock, stockpile.

**arms** n 1 WEAPONS, weaponry,
firearms, guns, artillery, instruments
of war, armaments, ordnance,
munitions, ammunition. 2 COAT-OF-
ARMS, armorial bearings, insignia,
heraldic device, escutcheon, shield,
crest, heraldry, blazonry.

**army** n armed force, military,
militia, land forces, soldiers, troops,
legions, cohorts, multitude, throng,

host, horde.

**aroma** *n* smell, odour, scent, perfume, fragrance, bouquet, savour.

**aromatic** *adj* perfumed, fragrant, sweet-smelling, balmy, redolent, savoury, spicy, pungent.

**around** *prep* 1 SURROUNDING, round, encircling, encompassing, enclosing, on all sides of, on every side of. 2 *around a dozen*: approximately, roughly, about, circa, more or less.
*adv* 1 EVERYWHERE, all over, in all directions, on all sides, about, here and there, to and fro. 2 CLOSE, close by, near, nearby, at hand.

**arouse** *v* rouse, startle, wake up, waken, awaken, instigate, summon up, call forth, spark, kindle, inflame, whet, sharpen, quicken, animate, excite, prompt, provoke, stimulate, galvanize, goad, spur, incite, agitate, stir up, whip up.
Ɛꓱ calm, lull, quieten.

**arrange** *v* 1 ORDER, tidy, range, array, marshal, dispose, distribute, position, set out, lay out, align, group, class, classify, categorize, sort (out), sift, file, systematize, methodize, regulate, adjust.
2 ORGANIZE, co-ordinate, prepare, fix, plan, project, design, devise, contrive, determine, settle. 3 *arrange music*: adapt, set, score, orchestrate, instrument, harmonize.
Ɛꓱ untidy, disorganize, muddle.

**arrangement** *n* 1 ORDER, array, display, disposition, layout, line-up, grouping, classification, structure, system, method, set-up, organization, preparation, planning, plan, scheme, design, schedule. 2 AGREEMENT, settlement, contract, terms, compromise. 3 ADAPTATION, version, interpretation, setting, score, orchestration, instrumentation, harmonization.

**array** *n* ARRANGEMENT, display, show, exhibition, exposition, assortment, collection, assemblage, muster, order, formation, line-up, parade.
*v* 1 ARRANGE, order, range, dispose, group, line up, align, draw up, marshal, assemble, muster, parade, display, show, exhibit. 2 CLOTHE, dress, robe, deck, adorn, decorate.

**arrest** *v* 1 *arrest a criminal*: capture, catch, seize, nick (*infml*), run in, apprehend, detain. 2 STOP, stem, check, restrain, inhibit, halt, interrupt, stall, delay, slow, retard, block, obstruct, impede, hinder.

**arrival** *n* appearance, entrance, advent, coming, approach, occurrence.
Ɛꓱ departure.

**arrive** *v* reach, get to, appear, materialize, turn up, show up (*infml*), roll up (*infml*), enter, come, occur, happen.
Ɛꓱ depart, leave.

**arrogant** *adj* haughty, supercilious, disdainful, scornful, contemptuous, superior, condescending, patronizing, high and mighty, lordly, overbearing, high-handed, imperious, self-important, presumptuous, assuming, insolent, proud, conceited, boastful.
Ɛꓱ humble, unassuming, bashful.

**art** *n* 1 FINE ART, painting, sculpture, drawing, artwork, craft, artistry, draughtsmanship, craftsmanship. 2 SKILL, knack, technique, method, aptitude, facility, dexterity, finesse, ingenuity, mastery, expertise, profession, trade. 3 ARTFULNESS, cunning, craftiness, slyness, guile, deceit, trickery, astuteness, shrewdness.

---

*Schools of art include*: abstract, action painting, Aestheticism, Art Deco, Art Nouveau, Barbizon, Baroque, Bohemian, Byzantine, classical revival, classicism, Conceptual Art, Constructivism, Cubism, Dadaism, Etruscan art,

# art and craft

Expressionism, Fauvism, Florentine, folk art, Futurism, Gothic, Hellenistic, Impressionism, junk art, Mannerism, medieval art, Minimal Art, Modernism, the Nabis, Naturalism, Neoclassicism, Neoexpressionism, Neoimpressionism, Neo-Plasticism, Op Art, plastic art, Pop Art, Postimpressionism, Post-Modernism, Purism, quattrocento, Realism, renaissance, Rococo, Romanesque, Romanticism, Suprematism, Surrealism, Symbolism, Venetian, Vorticism.

## art and craft

*Arts and crafts include*: painting, oil painting, watercolour, fresco, portraiture; architecture, drawing, sketching, caricature, illustration; graphics, film, video; sculpture, modelling, woodcarving, woodcraft, marquetry, metalwork, enamelling, cloisonné, engraving, etching, pottery, ceramics, mosaic, jewellery, stained glass, photography, lithography, calligraphy, collage, origami, spinning, weaving, batik, silk-screen printing, needlework, tapestry, embroidery, patchwork, crochet, knitting.

**artful** *adj* cunning, crafty, sly, foxy, wily, tricky, scheming, designing, deceitful, devious, subtle, sharp, shrewd, smart, clever, masterly, ingenious, resourceful, skilful, dexterous.
🔁 artless, naïve, ingenuous.
**article** *n* **1** *article in a magazine*: feature, report, story, account, piece, review, commentary, composition, essay, paper. **2** ITEM, thing, object, commodity, unit, part, constituent, piece, portion, division.
**articulate** *adj* distinct, well-spoken, clear, lucid, intelligible, comprehensible, understandable,

coherent, fluent, vocal, expressive, meaningful.
🔁 inarticulate, incoherent.
*v* say, utter, speak, talk, express, voice, vocalize, verbalize, state, pronounce, enunciate, breathe.
**articulation** *n* saying, utterance, speaking, talking, expression, voicing, vocalization, verbalization, pronunciation, enunciation, diction, delivery.
**artificial** *adj* false, fake, bogus, counterfeit, spurious, phoney (*infml*), pseudo, specious, sham, insincere, assumed, affected, mannered, forced, contrived, made-up, feigned, pretended, simulated, imitation, mock, synthetic, plastic, man-made, manufactured, non-natural, unnatural.
🔁 genuine, true, real, natural.
**artisan** *n* craftsman, craftswoman, artificer, journeyman, expert, skilled worker, mechanic, technician.
**artist**

*Types of artist include*: architect, graphic designer, designer, draughtsman, draughtswoman, illustrator, cartoonist, photographer, printer, engraver, goldsmith, silversmith, blacksmith, carpenter, potter, weaver, sculptor, painter; craftsman, craftswoman, master.

**artiste** *n* performer, entertainer, variety artist, vaudevillian, comic, comedian, comedienne, player, trouper, actor, actress.
**artistic** *adj* aesthetic, ornamental, decorative, beautiful, exquisite, elegant, stylish, graceful, harmonious, sensitive, tasteful, refined, cultured, cultivated, skilled, talented, creative, imaginative.
🔁 inelegant, tasteless.
**artistry** *n* craftsmanship, workmanship, skill, craft, talent, flair, brilliance, genius, finesse, style,

mastery, expertise, proficiency, accomplishment, deftness, touch, sensitivity, creativity.

F3 ineptitude.

**as** *conj, prep* **1** WHILE, when. **2** SUCH AS, for example, for instance, like, in the manner of. **3** BECAUSE, since, seeing that, considering that, inasmuch as, being.

**as for** with reference to, as regards, with regard to, on the subject of, in connection with, in relation to, with relation to, with respect to.

**ascend** *v* rise, take off, lift off, go up, move up, go upwards, climb, scale, mount, tower, float up, fly up, soar.

F3 descend, go down.

**ascent** *n* **1** ASCENDING, ascension, climb, climbing, scaling, escalation, rise, rising, mounting. **2** SLOPE, gradient, incline, ramp, hill, elevation.

F3 **1** descent.

**ascertain** *v* find out, learn, discover, determine, fix, establish, settle, locate, detect, identify, verify, confirm, make certain.

**ascribe** *v* attribute, credit, accredit, put down, assign, impute, charge, chalk up to.

**ashamed** *adj* sorry, apologetic, remorseful, contrite, guilty, conscience-stricken, sheepish, embarrassed, blushing, red-faced, mortified, humiliated, abashed, humbled, crestfallen, distressed, discomposed, confused, reluctant, hesitant, shy, self-conscious, bashful, modest, prudish.

F3 shameless, proud, defiant.

**aside** *adv* apart, on one side, in reserve, away, out of the way, separately, in isolation, alone, privately, secretly.

*n* digression, parenthesis, departure, soliloquy, stage whisper, whisper.

**ask** *v* **1** REQUEST, appeal, petition, sue, plead, beg, entreat, implore,

clamour, beseech, pray, supplicate, crave, demand, order, bid, require, seek, solicit, invite, summon. **2** INQUIRE, query, question, interrogate, quiz, press.

**asleep** *adj* sleeping, napping, snoozing, fast asleep, sound asleep, dormant, resting, inactive, inert, unconscious, numb, dozing.

**aspect** *n* angle, direction, elevation, side, facet, feature, face, expression, countenance, appearance, look, air, manner, bearing, attitude, condition, situation, position, standpoint, point of view, view, outlook, prospect, scene.

**aspiration** *n* aim, intent, purpose, endeavour, object, objective, goal, ambition, hope, dream, ideal, wish, desire, yearning, longing, craving, hankering.

**aspire** *v* aim, intend, purpose, seek, pursue, hope, dream, wish, desire, yearn, long, crave, hanker.

**aspiring** *adj* would-be, aspirant, striving, endeavouring, ambitious, enterprising, keen, eager, hopeful, optimistic, wishful, longing.

**assassin** *n* murderer, killer, slayer, cut-throat, executioner, hatchet man (*infml*), gunman, hit-man (*sl*), liquidator (*infml*).

**assassinate** *v* murder, kill, slay, dispatch, hit (*sl*), eliminate (*infml*), liquidate (*infml*).

**assault** *n* **1** ATTACK, offensive, onslaught, blitz, strike, raid, invasion, incursion, storm, storming, charge. **2** *charged with assault*: battery, grievous bodily harm, GBH (*infml*), mugging (*sl*), rape, abuse.

*v* attack, charge, invade, strike, hit, set upon, fall on, beat up (*infml*), mug (*sl*), rape, molest, abuse.

**assemble** *v* **1** GATHER, congregate, muster, rally, convene, meet, join up, flock, group, collect, accumulate, amass, bring together, round up, marshal, mobilize. **2** CONSTRUCT, build, put together, piece together, compose, make, fabricate, manufacture.

**F3 1** scatter, disperse. **2** dismantle.

**assembly** n **1** GATHERING, rally, meeting, convention, conference, convocation, congress, council, group, body, company, congregation, flock, crowd, multitude, throng, collection, assemblage.

**2** CONSTRUCTION, building, fabrication, manufacture.

**assert** v affirm, attest, swear, testify to, allege, claim, contend, maintain, insist, stress, protest, defend, vindicate, uphold, promote, declare, profess, state, pronounce, lay down, advance.

**F3** deny, refute.

**assertion** n affirmation, attestation, word, allegation, claim, contention, insistence, vindication, declaration, profession, statement, pronouncement.

**F3** denial.

**assertive** adj bold, confident, self-assured, forward, pushy, insistent, emphatic, forceful, firm, decided, strong-willed, dogmatic, opinionated, presumptuous, assuming, overbearing, domineering, aggressive.

**F3** timid, diffident.

**assess** v gauge, estimate, evaluate, appraise, review, judge, consider, weigh, size up, compute, determine, fix, value, rate, tax, levy, impose, demand.

**assessment** n gauging, estimation, estimate, evaluation, appraisal, review, judgement, opinion, consideration, calculation, determination, valuation, rating, taxation.

**asset** n strength, resource, virtue, plus (infml), benefit, advantage, blessing, boon, help, aid.

**F3** liability.

**assets** n estate, property,

possessions, goods, holdings, securities, money, wealth, capital, funds, reserves, resources, means.

**assign** v **1** ALLOCATE, apportion, grant, give, dispense, distribute, allot, consign, delegate, name, nominate, designate, appoint, choose, select, determine, set, fix, specify, stipulate. **2** ATTRIBUTE, accredit, ascribe, put down.

**assignment** n commission, errand, task, project, job, position, post, duty, responsibility, charge, appointment, delegation, designation, nomination, selection, allocation, consignment, grant, distribution.

**assist** v help, aid, abet, rally round, co-operate, collaborate, back, second, support, reinforce, sustain, relieve, benefit, serve, enable, facilitate, expedite, boost, further, advance.

**F3** hinder, thwart.

**assistance** n help, aid, succour, co-operation, collaboration, backing, support, reinforcement, relief, benefit, service, boost, furtherance.

**F3** hindrance, resistance.

**assistant** n helper, helpmate, aide, right-hand man, auxiliary, ancillary, subordinate, backer, second, supporter, accomplice, accessory, abettor, collaborator, colleague, partner, ally, confederate, associate.

**associate** v **1** AFFILIATE, confederate, ally, league, join, amalgamate, combine, unite, link, connect, correlate, relate, couple, pair, yoke. **2** associate with bad company: socialize, mingle, mix, fraternize, consort, hang around (infml).

n partner, ally, confederate, affiliate, collaborator, co-worker, mate, colleague, peer, compeer, fellow, comrade, companion, friend, sidekick (infml), assistant, follower.

**association** n **1** ORGANIZATION,

corporation, company, partnership, league, alliance, coalition, confederation, confederacy, federation, affiliation, consortium, cartel, syndicate, union, society, club, fraternity, fellowship, clique, group, band. **2** BOND, tie, connection, correlation, relation, relationship, involvement, intimacy, friendship, companionship, familiarity.

**assorted** *adj* miscellaneous, mixed, varied, different, differing, heterogeneous, diverse, sundry, various, several, manifold.

**assortment** *n* miscellany, medley, pot-pourri, jumble, mixture, variety, diversity, collection, selection, choice, arrangement, grouping.

**assume** *v* **1** PRESUME, surmise, accept, take for granted, expect, understand, deduce, infer, guess, postulate, suppose, think, believe, imagine, fancy. **2** AFFECT, take on, feign, counterfeit, simulate, put on, pretend. **3** *assume command*: undertake, adopt, embrace, seize, arrogate, commandeer, appropriate, usurp, take over.

**assumed** *adj* false, bogus, counterfeit, fake, phoney (*infml*), sham, affected, feigned, simulated, pretended, made-up, fictitious, hypothetical.
Ea true, real, actual.

**assumption** *n* presumption, surmise, inference, supposition, guess, conjecture, theory, hypothesis, premise, postulate, idea, notion, belief, fancy.

**assurance** *n* **1** ASSERTION, declaration, affirmation, guarantee, pledge, promise, vow, word, oath. **2** CONFIDENCE, self-confidence, aplomb, boldness, audacity, courage, nerve, conviction, sureness, certainty.
Ea **2** shyness, doubt, uncertainty.

**assure** *v* affirm, guarantee, warrant, pledge, promise, vow, swear, tell, convince, persuade, encourage,

hearten, reassure, soothe, comfort, boost, strengthen, secure, ensure, confirm.

**assured** *adj* **1** SURE, certain, indisputable, irrefutable, confirmed, positive, definite, settled, fixed, guaranteed, secure. **2** SELF-ASSURED, confident, self-confident, self-possessed, bold, audacious, assertive.
Ea **1** uncertain. **2** shy.

**astonish** *v* surprise, startle, amaze, astound, stun, stupefy, daze, stagger, floor (*infml*), dumbfound, flabbergast (*infml*), shock, confound, bewilder.

**astonishment** *n* surprise, amazement, shock, dismay, consternation, confusion, bewilderment, wonder.

**astounding** *adj* surprising, startling, amazing, astonishing, stunning, breathtaking, stupefying, overwhelming, staggering, shocking, bewildering.

**astray** *adv* adrift, off course, lost, amiss, wrong, off the rails (*infml*), awry, off the mark.

**astute** *adj* shrewd, prudent, sagacious, wise, canny, knowing, intelligent, sharp, penetrating, keen, perceptive, discerning, subtle, clever, crafty, cunning, sly, wily.
Ea stupid, slow.

**asylum** *n* haven, sanctuary, refuge, shelter, retreat, safety.

**asymmetric** *adj* unsymmetrical, unbalanced, uneven, crooked, awry, unequal, disproportionate, irregular.
Ea symmetrical.

**atheism** *n* unbelief, non-belief, disbelief, scepticism, irreligion, ungodliness, godlessness, impiety, infidelity, paganism, heathenism, free-thinking, rationalism.

**atheist** *n* unbeliever, non-believer, disbeliever, sceptic, infidel, pagan, heathen, free-thinker.

**athlete** *n* sportsman, sportswoman, runner, gymnast, competitor, contestant, contender.

**athletic** *adj* fit, energetic, vigorous, active, sporty, muscular, sinewy, brawny, strapping, robust, sturdy, strong, powerful, well-knit, well-proportioned, wiry.

**F3** puny.

**athletics** *n* sports, games, races, track events, field events, exercises, gymnastics.

**atmosphere** *n* **1** AIR, sky, aerospace, heavens, ether. **2** AMBIENCE, environment, surroundings, aura, feel, feeling, mood, spirit, tone, tenor, character, quality, flavour.

**atom** *n* molecule, particle, bit, morsel, crumb, grain, spot, speck, mite, shred, scrap, hint, trace, scintilla, jot, iota, whit.

> *Subatomic particles include:*
> photon, electron, positron, neutrino, anti-neutrino, muon, pion, kaon, proton, anti-proton, neutron, anti-neutron, lambda particle, sigma particle, omega particle, psi particle.

**atrocious** *adj* shocking, appalling, abominable, dreadful, terrible, horrible, hideous, ghastly, heinous, grievous, savage, vicious, monstrous, fiendish, ruthless.

**F3** admirable, fine.

**atrocity** *n* outrage, abomination, enormity, horror, monstrosity, savagery, barbarity, brutality, cruelty, viciousness, evil, villainy, wickedness, vileness, heinousness, hideousness, atrociousness.

**attach** *v* **1** *attach a label*: affix, stick, adhere, fasten, fix, secure, tie, bind, weld, join, unite, connect, link, couple, add, annex. **2** ASCRIBE, attribute, impute, assign, put, place, associate, relate to, belong.

**F3 1** detach, unfasten.

**attachment** *n* **1** ACCESSORY, fitting, fixture, extension, appendage, extra,

supplement, addition, adjunct, codicil. **2** FONDNESS, affection, tenderness, love, liking, partiality, loyalty, devotion, friendship, affinity, attraction, bond, tie, link.

**attack** *n* **1** OFFENSIVE, blitz, bombardment, invasion, incursion, foray, raid, strike, charge, rush, onslaught, assault, battery, aggression, criticism, censure, abuse. **2** SEIZURE, fit, convulsion, paroxysm, spasm, stroke.

*v* **1** invade, raid, strike, storm, charge, assail, assault, set about, set upon, fall on, lay into, do over (*sl*). **2** CRITICIZE, censure, blame, denounce, revile, malign, abuse.

**F3 1** defend, protect.

**attacker** *n* assailant, mugger (*sl*), aggressor, invader, raider, critic, detractor, reviler, abuser, persecutor.

**F3** defender, supporter.

**attain** *v* accomplish, achieve, fulfil, complete, effect, realize, earn, reach, touch, arrive at, grasp, get, acquire, obtain, procure, secure, gain, win, net.

**attainment** *n* accomplishment, achievement, feat, fulfilment, completion, consummation, realization, success, ability, capability, competence, proficiency, skill, art, talent, gift, aptitude, facility, mastery.

**attempt** *n* try, endeavour, shot (*infml*), go (*infml*), stab (*infml*), bash (*infml*), push, effort, struggle, bid, undertaking, venture, trial, experiment.

*v* try, endeavour, have a go (*infml*), aspire, seek, strive, undertake, tackle, venture, experiment.

**attend** *v* **1** *attend a meeting*: be present, go to, frequent, visit. **2** ESCORT, chaperon, accompany, usher, follow, guard, look after, take care of, care for, nurse, tend, minister to, help, serve, wait on. **3** PAY ATTENTION, listen, hear, heed, mind, mark, note, notice, observe.

**attend to** deal with, see to, take care of, look after, manage, direct, control, oversee, supervise.

**attendance** *n* presence, appearance, turnout, audience, house, crowd, gate.

**attendant** *n* aide, helper, assistant, auxiliary, steward, waiter, servant, page, retainer, guide, marshal, usher, escort, companion, follower, guard, custodian.
*adj* accompanying, attached, associated, related, incidental, resultant, consequent, subsequent.

**attention** *n* alertness, vigilance, concentration, heed, notice, observation, regard, mindfulness, awareness, recognition, thought, contemplation, consideration, concern, care, treatment, service.
**≋** inattention, disregard, carelessness.

**attentive** *adj* **1** ALERT, awake, vigilant, watchful, observant, concentrating, heedful, mindful, careful, conscientious.
**2** CONSIDERATE, thoughtful, kind, obliging, accommodating, polite, courteous, devoted.
**≋ 1** inattentive, heedless.
**2** inconsiderate.

**attitude** *n* feeling, disposition, mood, aspect, manner, bearing, pose, posture, stance, position, point of view, opinion, view, outlook, perspective, approach.

**attract** *v* pull, draw, lure, allure, entice, seduce, tempt, invite, induce, incline, appeal to, interest, engage, fascinate, enchant, charm, bewitch, captivate, excite.
**≋** repel, disgust.

**attraction** *n* pull, draw, magnetism, lure, allure, bait, enticement, inducement, seduction, temptation, invitation, appeal, interest, fascination, enchantment, charm, captivation.

**≋** repulsion.

**attractive** *adj* pretty, fair, fetching, good-looking, handsome, beautiful, gorgeous, stunning, glamorous, lovely, pleasant, pleasing, agreeable, appealing, winsome, winning, enticing, seductive, tempting, inviting, interesting, engaging, fascinating, charming, captivating, magnetic.
**≋** unattractive, repellent.

**attribute** *v* ascribe, accredit, credit, impute, assign, put down, blame, charge, refer, apply.
*n* property, quality, virtue, point, aspect, facet, feature, trait, characteristic, idiosyncrasy, peculiarity, quirk, note, mark, sign, symbol.

**auburn** *adj* red, chestnut, tawny, russet, copper, Titian.

**audible** *adj* clear, distinct, recognizable, perceptible, discernible, detectable, appreciable.
**≋** inaudible, silent, unclear.

**audience** *n* spectators, onlookers, house, auditorium, listeners, viewers, crowd, turnout, gathering, assembly, congregation, fans, devotees, regulars, following, public.

**audit** *n* examination, inspection, check, verification, investigation, scrutiny, analysis, review, statement, balancing.

**augur** *v* bode, forebode, herald, presage, portend, prophesy, predict, promise, signify.

**auspices** *n* aegis, authority, patronage, sponsorship, backing, support, protection, charge, care, supervision, control, influence, guidance.

**auspicious** *adj* favourable, propitious, encouraging, cheerful, bright, rosy, promising, hopeful, optimistic, fortunate, lucky, opportune, happy, prosperous.
**≋** inauspicious, ominous.

**austere** *adj* **1** STARK, bleak, plain,

simple, unadorned, grim, forbidding.
**2** SEVERE, stern, strict, cold, formal,
rigid, rigorous, exacting, hard, harsh,
spartan, grave, serious, solemn,
sober, abstemious, self-denying,
restrained, economical, frugal,
ascetic, self-disciplined, puritanical,
chaste.
**F3** 1 ornate, elaborate. 2 genial.

**austerity** n  plainness, simplicity,
severity, coldness, formality,
hardness, harshness, solemnity,
abstemiousness, abstinence,
economy, asceticism, puritanism.
**F3** elaborateness, materialism.

**authentic** adj  genuine, true, real,
actual, certain, bona fide, legitimate,
honest, valid, original, pure, factual,
accurate, true-to-life, faithful,
reliable, trustworthy.
**F3** false, fake, counterfeit, spurious.

**authenticate** v  guarantee, warrant,
vouch for, attest, authorize, accredit,
validate, certify, endorse, confirm,
verify, corroborate.

**authenticity** n  genuineness,
certainty, authoritativeness, validity,
truth, veracity, truthfulness, honesty,
accuracy, correctness, faithfulness,
fidelity, reliability, dependability,
trustworthiness.
**F3** spuriousness, invalidity.

**author** n  **1** WRITER, novelist,
dramatist, playwright, composer,
pen, penman, penwoman.
**2** CREATOR, founder, originator,
initiator, parent, prime mover,
mover, inventor, designer, architect,
planner, maker, producer.

**authoritarian** adj  strict,
disciplinarian, severe, harsh, rigid,
inflexible, unyielding, dogmatic,
doctrinaire, absolute, autocratic,
dictatorial, despotic, tyrannical,
oppressive, domineering, imperious.
**F3** liberal.

**authoritative** adj  scholarly, learned,
official, authorized, legitimate, valid,
approved, sanctioned, accepted,

definitive, decisive, authentic,
factual, true, truthful, accurate,
faithful, convincing, sound, reliable,
dependable, trustworthy.
**F3** unofficial, unreliable.

**authority** n  **1** SOVEREIGNTY,
supremacy, rule, sway, control,
dominion, influence, power, force,
government, administration,
officialdom. **2** AUTHORIZATION,
permission, sanction, permit,
warrant, licence, credentials, right,
prerogative. **3** an authority on
antiques: expert, pundit, connoisseur,
specialist, professional, master,
scholar.

**authorize** v  legalize, validate, ratify,
confirm, license, entitle, accredit,
empower, enable, commission,
warrant, permit, allow, consent to,
sanction, approve, give the go-ahead.

**autocracy** n  absolutism,
totalitarianism, dictatorship,
despotism, tyranny,
authoritarianism, fascism.
**F3** democracy.

**autocrat** n  absolutist, totalitarian,
dictator, despot, tyrant,
authoritarian, (little) Hitler (infml),
fascist.

**autocratic** adj  absolute, all-
powerful, totalitarian, despotic,
tyrannical, authoritarian, dictatorial,
domineering, overbearing, imperious.
**F3** democratic, liberal.

**automatic** adj  **1** AUTOMATED, self-
activating, mechanical, mechanized,
programmed, self-regulating,
computerized, push-button, robotic,
self-propelling, unmanned. **2**
SPONTANEOUS, reflex, involuntary,
unwilled, unconscious, unthinking,
natural, instinctive, routine,
necessary, certain, inevitable,
unavoidable, inescapable.

**autonomy** n  self-government, self-
rule, home rule, sovereignty,
independence, self-determination,
freedom, free will.

subjection, compulsion.

**auxiliary** *adj* ancillary, assistant, subsidiary, accessory, secondary, supporting, supportive, helping, assisting, aiding, extra, supplementary, spare, reserve, back-up, emergency, substitute.

**available** *adj* free, vacant, to hand, within reach, at hand, accessible, handy, convenient, on hand, ready, on tap, obtainable.
**F3** unavailable.

**avalanche** *n* landslide, landslip, cascade, torrent, deluge, flood, inundation, barrage.

**avant-garde** *adj* innovative, innovatory, pioneering, experimental, unconventional, far-out (*sl*), way-out (*sl*), progressive, advanced, forward-looking, enterprising, inventive.
**F3** conservative.

**avarice** *n* covetousness, rapacity, acquisitiveness, greed, greediness, meanness.
**F3** generosity, liberality.

**avaricious** *adj* covetous, grasping, rapacious, acquisitive, greedy, mercenary, mean, miserly.
**F3** generous.

**avenge** *v* take revenge for, take vengeance for, punish, requite, repay, retaliate.

**average** *n* mean, mid-point, norm, standard, rule, par, medium, run.
**F3** extreme, exception.
*adj* mean, medial, median, middle, intermediate, medium, moderate, satisfactory, fair, mediocre, middling, indifferent, so-so (*infml*), passable, tolerable, undistinguished, run-of-the-mill, ordinary, everyday, common, usual, normal, regular, standard, typical, unexceptional.
**F3** extreme, exceptional, remarkable.

**averse** *adj* reluctant, unwilling, loth, disinclined, ill-disposed, hostile, opposed, antagonistic, unfavourable.
**F3** willing, keen, sympathetic.

**aversion** *n* dislike, hate, hatred,

loathing, detestation, abhorrence, abomination, horror, phobia, reluctance, unwillingness, disinclination, distaste, disgust, revulsion, repugnance, repulsion, hostility, opposition, antagonism.
**F3** liking, sympathy, desire.

**avert** *v* turn away, deflect, turn aside, parry, fend off, ward off, stave off, forestall, frustrate, prevent, obviate, avoid, evade.

**aviation** *n* aeronautics, flying, flight, aircraft industry.

**avid** *adj* eager, earnest, keen, enthusiastic, fanatical, devoted, dedicated, zealous, ardent, fervent, intense, passionate, insatiable, ravenous, hungry, thirsty, greedy, grasping, covetous.
**F3** indifferent.

**avoid** *v* evade, elude, sidestep, dodge, shirk, duck (*infml*), escape, get out of, bypass, circumvent, balk, prevent, avert, shun, abstain from, refrain from, steer clear of.

**avoidable** *adj* escapable, preventable.
**F3** inevitable.

**avowed** *adj* sworn, declared, professed, self-proclaimed, self-confessed, confessed, admitted, acknowledged, open, overt.

**awake** *v* awaken, waken, wake, wake up, rouse, arouse.
*adj* wakeful, wide-awake, aroused, alert, vigilant, watchful, observant, attentive, conscious, aware, sensitive, alive.

**awakening** *n* awaking, wakening, waking, rousing, arousal, stimulation, animating, enlivening, activation, revival, birth.

**award** *v* give, present, distribute, dispense, bestow, confer, accord, endow, gift, grant, allot, apportion, assign, allow, determine.
*n* prize, trophy, decoration, medal, presentation, dispensation, bestowal, conferral, endowment, gift, grant,

allotment, allowance, adjudication, judgement, decision, order.

**aware** *adj* conscious, alive to, sensitive, appreciative, sentient, familiar, conversant, acquainted, informed, enlightened, au courant, knowing, knowledgeable, cognizant, mindful, heedful, attentive, observant, sharp, alert, on the ball (*infml*), shrewd, sensible.
**E3** unaware, oblivious, insensitive.

**awe** *n* wonder, veneration, reverence, respect, admiration, amazement, astonishment, fear, terror, dread, apprehension.
**E3** contempt.

**awe-inspiring** *adj* wonderful, sublime, magnificent, stupendous, overwhelming, breathtaking, stupefying, stunning, astonishing, amazing, impressive, imposing, majestic, solemn, moving, awesome, formidable, daunting, intimidating, fearsome.
**E3** contemptible, tame.

**awful** *adj* terrible, dreadful, fearful, frightful, ghastly, unpleasant, nasty, horrible, hideous, ugly, gruesome, dire, abysmal, atrocious, horrific, shocking, appalling, alarming, spine-chilling.

**E3** wonderful, excellent.

**awkward** *adj* **1** CLUMSY, gauche, inept, inexpert, unskilful, bungling, ham-fisted, unco-ordinated, ungainly, graceless, ungraceful, inelegant, cumbersome, unwieldy, inconvenient, difficult, fiddly, delicate, troublesome, perplexing. **2** *feeling awkward in their presence*: uncomfortable, ill at ease, embarrassed. **3** OBSTINATE, stubborn, unco-operative, irritable, touchy, prickly, rude, unpleasant.
**E3 1** graceful, elegant, convenient, handy. **2** comfortable, relaxed. **3** amenable, pleasant.

**axe** *n* hatchet, chopper, cleaver, tomahawk, battle-axe.
*v* **1** CUT (DOWN), fell, hew, chop, cleave, split. **2** CANCEL, terminate, discontinue, remove, withdraw, eliminate, get rid of, throw out, dismiss, discharge, sack (*infml*), fire (*infml*).

**axiom** *n* principle, fundamental, truth, truism, precept, dictum, byword, maxim, adage, aphorism.

**axis** *n* centre-line, vertical, horizontal, pivot, hinge.

**axle** *n* shaft, spindle, rod, pin, pivot.

# B

**babble** *v* **1** CHATTER, gabble, jabber, cackle, prate, mutter, mumble, murmur. **2** *the stream babbled*: burble, gurgle.
*n* chatter, gabble, clamour, hubbub, gibberish, burble, murmur.

**baby** *n* babe, infant, suckling, child, tiny, toddler.
*adj* miniature, small-scale, mini (*infml*), midget, small, little, tiny, minute, diminutive.

**babyish** *adj* childish, juvenile,

puerile, infantile, silly, foolish, soft (*infml*), sissy (*infml*), baby, young, immature, naïve.
**E3** mature, precocious.

**back** *n* rear, stern, end, tail, tail end, hind part, hindquarters, posterior, backside, reverse.
**E3** front, face.
*v* **1** GO BACKWARDS, reverse, recede, regress, backtrack, retreat, retire, withdraw, back away, recoil. **2** SUPPORT, sustain, assist, side with,

champion, advocate, encourage, promote, boost, favour, sanction, countenance, endorse, second, countersign, sponsor, finance, subsidize, underwrite.

**F3** 1 advance, approach. 2 discourage, weaken.

*adj* rear, end, tail, posterior, hind, hindmost, reverse.

**F3** 1 front.

**back down** concede, yield, give in, surrender, submit, retreat, withdraw, back-pedal.

**back out** abandon, give up, chicken out (*infml*), withdraw, pull out (*infml*), resign, recant, go back on, cancel.

**back up** confirm, corroborate, substantiate, endorse, second, champion, support, reinforce, bolster, assist, aid.

**F3** let down.

**backbone** *n* 1 SPINE, spinal column, vertebrae, vertebral column, mainstay, support, core, foundation, basis, character. 2 COURAGE, mettle, pluck, nerve, grit, determination, resolve, tenacity, steadfastness, toughness, stamina, strength, power.

**F3** 2 spinelessness, weakness.

**backfire** *v* recoil, rebound, ricochet, boomerang, miscarry, fail, flop.

**background** *n* 1 SETTING, surroundings, environment, context, circumstances. 2 HISTORY, record, credentials, experience, grounding, preparation, education, upbringing, breeding, culture, tradition.

**backing** *n* support, accompaniment, aid, assistance, helpers, championing, advocacy, encouragement, moral support, favour, sanction, promotion, endorsement, seconding, patronage, sponsorship, finance, funds, grant, subsidy.

**backlash** *n* reaction, response, repercussion, reprisal, retaliation, recoil, kickback, backfire, boomerang.

**backlog** *n* accumulation, stock,

supply, resources, reserve, reserves, excess.

**backsliding** *n* lapse, relapse, apostasy, defection, desertion, defaulting.

**backward** *adj* 1 *a backward step*: retrograde, retrogressive, regressive. 2 SHY, bashful, reluctant, unwilling, hesitant, hesitating, wavering, slow, behind, behindhand, late, immature, underdeveloped, retarded, subnormal, stupid.

**F3** 1 forward. 2 precocious.

**bacteria** *n* germs, bugs (*infml*), viruses, microbes, micro-organisms, bacilli.

**bad** *adj* 1 UNPLEASANT, disagreeable, nasty, undesirable, unfortunate, distressing, adverse, detrimental, harmful, damaging, injurious, serious, grave, severe, harsh. 2 EVIL, wicked, sinful, criminal, corrupt, immoral, vile. 3 *bad workmanship*: poor, inferior, substandard, imperfect, faulty, defective, deficient, unsatisfactory, useless. 4 ROTTEN, mouldy, decayed, spoilt, putrid, rancid, sour, off, tainted, contaminated. 5 *a bad child*: naughty, mischievous, ill-behaved, disobedient.

**F3** 1 good, pleasant, mild, slight. 2 virtuous. 3 skilled. 4 fresh. 5 well-behaved.

**badge** *n* identification, emblem, device, insignia, sign, mark, token, stamp, brand, trademark, logo.

**badly** *adv* 1 GREATLY, extremely, exceedingly, intensely, deeply, acutely, bitterly, painfully, seriously, desperately, severely, critically, crucially. 2 WICKEDLY, criminally, immorally, shamefully, unfairly. 3 WRONG, wrongly, incorrectly, improperly, defectively, faultily, imperfectly, inadequately, unsatisfactorily, poorly, incompetently, negligently, carelessly. 4 UNFAVOURABLY,

adversely, unfortunately, unsuccessfully.
**F3** 3 well.

**bad-tempered** *adj* irritable, cross, crotchety, crabbed, crabby, snappy, grumpy, querulous, petulant, fractious, stroppy (*infml*).
**F3** good-tempered, genial, equable.

**baffle** *v* puzzle, perplex, mystify, bemuse, bewilder, confuse, confound, bamboozle (*infml*), flummox (*infml*), daze, upset, disconcert, foil, thwart, frustrate, hinder, check, defeat, stump (*infml*).
**F3** enlighten, help.

**bag** *v* 1 CATCH, capture, trap, land, kill, shoot. 2 OBTAIN, acquire, get, gain, corner, take, grab, appropriate, commandeer, reserve.
*n* container, sack, case, suitcase, grip, carrier, hold-all, handbag, shoulder-bag, satchel, rucksack, haversack, pack.

**baggage** *n* luggage, suitcases, bags, belongings, things, equipment, gear, paraphernalia, impedimenta (*fml*).

**baggy** *adj* loose, slack, roomy, ill-fitting, billowing, bulging, floppy, sagging, droopy.
**F3** tight, firm.

**bail** *n* security, surety, pledge, bond, guarantee, warranty.

**bail out**[1] help, aid, assist, relieve, rescue, finance.

**bail out**[2], **bale out** withdraw, retreat, quit, back out, cop out (*sl*), escape.

**bait** *n* lure, incentive, inducement, bribe, temptation, enticement, allurement, attraction.
**F3** disincentive.
*v* tease, provoke, goad, irritate, annoy, irk, needle (*infml*), harass, persecute, torment.

**balance** *v* 1 STEADY, poise, stabilize, level, square, equalize, equate, match, counterbalance, counteract, neutralize, offset, adjust. 2 COMPARE, consider, weigh, estimate.

**F3** 1 unbalance, overbalance.
*n* 1 EQUILIBRIUM, steadiness, stability, evenness, symmetry, equality, parity, equity, equivalence, correspondence. 2 COMPOSURE, self-possession, poise, equanimity. 3 REMAINDER, rest, residue, surplus, difference.
**F3** 1 imbalance, instability.

**balcony** *n* terrace, veranda, gallery, upper circle, gods.

**bald** *adj* 1 BALD-HEADED, hairless, smooth, uncovered. 2 BARE, naked, unadorned, plain, simple, severe, stark, barren, treeless. 3 *a bald statement*: forthright, direct, straight, outright, downright, straightforward.
**F3** 1 hairy, hirsute. 2 adorned.

**bale** *n* bundle, truss, pack, package, parcel.

**bale out** *see* **bail out**[2].

**balk, baulk** *v* 1 FLINCH, recoil, shrink, jib, boggle, hesitate, refuse, resist, dodge, evade, shirk. 2 THWART, frustrate, foil, forestall, disconcert, baffle, hinder, obstruct, check, stall, bar, prevent, defeat, counteract.

**ball**[1] *n* sphere, globe, orb, globule, drop, conglomeration, pellet, pill, shot, bullet, slug (*infml*).

**ball**[2] *n* dance, dinner-dance, party, soirée, masquerade, carnival, assembly.

**ballad** *n* poem, song, folk-song, shanty, carol, ditty.

**ballet**

*Terms used in ballet include*: à pointe, arabesque, attitude, ballerina, prima ballerina, ballon, barre, battement, batterie, battu, bourrée, capriole, chassé, choreography, ciseaux, company, corps de ballet, coryphée, divertissement, écarté, élévation, entrechat, fish dive, five positions, fouetté, fouetté en tournant, glissade, jeté, grand jeté, leotard, pas de deux, pas de seul, pirouette, plié, pointes, sur les pointes, port de bras, principal male dancer, régisseur, répétiteur, ballet shoe, point shoe, splits, stulchak, tutu.

**ballot** n  poll, polling, vote, voting, election, referendum, plebiscite.

**ban** v  forbid, prohibit, disallow, proscribe, bar, exclude, ostracize, outlaw, banish, suppress, restrict.
**E3** allow, permit, authorize.
n  prohibition, embargo, veto, boycott, stoppage, restriction, suppression, censorship, outlawry, proscription, condemnation, denunciation, curse, taboo.
**E3** permission, dispensation.

**banal** adj  trite, commonplace, ordinary, everyday, humdrum, boring, unimaginative, hackneyed, clichéed, stock, stereotyped, corny (infml), stale, threadbare, tired, empty.
**E3** original, fresh, imaginative.

**band**¹ n  strip, belt, ribbon, tape, bandage, binding, tie, ligature, bond, strap, cord, chain.

**band**² n  **1** TROOP, gang, crew, group, herd, flock, party, body, association, company, society, club, clique. **2** the band played on: group, orchestra, ensemble.
v  group, gather, join, unite, ally, collaborate, consolidate, amalgamate, merge, affiliate, federate.
**E3** disband, disperse.

**bandage** n  dressing, plaster, compress, ligature, tourniquet, swathe, swaddle.
v  bind, dress, cover, swathe, swaddle.

**bandit** n  robber, thief, brigand, marauder, outlaw, highwayman, pirate, buccaneer, hijacker, cowboy, gunman, desperado, gangster.

**bandy**¹ v  exchange, swap, trade, barter, interchange, reciprocate, pass, toss, throw.

**bandy**² adj  bandy-legged, bow-

legged, curved, bowed, bent, crooked.

**bang** n  **1** BLOW, hit, knock, bump, crash, collision, smack, punch, thump, wallop (infml), stroke, whack (infml). **2** a loud bang: explosion, detonation, pop, boom, clap, peal, clang, clash, thud, thump, slam, noise, report, shot.
v  **1** STRIKE, hit, bash, knock, bump, rap, drum, hammer, pound, thump, stamp. **2** EXPLODE, burst, detonate, boom, echo, resound, crash, slam, clatter, clang, peal, thunder.
adv  straight, directly, headlong, right, precisely, slap, smack, hard, noisily, suddenly, abruptly.

**banish** v  expel, eject, evict, deport, transport, exile, outlaw, ban, bar, debar, exclude, shut out, ostracize, excommunicate, dismiss, oust, dislodge, remove, get rid of, discard, dispel, eliminate, eradicate.
**E3** recall, welcome.

**banishment** n  expulsion, eviction, deportation, expatriation, transportation, exile, outlawry, ostracism, excommunication.
**E3** return, recall, welcome.

**bank**¹ n  accumulation, fund, pool, reservoir, depository, repository, treasury, savings, reserve, store, stock, stockpile, hoard, cache.
v  deposit, save, keep, store, accumulate, stockpile.
**E3** spend.

**bank**² n  heap, pile, mass, mound, earthwork, ridge, rampart, embankment, side, slope, tilt, edge, shore.
v  **1** HEAP, pile, stack, mass, amass, accumulate, mound, drift. **2** SLOPE, incline, pitch, slant, tilt, tip.

**bank**³ n  array, panel, bench, group, tier, rank, line, row, series, succession, sequence, train.

**bankrupt** adj  insolvent, in liquidation, ruined, failed, beggared, destitute, impoverished, broke (*infml*), spent, exhausted, depleted, lacking.

🔁 solvent, wealthy.

*n* insolvent, debtor, pauper.

**banner** *n* flag, standard, colours, ensign, pennant, streamer.

**banquet** *n* feast, dinner, meal, repast (*fml*), treat.

**banter** *n* joking, jesting, pleasantry, badinage, repartee, word play, chaff, chaffing, kidding (*infml*), ribbing (*sl*), derision, mockery, ridicule.

**baptism** *n* christening, dedication, beginning, initiation, introduction, debut, launch, launching, immersion, sprinkling, purification.

**baptize** *v* christen, name, call, term, style, title, introduce, initiate, enrol, recruit, immerse, sprinkle, purify, cleanse.

**bar** *n* **1** PUBLIC HOUSE, pub (*infml*), inn, tavern, saloon, lounge, counter. **2** SLAB, block, lump, chunk, wedge, ingot, nugget. **3** ROD, stick, shaft, pole, stake, stanchion, batten, crosspiece, rail, railing, paling, barricade. **4** OBSTACLE, impediment, hindrance, obstruction, barrier, stop, check, deterrent.

*v* **1** EXCLUDE, debar, ban, forbid, prohibit, prevent, preclude, hinder, obstruct, restrain. **2** *bar the door*: barricade, lock, bolt, latch, fasten, secure.

**barbarian** *n* savage, brute, ruffian, hooligan, vandal, lout, oaf, boor, philistine, ignoramus, illiterate.

**barbaric** *adj* barbarous, primitive, wild, savage, fierce, ferocious, cruel, inhuman, brutal, brutish, uncivilized, uncouth, vulgar, coarse, crude, rude.

🔁 humane, civilized, gracious.

**barbarity** *n* barbarousness, wildness, savagery, ferocity, viciousness, cruelty, inhumanity, brutality, brutishness, rudeness.

🔁 civilization, humanity, civility.

**barbed** *adj* **1** PRICKLY, spiny, thorny, spiked, pronged, hooked,

jagged, toothed, pointed. **2** *a barbed remark*: cutting, caustic, acid, hurtful, unkind, nasty, snide, hostile, critical.

**bare** *adj* **1** NAKED, nude, unclothed, undressed, stripped, denuded, uncovered, exposed. **2** PLAIN, simple, unadorned, unfurnished, empty, barren, bald, stark, basic, essential.

🔁 **1** clothed. **2** decorated, detailed.

**barely** *adv* hardly, scarcely, only just, just, almost.

**bargain** *n* **1** DEAL, transaction, contract, treaty, pact, pledge, promise, agreement, understanding, arrangement, negotiation. **2** DISCOUNT, reduction, snip, giveaway, special offer.

*v* negotiate, haggle, deal, trade, traffic, barter, buy, sell, transact, contract, covenant, promise, agree.

**bargain for** expect, anticipate, plan for, include, reckon on, look for, foresee, imagine, contemplate, consider.

**barge** *v* bump, hit, collide, impinge, shove, elbow, push (in), muscle in, butt in, interrupt, gatecrash, intrude, interfere.

*n* canal-boat, flatboat, narrow-boat, houseboat, lighter.

**bark** *n* yap, woof, yelp, snap, snarl, growl, bay, howl.

*v* yap, woof, yelp, snap, snarl, growl, bay, howl.

**baroque** *adj* elaborate, ornate, rococo, florid, flamboyant, exuberant, vigorous, bold, convoluted, overdecorated, overwrought, extravagant, fanciful, fantastic, grotesque.

🔁 plain, simple.

**barracks** *n* garrison, camp, encampment, guardhouse, quarters, billet, lodging, accommodation.

**barrage** *n* bombardment, shelling, gunfire, cannonade, broadside, volley, salvo, burst, assault, attack, onset, onslaught, deluge, torrent, stream, storm, hail, rain, shower, mass, profusion.

**barrel** n cask, keg, tun, butt, water-butt.

**barren** adj **1** ARID, dry, desert, desolate, waste, empty, flat, dull, uninteresting, uninspiring, uninformative, uninstructive, unrewarding, unproductive, profitless, unfruitful, fruitless, pointless, useless, boring. **2** INFERTILE, sterile, childless, unprolific, unbearing.
**Ⓕ** **1** productive, fruitful, useful. **2** fertile.

**barricade** n blockade, obstruction, barrier, fence, stockade, bulwark, rampart, protection.
v block, obstruct, bar, fortify, defend, protect.

**barrier** n **1** WALL, fence, railing, barricade, blockade, boom, rampart, fortification, ditch, frontier, boundary, bar, check. **2** a barrier to success: obstacle, hurdle, stumbling-block, impediment, obstruction, hindrance, handicap, limitation, restriction, drawback, difficulty.

**bartender** n barman, barmaid, barkeeper, publican.

**barter** v exchange, swap, trade, traffic, deal, negotiate, bargain, haggle.

**base** n **1** the base of the statue: bottom, foot, pedestal, plinth, stand, rest, support, foundation, bed, groundwork. **2** BASIS, fundamental, essential, principal, key, heart, core, essence, root, origin, source.
**3** HEADQUARTERS, centre, post, station, camp, settlement, home, starting point.
v establish, found, ground, locate, station, build, construct, derive, depend, hinge.

**baseless** adj groundless, unfounded, unsupported, unsubstantiated, unauthenticated,

unconfirmed, unjustified, uncalled-for, gratuitous.
**Ⓕ** justifiable.

**bashful** adj shy, retiring, backward, reticent, reserved, unforthcoming, hesitant, shrinking, nervous, timid, coy, diffident, modest, inhibited, self-conscious, embarrassed, blushing, abashed, shamefaced, sheepish.
**Ⓕ** bold, confident, aggressive.

**basic** adj fundamental, elementary, primary, root, underlying, key, central, inherent, intrinsic, essential, indispensable, vital, necessary, important.
**Ⓕ** inessential, minor, peripheral.

**basically** adv fundamentally, at bottom, at heart, inherently, intrinsically, essentially, principally, primarily.

**basics** n fundamentals, rudiments, principles, essentials, necessaries, practicalities, brass tacks (infml), grass roots, bedrock, rock bottom, core, facts.

**basin** n bowl, dish, sink, crater, cavity, hollow, depression, dip.

**basis** n base, bottom, footing, support, foundation, ground, groundwork, fundamental, premise, principle, essential, heart, core, thrust.

**bask** v sunbathe, lie, lounge, relax, laze, wallow, revel, delight in, enjoy, relish, savour.

**basket** n hamper, creel, pannier, punnet, bassinet.

**bass** adj deep, low, low-toned, grave, resonant.

**bastion** n stronghold, citadel, fortress, defence, bulwark, mainstay, support, prop, pillar, rock.

**batch** n lot, consignment, parcel, pack, bunch, set, assortment, collection, assemblage, group, contingent, amount, quantity.

**bath** n wash, scrub, soak, shower, douche, tub, Jacuzzi®.
v bathe, wash, clean, soak, shower.

**bathe** v swim, wet, moisten, immerse, wash, cleanse, rinse, soak, steep, flood, cover, suffuse.
n swim, dip, paddle, wash, rinse, soak.

**battalion** n army, force, brigade, regiment, squadron, company, platoon, division, contingent, legion, horde, multitude, throng, host, mass, herd.

**batter** v beat, pound, pummel, buffet, smash, dash, pelt, lash, thrash, wallop (infml), abuse, maltreat, ill-treat, manhandle, maul, assault, hurt, injure, bruise, disfigure, mangle, distress, crush, demolish, destroy, ruin, shatter.

**battered** adj beaten, abused, ill-treated, injured, bruised, weather-beaten, dilapidated, tumbledown, ramshackle, crumbling, damaged, crushed.

**battle** n war, warfare, hostilities, action, conflict, strife, combat, fight, engagement, encounter, attack, fray, skirmish, clash, struggle, contest, campaign, crusade, row, disagreement, dispute, debate, controversy.
v fight, combat, war, feud, contend, struggle, strive, campaign, crusade, agitate, clamour, contest, argue, dispute.

**battle-cry** n war cry, war song, slogan, motto, watchword, catchword.

**baulk** see balk.

**bay**¹ n gulf, bight, arm, inlet, cove.

**bay**² n recess, alcove, niche, nook, opening, compartment, cubicle, booth, stall, carrel.

**bay**³ v howl, roar, bellow, bell, bawl, cry, holler (infml), bark.

**bazaar** n market, marketplace, mart, exchange, sale, fair, fête, bring-and-buy.

**be** v 1 EXIST, breathe, live, inhabit, reside, dwell. 2 STAY, remain, abide, last, endure, persist, continue, survive, stand, prevail, obtain. 3 HAPPEN, occur, arise, come about, take place, come to pass, befall, develop.

**beach** n sand, sands, shingle, shore, strand, seashore, seaside, water's edge, coast, seaboard.

**beacon** n signal, fire, watch fire, bonfire, light, beam, lighthouse, flare, rocket, sign.

**bead** n drop, droplet, drip, globule, glob (infml), blob, dot, bubble, pearl, jewel, pellet.

**beaker** n glass, tumbler, jar, cup, mug, tankard.

**beam** n 1 a beam of light: ray, shaft, gleam, glint, glimmer, glow. 2 PLANK, board, timber, rafter, joist, girder, spar, boom, bar, support.
v 1 EMIT, broadcast, transmit, radiate, shine, glare, glitter, glow, glimmer. 2 SMILE, grin.

**bear** v 1 CARRY, convey, transport, move, take, bring. 2 HOLD, support, shoulder, uphold, sustain, maintain, harbour, cherish. 3 bear children: give birth to, breed, propagate, beget, engender, produce, generate, develop, yield, bring forth, give up. 4 TOLERATE, stand, put up with, endure, abide, suffer, permit, allow, admit.

**bear on** refer to, relate to, affect, concern, involve.

**bear out** confirm, endorse, support, uphold, prove, demonstrate, corroborate, substantiate, vindicate, justify.

**bear up** persevere, soldier on, carry on, suffer, endure, survive, withstand.

**bear with** tolerate, put up with, endure, suffer, forbear, be patient with, make allowances for.

**bearable** adj tolerable, endurable, sufferable, supportable, sustainable, acceptable, manageable.
ⓔ unbearable, intolerable.

**bearded** adj unshaven, bristly, whiskered, tufted, hairy, hirsute, shaggy, bushy.

F3 beardless, clean-shaven, smooth.

**bearer** n carrier, conveyor, porter, courier, messenger, runner, holder, possessor.

**bearing** n 1 *have no bearing on the matter*: relevance, significance, connection, relation, reference. 2 DEMEANOUR, manner, mien, air, aspect, attitude, behaviour, comportment, poise, deportment, carriage, posture.

**bearings** n orientation, position, situation, location, whereabouts, course, track, way, direction, aim.

**beast** n animal, creature, brute, monster, savage, barbarian, pig, swine, devil, fiend.

**beat** v 1 WHIP, flog, lash, tan (*infml*), cane, strap, thrash, lay into, hit, punch, strike, swipe, knock, bang, wham, bash, pound, hammer, batter, buffet, pelt, bruise. 2 PULSATE, pulse, throb, thump, race, palpitate, flutter, vibrate, quiver, tremble, shake, quake. 3 DEFEAT, trounce, best, worst, hammer (*infml*), slaughter (*sl*), conquer, overcome, overwhelm, vanquish, subdue, surpass, excel, outdo, outstrip, outrun.
n 1 PULSATION, pulse, stroke, throb, thump, palpitation, flutter. 2 RHYTHM, time, tempo, metre, measure, rhyme, stress, accent. 3 *a policeman's beat*: round, rounds, territory, circuit, course, journey, way, path, route.

**beat up** (*infml*) attack, assault, knock about, knock around, batter, do over (*infml*).

**beaten** adj 1 HAMMERED, stamped, forged, wrought, worked, formed, shaped, fashioned. 2 WHISKED, whipped, mixed, blended, frothy, foamy.

**beating** n 1 CORPORAL PUNISHMENT, chastisement, whipping, flogging, caning,

thrashing. 2 DEFEAT, conquest, rout, ruin, downfall.

**beautiful** adj attractive, fair, pretty, lovely, good-looking, handsome, gorgeous, radiant, ravishing, stunning (*infml*), pleasing, appealing, alluring, charming, delightful, fine, exquisite.

F3 ugly, plain, hideous.

**beautify** v embellish, enhance, improve, grace, gild, garnish, decorate, ornament, deck, bedeck, adorn, array, glamorize, titivate (*infml*), tart up (*sl*).

F3 disfigure, spoil.

**beauty** n attractiveness, fairness, prettiness, loveliness, (good) looks, handsomeness, glamour, appeal, allure, charm, grace, elegance, symmetry, excellence.

F3 ugliness, repulsiveness.

**because** conj as, for, since, owing to, on account of, by reason of, thanks to.

**beckon** v summon, motion, gesture, signal, nod, wave, gesticulate, call, invite, attract, pull, draw, lure, allure, entice, tempt, coax.

**become** v 1 *become old-fashioned*: turn, grow, get, change into, develop into. 2 SUIT, befit, flatter, enhance, grace, embellish, ornament, set off, harmonize.

**bed** n 1 divan, couch, bunk, berth, cot, mattress, pallet, sack (*sl*). 2 LAYER, stratum, substratum, matrix, base, bottom, foundation, groundwork, watercourse, channel. 3 *bed of flowers*: garden, border, patch, plot.

**bedclothes** n bedding, bed-linen, sheets, pillowcases, pillowslips, covers, blankets, bedspreads, coverlets, quilts, eiderdowns, pillows.

**bedraggled** adj untidy, unkempt, dishevelled, disordered, scruffy, slovenly, messy, dirty, muddy, muddied, soiled, wet, sodden, drenched.

◨ neat, tidy, clean.

**before** *adv* ahead, in front, in advance, sooner, earlier, formerly, previously.
◨ after, later.

**beforehand** *adv* in advance, preliminarily, already, before, previously, earlier, sooner.

**befriend** *v* help, aid, assist, succour, back, support, stand by, uphold, sustain, comfort, encourage, welcome, favour, benefit, take under one's wing, make friends with, get to know.
◨ neglect, oppose.

**beg** *v* request, require, desire, crave, beseech, plead, entreat, implore, pray, supplicate, petition, solicit, cadge, scrounge, sponge.

**beggar** *n* mendicant, supplicant, pauper, down-and-out, tramp, vagrant, cadger, scrounger, sponger.

**begin** *v* start, commence, set about, embark on, set in motion, activate, originate, initiate, introduce, found, institute, instigate, arise, spring, emerge, appear.
◨ end, finish, cease.

**beginner** *n* novice, tiro, starter, learner, trainee, apprentice, student, freshman, fresher, recruit, cub, tenderfoot, fledgling.
◨ veteran, old hand, expert.

**beginning** *n* start, commencement, onset, outset, opening, preface, prelude, introduction, initiation, establishment, inauguration, inception, starting point, birth, dawn, origin, source, fountainhead, root, seed, emergence, rise.
◨ end, finish.

**begrudge** *v* resent, grudge, mind, object to, envy, covet, stint.
◨ allow.

**beguile** *v* 1 CHARM, enchant, bewitch, captivate, amuse, entertain, divert, distract, occupy, engross. 2 DECEIVE, fool, hoodwink, dupe, trick, cheat, delude, mislead.

**behalf** *n* sake, account, good, interest, benefit, advantage, profit, name, authority, side, support.

**behave** *v* act, react, respond, work, function, run, operate, perform, conduct oneself, acquit oneself, comport oneself (*fml*).

**behaviour** *n* conduct, comportment (*fml*), manner, manners, actions, doings, dealings, ways, habits, action, reaction, response, functioning, operation, performance.

**behead** *v* decapitate, execute, guillotine.

**behind** *prep* 1 FOLLOWING, after, later than, causing, responsible for, instigating, initiating. 2 SUPPORTING, backing, for.
*adv* after, following, next, subsequently, behindhand, late, overdue, in arrears, in debt.
*n* rump, rear, posterior (*infml*), buttocks, seat, bottom, backside (*infml*), bum (*sl*), butt (*US infml*), tail (*infml*).

**beige** *adj* buff, fawn, mushroom, camel, sandy, khaki, coffee, neutral.

**being** *n* 1 EXISTENCE, actuality, reality, life, animation, essence, substance, nature, soul, spirit. 2 CREATURE, animal, beast, human being, mortal, person, individual, thing, entity.

**belated** *adj* late, tardy, overdue, delayed, behindhand, unpunctual.
◨ punctual, timely.

**belch** *v* burp (*infml*), hiccup, emit, discharge, disgorge, spew.
*n* burp (*infml*), hiccup.

**beleaguered** *adj* harassed, pestered, badgered, bothered, worried, vexed, plagued, persecuted, surrounded, beset, besieged.

**belief** *n* 1 CONVICTION, persuasion, credit, trust, reliance, confidence, assurance, certainty, sureness, presumption, expectation, feeling, intuition, impression, notion, theory, view, opinion, judgement.

**2** IDEOLOGY, faith, creed, doctrine, dogma, tenet, principle.
🔁 **1** disbelief.

**believable** *adj* credible, imaginable, conceivable, acceptable, plausible, possible, likely, probable, authoritative, reliable, trustworthy.
🔁 unbelievable, incredible, unconvincing.

**believe** *v* accept, wear (*infml*), swallow (*infml*), credit, trust, count on, depend on, rely on, swear by, hold, maintain, postulate, assume, presume, gather, speculate, conjecture, guess, imagine, think, consider, reckon, suppose, deem, judge.
🔁 disbelieve, doubt.

**believer** *n* convert, proselyte, disciple, follower, adherent, devotee, zealot, supporter, upholder.
🔁 unbeliever, sceptic.

**belittle** *v* minimize, play down, dismiss, underrate, undervalue, underestimate, lessen, diminish, detract from, deprecate, decry, disparage, run down, deride, scorn, ridicule.
🔁 exaggerate, praise.

**belligerent** *adj* aggressive, militant, argumentative, quarrelsome, contentious, combative, pugnacious, violent, bullying, antagonistic, warring, warlike, bellicose.
🔁 peaceable.

**bellow** *v* roar, yell, shout, bawl, cry, scream, shriek, howl, clamour.

**belong** *v* fit, go with, be part of, attach to, link up with, tie up with, be connected with, relate to.

**belongings** *n* possessions, property, chattels, goods, effects, things, stuff (*infml*), gear (*infml*), paraphernalia.

**beloved** *adj* loved, adored, cherished, treasured, prized, precious, pet, favourite, dearest, dear, darling, admired, revered.

**below** *adv* beneath, under, underneath, down, lower, lower down.
🔁 above.
*prep* **1** UNDER, underneath, beneath.
**2** INFERIOR TO, lesser than, subordinate to, subject to.
🔁 above.

**belt** *n* **1** SASH, girdle, waistband, girth, strap. **2** STRIP, band, swathe, stretch, tract, area, region, district, zone, layer.

**bemused** *adj* confused, muddled, bewildered, puzzled, perplexed, dazed, befuddled, stupefied.
🔁 clear-headed, clear, lucid.

**bench** *n* **1** SEAT, form, settle, pew, ledge, counter, table, stall, workbench, worktable. **2** COURT, courtroom, tribunal, judiciary, judicature, judge, magistrate.

**bend** *v* curve, turn, deflect, swerve, veer, diverge, twist, contort, flex, shape, mould, buckle, bow, incline, lean, stoop, crouch.
🔁 straighten.
*n* curvature, curve, arc, bow, loop, hook, crook, elbow, angle, corner, turn, twist, zigzag.

**beneath** *adv* below, under, underneath, lower, lower down.
*prep* **1** UNDER, underneath, below, lower than. **2** UNWORTHY OF, unbefitting.

**benefactor** *n* philanthropist, patron, sponsor, angel (*infml*), backer, supporter, promoter, donor, contributor, subscriber, provider, helper, friend, well-wisher.
🔁 opponent, persecutor.

**beneficial** *adj* advantageous, favourable, useful, helpful, profitable, rewarding, valuable, improving, edifying, wholesome.
🔁 harmful, detrimental, useless.

**beneficiary** *n* payee, receiver, recipient, inheritor, legatee, heir, heiress, successor.

**benefit** *n* advantage, good, welfare, interest, favour, help, aid, assistance, service, use, avail, gain, profit, asset,

blessing.
☒ disadvantage, harm, damage.
*v* help, aid, assist, serve, avail,
advantage, profit, improve, enhance,
better, further, advance, promote.
☒ hinder, harm, undermine.

**benevolent** *adj* philanthropic,
humanitarian, charitable, generous,
liberal, munificent, altruistic, benign,
humane, kind, kindly, well-disposed,
compassionate, caring, considerate.
☒ mean, selfish, malevolent.

**benign** *adj* 1 BENEVOLENT, good,
gracious, gentle, kind, obliging,
friendly, amiable, genial,
sympathetic. 2 *a benign tumour*:
curable, harmless. 3 FAVOURABLE,
propitious, beneficial, temperate,
mild, warm, refreshing, restorative,
wholesome.
☒ 1 hostile. 2 malignant. 3 harmful,
unpleasant.

**bent** *adj* 1 ANGLED, curved, bowed,
arched, folded, doubled, twisted,
hunched, stooped. 2 (*infml*)
DISHONEST, crooked (*infml*), illegal,
criminal, corrupt, untrustworthy.
☒ 1 straight, upright. 2 honest.
*n* tendency, inclination, leaning,
preference, ability, capacity, faculty,
aptitude, facility, gift, talent, knack,
flair, forte.

**bent on** determined, resolved, set,
fixed, inclined, disposed.

**bequeath** *v* will, leave, bestow, gift,
endow, grant, settle, hand down, pass
on, impart, transmit, assign, entrust,
commit.

**bequest** *n* legacy, inheritance,
heritage, trust, bestowal, endowment,
gift, donation, estate, devisal,
settlement.

**bereavement** *n* loss, deprivation,
dispossession, death.

**bereft** *adj* deprived, robbed,
stripped, destitute, devoid, lacking,
wanting, minus.

**berserk** *adj* mad, crazy, demented,
insane, deranged, frantic, frenzied,

wild, raging, furious, violent, rabid,
raving.
☒ sane, calm.

**berth** *n* 1 BED, bunk, hammock,
billet. 2 MOORING, anchorage, quay,
wharf, dock, harbour, port.

**beside** *prep* alongside, abreast of,
next to, adjacent, abutting,
bordering, neighbouring, next door
to, close to, near, overlooking.

**besides** *adv* also, as well, too, in
addition, additionally, further,
furthermore, moreover.
*prep* apart from, other than, in
addition to, over and above.

**besiege** *v* 1 LAY SIEGE TO,
blockade, surround, encircle, confine.
2 TROUBLE, bother, importune,
assail, beset, beleaguer, harass,
pester, badger, nag, hound, plague.

**besotted** *adj* infatuated, doting,
obsessed, smitten, hypnotized,
spellbound, intoxicated.
☒ indifferent, disenchanted.

**best** *adj* optimum, optimal, first,
foremost, leading, unequalled,
unsurpassed, matchless,
incomparable, supreme, greatest,
highest, largest, finest, excellent,
outstanding, superlative, first-rate,
first-class, perfect.
☒ worst.
*adv* greatly, extremely, exceptionally,
excellently, superlatively.
☒ worst.
*n* finest, cream, prime, élite, top,
first, pick, choice, favourite.
☒ worst.

**bestow** *v* award, present, grant,
confer, endow, bequeath, commit,
entrust, impart, transmit, allot,
apportion, accord, give, donate,
lavish.
☒ withhold, deprive.

**bet** *n* wager, flutter (*infml*), gamble,
speculation, risk, venture, stake,
ante, bid, pledge.
*v* wager, gamble, punt, speculate,
risk, hazard, chance, venture, lay,

stake, bid, pledge.

**betray** v 1 *betray a friend*: inform on, shop (*sl*), sell (out), double-cross, desert, abandon, forsake.

2 DISCLOSE, give away, tell, divulge, expose, reveal, show, manifest.

**F3** 1 defend, protect. 2 conceal, hide.

**betrayal** n treachery, treason, sell-out, disloyalty, unfaithfulness, double-dealing, duplicity, deception, trickery, falseness.

**F3** loyalty, protection.

**betrayer** n traitor, Judas, informer, grass (*sl*), supergrass (*sl*), double-crosser, deceiver, conspirator, renegade, apostate.

**F3** protector, supporter.

**better** adj 1 SUPERIOR, bigger, larger, longer, greater, worthier, finer, surpassing, preferable.

2 IMPROVING, progressing, on the mend, recovering, fitter, healthier, stronger, recovered, restored.

**F3** 1 inferior. 2 worse.

v 1 IMPROVE, ameliorate, enhance, raise, further, promote, forward, reform, mend, correct. 2 SURPASS, top, beat, outdo, outstrip, overtake.

**F3** 1 worsen, deteriorate.

**between** prep mid, amid, amidst, among, amongst.

**beverage** n drink, draught, liquor, liquid, refreshment.

**bevy** n gathering, band, company, troupe, group, flock, gaggle, pack, bunch, crowd, throng.

**beware** v watch out, look out, mind, take heed, steer clear of, avoid, shun, guard against.

**bewilder** v confuse, muddle, disconcert, confound, bamboozle (*infml*), baffle, puzzle, perplex, mystify, daze, stupefy, disorient.

**bewildered** adj confused, muddled, uncertain, disoriented, nonplussed, bamboozled (*infml*), baffled, puzzled, perplexed, mystified, bemused, surprised, stunned.

**F3** unperturbed, collected.

**bewitch** v charm, enchant, allure, beguile, spellbind, possess, captivate, enrapture, obsess, fascinate, entrance, hypnotize.

**beyond** prep past, further than, apart from, away from, remote from, out of range of, out of reach of, above, over, superior to.

**bias** n slant, angle, distortion, bent, leaning, inclination, tendency, propensity, partiality, favouritism, prejudice, one-sidedness, unfairness, bigotry, intolerance.

**F3** impartiality, fairness.

**biased** adj slanted, angled, distorted, warped, twisted, loaded, weighted, influenced, swayed, partial, predisposed, prejudiced, one-sided, unfair, bigoted, blinkered, jaundiced.

**F3** impartial, fair.

**bicker** v squabble, row, quarrel, wrangle, argue, scrap, spar, fight, clash, disagree, dispute.

**F3** agree.

**bicycle** n cycle, bike (*infml*), two-wheeler, push-bike, racer, mountain-bike, tandem, penny-farthing.

**bid** v 1 ASK, request, desire, instruct, direct, command, enjoin, require, charge, call, summon, invite, solicit.

2 *he bid more than the painting was worth*: offer, proffer, tender, submit, propose.

n 1 OFFER, tender, sum, amount, price, advance, submission, proposal.

2 ATTEMPT, effort, try, go (*infml*), endeavour, venture.

**big** adj 1 LARGE, great, sizable, considerable, substantial, huge, enormous, immense, massive, colossal, gigantic, mammoth, burly, bulky, extensive, spacious, vast, voluminous. 2 IMPORTANT, significant, momentous, serious, main, principal, eminent, prominent, influential. 3 *that's big of you*: generous, magnanimous, gracious, unselfish.

**F3** 1 small, little. 2 insignificant,

unknown.

**bigot** *n* chauvinist, sectarian, racist, sexist, dogmatist, fanatic, zealot.
🔁 liberal, humanitarian.

**bigoted** *adj* prejudiced, biased, intolerant, illiberal, narrow-minded, narrow, blinkered, closed, dogmatic, opinionated, obstinate.
🔁 tolerant, liberal, broad-minded, enlightened.

**bigotry** *n* prejudice, discrimination, bias, injustice, unfairness, intolerance, narrow-mindedness, chauvinism, jingoism, sectarianism, racism, racialism, sexism, dogmatism, fanaticism.
🔁 tolerance.

**bilious** *adj* **1** IRRITABLE, choleric, cross, grumpy, crotchety, testy, grouchy, peevish. **2** SICK, queasy, nauseated, sickly, out of sorts (*infml*).

**bill** *n* **1** INVOICE, statement, account, charges, reckoning, tally, score.
**2** CIRCULAR, leaflet, handout, bulletin, handbill, broadsheet, advertisement, notice, poster, placard, playbill, programme.
**3** *parliamentary bill*: proposal, measure, legislation.
*v* invoice, charge, debit.

**billet** *n* **1** ACCOMMODATION, quarters, barracks, lodging, housing, berth. **2** EMPLOYMENT, post, occupation.

**billow** *v* swell, expand, bulge, puff out, fill out, balloon, rise, heave, surge, roll, undulate.

**bind** *v* **1** ATTACH, fasten, secure, clamp, stick, tie, lash, truss, strap, bandage, cover, dress, wrap. **2** OBLIGE, force, compel, constrain, necessitate, restrict, confine, restrain, hamper.

**binding** *adj* obligatory, compulsory, mandatory, necessary, requisite, permanent, conclusive, irrevocable, unalterable, indissoluble, unbreakable, strict.

*n* border, edging, trimming, tape, bandage, covering, wrapping.

**biography** *n* life story, life, history, autobiography, memoirs, recollections, curriculum vitae, account, record.

**biology**

*Biological terms include*: bacteriology, biochemistry, biology, bionics, botany, cybernetics, cytology, Darwinism, neo-Darwinism, ecology, embryology, endocrinology, evolution, Haeckel's law, genetics, Mendelism, Lamarckism, marine biology, natural history, palaeontology, pathology, physiology, systematics, taxonomy, zoology; amino acid, anatomy, animal behaviour, animal kingdom, bacillus, bacteria, biologist, botanist, cell, chromosome, class, coccus, conservation, corpuscle, cultivar, cytoplasm, deoxyribonucleic acid (DNA), diffusion, ecosystem, ectoplasm, embryo, endoplasmic reticulum (ER), enzyme, evolution, excretion, extinction, flora and fauna, food chain, fossil, gene, genetic engineering, genetic fingerprinting, population genetics, germ, Golgi apparatus, hereditary factor, homeostasis, living world, meiosis, membrane, metabolism, micro-organism, microbe, mitosis, molecule, mutation, natural selection, nuclear membrane, nucleus, nutrition, order, organism, osmosis, parasitism, photosynthesis, pollution, protein, protoplasm, reproduction, respiration, reticulum, ribonucleic acid (RNA), ribosome, secretion, survival of the fittest, symbiosis, virus.

**bird**

*Birds include*: sparrow, thrush, starling, blackbird, bluetit, chaffinch, greenfinch, bullfinch, dunnock, robin, wagtail, swallow, tit, wren, martin, swift, crow, magpie, dove, pigeon, skylark, nightingale, linnet, warbler, jay, jackdaw, rook, raven, cuckoo, woodpecker, yellowhammer; duck, mallard, eider, teal, swan, goose, heron, stork, flamingo, pelican, kingfisher, moorhen, coot, lapwing, peewit, plover, curlew, snipe, avocet, seagull, guillemot, tern, petrel, crane, bittern, petrel, albatross, gannet, cormorant, auk, puffin, dipper; eagle, owl, hawk, sparrowhawk, falcon, kestrel, osprey, buzzard, vulture, condor; emu, ostrich, kiwi, peacock, penguin; chicken, grouse, partridge, pheasant, quail, turkey; canary, budgerigar, budgie (*infml*), cockatiel, cockatoo, lovebird, parakeet, parrot, macaw, toucan, myna bird, mockingbird, kookaburra, bird of paradise.

**birth** *n* 1 CHILDBIRTH, parturition, confinement, delivery, nativity. 2 *of noble birth*: ancestry, family, parentage, descent, line, lineage, genealogy, pedigree, blood, stock, race, extraction, background, breeding. 3 BEGINNING, rise, emergence, origin, source, derivation.

**birthplace** *n* place of origin, native town, native country, fatherland, mother country, roots, provenance, source, fount.

**bisect** *v* halve, divide, separate, split, intersect, cross, fork, bifurcate.

**bit** *n* fragment, part, segment, piece, slice, crumb, morsel, scrap, atom, mite, whit, jot, iota, grain, speck.

**bit by bit** gradually, little by little, step by step, piecemeal.
F3 wholesale.

**bitchy** *adj* catty, snide, nasty, mean, spiteful, malicious, vindictive, backbiting, venomous, cruel, vicious.
F3 kind.

**bite** *v* 1 CHEW, masticate, munch,

gnaw, nibble, champ, crunch, crush. 2 *the dog bit her hand*: nip, pierce, wound, tear, rend. 3 SMART, sting, tingle. 4 GRIP, hold, seize, pinch, take effect.
*n* 1 NIP, wound, sting, smarting, pinch. 2 *a bite to eat*: snack, refreshment, mouthful, morsel, taste. 3 PUNGENCY, piquancy, kick (*infml*), punch.

**biting** *adj* 1 COLD, freezing, bitter, harsh, severe. 2 CUTTING, incisive, piercing, penetrating, raw, stinging, sharp, tart, caustic, scathing, cynical, hurtful.
F3 1 mild. 2 bland.

**bitter** *adj* 1 SOUR, tart, sharp, acid, acid, vinegary, unsweetened. 2 RESENTFUL, embittered, jaundiced, cynical, rancorous, acrimonious, acerbic, hostile. 3 INTENSE, severe, harsh, fierce, cruel, savage, merciless, painful, stinging, biting, freezing, raw.
F3 1 sweet. 2 contented. 3 mild.

**bizarre** *adj* strange, odd, queer, curious, weird, peculiar, eccentric, way-out (*infml*), outlandish, ludicrous, ridiculous, fantastic, extravagant, grotesque, freakish, abnormal, deviant, unusual, extraordinary.
F3 normal, ordinary.

**black** *adj* 1 JET-BLACK, coal-black, jet, ebony, sable, inky, sooty, dusky, swarthy. 2 DARK, unlit, moonless, starless, overcast, dingy, gloomy, sombre, funereal. 3 FILTHY, dirty, soiled, grimy, grubby.
F3 1 white. 2 bright. 3 clean.
*v* boycott, blacklist, ban, bar, taboo.

**black out** 1 FAINT, pass out, collapse, flake out (*infml*). 2 DARKEN, eclipse, cover up, conceal, suppress, withhold, censor, gag.

**blacken** *v* 1 DARKEN, dirty, soil, smudge, cloud. 2 DEFAME, malign, slander, libel, vilify, revile, denigrate, detract, smear, besmirch, sully, stain,

tarnish, taint, defile, discredit,
dishonour.
**F3** 2 praise, enhance.

**blackmail** n extortion, chantage,
hush money (infml), intimidation,
protection, pay-off, ransom.
v extort, bleed, milk, squeeze, hold
to ransom, threaten, lean on (infml),
force, compel, coerce, demand.

**blackout** n 1 a news blackout:
suppression, censorship, cover-up
(infml), concealment, secrecy. 2
FAINT, coma, unconsciousness,
oblivion. 3 power failure, power cut.

**blade** n edge, knife, dagger, sword,
scalpel, razor, vane.

**blame** n censure, criticism, stick (sl),
reprimand, reproof, reproach,
recrimination, condemnation,
accusation, charge, rap (sl),
incrimination, guilt, culpability,
fault, responsibility, accountability,
liability, onus.
v accuse, charge, tax, reprimand,
chide, reprove, upbraid, reprehend,
admonish, rebuke, reproach, censure,
criticize, find fault with, disapprove,
condemn.
**F3** exonerate, vindicate.

**blameless** adj innocent, guiltless,
clear, faultless, perfect, unblemished,
stainless, virtuous, sinless, upright,
above reproach, irreproachable,
unblamable, unimpeachable.
**F3** guilty, blameworthy.

**blanch** v blench, whiten, pale, fade,
bleach.
**F3** colour, blush, redden.

**bland** adv boring, monotonous,
humdrum, tedious, dull, uninspiring,
uninteresting, unexciting,
nondescript, characterless, flat,
insipid, tasteless, weak, mild,
smooth, soft, gentle, non-irritant.
**F3** lively, stimulating, sharp.

**blank** adj 1 a blank page: empty,
unfilled, void, clear, bare, unmarked,
plain, clean, white.
2 EXPRESSIONLESS, deadpan, poker-

faced, impassive, apathetic, glazed,
vacant, uncomprehending.
n space, gap, break, void, emptiness,
vacancy, vacuity, nothingness,
vacuum.

**blanket** n covering, coating, coat,
layer, film, carpet, rug, cloak,
mantle, cover, sheet, envelope,
wrapper, wrapping.
v cover, coat, eclipse, hide, conceal,
mask, cloak, surround, muffle,
deaden, obscure, cloud.

**blare** v trumpet, clamour, roar,
blast, boom, resound, ring, peal,
clang, hoot, toot, honk.

**blasé** adj nonchalant, offhand,
unimpressed, unmoved, unexcited,
jaded, weary, bored, uninterested,
uninspired, apathetic, indifferent,
cool, unconcerned.
**F3** excited, enthusiastic.

**blaspheme** v profane, desecrate,
swear, curse, imprecate, damn,
execrate, revile, abuse.

**blasphemous** adj profane, impious,
sacrilegious, imprecatory, godless,
ungodly, irreligious, irreverent.

**blasphemy** n profanity, curse,
expletive, imprecation, cursing,
swearing, execration, impiety,
irreverence, sacrilege, desecration,
violation, outrage.

**blast** n 1 EXPLOSION, detonation,
bang, crash, clap, crack, volley,
burst, outburst, discharge. 2 a blast
of cold air: draught, gust, gale,
squall, storm, tempest. 3 SOUND,
blow, blare, roar, boom, peal, hoot,
wail, scream, shriek.
v 1 EXPLODE, blow up, burst,
shatter, destroy, demolish, ruin, assail,
attack. 2 SOUND, blare, roar, boom,
peal, hoot, wail, scream, shriek.

**blatant** adj flagrant, brazen,
barefaced, arrant, open, overt,
undisguised, ostentatious, glaring,
conspicuous, obtrusive, prominent,
pronounced, obvious, sheer, outright,
unmitigated.

**blaze** *n* fire, flames, conflagration, bonfire, flare-up, explosion, blast, burst, outburst, radiance, brilliance, glare, flash, gleam, glitter, glow, light, flame.
*v* burn, flame, flare (up), erupt, explode, burst, fire, flash, gleam, glare, beam, shine, glow.

**bleach** *v* whiten, blanch, decolorize, fade, pale, lighten.

**bleak** *adj* **1** GLOOMY, sombre, leaden, grim, dreary, dismal, depressing, joyless, cheerless, comfortless, hopeless, discouraging, disheartening. **2** COLD, chilly, raw, weather-beaten, unsheltered, windy, windswept, exposed, open, barren, bare, empty, desolate, gaunt.
**F3** **1** bright, cheerful.

**bleed** *v* **1** HAEMORRHAGE, gush, spurt, flow, run, exude, weep, ooze, seep, trickle. **2** DRAIN, suck dry, exhaust, squeeze, milk, sap, reduce, deplete.

**blemish** *n* flaw, imperfection, defect, fault, deformity, disfigurement, birthmark, naevus, spot, mark, speck, smudge, blotch, blot, stain, taint, disgrace, dishonour.
*v* flaw, deface, disfigure, spoil, mar, damage, impair, spot, mark, blot, blotch, stain, sully, taint, tarnish.

**blend** *v* **1** MERGE, amalgamate, coalesce, compound, synthesize, fuse, unite, combine, mix, mingle.
**2** HARMONIZE, complement, fit, match.
**F3** **1** separate.
*n* compound, composite, alloy, amalgam, amalgamation, synthesis, fusion, combination, union, mix, mixture, concoction.

**bless** *v* **1** ANOINT, sanctify, consecrate, hallow, dedicate, ordain. **2** PRAISE, extol, magnify, glorify, exalt, thank. **3** APPROVE, countenance, favour, grace, bestow, endow, provide.
**F3** **1** curse. **2** condemn.

**blessed** *adj* **1** HOLY, sacred, hallowed, sanctified, revered, adored, divine. **2** HAPPY, contented, glad, joyful, joyous, lucky, fortunate, prosperous, favoured, endowed.
**F3** **1** cursed.

**blessing** *n* **1** CONSECRATION, dedication, benediction, grace, thanksgiving, invocation. **2** BENEFIT, advantage, favour, godsend, windfall, gift, gain, profit, help, service. **3** *give a proposal one's blessing*: approval, concurrence, backing, support, authority, sanction, consent, permission, leave.
**F3** **2** curse, blight. **3** condemnation.

**blight** *n* curse, bane, evil, scourge, affliction, disease, cancer, canker, fungus, mildew, rot, decay, pollution, contamination, corruption, infestation.
**F3** blessing, boon.
*v* spoil, mar, injure, undermine, ruin, wreck, crush, shatter, destroy, annihilate, blast, wither, shrivel, frustrate, disappoint.
**F3** bless.

**blind** *adj* **1** SIGHTLESS, unsighted, unseeing, eyeless, purblind, partially sighted. **2** IMPETUOUS, impulsive, hasty, rash, reckless, wild, mad, indiscriminate, careless, heedless, mindless, unthinking, unreasoning, irrational. **3** *blind to their needs*: ignorant, oblivious, unaware, unconscious, unobservant, inattentive, neglectful, indifferent, insensitive, thoughtless, inconsiderate. **4** CLOSED, obstructed, hidden, concealed, obscured.
**F3** **1** sighted. **2** careful, cautious. **3** aware, sensitive.
*n* screen, cover, cloak, mask, camouflage, masquerade, front, façade, distraction, smokescreen, cover-up (*infml*).

**bliss** *n* blissfulness, ecstasy, euphoria, rapture, joy, happiness, gladness, blessedness, paradise, heaven.

◪ misery, hell, damnation.

**blissful** adj ecstatic, euphoric, elated, enraptured, rapturous, delighted, enchanted, joyful, joyous, happy.

◪ miserable, wretched.

**blister** n sore, swelling, cyst, boil, abscess, ulcer, pustule, pimple, carbuncle.

**blizzard** n snowstorm, squall, storm, tempest.

**bloated** adj swollen, puffy, blown up, inflated, distended, dilated, expanded, enlarged, turgid, bombastic.

◪ thin, shrunken, shrivelled.

**blob** n drop, droplet, globule, glob (infml), bead, pearl, bubble, dab, spot, gob, lump, mass, ball, pellet, pill.

**block** n 1 a block of stone: piece, lump, mass, chunk, hunk, square, cube, brick, bar. 2 OBSTACLE, barrier, bar, jam, blockage, stoppage, resistance, obstruction, impediment, hindrance, let, delay.

v choke, clog, plug, stop up, dam up, close, bar, obstruct, impede, hinder, stonewall, stop, check, arrest, halt, thwart, scotch, deter.

**blockade** n barrier, barricade, siege, obstruction, restriction, stoppage, closure.

**blockage** n blocking, obstruction, stoppage, occlusion, block, clot, jam, log-jam, congestion, hindrance, impediment.

**blond, blonde** adj fair, flaxen, golden, fair-haired, golden-haired, light-coloured, bleached.

**blood** n extraction, birth, descent, lineage, family, kindred, relations, ancestry, descendants, kinship, relationship.

**bloodcurdling** adj horrifying, chilling, spine-chilling, hair-raising, terrifying, frightening, scary, dreadful, fearful, horrible, horrid,

horrendous.

**bloodshed** n killing, murder, slaughter, massacre, blood-bath, butchery, carnage, gore, bloodletting.

**bloodthirsty** adj murderous, homicidal, warlike, savage, barbaric, barbarous, brutal, ferocious, vicious, cruel, inhuman, ruthless.

**bloody** adj bleeding, bloodstained, gory, sanguinary, murderous, savage, brutal, ferocious, fierce, cruel.

**bloom** n 1 BLOSSOM, flower, bud. 2 PRIME, heyday, perfection, blush, flush, glow, rosiness, beauty, radiance, lustre, health, vigour, freshness.

v bud, sprout, grow, wax, develop, mature, blossom, flower, blow, open.

◪ fade, wither.

**blossom** n bloom, flower, bud.

v develop, mature, bloom, flower, blow, flourish, thrive, prosper, succeed.

◪ fade, wither.

**blot** n spot, stain, smudge, blotch, smear, mark, speck, blemish, flaw, fault, defect, taint, disgrace.

v spot, mark, stain, smudge, blur, sully, taint, tarnish, spoil, mar, disfigure, disgrace.

**blot out** obliterate, cancel, delete, erase, expunge, darken, obscure, shadow, eclipse.

**blotch** n patch, splodge, splotch, splash, smudge, blot, spot, mark, stain, blemish.

**blotchy** adj spotty, spotted, patchy, uneven, smeary, blemished, reddened, inflamed.

**blow**¹ v 1 BREATHE, exhale, pant, puff, waft, fan, flutter, float, flow, stream, rush, whirl, whisk, sweep, fling, buffet, drive, blast. 2 blow a horn: play, sound, pipe, trumpet, toot, blare.

n puff, draught, flurry, gust, blast, wind, gale, squall, tempest.

**blow over** die down, subside, end, finish, cease, pass, vanish, disappear, dissipate, fizzle out, peter out.

**blow up 1** EXPLODE, go off, detonate, burst, blast, bomb. **2** LOSE ONE'S TEMPER, blow one's top (*infml*), erupt, hit the roof (*infml*), rage, go mad (*infml*). **3** INFLATE, pump up, swell, fill (out), puff up, bloat, distend, dilate, expand, enlarge, magnify, exaggerate, overstate.

**blow²** *n* **1** *a blow on the head*: concussion, box, cuff, clip, clout, swipe, biff (*infml*), bash, slap, smack, whack (*infml*), wallop (*infml*), belt (*infml*), buffet, bang, clap, knock, rap, stroke, thump, punch. **2** MISFORTUNE, affliction, reverse, setback, comedown, disappointment, upset, jolt, shock, bombshell, calamity, catastrophe, disaster.

**blowy** *adj* breezy, windy, fresh, blustery, gusty, squally, stormy.

**bludgeon** *v* **1** BEAT, strike, club, batter, cosh (*sl*), cudgel. **2** FORCE, coerce, bulldoze, badger, hector, harass, browbeat, bully, terrorize, intimidate.

**blue** *adj* **1** AZURE, sapphire, cobalt, ultramarine, navy, indigo, aquamarine, turquoise, cyan. **2** DEPRESSED, low, down in the dumps (*infml*), dejected, downcast, dispirited, down-hearted, despondent, gloomy, glum, dismal, sad, unhappy, miserable, melancholy, morose, fed up (*infml*). **3** *a blue joke*: obscene, offensive, indecent, improper, coarse, vulgar, lewd, dirty, pornographic, bawdy, smutty, near the bone, near the knuckle, risqué.
**E₃ 2** cheerful, happy. **3** decent, clean.

**blueprint** *n* archetype, prototype, model, pattern, design, outline, draft, sketch, pilot, guide, plan, scheme, project.

**bluff** *v* lie, pretend, feign, sham, fake, deceive, delude, mislead, hoodwink, blind, bamboozle (*infml*), fool.
*n* lie, idle boast, bravado, humbug, pretence, show, sham, fake, fraud,

trick, subterfuge, deceit, deception.

**blunder** *n* mistake, error, solecism, howler (*infml*), bloomer (*infml*), clanger (*infml*), inaccuracy, slip, boob (*infml*), indiscretion, gaffe, faux pas, slip-up (*infml*), oversight, fault, cock-up (*sl*).
*v* stumble, flounder, bumble, err, slip up (*infml*), miscalculate, misjudge, bungle, botch, fluff (*infml*), mismanage, cock up (*sl*).

**blunt** *adj* **1** UNSHARPENED, dull, worn, pointless, rounded, stubbed. **2** FRANK, candid, direct, forthright, unceremonious, explicit, plain-spoken, honest, downright, outspoken, tactless, insensitive, rude, impolite, uncivil, brusque, curt, abrupt.
**E₃ 1** sharp, pointed. **2** subtle, tactful.
*v* dull, take the edge off, dampen, soften, deaden, numb, anaesthetize, alleviate, allay, abate, weaken.
**E₃** sharpen, intensify.

**blur** *v* smear, smudge, mist, fog, befog, cloud, becloud, blear, dim, darken, obscure, mask, conceal, soften.
*n* smear, smudge, blotch, haze, mist, fog, cloudiness, fuzziness, indistinctness, muddle, confusion, dimness, obscurity.

**blurred** *adj* out of focus, fuzzy, unclear, indistinct, vague, ill-defined, faint, hazy, misty, foggy, cloudy, bleary, dim, obscure, confused.
**E₃** clear, distinct.

**blurt out** *v* exclaim, cry, gush, spout, utter, tell, reveal, disclose, divulge, blab (*infml*), let out, leak, let slip, spill the beans (*infml*).
**E₃** bottle up, hush up.

**blush** *v* flush, redden, colour, glow.
**E₃** blanch.
*n* flush, reddening, rosiness, ruddiness, colour, glow.

**blushing** *adj* flushed, red, rosy, glowing, confused, embarrassed, ashamed, modest.

**⊟** pale, white, composed.

**bluster** v boast, brag, crow, talk big (*infml*), swagger, strut, vaunt, show off, rant, roar, storm, bully, hector.
n boasting, crowing, bravado, bluff, swagger.

**blustery** adj windy, gusty, squally, stormy, tempestuous, violent, wild, boisterous.

**⊟** calm.

**board** n 1 *a wooden board*: sheet, panel, slab, plank, beam, timber, slat. 2 COMMITTEE, council, panel, jury, commission, directorate, directors, trustees, advisers. 3 MEALS, food, provisions, rations.
v get on, embark, mount, enter, catch.

**boast** v brag, crow, swank (*infml*), claim, exaggerate, talk big (*infml*), bluster, trumpet, vaunt, strut, swagger, show off, exhibit, possess.

**⊟** belittle, deprecate.
n brag, swank (*infml*), claim, vaunt, pride, joy, gem, treasure.

**boastful** adj proud, conceited, vain, swollen-headed, big-headed (*infml*), puffed up, bragging, crowing, swanky (*infml*), cocky, swaggering.

**⊟** modest, self-effacing, humble.

**boats and ships**

*Types of boat or ship include*: canoe, dinghy, lifeboat, rowing-boat, kayak, coracle, skiff, punt, sampan, dhow, gondola, pedalo, catamaran, trimaran, yacht; cabin-cruiser, motor-boat, motor-launch, speedboat, trawler, barge, narrow boat, houseboat, dredger, junk, smack, lugger; hovercraft, hydrofoil; clipper, cutter, ketch, packet, brig, schooner, square-rigger, galleon; ferry, paddle-steamer, tug, freighter, liner, container-ship, tanker; warship, battleship, destroyer, submarine, U-boat, frigate, aircraft-carrier, cruiser, dreadnought, corvette, minesweeper, man-of-war.

**bob** v bounce, hop, skip, spring, jump, leap, twitch, jerk, jolt, shake, quiver, wobble, oscillate, nod, bow, curtsy.

**bob up** appear, emerge, arrive, show up (*infml*), materialize, rise, surface, pop up, spring up, crop up, arise.

**bodily** adj physical, corporeal, carnal, fleshly, real, actual, tangible, substantial, concrete, material.

**⊟** spiritual.
adv altogether, en masse, collectively, as a whole, completely, fully, wholly, entirely, totally, in toto.

**⊟** piecemeal.

**body** n 1 ANATOMY, physique, build, figure, trunk, torso. 2 CORPSE, cadaver, carcase, stiff (*sl*).
3 COMPANY, association, society, corporation, confederation, bloc, cartel, syndicate, congress, collection, group, band, crowd, throng, multitude, mob, mass.
4 CONSISTENCY, density, solidity, firmness, bulk, mass, substance, essence, fullness, richness.

**bodyguard** n guard, protector, minder (*infml*).

**bog** n marsh, swamp, fen, mire, quagmire, quag, slough, morass, quicksands, marshland, swampland, wetlands.

**bog down** encumber, hinder, impede, overwhelm, deluge, sink, stick, slow down, slow up, delay, retard, halt, stall.

**bogus** adj false, fake, counterfeit, forged, fraudulent, phoney (*infml*), spurious, sham, pseudo, artificial, imitation, dummy.

**⊟** genuine, true, real, valid.

**bohemian** adj artistic, arty (*infml*), unconventional, unorthodox, nonconformist, alternative, eccentric, offbeat, way-out (*sl*), bizarre, exotic.

**⊟** bourgeois, conventional, orthodox.
n beatnik, hippie, drop-out, nonconformist.

**⊟** bourgeois, conformist.

**boil**[1] v 1 SIMMER, stew, seethe, brew,

gurgle, bubble, fizz, effervesce, froth, foam, steam. **2** *boil with anger*: erupt, explode, rage, rave, storm, fulminate, fume.

**boil down** reduce, concentrate, distil, condense, digest, abstract, summarize, abridge.

**boil²** *n* pustule, abscess, gumboil, ulcer, tumour, pimple, carbuncle, blister, inflammation.

**boiling** *adj* **1** *boiling water*: turbulent, gurgling, bubbling, steaming. **2** HOT, baking, roasting, scorching, blistering. **3** ANGRY, indignant, incensed, infuriated, enraged, furious, fuming, flaming.

**boisterous** *adj* exuberant, rumbustious (*infml*), rollicking, bouncy, turbulent, tumultuous, loud, noisy, clamorous, rowdy, rough, disorderly, riotous, wild, unrestrained, unruly, obstreperous. ⊟ quiet, calm, restrained.

**bold** *adj* **1** FEARLESS, dauntless, daring, audacious, brave, courageous, valiant, heroic, gallant, intrepid, adventurous, venturesome, enterprising, plucky, spirited, confident, outgoing. **2** EYE-CATCHING, striking, conspicuous, prominent, strong, pronounced, bright, vivid, colourful, loud, flashy, showy, flamboyant. **3** BRAZEN, brash, forward, shameless, unabashed, cheeky (*infml*), impudent, insolent. ⊟ **1** cautious, timid, shy. **2** faint, restrained.

**bolt** *n* bar, rod, shaft, pin, peg, rivet, fastener, latch, catch, lock. *v* **1** FASTEN, secure, bar, latch, lock. **2** ABSCOND, escape, flee, fly, run, sprint, rush, dash, hurtle. **3** *bolt one's food*: gulp, wolf, gobble, gorge, devour, cram, stuff.

**bomb** *n* atom bomb, petrol bomb, shell, bombshell, explosive, charge, grenade, mine, torpedo, rocket, missile, projectile.

*v* bombard, shell, torpedo, attack, blow up, destroy.

**bombard** *v* attack, assault, assail, pelt, pound, strafe, blast, bomb, shell, blitz, besiege, hound, harass, pester.

**bombardment** *n* attack, assault, air-raid, bombing, shelling, blitz, barrage, cannonade, fusillade, salvo, fire, flak.

**bombastic** *adj* grandiloquent, magniloquent, grandiose, pompous, high-flown, inflated, bloated, windy, wordy, verbose.

**bond** *n* **1** CONNECTION, relation, link, tie, union, affiliation, attachment, affinity. **2** CONTRACT, covenant, agreement, pledge, promise, word, obligation. **3** FETTER, shackle, manacle, chain, cord, band, binding.
*v* connect, fasten, bind, unite, fuse, glue, gum, paste, stick, seal.

**bondage** *n* imprisonment, incarceration, captivity, confinement, restraint, slavery, enslavement, serfdom, servitude, subservience, subjection, subjugation, yoke. ⊟ freedom, independence.

**bone**

---

*Human bones include:* clavicle, coccyx, collar-bone, femur, fibula, hip-bone, humerus, ilium, ischium, mandible, maxilla, metacarpal, metatarsal, patella, pelvic girdle, pelvis, pubis, radius, rib, scapula, shoulder-blade, skull, sternum, stirrup-bone, temporal, thigh-bone, tibia, ulna, vertebra.

---

**bonus** *n* advantage, benefit, plus (*infml*), extra, perk (*infml*), perquisite, commission, dividend, premium, prize, reward, honorarium, tip, gratuity, gift, handout. ⊟ disadvantage, disincentive.

**bony** *adj* thin, lean, angular, lanky, gawky, gangling, skinny, scrawny, book 62

emaciated, rawboned, gaunt, drawn.
**F3** fat, plump.

**book** n volume, tome, publication, work, booklet, tract.

> *Types of book include*: hardback, paperback, bestseller; fiction, novel, story, thriller, romantic novel; children's book, primer, picture-book, annual; reference book, encyclopedia, dictionary, lexicon, thesaurus, concordance, anthology, compendium, omnibus, atlas, guidebook, gazetteer, directory, anthology, pocket companion, handbook, manual, cookbook, yearbook, almanac, catalogue; notebook, exercise book, textbook, scrapbook, album, sketchbook, diary, jotter, pad, ledger; libretto, manuscript, hymn-book, hymnal, prayer-book, psalter, missal, lectionary. *see also* **literature**.

v reserve, bag (*infml*), engage, charter, procure, order, arrange, organize, schedule, programme.
**F3** cancel.

**boom** v 1 BANG, crash, roar, thunder, roll, rumble, resound, reverberate, blast, explode.
2 FLOURISH, thrive, prosper, succeed, develop, grow, increase, gain, expand, swell, escalate, intensify, strengthen, explode.
**F3** 2 fail, collapse, slump.
n 1 BANG, clap, crash, roar, thunder, rumble, reverberation, blast, explosion, burst. 2 INCREASE, growth, expansion, gain, upsurge, jump, spurt, boost, upturn, improvement, advance, escalation, explosion.
**F3** 2 failure, collapse, slump, recession, depression.

**boon** n blessing, advantage, benefit, godsend, windfall, favour, kindness, gift, present, grant, gratuity.
**F3** disadvantage, blight.

**boorish** adj uncouth, oafish, loutish, ill-mannered, rude, coarse, crude, vulgar, unrefined, uncivilized, uneducated, ignorant.
**F3** polite, refined, cultured.

**boost** n improvement, enhancement, expansion, increase, rise, jump, increment, addition, supplement, booster, lift, hoist, heave, push, thrust, help, advancement, promotion, praise, encouragement, fillip, ego-trip (*sl*).
**F3** setback, blow.
v raise, elevate, improve, enhance, develop, enlarge, expand, amplify, increase, augment, heighten, lift, hoist, jack up, heave, push, thrust, help, aid, assist, advance, further, promote, advertise, plug (*infml*), praise, inspire, encourage, foster, support, sustain, bolster, supplement.
**F3** hinder, undermine.

**boot** n gumboot, wellington, welly (*infml*), galosh, overshoe, walking-boot, riding-boot, top-boot.

**booth** n kiosk, stall, stand, hut, box, compartment, cubicle, carrel.

**booty** n loot, plunder, pillage, spoils, swag (*sl*), haul, gains, takings, pickings, winnings.

**border** n 1 BOUNDARY, frontier, bound, bounds, confine, confines, limit, demarcation, borderline, margin, fringe, periphery, surround, perimeter, circumference, edge, rim, brim, verge, brink. 2 TRIMMING, frill, valance, skirt, hem, frieze.
**border on 1** ADJOIN, abut, touch, impinge, join, connect, communicate with. 2 RESEMBLE, approximate, approach, verge on.

**bore**¹ v drill, mine, pierce, perforate, penetrate, sink, burrow, tunnel, undermine, sap.

**bore**² v tire, weary, fatigue, jade, trouble, bother, worry, irritate, annoy, vex, irk.
**F3** interest, excite.
n (*infml*) nuisance, bother, bind

(*infml*), drag (*infml*), pain (*infml*), headache (*infml*).

**E3** pleasure, delight.

**boredom** *n* tedium, tediousness, monotony, dullness, apathy, listlessness, weariness, world-weariness.

**E3** interest, excitement.

**boring** *adj* tedious, monotonous, routine, repetitious, uninteresting, unexciting, uneventful, dull, dreary, humdrum, commonplace, trite, unimaginative, uninspired, dry, stale, flat, insipid.

**E3** interesting, exciting, stimulating, original.

**borrow** *v* steal, pilfer, filch, lift, plagiarize, crib, copy, imitate, mimic, echo, take, draw, derive, obtain, adopt, use, scrounge, cadge, sponge, appropriate, usurp.

**E3** lend.

**bosom** *n* 1 BUST, breasts, chest, breast. 2 HEART, core, centre, midst, protection, shelter, sanctuary.

**boss** *n* employer, governor, master, owner, captain, head, chief, leader, supremo, administrator, executive, director, manager, foreman, gaffer, superintendent, overseer, supervisor.

**boss around** order around, order about, domineer, tyrannize, bully, bulldoze, browbeat, push around, dominate.

**bossy** *adj* authoritarian, autocratic, tyrannical, despotic, dictatorial, domineering, overbearing, oppressive, lordly, high-handed, imperious, insistent, assertive, demanding, exacting.

**E3** unassertive.

**bother** *v* disturb, inconvenience, harass, hassle (*infml*), pester, plague, nag, annoy, irritate, irk, molest, trouble, worry, concern, alarm, dismay, distress, upset, vex.

*n* inconvenience, trouble, problem, difficulty, hassle (*infml*), fuss, bustle, flurry, nuisance, pest, annoyance,

irritation, aggravation (*infml*), vexation, worry, strain.

**bottle** *n* phial, flask, carafe, decanter, flagon, demijohn.

**bottle up** hide, conceal, restrain, curb, hold back, suppress, inhibit, restrict, enclose, contain.

**E3** unbosom, unburden.

**bottle-neck** *n* hold-up, traffic jam, snarl-up, congestion, clogging, blockage, obstruction, block, obstacle.

**bottom** *n* 1 UNDERSIDE, underneath, sole, base, foot, plinth, pedestal, support, foundation, substructure, ground, floor, bed, depths, nadir. 2 RUMP, rear, behind, posterior (*infml*), buttocks, seat, backside (*infml*), bum (*sl*), butt (*US infml*), tail (*infml*).

**E3** 1 top.

**bottomless** *adj* deep, profound, fathomless, unfathomed, unplumbed, immeasurable, measureless, infinite, boundless, limitless, unlimited, inexhaustible.

**E3** shallow, limited.

**bounce** *v* spring, jump, leap, bound, bob, ricochet, rebound, recoil.

*n* 1 SPRING, bound, springiness, elasticity, give, resilience, rebound, recoil. 2 EBULLIENCE, exuberance, vitality, vivacity, energy, vigour, go (*infml*), zip (*infml*), animation, liveliness.

**bound**[1] *adj* 1 FASTENED, secured, fixed, tied (up), chained, held, restricted, bandaged. 2 LIABLE, committed, duty-bound, obliged, required, forced, compelled, constrained, destined, fated, doomed, sure, certain.

**bound**[2] *v* jump, leap, vault, hurdle, spring, bounce, bob, hop, skip, frisk, gambol, frolic, caper, prance.

*n* jump, leap, vault, spring, bounce, bob, hop, skip, gambol, frolic, caper, dance, prance.

**boundary** *n* border, frontier,

barrier, line, borderline, demarcation, bounds, confines, limits, margin, fringe, verge, brink, edge, perimeter, extremity, termination.

**boundless** *adj* unbounded, limitless, unlimited, unconfined, countless, untold, incalculable, vast, immense, measureless, immeasurable, infinite, endless, unending, interminable, inexhaustible, unflagging, indefatigable.
**F3** limited, restricted.

**bounds** *n* confines, limits, borders, marches, margins, fringes, periphery, circumference, edges, extremities.

**bounty** *n* 1 GENEROSITY, liberality, munificence, largesse, almsgiving, charity, philanthropy, beneficence, kindness. 2 REWARD, recompense, premium, bonus, gratuity, gift, present, donation, grant, allowance.

**bouquet** *n* 1 *bouquet of flowers*: bunch, posy, nosegay, spray, corsage, buttonhole, wreath, garland.
2 AROMA, smell, odour, scent, perfume, fragrance.

**bourgeois** *adj* middle-class, materialistic, conservative, traditional, conformist, conventional, hide-bound, unadventurous, dull, humdrum, banal, commonplace, trite, unoriginal, unimaginative.
**F3** bohemian, unconventional, original.

**bout** *n* 1 FIGHT, battle, engagement, encounter, struggle, set-to, match, contest, competition, round, heat. 2 PERIOD, spell, time, stint, turn, go (*infml*), term, stretch, run, course, session, spree, attack, fit.

**bow** *v* 1 *bow one's head*: incline, bend, nod, bob, curtsy, genuflect (*fml*), kowtow, salaam, stoop. 2 YIELD, give in, consent, surrender, capitulate, submit, acquiesce, concede, accept, comply, defer. 3 SUBDUE, overpower, conquer, vanquish, crush, subjugate.

*n* inclination, bending, nod, bob, curtsy, genuflexion (*fml*), kowtow, salaam, obeisance (*fml*), salutation, acknowledgement.

**bow out** withdraw, pull out, desert, abandon, defect, back out, chicken out (*infml*), retire, resign, quit, stand down, step down, give up.

**bowels** *n* 1 INTESTINES, viscera, entrails, guts, insides, innards (*infml*). 2 DEPTHS, interior, inside, middle, centre, core, heart.

**bowl¹** *n* receptacle, container, vessel, dish, basin, sink.

**bowl²** *v* throw, hurl, fling, pitch, roll, spin, whirl, rotate, revolve.

**bowl over** surprise, amaze, astound, astonish, stagger, stun, dumbfound, flabbergast (*infml*), floor (*infml*).

**box¹** *n* container, receptacle, case, crate, carton, packet, pack, package, present, chest, coffer, trunk, coffin.
*v* case, encase, package, pack, wrap.

**box in** enclose, surround, circumscribe, cordon off, hem in, corner, trap, confine, restrict, imprison, cage, coop up, contain.

**box²** *v* fight, spar, punch, hit, strike, slap, buffet, cuff, clout, sock (*sl*), wallop (*infml*), whack (*infml*).

**boxer** *n* pugilist, fighter, prizefighter, sparring partner, flyweight, featherweight, lightweight, welterweight, middleweight, heavyweight.

**boxing** *n* pugilism, prizefighting, fisticuffs, sparring.

**boy** *n* son, lad, youngster, kid (*infml*), nipper (*infml*), stripling, youth, fellow.

**boycott** *v* refuse, reject, embargo, black, ban, prohibit, disallow, bar, exclude, blacklist, outlaw, ostracize, cold-shoulder, ignore, spurn.
**F3** encourage, support.

**boyfriend** *n* young man, man, fellow (*infml*), bloke (*infml*), admirer, date, sweetheart, lover, fiancé.

**brace** *n* pair, couple, twosome, duo.

*v* strengthen, reinforce, fortify, bolster, buttress, prop, shore (up), support, steady, tighten, fasten, tie, strap, bind, bandage.

**bracing** *adj* fresh, crisp, refreshing, reviving, strengthening, fortifying, tonic, rousing, stimulating, exhilarating, invigorating, enlivening, energizing, brisk, energetic, vigorous.
**F3** weakening, debilitating.

**braid** *v* plait, interweave, interlace, intertwine, weave, lace, twine, entwine, ravel, twist, wind.
**F3** undo, unravel.

**brain** *n* 1 CEREBRUM, grey matter, head, mind, intellect, nous, brains (*infml*), intelligence, wit, reason, sense, common sense, shrewdness, understanding. 2 MASTERMIND, intellectual, highbrow, egghead (*infml*), scholar, expert, boffin, genius, prodigy.
**F3** 2 simpleton.

*Parts of the brain include:* brainstem, cerebellum, cerebral cortex (grey matter), cerebrum, corpus callosum, forebrain, frontal lobe, hindbrain, hypothalamus, medulla oblongata, mesencephalon, midbrain, occipital lobe, optic thalamus, parietal lobe, pineal body, pituitary gland, pons, spinal cord, temporal lobe, thalamus.

**brainy** (*infml*) *adj* intellectual, intelligent, clever, smart, bright, brilliant.
**F3** dull.

**brake** *n* check, curb, rein, restraint, control, restriction, constraint, drag.
*v* slow, decelerate, retard, drag, slacken, moderate, check, halt, stop, pull up.
**F3** accelerate.

**branch** *n* 1 BOUGH, limb, sprig, shoot, offshoot, arm, wing, prong. 2 *a different branch of the company:* department, office, part, section, division, subsection, subdivision.

**branch out** diversify, vary, develop, expand, enlarge, extend, broaden out, increase, multiply, proliferate, ramify.

**brand** *n* make, brand-name, tradename, trademark, logo, mark, symbol, sign, emblem, label, stamp, hallmark, grade, quality, class, kind, type, sort, line, variety, species.
*v* mark, stamp, label, type, stigmatize, burn, scar, stain, taint, disgrace, discredit, denounce, censure.

**brandish** *v* wave, flourish, shake, raise, swing, wield, flash, flaunt, exhibit, display, parade.

**brash** *adj* 1 BRAZEN, forward, impertinent, impudent, insolent, rude, cocky, assured, bold, audacious. 2 RECKLESS, rash, impetuous, impulsive, hasty, precipitate, foolhardy, incautious, indiscreet.
**F3** 1 reserved. 2 cautious.

**bravado** *n* swagger, boasting, bragging, bluster, bombast, talk, boast, vaunting, showing off, parade, show, pretence.
**F3** modesty, restraint.

**brave** *adj* courageous, plucky, unafraid, fearless, dauntless, undaunted, bold, audacious, daring, intrepid, stalwart, hardy, stoical, resolute, stout-hearted, valiant, gallant, heroic, indomitable.
**F3** cowardly, afraid, timid.
*v* face, confront, defy, challenge, dare, stand up to, face up to, suffer, endure, bear, withstand.
**F3** capitulate.

**bravery** *n* courage, pluck, guts (*infml*), fearlessness, dauntlessness, boldness, audacity, daring, intrepidity, stalwartness, hardiness, fortitude, resolution, stout-heartedness, valiance, valour, gallantry, heroism, indomitability, grit, mettle, spirit.
**F3** cowardice, faint-heartedness, timidity.

**brawl** n fight, punch-up (infml), scrap, scuffle, dust-up (infml), mêlée, free-for-all, fray, affray, broil, fracas, rumpus, disorder, row, argument, quarrel, squabble, altercation, dispute, clash.

v fight, scrap, scuffle, wrestle, tussle, row, argue, quarrel, squabble, wrangle, dispute.

**brawny** adj muscular, sinewy, athletic, well-built, burly, beefy, hefty, solid, bulky, hulking, massive, strapping, strong, powerful, vigorous, sturdy, robust, hardy, stalwart.

Ea slight, frail.

**brazen** adj blatant, flagrant, brash, brassy, bold, forward, saucy, pert, barefaced, impudent, insolent, defiant, shameless, unashamed, unabashed, immodest.

Ea shy, shamefaced, modest.

**breach** n 1 a breach of the rules: violation, contravention, infringement, trespass, disobedience, offence, transgression, lapse, disruption. 2 QUARREL, disagreement, dissension, difference, variance, schism, rift, rupture, split, division, separation, parting, estrangement, alienation, disaffection, dissociation. 3 BREAK, crack, rift, rupture, fissure, cleft, crevice, opening, aperture, gap, space, hole, chasm.

**bread** n loaf, roll, food, provisions, diet, fare, nourishment, nutriment, sustenance, subsistence, necessities.

**breadth** n width, broadness, wideness, latitude, thickness, size, magnitude, measure, scale, range, reach, scope, compass, span, sweep, extent, expanse, spread, comprehensiveness, extensiveness, vastness.

**break** v 1 FRACTURE, crack, snap, split, sever, separate, divide, rend, smash, disintegrate, splinter, shiver, shatter, ruin, destroy, demolish.

2 break the law: violate, contravene, infringe, breach, disobey, flout. 3 PAUSE, halt, stop, discontinue, interrupt, suspend, rest. 4 SUBDUE, tame, weaken, enfeeble, impair, undermine, demoralize. 5 break the news: tell, inform, impart, divulge, disclose, reveal, announce. 6 break a record: exceed, beat, better, excel, surpass, outdo, outstrip.

Ea 1 mend. 2 keep, observe, abide by. 4 strengthen.

n 1 FRACTURE, crack, split, rift, rupture, schism, separation, tear, gash, fissure, cleft, crevice, opening, gap, hole, breach. 2 INTERVAL, intermission, interlude, interruption, pause, halt, lull, let-up (infml), respite, rest, breather (infml), time out, holiday. 3 OPPORTUNITY, chance, advantage, fortune, luck.

**break away** separate, split, part company, detach, secede, leave, depart, quit, run away, escape, flee, fly.

**break down** 1 the van broke down: fail, stop, pack up (infml), conk out (sl), seize up, give way, collapse, crack up (infml). 2 ANALYSE, dissect, separate, itemize, detail.

**break in** 1 INTERRUPT, butt in, interpose, interject, intervene, intrude, encroach, impinge. 2 BURGLE, rob, raid, invade.

**break off** 1 DETACH, snap off, sever, separate, part, divide, disconnect. 2 PAUSE, interrupt, suspend, discontinue, halt, stop, cease, end, finish, terminate.

**break out** 1 START, begin, commence, arise, emerge, happen, occur, erupt, flare up, burst out. 2 ESCAPE, abscond, bolt, flee.

**break up** 1 DISMANTLE, take apart, demolish, destroy, disintegrate, splinter, sever, divide, split, part, separate, divorce. 2 DISBAND, disperse, dissolve, adjourn, suspend, stop, finish, terminate.

**breakable** adj brittle, fragile,

delicate, flimsy, insubstantial, frail.
**F3** unbreakable, durable, sturdy.

**breakdown** n **1** FAILURE, collapse, disintegration, malfunction, interruption, stoppage. **2** ANALYSIS, dissection, itemization, classification, categorization.

**break-in** n burglary, house-breaking, robbery, raid, invasion, intrusion, trespass.

**breakthrough** n discovery, find, finding, invention, innovation, advance, progress, headway, step, leap, development, improvement.

**break-up** n divorce, separation, parting, split, rift, finish, termination, dissolution, dispersal, disintegration, crumbling.

**breakwater** n groyne, mole, jetty, pier, quay, wharf, dock.

**breath** n **1** AIR, breathing, respiration, inhalation, exhalation, sigh, gasp, pant, gulp. **2** BREEZE, puff, waft, gust. **3** AROMA, smell, odour, whiff. **4** HINT, suggestion, suspicion, undertone, whisper, murmur.

**breathe** v **1** RESPIRE, inhale, exhale, expire, sigh, gasp, pant, puff. **2** SAY, utter, express, voice, articulate, murmur, whisper, impart, tell.
**3** INSTIL, imbue, infuse, inject, inspire.

**breathless** adj **1** SHORT-WINDED, out of breath, panting, puffing, puffed (out), exhausted, winded, gasping, wheezing, choking.
**2** breathless anticipation: expectant, impatient, eager, agog, excited, feverish, anxious.

**breathtaking** adj awe-inspiring, impressive, magnificent, overwhelming, amazing, astonishing, stunning, exciting, thrilling, stirring, moving.

**breed** v **1** REPRODUCE, procreate, multiply, propagate, hatch, bear, bring forth, rear, raise, bring up, educate, train, instruct. **2** PRODUCE,

create, originate, arouse, cause, occasion, engender, generate, make, foster, nurture, nourish, cultivate, develop.
n species, strain, variety, family, ilk, sort, kind, type, stamp, stock, race, progeny, line, lineage, pedigree.

**breeding** n **1** REPRODUCTION, procreation, nurture, development, rearing, raising, upbringing, education, training, background, ancestry, lineage, stock. **2** MANNERS, politeness, civility, gentility, urbanity, refinement, culture, polish.
**F3 2** vulgarity.

**breeze** n wind, gust, flurry, waft, puff, breath, draught, air.

**breezy** adj **1** WINDY, blowing, fresh, airy, gusty, blustery, squally.
**2** ANIMATED, lively, vivacious, jaunty, buoyant, blithe, debonair, carefree, cheerful, easy-going (infml) casual, informal, light, bright, exhilarating.
**F3 1** still. **2** staid, serious.

**brevity** n briefness, shortness, terseness, conciseness, succinctness, pithiness, crispness, incisiveness, abruptness, curtness, impermanence, ephemerality, transience, transitoriness.
**F3** verbosity, permanence, longevity.

**brew** v **1** INFUSE, stew, boil, seethe, ferment, prepare, soak, steep, mix, cook. **2** PLOT, scheme, plan, project, devise, contrive, concoct, hatch, excite, foment, build up, gather, develop.
n infusion, drink, beverage, liquor, potion, broth, gruel, stew, mixture, blend, concoction, preparation, fermentation, distillation.

**bribe** n incentive, inducement, allurement, enticement, back-hander (infml), kickback, payola, refresher (infml), sweetener (infml), hush money (infml), protection money.
v corrupt, suborn, buy off, reward.

**bribery** n corruption, graft (sl),

palm-greasing, inducement, lubrication.

**bric-à-brac** n  knick-knacks, ornaments, curios, antiques, trinkets, baubles.

**bridal** adj  wedding, nuptial, marriage, matrimonial, marital, conjugal.

**bridge** n  arch, span, causeway, link, connection, bond, tie.

> *Types of bridge include*: suspension bridge, arch bridge, cantilever bridge, flying bridge, flyover, overpass, footbridge, railway bridge, viaduct, aqueduct, humpback bridge, toll bridge, pontoon bridge, Bailey bridge, rope bridge, drawbridge, swing bridge.

v  span, cross, traverse, fill, link, connect, couple, join, unite, bind.

**bridle** v  check, curb, restrain, control, govern, master, subdue, moderate, repress, contain.

**brief** adj  **1** SHORT, terse, succinct, concise, pithy, crisp, compressed, thumbnail, laconic, abrupt, sharp, brusque, blunt, curt, surly. **2** SHORT-LIVED, momentary, ephemeral, transient, fleeting, passing, transitory, temporary, limited, cursory, hasty, quick, swift, fast.
**F3** 1 long. 2 lengthy.
n  **1** ORDERS, instructions, directions, remit, mandate, directive, advice, briefing, data, information.
**2** OUTLINE, summary, précis, dossier, case, defence, argument.
v  instruct, direct, explain, guide, advise, prepare, prime, inform, fill in (infml), gen up (sl).

**briefing** n  meeting, conference, preparation, priming, filling-in (infml), gen (sl), low-down (sl), information, advice, guidance, directions, instructions, orders.

**bright** adj  **1** LUMINOUS, illuminated, radiant, shining, beaming, flashing, gleaming, glistening, glittering, sparkling, twinkling, shimmering, glowing, brilliant, resplendent, glorious, splendid, dazzling, glaring, blazing, intense, vivid. **2** HAPPY, cheerful, glad, joyful, merry, jolly, lively, vivacious. **3** *the future looks bright*: promising, propitious, auspicious, favourable, rosy, optimistic, hopeful, encouraging.
**4** CLEVER, brainy (infml), smart, intelligent, quick-witted, quick, sharp, acute, keen, astute, perceptive.
**5** CLEAR, transparent, translucent, lucid. **6** *a bright day*: fine, sunny, cloudless, unclouded.
**F3** 1 dull. 2 sad. 3 depressing.
4 stupid. 5 muddy. 6 dark.

**brighten** v  **1** LIGHT UP, illuminate, lighten, clear up. **2** POLISH, burnish, rub up, shine, gleam, glow. **3** CHEER UP, gladden, hearten, encourage, enliven, perk up.
**F3** 1 darken. 2 dull, tarnish.

**brilliance** n  **1** TALENT, virtuosity, genius, greatness, distinction, excellence, aptitude, cleverness. **2** RADIANCE, brightness, sparkle, dazzle, intensity, vividness, gloss, lustre, sheen, glamour, glory, magnificence, splendour.

**brilliant** adj  **1** *a brilliant pianist*: gifted, talented, accomplished, expert, skilful, masterly, exceptional, outstanding, superb, illustrious, famous, celebrated. **2** SPARKLING, glittering, scintillating, dazzling, glaring, blazing, intense, vivid, bright, shining, glossy, showy, glorious, magnificent, splendid. **3** CLEVER, brainy (infml), intelligent, quick, astute.
**F3** 1 undistinguished. 2 dull. 3 stupid.

**brim** n  rim, perimeter, circumference, lip, edge, margin, border, brink, verge, top, limit.

**bring** v  **1** CARRY, bear, convey, transport, fetch, take, deliver, escort, accompany, usher, guide, conduct, lead. **2** CAUSE, produce, engender,

**create**, prompt, provoke, force, attract, draw.

**bring about** cause, occasion, create, produce, generate, effect, accomplish, achieve, fulfil, realize, manage, engineer, manoeuvre, manipulate.

**bring in** earn, net, gross, produce, yield, fetch, return, accrue, realize.

**bring off** achieve, accomplish, fulfil, execute, discharge, perform, succeed, win.

**bring on** cause, occasion, induce, lead to, give rise to, generate, inspire, prompt, provoke, precipitate, expedite, accelerate, advance.
**E3** inhibit.

**bring out** 1 EMPHASIZE, stress, highlight, enhance, draw out.
2 PUBLISH, print, issue, launch, introduce.

**bring up** 1 REAR, raise, foster, nurture, educate, teach, train, form. 2 *bring up a subject*: introduce, broach, mention, submit, propose. 3 VOMIT, regurgitate, throw up (*infml*).

**brink** *n* verge, threshold, edge, margin, fringe, border, boundary, limit, extremity, lip, rim, brim, bank.

**brisk** *adj* 1 ENERGETIC, vigorous, quick, snappy, lively, spirited, active, busy, bustling, agile, nimble, alert.
2 INVIGORATING, exhilarating, stimulating, bracing, refreshing, fresh, crisp.
**E3** 1 lazy, sluggish.

**bristle** *n* hair, whisker, stubble, spine, prickle, barb, thorn.

**bristly** *adj* hairy, whiskered, bearded, unshaven, stubbly, rough, spiny, prickly, spiky, thorny.
**E3** clean-shaven, smooth.

**brittle** *adj* breakable, fragile, delicate, frail, crisp, crumbly, crumbling, friable, shattery, shivery.
**E3** durable, resilient.

**broad** *adj* 1 WIDE, large, vast, roomy, spacious, capacious, ample, extensive, widespread. 2 WIDE-RANGING, far-reaching, encyclopedic, catholic, eclectic, all-embracing, inclusive, comprehensive, general, sweeping, universal, unlimited.
**E3** 1 narrow. 2 restricted.

**broadcast** *v* air, show, transmit, beam, relay, televise, report, announce, publicize, advertise, publish, circulate, promulgate, disseminate, spread.
*n* transmission, programme, show.

**broaden** *v* widen, thicken, swell, spread, enlarge, expand, extend, stretch, increase, augment, develop, open up, branch out, diversify.

**broadminded** *adj* liberal, tolerant, permissive, enlightened, free-thinking, open-minded, receptive, unbiased, unprejudiced.
**E3** narrow-minded, intolerant, biased.

**brochure** *n* leaflet, booklet, pamphlet, prospectus, broadsheet, handbill, circular, handout, folder.

**broke** (*infml*) *adj* insolvent, penniless, bankrupt, bust, ruined, impoverished, destitute.
**E3** solvent, rich, affluent.

**broken** *adj* 1 FRACTURED, burst, ruptured, severed, separated, faulty, defective, out of order, shattered, destroyed, demolished.
2 DISJOINTED, disconnected, fragmentary, discontinuous, interrupted, intermittent, spasmodic, erratic, hesitating, stammering, halting, imperfect. 3 *a broken man*: beaten, defeated, crushed, demoralized, down, weak, feeble, exhausted, tamed, subdued, oppressed.
**E3** 1 mended. 2 fluent.

**broken-down** *adj* dilapidated, worn-out, ruined, collapsed, decayed, inoperative, out of order.

**broken-hearted** *adj* heartbroken, inconsolable, devastated, grief-stricken, desolate, despairing, miserable, wretched, mournful, sorrowful, sad, unhappy, dejected,

**brooch** *n* badge, pin, clip, clasp.

**brood** *v* ponder, ruminate, meditate, muse, mull over, go over, rehearse, dwell on, agonize, fret, mope.
*n* clutch, chicks, hatch, litter, young, offspring, issue, progeny, children, family.

**brook** *n* stream, rivulet, beck, burn, watercourse, channel.

**brother** *n* sibling, relation, relative, comrade, friend, mate, partner, colleague, associate, fellow, companion, monk, friar.

**brotherhood** *n* fraternity, association, society, league, confederation, confederacy, alliance, union, guild, fellowship, community, clique.

**browbeat** *v* bully, coerce, dragoon, bulldoze, awe, cow, intimidate, threaten, tyrannize, domineer, overbear, oppress, hound.
**E3** coax.

**brown** *adj* mahogany, chocolate, coffee, hazel, bay, chestnut, umber, sepia, tan, tawny, russet, rust, rusty, brunette, dark, dusky, sunburnt, tanned, bronzed, browned, toasted.

**browse** *v* 1 LEAF THROUGH, flick through, dip into, skim, survey, scan, peruse. 2 GRAZE, pasture, feed, eat, nibble.

**bruise** *v* discolour, blacken, mark, blemish, pound, pulverize, crush, hurt, injure, insult, offend, grieve.
*n* contusion, discoloration, black eye, shiner (*sl*), mark, blemish, injury.

**brush**[1] *n* broom, sweeper, besom.
*v* 1 CLEAN, sweep, flick, burnish, polish, shine. 2 TOUCH, contact, graze, kiss, stroke, rub, scrape.
**brush aside** dismiss, pooh-pooh, belittle, disregard, ignore, flout, override.
**brush off** disregard, ignore, slight, snub, cold-shoulder, rebuff, dismiss, spurn, reject, repulse, disown,

repudiate.
**brush up** 1 REVISE, relearn, improve, polish up, study, read up, swot (*infml*). 2 REFRESH, freshen up, clean, tidy.

**brush**[2] *n* scrub, thicket, bushes, shrubs, brushwood, undergrowth, ground cover.

**brush**[3] *n* confrontation, encounter, clash, conflict, fight, scrap, skirmish, set-to, tussle, dust-up (*infml*), fracas.

**brusque** *adj* abrupt, sharp, short, terse, curt, gruff, surly, discourteous, impolite, uncivil, blunt, tactless, undiplomatic.
**E3** courteous, polite, tactful.

**brutal** *adj* animal, bestial, beastly, brutish, inhuman, savage, bloodthirsty, vicious, ferocious, cruel, inhumane, remorseless, pitiless, merciless, ruthless, callous, insensitive, unfeeling, heartless, harsh, gruff, rough, coarse, crude, rude, uncivilized, barbarous.
**E3** kindly, humane, civilized.

**brutality** *n* savagery, bloodthirstiness, viciousness, ferocity, cruelty, inhumanity, violence, atrocity, ruthlessness, callousness, roughness, coarseness, barbarism, barbarity.
**E3** gentleness, kindness.

**brute** *n* animal, beast, swine, creature, monster, ogre, devil, fiend, savage, sadist, bully, lout.

**bubble** *n* blister, vesicle, globule, ball, drop, droplet, bead.
*v* effervesce, fizz, sparkle, froth, foam, seethe, boil, burble, gurgle.

**bubbly** *adj* 1 EFFERVESCENT, fizzy, sparkling, carbonated, frothy, foaming, sudsy. 2 LIVELY, bouncy, happy, merry, elated, excited.
**E3** 1 flat, still. 2 lethargic.

**bucket** *n* pail, can, bail, scuttle, vessel.

**buckle** *n* clasp, clip, catch, fastener.
*v* 1 *buckle one's belt*: fasten, clasp, catch, hook, hitch, connect, close, secure. 2 BEND, warp, twist, distort,

bulge, cave in, fold, wrinkle, crumple, collapse.

**bud** n shoot, sprout, germ, embryo.

v shoot, sprout, burgeon, develop, grow.

**F3** wither, waste away.

**budding** adj potential, promising, embryonic, burgeoning, developing, growing, flowering.

**budge** v move, stir, shift, remove, dislodge, push, roll, slide, propel, sway, influence, persuade, convince, change, bend, yield, give (way).

**budget** n finances, funds, resources, means, allowance, allotment, allocation, estimate.

v plan, estimate, alow, allot, allocate, apportion, ration.

**buff**[1] adj yellowish-brown, straw, sandy, fawn, khaki.

v polish, burnish, shine, smooth, rub, brush.

**buff**[2] (infml) n expert, connoisseur, enthusiast, fan, admirer, devotee, addict, fiend, freak.

**buffer** n shock-absorber, bumper, fender, pad, cushion, pillow, intermediary, screen, shield.

**buffet**[1] n snack-bar, counter, café, cafeteria.

**buffet**[2] v batter, hit, strike, knock, bang, bump, push, shove, pound, pummel, beat, thump, box, cuff, clout, slap.

n blow, knock, bang, bump, jar, jolt, push, shove, thump, box, cuff, clout, slap, smack.

**bug** n 1 VIRUS, bacterium, germ, microbe, micro-organism, infection, disease. 2 FAULT, defect, flaw, blemish, imperfection, failing, error, gremlin (infml).

v (infml) annoy, irritate, vex, irk, needle (infml), bother, disturb, harass, badger.

**build** v 1 ERECT, raise, construct, fabricate, make, form, constitute, assemble, knock together, develop, enlarge, extend, increase, augment,

escalate, intensify. 2 BASE, found, establish, institute, inaugurate, initiate, begin.

**F3** 1 destroy, demolish, knock down, lessen.

n physique, figure, body, form, shape, size, frame, structure.

**build up** strengthen, reinforce, fortify, extend, expand, develop, amplify, increase, escalate, intensify, heighten, boost, improve, enhance, publicize, advertise, promote, plug (infml), hype (sl).

**F3** weaken, lessen.

**building** n edifice, dwelling, erection, construction, fabrication, structure, architecture.

> *Types of building include*: house, bungalow, cottage, block of flats, cabin, farmhouse, villa, mansion, chateau, castle, palace; church, chapel, cathedral, abbey, monastery, temple, pagoda, mosque, synagogue; shop, store, garage, factory, warehouse, silo, office block, tower block, skyscraper, theatre, cinema, gymnasium, sports hall, restaurant, café, hotel, pub (infml), public house, inn, school, college, museum, library, hospital, prison, power station, observatory; barracks, fort, fortress, monument, mausoleum; shed, barn, outhouse, stable, mill, lighthouse, pier, pavilion, boat-house, beach-hut, summerhouse, gazebo, dovecote, windmill. *see also* **house**; **shop**.

**build-up** n 1 ENLARGEMENT, expansion, development, increase, gain, growth, escalation, publicity, promotion, plug (infml), hype (sl). 2 ACCUMULATION, mass, load, heap, stack, store, stockpile.

**F3** 1 reduction, decrease.

**bulbs and corms**

> *Plants grown from bulbs and corms include*: acidanthera, allium,

amaryllis, anemone, bluebell (endymion), chincherinchee, chionodoxa, crocosmia, crocus, autumn crocus (colchicum), cyclamen, daffodil, crown imperial (fritillaria), galtonia, garlic, gladiolus, grape hyacinth (muscari), hyacinth, iris, ixia, jonquil, lily, montbretia, narcissus, nerine, ranunculus, scilla, snowdrop (galanthus), sparaxis, tulip, winter aconite.

**bulge** n 1 SWELLING, bump, lump, hump, distension, protuberance, projection. 2 RISE, increase, surge, upsurge, intensification.
v swell, puff out, bulb, hump, dilate, expand, enlarge, distend, protrude, project.

**bulk** n size, magnitude, dimensions, extent, amplitude, bigness, largeness, immensity, volume, mass, weight, substance, body, preponderance, majority, most.

**bulky** adj substantial, big, large, huge, enormous, immense, mammoth, massive, colossal, hulking, hefty, heavy, weighty, unmanageable, unwieldy, awkward, cumbersome.
🔁 insubstantial, small, handy.

**bullet** n shot, pellet, ball, slug (infml), missile, projectile.

**bulletin** n report, newsflash, dispatch, communiqué, statement, announcement, notification, communication, message.

**bully** n persecutor, tormentor, browbeater, intimidator, bully-boy, heavy (sl), ruffian, tough.
v persecute, torment, terrorize, bulldoze, coerce, browbeat, bullyrag, intimidate, cow, tyrannize, domineer, overbear, oppress, push around.

**bump** v 1 HIT, strike, knock, bang, crash, collide (with). 2 JOLT, jerk, jar, jostle, rattle, shake, bounce.
n 1 BLOW, hit, knock, bang, thump, thud, smash, crash, collision, impact,

jolt, jar, shock. 2 LUMP, swelling, bulge, hump, protuberance.
**bump into** meet, encounter, run into, chance upon, come across.
**bump off** (infml) kill, murder, assassinate, eliminate (sl), liquidate (sl), do in (sl), top (sl).

**bumper** adj plentiful, abundant, large, great, enormous, massive, excellent, exceptional.
🔁 small.

**bumptious** adj self-important, pompous, officious, overbearing, pushy, assertive, over-confident, presumptuous, forward, impudent, arrogant, cocky, conceited, swaggering, boastful, full of oneself, egotistic.
🔁 humble, modest.

**bumpy** adj jerky, jolting, bouncy, choppy, rough, lumpy, knobbly, knobby, uneven, irregular.
🔁 smooth, even.

**bunch** n 1 BUNDLE, sheaf, tuft, clump, cluster, batch, lot, heap, pile, stack, mass, number, quantity, collection, assortment. 2 bunch of flowers: bouquet, posy, spray. 3 GANG, band, troop, crew, team, party, gathering, flock, swarm, crowd, mob, multitude.
v group, bundle, cluster, collect, assemble, congregate, gather, flock, herd, crowd, mass, pack, huddle.
🔁 disperse, scatter, spread out.

**bundle** n bunch, sheaf, roll, bale, truss, parcel, package, packet, carton, box, bag, pack, batch, consignment, group, set, collection, assortment, quantity, mass, accumulation, pile, stack, heap.
v pack, wrap, bale, truss, bind, tie, fasten.

**bungle** v mismanage, cock up (sl), screw up (sl), foul up (infml), mess up (infml), ruin, spoil, mar, botch, fudge, blunder.

**buoy** n float, marker, signal, beacon.
**buoy up** support, sustain, raise, lift,

boost, encourage, cheer, hearten.
**F3** depress, discourage.

**buoyant** adj **1** in buoyant mood:
light-hearted, carefree, bright,
cheerful, happy, joyful, lively,
animated, bouncy. **2** FLOATABLE,
floating, afloat, light, weightless.
**F3 1** depressed. **2** heavy.

**burden** n cargo, load, weight, dead-
weight, encumbrance, millstone,
onus, responsibility, obligation, duty,
strain, stress, worry, anxiety, care,
trouble, trial, affliction, sorrow.
v load, weigh down, encumber,
handicap, bother, worry, tax, strain,
overload, lie heavy on, oppress,
overwhelm.
**F3** unburden, relieve.

**bureau** n service, agency, office,
branch, department, division,
counter, desk.

**bureaucracy** n administration,
government, ministry, civil service,
the authorities, the system,
officialdom, red tape, regulations.

**burglar** n housebreaker, robber,
thief, pilferer, trespasser.

**burglary** n housebreaking, break-in,
robbery, theft, stealing, trespass.

**burial** n burying, interment,
entombment, funeral, obsequies.

**burly** adj big, well-built, hulking,
hefty, heavy, stocky, sturdy, brawny,
beefy, muscular, athletic, strapping,
strong, powerful.
**F3** small, puny, thin, slim.

**burn** v **1** FLAME, blaze, flare, flash,
glow, flicker, smoulder, smoke, fume,
simmer, seethe. **2** IGNITE, light,
kindle, incinerate, cremate, consume,
corrode. **3** SCALD, scorch, parch,
shrivel, singe, char, toast, brand,
sear, smart, sting, bite, hurt, tingle.

**burning** adj **1** ABLAZE, aflame,
afire, fiery, flaming, blazing,
flashing, gleaming, glowing,
smouldering, alight, lit, illuminated.
**2** HOT, scalding, scorching, searing,
piercing, acute, smarting, stinging,

prickling, tingling, biting, caustic,
pungent. **3** burning desire: ardent,
fervent, eager, earnest, intense,
vehement, passionate, impassioned,
frantic, frenzied, consuming.
**4** burning issue: urgent, pressing,
important, significant, crucial,
essential, vital.
**F3 2** cold. **3** apathetic. **4** unimportant.

**burrow** n warren, hole, earth, set,
den, lair, retreat, shelter, tunnel.
v tunnel, dig, delve, excavate, mine,
undermine.

**burst** v puncture, rupture, tear, split,
crack, break, fragment, shatter,
shiver, disintegrate, explode, blow
up, erupt, gush, spout, rush, run.
n **1** PUNCTURE, blow-out (infml),
rupture, split, crack, break, breach,
explosion, blast, bang, eruption. **2**
DISCHARGE, gush, spurt, surge, rush,
spate, torrent, outpouring, outburst,
outbreak, fit.

**bury** v **1** bury the dead: inter,
entomb, lay to rest, shroud. **2** SINK,
submerge, immerse, plant, implant,
embed, conceal, hide, cover,
enshroud, engulf, enclose, engross,
occupy, engage, absorb.
**F3 1** disinter, exhume. **2** uncover.

**bush** n **1** SHRUB, hedge, thicket. **2**
SCRUB, brush, scrubland,
backwoods, wilds.

**business** n **1** TRADE, commerce,
industry, manufacturing, dealings,
transactions, bargaining, trading,
buying, selling. **2** COMPANY, firm,
corporation, establishment,
organization, concern, enterprise,
venture. **3** JOB, occupation, work,
employment, trade, profession, line,
calling, career, vocation, duty, task,
responsibility. **4** AFFAIR, matter,
issue, subject, topic, question,
problem, point.

**businesslike** adj professional,
efficient, thorough, systematic,
methodical, organized, orderly, well-
ordered, practical, matter-of-fact,

precise, correct, formal, impersonal.
**F3** inefficient, disorganized.

**businessman, businesswoman** n
entrepreneur, industrialist, trader,
merchant, tycoon, magnate,
capitalist, financier, employer,
executive.

**bust** n **1** SCULPTURE, head, torso,
statue. **2** BOSOM, beasts, chest, breast.

**bustle** v dash, rush, scamper, scurry,
hurry, hasten, scramble, fuss.
n activity, stir, commotion, tumult,
agitation, excitement, fuss, ado, flurry,
hurry, haste.

**busy** adj occupied, engaged, tied up
(*infml*), employed, working, slaving,
stirring, restless, tireless, diligent,
industrious, active, lively, energetic,
strenuous, tiring, full, crowded,
swarming, teeming, bustling, hectic,
eventful.
**F3** idle, lazy, quiet.
v occupy, engage, employ, engross,
absorb, immerse, interest, concern,
bother.

**busybody** n meddler, nosey parker
(*infml*), intruder, pry, gossip,
eavesdropper, snoop, snooper,
troublemaker.

**butt**[1] n stub, end, tip, tail, base, foot,
shaft, stock, handle, haft.

**butt**[2] n target, mark, object, subject,
victim, laughing-stock, dupe.

**butt**[3] v, n hit, bump, knock, buffet,
push, shove, ram, thrust, punch, jab,
prod, poke.
**butt in** interrupt, cut in, interpose,
intrude, meddle, interfere.

**butterflies and moths**

*Types of butterfly include:* red
admiral, white admiral, apollo,
cabbage white, chalkhill blue,
common blue, brimstone, meadow
brown, Camberwell beauty, clouded
yellow, comma, large copper, small
copper, fritillary, Duke of Burgundy
fritillary, heath fritillary, gatekeeper,
grayling, hairstreak, purple
hairstreak, white letter hairstreak,
hermit, monarch, orange-tip, painted
lady, peacock, purple emperor,
ringlet, grizzled skipper, swallowtail,
tortoiseshell.
*Types of moth include:* brown-tail,
buff-tip, burnet, six-spot, carpet,
cinnabar, clothes, emperor, garden
tiger, gypsy, death's head hawkmoth,
privet hawkmoth, Kentish glory,
lackey, lappet, leopard, lobster,
magpie, oak hook-tip, pale tussock,
peach blossom, peppered, puss, red
underwing, silkworm, silver-Y,
swallowtail, turnip, wax, winter.

**buttocks** n rump, hindquarters, rear,
posterior (*infml*), seat, bottom,
behind, backside (*infml*), arse (*sl*).

**buttonhole** v accost, waylay, catch,
grab, nab, detain, importune.

**buttress** n support, prop, shore,
stay, brace, pier, strut, stanchion,
mainstay, reinforcement.
v support, prop up, shore up, hold
up, brace, strengthen, reinforce,
bolster up, sustain.
**F3** undermine, weaken.

**buy** v purchase, invest in (*infml*), pay
for, procure, acquire, obtain, get.
**F3** sell.
n purchase, acquisition, bargain, deal.

**buyer** n purchaser, shopper,
consumer, customer, vendee, emptor.
**F3** seller, vendor.

**by** prep near, next to, beside, along,
over, through, via, past.
adv near, close, handy, at hand, past,
beyond, away, aside.

**bypass** v avoid, dodge, sidestep,
skirt, circumvent, ignore, neglect,
omit.
n ring road, detour, diversion.

**by-product** n consequence, result,
side-effect, fallout (*infml*),
repercussion, after-effect.

**bystander** n spectator, onlooker,
looker-on, watcher, observer,
witness, eye-witness, passer-by.

# C

**cabin** *n* **1** BERTH, quarters, compartment, room. **2** HUT, shack, shanty, lodge, chalet, cottage, shed, shelter.

**cabinet** *n* cupboard, closet, dresser, case, locker.

**cable** *n* line, rope, cord, chain, wire, flex, lead.

**cadge** *v* scrounge, sponge, beg, hitch.

**café** *n* coffee shop, tea shop, tea room, coffee bar, cafeteria, snackbar, bistro, brasserie, restaurant.

**cage** *v* encage, coop up, shut up, confine, restrain, fence in, imprison, impound, incarcerate, lock up.
**F∃** release, let out, free.
*n* aviary, coop, hutch, enclosure, pen, pound, corral.

**cajole** *v* coax, persuade, wheedle, flatter, sweet-talk (*infml*), butter up (*infml*), tempt, lure, seduce, entice, beguile, mislead, dupe.
**F∃** bully, force, compel.

**cake** *v* coat, cover, encrust, dry, harden, solidify, consolidate, coagulate, congeal, thicken.
*n* **1** *tea and cakes*: gâteau, fancy, madeleine, bun, pie, flan. **2** LUMP, mass, bar, slab, block, loaf.

**calamitous** *adj* disastrous, catastrophic, ruinous, devastating, deadly, fatal, dire, ghastly, dreadful, tragic, woeful, grievous.
**F∃** good, fortunate, happy.

**calamity** disaster, catastrophe, mishap, misadventure, mischance, misfortune, adversity, reverse, trial, tribulation, affliction, distress, tragedy, ruin, downfall.
**F∃** blessing, godsend.

**calculate** *v* compute, work out, count, enumerate, reckon, figure, determine, weigh, rate, value, estimate, gauge, judge, consider, plan, intend, aim.

**calculating** *adj* crafty, cunning, sly, devious, scheming, designing, contriving, sharp, shrewd.
**F∃** artless, naïve.

**calculation** *n* sum, computation, answer, result, reckoning, figuring, estimate, forecast, judgement, planning, deliberation.

**calibre** *n* **1** DIAMETER, bore, gauge, size, measure. **2** *candidates of the right calibre*: talent, gifts, strength, worth, merit, quality, character, ability, capacity, faculty, stature, distinction.

**call** *v* **1** NAME, christen, baptize, title, entitle, dub, style, term, label, designate. **2** SHOUT, yell, exclaim, cry. **3** SUMMON, invite, bid, convene, assemble. **4** TELEPHONE, phone, ring (up), contact.
*n* **1** CRY, exclamation, shout, yell, scream. **2** VISIT, ring, summons, invitation. **3** *there's no call for it*: demand, need, occasion, cause, excuse, justification, reason, grounds, right. **4** APPEAL, request, plea, order, command, claim, announcement, signal.

**call for 1** DEMAND, require, need, necessitate, involve, entail, occasion, suggest. **2** FETCH, collect, pick up.

**call off** cancel, drop, abandon, discontinue, break off, withdraw.

**calling** *n* mission, vocation, career, profession, occupation, job, trade, business, line, work, employment, field, province, pursuit.

**callous** *adj* heartless, hard-hearted,

cold, indifferent, uncaring, unsympathetic, unfeeling, insensitive, hardened, thick-skinned.

**E3** kind, caring, sympathetic, sensitive.

**calm** adj 1 COMPOSED, self-possessed, collected, cool, dispassionate, unemotional, impassive, unmoved, placid, sedate, imperturbable, unflappable, unexcitable, laid back (sl), relaxed, unexcited, unruffled, unflustered, unperturbed, undisturbed, untroubled, unapprehensive. 2 calm waters: smooth, still, windless, unclouded, mild, tranquil, serene, peaceful, quiet, uneventful, restful.

**E3** 1 excitable, worried, anxious. 2 rough, wild, stormy.

v compose, soothe, relax, sedate, tranquillize, hush, quieten, placate, pacify.

**E3** excite, worry.

n calmness, stillness, tranquillity, serenity, peacefulness, peace, quiet, hush, repose.

**E3** storminess, restlessness.

**camera**

> Types of camera include:
> automatic, bellows, binocular, box Brownie®, camcorder, camera obscura, cine, cinematographic, compact, daguerreotype, disc, disposable, film, Instamatic®, large-format, miniature, subminiature, panoramic, plate, dry-plate, half-plate, quarter-plate, wet-plate, point-and-press, Polaroid®, press, reflex, folding reflex, single-lens reflex (SLR), twin-lens reflex (TLR), security, sliding box, sound, still, stereo, Super 8®, TV, video.

**camouflage** n disguise, guise, masquerade, mask, cloak, screen, blind, front, cover, concealment, deception.

v disguise, mask, cloak, veil, screen, cover, conceal, hide, obscure.

**E3** uncover, reveal.

**campaign** n crusade, movement, promotion, drive, push, offensive, attack, battle, expedition, operation.

v crusade, promote, push, advocate, fight, battle.

**cancel** v call off, abort, abandon, drop, abolish, annul, quash, rescind, revoke, repeal, countermand, delete, erase, obliterate, eliminate, offset, compensate, redeem, neutralize, nullify.

**cancer** n 1 EVIL, blight, canker, pestilence, sickness, corruption, rot. 2 TUMOUR, growth, malignancy, carcinoma.

**candid** adj frank, open, truthful, honest, sincere, forthright, straightforward, ingenuous, guileless, simple, plain, clear, unequivocal, blunt, outspoken.

**E3** guarded, evasive, devious.

**candidate** n applicant, aspirant, contender, contestant, competitor, entrant, runner, possibility, nominee, claimant, pretender, suitor.

**candour** n frankness, openness, truthfulness, honesty, plain-dealing, sincerity, straightforwardness, directness, ingenuousness, guilelessness, naïvety, artlessness, simplicity, plainness, bluntness, unequivocalness, outspokenness.

**E3** evasiveness, deviousness.

**canonical hours**

> Names of canonical hours include:
> compline, lauds, matins, none, prime, sext, terce, vespers.

**canopy** n awning, covering, shade, shelter, sunshade, umbrella.

**cantankerous** adj irritable, irascible, grumpy, grouchy, crusty, crotchety, crabbed, crabby, testy, bad-tempered, ill-humoured, cross, peevish, difficult, perverse, contrary, quarrelsome.

**F3** good-natured, easy-going (*infml*).

**canvass** *v* **1** ELECTIONEER, agitate, campaign, solicit, ask for, seek, poll. **2** EXAMINE, inspect, scrutinize, study, scan, investigate, analyse, sift, discuss, debate.
*n* poll, survey, examination, scrutiny, investigation, inquiry.

**canyon** *n* gorge, ravine, gully, valley.

**cap** *v* exceed, surpass, transcend, better, beat, outdo, outstrip, eclipse, complete, finish, crown, top, cover.
*n* **1** HAT, skullcap, beret, tam-o'-shanter. **2** LID, top, cover.

**capability** *n* ability, capacity, faculty, power, potential, means, facility, competence, qualification, skill, proficiency, talent.
**F3** inability, incompetence.

**capable** *adj* able, competent, efficient, qualified, experienced, accomplished, skilful, proficient, gifted, talented, masterly, clever, intelligent, fitted, suited, apt, liable, disposed.
**F3** incapable, incompetent, useless.

**capacity** *n* **1** VOLUME, space, room, size, dimensions, magnitude, extent, compass, range, scope. **2** CAPABILITY, ability, faculty, power, potential, competence, efficiency, skill, gift, talent, genius, cleverness, intelligence, aptitude, readiness. **3** *in her capacity as president*: role, function, position, office, post, appointment, job.

**cape**[1] *n* headland, head, promontory, point, ness, peninsula.

**cape**[2] *n* cloak, shawl, wrap, robe, poncho, coat.

**capital** *n* funds, finance, principal, money, cash, savings, investment(s), wealth, means, wherewithal, resources, assets, property, stock.

**capitalize on** *v* profit from, take advantage of, exploit, cash in on.

**capitulate** *v* surrender, throw in the towel, yield, give in, relent, submit, succumb.
**F3** fight on.

**capsize** *v* overturn, turn over, turn turtle, invert, keel over, upset.

**capsule** *n* pill, tablet, lozenge, receptacle, shell, sheath, pod, module.

**captain** *n* commander, master, skipper, pilot, head, chief, leader, boss, officer.

**captivate** *v* charm, enchant, bewitch, beguile, fascinate, enthral, hypnotize, mesmerize, lure, allure, seduce, win, attract, enamour, infatuate, enrapture, dazzle.
**F3** repel, disgust, appal.

**captive** *n* prisoner, hostage, slave, detainee, internee, convict.
*adj* imprisoned, caged, confined, restricted, secure, locked up, enchained, enslaved, ensnared.
**F3** free.

**captivity** *n* custody, detention, imprisonment, incarceration, internment, confinement, restraint, bondage, duress, slavery, servitude.
**F3** freedom.

**capture** *v* catch, trap, snare, take, seize, arrest, apprehend, imprison, secure.
*n* catching, trapping, taking, seizure, arrest, imprisonment.

**car** *n* automobile, motor car, motor, vehicle.

> *Types of car include*: saloon, hatchback, fastback, estate, sports car, cabriolet, convertible, limousine, limo (*infml*), wheels (*sl*), banger (*infml*), Mini, bubble-car, coupé, station wagon, shooting brake, veteran car, vintage car, Beetle (*infml*), four-wheel drive, Jeep®, buggy, Land Rover, Range Rover, panda car, patrol car, taxi, cab.

**carcase** *n* body, corpse, cadaver, remains, relics, skeleton, shell, structure, framework, hulk.

**care** *n* **1** WORRY, anxiety, stress,

strain, pressure, concern, trouble, distress, affliction, tribulation, vexation. **2** CAREFULNESS, caution, prudence, forethought, vigilance, watchfulness, pains, meticulousness, attention, heed, regard, consideration, interest. **3** *in their care*: keeping, custody, guardianship, protection, ward, charge, responsibility, control, supervision. **F3** **2** carelessness, thoughtlessness, inattention, neglect.
*v* worry, mind, bother.

**care for 1** LOOK AFTER, nurse, tend, mind, watch over, protect, minister to, attend. **2** LIKE, be fond of, love, be keen on, enjoy, delight in, want, desire.

**career** *n* vocation, calling, life-work, occupation, pursuit, profession, trade, job, employment, livelihood.
*v* rush, dash, tear, hurtle, race, run, gallop, speed, shoot, bolt.

**carefree** *adj* unworried, untroubled, unconcerned, blithe, breezy, happy-go-lucky, cheery, light-hearted, cheerful, happy, easy-going (*infml*), laid back (*infml*).
**F3** worried, anxious, despondent.

**careful** *adj* **1** CAUTIOUS, prudent, circumspect, judicious, wary, chary, vigilant, watchful, alert, attentive, mindful. **2** METICULOUS, painstaking, conscientious, scrupulous, thorough, detailed, punctilious, particular, accurate, precise, thoughtful.
**F3** **1** careless, inattentive, thoughtless, reckless. **2** careless.

**careless** *adj* **1** UNTHINKING, thoughtless, inconsiderate, uncaring, unconcerned, heedless, unmindful, forgetful, remiss, negligent, irresponsible, unguarded. **2** *careless work*: inaccurate, messy, untidy, disorderly, sloppy, neglectful, slipshod, slap-dash, hasty, cursory, offhand, casual.
**F3** **1** thoughtful, prudent. **2** careful, accurate, meticulous.

**caress** *v* stroke, pet, fondle, cuddle, hug, embrace, kiss, touch, rub.
*n* stroke, pat, fondle, cuddle, hug, embrace, kiss.

**caretaker** *n* janitor, porter, watchman, keeper, custodian, curator, warden, superintendent.

**cargo** *n* freight, load, pay-load, lading, tonnage, shipment, consignment, contents, goods, merchandise, baggage.

**caricature** *n* cartoon, parody, lampoon, burlesque, satire, send-up, take-off, imitation, representation, distortion, travesty.
*v* parody, mock, ridicule, satirize, send up, take off, mimic, distort, exaggerate.

**carnage** *n* bloodshed, blood-bath, butchery, slaughter, killing, murder, massacre, holocaust.

**carnival** *n* festival, fiesta, gala, jamboree, fête, fair, holiday, jubilee, celebration, merrymaking, revelry.

**carriage** *n* **1** COACH, wagon, car, vehicle. **2** DEPORTMENT, posture, bearing, air, manner, mien, demeanour, behaviour, conduct. **3** CARRYING, conveyance, transport, transportation, delivery, postage.

**carry** *v* **1** BRING, convey, transport, haul, move, transfer, relay, release, conduct, take, fetch. **2** BEAR, shoulder, support, underpin, maintain, uphold, sustain, suffer, stand.

**carry on 1** CONTINUE, proceed, last, endure, maintain, keep on, persist, persevere. **2** *carry on a business*: operate, run, manage, administer.
**F3** **1** stop, finish.

**carry out** do, perform, undertake, discharge, conduct, execute, implement, fulfil, accomplish, achieve, realize, bring off.

**cart** *n* barrow, handcart, wheel-barrow, wagon, truck.
*v* move, convey, transport, haul, lug (*infml*), hump (*infml*), bear, carry.

**carton** n  box, packet, pack, case, container, package, parcel.

**cartoon** n  comic strip, animation, sketch, drawing, caricature, parody.

**cartridge** n  cassette, canister, cylinder, tube, container, case, capsule, shell, magazine, round, charge.

**carve** v  cut, slice, hack, hew, chisel, chip, sculpt, sculpture, shape, form, fashion, mould, etch, engrave, incise, indent.

**cascade** n  rush, gush, outpouring, flood, deluge, torrent, avalanche, cataract, waterfall, falls, fountain, shower.

**E3** trickle.

v  rush, gush, surge, flood, overflow, spill, tumble, fall, descend, shower, pour, plunge, pitch.

**case**[1] n  container, receptacle, holder, suitcase, trunk, crate, box, carton, casket, chest, cabinet, showcase, casing, cartridge, shell, capsule, sheath, cover, jacket, wrapper.

**case**[2] n  **1** CIRCUMSTANCES, context, state, condition, position, situation, contingency, occurrence, occasion, event, specimen, example, instance, illustration, point.
**2** LAWSUIT, suit, trial, proceedings, action, process, cause, argument, dispute.

**cash** n  money, hard money, ready money, bank-notes, notes, coins, change, legal tender, currency, hard currency, bullion, funds, resources, wherewithal.

v  encash, exchange, realize, liquidate.

**cashier** n  clerk, teller, treasurer, bursar, purser, banker, accountant.

**cask** n  barrel, tun, hogshead, firkin, vat, tub, butt.

**cast** v  **1** THROW, hurl, lob, pitch, fling, toss, sling, shy, launch, impel, drive, direct, project, shed, emit, diffuse, spread, scatter. **2** MOULD, shape, form, model, found.

n  **1** COMPANY, troupe, actors, players, performers, entertainers, characters, dramatis personae.
**2** CASTING, mould, shape, form.

**cast down** depress, discourage, dishearten, deject, sadden, crush, desolate.

**E3** cheer up, encourage.

**castle** n  stronghold, fortress, citadel, keep, tower, château, palace, mansion, stately home, country house.

*Parts of a castle include*: approach, bailey, barbican, bartizan, bastion, battlements, brattice, buttress, chapel, corbel, courtyard, crenel, crenellation, curtain wall, ditch, donjon, drawbridge, dungeon, embrasure, enclosure wall, fosse, gatehouse, inner wall, keep, merlon, moat, motte, mound, outer bailey, parapet, portcullis, postern, rampart, scarp, stockade, tower, lookout tower, turret, ward, watchtower.

**casual** adj  **1** *a casual meeting*: chance, fortuitous, accidental, unintentional, unpremeditated, unexpected, unforeseen, irregular, random, occasional, incidental, superficial, cursory.
**2** NONCHALANT, blasé, lackadaisical, negligent, couldn't-care-less (*infml*), apathetic, indifferent, unconcerned, informal, offhand, relaxed, laid back (*infml*).

**E3** **1** deliberate, planned. **2** formal.

**casualty** n  injury, loss, death, fatality, victim, sufferer, injured person, wounded, dead person.

**cat**

*Breeds of cat include*: Abyssinian, American shorthair, Balinese, Birman, Bombay, British shorthair, British longhair, Burmese, Carthusian, chinchilla, Cornish rex, Cymric, Devon rex, domestic tabby,

Egyptian Mau, Exotic shorthair, Foreign Blue, Foreign spotted shorthair, Foreign White, Havana, Himalayan, Japanese Bobtail, Korat, Maine Coon, Manx, Norwegian Forest, Persian, rag-doll, rex, Russian Blue, Scottish Fold, Siamese, silver tabby, Singapura, Somali, Tiffany, Tonkinese, Tortoiseshell, Turkish Angora, Turkish Van.

**catalogue** n list, inventory, roll, register, roster, schedule, record, table, index, directory, gazetteer, brochure, prospectus.
  v list, register, record, index, classify, alphabetize, file.

**catapult** v hurl, fling, throw, pitch, toss, sling, launch, propel, shoot, fire.

**cataract** n waterfall, falls, rapids, force, cascade, downpour, torrent, deluge.

**catastrophe** n disaster, calamity, cataclysm, debacle, fiasco, failure, ruin, devastation, tragedy, blow, reverse, mischance, misfortune, adversity, affliction, trouble, upheaval.

**catch** v 1 SEIZE, grab, take, hold, grasp, grip, clutch, capture, trap, entrap, snare, ensnare, hook, net, arrest, apprehend. 2 HEAR, understand, perceive, recognize. 3 SURPRISE, expose, unmask, find (out), discover, detect, discern. 4 *catch a cold*: contract, get, develop, go down with.
  ⊟ 1 drop, release, free. 2 miss.
  n 1 FASTENER, clip, hook, clasp, hasp, latch, bolt. 2 DISADVANTAGE, drawback, snag, hitch, obstacle, problem.

**catch up** gain on, draw level with, overtake.

**catching** adj infectious, contagious, communicable, transmittable.

**catchword** n catch-phrase, slogan, motto, watchword, byword, password.

**catchy** adj memorable, haunting, popular, melodic, tuneful, attractive, captivating.
  ⊟ dull, boring.

**categorical** adj absolute, total, utter, unqualified, unreserved, unconditional, downright, positive, definite, emphatic, unequivocal, clear, explicit, express, direct.
  ⊟ tentative, qualified, vague.

**categorize** v class, classify, group, sort, grade, rank, order, list.

**category** n class, classification, group, grouping, sort, type, section, division, department, chapter, head, heading, grade, rank, order, list.

**cater** v provision, victual, provide, supply, furnish, serve, indulge, pander.

**catholic** adj broad, wide, wide-ranging, universal, global, general, comprehensive, inclusive, all-inclusive, all-embracing, liberal, tolerant, broad-minded.
  ⊟ narrow, limited, narrow-minded.

**cattle** n cows, bulls, oxen, livestock, stock, beasts.

*Breeds of cattle include*: Aberdeen Angus, Africander, Alderney, Ankole, Ayrshire, Blonde d'Aquitaine, Brahman, Brown Swiss, cattabu, cattalo, Charolais, Chillingham, Devon, dexter, Durham, Friesian, Galloway, Guernsey, Hereford, Highland, Holstein, Jersey, Latvian, Limousin, Longhorn, Luing, Red Poll, Romagnola, Santa Gertrudis, Shetland, Shorthorn, Simmenthaler, Teeswater, Ukrainian, Welsh Black.

**cause** n 1 SOURCE, origin, beginning, root, basis, spring, originator, creator, producer, maker, agent, agency. 2 REASON, motive, grounds, motivation, stimulus, incentive, inducement, impulse. 3 *a worthy cause*: object, purpose, end, ideal, belief, conviction, movement, undertaking, enterprise.

**E3** 1 effect, result, consequence.

*v* begin, give rise to, lead to, result in, occasion, bring about, effect, produce, generate, create, precipitate, motivate, stimulate, provoke, incite, induce, force, compel.

**E3** stop, prevent.

**caustic** *adj* corrosive, acid, burning, stinging, biting, cutting, mordant, trenchant, keen, pungent, bitter, acrimonious, sarcastic, scathing, virulent, severe.

**E3** soothing, mild.

**caution** *n* 1 CARE, carefulness, prudence, vigilance, watchfulness, alertness, heed, discretion, forethought, deliberation, wariness. 2 WARNING, caveat, injunction, admonition, advice, counsel.

**E3** 1 carelessness, recklessness.

*v* warn, admonish, advise, urge.

**cautious** *adj* careful, prudent, circumspect, judicious, vigilant, watchful, alert, heedful, discreet, tactful, chary, wary, cagey (*infml*), guarded, tentative, softly-softly, unadventurous.

**E3** incautious, imprudent, heedless, reckless.

**cavalcade** *n* procession, parade, march-past, troop, array, retinue, train.

**cavalier** *n* horseman, equestrian, knight, gentleman, gallant, escort, partner.

*adj* supercilious, condescending, lordly, haughty, lofty, arrogant, swaggering, insolent, scornful, disdainful, curt, offhand, free-and-easy.

**cave** *n* cavern, grotto, hole, pothole, hollow, cavity.

**cave in** collapse, subside, give way, yield, fall, slip.

**cavernous** *adj* hollow, concave, gaping, yawning, echoing, resonant, deep, sunken.

**cavity** *n* hole, gap, dent, hollow, crater, pit, well, sinus, ventricle.

**cavort** *v* caper, frolic, gambol, prance, skip, dance, frisk, sport, romp.

**cease** *v* stop, desist, refrain, pack in (*sl*), halt, call a halt, break off, discontinue, finish, end, conclude, terminate, fail, die.

**E3** begin, start, commence.

**ceaseless** *adj* endless, unending, never-ending, eternal, everlasting, continuous, non-stop, incessant, interminable, constant, perpetual, continual, persistent, untiring, unremitting.

**E3** occasional, irregular.

**cede** *v* surrender, give up, resign, abdicate, renounce, abandon, yield, relinquish, convey, transfer, hand over, grant, allow, concede.

**celebrate** *v* commemorate, remember, observe, keep, rejoice, toast, drink to, honour, exalt, glorify, praise, extol, eulogize, commend, bless, solemnize.

**celebrated** *adj* famous, well-known, famed, renowned, illustrious, glorious, eminent, distinguished, notable, prominent, outstanding, popular, acclaimed, exalted, revered.

**E3** unknown, obscure, forgotten.

**celebration** *n* commemoration, remembrance, observance, anniversary, jubilee, festival, gala, merrymaking, jollification, revelry, festivity, party, rave-up (*infml*).

---

*Celebrations include*: anniversary, banquet, baptism, bar mitzvah, birthday, centenary, christening, coming-of-age, commemoration, feast, fête, festival, gala, graduation, harvest festival, homecoming, Independence Day, jubilee, marriage, May Day, name-day, party, reception, remembrance, retirement, reunion, saint's day, thanksgiving, tribute, wedding. *see also* **anniversary**; **party**.

**celebrity** *n* personage, dignitary, VIP (*infml*), luminary, worthy, personality, name, big name, star, superstar.
Fa nobody, nonentity.

**celibacy** *n* singleness, bachelorhood, spinsterhood, virginity, chastity, purity, abstinence, continence.

**cell** *n* dungeon, prison, room, cubicle, chamber, compartment, cavity, unit.

**cellar** *n* basement, crypt, vault, storeroom, wine cellar.

**cement** *v* stick, bond, weld, solder, join, unite, bind, combine.
*n* plaster, mortar, concrete.

**cemetery** *n* burial-ground, graveyard, churchyard.

**censor** *v* cut, edit, blue-pencil, bowdlerize, expurgate.

**censorious** *adj* condemnatory, disapproving, disparaging, fault-finding, carping, cavilling, critical, hypercritical, severe.
Fa complimentary, approving.

**censure** *n* condemnation, blame, disapproval, criticism, admonishment, admonition, reprehension, reproof, reproach, rebuke, reprimand, telling-off (*infml*).
Fa praise, compliments, approval.
*v* condemn, denounce, blame, criticize, castigate, admonish, reprehend, reprove, upbraid, reproach, rebuke, reprimand, scold, tell off (*infml*).
Fa praise, compliment, approve.

**central** *adj* middle, mid, inner, interior, focal, main, chief, key, principal, primary, fundamental, vital, essential, important.
Fa peripheral, minor, secondary.

**centre** *n* middle, mid-point, bull's-eye, heart, core, nucleus, pivot, hub, focus, crux.
Fa edge, periphery, outskirts.
*v* focus, concentrate, converge, gravitate, revolve, pivot, hinge.

**ceremonial** *adj* formal, official, stately, solemn, ritual, ritualistic.
Fa informal, casual.
*n* ceremony, formality, protocol, solemnity, ritual, rite.

**ceremonious** *adj* stately, dignified, grand, solemn, ritual, civil, polite, courteous, deferential, courtly, formal, stiff, starchy, exact, precise, punctilious.
Fa unceremonious, informal, relaxed.

**ceremony** *n* *wedding ceremony*: service, rite, commemoration, observance, celebration, function, parade. **2** ETIQUETTE, protocol, decorum, propriety, formality, form, niceties, ceremonial, ritual, pomp, show.

**certain** *adj* **1** SURE, positive, assured, confident, convinced, undoubted, indubitable, unquestionable, incontrovertible, undeniable, irrefutable, plain, conclusive, absolute, convincing, true. **2** INEVITABLE, unavoidable, bound, destined, fated. **3** SPECIFIC, special, particular, individual, precise, express, fixed, established, settled, decided, definite. **4** DEPENDABLE, reliable, trustworthy, constant, steady, stable.
Fa **1** uncertain, unsure, hesitant, doubtful. **2** unlikely. **4** unreliable.

**certainly** *adv* of course, naturally, definitely, for sure, undoubtedly, doubtlessly.

**certainty** *n* sureness, positiveness, assurance, confidence, conviction, faith, trust, truth, validity, fact, reality, inevitability.
Fa uncertainty, doubt, hesitation.

**certificate** *n* document, award, diploma, qualification, credentials, testimonial, guarantee, endorsement, warrant, licence, authorization, pass, voucher.

**certify** *v* declare, attest, aver, assure, guarantee, endorse, corroborate, confirm, vouch, testify, witness, verify, authenticate, validate, authorize, license.

**chain** n 1 FETTER, manacle, restraint, bond, link, coupling, union. **2** *chain of events*: sequence, succession, progression, string, train, series, set.
v tether, fasten, secure, bind, restrain, confine, fetter, shackle, manacle, handcuff, enslave.
**Ea** release, free.

**chairman, chairwoman** n chairperson, chair, president, convenor, organizer, director, master of ceremonies, MC, toastmaster, speaker.

**challenge** v 1 DARE, defy, throw down the gauntlet, confront, brave, accost, provoke, test, tax, try.
**2** DISPUTE, question, query, protest, object to.
n dare, defiance, confrontation, provocation, test, trial, hurdle, obstacle, question, ultimatum.

**champion** n winner, victor, conqueror, hero, guardian, protector, defender, vindicator, patron, backer, supporter, upholder, advocate.
v defend, stand up for, back, support, maintain, uphold, espouse, advocate, promote.

**chance** n 1 ACCIDENT, fortuity, coincidence, fluke (*infml*), luck, fortune, providence, fate, destiny, risk, gamble, speculation, possibility, prospect, probability, likelihood, odds. **2** *a second chance*: opportunity, opening, occasion, time.
**Ea** 1 certainty.
v 1 RISK, hazard, gamble, wager, stake, try, venture. **2** HAPPEN, occur.
adj fortuitous, casual, accidental, inadvertent, unintentional, unintended, unforeseen, unlooked-for, random, haphazard, incidental.
**Ea** deliberate, intentional, foreseen, certain.

**change** v alter, modify, convert, reorganize, reform, remodel, restyle, transform, transfigure, metamorphose, mutate, vary, fluctuate, vacillate, shift, displace, swap, exchange, trade, switch, transpose, substitute, replace, alternate, interchange.
n alteration, modification, conversion, transformation, metamorphosis, mutation, variation, fluctuation, shift, exchange, transposition, substitution, interchange, difference, diversion, novelty, innovation, variety, transition, revolution, upheaval.

**changeable** adj variable, mutable, fluid, kaleidoscopic, shifting, mobile, unsettled, uncertain, unpredictable, unreliable, erratic, irregular, inconstant, fickle, capricious, volatile, unstable, unsteady, wavering, vacillating.
**Ea** constant, reliable.

**channel** n 1 DUCT, conduit, main, groove, furrow, trough, gutter, canal, flume, watercourse, waterway, strait, sound. **2** *channel of communication*: route, course, path, avenue, way, means, medium, approach, passage.
v direct, guide, conduct, convey, send, transmit, force.

**chant** n plainsong, psalm, song, melody, chorus, refrain, slogan, war cry.
v recite, intone, sing, chorus.

**chaos** n disorder, confusion, disorganization, anarchy, lawlessness, tumult, pandemonium, bedlam.
**Ea** order.

**chaotic** adj disordered, confused, disorganized, topsy-turvy, deranged, anarchic, lawless, riotous, tumultuous, unruly, uncontrolled.
**Ea** ordered, organized.

**chap** (*infml*) n fellow, bloke (*infml*), guy (*infml*), man, boy, person, individual, character, sort, type.

**chapter** n part, section, division, clause, topic, episode, period, phase, stage.

**character** n **1** PERSONALITY,
nature, disposition, temperament,
temper, constitution, make-up,
individuality, peculiarity, feature,
attributes, quality, type, stamp,
calibre, reputation, status, position,
trait. **2** LETTER, figure, symbol, sign,
mark, type, cipher, rune, hieroglyph,
ideograph. **3** INDIVIDUAL, person,
sort, type, role, part.

**characteristic** adj distinctive,
distinguishing, individual,
idiosyncratic, peculiar, specific,
special, typical, representative,
symbolic, symptomatic.
**E3** uncharacteristic, untypical.
n peculiarity, idiosyncrasy,
mannerism, feature, trait, attribute,
property, quality, hallmark, mark,
symptom.

**characterize** v typify, mark, stamp,
brand, identify, distinguish, indicate,
represent, portray.

**charge** v **1** charge a high price: ask,
demand, levy, exact, debit.
**2** ACCUSE, indict, impeach,
incriminate, blame. **3** ATTACK,
assail, storm, rush.
n **1** PRICE, cost, fee, rate, amount,
expense, expenditure, outlay, payment.
**2** ACCUSATION, indictment,
allegation, imputation. **3** ATTACK,
assault, onslaught, sortie, rush. **4** in
your charge: custody, keeping, care,
safekeeping, guardianship, ward,
trust, responsibility, duty.

**charitable** adj philanthropic,
humanitarian, benevolent, benign,
kind, compassionate, sympathetic,
understanding, considerate,
generous, magnanimous, liberal,
tolerant, broad-minded, lenient,
forgiving, indulgent, gracious.
**E3** uncharitable, inconsiderate,
unforgiving.

**charity** n **1** GENEROSITY,
bountifulness, alms-giving,
beneficence, philanthropy,

unselfishness, altruism, benevolence,
benignness, kindness, goodness,
humanity, compassion, tender-
heartedness, love, affection,
clemency, indulgence. **2** ALMS, gift,
handout, aid, relief, assistance.
**E3 1** selfishness, malice.

**charm** v please, delight, enrapture,
captivate, fascinate, beguile, enchant,
bewitch, mesmerize, attract, allure,
cajole, win, enamour.
**E3** repel.
n **1** ATTRACTION, allure,
magnetism, appeal, desirability,
fascination, enchantment, spell,
sorcery, magic. **2** lucky charm: trinket,
talisman, amulet, fetish, idol.

**charming** adj pleasing, delightful,
pleasant, lovely, captivating,
enchanting, attractive, fetching,
appealing, sweet, winsome, seductive,
winning, irresistible.
**E3** ugly, unattractive, repulsive.

**chart** n diagram, table, graph, map,
plan, blueprint.
v map, map out, sketch, draw, draft,
outline, delineate, mark, plot, place.

**charter** n right, privilege,
prerogative, authorization, permit,
licence, franchise, concession,
contract, indenture, deed, bond,
document.
v hire, rent, lease, commission,
engage, employ, authorize, sanction,
license.

**chase** v pursue, follow, hunt, track,
drive, expel, rush, hurry.

**chasm** n gap, opening, gulf, abyss,
void, hollow, cavity, crater, breach,
rift, split, cleft, fissure, crevasse,
canyon, gorge, ravine.

**chaste** adj pure, virginal, unsullied,
undefiled, immaculate, abstinent,
continent, celibate, virtuous, moral,
innocent, wholesome, modest,
decent, plain, simple, austere.
**E3** corrupt, lewd, vulgar, indecorous.

**chasten** v humble, humiliate, tame,
subdue, repress, curb, moderate,

soften, discipline, punish, correct,
chastise, castigate, reprove.

**chastise** *v* punish, discipline,
correct, beat, flog, whip, lash,
scourge, smack, spank, castigate,
reprove, admonish, scold, upbraid,
berate, censure.

**chat** *n* talk, conversation, natter
(*infml*), gossip, chinwag (*infml*), tête-
à-tête, heart-to-heart.
  *v* talk, crack, natter (*infml*), gossip,
chatter, rabbit (on) (*infml*).

**chatter** *v*, *n* prattle, babble, chat,
natter (*infml*), gossip, tattle.

**chatty** *adj* talkative, gossipy, newsy,
friendly, informal, colloquial,
familiar.
  ▣ quiet.

**cheap** *adj* 1 INEXPENSIVE,
reasonable, dirt-cheap, bargain,
reduced, cut-price, knock-down,
budget, economy, economical.
  2 TAWDRY, tatty, cheapo (*sl*),
shoddy, inferior, second-rate,
worthless, vulgar, common, poor,
paltry, mean, contemptible,
despicable, low.
  ▣ 1 expensive, costly. 2 superior,
noble, admirable.

**cheapen** *v* devalue, degrade, lower,
demean, depreciate, belittle,
disparage, denigrate, downgrade.

**cheat** *v* defraud, swindle, diddle,
short-change, do (*infml*), rip off (*sl*),
fleece, con (*infml*), double-cross,
mislead, deceive, dupe, fool, trick,
hoodwink, bamboozle (*infml*),
beguile.
  *n* cheater, dodger, fraud, swindler,
shark (*infml*), con man (*infml*),
extortioner, double-crosser, impostor,
charlatan, deceiver, trickster, rogue.

**check** *v* 1 EXAMINE, inspect,
scrutinize, give the once-over (*infml*),
investigate, probe, test, monitor,
study, research, compare, cross-
check, confirm, verify. 2 *check an
impulse*: curb, bridle, restrain,
control, limit, repress, inhibit, damp,

thwart, hinder, impede, obstruct, bar,
retard, delay, stop, arrest, halt.
  *n* 1 EXAMINATION, inspection,
scrutiny, once-over (*infml*), check-up,
investigation, audit, test, research.
  2 CURB, restraint, control, limitation,
constraint, inhibition, damper, blow,
disappointment, reverse, setback,
frustration, hindrance, impediment,
obstruction, stoppage.

**cheek** (*infml*) *n* impertinence,
impudence, insolence, disrespect,
effrontery, brazenness, temerity,
audacity, nerve (*infml*), gall.

**cheeky** (*infml*) *adj* impertinent,
impudent, insolent, disrespectful,
forward, brazen, pert, saucy (*infml*),
audacious.
  ▣ respectful, polite.

**cheer** *v* 1 ACCLAIM, hail, clap,
applaud. 2 COMFORT, console,
brighten, gladden, warm, uplift,
elate, exhilarate, encourage, hearten.
  ▣ 1 boo, jeer. 2 dishearten.
  *n* acclamation, hurrah, bravo,
applause, ovation.
  **cheer up** encourage, hearten, take
heart, rally, buck up (*infml*), perk up
(*infml*).

**cheerful** *adj* happy, glad, contented,
joyful, joyous, blithe, carefree, light-
hearted, cheery, good-humoured,
sunny, optimistic, enthusiastic,
hearty, genial, jovial, jolly, merry,
lively, animated, bright, chirpy,
breezy, jaunty, buoyant, sparkling.
  ▣ sad, dejected, depressed.

**cheese**

*Varieties of cheese include:*
Amsterdam, Bel Paese, Bleu
d'Auvergne, Blue Cheshire, Blue Vinny,
Boursin, Brie, Caboc, Caerphilly,
Camembert, Carré, Cheddar,
Cheshire, Churnton, cottage cheese,
cream cheese, Crowdie, curd cheese,
Danish blue, Derby, Dolcelatte,
Dorset Blue, Double Gloucester,
Dunlop, Edam, Emmental,

Emmentaler, ewe-cheese, Feta, fromage frais, Gloucester, Gorgonzola, Gouda, Gruyère, Huntsman, Jarlsberg, Killarney, Lancashire, Leicester, Limburg(er), Lymeswold, mascarpone, mouse-trap, mozzarella, Neufchâtel, Orkney, Parmesan, Petit Suisse, Pont-l'Éveque, Port Salut, processed cheese, quark, Red Leicester, Red Windsor, ricotta, Roquefort, sage Derby, Saint-Paulin, Stilton, stracchino, vegetarian cheese, Vacherin, Wensleydale.

## chemical elements

*The chemical elements (with their symbols) are*: actinium (Ac), aluminium (Al), americium (Am), antimony (Sb), argon (Ar), arsenic (As), astatine (At), barium (Ba), berkelium (Bk), beryllium (Be), bismuth (Bi), boron (B), bromine (Br), cadmium (Cd), caesium (Cs), calcium (Ca), californium (Cf), carbon (C), cerium (Ce), chlorine (Cl), chromium (Cr), cobalt (Co), copper (Cu), curium (Cm), dysprosium (Dy), einsteinium (Es), erbium (Er), europium (Eu), fermium (Fm), fluorine (F), francium (Fr), gadolinium (Gd), gallium (Ga), germanium (Ge), gold (Au), hafnium (Hf), hahnium (Ha), helium (He), holmium (Ho), hydrogen (H), indium (In), iodine (I), iridium (Ir), iron (Fe), krypton (Kr), lanthanum (La), lawrencium (Lr), lead (Pb), lithium (Li), lutetium (Lu), magnesium (Mg), manganese (Mn), mendelevium (Md), mercury (Hg), molybdenum (Mo), neodymium (Nd), neon (Ne), neptunium (Np), nickel (Ni), niobium (Nb), nitrogen (N), nobelium (No), osmium (Os), oxygen (O), palladium (Pd), phosphorus (P), platinum (Pt), plutonium (Pu), polonium (Po), potassium (K), praseodymium (Pr), promethium (Pm), protactinium (Pa),

radium (Ra), radon (Rn), rhenium (Re), rhodium (Rh), rubidium (Rb), ruthenium (Ru), rutherfordium (Rf), samarium (Sm), scandium (Sc), selenium (Se), silicon (Si), silver (Ag), sodium (Na), strontium (Sr), sulphur (S), tantalum (Ta), technetium (Tc), tellurium (Te), terbium (Tb), thallium (Tl), thorium (Th), thulium (Tm), tin (Sn), titanium (Ti), tungsten (W), uranium (U), vanadium (V), xenon (Xe), ytterbium (Yb), yttrium (Y), zinc (Zn), zirconium (Zr).

## chemistry

*Terms used in chemistry include*: analytical chemistry, biochemistry, inorganic chemistry, organic chemistry, physical chemistry; acid, alkali, analysis, atom, atomic number, atomic structure, subatomic particles, base, bond, buffer, catalysis, catalyst, chain reaction, chemical bond, chemical compound, chemical element, chemical equation, chemical reaction, chemist, chlorination, combustion, compound, corrosion, covalent bond, crystal, cycle, decomposition, diffusion, dissociation, distillation, electrochemical cell, electrode, electron, electrolysis, emulsion, fermentation, fixation, formula, free radical, gas, halogen, hydrolysis, immiscible, indicator, inert gas, ion, ionic bond, isomer, isotope, lipid, liquid, litmus paper, litmus test, mass, matter, metallic bond, mixture, mole, molecule, neutron, noble gas, nucleus, oxidation, periodic table, pH, polymer, proton, radioactivity, reaction, reduction, respiration, salt, solids, solution, solvent, substance, suspension, symbol, synthesis, valency, zwitterion.

**cherish** *v* foster, care for, look after, nurse, nurture, nourish, sustain, support, harbour, shelter, entertain, hold dear, value, prize, treasure.

**chest** n trunk, crate, box, case, casket, coffer, strongbox.

**chew** v masticate, gnaw, munch, champ, crunch, grind.

**chief** adj leading, foremost, uppermost, highest, supreme, grand, arch, premier, principal, main, key, central, prime, prevailing, predominant, pre-eminent, outstanding, vital, essential, primary, major.

🔁 minor, unimportant.

n ruler, chieftain, lord, master, supremo, head, principal, leader, commander, captain, governor, boss, director, manager, superintendent, superior, ringleader.

**chiefly** adv mainly, mostly, for the most part, predominantly, principally, primarily, essentially, especially, generally, usually.

**child** n youngster, kid (infml), nipper (infml), brat (infml), baby, infant, toddler, tot (infml), minor, juvenile, offspring, issue, progeny, descendant.

**childhood** n babyhood, infancy, boyhood, girlhood, schooldays, youth, adolescence, minority, immaturity.

**childish** adj babyish, boyish, girlish, infantile, puerile, juvenile, immature, silly, foolish, frivolous.

🔁 mature, sensible.

**childlike** adj innocent, naïve, ingenuous, artless, guileless, credulous, trusting, trustful, simple, natural.

**chill** v 1 COOL, refrigerate, freeze, ice. 2 FRIGHTEN, terrify, dismay, dishearten, discourage, depress, dampen.

🔁 1 warm, heat.

n coolness, cold, coldness, frigidity, rawness, bite, nip, crispness.

🔁 warmth.

**chilly** adj 1 chilly weather: cold, fresh, brisk, crisp, nippy (infml),

wintry. 2 a chilly response: cool, frigid, unsympathetic, unwelcoming, aloof, stony, unfriendly, hostile.

🔁 1 warm. 2 friendly.

**chime** v sound, strike, toll, ring, peal, clang, dong, jingle, tinkle.

**china** adj porcelain, ceramic, pottery, earthenware, terracotta.

**Chinese calendar**

> *The animals representing the years in which people are born:* rat, buffalo, tiger, rabbit (or hare), dragon, snake, horse, goat (or sheep), monkey, rooster, dog, pig.

**chink** n crack, rift, cleft, fissure, crevice, slot, opening, aperture, gap, space.

**chip** n 1 NOTCH, nick, scratch, dent, flaw. 2 FRAGMENT, scrap, wafer, sliver, flake, shaving, paring.

v chisel, whittle, nick, notch, gash, damage.

**chirp** v, n chirrup, tweet, cheep, peep, twitter, warble, sing, pipe, whistle.

**chivalrous** adj gentlemanly, polite, courteous, gallant, heroic, valiant, brave, courageous, bold, noble, honourable.

🔁 ungallant, cowardly.

**chivalry** n gentlemanliness, politeness, courtesy, gallantry, bravery, courage, boldness.

**choice** n option, alternative, selection, variety, pick, preference, say, decision, dilemma, election, discrimination, choosing, opting.

adj best, superior, prime, plum, excellent, fine, exquisite, exclusive, select, hand-picked, special, prize, valuable, precious.

🔁 inferior, poor.

**choke** v 1 THROTTLE, strangle, asphyxiate, suffocate, stifle, smother, suppress. 2 OBSTRUCT, constrict, congest, clog, block, dam, bar, close, stop. 3 COUGH, gag, retch.

**choose** v pick, select, single out, designate, predestine, opt for, plump for, vote for, settle on, fix on, adopt, elect, prefer, wish, desire, see fit.

**choosy** (infml) adj selective, discriminating, picky (infml), fussy, particular, finicky, fastidious, exacting.
Fa undemanding.

**chop** v cut, hack, hew, lop, sever, truncate, cleave, divide, split, slash.
**chop up** cut (up), slice (up), divide, cube, dice, mince.

**choppy** adj rough, turbulent, tempestuous, stormy, squally, ruffled, wavy, uneven, broken.
Fa calm, still.

**chore** n task, job, errand, duty, burden.

**chorus** n 1 REFRAIN, burden, response, call, shout. 2 CHOIR, choristers, singers, vocalists, ensemble.

**christen** v baptize, name, call, dub, title, style, term, designate, inaugurate, use.

**Christmas** n Xmas, Noel, Yule, Yuletide.

**chronic** adj 1 INCURABLE, deep-seated, recurring, incessant, persistent, inveterate, confirmed, habitual, ingrained, deep-rooted. 2 (infml) a chronic film: awful, terrible, dreadful, appalling, atrocious.
Fa 1 acute, temporary.

**chronological** adj historical, consecutive, sequential, progressive, ordered.

**chubby** adj plump, podgy, fleshy, flabby, stout, portly, rotund, round, tubby, paunchy.
Fa slim, skinny.

**chuckle** v laugh, giggle, titter, snigger, chortle, snort, crow.

**chunk** n lump, hunk, mass, wodge (infml), wedge, block, slab, piece, portion.

**church** n chapel, house of God, cathedral, minster, abbey, temple.

> *Names of church services include:* baptism, christening, Christingle, communion, Holy Communion, confirmation, dedication, Eucharist, evening service, evensong, funeral, Lord's Supper, marriage, Mass, High Mass, Midnight Mass, nuptial Mass, Requiem Mass, Holy Matrimony, memorial service, morning prayers, morning service. *see also* **canonical hours**.

**cinema** n 1 films, pictures, movies (infml), flicks (sl), big screen. 2 picture-house, picture-palace, fleapit (infml).

**circle** n 1 RING, hoop, loop, round, disc, sphere, globe, orb, cycle, turn, revolution, circuit, orbit, circumference, perimeter, coil, spiral. 2 circle of friends: group, band, company, crowd, set, clique, coterie, club, society, fellowship, fraternity. v 1 RING, loop, encircle, surround, gird, encompass, enclose, hem in, circumscribe, circumnavigate. 2 ROTATE, revolve, pivot, gyrate, whirl, turn, coil, wind.

> *Types of circle include:* annulus, ball, band, belt, circuit, circumference, coil, cordon, coronet, crown, curl, cycle, disc, discus, ellipse, girdle, globe, halo, hoop, lap, loop, orb, orbit, oval, perimeter, plate, revolution, ring, rotation, round, saucer, sphere, spiral, turn, tyre, wheel, wreath.

**circuit** n lap, orbit, revolution, tour, journey, course, route, track, round, beat, district, area, region, circumference, boundary, bounds, limit, range, compass, ambit.

**circuitous** adj roundabout, periphrastic, indirect, oblique, devious, tortuous, winding,

meandering, rambling, labyrinthine.
**F3** direct, straight.

**circular** *adj* round, annular, ring-shaped, hoop-shaped, disc-shaped.
*n* handbill, leaflet, pamphlet, notice, announcement, advertisement, letter.

**circulate** *v* **1** *circulate information*: spread, diffuse, broadcast, publicize, publish, issue, propagate, pass round, distribute. **2** GO ROUND, rotate, revolve, gyrate, whirl, swirl, flow.

**circulation** *n* **1** BLOOD-FLOW, flow, motion, rotation, circling. **2** SPREAD, transmission, publication, dissemination, distribution.

**circumference** *n* circuit, perimeter, rim, edge, outline, boundary, border, bounds, limits, extremity, margin, verge, fringe, periphery.

**circumstances** *n* details, particulars, facts, items, elements, factors, conditions, state, state of affairs, situation, position, status, lifestyle, means, resources.

**cistern** *n* tank, reservoir, sink, basin, vat.

**citadel** *n* fortress, stronghold, bastion, castle, keep, tower, fortification, acropolis.

**cite** *v* quote, adduce, name, specify, enumerate, mention, refer to, advance, bring up.

**citizen** *n* city-dweller, townsman, townswoman, inhabitant, denizen, resident, householder, taxpayer, subject.

**city** *n* metropolis, town, municipality, conurbation.

**civic** *adj* city, urban, municipal, borough, community, local, public, communal.

**civil** *adj* **1** POLITE, courteous, well-mannered, well-bred, courtly, refined, civilized, polished, urbane, affable, complaisant, obliging, accommodating. **2** *civil affairs*: domestic, home, national, internal, interior, state, municipal, civic.
**F3 1** uncivil, discourteous, rude.

**2** international, military.

**civility** *n* politeness, courteousness, courtesy, breeding, refinement, urbanity, graciousness, affability, amenity.
**F3** discourtesy, rudeness.

**civilization** *n* progress, advancement, development, education, enlightenment, cultivation, culture, refinement, sophistication, urbanity.
**F3** barbarity, primitiveness.

**civilize** *v* tame, humanize, educate, enlighten, cultivate, refine, polish, sophisticate, improve, perfect.

**civilized** *adj* advanced, developed, educated, enlightened, cultured, refined, sophisticated, urbane, polite, sociable.
**F3** uncivilized, barbarous, primitive.

**claim** *v* **1** ALLEGE, pretend, profess, state, affirm, assert, maintain, contend, hold, insist. **2** *claim a refund*: ask, request, require, need, demand, exact, take, collect.
*n* **1** ALLEGATION, pretension, affirmation, assertion, contention, insistence. **2** APPLICATION, petition, request, requirement, demand, call, right, privilege.

**clairvoyant** *adj* psychic, prophetic, visionary, telepathic, extra-sensory.
*n* psychic, fortune-teller, prophet, prophetess, visionary, seer, soothsayer, augur, oracle, diviner, telepath.

**clammy** *adj* damp, moist, sweaty, sweating, sticky, slimy, dank, muggy, heavy, close.

**clamp** *n* vice, grip, press, brace, bracket, fastener.
*v* fasten, secure, fix, clinch, grip, brace.

**clan** *n* tribe, family, house, race, society, brotherhood, fraternity, confraternity, sect, faction, group, band, set, clique, coterie.

**clap** *v* **1** APPLAUD, acclaim, cheer. **2** SLAP, smack, pat, wallop (*infml*), whack (*infml*), bang.

**clarify** v **1** EXPLAIN, throw light on, illuminate, elucidate, gloss, define, simplify, resolve, clear up. **2** REFINE, purify, filter, clear.

**Ea** obscure, confuse. **2** cloud.

**clarity** n clearness, transparency, lucidity, simplicity, intelligibility, comprehensibility, explicitness, unambiguousness, obviousness, definition, precision.

**Ea** obscurity, vagueness, imprecision.

**clash** v **1** CRASH, bang, clank, clang, jangle, clatter, rattle, jar.
**2** CONFLICT, disagree, quarrel, wrangle, grapple, fight, feud, war.
n **1** CRASH, bang, jangle, clatter, noise. **2** a clash with the police: confrontation, showdown, conflict, disagreement, fight, brush.

**clasp** n **1** FASTENER, buckle, clip, pin, hasp, hook, catch. **2** HOLD, grip, grasp, embrace, hug.
v **1** HOLD, grip, grasp, clutch, embrace, enfold, hug, squeeze, press.
**2** FASTEN, connect, attach, grapple, hook, clip, pin.

**class** n **1** CATEGORY, classification, group, set, section, division, department, sphere, grouping, order, league, rank, status, caste, quality, grade, type, genre, sort, kind, species, genus, style. **2** a French class: lesson, lecture, seminar, tutorial, course.

> Social classes/groups include:
> aristocracy, nobility, gentry, landed
> gentry, gentlefolk, élite, nob (sl), high
> society, top drawer (infml), upper
> class, Sloane Ranger (sl), ruling class,
> jet set, middle class, lower class,
> working class, bourgeoisie, proletariat,
> hoi-polloi, commoner, serf, plebeian,
> pleb (infml).

v categorize, classify, group, sort, rank, grade, rate, designate, brand.

**classic** adj typical, characteristic, standard, regular, usual, traditional, time-honoured, established, archetypal, model, exemplary, ideal, best, finest, first-rate, consummate, definitive, masterly, excellent, ageless, immortal, undying, lasting, enduring, abiding.

**Ea** unrepresentative, second-rate.
n standard, model, prototype, exemplar, masterwork, masterpiece, pièce de résistance.

**classical** adj elegant, refined, pure, traditional, excellent, well-proportioned, symmetrical, harmonious, restrained.

**Ea** modern, inferior.

**classification** n categorization, taxonomy, sorting, grading, arrangement, systematization, codification, tabulation, cataloguing.

**classify** v categorize, class, group, pigeonhole, sort, grade, rank, arrange, dispose, distribute, systematize, codify, tabulate, file, catalogue.

**clause** n article, item, part, section, subsection, paragraph, heading, chapter, passage, condition, proviso, provision, specification, point.

**claw** n talon, nail, pincer, nipper, gripper.
v scratch, scrabble, scrape, graze, tear, rip, lacerate, maul, mangle.

**clean** adj **1** WASHED, laundered, sterile, aseptic, antiseptic, hygienic, sanitary, sterilized, decontaminated, purified, pure, unadulterated, fresh, unpolluted, uncontaminated, immaculate, spotless, unspotted, unstained, unsoiled, unsullied, perfect, faultless, flawless, unblemished. **2** a clean life: innocent, guiltless, virtuous, upright, moral, honest, honourable, respectable, decent, chaste. **3** SMOOTH, regular, straight, neat, tidy.

**Ea** **1** dirty, polluted. **2** dishonourable, indecent. **3** rough.

v wash, bath, launder, rinse, wipe, sponge, scrub, scour, mop, swab, sweep, vacuum, dust, freshen,

91     **clip**

deodorize, cleanse, purge, purify,
decontaminate, disinfect, sanitize,
sterilize, clear, filter.
**F∃** dirty, defile.

**cleanser** *n* soap, soap powder,
detergent, cleaner, solvent, scourer,
scouring powder, purifier,
disinfectant.

**clear** *adj* **1** PLAIN, distinct,
comprehensible, intelligible,
coherent, lucid, explicit, precise,
unambiguous, well-defined,
apparent, evident, patent, obvious,
manifest, conspicuous, unmistakable,
unquestionable. **2** SURE, certain,
positive, definite, convinced. **3** *clear
water*: transparent, limpid,
crystalline, glassy, see-through, clean,
unclouded, colourless. **4** *a clear day*:
cloudless, unclouded, fine, bright,
sunny, light, luminous, undimmed.
**5** UNOBSTRUCTED, unblocked, open,
free, empty, unhindered, unimpeded.
**6** AUDIBLE, perceptible, pronounced,
distinct, recognizable.
**F∃** **1** unclear, vague, ambiguous,
confusing. **2** unsure, muddled.
**3** opaque, cloudy. **4** dull. **5** blocked. **6**
inaudible, indistinct.
*v* **1** UNBLOCK, unclog, decongest,
free, rid, extricate, disentangle, loosen.
**2** CLEAN, wipe, erase, cleanse, refine,
filter, tidy, empty, unload. **3** ACQUIT,
exculpate, exonerate, absolve,
vindicate, excuse, justify, free, liberate,
release, let go.
**F∃** **1** block. **2** dirty, defile. **3** condemn.

**clear up** **1** EXPLAIN, clarify, elucidate,
unravel, solve, resolve, answer.
**2** TIDY, order, sort, rearrange,
remove.

**clearance** *n* **1** AUTHORIZATION,
sanction, endorsement, permission,
consent, leave, OK (*infml*), go-ahead,
green light (*infml*). **2** SPACE, gap,
headroom, margin, allowance.

**clearing** *n* space, gap, opening,
glade, dell.

**clergy** *n* clergymen, churchmen,

clerics, the church, the cloth,
ministry, priesthood.

**clergyman** *n* churchman, cleric,
ecclesiastic, divine, man of God,
minister, priest, reverend, father,
vicar, pastor, padre, parson, rector,
canon, dean, deacon, chaplain,
curate, presbyter, rabbi.

**clerical** *adj* **1** OFFICE, secretarial,
white-collar, official, administrative.
**2** ECCLESIASTIC(AL), pastoral,
ministerial, priestly, episcopal,
canonical, sacerdotal.

**clever** *adj* intelligent, brainy (*infml*),
bright, smart, witty, gifted, expert,
knowledgeable, adroit, apt, able,
capable, quick, quick-witted, sharp,
keen, shrewd, knowing, discerning,
cunning, ingenious, inventive,
resourceful, sensible, rational.
**F∃** foolish, stupid, senseless, ignorant.

**cliché** *n* platitude, commonplace,
banality, truism, bromide, chestnut,
stereotype.

**client** *n* customer, patron, regular,
buyer, shopper, consumer, user,
patient, applicant.

**cliff** *n* bluff, face, rock-face, scar,
scarp, escarpment, crag, overhang,
precipice.

**climate** *n* weather, temperature,
setting, milieu, environment,
ambience, atmosphere, feeling,
mood, temper, disposition, tendency,
trend.

**climax** *n* culmination, height, high
point, highlight, acme, zenith, peak,
summit, top, head.
**F∃** nadir.

**climb** *v* ascend, scale, shin up,
clamber, mount, rise, soar, top.

**climb down** retract, eat one's words,
back down, retreat.

**cling** *v* clasp, clutch, grasp, grip,
stick, adhere, cleave, fasten, embrace,
hug.

**clip¹** *v* trim, snip, cut, prune, pare,
shear, crop, dock, poll, truncate,
curtail, shorten, abbreviate.

**clip²** *v* pin, staple, fasten, attach, fix, hold.

**clipping** *n* cutting, snippet, quotation, citation, passage, section, excerpt, extract, clip.

**clique** *n* circle, set, coterie, group, bunch, pack, gang, crowd, faction, clan.

**cloak** *n* cape, mantle, robe, wrap, coat, cover, shield, mask, front, pretext.
*v* cover, veil, mask, screen, hide, conceal, obscure, disguise, camouflage.

**clocks and watches**

---

*Types of clock or watch include*: alarm-clock, digital clock, mantel clock, bracket clock, carriage clock, cuckoo-clock, longcase clock, grandfather clock, grandmother clock, speaking clock, Tim (*infml*); wrist-watch, fob-watch, repeating watch, chronograph, pendant watch, ring-watch, stop-watch; chronometer; sundial.

---

**clog** *v* block, choke, stop up, bung up, dam, congest, jam, obstruct, impede, hinder, hamper, burden.
**F3** unblock.

**close¹** *v* **1** SHUT, fasten, secure, lock, bar, obstruct, block, clog, plug, cork, stop up, fill, seal, fuse, join, unite. **2** END, finish, complete, conclude, terminate, wind up, stop, cease.
**F3 1** open, separate. **2** start.
*n* end, finish, completion, conclusion, culmination, ending, finale, dénouement, termination, cessation, stop, pause.

**close²** *adj* **1** NEAR, nearby, at hand, neighbouring, adjacent, adjoining, impending, imminent. **2** INTIMATE, dear, familiar, attached, devoted, loving. **3** OPPRESSIVE, heavy, muggy, humid, sultry, sweltering, airless, stifling, suffocating, stuffy,

unventilated. **4** MISERLY, mean, parsimonious, tight (*infml*), stingy, niggardly. **5** SECRETIVE, uncommunicative, taciturn, private, secret, confidential. **6** *a close translation*: exact, precise, accurate, strict, literal, faithful. **7** *pay close attention*: fixed, concentrated, intense, keen. **8** DENSE, solid, packed, cramped.
**F3 1** far, distant. **2** cool, unfriendly. **3** fresh, airy. **4** generous. **5** open. **6** rough.

**clot** *n* lump, mass, thrombus, thrombosis, clotting, coagulation.
*v* coalesce, curdle, coagulate, congeal, thicken, solidify, set, gel.

**cloth** *n* **1** FABRIC, material, stuff, textile. **2** RAG, face-cloth, flannel, dish-cloth, floorcloth, duster, towel.

**clothe** *v* dress, put on, robe, attire, deck, outfit, rig, vest, invest, drape, cover.
**F3** undress, strip, disrobe.

**clothes** *n* clothing, garments, wear, attire, garb, gear (*infml*), togs (*infml*), outfit, get-up (*infml*), dress, costume, wardrobe.

---

*Clothes include*: suit, trouser suit, dress suit, catsuit, jumpsuit, tracksuit, shell suit, wet suit; dress, frock, evening-dress, shirtwaister, caftan, kimono, sari; skirt, mini skirt, dirndl, pencil-skirt, pinafore-skirt, divided-skirt, culottes, kilt, sarong; cardigan, jumper, jersey, sweater, polo-neck, turtle-neck, guernsey, pullover, twin-set, shirt, dress-shirt, sweat-shirt, tee-shirt, T-shirt, tunic, waistcoat, blouse, smock, tabard, tunic; trousers, jeans, Levis®, denims, slacks, cords, flannels, drainpipes, bell-bottoms, dungarees, leggings, pedal-pushers, breeches, plus-fours, jodhpurs, Bermuda shorts, hot pants, shorts; bra, brassière, body stocking, camisole, liberty bodice, corset, girdle, garter, suspender belt, suspenders, shift, slip, petticoat, teddy, basque, briefs, pants, panties, French knickers, camiknickers, pantihose, tights, stockings; underpants, boxer-shorts, Y-fronts, vest, string vest, singlet; swimsuit, bathing-costume, bikini, swimming costume, swimming trunks, leotard, salopette; nightdress, nightie (*infml*) pyjamas, bed-jacket, bedsocks, dressing-gown, housecoat, negligee; scarf, glove, mitten, muffler, earmuffs, leg-warmers, sock, tie, bow-tie, cravat, stole, shawl, belt, braces, cummerbund, veil, yashmak. *see also* **coat**; **footwear**; **hat**.

**cloud** *n* vapour, haze, mist, fog, gloom, darkness, obscurity.
*v* mist, fog, blur, dull, dim, darken, shade, shadow, overshadow, eclipse, veil, shroud, obscure, muddle, confuse, obfuscate.
**F3** clear.

*Types of cloud include*: cirrus, cirrostratus, cirrocumulus, altocumulus, altostratus, cumulus, stratocumulus, nimbostratus, fractostratus, fractocumulus, cumulonimbus, stratus.

**cloudy** *adj* nebulous, hazy, misty, foggy, blurred, blurry, opaque, milky, muddy, dim, indistinct, obscure, dark, murky, sombre, leaden, lowering, overcast, dull, sunless.
**F3** clear, bright, sunny, cloudless.

**clown** *n* buffoon, comic, comedian, joker, jester, fool, harlequin, pierrot.

**club** *n* **1** ASSOCIATION, society, company, league, guild, order, union, fraternity, group, set, circle, clique.
**2** BAT, stick, mace, bludgeon, truncheon, cosh (*sl*).
*v* hit, strike, beat, bash, clout, clobber (*sl*), bludgeon, cosh (*sl*), batter,
pummel.

**clue** *n* hint, tip, suggestion, idea, notion, lead, tip-off, pointer, sign, indication, evidence, trace, suspicion, inkling, intimation.

**clump** *n* cluster, bundle, bunch, mass, tuft, thicket.
*v* tramp, clomp, stamp, stomp, plod, lumber, thump, thud.

**clumsy** *adj* bungling, ham-fisted, unhandy, unskilful, inept, bumbling, blundering, lumbering, gauche, ungainly, gawky (*infml*), unco-ordinated, awkward, ungraceful, uncouth, rough, crude, ill-made, shapeless, unwieldy, heavy, bulky, cumbersome.
**F3** careful, graceful, elegant.

**cluster** *n* bunch, clump, batch, group, knot, mass, crowd, gathering, collection, assembly.
*v* bunch, group, gather, collect, assemble, flock.

**clutch** *v* hold, clasp, grip, hang on to, grasp, seize, snatch, grab, catch, grapple, embrace.

**clutter** *n* litter, mess, jumble, untidiness, disorder, disarray, muddle, confusion.
*v* litter, encumber, fill, cover, strew, scatter.

**coach** *n* trainer, instructor, tutor, teacher.
*v* train, drill, instruct, teach, tutor, cram, prepare.

**coagulate** *v* clot, curdle, congeal, thicken, solidify, gel.
**F3** melt.

**coalition** *n* merger, amalgamation, combination, integration, fusion, alliance, league, bloc, compact, federation, confederation, confederacy, association, affiliation, union.

**coarse** *adj* **1** ROUGH, unpolished, unfinished, uneven, lumpy, unpurified, unrefined, unprocessed.
**2** *coarse humour*: bawdy, ribald, earthy, smutty, vulgar, crude,

offensive, foul-mouthed, boorish, loutish, rude, impolite, indelicate, improper, indecent, immodest.

**E3** 1 smooth, fine. 2 refined, sophisticated, polite.

**coast** n coastline, seaboard, shore, beach, seaside.

v free-wheel, glide, slide, sail, cruise, drift.

**coat** n 1 FUR, hair, fleece, pelt, hide, skin. 2 LAYER, coating, covering.

> *Types of coat include*: overcoat, greatcoat, car-coat, duffel coat, Afghan, blanket, frock-coat, tail-coat, jacket, bomber jacket, dinner-jacket, donkey-jacket, hacking-jacket, reefer, pea-jacket, shooting-jacket, safari jacket, Eton jacket, matinee jacket, tuxedo, blazer, raincoat, trench-coat, mackintosh, mac (*infml*), Burberry, parka, anorak, cagoul, windcheater, jerkin, blouson, cape, cloak, poncho.

v cover, paint, spread, smear, plaster.

**coating** n covering, layer, dusting, wash, coat, blanket, sheet, membrane, film, glaze, varnish, finish, veneer, lamination, overlay.

**coax** v persuade, cajole, wheedle, sweet-talk (*infml*), soft-soap, flatter, beguile, allure, entice, tempt.

**cocky** adj arrogant, bumptious, self-important, conceited, vain, swollen-headed, egotistical, swaggering, brash, cocksure, self-assured, self-confident, overconfident.

**E3** humble, modest, shy.

**code** n 1 ETHICS, rules, regulations, principles, system, custom, convention, etiquette, manners. 2 *written in code*: cipher, secret language.

**coerce** v force, drive, compel, constrain, pressurize, bully, intimidate, browbeat, bludgeon, bulldoze, dragoon, press-gang.

**coercion** n force, duress, compulsion, constraint, pressure,

bullying, intimidation, threats, browbeating.

**coffer** n casket, case, box, chest, trunk, strongbox, treasury, repository.

**cognition** n perception, awareness, knowledge, apprehension, discernment, insight, comprehension, understanding, intelligence, reasoning.

**cohere** v 1 STICK, adhere, cling, fuse, unite, bind, combine, coalesce, consolidate. 2 *the argument does not cohere*: agree, square, correspond, harmonize, hold, hang together.

**E3** 1 separate.

**coherent** adj articulate, intelligible, comprehensible, meaningful, lucid, consistent, logical, reasoned, rational, sensible, orderly, systematic, organized.

**E3** incoherent, unintelligible, meaningless.

**coil** v wind, spiral, convolute, curl, loop, twist, writhe, snake, wreathe, twine, entwine.

n roll, curl, loop, ring, convolution, spiral, corkscrew, helix, twist.

**coin** v invent, make up, think up, conceive, devise, formulate, originate, create, fabricate, produce, mint, forge.

n piece, bit, money, cash, change, small change, loose change, silver, copper.

**coincide** v coexist, synchronize, agree, concur, correspond, square, tally, accord, harmonize, match.

**coincidence** n 1 CHANCE, accident, eventuality, fluke (*infml*), luck, fortuity. 2 COEXISTENCE, conjunction, concurrence, correspondence, correlation.

**coincidental** adj 1 CHANCE, accidental, casual, unintentional, unplanned, flukey (*infml*), lucky, fortuitous. 2 COINCIDENT, coexistent, concurrent, simultaneous, synchronous.

**E3** 1 deliberate, planned.

**cold** adj **1** UNHEATED, cool, chilled, chilly, chill, shivery, nippy, parky (*infml*), raw, biting, bitter, wintry, frosty, icy, glacial, freezing, frozen, arctic, polar. **2** UNSYMPATHETIC, unmoved, unfeeling, stony, frigid, unfriendly, distant, aloof, standoffish, reserved, undemonstrative, unresponsive, indifferent, lukewarm.

**E3** 1 hot, warm. 2 friendly, responsive.

n  coldness, chill, chilliness, coolness, frigidity, iciness.

**E3** warmth.

**cold-blooded** adj cruel, inhuman, brutal, savage, barbaric, barbarous, merciless, pitiless, callous, unfeeling, heartless.

**E3** compassionate, merciful.

**collaborate** v conspire, collude, work together, co-operate, join forces, team up, participate.

**collaboration** n conspiring, collusion, association, alliance, partnership, teamwork, co-operation.

**collaborator** n co-worker, associate, partner, team-mate, colleague, assistant, accomplice, traitor, turncoat.

**collapse** v **1** *collapse with exhaustion*: faint, pass out, crumple. **2** FALL, sink, founder, fail, fold (*infml*), fall apart, disintegrate, crumble, subside, cave in.

n  failure, breakdown, flop, debacle, downfall, ruin, disintegration, subsidence, cave-in, faint, exhaustion.

**colleague** n workmate, co-worker, team-mate, partner, collaborator, ally, associate, confederate, confrère, comrade, companion, aide, helper, assistant, auxiliary.

**collect** v gather, assemble, congregate, convene, muster, rally, converge, cluster, aggregate, accumulate, amass, heap, hoard, stockpile, save, acquire, obtain, secure.

**E3** disperse, scatter.

**collected** adj composed, self-possessed, placid, serene, calm, unruffled, unperturbed, imperturbable, cool.

**E3** anxious, worried, agitated.

**collection** n **1** GATHERING, assembly, convocation, congregation, crowd, group, cluster, accumulation, conglomeration, mass, heap, pile, hoard, stockpile, store. **2** SET, assemblage, assortment, job-lot, anthology, compilation.

**collective** adj united, combined, concerted, co-operative, joint, common, shared, corporate, democratic, composite, aggregate, cumulative.

**E3** individual.

**collective nouns**

---

*Collective nouns (by animal) include*: shrewdness of *apes*, cete of *badgers*, sloth of *bears*, swarm of *bees*, obstinacy of *buffaloes*, clowder of *cats*, drove of *cattle*, brood of *chickens*, bask of *crocodiles*, murder of *crows*, herd of *deer*, pack of *dogs*, school of *dolphins*, dole of *doves*, team of *ducks*, parade of *elephants*, busyness of *ferrets*, charm of *finches*, shoal of *fish*, skulk of *foxes*, army of *frogs*, gaggle/skein of *geese*, tribe of *goats*, husk of *hares*, cast of *hawks*, brood of *hens*, bloat of *hippopotamuses*, string of *horses*, pack of *hounds*, troop of *kangaroos*, kindle of *kittens*, exaltation of *larks*, leap of *leopards*, pride of *lions*, swarm of *locusts*, tittering of *magpies*, troop of *monkeys*, watch of *nightingales*, family of *otters*, parliament of *owls*, pandemonium of *parrots*, covey of *partridges*, muster of *peacocks*, rookery of *penguins*, nye of *pheasants*, litter of *pigs*, school of *porpoises*, bury of *rabbits*, colony of *rats*, unkindness of *ravens*, crash of *rhinoceroses*, building of *rooks*, pod of *seals*, flock of *sheep*, murmuration of *starlings*, ambush of *tigers*, rafter of *turkeys*, turn of *turtles*, descent of *woodpeckers*, gam of *whales*, rout of *wolves*, zeal of *zebras*.

## collectors and enthusiasts

*Names of collectors and enthusiasts include:* zoophile (*animals*), antiquary (*antiques*), tegestologist (*beer mats*), campanologist (*bell-ringing*), ornithologist (*birds*), bibliophile (*books*), audiophile (*broadcast and recorded sound*), lepidopterist (*butterflies*), cartophilist (*cigarette cards*), numismatist (*coins/medals*), conservationist (*countryside*), environmentalist (*the environment*), xenophile (*foreigners*), gourmet (*good food*), gastronome (*good-living*), discophile (*gramophone records*), chirographist (*hand-writing*), hippophile (*horses*), entomologist (*insects*), phillumenist (*matches/matchboxes*), monarchist (*the monarchy*), deltiologist (*postcards*), arachnologist (*spiders/arachnids*), philatelist (*stamps*), arctophile (*teddy bears*), etymologist (*words*).

**collide** *v* crash, bump, smash, clash, conflict, confront, meet.

**collision** *n* impact, crash, bump, smash, accident, pile-up, clash, conflict, confrontation, opposition.

**colloquial** *adj* conversational, informal, familiar, everyday, vernacular, idiomatic.
**Ⓔ** formal.

**collude** *v* conspire, plot, connive, collaborate, scheme, machinate, intrigue.

**colonist** *n* colonial, settler, immigrant, emigrant, pioneer.

**colonize** *v* settle, occupy, people, populate.

**colony** *n* settlement, outpost,

dependency, dominion, possession, territory, province.

**colossal** *adj* huge, enormous, immense, vast, massive, gigantic, mammoth, monstrous, monumental.
**Ⓔ** tiny, minute.

**colour** *n* **1** HUE, shade, tinge, tone, tincture, tint, dye, paint, wash, pigment, pigmentation, coloration, complexion. **2** VIVIDNESS, brilliance, rosiness, ruddiness, glow, liveliness, animation.

*The range of colours includes:* red, crimson, scarlet, vermilion, cherry, cerise, magenta, maroon, burgundy, ruby, orange, tangerine, apricot, coral, salmon, peach, amber, brown, chestnut, mahogany, bronze, auburn, rust, copper, cinnamon, chocolate, tan, sepia, taupe, beige, fawn, yellow, lemon, canary, ochre, saffron, topaz, gold, chartreuse, green, eau de nil, emerald, jade, bottle, avocado, sage, khaki, turquoise, aquamarine, cobalt, blue, sapphire, gentian, indigo, navy, violet, purple, mauve, plum, lavender, lilac, pink, rose, magnolia, cream, ecru, milky, white, grey, silver, charcoal, ebony, jet, black.

*v* **1** PAINT, crayon, dye, tint, stain, tinge. **2** BLUSH, flush, redden. **3** *colour one's judgement:* affect, bias, prejudice, distort, pervert, exaggerate, falsify.

**colourful** *adj* **1** MULTICOLOURED, kaleidoscopic, variegated, parti-coloured, vivid, bright, brilliant, rich, intense. **2** *a colourful description:* vivid, graphic, picturesque, lively, stimulating, exciting, interesting.
**Ⓔ** **1** colourless, drab.

**colourless** *adj* **1** TRANSPARENT, neutral, bleached, washed out, faded, pale, ashen, sickly, anaemic.
**2** INSIPID, lacklustre, dull, dreary, drab, plain, characterless, unmemorable, uninteresting, tame.

🖪 1 colourful. 2 bright, exciting.

**column** n 1 PILLAR, post, shaft, upright, support, obelisk. 2 LIST, line, row, rank, file, procession, queue, string.

**comb** v 1 *comb one's hair*: groom, neaten, tidy, untangle. 2 SEARCH, hunt, scour, sweep, sift, screen, rake, rummage, ransack.

**combat** n war, warfare, hostilities, action, battle, fight, skirmish, struggle, conflict, clash, encounter, engagement, contest, bout, duel.
v fight, battle, strive, struggle, contend, contest, oppose, resist, withstand, defy.

**combination** n 1 BLEND, mix, mixture, composite, amalgam, synthesis, compound. 2 MERGER, amalgamation, unification, alliance, coalition, association, federation, confederation, confederacy, combine, consortium, syndicate, union, integration, fusion, coalescence, connection.

**combine** v merge, amalgamate, unify, blend, mix, integrate, incorporate, synthesize, compound, fuse, bond, bind, join, connect, link, marry, unite, pool, associate, co-operate.
🖪 divide, separate, detach.

**come** v advance, move towards, approach, near, draw near, reach, attain, arrive, enter, appear, materialize, happen, occur.
🖪 go, depart, leave.

**come about** happen, occur, come to pass, transpire, result, arise.

**come across** find, discover, chance upon, happen upon, bump into, meet, encounter, notice.

**come along** arrive, happen, develop, improve, progress, rally, mend, recover, recuperate.

**come apart** disintegrate, fall to bits, break, separate, split, tear.

**come between** separate, part, divide, split up, disunite, estrange, alienate.

**come down** descend, fall, reduce, decline, deteriorate, worsen, degenerate.

**come in** enter, appear, show up (*infml*), arrive, finish.

**come off** happen, occur, take place, succeed.

**come on** begin, appear, advance, proceed, progress, develop, improve, thrive, succeed.

**come out** result, end, conclude, terminate.

**come out with** say, state, affirm, declare, exclaim, disclose, divulge.

**come round** 1 *come round from the anaesthetic*: recover, wake, awake. 2 YIELD, relent, concede, allow, grant, accede.

**come through** endure, withstand, survive, prevail, triumph, succeed, accomplish, achieve.

**come up** rise, arise, happen, occur, crop up.

**comeback** n return, reappearance, resurgence, revival, recovery.

**comedian** n comic, clown, humorist, wit, joker, wag.

**comedown** n anticlimax, let-down, disappointment, deflation, blow, reverse, decline, descent, demotion, humiliation, degradation.

**comedy** n farce, slapstick, clowning, hilarity, drollery, humour, wit, joking, jesting, facetiousness.

**comfort** v ease, soothe, relieve, alleviate, assuage, console, cheer, gladden, reassure, hearten, encourage, invigorate, strengthen, enliven, refresh.
n 1 CONSOLATION, compensation, cheer, reassurance, encouragement, alleviation, relief, help, aid, support. 2 EASE, relaxation, luxury, snugness, cosiness, wellbeing, satisfaction, contentment, enjoyment.
🖪 1 distress. 2 discomfort.

**comfortable** adj 1 SNUG, cosy, comfy (*infml*), relaxing, restful, easy, convenient, pleasant, agreeable,

enjoyable, delightful. **2** AT EASE, relaxed, contented, happy.
**3** AFFLUENT, well-off, well-to-do, prosperous.
**E₃** **1** uncomfortable, unpleasant. **2** uneasy, nervous. **3** poor.

**comic** *adj* funny, hilarious, side-splitting, comical, droll, humorous, witty, amusing, entertaining, diverting, joking, facetious, light, farcical, ridiculous, ludicrous, absurd, laughable, priceless (*infml*), rich (*infml*).
**E₃** tragic, serious.
*n* comedian, gagster (*infml*), joker, jester, clown, buffoon, humorist, wit, wag.

**coming** *adj* next, forthcoming, impending, imminent, due, approaching, near, future, aspiring, rising, up-and-coming.
*n* advent, approach, arrival, accession.

**command** *v* **1** ORDER, bid, charge, enjoin, direct, instruct, require, demand, compel. **2** LEAD, head, rule, reign, govern, control, dominate, manage, supervise.
*n* **1** COMMANDMENT, decree, edict, precept, mandate, order, bidding, charge, injunction, directive, direction, instruction, requirement. **2** *be in command*: power, authority, leadership, control, domination, dominion, rule, sway, government, management.

**commander** *n* leader, head, chief, boss, commander-in-chief, general, admiral, captain, commanding officer, officer.

**commemorate** *v* celebrate, solemnize, remember, memorialize, mark, honour, salute, immortalize, observe, keep.

**commemoration** *n* celebration, observance, remembrance, tribute, honouring, ceremony.

**commence** *v* begin, start, embark on, originate, initiate, inaugurate,

open, launch.
**E₃** finish, end, cease.

**commend** *v* **1** PRAISE, compliment, acclaim, extol, applaud, approve, recommend. **2** COMMIT, entrust, confide, consign, deliver, yield.
**E₃** **1** criticize, censure.

**comment** *v* say, mention, interpose, interject, remark, observe, note, annotate, interpret, explain, elucidate, criticize.
*n* statement, remark, observation, note, annotation, footnote, marginal note, explanation, elucidation, illustration, exposition, commentary, criticism.

**commentary** *n* narration, voice-over, analysis, description, review, critique, explanation, notes, treatise.

**commentator** *n* sportscaster, broadcaster, reporter, narrator, commenter, critic, annotator, interpreter.

**commerce** *n* trade, traffic, business, dealings, relations, dealing, trafficking, exchange, marketing, merchandising.

**commercial** *adj* trade, trading, business, sales, profit-making, profitable, sellable, saleable, popular, monetary, financial, mercenary, venal.

**commission** *n* **1** ASSIGNMENT, mission, errand, task, job, duty, function, appointment, employment, mandate, warrant, authority, charge, trust. **2** COMMITTEE, board, delegation, deputation, representative. **3** *commission on a sale*: percentage, cut (*infml*), rake-off (*infml*), allowance, fee.
*v* nominate, select, appoint, engage, employ, authorize, empower, delegate, depute, send, order, request, ask for.

**commit** *v* **1** *commit a crime*: do, perform, execute, enact, perpetrate. **2** ENTRUST, confide, commend, consign, deliver, hand over, give, deposit. **3** BIND, obligate, pledge, engage, involve.

**commit oneself** decide, undertake, promise, pledge, bind oneself.

**commitment** n undertaking, guarantee, assurance, promise, word, pledge, vow, engagement, involvement, dedication, devotion, adherence, loyalty, tie, obligation, duty, responsibility, liability.
**F3** vacillation, wavering.

**committee** n council, board, panel, jury, commission, advisory group, think-tank, working party, task force.

**common** adj **1** FAMILIAR, customary, habitual, usual, daily, everyday, routine, regular, frequent, widespread, prevalent, general, universal, standard, average, ordinary, plain, simple, workaday, run-of-the-mill, undistinguished, unexceptional, conventional, accepted, popular, commonplace.
**2** VULGAR, coarse, unrefined, crude, inferior, low, ill-bred, loutish, plebeian. **3** COMMUNAL, public, shared, mutual, joint, collective.
**F3 1** uncommon, unusual, rare, noteworthy. **2** tasteful, refined.

**commonplace** adj ordinary, everyday, common, humdrum, pedestrian, banal, trite, widespread, frequent, hackneyed, stock, stale, obvious, worn out, boring, uninteresting, threadbare.
**F3** memorable, exceptional.

**commonsense** adj commonsensical, matter-of-fact, sensible, level-headed, sane, sound, reasonable, practical, down-to-earth, pragmatic, hard-headed, realistic, shrewd, astute, prudent, judicious.
**F3** foolish, unreasonable, unrealistic.

**commotion** n agitation, hurly-burly, turmoil, tumult, excitement, ferment, fuss, bustle, ado, to-do (infml), uproar, furore, ballyhoo (infml), hullaballoo (infml), racket, hubbub, rumpus, fracas, disturbance, bust-up

(infml), disorder, riot.

**communal** adj public, community, shared, joint, collective, general, common.
**F3** private, personal.

**commune** n collective, co-operative, kibbutz, community, fellowship, colony, settlement.
v converse, discourse, communicate, make contact.

**communicate** v **1** ANNOUNCE, declare, proclaim, report, reveal, disclose, divulge, impart, inform, acquaint, intimate, notify, publish, disseminate, spread, diffuse, transmit, convey. **2** TALK, converse, commune, correspond, write, phone, telephone, contact.

**communication** n information, intelligence, intimation, disclosure, contact, connection, transmission, dissemination.

---

*Forms of communication include:* broadcasting, radio, wireless, television, TV, cable TV, satellite, video, teletext; newspaper, press, news, newsflash, magazine, journal, advertising, publicity, poster, leaflet, pamphlet, brochure, catalogue; post, dispatch, correspondence, letter, postcard, aerogram, telegram, cable, wire (infml), chain letter, junk mail, mailshot; conversation, word, message, dialogue, speech, gossip, grapevine (infml); notice, bulletin, announcement, communiqué, circular, memo, note, report; telephone, intercom, answering machine, walkie-talkie, bleeper, tannoy, telex, teleprinter, facsimile, fax, computer, word processor, typewriter, dictaphone, megaphone, loud-hailer; radar, Morse code, semaphore, Braille, sign language.

---

**communicative** adj talkative, voluble, expansive, informative, chatty, sociable, friendly,

forthcoming, outgoing, extrovert, unreserved, free, open, frank, candid.
**F3** quiet, reserved, reticent, secretive.

**community** n district, locality, population, people, populace, public, residents, nation, state, colony, commune, kibbutz, society, association, fellowship, brotherhood, fraternity.

**commute** v **1** REDUCE, decrease, shorten, curtail, lighten, soften, mitigate, remit, adjust, modify, alter, change, exchange, alternate.
**2** *commute by train*: travel, journey.

**compact** adj small, short, brief, terse, succinct, concise, condensed, compressed, close, dense, impenetrable, solid, firm.
**F3** large, rambling, diffuse.

**companion** n fellow, comrade, friend, buddy (*infml*), crony (*infml*), intimate, confidant(e), ally, confederate, colleague, associate, partner, mate, consort, escort, chaperon, attendant, aide, assistant, accomplice, follower.

**companionship** n fellowship, comradeship, camaraderie, esprit de corps, support, friendship, company, togetherness, conviviality, sympathy, rapport.

**company** n **1** *a manufacturing company*: firm, business, concern, association, corporation, establishment, house, partnership, syndicate, cartel, consortium.
**2** TROUPE, group, band, ensemble, set, circle, crowd, throng, body, troop, crew, party, assembly, gathering, community, society.
**3** GUESTS, visitors, callers, society, companionship, fellowship, support, attendance, presence.

**comparable** adj similar, alike, related, akin, cognate, corresponding, analogous, equivalent, tantamount, proportionate, commensurate, parallel, equal.

**F3** dissimilar, unlike, unequal.

**compare** v liken, equate, contrast, juxtapose, balance, weigh, correlate, resemble, match, equal, parallel.

**comparison** n juxtaposition, analogy, parallel, correlation, relationship, likeness, resemblance, similarity, comparability, contrast, distinction.

**compartment** n section, division, subdivision, category, pigeonhole, cubbyhole, niche, alcove, bay, area, stall, booth, cubicle, locker, carrel, cell, chamber, berth, carriage.

**compassion** n kindness, tenderness, fellow-feeling, humanity, mercy, pity, sympathy, commiseration, condolence, sorrow, concern, care.
**F3** cruelty, indifference.

**compassionate** adj kind-hearted, kindly, tender-hearted, tender, caring, warm-hearted, benevolent, humanitarian, humane, merciful, clement, lenient, pitying, sympathetic, understanding, supportive.
**F3** cruel, indifferent.

**compatible** adj harmonious, consistent, congruous, matching, consonant, accordant, suitable, reconcilable, adaptable, conformable, sympathetic, like-minded, well-matched, similar.
**F3** incompatible, antagonistic, contradictory.

**compel** v force, make, constrain, oblige, necessitate, drive, urge, impel, coerce, pressurize, hustle, browbeat, bully, strongarm, bulldoze, press-gang, dragoon.

**compelling** adj forceful, coercive, imperative, urgent, pressing, irresistible, overriding, powerful, cogent, persuasive, convincing, conclusive, incontrovertible, irrefutable, gripping, enthralling, spellbinding, mesmeric, compulsive.
**F3** weak, unconvincing, boring.

**compensate** v balance,

counterbalance, cancel, neutralize, counteract, offset, redress, satisfy, requite, repay, refund, reimburse, indemnify, recompense, reward, remunerate, atone, redeem, make good, restore.

**compensation** n amends, redress, satisfaction, requital, repayment, refund, reimbursement, indemnification, indemnity, damages, reparation, recompense, reward, payment, remuneration, return, restoration, restitution, consolation, comfort.

**compete** v vie, contest, fight, battle, struggle, strive, oppose, challenge, rival, emulate, contend, participate, take part.

**competent** adj capable, able, adept, efficient, trained, qualified, well-qualified, skilled, experienced, proficient, expert, masterly, equal, fit, suitable, appropriate, satisfactory, adequate, sufficient.
**E3** incompetent, incapable, unable, inefficient.

**competition** n **1** CONTEST, championship, tournament, cup, event, race, match, game, quiz. **2** RIVALRY, opposition, challenge, contention, conflict, struggle, strife, competitiveness, combativeness. **3** COMPETITORS, rivals, opponents, challengers, field.

**competitive** adj combative, contentious, antagonistic, aggressive, pushy, ambitious, keen, cut-throat.

**competitor** n contestant, contender, entrant, candidate, challenger, opponent, adversary, antagonist, rival, emulator, competition, opposition.

**compile** v compose, put together, collect, gather, garner, cull, accumulate, amass, assemble, marshal, organize, arrange.

**complacent** adj smug, self-satisfied, gloating, triumphant, proud, self-righteous, unconcerned, serene, self-assured, pleased, gratified, contented, satisfied.
**E3** diffident, concerned, discontented.

**complain** v protest, grumble, grouse, gripe, beef, carp, fuss, lament, bemoan, bewail, moan, whine, groan, growl.

**complaint** n **1** PROTEST, objection, grumble, grouse, gripe, beef, moan, grievance, dissatisfaction, annoyance, fault-finding, criticism, censure, accusation, charge. **2** a chest complaint: ailment, illness, sickness, disease, malady, malaise, indisposition, affliction, disorder, trouble, upset.

**complementary** adj reciprocal, interdependent, correlative, interrelated, corresponding, matching, twin, fellow, companion.
**E3** contradictory, incompatible.

**complete** adj **1** UTTER, total, absolute, downright, out-and-out, thorough, perfect. **2** FINISHED, ended, concluded, over, done, accomplished, achieved. **3** UNABRIDGED, unabbreviated, unedited, unexpurgated, integral, whole, entire, full, undivided, intact.
**E3** **1** partial. **2** incomplete. **3** abridged.
v finish, end, close, conclude, wind up, terminate, finalize, settle, clinch, perform, discharge, execute, fulfil, realize, accomplish, achieve, consummate, crown, perfect.

**completion** n finish, end, close, conclusion, termination, finalization, settlement, discharge, fulfilment, realization, accomplishment, achievement, attainment, fruition, culmination, consummation, perfection.

**complex** adj complicated, intricate, elaborate, involved, convoluted, circuitous, tortuous, devious, mixed, varied, diverse, multiple, composite, compound, ramified.
**E3** simple, easy.
n **1** NETWORK, structure, system,

scheme, organization, establishment, institute, development. **2** FIXATION, obsession, preoccupation, hang-up (*infml*), phobia.

**complexion** *n* **1** skin, colour, colouring, pigmentation. **2** look, appearance, aspect, light, character, nature, type, kind.

**complicate** *v* compound, elaborate, involve, muddle, mix up, confuse, tangle, entangle.
€3 simplify.

**complicated** *adj* complex, intricate, elaborate, involved, convoluted, tortuous, difficult, problematic, puzzling, perplexing.
€3 simple, easy.

**complication** *n* difficulty, drawback, snag, obstacle, problem, ramification, repercussion, complexity, intricacy, elaboration, convolution, tangle, web, confusion, mixture.

**compliment** *n* flattery, admiration, favour, approval, congratulations, tribute, honour, accolade, bouquet, commendation, praise, eulogy.
€3 insult, criticism.
*v* flatter, admire, commend, praise, extol, congratulate, applaud, salute.
€3 insult, condemn.

**complimentary** *adj* **1** FLATTERING, admiring, favourable, approving, appreciative, congratulatory, commendatory, eulogistic.
**2** *complimentary ticket*: free, gratis, honorary, courtesy.
€3 **1** insulting, unflattering, critical.

**comply** *v* agree, consent, assent, accede, yield, submit, defer, respect, observe, obey, fall in, conform, follow, perform, discharge, fulfil, satisfy, meet, oblige, accommodate.
€3 defy, disobey.

**component** *n* part, constituent, ingredient, element, factor, item, unit, piece, bit, spare part.

**compose** *v* **1** CONSTITUTE, make up, form. **2** CREATE, invent, devise,

write, arrange, produce, make, form, fashion, build, construct, frame.
**3** CALM, soothe, quiet, still, settle, tranquillize, quell, pacify, control, regulate.

**composed** *adj* calm, tranquil, serene, relaxed, unworried, unruffled, level-headed, cool, collected, self-possessed, confident, imperturbable, unflappable, placid.
€3 agitated, worried, troubled.

**composition** *n* **1** MAKING, production, formation, creation, invention, design, formulation, writing, compilation, proportion.
**2** CONSTITUTION, make-up, combination, mixture, form, structure, configuration, layout, arrangement, organization, harmony, consonance, balance, symmetry. **3** *a musical composition*: work, opus, piece, study, exercise.

**composure** *n* calm, tranquillity, serenity, ease, coolness, self-possession, confidence, assurance, self-assurance, aplomb, poise, dignity, imperturbability, placidity, equanimity, dispassion, impassivity.
€3 agitation, nervousness, discomposure.

**compound** *v* **1** COMBINE, amalgamate, unite, fuse, coalesce, synthesize, alloy, blend, mix, mingle, intermingle. **2** WORSEN, exacerbate, aggravate, complicate, intensify, heighten, magnify, increase, augment.
*n* alloy, blend, mixture, medley, composite, amalgam, synthesis, fusion, composition, amalgamation, combination.
*adj* composite, mixed, multiple, complex, complicated, intricate.

**comprehend** *v* **1** UNDERSTAND, conceive, see, grasp, fathom, penetrate, tumble to (*infml*), realize, appreciate, know, apprehend, perceive, discern, take in, assimilate.
**2** INCLUDE, comprise, encompass,

embrace, cover.
🗲 1 misunderstand.

**comprehensible** *adj*
understandable, intelligible, coherent,
explicit, clear, lucid, plain, simple,
straightforward.
🗲 incomprehensible, obscure.

**comprehension** *n* understanding,
conception, grasp, realization,
appreciation, knowledge,
apprehension, perception,
discernment, judgement, sense,
intelligence.
🗲 incomprehension, unawareness.

**comprehensive** *adj* thorough,
exhaustive, full, complete,
encyclopedic, compendious, broad,
wide, extensive, sweeping, general,
blanket, inclusive, all-inclusive, all-
embracing, across-the-board.
🗲 partial, incomplete, selective.

**compress** *v* press, squeeze, crush,
squash, flatten, jam, wedge, cram,
stuff, compact, concentrate,
condense, contract, telescope,
shorten, abbreviate, summarize.
🗲 expand, diffuse.

**comprise** *v* consist of, include,
contain, incorporate, embody,
involve, encompass, embrace, cover.

**compromise** *v* **1** NEGOTIATE,
bargain, arbitrate, settle, agree,
concede, make concessions, meet
halfway, adapt, adjust. **2** *compromise
one's principles*: weaken, undermine,
expose, endanger, imperil,
jeopardize, risk, prejudice.
**3** DISHONOUR, discredit, embarrass,
involve, implicate.
*n* bargain, trade-off, settlement,
agreement, concession, give and take,
co-operation, accommodation,
adjustment.
🗲 disagreement, intransigence.

**compulsive** *adj* **1** IRRESISTIBLE,
overwhelming, overpowering,
uncontrollable, compelling, driving,
urgent. **2** *a compulsive gambler*:
obsessive, hardened, incorrigible,

irredeemable, incurable, hopeless.

**compulsory** *adj* obligatory,
mandatory, imperative, forced,
required, requisite, set, stipulated,
binding, contractual.
🗲 optional, voluntary, discretionary.

**computer** *n* personal computer, PC,
mainframe, processor, word-
processor, data processor, calculator,
adding machine.

---

*Computing terms include*:
mainframe, microcomputer,
minicomputer, PC (personal
computer), Applemac®; hardware,
CPU (central processing unit), disk
drive, joystick, keyboard, lap-top,
light pen, microprocessor, modem,
monitor, mouse, mouse mat,
notebook computer, printer,
bubblejet printer, daisywheel printer,
dot-matrix printer, ink-jet printer,
laser printer, screen, VDU (visual
display unit); software, program,
Windows®, WordPerfect®,
Wordstar®; disk, magnetic disk,
floppy disk, hard disk, optical disk,
magnetic tape; programming
language, BASIC, COBOL,
FORTRAN; memory, backing
storage, external memory, immediate
access memory, internal memory,
RAM (Random Access Memory),
ROM (Read Only Memory), CD-
ROM (Compact Disc Read Only
Memory); access, ASCII, backup, bit,
boot, buffer, byte, kilobyte, megabyte,
character, chip, silicon chip, computer
game, computer graphics, computer
literate, computer simulation,
computer terminal, cursor, data,
databank, database, default, desktop
publishing (DTP), digitizer, directory,
DOS (disk operating system),
electronic mail, E-mail, format,
function, grammar checker, graphics,
hacking, interface, macro, menu,
MSDOS (Microsoft® disk operating
system), network, peripheral, pixel,

scrolling, spellchecker, spreadsheet, template, toggle, toolbar, user-friendly, user interface, video game, virtual reality, virus, window, word-processing, work station, WYSIWYG (what you see is what you get).

**con** (*infml*) *v* trick, hoax, dupe, deceive, mislead, inveigle, hoodwink, bamboozle (*infml*), cheat, double-cross, swindle, defraud, rip off (*sl*), rook.
*n* confidence trick, trick, bluff, deception, swindle, fraud.

**concave** *adj* hollow, hollowed, cupped, scooped, excavated, sunken, depressed.
**F3** convex.

**conceal** *v* hide, obscure, disguise, camouflage, mask, screen, veil, cloak, cover, bury, submerge, smother, suppress, keep dark, keep quiet, hush up (*infml*).
**F3** reveal, disclose, uncover.

**concede** *v* 1 ADMIT, confess, acknowledge, recognize, own, grant, allow, accept. 2 YIELD, give up, surrender, relinquish, forfeit, sacrifice.
**F3** 1 deny.

**conceit** *n* conceitedness, vanity, boastfulness, swagger, egotism, self-love, self-importance, cockiness, self-satisfaction, complacency, pride, arrogance.
**F3** modesty, diffidence.

**conceited** *adj* vain, boastful, swollen-headed, bigheaded (*infml*), egotistical, self-important, cocky, self-satisfied, complacent, smug, proud, arrogant, stuck-up (*infml*), toffee-nosed (*infml*).
**F3** modest, self-effacing, diffident, humble.

**conceivable** *adj* imaginable, credible, believable, thinkable, tenable, possible, likely, probable.
**F3** inconceivable, unimaginable.

**conceive** *v* 1 IMAGINE, envisage,

visualize, see, grasp, understand, comprehend, realize, appreciate, believe, think, suppose. 2 INVENT, design, devise, formulate, create, originate, form, produce, develop.

**concentrate** *v* 1 FOCUS, converge, centre, cluster, crowd, congregate, gather, collect, accumulate. 2 APPLY ONESELF, think, pay attention, attend. 3 CONDENSE, evaporate, reduce, thicken, intensify.
**F3** 1 disperse. 3 dilute.

**concentrated** *adj* 1 *concentrated liquid*: condensed, evaporated, reduced, thickened, dense, rich, strong, undiluted. 2 INTENSE, intensive, all-out, concerted, hard, deep.
**F3** 1 diluted. 2 half-hearted.

**concentration** *n* 1 CONVERGENCE, centralization, cluster, crowd, grouping, collection, accumulation, agglomeration, conglomeration. 2 ATTENTION, heed, absorption, application, single-mindedness, intensity. 3 COMPRESSION, reduction, consolidation, denseness, thickness.
**F3** 1 dispersal. 2 distraction. 3 dilution.

**concept** *n* idea, notion, plan, theory, hyphothesis, thought, abstraction, conception, conceptualization, visualization, image, picture, impression.

**conception** *n* 1 CONCEPT, idea, notion, thought. 2 KNOWLEDGE, understanding, appreciation, perception, visualization, image, picture, impression, inkling, clue. 3 INVENTION, design, birth, beginning, origin, outset, initiation, inauguration, formation. 4 *from conception to birth*: impregnation, insemination, fertilization.

**concern** *v* 1 UPSET, distress, trouble, disturb, bother, worry. 2 RELATE TO, refer to, regard, involve, interest, affect, touch.

*n* **1** *a cause for concern*: anxiety, worry, unease, disquiet, care, sorrow, distress. **2** REGARD, consideration, attention, heed, thought. **3** *it's not my concern*: duty, responsibility, charge, job, task, field, business, affair, matter, problem, interest, involvement. **4** COMPANY, firm, business, corporation, establishment, enterprise, organization.
**F3** 1 joy. 2 indifference.

**concerned** *adj* **1** ANXIOUS, worried, uneasy, apprehensive, upset, unhappy, distressed, troubled, disturbed, bothered, attentive, caring. **2** CONNECTED, related, involved, implicated, interested, affected.
**F3** 1 unconcerned, indifferent, apathetic.

**concerning** *prep* about, regarding, with regard to, as regards, respecting, with reference to, relating to, in the matter of.

**concerted** *adj* combined, united, joint, collective, shared, collaborative, co-ordinated, organized, prearranged, planned.
**F3** separate, unco-ordinated, disorganized.

**concession** *n* compromise, adjustment, grant, allowance, exception, privilege, favour, indulgence, permit, admission, acknowledgement.

**concise** *adj* short, brief, terse, succinct, pithy, compendious, compact, compressed, condensed, abridged, abbreviated, summary, synoptic.
**F3** diffuse, wordy.

**conclude** *v* **1** INFER, deduce, assume, surmise, suppose, reckon, judge. **2** END, close, finish, complete, consummate, cease, terminate, culminate. **3** SETTLE, resolve, decide, establish, determine, clinch.
**F3** 2 start, commence.

**conclusion** *n* **1** INFERENCE,

deduction, assumption, opinion, conviction, judgement, verdict, decision, resolution, settlement, result, consequence, outcome, upshot, answer, solution. **2** END, close, finish, completion, consummation, termination, culmination, finale.

**conclusive** *adj* final, ultimate, definitive, decisive, clear, convincing, definite, undeniable, irrefutable, indisputable, incontrovertible, unarguable, unanswerable, clinching.
**F3** inconclusive, questionable.

**concoct** *v* fabricate, invent, devise, contrive, formulate, plan, plot, hatch, brew, prepare, develop.

**concoction** *n* brew, potion, preparation, mixture, blend, compound, creation, contrivance.

**concrete** *adj* real, actual, factual, solid, physical, material, substantial, tangible, touchable, perceptible, visible, firm, definite, specific, explicit.
**F3** abstract, vague.

**concurrent** *adj* simultaneous, synchronous, contemporaneous, coinciding, coincident, concomitant, coexisting, coexistent.

**condemn** *v* disapprove, reprehend, reprove, upbraid, reproach, castigate, blame, disparage, revile, denounce, censure, slam (*infml*), slate (*infml*), damn, doom, convict.
**F3** praise, approve.

**condemnation** *n* disapproval, reproof, reproach, castigation, blame, disparagement, denunciation, censure, thumbs-down (*infml*), damnation, conviction, sentence, judgement.
**F3** praise, approval.

**condensation** *n* **1** *condensation of liquid*: distillation, liquefaction, precipitation, concentration, evaporation, reduction, consolidation. **2** ABRIDGEMENT, précis, synopsis, digest, contraction,

**condense** 106

compression, curtailment.

**condense** v **1** *condense a book*:
shorten, curtail, abbreviate, abridge,
précis, summarize, encapsulate,
contract, compress, compact.
**2** DISTIL, precipitate, concentrate,
evaporate, reduce, thicken, solidify,
coagulate.
**E3** **1** expand. **2** dilute.

**condescend** v deign, see fit, stoop,
bend, lower oneself, patronize, talk
down.

**condescending** adj patronizing,
disdainful, supercilious, snooty,
snobbish, haughty, lofty, superior,
lordly, imperious.
**E3** gracious, humble.

**condition** n **1** CASE, state,
circumstances, position, situation,
predicament, plight.
**2** REQUIREMENT, obligation,
prerequisite, terms, stipulation,
proviso, qualification, limitation,
restriction, rule. **3** *a heart condition*:
disorder, defect, weakness, infirmity,
problem, complaint, disease. **4** *out of
condition*: fitness, health, state,
shape, form, fettle, nick (*sl*).
v indoctrinate, brainwash, influence,
mould, educate, train, groom, equip,
prepare, prime, accustom, season,
temper, adapt, adjust, tune.

**conditional** adj provisional,
qualified, limited, restricted, tied,
relative, dependent, contingent.
**E3** unconditional, absolute.

**conditions** n surroundings,
environment, milieu, setting,
atmosphere, background, context,
circumstances, situation, state.

**condom** n sheath, French letter (*sl*),
johnnie (*sl*), rubber (*sl*), protective.

**condone** v forgive, pardon, excuse,
overlook, ignore, disregard, tolerate,
brook, allow.
**E3** condemn, censure.

**conducive** adj leading, tending,
contributory, productive,
advantageous, beneficial, favourable,

helpful, encouraging.
**E3** detrimental, adverse, unfavourable.

**conduct** n **1** *good conduct*:
behaviour, comportment, actions,
ways, manners, bearing, attitude. **2**
ADMINISTRATION, management,
direction, running, organization,
operation, control, supervision,
leadership, guidance.
v **1** ADMINISTER, manage, run,
organize, orchestrate, chair, control,
handle, regulate. **2** ACCOMPANY,
escort, usher, lead, guide, direct,
pilot, steer. **3** *conduct heat*: convey,
carry, bear, transmit. **4** *conduct
oneself*: behave, acquit, comport, act.

**confer** v **1** DISCUSS, debate,
deliberate, consult, talk, converse.
**2** BESTOW, award, present, give,
grant, accord, impart, lend.

**conference** n meeting, convention,
congress, convocation, symposium,
forum, discussion, debate,
consultation.

**confess** v admit, confide, own (up),
come clean (*infml*), grant, concede,
acknowledge, recognize, affirm,
assert, profess, declare, disclose,
divulge, expose.
**E3** deny, conceal.

**confession** n admission,
acknowledgement, affirmation,
assertion, profession, declaration,
disclosure, divulgence, revelation,
unburdening.
**E3** denial, concealment.

**confide** v confess, admit, reveal,
disclose, divulge, whisper, breathe,
tell, impart, unburden.
**E3** hide, suppress.

**confidence** n certainty, faith,
credence, trust, reliance, dependence,
assurance, composure, calmness, self-
possession, self-confidence, self-
reliance, self-assurance, boldness,
courage.
**E3** distrust, diffidence.

**confident** adj sure, certain, positive,
convinced, assured, composed, self-

possessed, cool, self-confident, self-reliant, self-assured, unselfconscious, bold, fearless, dauntless, unabashed.
**E3** doubtful, diffident.

**confidential** *adj* secret, top secret, classified, restricted, hush-hush (*infml*), off-the-record, private, personal, intimate, privy.

**confine** *v* enclose, circumscribe, bound, limit, restrict, cramp, constrain, imprison, incarcerate, intern, cage, shut up, immure, bind, shackle, trammel, restrain, repress, inhibit.
**E3** free.

**confinement** *n* **1** IMPRISONMENT, incarceration, internment, custody, detention, house arrest.
**2** CHILDBIRTH, birth, labour, delivery.
**E3 1** freedom, liberty.

**confines** *n* limits, bounds, border, boundary, frontier, circumference, perimeter, edge.

**confirm** *v* **1** ENDORSE, back, support, reinforce, strengthen, fortify, validate, authenticate, corroborate, substantiate, verify, prove, evidence. **2** ESTABLISH, fix, settle, clinch, ratify, sanction, approve.
**E3 1** refute, deny.

**confirmation** *n* ratification, sanction, approval, assent, acceptance, agreement, endorsement, backing, support, validation, authentication, corroboration, substantiation, verification, proof, evidence, testimony.
**E3** denial.

**confirmed** *adj* inveterate, entrenched, dyed-in-the-wool, rooted, established, long-established, long-standing, habitual, chronic, seasoned, hardened, incorrigible, incurable.

**confiscate** *v* seize, appropriate, expropriate, remove, take away, impound, sequester, commandeer.

**E3** return, restore.

**conflict** *n* **1** DIFFERENCE, variance, discord, contention, disagreement, dissension, dispute, opposition, antagonism, hostility, friction, strife, unrest, confrontation. **2** BATTLE, war, warfare, combat, fight, contest, engagement, skirmish, set-to, fracas, brawl, quarrel, feud, encounter, clash.
**E3 1** agreement, harmony, concord.
*v* differ, clash, collide, disagree, contradict, oppose, contest, fight, combat, battle, war, strive, struggle, contend.
**E3** agree, harmonize.

**conform** *v* agree, accord, harmonize, match, correspond, tally, square, adapt, adjust, accommodate, comply, obey, follow.
**E3** differ, conflict, rebel.

**conformity** *n* conventionality, orthodoxy, traditionalism, compliance, observance, allegiance, affinity, agreement, consonance, harmony, correspondence, congruity, likeness, similarity, resemblance.
**E3** nonconformity, rebellion, difference.

**confound** *v* **1** CONFUSE, bewilder, baffle, perplex, mystify, bamboozle (*infml*), nonplus, surprise, amaze, astonish, astound, flabbergast (*infml*), dumbfound, stupefy.
**2** *confound their plans*: thwart, upset, defeat, overwhelm, overthrow, destroy, demolish, ruin.

**confront** *v* face, meet, encounter, accost, address, oppose, challenge, defy, brave, beard.
**E3** evade.

**confrontation** *n* encounter, clash, collision, showdown, conflict, disagreement, fight, battle, quarrel, set-to, engagement, contest.

**confuse** *v* **1** PUZZLE, baffle, perplex, mystify, confound, bewilder, disorient, disconcert, fluster, discompose, upset, embarrass,

mortify. **2** MUDDLE, mix up, mistake, jumble, disarrange, disorder, tangle, entangle, involve, mingle.
**E3 1** enlighten, clarify.

**confused** *adj* **1** MUDDLED, jumbled, disarranged, disordered, untidy, disorderly, higgledy-piggledy (*infml*), chaotic, disorganized. **2** PUZZLED, baffled, perplexed, flummoxed (*infml*), nonplussed, bewildered, disorientated.
**E3 1** orderly.

**confusion** *n* **1** DISORDER, disarray, untidiness, mess, clutter, jumble, muddle, mix-up, disorganization, chaos, turmoil, commotion, upheaval. **2** MISUNDERSTANDING, puzzlement, perplexity, mystification, bewilderment.
**E3 1** order. **2** clarity.

**congeal** *v* clot, curdle, coalesce, coagulate, thicken, stiffen, harden, solidify, set, gel, freeze.
**E3** dissolve, melt.

**congested** *adj* clogged, blocked, jammed, packed, stuffed, crammed, full, crowded, overcrowded, overflowing, teeming.
**E3** clear.

**congestion** *n* clogging, blockage, overcrowding, jam, traffic jam, snarl-up, gridlock, bottle-neck.

**conglomeration** *n* mass, agglomeration, aggregation, accumulation, collection, assemblage, composite, medley, hotchpotch.

**congratulate** *v* praise, felicitate, compliment, wish well.
**E3** commiserate.

**congregate** *v* gather, assemble, collect, muster, rally, rendezvous, meet, convene, converge, flock, crowd, throng, mass, accumulate, cluster, clump, conglomerate.
**E3** disperse.

**congregation** *n* assembly, crowd, throng, multitude, host, flock, parishioners, parish, laity, fellowship.

**conical** *adj* cone-shaped, pyramidal, tapering, tapered, pointed.

**conjecture** *v* speculate, theorize, hypothesize, guess, estimate, reckon, suppose, surmise, assume, infer, imagine, suspect.
*n* speculation, theory, hypothesis, notion, guesswork, guess, estimate, supposition, surmise, assumption, presumption, conclusion, inference, extrapolation, projection.

**conjure** *v* summon, invoke, rouse, raise, bewitch, charm, fascinate, compel.
**conjure up** evoke, create, produce, excite, awaken, recollect, recall.

**connect** *v* join, link, unite, couple, combine, fasten, affix, attach, relate, associate, ally.
**E3** disconnect, cut off, detach.

**connected** *adj* joined, linked, united, coupled, combined, related, akin, associated, affiliated, allied.
**E3** disconnected, unconnected.

**connection** *n* junction, coupling, fastening, attachment, bond, tie, link, association, alliance, relation, relationship, interrelation, contact, communication, correlation, correspondence, relevance.
**E3** disconnection.

**connoisseur** *n* authority, specialist, expert, judge, devotee, buff (*infml*), gourmet, epicure.

**connotation** *n* implication, suggestion, hint, nuance, undertone, overtone, colouring, association.

**conquer** *v* **1** DEFEAT, beat, overthrow, vanquish, rout, overrun, best, worst, get the better of, overcome, surmount, win, succeed, triumph, prevail, overpower, master, crush, subdue, quell, subjugate, humble. **2** SEIZE, take, annex, occupy, possess, acquire, obtain.
**E3 1** surrender, yield, give in.

**conqueror** *n* victor, winner, champion, champ (*infml*), hero, vanquisher, master, lord.

**conquest** n victory, triumph, defeat, overthrow, coup, rout, mastery, subjugation, subjection, invasion, occupation, capture, appropriation, annexation, acquisition.

**conscience** n principles, standards, morals, ethics, scruples, qualms.

**conscientious** adj diligent, hard-working, scrupulous, painstaking, thorough, meticulous, punctilious, particular, careful, attentive, responsible, upright, honest, faithful, dutiful.
Ea careless, irresponsible, unreliable.

**conscious** adj 1 AWAKE, alive, responsive, sentient, sensible, rational, reasoning, alert. 2 AWARE, self-conscious, heedful, mindful, knowing, deliberate, intentional, calculated, premeditated, studied, wilful, voluntary.
Ea 1 unconscious. 2 unaware.

**consciousness** n awareness, sentience, sensibility, knowledge, intuition, realization, recognition.
Ea unconsciousness.

**consecrate** v sanctify, hallow, bless, dedicate, devote, ordain, venerate, revere, exalt.

**consecutive** adj sequential, successive, continuous, unbroken, uninterrupted, following, succeeding, running.
Ea discontinuous.

**consent** v agree, concur, accede, assent, approve, permit, allow, grant, admit, concede, acquiesce, yield, comply.
Ea refuse, decline, oppose.
n agreement, concurrence, assent, approval, permission, go-ahead, green light (infml), sanction, concession, acquiescence, compliance.
Ea disagreement, refusal, opposition.

**consequence** n 1 RESULT, outcome, issue, end, upshot, effect, side effect, repercussion. 2 of no consequence: importance,

significance, concern, value, weight, note, eminence, distinction.
Ea 1 cause. 2 unimportance, insignificance.

**consequent** adj resultant, resulting, ensuing, subsequent, following, successive, sequential.

**conservation** n keeping, safe-keeping, custody, saving, economy, husbandry, maintenance, upkeep, preservation, protection, safeguarding, ecology, environmentalism.
Ea destruction.

**conservative** adj Tory, right-wing, hidebound, die-hard, reactionary, establishmentarian, unprogressive, conventional, traditional, moderate, middle-of-the-road, cautious, guarded, sober.
Ea left-wing, radical, innovative.
n Tory, right-winger, die-hard, stick-in-the-mud, reactionary, traditionalist, moderate.
Ea left-winger, radical.

**conservatory** n greenhouse, glasshouse, hothouse.

**conserve** v keep, save, store up, hoard, maintain, preserve, protect, guard, safeguard.
Ea use, waste, squander.

**consider** v 1 PONDER, deliberate, reflect, contemplate, meditate, muse, mull over, chew over, examine, study, weigh, respect, remember, take into account. 2 consider it an honour: regard, deem, think, believe, judge, rate, count.

**considerable** adj great, large, big, sizable, substantial, tidy (infml), ample, plentiful, abundant, lavish, marked, noticeable, perceptible, appreciable, reasonable, tolerable, respectable, important, significant, noteworthy, distinguished, influential.
Ea small, slight, insignificant, unremarkable.

**considerate** adj kind, thoughtful,

caring, attentive, obliging, helpful, charitable, unselfish, altruistic, gracious, sensitive, tactful, discreet.
**E3** inconsiderate, thoughtless, selfish.

**consideration** n 1 THOUGHT, deliberation, reflection, contemplation, meditation, examination, analysis, scrutiny, review, attention, notice, regard. 2 KINDNESS, thoughtfulness, care, attention, regard, respect.
**E3** 1 disregard. 2 thoughtlessness.

**consign** v entrust, commit, devote, hand over, transfer, deliver, convey, ship, banish, relegate.

**consignment** n cargo, shipment, load, batch, delivery, goods.

**consist of** comprise, be composed of, contain, include, incorporate, embody, embrace, involve, amount to.

**consistency** n 1 of the consistency of porridge: viscosity, thickness, density, firmness. 2 STEADINESS, regularity, evenness, uniformity, sameness, identity, constancy, steadfastness. 3 AGREEMENT, accordance, correspondence, congruity, compatibility, harmony.
**E3** 3 inconsistency.

**consistent** adj 1 STEADY, stable, regular, uniform, unchanging, undeviating, constant, persistent, unfailing, dependable. 2 AGREEING, accordant, consonant, congruous, compatible, harmonious, logical.
**E3** 1 irregular, erratic. 2 inconsistent.

**console** v comfort, cheer, hearten, encourage, relieve, soothe, calm.
**E3** upset, agitate.

**consolidate** v reinforce, strengthen, secure, stabilize, unify, unite, join, combine, amalgamate, fuse, cement, compact, condense, thicken, harden, solidify.

**conspicuous** adj apparent, visible, noticeable, marked, clear, obvious, evident, patent, manifest, prominent, striking, blatant, flagrant, glaring,

ostentatious, showy, flashy, garish.
**E3** inconspicuous, concealed, hidden.

**conspiracy** n plot, scheme, intrigue, machination, fix (infml), frame-up (infml), collusion, league, treason.

**conspirator** n conspirer, plotter, schemer, intriguer, traitor.

**conspire** v plot, scheme, intrigue, manoeuvre, connive, collude, hatch, devise.

**constancy** n 1 STABILITY, steadiness, permanence, firmness, regularity, uniformity, resolution, perseverance, tenacity. 2 LOYALTY, faithfulness, fidelity, devotion.
**E3** 1 change, irregularity. 2 fickleness.

**constant** adj 1 CONTINUOUS, unbroken, never-ending, non-stop, endless, interminable, ceaseless, incessant, eternal, everlasting, perpetual, continual, unremitting, relentless, persistent, resolute, persevering, unflagging, unwavering, stable, steady, unchanging, unvarying, changeless, immutable, invariable, unalterable, fixed, permanent, firm, even, regular, uniform. 2 a constant friend: loyal, faithful, staunch, steadfast, dependable, trustworthy, true, devoted.
**E3** 1 variable, irregular, fitful, occasional. 2 disloyal, fickle.

**constituent** adj component, integral, essential, basic, intrinsic, inherent.
n ingredient, element, factor, principle, component, part, bit, section, unit.
**E3** whole.

**constitute** v represent, make up, compose, comprise, form, create, establish, set up, found.

**constrain** v 1 FORCE, compel, oblige, necessitate, drive, impel, urge. 2 limit, confine, constrict, restrain, check, curb, bind.

**constrained** adj uneasy, embarrassed, inhibited, reticent,

reserved, guarded, stiff, forced, unnatural.
**F3** relaxed, free.

**constraint** n **1** FORCE, duress, compulsion, coercion, pressure, necessity, deterrent. **2** RESTRICTION, limitation, hindrance, restraint, check, curb, damper.

**constrict** v squeeze, compress, pinch, cramp, narrow, tighten, contract, shrink, choke, strangle, inhibit, limit, restrict.
**F3** expand.

**construct** v build, erect, raise, elevate, make, manufacture, fabricate, assemble, put together, compose, form, shape, fashion, model, design, engineer, create, found, establish, formulate.
**F3** demolish.

**construction** n building, edifice, erection, structure, fabric, form, shape, figure, model, manufacture, fabrication, assembly, composition, constitution, formation, creation.
**F3** destruction.

**constructive** adj practical, productive, positive, helpful, useful, valuable, beneficial, advantageous.
**F3** destructive, negative, unhelpful.

**consult** v refer to, ask, question, interrogate, confer, discuss, debate, deliberate.

**consultant** n adviser, expert, authority, specialist.

**consultation** n discussion, deliberation, dialogue, conference, meeting, hearing, interview, examination, appointment, session.

**consume** v **1** EAT, drink, swallow, devour, gobble. **2** USE, absorb, spend, expend, deplete, drain, exhaust, use up, dissipate, squander, waste. **3** DESTROY, demolish, annihilate, devastate, ravage.

**consumer** n user, end-user, customer, buyer, purchaser, shopper.

**consumption** n use, utilization, spending, expenditure, depletion, exhaustion, waste.

**contact** n touch, impact, juxtaposition, contiguity, communication, meeting, junction, union, connection, association.
v approach, apply to, reach, get hold of, get in touch with, telephone, phone, ring, call, notify.

**contagious** adj infectious, catching, communicable, transmissible, spreading, epidemic.

**contain** v **1** INCLUDE, comprise, incorporate, embody, involve, embrace, enclose, hold, accommodate, seat. **2** contain one's feelings: repress, stifle, restrain, control, check, curb, limit.
**F3 1** exclude.

**container** n receptacle, vessel, holder.

**contaminate** v infect, pollute, adulterate, taint, soil, sully, defile, corrupt, deprave, debase, stain, tarnish.
**F3** purify.

**contemplate** v **1** MEDITATE, reflect on, ponder, mull over, deliberate, consider, regard, view, survey, observe, study, examine, inspect, scrutinize. **2** EXPECT, foresee, envisage, plan, design, propose, intend, mean.

**contemporary** adj **1** MODERN, current, present, present-day, recent, latest, up-to-date, fashionable, up-to-the-minute, ultra-modern.
**2** CONTEMPORANEOUS, coexistent, concurrent, synchronous, simultaneous.
**F3 1** out-of-date, old-fashioned.

**contempt** n scorn, disdain, condescension, derision, ridicule, mockery, disrespect, dishonour, disregard, neglect, dislike, loathing, detestation.
**F3** admiration, regard.

**contemptible** adj despicable, shameful, ignominious, low, mean, vile, detestable, loathsome, abject,

wretched, pitiful, paltry, worthless.
**E3** admirable, honourable.

**contemptuous** *adj* scornful,
disdainful, sneering, supercilious,
condescending, arrogant, haughty,
high and mighty, cynical, derisive,
insulting, disrespectful, insolent.
**E3** humble, respectful.

**contend** *v* **1** MAINTAIN, hold, argue,
allege, assert, declare, affirm.
**2** COMPETE, vie, contest, dispute,
clash, wrestle, grapple, struggle,
strive, cope.

**content** *v* satisfy, humour, indulge,
gratify, please, delight, appease,
pacify, placate.
**E3** displease.
*n* **1** SUBSTANCE, matter, essence,
gist, meaning, significance, text,
subject matter, ideas, contents, load,
burden. **2** CAPACITY, volume, size,
measure.
*adj* satisfied, fulfilled, contented,
untroubled, pleased, happy, willing.
**E3** dissatisfied, troubled.

**contented** *adj* happy, glad, pleased,
cheerful, comfortable, relaxed,
content, satisfied.
**E3** discontented, unhappy, annoyed.

**contentment** *n* contentedness,
happiness, gladness, pleasure,
gratification, comfort, ease,
complacency, peace, peacefulness,
serenity, equanimity, content,
satisfaction, fulfilment.
**E3** unhappiness, discontent,
dissatisfaction.

**contents** *n* **1** *the contents of the
package*: constituents, parts,
elements, ingredients, content, load,
items. **2** CHAPTERS, divisions,
subjects, topics, themes.

**contest** *n* competition, game, match,
tournament, encounter, fight, battle,
set-to, combat, conflict, struggle,
dispute, debate, controversy.
*v* **1** DISPUTE, debate, question,
doubt, challenge, oppose, argue
against, litigate, deny, refute.

**2** COMPETE, vie, contend, strive,
fight.
**E3** **1** accept.

**contestant** *n* competitor, contender,
player, participant, entrant,
candidate, aspirant, rival, opponent.

**context** *n* background, setting,
surroundings, framework, frame of
reference, situation, position,
circumstances, conditions.

**contingent** *n* body, company,
deputation, delegation, detachment,
section, group, set, batch, quota,
complement.

**continual** *adj* constant, perpetual,
incessant, interminable, eternal,
everlasting, regular, frequent,
recurrent, repeated.
**E3** occasional, intermittent,
temporary.

**continuation** *n* resumption,
maintenance, prolongation,
extension, development, furtherance,
addition, supplement.
**E3** cessation, termination.

**continue** *v* resume, recommence,
carry on, go on, proceed, persevere,
stick at, persist, last, endure, survive,
remain, abide, stay, rest, pursue,
sustain, maintain, lengthen, prolong,
extend, project.
**E3** discontinue, stop.

**continuity** *n* flow, progression,
succession, sequence, linkage,
interrelationship, connection,
cohesion.
**E3** discontinuity.

**continuous** *adj* unbroken,
uninterrupted, consecutive, non-stop,
endless, ceaseless, unending,
unceasing, constant, unremitting,
prolonged, extended, continued,
lasting.
**E3** discontinuous, broken, sporadic.

**contort** *v* twist, distort, warp,
wrench, disfigure, deform, misshape,
convolute, gnarl, knot, writhe,
squirm, wriggle.

**contour** *n* outline, silhouette, shape,

form, figure, curve, relief, profile, character, aspect.

**contract** v 1 SHRINK, lessen, diminish, reduce, shorten, curtail, abbreviate, abridge, condense, compress, constrict, narrow, tighten, tense, shrivel, wrinkle. 2 *contract pneumonia*: catch, get, go down with, develop. 3 PLEDGE, promise, undertake, agree, stipulate, arrange, negotiate, bargain.
**F3** 1 expand, enlarge, lengthen.
n bond, commitment, engagement, covenant, treaty, convention, pact, compact, agreement, transaction, deal, bargain, settlement, arrangement, understanding.

**contradict** v deny, disaffirm, confute, challenge, oppose, impugn, dispute, counter, negate, gainsay.
**F3** agree, confirm, corroborate.

**contradictory** adj contrary, opposite, paradoxical, conflicting, discrepant, inconsistent, incompatible, antagonistic, irreconcilable, opposed, repugnant.
**F3** consistent.

**contraption** n contrivance, device, gadget, apparatus, rig, machine, mechanism.

**contrary** adj 1 OPPOSITE, counter, reverse, conflicting, antagonistic, opposed, adverse, hostile. 2 PERVERSE, awkward, disobliging, difficult, wayward, obstinate, intractable, cantankerous, stroppy (*infml*).
**F3** 1 like. 2 obliging.
n opposite, converse, reverse.

**contrast** n difference, dissimilarity, disparity, divergence, distinction, differentiation, comparison, foil, antithesis, opposition.
**F3** similarity.
v compare, differentiate, distinguish, discriminate, differ, oppose, clash, conflict.

**contravene** v infringe, violate, break, breach, disobey, defy, flout,

transgress.
**F3** uphold, observe, obey.

**contribute** v donate, subscribe, chip in (*infml*), add, give, bestow, provide, supply, furnish, help, lead, conduce.
**F3** withhold.

**contribution** n donation, subscription, gift, gratuity, handout, grant, offering, input, addition.

**contributor** n 1 DONOR, subscriber, giver, patron, benefactor, sponsor, backer, supporter. 2 WRITER, journalist, reporter, correspondent, freelance.

**contrite** adj sorry, regretful, remorseful, repentant, penitent, conscience-stricken, chastened, humble, ashamed.

**contrivance** n 1 INVENTION, device, contraption, gadget, implement, appliance, machine, mechanism, apparatus, equipment, gear. 2 STRATAGEM, ploy, trick, dodge, ruse, expedient, plan, design, project, scheme, plot, intrigue, machination.

**contrived** adj unnatural, artificial, false, forced, strained, laboured, mannered, elaborate, overdone.
**F3** natural, genuine.

**control** v 1 LEAD, govern, rule, command, direct, manage, oversee, supervise, superintend, run, operate. 2 *control the temperature*: regulate, adjust, monitor, verify. 3 *control one's temper*: restrain, check, curb, subdue, repress, hold back, contain.
n 1 POWER, charge, authority, command, mastery, government, rule, direction, management, oversight, supervision, superintendence, discipline, guidance. 2 RESTRAINT, check, curb, repression.
3 INSTRUMENT, dial, switch, button, knob, lever.

**controversial** adj contentious, polemical, disputed, doubtful, questionable, debatable, disputable.

**controversy** n debate, discussion,

war of words, polemic, dispute, disagreement, argument, quarrel, squabble, wrangle, strife, contention, dissension.

F3 accord, agreement.

**convenience** n 1 ACCESSIBILITY, availability, handiness, usefulness, use, utility, serviceability, service, benefit, advantage, help, suitability, fitness. 2 *all modern conveniences*: facility, amenity, appliance.

F3 1 inconvenience.

**convenient** adj nearby, at hand, accessible, available, handy, useful, commodious, beneficial, helpful, labour-saving, adapted, fitted, suited, suitable, fit, appropriate, opportune, timely, well-timed.

F3 inconvenient, awkward.

**convention** n 1 CUSTOM, tradition, practice, usage, protocol, etiquette, formality, matter of form, code. 2 ASSEMBLY, congress, conference, meeting, council, delegates, representatives.

**conventional** adj traditional, orthodox, formal, correct, proper, prevalent, prevailing, accepted, received, expected, unoriginal, ritual, routine, usual, customary, regular, standard, normal, ordinary, straight, stereotyped, hidebound, pedestrian, commonplace, common, run-of-the-mill.

F3 unconventional, unusual, exotic.

**converge** v focus, concentrate, approach, merge, coincide, meet, join, combine, gather.

F3 diverge, disperse.

**convergence** n concentration, approach, merging, confluence, blending, meeting, coincidence, junction, intersection, union.

F3 divergence, separation.

**conversation** n talk, chat, gossip, discussion, discourse, dialogue, exchange, communication.

**converse** n opposite, reverse, contrary, antithesis, obverse.

adj opposite, reverse, counter, contrary, reversed, transposed.

**conversion** n alteration, change, transformation, adaptation, modification, remodelling, reconstruction, reorganization, reformation, regeneration, rebirth.

**convert** v 1 ALTER, change, turn, transform, adapt, modify, remodel, restyle, revise, reorganize. 2 WIN OVER, convince, persuade, reform, proselytize.

**convex** adj rounded, bulging, protuberant.

F3 concave.

**convey** v carry, bear, bring, fetch, move, transport, send, forward, deliver, transfer, conduct, guide, transmit, communicate, impart, tell, relate, reveal.

**convict** v condemn, sentence, imprison.

n criminal, felon, culprit, prisoner.

**conviction** n assurance, confidence, fervour, earnestness, certainty, firmness, persuasion, view, opinion, belief, faith, creed, tenet, principle.

**convince** v assure, persuade, sway, win over, bring round, reassure, satisfy.

**convincing** adj persuasive, cogent, powerful, telling, impressive, credible, plausible, likely, probable, conclusive, incontrovertible.

F3 unconvincing, improbable.

**convoluted** adj twisting, winding, meandering, tortuous, involved, complicated, complex, tangled.

F3 straight, straightforward.

**convoy** n fleet, escort, guard, protection, attendance, train.

**convulsion** n 1 FIT, seizure, paroxysm, spasm, cramp, contraction, tic, tremor.

2 ERUPTION, outburst, furore, disturbance, commotion, tumult, agitation, turbulence, upheaval.

**convulsive** adj jerky, spasmodic, fitful, sporadic, uncontrolled, violent.

*Ways of cooking include*: bake, barbecue, boil, braise, broil, casserole, coddle, deep-fry, fry, grill, microwave, poach, pot-roast, roast, sauté, scramble, simmer, spit-roast, steam, stew, stir-fry, toast; prepare, heat.

**cook up** concoct, prepare, brew, invent, fabricate, contrive, devise, plan, plot, scheme.

**cool** *adj* **1** CHILLY, fresh, breezy, nippy, cold, chilled, iced, refreshing. **2** CALM, unruffled, unexcited, composed, self-possessed, level-headed, unemotional, quiet, relaxed, laid-back (*infml*). **3** *a cool reception*: unfriendly, unwelcoming, cold, frigid, lukewarm, half-hearted, unenthusiastic, apathetic, uninterested, unresponsive, uncommunicative, reserved, distant, aloof, standoffish.
**F3 1** warm, hot. **2** excited, angry. **3** friendly, welcoming.
*v* **1** CHILL, refrigerate, ice, freeze, fan. **2** MODERATE, lessen, temper, dampen, quiet, abate, calm, allay, assuage.
**F3 1** warm, heat. **2** excite.
*n* coolness, calmness, collectedness, composure, poise, self-possession, self-discipline, self-control, control, temper.

**co-operate** *v* collaborate, work together, play ball (*infml*), help, assist, aid, contribute, participate, combine, unite, conspire.

**co-operation** *n* helpfulness, assistance, participation, collaboration, teamwork, unity, co-ordination, give-and-take.
**F3** opposition, rivalry, competition.

**co-operative** *adj* **1** HELPFUL, supportive, obliging, accommodating, willing. **2** COLLECTIVE, joint, shared, combined, united, concerted, co-ordinated.
**F3 1** unco-operative, rebellious.

**co-ordinate** *v* organize, arrange, systematize, tabulate, integrate, mesh, synchronize, harmonize, match, correlate, regulate.

**cope** *v* manage, carry on, survive, get by, make do.
**cope with** deal with, encounter, contend with, struggle with, grapple with, wrestle with, handle, manage, weather.

**copious** *adj* abundant, plentiful, inexhaustible, overflowing, profuse, rich, lavish, bountiful, liberal, full, ample, generous, extensive, great, huge.
**F3** scarce, meagre.

**copy** *n* duplicate, carbon copy, photocopy, Photostat®, Xerox®, facsimile, reproduction, print, tracing, transcript, transcription, replica, model, pattern, archetype, representation, image, likeness, counterfeit, forgery, fake, imitation, borrowing, plagiarism, crib.
**F3** original.
*v* duplicate, photocopy, reproduce, print, trace, transcribe, forge, counterfeit, simulate, imitate, impersonate, mimic, ape, parrot, repeat, echo, mirror, follow, emulate, borrow, plagiarize, crib.

**cord** *n* string, twine, rope, line, cable, flex, connection, link, bond, tie.

**core** *n* kernel, nucleus, heart, centre, middle, nub, crux, essence, gist, nitty-gritty (*infml*).
**F3** surface, exterior.

**corner** *n* **1** *round the corner*: angle, joint, crook, bend, turning. **2** NOOK, cranny, niche, recess, cavity, hole, hideout, hide-away, retreat.

**corporation** *n* council, authorities, association, society, organization, company, firm, combine, conglomerate.

**corpse** *n* body, stiff (*sl*), carcase,

skeleton, remains.

**correct** v 1 *correct an error*: rectify, put right, right, emend, remedy, cure, debug, redness, adjust, regulate, improve, amend. 2 PUNISH, discipline, reprimand, reprove, reform.
*adj* 1 *the correct answer*: right, accurate, precise, exact, strict, true, truthful, word-perfect, faultless, flawless. 2 PROPER, acceptable, OK (*infml*), standard, regular, just, appropriate, fitting.
**F3** incorrect, wrong, inaccurate.

**correction** n rectification, emendation, adjustment, alteration, modification, amendment, improvement.

**correspond** v 1 MATCH, fit, answer, conform, tally, square, agree, concur, coincide, correlate, accord, harmonize, dovetail, complement. 2 COMMUNICATE, write.

**correspondence** n 1 COMMUNICATION, writing, letters, post, mail. 2 CONFORMITY, agreement, concurrence, coincidence, correlation, relation, analogy, comparison, comparability, similarity, resemblance, congruity, equivalence, harmony, match.
**F3** divergence, incongruity.

**correspondent** n journalist, reporter, contributor, writer.

**corresponding** adj matching, complementary, reciprocal, interrelated, analogous, equivalent, similar, identical.

**corridor** n aisle, passageway, passage, hallway, hall, lobby.

**corroborate** v confirm, prove, bear out, support, endorse, ratify, substantiate, validate, authenticate, document, underpin, sustain.
**F3** contradict.

**corrode** v erode, wear away, eat away, consume, waste, rust, oxidize, tarnish, impair, deteriorate, crumble, disintegrate.

**corrosive** adj corroding, acid, caustic, cutting, abrasive, erosive, wearing, consuming, wasting.

**corrugated** adj ridged, fluted, grooved, channelled, furrowed, wrinkled, crinkled, rumpled, creased.

**corrupt** adj rotten, unscrupulous, unprincipled, unethical, immoral, fraudulent, shady (*infml*), dishonest, bent (*infml*), crooked (*infml*), untrustworthy, depraved, degenerate, dissolute.
**F3** ethical, virtuous, upright, honest, trustworthy.
*v* contaminate, pollute, adulterate, taint, defile, debase, pervert, deprave, lead astray, lure, bribe, suborn.
**F3** purify.

**corruption** n unscrupulousness, immorality, impurity, depravity, degeneration, degradation, perversion, distortion, dishonesty, crookedness (*infml*), fraud, shadiness (*infml*), bribery, extortion, vice, wickedness, iniquity, evil.
**F3** honesty, virtue.

**cosmetic** adj superficial, surface.
**F3** essential.

**cosmetics** n make-up, grease paint.

---

*Types of cosmetics include*: blusher, cleanser, eyebrow pencil, eyelash dye, eyeliner, eye shadow, face cream, face mask, face pack, face powder, false eyelashes, foundation, kohl pencil, lip gloss, lip liner, lipstick, loose powder, mascara, moisturizer, nail polish, nail varnish, Pan-cake®, pressed powder, rouge, toner.

---

**cosmopolitan** adj worldly, worldly-wise, well-travelled, sophisticated, urbane, international, universal.
**F3** insular, parochial, rustic.

**cosset** v coddle, mollycoddle, baby, pamper, indulge, spoil, pet, fondle, cuddle, cherish.

**cost** n 1 EXPENSE, outlay, payment, disbursement, expenditure, charge,

price, rate, amount, figure, worth. **2**
DETRIMENT, harm, injury, hurt, loss,
deprivation, sacrifice, penalty, price.

**costly** *adj* **1** EXPENSIVE, dear, pricey
(*infml*), exorbitant, excessive, lavish,
rich, splendid, valuable, precious,
priceless. **2** HARMFUL, damaging,
disastrous, catastrophic, loss-making.
**F3** **1** cheap, inexpensive.

**costume** *n* outfit, uniform, livery,
robes, vestments, dress, clothing, get-
up (*infml*), fancy dress.

**cosy** *adj* snug, comfortable, comfy
(*infml*), warm, sheltered, secure,
homely, intimate.
**F3** uncomfortable, cold.

**cottage** *n* lodge, chalet, bungalow,
hut, cabin, shack.

**couch** *n* sofa, settee, chesterfield,
chaise-longue, ottoman, divan, bed.

**council** *n* committee, panel, board,
cabinet, ministry, parliament,
congress, assembly, convention,
conference.

**counsel** *n* **1** ADVICE, suggestion,
recommendation, guidance,
direction, information, consultation,
deliberation, consideration,
forethought. **2** *counsel for the
defence*: lawyer, advocate, solicitor,
attorney, barrister.
*v* advise, warn, caution, suggest,
recommend, advocate, urge, exhort,
guide, direct, instruct.

**count** *v* **1** NUMBER, enumerate, list,
include, reckon, calculate, compute,
tell, check, add, total, tot up, score.
**2** MATTER, signify, qualify. **3** *count
yourself lucky*: consider, regard,
deem, judge, think, reckon, hold.
*n* numbering, enumeration, poll,
reckoning, calculation, computation,
sum, total, tally.

**count on** depend on, rely on, bank on,
reckon on, expect, believe, trust.

**counter** *adv* against, in opposition,
conversely.
*adj* contrary, opposite, opposing,
conflicting, contradictory, contrasting,

opposed, against, adverse.
*v* parry, resist, offset, answer,
respond, retaliate, retort, return,
meet.

**counteract** *v* neutralize,
counterbalance, offset, countervail,
act against, oppose, resist, hinder,
check, thwart, frustrate, foil, defeat,
undo, negate, annul, invalidate.
**F3** support, assist.

**counterfeit** *v* fake, forge, fabricate,
copy, imitate, impersonate, pretend,
feign, simulate, sham.
*adj* fake, false, phoney (*infml*),
forged, copied, fraudulent, bogus,
pseudo, sham, spurious, imitation,
artificial, simulated, feigned,
pretended.
**F3** genuine, authentic, real.
*n* fake, forgery, copy, reproduction,
imitation, fraud, sham.

**counterpart** *n* equivalent, opposite
number, complement, supplement,
match, fellow, mate, twin, duplicate,
copy.

**countless** *adj* innumerable, myriad,
numberless, unnumbered, untold,
incalculable, infinite, endless,
immeasurable, measureless, limitless.
**F3** finite, limited.

**country** *n* **1** STATE, nation, people,
kingdom, realm, principality.
**2** COUNTRYSIDE, green belt,
farmland, provinces, sticks (*infml*),
backwoods, wilds. **3** TERRAIN, land,
territory, region, area, district.
**F3** **2** town, city.
*adj* rural, provincial, agrarian,
agricultural, pastoral, rustic, bucolic,
landed.
**F3** urban.

**countryside** *n* landscape, scenery,
country, green belt, farmland,
outdoors.

**county** *n* shire, province, region,
area, district.

**couple** *n* pair, brace, twosome, duo.
*v* pair, match, marry, wed, unite,
join, link, connect, fasten, hitch,

clasp, buckle, yoke.

**coupon** *n* voucher, token, slip, check, ticket, certificate.

**courage** *n* bravery, pluck, guts (*infml*), fearlessness, dauntlessness, heroism, gallantry, valour, boldness, audacity, nerve, daring, resolution, fortitude, spirit, mettle.

　🔁 cowardice, fear.

**courageous** *adj* brave, plucky, fearless, dauntless, indomitable, heroic, gallant, valiant, lion-hearted, hardy, bold, audacious, daring, intrepid, resolute.

　🔁 cowardly, afraid.

**course** *n* 1 CURRICULUM, syllabus, classes, lessons, lectures, studies. 2 FLOW, movement, advance, progress, development, furtherance, order, sequence, series, succession, progression. 3 DURATION, time, period, term, passage. 4 DIRECTION, way, path, track, road, route, channel, trail, line, circuit, orbit, trajectory, flight path. 5 *course of action*: plan, schedule, programme, policy, procedure, method, mode.

**court** *n* 1 LAW-COURT, bench, bar, tribunal, trial, session. 2 COURTYARD, yard, quadrangle, square, cloister, forecourt, enclosure. 3 ENTOURAGE, attendants, retinue, suite, train, cortège.

**courteous** *adj* polite, civil, respectful, well-mannered, well-bred, ladylike, gentlemanly, gracious, obliging, considerate, attentive, gallant, courtly, urbane, debonair, refined, polished.

　🔁 discourteous, impolite, rude.

**courtesy** *n* politeness, civility, respect, manners, breeding, graciousness, consideration, attention, gallantry, urbanity.

　🔁 discourtesy, rudeness.

**courtier** *n* noble, nobleman, lord, lady, steward, page, attendant, follower, flatterer, sycophant, toady.

**courtyard** *n* yard, quadrangle, quad

(*infml*), area, enclosure, court.

**cove** *n* bay, bight, inlet, estuary, firth, fiord, creek.

**cover** *v* 1 HIDE, conceal, obscure, shroud, veil, screen, mask, disguise, camouflage. 2 *covered with mud*: coat, spread, daub, plaster, encase, wrap, envelop, clothe, dress. 3 SHELTER, protect, shield, guard, defend. 4 *cover a topic*: deal with, treat, consider, examine, investigate, encompass, embrace, incorporate, embody, involve, include, contain, comprise.

　🔁 1 uncover. 2 strip. 3 expose. 4 exclude.

*n* 1 COATING, covering, top, lid, cup, veil, screen, mask, front, façade, jacket, wrapper, case, envelope, clothing, dress, bedspread, canopy. 2 SHELTER, refuge, protection, shield, guard, defence, concealment, disguise, camouflage.

**cover up** (*infml*) conceal, hide, whitewash, dissemble, suppress, hush up, keep dark, repress.

　🔁 disclose, reveal.

**covering** *n* layer, coat, coating, blanket, film, veneer, skin, crust, shell, casing, housing, wrapping, clothing, protection, mask, overlay, cover, top, shelter, roof.

**cover-up** (*infml*) *n* concealment, whitewash, smokescreen, front, façade, pretence, conspiracy, complicity.

**covet** *v* envy, begrudge, crave, long for, yearn for, hanker for, want, desire, fancy (*infml*), lust after.

**coward** *n* craven, faint-heart, chicken (*infml*), scaredy-cat, yellow-belly (*sl*), wimp (*infml*), renegade, deserter.

　🔁 hero.

**cowardice** *n* cowardliness, faint-heartedness, timorousness, spinelessness.

　🔁 courage, valour.

**cowardly** *adj* faint-hearted, craven,

**crave**

fearful, timorous, scared, unheroic, chicken-hearted, chicken-livered, chicken (infml), yellow-bellied (sl), yellow (sl), spineless, weak, weak-kneed, soft.

**E3** brave, courageous, bold.

**cower** v crouch, grovel, skulk, shrink, flinch, cringe, quail, tremble, shake, shiver.

**coy** adj modest, demure, prudish, diffident, shy, bashful, timid, shrinking, backward, retiring, self-effacing, reserved, evasive, arch, flirtatious, coquettish, skittish, kittenish.

**E3** bold, forward.

**crack** v 1 SPLIT, burst, fracture, break, snap, shatter, splinter, chip. 2 EXPLODE, burst, pop, crackle, snap, crash, clap, slap, whack (infml). 3 crack a code: decipher, work out, solve.

n 1 BREAK, fracture, split, rift, gap, crevice, fissure, chink, line, flaw, chip. 2 EXPLOSION, burst, pop, snap, crash, clap, blow, smack, slap, whack (infml). 3 JOKE, quip, witticism, gag (infml), wisecrack, gibe, dig.

adj (infml) first-class, first-rate, top-notch (infml), excellent, superior, choice, hand-picked.

**crack down on** clamp down on, end, stop, put a stop to, crush, suppress, check, repress, act against.

**crack up** go mad, go to pieces, break down, collapse.

**cradle** n 1 COT, crib, bed. 2 SOURCE, origin, spring, wellspring, fount, fountain-head, birthplace, beginning.

v hold, support, rock, lull, nurse, nurture, tend.

**craft** n 1 SKILL, expertise, mastery, talent, knack, ability, aptitude, dexterity, cleverness, art, handicraft, handiwork. 2 TRADE, business, calling, vocation, job, occupation, work, employment. 3 VESSEL, boat, ship, aircraft, spacecraft, spaceship.

**craftsman, craftswoman** n artisan, technician, master, maker, wright, smith.

**craftsmanship** n artistry, workmanship, technique, dexterity, expertise, mastery.

**crafty** adj sly, cunning, artful, wily, devious, subtle, scheming, calculating, designing, deceitful, fraudulent, sharp, shrewd, astute, canny.

**E3** artless, naïve.

**cram** v stuff, jam, ram, force, press, squeeze, crush, compress, pack, crowd, overfill, glut, gorge.

**cramp**[1] v hinder, hamper, obstruct, impede, inhibit, handicap, thwart, frustrate, check, restrict, confine, shackle, tie.

**cramp**[2] n pain, ache, twinge, pang, contraction, convulsion, spasm, crick, stitch, pins and needles, stiffness.

**cramped** adj narrow, tight, uncomfortable, restricted, confined, crowded, packed, squashed, squeezed, overcrowded, jam-packed, congested.

**E3** spacious.

**crash** n 1 car crash: accident, collision, bump, smash, pile-up, smash-up (infml), wreck. 2 BANG, clash, clatter, clang, thud, thump, boom, thunder, racket, din. 3 stock-market crash: collapse, failure, ruin, downfall, bankruptcy, depression.

v 1 COLLIDE, hit, knock, bump, bang. 2 BREAK, fracture, smash, dash, shatter, splinter, shiver, fragment, disintegrate. 3 FALL, topple, pitch, plunge, collapse, fail, fold (up), go under, go bust (infml).

**crate** n container, box, case, tea-chest, packing-box, packing-case.

**crave** v hunger for, thirst for, long for, yearn for, pine for, hanker after, fancy (infml), desire, want, need, require.

**E3** dislike.

**craving** n appetite, hunger, thirst, longing, yearning, hankering, lust, desire, urge.
**F3** dislike, distaste.

**crawl** v 1 CREEP, inch, edge, slither, wriggle. 2 GROVEL, cringe, toady, fawn, flatter, suck up (sl).

**craze** n fad, novelty, fashion, vogue, mode, trend, rage (infml), thing (infml), obsession, preoccupation, mania, frenzy, passion, infatuation, enthusiasm.

**crazy** adj 1 MAD, insane, lunatic, unbalanced, deranged, demented, crazed, potty (infml), barmy (infml), daft (infml), silly, foolish, idiotic, senseless, unwise, imprudent, nonsensical, absurd, ludicrous, ridiculous, preposterous, outrageous, half-baked, impracticable, irresponsible, wild, berserk. 2 (infml) crazy about golf: enthusiastic, fanatical, zealous, ardent, passionate, infatuated, enamoured, smitten, mad, wild.
**F3** 1 sane, sensible. 2 indifferent.

**creak** v squeak, groan, grate, scrape, rasp, scratch, grind, squeal, screech.

**cream** n 1 PASTE, emulsion, oil, lotion, ointment, salve, cosmetic. 2 BEST, pick, élite, prime.

**creamy** adj 1 CREAM-COLOURED, off-white, yellowish-white. 2 MILKY, buttery, oily, smooth, velvety, rich, thick.

**crease** v fold, pleat, wrinkle, pucker, crumple, rumple, crinkle, crimp, corrugate, ridge.
n fold, line, pleat, tuck, wrinkle, pucker, ruck, crinkle, corrugation, ridge, groove.

**create** v invent, coin, formulate, compose, design, devise, concoct, hatch, originate, initiate, found, establish, set up, institute, cause, occasion, produce, generate, engender, make, form, appoint, install, invest, ordain.
**F3** destroy.

**creation** n 1 MAKING, formation, constitution, invention, concoction, origination, foundation, establishment, institution, production, generation, procreation, conception, birth. 2 INVENTION, brainchild, concept, product, handiwork, chef d'oeuvre, achievement.
**F3** 1 destruction.

**creative** adj artistic, inventive, original, imaginative, inspired, visionary, talented, gifted, clever, ingenious, resourceful, fertile, productive.
**F3** unimaginative.

**creator** n maker, inventor, designer, architect, author, originator, initiator.

**creature** n animal, beast, bird, fish, organism, being, mortal, individual, person, man, woman, body, soul.

**credentials** n diploma, certificate, reference, testimonial, recommendation, accreditation, authorization, warrant, licence, permit, passport, identity card, papers, documents, deed, title.

**credibility** n integrity, reliability, trustworthiness, plausibility, probability.
**F3** implausibility.

**credible** adj believable, imaginable, conceivable, thinkable, tenable, plausible, likely, probable, possible, reasonable, persuasive, convincing, sincere, honest, trustworthy, reliable, dependable.
**F3** incredible, unbelievable, implausible, unreliable.

**credit** n acknowledgement, recognition, thanks, approval, commendation, praise, acclaim, tribute, glory, fame, prestige, distinction, honour, reputation, esteem, estimation.
**F3** discredit, shame.
v believe, swallow (infml), accept, subscribe to, trust, rely on.

**E3** disbelieve.

**creditable** *adj* honourable, reputable, respectable, estimable, admirable, commendable, praiseworthy, good, excellent, exemplary, worthy, deserving.
**E3** shameful, blameworthy.

**credulous** *adj* naïve, gullible, wide-eyed, trusting, unsuspecting, uncritical.
**E3** sceptical, suspicious.

**creed** *n* belief, faith, persuasion, credo, catechism, doctrine, principles, tenets, articles, canon, dogma.

**creek** *n* inlet, estuary, cove, bay, bight.

**creep** *v* inch, edge, tiptoe, steal, sneak, slink, crawl, slither, worm, wriggle, squirm, grovel, writhe.

**creepy** *adj* eerie, spooky, sinister, threatening, frightening, scary, terrifying, hair-raising, nightmarish, macabre, gruesome, horrible, unpleasant, disturbing.

**crest** *n* **1** *the crest of the hill*: ridge, crown, top, peak, summit, pinnacle, apex, head. **2** TUFT, tassel, plume, comb, mane. **3** INSIGNIA, device, symbol, emblem, badge.

**crevice** *n* crack, fissure, split, rift, cleft, slit, chink, cranny, gap, hole, opening, break.

**crew** *n* team, party, squad, troop, corps, company, gang, band, bunch, crowd, mob, set, lot.

**crime** *n* law-breaking, lawlessness, delinquency, offence, felony, misdemeanour, misdeed, wrongdoing, misconduct, transgression, violation, sin, iniquity, vice, villainy, wickedness, atrocity, outrage.

*Crimes include*: theft, robbery, burglary, larceny, pilfering, mugging, poaching; assault, rape, grievous bodily harm, GBH (*infml*), battery, manslaughter, homicide, murder, assassination; fraud, bribery, corruption, embezzlement, extortion, blackmail; arson, treason, terrorism, hijack, piracy, kidnapping, sabotage, vandalism, hooliganism, drug-smuggling, forgery, counterfeiting, perjury, joy-riding, drink-driving, drunk and disorderly.

**criminal** *n* law-breaker, crook, felon, delinquent, offender, wrongdoer, miscreant, culprit, convict, prisoner.
*adj* illegal, unlawful, illicit, lawless, wrong, culpable, indictable, crooked (*infml*), bent (*infml*), dishonest, corrupt, wicked, scandalous, deplorable.
**E3** legal, lawful, honest, upright.

**cringe** *v* shrink, recoil, shy, flinch, wince, quail, tremble, quiver, cower, crouch, bend, bow, stoop, grovel, crawl, creep.

**cripple** *v* lame, paralyse, disable, handicap, injure, maim, mutilate, damage, impair, spoil, ruin, destroy, sabotage, incapacitate, weaken, debilitate.

**crippled** *adj* lame, paralysed, disabled, handicapped, incapacitated.

**crisis** *n* emergency, extremity, crunch (*infml*), catastrophe, disaster, calamity, dilemma, quandary, predicament, difficulty, trouble, problem.

**crisp** *adj* **1** *a crisp biscuit*: crispy, crunchy, brittle, crumbly, firm, hard. **2** BRACING, invigorating, refreshing, fresh, brisk. **3** TERSE, pithy, snappy, brief, short, clear, incisive.
**E3** **1** soggy, limp, flabby. **2** muggy. **3** wordy, vague.

**criterion** *n* standard, norm, touchstone, benchmark, yardstick, measure, gauge, rule, principle, canon, test.

**critic** *n* reviewer, commentator, analyst, pundit, authority, expert, judge, censor, carper, fault-finder, attacker, knocker (*infml*).

**critical** *adj* **1** *at the critical moment*: crucial, vital, essential, all-important, momentous, decisive, urgent, pressing, serious, grave, dangerous, perilous. **2** ANALYTICAL, diagnostic, penetrating, probing, discerning, perceptive. **3** UNCOMPLIMENTARY, derogatory, disparaging, disapproving, censorious, carping, fault-finding, cavilling, nit-picking (*infml*).

**F3** **1** unimportant. **3** complimentary, appreciative.

**criticism** *n* **1** CONDEMNATION, disapproval, disparagement, fault-finding, censure, blame, brickbat, flak (*infml*). **2** REVIEW, critique, assessment, evaluation, appraisal, judgement, analysis, commentary, appreciation.

**F3** **1** praise, commendation.

**criticize** *v* **1** CONDEMN, slate (*infml*), slam (*infml*), knock (*infml*), disparage, carp, find fault, censure, blame. **2** REVIEW, assess, evaluate, appraise, judge, analyse.

**F3** **1** praise, commend.

**crockery** *n* dishes, tableware, china, porcelain, earthenware, stoneware, pottery.

> *Items of crockery include*: cup, saucer, coffee cup, mug, beaker, plate, side plate, dinner plate, bowl, cereal bowl, soup bowl, salad-bowl, sugar bowl, jug, milk-jug, basin, pot, teapot, coffee pot, percolator, cafetière, cakestand, meat dish, butter-dish, tureen, gravy boat, cruet, teaset, dinner service.

**crook** *n* criminal, thief, robber, swindler, cheat, shark (*infml*), rogue, villain.

**crooked** *adj* **1** ASKEW, skew-whiff (*infml*), awry, lopsided, asymmetric, irregular, uneven, off-centre, tilted, slanting, bent, angled, hooked,

curved, bowed, warped, distorted, misshapen, deformed, twisted, tortuous, winding, zigzag. **2** (*infml*) ILLEGAL, unlawful, illicit, criminal, nefarious, dishonest, deceitful, bent (*infml*), corrupt, fraudulent, shady (*infml*), shifty, underhand, treacherous, unscrupulous, unprincipled, unethical.

**F3** **1** straight. **2** honest.

**crop** *n* growth, yield, produce, fruits, harvest, vintage, gathering.

*v* cut, snip, clip, shear, trim, pare, prune, lop, shorten, curtail.

**crop up** arise, emerge, appear, arrive, occur, happen.

**cross** *adj* **1** IRRITABLE, annoyed, angry, vexed, shirty (*infml*), bad-tempered, ill-tempered, crotchety, grumpy, grouchy, irascible, crabby, short, snappy, snappish, surly, sullen, fractious, fretful, impatient.

**2** TRANSVERSE, crosswise, oblique, diagonal, intersecting, opposite, reciprocal.

**F3** placid, pleasant.

*v* **1** *cross the river*: go across, traverse, ford, bridge, span. **2** INTERSECT, meet, criss-cross, lace, intertwine. **3** CROSSBREED, interbreed, mongrelize, hybridize, cross-fertilize, cross-pollinate, blend, mix. **4** THWART, frustrate, foil, hinder, impede, obstruct, block, oppose. *n* **1** BURDEN, load, affliction, misfortune, trouble, worry, trial, tribulation, grief, misery, woe. **2** CROSSBREED, hybrid, mongrel, blend, mixture, amalgam, combination. **3** crucifix.

**crouch** *v* squat, kneel, stoop, bend, bow, hunch, duck, cower, cringe.

**crowd** *n* **1** THRONG, multitude, host, mob, masses, populace, people, public, riff-raff, rabble, horde, swarm, flock, herd, pack, press, crush, squash, assembly, company, group, bunch, lot, set, circle, clique. **2** SPECTATORS, gate, attendance, audience.

*v* gather, congregate, muster, huddle, mass, throng, swarm, flock, surge, stream, push, shove, elbow, jostle, press, squeeze, bundle, pile, pack, congest, cram, compress.

**crowded** *adj* full, filled, packed, jammed, jam-packed, congested, cramped, overcrowded, overpopulated, busy, teeming, swarming, overflowing.

Fa empty, deserted.

**crown** *n* **1** CORONET, diadem, tiara, circlet, wreath, garland. **2** PRIZE, trophy, reward, honour, laurels. **3** SOVEREIGN, monarch, king, queen, ruler, sovereignty, monarchy, royalty. **4** TOP, tip, apex, crest, summit, pinnacle, peak, acme.

*v* **1** ENTHRONE, anoint, adorn, festoon, honour, dignify, reward. **2** TOP, cap, complete, fulfil, consummate, perfect.

**crucial** *adj* urgent, pressing, vital, essential, key, pivotal, central, important, momentous, decisive, critical, trying, testing, searching.

Fa unimportant, trivial.

**crude** *adj* **1** RAW, unprocessed, unrefined, rough, unfinished, unpolished, natural, primitive. **2** *a crude remark*: VULGAR, coarse, rude, indecent, obscene, gross, dirty, lewd.

Fa **1** refined, finished. **2** polite, decent.

**cruel** *adj* fierce, ferocious, vicious, savage, barbarous, bloodthirsty, murderous, cold-blooded, sadistic, brutal, inhuman, inhumane, unkind, malevolent, spiteful, callous, heartless, unfeeling, merciless, pitiless, flinty, hard-hearted, stony-hearted, implacable, ruthless, remorseless, relentless, unrelenting, inexorable, grim, hellish, atrocious, bitter, harsh, severe, cutting, painful, excruciating.

Fa kind, compassionate, merciful.

**cruelty** *n* ferocity, viciousness, savagery, barbarity, bloodthirstiness,

murderousness, violence, sadism, brutality, bestiality, inhumanity, spite, venom, callousness, heartlessness, hard-heartedness, mercilessness, ruthlessness, tyranny, harshness, severity.

Fa kindness, compassion, mercy.

**crumble** *v* fragment, break up, decompose, disintegrate, decay, degenerate, deteriorate, collapse, crush, pound, grind, powder, pulverize.

**crumple** *v* crush, wrinkle, pucker, crinkle, rumple, crease, fold, collapse.

**crunch** *v* munch, chomp, champ, masticate, grind, crush.

**crusade** *n* campaign, drive, push, movement, cause, undertaking, expedition, holy war, jihad.

**crush** *v* **1** SQUASH, compress, squeeze, press, pulp, break, smash, pound, pulverize, grind, crumble, crumple, wrinkle. **2** *the rebels were crushed*: conquer, vanquish, demolish, devastate, overpower, overwhelm, overcome, quash, quell, subdue, put down, humiliate, shame, abash.

**crust** *n* surface, exterior, outside, covering, coat, coating, layer, film, skin, rind, shell, scab, incrustation, caking, concretion.

**crux** *n* nub, heart, core, essence.

**cry** *v* **1** WEEP, sob, blubber, wail, bawl, whimper, snivel. **2** SHOUT, call, exclaim, roar, bellow, yell, scream, shriek, screech.

*n* **1** WEEP, sob, blubber, wail, bawl, whimper, snivel. **2** SHOUT, call, plea, exclamation, roar, bellow, yell, scream, shriek.

**cryptic** *adj* enigmatic, ambiguous, equivocal, puzzling, perplexing, mysterious, strange, bizarre, secret, hidden, veiled, obscure, abstruse, esoteric, dark, occult.

Fa straightforward, clear, obvious.

**cuddle** *v* hug, embrace, clasp, hold,

nurse, nestle, snuggle, pet, fondle, caress.

**cuddly** *adj* cuddlesome, lovable, huggable, plump, soft, warm, cosy.

**cue** *n* signal, sign, nod, hint, suggestion, reminder, prompt, incentive, stimulus.

**cuff** *v* hit, thump, box, clip, knock, biff (*infml*), buffet, slap, smack, strike, clout, clobber (*sl*), belt (*infml*), beat, whack (*infml*).

**culminate** *v* climax, end (up), terminate, close, conclude, finish, consummate.
**F3** start, begin.

**culmination** *n* climax, height, peak, pinnacle, summit, top, crown, perfection, consummation, finale, conclusion, completion.
**F3** start, beginning.

**culprit** *n* guilty party, offender, wrongdoer, miscreant, law-breaker, criminal, felon, delinquent.

**cult** *n* **1** SECT, denomination, school, movement, party, faction. **2** CRAZE, fad, fashion, vogue, trend.

**cultivate** *v* **1** FARM, till, work, plough, grow, sow, plant, tend, harvest. **2** FOSTER, nurture, cherish, help, aid, support, encourage, promote, further, work on, develop, train, prepare, polish, refine, improve, enrich.
**F3 2** neglect.

**cultural** *adj* artistic, aesthetic, liberal, civilizing, humanizing, enlightening, educational, edifying, improving, enriching, elevating.

**culture** *n* **1** CIVILIZATION, society, lifestyle, way of life, customs, mores, the arts. **2** CULTIVATION, taste, education, enlightenment, breeding, gentility, refinement, politeness, urbanity.

**cultured** *adj* cultivated, civilized, advanced, enlightened, educated, well-read, well-informed, scholarly, highbrow, well-bred, refined, polished, genteel, urbane.

**F3** uncultured, uneducated, ignorant.

**cumbersome** *adj* awkward, inconvenient, bulky, unwieldy, unmanageable, burdensome, onerous, heavy, weighty.
**F3** convenient, manageable.

**cunning** *adj* crafty, sly, artful, wily, tricky, devious, subtle, deceitful, guileful, sharp, shrewd, astute, canny, knowing, deep, imaginative, ingenious, skilful, deft, dexterous.
**F3** naïve, ingenuous, gullible.
*n* craftiness, slyness, artfulness, trickery, deviousness, subtlety, deceitfulness, guile, sharpness, shrewdness, astuteness, ingenuity, cleverness, adroitness.

**cup** *n* mug, tankard, beaker, goblet, chalice, trophy.

**cupboard** *n* cabinet, locker, closet, wardrobe.

**curb** *v* restrain, constrain, restrict, contain, control, check, moderate, bridle, muzzle, suppress, subdue, repress, inhibit, hinder, impede, hamper, retard.
**F3** encourage, foster.

**curdle** *v* coagulate, congeal, clot, thicken, turn, sour, ferment.

**cure** *v* **1** HEAL, remedy, correct, restore, repair, mend, relieve, ease, alleviate, help. **2** PRESERVE, dry, smoke, salt, pickle, kipper.
*n* remedy, antidote, panacea, medicine, specific, corrective, restorative, healing, treatment, therapy, alleviation, recovery.

**curiosity** *n* **1** INQUISITIVENESS, nosiness, prying, snooping, interest. **2** CURIO, objet d'art, antique, bygone, novelty, trinket, knick-knack. **3** ODDITY, rarity, freak, phenomenon, spectacle.

**curious** *adj* **1** INQUISITIVE, nosey, prying, meddlesome, questioning, inquiring, interested. **2** *a curious sight*: ODD, queer, funny (*infml*), strange, peculiar, bizarre, mysterious, puzzling, extraordinary, unusual,

rare, unique, novel, exotic,
unconventional, unorthodox, quaint.
**F3 1** uninterested, indifferent.
**2** ordinary, usual, normal.

**curl** *v* crimp, frizz, wave, ripple,
bend, curve, meander, loop, turn,
twist, wind, wreathe, twine, coil,
spiral, corkscrew, scroll.
**F3** uncurl.
*n* wave, kink, swirl, twist, ringlet,
coil, spiral, whorl.

**curly** *adj* wavy, kinky, curling,
spiralled, corkscrew, curled, crimped,
permed, frizzy, fuzzy.
**F3** straight.

**currency** *n* **1** MONEY, legal tender,
coinage, coins, notes, bills.
**2** ACCEPTANCE, publicity,
popularity, vogue, circulation,
prevalence, exposure.

---

*Currencies of the world include*: baht
(Thailand), bolívar (Venezuela), cent
(US, Canada, Australia, NZ, S Africa,
etc), centavo (Portugal, Brazil,
Mexico, etc), centime (France,
Belgium, Algeria, etc), cruzeiro
(Brazil), dinar (Iraq, Jordan, etc),
dirham (Morocco), dollar (US,
Canada, Australia, NZ, etc), dong
(Vietnam), drachma (Greece), ecu
(EC), escudo (Portugal), fils (Iraq,
Jordan, etc), guilder (Netherlands),
franc (France, Belgium, Switzerland,
etc), karbovanets (Ukraine), kopeck
(Russia), koruna (Czech Republic,
Slovakia), krona (Sweden), króna
(Iceland), krone (Denmark, Norway),
kyat (Myanmar), lek (Albania), leu
(Romania), lev (Bulgaria), lira (Italy),
mark (Germany), pence (UK), peseta
(Spain), peso (Mexico, Chile, etc),
pfennig (Germany), piastre (Egypt,
Syria, etc), pound (UK, Egypt, etc),
punt (Ireland), rand (S Africa), rial
(Iran), riyal (Saudi Arabia), rouble
(Russia), rupee (India, Pakistan, etc),
schilling (Austria), shekel (Israel),
shilling (Kenya, Uganda, etc), som

(Uzbekistan), sterling (UK), sucre
(Ecuador), tolar (Slovenia), won (N
Korea, S Korea), yen (Japan), yuan
(China), zaïre (Zaire), zloty (Poland).

---

**current** *adj* present, on-going,
existing, contemporary, present-day,
modern, fashionable, up-to-date, up-
to-the-minute, trendy (*infml*),
popular, widespread, prevalent,
common, general, prevailing,
reigning, accepted.
**F3** obsolete, old-fashioned.
*n* draught, stream, jet, flow, drift,
tide, course, trend, tendency,
undercurrent, mood, feeling.

**curse** *n* **1** SWEAR-WORD, oath,
expletive, obscenity, profanity,
blasphemy. **2** JINX, anathema, bane,
evil, plague, scourge, affliction,
trouble, torment, ordeal, calamity,
disaster.
**F3 2** blessing, advantage.
*v* **1** SWEAR, blaspheme, damn,
condemn, denounce, fulminate.
**2** BLIGHT, plague, scourge, afflict,
trouble, torment.
**F3 2** bless.

**curtail** *v* shorten, truncate, cut, trim,
abridge, abbreviate, lessen, decrease,
reduce, restrict.
**F3** lengthen, extend, prolong.

**curtain** *n* blind, screen, backdrop,
hanging, drapery, tapestry.

**curve** *v* bend, arch, arc, bow, bulge,
hook, crook, turn, wind, twist, spiral,
coil.
*n* bend, turn, arc, trajectory, loop,
camber, curvature.

**curved** *adj* bent, arched, bowed,
rounded, humped, convex, concave,
crooked, twisted, sweeping, sinuous,
serpentine.
**F3** straight.

**cushion** *n* pad, buffer, shock
absorber, bolster, pillow, headrest,
hassock.
*v* soften, deaden, dampen, absorb,
muffle, stifle, suppress, lessen,

mitigate, protect, bolster, buttress, support.

**custody** n **1** KEEPING, possession, charge, care, safe-keeping, protection, preservation, custodianship, trusteeship, guardianship, supervision. **2** DETENTION, confinement, imprisonment, incarceration.

**custom** n tradition, usage, use, habit, routine, procedure, practice, policy, way, manner, style, form, convention, etiquette, formality, observance, ritual.

**customary** adj traditional, conventional, accepted, established, habitual, routine, regular, usual, normal, ordinary, everyday, familiar, common, general, popular, fashionable, prevailing.

**E3** unusual, rare.

**customer** n client, patron, regular, punter (infml), consumer, shopper, buyer, purchaser, prospect.

**cut** v **1** CLIP, trim, crop, shear, mow, shave, pare, chop, hack, hew, slice, carve, divide, part, split, bisect, dock, lop, sever, prune, excise, incise, penetrate, pierce, stab, wound, nick, gash, slit, slash, lacerate, score, engrave, chisel, sculpt. **2** REDUCE, decrease, lower, shorten, curtail, abbreviate, abridge, condense, précis, edit, delete. **3** IGNORE, cold-shoulder, spurn, avoid, snub, slight, rebuff, insult.

n **1** INCISION, wound, nick, gash, slit, slash, rip, laceration. **2** spending cuts: REDUCTION, decrease, lowering, cutback, saving, economy.

**cut down 1** cut down a tree: fell, hew, lop, level, raze. **2** REDUCE, decrease, lower, lessen, diminish.

**cut in** interrupt, butt in, interject, interpose, intervene, intrude.

**cut off 1** SEVER, amputate, separate, isolate, disconnect, block, obstruct, intercept. **2** STOP, end, halt, suspend, discontinue, disown, disinherit.

**cut out** excise, extract, remove, delete, eliminate, exclude, debar, stop, cease.

**cut up** chop, dice, mince, dissect, divide, carve, slice, slash.

**cutback** n cut, saving, economy, retrenchment, reduction, decrease, lowering, lessening.

**cutlery**

> *Items of cutlery include*: knife, butter-knife, carving-knife, fish knife, steak knife, cheese knife, breadknife, vegetable knife, fork, fish fork, carving fork, spoon, dessert-spoon, tablespoon, teaspoon, soup-spoon, caddy spoon, salt spoon, apostle spoon, ladle, salad servers, fish slice, cake server, sugar tongs, chopsticks, canteen of cutlery.

**cut-price** adj reduced, sale, discount, bargain, cheap, low-priced.

**cutter**

> *Types of cutter include*: axe, billhook, blade, chisel, chopper, clippers, guillotine, hedgetrimmer, knife, flick knife, penknife, pocket knife, Stanley knife®, Swiss army knife, lopper, machete, mower, lawnmower, plane, razor, saw, chainsaw, fretsaw, hacksaw, jigsaw, scalpel, scissors, scythe, secateurs, shears, pinking shears, sickle, Strimmer®, sword.

**cutting** adj sharp, keen, pointed, trenchant, incisive, penetrating, piercing, wounding, stinging, biting, mordant, caustic, acid, scathing, sarcastic, malicious, bitter, raw, chill. n clipping, extract, piece.

**cycle** n circle, round, rotation, revolution, series, sequence, phase, period, era, age, epoch, aeon.

**cylinder** n column, barrel, drum, reel, bobbin, spool, spindle.

**cynic** n sceptic, doubter, pessimist, killjoy, spoilsport (infml), scoffer, knocker (*infml*).

**cynical** *adj* sceptical, doubtful,
distrustful, pessimistic, negative,
scornful, derisive, contemptuous,
sneering, scoffing, mocking,
sarcastic, sardonic, ironic.

**cynicism** *n* scepticism, doubt,
disbelief, distrust, pessimism, scorn,
sarcasm, irony.

# D

**dab** *v* pat, tap, daub, swab, wipe.
*n* **1** BIT, dollop (*infml*), drop, speck,
spot, trace, smear, smudge, fleck.
**2** TOUCH, pat, stroke, tap.

**dabble** *v* **1** TRIFLE, tinker, toy,
dally, potter. **2** PADDLE, moisten,
wet, sprinkle, splash.

**dabbler** *n* amateur, dilettante,
trifler.
**F3** professional, expert.

**daft** *adj* **1** FOOLISH, crazy, silly,
stupid, absurd, dotty (*infml*), idiotic,
inane. **2** INSANE, mad, lunatic,
simple, crazy, mental. **3** (*infml*)
INFATUATED.
**F3 1** sensible. **2** sane.

**daily** *adj* **1** REGULAR, routine,
everyday, customary, common,
commonplace, ordinary.
**2** EVERYDAY, diurnal (*fml*).

**dainty** *adj* **1** DELICATE, elegant,
exquisite, refined, fine, graceful, neat,
charming, delectable. **2** FASTIDIOUS,
fussy, particular, scrupulous, nice
(*fml*).
**F3 1** gross, clumsy.

**dam** *n* barrier, barrage,
embankment, blockage, obstruction,
hindrance.
*v* block, confine, restrict, check,
barricade, staunch, stem, obstruct.

**damage** *n* harm, injury, hurt,
destruction, devastation, loss,
suffering, mischief, mutilation,
impairment, detriment.
**F3** repair.
*v* harm, injure, hurt, spoil, ruin,
impair, mar, wreck, deface, mutilate,

weaken, tamper with, play havoc
with, incapacitate.
**F3** mend, repair, fix.

**damn** *v* **1** CURSE, swear, blast,
imprecate, blaspheme. **2** ABUSE,
revile, denounce, criticise, censure,
slate (*infml*), denunciate, execrate,
castigate, slam (*infml*). **3** CONDEMN,
doom, sentence.
**F3 1** bless.

**damnation** *n* condemnation, doom,
denunciation, perdition,
excommunication, anathema.

**damp** *n* dampness, moisture,
clamminess, dankness, humidity, wet,
dew, drizzle, fog, mist, vapour.
**F3** dryness.
*adj* moist, wet, clammy, dank,
humid, dewy, muggy, drizzly, misty,
soggy.
**F3** dry, arid.

**dampen** *v* **1** MOISTEN, wet, spray. **2**
DISCOURAGE, dishearten, deter,
dash, dull, deaden, restrain, check,
depress, dismay, reduce, lessen,
moderate, decrease, diminish, muffle,
stifle, smother.
**F3 1** dry. **2** encourage.

**dance** *n* ball, hop (*infml*), knees-up
(*infml*), social, shindig (*infml*).

*Dances include*: waltz, quickstep,
foxtrot, tango, polka, one-step,
military two-step, valeta, Lancers,
rumba, samba, mambo, bossanova,
beguine, fandango, flamenco,
mazurka, bolero, paso doble, can-can;
rock 'n' roll, jive, twist, stomp, bop,

jitterbug, mashed potato; black bottom, Charleston, cha-cha, turkey-trot; Circassian circle, Paul Jones, jig, reel, quadrille, Highland fling, morris-dance, clog dance, hoe-down, hokey-cokey, Lambeth Walk, conga, belly-dance; galliard, gavotte, minuet.

*Types of dancing include*: ballet, tap, ballroom, old-time, disco, folk, country, Irish, Highland, Latin-American, flamenco, clog-dancing, morris dancing, limbo-dancing, break-dancing, robotics.

*Dance functions include*: disco, dance, social, tea dance, barn dance, ball, fancy dress ball, charity ball, hunt ball, hop (*infml*), knees-up (*sl*), shindig (*infml*), rave (*infml*), prom (*US*), ceilidh.

**danger** *n* **1** *in danger of falling*: insecurity, endangerment, jeopardy, precariousness, liability, vulnerability. **2** *the dangers of smoking*: risk, threat, peril, hazard, menace.
**1** safety, security. **2** safety.

**dangerous** *adj* unsafe, insecure, risky, threatening, breakneck, hairy (*infml*), hazardous, perilous, precarious, reckless, treacherous, vulnerable, menacing, exposed, alarming, critical, severe, serious, grave, daring, nasty.
**safe**, secure, harmless.

**dangle** *v* **1** HANG, droop, swing, sway, flap, trail. **2** TEMPT, entice, flaunt, flourish, lure, tantalize.

**dank** *adj* damp, moist, clammy, dewy, slimy, soggy.
**dry**.

**dappled** *adj* speckled, mottled, spotted, stippled, dotted, flecked, freckled, variegated, bespeckled, piebald, checkered.

**dare** *v* **1** RISK, venture, brave, hazard, adventure, endanger, stake, gamble. **2** CHALLENGE, goad, provoke, taunt. **3** DEFY, presume.
*n* challenge, provocation, taunt, gauntlet.

**daredevil** *n* adventurer, desperado, madcap.
**coward**.

**daring** *adj* bold, adventurous, intrepid, fearless, brave, plucky, audacious, dauntless, reckless, rash, impulsive, valiant.
**cautious**, timid, afraid.
*n* boldness, fearlessness, courage, bravery, nerve, audacity, guts (*infml*), intrepidity, defiance, pluck, rashness, spirit, grit, gall, prowess.
**caution**, timidity, cowardice.

**dark** *adj* **1** *a dark room*: unlit, overcast, black, dim, unilluminated, shadowy, murky, cloudy, dusky, dingy. **2** *a dark manner*: gloomy, grim, cheerless, dismal, bleak, forbidding, sombre, sinister, mournful, ominous, menacing, drab. **3** *dark secrets*: hidden, mysterious, obscure, secret, unintelligible, enigmatic, cryptic, abstruse.
**1** light. **2** bright, cheerful. **3** comprehensible.
*n* **1** DARKNESS, dimness, night, night-time, nightfall, gloom, dusk, twilight, murkiness.
**2** CONCEALMENT, secrecy, obscurity.
**1** light. **2** openness.

**darken** *v* **1** DIM, obscure, blacken, cloud (over), shadow, overshadow, eclipse. **2** DEPRESS, sadden.
**1** lighten. **2** brighten.

**darling** *n* beloved, dear, dearest, favourite, sweetheart, love, pet.
*adj* dear, beloved, adored, cherished, precious, treasured.

**dart** *v* **1** DASH, bound, sprint, flit, flash, fly, rush, run, race, spring, tear. **2** THROW, hurl, fling, shoot, sling, launch, propel, send.
*n* bolt, arrow, barb, shaft.

**dash** v 1 RUSH, dart, hurry, race, sprint, run, bolt, tear. 2 FLING, throw, crash, hurl. 3 DISCOURAGE, disappoint, dampen, confound, blight, ruin, destroy, spoil, frustrate, smash, shatter.

n 1 DROP, pinch, touch, flavour, soupçon, suggestion, hint, bit, little. 2 SPRINT, dart, bolt, rush, spurt, race, run.

**dashing** adj 1 LIVELY, vigorous, spirited, gallant, daring, bold, plucky, exuberant. 2 SMART, stylish, elegant, debonair, showy, flamboyant.

F3 1 lethargic. 2 dowdy.

**data** n information, documents, facts, input, statistics, figures, details, materials.

**date** n 1 TIME, age, period, era, stage, epoch. 2 APPOINTMENT, engagement, assignation, meeting, rendezvous. 3 ESCORT, steady (infml), partner, friend.

**out-of-date** adj old-fashioned, unfashionable, outdated, obsolete, dated, outmoded, antiquated, passé.

F3 fashionable, modern.

**up-to-date** adj fashionable, modern, current, contemporary.

F3 old-fashioned, dated.

**daunt** v 1 DISCOURAGE, dishearten, put off, dispirit, deter. 2 INTIMIDATE, overawe, unnerve, alarm, dismay, frighten, scare.

F3 1 encourage.

**dauntless** adj fearless, undaunted, resolute, brave, courageous, bold, intrepid, daring, plucky, valiant.

F3 discouraged, disheartened.

**dawdle** v delay, loiter, lag, hang about, dally, trail, potter, dilly-dally (infml).

F3 hurry.

**dawn** n 1 SUNRISE, daybreak, morning, daylight. 2 BEGINNING, start, emergence, onset, origin, birth, advent.

F3 1 dusk. 2 end.

v 1 BREAK, brighten, lighten, gleam, glimmer. 2 BEGIN, appear, emerge, open, develop, originate, rise.

**day** n 1 DAYTIME, daylight. 2 AGE, period, time, date, era, generation, epoch.

F3 1 night.

**day after day** regularly, continually, endlessly, persistently, monotonously, perpetually, relentlessly.

**day by day** gradually, progressively, slowly but surely, steadily.

**daydream** n fantasy, imagining, reverie, castles in the air, pipe dream, vision, musing, wish, dream, figment.

v fantasize, imagine, muse, fancy, dream.

**daze** v 1 STUN, stupefy, shock. 2 DAZZLE, bewilder, blind, confuse, baffle, dumbfound, amaze, surprise, startle, perplex, astonish, flabbergast (infml), astound, stagger.

n bewilderment, confusion, stupor, trance, shock, distraction.

**dazzle** v 1 DAZE, blind, confuse, blur. 2 SPARKLE, fascinate, impress, overwhelm, awe, overawe, scintillate, bedazzle, amaze, astonish, bewitch, stupefy.

n sparkle, brilliance, magnificence, splendour, scintillation, glitter, glare.

**dead** adj 1 LIFELESS, deceased, inanimate, defunct, departed, late, gone. 2 UNRESPONSIVE, apathetic, dull, indifferent, insensitive, numb, cold, frigid, lukewarm, torpid.

3 EXHAUSTED, tired, worn out, dead-beat (infml). 4 EXACT, absolute, perfect, unqualified, utter, outright, complete, entire, total, downright.

F3 1 alive. 2 lively. 3 refreshed.

**deaden** v reduce, blunt, muffle, lessen, quieten, suppress, weaken, numb, diminish, stifle, alleviate, anaesthetize, desensitize, smother, check, abate, allay, dampen, hush, mute, paralyse.

F3 heighten.

**deadlock** n  standstill, stalemate, impasse, halt.

**deadly** adj  1 *deadly poison*: lethal, fatal, dangerous, venomous, destructive, pernicious, malignant, murderous, mortal. 2 *a deadly lecture*: dull, boring, uninteresting, tedious, monotonous. 3 *deadly aim*: unerring, effective, true.
🖛 1 harmless. 2 exciting.

**deaf** adj  1 HARD OF HEARING, stone-deaf. 2 UNCONCERNED, indifferent, unmoved, oblivious, heedless, unmindful.
🖛 2 aware, conscious.

**deafening** adj  piercing, ear-splitting, booming, resounding, thunderous, ringing, roaring.
🖛 quiet.

**deal** v  1 APPORTION, distribute, share, dole out, divide, allot, dispense, assign, mete out, give, bestow. 2 TRADE, negotiate, traffic, bargain, treat.
n  1 QUANTITY, amount, extent, degree, portion, share.
2 AGREEMENT, contract, understanding, pact, transaction, bargain, buy. 3 ROUND, hand, distribution.
**deal with** attend to, concern, see to, manage, handle, cope with, treat, consider, oversee.

**dealer** n  trader, merchant, wholesaler, marketer, merchandizer.

**dear** adj  1 LOVED, beloved, treasured, valued, cherished, precious, favourite, esteemed, intimate, close, darling, familiar. 2 EXPENSIVE, high-priced, costly, overpriced, pric(e)y (*infml*).
🖛 1 disliked, hated. 2 cheap.
n  beloved, loved one, precious, darling, treasure.

**dearly** adv  1 *he loves her dearly*: fondly, affectionately, lovingly, devotedly, tenderly. 2 *I wish it dearly*: greatly, extremely, profoundly.

**dearth** n  scarcity, shortage, insufficiency, inadequacy, deficiency, lack, want, absence, scantiness, sparsity, need, paucity, poverty, famine.
🖛 excess, abundance.

**death** n  1 DECEASE, end, finish, loss, demise, departure, fatality, cessation, passing, expiration, dissolution.
2 DESTRUCTION, ruin, undoing, annihilation, downfall, extermination, extinction, obliteration, eradication.
🖛 1 life, birth.

**deathly** adj  1 ASHEN, grim, haggard, pale, pallid, ghastly, wan. 2 FATAL, deadly, mortal, intense.

**debase** v  1 DEGRADE, demean, devalue, disgrace, dishonour, shame, humble, humiliate, lower, reduce, abase, defile. 2 CONTAMINATE, pollute, corrupt, adulterate, taint.
🖛 1 elevate. 2 purify.

**debatable** adj  questionable, uncertain, disputable, contestable, controversial, arguable, open to question, doubtful, contentious, undecided, unsettled, problematical, dubious, moot.
🖛 unquestionable, certain, incontrovertible.

**debate** v  1 DISPUTE, argue, discuss, contend, wrangle. 2 CONSIDER, deliberate, ponder, reflect, meditate on, mull over, weigh.
n  discussion, argument, controversy, disputation, deliberation, consideration, contention, dispute, reflection, polemic.

**debauchery** n  depravity, intemperance, overindulgence, dissipation, licentiousness, dissoluteness, excess, decadence, wantonness, lewdness, carousal, orgy, revel, lust, riot.
🖛 restraint, temperance.

**debilitate** v  weaken, enervate, undermine, sap, incapacitate, wear out, exhaust, impair.

**F3** strengthen, invigorate, energize.

**debris** *n* remains, ruins, rubbish, waste, wreck, wreckage, litter, fragments, rubble, trash, pieces, bits, sweepings, drift.

**debt** *n* indebtedness, obligation, debit, arrears, due, liability, duty, bill, commitment, claim, score.
**F3** credit, asset.

**debtor** *n* borrower, bankrupt, insolvent, defaulter, mortgagor.
**F3** creditor.

**debunk** *v* expose, deflate, show up, ridicule, mock, explode, lampoon.

**debut** *n* introduction, launching, beginning, entrance, presentation, inauguration, première, appearance, initiation.

**decadent** *adj* 1 CORRUPT, debased, debauched, depraved, dissolute, immoral, degenerate, degraded, self-indulgent. 2 DECAYING, declining.
**F3** 1 moral.

**decay** *v* 1 ROT, go bad, putrefy, decompose, spoil, perish, mortify. 2 DECLINE, deteriorate, disintegrate, corrode, crumble, waste away, degenerate, wear away, dwindle, shrivel, wither, sink.
**F3** 2 flourish, grow.
*n* 1 ROT, decomposition, rotting, perishing. 2 DECLINE, deterioration, disintegration, degeneration, collapse, decadence, wasting, failing, withering, fading.

**decease** *n* death, dying, demise, departure, passing, dissolution.

**deceased** *adj* dead, departed, former, late, lost, defunct, expired, gone, finished, extinct.
*n* dead, departed.

**deceit** *n* deception, pretence, cheating, misrepresentation, fraud, duplicity, trickery, fraudulence, double-dealing, underhandedness, fake, guile, sham, subterfuge, swindle, treachery, hypocrisy, artifice, ruse, cunning, slyness, craftiness, stratagem, wile,

imposition, feint, shift, abuse.
**F3** honesty, openness, frankness.

**deceitful** *adj* dishonest, deceptive, deceiving, false, insincere, untrustworthy, double-dealing, fraudulent, two-faced (*infml*), treacherous, duplicitous, guileful, tricky (*infml*), underhand, sneaky, counterfeit, crafty, hypocritical, designing, illusory, knavish.
**F3** honest, open.

**deceive** *v* mislead, delude, cheat, betray, fool, take in (*infml*), trick, dissemble, hoax, con (*infml*), have on (*infml*), take for a ride (*infml*), double-cross (*infml*), dupe, kid (*infml*), swindle, impose upon, bamboozle (*infml*), two-time (*infml*), lead on, outwit, hoodwink, beguile, ensnare, camouflage, abuse, befool, gull.

**decency** *n* propriety, courtesy, modesty, decorum, respectability, civility, correctness, fitness, etiquette, helpfulness.
**F3** impropriety, discourtesy.

**decent** *adj* 1 RESPECTABLE, proper, fitting, decorous, chaste, seemly, suitable, modest, appropriate, presentable, pure, fit, becoming, befitting, nice. 2 KIND, obliging, courteous, helpful, generous, polite, gracious. 3 ADEQUATE, acceptable, satisfactory, reasonable, sufficient, tolerable, competent.
**F3** 1 indecent. 2 disobliging.

**deception** *n* deceit, pretence, trick, cheat, fraud, imposture, lie, dissembling, deceptiveness, insincerity, con (*infml*), sham, subterfuge, artifice, hypocrisy, bluff, treachery, hoax, fraudulence, duplicity, ruse, snare, stratagem, leg-pull (*infml*), illusion, wile, guile, craftiness, cunning.
**F3** openness, honesty.

**deceptive** *adj* dishonest, false, fraudulent, misleading, unreliable, illusive, fake, illusory, spurious, mock, fallacious, ambiguous, specious.

**F3** genuine, artless, open.

**decide** *v* choose, determine, resolve, reach a decision, settle, elect, opt, judge, adjudicate, conclude, fix, purpose, decree.

**decided** *adj* **1** DEFINITE, certain, undeniable, indisputable, absolute, clear-cut, undisputed, unmistakable, unquestionable, positive, unambiguous, categorical, distinct, emphatic. **2** RESOLUTE, decisive, determined, firm, unhesitating, deliberate, forthright.

**F3** **1** inconclusive. **2** irresolute.

**decipher** *v* decode, unscramble, crack, construe, interpret, make out (*infml*), figure out (*infml*), understand, transliterate.

**F3** encode.

**decision** *n* **1** RESULT, conclusion, outcome, verdict, finding, settlement, judgement, arbitration, ruling.
**2** DETERMINATION, decisiveness, firmness, resolve, purpose.

**decisive** *adj* **1** CONCLUSIVE, definite, definitive, absolute, final.
**2** DETERMINED, resolute, decided, positive, firm, forceful, forthright, strong-minded. **3** SIGNIFICANT, critical, crucial, influential, momentous, fateful.

**F3** **1** inconclusive. **2** indecisive.
**3** insignificant.

**declaration** *n* **1** AFFIRMATION, acknowledgement, assertion, statement, testimony, attestation, disclosure, profession, revelation.
**2** ANNOUNCEMENT, notification, pronouncement, proclamation, edict, manifesto, promulgation.

**declare** *v* **1** AFFIRM, assert, claim, profess, maintain, state, attest, certify, confess, confirm, disclose, reveal, show, aver, swear, testify, witness, validate. **2** ANNOUNCE, proclaim, pronounce, decree, broadcast.

**decline** *v* **1** REFUSE, reject, deny, forgo, avoid, balk. **2** DIMINISH, decrease, dwindle, lessen, fall, sink, wane. **3** DECAY, deteriorate, worsen, degenerate. **4** DESCEND, sink, slope, dip, slant.

**F3** **3** improve. **4** rise.

*n* **1** DETERIORATION, dwindling, lessening, decay, degeneration, weakening, worsening, failing, downturn, diminution, falling-off, recession, slump, abatement.
**2** DESCENT, dip, declivity, declination, hill, slope, incline, divergence, deviation.

**F3** **1** improvement. **2** rise.

**decode** *v* decipher, interpret, unscramble, translate, transliterate, uncipher.

**F3** encode.

**decompose** *v* disintegrate, rot, decay, putrefy, break down, break up, crumble, spoil, dissolve, separate, fester.

**décor** *n* decoration, furnishings, colour scheme, ornamentation, scenery.

**decorate** *v* **1** ORNAMENT, adorn, beautify, embellish, trim, deck, tart up (*sl*), grace, enrich, prettify, trick out. **2** RENOVATE, do up (*infml*), paint, paper, colour, refurbish.
**3** HONOUR, crown, cite, garland, bemedal.

**decoration** *n* **1** ORNAMENT, adornment, ornamentation, trimming, embellishment, beautification, garnish, flourish, enrichment, elaboration, frill, scroll, bauble. **2** AWARD, medal, order, badge, garland, crown, colours, ribbon, laurel, star, emblem.

**decorative** *adj* ornamental, fancy, adorning, beautifying, embellishing, non-functional, pretty, ornate, enhancing.

**F3** plain.

**decorum** *n* propriety, seemliness, etiquette, good manners, respectability, protocol, behaviour, decency, dignity, deportment, restraint, politeness, modesty, grace, breeding.

**E3** impropriety, indecorum, bad manners.

**decoy** *n* lure, trap, enticement, inducement, ensnarement, pretence, attraction, bait.
*v* bait, lure, entrap, entice, ensnare, allure, tempt, deceive, attract, seduce, lead, draw.

**decrease** *v* lessen, lower, diminish, dwindle, decline, fall off, reduce, subside, abate, cut down, contract, drop, ease, shrink, taper, wane, slim, slacken, peter out, curtail.

**E3** increase.
*n* lessening, reduction, decline, falling-off, dwindling, loss, diminution, abatement, cutback, contraction, downturn, ebb, shrinkage, subsidence, step-down.

**E3** increase.

**decree** *n* order, command, law, ordinance, regulation, ruling, statute, act, enactment, edict, proclamation, mandate, precept, interlocution.
*v* order, command, rule, lay down, dictate, decide, determine, ordain, prescribe, proclaim, pronounce, enact.

**decrepit** *adj* dilapidated, run-down, rickety, broken-down, worn-out, tumble-down.

**dedicate** *v* 1 DEVOTE, commit, assign, give over to, pledge, present, offer, sacrifice, surrender. 2 CONSECRATE, bless, sanctify, set apart, hallow. 3 *dedicate a book*: inscribe, address.

**dedicated** *adj* devoted, committed, enthusiastic, single-minded, whole-hearted, single-hearted, zealous, given over to, purposeful.

**E3** uncommitted, apathetic.

**dedication** *n* 1 COMMITMENT, devotion, single-mindedness, whole-heartedness, allegiance, attachment,

adherence, faithfulness, loyalty, self-sacrifice. 2 CONSECRATION, hallowing, presentation. 3 INSCRIPTION, address.

**E3** 1 apathy.

**deduce** *v* derive, infer, gather, conclude, reason, surmise, understand, draw, glean.

**deduct** *v* subtract, take away, remove, reduce by, decrease by, knock off (*infml*), withdraw.

**E3** add.

**deduction** *n* 1 INFERENCE, reasoning, finding, conclusion, corollary, assumption, result. 2 SUBTRACTION, reduction, decrease, diminution, abatement, withdrawal, discount, allowance.

**E3** 2 addition, increase.

**deed** *n* 1 ACTION, act, achievement, performance, exploit, feat, fact, truth, reality. 2 DOCUMENT, contract, record, title, transaction, indenture (*fml*).

**deep** *adj* 1 PROFOUND, bottomless, unplumbed, fathomless, yawning, immersed. 2 OBSCURE, mysterious, difficult, recondite, abstruse, esoteric. 3 WISE, perceptive, discerning, profound, learned, astute. 4 INTENSE, serious, earnest, extreme. 5 LOW, bass, resonant, booming.

**E3** 1 shallow, open. 2 clear, plain, open. 3 superficial. 4 light. 5 high.

**deepen** *v* 1 INTENSIFY, grow, increase, strengthen, reinforce, magnify. 2 HOLLOW, scoop out.

**deep-seated** *adj* ingrained, entrenched, deep-rooted, fixed, confirmed, deep, settled.

**E3** eradicable, temporary.

**deface** *v* damage, spoil, disfigure, blemish, impair, mutilate, mar, sully, tarnish, vandalize, deform, obliterate, injure, destroy.

**E3** repair.

**defamation** (*fml*) *n* vilification, aspersion (*fml*), slander, libel, disparagement, slur, smear, innuendo, scandal.

🔁 commendation, praise.

**defamatory** (*fml*) *adj* vilifying, slanderous, libellous, denigrating, disparaging, pejorative, insulting, injurious, derogatory.

🔁 complimentary, appreciative.

**default** *n* failure, absence, neglect, non-payment, omission, deficiency, lapse, fault, want, lack, defect.

*v* fail, evade, defraud, neglect, dodge, swindle, backslide.

**defaulter** *n* non-payer, offender.

**defeat** *v* 1 CONQUER, beat, overpower, subdue, overthrow, worst, repel, subjugate, overwhelm, rout, ruin, thump (*infml*), quell, vanquish (*fml*). 2 FRUSTRATE, confound, balk, get the better of, disappoint, foil, thwart, baffle, checkmate.

*n* 1 CONQUEST, beating, overthrow, rout, subjugation, vanquishment (*fml*). 2 FRUSTRATION, failure, setback, reverse, disappointment, checkmate.

**defeatist** *n* pessimist, quitter, prophet of doom.

🔁 optimist.

*adj* pessimistic, resigned, fatalistic, despondent, helpless, hopeless, despairing, gloomy.

🔁 optimistic.

**defect** *n* imperfection, fault, flaw, deficiency, failing, mistake, inadequacy, blemish, error, bug (*infml*), shortcoming, want, weakness, frailty, lack, spot, absence, taint.

*v* desert, break faith, rebel, apostatize (*fml*), revolt, renegue.

**defective** *adj* faulty, imperfect, out of order, flawed, deficient, broken, abnormal.

🔁 in order, operative.

**defence** *n* 1 PROTECTION, resistance, security, fortification, cover, safeguard, shelter, guard, shield, deterrence, barricade, bastion, immunity, bulwark, rampart,

buttress. 2 JUSTIFICATION, explanation, excuse, argument, exoneration, plea, vindication, apologia (*fml*), pleading, alibi, case.

🔁 1 attack, assault. 2 accusation.

**defenceless** *adj* unprotected, undefended, unarmed, unguarded, vulnerable, exposed, helpless, powerless.

🔁 protected, guarded.

**defend** *v* 1 PROTECT, guard, safeguard, shelter, fortify, secure, shield, screen, cover, contest. 2 SUPPORT, stand up for, stand by, uphold, endorse, vindicate, champion, argue for, speak up for, justify, plead.

🔁 1 attack. 2 accuse.

**defendant** *n* accused, offender, prisoner, respondent.

**defender** *n* 1 PROTECTOR, guard, bodyguard. 2 SUPPORTER, advocate, vindicator, champion, patron, sponsor, counsel.

🔁 1 attacker. 2 accuser.

**defensive** *adj* 1 PROTECTIVE, defending, safeguarding, wary, opposing, cautious, watchful. 2 SELF-JUSTIFYING, apologetic.

**defer**¹ *v* delay, postpone, put off, adjourn, hold over, shelve, suspend, procrastinate, prorogue (*fml*), protract, waive.

**defer**² *v* yield, give way, comply, submit, accede, capitulate, respect, bow.

**deference** *n* 1 SUBMISSION, submissiveness, compliance, acquiescence, obedience, yielding. 2 RESPECT, regard, honour, esteem, reverence, courtesy, civility, politeness, consideration.

🔁 1 resistance. 2 contempt.

**defiance** *n* opposition, confrontation, resistance, challenge, disobedience, rebelliousness, contempt, insubordination, disregard, insolence.

🔁 compliance, acquiescence,

submissiveness.

**defiant** adj challenging, resistant, antagonistic, aggressive, rebellious, insubordinate, disobedient, intransigent, bold, contumacious (fml), insolent, obstinate, unco-operative, provocative.
⊞ compliant, acquiescent, submissive.

**deficiency** n 1 SHORTAGE, lack, inadequacy, scarcity, insufficiency, dearth, want, scantiness, absence, deficit. 2 IMPERFECTION, shortcoming, weakness, fault, defect, flaw, failing, frailty.
⊞ 1 excess, surfeit. 2 perfection.

**deficient** adj 1 INADEQUATE, insufficient, scarce, short, lacking, wanting, meagre, scanty, skimpy, incomplete. 2 IMPERFECT, impaired, flawed, faulty, defective, unsatisfactory, inferior, weak.
⊞ 1 excessive. 2 perfect.

**deficit** n shortage, shortfall, deficiency, loss, arrears, lack, default.
⊞ excess.

**defile** v pollute, violate, contaminate, degrade, dishonour, desecrate, debase, soil, stain, sully, tarnish, taint, profane, corrupt, disgrace.

**define** v 1 define the boundaries: bound, limit, delimit, demarcate, mark out. 2 define the meaning: explain, characterize, describe, interpret, expound, determine, designate, specify, spell out, detail.

**definite** adj 1 CERTAIN, settled, sure, positive, fixed, decided, determined, assured, guaranteed. 2 CLEAR, clear-cut, exact, precise, specific, explicit, particular, obvious, marked.
⊞ 1 indefinite. 2 vague.

**definitely** adv positively, surely, unquestionably, absolutely, certainly, categorically, undeniably, clearly, doubtless, unmistakably, plainly, obviously, indeed, easily.

**definition** n 1 DELINEATION,

demarcation, delimitation. 2 EXPLANATION, description, interpretation, exposition, clarification, elucidation, determination. 3 DISTINCTNESS, clarity, precision, clearness, focus, contrast, sharpness.

**definitive** adj decisive, conclusive, final, authoritative, standard, correct, ultimate, reliable, exhaustive, perfect, exact, absolute, complete.
⊞ interim.

**deflate** v 1 FLATTEN, puncture, collapse, exhaust, squash, empty, contract, void, shrink, squeeze. 2 DEBUNK, humiliate, put down (infml), dash, dispirit, humble, mortify, disconcert. 3 DECREASE, devalue, reduce, lessen, lower, diminish, depreciate, depress.
⊞ 1 inflate. 2 boost. 3 increase.

**deflect** v deviate, diverge, turn (aside), swerve, veer, sidetrack, twist, avert, wind, glance off, bend, ricochet.

**deform** v distort, contort, disfigure, warp, mar, pervert, ruin, spoil, twist.

**deformed** adj distorted, misshapen, contorted, disfigured, crippled, crooked, bent, twisted, warped, buckled, defaced, mangled, maimed, marred, ruined, mutilated, perverted, corrupted.

**deformity** n distortion, misshapenness, malformation, disfigurement, abnormality, irregularity, misproportion, defect, ugliness, monstrosity, corruption.

**defraud** v cheat, swindle, dupe, fleece, sting (infml), rip off (infml), do (infml), diddle (infml), rob, trick, con (infml), rook, deceive, delude, embezzle, beguile.

**deft** adj adept, handy, dexterous, nimble, skilful, adroit, agile, expert, nifty, proficient, able, neat, clever.
⊞ clumsy, awkward.

**defunct** adj 1 DEAD, deceased, departed, gone, expired, extinct.

2 OBSOLETE, invalid, inoperative, expired.

**F3** 1 alive, live. 2 operative.

**defy** v 1 *defy the authorities*: challenge, confront, resist, dare, brave, face, repel, spurn, beard, flout, withstand, disregard, scorn, despise, defeat, provoke, thwart. 2 *her writings defy categorization*: elude, frustrate, baffle, foil.

**F3** 1 obey. 2 permit.

**degenerate** adj dissolute, debauched, depraved, degraded, debased, base, low, decadent, corrupt, fallen, immoral, mean, degenerated, perverted, deteriorated.

**F3** moral, upright.

v decline, deteriorate, sink, decay, rot, slip, worsen, regress, fall off, lapse, decrease.

**F3** improve.

**degradation** n 1 DETERIORATION, degeneration, decline, downgrading, demotion. 2 ABASEMENT, humiliation, mortification, dishonour, disgrace, shame, ignominy, decadence.

**F3** 1 virtue. 2 enhancement.

**degrade** v 1 DISHONOUR, disgrace, debase, abase, shame, humiliate, humble, discredit, demean, lower, weaken, impair, deteriorate, cheapen, adulterate, corrupt. 2 DEMOTE, depose, downgrade, deprive, cashier.

**F3** 1 exalt. 2 promote.

**degree** n 1 GRADE, class, rank, order, position, standing, status. 2 EXTENT, measure, range, stage, step, level, intensity, standard. 3 LEVEL, limit, unit, mark.

**deify** v exalt, elevate, worship, glorify, idolize, extol, venerate, immortalize, ennoble, idealize.

**deign** v condescend, stoop, lower oneself, consent, demean oneself.

**deity** n god, goddess, divinity, godhead, idol, demigod, demigoddess, power, immortal.

**dejected** adj downcast, despondent,

depressed, downhearted, disheartened, down, low, melancholy, disconsolate, sad, miserable, cast down, gloomy, glum, crestfallen, dismal, wretched, doleful, morose, spiritless.

**F3** cheerful, high-spirited, happy.

**delay** v 1 OBSTRUCT, hinder, impede, hold up, check, hold back, set back, stop, halt, detain. 2 DEFER, put off, postpone, procrastinate, suspend, shelve, hold over, stall. 3 DAWDLE, linger, lag, loiter, dilly-dally (*infml*), tarry.

**F3** 1 accelerate. 2 bring forward. 3 hurry.

n 1 OBSTRUCTION, hindrance, impediment, hold-up, check, setback, stay, stoppage. 2 DEFERMENT, postponement, procrastination, suspension. 3 DAWDLING, lingering, tarrying. 4 INTERRUPTION, lull, interval, wait.

**F3** 1 hastening. 3 hurry. 4 continuation.

**delegate** n representative, agent, envoy, messenger, deputy, ambassador, commissioner.

v authorize, appoint, depute, charge, commission, assign, empower, entrust, devolve, consign, designate, nominate, name, hand over.

**delegation** n 1 DEPUTATION, commission, legation, mission, contingent, embassy. 2 AUTHORIZATION, commissioning, assignment.

**delete** v erase, remove, cross out, cancel, rub out, strike (out), obliterate, edit (out), blot out, efface.

**F3** add, insert.

**deliberate** v consider, ponder, reflect, think, cogitate, meditate, mull over, debate, discuss, weigh, consult.

adj 1 INTENTIONAL, planned, calculated, prearranged, premeditated, willed, conscious, designed, considered, advised. 2

CAREFUL, unhurried, thoughtful, methodical, cautious, circumspect, studied, prudent, slow, ponderous, measured, heedful.

**E3** 1 unintentional, accidental. 2 hasty.

**deliberation** n 1 CONSIDERATION, reflection, thought, calculation, forethought, meditation, rumination, study, debate, discussion, consultation, speculation. 2 CARE, carefulness, caution, circumspection, prudence.

**delicacy** n 1 DAINTINESS, fineness, elegance, exquisiteness, lightness, precision. 2 REFINEMENT, sensitivity, subtlety, finesse, discrimination, tact, niceness. 3 TITBIT, dainty, taste, sweetmeat, savoury, relish.

**E3** 1 coarseness, roughness.
2 tactlessness.

**delicate** adj 1 FINE, fragile, dainty, exquisite, flimsy, elegant, graceful.
2 FRAIL, weak, ailing, faint.
3 SENSITIVE, scrupulous, discriminating, careful, accurate, precise. 4 SUBTLE, muted, pastel, soft.

**E3** 1 coarse, clumsy. 2 healthy.

**delicious** adj 1 ENJOYABLE, pleasant, agreeable, delightful.
2 APPETIZING, palatable, tasty, delectable, scrumptious (infml), mouth-watering, succulent, savoury.

**E3** 1 unpleasant. 2 unpalatable.

**delight** n bliss, happiness, joy, pleasure, ecstasy, enjoyment, gladness, rapture, transport, gratification, jubilation.

**E3** disgust, displeasure.

v please, charm, gratify, enchant, tickle, thrill, ravish.

**E3** displease, dismay.

**delight in** enjoy, relish, like, love, appreciate, revel in, take pride in, glory in, savour.

**E3** dislike, hate.

**delighted** adj charmed, elated, happy, pleased, enchanted, captivated, ecstatic, thrilled,

overjoyed, jubilant, joyous.

**E3** disappointed, dismayed.

**delightful** adj charming, enchanting, captivating, enjoyable, pleasant, thrilling, agreeable, pleasurable, engaging, attractive, pleasing, gratifying, entertaining, fascinating.

**E3** nasty, unpleasant.

**delinquency** n crime, offence, wrong-doing, misbehaviour, misconduct, law-breaking, misdemeanour, criminality.

**delinquent** n offender, criminal, wrong-doer, law-breaker, hooligan, culprit, miscreant (fml).

**delirious** adj demented, raving, incoherent, beside oneself, deranged, frenzied, light-headed, wild, mad, frantic, insane, crazy, ecstatic.

**E3** sane.

**deliver** v 1 deliver a parcel: convey, bring, send, give, carry, supply.
2 SURRENDER, hand over, relinquish, yield, transfer, grant, entrust, commit. 3 UTTER, speak, proclaim, pronounce.
4 ADMINISTER, inflict, direct. 5 SET FREE, liberate, release, emancipate.

**delivery** n 1 CONVEYANCE, consignment, dispatch, transmission, transfer, surrender.
2 ARTICULATION, enunciation, speech, utterance, intonation, elocution. 3 CHILDBIRTH, labour, confinement.

**delude** v deceive, mislead, beguile, dupe, take in, trick, hoodwink, hoax, cheat, misinform.

**deluge** n flood, inundation, downpour, torrent, spate, rush.

v flood, inundate, drench, drown, overwhelm, soak, swamp, engulf, submerge.

**delusion** n illusion, hallucination, fancy, misconception, misapprehension, deception, misbelief, fallacy.

**demand** v 1 ASK, request, call for, insist on, solicit, claim, exact,

inquire, question, interrogate. **2**
NECESSITATE, need, require, involve.
n **1** REQUEST, question, claim, order,
inquiry, desire, interrogation. **2** NEED,
necessity, call.

**demanding** adj hard, difficult,
challenging, exacting, taxing, tough,
exhausting, wearing, back-breaking,
insistent, pressing, urgent, trying.
Ⓔ easy, undemanding, easy-going.

**demean** v lower, humble, degrade,
humiliate, debase, abase, descend,
stoop, condescend.
Ⓔ exalt, enhance.

**demeanour** n bearing, manner,
deportment, conduct, behaviour, air.

**demented** adj mad, insane, lunatic,
out of one's mind, crazy, loony (sl),
deranged, unbalanced, frenzied.
Ⓔ sane.

**demise** n **1** DEATH, decease, end,
passing, departure, termination,
expiration. **2** DOWNFALL, fall,
collapse, failure, ruin. **3** TRANSFER,
conveyance, inheritance,
transmission, alienation.

**democracy** n self-government,
commonwealth, autonomy, republic.

**democratic** adj self-governing,
representative, egalitarian,
autonomous, popular, populist,
republican.

**demolish** v **1** DESTROY, dismantle,
knock down, pull down, flatten,
bulldoze, raze, tear down, level.
**2** RUIN, defeat, destroy, annihilate,
wreck, overturn, overthrow.
Ⓔ **1** build up.

**demolition** n destruction,
dismantling, levelling, razing.

**demon** n **1** DEVIL, fiend, evil spirit,
fallen angel, imp. **2** VILLAIN, devil,
rogue, monster.

**demonstrable** adj verifiable,
provable, arguable, attestable, self-
evident, obvious, evident, certain,
clear, positive.
Ⓔ unverifiable.

**demonstrate** v **1** SHOW, display,

prove, establish, exhibit,
substantiate, manifest, testify to,
indicate. **2** EXPLAIN, illustrate,
describe, teach. **3** PROTEST, march,
parade, rally, picket, sit in.

**demonstration** n **1** DISPLAY,
exhibition, manifestation, proof,
confirmation, affirmation,
substantiation, validation, evidence,
testimony, expression.
**2** EXPLANATION, illustration,
description, exposition, presentation,
test, trial. **3** PROTEST, march, demo
(infml), rally, picket, sit-in, parade.

**demonstrative** adj affectionate,
expressive, expansive, emotional,
open, loving.
Ⓔ reserved, cold, restrained.

**demoralize** v **1** DISCOURAGE,
dishearten, dispirit, undermine,
depress, deject, crush, lower,
disconcert. **2** CORRUPT, deprave,
debase.
Ⓔ **1** encourage. **2** improve.

**demote** v downgrade, degrade,
relegate, reduce, cashier.
Ⓔ promote, upgrade.

**demur** v disagree, dissent, object,
take exception, refuse, protest,
dispute, balk, scruple, doubt,
hesitate.

**demure** adj modest, reserved,
reticent, prim, coy, shy, retiring,
prissy, grave, prudish, sober, strait-
laced, staid.
Ⓔ wanton, forward.

**den** n lair, hide-out, hole, retreat,
study, hide-away, shelter, sanctuary,
haunt.

**denial** n **1** CONTRADICTION,
negation, dissent, repudiation,
disavowal, disclaimer, dismissal,
renunciation. **2** REFUSAL, rebuff,
rejection, prohibition, veto.

**denigrate** v disparage, run down,
slander, revile, defame, malign, vilify,
decry, besmirch, impugn, belittle,
abuse, assail, criticize.
Ⓔ praise, acclaim.

**denomination** n 1
CLASSIFICATION, category, class,
kind, sort. 2 RELIGION, persuasion,
sect, belief, faith, creed, communion,
school.

**denote** v indicate, stand for, signify,
represent, symbolize, mean, express,
designate, typify, mark, show, imply.

**dénouement** n climax, culmination,
conclusion, outcome, upshot, pay-off
(infml), finale, resolution, finish,
solution, close.

**denounce** v condemn, censure,
accuse, revile, decry, attack, inform
against, betray, impugn, vilify,
fulminate.
**E3** acclaim, praise.

**dense** adj 1 COMPACT, thick,
compressed, condensed, close, close-
knit, heavy, solid, opaque,
impenetrable, packed, crowded.
2 STUPID, thick (infml), crass, dull,
slow, slow-witted.
**E3** 1 thin, sparse. 2 quick-witted,
clever.

**dent** n hollow, depression, dip,
concavity, indentation, crater,
dimple, dint, pit.
v depress, gouge, push in, indent.

**denude** v strip, divest, expose,
uncover, bare, deforest.
**E3** cover, clothe.

**denunciation** n condemnation,
denouncement, censure, accusation,
incrimination, invective, criticism.
**E3** praise.

**deny** v 1 deny God's existence:
contradict, oppose, refute, disagree
with, disaffirm, disprove. 2 deny
one's parentage: disown, disclaim,
renounce, repudiate, recant. 3 deny
their human rights: refuse, turn
down, forbid, reject, withhold,
rebuff, veto.
**E3** 1 admit. 3 allow.

**depart** v 1 GO, leave, withdraw, exit,
make off, quit, decamp, take one's
leave, absent oneself, set off, remove,
retreat, migrate, escape, disappear,

retire, vanish. 2 DEVIATE, digress,
differ, diverge, swerve, veer.
**E3** 1 arrive, return. 2 keep to.

**departed** adj dead, deceased, gone,
late, expired.

**department** n 1 DIVISION, branch,
subdivision, section, sector, office,
station, unit, region, district.
2 SPHERE, realm, province, domain,
field, area, concern, responsibility,
speciality, line.

**departure** n 1 EXIT, going, leave-
taking, removal, withdrawal,
retirement, exodus. 2 DEVIATION,
digression, divergence, variation,
innovation, branching (out),
difference, change, shift, veering.
**E3** 1 arrival, return.

**depend on** 1 RELY UPON, count on,
bank on (infml), calculate on, reckon
on (infml), build upon, trust in, lean
on, expect. 2 HINGE ON, rest on,
revolve around, be contingent upon,
hang on.

**dependable** adj reliable,
trustworthy, steady, trusty,
responsible, faithful, unfailing, sure,
honest, conscientious, certain.
**E3** unreliable, fickle.

**dependence** n 1 RELIANCE,
confidence, faith, trust, need,
expectation. 2 SUBORDINATION,
attachment, subservience,
helplessness, addiction.
**E3** 2 independence.

**dependent** adj 1 RELIANT, helpless,
weak, immature, subject,
subordinate, vulnerable.
2 CONTINGENT, conditional,
determined by, relative.
**E3** 1 independent.

**depict** v portray, illustrate,
delineate, sketch, outline, draw,
picture, paint, trace, describe,
characterize, detail.

**deplete** v empty, drain, exhaust,
evacuate, use up, expend, run down,
reduce, lessen, decrease.

**deplorable** adj 1 GRIEVOUS,

lamentable, pitiable, regrettable, unfortunate, wretched, distressing, sad, miserable, heartbreaking, melancholy, disastrous, dire, appalling. **2** REPREHENSIBLE, disgraceful, scandalous, shameful, dishonourable, disreputable.
**F3 1** excellent. **2** commendable.

**deplore** v **1** GRIEVE FOR, lament, mourn, regret, bemoan, rue. **2** CENSURE, condemn, denounce, deprecate.
**F3 2** extol.

**deploy** v dispose, arrange, position, station, use, utilize, distribute.

**deport** v expel, banish, exile, extradite, transport, expatriate, oust, ostracize.

**depose** v demote, dethrone, downgrade, dismiss, unseat, topple, disestablish, displace, oust.

**deposit** v **1** LAY, drop, place, put, settle, dump (infml), park, precipitate, sit, locate. **2** SAVE, store, hoard, bank, amass, consign, entrust, lodge, file.
n **1** SEDIMENT, accumulation, dregs, precipitate, lees, silt. **2** SECURITY, stake, down payment, pledge, retainer, instalment, part payment, money.

**depot** n military depot: storehouse, store, warehouse, depository, repository, arsenal. **2** bus depot: station, garage, terminus.

**deprave** v corrupt, debauch, debase, degrade, pervert, subvert, infect, demoralize, seduce.
**F3** improve, reform.

**depraved** adj corrupt, debauched, degenerate, perverted, debased, dissolute, immoral, base, shameless, licentious, wicked, sinful, vile, evil.
**F3** moral, upright.

**deprecate** (fml) v deplore, condemn, censure, disapprove of, object to, protest at, reject.
**F3** approve, commend.

**depreciate** v **1** DEVALUE, deflate, downgrade, decrease, reduce, lower,

drop, fall, lessen, decline, slump. **2** DISPARAGE, belittle, undervalue, underestimate, underrate, slight.
**F3 1** appreciate. **2** overrate.

**depreciation** n **1** DEVALUATION, deflation, depression, slump, fall. **2** DISPARAGEMENT, belittlement, underestimation.

**depress** v **1** DEJECT, sadden, dishearten, discourage, oppress, upset, daunt, burden, overburden. **2** WEAKEN, undermine, sap, tire, drain, exhaust, weary, impair, reduce, lessen, press, lower, level. **3** DEVALUE, bring down, lower.
**F3 1** cheer. **2** fortify. **3** increase, raise.

**depressed** adj **1** DEJECTED, low-spirited, melancholy, dispirited, sad, unhappy, low, down, downcast, disheartened, fed up (infml), miserable, moody, cast down, discouraged, glum, downhearted, distressed, despondent, morose, crestfallen, pessimistic. **2** POOR, disadvantaged, deprived, destitute. **3** SUNKEN, recessed, concave, hollow, indented, dented.
**F3 1** cheerful. **2** affluent. **3** convex, protuberant.

**depressing** adj dejecting, dismal, bleak, gloomy, saddening, cheerless, dreary, disheartening, sad, melancholy, sombre, grey, black, daunting, discouraging, heartbreaking, distressing, hopeless.
**F3** cheerful, encouraging.

**depression** n **1** DEJECTION, despair, despondency, melancholy, low spirits, sadness, gloominess, doldrums, blues (infml), glumness, dumps (infml). **2** RECESSION, slump, stagnation, hard times, decline, inactivity. **3** INDENTATION, hollow, dip, concavity, dent, dimple, valley, pit, sink, dint, bowl, cavity, basin, impression, dish, excavation.
**F3 1** cheerfulness. **2** prosperity, boom. **3** convexity, protuberance.

**deprive** v 1 DISPOSSESS, strip, divest, denude, bereave, expropriate, rob. 2 DENY, withhold, refuse.
🗲 1 endow. 2 provide.

**deprived** adj poor, needy, underprivileged, disadvantaged, impoverished, destitute, lacking, bereft.
🗲 prosperous.

**depth** n 1 DEEPNESS, profoundness, extent, measure, drop. 2 MIDDLE, midst, abyss, deep, gulf. 3 WISDOM, insight, discernment, penetration. 4 INTENSITY, strength.
🗲 1 shallowness. 2 surface.

**deputation** n commission, delegation, embassy, mission, representatives, legation.

**deputise** n 1 REPRESENT, stand in for, substitute, replace, understudy, double. 2 DELEGATE, commission.

**deputy** n representative, agent, delegate, proxy, substitute, second-in-command, ambassador, commissioner, lieutenant, surrogate, subordinate, assistant, locum.

**deranged** adj disordered, demented, crazy, mad, lunatic, insane, unbalanced, disturbed, confused, frantic, delirious, distraught, berserk.
🗲 sane, calm.

**derelict** adj abandoned, neglected, deserted, forsaken, desolate, discarded, dilapidated, ruined.

**deride** v ridicule, mock, scoff, scorn, jeer, sneer, satirize, knock (*infml*), gibe, disparage, insult, belittle, disdain, taunt.
🗲 respect, praise.

**derision** n ridicule, mockery, scorn, contempt, scoffing, satire, sneering, disrespect, insult, disparagement, disdain.
🗲 respect, praise.

**derisive** adj mocking, scornful, contemptuous, disrespectful, irreverent, jeering, disdainful, taunting.
🗲 respectful, flattering.

**derivation** n source, origin, root, beginning, etymology, extraction, foundation, genealogy, ancestry, basis, descent, deduction, inference.

**derivative** adj unoriginal, acquired, copied, borrowed, derived, imitative, obtained, second-hand, secondary, plagiarized, cribbed (*infml*), hackneyed, trite.
n derivation, offshoot, by-product, development, branch, outgrowth, spin-off, product, descendant.

**derive** v 1 GAIN, obtain, get, draw, extract, receive, procure, acquire, borrow. 2 ORIGINATE, arise, spring, flow, emanate, descend, proceed, stem, issue, follow, develop. 3 INFER, deduce, trace, gather, glean.

**derogatory** adj insulting, pejorative, offensive, disparaging, depreciative, critical, defamatory, injurious.
🗲 flattering.

**descend** v 1 DROP, go down, fall, plummet, plunge, tumble, swoop, sink, arrive, alight, dismount, dip, slope, subside. 2 DEGENERATE, deteriorate. 3 CONDESCEND, deign, stoop. 4 ORIGINATE, proceed, spring, stem.
🗲 1 ascend, rise.

**descendants** n offspring, children, issue, progeny, successors, lineage, line, seed (*fml*).

**descent** n 1 FALL, drop, plunge, dip, decline, incline, slope. 2 COMEDOWN, debasement, degradation. 3 ANCESTRY, parentage, heredity, family tree, genealogy, lineage, extraction, origin.
🗲 1 ascent, rise.

**describe** v portray, depict, delineate, illustrate, characterize, specify, draw, define, detail, explain, express, tell, narrate, outline, relate, recount, present, report, sketch, mark out, trace.

**description** n 1 PORTRAYAL, representation, characterization, account, delineation, depiction, sketch, presentation, report, outline, explanation, exposition, narration. **2** SORT, type, kind, variety, specification, order.

**descriptive** *adj* illustrative, explanatory, expressive, detailed, graphic, colourful, pictorial, vivid.

**desert¹** *n* wasteland, wilderness, wilds, void.
*adj* bare, barren, waste, wild, uninhabited, uncultivated, dry, arid, infertile, desolate, sterile, solitary.

**desert²** *v* abandon, forsake, leave, maroon, strand, decamp, defect, give up, renounce, relinquish, jilt, abscond, quit.
 stand by, support.

**desert³** *n* **1** DUE, right, reward, deserts, return, retribution, come-uppance (*infml*), payment, recompense, remuneration.
**2** WORTH, merit, virtue.

**deserted** *adj* abandoned, forsaken, empty, derelict, desolate, godforsaken, neglected, underpopulated, stranded, isolated, bereft, vacant, betrayed, lonely, solitary, unoccupied.
 populous.

**deserter** *n* runaway, absconder, escapee, truant, renegade, defector, rat (*infml*), traitor, fugitive, betrayer, apostate, backslider, delinquent.

**deserve** *v* earn, be worthy of, merit, be entitled to, warrant, justify, win, rate, incur.

**deserved** *adj* due, earned, merited, justifiable, warranted, right, rightful, well-earned, suitable, proper, fitting, fair, just, appropriate, apt, legitimate, apposite, meet (*fml*).
 gratuitous, undeserved.

**deserving** *adj* worthy, estimable, exemplary, praiseworthy, admirable, commendable, laudable, righteous.
 undeserving, unworthy.

**design** *n* **1** BLUEPRINT, draft, pattern, plan, prototype, sketch, drawing, outline, model, guide.

**2** STYLE, shape, form, figure, structure, organization, arrangement, composition, construction, motif.
**3** AIM, intention, goal, purpose, plan, end, object, objective, scheme, plot, project, meaning, target, undertaking.
*v* **1** PLAN, plot, intend, devise, purpose, aim, scheme, shape, project, propose, tailor, mean. **2** SKETCH, draft, outline, draw (up). **3** INVENT, originate, conceive, create, think up, develop, construct, fashion, form, model, fabricate, make.

**designation** *n* **1** NAME, title, label, epithet, nickname. **2** INDICATION, specification, description, definition, classification, category.
**3** NOMINATION, appointment, selection.

**designer** *n* deviser, originator, maker, stylist, inventor, creator, contriver, fashioner, architect, author.

**designing** *adj* artful, crafty, scheming, conspiring, devious, intriguing, plotting, tricky, wily, sly, deceitful, cunning, guileful, underhand, sharp, shrewd.
 artless, naïve.

**desirable** *adj* **1** ADVANTAGEOUS, profitable, worthwhile, advisable, appropriate, expedient, beneficial, preferable, sensible, eligible, good, pleasing. **2** ATTRACTIVE, alluring, sexy (*infml*), seductive, fetching, tempting.
 **1** undesirable. **2** unattractive.

**desire** *v* **1** ASK, request, petition, solicit. **2** WANT, wish for, covet, long for, need, crave, hunger for, yearn for, fancy (*infml*), hanker after.
*n* **1** WANT, longing, wish, need, yearning, craving, hankering, appetite, aspiration. **2** LUST, passion, concupiscence (*fml*), ardour.
**3** REQUEST, petition, appeal, supplication.

**desist** *v* stop, cease, leave off,

refrain, discontinue, end, break off,
give up, halt, abstain, suspend,
pause, peter out, remit, forbear (*fml*).
**F3** continue, resume.

**desolate** *adj* **1** DESERTED,
uninhabited, abandoned,
unfrequented, barren, bare, arid,
bleak, gloomy, dismal, dreary,
lonely, god-forsaken, forsaken,
waste, depressing. **2** FORLORN,
bereft, depressed, dejected, forsaken,
despondent, distressed, melancholy,
miserable, lonely, gloomy,
disheartened, dismal, downcast,
solitary, wretched.
**F3** **1** populous. **2** cheerful.
*v* devastate, lay waste, destroy,
despoil, spoil, wreck, denude,
depopulate, ruin, waste, ravage,
plunder, pillage.

**desolation** *n* **1** DESTRUCTION, ruin,
devastation, ravages. **2** DEJECTION,
despair, despondency, gloom, misery,
sadness, melancholy, sorrow,
unhappiness, anguish, grief, distress,
wretchedness. **3** BARRENNESS,
bleakness, emptiness, forlornness,
loneliness, isolation, solitude,
wildness.

**despair** *v* lose heart, lose hope, give
up, give in, collapse, surrender.
**F3** hope.
*n* despondency, gloom, hopelessness,
desperation, anguish,
inconsolableness, melancholy, misery,
wretchedness.
**F3** cheerfulness, resilience.

**despairing** *adj* despondent,
distraught, inconsolable, desolate,
desperate, heart-broken, suicidal,
grief-stricken, hopeless, disheartened,
dejected, miserable, wretched,
sorrowful, dismayed, downcast.
**F3** cheerful, hopeful.

**despatch** *see* **dispatch**.

**desperado** *n* bandit, criminal,
brigand, gangster, hoodlum (*infml*),
outlaw, ruffian, thug, cut-throat,
law-breaker.

**desperate** *adj* **1** HOPELESS,
inconsolable, wretched, despondent,
abandoned. **2** RECKLESS, rash,
impetuous, audacious, daring,
dangerous, do-or-die, foolhardy,
risky, hazardous, hasty, precipitate,
wild, violent, frantic, frenzied,
determined. **3** CRITICAL, acute,
serious, severe, extreme, urgent.
**F3** **1** hopeful. **2** cautious.

**desperately** *adv* dangerously,
critically, gravely, hopelessly,
seriously, severely, badly, dreadfully,
fearfully, frightfully.

**desperation** *n* **1** DESPAIR,
despondency, anguish, hopelessness,
misery, agony, distress, pain, sorrow,
trouble, worry, anxiety.
**2** RECKLESSNESS, rashness, frenzy,
madness, hastiness.

**despicable** *adj* contemptible, vile,
worthless, detestable, disgusting,
mean, wretched, disgraceful,
disreputable, shameful, reprobate.
**F3** admirable, noble.

**despise** *v* scorn, deride, look down
on, disdain, condemn, spurn,
undervalue, slight, revile, deplore,
dislike, detest, loathe.
**F3** admire.

**despite** *prep* in spite of,
notwithstanding, regardless of, in the
face of, undeterred by, against,
defying.

**despondent** *adj* depressed, dejected,
disheartened, downcast, down, low,
gloomy, glum, discouraged,
miserable, melancholy, sad,
sorrowful, doleful, despairing, heartbroken, inconsolable, mournful,
wretched.
**F3** cheerful, heartened, hopeful.

**despot** *n* autocrat, tyrant, dictator,
oppressor, absolutist, boss.

**despotic** *adj* autocratic, tyrannical,
imperious, oppressive, dictatorial,
authoritarian, domineering, absolute,
overbearing, arbitrary, arrogant.
**F3** democratic, egalitarian, liberal,

tolerant.

**despotism** n autocracy, totalitarianism, tyranny, dictatorship, absolutism, oppression, repression.

**E3** democracy, egalitarianism, liberalism, tolerance.

**destination** n 1 GOAL, aim, objective, object, purpose, target, end, intention, aspiration, design, ambition. 2 JOURNEY'S END, terminus, station, stop.

**destined** adj 1 FATED, doomed, inevitable, predetermined, ordained, certain, foreordained, meant, unavoidable, inescapable, intended, designed, appointed. 2 BOUND, directed, en route, headed, heading, scheduled, assigned, booked.

**destiny** n fate, doom, fortune, karma, lot (fml), portion (fml), predestiny, kismet.

**destitute** adj 1 LACKING, needy, wanting, devoid of, bereft, innocent of, deprived, deficient, depleted. 2 POOR, penniless, poverty-stricken, impoverished, down and out (infml), distressed, bankrupt.

**E3** prosperous, rich.

**destroy** v 1 DEMOLISH, ruin, shatter, wreck, devastate, smash, break, crush, overthrow, sabotage, undo, dismantle, thwart, undermine, waste, gut, level, ravage, raze, torpedo, unshape. 2 KILL, annihilate, eliminate, extinguish, eradicate, dispatch, slay (fml), nullify.

**E3** 1 build up. 2 create.

**destruction** n 1 RUIN, devastation, shattering, crushing, wreckage, demolition, defeat, downfall, overthrow, ruination, desolation, undoing, wastage, havoc, ravagement. 2 ANNIHILATION, extermination, eradication, elimination, extinction, slaughter, massacre, end, liquidation, nullification.

**E3** 2 creation.

**destructive** adj 1 destructive storms: devastating, damaging, catastrophic, disastrous, deadly, harmful, fatal, disruptive, lethal, ruinous, detrimental, hurtful, malignant, mischievous, nullifying, slaughterous. 2 destructive criticism: adverse, hostile, negative, discouraging, disparaging, contrary, undermining, subversive, vicious.

**E3** 1 creative. 2 constructive.

**desultory** adj random, erratic, aimless, disorderly, haphazard, irregular, spasmodic, inconsistent, undirected, unco-ordinated, unsystematic, unmethodical, fitful, disconnected, loose, capricious.

**E3** systematic, methodical.

**detach** v separate, disconnect, unfasten, disjoin, cut off, disengage, remove, undo, uncouple, sever, dissociate, isolate, loosen, free, unfix, unhitch, segregate, divide, disentangle, estrange.

**E3** attach.

**detached** adj 1 SEPARATE, disconnected, dissociated, severed, free, loose, divided, discrete. 2 ALOOF, dispassionate, impersonal, neutral, impartial, independent, disinterested, objective.

**E3** 1 connected. 2 involved.

**detachment** n 1 ALOOFNESS, remoteness, coolness, unconcern, indifference, impassivity, disinterestedness, neutrality, impartiality, objectivity, fairness. 2 SEPARATION, disconnection, disunion, disengagement. 3 SQUAD, unit, force, corps, brigade, patrol, task force.

**detail** n particular, item, factor, element, aspect, component, feature, point, specific, ingredient, attribute, count, respect, technicality, complication, intricacy, triviality, fact, thoroughness, elaboration, meticulousness, refinement, nicety.

*v* **1** LIST, enumerate, itemize, specify, catalogue, recount, relate. **2** ASSIGN, appoint, charge, delegate, commission.

**detailed** *adj* comprehensive, exhaustive, full, blow-by-blow (*infml*), thorough, minute, exact, specific, particular, itemized, intricate, elaborate, complex, complicated, meticulous, descriptive.
**F3** cursory, general.

**detain** *v* **1** DELAY, hold (up), hinder, impede, check, retard, slow, stay, stop. **2** CONFINE, arrest, intern, hold, restrain, keep.
**F3 2** release.

**detect** *v* **1** NOTICE, ascertain, note, observe, perceive, recognize, discern, distinguish, identify, sight, spot, spy. **2** UNCOVER, catch, discover, disclose, expose, find, track down, unmask, reveal.

**detective** *n* investigator, private eye (*infml*), sleuth (*infml*), sleuth-hound (*infml*).

**detention** *n* **1** DETAINMENT, custody, confinement, imprisonment, restraint, incarceration, constraint, quarantine. **2** DELAY, hindrance, holding back.
**F3 1** release.

**deter** *v* discourage, put off, inhibit, intimidate, dissuade, daunt, turn of (*infml*), check, caution, warn, restrain, hinder, frighten, disincline, prevent, prohibit, stop.
**F3** encourage.

**deteriorate** *v* **1** WORSEN, decline, degenerate, depreciate, go downhill (*infml*), fail, fall off, lapse, slide, relapse, slip. **2** DECAY, disintegrate, decompose, weaken, fade.
**F3 1** improve. **2** progress.

**determination** *n* **1** RESOLUTENESS, tenacity, firmness, will-power, perseverance, persistence, purpose, backbone, guts (*infml*), grit (*infml*), steadfastness, single-mindedness, will, insistence, conviction,

dedication, drive, fortitude. **2** DECISION, judgement, settlement, resolution, conclusion.
**F3 1** irresolution.

**determine** *v* **1** DECIDE, settle, resolve, make up one's mind, choose, conclude, fix on, elect, clinch, finish. **2** DISCOVER, establish, find out, ascertain, identify, check, detect, verify. **3** AFFECT, influence, govern, control, dictate, direct, guide, regulate, ordain.

**determined** *adj* resolute, firm, purposeful, strong-willed, single-minded, persevering, persistent, strong-minded, steadfast, tenacious, dogged, insistent, intent, fixed, convinced, decided, unflinching.
**F3** irresolute, wavering.

**deterrent** *n* hindrance, impediment, obstacle, repellent, check, bar, discouragement, obstruction, curb, restraint, difficulty.
**F3** incentive, encouragement.

**detest** *v* hate, abhor, loathe, abominate, execrate (*fml*), dislike, recoil from, deplore, despise.
**F3** adore, love.

**detestable** *adj* hateful, loathsome, abhorrent, abominable, repellent, obnoxious, execrable (*fml*), despicable, revolting, repulsive, repugnant, offensive, vile, disgusting, accursed (*fml*), heinous, shocking, sordid.
**F3** adorable, admirable.

**detour** *n* deviation, diversion, indirect route, circuitous route, roundabout route, digression, byroad, byway, bypath, bypass.

**detract (from)** *v* diminish, subtract from, take away from, reduce, lessen, lower, devaluate, depreciate, belittle, disparage.
**F3** add to, enhance, praise.

**detriment** *n* damage, harm, hurt, disadvantage, loss, ill, injury, disservice, evil, mischief, prejudice.
**F3** advantage, benefit.

**detrimental** adj damaging, harmful, hurtful, adverse, disadvantageous, injurious, prejudicial, mischievous, destructive.
🔁 advantageous, favourable, beneficial.

**devastate** v 1 DESTROY, desolate, lay waste, demolish, spoil, despoil, wreck, ruin, ravage, waste, ransack, plunder, level, raze, pillage, sack. 2 DISCONCERT, overwhelm, take aback, confound, shatter (infml), floor (infml), nonplus, discomfit.

**devastating** adj 1 devastating storms: destructive, disastrous. 2 a devastating argument: effective, incisive, overwhelming, stunning.

**devastation** n destruction, desolation, havoc, ruin, wreckage, ravages, demolition, annihilation, pillage, plunder, spoliation.

**develop** v 1 ADVANCE, evolve, expand, progress, foster, flourish, mature, prosper, branch out. 2 ELABORATE, amplify, argument, enhance, unfold. 3 ACQUIRE, contract, begin, generate, create, invent. 4 RESULT, come about, grow, ensue, arise, follow, happen.

**development** n 1 GROWTH, evolution, advance, blossoming, elaboration, furtherance, progress, unfolding, expansion, extension, spread, increase, improvement, maturity, promotion, refinement, issue. 2 OCCURRENCE, happening, event, change, outcome, situation, result, phenomenon.

**deviate** v diverge, veer, turn (aside), digress, swerve, vary, differ, depart, stray, yaw, wander, err, go astray, go off the rails (infml), drift, part.

**deviation** n divergence, aberration, departure, abnormality, irregularity, variance, variation, digression, eccentricity, anomaly, deflection, alteration, disparity, discrepancy, detour, fluctuation, change, quirk, shift, freak.

🔁 conformity, regularity.

**device** n 1 TOOL, implement, appliance, gadget, contrivance, contraption (infml), apparatus, utensil, instrument, machine. 2 SCHEME, ruse, strategy, plan, plot, gambit, manoeuvre, wile, trick, dodge (infml), machination. 3 EMBLEM, symbol, motif, logo (infml), design, insignia, crest, badge, shield.

**devil** n 1 DEMON, Satan, fiend, evil spirit, arch-fiend, Lucifer, imp, Evil One, Prince of Darkness, Adversary, Beelzebub, Mephistopheles, Old Nick (infml), Old Harry (infml). 2 BRUTE, rogue, monster, ogre.

**devious** adj 1 UNDERHAND, deceitful, dishonest, disingenuous, double-dealing, scheming, tricky (infml), insidious, insincere, calculating, cunning, evasive, wily, sly, slippery (infml), surreptitious, treacherous, misleading. 2 INDIRECT, circuitous, rambling, roundabout, wandering, winding, tortuous, erratic.
🔁 straightforward.

**devise** v invent, contrive, plan, plot, design, conceive, arrange, formulate, imagine, scheme, construct, concoct, forge, frame, project, shape, form.

**devoid** adj lacking, wanting, without, free, bereft, destitute, deficient, deprived, barren, empty, vacant, void.
🔁 endowed.

**devote** v dedicate, consecrate, commit, give oneself, set apart, set aside, reserve, apply, allocate, allot, sacrifice, enshrine, assign, appropriate, surrender, pledge.

**devoted** adj dedicated, ardent, committed, loyal, faithful, devout, loving, staunch, steadfast, true, constant, fond, unswerving, tireless, concerned, attentive, caring.
🔁 indifferent, disloyal.

**devotee** n enthusiast, fan (infml), fanatic, addict, aficionado, follower, supporter, zealot, adherent, admirer, disciple, buff (*infml*), freak (*infml*), merchant (*infml*), fiend (*infml*), hound.

**devotion** *n* 1 DEDICATION, commitment, consecration, ardour, loyalty, allegiance, adherence, zeal, support, love, passion, fervour, fondness, attachment, adoration, affection, faithfulness, reverence, steadfastness, regard, earnestness. 2 DEVOUTNESS, piety, godliness, faith, holiness, spirituality. 3 PRAYER, worship.
**F₃** 1 inconstancy. 2 irreverence.

**devour** *v* 1 EAT, consume, guzzle, gulp, gorge, gobble, bolt, wolf down, swallow, stuff (*infml*), cram, polish off (*infml*), gormandize, feast on, relish, revel in. 2 DESTROY, consume, absorb, engulf, ravage, dispatch.

**devout** *adj* 1 SINCERE, earnest, devoted, fervent, genuine, staunch, steadfast, ardent, passionate, serious, whole-hearted, constant, faithful, intense, heartfelt, zealous, unswerving, deep, profound. 2 PIOUS, godly, religious, reverent, prayerful, saintly, holy, orthodox.
**F₃** 1 insincere. 2 irreligious.

**dexterous** *adj* deft, adroit, agile, able, nimble, proficient, skilful, clever, expert, nifty, nippy, handy, facile, nimble-fingered, neat-handed.
**F₃** clumsy, inept, awkward.

**diabolical** *adj* devilish, fiendish, demonic, hellish, damnable, evil, infernal, wicked, vile, dreadful, outrageous, shocking, disastrous, excruciating, atrocious.

**diagnose** *v* identify, determine, recognize, pinpoint, distinguish, analyse, explain, isolate, interpret, investigate.

**diagnosis** *n* identification, verdict, explanation, conclusion, answer, interpretation, analysis, opinion, investigation, examination, scrutiny.

**diagonal** *adj* oblique, slanting, cross, crosswise, sloping, crooked, angled, cornerways.

**diagram** *n* plan, sketch, chart, drawing, figure, representation, schema, illustration, outline, graph, picture, layout, table.

**dial** *n* circle, disc, face, clock, control.
*v* phone, ring, call (up).

**dialect** *n* idiom, language, regionalism, patois, provincialism, vernacular, argot, jargon, accent, lingo (*infml*), speech, diction.

**dialectic** *adj* dialectical, logical, rational, argumentative, analytical, rationalistic, logistic, polemical, inductive, deductive.
*n* dialectics, logic, reasoning, rationale, disputation, analysis, debate, argumentation, contention, discussion, polemics, induction, deduction.

**dialogue** *n* 1 CONVERSATION, interchange, discourse, communication, talk, exchange, discussion, converse, debate, conference. 2 LINES, script.

**diametric** *adj* diametrical, opposed, opposite, contrary, counter, contrasting, antithetical.

**diary** *n* journal, day-book, logbook, chronicle, year-book, appointment book, engagement book.

**diatribe** *n* tirade, invective, abuse, harangue, attack, onslaught, denunciation, criticism, insult, reviling, upbraiding.
**F₃** praise, eulogy.

**dicey** (*infml*) *adj* risky, chancy, unpredictable, tricky, problematic, dangerous, difficult, iffy (*infml*), dubious, hairy (*infml*).
**F₃** certain.

**dictate** *v* 1 SAY, speak, utter, announce, pronounce, transmit. 2 COMMAND, order, direct, decree, instruct, rule.
*n* command, decree, precept, principle, rule, direction, injunction,

edict, order, ruling, statute, requirement, ordinance, law, bidding, mandate, ultimatum, word.

**dictator** n despot, autocrat, tyrant, supremo (*infml*), Big Brother (*infml*).

**dictatorial** adj tyrannical, despotic, totalitarian, authoritarian, autocratic, oppressive, imperious, domineering, bossy (*infml*), absolute, repressive, overbearing, arbitrary, dogmatic.

Ea democratic, egalitarian, liberal.

**diction** n speech, articulation, language, elocution, enunciation, intonation, pronunciation, inflection, fluency, delivery, expression, phrasing.

**dictionary** n lexicon, glossary, thesaurus, vocabulary, wordbook, encyclopaedia, concordance.

**dictum** n pronouncement, ruling, maxim, decree, dictate, edict, fiat (*fml*), precept, axiom, command, order, utterance.

**didactic** adj instructive, educational, educative, pedagogic, prescriptive, pedantic, moralizing, moral.

**die** v 1 DECEASE, perish, pass away, expire, depart, breathe one's last, peg out (*infml*), snuff it (*sl*), bite the dust (*infml*), kick the bucket (*sl*).
2 DWINDLE, fade, ebb, sink, wane, wilt, wither, peter out, decline, decay, finish, lapse, end, disappear, vanish, subside. 3 LONG FOR, pine for, yearn, desire.

Ea 1 live.

**die-hard** n reactionary, intransigent, hardliner, blimp (*infml*), ultra-conservative, old fogey (*infml*), stick-in-the-mud (*infml*), rightist, fanatic.

**diet** n 1 FOOD, nutrition, provisions, sustenance, rations, foodstuffs, subsistence. 2 FAST, abstinence, regimen.
v lose weight, slim, fast, reduce, abstain, weight-watch (*infml*).

**differ** v 1 VARY, diverge, deviate, depart from, contradict, contrast.

2 DISAGREE, argue, conflict, oppose, dispute, dissent, be at odds with, clash, quarrel, fall out, debate, contend, take issue.

Ea 1 conform. 2 agree.

**difference** n 1 DISSIMILARITY, unlikeness, discrepancy, divergence, diversity, variation, variety, distinctness, distinction, deviation, differentiation, contrast, disparity, singularity, exception.
2 DISAGREEMENT, clash, dispute, conflict, contention, controversy.
3 REMAINDER, rest.

Ea 1 conformity. 2 agreement.

**different** adj 1 DISSIMILAR, unlike, contrasting, divergent, inconsistent, deviating, at odds, clashing, opposed.
2 VARIED, various, diverse, miscellaneous, assorted, disparate, many, numerous, several, sundry, other. 3 UNUSUAL, unconventional, unique, distinct, distinctive, extraordinary, individual, original, special, strange, separate, peculiar, rare, bizarre, anomalous.

Ea 1 similar. 2 same. 3 conventional.

**differentiate** v distinguish, tell apart, discriminate, contrast, separate, mark off, individualize, particularize.

**difficult** adj 1 HARD, laborious, demanding, arduous, strenuous, tough, wearisome, uphill, formidable.
2 COMPLEX, complicated, intricate, involved, abstruse, obscure, dark, knotty, thorny, problematical, perplexing, abstract, baffling, intractable. 3 UNMANAGEABLE, perverse, troublesome, trying, unco-operative, tiresome, stubborn, obstinate, intractable.

Ea 1 easy. 2 straightforward.
3 manageable.

**difficulty** n 1 HARDSHIP, trouble, labour, arduousness, painfulness, trial, tribulation, awkwardness. 2 PROBLEM, predicament, dilemma, quandary, perplexity, embarrassment, plight, distress, fix (*infml*), mess (*infml*), jam (*infml*), spot (*infml*), hiccup (*infml*), hang-up. **3** OBSTACLE, hindrance, hurdle, impediment, objection, opposition, block, complication, pitfall, protest, stumbling-block.

**F∃** 1 ease.

**diffidence** *n* unassertiveness, modesty, shyness, self-consciousness, self-effacement, timidity, insecurity, reserve, bashfulness, humility, inhibition, meekness, self-distrust, self-doubt, hesitancy, reluctance, backwardness.

**F∃** confidence.

**diffident** *adj* unassertive, modest, shy, timid, self-conscious, self-effacing, insecure, bashful, abashed, meek, reserved, withdrawn, tentative, shrinking, inhibited, hesitant, reluctant, unsure, shamefaced.

**F∃** assertive, confident.

**diffuse** *adj* **1** *diffuse outbreaks of rain*: scattered, unconcentrated, diffused, dispersed, disconnected. **2** *a diffuse prose style*: verbose, imprecise, wordy, rambling, long-winded, waffling (*infml*), vague, discursive.

**F∃** 1 concentrated. 2 succinct.

*v* spread, scatter, disperse, distribute, propagate, dispense, disseminate, circulate, dissipate.

**F∃** concentrate.

**dig** *v* **1** EXCAVATE, penetrate, burrow, mine, quarry, scoop, tunnel, till, gouge, delve, pierce. **2** POKE, prod. **3** INVESTIGATE, probe, go into, research, search.

*n* gibe, jeer, sneer, taunt, crack, insinuation, insult, wisecrack.

**F∃** compliment.

**dig up** discover, unearth, uncover, disinter, expose, extricate, exhume, find, retrieve, track down.

**F∃** bury, obscure.

**digest** *v* **1** ABSORB, assimilate, incorporate, process, dissolve.

**2** TAKE IN, absorb, understand, assimilate, grasp, study, consider, contemplate, meditate, ponder. **3** SHORTEN, summarize, condense, compress, reduce.

*n* summary, abridgement, abstract, précis, synopsis, résumé, reduction, abbreviation, compression, compendium.

**dignified** *adj* stately, solemn, imposing, majestic, noble, august, lordly, lofty, exalted, formal, distinguished, grave, impressive, reserved, honourable.

**F∃** undignified, lowly.

**dignitary** *n* worthy, notable, VIP (*infml*), high-up, personage, bigwig (*infml*).

**dignity** *n* stateliness, propriety, solemnity, decorum, courtliness, grandeur, loftiness, majesty, honour, eminence, importance, nobility, self-respect, self-esteem, standing, poise, respectability, greatness, status, pride.

**digress** *v* diverge, deviate, stray, wander, go off at a tangent, drift, depart, ramble.

**dilapidated** *adj* ramshackle, shabby, broken-down, neglected, tumble-down, uncared-for, rickety, decrepit, crumbling, run-down, worn-out, ruined, decayed, decaying.

**dilate** *v* distend, enlarge, expand, spread, broaden, widen, increase, extend, stretch, swell.

**F∃** contract.

**dilatory** *adj* delaying, procrastinating, slow, tardy, tarrying, sluggish, lingering, lackadaisical, slack.

**F∃** prompt.

**dilemma** *n* quandary, conflict, predicament, problem, catch-22 (*infml*), difficulty, puzzle, embarrassment, perplexity, plight.

**diligent** *adj* assiduous, industrious, hard-working, conscientious, painstaking, busy, attentive, tireless, careful, meticulous, persevering, persistent, studious.

**Ⓔ** negligent, lazy.

**dilute** *v* adulterate, water down, thin (out), attenuate, weaken, diffuse, diminish, decrease, lessen, reduce, temper, mitigate.

**Ⓔ** concentrate.

**dim** *adj* **1** DARK, dull, dusky, cloudy, shadowy, gloomy, sombre, dingy, lack-lustre, feeble, imperfect. **2** INDISTINCT, blurred, hazy, ill-defined, obscure, misty, unclear, foggy, fuzzy, vague, faint, weak. **3** STUPID, dense, obtuse, thick (*infml*), doltish.

**Ⓔ** **1** bright. **2** distinct. **3** bright, intelligent.

*v* darken, dull, obscure, cloud, blur, fade, tarnish, shade.

**Ⓔ** brighten, illuminate.

**dimension(s)** *n* extent, measurement, measure, size, scope, magnitude, largeness, capacity, mass, scale, range, bulk, importance, greatness.

**diminish** *v* **1** DECREASE, lessen, reduce, lower, contract, decline, dwindle, shrink, recede, taper off, wane, weaken, abate, fade, sink, subside, ebb, slacken, cut. **2** BELITTLE, disparage, deprecate, devalue.

**Ⓔ** **1** increase. **2** exaggerate.

**diminutive** *adj* undersized, small, tiny, little, miniature, minute, infinitesimal, wee, petite, midget, mini (*infml*), teeny (*infml*), teeny-weeny (*infml*), Lilliputian, dinky (*infml*), pint-size(d) (*infml*), pocket(-sized), pygmy.

**Ⓔ** big, large, oversized.

**din** *n* noise, row, racket, clash, clatter, clamour, pandemonium, uproar, commotion, crash, hullabaloo (*infml*), hubbub, outcry, shout, babble.

**Ⓔ** quiet, calm.

**dine** *v* eat, feast, sup, lunch,

banquet, feed.

**dingy** *adj* dark, drab, grimy, murky, faded, dull, dim, shabby, soiled, discoloured, dirty, dreary, gloomy, seedy, sombre, obscure, run-down, colourless, dusky, worn.

**Ⓔ** bright, clean.

**dinner** *n* meal, supper, tea (*infml*), banquet, feast, spread, repast (*fml*).

**dinosaur**

---

*Dinosaurs include*: Ornithischia, Saurischia; Allosaurus, Ankylosaurus, Apatosaurus, Barosaurus, Brachiosaurus, Brontosaurus, Camptosaurus, Coelophysis, Compsognathus, Corythosaurus, Deinonychus, Diplodocus, Heterodontosaurus, Iguanodon, Ophiacodon, Ornithomimus, Pachycephalosaurus, Parasaurolophus, Plateosaurus, Stegosaurus, Styracosaurus, Triceratops, Tyrannosaurus.

---

**dip** *v* **1** PLUNGE, immerse, submerge, duck, dunk, bathe, douse, sink. **2** DESCEND, decline, drop, fall, subside, slump, sink, lower.

*n* **1** HOLLOW, basin, decline, hole, concavity, incline, depression, fall, slope, slump, lowering. **2** BATHE, immersion, plunge, soaking, ducking, swim, drenching, infusion, dive.

**diplomacy** *n* **1** TACT, tactfulness, finesse, delicacy, discretion, savoir-faire, subtlety, skill, craft. **2** STATECRAFT, statesmanship, politics, negotiation, manoeuvring.

**diplomat** *n* go-between, mediator, negotiator, ambassador, envoy, conciliator, peacemaker, moderator, politician.

**diplomatic** *adj* tactful, politic, discreet, judicious, subtle, sensitive, prudent, discreet.

**Ⓔ** tactless.

**dire** *adj* **1** DISASTROUS, dreadful, awful, appalling, calamitous, catastrophic. **2** DESPERATE, urgent, grave, drastic, crucial, extreme, alarming, ominous.

**direct** v **1** CONTROL, manage, run, administer, organize, lead, govern, regulate, superintend, supervise. **2** INSTRUCT, command, order, charge. **3** GUIDE, lead, conduct, point. **4** AIM, point, focus, turn.
adj **1** STRAIGHT, undeviating, through, uninterrupted.
**2** STRAIGHTFORWARD, outspoken, blunt, frank, unequivocal, sincere, candid, honest, explicit.
**3** IMMEDIATE, first-hand, face-to-face, personal.
**F3** 1 circuitous. **2** equivocal. **3** indirect.

**direction** n **1** CONTROL, administration, management, government, supervision, guidance, leadership. **2** ROUTE, way, line, road.

**directions** n instructions, guidelines, orders, briefing, guidance, recommendations, indication, plan.

**directive** n command, instruction, order, regulation, ruling, imperative, dictate, decree, charge, mandate, injunction, ordinance, edict, fiat, notice.

**directly** adv **1** IMMEDIATELY, instantly, promptly, right away, speedily, forthwith, instantaneously, quickly, soon, presently, straightaway, straight. **2** FRANKLY, bluntly, candidly, honestly.

**director** n manager, head, boss, chief, controller, executive, principal, governor, leader, organizer, supervisor, administrator, producer, conductor.

**dirt** n **1** EARTH, soil, clay, dust, mud. **2** FILTH, grime, muck, mire, excrement, stain, smudge, slime, tarnish. **3** INDECENCY, impurity, obscenity, pornography.

**dirty** adj **1** FILTHY, grimy, grubby, mucky, soiled, unwashed, foul, messy, muddy, polluted, squalid, dull, miry, scruffy, shabby, sullied, clouded, dark. **2** INDECENT, obscene, filthy, smutty, sordid, salacious, vulgar, pornographic, corrupt.
**F3** 1 clean. **2** decent.
v pollute, soil, stain, foul, mess up, defile, smear, smirch, spoil, smudge, sully, muddy, blacken.
**F3** clean, cleanse.

**disability** n handicap, impairment, disablement, disorder, inability, incapacity, infirmity, defect, unfitness, disqualification, affliction, ailment, complaint, weakness.

**disable** v cripple, lame, incapacitate, damage, handicap, impair, debilitate, disqualify, weaken, immobilize, invalidate, paralyse, prostrate.

**disabled** adj handicapped, incapacitated, impaired, infirm, crippled, lame, immobilized, maimed, weak, weakened, paralysed, wrecked.
**F3** able, able-bodied.

**disadvantage** n **1** HARM, damage, detriment, hurt, injury, loss, prejudice. **2** DRAWBACK, snag, hindrance, handicap, impediment, inconvenience, flaw, nuisance, weakness, trouble.
**F3** 2 advantage, benefit.

**disadvantaged** adj deprived, underprivileged, poor, handicapped, impoverished, struggling.
**F3** privileged.

**disadvantageous** adj harmful, detrimental, inopportune, unfavourable, prejudicial, adverse, damaging, hurtful, injurious, inconvenient, ill-timed.
**F3** advantageous, auspicious.

**disaffected** adj disloyal, hostile, estranged, alienated, antagonistic, rebellious, dissatisfied, disgruntled, discontented.
**F3** loyal.

**disaffection** n disloyalty, hostility, alienation, discontentment, resentment, ill-will, dissatisfaction, animosity, coolness, unfriendliness,

**disagree** *v* **1** DISSENT, oppose, quarrel, argue, bicker, fall out (*infml*), wrangle, fight, squabble, contend, dispute, contest, object. **2** CONFLICT, clash, diverge, contradict, counter, differ, deviate, depart, run counter to, vary.
**F3** **1** agree. **2** correspond.

**disagreeable** *adj* **1** *disagreeable old man*: bad-tempered, ill-humoured, difficult, peevish, rude, surly, churlish, irritable, contrary, cross, brusque. **2** *a disagreeable taste*: disgusting, offensive, repulsive, repellent, obnoxious, unsavoury, objectionable, nasty.
**F3** **1** amiable, pleasant. **2** agreeable.

**disagreement** *n* **1** DISPUTE, argument, conflict, altercation (*fml*), quarrel, clash, dissent, falling-out, contention, strife, misunderstanding, squabble, tiff (*infml*), wrangle.
**2** DIFFERENCE, variance, unlikeness, disparity, discrepancy, deviation, discord, dissimilarity, incompatibility, divergence, diversity, incongruity.
**F3** **1** agreement, harmony. **2** similarity.

**disappear** *v* **1** VANISH, wane, recede, fade, evaporate, dissolve, ebb. **2** GO, depart, withdraw, retire, flee, fly, escape, scarper (*infml*), hide. **3** END, expire, perish, pass.
**F3** **1** appear. **3** emerge.

**disappearance** *n* vanishing, fading, evaporation, departure, loss, going, passing, melting, desertion, flight.
**F3** appearance, manifestation.

**disappoint** *v* fail, dissatisfy, let down, disillusion, dash, dismay, disenchant, sadden, thwart, vex, frustrate, foil, dishearten, disgruntle, disconcert, hamper, hinder, deceive, defeat, delude.
**F3** satisfy, please, delight.

**disappointed** *adj* let down,

frustrated, thwarted, disillusioned, dissatisfied, miffed (*infml*), upset, discouraged, disgruntled, disheartened, distressed, down-hearted, saddened, despondent, depressed.
**F3** pleased, satisfied.

**disappointment** *n*
**1** FRUSTRATION, dissatisfaction, failure, disenchantment, disillusionment, displeasure, discouragement, distress, regret.
**2** FAILURE, let-down, setback, comedown, blow, misfortune, fiasco, disaster, calamity, washout (*infml*), damp squib (*infml*), swiz (*infml*), swizzle (*infml*).
**F3** **1** pleasure, satisfaction, delight.
**2** success.

**disapproval** *n* censure, disapprobation (*fml*), condemnation, criticism, displeasure, reproach, objection, dissatisfaction, denunciation, dislike.
**F3** approbation (*fml*), approval.

**disapprove of** censure, condemn, blame, take exception to, object to, deplore, denounce, disparage, dislike, reject, spurn.
**F3** approve of.

**disarm** *v* **1** DISABLE, unarm, demilitarize, demobilize, deactivate, disband. **2** APPEASE, conciliate, win, mollify, persuade.
**F3** **1** arm.

**disarray** *n* disorder, confusion, chaos, mess, muddle, shambles (*infml*), disorganization, clutter, untidiness, unruliness, jumble, indiscipline, tangle, upset.
**F3** order.

**disaster** *n* calamity, catastrophe, misfortune, reverse, tragedy, blow, accident, act of God, cataclysm, debacle, mishap, failure, flop (*infml*), fiasco, ruin, stroke, trouble, mischance, ruination.
**F3** success, triumph.

**disastrous** *adj* calamitous,

catastrophic, cataclysmic, devastating, ruinous, tragic, unfortunate, dreadful, dire, terrible, destructive, ill-fated, fatal, miserable. **Ⓕ** successful, auspicious.

**disband** v disperse, break up, scatter, dismiss, demobilize, part company, separate, dissolve. **Ⓕ** assemble, muster.

**disbelief** n unbelief, incredulity, doubt, scepticism, suspicion, distrust, mistrust, rejection. **Ⓕ** belief.

**disbelieve** v discount, discredit, repudiate, reject, mistrust, suspect. **Ⓕ** believe, trust.

**disc** n 1 CIRCLE, face, plate, ring. 2 RECORD, album, LP, CD. 3 DISK, diskette, hard disk, floppy disk, CD-ROM.

**discard** v reject, abandon, dispose of, get rid of, jettison, dispense with, cast aside, ditch (*infml*), dump (*infml*), drop, scrap, shed, remove, relinquish. **Ⓕ** retain, adopt.

**discern** v 1 PERCEIVE, make out, observe, detect, recognize, see, ascertain, notice, determine, discover, descry. 2 DISCRIMINATE, distinguish, differentiate, judge.

**discernible** adj perceptible, noticeable, detectable, appreciable, distinct, observable, recognizable, visible, apparent, clear, obvious, plain, patent, manifest, discoverable. **Ⓕ** imperceptible.

**discerning** adj discriminating, perceptive, astute, clear-sighted, sensitive, shrewd, wise, sharp, subtle, sagacious, penetrating, acute, piercing, critical, eagle-eyed. **Ⓕ** dull, obtuse.

**discharge** v 1 LIBERATE, free, pardon, release, clear, absolve, exonerate, acquit, relieve, dismiss. 2 EXECUTE, carry out, perform, fulfil, dispense. 3 FIRE, shoot, let off, detonate, explode. 4 EMIT, sack

(*infml*), remove, fire (*infml*), expel, oust, eject. **Ⓕ** 1 detain. 2 neglect. 4 appoint. n 1 LIBERATION, release, acquittal, exoneration. 2 EMISSION, secretion, ejection. 3 EXECUTION, accomplishment, fulfilment. **Ⓕ** 1 confinement, detention. 2 absorption. 3 neglect.

**disciple** n follower, convert, proselyte, adherent, believer, devotee, supporter, learner, pupil, student.

**disciplinarian** n authoritarian, taskmaster, autocrat, stickler, despot, tyrant.

**discipline** n 1 TRAINING, exercise, drill, practice. 2 PUNISHMENT, chastisement, correction. 3 STRICTNESS, restraint, regulation, self-control, orderliness. **Ⓕ** 3 indiscipline. v 1 TRAIN, instruct, drill, educate, exercise, break in. 2 CHECK, control, correct, restrain, govern. 3 PUNISH, chastize, chasten, penalize, reprimand, castigate.

**disclaim** v deny, disown, repudiate, abandon, renounce, reject, abjure (*fml*). **Ⓕ** accept, confess.

**disclose** v 1 DIVULGE, make known, reveal, tell, confess, let slip, relate, publish, communicate, impart, leak (*infml*). 2 EXPOSE, reveal, uncover, lay bare, unveil, discover. **Ⓕ** conceal.

**disclosure** n divulgence, exposure, exposé, revelation, uncovering, publication, leak (*infml*), discovery, admission, acknowledgement, announcement, declaration.

**discomfort** n ache, pain, uneasiness, malaise, trouble, distress, disquiet, hardship, vexation, irritation, annoyance. **Ⓕ** comfort, ease.

**disconcerting** adj disturbing, confusing, upsetting, unnerving, alarming, bewildering, off-putting (*infml*), distracting, embarrassing, awkward, baffling, perplexing, dismaying, bothersome.

**disconnect** *v* cut off, disengage, uncouple, sever, separate, detach, unplug, unhook, part, divide.
**F3** attach, connect.

**disconnected** *adj* confused, incoherent, rambling, unco-ordinated, unintelligible, loose, irrational, disjointed, illogical, jumbled.
**F3** coherent, connected.

**disconsolate** *adj* desolate, dejected, dispirited, sad, melancholy, unhappy, wretched, miserable, gloomy, forlorn, inconsolable, crushed, heavy-hearted, hopeless.
**F3** cheerful, joyful.

**discontent** *n* uneasiness, dissatisfaction, disquiet, restlessness, fretfulness, unrest, impatience, vexation, regret.
**F3** content.

**discontented** *adj* dissatisfied, fed up (*infml*), disgruntled, unhappy, browned off (*infml*), cheesed off (*infml*), disaffected, miserable, exasperated, complaining.
**F3** contented, satisfied.

**discontinue** *v* stop, end, finish, cease, break off, terminate, halt, drop, suspend, abandon, cancel, interrupt.
**F3** continue.

**discord** *n* **1** DISSENSION, disagreement, discordance, clashing, disunity, incompatibility, conflict, difference, dispute, contention, friction, division, opposition, strife, split, wrangling. **2** DISSONANCE, disharmony, cacophony (*fml*), jangle, jarring, harshness.
**F3 1** concord, agreement. **2** harmony.

**discordant** *adj* **1** DISAGREEING, conflicting, at odds, clashing, contradictory, incongruous, incompatible, inconsistent.

**2** DISSONANT, cacophonous (*fml*), grating, jangling, jarring, harsh.
**F3 1** harmonious. **2** harmonious.

**discount**[1] *v* **1** DISREGARD, ignore, overlook, disbelieve, gloss over. **2** REDUCE, deduct, mark down, knock off (*infml*).

**discount**[2] *n* reduction, rebate, allowance, cut, concession, deduction, mark-down.

**discourage** *v* **1** DISHEARTEN, dampen, dispirit, depress, demoralize, dismay, unnerve, deject, disappoint. **2** DETER, dissuade, hinder, put off, restrain, prevent.
**F3 1** hearten. **2** encourage.

**discouragement** *n*
**1** DOWNHEARTEDNESS, despondency, pessimism, dismay, depression, dejection, despair, disappointment. **2** DETERRENT, damper, setback, impediment, obstacle, opposition, hindrance, restraint, rebuff.
**F3 1** encouragement. **2** incentive.

**discourse** *n* **1** CONVERSATION, dialogue, chat, communication, talk, converse, discussion. **2** SPEECH, address, oration (*fml*), lecture, sermon, essay, treatise, dissertation, homily.
*v* converse, talk, discuss, debate, confer, lecture.

**discourteous** *adj* rude, bad-mannered, ill-mannered, impolite, boorish, disrespectful, ill-bred, uncivil, unceremonious, insolent, offhand, curt, brusque, abrupt.
**F3** courteous, polite.

**discover** *v* **1** FIND, uncover, unearth, dig up, disclose, reveal, light on, locate. **2** ASCERTAIN, determine, realize, notice, recognize, perceive, see, find out, spot, discern, learn, detect. **3** ORIGINATE, invent, pioneer.
**F3 1** miss. **2** conceal, cover (up).

**discovery** *n* **1** BREAKTHROUGH, find, origination, introduction,

innovation, invention, exploration.
2 DISCLOSURE, detection, revelation, location.

**discredit** v 1 DISBELIEVE, distrust, doubt, question, mistrust, challenge.
2 DISPARAGE, dishonour, degrade, defame, disgrace, slander, slur, smear, reproach, vilify.
**E3** 1 believe. 2 honour.
n 1 DISBELIEF, distrust, doubt, mistrust, scepticism, suspicion.
2 DISHONOUR, disrepute, censure, aspersion, disgrace, blame, shame, reproach, slur, smear, scandal.
**E3** 1 belief. 2 credit.

**discreditable** adj dishonourable, disreputable, disgraceful, reprehensible, scandalous, blameworthy, shameful, infamous, degrading, improper.
**E3** creditable.

**discreet** adj tactful, careful, diplomatic, politic, prudent, cautious, delicate, judicious, reserved, wary, sensible.
**E3** tactless, indiscreet.

**discrepancy** n difference, disparity, variance, variation, inconsistency, dissimilarity, discordance, divergence, disagreement, conflict, inequality.

**discretion** n 1 TACT, diplomacy, judiciousness, caution, prudence, wisdom, circumspection, discernment, judgement, care, carefulness, consideration, wariness.
2 CHOICE, freedom, preference, will, wish.
**E3** 1 indiscretion.

**discriminate** v distinguish, differentiate, discern, tell apart, make a distinction, segregate, separate.
**E3** confuse, confound.

**discriminate (against)** be prejudiced, be biased, victimize.

**discriminating** adj discerning, fastidious, selective, critical, perceptive, particular, tasteful, astute, sensitive, cultivated.

**discrimination** n 1 BIAS, prejudice, intolerance, unfairness, bigotry, favouritism, inequity, racism, sexism.
2 DISCERNMENT, judgement, acumen, perception, acuteness, insight, penetration, subtlety, keenness, refinement, taste.

**discursive** adj rambling, digressing, wandering, long-winded, meandering, wide-ranging, circuitous.
**E3** terse.

**discuss** v debate, talk about, confer, argue, consider, deliberate, converse, consult, examine.

**discussion** n debate, conference, argument, conversation, dialogue, exchange, consultation, discourse, deliberation, consideration, analysis, review, examination, scrutiny, seminar, symposium.

**disdain** n scorn, contempt, arrogance, haughtiness, derision, sneering, dislike, snobbishness.
**E3** admiration, respect.

**disdainful** adj scornful, contemptuous, derisive, haughty, aloof, arrogant, supercilious, sneering, superior, proud, insolent.
**E3** respectful.

**disease** n illness, sickness, ill-health, infirmity, complaint, disorder, ailment, indisposition, malady, condition, affliction, infection, epidemic.
**E3** health.

**diseased** adj sick, ill, unhealthy, ailing, unsound, contaminated, infected.
**E3** healthy.

**disembark** v land, arrive, alight, debark.
**E3** embark.

**disembodied** adj bodiless, incorporeal (fml), ghostly, phantom, spiritual, immaterial, intangible.

**disengage** v disconnect, detach, loosen, free, extricate, undo, release, liberate, separate, disentangle, untie, withdraw.

**E3** connect, engage.

**disentangle** v **1** LOOSE, free, extricate, disconnect, untangle, disengage, detach, unravel, separate, unfold. **2** RESOLVE, clarify, simplify.

**E3** 1 entangle.

**disfigure** v deface, blemish, mutilate, scar, mar, deform, distort, damage, spoil.

**E3** adorn, embellish.

**disgrace** n shame, ignominy, disrepute, dishonour, disfavour, humiliation, defamation, discredit, scandal, reproach, slur, stain.

**E3** honour, esteem.

v shame, dishonour, abase, defame, humiliate, disfavour, stain, discredit, reproach, slur, sully, taint, stigmatize.

**E3** honour, respect.

**disgraceful** adj shameful, dishonourable, disreputable, ignominious, scandalous, shocking, unworthy, dreadful, appalling.

**E3** honourable, respectable.

**disguise** v **1** CONCEAL, cover, camouflage, mask, hide, dress up, cloak, screen, veil, shroud. **2** FALSIFY, deceive, dissemble, misrepresent, fake, fudge.

**E3** 1 reveal, expose.

n concealment, camouflage, cloak, cover, costume, mask, front, façade, masquerade, deception, pretence, travesty, screen, veil.

**disgust** v offend, displease, nauseate, revolt, sicken, repel, outrage, put off.

**E3** delight, please.

n revulsion, repulsion, repugnance, distaste, aversion, abhorrence, nausea, loathing, detestation, hatred.

**disgusted** adj repelled, repulsed, revolted, offended, appalled, outraged.

**E3** attracted, delighted.

**disgusting** adj repugnant, repellent, revolting, offensive, sickening, nauseating, odious, foul,

unappetizing, unpleasant, vile, obscene, abominable, detestable, objectionable, nasty.

**E3** delightful, pleasant.

**dish** n plate, bowl, platter, food, recipe.

**dish out** distribute, give out, hand out, hand round, dole out, allocate, mete out, inflict.

**dish up** serve, present, ladle, spoon, dispense, scoop.

**dishearten** v discourage, dispirit, dampen, cast down, depress, dismay, dash, disappoint, deject, daunt, crush, deter.

**E3** encourage, hearten.

**dishevelled** adj tousled, unkempt, uncombed, untidy, bedraggled, messy, ruffled, slovenly, disordered.

**E3** neat, tidy.

**dishonest** adj untruthful, fraudulent, deceitful, false, lying, deceptive, double-dealing, cheating, crooked (infml), treacherous, unprincipled, swindling, shady (infml), corrupt, disreputable.

**E3** honest, trustworthy, scrupulous.

**dishonesty** n deceit, falsehood, falsity, fraudulence, fraud, criminality, insincerity, treachery, cheating, crookedness (infml), corruption, unscrupulousness, trickery.

**E3** honesty, truthfulness.

**dishonour** v disgrace, shame, humiliate, debase, defile, degrade, defame, discredit, demean, debauch.

**E3** honour.

n disgrace, abasement, humiliation, shame, degradation, discredit, disrepute, indignity, ignominy, reproach, slight, slur, scandal, insult, disfavour, outrage, aspersion, abuse, discourtesy.

**E3** honour.

**disillusioned** adj disenchanted, disabused, undeceived, disappointed.

**disinclined** adj averse, reluctant, resistant, indisposed, loath, opposed,

hesitant.
**F3** inclined, willing.

**disinfect** v sterilize, fumigate, sanitize, decontaminate, cleanse, purify, purge, clean.
**F3** contaminate, infect.

**disinfectant** n sterilizer, antiseptic, sanitizer.

**disintegrate** v break up, decompose, fall apart, crumble, rot, moulder, separate, splinter.

**disinterest** n disinterestedness, impartiality, neutrality, detachment, unbiasedness, dispassionateness, fairness.

**disinterested** adj unbiased, neutral, impartial, unprejudiced, dispassionate, detached, uninvolved, open-minded, equitable, even-handed, unselfish.
**F3** biased, concerned.

**disjointed** adj 1 DISCONNECTED, dislocated, divided, separated, disunited, displaced, broken, fitful, split, disarticulated. 2 INCOHERENT, aimless, confused, disordered, loose, unconnected, bitty, rambling, spasmodic.
**F3** 2 coherent.

**dislike** n aversion, hatred, repugnance, hostility, distaste, disinclination, disapproval, disapprobation, displeasure, animosity, antagonism, enmity, detestation, disgust, loathing.
**F3** liking, predilection.
v hate, detest, object to, loathe, abhor, abominate, disapprove, shun, despise, scorn.
**F3** like, favour.

**dislocate** v disjoint, displace, misplace, disengage, put out (infml), disorder, shift, disconnect, disrupt, disunite.

**dislodge** v displace, eject, remove, oust, extricate, shift, move, uproot.

**disloyal** adj treacherous, faithless, false, traitorous, two-faced (infml), unfaithful, apostate, unpatriotic.

**F3** loyal, trustworthy.

**dismal** adj dreary, gloomy, depressing, bleak, cheerless, dull, drab, low-spirited, melancholy, sad, sombre, lugubrious, forlorn, despondent, dark, sorrowful, long-faced (infml), hopeless, discouraging.
**F3** cheerful, bright.

**dismantle** v demolish, take apart, disassemble, strip.
**F3** assemble, put together.

**dismay** v alarm, daunt, frighten, unnerve, unsettle, scare, put off, dispirit, distress, disconcert, dishearten, discourage, disillusion, depress, horrify, disappoint.
**F3** encourage, hearten.
n consternation, alarm, distress, apprehension, agitation, dread, fear, trepidation, fright, horror, terror, discouragement, disappointment.
**F3** boldness, encouragement.

**dismember** v disjoint, amputate, dissect, dislocate, divide, mutilate, sever.
**F3** assemble, join.

**dismiss** v 1 the class was dismissed: discharge, free, let go, release, send away, remove, drop, discord, banish. 2 dismiss employees: sack (infml), make redundant, lay off, fire (infml), relegate. 3 dismiss it from your mind: discount, disregard, reject, repudiate, set aside, shelve, spurn.
**F3** 1 retain. 2 appoint. 3 accept.

**disobey** v contravene, infringe, violate, transgress, flout, disregard, defy, ignore, resist, rebel.
**F3** obey.

**disorder** n 1 CONFUSION, chaos, muddle, disarray, mess, untidiness, shambles (infml), clutter, disorganization, jumble.
2 DISTURBANCE, tumult, riot, confusion, commotion, uproar, fracas, brawl, fight, clamour, quarrel.
3 ILLNESS, complaint, disease, sickness, disability, ailment, malady, affliction.

**≠ 1** neatness, order. **2** law and order, peace.

*v* disturb, mess up, disarrange, mix up, muddle, upset, disorganize, confuse, confound, clutter, jumble, discompose, scatter, unsettle.

**≠** arrange, organize.

**disorderly** *adj* **1** DISORGANIZED, confused, chaotic, irregular, messy, untidy. **2** UNRULY, undisciplined, unmanageable, obstreperous, rowdy, turbulent, rebellious, lawless.

**≠ 1** neat, tidy. **2** well-behaved.

**disorganize** *v* disorder, disrupt, disturb, disarrange, muddle, upset, confuse, discompose, jumble, play havoc with, unsettle, break up, destroy.

**≠** organize.

**disown** *v* repudiate, renounce, disclaim, deny, cast off, disallow, reject, abandon.

**≠** accept, acknowledge.

**disparaging** *adj* derisive, derogatory, mocking, scornful, critical, insulting, snide (*infml*).

**≠** flattering, praising.

**dispassionate** *adj* detached, objective, impartial, neutral, disinterested, impersonal, fair, cool, calm, composed.

**≠** biased, emotional.

**dispatch, despatch** *v* **1** SEND, express, transmit, forward, consign, expedite, accelerate. **2** DISPOSE OF, finish, perform, discharge, conclude. **3** KILL, murder, execute.

**≠ 1** receive.

*n* **1** COMMUNICATION, message, report, bulletin, communiqué, news, letter, account. **2** PROMPTNESS, speed, alacrity, expedition, celerity, haste, rapidity, swiftness.

**≠ 2** slowness.

**dispense** *v* **1** DISTRIBUTE, give out, apportion, allot, allocate, assign, share, mete out. **2** ADMINISTER, apply, implement, enforce, discharge, execute, operate.

**dispense with** dispose of, get rid of, abolish, discard, omit, disregard, cancel, forgo, ignore, waive.

**disperse** *v* scatter, dispel, spread, distribute, diffuse, dissolve, break up, dismiss, separate.

**≠** gather.

**displace** *v* **1** DISLODGE, move, shift, misplace, disturb, dislocate. **2** DEPOSE, oust, remove, replace, dismiss, discharge, supplant, eject, evict, succeed, supersede.

**display** *v* **1** SHOW, present, demonstrate, exhibit. **2** BETRAY, disclose, reveal, show, expose. **3** SHOW OFF, flourish, parade, flaunt.

**≠ 1** conceal. **2** disguise.

*n* show, exhibition, demonstration, presentation, parade, spectacle, revelation.

**displease** *v* offend, annoy, irritate, anger, upset, put out (*infml*), infuriate, exasperate, incense.

**≠** please.

**displeasure** *n* offence, annoyance, disapproval, irritation, resentment, disfavour, anger, indignation, wrath.

**≠** pleasure.

**disposal** *n* **1** ARRANGEMENT, grouping, order. **2** CONTROL, direction, command. **3** REMOVAL, riddance, discarding, jettisoning.

**dispose of 1** DEAL WITH, decide, settle. **2** GET RID OF, discard, scrap, destroy, dump (*infml*), jettison.

**≠ 2** keep.

**disposed** *adj* liable, inclined, predisposed, prone, likely, apt, minded, subject, ready, willing.

**≠** disinclined.

**disposition** *n* character, nature, temperament, inclination, make-up, bent, leaning, predisposition, constitution, habit, spirit, tendency, proneness.

**disproportionate** *adj* unequal, uneven, incommensurate, excessive, unreasonable.

**E3** balanced.

**disprove** v refute, rebut, confute, discredit, invalidate, contradict, expose.
**E3** confirm, prove.

**dispute** v argue, debate, question, contend, challenge, discuss, doubt, contest, contradict, deny, quarrel, clash, wrangle, squabble.
**E3** agree.
n argument, debate, disagreement, controversy, conflict, contention, quarrel, wrangle, feud, strife, squabble.
**E3** agreement, settlement.

**disqualify** v 1 INCAPACITATE, disable, invalidate. 2 DEBAR, preclude, rule out, disentitle, eliminate, prohibit.
**E3** 2 qualify, accept.

**disquiet** n anxiety, worry, concern, nervousness, uneasiness, restlessness, alarm, distress, fretfulness, fear, disturbance, trouble.
**E3** calm, reassurance.

**disregard** v 1 IGNORE, overlook, discount, neglect, pass over, disobey, make light of, turn a blind eye to (*infml*), brush aside. 2 SLIGHT, snub, despise, disdain, disparage.
**E3** 1 heed, pay attention to. 2 respect.
n neglect, negligence, inattention, oversight, indifference, disrespect, contempt, disdain, brush-off (*infml*).
**E3** attention, heed.

**disrepair** n dilapidation, deterioration, decay, collapse, ruin, shabbiness.
**E3** good repair.

**disreputable** adj 1 DISGRACEFUL, discreditable, dishonourable, unrespectable, notorious, scandalous, shameful, shady, base, contemptible, low, mean, shocking. 2 SCRUFFY, shabby, seedy, unkempt.
**E3** 1 respectable. 2 smart.

**disrespectful** adj rude, discourteous, impertinent, impolite, impudent, insolent, uncivil,

unmannerly, cheeky, insulting, irreverent, contemptuous.
**E3** polite, respectful.

**disrupt** v disturb, disorganize, confuse, interrupt, break up, unsettle, intrude, upset.

**dissatisfaction** n discontent, displeasure, dislike, discomfort, disappointment, frustration, annoyance, irritation, exasperation, regret, resentment.
**E3** satisfaction.

**dissect** v 1 DISMEMBER, anatomize. 2 ANALYSE, investigate, scrutinize, examine, inspect, pore over.

**dissension** n disagreement, discord, dissent, dispute, contention, conflict, strife, friction, quarrel.
**E3** agreement.

**dissent** v disagree, differ, protest, object, refuse, quibble.
**E3** assent.
n disagreement, difference, dissension, discord, resistance, opposition, objection.
**E3** agreement, conformity.

**disservice** n disfavour, injury, wrong, bad turn, harm, unkindness, injustice.
**E3** favour.

**dissident** adj disagreeing, differing, dissenting, discordant, nonconformist, heterodox (*fml*).
**E3** acquiescent, orthodox.
n dissenter, protestor, noncomformist, rebel, agitator, revolutionary, schismatic, recusant.
**E3** assenter.

**dissimilar** adj unlike, different, divergent, disparate, unrelated, incompatible, mismatched, diverse, various, heterogeneous.
**E3** similar, like.

**dissipate** v 1 *he dissipated his inheritance*: spend, waste, squander, expend, consume, deplete, fritter away, burn up. 2 *the clouds dissipated*: disperse, vanish, disappear, dispel, diffuse, evaporate, dissolve.

**🖙 1** accumulate. **2** appear.

**dissociate** *v* separate, detach, break off, disunite, disengage, disconnect, cut off, disband, divorce, disrupt, isolate, segregate.

**🖙** associate, join.

**dissolute** *adj* dissipated, debauched, degenerate, depraved, wanton, abandoned, corrupt, immoral, licentious, lewd, wild.

**🖙** restrained, virtuous.

**dissolution** *n* **1** DISINTEGRATION, decomposition, separation, resolution, division. **2** ENDING, termination, conclusion, finish, discontinuation, divorce, dismissal, dispersal, destruction, overthrow. **3** EVAPORATION, disappearance.

**dissolve** *v* **1** EVAPORATE, disintegrate, liquefy, melt. **2** DECOMPOSE, disintegrate, disperse, break up, disappear, crumble. **3** END, terminate, separate, sever, divorce.

**dissuade** *v* deter, discourage, put off, disincline.

**🖙** persuade.

**distance** *n* **1** SPACE, interval, gap, extent, range, reach, length, width. **2** ALOOFNESS, reserve, coolness, coldness, remoteness.

**🖙 1** closeness. **2** approachability.

**distant** *adj* **1** FAR, faraway, far-flung, out-of-the-way, remote, outlying, abroad, dispersed. **2** ALOOF, cool, reserved, stand-offish (*infml*), formal, cold, restrained, stiff.

**🖙 1** close. **2** approachable.

**distaste** *n* dislike, aversion, repugnance, disgust, revulsion, loathing, abhorrence.

**🖙** liking.

**distasteful** *adj* disagreeable, offensive, unpleasant, objectionable, repulsive, obnoxious, repugnant, unsavoury, loathsome, abhorrent.

**🖙** pleasing.

**distinct** *adj* **1** SEPARATE, different, detached, individual, dissimilar.

**2** CLEAR, plain, evident, obvious, apparent, marked, definite, noticeable, recognizable.

**🖙 2** indistinct, vague.

**distinction** *n* **1** DIFFERENTIATION, discrimination, discernment, separation, difference, dissimilarity, contrast. **2** CHARACTERISTIC, peculiarity, individuality, feature, quality, mark. **3** RENOWN, fame, celebrity, prominence, eminence, importance, reputation, greatness, honour, prestige, repute, superiority, worth, merit, excellence, quality.

**🖙 3** unimportance, obscurity.

**distinctive** *adj* characteristic, distinguishing, individual, peculiar, different, unique, singular, special, original, extraordinary, idiosyncratic.

**🖙** ordinary, common.

**distinguish** *v* **1** DIFFERENTIATE, tell apart, discriminate, determine, categorize, characterize, classify. **2** DISCERN, perceive, identify, ascertain, make out, recognize, see, discriminate.

**distinguished** *adj* famous, eminent, celebrated, well-known, acclaimed, illustrious, notable, noted, renowned, famed, honoured, outstanding, striking, marked, extraordinary, conspicuous.

**🖙** insignificant, obscure, unimpressive.

**distort** *v* **1** DEFORM, contort, bend, misshape, disfigure, twist, warp. **2** FALSIFY, misrepresent, pervert, slant, colour, garble.

**distract** *v* **1** DIVERT, sidetrack, deflect. **2** CONFUSE, disconcert, bewilder, confound, disturb, perplex, puzzle. **3** AMUSE, occupy, divert, engross.

**distraught** *adj* agitated, anxious, overwrought, upset, distressed, distracted, beside oneself, worked up, frantic, hysterical, raving, mad, wild, crazy.

**🖙** calm, untroubled.

**distress** *n* **1** ANGUISH, grief, misery, sorrow, heartache, affliction, suffering, torment, wretchedness, sadness, worry, anxiety, desolation, pain, agony. **2** ADVERSITY, hardship, poverty, need, privation, destitution, misfortune, trouble, difficulties, trial.
**F3** **1** content. **2** comfort, ease.
*v* upset, afflict, grieve, disturb, trouble, sadden, worry, torment, harass, harrow, pain, agonize, bother.
**F3** comfort.

**distribute** *v* **1** DISPENSE, allocate, dole out, dish out, share, deal, divide, apportion. **2** DELIVER, hand out, spread, issue, circulate, diffuse, disperse, scatter.
**F3** **2** collect.

**distribution** *n* **1** ALLOCATION, apportionment, division, sharing. **2** CIRCULATION, spreading, scattering, delivery, dissemination, supply, dealing, handling. **3** ARRANGEMENT, grouping, classification, organization.
**F3** **2** collection.

**district** *n* region, area, quarter, neighbourhood, locality, sector, precinct, parish, locale, community, vicinity, ward.

**distrust** *v* mistrust, doubt, disbelieve, suspect, question.
**F3** trust.
*n* mistrust, doubt, disbelief, suspicion, misgiving, wariness, scepticism, question, qualm.
**F3** trust.

**disturb** *v* **1** DISRUPT, interrupt, distract. **2** AGITATE, unsettle, upset, distress, worry, fluster, annoy, bother. **3** DISARRANGE, disorder, confuse, upset.
**F3** **2** reassure. **3** order.

**disturbance** *n* **1** DISRUPTION, agitation, interruption, intrusion, upheaval, upset, confusion, annoyance, bother, trouble, hindrance. **2** DISORDER, uproar, commotion, tumult, turmoil, fracas, fray, brawl, riot.
**F3** **1** peace. **2** order.

**disuse** *n* neglect, desuetude (*fml*), abandonment, discontinuance, decay.
**F3** use.

**ditch** *n* trench, dyke, channel, gully, furrow, moat, drain, level, watercourse.

**dither** *v* hesitate, shilly-shally (*infml*), waver, vacillate.

**dive** *v* plunge, plummet, dip, submerge, jump, leap, nose-dive, fall, drop, swoop, descend, pitch.
*n* **1** PLUNGE, lunge, header, jump, leap, nose-dive, swoop, dash, spring. **2** (*infml*) BAR, club, saloon.

**diverge** *v* **1** DIVIDE, branch, fork, separate, spread, split. **2** DEVIATE, digress, stray, wander. **3** DIFFER, vary, disagree, dissent, conflict.
**F3** **1** converge. **3** agree.

**diverse** *adj* various, varied, varying, sundry, different, differing, assorted, dissimilar, miscellaneous, discrete, separate, several, distinct.
**F3** similar, identical.

**diversify** *v* vary, change, expand, branch out, spread out, alter, mix, assort.

**diversion** *n* **1** DEVIATION, detour. **2** AMUSEMENT, entertainment, distraction, pastime, recreation, relaxation, play, game. **3** ALTERATION, change.

**diversity** *n* variety, dissimilarity, difference, variance, assortment, range, medley.
**F3** similarity, likeness.

**divert** *v* **1** DEFLECT, redirect, reroute, side-track, avert, distract, switch. **2** AMUSE, entertain, occupy, distract, interest.

**divide** *v* **1** SPLIT, separate, part, cut, break up, detach, bisect, disconnect. **2** DISTRIBUTE, share, allocate, deal out, allot, apportion. **3** DISUNITE, separate, estrange, alienate. **4** CLASSIFY, group, sort, grade, segregate.

**⊟** 1 join. 2 collect. 3 unite.

**divine** adj 1 GODLIKE, superhuman, supernatural, celestial, heavenly, angelic, spiritual. 2 HOLY, sacred, sanctified, consecrated, transcendent, exalted, glorious, religious, supreme.

**⊟** 1 human. 2 mundane.

**divinity** n god, goddess, deity, godliness, holiness, sanctity, godhead, spirit.

**division** n 1 SEPARATION, detaching, parting, cutting, disunion. 2 BREACH, rupture, split, schism, disunion, estrangement, disagreement, feud. 3 DISTRIBUTION, sharing, allotment, apportionment. 4 SECTION, sector, segment, part, department, category, class, compartment, branch.

**⊟** 1 union. 2 unity. 3 collection. 4 whole.

**divorce** n dissolution, annulment, break-up, split-up, rupture, separation, breach, disunion. v separate, part, annul, split up, sever, dissolve, divide, dissociate.

**⊟** marry, unite.

**divulge** v disclose, reveal, communicate, tell, leak (infml), impart, confess, betray, uncover, let slip, expose, publish, proclaim.

**dizzy** adj 1 GIDDY, faint, light-headed, woozy (infml), shaky, reeling. 2 CONFUSED, bewildered, dazed, muddled.

**do** v 1 PERFORM, carry out, execute, accomplish, achieve, fulfil, implement, complete, undertake, work, put on, present, conclude, end, finish. 2 BEHAVE, act, conduct oneself. 3 FIX, prepare, organize, arrange, deal with, look after, manage, produce, make, create, cause, proceed. 4 SUFFICE, satisfy, serve.

n (infml) function, affair, event, gathering, party, occasion.

**do away with** get rid of, dispose of, exterminate, eliminate, abolish,

discontinue, remove, destroy, discard, kill, murder.

**do up** 1 FASTEN, tie, lace, pack. 2 RENOVATE, restore, decorate, redecorate, modernize, repair.

**do without** dispense with, abstain from, forgo, give up, relinquish.

**docile** adj tractable, co-operative, manageable, submissive, obedient, amenable, controlled, obliging.

**⊟** truculent, unco-operative.

**dock**¹ n harbour, wharf, quay, boat-yard, pier, waterfront, marina. v anchor, moor, drop anchor, land, berth, put in, tie up.

**dock**² v crop, clip, cut, shorten, curtail, deduct, reduce, lessen, withhold, decrease, subtract, diminish.

**doctor** n physician, general practitioner, GP, medic (infml), medical officer, consultant, clinician.

> *Types of medical doctor include:*
> general practitioner, GP, family
> doctor, family practitioner, locum,
> hospital doctor, houseman, intern,
> resident, registrar, consultant,
> medical officer (MO), doc (infml),
> bones (infml), quack (infml), dentist,
> veterinary surgeon, vet (infml).

v 1 ALTER, tamper with, falsify, misrepresent, pervert, adulterate, change, disguise, dilute. 2 REPAIR, fix, patch up.

**doctrine** n dogma, creed, belief, tenet, principle, teaching, precept, conviction, opinion, canon.

**document** n paper, certificate, deed, record, report, form, instrument (fml). v 1 RECORD, report, chronicle, list, detail, cite. 2 SUPPORT, prove, corroborate, verify.

**dodge** v avoid, elude, evade, swerve, side-step, shirk, shift. n trick, ruse, ploy, wile, scheme, stratagem, machination, manoeuvre.

**dog** *n* hound, cur, mongrel, canine, puppy, pup, bitch, mutt (*infml*), pooch (*infml*).

> *Breeds of dog include*: Afghan hound, alsatian, basset-hound, beagle, Border collie, borzoi, bull-mastiff, bulldog, bull-terrier, cairn terrier, chihuahua, chow, cocker spaniel, collie, corgi, dachshund, Dalmatian, Doberman pinscher, foxhound, fox-terrier, German Shepherd, golden retriever, Great Dane, greyhound, husky, Irish wolfhound, Jack Russell, King Charles spaniel, Labrador, lhasa apso, lurcher, Maltese, Old English sheepdog, Pekingese, pit bull terrier, pointer, poodle, pug, Rottweiler, saluki, sausage-dog (*infml*), schnauzer, Scottie (*infml*), Scottish-terrier, Sealyham, setter, sheltie, shih tzu, springer spaniel, St Bernard, terrier, whippet, West Highland terrier, Westie (*infml*), wolf-hound, Yorkshire terrier.

*v* pursue, follow, trail, track, tail, hound, shadow, plague, harry, haunt, trouble, worry.

**dogged** *adj* determined, resolute, persistent, persevering, intent, tenacious, firm, steadfast, staunch, single-minded, indefatigable, steady, unshakable, stubborn, obstinate, relentless, unyielding.
**F₃** irresolute, apathetic.

**dogma** *n* doctrine, creed, belief, precept, principle, article (of faith), credo, tenet, conviction, teaching, opinion.

**dogmatic** *adj* opinionated, assertive, authoritative, positive, doctrinaire, dictatorial, doctrinal, categorical, emphatic, overbearing, arbitrary.

**dole out** *v* distribute, allocate, hand out, dish out, apportion, allot, mete out, share, divide, deal, issue, ration, dispense, administer, assign.

**domain** *n* **1** DOMINION, kingdom,

realm, territory, region, empire, lands, province. **2** FIELD, area, speciality, concern, department, sphere, discipline, jurisdiction.

**domestic** *adj* **1** HOME, family, household, home-loving, stay-at-home, homely, house-trained, tame, pet, private. **2** INTERNAL, indigenous, native.
*n* servant, maid, charwoman, char, daily help, daily, au pair.

**domesticate** *v* tame, house-train, break, train, accustom, familiarize.

**dominant** *adj* **1** AUTHORITATIVE, controlling, governing, ruling, powerful, assertive, influential.
**2** PRINCIPAL, main, outstanding, chief, important, predominant, primary, prominent, leading, pre-eminent, prevailing, prevalent, commanding.
**F₃ 1** submissive. **2** subordinate.

**dominate** *v* **1** CONTROL, domineer, govern, rule, direct, monopolize, master, lead, overrule, prevail, overbear, tyrannize.
**2** OVERSHADOW, eclipse, dwarf.

**domineering** *adj* overbearing, authoritarian, imperious, autocratic, bossy (*infml*), dictatorial, despotic, masterful, high-handed, oppressive, tyrannical, arrogant.
**F₃** meek, servile.

**dominion** *n* **1** POWER, authority, domination, command, control, rule, sway, jurisdiction, government, lordship, mastery, supremacy, sovereignty. **2** DOMAIN, country, territory, province, colony, realm, kingdom, empire.

**donate** *v* give, contribute, present, bequeath, cough up (*infml*), fork out (*infml*), bestow (*fml*), confer (*fml*), subscribe.
**F₃** receive.

**donation** *n* gift, present, offering, grant, gratuity, largess(e), contribution, presentation, subscription, alms, benefaction (*fml*), bequest.

**done** *adj* **1** FINISHED, over, accomplished, completed, ended, concluded, settled, realized, executed. **2** CONVENTIONAL, acceptable, proper. **3** COOKED, ready.

**donor** *n* giver, donator, benefactor, contributor, philanthropist, provider, fairy godmother (*infml*).
**E3** beneficiary.

**doom** *n* **1** FATE, fortune, destiny, portion, lot. **2** DESTRUCTION, catastrophe, downfall, ruin, death, death-knell. **3** CONDEMNATION, judgement, sentence, verdict.
*v* condemn, damn, consign, judge, sentence, destine.

**doomed** *adj* condemned, damned, fated, ill-fated, ill-omened, cursed, destined, hopeless, luckless, ill-starred.

**door** *n* opening, entrance, entry, exit, doorway, portal, hatch.

**dope** (*infml*) *n* **1** NARCOTIC, drugs, marijuana, cannabis, opiate, hallucinogen. **2** FOOL, dolt, idiot, half-wit (*infml*), dimwit (*infml*), dunce, simpleton, clot (*infml*), blockhead. **3** INFORMATION, facts, low-down (*infml*), details.
*v* drug, sedate, anaesthetize, stupefy, medicate, narcotize, inject, doctor.

**dormant** *adj* **1** INACTIVE, asleep, sleeping, inert, resting, slumbering, sluggish, torpid, hibernating, fallow, comatose. **2** LATENT, unrealized, potential, undeveloped, undisclosed.
**E3** **1** active, awake. **2** realized, developed.

**dose** *n* measure, dosage, amount, portion, quantity, draught, potion, prescription, shot.
*v* medicate, administer, prescribe, dispense, treat.

**dot** *n* point, spot, speck, mark, fleck, circle, pin-point, atom, decimal point, full stop, iota, jot.
*v* spot, sprinkle, stud, dab, punctuate.

**dote on** adore, idolize, treasure, admire, indulge.

**double** *adj* dual, twofold, twice, duplicate, twin, paired, doubled, coupled.
**E3** single, half.
*v* duplicate, enlarge, increase, repeat, multiply, fold, magnify.
*n* twin, duplicate, copy, clone, replica, doppelgänger, lookalike, spitting image (*infml*), ringer (*infml*), image, counterpart, impersonator.
**at the double** immediately, at once, quickly, without delay.

**double-cross** *v* cheat, swindle, defraud, trick, con (*infml*), hoodwink, betray, two-time (*infml*), mislead.

**doubt** *v* **1** DISTRUST, mistrust, query, question, suspect, fear. **2** BE UNCERTAIN, be dubious, hesitate, vacillate, waver.
**E3** **1** believe, trust.
*n* **1** DISTRUST, suspicion, mistrust, scepticism, reservation, misgiving, incredulity, apprehension, hesitation. **2** UNCERTAINTY, difficulty, confusion, ambiguity, problem, indecision, perplexity, dilemma, quandary.
**E3** **1** trust, faith. **2** certainty, belief.

**doubtful** *adj* **1** *doubtful about his future*: uncertain, unsure, undecided, suspicious, irresolute, wavering, hesitant, vacillating, tentative, sceptical. **2** *writing of doubtful origin*: dubious, questionable, unclear, ambiguous, vague, obscure, debatable.
**E3** **1** certain, decided. **2** definite, settled.

**doubtless** *adv* **1** CERTAINLY, without doubt, undoubtedly, unquestionably, indisputably, no doubt, clearly, surely, of course, truly, precisely. **2** PROBABLY, presumably, most likely, seemingly, supposedly.

**dour** *adj* **1** GLOOMY, dismal,

forbidding, grim, morose, unfriendly, dreary, austere, sour, sullen. **2** HARD, inflexible, unyielding, rigid, severe, rigorous, strict, obstinate.
**E3** cheerful, bright. **2** easy-going.

**douse, dowse** v **1** SOAK, saturate, steep, submerge, immerse, immerge, dip, duck, drench, dunk, plunge. **2** EXTINGUISH, put out, blow out, smother, snuff.

**dowdy** adj unfashionable, ill-dressed, frumpish, drab, shabby, tatty (infml), frowsy, tacky (infml), dingy, old-fashioned, slovenly.
**E3** fashionable, smart.

**down** v **1** KNOCK DOWN, fell, floor, prostrate, throw, topple.
**2** SWALLOW, drink, gulp, swig (infml), knock back (infml).
**down and out** destitute, impoverished, penniless, derelict, ruined.

**downcast** adj dejected, depressed, despondent, sad, unhappy, miserable, down, low, disheartened, dispirited, blue (infml), fed up (infml), discouraged, disappointed, crestfallen, dismayed.
**E3** cheerful, happy, elated.

**downfall** n fall, ruin, failure, collapse, destruction, disgrace, debacle, undoing, overthrow.

**downgrade** v **1** DEGRADE, demote, lower, humble. **2** DISPARAGE, denigrate, belittle, run down, decry.
**E3 1** upgrade, improve. **2** praise.

**downhearted** adj depressed, dejected, despondent, sad, downcast, discouraged, disheartened, low-spirited, unhappy, gloomy, glum, dismayed.
**E3** cheerful, enthusiastic.

**downpour** n cloudburst, deluge, rainstorm, flood, inundation, torrent.

**downright** adj, adv absolute(ly), outright, plain(ly), utter(ly), clear(ly), complete(ly), out-and-out, frank(ly), explicit(ly).

**down-trodden** adj oppressed, subjugated, subservient, exploited, trampled on, abused, tyrannized, victimized, helpless.

**downward** adj descending, declining, downhill, sliding, slipping.
**E3** upward.

**dowse** see **douse**.

**doze** v sleep, nod off, drop off, snooze (infml), kip (infml), zizz (sl).
n nap, catnap, siesta, snooze (infml), forty winks (infml), kip (infml), shut-eye (infml), zizz (sl).

**drab** adj dull, dingy, dreary, dismal, gloomy, flat, grey, lacklustre, cheerless, sombre, shabby.
**E3** bright, cheerful.

**draft**[1] v draw (up), outline, sketch, plan, design, formulate, compose.
n outline, sketch, plan, delineation, abstract, rough, blueprint, protocol (fml).

**draft**[2] n bill of exchange, cheque, money order, letter of credit, postal order.

**drag** v **1** DRAW, pull, haul, lug, tug, trail, tow. **2** GO SLOWLY, creep, crawl, lag.
n (infml) bore, annoyance, nuisance, pain (infml), bother.

**drain** v **1** EMPTY, remove, evacuate, draw off, strain, dry, milk, bleed.
**2** DISCHARGE, trickle, flow out, leak, ooze. **3** EXHAUST, consume, sap, use up, deplete, drink up, swallow.
**E3 1** fill.
n **1** CHANNEL, conduit, culvert, duct, outlet, trench, ditch, pipe, sewer.
**2** DEPLETION, exhaustion, sap, strain.

**drama** n **1** PLAY, acting, theatre, show, spectacle, stage-craft, scene, melodrama. **2** EXCITEMENT, crisis, turmoil.

**dramatic** adj **1** EXCITING, striking, stirring, thrilling, marked, significant, expressive, impressive.
**2** HISTRIONIC, exaggerated, melodramatic, flamboyant.

**dramatize** v **1** STAGE, put on, adapt. **2** ACT, play-act, exaggerate, overdo, overstate.

**drape** v cover, wrap, hang, fold, drop, suspend.

**drastic** adj extreme, radical, strong, forceful, severe, harsh, far-reaching, desperate, dire.
F3 moderate, cautious.

**draught** n 1 PUFF, current, influx, flow. 2 DRINK, potion, quantity. 3 PULLING, traction.

**draw** v 1 ATTRACT, allure, entice, bring in, influence, persuade, elicit. 2 PULL, drag, haul, tow, tug. 3 DELINEATE, map out, sketch, portray, trace, pencil, depict, design. 4 TIE, be equal, be even.
F3 1 repel. 2 push.
n 1 ATTRACTION, enticement, lure, appeal, bait, interest. 2 TIE, stalemate, dead-heat.

**draw out** protract, extend, prolong, drag out, spin out, elongate, stretch, lengthen, string out.
F3 shorten.

**draw up** 1 DRAFT, compose, formulate, prepare, frame, write out. 2 PULL UP, stop, halt, run in.

**drawback** n disadvantage, snag, hitch, obstacle, impediment, hindrance, difficulty, flaw, fault, fly in the ointment (infml), catch, stumbling block, nuisance, trouble, defect, handicap, deficiency, imperfection.
F3 advantage, benefit.

**drawing** n sketch, picture, outline, representation, delineation, portrayal, illustration, cartoon, graphic, portrait.

**dread** v fear, shrink from, quail, cringe at, flinch, shy, shudder, tremble.
n fear, apprehension, misgiving, trepidation, dismay, alarm, horror, terror, fright, disquiet, worry, quietly, qualm.
F3 confidence, security.

**dreadful** adj awful, terrible, frightful, horrible, appalling, dire,

shocking, ghastly, horrendous, tragic, grievous, hideous, tremendous.
F3 wonderful, comforting.

**dream** n 1 VISION, illusion, reverie, trance, fantasy, daydream, nightmare, hallucination, delusion, imagination. 2 ASPIRATION, wish, hope, ambition, desire, pipe-dream, ideal, goal, design, speculation.
v imagine, envisage, fancy, fantasize, daydream, hallucinate, conceive, visualize, conjure up, muse.

**dream up** invent, devise, conceive, think up, imagine, concoct, hatch, create, spin, contrive.

**dreamer** n idealist, visionary, fantasizes, romancer, daydreamer, star-gazer, theorizer.
F3 realist, pragmatist.

**dreamy** adj 1 FANTASTIC, unreal, imaginary, shadowy, vague, misty. 2 IMPRACTICAL, fanciful, daydreaming, romantic, visionary, faraway, absent, musing, pensive.
F3 1 real. 2 practical, down-to-earth.

**dreary** adj 1 a dreary job: boring, tedious, uneventful, dull, humdrum, routine, monotonous, wearisome, commonplace, colourless, lifeless. 2 a dreary landscape: gloomy, depressing, drab, dismal, bleak, sombre, sad, mournful.
F3 1 interesting. 2 cheerful.

**dregs** n 1 SEDIMENT, deposit, residue, lees, grounds, scum, dross, trash, waste. 2 OUTCASTS, rabble, riff-raff, scum, down-and-outs.

**drench** v soak, saturate, steep, wet, douse, souse, immerse, inundate, duck, flood, imbue, drown.

**dress** n 1 FROCK, gown, robe. 2 CLOTHES, clothing, garment(s), outfit, costume, garb, get-up (infml), gear (infml), togs (infml).
v 1 CLOTHE, put on, garb, rig, robe, wear, don, decorate, deck, garnish, trim, adorn, fit, drape. 2 ARRANGE, adjust, dispose, prepare, groom, straighten. 3 BANDAGE, tend, treat.

**⊟ 1** strip, undress.

**dress up** beautify, adorn, embellish, improve, deck, doll up, tart up (*infml*), gild, disguise.

**dribble** *v* **1** TRICKLE, drip, leak, run, seep, drop, ooze. **2** DROOL, slaver, slobber, drivel.

**drift** *v* **1** WANDER, waft, stray, float, freewheel, coast. **2** GATHER, accumulate, pile up, drive.

*n* **1** ACCUMULATION, mound, pile, bank, mass, heap. **2** TREND, tendency, course, direction, flow, movement, current, rush, sweep. **3** MEANING, intention, implication, gist, tenor, thrust, significance, aim, design, scope.

**drill** *v* **1** TEACH, train, instruct, coach, practise, school, rehearse, exercise, discipline. **2** BORE, pierce, penetrate, puncture, perforate.

*n* **1** INSTRUCTION, training, practice, coaching, exercise, repetition, tuition, preparation, discipline. **2** BORER, awl, bit, gimlet.

**drink** *v* **1** IMBIBE, swallow, sip, drain, down, gulp, swig (*infml*), knock back (*infml*), sup, quaff, absorb, guzzle, partake of (*fml*), swill. **2** GET DRUNK, booze (*infml*), tipple (*infml*), indulge, carouse, revel, tank up (*infml*).

*n* **1** BEVERAGE, liquid, refreshment, draught, sip, swallow, swig (*infml*), gulp. **2** ALCOHOL, spirits, booze (*infml*), liquor, tipple (*infml*), tot, the bottle (*infml*), stiffener (*infml*).

*Alcoholic drinks include*: ale, beer, cider, lager, shandy, stout, Guinness®; aquavit, Armagnac, bourbon, brandy, Calvados, Cognac, gin, gin-and-tonic, pink gin, sloe gin, rum, grog, rye, vodka, whisky, Scotch and soda, hot toddy; wine, red wine, vin rouge, vin rosé, white wine, vin blanc, Beaujolais, Beaune, Bordeaux, burgundy, claret, mulled wine, muscatel, Chianti, Graves, Rioja,

Chablis, champagne, bubbly (*infml*), hock, Moselle, Riesling, Sauterne, mead, perry, vino (*infml*), plonk (*infml*); absinthe, advocaat, Benedictine, Chartreuse, black velvet, bloody Mary, Buck's fizz, Campari, cherry brandy, cocktail, Cointreau®, crème de menthe, daiquiri, eggnog, ginger wine, kirsch, Marsala, Martini®, ouzo, Pernod®, piña colada, port, punch, retsina, sake, sangria, schnapps, sherry, snowball, tequila, Tom Collins, vermouth.

**drip** *v* drop, dribble, trickle, plop, perculate, drizzle, splash, sprinkle, weep.

*n* **1** DROP, trickle, dribble, leak, bead, tear. **2** (*infml*) WEAKLING, wimp (*infml*), softy (*infml*), bore, wet (*infml*), ninny (*infml*).

**drive** *v* **1** DIRECT, control, manage, operate, run, handle, motivate. **2** FORCE, compel, impel, coerce, constrain, press, push, urge, dragoon, gpad, goad, oblige. **3** STEER, motor, propel, ride, travel.

*n* **1** ENERGY, enterprise, ambition, initiative, get-up-and-go (*infml*), vigour, motivation, determination. **2** CAMPAIGN, crusade, appeal, effort, action. **3** EXCURSION, outing, journey, ride, spin, trip, jaunt. **4** URGE, instinct, impulse, need, desire.

**drive at** imply, allude to, intimate, mean, suggest, hint, get at, intend, refer to, signify, insinuate, indicate.

**driving** *adj* compelling, forceful, vigorous, dynamic, energetic, forthright, heavy, violent, sweeping.

**drizzle** *n* mist, mizzle, rain, spray, shower.

*v* spit, sprinkle, rain, spot, shower.

**droop** *v* **1** HANG (DOWN), dangle, sag, bend. **2** LANGUISH, decline, flag, falter, slump, lose heart, wilt, wither, drop, faint, fall down, fade, slouch. **3** sink.

**E3 1** straighten. **2** flourish, rise.

**drop** *n* **1** DROPLET, bead, tear, drip, bubble, globule, trickle. **2** DASH, pinch, spot, sip, trace, dab. **3** FALL, decline, falling-off, lowering, downturn, decrease, reduction, slump, plunge, deterioration.

**4** DESCENT, precipice, slope, chasm, abyss.

*v* **1** FALL, sink, decline, plunge, plummet, tumble, dive, descend, lower, droop, depress, diminish.

**2** ABANDON, forsake, desert, give up, relinquish, reject, jilt, leave, renounce, throw over, repudiate, cease, discontinue, quit.

**E3 1** rise.

**drop off 1** NOD OFF, doze, snooze (*infml*), have forty winks (*infml*).

**2** DECLINE, fall off, decrease, dwindle, lessen, diminish, slacken. **3** DELIVER, set down, leave.

**E3 1** wake up. **2** increase. **3** pick up.

**drop out** back out, abandon, cry off, withdraw, forsake, leave, quit.

**drought** *n* dryness, aridity, parchedness, dehydration, desiccation, shortage, want.

**drove** *n* herd, horde, gathering, crowd, multitude, swarm, throng, flock, company, mob, press.

**drown** *v* **1** SUBMERGE, immerse, inundate, go under, flood, sink, deluge, engulf, drench.

**2** OVERWHELM, overpower, overcome, swamp, wipe out, extinguish.

**drowsy** *adj* sleepy, tired, lethargic, nodding, dreamy, dozy, somnolent (*fml*).

**E3** alert, awake.

**drudge** *n* toiler, menial, dogsbody (*infml*), hack, servant, slave, factotum, worker, skivvy (*infml*), galley-slave, lackey.

*v* plod, toil, work, slave, plug away (*infml*), grind (*infml*), labour, beaver (*infml*).

**E3** idle, laze.

**drudgery** *n* labour, donkey-work (*infml*), hack-work, slog (*infml*), grind (*infml*), slavery, sweat, sweated labour, toil, skivvying, chore.

**drug** *n* medication, medicine, remedy, potion.

> *Types of drug include*: anaesthetic, analgesic, antibiotic, antidepressant, antihistamine, barbiturate, narcotic, opiate, hallucinogenic, sedative, steroid, stimulant, tranquillizer; chloroform, aspirin, codeine, paracetamol, morphine, penicillin, diazepam, Valium®, cortisone, insulin, digitalis, laudanum, quinine, progesterone, oestrogen, cannabis, marijuana, smack, LSD, acid, ecstasy, E (*sl*), heroin, opium, cocaine, crack, dope (*infml*). *see also* **medicine**.

*v* medicate, sedate, tranquillize, dope (*infml*), anaesthetize, dose, knock out (*infml*), stupefy, deaden, numb.

**drum** *v* beat, pulsate, tap, throb, thrum, tattoo, reverberate, rap.

**drum up** obtain, round up, collect, gather, solicit, canvass, petition, attract.

**drunk** *adj* inebriated, intoxicated, under the influence, drunken, stoned (*sl*), legless (*sl*), paralytic (*infml*), sloshed (*infml*), merry (*infml*), tight (*infml*), tipsy (*infml*), tanked up (*infml*), tiddly (*infml*), plastered (*infml*), loaded (*infml*), lit up (*infml*), sozzled (*infml*), well-oiled (*infml*), canned (*sl*), blotto (*sl*).

**E3** sober, temperate, abstinent, teetotal.

**drunkard** *n* drunk, inebriate, alcoholic, dipsomaniac, boozer (*infml*), wino (*infml*), tippler (*infml*), soak (*infml*), lush (*infml*), sot (*infml*).

**dry** *adj* **1** ARID, parched, thirsty, dehydrated, desiccated, barren.

**2** BORING, dull, dreary, tedious,

monotonous. **3** *dry humour*: ironic, cynical, droll, deadpan, sarcastic, cutting.

**⊟ 1** wet. **2** interesting.

*v* dehydrate, parch, desiccate, drain, shrivel, wither.

**⊟** soak.

**dual** *adj* double, twofold, duplicate, duplex, binary, combined, paired, twin, matched.

**dubious** *adj* **1** DOUBTFUL, uncertain, undecided, unsure, wavering, unsettled, suspicious, sceptical, hesitant. **2** QUESTIONABLE, debatable, unreliable, ambiguous, suspect, obscure, fishy (*infml*), shady (*infml*).

**⊟ 1** certain. **2** trustworthy.

**duck** *v* **1** CROUCH, stoop, bob, bend. **2** AVOID, dodge, evade, shirk, sidestep. **3** DIP, immerse, plunge, dunk, dive, submerge, douse, souse, wet, lower.

**due** *adj* **1** OWED, owing, payable, unpaid, outstanding, in arrears. **2** RIGHTFUL, fitting, appropriate, proper, merited, deserved, justified, suitable. **3** ADEQUATE, enough, sufficient, ample, plenty of. **4** EXPECTED, scheduled.

**⊟ 1** paid. **3** inadequate.

*adv* exactly, direct(ly), precisely, straight, dead (*infml*).

**duel** *n* affair of honour, combat, contest, fight, clash, competition, rivalry, encounter.

**dull** *adj* **1** BORING, uninteresting, unexciting, flat, dreary, monotonous, tedious, uneventful, humdrum, unimaginative, dismal, lifeless, plain, insipid, heavy. **2** DARK, gloomy, drab, murky, indistinct, grey, cloudy, lack-lustre, opaque, dim, overcast. **3** UNINTELLIGENT, dense, dim, dimwitted (*infml*), thick (*infml*), stupid, slow.

**⊟ 1** interesting, exciting. **2** bright. **3** intelligent, clever.

*v* **1** BLUNT, alleviate, mitigate,

moderate, lessen, relieve, soften. **2** DEADEN, numb, paralyse. **3** DISCOURAGE, dampen, subdue, sadden. **4** DIM, obscure, fade.

**dumb** *adj* silent, mute, soundless, speechless, tongue-tied, inarticulate, mum (*infml*).

**dumbfounded** *adj* astonished, amazed, astounded, overwhelmed, speechless, taken aback, thrown (*infml*), startled, overcome, confounded, flabbergasted (*infml*), staggered, confused, bowled over, dumb, floored (*infml*), paralysed.

**dummy** *n* **1** COPY, duplicate, imitation, counterfeit, substitute. **2** MODEL, lay-figure, mannequin, figure, form. **3** TEAT, pacifier.

*adj* **1** ARTIFICIAL, fake, imitation, false, bogus, mock, sham, phoney. **2** SIMULATED, practice, trial.

**dump** *v* **1** DEPOSIT, drop, offload, throw down, let fall, unload, empty out, discharge, park. **2** GET RID OF, scrap, throw away, dispose of, ditch, tip, jettison.

*n* **1** RUBBISH-TIP, junk-yard, rubbish-heap, tip. **2** HOVEL, slum, shack, shanty, hole (*infml*), joint (*infml*), pigsty, mess.

**dungeon** *n* cell, prison, jail, gaol, cage, lock-up, keep, oubliette, vault.

**dupe** *n* victim, sucker (*infml*), fool, gull, mug (*infml*), push-over (*infml*), fall guy (*infml*), pawn, puppet, instrument, stooge (*infml*), simpleton.

*v* deceive, delude, fool, trick, outwit, con (*infml*), cheat, hoax, swindle, rip off (*infml*), take in, hoodwink, defraud, bamboozle (*infml*).

**duplicate** *adj* identical, matching, twin, twofold, corresponding, matched.

*n* copy, replica, reproduction, photocopy, carbon (copy), match, facsimile.

*v* copy, reproduce, repeat, photocopy, double, clone, echo.

**durable** *adj* lasting, enduring, long-lasting, abiding, hard-wearing, strong, sturdy, tough, unfading, substantial, sound, reliable, dependable, stable, resistant, persistent, constant, permanent, firm, fixed, fast.
**F3** perishable, weak, fragile.

**duress** *n* constraint, coercion, compulsion, pressure, restraint, threat, force.

**dusk** *n* twilight, sunset, nightfall, evening, sundown, gloaming, darkness, dark, gloom, shadows, shade.
**F3** dawn, brightness.

**dust** *n* powder, particles, dirt, earth, soil, ground, grit, grime.

**dusty** *adj* **1** DIRTY, grubby, filthy. **2** POWDERY, granular, crumbly, chalky, sandy.
**F3** **1** clean. **2** solid, hard.

**dutiful** *adj* obedient, respectful, conscientious, devoted, filial, reverential, submissive.

**duty** *n* **1** OBLIGATION, responsibility, assignment, calling, charge, role, task, job, business, function, work, office, service. **2** OBEDIENCE, respect, loyalty. **3** TAX, toll, tariff, levy, customs, excise.
**on duty** at work, engaged, busy.

**dwarf** *n* **1** PERSON OF RESTRICTED GROWTH, midget, pygmy, Tom Thumb, Lilliputian. **2** GNOME, goblin.
*adj* miniature, small, tiny, pocket, mini (*infml*), diminutive, petite, Lilliputian, baby.
**F3** large.
*v* **1** STUNT, retard, check. **2** OVERSHADOW, tower over, dominate.

**dwell** *v* live, inhabit, reside, stay, settle, populate, people, lodge, rest, abide (*fml*).

**dwindle** *v* diminish, decrease, decline, lessen, subside, ebb, fade, weaken, taper off, tail off, shrink, peter out, fall, wane, waste away, die out, wither, shrivel, disappear.
**F3** increase, grow.

**dye** *n* colour, colouring, stain, pigment, tint, tinge.
*v* colour, tint, stain, pigment, tinge, imbue.

**dying** *adj* moribund, passing, final, going, mortal, not long for this world, perishing, failing, fading, vanishing.
**F3** reviving.

**dynamic** *adj* forceful, powerful, energetic, vigorous, go-ahead, high-powered, driving, self-starting, spirited, vital, lively, active.
**F3** inactive, apathetic.

**dynasty** *n* house, line, succession, dominion, regime, government, rule, empire, sovereignty.

# E

**eager** *adj* **1** KEEN, enthusiastic, fervent, intent, earnest, zealous. **2** LONGING, yearning.
**F3** **1** unenthusiastic, indifferent.

**ear** *n* **1** ATTENTION, heed, notice, regard. **2** *an ear for language*: perception, sensitivity, discrimination, appreciation, hearing, skill, ability.

*Parts of the ear include*: anvil (incus), auditory canal, auditory nerve, auricle, cochlea, concha, eardrum, eustachian tube, hammer (malleus), helix, labyrinth, lobe, oval window, pinna, round window, semicircular canal, stirrup (stapes), tragus, tympanum, vestibular nerve, vestibule.

**early** adj **1** *early symptoms*: forward, advanced, premature, untimely, undeveloped. **2** *early theatre*: primitive, ancient, primeval.
adv ahead of time, in good time, beforehand, in advance, prematurely.
**F∃** late.

**earn** v **1** *earn a good salary*: receive, obtain, make, get, draw, bring in (*infml*), gain, realize, gross, reap. **2** *earn one's reputation*: deserve, merit, warrant, win, rate.
**F∃** **1** spend, lose.

**earnest** adj **1** RESOLUTE, devoted, ardent, conscientious, intent, keen, fervent, firm, fixed, eager, enthusiastic, steady. **2** SERIOUS, sincere, solemn, grave, heartfelt.
**F∃** **1** apathetic. **2** frivolous, flippant.

**earnings** n pay, income, salary, wages, profits, gain, proceeds, reward, receipts, return, revenue, remuneration, stipend.
**F∃** expenditure, outgoings.

**earth** n **1** WORLD, planet, globe, sphere. **2** LAND, ground, soil, clay, loam, sod, humus.

**earthenware** n pottery, ceramics, crockery, pots.

**earthly** adj **1** *our earthly life*: material, physical, human, worldly, mortal, mundane, fleshly, secular, sensual, profane, temporal. **2** *no earthly explanation*: possible, likely, conceivable, slightest.
**F∃** **1** spiritual, heavenly.

**earthy** adj crude, coarse, vulgar, bawdy, rough, raunchy (*infml*), down-to-earth, ribald, robust.
**F∃** refined, modest.

**ease** n **1** FACILITY, effortlessness, skilfulness, deftness, dexterity, naturalness, cleverness. **2** COMFORT, contentment, peace, affluence, repose, leisure, relaxation, rest, quiet,

happiness.
**F∃** **1** difficulty. **2** discomfort.
v **1** *ease the pain*: alleviate, moderate, lessen, lighten, relieve, mitigate, abate, relent, allay, assuage, relax, comfort, calm, soothe, facilitate, smooth.
**2** *ease it into position*: inch, steer, slide, still.
**F∃** **1** aggravate, intensify, worsen.

**easily** adv **1** EFFORTLESSLY, comfortably, readily, simply. **2** BY FAR, undoubtedly, indisputably, definitely, certainly, doubtlessly, clearly, far and away, undeniably, simply, surely, probably, well.
**F∃** **1** laboriously.

**easy** adj **1** EFFORTLESS, simple, uncomplicated, undemanding, straightforward, manageable, cushy (*infml*). **2** RELAXED, carefree, easy-going, comfortable, informal, calm, natural, leisurely.
**F∃** **1** difficult, demanding, exacting.
**2** tense, uneasy.

**easy-going** adj relaxed, tolerant, laid-back (*infml*), amenable, happy-go-lucky (*infml*), carefree, calm, even-tempered, serene.
**F∃** strict, intolerant, critical.

**eat** v **1** CONSUME, feed, swallow, devour, chew, scoff (*infml*), munch, dine. **2** CORRODE, erode, wear away, decay, rot, crumble, dissolve.

**eatable** adj edible, palatable, good, wholesome, digestible, comestible (*fml*), harmless.
**F∃** inedible, unpalatable.

**eavesdrop** v listen in, spy, overhear, snoop (*infml*), tap (*infml*), bug (*infml*), monitor.

**eccentric** adj odd, peculiar, abnormal, unconventional, strange, quirky, weird, way-out (*infml*), queer, outlandish, idiosyncratic, bizarre, freakish, erratic, singular, dotty.
**F∃** conventional, orthodox, normal.
n nonconformist, oddball (*infml*), oddity, crank (*infml*), freak (*infml*),

character (*infml*).

**eccentricity** *n*
UNCONVENTIONALITY, strangeness,
peculiarity, nonconformity,
abnormality, oddity, weirdness,
idiosyncrasy, singularity, quirk,
freakishness, aberration, anomaly,
capriciousness.
☒ conventionality, ordinariness.

**ecclesiastical** *adj* church, churchly,
religious, clerical, priestly, divine,
spiritual.

**echo** *v* 1 REVERBERATE, resound,
repeat, reflect, reiterate, ring.
2 IMITATE, copy, reproduce, mirror,
resemble, mimic.
*n* 1 REVERBERATION, reiteration,
repetition, reflection. 2 IMITATION,
copy, reproduction, mirror image,
image, parallel.

**eclipse** *v* 1 BLOT OUT, obscure,
cloud, veil, darken, dim. 2 OUTDO,
overshadow, outshine, surpass,
transcend.
*n* 1 OBSCURATION, overshadowing,
darkening, shading, dimming.
2 DECLINE, failure, fall, loss.

**economic** *adj* 1 COMMERCIAL,
business, industrial. 2 FINANCIAL,
budgetary, fiscal, monetary.
3 PROFITABLE, profit-making,
money-making, productive, cost-
effective, viable.

**economical** *adj* 1 THRIFTY, careful,
prudent, saving, sparing, frugal.
2 CHEAP, inexpensive, low-priced,
reasonable, cost-effective, modest,
efficient.
☒ 1 wasteful. 2 expensive,
uneconomical.

**economize** *v* save, cut back, tighten
one's belt (*infml*), cut costs.
☒ waste, squander.

**economy** *n* thrift, saving, restraint,
prudence, frugality, parsimony,
providence, husbandry.
☒ extravagance.

**ecstasy** *n* delight, rapture, bliss,
elation, joy, euphoria, frenzy,

exaltation, fervour.
☒ misery, torment.

**ecstatic** *adj* elated, blissful, joyful,
rapturous, overjoyed, euphoric,
delirious, frenzied, fervent.
☒ downcast.

**eddy** *n* whirlpool, swirl, vortex,
twist.
*v* swirl, whirl.

**edge** *n* 1 BORDER, rim, boundary,
limit, brim, threshold, brink, fringe,
margin, outline, side, verge, line,
perimeter, periphery, lip.
2 ADVANTAGE, superiority, force.
3 SHARPNESS, acuteness, keenness,
incisiveness, pungency, zest.
*v* creep, inch, ease, sidle.

**edgy** *adj* on edge, nervous, tense,
anxious, ill at ease, keyed-up, touchy,
irritable.
☒ calm.

**edible** *adj* eatable, palatable,
digestible, wholesome, good,
harmless.
☒ inedible.

**edict** *n* command, order,
proclamation, law, decree,
regulation, pronouncement, ruling,
mandate, statute, injunction,
manifesto.

**edifice** *n* building, construction,
structure, erection.

**edify** *v* instruct, improve, enlighten,
inform, guide, educate, nurture,
teach.

**edit** *v* correct, emend, revise, rewrite,
reorder, rearrange, adapt, check,
compile, rephrase, select, polish,
annotate, censor.

**edition** *n* copy, volume, impression,
printing, issue, version, number.

**educate** *v* teach, train, instruct,
tutor, coach, school, inform,
cultivate, edify, drill, improve,
discipline, develop.

**educated** *adj* learned, taught,
schooled, trained, knowledgeable,
informed, instructed, lettered,
cultured, civilized, tutored, refined,

well-bred.

≠ uneducated, uncultured.

**education** *n* teaching, training, schooling, tuition, tutoring, coaching, guidance, instruction, cultivation, culture, scholarship, improvement, enlightenment, knowledge, nurture, development.

*Educational establishments include*: kindergarten, nursery school, infant school, primary school, middle school, combined school, secondary school, secondary modern, upper school, high school, grammar school, grant-maintained school, preparatory school, public school, private school, boarding-school, college, sixth-form college, polytechnic, poly, city technical college, CTC, technical college, university, adult-education centre, academy, seminary, finishing school, business school, secretarial college, Sunday school, convent school, summer-school.

*Educational terms include*: adult education, assisted places scheme, A-level, baccalaureate, board of governors, break time, bursar, campus, catchment area, certificate, classroom, coeducation, common entrance, course, curriculum, degree, diploma, double-first, eleven-plus, enrolment, examination, exercise book, final exam, finals, further education, GCSE (General Certificate of Secondary Education), governor, graduation, half-term, head boy, head girl, head teacher, higher education, homework, intake, invigilator, lecture, literacy, matriculation, matron, mixed-ability teaching, modular course, national curriculum, NVQ (national vocational qualification), numeracy, O-level, opting out, parent governor, PTA (parent teacher association), playground, playtime, prefect, primary education, proctor, professor, pupil, quadrangle, qualification, refresher course, register, report, scholarship, school term, secondary education, special education, statemented, streaming, student, student grant, student loan, study, subject, syllabus, teacher, teacher training, test paper, textbook, thesis, timetable, truancy, university entrance, work experience, YTS (Youth Training Scheme).

**eerie** *adj* weird, strange, uncanny, spooky (*infml*), creepy, frightening, scary, spine-chilling.

**effect** *n* **1** OUTCOME, result, conclusion, consequence, upshot, aftermath, issue. **2** POWER, force, impact, efficacy, impression, strength. **3** MEANING, significance, import.

*v* cause, execute, create, achieve, accomplish, perform, produce, make, initiate, fulfil, complete.

**in effect** in fact, actually, really, in reality, to all intents and purposes, for all practical purposes, essentially, effectively, virtually.

**take effect** be effective, become operative, come into force, come into operation, be implemented, begin, work.

**effective** *adj* **1** EFFICIENT, efficacious, productive, adequate, capable, useful. **2** OPERATIVE, in force, functioning, current, active. **3** STRIKING, impressive, forceful, cogent, powerful, persuasive, convincing, telling.

≠ **1** ineffective, powerless.

**effects** *n* belongings, possessions, property, goods, gear (*infml*), movables, chattels (*fml*), things, trappings.

**effeminate** *adj* unmanly, womanly, womanish, feminine, sissy (*infml*), delicate.

**Ea** manly.

**effervescent** adj **1** BUBBLY, sparkling, fizzy, frothy, carbonated, foaming. **2** LIVELY, ebullient, vivacious, animated, buoyant, exhilarated, enthusiastic, exuberant, excited, vital.
**Ea 1** flat. **2** dull.

**efficiency** n effectiveness, competence, proficiency, skill, expertise, skilfulness, capability, ability, productivity.
**Ea** inefficiency, incompetence.

**efficient** adj effective, competent, proficient, skilful, capable, able, productive, well-organized, businesslike, powerful, well-conducted.
**Ea** inefficient, incompetent.

**effort** n **1** EXERTION, strain, application, struggle, trouble, energy, toil, striving, pains, travail (*fml*). **2** ATTEMPT, try, go (*infml*), endeavour, shot, stab. **3** ACHIEVEMENT, accomplishment, feat, exploit, production, creation, deed, product, work.

**effortless** adj easy, simple, undemanding, facile, painless, smooth.
**Ea** difficult.

**effrontery** n audacity, impertinence, insolence, cheek (*infml*), impudence, temerity, boldness, brazenness, cheekiness, gall, nerve, presumption, disrespect, arrogance, brashness.
**Ea** respect, timidity.

**effusive** adj fulsome, gushing, unrestrained, expansive, ebullient, demonstrative, profuse, overflowing, enthusiastic, exuberant, extravagant, lavish, talkative, voluble.
**Ea** reserved, restrained.

**egotism** n egoism, egomania, self-centredness, self-importance, conceitedness, self-regard, self-love, self-conceit, narcissism, self-admiration, vanity, bigheadedness (*infml*).

**Ea** humility.

**egotistic** adj egoistic, egocentric, self-centred, self-important, conceited, vain, swollen-headed (*infml*), bigheaded (*infml*), boasting, bragging.
**Ea** humble.

**ejaculate** v **1** DISCHARGE, eject, spurt, emit. **2** EXCLAIM, call, blurt (out), cry, shout, yell, utter, scream.

**eject** v **1** EMIT, expel, discharge, spout, spew, evacuate, vomit. **2** OUST, evict, throw out, drive out, turn out, expel, remove, banish, deport, dismiss, exile, kick out, fire (*infml*), sack (*infml*).

**elaborate** adj **1** *elaborate plans*: detailed, careful, thorough, exact, extensive, painstaking, precise, perfected, minute, laboured, studied. **2** *elaborate design*: intricate, complex, complicated, involved, ornamental, ornate, fancy, decorated, ostentatious, showy, fussy.
**Ea 2** simple, plain.
v amplify, develop, enlarge, expand, flesh out, polish, improve, refine, devise, explain.
**Ea** précis, simplify.

**elapse** v pass, lapse, go by, slip away.

**elastic** adj **1** PLIABLE, flexible, stretchable, supple, resilient, yielding, springy, rubbery, pliant, plastic, bouncy, buoyant. **2** ADAPTABLE, accommodating, flexible, tolerant, adjustable.
**Ea 1** rigid. **2** inflexible.

**elasticity** n **1** PLIABILITY, flexibility, resilience, stretch, springiness, suppleness, give, plasticity, bounce, buoyancy. **2** ADAPTABILITY, flexibility, tolerance, adjustability.
**Ea 1** rigidity. **2** inflexibility.

**elated** adj exhilarated, excited, euphoric, ecstatic, exultant, jubilant, overjoyed, joyful.

**ES** despondent, downcast.

**elbow** v jostle, nudge, push, shove, bump, crowd, knock, shoulder.

**elder** adj older, senior, first-born, ancient.
**ES** younger.

**elderly** adj aging, aged, old, hoary, senile.
**ES** young, youthful.

**elect** v choose, pick, opt for, select, vote for, prefer, adopt, designate, appoint, determine.
adj choice, elite, chosen, designated, designate, picked, prospective, selected, to be, preferred, hand-picked.

**election** n choice, selection, voting, ballot, poll, appointment, determination, decision, preference.

**elector** n selector, voter, constituent.

**electric** adj electrifying, exciting, stimulating, thrilling, charged, dynamic, stirring, tense, rousing.
**ES** unexciting, flat.

**electrify** v thrill, excite, shock, invigorate, animate, stimulate, stir, rouse, fire, jolt, galvanize, amaze, astonish, astound, stagger.
**ES** bore.

**elegant** adj stylish, chic, fashionable, modish, smart, refined, polished, genteel, smooth, tasteful, fine, exquisite, beautiful, graceful, handsome, delicate, neat, artistic.
**ES** inelegant, unrefined, unfashionable.

**elegy** n dirge, lament, requiem, plaint.

**element** n factor, component, constituent, ingredient, member, part, piece, fragment, feature, trace.
**ES** whole.

**elementary** adj basic, fundamental, rudimentary, principal, primary, clear, easy, introductory, straightforward, uncomplicated, simple.
**ES** advanced.

**elements** n basics, fundamentals,

foundations, principles, rudiments, essentials.

**elevate** v 1 LIFT, raise, hoist, heighten, intensify, magnify. 2 EXALT, advance, promote, aggrandize, upgrade. 3 UPLIFT, rouse, boost, brighten.
**ES** 1 lower. 2 downgrade.

**elevated** adj raised, lofty, exalted, high, grand, noble, dignified, sublime.
**ES** base.

**elevation** n 1 RISE, promotion, advancement, preferment, aggrandizement. 2 EXALTATION, loftiness, grandeur, eminence, nobility. 3 HEIGHT, altitude, hill, rise.
**ES** 1 demotion. 2 dip.

**elicit** v evoke, draw out, derive, extract, obtain, exact, extort, cause.

**eligible** adj qualified, fit, appropriate, suitable, acceptable, worthy, proper, desirable.
**ES** ineligible.

**eliminate** v remove, get rid of, cut out, take out, exclude, delete, dispense with, rub out, omit, reject, disregard, dispose of, drop, do away with, eradicate, expel, extinguish, stamp out, exterminate, knock out, kill, murder.
**ES** include, accept.

**elite** n best, elect, aristocracy, upper classes, nobility, gentry, crème de la crème, establishment, high society.
adj choice, best, exclusive, selected, first-class, aristocratic, noble, upper-class.

**elocution** n delivery, articulation, diction, enunciation, pronunciation, oratory, rhetoric, speech, utterance.

**elongated** adj lengthened, extended, prolonged, protracted, stretched, long.

**elope** v run off, run away, decamp, bolt, abscond, do a bunk (infml), escape, steal away, leave, disappear.

**eloquent** adj articulate, fluent, well-

**elucidate** v explain, clarify, clear up, interpret, spell out, illustrate, unfold.
Fa confuse.

**elude** v 1 AVOID, escape, evade, dodge, shirk, duck (*infml*), flee. 2 PUZZLE, frustrate, baffle, confound, thwart, stump, foil.

**elusive** adj 1 INDEFINABLE, intangible, unanalysable, subtle, puzzling, baffling, transient, transitory. 2 EVASIVE, shifty, slippery, tricky.

**emaciated** adj thin, gaunt, lean, haggard, wasted, scrawny, skeletal, pinched, attenuated, meagre, lank.
Fa plump, well-fed.

**emanate** v 1 ORIGINATE, proceed, arise, derive, issue, spring, stem, flow, come, emerge. 2 DISCHARGE, send out, emit, give out, give off, radiate.

**emancipate** v free, liberate, release, set free, enfranchise, deliver, discharge, loose, unchain, unshackle, unfetter.
Fa enslave.

**embankment** n causeway, dam, rampart, levee, earthwork.

**embargo** n restriction, ban, prohibition, restraint, proscription, bar, barrier, interdiction (*fml*), impediment, check, hindrance, blockage, stoppage, seizure.

**embark** v board (ship), go aboard, take ship.
Fa disembark.

**embark on** begin, start, commence, set about, launch, undertake, enter, initiate, engage.
Fa complete, finish.

**embarrass** v disconcert, mortify, show up, discompose, fluster, humiliate, shame, distress.

**embarrassment** n

1 DISCOMPOSURE, self-consciousness, chagrin, mortification, humiliation, shame, awkwardness, confusion, bashfulness. 2 DIFFICULTY, constraint, predicament, distress, discomfort.

**embellish** v adorn, ornament, decorate, deck, dress up, beautify, gild, garnish, festoon, elaborate, embroider, enrich, exaggerate, enhance, varnish, grace.
Fa simplify, denude.

**embellishment** n adornment, ornament, ornamentation, decoration, elaboration, garnish, trimming, gilding, enrichment, enhancement, embroidery, exaggeration.

**embezzle** v appropriate, misappropriate, steal, pilfer, filch, pinch (*infml*).

**embezzlement** n appropriation, misappropriation, pilfering, fraud, stealing, theft, filching.

**embittered** adj bitter, disaffected, sour, disillusioned.

**emblem** n symbol, sign, token, representation, logo, insignia, device, crest, mark, badge, figure.

**embodiment** n incarnation, personification, exemplification, expression, epitome, example, incorporation, realization, representation, manifestation, concentration.

**embody** v 1 PERSONIFY, exemplify, represent, stand for, symbolize, incorporate, express, manifest. 2 INCLUDE, contain, integrate.

**embrace** v 1 HUG, clasp, cuddle, hold, grasp, squeeze. 2 INCLUDE, encompass, incorporate, contain, comprise, cover, involve. 3 ACCEPT, take up, welcome.
n hug, cuddle, clasp, clinch (*infml*).

**embroil** v involve, implicate, entangle, enmesh, mix up, incriminate.

**embryo** n nucleus, germ, beginning,

root.

**embryonic** *adj* undeveloped, rudimentary, immature, early, germinal, primary.
🖙 developed.

**emerge** *v* 1 ARISE, rise, surface, appear, develop, crop up (*infml*), transpire, turn up, materialize.
2 EMANATE, issue, proceed.
🖙 1 disappear.

**emergence** *n* appearance, rise, advent, coming, dawn, development, arrival, disclosure, issue.
🖙 disappearance.

**emergency** *n* crisis, danger, difficulty, exigency (*fml*), predicament, plight, pinch, strait, quandary.

**emigrate** *n* migrate, relocate, move, depart.

**eminence** *n* distinction, fame, pre-eminence, prominence, renown, reputation, greatness, importance, esteem, note, prestige, rank.

**eminent** *adj* distinguished, famous, prominent, illustrious, outstanding, notable, pre-eminent, prestigious, celebrated, renowned, noteworthy, conspicuous, esteemed, important, well-known, elevated, respected, great, high-ranking, grand, superior.
🖙 unknown, obscure, unimportant.

**emissary** *n* ambassador, agent, envoy, messenger, delegate, herald, courier, representative, scout, deputy, spy.

**emission** *n* discharge, issue, ejection, emanation, ejaculation, diffusion, transmission, exhalation, radiation, release, exudation, vent.

**emit** *v* discharge, issue, eject, emanate, exude, give out, give off, diffuse, radiate, release, shed, vent.
🖙 absorb.

**emotion** *n* feeling, passion, sensation, sentiment, ardour, fervour, warmth, reaction, vehemence, excitement.

**emotional** *adj* 1 FEELING,

passionate, sensitive, responsive, ardent, tender, warm, roused, demonstrative, excitable, enthusiastic, fervent, impassioned, moved, sentimental, zealous, hot-blooded, heated, tempestuous, overcharged, temperamental, fiery.
2 EMOTIVE, moving, poignant, thrilling, touching, stirring, heart-warming, exciting, pathetic.
🖙 1 unemotional, cold, detached, calm.

**emphasis** *n* stress, weight, significance, importance, priority, underscoring, accent, force, power, prominence, pre-eminence, attention, intensity, strength, urgency, positiveness, insistence, mark, moment.

**emphasize** *v* stress, accentuate, underline, highlight, accent, feature, dwell on, weight, point up, spotlight, play up, insist on, press home, intensify, strengthen, punctuate.
🖙 play down, understate.

**emphatic** *adj* forceful, positive, insistent, certain, definite, decided, unequivocal, absolute, categorical, earnest, marked, pronounced, significant, strong, striking, vigorous, distinct, energetic, forcible, important, impressive, momentous, powerful, punctuated, telling, vivid, graphic, direct.
🖙 tentative, hesitant, understated.

**empire** *n* 1 SUPREMACY, sovereignty, rule, authority, command, government, jurisdiction, control, power, sway. 2 DOMAIN, dominion, kingdom, realm, commonwealth, territory.

**employ** *v* 1 ENGAGE, hire, take on, recruit, enlist, commission, retain, fill, occupy, take up. 2 USE, utilize, make use of, apply, bring to bear, ply, exercise.

**employee** *n* worker, member of staff, job-holder, hand, wage-earner.

**employer** *n* boss, proprietor, owner,

manager, gaffer (*infml*), management, company, firm, business, establishment.

**employment** n 1 JOB, work, occupation, situation, business, calling, profession, line (*infml*), vocation, trade, pursuit, craft. 2 ENLISTMENT, employ, engagement, hire.
≠ 1 unemployment.

**empower** v authorize, warrant, enable, license, sanction, permit, entitle, commission, delegate, qualify.

**emptiness** n 1 VACUUM, vacantness, void, hollowness, hunger, bareness, barrenness, desolation. 2 FUTILITY, meaninglessness, worthlessness, aimlessness, ineffectiveness, unreality.
≠ 1 fullness.

**empty** adj 1 VACANT, void, unoccupied, uninhabited, unfilled, deserted, bare, hollow, desolate, blank, clear. 2 FUTILE, aimless, meaningless, senseless, trivial, vain, worthless, useless, insubstantial, ineffective, insincere. 3 VACUOUS, inane, expressionless, blank, vacant.
≠ 1 full. 2 meaningful.
v drain, exhaust, discharge, clear, evacuate, vacate, pour out, unload, void, gut.
≠ fill.

**empty-headed** adj inane, silly, frivolous, scatter-brained (*infml*), feather-brained (*infml*).

**emulate** v match, copy, mimic, follow, imitate, echo, compete with, contend with, rival, vie with.

**enable** v equip, qualify, empower, authorize, sanction, warrant, allow, permit, prepare, fit, facilitate, license, commission, endue.
≠ prevent, inhibit, forbid.

**enact** v 1 DECREE, ordain, order, authorize, command, legislate, sanction, ratify, pass, establish. 2 ACT (OUT), perform, play,

portray, represent, depict.
≠ 1 repeal, rescind.

**enamoured** adj charmed, infatuated, in love with, enchanted, captivated, entranced, smitten, keen, taken, fascinated, fond.

**enchant** v 1 CAPTIVATE, charm, fascinate, enrapture, attract, allure, appeal, delight, thrill. 2 ENTRANCE, enthral, bewitch, spellbind, hypnotize, mesmerize.
≠ 1 repel.

**enclose** v encircle, encompass, surround, fence, hedge, hem in, bound, encase, embrace, envelop, confine, hold, shut in, wrap, pen, cover, circumscribe, incorporate, include, insert, contain, comprehend.

**enclosure** n pen, pound, compound, paddock, fold, stockade, sty, arena, corral, court, ring, cloister.

**encompass** v 1 ENCIRCLE, circle, ring, surround, gird, envelop, circumscribe, hem in, enclose, hold. 2 INCLUDE, cover, embrace, contain, comprise, admit, incorporate, involve, embody, comprehend.

**encounter** v 1 MEET, come across, run into (*infml*), happen on, chance upon, run across, confront, face, experience. 2 FIGHT, clash with, combat, cross swords with (*infml*), engage, grapple with, struggle, strive, contend.
n 1 MEETING, brush, confrontation. 2 CLASH, fight, combat, conflict, contest, battle, set-to (*infml*), dispute, engagement, action, skirmish, run-in, collision.

**encourage** v 1 HEARTEN, exhort, stimulate, spur, reassure, rally, inspire, incite, egg on (*infml*), buoy up, cheer, urge, rouse, comfort, console. 2 PROMOTE, advance, aid, boost, forward, further, foster, support, help, strengthen.
≠ 1 discourage, depress. 2 discourage.

**encouragement** n 1

REASSURANCE, inspiration, cheer, exhortation, incitement, pep talk (*infml*), urging, stimulation, consolation, succour (*fml*).
**2** PROMOTION, help, aid, boost, shot in the arm (*infml*), incentive, support, stimulus.
☒ discouragement, disapproval.

**encouraging** *adj* heartening, promising, hopeful, reassuring, stimulating, uplifting, auspicious, cheering, comforting, bright, rosy, cheerful, satisfactory.
☒ discouraging.

**encroach** *v* intrude, invade, impinge, trespass, infringe, usurp, overstep, make inroads, muscle in (*infml*).

**encumber** *v* burden, overload, weigh down, saddle, oppress, handicap, hamper, hinder, impede, slow down, obstruct, inconvenience, prevent, retard, cramp.

**encumbrance** *n* burden, cumbrance, load, cross, millstone, albatross, difficulty, handicap, impediment, obstruction, obstacle, inconvenience, hindrance, liability.

**end** *n* **1** FINISH, conclusion, termination, close, completion, cessation, culmination, dénouement.
**2** EXTREMITY, boundary, edge, limit, tip. **3** REMAINDER, tip, butt, left-over, remnant, stub, scrap, fragment. **4** AIM, object, objective, purpose, intention, goal, point, reason, design. **5** RESULT, outcome, consequence, upshot. **6** DEATH, demise, destruction, extermination, downfall, doom, ruin, dissolution.
☒ **1** beginning, start. **6** birth.
*v* **1** FINISH, close, cease, conclude, stop, terminate, complete, culminate, wind up. **2** DESTROY, annihilate, exterminate, extinguish, ruin, abolish, dissolve.
☒ **1** begin, start.

**endanger** *v* imperil, hazard, jeopardize, risk, expose, threaten,

compromise.
☒ protect.

**endearing** *adj* lovable, charming, appealing, attractive, winsome, delightful, enchanting.

**endeavour** *n* attempt, effort, go (*infml*), try, shot (*infml*), stab (*infml*), undertaking, enterprise, aim, venture.
*v* attempt, try, strive, aim, aspire, undertake, venture, struggle, labour, take pains.

**ending** *n* end, close, finish, completion, termination, conclusion, culmination, climax, resolution, consummation, dénouement, finale, epilogue.
☒ beginning, start.

**endless** *adj* **1** INFINITE, boundless, unlimited, measureless.
**2** EVERLASTING, ceaseless, perpetual, constant, continual, continuous, undying, eternal, interminable, monotonous.
☒ **1** finite, limited. **2** temporary.

**endorse** *v* **1** APPROVE, sanction, authorize, support, back, affirm, ratify, confirm, vouch for, advocate, warrant, recommend, subscribe to, sustain, adopt. **2** SIGN, countersign.

**endorsement** *n* **1** APPROVAL, sanction, authorization, support, backing, affirmation, ratification, confirmation, advocacy, warrant, recommendation, commendation, seal of approval, testimonial, OK (*infml*). **2** SIGNATURE, countersignature.

**endow** *v* bestow, bequeath, leave, will, give, donate, endue (*fml*), confer, grant, present, award, finance, fund, support, make over, furnish, provide, supply.

**endowment** *n* **1** BEQUEST, legacy, award, grant, fund, gift, provision, settlement, donation, bestowal, benefaction, dowry, income, revenue.
**2** TALENT, attribute, faculty, gift, ability, quality, flair, genius, qualification.

**endurance** n fortitude, patience, staying power, stamina, resignation, stoicism, tenacity, perseverance, resolution, stability, persistence, strength, toleration.

**endure** v 1 *endure hardship*: bear, stand, put up with, tolerate, weather, brave, cope with, face, go through, experience, submit to, suffer, sustain, swallow, undergo, withstand, stick, stomach, allow, permit, support. 2 *a peace that will endure for ever*: last, abide (*fml*), remain, live, survive, stay, persist, hold, prevail.

**enemy** n adversary, opponent, foe (*fml*), rival, antagonist, the opposition, competitor, opposer, other side.
**Ea** friend, ally.

**energetic** adj lively, vigorous, active, animated, dynamic, spirited, tireless, zestful, brisk, strong, forceful, potent, powerful, strenuous, high-powered.
**Ea** lethargic, sluggish, inactive, idle.

**energy** n liveliness, vigour, activity, animation, drive, dynamism, get-up-and-go (*infml*), life, spirit, verve, vivacity, vitality, zest, zeal, ardour, fire, efficiency, force, forcefulness, zip (*infml*), strength, power, intensity, exertion, stamina.
**Ea** lethargy, inertia, weakness.

**enforce** v impose, administer, implement, apply, execute, discharge, insist on, compel, oblige, urge, carry out, constrain, require, coerce, prosecute, reinforce.

**engage** v 1 PARTICIPATE, take part, embark on, take up, practise, involve. 2 ATTRACT, allure, draw, captivate, charm, catch. 3 OCCUPY, engross, absorb, busy, tie up, grip. 4 EMPLOY, hire, appoint, take on, enlist, enrol, commission, recruit, contract. 5 INTERLOCK, mesh, interconnect, join, interact, attach. 6 FIGHT, battle with, attack, take on, encounter, assail, combat.

**Ea** 2 repel. 4 dismiss, discharge. 5 disengage.

**engaged** adj 1 *engaged in his work*: occupied, busy, engrossed, immersed, absorbed, preoccupied, involved, employed. 2 *engaged to be married*: promised, betrothed (*fml*), pledged, spoken for, committed. 3 *the phone is engaged*: busy, tied up, unavailable.

**engagement** n 1 APPOINTMENT, meeting, date, arrangement, assignation, fixture, rendezvous. 2 PROMISE, pledge, betrothal (*fml*), commitment, obligation, assurance, vow, troth (*fml*). 3 FIGHT, battle, combat, conflict, action, encounter, confrontation, contest.

**engaging** adj charming, attractive, appealing, captivating, pleasing, delightful, winsome, lovable, likable, pleasant, fetching, fascinating, agreeable.
**Ea** repulsive, repellant.

**engine** n motor, machine, mechanism, appliance, contraption, apparatus, device, instrument, tool, locomotive, dynamo.

*Types of engine include:* diesel, donkey, fuel-injection, internal-combustion, jet, petrol, steam, turbine, turbojet, turboprop, V-engine.

**engineer** n 1 MECHANIC, technician, engine driver. 2 DESIGNER, originator, planner, inventor, deviser, mastermind, architect.
v plan, contrive, devise, manoeuvre, cause, manipulate, control, bring about, mastermind, originate, orchestrate, effect, plot, scheme, manage, create, rig.

**engrave** v 1 INSCRIBE, cut, carve, chisel, etch, chase. 2 *engraved on her mind*: imprint, impress, fix, stamp, lodge, ingrain.

**engraving** n print, impression, inscription, carving, etching, woodcut, plate, block, cutting, chiselling, mark.

**engross** v absorb, occupy, engage, grip, hold, preoccupy, rivet, fascinate, captivate, enthral, arrest, involve, intrigue.
🔁 bore.

**enhance** v heighten, intensify, increase, improve, elevate, magnify, swell, exalt, raise, lift, boost, strengthen, reinforce, embellish.
🔁 reduce, minimize.

**enigma** n mystery, riddle, puzzle, conundrum, problem, poser (*infml*), brain-teaser.

**enigmatic** adj mysterious, puzzling, cryptic, obscure, strange, perplexing.
🔁 simple, straightforward.

**enjoy** v take pleasure in, delight in, appreciate, like, relish, revel in, rejoice in, savour.
🔁 dislike, hate.

**enjoy oneself** have a good time, have fun, make merry.

**enjoyable** adj pleasant, agreeable, delightful, pleasing, gratifying, entertaining, amusing, fun, delicious, good, satisfying.
🔁 disagreeable.

**enjoyment** n 1 PLEASURE, delight, amusement, gratification, entertainment, relish, joy, fun, happiness, diversion, indulgence, recreation, zest, satisfaction.
2 POSSESSION, use, advantage, benefit.
🔁 1 displeasure.

**enlarge** v increase, expand, augment, add to, grow, extend, magnify, inflate, swell, wax, stretch, multiply, develop, amplify, blow up, widen, broaden, lengthen, heighten, elaborate.
🔁 diminish, shrink.

**enlighten** v instruct, edify, educate, inform, illuminate, teach, counsel, apprise, advise.
🔁 confuse.

**enlightened** adj informed, aware,

knowledgeable, educated, civilized, cultivated, refined, sophisticated, conversant, wise, reasonable, liberal, open-minded, literate.
🔁 ignorant, confused.

**enlist** v engage, enrol, register, sign up, recruit, conscript, employ, volunteer, join (up), gather, muster, secure, obtain, procure, enter.

**enmity** n animosity, hostility, antagonism, discord, strife, feud, antipathy, acrimony, bitterness, hatred, aversion, ill-will, bad blood, rancour, malevolence, malice, venom.
🔁 friendship.

**enormity** n atrocity, outrage, iniquity, horror, evil, crime, abomination, monstrosity, wickedness, vileness, depravity, atrociousness, viciousness.

**enormous** adj huge, immense, vast, gigantic, massive, colossal, gross, gargantuan, monstrous, mammoth, jumbo (*infml*), tremendous, prodigious.
🔁 small, tiny.

**enough** adj sufficient, adequate, ample, plenty, abundant.
n sufficiency, adequacy, plenty, abundance.
adv sufficiently, adequately, reasonably, tolerably, passably, moderately, fairly, satisfactorily, amply.

**enquire** *see* inquire.

**enquiry** *see* inquiry.

**enrage** v incense, infuriate, anger, madden, provoke, incite, inflame, exasperate, irritate, rile.
🔁 calm, placate.

**enrich** v 1 ENDOW, enhance, improve, refine, develop, cultivate, augment. 2 ADORN, ornament, beautify, embellish, decorate, grace.
🔁 1 impoverish.

**enrol** v 1 REGISTER, enlist, sign on, sign up, join up, recruit, engage, admit. 2 RECORD, list, note, inscribe.

**enrolment** n registration,

recruitment, enlistment, admission, acceptance.

**ensemble** n 1 WHOLE, total, entirety, sum, aggregate, set, collection. 2 OUTFIT, costume, get-up (*infml*), rig-out (*infml*). 3 GROUP, band, company, troupe, chorus.

**ensign** n banner, standard, flag, colours, pennant, jack, badge.

**enslave** v subjugate, subject, dominate, bind, enchain, yoke.
**E3** free, emancipate.

**ensue** v follow, issue, proceed, succeed, result, arise, happen, turn out, befall, flow, derive, stem.
**E3** precede.

**ensure** v 1 CERTIFY, guarantee, warrant. 2 PROTECT, guard, safeguard, secure.

**entail** v involve, necessitate, occasion, require, demand, cause, give rise to, lead to, result in.

**entangle** v enmesh, ensnare, embroil, involve, implicate, snare, tangle, entrap, trap, catch, mix up, knot, ravel, muddle.
**E3** disentangle.

**enter** v 1 COME IN, go in, arrive, insert, introduce, board, penetrate. 2 RECORD, log, note, register, take down, inscribe. 3 JOIN, embark upon, enrol, enlist, set about, sign up, participate, commence, start, begin.
**E3** 1 depart. 2 delete.

**enterprise** n 1 UNDERTAKING, venture, project, plan, effort, operation, programme, endeavour. 2 INITIATIVE, resourcefulness, drive, adventurousness, boldness, get-up-and-go (*infml*), push, energy, enthusiasm, spirit. 3 BUSINESS, company, firm, establishment, concern.
**E3** 2 apathy.

**enterprising** adj venturesome, adventurous, bold, daring, go-ahead, imaginative, resourceful, self-reliant, enthusiastic, energetic, keen,
ambitious, aspiring, spirited, active.
**E3** unenterprising, lethargic.

**entertain** v 1 AMUSE, divert, please, delight, cheer. 2 RECEIVE, have guests, accommodate, put up, treat. 3 HARBOUR, countenance, contemplate, consider, imagine, conceive.
**E3** 1 bore. 3 reject.

**entertainer**

---

*Entertainers include*: acrobat, actor, actress, busker, chat-show host, clown, comedian, comic, conjuror, dancer, disc jockey, DJ (*infml*), escapologist, game-show host, hypnotist, ice-skater, impressionist, jester, juggler, magician, mimic, mind-reader, minstrel, musician, presenter, singer, song-and-dance act, stand-up comic, striptease-artist, stripper (*infml*), trapeze-artist, tight-rope walker, ventriloquist; performer, artiste *see also* **musician; singer**.

---

**entertaining** adj amusing, diverting, fun, delightful, interesting, pleasant, pleasing, humorous, witty.
**E3** boring.

**entertainment** n 1 AMUSEMENT, diversion, recreation, enjoyment, play, pastime, fun, sport, distraction, pleasure. 2 SHOW, spectacle, performance, extravaganza.

---

*Forms of entertainment include*: cinema, cartoon show, video, radio, television, theatre, pantomime; dance, disco, discothèque, concert, recital, musical, opera, variety show, music hall, revue, karaoke, cabaret, night-club, casino; magic-show, puppet show, Punch-and-Judy show, circus, gymkhana, waxworks, laser-light show, zoo, rodeo, carnival, pageant, fête, festival, firework party, barbecue.

---

**enthral** v captivate, entrance, enchant, fascinate, charm, beguile, thrill, intrigue, hypnotize, mesmerize, engross.

**F3** bore.

**enthusiasm** n zeal, ardour, fervour, passion, keenness, eagerness, vehemence, warmth, frenzy, excitement, earnestness, relish, spirit, devotion, craze, mania, rage.

**F3** apathy.

**enthusiast** n devotee, zealot, admirer, fan (infml), supporter, follower, buff (infml), freak (infml), fanatic, fiend (infml), lover.

**enthusiastic** adj keen, ardent, eager, fervent, vehement, passionate, warm, whole-hearted, zealous, vigorous, spirited, earnest, devoted, avid, excited, exuberant.

**F3** unenthusiastic, apathetic.

**entice** v tempt, lure, attract, seduce, lead on, draw, coax, persuade, induce, sweet-talk (infml).

**entire** adj complete, whole, total, full, intact, perfect.

**F3** incomplete, partial.

**entirely** adv completely, wholly, totally, fully, utterly, unreservedly, absolutely, in toto, thoroughly, altogether, perfectly, solely, exclusively, every inch.

**F3** partially.

**entitle** v 1 AUTHORIZE, qualify, empower, enable, allow, permit, license, warrant. 2 NAME, call, term, title, style, christen, dub, label, designate.

**entity** n being, existence, thing, body, creature, individual, organism, substance.

**entrance**¹ n 1 ACCESS, admission, admittance, entry, entrée.

2 ARRIVAL, appearance, debut, initiation, introduction, start.

3 OPENING, way in, door, doorway, gate.

**F3** 2 departure. 3 exit.

**entrance**² v charm, enchant, enrapture, bewitch, spellbind, fascinate, delight, ravish,

transport, hypnotize, mesmerize.

**F3** repel.

**entrant** n 1 NOVICE, beginner, newcomer, initiate, convert, probationer. 2 COMPETITOR, candidate, contestant, contender, entry, participant, player.

**entreat** v beg, implore, plead with, beseech, crave, supplicate, pray, invoke, ask, petition, request, appeal to.

**entreaty** n appeal, plea, prayer, petition, supplication, suit, invocation, cry, solicitation, request.

**entrench** v establish, fix, embed, dig in, ensconce, install, lodge, root, ingrain, settle, seat, plant, anchor, set.

**F3** dislodge.

**entrust** v trust, commit, confide, consign, authorize, charge, assign, turn over, commend, depute, invest, delegate, deliver.

**entry** n 1 ENTRANCE, appearance, admittance, admission, access, entrée, introduction. 2 OPENING, entrance, door, doorway, access, threshold, way in, passage, gate. 3 RECORD, item, minute, note, memorandum, statement, account. 4 ENTRANT, competitor, contestant, candidate, participant, player.

**F3** 2 exit.

**enumerate** v list, name, itemize, cite, detail, specify, count, number, relate, recount, spell out, tell, mention, calculate, quote, recite, reckon.

**enunciate** v 1 ARTICULATE, pronounce, vocalize, voice, express, say, speak, utter, sound. 2 STATE, declare, proclaim, announce, propound.

**envelop** v wrap, enfold, enwrap, encase, cover, swathe, shroud, engulf, enclose, encircle, encompass, surround, cloak, veil, blanket, conceal, obscure, hide.

**envelope** n wrapper, wrapping,

cover, case, casing, sheath, covering, shell, skin, jacket, coating.

**enviable** *adj* desirable, privileged, favoured, blessed, fortunate, lucky, advantageous, sought-after, excellent, fine.
**F3** unenviable.

**envious** *adj* covetous, jealous, resentful, green (with envy), dissatisfied, grudging, jaundiced, green-eyed (*infml*).

**environment** *n* surroundings, conditions, circumstances, milieu, atmosphere, habitat, situation, element, medium, background, ambience, setting, context, territory, domain.

**envisage** *v* visualize, imagine, picture, envision, conceive of, preconceive, predict, anticipate, foresee, image, see, contemplate.

**envoy** *n* agent, representative, ambassador, diplomat, messenger, legate, emissary, minister, delegate, deputy, courier, intermediary.

**envy** *n* covetousness, jealousy, resentfulness, resentment, dissatisfaction, grudge, ill-will, malice, spite.
*v* covet, resent, begrudge, grudge, crave.

**epidemic** *adj* widespread, prevalent, rife, rampant, pandemic, sweeping, wide-ranging, prevailing.
*n* plague, outbreak, spread, rash, upsurge, wave.

**epilogue** *n* afterword, postscript, coda, conclusion.
**F3** foreword, prologue, preface.

**episode** *n* 1 INCIDENT, event, occurrence, happening, occasion, circumstance, experience, adventure, matter, business. 2 INSTALMENT, part, chapter, passage, section, scene.

**epitome** *n* 1 PERSONIFICATION, embodiment, representation, model, archetype, type, essence.
2 SUMMARY, abstract, abridgement, digest.

**epoch** *n* age, era, period, time, date.

**equable** *adj* 1 *an equable person*: even-tempered, placid, calm, serene, unexcitable, tranquil, unflappable, composed, level-headed, easy-going. 2 *an equable climate*: uniform, even, consistent, constant, regular, temperate, unvarying, steady, stable, smooth.
**F3** 1 excitable. 2 variable.

**equal** *adj* 1 IDENTICAL, the same, alike, like, equivalent, corresponding, commensurate, comparable. 2 EVEN, uniform, regular, unvarying, balanced, matched. 3 COMPETENT, able, adequate, fit, capable, suitable.
**F3** 1 different. 2 unequal. 3 unsuitable.
*n* peer, counterpart, equivalent, coequal, match, parallel, twin, fellow.
*v* match, parallel, correspond to, balance, square with, tally with, equalize, equate, rival, level, even.

**equality** *n* 1 UNIFORMITY, evenness, equivalence, correspondence, balance, parity, par, symmetry, proportion, identity, sameness, likeness. 2 IMPARTIALITY, fairness, justice, egalitarianism.
**F3** 2 inequality.

**equalize** *v* level, even up, match, equal, equate, draw level, balance, square, standardize, compensate, smooth.

**equate** *v* compare, liken, match, pair, correspond to, correspond with, balance, parallel, equalize, offset, square, agree, tally, juxtapose.

**equation** *n* equality, correspondence, equivalence, balancing, agreement, parallel, pairing, comparison, match, likeness, juxtaposition.

**equilibrium** *n* 1 BALANCE, poise, symmetry, evenness, stability.
2 EQUANIMITY, self-possession, composure, calmness, coolness, serenity.
**F3** 1 imbalance.

**equip** *v* provide, fit out, supply,

furnish, prepare, arm, fit up, kit out, stock, endow, rig, dress, array, deck out.

**equipment** n apparatus, gear, supplies, tackle, rig-out (*infml*), tools, material, furnishings, baggage, outfit, paraphernalia, stuff, things, accessories, furniture.

**equivalence** n identity, parity, correspondence, agreement, likeness, interchangeability, similarity, substitutability, correlation, parallel, conformity, sameness.
🖃 unlikeness, dissimilarity.

**equivalent** adj equal, same, similar, substitutable, corresponding, alike, comparable, interchangeable, even, tantamount, twin.
🖃 unlike, different.

**equivocal** adj ambiguous, uncertain, obscure, vague, evasive, oblique, misleading, dubious, confusing, indefinite.
🖃 unequivocal, clear.

**equivocate** v prevaricate, evade, dodge, fence, beat about the bush (*infml*), hedge, mislead.

**era** n age, epoch, period, date, day, days, time, aeon, stage, century.

**eradicate** v eliminate, annihilate, get rid of, remove, root out, suppress, destroy, exterminate, extinguish, weed out, stamp out, abolish, erase, obliterate.

**erase** v obliterate, rub out, expunge (*fml*), delete, blot out, cancel, efface, get rid of, remove, eradicate.

**erect** adj upright, straight, vertical, upstanding, standing, raised, rigid, stiff.
v build, construct, put up, establish, set up, elevate, assemble, found, form, institute, initiate, raise, rear, lift, mount, pitch, create.

**erode** v wear away, eat away, wear down, corrode, abrade, consume, grind down, disintegrate, deteriorate, spoil.

**erosion** n wear, corrosion, abrasion,

attrition, denudation, disintegration, deterioration, destruction, undermining.

**erotic** adj aphrodisiac, seductive, sexy, sensual, titillating, pornographic, lascivious, stimulating, suggestive, amorous, amatory, venereal, carnal, lustful, voluptuous.

**err** v 1 MAKE A MISTAKE, be wrong, miscalculate, mistake, misjudge, slip up, blunder, misunderstand. 2 DO WRONG, sin, misbehave, go astray, offend, transgress, deviate.

**errand** n commission, charge, mission, assignment, message, task, job, duty.

**erratic** adj changeable, variable, fitful, fluctuating, inconsistent, irregular, unstable, shifting, inconstant, unpredictable, unreliable, aberrant, abnormal, eccentric, desultory, meandering.
🖃 steady, consistent, stable.

**erroneous** adj incorrect, wrong, mistaken, false, untrue, inaccurate, inexact, invalid, illogical, unfounded, faulty, flawed.
🖃 correct, right.

**error** n mistake, inaccuracy, slip, slip-up, blunder, howler (*infml*), gaffe, faux pas, solecism, lapse, miscalculation, misunderstanding, misconception, misapprehension, misprint, oversight, omission, fallacy, flaw, fault, wrong.

**erudite** adj learned, scholarly, well-educated, knowledgeable, lettered, educated, well-read, literate, academic, cultured, wise, highbrow, profound.
🖃 illiterate, ignorant.

**erupt** v break out, explode, belch, discharge, burst, gush, spew, spout, eject, expel, emit, flare up, vomit, break.

**eruption** n 1 OUTBURST, discharge, ejection, emission, explosion, flare-up. 2 RASH, outbreak, inflammation.

**escalate** v increase, intensify, grow,

accelerate, rise, step up, heighten, raise, spiral, magnify, enlarge, expand, extend, mount, ascend, climb, amplify.
**F3** decrease, diminish.

**escapade** n adventure, exploit, fling, prank, caper, romp, spree, lark (*infml*), antic, stunt, trick.

**escape** v 1 GET AWAY, break free, run away, bolt, abscond, flee, fly, decamp, break loose, break out, do a bunk (*infml*), flit, slip away, shake off, slip. 2 AVOID, evade, elude, dodge, skip, shun. 3 LEAK, seep, flow, drain, gush, issue, discharge, ooze, trickle, pour forth, pass.
n 1 GETAWAY, flight, bolt, flit, breakout, decampment, jail-break. 2 AVOIDANCE, evasion. 3 LEAK, seepage, leakage, outflow, gush, drain, discharge, emission, spurt, outpour, emanation. 4 ESCAPISM, diversion, distraction, recreation, relaxation, pastime, safety-valve.

**escapist** n dreamer, daydreamer, fantasizer, wishful thinker, nonrealist, ostrich (*infml*).
**F3** realist.

**escort** n 1 COMPANION, chaperon(e), partner, attendant, aide, squire, guide, bodyguard, protector. 2 ENTOURAGE, company, retinue, suite, train, guard, convoy, cortège.
v accompany, partner, chaperon(e), guide, lead, usher, conduct, guard, protect.

**esoteric** adj recondite, obscure, abstruse, cryptic, inscrutable, mysterious, mystic, mystical, occult, hidden, secret, confidential, private, inside.
**F3** well-known, familiar.

**especially** adv 1 CHIEFLY, mainly, principally, primarily, pre-eminently, above all. 2 PARTICULARLY, specially, markedly, notably, exceptionally, outstandingly, expressly, supremely, uniquely, unusually, strikingly, very.

**essay** n composition, dissertation, paper, article, assignment, thesis, piece, commentary, critique, discourse, treatise, review, leader, tract.

**essence** n 1 NATURE, being, quintessence, substance, soul, spirit, core, centre, heart, meaning, quality, significance, life, entity, crux, kernel, marrow, pith, character, characteristics, attributes, principle. 2 CONCENTRATE, extract, distillation, spirits.

**essential** adj 1 FUNDAMENTAL, basic, intrinsic, inherent, principal, main, key, characteristic, definitive, typical, constituent. 2 CRUCIAL, indispensable, necessary, vital, requisite, required, needed, important.
**F3** 1 incidental. 2 dispensable, inessential.
n necessity, prerequisite, must, requisite, sine qua non (*fml*), requirement, basic, fundamental, necessary, principle.
**F3** inessential.

**establish** v 1 SET UP, found, start, form, institute, create, organize, inaugurate, introduce, install, plant, settle, secure, lodge, base. 2 PROVE, substantiate, demonstrate, authenticate, ratify, verify, validate, certify, confirm, affirm.
**F3** 1 uproot. 2 refute.

**establishment** n 1 FORMATION, setting up, founding, creation, foundation, installation, institution, inauguration. 2 BUSINESS, company, firm, institute, organization, concern, institution, enterprise. 3 RULING CLASS, the system, the authorities, the powers that be.

**estate** n 1 POSSESSIONS, effects, assets, belongings, holdings, property, goods, lands. 2 AREA, development, land, manor. 3 (*fml*) STATUS, standing, situation, position, class, place, condition, state, rank.

**estimate** v  assess, reckon, evaluate, calculate, gauge, guess, value, conjecture, consider, judge, think, number, count, compute, believe.
n  reckoning, valuation, judgement, guess, approximation, assessment, estimation, evaluation, computation, opinion.

**estimation** n  **1** JUDGEMENT, opinion, belief, consideration, estimate, view, evaluation, assessment, reckoning, conception, calculation, computation.
**2** RESPECT, regard, appreciation, esteem, credit.

**estranged** adj  divided, separate, alienated, disaffected, antagonized.
**E3** reconciled, united.

**estuary** n  inlet, mouth, firth, fjord, creek, arm, sea-loch.

**eternal** adj  **1** eternal bliss: unending, endless, ceaseless, everlasting, never-ending, infinite, limitless, immortal, undying, imperishable. **2** eternal truths: unchanging, timeless, enduring, lasting, perennial, abiding. **3** (infml) eternal quarrelling: constant, continuous, perpetual, incessant, interminable.
**E3 1** ephemeral, temporary.
**2** changeable.

**eternity** n  **1** EVERLASTINGNESS, endlessness, everlasting, imperishability, infinity, timelessness, perpetuity, immutability, ages, age, aeon. **2** AFTER-LIFE, hereafter, immortality, heaven, paradise, next world, world to come.

**ethical** adj  moral, principled, just, right, proper, virtuous, honourable, fair, upright, righteous, seemly, honest, good, correct, commendable, fitting, noble, meet (fml).
**E3** unethical.

**ethics** n  moral values, morality, principles, standards, code, moral philosophy, rules, beliefs, propriety, conscience, equity.

**ethnic** adj  racial, native, indigenous, traditional, tribal, folk, cultural, national, aboriginal.

**ethos** n  attitude, beliefs, standards, manners, ethics, morality, code, principles, spirit, tenor, rationale, character, disposition.

**etiquette** n  code, formalities, standards, correctness, conventions, customs, protocol (fml), rules, manners, politeness, courtesy, civility, decorum, ceremony, decency.

**euphemism** n  evasion, polite term, substitution, genteelism, politeness, understatement.

**euphoria** n  elation, ecstasy, bliss, rapture, high spirits, well-being, high (infml) exhilaration, exultation, joy, intoxication, jubilation, transport, glee, exaltation, enthusiasm, cheerfulness.
**E3** depression, despondency.

**evacuate** v  **1** LEAVE, depart, withdraw, quit, remove, retire from, clear (out) (infml), abandon, desert, forsake, vacate, decamp, relinquish. **2** EMPTY, eject, void, expel, discharge, eliminate, defecate, purge.

**evacuation** n  **1** DEPARTURE, withdrawal, retreat, exodus, removal, quitting, desertion, abandonment, clearance, relinquishment, retirement, vacation. **2** EMPTYING, expulsion, ejection, discharge, elimination, defecation, urination.

**evade** v  **1** evade one's duties: elude, avoid, escape, dodge, shirk, steer clear of, shun, sidestep, duck (infml), balk, skive (infml), fend off, chicken out (infml), cop out (infml). **2** evade a question: prevaricate, equivocate, fence, fudge, parry, quibble, hedge.
**E3 1** confront, face.

**evaluate** v  value, assess, appraise, estimate, reckon, calculate, gauge, judge, rate, size up, weigh, compute, rank.

**evaluation** n  valuation, appraisal, assessment, estimation, estimate, judgement, reckoning, calculation, opinion, computation.

**evaporate** v 1 DISAPPEAR, dematerialize, vanish, melt (away), dissolve, disperse, dispel, dissipate, fade. 2 VAPORIZE, dry, dehydrate, exhale.

**evasion** n avoidance, escape, dodge, equivocation, excuse, prevarication, put-off, trickery, subterfuge, shirking.
F3 frankness, directness.

**evasive** adj equivocating, indirect, prevaricating, devious, shifty (infml), unforthcoming, slippery (infml), misleading, deceitful, deceptive, cagey (infml), oblique, secretive, tricky, cunning.
F3 direct, frank.

**eve** n day before, verge, brink, edge, threshold.

**even** adj 1 LEVEL, flat, smooth, horizontal, flush, parallel, plane. 2 STEADY, unvarying, constant, regular, uniform. 3 EQUAL, balanced, matching, same, similar, like, symmetrical, fifty-fifty, level, side by side, neck and neck (infml). 4 EVEN-TEMPERED, calm, placid, serene, tranquil, composed, unruffled. 5 EVEN-HANDED, balanced, equitable, fair, impartial.
F3 1 uneven. 3 unequal.
v smooth, flatten, level, match, regularize, balance, equalize, align, square, stabilize, steady, straighten.

**evening** n nightfall, dusk, eve, eventide, twilight, sunset, sundown.

**event** n 1 HAPPENING, occurrence, incident, occasion, affair, circumstance, episode, eventuality, experience, matter, case, adventure, business, fact, possibility, milestone. 2 CONSEQUENCE, result, outcome, conclusion, end, effect, issue, termination. 3 GAME, match, competition, contest, tournament, engagement.

**even-tempered** adj calm, level-headed, placid, stable, tranquil, serene, composed, cool, steady, peaceful, peaceable.
F3 excitable, erratic.

**eventful** adj busy, exciting, lively, active, full, interesting, remarkable, significant, memorable, momentous, notable, noteworthy, unforgettable.
F3 dull, ordinary.

**eventual** adj final, ultimate, resulting, concluding, ensuing, future, later, subsequent, prospective, projected, planned, impending.

**eventually** adv finally, ultimately, at last, in the end, at length, subsequently, after all, sooner or later.

**ever** adv 1 ALWAYS, evermore, for ever, perpetually, constantly, at all times, continually, endlessly. 2 AT ANY TIME, in any case, in any circumstances, at all, on any account.
F3 1 never.

**everlasting** adj eternal, undying, never-ending, endless, immortal, infinite, imperishable, constant, permanent, perpetual, indestructible, timeless.
F3 temporary, transient.

**everyday** adj ordinary, common, commonplace, day-to-day, familiar, run-of-the-mill, regular, plain, routine, usual, workaday, common-or-garden (infml), normal, customary, stock, accustomed, conventional, daily, habitual, monotonous, frequent, simple, informal.
F3 unusual, exceptional, special.

**everyone** n everybody, one and all, each one, all and sundry, the whole world.

**everywhere** adv all around, all over, throughout, far and near, far and wide, high and low, ubiquitous, left, right and centre (infml).

**evict** v expel, eject, dispossess, put out, turn out, turf out (infml), kick out (infml), force out, remove, cast

out, chuck out (*infml*), oust, dislodge,
expropriate.

**evidence** *n* 1 PROOF, verification,
confirmation, affirmation, grounds,
substantiation, documentation, data.
2 TESTIMONY, declaration.
3 INDICATION, manifestation,
suggestion, sign, mark, hint,
demonstration, token.

**evident** *adj* clear, obvious, manifest,
apparent, plain, patent, visible,
conspicuous, noticeable, clear-cut,
unmistakable, perceptible, distinct,
discernible, tangible, incontestable,
indisputable, incontrovertible.

**evidently** *adv* clearly, apparently,
plainly, patently, manifestly,
obviously, seemingly, undoubtedly,
doubtless(ly), indisputably.

**evil** *adj* 1 WICKED, wrong, sinful,
bad, immoral, vicious, vile,
malevolent, iniquitous, cruel, base,
corrupt, heinous, malicious,
malignant, devilish, depraved,
mischievous. 2 HARMFUL,
pernicious, destructive, deadly,
detrimental, hurtful, poisonous.
3 DISASTROUS, ruinous, calamitous,
catastrophic, adverse, dire,
inauspicious. 4 OFFENSIVE, noxious,
foul.
*n* 1 WICKEDNESS, wrong-doing,
wrong, immorality, badness, sin,
sinfulness, vice, viciousness, iniquity,
depravity, baseness, corruption,
malignity, mischief, heinousness.
2 ADVERSITY, affliction, calamity,
disaster, misfortune, suffering, sorrow,
ruin, catastrophe, blow, curse, distress,
hurt, harm, ill, injury, misery, woe.

**evoke** *v* summon (up), call, elicit,
invoke, arouse, stir, raise, stimulate,
call forth, call up, conjure up,
awaken, provoke, excite, recall.
F3 suppress.

**evolution** *n* development, growth,
progression, progress, expansion,
increase, ripening, derivation,
descent.

**evolve** *v* develop, grow, increase,
mature, progress, unravel, expand,
enlarge, emerge, descend, derive,
result, elaborate.

**exact** *adj* 1 PRECISE, accurate,
correct, faithful, literal, flawless,
faultless, right, true, veracious,
definite, explicit, detailed, specific,
strict, unerring, close, factual,
identical, express, word-perfect,
blow-by-blow (*infml*). 2 CAREFUL,
scrupulous, particular, rigorous,
methodical, meticulous, orderly,
painstaking.
F3 1 inexact, imprecise.
*v* extort, extract, claim, insist on,
wrest, wring, compel, demand,
command, force, impose, require,
squeeze, milk (*infml*).

**exacting** *adj* demanding, difficult,
hard, laborious, arduous, rigorous,
taxing, tough, harsh, painstaking,
severe, strict, unsparing.
F3 easy.

**exactly** *adv* 1 PRECISELY,
accurately, literally, faithfully,
correctly, specifically, rigorously,
scrupulously, veraciously, verbatim,
carefully, faultlessly, unerringly,
strictly, to the letter, particularly,
methodically, explicitly, expressly,
dead (*infml*). 2 ABSOLUTELY,
definitely, precisely, indeed,
certainly, truly, quite, just,
unequivocally.
F3 1 inaccurately, roughly.

**exaggerate** *v* overstate, overdo,
magnify, overemphasize, emphasize,
embellish, embroider, enlarge,
amplify, oversell, pile it on (*infml*).
F3 understate.

**examination** *n* 1 INSPECTION,
enquiry, scrutiny, study, survey,
search, analysis, exploration,
investigation, probe, appraisal,
observation, research, review, scan,
once-over (*infml*), perusal, check,
check-up, audit, critique. 2 TEST,
exam, quiz, questioning, cross-

examination, cross-questioning, trial, inquisition, interrogation, viva.

**examine** v 1 INSPECT, investigate, scrutinize, study, survey, analyse, explore, enquire, consider, probe, review, scan, check (out), ponder, pore over, sift, vet, weigh up, appraise, assay, audit, peruse, case (*sl*). 2 TEST, quiz, question, cross-examine, cross-question, interrogate, grill (*infml*), catechize (*fml*).

**example** n instance, case, case in point, illustration, exemplification, sample, specimen, model, pattern, ideal, archetype, prototype, standard, type, lesson, citation.

**exasperate** v infuriate, annoy, anger, incense, irritate, madden, provoke, get on someone's nerves, enrage, irk, rile, rankle, rouse, get to (*infml*), goad, vex.
Ⓔ appease, pacify.

**excavate** v dig (out), dig up, hollow, burrow, tunnel, delve, unearth, mine, quarry, disinter, gouge, scoop, exhume, uncover.

**excavation** n hole, hollow, pit, quarry, mine, dugout, dig, diggings, burrow, cavity, crater, trench, trough, shaft, ditch, cutting.

**exceed** v surpass, outdo, outstrip, beat, better, pass, overtake, top, outshine, eclipse, outreach, outrun, transcend, cap, overdo, overstep.

**excel** v 1 SURPASS, outdo, beat, outclass, outperform, outrank, eclipse, better. 2 BE EXCELLENT, succeed, shine, stand out, predominate.

**excellence** n superiority, pre-eminence, distinction, merit, supremacy, quality, worth, fineness, eminence, goodness, greatness, virtue, perfection, purity.

**excellent** adj superior, first-class, first-rate, prime, superlative, unequalled, outstanding, surpassing, remarkable, distinguished, great, good, exemplary, select, superb,

admirable, commendable, top-notch (*infml*), splendid, noteworthy, notable, fine, wonderful, worthy.
Ⓔ inferior, second-rate.

**except** prep excepting, but, apart from, other than, save, omitting, not counting, leaving out, excluding, except for, besides, bar, minus, less.
v leave out, omit, bar, exclude, reject, rule out.

**exception** n oddity, anomaly, deviation, abnormality, irregularity, peculiarity, inconsistency, rarity, special case, quirk.

**exceptional** adj 1 ABNORMAL, unusual, anomalous, strange, odd, irregular, extraordinary, peculiar, special, rare, uncommon. 2 OUTSTANDING, remarkable, phenomenal, prodigious, notable, noteworthy, superior, unequalled, marvellous.
Ⓔ 1 normal. 2 mediocre.

**excerpt** n extract, passage, portion, section, selection, quote, quotation, part, citation, scrap, fragment.

**excess** n 1 SURFEIT, overabundance, glut, plethora, superfluity, superabundance, surplus, overflow, overkill, remainder, left-over. 2 OVERINDULGENCE, dissipation, immoderateness, intemperance, extravagance, unrestraint, debauchery.
Ⓔ 1 deficiency. 2 restraint.
adj extra, surplus, spare, redundant, remaining, residual, left-over, additional, superfluous, supernumerary.
Ⓔ inadequate.

**excessive** adj immoderate, inordinate, extreme, undue, uncalled-for, disproportionate, unnecessary, unneeded, superfluous, unreasonable, exorbitant, extravagant, steep (*infml*).
Ⓔ insufficient.

**exchange** v barter, change, trade, swap, switch, replace, interchange,

convert, commute, substitute, reciprocate, bargain, bandy.
*n* **1** CONVERSATION, discussion, chat. **2** TRADE, commerce, dealing, market, traffic, barter, bargain. **3** INTERCHANGE, swap, switch, replacement, substitution, reciprocity.

**excitable** *adj* temperamental, volatile, passionate, emotional, highly-strung, fiery, hot-headed, hasty, nervous, hot-tempered, irascible, quick-tempered, sensitive, susceptible.
F∃ calm, stable.

**excite** *v* **1** MOVE, agitate, disturb, upset, touch, stir up, thrill, elate, turn on (*infml*), impress. **2** AROUSE, rouse, animate, awaken, fire, inflame, kindle, motivate, stimulate, engender, inspire, instigate, incite, induce, ignite, galvanize, generate, provoke, sway, quicken, evoke.
F∃ **1** calm.

**excited** *adj* aroused, roused, stimulated, stirred, thrilled, elated, enthusiastic, eager, moved, high (*infml*), worked up, wrought-up, overwrought, restless, frantic, frenzied, wild.
F∃ calm, apathetic.

**excitement** *n* **1** UNREST, ado, action, activity, commotion, fuss, tumult, flurry, furore, adventure. **2** DISCOMPOSURE, agitation, passion, thrill, animation, elation, enthusiasm, restlessness, kicks (*infml*), ferment, fever, eagerness, stimulation.
F∃ **1** calm. **2** apathy.

**exciting** *adj* stimulating, stirring, intoxicating, exhilarating, thrilling, rousing, moving, enthralling, electrifying, nail-biting (*infml*), cliff-hanging (*infml*), striking, sensational, provocative, inspiring, interesting.
F∃ dull, unexciting.

**exclaim** *v* cry (out), declare, blurt (out), call, yell, shout, proclaim, utter.

**exclamation** *n* cry, call, yell, shout, expletive, interjection, ejaculation, outcry, utterance.

**exclude** *v* **1** BAN, bar, prohibit, disallow, veto, proscribe, forbid, blacklist. **2** OMIT, leave out, keep out, refuse, reject, ignore, shut out, rule out, ostracize, eliminate. **3** EXPEL, eject, evict, excommunicate.
F∃ **1** admit. **2** include.

**exclusive** *adj* **1** SOLE, single, unique, only, undivided, unshared, whole, total, peculiar.
**2** RESTRICTED, limited, closed, private, narrow, restrictive, choice, select, discriminative, cliquey, chic, classy (*infml*), elegant, fashionable, posh (*infml*), snobbish.

**excruciating** *adj* agonizing, painful, severe, tormenting, unbearable, insufferable, acute, intolerable, intense, sharp, piercing, extreme, atrocious, racking, harrowing, savage, burning, bitter.

**excursion** *n* outing, trip, jaunt, expedition, day trip, journey, tour, airing, breather, junket (*infml*), ride, drive, walk, ramble.

**excuse** *v* **1** FORGIVE, pardon, overlook, absolve, acquit, exonerate, tolerate, ignore, indulge. **2** RELEASE, free, discharge, liberate, let off, relieve, spare, exempt. **3** CONDONE, explain, mitigate, justify, vindicate, defend, apologize for.
F∃ **1** criticize. **2** punish.
*n* justification, explanation, grounds, defence, plea, alibi, reason, apology, pretext, pretence, exoneration, evasion, cop-out (*infml*), shift, substitute.

**execute** *v* **1** PUT TO DEATH, kill, liquidate, hang, electrocute, shoot, guillotine, decapitate, behead. **2** CARRY OUT, perform, do, accomplish, achieve, fulfil, complete, discharge, effect, enact, deliver, enforce, finish, implement, administer, consummate, realize, dispatch, expedite, validate, serve, render, sign.

**execution** n **1** DEATH PENALTY, capital punishment, killing, hanging, electrocution, firing squad, shooting, guillotining, decapitation, beheading. **2** ACCOMPLISHMENT, operation, performance, completion, achievement, administration, effect, enactment, implementation, realization, discharge, dispatch, consummation, enforcement. **3** STYLE, technique, rendition, delivery, performance, manner, mode.

**executive** n **1** ADMINISTRATION, management, government, leadership, hierarchy. **2** ADMINISTRATOR, manager, organizer, leader, controller, director, governor, official. *adj* administrative, managerial, controlling, supervisory, regulating, decision-making, governing, organizing, directing, directorial, organizational, leading, guiding.

**exemplary** adj **1** MODEL, ideal, perfect, admirable, excellent, faultless, flawless, correct, good, commendable, praiseworthy, worthy, laudable, estimable, honourable. **2** CAUTIONARY, warning.
E3 **1** imperfect, unworthy.

**exemplify** v illustrate, demonstrate, show, instance, represent, typify, manifest, embody, epitomize, exhibit, depict, display.

**exempt** v excuse, release, relieve, let off, free, absolve, discharge, dismiss, liberate, spare. *adj* excused, not liable, immune, released, spared, absolved, discharged, excluded, free, liberated, clear.
E3 liable.

**exercise** v **1** USE, utilize, employ, apply, exert, practise, wield, try, discharge. **2** TRAIN, drill, practise, work out (*infml*), keep fit. **3** WORRY, disturb, trouble, upset, burden,

distress, vex, annoy, agitate, afflict. n **1** TRAINING, drill, practice, effort, exertion, task, lesson, work, discipline, activity, physical jerks (*infml*), work-out (*infml*), aerobics, labour. **2** USE, utilization, employment, application, implementation, practice, operation, discharge, assignment, fulfilment, accomplishment.

**exert** v use, utilize, employ, apply, exercise, bring to bear, wield, expend. **exert oneself** strive, struggle, strain, make every effort, take pains, toil, labour, work, sweat (*infml*), endeavour, apply oneself.

**exertion** n **1** EFFORT, industry, labour, toil, work, struggle, diligence, assiduousness, perseverance, pains, endeavour, attempt, strain, travail (*fml*), trial. **2** USE, utilization, employment, application, exercise, operation, action.
E3 **1** idleness, rest.

**exhaust** v **1** CONSUME, empty, deplete, drain, sap, spend, waste, squander, dissipate, impoverish, use up, finish, dry, bankrupt. **2** TIRE (OUT), weary, fatigue, tax, strain, weaken, overwork, wear out.
E3 **1** renew. **2** refresh.
n emission, exhalation, discharge, fumes.

**exhausted** adj **1** EMPTY, finished, depleted, spent, used up, drained, dry, worn out, void. **2** TIRED (OUT), dead tired, dead-beat (*infml*), all in (*infml*), done (in) (*infml*), fatigued, weak, washed-out, whacked (*infml*), knackered (*infml*), jaded.
E3 **1** fresh. **2** vigorous.

**exhausting** adj tiring, strenuous, taxing, gruelling, arduous, hard, laborious, backbreaking, draining, severe, testing, punishing, formidable, debilitating.
E3 refreshing.

**exhaustion** n fatigue, tiredness, weariness, debility, feebleness, jet-

lag.
ᴇᴀ freshness, liveliness.

**exhaustive** adj comprehensive, all-embracing, all-inclusive, far-reaching, complete, extensive, encyclopedic, full-scale, thorough, full, in-depth, intensive, detailed, definitive, all-out, sweeping.
ᴇᴀ incomplete, restricted.

**exhibit** v display, show, present, demonstrate, manifest, expose, parade, reveal, express, disclose, indicate, air, flaunt, offer.
ᴇᴀ conceal.
n display, exhibition, show, illustration, model.

**exhibition** n display, show, demonstration, exhibit, presentation, manifestation, spectacle, exposition, expo (infml), showing, fair, performance, airing, representation, showcase.

**exhilarate** v thrill, excite, elate, animate, enliven, invigorate, vitalize, stimulate.
ᴇᴀ bore.

**exile** n 1 BANISHMENT, deportation, expatriation, expulsion, ostracism, transportation. 2 EXPATRIATE, refugee, émigré, deportee, outcast.
v banish, expel, deport, expatriate, drive out, ostracize, oust.

**exist** v 1 BE, live, abide, continue, endure, have one's being, breathe, prevail. 2 SUBSIST, survive. 3 BE PRESENT, occur, happen, be available, remain.

**existence** n 1 BEING, life, reality, actuality, continuance, continuation, endurance, survival, breath, subsistence. 2 CREATION, the world. 3 (fml) ENTITY, creature, thing.
ᴇᴀ 1 death, non-existence.

**exit** n 1 DEPARTURE, going, retreat, withdrawal, leave-taking, retirement, farewell, exodus. 2 DOOR, way out, doorway, gate, vent.
ᴇᴀ 1 entrance, arrival. 2 entrance.
v depart, leave, go, retire, withdraw,

take one's leave, retreat, issue.
ᴇᴀ arrive, enter.

**exonerate** v 1 ABSOLVE, acquit, clear, vindicate, exculpate (fml), justify, pardon, discharge. 2 EXEMPT, excuse, spare, let off, release, relieve.
ᴇᴀ 1 incriminate.

**exorbitant** adj excessive, unreasonable, unwarranted, undue, inordinate, immoderate, extravagant, extortionate, enormous, preposterous.
ᴇᴀ reasonable, moderate.

**exotic** adj 1 FOREIGN, alien, imported, introduced. 2 UNUSUAL, striking, different, unfamiliar, extraordinary, bizarre, curious, strange, fascinating, colourful, peculiar, outlandish.
ᴇᴀ 1 native. 2 ordinary.

**expand** v 1 STRETCH, swell, widen, lengthen, thicken, magnify, multiply, inflate, broaden, blow up, open out, fill out, fatten. 2 INCREASE, grow, extend, enlarge, develop, amplify, spread, branch out, diversify, elaborate.
ᴇᴀ 1 contract.

**expanse** n extent, space, area, breadth, range, stretch, sweep, field, plain, tract.

**expansive** adj 1 FRIENDLY, genial, outgoing, open, affable, sociable, talkative, warm, communicative, effusive. 2 EXTENSIVE, broad, comprehensive, wide-ranging, all-embracing, thorough.
ᴇᴀ 1 reserved, cold. 2 restricted, narrow.

**expect** v 1 expect the money soon: anticipate, await, look forward to, hope for, look for, bank on, bargain for, envisage, predict, forecast, contemplate, project, foresee. 2 expect you to comply: require, want, wish, insist on, demand, rely on, count on. 3 expect you're right: suppose, surmise, assume, believe, think, presume, imagine, reckon, guess (*infml*), trust.

**expectant** *adj* **1** AWAITING, anticipating, hopeful, in suspense, ready, apprehensive, anxious, watchful, eager, curious.
**2** PREGNANT, expecting (*infml*), with child (*fml*).

**expedition** *n* **1** JOURNEY, excursion, trip, voyage, tour, exploration, trek, safari, hike, sail, ramble, raid, quest, pilgrimage, mission, crusade. **2** (*fml*) PROMPTNESS, speed, alacrity, haste.

**expel** *v* **1** DRIVE OUT, eject, evict, banish, throw out, ban, bar, oust, exile, expatriate. **2** DISCHARGE, evacuate, void, cast out.
**E3** **1** welcome.

**expend** *v* **1** SPEND, pay, disburse (*fml*), fork out (*infml*). **2** CONSUME, use (up), dissipate, exhaust, employ.
**E3** **1** save. **2** conserve.

**expenditure** *n* spending, expense, outlay, outgoings, disbursement (*fml*), payment, output.
**E3** income.

**expense** *n* spending, expenditure, disbursement (*fml*), outlay, payment, loss, cost, charge.

**expensive** *adj* dear, high-priced, costly, exorbitant, extortionate, steep (*infml*), extravagant, lavish.
**E3** cheap, inexpensive.

**experience** *n* **1** KNOWLEDGE, familiarity, know-how, involvement, participation, practice, understanding. **2** INCIDENT, event, episode, happening, encounter, occurrence, adventure.
**E3** **1** inexperience.
*v* undergo, go through, live through, suffer, feel, endure, encounter, face, meet, know, try, perceive, sustain.

**experienced** *adj* **1** PRACTISED, knowledgeable, familiar, capable, competent, well-versed, expert, accomplished, qualified, skilled, tried, trained, professional.
**2** MATURE, seasoned, wise, veteran.

**E3** **1** inexperienced, unskilled.

**experiment** *n* trial, test, investigation, experimentation, research, examination, trial run, venture, trial and error, attempt, procedure, proof.
*v* try, test, investigate, examine, research, sample, verify.

**experimental** *adj* trial, test, exploratory, empirical (*fml*), tentative, provisional, speculative, pilot, preliminary, trial-and-error.

**expert** *n* specialist, connoisseur, authority, professional, pro (*infml*), dab hand (*infml*), maestro, virtuoso.
*adj* proficient, adept, skilled, skilful, knowledgeable, experienced, able, practised, professional, masterly, specialist, qualified, virtuoso.
**E3** amateurish, novice.

**expertise** *n* expertness, proficiency, skill, skilfulness, know-how, knack (*infml*), knowledge, mastery, dexterity, virtuosity.
**E3** inexperience.

**expire** *v* end, cease, finish, stop, terminate, close, conclude, discontinue, run out, lapse, die, depart, decease, perish.
**E3** begin.

**explain** *v* **1** INTERPRET, clarify, describe, define, make clear, elucidate, simplify, resolve, solve, spell out, translate, unfold, unravel, untangle, illustrate, demonstrate, disclose, expound, teach. **2** JUSTIFY, excuse, account for, rationalize.
**E3** **1** obscure, confound.

**explanation** *n* **1** INTERPRETATION, clarification, definition, elucidation, illustration, demonstration, account, description, exegesis (*fml*).
**2** JUSTIFICATION, excuse, warrant, rationalization. **3** ANSWER, meaning, motive, reason, key, sense, significance.

**explanatory** *adj* descriptive, interpretive, explicative, demonstrative, expository (*fml*), justifying.

**explicit** *adj* **1** CLEAR, distinct, exact, categorical, absolute, certain, positive, precise, specific, unambiguous, express, definite, declared, detailed, stated. **2** OPEN, direct, frank, outspoken, straightforward, unreserved, plain.
**F3 1** implicit, unspoken, vague.

**explode** *v* **1** BLOW UP, burst, go off, set off, detonate, discharge, blast, erupt. **2** DISCREDIT, disprove, give the lie to, debunk, invalidate, refute, rebut, repudiate.
**F3 2** prove, confirm.

**exploit** *n* deed, feat, adventure, achievement, accomplishment, attainment, stunt.
*v* **1** USE, utilize, capitalize on, profit by, turn to account, take advantage of, cash in on, make capital out of.
**2** MISUSE, abuse, oppress, ill-treat, impose on, manipulate, rip off (*infml*), fleece (*infml*).

**exploration** *n* **1** INVESTIGATION, examination, enquiry, research, scrutiny, study, inspection, analysis, probe. **2** EXPEDITION, survey, reconnaissance, search, trip, tour, voyage, travel, safari.

**explore** *v* **1** INVESTIGATE, examine, inspect, research, scrutinize, probe, analyse. **2** TRAVEL, tour, search, reconnoitre, prospect, scout, survey.

**explosion** *n* detonation, blast, burst, outburst, discharge, eruption, bang, outbreak, clap, crack, fit, report.

**explosive** *adj* unstable, volatile, sensitive, tense, fraught, charged, touchy, overwrought, dangerous, hazardous, perilous, stormy.
**F3** stable, calm.

**expose** *v* **1** REVEAL, show, exhibit, display, disclose, uncover, bring to light, present, manifest, detect, divulge, unveil, unmask, denounce.
**2** ENDANGER, jeopardize, imperil, risk, hazard.

**F3 1** conceal. **2** cover up.

**exposed** *adj* bare, open, revealed, laid bare, unprotected, vulnerable, exhibited, on display, on show, on view, shown, susceptible.
**F3** covered, sheltered.

**exposure** *n* **1** REVELATION, uncovering, disclosure, exposé, showing, unmasking, unveiling, display, airing, exhibition, presentation, publicity, manifestation, discovery, divulgence. **2** FAMILIARITY, experience, knowledge, contact. **3** JEOPARDY, danger, hazard, risk, vulnerability.

**express** *v* **1** ARTICULATE, verbalize, utter, voice, say, speak, state, communicate, pronounce, tell, assert, declare, put across, formulate, intimate, testify, convey. **2** SHOW, manifest, exhibit, disclose, reveal, indicate, denote, depict, embody. **3** SYMBOLIZE, stand for, represent, signify, designate.
*adj* **1** SPECIFIC, explicit, exact, definite, clear, categorical, precise, distinct, clear-cut, certain, plain, manifest, particular, stated, unambiguous. **2** FAST, speedy, rapid, quick, high-speed, non-stop.
**F3 1** vague.

**expression** *n* **1** LOOK, air, aspect, countenance, appearance, mien (*fml*). **2** REPRESENTATION, manifestation, demonstration, indication, exhibition, embodiment, show, sign, symbol, style. **3** UTTERANCE, verbalization, communication, articulation, statement, assertion, announcement, declaration, pronouncement, speech. **4** TONE, intonation, delivery, diction, enunciation, modulation, wording. **5** PHRASE, term, turn of phrase, saying, set phrase, idiom.

**expressionless** *adj* dull, blank, dead-pan, impassive, straight-faced, poker-faced (*infml*), inscrutable, empty, vacuous, glassy.

**expressive.**

**expressive** *adj* eloquent, meaningful, forceful, telling, revealing, informative, indicative, communicative, demonstrative, emphatic, moving, poignant, lively, striking, suggestive, significant, thoughtful, vivid, sympathetic.

**expulsion** *n* ejection, eviction, exile, banishment, removal, discharge, exclusion, dismissal.

**exquisite** *adj* **1** BEAUTIFUL, attractive, dainty, delicate, charming, elegant, delightful, lovely, pleasing. **2** PERFECT, flawless, fine, excellent, choice, precious, rare, outstanding. **3** REFINED, discriminating, meticulous, sensitive, impeccable. **4** INTENSE, keen, sharp, poignant.
**✍ 1** ugly. **2** flawed. **3** unrefined.

**extend** *v* **1** SPREAD, stretch, reach, continue. **2** ENLARGE, increase, expand, develop, amplify, lengthen, widen, elongate, draw out, protract, prolong, spin out, unwind. **3** OFFER, give, grant, hold out, impart, present, bestow, confer.
**✍ 2** contract, shorten. **3** withhold.

**extension** *n* **1** ENLARGEMENT, increase, stretching, broadening, widening, lengthening, expansion, elongation, development, enhancement, protraction, continuation. **2** ADDITION, supplement, appendix, annexe, addendum (*fml*). **3** DELAY, postponement.

**extensive** *adj* **1** BROAD, comprehensive, far-reaching, large-scale, thorough, widespread, universal, extended, all-inclusive, general, pervasive, prevalent. **2** LARGE, huge, roomy, spacious, vast, voluminous, long, lengthy, wide.
**✍ 1** restricted, narrow. **2** small.

**extent** *n* **1** DIMENSION(S), amount, magnitude, expanse, size, area, bulk, degree, breadth, quantity, spread, stretch, volume, width, measure, duration, term, time. **2** LIMIT, bounds, lengths, range, reach, scope, compass, sphere, play, sweep.

**exterior** *n* outside, surface, covering, coating, face, façade, shell, skin, finish, externals, appearance.
**✍** inside, interior.
*adj* outer, outside, outermost, surface, external, superficial, surrounding, outward, peripheral, extrinsic.
**✍** inside, interior.

**exterminate** *v* annihilate, eradicate, destroy, eliminate, massacre, abolish, wipe out.

**external** *adj* outer, surface, outside, exterior, superficial, outward, outermost, apparent, visible, extraneous, extrinsic, extramural, independent.
**✍** internal.

**extinct** *adj* **1** DEFUNCT, dead, gone, obsolete, ended, exterminated, terminated, vanished, lost, abolished. **2** EXTINGUISHED, quenched, inactive, out.
**✍ 1** living.

**extinction** *n* annihilation, extermination, death, eradication, obliteration, destruction, abolition, excision.

**extinguish** *v* **1** PUT OUT, blow out, snuff out, stifle, smother, douse, quench. **2** ANNIHILATE, exterminate, eliminate, destroy, kill, eradicate, erase, expunge, abolish, remove, end, suppress.

**extort** *v* extract, wring, exact, coerce, force, milk (*infml*), blackmail, squeeze, bleed (*infml*), bully.

**extortionate** *v* exorbitant, excessive, grasping, exacting, immoderate, rapacious, unreasonable, oppressive, blood-sucking (*infml*), rigorous, severe, hard, harsh, inordinate.

**extra** *adj* **1** ADDITIONAL, added, auxiliary, supplementary, new, more,

further, ancillary, fresh, other. **2**
EXCESS, spare, superfluous,
supernumerary, surplus, unused,
unneeded, leftover, reserve,
redundant.
 **1** integral. **2** essential.
*n* addition, supplement, extension,
accessory, appendage, bonus,
complement, adjunct, addendum
(*fml*), attachment.
*adv* especially, exceptionally,
extraordinarily, particularly, unusually,
remarkably, extremely.

**extract** *v* **1** REMOVE, take out, draw
out, exact, uproot, withdraw.
**2** DERIVE, draw, distil, obtain, get,
gather, glean, wrest, wring, elicit.
**3** CHOOSE, select, cull, abstract, cite,
quote.
 **1** insert.
*n* **1** DISTILLATION, essence, juice. **2**
EXCERPT, passage, selection, clip,
cutting, quotation, abstract, citation.

**extraordinary** *adj* remarkable,
unusual, exceptional, notable,
noteworthy, outstanding, unique,
special, strange, peculiar, rare,
surprising, amazing, wonderful,
unprecedented, marvellous, fantastic,
significant, particular.
 commonplace, ordinary.

**extravagance** *n* **1** OVERSPENDING,
profligacy, squandering, waste.
**2** EXCESS, immoderation,
recklessness, profusion,
outrageousness, folly.
 **1** thrift. **2** moderation.

**extravagant** *adj* **1** PROFLIGATE,
prodigal, spendthrift, thriftless,
wasteful, reckless. **2** IMMODERATE,
flamboyant, preposterous,
outrageous, ostentatious, pretentious,
lavish, ornate, flashy (*infml*),
fanciful, fantastic, wild. **3**
OVERPRICED, exorbitant, expensive,
excessive, costly.
 **1** thrifty. **2** moderate. **3** reasonable.

**extreme** *adj* **1** INTENSE, great,
immoderate, inordinate, utmost,

utter, out-and-out, maximum, acute,
downright, extraordinary,
exceptional, greatest, highest,
unreasonable, remarkable.
**2** FARTHEST, far-off, faraway,
distant, endmost, outermost,
remotest, uttermost, final, last,
terminal, ultimate. **3** RADICAL,
zealous, extremist, fanatical.
**4** DRASTIC, dire, uncompromising,
stern, strict, rigid, severe, harsh.
 **1** mild. **3** moderate.
*n* extremity, limit, maximum,
ultimate, utmost, excess, top,
pinnacle, peak, height, end, climax,
depth, edge, termination.

**extremity** *n* **1** EXTREME, limit,
boundary, brink, verge, bound,
border, apex, height, tip, top, edge,
excess, end, acme, termination, peak,
pinnacle, margin, terminal, terminus,
ultimate, pole, maximum, minimum,
frontier, depth. **2** CRISIS, danger,
emergency, plight, hardship.

**extricate** *v* disentangle, clear,
disengage, free, deliver, liberate,
release, rescue, relieve, remove,
withdraw.
 involve.

**extroverted** *adj* outgoing, friendly,
sociable, amicable, amiable,
exuberant.
 introverted.

**exuberant** *adj* **1** LIVELY, vivacious,
spirited, zestful, high-spirited,
effervescent, ebullient, enthusiastic,
sparkling, excited, exhilarated,
effusive, cheerful, fulsome. **2**
PLENTIFUL, lavish, overflowing,
plenteous.
 **1** apathetic. **2** scarce.

**exult** *v* rejoice, revel, delight, glory,
celebrate, relish, crow, gloat,
triumph.

**eye** *n* **1** APPRECIATION,
discrimination, discernment,
perception, recognition.
**2** VIEWPOINT, opinion, judgement,
mind. **3** WATCH, observation,

lookout.

> *Parts of the eye include*: anterior
> chamber, aqueous humour, blind
> spot, choroid, ciliary body, cone,
> conjunctiva, cornea, eyelash, fovea,
> iris, lacrimal duct, lens, lower eyelid,
> ocular muscle, optic nerve, papilla,
> pupil, posterior chamber, retina, rod,
> sclera, suspension ligament, upper
> eyelid, vitreous humour.

*v* look at, watch, regard, observe,

stare at, gaze at, glance at, view,
scrutinize, scan, examine, peruse,
study, survey, inspect, contemplate.

**eyesight** *n* vision, sight, perception,
observation, view.

**eyesore** *n* ugliness, blemish,
monstrosity, blot on the landscape,
disfigurement, horror, blight,
atrocity, mess.

**eye-witness** *n* witness, observer,
spectator, looker-on, onlooker,
bystander, viewer, passer-by.

# F

**fable** *n* allegory, parable, story, tale,
yarn, myth, legend, fiction,
fabrication, invention, lie, untruth,
falsehood, tall story, old wives' tale.

**fabric** *n* **1** CLOTH, material, textile,
stuff, web, texture. **2** STRUCTURE,
framework, construction, make-up,
constitution, organization,
infrastructure, foundations.

> *Fabrics include*: alpaca, angora,
> astrakhan, barathea, bouclé,
> cashmere, chenille, duffel, felt, flannel,
> fleece, Harris tweed®, mohair,
> paisley, serge, sheepskin, Shetland
> wool, tweed, vicuña, wool, worsted;
> brocade, buckram, calico, cambric,
> candlewick, canvas, chambray,
> cheesecloth, chino, chintz, cord,
> corduroy, cotton, crepe, denim, drill,
> jean, flannelette, gaberdine, gingham,
> jersey, lawn, linen, lisle, madras,
> moleskin, muslin, needlecord, piqué,
> poplin, sateen, seersucker, terry
> towelling, ticking, Viyella®, webbing,
> winceyette; brocade, grosgrain,
> damask, Brussels lace, chiffon,
> georgette, gossamer, voile, organza,
> organdie, tulle, net, crepe de Chine,
> silk, taffeta, shantung, velvet, velour;

> polycotton, polyester, rayon, nylon,
> Crimplene®, Terylene®, Lurex®,
> lamé; hessian, horsehair, chamois,
> kid, leather, leather-cloth, sharkskin,
> suede.

**fabricate** *v* **1** FAKE, falsify, forge,
invent, make up, trump up, concoct.
**2** MAKE, manufacture, construct,
assemble, build, erect, form, shape,
fashion, create, devise.
**F3 2** demolish, destroy.

**fabulous** *adj* **1** WONDERFUL,
marvellous, fantastic, superb,
breathtaking, spectacular,
phenomenal, amazing, astounding,
unbelievable, incredible,
inconceivable. **2** *a fabulous beast*:
mythical, legendary, fabled, fantastic,
fictitious, invented, imaginary.
**F3 2** real.

**face** *n* **1** FEATURES, countenance,
visage, physiognomy. **2** EXPRESSION,
look, appearance, air. **3** *pull a face*:
grimace, frown, scowl, pout. **4**
EXTERIOR, outside, surface, cover,
front, façade, aspect, side.
*v* **1** BE OPPOSITE, give on to, front,
overlook. **2** CONFRONT, face up to,
deal with, cope with, tackle, brave,

defy, oppose, encounter, meet,
experience. **3** COVER, coat, dress,
clad, overlay, veneer.

**face to face** opposite, eye to eye,
eyeball to eyeball, in confrontation.

**face up to** accept, come to terms with,
acknowledge, recognize, cope with,
deal with, confront, meet head-on,
stand up to.

**facet** *n* surface, plane, side, face,
aspect, angle, point, feature,
characteristic.

**facetious** *adj* flippant, frivolous,
playful, jocular, jesting, tongue-in-
cheek, funny, amusing, humorous,
comical, witty.
**E3** serious.

**facile** *adj* easy, simple, simplistic,
ready, quick, hasty, glib, fluent,
smooth, slick, plausible, shallow,
superficial.
**E3** complicated, profound.

**facilitate** *v* ease, help, assist, further,
promote, forward, expedite, speed
up.

**facilities** *n* amenities, services,
conveniences, resources,
prerequisites, equipment, mod cons
(*infml*), means, opportunities.

**facility** *n* ease, effortlessness,
readiness, quickness, fluency,
proficiency, skill, skilfulness, talent,
gift, knack, ability.

**fact** *n* **1** *facts and figures*:
information, datum, detail,
particular, specific, point, item,
circumstance, event, incident,
occurrence, happening, act, deed, fait
accompli. **2** REALITY, actuality,
truth.
**E3 2** fiction.

**in fact** actually, in actual fact, in point
of fact, as a matter of fact, in reality,
really, indeed.

**faction** *n* splinter group, ginger
group, minority, division, section,
contingent, party, camp, set, clique,
coterie, cabal, junta, lobby, pressure
group.

**factor** *n* cause, influence,
circumstance, contingency,
consideration, element, ingredient,
component, part, point, aspect, fact,
item, detail.

**factory** *n* works, plant, mill, shop
floor, assembly line, manufactory.

**factual** *adj* true, historical, actual,
real, genuine, authentic, correct,
accurate, precise, exact, literal,
faithful, close, detailed, unbiased,
objective.
**E3** false, fictitious, imaginary,
fictional.

**faculties** *n* wits, senses, intelligence,
reason, powers, capabilities.

**faculty** *n* ability, capability,
capacity, power, facility, knack, gift,
talent, skill, aptitude, bent.

**fad** *n* craze, rage (*infml*), mania,
fashion, mode, vogue, trend, whim,
fancy, affectation.

**fade** *v* **1** DISCOLOUR, bleach,
blanch, blench, pale, whiten, dim,
dull. **2** DECLINE, fall, diminish,
dwindle, ebb, wane, disappear,
vanish, flag, weaken, droop, wilt,
wither, shrivel, perish, die.

**fail** *v* **1** GO WRONG, miscarry,
misfire, flop, miss, flunk (*sl*), fall
through, come to grief, collapse, fold
(*infml*), go bankrupt, go bust, go
under, founder, sink, decline, fail,
weaken, dwindle, fade, wane, peter
out, cease, die. **2** *fail to pay a bill*:
omit, neglect, forget. **3** LET DOWN,
disappoint, leave, desert, abandon,
forsake.
**E3** succeed, prosper.

**failing** *n* weakness, foible, fault,
defect, imperfection, flaw, blemish,
drawback, deficiency, shortcoming,
failure, lapse, error.
**E3** strength, advantage.

**failure** *n* **1** MISCARRIAGE, flop,
wash-out (*infml*), fiasco,
disappointment, loss, defeat,
downfall, decline, decay,
deterioration, ruin, bankruptcy,

crash, collapse, breakdown,
stoppage. **2** OMISSION, slip-up
(*infml*), neglect, negligence, failing,
shortcoming, deficiency.
**F3 1** success, prosperity.

**faint** *adj* **1** SLIGHT, weak, feeble,
soft, low, hushed, muffled, subdued,
faded, bleached, light, pale, dull,
dim, hazy, indistinct, vague. **2** *I feel
faint*: dizzy, giddy, woozy (*infml*),
light-headed, weak, feeble,
exhausted.
**F3 1** strong, clear.
*v* black out, pass out, swoon,
collapse, flake out (*infml*), keel over
(*infml*), drop.
*n* blackout, swoon, collapse,
unconsciousness.

**fair**[1] *adj* **1** JUST, equitable, square,
even-handed, dispassionate,
impartial, objective, disinterested,
unbiased, unprejudiced, right,
proper, lawful, legitimate, honest,
trustworthy, upright, honourable.
**2** FAIR-HAIRED, fair-headed,
blond(e), light. **3** *fair weather*: fine,
dry, sunny, bright, clear, cloudless,
unclouded. **4** AVERAGE, moderate,
middling, not bad, all right, OK
(*infml*), satisfactory, adequate,
acceptable, tolerable, reasonable,
passable, mediocre, so-so (*infml*).
**F3 1** unfair. **2** dark. **3** inclement,
cloudy. **4** excellent, poor.

**fair**[2] *n* show, exhibition, exposition,
expo (*infml*), market, bazaar, fête,
festival, carnival, gala.

**faith** *n* **1** BELIEF, credit, trust,
reliance, dependence, conviction,
confidence, assurance. **2** RELIGION,
denomination, persuasion, church,
creed, dogma. **3** FAITHFULNESS,
fidelity, loyalty, allegiance, honour,
sincerity, honesty, truthfulness.
**F3 1** mistrust. **3** unfaithfulness,
treachery.

**faithful** *adj* **1** LOYAL, devoted,
staunch, steadfast, constant, trusty,
reliable, dependable, true. **2** *a faithful

description*: accurate, precise, exact,
strict, close, true, truthful.
**F3 1** disloyal, treacherous.
**2** inaccurate, vague.

**fake** *v* forge, fabricate, counterfeit,
copy, imitate, simulate, feign, sham,
pretend, put on, affect, assume.
*n* forgery, copy, reproduction,
replica, imitation, simulation, sham,
hoax, fraud, phoney (*infml*), impostor,
charlatan.
*adj* forged, counterfeit, false,
spurious, phoney (*infml*), pseudo,
bogus, assumed, affected, sham,
artificial, simulated, mock, imitation,
reproduction.
**F3** genuine.

**fall** *v* **1** TUMBLE, stumble, trip,
topple, keel over, collapse, slump,
crash. **2** DESCEND, go down, drop,
slope, incline, slide, sink, dive,
plunge, plummet, nose-dive, pitch.
**3** DECREASE, lessen, decline,
diminish, dwindle, fall off, subside.
**F3 2** rise. **3** increase.
*n* **1** TUMBLE, descent, slope, incline,
dive, plunge, decrease, reduction,
lessening, drop, decline, dwindling,
slump, crash. **2** *the fall of Rome*:
defeat, conquest, overthrow, downfall,
collapse, surrender, capitulation.

**fall apart** break, go to pieces, shatter,
disintegrate, crumble, decompose,
decay, rot.

**fall asleep** drop off, doze off, nod off
(*infml*).

**fall back on** resort to, have recourse to,
use, turn to, look to.

**fall behind** lag, trail, drop back.

**fall in** cave in, come down, collapse,
give way, subside, sink.

**fall in with** agree with, assent to, go
along with, accept, comply with, co-
operate with.

**fall off** decrease, lessen, drop, slump,
decline, deteriorate, worsen, slow,
slacken.

**fall out** quarrel, argue, squabble,
bicker, fight, clash, disagree, differ.

**agree.**

**fall through** come to nothing, fail, miscarry, founder, collapse.
☒ come off, succeed.

**fallacy** n misconception, delusion, mistake, error, flaw, inconsistency, falsehood.
☒ truth.

**fallow** adj uncultivated, unplanted, unsown, undeveloped, unused, idle, inactive, dormant, resting.

**false** adj 1 wrong, incorrect, mistaken, erroneous, inaccurate, inexact, misleading, faulty, fallacious, invalid. 2 UNREAL, artificial, synthetic, imitation, simulated, mock, fake, counterfeit, forged, feigned, pretended, sham, bogus, assumed, fictitious. 3 *false friends*: disloyal, unfaithful, faithless, lying, deceitful, insincere, hypocritical, two-faced, double-dealing, treacherous, unreliable.
☒ 1 true, right. 2 real, genuine. 3 faithful, reliable.

**falsehood** n untruth, lie, fib, story, fiction, fabrication, perjury, untruthfulness, deceit, deception, dishonesty.
☒ truth, truthfulness.

**falsify** v alter, cook (*infml*), tamper with, doctor, distort, pervert, misrepresent, misstate, forge, counterfeit, fake.

**falter** v totter, stumble, stammer, stutter, hesitate, waver, vacillate, flinch, quail, shake, tremble, flag, fail.

**fame** n renown, celebrity, stardom, prominence, eminence, illustriousness, glory, honour, esteem, reputation, name.

**familiar** adj 1 EVERYDAY, routine, household, common, ordinary, well-known, recognizable. 2 INTIMATE, close, confidential, friendly, informal, free, free-and-easy, relaxed.
3 *familiar with the procedure*: aware, acquainted, abreast, knowledgeable,

versed, conversant.
☒ 1 unfamiliar, strange. 2 formal, reserved. 3 unfamiliar, ignorant.

**familiarity** n 1 INTIMACY, liberty, closeness, friendliness, sociability, openness, naturalness, informality.
2 AWARENESS, acquaintance, experience, knowledge, understanding, grasp.

**familiarize** v accustom, acclimatize, school, train, coach, instruct, prime, brief.

**family** n 1 RELATIVES, relations, kin, kindred, kinsmen, people, folk (*infml*), ancestors, forebears, children, offspring, issue, progeny, descendants. 2 CLAN, tribe, race, dynasty, house, pedigree, ancestry, parentage, descent, line, lineage, extraction, blood, stock, birth.
3 CLASS, group, classification.

> *Members of a family include*: ancestor, forebear, forefather, descendant, offspring, heir; husband, wife, spouse, parent, father, dad (*infml*), daddy (*infml*), old man (*infml*), mother, mum (*infml*), mummy (*infml*), mom (*US infml*), grandparent, grandfather, grandmother, granny (*infml*), nanny (*infml*), grandchild, son, daughter, brother, half-brother, sister, half-sister, sibling, uncle, aunt, nephew, niece, cousin, godfather, godmother, godchild, stepfather, stepmother, foster-parent, foster-child.

**family tree** ancestry, pedigree, genealogy, line, lineage, extraction.

**famine** n starvation, hunger, destitution, want, scarcity, death.
☒ plenty.

**famous** adj well-known, famed, renowned, celebrated, noted, great, distinguished, illustrious, eminent, honoured, acclaimed, glorious, legendary, remarkable, notable, prominent, signal.
☒ unheard-of, unknown, obscure.

**fan¹** *v* **1** COOL, ventilate, air, air-
condition, air-cool, blow, refresh.
**2** INCREASE, provoke, stimulate,
rouse, arouse, excite, agitate, stir up,
work up, whip up.
*n* extractor fan, ventilator, air-
conditioner, blower, propeller, vane.

**fan²** *n* enthusiast, admirer,
supporter, follower, adherent,
devotee, lover, buff (*infml*), fiend,
freak.

**fanatic** *n* zealot, devotee, enthusiast,
addict, fiend, freak, maniac,
visionary, bigot, extremist, militant,
activist.

**fanatical** *adj* overenthusiastic,
extreme, passionate, zealous, fervent,
burning, mad, wild, frenzied, rabid,
obsessive, single-minded, bigoted,
visionary.
🔁 moderate, unenthusiastic.

**fanaticism** *n* extremism,
monomania, single-mindedness,
obsessiveness, madness, infatuation,
bigotry, zeal, fervour, enthusiasm,
dedication.
🔁 moderation.

**fanciful** *adj* imaginary, mythical,
fabulous, fantastic, visionary,
romantic, fairy-tale, airy-fairy,
vaporous, whimsical, wild,
extravagant, curious.
🔁 real, ordinary.

**fancy** *v* **1** LIKE, be attracted to, take
a liking to, take to, go for, prefer,
favour, desire, wish for, long for,
yearn for. **2** THINK, conceive,
imagine, dream of, picture,
conjecture, believe, suppose, reckon,
guess.
🔁 **1** dislike.
*n* **1** DESIRE, craving, hankering, urge,
liking, fondness, inclination,
preference. **2** NOTION, thought,
impression, imagination, dream,
fantasy.
🔁 **1** dislike, aversion. **2** fact, reality.
*adj* elaborate, ornate, decorated,
ornamented, rococo, baroque,
elegant, extravagant, fantastic,
fanciful, far-fetched.
🔁 plain.

**fantastic** *adj* **1** WONDERFUL,
marvellous, sensational, superb,
excellent, first-rate, tremendous,
terrific, great, incredible,
unbelievable, overwhelming,
enormous, extreme.
**2** STRANGE, weird, odd, exotic,
outlandish, fanciful, fabulous,
imaginative, visionary.
🔁 **1** ordinary. **2** real.

**fantasy** *n* dream, daydream, reverie,
pipe-dream, nightmare, vision,
hallucination, illusion, mirage,
apparition, invention, fancy, flight of
fancy, delusion, misconception,
imagination, unreality.
🔁 reality.

**far** *adv* a long way, a good way,
miles (*infml*), much, greatly,
considerably, extremely, decidedly,
incomparably.
🔁 near, close.
*adj* distant, far-off, faraway, far-flung,
outlying, remote, out-of-the-way, god-
forsaken, removed, far-removed,
further, opposite, other.
🔁 nearby, close.

**farce** *n* **1** COMEDY, slapstick,
buffoonery, satire, burlesque.
**2** TRAVESTY, sham, parody, joke,
mockery, ridiculousness, absurdity,
nonsense.

**fare** *n* **1** *pay one's fare*: charge, cost,
price, fee, passage. **2** FOOD, eatables
(*infml*), provisions, rations,
sustenance, meals, diet, menu, board,
table.

**far-fetched** *adj* implausible,
improbable, unlikely, dubious,
incredible, unbelievable, fantastic,
preposterous, crazy, unrealistic.
🔁 plausible.

**farm** *n* ranch, farmstead, grange,
homestead, station, land, holding,
acreage, acres.

*Types of farm include*: arable farm, cattle ranch, dairy farm, fish farm, mixed farm, organic farm, pig farm, sheep station, croft, smallholding, estate, plantation.

*v* cultivate, till, work the land, plant, operate.

**farmer** *n* agriculturist, crofter, smallholder, husbandman, yeoman.

**farming** *n* agriculture, cultivation, husbandry, crofting.

**far-reaching** *adj* broad, extensive, widespread, sweeping, important, momentous.
🔁 insignificant.

**fascinate** *v* absorb, engross, intrigue, delight, charm, captivate, spellbind, enthral, rivet, transfix, hypnotize, mesmerize.
🔁 bore, repel.

**fascination** *n* interest, attraction, lure, magnetism, pull, charm, enchantment, spell, sorcery, magic.
🔁 boredom, repulsion.

**fashion** *n* **1** MANNER, way, method, mode, style, shape, form, pattern, line, cut, look, appearance, type, sort, kind. **2** VOGUE, trend, mode, style, fad, craze, rage (*infml*), latest (*infml*), custom, convention.
*v* create, form, shape, mould, model, design, fit, tailor, alter, adjust, adapt, suit.

**fashionable** *adj* chic, smart, elegant, stylish, modish, à la mode, in vogue, trendy (*infml*), in, all the rage (*infml*), popular, prevailing, current, latest, up-to-the-minute, contemporary, modern, up-to-date.
🔁 unfashionable.

**fast¹** *adj* **1** QUICK, swift, rapid, brisk, accelerated, speedy, nippy (*infml*), hasty, hurried, flying. **2** FASTENED, secure, fixed, immovable, immobile, firm, tight.
🔁 **1** slow, unhurried. **2** loose.
*adv* quickly, swiftly, rapidly, speedily, like a flash, like a shot, hastily,

hurriedly, apace, presto.
🔁 slowly, gradually.

**fast²** *v* go hungry, diet, starve, abstain.
*n* fasting, diet, starvation, abstinence.
🔁 gluttony, self-indulgence.

**fasten** *v* fix, attach, clamp, grip, anchor, rivet, nail, seal, close, shut, lock, bolt, secure, tie, bind, chain, link, interlock, connect, join, unite, do up, button, lace, buckle.
🔁 unfasten, untie.

**fat** *adj* plump, obese, tubby, stout, corpulent, portly, round, rotund, paunchy, pot-bellied, overweight, heavy, beefy, solid, chubby, podgy, fleshy, flabby, gross.
🔁 thin, slim, poor.
*n* fatness, obesity, overweight, corpulence, paunch, pot (belly), blubber, flab (*infml*).

**fatal** *adj* deadly, lethal, mortal, killing, incurable, malignant, terminal, final, destructive, calamitous, catastrophic, disastrous.
🔁 harmless.

**fatality** *n* death, mortality, loss, casualty, deadliness, lethality, disaster.

**fate** *n* destiny, providence, chance, future, fortune, horoscope, stars, lot, doom, end, outcome, ruin, destruction, death.

**fated** *adj* destined, predestined, preordained, foreordained, doomed, unavoidable, inevitable, inescapable, certain, sure.
🔁 avoidable.

**fateful** *adj* crucial, critical, decisive, important, momentous, significant, fatal, lethal, disastrous.
🔁 unimportant.

**father** *n* **1** PARENT, begetter, procreator, progenitor, sire (*fml*), papa, dad (*infml*), daddy (*infml*), old man (*infml*), patriarch, elder, forefather, ancestor, forebear, predecessor. **2** FOUNDER, creator,

originator, inventor, maker,
architect, author, patron, leader,
prime mover. **3** PRIEST, padre, abbé,
curé.

*v* beget, procreate, sire, produce.

**fathom** *v* **1** MEASURE, gauge, plumb,
sound, probe, penetrate.
**2** UNDERSTAND, comprehend, grasp,
see, work out, get to the bottom of,
interpret.

**fatigue** *n* tiredness, weariness,
exhaustion, lethargy, listlessness,
lassitude, weakness, debility.
🖃 energy.

*v* tire, wear out, weary, exhaust,
drain, weaken, debilitate.

**fatten** *v* feed, nourish, build up,
overfeed, cram, stuff, bloat, swell, fill
out, spread, expand, thicken.

**fatty** *adj* fat, greasy, oily.

**fault** *n* **1** DEFECT, flaw, blemish,
imperfection, deficiency,
shortcoming, weakness, failing,
foible, negligence, omission,
oversight. **2** ERROR, mistake,
blunder, slip-up (*infml*), slip, lapse,
misdeed, offence, wrong, sin. **3** *it's
your fault*: responsibility,
accountability, liability, culpability.
*v* find fault with, pick holes in,
criticize, knock (*infml*), impugn,
censure, blame, call to account.
🖃 praise.

**at fault** (in the) wrong, blameworthy,
to blame, responsible, guilty, culpable.

**faultless** *adj* perfect, flawless,
unblemished, spotless, immaculate,
unsullied, pure, blameless,
exemplary, model, correct, accurate.
🖃 faulty, imperfect, flawed.

**faulty** *adj* imperfect, defective,
flawed, blemished, damaged,
impaired, out of order, broken,
wrong.
🖃 faultless.

**favour** *n* **1** APPROVAL, esteem,
support, backing, sympathy,
goodwill, patronage, favouritism,
preference, partiality. **2** *he did me a*

*favour*: kindness, service, good turn,
courtesy.
🖃 **1** disapproval.
*v* **1** PREFER, choose, opt for, like,
approve, support, back, advocate,
champion. **2** HELP, assist, aid,
benefit, promote, encourage, pamper,
spoil.
🖃 **1** dislike. **2** mistreat.

**in favour of** for, supporting, on the side
of.
🖃 against.

**favourable** *adj* beneficial,
advantageous, helpful, fit, suitable,
convenient, timely, opportune, good,
fair, promising, auspicious, hopeful,
positive, encouraging,
complimentary, enthusiastic,
friendly, amicable, well-disposed,
kind, sympathetic, understanding,
reassuring.
🖃 unfavourable, unhelpful, negative.

**favourite** *adj* preferred, favoured,
pet, best-loved, dearest, beloved,
esteemed, chosen.
🖃 hated.
*n* preference, choice, pick, pet, blue-
eyed boy, teacher's pet, the apple of
one's eye, darling, idol.
🖃 bête noire, pet hate.

**favouritism** *n* nepotism, preferential
treatment, preference, partiality, one-
sidedness, partisanship, bias,
injustice.
🖃 impartiality.

**fear** *n* alarm, fright, terror, horror,
panic, agitation, worry, anxiety,
consternation, concern, dismay,
distress, uneasiness, qualms,
misgivings, apprehension,
trepidation, dread, foreboding, awe,
phobia, nightmare.
🖃 courage, bravery, confidence.
*v* take fright, shrink from, dread,
shudder at, tremble, worry, suspect,
anticipate, expect, foresee, respect,
venerate.

**fearful** *adj* **1** FRIGHTENED, afraid,
scared, alarmed, nervous, anxious,

tense, uneasy, apprehensive, hesitant, nervy, panicky. **2** TERRIBLE, fearsome (*fml*), dreadful, awful, frightful, atrocious, shocking, appalling, monstrous, gruesome, hideous, ghastly, horrible.
**F3 1** brave, courageous, fearless.
**2** wonderful, delightful.

**feasible** *adj* practicable, practical, workable, achievable, attainable, realizable, viable, reasonable, possible, likely.
**F3** impossible.

**feast** *n* **1** BANQUET, dinner, spread, blow-out (*sl*), binge (*infml*), beano (*infml*), junket. **2** FESTIVAL, holiday, gala, fête, celebration, revels.
*v* gorge, eat one's fill, wine and dine, treat, entertain.

**feat** *n* exploit, deed, act, accomplishment, achievement, attainment, performance.

**feature** *n* **1** ASPECT, facet, point, factor, attribute, quality, property, trait, lineament, characteristic, peculiarity, mark, hallmark, speciality, highlight. **2** *a magazine feature*: column, article, report, story, piece, item, comment.
*v* **1** EMPHASIZE, highlight, spotlight, play up, promote, show, present.
**2** APPEAR, figure, participate, act, perform, star.

**fee** *n* charge, terms, bill, account, pay, remuneration, payment, retainer, subscription, reward, recompense, hire, toll.

**feeble** *adj* **1** WEAK, faint, exhausted, frail, delicate, puny, sickly, infirm, powerless, helpless. **2** INADEQUATE, lame, poor, thin, flimsy, ineffective, incompetent, indecisive.
**F3 1** strong, powerful.

**feed** *v* nourish, cater for, provide for, supply, sustain, suckle, nurture, foster, strengthen, fuel, graze, pasture, eat, dine.
*n* food, fodder, forage, pasture, silage.

**feed on** eat, consume, devour, live on, exist on.

**feel** *v* **1** EXPERIENCE, go through, undergo, suffer, endure, enjoy.
**2** TOUCH, finger, handle, manipulate, hold, stroke, caress, fondle, paw, fumble, grope. **3** *feel soft*: seem, appear. **4** THINK, believe, consider, reckon, judge. **5** SENSE, perceive, notice, observe, know.
*n* texture, surface, finish, touch, knack, sense, impression, feeling, quality.

**feel for** pity, sympathize (with), commiserate (with), be sorry for.

**feel like** fancy, want, desire.

**feeling** *n* **1** SENSATION, perception, sense, instinct, hunch, suspicion, inkling, impression, idea, notion, opinion, view, point of view.
**2** EMOTION, passion, intensity, warmth, compassion, sympathy, understanding, pity, concern, affection, fondness, sentiment, sentimentality, susceptibility, sensibility, sensitivity, appreciation.
**3** AIR, aura, atmosphere, mood, quality.

**fell** *v* cut down, hew, knock down, strike down, floor, level, flatten, raze, demolish.

**fellow** *n* **1** PERSON, man, boy, chap (*infml*), bloke (*infml*), guy (*infml*), individual, character. **2** PEER, compeer, equal, partner, associate, colleague, co-worker, companion, comrade, friend, counterpart, match, mate, twin, double.
*adj* co-, associate, associated, related, like, similar.

**fellowship** *n* **1** COMPANIONSHIP, camaraderie, communion, familiarity, intimacy.
**2** ASSOCIATION, league, guild, society, club, fraternity, brotherhood, sisterhood, order.

**female** *adj* feminine, she-, girlish, womanly.
**F3** male.

*Female terms include*: girl, lass, maiden, woman, lady, daughter, sister, girlfriend, fiancée, bride, wife, mother, aunt, niece, grandmother, matriarch, godmother, widow, dowager, dame, madam, mistress, virgin, spinster, old-maid, bird (*sl*), chick (*sl*), lesbian, bitch (*sl*), prostitute, whore, harlot; cow, heifer, bitch, doe, ewe, hen, mare, filly, nanny-goat, sow, tigress, vixen.

**feminine** *adj* **1** FEMALE, womanly, ladylike, graceful, gentle, tender. **2** EFFEMINATE, unmanly, womanish, girlish, sissy.
**F3** **1** masculine. **2** manly.

**feminism** *n* women's movement, women's lib(eration), female emancipation, women's rights.

**fence** *n* barrier, railing, paling, wall, hedge, windbreak, guard, defence, barricade, stockade, rampart.
*v* **1** SURROUND, encircle, bound, hedge, wall, enclose, pen, coop, confine, restrict, separate, protect, guard, defend, fortify. **2** PARRY, dodge, evade, hedge, equivocate, quibble, pussyfoot, stonewall.

**fencing**

*Fencing terms include*: appel, attack, balestra, barrage, coquille, disengage, en garde, épée, feint, flèche, foible, foil, forte, hit, lunge, on guard, parry, counter-parry, pink, piste, plastron, remise, reprise, riposte, counter-riposte, sabre, tac-au-tac, thrust, touch, touché, volt.

**fend for** look after, take care of, shift for, support, maintain, sustain, provide for.

**fend off** ward off, beat off, parry, deflect, avert, resist, repel, repulse, hold at bay, keep off, shut out.

**ferment** *v* **1** BUBBLE, effervesce, froth, foam, boil, seethe, smoulder, fester, brew, rise. **2** ROUSE, stir up,
excite, work up, agitate, foment, incite, provoke, inflame, heat.
*n* unrest, agitation, turbulence, stir, excitement, turmoil, disruption, commotion, tumult, hubbub, uproar, furore, frenzy, fever, glow.
**F3** calm.

**ferocious** *adj* vicious, savage, fierce, wild, barbarous, barbaric, brutal, inhuman, cruel, sadistic, murderous, bloodthirsty, violent, merciless, pitiless, ruthless.
**F3** gentle, mild, tame.

**ferocity** *n* viciousness, savagery, fierceness, wildness, barbarity, brutality, inhumanity, cruelty, sadism, bloodthirstiness, violence, ruthlessness.
**F3** gentleness, mildness.

**ferry** *n* ferry-boat, car ferry, ship, boat, vessel.
*v* transport, ship, convey, carry, take, shuttle, taxi, drive, run, move, shift.

**fertile** *adj* fruitful, productive, generative, yielding, prolific, teeming, abundant, plentiful, rich, lush, luxuriant, fat.
**F3** infertile, barren, sterile, unproductive.

**fertilize** *v* **1** IMPREGNATE, inseminate, pollinate. **2** *fertilize land*: enrich, feed, dress, compost, manure, dung.

**fertilizer** *n* dressing, compost, manure, dung.

**fervent** *adj* ardent, earnest, eager, enthusiastic, whole-hearted, excited, energetic, vigorous, fiery, spirited, intense, vehement, passionate, full-blooded, zealous, devout, heartfelt, impassioned, emotional, warm.
**F3** cool, indifferent, apathetic.

**fervour** *n* ardour, eagerness, enthusiasm, excitement, animation, energy, vigour, spirit, verve, intensity, vehemence, passion, zeal, warmth.
**F3** apathy.

**fester** *v* ulcerate, gather, suppurate,

discharge, putrefy, rot, decay, rankle, smoulder.

**festival** n celebration, commemoration, anniversary, jubilee, holiday, feast, gala, fête, carnival, fiesta, party, merrymaking, entertainment, festivities.

**festive** adj celebratory, festal, holiday, gala, carnival, happy, joyful, merry, hearty, cheery, jolly, jovial, cordial, convivial.
**F3** gloomy, sombre, sober.

**festivity** n celebration, jubilation, feasting, banqueting, fun, enjoyment, pleasure, entertainment, sport, amusement, merriment, merrymaking, revelry, jollity, joviality, conviviality.

**festoon** v adorn, deck, bedeck, garland, wreathe, drape, hang, swathe, decorate, garnish.

**fetch** v 1 *fetch a bucket*: get, collect, bring, carry, transport, deliver, escort. 2 SELL FOR, go for, bring in, yield, realize, make, earn.

**fetching** adj attractive, pretty, sweet, cute, charming, enchanting, fascinating, captivating.
**F3** repellent.

**fête** n fair, bazaar, sale of work, garden party, gala, carnival, festival.
v entertain, treat, regale, welcome, honour, lionize.

**feud** n vendetta, quarrel, row, argument, disagreement, dispute, conflict, strife, discord, animosity, ill will, bitterness, enmity, hostility, antagonism, rivalry.
**F3** agreement, peace.

**fever** n 1 FEVERISHNESS, (high) temperature, delirium.
2 EXCITEMENT, agitation, turmoil, unrest, restlessness, heat, passion, ecstasy.

**feverish** adj 1 DELIRIOUS, hot, burning, flushed. 2 EXCITED, impatient, agitated, restless, nervous, overwrought, frenzied, frantic, hectic, hasty, hurried.

**F3** 1 cool. 2 calm.

**few** adj scarce, rare, uncommon, sporadic, infrequent, sparse, thin, scant, scanty, meagre, inconsiderable, inadequate, insufficient, in short supply.
**F3** many.
pron not many, hardly any, one or two, a couple, scattering, sprinkling, handful, some.
**F3** many.

**fibre** n 1 FILAMENT, strand, thread, nerve, sinew, pile, texture. 2 *moral fibre*: character, calibre, backbone, strength, stamina, toughness, courage, resolution, determination.

**fickle** adj inconstant, disloyal, unfaithful, faithless, treacherous, unreliable, unpredictable, changeable, capricious, mercurial, irresolute, vacillating.
**F3** constant, steady, stable.

**fiction** n 1 FANTASY, fancy, imagination, figment, invention, fabrication, concoction, improvisation, story-telling.
2 NOVEL, romance, story, tale, yarn, fable, parable, legend, myth, lie.
**F3** 2 non-fiction, fact, truth.

**fictional** adj literary, invented, made-up, imaginary, make-believe, legendary, mythical, mythological, fabulous, non-existent, unreal.
**F3** factual, real.

**fictitious** adj false, untrue, invented, made-up, fabricated, apocryphal, imaginary, non-existent, bogus, counterfeit, spurious, assumed, supposed.
**F3** true, genuine.

**fiddle** v 1 *fiddling with her necklace*: play, tinker, toy, trifle, tamper, mess around, meddle, interfere, fidget.
2 CHEAT, swindle, diddle, cook the books (*infml*), juggle, manoeuvre, racketeer, graft (*sl*).
n swindle, con (*infml*), rip-off (*sl*), fraud, racket, sharp practice, graft (*sl*).

**fiddling** adj trifling, petty, trivial,

insignificant, negligible, paltry.
**F3** important, significant.

**fidelity** n 1 FAITHFULNESS, loyalty, allegiance, devotion, constancy, reliability. 2 ACCURACY, exactness, precision, closeness, adherence.
**F3** 1 infidelity, inconstancy, treachery. 2 inaccuracy.

**fidget** v squirm, wriggle, shuffle, twitch, jerk, jump, fret, fuss, bustle, fiddle, mess about, play around.

**fidgety** adj restless, impatient, uneasy, nervous, agitated, jittery, jumpy, twitchy, on edge.
**F3** still.

**field** n 1 GRASSLAND, meadow, pasture, paddock, playing-field, ground, pitch, green, lawn. 2 RANGE, scope, bounds, limits, confines, territory, area, province, domain, sphere, environment, department, discipline, speciality, line, forte. 3 PARTICIPANTS, entrants, contestants, competitors, contenders, runners, candidates, applicants, opponents, opposition, competition.

**fiend** n 1 EVIL SPIRIT, demon, devil, monster. 2 a health fiend: enthusiast, fanatic, addict, devotee, freak (infml), nut (infml).

**fiendish** adj devilish, diabolical, infernal, wicked, malevolent, cunning, cruel, inhuman, savage, monstrous, unspeakable.

**fierce** adj ferocious, vicious, savage, cruel, brutal, merciless, aggressive, dangerous, murderous, frightening, menacing, threatening, stern, grim, relentless, raging, wild, passionate, intense, strong, powerful.
**F3** gentle, kind, calm.

**fiery** adj 1 BURNING, afire, flaming, aflame, blazing, ablaze, red-hot, glowing, aglow, flushed, hot, torrid, sultry. 2 PASSIONATE, inflamed, ardent, fervent, impatient, excitable, impetuous, impulsive, hot-headed, fierce, violent, heated.
**F3** 1 cold. 2 impassive.

**fight** v 1 WRESTLE, box, fence, joust, brawl, scrap, scuffle, tussle, skirmish, combat, battle, do battle, war, wage war, clash, cross swords, engage, grapple, struggle, strive, contend. 2 QUARREL, argue, dispute, squabble, bicker, wrangle. 3 OPPOSE, contest, campaign against, resist, withstand, defy, stand up to.
n 1 BOUT, contest, duel, combat, action, battle, war, hostilities, brawl, scrap, scuffle, tussle, struggle, skirmish, set-to, clash, engagement, brush, encounter, conflict, fray, free-for-all, fracas, riot. 2 QUARREL, row, argument, dispute, dissension.

**fight back** 1 RETALIATE, defend oneself, resist, put up a fight, retort, reply. 2 fight back the tears: hold back, restrain, curb, control, repress, bottle up, contain, suppress.

**fight off** hold off, keep at bay, ward off, stave off, resist, repel, rebuff, beat off, rout, put to flight.

**fighter** n combatant, contestant, contender, disputant, boxer, wrestler, pugilist, prizefighter, soldier, trouper, mercenary, warrior, man-at-arms, swordsman, gladiator.

**figurative** adj metaphorical, symbolic, emblematic, representative, allegorical, parabolic, descriptive, pictorial.
**F3** literal.

**figure** n 1 NUMBER, numeral, digit, integer, sum, amount. 2 SHAPE, form, outline, silhouette, body, frame, build, physique. 3 public figure: dignitary, celebrity, personality, character, person. 4 DIAGRAM, illustration, picture, drawing, sketch, image, representation, symbol.
v 1 RECKON, guess, estimate, judge, think, believe. 2 FEATURE, appear, crop up.

**figure out** work out, calculate, compute, reckon, puzzle out, resolve, fathom, understand, see, make out, decipher.

**figurehead** *n* mouthpiece, front man, name, dummy, puppet.

**filament** *n* fibre, strand, thread, hair, whisker, wire, string, pile.

**file**[1] *v* rub (down), sand, abrade, scour, scrape, grate, rasp, hone, whet, shave, plane, smooth, polish.

**file**[2] *n* folder, dossier, portfolio, binder, case, record, documents, data, information.
*v* record, register, note, enter, process, store, classify, categorize, pigeonhole, catalogue.

**file**[3] *n* line, queue, column, row, procession, cortège, train, string, stream, trail.
*v* march, troop, parade, stream, trail.

**fill** *v* 1 REPLENISH, stock, supply, furnish, satisfy, pack, crowd, cram, stuff, congest, block, clog, plug, bung, cork, stop, close, seal. 2 PERVADE, imbue, permeate, soak, impregnate. 3 *fill a post*: take up, hold, occupy, discharge, fulfil.
£ɜ empty, drain.

**fill in** 1 *fill in a form*: complete, fill out, answer. 2 (*infml*) STAND IN, deputize, understudy, substitute, replace, represent, act for. 3 (*infml*) BRIEF, inform, advise, acquaint, bring up to date.

**filling** *n* contents, inside, stuffing, padding, wadding, filler.
*adj* satisfying, nutritious, square, solid, substantial, heavy, large, big, generous, ample.
£ɜ insubstantial.

**film** *n* 1 MOTION PICTURE, picture, movie (*infml*), video, feature film, short, documentary. 2 LAYER, covering, dusting, coat, coating, glaze, skin, membrane, tissue, sheet, veil, screen, cloud, mist, haze.
*v* photograph, shoot, video, videotape.

**filter** *v* strain, sieve, sift, screen, refine, purify, clarify, percolate, ooze, seep, leak, trickle, dribble.

*n* strainer, sieve, sifter, colander, mesh, gauze, membrane.

**filth** *n* 1 DIRT, grime, muck, dung, excrement, faeces, sewage, refuse, rubbish, garbage, trash, slime, sludge, effluent, pollution, contamination, corruption, impurity, uncleanness, foulness, sordidness, squalor. 2 OBSCENITY, pornography, smut, indecency, vulgarity, coarseness.
£ɜ 1 cleanness, cleanliness, purity.

**filthy** *adj* 1 DIRTY, soiled, unwashed, grimy, grubby, mucky, muddy, slimy, sooty, unclean, impure, foul, gross, sordid, squalid, vile, low, mean, base, contemptible, despicable. 2 OBSCENE, pornographic, smutty, bawdy, suggestive, indecent, offensive, foul-mouthed, vulgar, coarse, corrupt, depraved.
£ɜ 1 clean, pure. 2 decent.

**final** *adj* last, latest, closing, concluding, finishing, end, ultimate, terminal, dying, last-minute, eventual, conclusive, definitive, decisive, definite, incontrovertible.
£ɜ first, initial.

**finale** *n* climax, dénouement, culmination, crowning glory, end, conclusion, close, curtain, epilogue.

**finalize** *v* conclude, finish, complete, round off, resolve, settle, agree, decide, close, clinch, sew up (*infml*), wrap up (*infml*).

**finally** *adv* lastly, in conclusion, ultimately, eventually, at last, at length, in the end, conclusively, once and for all, for ever, irreversibly, irrevocably, definitely.

**finance** *n* economics, money management, accounting, banking, investment, stock market, business, commerce, trade, money, funding, sponsorship, subsidy.
*v* pay for, fund, sponsor, back, support, underwrite, guarantee, subsidize, capitalize, float, set up.

**finances** *n* accounts, affairs, budget,

bank account, income, revenue, liquidity, resources, assets, capital, wealth, money, cash, funds, wherewithal.

**financial** adj monetary, money, pecuniary, economic, fiscal, budgetary, commercial.

**financier** n financialist, banker, stockbroker, money-maker, investor, speculator.

**find** v 1 DISCOVER, locate, track down, trace, retrieve, recover, unearth, uncover, expose, reveal, come across, chance on, stumble on, meet, encounter, detect, recognize, notice, observe, perceive, realize, learn. 2 ATTAIN, achieve, win, reach, gain, obtain, get. 3 *find it difficult:* consider, think, judge, declare.
F3 1 lose.

**find out** 1 LEARN, ascertain, discover, detect, note, observe, perceive, realize. 2 UNMASK, expose, show up, uncover, reveal, disclose, catch, suss out (*sl*), rumble (*sl*), tumble to (*infml*).

**finding** n 1 FIND, discovery, breakthrough. 2 DECISION, conclusion, judgement, verdict, pronouncement, decree, recommendation, award.

**fine**[1] adj 1 EXCELLENT, outstanding, exceptional, superior, exquisite, splendid, magnificent, brilliant, beautiful, handsome, attractive, elegant, lovely, nice, good. 2 THIN, slender, sheer, gauzy, powdery, flimsy, fragile, delicate, dainty. 3 SATISFACTORY, acceptable, all right, OK (*infml*). 4 *fine weather:* bright, sunny, clear, cloudless, dry, fair.
F3 1 mediocre. 2 thick, coarse. 4 cloudy.

**fine**[2] n penalty, punishment, forfeit, forfeiture, damages.

**finger** v touch, handle, manipulate, feel, stroke, caress, fondle, paw, fiddle with, toy with, play about with, meddle with.

**finicky** adj 1 PARTICULAR, finickety, pernickety, fussy, choosy (*infml*), fastidious, meticulous, scrupulous, critical, hypercritical, nit-picking. 2 FIDDLY, intricate, tricky, difficult, delicate.
F3 1 easy-going. 2 easy.

**finish** v 1 END, terminate, stop, cease, complete, accomplish, achieve, fulfil, discharge, deal with, do, conclude, wind up, settle, round off, culminate, perfect. 2 DESTROY, ruin, exterminate, get rid of, annihilate, defeat, overcome, rout, overthrow. 3 USE (UP), consume, devour, eat, drink, exhaust, drain, empty.
F3 1 begin, start.
n 1 END, termination, completion, conclusion, close, ending, finale, culmination. 2 SURFACE, appearance, texture, grain, polish, shine, gloss, lustre, smoothness.
F3 1 beginning, start, commencement.

**finite** adj limited, restricted, bounded, demarcated, terminable, definable, fixed, measurable, calculable, countable, numbered.
F3 infinite.

**fire** n 1 FLAMES, blaze, bonfire, conflagration, inferno, burning, combustion. 2 PASSION, feeling, excitement, enthusiasm, spirit, intensity, heat, radiance, sparkle.
v 1 IGNITE, light, kindle, set fire to, set on fire, set alight. 2 *fire a missile:* shoot, launch, set off, let off, detonate, explode. 3 DISMISS, discharge, sack (*infml*), eject. 4 EXCITE, whet, enliven, galvanize, electrify, stir, arouse, rouse, stimulate, inspire, incite, spark off, trigger off.

**on fire** burning, alight, ignited, flaming, in flames, aflame, blazing, ablaze, fiery.

**firm**[1] adj 1 *firm ground:* dense, compressed, compact, concentrated, set, solid, hard, unyielding, stiff, rigid, inflexible. 2 FIXED, embedded, fast, tight, secure, fastened, anchored, immovable, motionless, stationary, steady, stable, sturdy, strong. **3** ADAMANT, unshakable, resolute, determined, dogged, unwavering, strict, constant, steadfast, staunch, dependable, true, sure, convinced, definite, settled, committed.

🖃 **1** soft, flabby. **2** unsteady. **3** hesitant.

**firm²** *n* company, corporation, business, enterprise, concern, house, establishment, institution, organization, association, partnership, syndicate, conglomerate.

**first** *adj* **1** INITIAL, opening, introductory, preliminary, elementary, primary, basic, fundamental. **2** ORIGINAL, earliest, earlier, prior, primitive, primeval, oldest, eldest, senior. **3** CHIEF, main, key, cardinal, principal, head, leading, ruling, sovereign, highest, uppermost, paramount, prime, predominant, pre-eminent.

🖃 **1** last, final.

*adv* initially, to begin with, to start with, at the outset, beforehand, originally, in preference, rather, sooner.

**first name** forename, Christian name, baptismal name, given name.

**first-rate** *adj* first-class, A1, second-to-none, matchless, coley, peerless, top, top-notch (*infml*), top-flight, leading, supreme, superior, prime, excellent, outstanding, superlative, exceptional, splendid, superb, fine, admirable.

🖃 inferior.

**fish**

> *Types of fish include*: bloater, brisling, cod, coley, Dover sole, haddock, hake, halibut, herring, jellied eel, kipper, mackerel, pilchard, plaice, rainbow trout, salmon, sardine, sole, sprat, trout, tuna, turbot, whitebait; bass, Bombay duck, bream, brill, carp, catfish, chub, conger eel, cuttlefish, dab, dace, dogfish, dory, eel, goldfish, guppy, marlin, minnow, monkfish, mullet, octopus, perch, pike, piranha, roach, shark, skate, snapper, squid, stickleback, stingray, sturgeon, swordfish, tench, whiting; clam, cockle, crab, crayfish (*US*), kingprawn, lobster, mussel, oyster, prawn, scallop, shrimp, whelk.

*v* angle, trawl, delve, hunt, seek, invite, solicit.

**fish out** produce, take out, extract, find, come up with, dredge up, haul up.

**fishing** *n* angling, trawling.

**fit¹** *adj* **1** SUITABLE, appropriate, apt, fitting, correct, right, proper, ready, prepared, able, capable, competent, qualified, eligible, worthy. **2** HEALTHY, well, able-bodied, in good form, in good shape, sound, sturdy, strong, robust, hale and hearty.

🖃 **1** unsuitable, unworthy. **2** unfit.

*v* **1** MATCH, correspond, conform, follow, agree, concur, tally, suit, harmonize, go, belong, dovetail, interlock, join, meet, arrange, place, position, accommodate. **2** ALTER, modify, change, adjust, adapt, tailor, shape, fashion.

**fit out** equip, rig out, kit out, outfit, provide, supply, furnish, prepare, arm.

**fit²** *n* seizure, convulsion, spasm, paroxysm, attack, outbreak, bout, spell, burst, surge, outburst, eruption, explosion.

**fitful** *adj* sporadic, intermittent, occasional, spasmodic, erratic, irregular, uneven, broken, disturbed.

🖃 steady, regular.

**fitted** *adj* **1** *fitted wardrobe*: built-in, permanent. **2** EQUIPPED, rigged out, provided, furnished, appointed, prepared, armed. **3** SUITED, right, suitable, fit, qualified.

**fitting** *adj* apt, appropriate, suitable, fit, correct, right, proper, seemly, meet (*fml*), desirable, deserved.

**F3** unsuitable, improper.

*n* connection, attachment, accessory, part, component, piece, unit, fitment.

**fittings** *n* equipment, furnishings, furniture, fixtures, installations, fitments, accessories, extras.

**fix** *v* **1** FASTEN, secure, tie, bind, attach, join, connect, link, couple, anchor, pin, nail, rivet, stick, glue, cement, set, harden, solidify, stiffen, stabilize, plant, root, implant, embed, establish, install, place, locate, position. **2** *fix a date*: arrange, set, specify, define, agree on, decide, determine, settle, resolve, finalize. **3** MEND, repair, correct, rectify, adjust, restore.

**F3** **1** move, shift. **3** damage.

*n* (*infml*) dilemma, quandary, predicament, plight, difficulty, hole (*infml*), corner, spot (*infml*), mess, muddle.

**fix up** arrange, organize, plan, lay on, provide, supply, furnish, equip, settle, sort out, produce, bring about.

**fixation** *n* preoccupation, obsession, mania, fetish, thing (*infml*), infatuation, compulsion, hang-up (*infml*), complex.

**fixed** *adj* decided, settled, established, definite, arranged, planned, set, firm, rigid, inflexible, steady, secure, fast, rooted, permanent.

**F3** variable.

**fizz** *v* effervesce, sparkle, bubble, froth, foam, fizzle, hiss, sizzle, sputter, spit.

**fizzy** *adj* effervescent, sparkling, aerated, carbonated, gassy, bubbly, bubbling, frothy, foaming.

**flabbergasted** (*infml*) *adj* amazed, confounded, astonished, astounded, staggered, dumbfounded, speechless, stunned, dazed, overcome, overwhelmed, bowled over.

**flabby** *adj* fleshy, soft, yielding, flaccid, limp, floppy, drooping,

hanging, sagging, slack, loose, lax, weak, feeble.

**F3** firm, strong.

**flag**[1] *v* lessen, diminish, decline, fall (off), abate, subside, sink, slump, dwindle, peter out, fade, fail, weaken, slow, falter, tire, weary, wilt, droop, sag, flop, faint, die.

**F3** revive.

**flag**[2] *n* ensign, jack, pennant, colours, standard, banner, streamer.

> *Types of flag include*: banner, bunting, burgee, colours, cornet, gonfalon, jack, oriflamme, pennant, pilot flag, signal flag, standard, streamer, swallow tail.
> *Names of flag include*: Blue Ensign, Blue Peter, Crescent, Hammer and Sickle, Jolly Roger, Old Glory, Olympic Flag, Red Ensign, Rising Sun, Skull and Crossbones, Star Spangled Banner, Stars and Stripes, Tricolour, Union Jack, White Ensign, Yellow Jack.

*v* **1** SIGNAL, wave, salute, motion. **2** MARK, indicate, label, tag, note.

**flail** *v* thresh, thrash, beat, whip.

**flair** *n* skill, ability, aptitude, faculty, gift, talent, facility, knack, mastery, genius, feel, taste, discernment, acumen, style, elegance, stylishness, panache.

**F3** inability, ineptitude.

**flake** *n* scale, peeling, paring, shaving, sliver, wafer, chip, splinter.

*v* scale, peel, chip, splinter.

**flamboyant** *adj* showy, ostentatious, flashy, gaudy, colourful, brilliant, dazzling, striking, extravagant, rich, elaborate, ornate, florid.

**F3** modest, restrained.

**flame** *v* burn, flare, blaze, glare, flash, beam, shine, glow, radiate.

*n* **1** FIRE, blaze, light, brightness, heat, warmth. **2** PASSION, ardour, fervour, enthusiasm, zeal, intensity, radiance.

**flaming** adj 1 a flaming torch: burning, alight, aflame, blazing, fiery, brilliant, scintillating, red-hot, glowing, smouldering. 2 INTENSE, vivid, aroused, impassioned, hot, raging, frenzied.

**flammable** adj inflammable, ignitable, combustible.
**Ea** non-flammable, incombustible, flameproof, fire-resistant.

**flank** n side, edge, quarter, wing, loin, hip, thigh.
  v edge, fringe, skirt, line, border, bound, confine, wall, screen.

**flap** v flutter, vibrate, wave, agitate, shake, wag, swing, swish, thrash, beat.
  n 1 FOLD, fly, lapel, tab, lug, tag, tail, skirt, aileron. 2 (infml) PANIC, state (infml), fuss, commotion, fluster, agitation, flutter, dither, tizzy (infml).

**flare** v 1 FLAME, burn, blaze, glare, flash, flicker, burst, explode, erupt. 2 BROADEN, widen, flare out, spread out, splay.
  n 1 FLAME, blaze, glare, flash, flicker, burst. 2 BROADENING, widening, splay.

**flare up** erupt, break out, explode, blow up.

**flash** v 1 BEAM, shine, light up, flare, blaze, glare, gleam, glint, flicker, twinkle, sparkle, glitter, shimmer. 2 the train flashed past: streak, fly, dart, race, dash.
  n beam, ray, shaft, spark, blaze, flare, burst, streak, gleam, glint, flicker, twinkle, sparkle, shimmer.

**flashy** adj showy, ostentatious, flamboyant, glamorous, bold, loud, garish, gaudy, jazzy, flash, tawdry, cheap, vulgar, tasteless.
**Ea** plain, tasteful.

**flat¹** adj 1 LEVEL, plane, even, smooth, uniform, unbroken, horizontal, outstretched, prostrate, prone, recumbent, reclining, low. 2 DULL, boring, monotonous, tedious, uninteresting, unexciting,

stale, lifeless, dead, spiritless, lacklustre, vapid, insipid, weak, watery, empty, pointless. 3 a flat refusal: absolute, utter, total, unequivocal, categorical, positive, unconditional, unqualified, point-blank, direct, straight, explicit, plain, final. 4 a flat tyre: punctured, burst, deflated, collapsed.
**Ea** 1 bumpy, vertical. 2 exciting, full. 3 equivocal.

**flat out** at top speed, at full speed, all out, for all one is worth.

**flat²** n apartment, penthouse, maisonnette, tenement, flatlet, rooms, suite, bed-sit(ter).

**flatten** v 1 SMOOTH, iron, press, roll, crush, squash, compress, level, even out. 2 KNOCK DOWN, prostrate, floor, fell, demolish, raze, overwhelm, subdue.

**flatter** v praise, compliment, sweet-talk (infml), adulate, fawn, butter up (infml), wheedle, humour, play up to, court, curry favour with.
**Ea** criticize.

**flattery** n adulation, eulogy, sweet talk (infml), soft soap (infml), flannel (infml), blarney, cajolery, fawning, toadyism, sycophancy, ingratiation, servility.
**Ea** criticism.

**flavour** n 1 TASTE, tang, smack, savour, relish, zest, zing (infml), aroma, odour. 2 QUALITY, property, character, style, aspect, feeling, feel, atmosphere. 3 HINT, suggestion, touch, tinge, tone.
  v season, spice, ginger up, infuse, imbue.

**flavouring** n seasoning, zest, essence, flavour, additive.

**flaw** n defect, imperfection, fault, blemish, spot, mark, speck, crack, crevice, fissure, cleft, split, rift, break, fracture, weakness, shortcoming, failing, fallacy, lapse, slip, error, mistake.

**flawed** adj imperfect, defective,

faulty, blemished, marked, damaged,
spoilt, marred, cracked, chipped,
broken, unsound, fallacious,
erroneous.
**E3** flawless, perfect.

**flawless** *adj* perfect, faultless,
unblemished, spotless, immaculate,
stainless, sound, intact, whole,
unbroken, undamaged.
**E3** flawed, imperfect.

**fleck** *v* dot, spot, mark, speckle,
dapple, mottle, streak, sprinkle, dust.
*n* dot, point, spot, mark, speck,
speckle, streak.

**flee** *v* run away, bolt, fly, take flight,
take off, make off, cut and run,
escape, get away, decamp, abscond,
leave, depart, withdraw, retreat,
vanish, disappear.
**E3** stay.

**fleet** *n* flotilla, armada, navy, task
force, squadron.

**fleeting** *adj* short, brief, flying,
short-lived, momentary, ephemeral,
transient, transitory, passing,
temporary.
**E3** lasting, permanent.

**flesh** *n* body, tissue, fat, muscle,
brawn, skin, meat, pulp, substance,
matter, physicality.

**flex** *v* bend, bow, curve, angle, ply,
double up, tighten, contract.
**E3** straighten, extend.
*n* cable, wire, lead, cord.

**flexible** *adj* **1** BENDABLE, bendy
(*infml*), pliable, pliant, plastic,
malleable, mouldable, elastic,
stretchy, springy, yielding, supple,
lithe, limber, double-jointed, mobile.
**2** ADAPTABLE, adjustable,
amenable, accommodating, variable,
open.
**E3 1** inflexible, rigid.

**flick** *v* hit, strike, rap, tap, touch,
dab, flip, jerk, whip, lash.
*n* rap, tap, touch, dab, flip, jerk,
click.

**flick through** flip through, thumb
through, leaf through, glance at, skim,

scan.

**flicker** *v* flash, blink, wink, twinkle,
sparkle, glimmer, shimmer, gutter,
flutter, vibrate, quiver, waver.
*n* flash, gleam, glint, twinkle,
glimmer, spark, trace, drop, iota,
atom, indication.

**flight**[1] *n* **1** FLYING, aviation,
aeronautics, air transport, air travel.
**2** JOURNEY, trip, voyage.

**flight**[2] *n* fleeing, escape, getaway,
breakaway, exit, departure, exodus,
retreat.

**flimsy** *adj* thin, fine, light, slight,
insubstantial, ethereal, fragile,
delicate, shaky, rickety, makeshift,
weak, feeble, meagre, inadequate,
shallow, superficial, trivial, poor,
unconvincing, implausible.
**E3** sturdy.

**flinch** *v* wince, start, cringe, cower,
quail, tremble, shake, quake,
shudder, shiver, shrink, recoil, draw
back, balk, shy away, duck, shirk,
withdraw, retreat, flee.

**fling** *v* throw, hurl, pitch, lob, toss,
chuck (*infml*), cast, sling, catapult,
launch, propel, send, let fly, heave,
jerk.

**flip** *v* flick, spin, twirl, twist, turn,
toss, throw, cast, pitch, jerk, flap.
*n* flick, spin, twirl, twist, turn, toss,
jerk, flap.

**flippant** *adj* facetious, light-hearted,
frivolous, superficial, offhand, flip,
glib, pert, saucy (*infml*), cheeky
(*infml*), impudent, impertinent, rude,
disrespectful, irreverent.
**E3** serious, respectful.

**flirt** *v* chat up, make up to, lead on,
philander, dally.
**flirt with** consider, entertain, toy with,
play with, trifle with, dabble in, try.

**flit** *v* dart, speed, flash, fly, wing,
flutter, whisk, skim, slip, pass, bob,
dance.

**float** *v* **1** GLIDE, sail, swim, bob,
drift, waft, hover, hang. **2** LAUNCH,
initiate, set up, promote.

**⊞ 1** sink.

**floating** *adj* **1** AFLOAT, buoyant, unsinkable, sailing, swimming, bobbing, drifting. **2** VARIABLE, fluctuating, movable, migratory, transitory, wandering, unattached, free, uncommitted.

**⊞ 1** sinking. **2** fixed.

**flock** *v* herd, swarm, troop, converge, mass, bunch, cluster, huddle, crowd, throng, group, gather, collect, congregate.
*n* herd, pack, crowd, throng, multitude, mass, bunch, cluster, group, gathering, assembly, congregation.

**flog** *v* beat, whip, lash, flagellate, scourge, birch, cane, flay, drub, thrash, whack (*infml*), chastise, punish.

**flogging** *n* beating, whipping, lashing, flagellation, scourging, birching, caning, flaying, thrashing, hiding.

**flood** *v* **1** DELUGE, inundate, soak, drench, saturate, fill, overflow, immerse, submerge, engulf, swamp, overwhelm, drown. **2** FLOW, pour, stream, rush, surge, gush.
*n* deluge, inundation, downpour, torrent, flow, tide, stream, rush, spate, outpouring, overflow, glut, excess, abundance, profusion.

**⊞** drought, trickle, dearth.

**floor** *n* **1** FLOORING, ground, base, basis. **2** *on the third floor*: storey, level, stage, landing, deck, tier.
*v* (*infml*) defeat, overwhelm, beat, stump (*infml*), frustrate, confound, perplex, baffle, puzzle, bewilder, disconcert, throw.

**flop** *v* **1** DROOP, hang, dangle, sag, drop, fall, topple, tumble, slump, collapse. **2** FAIL, misfire, fall flat, founder, fold.
*n* failure, non-starter, fiasco, debacle, wash-out (*infml*), disaster.

**floppy** *adj* droopy, hanging, dangling, sagging, limp, loose, baggy, soft, flabby.

**⊞** firm.

**florid** *adj* **1** FLOWERY, ornate, elaborate, fussy, overelaborate, baroque, rococo, flamboyant, grandiloquent. **2** *a florid complexion*: ruddy, red, purple.

**⊞ 1** plain, simple. **2** pale.

**flotsam** *n* jetsam, wreckage, debris, rubbish, junk, oddments.

**flounder** *v* wallow, struggle, grope, fumble, blunder, stagger, stumble, falter.

**flourish** *v* **1** THRIVE, grow, wax, increase, flower, blossom, bloom, develop, progress, get on, do well, prosper, succeed, boom.
**2** BRANDISH, wave, shake, twirl, swing, display, wield, flaunt, parade, vaunt.

**⊞ 1** decline, languish, fail.
*n* display, parade, show, gesture, wave, sweep, fanfare, ornament, decoration, panache, pizzazz (*infml*).

**flourishing** *adj* thriving, blooming, prosperous, successful, booming.

**flout** *v* defy, disobey, violate, break, disregard, spurn, reject, scorn, jeer at, scoff at, mock, ridicule.

**⊞** obey, respect, regard.

**flow** *v* **1** CIRCULATE, ooze, trickle, ripple, bubble, well, spurt, squirt, gush, spill, run, pour, cascade, rush, stream, teem, flood, overflow, surge, sweep, move, drift, slip, slide, glide, roll, swirl. **2** ORIGINATE, derive, arise, spring, emerge, issue, result, proceed, emanate.
*n* course, flux, tide, current, drift, outpouring, stream, deluge, cascade, spurt, gush, flood, spate, abundance, plenty.

**flower** *n* **1** BLOOM, blossom, bud, floret.

*Flowers include*: African violet, alyssum, anemone, aster, aubrietia, azalea, begonia, bluebell, busy lizzie (impatiens), calendula, candytuft, carnation, chrysanthemum, cornflower, cowslip, crocus, cyclamen, daffodil, dahlia, daisy, delphinium, forget-me-not, foxglove (digitalis), freesia, fuchsia, gardenia, geranium, gladioli, hollyhock, hyacinth, iris (flag), lily, lily-of-the-valley, lobelia, lupin, marigold, narcissus, nasturtium, nemesia, nicotiana, night-scented stock, orchid, pansy, petunia, pink (dianthus), phlox, poinsettia, polyanthus, poppy, primrose, primula, rose, salvia, snapdragon (antirrhinum), snowdrop, stock, sunflower, sweet pea, sweet william, tulip, verbena, viola, violet, wallflower, zinnia. *see also* **plant**; **shrub**.

*Parts of a flower include*: anther, calyx, capitulum, carpel, corolla, corymb, dichasium, filament, gynoecium, monochasium, nectary, ovary, ovule, panicle, pedicel, petal, pistil, raceme, receptacle, sepal, spadix, spike, stalk, stamen, stigma, style, thalamus, torus, umbel.

2 BEST, cream, pick, choice, élite.

*v* bud, burgeon, bloom, blossom, open, come out.

**flowery** *adj* florid, ornate, elaborate, fancy, baroque, rhetorical.
F3 plain, simple.

**fluctuate** *v* vary, change, alter, shift, rise and fall, seesaw, ebb and flow, alternate, swing, sway, oscillate, vacillate, waver.

**fluent** *adj* flowing, smooth, easy, effortless, articulate, eloquent, voluble, glib, ready.
F3 broken, inarticulate, tongue-tied.

**fluff** *n* down, nap, pile, fuzz, floss, lint, dust.

**fluffy** *adj* furry, fuzzy, downy, feathery, fleecy, woolly, hairy, shaggy, velvety, silky, soft.

**fluid** *adj* 1 LIQUID, liquefied, aqueous, watery, running, runny, melted, molten. 2 *a fluid situation*: variable, changeable, unstable, inconstant, shifting, mobile, adjustable, adaptable, flexible, open. 3 *fluid movements*: flowing, smooth, graceful.
F3 1 solid. 2 stable.
*n* liquid, solution, liquor, juice, gas, vapour.

**flurry** *n* 1 BURST, outbreak, spell, spurt, gust, blast, squall. 2 BUSTLE, hurry, fluster, fuss, to-do, commotion, tumult, whirl, disturbance, stir, flap (*infml*).

**flush**[1] *v* 1 BLUSH, go red, redden, crimson, colour, burn, glow, suffuse. 2 CLEANSE, wash, rinse, hose, swab, clear, empty, evacuate.
*adj* 1 ABUNDANT, lavish, generous, full, overflowing, rich, wealthy, moneyed, prosperous, well-off, well-heeled, well-to-do. 2 LEVEL, even, smooth, flat, plane, square, true.

**flush**[2] *v* start, rouse, disturb, drive out, force out, expel, eject, run to earth, discover, uncover.

**fluster** *v* bother, upset, embarrass, disturb, perturb, agitate, ruffle, discompose, confuse, confound, unnerve, disconcert, rattle (*infml*), put off, distract.
F3 calm.
*n* flurry, bustle, commotion, disturbance, turmoil, state (*infml*), agitation, embarrassment, flap (*infml*), dither, tizzy (*infml*).
F3 calm.

**fluted** *adj* grooved, furrowed, channelled, corrugated, ribbed, ridged.

**flutter** *v* flap, wave, beat, bat, flicker, vibrate, palpitate, agitate, shake, tremble, quiver, shiver, ruffle, ripple, twitch, toss, waver, fluctuate.
*n* flapping, beat, flicker, vibration, palpitation, tremble, tremor, quiver, shiver, shudder, twitch.

**folly**

**flux** *n* fluctuation, instability, change, alteration, modification, fluidity, flow, movement, motion, transition, development.
**F3** stability, rest.

**fly** *v* **1** TAKE OFF, rise, ascend, mount, soar, glide, float, hover, flit, wing. **2** RACE, sprint, dash, tear, rush, hurry, speed, zoom, shoot, dart, career.
**fly at** attack, go for, fall upon.

**foam** *n* froth, lather, suds, head, bubbles, effervescence.
*v* froth, lather, bubble, effervesce, fizz, boil, seethe.

**fob off** foist, pass off, palm off (*infml*), get rid of, dump, unload, inflict, impose, deceive, put off.

**focus** *n* focal point, target, centre, heart, core, nucleus, kernel, crux, hub, axis, linchpin, pivot, hinge.
*v* converge, meet, join, centre, concentrate, aim, direct, fix, spotlight, home in, zoom in, zero in (*infml*).

**fog** *n* **1** MIST, haze, cloud, gloom, murkiness, smog, pea-souper.
**2** PERPLEXITY, puzzlement, confusion, bewilderment, daze, trance, vagueness, obscurity.
*v* mist, steam up, cloud, dull, dim, darken, obscure, blur, confuse, muddle.

**foggy** *adj* misty, hazy, smoggy, cloudy, murky, dark, shadowy, dim, indistinct, obscure.
**F3** clear.

**foil**[1] *v* defeat, outwit, frustrate, thwart, baffle, counter, nullify, stop, check, obstruct, block, circumvent, elude.
**F3** abet.

**foil**[2] *n* setting, background, relief, contrast, complement, balance.

**fold** *v* **1** BEND, ply, double, overlap, tuck, pleat, crease, crumple, crimp, crinkle. **2** (*infml*) *the business folded*: fail, go bust, shut down, collapse, crash. **3** ENFOLD, embrace, hug, clasp, envelop, wrap (up), enclose, entwine, intertwine.
*n* bend, turn, layer, ply, overlap, tuck, pleat, crease, knife-edge, line, wrinkle, furrow, corrugation.

**folder** *n* file, binder, folio, portfolio, envelope, holder.

**folk** *n* people, society, nation, race, tribe, clan, family, kin, kindred.
*adj* ethnic, national, traditional, native, indigenous, tribal, ancestral.

**follow** *v* **1** *night follows day*: come after, succeed, come next, replace, supersede, supplant. **2** CHASE, pursue, go after, hunt, track, trail, shadow, tail, hound, catch.
**3** ACCOMPANY, go (along) with, escort, attend. **4** RESULT, ensue, develop, emanate, arise. **5** OBEY, comply with, adhere to, heed, mind, observe, conform to, carry out, practise. **6** GRASP, understand, comprehend, fathom.
**F3** 1 precede. 3 abandon, desert. 5 disobey.

**follow through** continue, pursue, see through, finish, complete, conclude, fulfil, implement.

**follow up** investigate, check out, continue, pursue, reinforce, consolidate.

**follower** *n* attendant, retainer, helper, companion, sidekick (*infml*), apostle, disciple, pupil, imitator, emulator, adherent, hanger-on, believer, convert, backer, supporter, admirer, fan, devotee, freak (*infml*), buff (*infml*).
**F3** leader, opponent.

**following** *adj* subsequent, next, succeeding, successive, resulting, ensuing, consequent, later.
**F3** previous.
*n* followers, suite, retinue, entourage, circle, fans, supporters, support, backing, patronage, clientele, audience, public.

**folly** *n* foolishness, stupidity, senselessness, rashness, recklessness, irresponsibility, indiscretion, craziness, madness, lunacy, insanity, idiocy, imbecility, silliness, absurdity, nonsense.

☒ wisdom, prudence, sanity.

**fond** *adj* affectionate, warm, tender, caring, loving, adoring, devoted, doting, indulgent.

**fond of** partial to, attached to, enamoured of, keen on, addicted to, hooked on.

**fondle** *v* caress, stroke, pat, pet, cuddle.

**food** *n* foodstuffs, comestibles, eatables (*infml*), provisions, stores, rations, eats (*infml*), grub (*sl*), nosh (*sl*), refreshment, sustenance, nourishment, nutrition, nutriment, subsistence, feed, fodder, diet, fare, cooking, cuisine, menu, board, table, larder.

*Kinds of food include*: soup, broth, minestrone, bouillabaisse, borsch, cockaleckie, consommé, gazpacho, goulash, vichyssoise; chips, French fries, ratatouille, sauerkraut, bubble-and-squeak, nut cutlet, cauliflower cheese, chiladas, hummus, macaroni cheese; pasta, cannelloni, fettuccine, ravioli, spaghetti bolognese, tortellini, lasagne; fish and chips, fishcake, fish-finger, fisherman's pie, kedgeree, gefilte fish, kipper, pickled herring, scampi, calamari, prawn cocktail, caviar; meat, casserole, cassoulet, hotpot, shepherd's pie, cottage pie, chilli con carne, biriyani, chop suey, moussaka, paella, samosa, pizza, ragout, risotto, tandoori, vindaloo, Wiener schnitzel, smöga[an]sbord, stroganoff, Scotch woodcock, welsh rarebit, faggot, haggis, sausage, frankfurter, hot dog, fritter, hamburger, McDonald's®, Big Mac®, Wimpy®, bacon, egg, omelette, quiche, tofu, Quorn®, Yorkshire pudding, toad-in-the-hole; ice cream, charlotte russe, egg custard, fruit salad, fruit cocktail,

gateau, millefeuilles, pavlova, profiterole, Sachertorte, soufflé, summer pudding, Bakewell tart, trifle, yogurt, sundae, syllabub, queen of puddings, Christmas pudding, tapioca, rice pudding, roly-poly pudding, spotted dick, zabaglione; doughnut, Chelsea bun, Eccles cake, éclair, flapjack, fruitcake, Danish pastry, Genoa cake, Battenburg cake, Madeira cake, lardy cake, hot-cross-bun, ginger nut, gingerbread, shortbread, ginger snap, macaroon, Garibaldi biscuit; bread, French bread, French toast, pumpernickel, cottage loaf, croissant; gravy, fondue, salad cream, mayonnaise, French dressing; sauces: tartare, Worcestershire, bechamel, white, barbecue, tomato ketchup, hollandaise, Tabasco®, apple, mint, cranberry, horseradish, pesto. *see also* **cheese; fish; fruit; meat; nut; sweets; vegetable**.

**fool** *n* blockhead, fat-head, nincompoop (*infml*), ass (*infml*), chump (*infml*), ninny (*infml*), clot (*infml*), dope (*infml*), wally (*sl*), twit (*infml*), nitwit (*infml*), nit (*infml*), dunce, dimwit, simpleton, halfwit, idiot, imbecile, moron, dupe; sucker (*infml*), mug (*infml*), stooge, clown, buffoon, jester.

*v* deceive, take in, delude, mislead, dupe, gull, hoodwink, put one over on, trick, hoax, con (*infml*), cheat, swindle, diddle (*infml*), string along (*infml*), have on (*infml*), kid (*infml*), tease, joke, jest.

**fool about** lark about, horse around (*sl*), play about, mess about (*infml*), mess around (*infml*).

**foolhardy** *adj* rash, reckless, imprudent, ill-advised, irresponsible.

☒ cautious, prudent.

**foolish** *adj* stupid, senseless, unwise, ill-advised, ill-considered, short-sighted, half-baked, daft (*infml*), crazy, mad, insane, idiotic, moronic, hare-brained, half-witted, simple-minded, simple, unintelligent, inept, inane, silly, absurd, ridiculous, ludicrous, nonsensical.

**F3** wise, prudent.

**foolproof** *adj* idiot-proof, infallible, fail-safe, sure, certain, sure-fire (*infml*), guaranteed.

**F3** unreliable.

**footing** *n* base, foundation, basis, ground, relations, relationship, terms, conditions, state, standing, status, grade, rank, position, balance, foothold, purchase.

**footprint** *n* footmark, track, trail, trace, vestige.

**footwear**

*Types of footwear include:* shoe, court-shoe, brogue, casual, lace-up (*infml*), slip-on (*infml*), slingback, sandal, espadrille, stiletto heel, platform heel, moccasin, Doc Martens®, slipper, flip-flop (*infml*), boot, bootee, wellington boot, welly (*infml*), galosh, gumboot, football boot, rugby boot, tennis shoe, plimsoll, pump, sneaker, trainer, ballet shoe, clog, sabot, snow-shoe, beetle-crushers (*sl*), brothel-creepers (*sl*).

**forage** *n* fodder, pasturage, feed, food, foodstuffs.

*v* rummage, search, cast about, scour, hunt, scavenge, ransack, plunder, raid.

**forbid** *v* prohibit, disallow, ban, proscribe, interdict, veto, refuse, deny, outlaw, debar, exclude, rule out, preclude, prevent, block, hinder, inhibit.

**F3** allow, permit, approve.

**forbidden** *adj* prohibited, banned, proscribed, taboo, vetoed, outlawed, out of bounds.

**forbidding** *adj* stern, formidable, awesome, daunting, off-putting, uninviting, menacing, threatening, ominous, sinister, frightening.

**F3** approachable, congenial.

**force** *n* **1** COMPULSION, impulse, influence, coercion, constraint, pressure, duress, violence, aggression. **2** POWER, might, strength, intensity, effort, energy, vigour, drive, dynamism, stress, emphasis. **3** ARMY, troop, body, corps, regiment, squadron, battalion, division, unit, detachment, patrol.

**F3** **2** weakness.

*v* **1** COMPEL, make, oblige, necessitate, urge, coerce, constrain, press, pressurize, lean on (*infml*), press-gang, bulldoze, drive, propel, push, thrust. **2** PRISE, wrench, wrest, extort, exact, wring.

**forced** *adj* unnatural, stiff, wooden, stilted, laboured, strained, false, artificial, contrived, feigned, affected, insincere.

**F3** spontaneous, sincere.

**forceful** *adj* strong, mighty, powerful, potent, effective, compelling, convincing, persuasive, cogent, telling, weighty, urgent, emphatic, vehement, forcible, dynamic, energetic, vigorous.

**F3** weak, feeble.

**forebear** *n* ancestor, forefather, father, predecessor, forerunner, antecedent.

**F3** descendant.

**foreboding** *n* misgiving, anxiety, worry, apprehension, dread, fear, omen, sign, token, premonition, warning, prediction, prognostication, intuition, feeling.

**forecast** *v* predict, prophesy, foretell, foresee, anticipate, expect, estimate, calculate.

*n* prediction, prophecy, expectation, prognosis, outlook, projection, guess, guesstimate (*infml*).

**forefront** *n* front, front line, firing line, van, vanguard, lead, fore, avant-garde.

🔄 rear.

**foregoing** *adj* preceding, antecedent, above, previous, earlier, former, prior.
🔄 following.

**foreign** *adj* alien, immigrant, imported, international, external, outside, overseas, exotic, faraway, distant, remote, strange, unfamiliar, unknown, uncharacteristic, incongruous, extraneous, borrowed.
🔄 native, indigenous.

**foreigner** *n* alien, immigrant, incomer, stranger, newcomer, visitor.
🔄 native.

**foremost** *adj* first, leading, front, chief, main, principal, primary, cardinal, paramount, central, highest, uppermost, supreme, prime, pre-eminent.

**forerunner** *n* predecessor, ancestor, antecedent, precursor, harbinger, herald, envoy, sign, token.
🔄 successor, follower.

**foresee** *v* envisage, anticipate, expect, forecast, predict, prophesy, prognosticate, foretell, forebode, divine.

**foreshadow** *v* prefigure, presage, augur, predict, prophesy, signal, indicate, promise.

**foresight** *n* anticipation, planning, forethought, far-sightedness, vision, caution, prudence, circumspection, care, readiness, preparedness, provision, precaution.
🔄 improvidence.

**forestall** *v* pre-empt, anticipate, preclude, obviate, avert, head off, ward off, parry, balk, frustrate, thwart, hinder, prevent.

**foretaste** *n* preview, trailer, sample, specimen, example, whiff, indication, warning, premonition.

**foretell** *v* prophesy, forecast, predict, prognosticate, augur, presage, signify, foreshadow, forewarn.

**forethought** *n* preparation,

planning, forward planning, provision, precaution, anticipation, foresight, far-sightedness, circumspection, prudence, caution.
🔄 improvidence, carelessness.

**forever** *adv* continually, constantly, persistently, incessantly, perpetually, endlessly, eternally, always, evermore, for all time, permanently.

**foreword** *n* preface, introduction, prologue.
🔄 appendix, postscript, epilogue.

**forfeit** *n* loss, surrender, confiscation, sequestration, penalty, fine, damages.
*v* lose, give up, surrender, relinquish, sacrifice, forgo, renounce, abandon.

**forge** *v* **1** MAKE, mould, cast, shape, form, fashion, beat out, hammer out, work, create, invent. **2** *forge a document*: fake, counterfeit, falsify, copy, imitate, simulate, feign.

**forgery** *n* fake, counterfeit, copy, replica, reproduction, imitation, dud (*infml*), phoney (*infml*), sham, fraud.
🔄 original.

**forget** *v* omit, fail, neglect, let slip, overlook, disregard, ignore, lose sight of, dismiss, think no more of, unlearn.
🔄 remember, recall, recollect.

**forgetful** *adj* absent-minded, dreamy, inattentive, oblivious, negligent, lax, heedless.
🔄 attentive, heedful.

**forgive** *v* pardon, absolve, excuse, exonerate, exculpate, acquit, remit, let off, overlook, condone.
🔄 punish, censure.

**forgiveness** *n* pardon, absolution, exoneration, acquittal, remission, amnesty, mercy, clemency, leniency.
🔄 punishment, censure, blame.

**forgiving** *adj* merciful, clement, lenient, tolerant, forbearing, indulgent, kind, humane, compassionate, soft-hearted, mild.
🔄 merciless, censorious, harsh.

**forgo** *v* give up, yield, surrender,

relinquish, sacrifice, forfeit, waive, renounce, abandon, resign, pass up, do without, abstain from, refrain from.

**Ⅎ** claim, indulge in.

**fork** v split, divide, part, separate, diverge, branch (off).

**forlorn** adj deserted, abandoned, forsaken, forgotten, bereft, friendless, lonely, lost, homeless, destitute, desolate, hopeless, unhappy, miserable, wretched, helpless, pathetic, pitiable.

**Ⅎ** cheerful.

**form** v 1 SHAPE, mould, model, fashion, make, manufacture, produce, create, found, establish, build, construct, assemble, put together, arrange, organize. 2 COMPRISE, constitute, make up, compose. 3 APPEAR, take shape, materialize, crystallize, grow, develop.

n 1 APPEARANCE, shape, mould, cast, cut, outline, silhouette, figure, build, frame, structure, format, model, pattern, design, arrangement, organization, system. 2 *a form of punishment*: type, kind, sort, order, species, variety, genre, style, manner, nature, character, description. 3 CLASS, year, grade, stream. 4 *on top form*: health, fitness, fettle, condition, spirits. 5 ETIQUETTE, protocol, custom, convention, ritual, behaviour, manners. 6 QUESTIONNAIRE, document, paper, sheet.

**formal** adj 1 OFFICIAL, ceremonial, stately, solemn, conventional, orthodox, correct, fixed, set, regular. 2 PRIM, starchy, stiff, strict, rigid, precise, exact, punctilious, ceremonious, stilted, reserved.

**Ⅎ** 2 informal, casual.

**formality** n custom, convention, ceremony, ritual, procedure, matter of form, bureaucracy, red tape, protocol, etiquette, form, correctness, propriety, decorum, politeness.

**Ⅎ** informality.

**formation** n 1 STRUCTURE, construction, composition, constitution, configuration, format, organization, arrangement, grouping, pattern, design, figure. 2 CREATION, generation, production, manufacture, appearance, development, establishment.

**former** adj past, ex-, one-time, sometime, late, departed, old, old-time, ancient, bygone, earlier, prior, previous, preceding, antecedent, foregoing, above.

**Ⅎ** current, present, future, following.

**formerly** adv once, previously, earlier, before, at one time, lately.

**Ⅎ** currently, now, later.

**formidable** adj daunting, challenging, intimidating, threatening, frightening, terrifying, terrific, frightful, fearful, great, huge, tremendous, prodigious, impressive, awesome, overwhelming, staggering.

**formula** n recipe, prescription, proposal, blueprint, code, wording, rubric, rule, principle, form, procedure, technique, method, way.

**formulate** v create, invent, originate, found, form, devise, work out, plan, design, draw up, frame, define, express, state, specify, detail, develop, evolve.

**forsake** v desert, abandon, jilt, throw over, discard, jettison, reject, disown, leave, quit, give up, surrender, relinquish, renounce, forgo.

**fort** n fortress, castle, tower, citadel, stronghold, fortification, garrison, station, camp.

**forthcoming** adj 1 *their forthcoming wedding*: impending, imminent, approaching, coming, future, prospective, projected, expected. 2 COMMUNICATIVE, talkative, chatty, conversational, sociable, informative, expansive, open, frank, direct.

**≣ 2** reticent, reserved.

**forthright** *adj* direct, straightforward, blunt, frank, candid, plain, open, bold, outspoken.

**≣** devious, secretive.

**fortify** *v* **1** STRENGTHEN, reinforce, brace, shore up, buttress, garrison, defend, protect, secure. **2** INVIGORATE, sustain, support, boost, encourage, hearten, cheer, reassure.

**≣ 1** weaken.

**fortitude** *n* courage, bravery, valour, grit, pluck, resolution, determination, perseverance, firmness, strength of mind, willpower, hardihood, endurance, stoicism.

**≣** cowardice, fear.

**fortuitous** *adj* accidental, chance, random, arbitrary, casual, incidental, unforeseen, lucky, fortunate, providential.

**≣** intentional, planned.

**fortunate** *adj* lucky, providential, happy, felicitous, prosperous, successful, well-off, timely, well-timed, opportune, convenient, propitious, advantageous, favourable, auspicious.

**≣** unlucky, unfortunate, unhappy.

**fortune** *n* **1** WEALTH, riches, treasure, mint (*infml*), pile (*infml*), income, means, assets, estate, property, possessions, affluence, prosperity, success. **2** LUCK, chance, accident, providence, fate, destiny, doom, lot, portion, life, history, future.

**forward** *adj* **1** FIRST, head, front, fore, foremost, leading, onward, progressive, go-ahead, forward-looking, enterprising. **2** CONFIDENT, assertive, pushy, bold, audacious, brazen, brash, barefaced, cheeky (*infml*), impudent, impertinent, fresh (*sl*), familiar, presumptuous.

**3** EARLY, advance, precocious, premature, advanced, well-advanced, well-developed.

**≣ 1** backward, retrograde. **2** shy,

modest. **3** late, retarded.

*adv* forwards, ahead, on, onward, out, into view.

*v* advance, promote, further, foster, encourage, support, back, favour, help, assist, aid, facilitate, accelerate, speed, hurry, hasten, expedite, dispatch, send (on), post, transport, ship.

**≣** impede, obstruct, hinder, slow.

**foster** *v* raise, rear, bring up, nurse, care for, take care of, nourish, feed, sustain, support, promote, advance, encourage, stimulate, cultivate, nurture, cherish, entertain, harbour.

**≣** neglect, discourage.

**foul** *adj* **1** DIRTY, filthy, unclean, tainted, polluted, contaminated, rank, fetid, stinking, smelly, putrid, rotten, nauseating, offensive, repulsive, revolting, disgusting, squalid. **2** *foul language*: obscene, lewd, smutty, indecent, coarse, vulgar, gross, blasphemous, abusive. **3** NASTY, disagreeable, wicked, vicious, vile, base, abhorrent, disgraceful, shameful. **4** *foul weather*: bad, unpleasant, rainy, wet, stormy, rough.

**≣ 1** clean. **4** fine.

*v* **1** DIRTY, soil, stain, sully, defile, taint, pollute, contaminate. **2** BLOCK, obstruct, clog, choke, foul up. **3** ENTANGLE, catch, snarl, twist, ensnare.

**≣ 1** clean. **2** clear. **3** disentangle.

**found** *v* **1** START, originate, create, initiate, institute, inaugurate, set up, establish, endow, organize. **2** BASE, ground, bottom, rest, settle, fix, plant, raise, build, erect, construct.

**foundation** *n* **1** BASE, foot, bottom, ground, bedrock, substance, basis, footing. **2** SETTING UP, establishment, institution, inauguration, endowment, organization, groundwork.

**founder**[1] *n* originator, initiator, father, mother, benefactor, creator, author, architect, designer, inventor, maker, builder, constructor, organizer.

**founder**[2] *v* sink, go down, submerge, subside, collapse, break down, fall, come to grief, fail, misfire, miscarry, abort, fall through, come to nothing.

**fountain** *n* 1 SPRAY, jet, spout, spring, well, wellspring, reservoir, waterworks. 2 SOURCE, origin, fount, font, fountain-head, wellhead.

**fracture** *n* break, crack, fissure, cleft, rupture, split, rift, rent, schism, breach, gap, opening.
*v* break, crack, rupture, split, splinter, chip.
**F3** join.

**fragile** *adj* brittle, breakable, frail, delicate, flimsy, dainty, fine, slight, insubstantial, weak, feeble, infirm.
**F3** robust, tough, durable.

**fragment** *n* piece, bit, part, portion, fraction, particle, crumb, morsel, scrap, remnant, shred, chip, splinter, shiver, sliver, shard.
*v* break, shatter, splinter, shiver, crumble, disintegrate, come to pieces, come apart, break up, divide, split (up), disunite.
**F3** hold together, join.

**fragmentary** *adj* bitty, piecemeal, scrappy, broken, disjointed, disconnected, separate, scattered, sketchy, partial, incomplete.
**F3** whole, complete.

**fragrance** *n* perfume, scent, smell, odour, aroma, bouquet.

**fragrant** *adj* perfumed, scented, sweet-smelling, sweet, balmy, aromatic, odorous.
**F3** unscented.

**frail** *adj* delicate, brittle, breakable, fragile, flimsy, insubstantial, slight, puny, weak, feeble, infirm, vulnerable.
**F3** robust, tough, strong.

**frailty** *n* weakness, foible, failing, deficiency, shortcoming, fault, defect,

flaw, blemish, imperfection, fallibility, susceptibility.
**F3** strength, robustness, toughness.

**frame** *v* 1 COMPOSE, formulate, conceive, devise, contrive, concoct, cook up, plan, map out, sketch, draw up, draft, shape, form, model, fashion, mould, forge, assemble, put together, build, construct, fabricate, make. 2 SURROUND, enclose, box in, case, mount. 3 *I've been framed*: set up, fit up (*sl*), trap.
*n* 1 STRUCTURE, fabric, framework, skeleton, carcase, shell, casing, chassis, construction, bodywork, body, build, form. 2 MOUNT, mounting, setting, surround, border, edge.

**frame of mind** state of mind, mood, humour, temper, disposition, spirit, outlook, attitude.

**framework** *n* structure, fabric, bare bones, skeleton, shell, frame, outline, plan, foundation, groundwork.

**franchise** *n* concession, licence, charter, authorization, privilege, right, suffrage, liberty, freedom, immunity, exemption.

**frank** *adj* honest, truthful, sincere, candid, blunt, open, free, plain, direct, forthright, straight, straightforward, downright, outspoken.
**F3** insincere, evasive.

**frankly** *adv* to be frank, to be honest, in truth, honestly, candidly, bluntly, openly, freely, plainly, directly, straight.
**F3** insincerely, evasively.

**frantic** *adj* agitated, overwrought, fraught, desperate, beside oneself, furious, raging, mad, wild, raving, frenzied, berserk, hectic.
**F3** calm, composed.

**fraternize** *v* mix, mingle, socialize, consort, associate, affiliate, unite, sympathize.
**F3** shun, ignore.

**fraud** *n* 1 DECEIT, deception, guile,

cheating, swindling, double-dealing, sharp practice, fake, counterfeit, forgery, sham, hoax, trick. **2** (*infml*) CHARLATAN, impostor, pretender, phoney (*infml*), bluffer, hoaxer, cheat, swindler, double-dealer, con man (*infml*).

**fraudulent** *adj* dishonest, crooked (*infml*), criminal, deceitful, deceptive, false, bogus, phoney (*infml*), sham, counterfeit, swindling, double-dealing.

**Ea** honest, genuine.

**fray** *n* brawl, scuffle, dust-up (*infml*), free-for-all, set-to, clash, conflict, fight, combat, battle, quarrel, row, rumpus, disturbance, riot.

**frayed** *adj* ragged, tattered, worn, threadbare, unravelled.

**freak** *n* **1** MONSTER, mutant, monstrosity, malformation, deformity, irregularity, anomaly, abnormality, aberration, oddity, curiosity, quirk, caprice, vagary, twist, turn. **2** ENTHUSIAST, fanatic, addict, devotee, fan, buff (*infml*), fiend (*infml*), nut (*infml*).
*adj* abnormal, atypical, unusual, exceptional, odd, queer, bizarre, aberrant, capricious, erratic, unpredictable, unexpected, surprise, chance, fortuitous, flukey.

**Ea** normal, common.

**free** *adj* **1** AT LIBERTY, at large, loose, unattached, unrestrained, liberated, emancipated, independent, democratic, self-governing. **2** *free time*: spare, available, idle, unemployed, unoccupied, vacant, empty. **3** *free tickets*: gratis, without charge, free of charge, complimentary, on the house. **4** CLEAR, unobstructed, unimpeded, open. **5** GENEROUS, liberal, open-handed, lavish, charitable, hospitable.

**Ea 1** imprisoned, confined, restricted. **2** busy, occupied.

*v* release, let go, loose, turn loose, set

free, untie, unbind, unchain, unleash, liberate, emancipate, rescue, deliver, save, ransom, disentangle, disengage, extricate, clear, rid, relieve, unburden, exempt, absolve, acquit.

**Ea** imprison, confine.

**free of** lacking, devoid of, without, unaffected by, immune to, exempt from, safe from.

**freedom** *n* **1** LIBERTY, emancipation, deliverance, release, exemption, immunity, impunity.
**2** INDEPENDENCE, autonomy, self-government, home rule. **3** RANGE, scope, play, leeway, latitude, licence, privilege, power, free rein, free hand, opportunity, informality.

**Ea 1** captivity, confinement.
**3** restriction.

**freely** *adv* **1** READILY, willingly, voluntarily, spontaneously, easily.
**2** *give freely*: generously, liberally, lavishly, extravagantly, amply, abundantly. **3** *speak freely*: frankly, candidly, unreservedly, openly, plainly.

**Ea 2** grudgingly. **3** evasively, cautiously.

**freeze** *v* **1** ICE OVER, ice up, glaciate, congeal, solidify, harden, stiffen. **2** DEEP-FREEZE, ice, refrigerate, chill, cool. **3** STOP, suspend, fix, immobilize, hold.
*n* **1** FROST, freeze-up. **2** STOPPAGE, halt, standstill, shutdown, suspension, interruption, postponement, stay, embargo, moratorium.

**freezing** *adj* icy, frosty, glacial, arctic, polar, Siberian, wintry, raw, bitter, biting, cutting, penetrating, numbing, cold, chilly.

**Ea** hot, warm.

**freight** *n* cargo, load, lading, pay-load, contents, goods, merchandise, consignment, shipment, transportation, conveyance, carriage, haulage.

**frenzied** *adj* frantic, frenetic, hectic, feverish, desperate, furious, wild, uncontrolled, mad, demented, hysterical.

$\boxtimes$ calm, composed.

**frenzy** n 1 TURMOIL, agitation, distraction, derangement, madness, lunacy, mania, hysteria, delirium, fever. 2 BURST, fit, spasm, paroxysm, convulsion, seizure, outburst, transport, passion, rage, fury.

$\boxtimes$ 1 calm, composure.

**frequent** adj 1 NUMEROUS, countless, incessant, constant, continual, persistent, repeated, recurring, regular. 2 COMMON, commonplace, everyday, familiar, usual, customary.

$\boxtimes$ 1 infrequent.

v visit, patronize, attend, haunt, hang out at (infml), associate with, hang about with (infml), hang out with (infml).

**fresh** adj 1 ADDITIONAL, supplementary, extra, more, further, other. 2 NEW, novel, innovative, original, different, unconventional, modern, up-to-date, recent, latest. 3 REFRESHING, bracing, invigorating, brisk, crisp, keen, cool, fair, bright, clear, pure. 4 fresh fruit: raw, natural, unprocessed, crude. 5 REFRESHED, revived, restored, renewed, rested, invigorated, energetic, vigorous, lively, alert. 6 PERT, saucy (infml), cheeky (infml), disrespectful, impudent, insolent, bold, brazen, forward, familiar, presumptuous.

$\boxtimes$ 2 old, hackneyed. 3 stale. 4 processed. 5 tired.

**freshen** v 1 AIR, ventilate, purify. 2 REFRESH, restore, revitalize, reinvigorate, liven, enliven, spruce up, tart up (infml).

$\boxtimes$ 2 tire.

**fret** v 1 WORRY, agonize, brood, pine. 2 VEX, irritate, nettle, bother, trouble, torment.

**friction** n 1 DISAGREEMENT, dissension, dispute, disharmony, conflict, antagonism, hostility, opposition, rivalry, animosity, ill feeling, bad blood, resentment. 2 RUBBING, chafing, irritation, abrasion, scraping, grating, rasping, erosion, wearing away, resistance.

**friend** n mate (infml), pal (infml), chum (infml), buddy (infml), crony (infml), intimate, confidant(e), bosom friend, soul mate, comrade, ally, partner, associate, companion, playmate, pen-friend, acquaintance, well-wisher, supporter.

$\boxtimes$ enemy, opponent.

**friendly** adj 1 AMIABLE, affable, genial, kind, kindly, neighbourly, helpful, sympathetic, fond, affectionate, familiar, intimate, close, matey (infml), pally (infml), chummy (infml), companionable, sociable, outgoing, approachable, receptive, comradely, amicable, peaceable, well-disposed, favourable. 2 a friendly atmosphere: convivial, congenial, cordial, welcoming, warm.

$\boxtimes$ 1 hostile, unsociable. 2 cold.

**friendship** n closeness, intimacy, familiarity, affinity, rapport, attachment, affection, fondness, love, harmony, concord, goodwill, friendliness, alliance, fellowship, comradeship.

$\boxtimes$ enmity, animosity.

**fright** n shock, scare, alarm, consternation, dismay, dread, apprehension, trepidation, fear, terror, horror, panic.

**frighten** v alarm, daunt, unnerve, dismay, intimidate, terrorize, scare, startle, scare stiff, terrify, petrify, horrify, appal, shock.

$\boxtimes$ reassure, calm.

**frightening** adj alarming, daunting, formidable, fearsome, scary, terrifying, hair-raising, bloodcurdling, spine-chilling, petrifying, traumatic.

**frightful** adj unpleasant, disagreeable, awful, dreadful, fearful, terrible, appalling, shocking, harrowing, unspeakable, dire, grim, ghastly, hideous, horrible, horrid, grisly, macabre, gruesome. **F3** pleasant, agreeable.

**frigid** adj **1** UNFEELING, unresponsive, passionless, unloving, cool, aloof, passive, lifeless. **2** FROZEN, icy, frosty, glacial, arctic, cold, chill, chilly, wintry. **F3 1** responsive. **2** hot.

**frilly** adj ruffled, crimped, gathered, frilled, trimmed, lacy, fancy, ornate. **F3** plain.

**fringe** n **1** MARGIN, periphery, outskirts, edge, perimeter, limits, borderline. **2** BORDER, edging, trimming, tassel, frill, valance. adj unconventional, unorthodox, unofficial, alternative, avant-garde. **F3** conventional, mainstream.

**frisk** v jump, leap, skip, hop, bounce, caper, dance, gambol, frolic, romp, play, sport.

**frisky** adj lively, spirited, high-spirited, frolicsome, playful, romping, rollicking, bouncy. **F3** quiet.

**fritter** v waste, squander, dissipate, idle, misspend, blow (sl).

**frivolity** n fun, gaiety, flippancy, facetiousness, jest, light-heartedness, levity, triviality, superficiality, silliness, folly, nonsense. **F3** seriousness.

**frivolous** adj trifling, trivial, unimportant, shallow, superficial, light, flippant, jocular, light-hearted, juvenile, puerile, foolish, silly, idle, vain, pointless. **F3** serious, sensible.

**frolic** v gambol, caper, romp, play, lark around, rollick, make merry, frisk, prance, cavort, dance. n fun, amusement, sport, gaiety, jollity, merriment, revel, romp, prank, lark, caper, high jinks, antics.

**front** n **1** at the front: face, aspect, frontage, façade, outside, exterior,

facing, cover, obverse, top, head, lead, vanguard, forefront, front line, foreground, forepart, bow. **2** PRETENCE, show, air, appearance, look, expression, manner, façade, cover, mask, disguise, pretext, cover-up. **F3 1** back, rear. adj fore, leading, foremost, head, first. **F3** back, rear, last. **in front** ahead, leading, first, in advance, before, preceding. **F3** behind.

**frontier** n border, boundary, borderline, limit, edge, perimeter, confines, marches, bounds, verge.

**frosty** adj **1** ICY, frozen, freezing, frigid, wintry, cold, chilly. **2** UNFRIENDLY, unwelcoming, cool, aloof, standoffish, stiff, discouraging. **F3** warm.

**froth** n bubbles, effervescence, foam, lather, suds, head, scum. v foam, lather, ferment, fizz, effervesce, bubble.

**frown** v scowl, glower, lour, glare, grimace. n scowl, glower, dirty look (infml), glare, grimace. **frown on** disapprove of, object to, dislike, discourage. **F3** approve of.

**frozen** adj iced, chilled, icy, icebound, arctic, ice-cold, frigid, freezing, numb, solidified, stiff, rigid, fixed. **F3** warm.

**frugal** adj thrifty, penny-wise, parsimonious, careful, provident, saving, economical, sparing, meagre. **F3** wasteful, generous.

**fruit**

---

*Varieties of fruit include*: apple, Bramley, Cox's Orange Pippin, Golden Delicious, Granny Smith, crab apple; pear, William, Conference; orange, Jaffa, mandarin, mineola,

clementine, satsuma, tangerine,
Seville; apricot, peach, plum,
nectarine, cherry, sloe, damson,
greengage, grape, gooseberry,
goosegog (*infml*), rhubarb, tomato;
banana, pineapple, olive, lemon, lime,
ugli fruit, star fruit, lychee, date, fig,
grapefruit, kiwi fruit, mango, avocado;
melon, honeydew, cantaloupe,
watermelon; strawberry, raspberry,
blackberry, bilberry, loganberry,
elderberry, blueberry, boysenberry,
cranberry; redcurrant, blackcurrant.

**fruitful** *adj* **1** FERTILE, rich, teeming,
plentiful, abundant, prolific,
productive. **2** REWARDING,
profitable, advantageous, beneficial,
worthwhile, well-spent, useful,
successful.
**E3 1** barren. **2** fruitless.

**fruition** *n* realization, fulfilment,
attainment, achievement, completion,
maturity, ripeness, consummation,
perfection, success, enjoyment.

**fruitless** *adj* unsuccessful, abortive,
useless, futile, pointless, vain, idle,
hopeless, barren, sterile.
**E3** fruitful, successful, profitable.

**frustrate** *v* **1** THWART, foil, balk,
baffle, block, check, spike, defeat,
circumvent, forestall, counter,
nullify, neutralize, inhibit.
**2** DISAPPOINT, discourage,
dishearten, depress.
**E3 1** further, promote. **2** encourage.

**fuel** *n* **1** *a tax on fuel*: combustible,
propellant, motive power.
**2** PROVOCATION, incitement,
encouragement, ammunition,
material.

*Fuels include*: gas, calor gas®,
propane, butane, methane, acetylene,
electricity, coal, coke, anthracite,
charcoal, oil, petrol, gasoline, diesel,
derv, paraffin, kerosine, methylated
spirit, wood, logs, peat, nuclear
power.

*v* incite, inflame, fire, encourage, fan,
feed, nourish, sustain, stoke up.
**E3** discourage, damp down.

**fugitive** *n* escapee, runaway,
deserter, refugee.
*adj* fleeting, transient, transitory,
passing, short, brief, flying,
temporary, ephemeral, elusive.
**E3** permanent.

**fulfil** *v* complete, finish, conclude,
consummate, perfect, realize,
achieve, accomplish, perform,
execute, discharge, implement, carry
out, comply with, observe, keep,
obey, conform to, satisfy, fill,
answer.
**E3** fail, break.

**fulfilment** *n* completion, perfection,
consummation, realization,
achievement, accomplishment,
success, performance, execution,
discharge, implementation,
observance, satisfaction.
**E3** failure.

**full** *adj* **1** FILLED, loaded, packed,
crowded, crammed, stuffed, jammed.
**2** ENTIRE, whole, intact, total,
complete, unabridged, unexpurgated.
**3** THOROUGH, comprehensive,
exhaustive, all-inclusive, broad, vast,
extensive, ample, generous,
abundant, plentiful, copious, profuse.
**4** *a full sound*: rich, resonant, loud,
deep, clear, distinct. **5** *at full speed*:
maximum, top, highest, greatest,
utmost.
**E3 1** empty. **2** partial, incomplete.
**3** superficial.

**full-grown** *adj* adult, grown-up, of
age, mature, ripe, developed, full-
blown, full-scale.
**E3** young, undeveloped.

**fully** *adv* completely, totally, utterly,
wholly, entirely, thoroughly,
altogether, quite, positively, without
reserve, perfectly.
**E3** partly.

**fumble** *v* grope, feel, bungle, botch,
mishandle, mismanage.

**fume** v 1 SMOKE, smoulder, boil, steam. 2 RAGE, storm, rant, rave, seethe.

**fumes** n exhaust, smoke, gas, vapour, haze, fog, smog, pollution.

**fumigate** v deodorize, disinfect, sterilize, purify, cleanse.

**fun** n enjoyment, pleasure, amusement, entertainment, diversion, distraction, recreation, play, sport, game, foolery, tomfoolery, horseplay, skylarking, romp, merrymaking, mirth, jollity, jocularity, joking, jesting.

**make fun of** rag, jeer at, ridicule, laugh at, mock, taunt, tease, rib (*sl*).

**function** n 1 ROLE, part, office, duty, charge, responsibility, concern, job, task, occupation, business, activity, purpose, use. 2 RECEPTION, party, gathering, affair, do (*infml*), dinner, luncheon.

*v* work, operate, run, go, serve, act, perform, behave.

**functional** adj working, operational, practical, useful, utilitarian, utility, plain, hard-wearing.

**F3** useless, decorative.

**fund** n pool, kitty, treasury, repository, storehouse, store, reserve, stock, hoard, cache, stack, mine, well, source, supply.

*v* finance, capitalize, endow, subsidize, underwrite, sponsor, back, support, promote, float.

**fundamental** adj basic, primary, first, rudimentary, elementary, underlying, integral, central, principal, cardinal, prime, main, key, essential, indispensable, vital, necessary, crucial, important.

**funds** n money, finance, backing, capital, resources, savings, wealth, cash.

**funeral** n burial, interment, entombment, cremation, obsequies, wake.

**fungus**

*Types of fungus include*: black spot, blight, botritis, brown rot, candida, downy mildew, ergot, grey mould, mushroom, orange-peel fungus, penicillium, potato blight, powdery mildew, rust, scab, smut, sooty mould, toadstool, yeast, brewer's yeast. *see also* **mushrooms and toadstools**.

**funnel** v channel, direct, convey, move, transfer, pass, pour, siphon, filter.

**funny** adj 1 HUMOROUS, amusing, entertaining, comic, comical, hilarious, witty, facetious, droll, farcical, laughable, ridiculous, absurd, silly. 2 ODD, strange, peculiar, curious, queer, weird, unusual, remarkable, puzzling, perplexing, mysterious, suspicious, dubious.

**F3** 1 serious, solemn, sad. 2 normal, ordinary, usual.

**furious** adj 1 ANGRY, mad (*infml*), up in arms (*infml*), livid, enraged, infuriated, incensed, raging, fuming, boiling. 2 VIOLENT, wild, fierce, intense, vigorous, frantic, boisterous, stormy, tempestuous.

**F3** 1 calm, pleased.

**furnish** v equip, fit out, decorate, rig, stock, provide, supply, afford, grant, give, offer, present.

**F3** divest.

**furniture** n equipment, appliances, furnishings, fittings, fitments, household goods, movables, possessions, effects, things.

*Types of furniture include*: table, dining-table, gateleg table, refectory table, lowboy, side-table, coffee-table, card table; chair, easy chair, armchair, rocking-chair, recliner, dining-chair, carver, kitchen chair, stool, swivel-chair, high-chair, suite, settee, sofa, couch, studio couch, chesterfield, pouffe, footstool, bean-bag; bed, four-poster, chaise-longue, daybed, bed-settee, divan, camp-bed, bunk, water-bed, cot, cradle; desk, bureau, secretaire, bookcase, cupboard, cabinet, china cabinet, Welsh dresser, sideboard, buffet, dumb-waiter, fireplace, overmantel, fender, firescreen, hallstand, umbrella-stand, mirror, magazine rack; wardrobe, armoire, dressing-table, vanity unit, washstand, chest-of-drawers, tallboy, chiffonier, commode, ottoman, chest, coffer, blanket box.

**furrow** n groove, channel, trench, hollow, rut, track, line, crease, wrinkle.
v seam, flute, corrugate, groove, crease, wrinkle, draw together, knit.

**further** adj more, additional, supplementary, extra, fresh, new, other.
v advance, forward, promote, champion, push, encourage, foster, help, aid, assist, ease, facilitate, speed, hasten, accelerate, expedite.
**F3** stop, frustrate.

**furthermore** adv moreover, what's more, in addition, further, besides, also, too, as well, additionally.

**furthest** adj farthest, furthermost, remotest, outermost, outmost, extreme, ultimate, utmost, uttermost.
**F3** nearest.

**furtive** adj surreptitious, sly, stealthy, secretive, underhand, hidden, covert, secret.
**F3** open.

**fury** n anger, rage, wrath, frenzy, madness, passion, vehemence, fierceness, ferocity, violence, wildness, turbulence, power.
**F3** calm, peacefulness.

**fusion** n melting, smelting, welding, union, synthesis, blending, coalescence, amalgamation, integration, merger, federation.

**fuss** n bother, trouble, hassle (infml), palaver, to-do (infml), hoo-ha (infml), furore, squabble, row, commotion, stir, fluster, confusion, upset, worry, agitation, flap (infml), excitement, bustle, flurry, hurry.
**F3** calm.
v complain, grumble, fret, worry, flap (infml), take pains, bother, bustle, fidget.

**fussy** adj 1 PARTICULAR, fastidious, scrupulous, finicky, pernickety, difficult, hard to please, choosy (infml), discriminating.
2 FANCY, elaborate, ornate, cluttered.
**F3** 1 casual, uncritical. 2 plain.

**futile** adj pointless, useless, worthless, vain, idle, wasted, fruitless, profitless, unavailing, unsuccessful, abortive, unprofitable, unproductive, barren, empty, hollow, forlorn.
**F3** fruitful, profitable.

**futility** n pointlessness, uselessness, worthlessness, vanity, emptiness, hollowness, aimlessness.
**F3** use, purpose.

**future** n hereafter, tomorrow, outlook, prospects, expectations.
**F3** past.
adj prospective, designate, to be, fated, destined, to come, forthcoming, in the offing, impending, coming, approaching, expected, planned, unborn, later, subsequent, eventual.
**F3** past.

**fuzzy** adj 1 FRIZZY, fluffy, furry, woolly, fleecy, downy, velvety, napped. 2 BLURRED, unfocused, ill-defined, unclear, vague, faint, hazy, shadowy, woolly, muffled, distorted.
**F3** 2 clear, distinct.

# G

**gadget** *n* tool, appliance, device, contrivance, contraption, thing, thingumajig (*infml*), invention, novelty, gimmick.

**gag**[1] mufle, muzzle, silence, quiet, stifle, throttle, suppress, curb, check, still.

**gag**[2] (*infml*) joke, jest, quip, crack, wisecrack, one-liner, pun, witticism, funny (*infml*).

**gaiety** *n* happiness, glee, cheerfulness, joie de vivre, jollity, merriment, mirth, hilarity, fun, merrymaking, revelry, festivity, joviality, good humour, high spirits, light-heartedness, liveliness, brightness, brilliance, sparkle, colour, colourfulness, show, showiness.
**F3** sadness, drabness.

**gaily** *adv* happily, joyfully, merrily, blithely, brightly, brilliantly, colourfully, flamboyantly.
**F3** sadly, dully.

**gain** *v* 1 EARN, make, produce, gross, net, clear, profit, yield, bring in, reap, harvest, win, capture, secure, net, obtain, acquire, procure. 2 REACH, arrive at, come to, get to, attain, achieve, realize. 3 *gain speed*: increase, pick up, gather, collect, advance, progress, improve.
**F3** 1 lose. 3 lose.

*n* earnings, proceeds, income, revenue, winnings, profit, return, yield, dividend, growth, increase, increment, rise, advance, progress, headway, improvement, advantage, benefit, attainment, achievement, acquisition.
**F3** loss.

**gain on** close with, narrow the gap, approach, catch up, level with, overtake, outdistance, leave behind.

**gala** *n* festivity, celebration, festival, carnival, jubilee, jamboree, fête, fair, pageant, procession.

**gale** *n* 1 WIND, squall, storm, hurricane, tornado, typhoon, cyclone. 2 BURST, outburst, outbreak, fit, eruption, explosion, blast.

**gallant** *adj* chivalrous, gentlemanly, courteous, polite, gracious, courtly, noble, dashing, heroic, valiant, brave, courageous, fearless, dauntless, bold, daring.
**F3** ungentlemanly, cowardly.

**gallery** *n* art gallery, museum, arcade, passage, walk, balcony, circle, gods (*infml*), spectators.

**gallop** *v* bolt, run, sprint, race, career, fly, dash, tear, speed, zoom, shoot, dart, rush, hurry, hasten.
**F3** amble.

**galvanize** *v* electrify, shock, jolt, prod, spur, provoke, stimulate, stir, move, arouse, excite, fire, invigorate, vitalize.

**gamble** *v* bet, wager, have a flutter (*infml*), try one's luck, punt, play, game, stake, chance, take a chance, risk, hazard, venture, speculate, back.

*n* bet, wager, flutter (*infml*), punt, lottery, chance, risk, venture, speculation.

**gambler** *n* better, punter.

**gambol** *v* caper, frolic, frisk, skip, jump, bound, hop, bounce.

**game**[1] *n* 1 RECREATION, play, sport, pastime, diversion, distraction, entertainment, amusement, fun, frolic, romp, joke, jest.

*Types of indoor game include*:
board game, backgammon, checkers (*North Amer.*), chess, Cluedo®, draughts, halma, ludo, mah-jong, Monopoly®, nine men's morris, Scrabble®, snakes and ladders, Trivial Pursuit®; card game, baccarat, beggar-my-neighbour, bezique, blackjack, brag, bridge, canasta, chemin de fer, crib (*infml*), cribbage, faro, gin rummy, rummy, happy families, nap (*infml*), napoleon, newmarket, old maid, patience, Pelmanism, picquet, poker, draw poker, stud poker, pontoon, vingt-et-un, snap, solitaire, twenty-one, whist, partner whist, solo whist; bagatelle, pinball, billiards, pool, snooker, bowling, ten-pin bowling, bowls, darts, dice, craps, dominoes, roulette, shove ha'penny, table tennis, ping pong.

*Types of children's games include*:
battleships, blind man's buff, charades, Chinese whispers, consequences, fivestones, forfeits, hangman, hide-and-seek, I-spy, jacks, jackstraws, musical chairs, noughts and crosses, pass the parcel, piggy-in-the-middle, pin the tail on the donkey, postman's knock, sardines, Simon says, spillikins, spin the bottle, tiddlywinks.

**2** COMPETITION, contest, match, round, tournament, event, meeting. **3** GAME BIRDS, animals, meat, flesh, prey, quarry, bag, spoils.

*Types of game (killed for sport) include*: antelope, badger, bear, blackcock, boar, wild boar, caribou, deer, fallow deer, red deer, roe deer, duck, elk, fox, grouse, hazel grouse, wood grouse, hare, lion, moose, mountain lion, partridge, pheasant, quail, rabbit, snipe, squirrel, stag, tiger, waterfowl.

**game²** *adj* (*infml*) **1** game for anything: willing, inclined, ready, prepared, eager. **2** BOLD, daring, intrepid, brave, courageous, fearless, resolute, spirited.
 ⊟ **1** unwilling. **2** cowardly.

**gamut** *n* scale, series, range, sweep, scope, compass, spectrum, field, area.

**gang** *n* group, band, ring, pack, herd, mob, crowd, circle, clique, coterie, set, lot, team, crew, squad, shift, party.

**gangster** *n* mobster, desperado, hoodlum, ruffian, rough, tough, thug, heavy (*sl*), racketeer, bandit, brigand, robber, criminal, crook (*infml*).

**gaol** *see* **jail**.

**gaoler** *see* **jailer**.

**gap** *n* **1** SPACE, blank, void, hole, opening, crack, chink, crevice, cleft, breach, rift, divide, divergence, difference. **2** INTERRUPTION, break, recess, pause, lull, interlude, intermission, interval.

**gape** *v* **1** STARE, gaze, gawp (*infml*), goggle, gawk (*infml*). **2** OPEN, yawn, part, split, crack.

**gaping** *adj* open, yawning, broad, wide, vast, cavernous.
 ⊟ tiny.

**garage** *n* lock-up, petrol station, service station.

**garble** *v* confuse, muddle, jumble, scramble, mix up, twist, distort, pervert, slant, misrepresent, falsify.
 ⊟ decipher.

**garden** *n* yard, backyard, plot, allotment, flowers, orchard, park.

**garish** *adj* gaudy, lurid, loud, glaring, flashy, showy, tawdry, vulgar, tasteless.
 ⊟ quiet, tasteful.

**garland** *n* wreath, festoon, decoration, flowers, laurels, honours.
 *v* wreathe, festoon, deck, adorn, crown.

**garments** *n* clothes, clothing, wear, attire, gear (*infml*), togs (*infml*), outfit, get-up (*infml*), dress, costume, uniform.

**garnish** v decorate, adorn, ornament, trim, embellish, enhance, grace, set off.
**E3** divest.
n decoration, ornament, trimming, embellishment, enhancement, relish.

**gash** v cut, wound, slash, slit, incise, lacerate, tear, rend, split, score, gouge.
n cut, wound, slash, slit, incision, laceration, tear, rent, split, score, gouge.

**gasp** v pant, puff, blow, breathe, wheeze, choke, gulp.
n pant, puff, blow, breath, gulp, exclamation.

**gate** n barrier, door, doorway, gateway, opening, entrance, exit, access, passage.

**gather** v 1 CONGREGATE, convene, muster, rally, round up, assemble, collect, group, amass, accumulate, hoard, stockpile, heap, pile up, build. 2 INFER, deduce, conclude, surmise, assume, understand, learn, hear. 3 FOLD, pleat, tuck, pucker. 4 *gather flowers*: pick, pluck, cull, select, reap, harvest, glean.
**E3** 1 scatter, dissipate.

**gathering** n assembly, convocation, convention, meeting, round-up, rally, get-together, jamboree, party, group, company, congregation, mass, crowd, throng, turnout.

**gaudy** adj bright, brilliant, glaring, garish, loud, flashy, showy, ostentatious, tinselly, glitzy (*infml*), tawdry, vulgar, tasteless.
**E3** drab, plain.

**gauge** v estimate, guess, judge, assess, evaluate, value, rate, reckon, figure, calculate, compute, count, measure, weigh, determine, ascertain.
n 1 STANDARD, norm, criterion, benchmark, yardstick, rule, guideline, indicator, measure, meter, test, sample, example, model, pattern.

2 SIZE, magnitude, measure, capacity, bore, calibre, thickness, width, span, extent, scope, height, depth, degree.

**gaunt** adj 1 HAGGARD, hollow-eyed, angular, bony, thin, lean, lank, skinny, scraggy, scrawny, skeletal, emaciated, wasted. 2 BLEAK, stark, bare, desolate, forlorn, dismal, dreary, grim, harsh.
**E3** 1 plump.

**gawky** adj awkward, clumsy, maladroit, gauche, inept, oafish, ungainly, gangling, unco-ordinated, graceless.
**E3** graceful.

**gay** adj 1 HAPPY, joyful, jolly, merry, cheerful, blithe, sunny, carefree, debonair, fun-loving, pleasure-seeking, vivacious, lively, animated, playful, light-hearted. 2 *gay colours*: vivid, rich, bright, brilliant, sparkling, festive, colourful, gaudy, garish, flashy, showy, flamboyant. 3 HOMOSEXUAL, lesbian, queer (*sl*).
**E3** 1 sad, gloomy. 3 heterosexual, straight (*sl*).
n homosexual, queer (*sl*), poof (*sl*), lesbian, dike (*sl*).
**E3** heterosexual.

**gaze** v stare, contemplate, regard, watch, view, look, gape, wonder.
n stare, look.

**gear** n 1 EQUIPMENT, kit, outfit, tackle, apparatus, tools, instruments, accessories. 2 GEARWHEEL, cogwheel, cog, gearing, mechanism, machinery, works. 3 (*infml*) BELONGINGS, possessions, things, stuff, baggage, luggage, paraphernalia. 4 (*infml*) CLOTHES, clothing, garments, attire, dress, garb (*infml*), togs (*infml*), get-up (*infml*).

**gel, jell** v set, congeal, coagulate, crystallize, harden, thicken, solidify, materialize, come together, finalize, form, take shape.

**gelatinous** adj jelly-like, jellied, congealed, rubbery, glutinous, gummy, gluey, gooey (*infml*), sticky, viscous.

**gem** *n* gemstone, precious stone, stone, jewel, treasure, prize, masterpiece, pièce de résistance.

*Gems and gemstones include*:
diamond, white sapphire, zircon, cubic zirconia, marcasite, rhinestone, pearl, moonstone, onyx, opal, mother-of-pearl, amber, citrine, fire opal, topaz, agate, tiger's eye, jasper, morganite, ruby, garnet, rose quartz, beryl, cornelian, coral, amethyst, sapphire, turquoise, lapis lazuli, emerald, aquamarine, bloodstone, jade, peridot, tourmaline, jet.

**genealogy** *n* family tree, pedigree, lineage, ancestry, descent, derivation, extraction, family, line.

**general** *adj* **1** *a general statement*: broad, sweeping, blanket, all-inclusive, comprehensive, universal, global, total, across-the-board, widespread, prevalent, extensive, overall, panoramic. **2** VAGUE, ill-defined, indefinite, imprecise, inexact, approximate, loose, unspecific. **3** USUAL, regular, normal, typical, ordinary, everyday, customary, conventional, common, public.
**F3** **1** particular, limited. **2** specific.
**3** rare.

**generally** *adv* usually, normally, as a rule, by and large, on the whole, mostly, mainly, chiefly, broadly, commonly, universally.

**generate** *v* produce, engender, whip up, arouse, cause, bring about, give rise to, create, originate, initiate, make, form, breed, propagate.
**F3** prevent.

**generation** *n* **1** AGE GROUP, age, era, epoch, period, time.
**2** PRODUCTION, creation, origination, formation, genesis, procreation, reproduction,

propagation, breeding.

**generosity** *n* liberality, munificence, open-handedness, bounty, charity, magnanimity, philanthropy, kindness, big-heartedness, benevolence, goodness.
**F3** meanness, selfishness.

**generous** *adj* **1** LIBERAL, free, bountiful, open-handed, unstinting, unsparing, lavish. **2** MAGNANIMOUS, charitable, philanthropic, public-spirited, unselfish, kind, big-hearted, benevolent, good, high-minded, noble. **3** AMPLE, full, plentiful, abundant, copious, overflowing.
**F3** **1** mean, miserly. **2** selfish.
**3** meagre.

**genial** *adj* affable, amiable, friendly, convivial, cordial, kindly, kind, warm-hearted, warm, hearty, jovial, jolly, cheerful, happy, good-natured, easy-going (*infml*), agreeable, pleasant.
**F3** cold.

**genius** *n* **1** VIRTUOSO, maestro, master, past master, expert, adept, egghead (*infml*), intellectual, mastermind, brain, intellect.
**2** INTELLIGENCE, brightness, brilliance, ability, aptitude, gift, talent, flair, knack, bent, inclination, propensity, capacity, faculty.

**gentle** *adj* **1** KIND, kindly, amiable, tender, soft-hearted, compassionate, sympathetic, merciful, mild, placid, calm, tranquil. **2** *a gentle slope*: gradual, slow, easy, smooth, moderate, slight, light, imperceptible.
**3** SOOTHING, peaceful, serene, quiet, soft, balmy.
**F3** unkind, rough, harsh, wild.

**genuine** *adj* real, actual, natural, pure, original, authentic, veritable, true, bona fide, legitimate, honest, sincere, frank, candid, earnest.
**F3** artificial, false, insincere.

**germ** *n* **1** MICRO-ORGANISM, microbe, bacterium, bacillus, virus, bug (*infml*). **2** BEGINNING, start, origin, source, cause, spark, rudiment, nucleus, root, seed, embryo, bud, sprout.

**germinate** v bud, sprout, shoot, develop, grow, swell.

**gesticulate** v wave, signal, gesture, indicate, sign.

**gesture** n act, action, movement, motion, indication, sign, signal, wave, gesticulation.
v indicate, sign, motion, beckon, point, signal, wave, gesticulate.

**get** v 1 OBTAIN, acquire, procure, come by, receive, earn, gain, win, secure, achieve, realize. 2 *it's getting dark*: become, turn, go, grow. 3 *get him to help*: persuade, coax, induce, urge, influence, sway. 4 MOVE, go, come up, reach, arrive. 5 FETCH, collect, pick up, take, catch, capture, seize, grab. 6 CONTRACT, catch, pick up, develop, come down with.
**E3** 1 lose. 4 leave.

**get across** communicate, transmit, convey, impart, put across, bring home to.

**get ahead** advance, progress, get on, go places (*infml*), thrive, flourish, prosper, succeed, make good, make it, get there (*infml*).
**E3** fall behind, fail.

**get along** 1 COPE, manage, get by, survive, fare, progress, develop. 2 AGREE, harmonize, get on, hit it off.

**get at** 1 REACH, attain, find, discover. 2 (*infml*) BRIBE, suborn, corrupt, influence. 3 (*infml*) MEAN, intend, imply, insinuate, hint, suggest. 4 (*infml*) CRITICIZE, find fault with, pick on, attack, make fun of.

**get away** escape, get out, break out, break away, run away, flee, depart, leave.

**get back** recover, regain, recoup, repossess, retrieve.

**get down** 1 DEPRESS, sadden, dishearten, dispirit. 2 DESCEND, dismount, disembark, alight, get off.
**E3** 1 encourage. 2 board.

**get in** enter, penetrate, infiltrate, arrive, come, land, embark.

**get off** 1 *get off a train*: alight, disembark, dismount, descend. 2 REMOVE, detach, separate, shed, get down.
**E3** 1 get on. 2 put on.

**get on** 1 BOARD, embark, mount, ascend. 2 COPE, manage, fare, get along, make out, prosper, succeed. 3 CONTINUE, proceed, press on, advance, progress.
**E3** 1 get off.

**get out** 1 ESCAPE, flee, break out, extricate oneself, free oneself, leave, quit, vacate, evacuate, clear out, clear off (*infml*). 2 *she got out a pen*: take out, produce.

**get over** 1 RECOVER FROM, shake off, survive. 2 SURMOUNT, overcome, defeat, deal with. 3 COMMUNICATE, get across, convey, put over, impart, explain.

**get round** 1 CIRCUMVENT, bypass, evade, avoid. 2 PERSUADE, win over, talk round, coax, prevail upon.

**get together** assemble, collect, gather, congregate, rally, meet, join, unite, collaborate.

**get up** stand (up), arise, rise, ascend, climb, mount, scale.

**ghastly** adj awful, dreadful, frightful, terrible, grim, gruesome, hideous, horrible, horrid, loathsome, repellent, shocking, appalling.
**E3** delightful, attractive.

**ghost** n spectre, phantom, spook (*infml*), apparition, visitant, spirit, wraith, soul, shade, shadow.

**ghostly** adj eerie, spooky (*infml*), creepy, supernatural, unearthly, ghostlike, spectral, wraith-like, phantom, illusory.

**giant** n monster, titan, colossus, Goliath, Hercules.
adj gigantic, colossal, titanic, mammoth, jumbo (*infml*), king-size, huge, enormous, immense, vast, large.

**gibe, jibe** n jeer, sneer, mockery,

ridicule, taunt, derision, scoff, dig
(*infml*), crack (*infml*), poke, quip.

**giddy** *adj* 1 DIZZY, faint, light-
headed, unsteady, reeling,
vertiginous. 2 SILLY, flighty, wild.

**gift** *n* 1 PRESENT, offering, donation,
contribution, bounty, largess,
gratuity, tip, bonus, freebie (*sl*),
legacy, bequest, endowment.
2 TALENT, genius, flair, aptitude,
bent, knack, power, faculty,
attribute, ability, capability,
capacity.

**gifted** *adj* talented, adept, skilful,
expert, masterly, skilled,
accomplished, able, capable, clever,
intelligent, bright, brilliant.

**gigantic** *adj* huge, enormous,
immense, vast, giant, colossal,
titanic, mammoth, gargantuan,
Brobdingnagian.
**E3** tiny, Lilliputian.

**giggle** *v, n* titter, snigger, chuckle,
chortle, laugh.

**gilded** *adj* gilt, gold, golden, gold-
plated.

**gimmick** *n* attraction, ploy,
stratagem, ruse, scheme, trick, stunt,
dodge, device, contrivance, gadget.

**gingerly** *adv* tentatively, hesitantly,
warily, cautiously, carefully,
delicately.
**E3** boldly, carelessly.

**gipsy** *see* **gypsy**.

**girdle** *n* belt, sash, band, waistband,
corset.

**girl** *n* lass, young woman, girlfriend,
sweetheart, daughter.

**girth** *n* circumference, perimeter,
measure, size, bulk, strap, band.

**gist** *n* pith, essence, marrow,
substance, matter, meaning,
significance, import, sense, idea,
drift, direction, point, nub, core,
quintessence.

**give** *v* 1 PRESENT, award, confer,
offer, lend, donate, contribute,
provide, supply, furnish, grant,
bestow, endow, gift, make over, hand

over, deliver, entrust, commit,
devote. 2 *give news*: communicate,
transmit, impart, utter, announce,
declare, pronounce, publish, set
forth. 3 CONCEDE, allow, admit,
yield, give way, surrender. 4 *give
trouble*: cause, occasion, make,
produce, do, perform. 5 SINK, yield,
bend, give way, break, collapse, fall.
**E3** take, withhold. 5 withstand.

**give away** betray, inform on, expose,
uncover, divulge, let slip, disclose,
reveal, leak, let out.

**give in** surrender, capitulate, submit,
yield, give way, concede, give up, quit.
**E3** hold out.

**give off** emit, discharge, release, give
out, send out, throw out, pour out,
exhale, exude, produce.

**give out** 1 DISTRIBUTE, hand out, dole
out, deal. 2 ANNOUNCE, declare,
broadcast, publish, disseminate,
communicate, transmit, impart,
notify, advertise.

**give up** 1 STOP, cease, quit, resign,
abandon, renounce, relinquish, waive.
2 SURRENDER, capitulate, give in.
**E3** 1 start. 2 hold out.

**given** *adj* 1 *a given number*:
specified, particular, definite.
2 INCLINED, disposed, likely, liable,
prone.

**glad** *adj* 1 PLEASED, delighted,
gratified, contented, happy, joyful,
merry, cheerful, cheery, bright. 2
WILLING, eager, keen, ready,
inclined, disposed.
**E3** 1 sad, unhappy. 2 unwilling,
reluctant.

**glamorous** *adj* smart, elegant,
attractive, beautiful, gorgeous,
enchanting, captivating, alluring,
appealing, fascinating, exciting,
dazzling, glossy, colourful.
**E3** plain, drab, boring.

**glamour** *n* attraction, allure, appeal,
fascination, charm, magic, beauty,
elegance, glitter, prestige.

**glance** *v* peep, peek, glimpse, view,

look, scan, skim, leaf, flip, thumb, dip, browse.

*n* peep, peek, glimpse, look.

**glare** *v* 1 GLOWER, look daggers, frown, scowl, stare. 2 DAZZLE, blaze, flame, flare, shine, reflect.

*n* 1 BLACK LOOK, dirty look (*infml*), frown, scowl, stare, look.

2 BRIGHTNESS, brilliance, blaze, flame, dazzle, spotlight.

**glaring** *adj* blatant, flagrant, open, conspicuous, manifest, patent, obvious, outrageous, gross.

🖃 hidden, concealed, minor.

**glassy** *adj* 1 GLASSLIKE, smooth, slippery, icy, shiny, glossy, transparent, clear. 2 *a glassy stare:* expressionless, blank, empty, vacant, dazed, fixed, glazed, cold, lifeless, dull.

**glaze** *v* coat, enamel, gloss, varnish, lacquer, polish, burnish.

*n* coat, coating, finish, enamel, varnish, lacquer, polish, shine, lustre, gloss.

**gleam** *n* glint, flash, beam, ray, flicker, glimmer, shimmer, sparkle, glitter, gloss, glow.

*v* glint, flash, glance, flare, shine, glisten, flash, glitter, sparkle, shimmer, glow.

**glib** *adj* fluent, easy, facile, quick, ready, talkative, plausible, insincere, smooth, slick, suave, smooth-tongued.

🖃 tongue-tied, implausible.

**glide** *v* slide, slip, skate, skim, fly, float, drift, sail, coast, roll, run, flow.

**glimmer** *v* glow, shimmer, glisten, glitter, sparkle, twinkle, wink, blink, flicker, gleam, shine.

*n* 1 GLOW, shimmer, sparkle, twinkle, flicker, glint, gleam.

2 TRACE, hint, suggestion, grain.

**glimpse** *n* peep, peek, squint, glance, look, sight, sighting, view.

*v* spy, espy, spot, catch sight of, sight, view.

**glint** *v* flash, gleam, shine, reflect,

glitter, sparkle, twinkle, glimmer.

*n* flash, gleam, shine, reflection, glitter, sparkle, twinkle, glimmer.

**glisten** *v* shine, gleam, glint, glitter, sparkle, twinkle, glimmer, shimmer.

**glitter** *v* sparkle, spangle, scintillate, twinkle, shimmer, glimmer, glisten, glint, gleam, flash, shine.

*n* sparkle, coruscation, scintillation, twinkle, shimmer, glimmer, glint, gleam, flash, shine, lustre, sheen, brightness, radiance, brilliance, splendour, showiness, glamour, tinsel.

**gloat** *v* triumph, glory, exult, rejoice, revel in, relish, crow, boast, vaunt, rub it in (*infml*).

**global** *adj* universal, worldwide, international, general, all-encompassing, total, thorough, exhaustive, comprehensive, all-inclusive, encyclopedic, wide-ranging.

🖃 parochial, limited.

**globe** *n* world, earth, planet, sphere, ball, orb, round.

**gloom** *n* 1 DEPRESSION, low spirits, despondency, dejection, sadness, unhappiness, glumness, melancholy, misery, desolation, despair. 2 DARK, darkness, shade, shadow, dusk, twilight, dimness, obscurity, cloud, cloudiness, dullness.

🖃 1 cheerfulness, happiness. 2 brightness.

**gloomy** *adj* 1 DEPRESSED, down, low, despondent, dejected, downcast, dispirited, down-hearted, sad, miserable, glum, morose, pessimistic, cheerless, dismal, depressing.

2 DARK, sombre, shadowy, dim, obscure, overcast, dull, dreary.

🖃 1 cheerful. 2 bright.

**glorious** *adj* 1 ILLUSTRIOUS, eminent, distinguished, famous, renowned, noted, great, noble, splendid, magnificent, grand, majestic, triumphant. 2 FINE, bright, radiant, shining, brilliant, dazzling, beautiful, gorgeous, superb, excellent, wonderful, marvellous, delightful, heavenly.

☞ 1 unknown.

**glory** n 1 FAME, renown, celebrity, illustriousness, greatness, eminence, distinction, honour, prestige, kudos, triumph. 2 PRAISE, homage, tribute, worship, veneration, adoration, exaltation, blessing, thanksgiving, gratitude. 3 BRIGHTNESS, radiance, brilliance, beauty, splendour, resplendence, magnificence, grandeur, majesty, dignity.

**gloss**¹ n polish, varnish, lustre, sheen, shine, brightness, brilliance, show, appearance, semblance, surface, front, façade, veneer, window-dressing.

   **gloss over** conceal, hide, veil, mask, disguise, camouflage, cover up, whitewash, explain away.

**gloss**² n annotation, note, footnote, explanation, elucidation, interpretation, translation, definition, comment, commentary.

   v annotate, define, explain, elucidate, interpret, construe, translate, comment.

**glossy** adj shiny, sheeny, lustrous, sleek, silky, smooth, glassy, polished, burnished, glazed, enamelled, bright, shining, brilliant.

☞ matt.

**glow** n 1 LIGHT, gleam, glimmer, radiance, luminosity, brightness, vividness, brilliance, splendour. 2 ARDOUR, fervour, intensity, warmth, passion, enthusiasm, excitement. 3 FLUSH, blush, rosiness, redness, burning.

   v 1 SHINE, radiate, gleam, glimmer, burn, smoulder. 2 *their faces glowed*: flush, blush, colour, redden.

**glower** v glare, look daggers, frown, scowl.

   n glare, black look, dirty look (*infml*), frown, scowl, stare, look.

**glowing** adj 1 BRIGHT, luminous, vivid, vibrant, rich, warm, flushed, red, flaming. 2 *a glowing review*:

complimentary, enthusiastic, ecstatic, rhapsodic, rave (*infml*).

☞ 1 dull, colourless. 2 restrained.

**glue** n adhesive, gum, paste, size, cement.

   v stick, affix, gum, paste, seal, bond, cement, fix.

**glut** n surplus, excess, superfluity, surfeit, overabundance, superabundance, saturation, overflow.

☞ scarcity, lack.

**glutton** n gourmand, gormandizer, guzzler, gorger, gobbler, pig.

☞ ascetic.

**gluttony** n gourmandise, gourmandism, greed, greediness, voracity, insatiability, piggishness.

☞ abstinence, asceticism.

**gnarled** adj gnarly, knotted, knotty, twisted, contorted, distorted, rough, rugged, weather-beaten.

**gnaw** v 1 BITE, nibble, munch, chew, eat, devour, consume, erode, wear, haunt. 2 WORRY, niggle, fret, trouble, plague, nag, prey.

**go** v 1 MOVE, pass, advance, progress, proceed, make for, travel, journey, start, begin, depart, leave, take one's leave, retreat, withdraw, disappear, vanish. 2 OPERATE, function, work, run, act, perform. 3 EXTEND, spread, stretch, reach, span, continue, unfold. 4 *time goes quickly*: pass, elapse, lapse, roll on.

☞ 2 break down, fail.

   n (*infml*) 1 *have a go*: attempt, try, shot (*infml*), bash (*infml*), stab (*infml*), turn. 2 ENERGY, get-up-and-go (*infml*), vitality, life, spirit, dynamism, effort.

   **go about** approach, begin, set about, address, tackle, attend to, undertake, engage in, perform.

   **go ahead** begin, proceed, carry on, continue, advance, progress, move.

   **go away** depart, leave, clear off (*infml*), withdraw, retreat, disappear, vanish.

**go back** return, revert, backslide, retreat.

**go by 1** PASS, elapse, flow. **2** *go by the rules*: observe, follow, comply with, heed.

**go down** descend, sink, set, fall, drop, decrease, decline, deteriorate, degenerate, fail, founder, go under, collapse, fold (*infml*).

**go for 1** (*infml*) CHOOSE, prefer, favour, like, admire, enjoy. **2** ATTACK, assail, set about, lunge at.

**go in for** enter, take part in, participate in, engage in, take up, embrace, adopt, undertake, practise, pursue, follow.

**go into** discuss, consider, review, examine, study, scrutinize, investigate, inquire into, check out, probe, delve into, analyse, dissect.

**go off 1** DEPART, leave, quit, abscond, vanish, disappear. **2** EXPLODE, blow up, detonate. **3** *the milk has gone off*: deteriorate, turn, sour, go bad, rot.

**go on 1** CONTINUE, carry on, proceed, persist, stay, endure, last. **2** CHATTER, rabbit (*infml*), witter (*infml*), ramble on. **3** HAPPEN, occur, take place.

**go out** exit, depart, leave.

**go over** examine, peruse, study, revise, scan, read, inspect, check, review, repeat, rehearse, list.

**go through 1** SUFFER, undergo, experience, bear, tolerate, endure, withstand. **2** INVESTIGATE, check, examine, look, search, hunt, explore. **3** USE, consume, exhaust, spend, squander.

**go together** match, harmonize, accord, fit.

**go with 1** MATCH, harmonize, co-ordinate, blend, complement, suit, fit, correspond. **2** ACCOMPANY, escort, take, usher.
**Ǝ 1** clash.

**go without** abstain, forgo, do without, manage without, lack, want.

**goad** *v* prod, prick, spur, impel, push, drive, provoke, incite, instigate, arouse, stimulate, prompt, urge, nag, hound, harass, annoy, irritate, vex.

**go-ahead** *n* permission, authorization, clearance, green light (*infml*), sanction, assent, consent, OK (*infml*), agreement.
**Ǝ** ban, veto, embargo.
*adj* enterprising, pioneering, progressive, ambitious, up-and-coming, dynamic, energetic.
**Ǝ** unenterprising, sluggish.

**goal** *n* target, mark, objective, aim, intention, object, purpose, end, ambition, aspiration.

**gobble** *v* bolt, guzzle, gorge, cram, stuff, devour, consume, put away (*infml*), swallow, gulp.

**go-between** *n* intermediary, mediator, liaison, contact, middleman, broker, dealer, agent, messenger, medium.

**God** *n* Supreme Being, Creator, Providence, Lord, Almighty, Holy One, Jehovah, Yahweh, Allah, Brahma, Zeus.

**god, goddess** *n* deity, divinity, idol, spirit, power.

**god-forsaken** *adj* remote, isolated, lonely, bleak, desolate, abandoned, deserted, forlorn, dismal, dreary, gloomy, miserable, wretched.

**godless** *adj* ungodly, atheistic, heathen, pagan, irreligious, unholy, impious, sacrilegious, profane, irreverent, bad, evil, wicked.
**Ǝ** godly, pious.

**godly** *adj* religious, holy, pious, devout, God-fearing, righteous, good, virtuous, pure, innocent.
**Ǝ** godless, impious.

**godsend** *n* blessing, boon, stroke of luck, windfall, miracle.
**Ǝ** blow, setback.

**golden** *adj* **1** GOLD, gilded, gilt, yellow, blond(e), fair, bright, shining, lustrous, resplendent. **2** PROSPEROUS, successful, glorious, excellent, happy, joyful, favourable, auspicious, promising, rosy.

**good** *adj* **1** ACCEPTABLE,

satisfactory, pleasant, agreeable, nice, enjoyable, pleasing, commendable, excellent, great (*infml*), super (*infml*), first-class, first-rate, superior, advantageous, beneficial, favourable, auspicious, helpful, useful, worthwhile, profitable, appropriate, suitable, fitting. **2** *good at her job*: competent, proficient, skilled, expert, accomplished, professional, skilful, clever, talented, gifted, fit, able, capable, dependable, reliable. **3** KIND, considerate, gracious, benevolent, charitable, philanthropic. **4** VIRTUOUS, exemplary, moral, upright, honest, trustworthy, worthy, righteous. **5** WELL-BEHAVED, obedient, well-mannered. **6** THOROUGH, complete, whole, substantial, considerable.

**Ea 1** bad, poor. **2** incompetent. **3** unkind, inconsiderate. **4** wicked, immoral. **5** naughty, disobedient.

*n* **1** VIRTUE, morality, goodness, righteousness, right. **2** USE, purpose, avail, advantage, profit, gain, worth, merit, usefulness, service. **3** *for your own good*: welfare, wellbeing, interest, sake, behalf, benefit, convenience.

**good-bye** *n* farewell, adieu, au revoir, valediction, leave-taking, parting.

**good-humoured** *adj* cheerful, happy, jovial, genial, affable, amiable, friendly, congenial, pleasant, good-tempered, approachable.

**Ea** ill-humoured.

**good-looking** *adj* attractive, handsome, beautiful, fair, pretty, personable, presentable.

**Ea** ugly, plain.

**good-natured** *adj* kind, kindly, kind-hearted, sympathetic, benevolent, helpful, neighbourly, gentle, good-tempered, friendly, tolerant, patient.

**Ea** ill-natured.

**goodness** *n* virtue, uprightness, rectitude, honesty, probity, kindness, compassion, graciousness, goodwill, benevolence, unselfishness, generosity, friendliness, helpfulness.

**Ea** badness, wickedness.

**goods** *n* **1** PROPERTY, chattels, effects, possessions, belongings, paraphernalia, stuff, things, gear (*infml*). **2** MERCHANDISE, wares, commodities, stock, freight.

**goodwill** *n* benevolence, kindness, generosity, favour, friendliness, friendship, zeal.

**Ea** ill-will.

**gore** *v* pierce, penetrate, stab, spear, stick, impale, wound.

**gorge** *n* canyon, ravine, gully, defile, chasm, abyss, cleft, fissure, gap, pass.

*v* feed, guzzle, gobble, devour, bolt, wolf, gulp, swallow, cram, stuff, fill, sate, surfeit, glut, overeat.

**Ea** fast.

**gorgeous** *adj* magnificent, splendid, grand, glorious, superb, fine, rich, sumptuous, luxurious, brilliant, dazzling, showy, glamorous, attractive, beautiful, handsome, good-looking, delightful, pleasing, lovely, enjoyable, good.

**Ea** dull, plain.

**gory** *adj* bloody, sanguinary, bloodstained, blood-soaked, grisly, brutal, savage, murderous.

**gossip** *n* **1** IDLE TALK, prattle, chitchat, tittle-tattle, rumour, hearsay, report, scandal. **2** GOSSIP-MONGER, scandalmonger, whisperer, prattler, babbler, chatterbox, nosey parker (*infml*), busybody, talebearer, tell-tale, tattler.

*v* talk, chat, natter, chatter, gabble, prattle, tattle, tell tales, whisper, rumour.

**gouge** *v* chisel, cut, hack, incise, score, groove, scratch, claw, gash, slash, dig, scoop, hollow, extract.

**gourmet** *n* gastronome, epicure,

epicurean, connoisseur, bon vivant.

**govern** v **1** RULE, reign, direct, manage, superintend, supervise, oversee, preside, lead, head, command, influence, guide, conduct, steer, pilot. **2** *govern one's temper*: dominate, master, control, regulate, curb, check, restrain, contain, quell, subdue, tame, discipline.

**government** n **1** *blame the government*: administration, executive, ministry, Establishment, authorities, powers that be, state, régime. **2** RULE, sovereignty, sway, direction, management, superintendence, supervision, surveillance, command, charge, authority, guidance, conduct, domination, dominion, control, regulation, restraint.

**government systems**

Government systems include:
absolutism, autocracy, commonwealth, communism, democracy, despotism, dictatorship, empire, federation, hierocracy, junta, kingdom, monarchy, plutocracy, puppet government, republic, theocracy, triumvirate. *see also* **parliaments and political assemblies**.

**governor** n ruler, commissioner, administrator, executive, director, manager, leader, head, chief, commander, superintendent, supervisor, overseer, controller, boss.

**gown** n robe, dress, frock, dressing-gown, habit, costume.

**grab** v seize, snatch, take, nab (*infml*), pluck, snap up, catch hold of, grasp, clutch, grip, catch, bag, capture, collar (*infml*), commandeer, appropriate, usurp, annex.

**grace** n **1** GRACEFULNESS, poise, beauty, attractiveness, loveliness, shapeliness, elegance, tastefulness, refinement, polish, breeding, manners, etiquette, decorum,

decency, courtesy, charm. **2** KINDNESS, kindliness, compassion, consideration, goodness, virtue, generosity, charity, benevolence, goodwill, favour, forgiveness, indulgence, mercy, leniency, pardon, reprieve. **3** *say grace*: blessing, benediction, thanksgiving, prayer. **F∃ 2** cruelty, harshness.
v favour, honour, dignify, distinguish, embellish, enhance, set off, trim, garnish, decorate, ornament, adorn.
**F∃** spoil, detract from.

**graceful** adj easy, flowing, smooth, supple, agile, deft, natural, slender, fine, tasteful, elegant, beautiful, charming, suave.
**F∃** graceless, awkward, clumsy, ungainly.

**gracious** adj elegant, refined, polite, courteous, well-mannered, considerate, sweet, obliging, accommodating, kind, compassionate, kindly, benevolent, generous, magnanimous, charitable, hospitable, forgiving, indulgent, lenient, mild, clement, merciful.
**F∃** ungracious.

**grade** n rank, status, standing, station, place, position, level, stage, degree, step, rung, notch, mark, brand, quality, standard, condition, size, order, group, class, category.
v sort, arrange, categorize, order, group, class, rate, size, rank, range, classify, evaluate, assess, value, mark, brand, label, pigeonhole, type.

**gradient** n slope, incline, hill, bank, rise, declivity.

**gradual** adj slow, leisurely, unhurried, easy, gentle, moderate, regular, even, measured, steady, continuous, progressive, step-by-step.
**F∃** sudden, precipitate.

**gradually** adv little by little, bit by bit, imperceptibly, inch by inch, step by step, progressively, by degrees, piecemeal, slowly, gently, cautiously, gingerly, moderately, evenly, steadily.

**graduate** *v* 1 *graduate from medical school*: pass, qualify. 2 CALIBRATE, mark off, measure out, proportion, grade, arrange, range, order, rank, sort, group, classify.

**graft** *n* implant, implantation, transplant, splice, bud, sprout, shoot, scion.

*v* engraft, implant, insert, transplant, join, splice.

**grain** *n* 1 BIT, piece, fragment, scrap, morsel, crumb, granule, particle, molecule, atom, jot, iota, mite, speck, modicum, trace. 2 SEED, kernel, corn, cereals. 3 TEXTURE, fibre, weave, pattern, marking, surface.

**grand** *adj* 1 MAJESTIC, regal, stately, splendid, magnificent, glorious, superb, sublime, fine, excellent, outstanding, first-rate, impressive, imposing, striking, monumental, large, noble, lordly, lofty, pompous, pretentious, grandiose, ambitious. 2 SUPREME, pre-eminent, leading, head, chief, arch, highest, senior, great, illustrious.

Ea 1 humble, common, poor.

**grandeur** *n* majesty, stateliness, pomp, state, dignity, splendour, magnificence, nobility, greatness, illustrious, importance.

Ea humbleness, lowliness, simplicity.

**grandiose** *adj* pompous, pretentious, high-flown, lofty, ambitious, extravagant, ostentatious, showy, flamboyant, grand, majestic, stately, magnificent, impressive, imposing, monumental.

Ea unpretentious.

**grant** *v* 1 GIVE, donate, present, award, confer, bestow, impart, transmit, dispense, apportion, assign, allot, allocate, provide, supply. 2 ADMIT, acknowledge, concede, allow, permit, consent to, agree to, accede to.

Ea 1 withhold. 2 deny.

*n* allowance, subsidy, concession, award, bursary, scholarship, gift, donation, endowment, bequest, annuity, pension, honorarium.

**granular** *adj* grainy, granulated, gritty, sandy, lumpy, rough, crumbly, friable.

**graph** *n* diagram, chart, table, grid.

**graphic** *adj* vivid, descriptive, expressive, striking, telling, lively, realistic, explicit, clear, lucid, specific, detailed, blow-by-blow, visual, pictorial, diagrammatic, illustrative.

Ea vague, impressionistic.

**grapple** *v* seize, grasp, snatch, grab, grip, clutch, clasp, hold, wrestle, tussle, struggle, contend, fight, combat, clash, engage, encounter, face, confront, tackle, deal with, cope with.

Ea release, avoid, evade.

**grasp** *v* 1 HOLD, clasp, clutch, grip, grapple, seize, snatch, grab, catch. 2 *grasp a concept*: understand, comprehend, get (*infml*), follow, see, realize.

*n* 1 GRIP, clasp, hold, embrace, clutches, possession, control, power. 2 UNDERSTANDING, comprehension, apprehension, mastery, familiarity, knowledge.

**grasping** *adj* avaricious, greedy, rapacious, acquisitive, mercenary, mean, selfish, miserly, close-fisted, tight-fisted, parsimonious.

Ea generous.

**grass** *n* turf, lawn, green, grassland, field, meadow, pasture, prairie, pampas, savanna, steppe.

*Types of grass include:* bamboo, barley, beard grass, bent, buckwheat, cane, cocksfoot, corn, couch grass, English ryegrass, esparto, fescue, Italian ryegrass, Kentucky bluegrass, kangaroo grass, knot grass, maize, marijuana, marram grass, meadow foxtail, meadow grass, millet, oats, paddy, pampas grass, papyrus, rattan, reed, rice, rye, ryegrass, sorghum, squirrel-tail grass, sugar cane, switch grass, twitch grass, wheat, wild oat.

**grate** v 1 GRIND, shred, mince, pulverize, rub, rasp, scrape. 2 JAR, set one's teeth on edge, annoy, irritate, aggravate (*infml*), get on one's nerves, vex, irk, exasperate.

**grateful** adj thankful, appreciative, indebted, obliged, obligated, beholden.
✎ ungrateful.

**gratify** v satisfy, fulfil, indulge, pander to, humour, favour, please, gladden, delight, thrill.
✎ frustrate, thwart.

**grating**[1] adj harsh, rasping, scraping, squeaky, strident, discordant, jarring, annoying, irritating, unpleasant, disagreeable.
✎ harmonious, pleasing.

**grating**[2] n grate, grill, grid, lattice, trellis.

**gratitude** n gratefulness, thankfulness, thanks, appreciation, acknowledgement, recognition, indebtedness, obligation.
✎ ingratitude, ungratefulness.

**gratuitous** adj wanton, unnecessary, needless, superfluous, unwarranted, unjustified, groundless, undeserved, unprovoked, uncalled-for, unasked-for, unsolicited, voluntary, free, gratis, complimentary.
✎ justified, provoked.

**gratuity** n tip, bonus, perk (*infml*), gift, present, donation, reward, recompense.

**grave**[1] n burial-place, tomb, vault, crypt, sepulchre, mausoleum, pit, barrow, tumulus, cairn.

**grave**[2] adj 1 *a grave mistake*: important, significant, weighty, momentous, serious, critical, vital, crucial, urgent, acute, severe,

dangerous, hazardous. 2 SOLEMN, dignified, sober, sedate, serious, thoughtful, pensive, grim, long-faced, quiet, reserved, subdued, restrained.
✎ 1 trivial, light, slight. 2 cheerful.

**graveyard** n cemetery, burial-ground, churchyard.

**gravity** n 1 IMPORTANCE, significance, seriousness, urgency, acuteness, severity, danger. 2 SOLEMNITY, dignity, sobriety, seriousness, thoughtfulness, sombreness, reserve, restraint. 3 GRAVITATION, attraction, pull, weight, heaviness.
✎ 1 triviality. 2 levity.

**graze** v scratch, scrape, skin, abrade, rub, chafe, shave, brush, skim, touch.
n scratch, scrape, abrasion.

**grease** n oil, lubrication, fat, lard, dripping, tallow.

**greasy** adj oily, fatty, lardy, buttery, smeary, slimy, slippery, smooth, waxy.

**great** adj 1 LARGE, big, huge, enormous, massive, colossal, gigantic, mammoth, immense, vast, impressive. 2 *with great care*: considerable, pronounced, extreme, excessive, inordinate. 3 FAMOUS, renowned, celebrated, illustrious, eminent, distinguished, prominent, noteworthy, notable, remarkable, outstanding, grand, glorious, fine. 4 IMPORTANT, significant, serious, major, principal, primary, main, chief, leading. 5 (*infml*) EXCELLENT, first-rate, superb, wonderful, marvellous, tremendous, terrific, fantastic, fabulous.
✎ 1 small. 2 slight. 3 unknown. 4 unimportant, insignificant.

**greed** n 1 HUNGER, ravenousness, gluttony, gourmandism, voracity, insatiability. 2 ACQUISITIVENESS, covetousness, desire, craving, longing, eagerness, avarice, selfishness.

1 abstemiousness, self-restraint.

**greedy** *adj* 1 HUNGRY, starving, ravenous, gluttonous, gormandizing, voracious, insatiable. 2 ACQUISITIVE, covetous, desirous, craving, eager, impatient, avaricious, grasping, selfish.

1 abstemious.

**green** *adj* 1 GRASSY, leafy, verdant, unripe, unseasoned, tender, fresh, budding, blooming, flourishing. 2 *green with envy*: envious, covetous, jealous, resentful. 3 IMMATURE, naïve, unsophisticated, ignorant, inexperienced, untrained, raw, new, recent, young. 4 ECOLOGICAL, environmental, eco-friendly, environmentally aware.
*n* common, lawn, grass, turf.

**greenhouse** *n* glasshouse, hothouse, conservatory, pavilion, vinery, orangery.

**greet** *v* hail, salute, acknowledge, address, accost, meet, receive, welcome.

ignore.

**greeting** *n* salutation, acknowledgement, wave, hallo, the time of day, address, reception, welcome.

**greetings** *n* regards, respects, compliments, salutations, best wishes, good wishes, love.

**gregarious** *adj* sociable, outgoing, extrovert, friendly, affable, social, convivial, cordial, warm.

unsociable.

**grey** *adj* 1 NEUTRAL, colourless, pale, ashen, leaden, dull, cloudy, overcast, dim, dark, murky. 2 GLOOMY, dismal, cheerless, depressing, dreary, bleak.

**grief** *n* sorrow, sadness, unhappiness, depression, dejection, desolation, distress, misery, woe, heartbreak, mourning, bereavement, heartache, anguish, agony, pain, suffering, affliction, trouble, regret, remorse.

happiness, delight.

**grievance** *n* complaint, moan (*infml*), grumble (*infml*), resentment, objection, protest, charge, wrong, injustice, injury, damage, trouble, affliction, hardship, trial, tribulation.

**grieve** *v* 1 SORROW, mope, lament, mourn, wail, cry, weep. 2 SADDEN, upset, dismay, distress, afflict, pain, hurt, wound.

1 rejoice. 2 please, gladden.

**grim** *adj* 1 UNPLEASANT, horrible, horrid, ghastly, gruesome, grisly, sinister, frightening, fearsome, terrible, shocking. 2 STERN, severe, harsh, dour, forbidding, surly, sullen, morose, gloomy, depressing, unattractive.

1 pleasant. 2 attractive.

**grimace** *n* frown, scowl, pout, smirk, sneer, face.
*v* make a face, pull a face, frown, scowl, pout, smirk, sneer.

**grime** *n* dirt, muck, filth, soot, dust.

**grimy** *adj* dirty, mucky, grubby, soiled, filthy, sooty, smutty, dusty, smudgy.

clean.

**grind** *v* crush, pound, pulverize, powder, mill, grate, scrape, gnash, rut, abrade, sand, file, smooth, polish, sharpen, whet.

**grip** *n* hold, grasp, clasp, embrace, clutches, control, power.
*v* 1 HOLD, grasp, clasp, clutch, seize, grab, catch. 2 FASCINATE, thrill, enthral, spellbind, mesmerize, hypnotize, rivet, engross, absorb, involve, engage, compel.

**grisly** *adj* gruesome, gory, grim, macabre, horrid, horrible, ghastly, awful, frightful, terrible, dreadful, abominable, appalling, shocking.

delightful.

**grit** *n* gravel, pebbles, shingle, sand, dust.
*v* clench, gnash, grate, grind.

**groan** *n* moan, sigh, cry, whine, wail, lament, complaint, objection,

protest, outcry.
≡ cheer.
*v* moan, sigh, cry, whine, wail,
lament, complain, object, protest.
≡ cheer.

**groom** *v* 1 SMARTEN, neaten, tidy,
spruce up, clean, brush, curry, preen,
dress. 2 *groomed for her new post*:
PREPARE, train, school, educate,
drill.

**groove** *n* furrow, rut, track, slot,
channel, gutter, trench, hollow,
indentation, score.
≡ ridge.

**grope** *v* feel, fumble, scrabble,
flounder, cast about, fish, search,
probe.

**gross** *adj* 1 *gross misconduct*:
serious, grievous, blatant, flagrant,
glaring, obvious, plain, sheer, utter,
outright, shameful, shocking.
2 OBSCENE, lewd, improper,
indecent, offensive, rude, coarse,
crude, vulgar, tasteless. 3 FAT, obese,
overweight, big, large, huge, colossal,
hulking, bulky, heavy. 4 *gross
earnings*: inclusive, all-inclusive,
total, aggregate, entire, complete,
whole.
≡ 3 slight. 4 net.

**grotesque** *adj* bizarre, odd, weird,
unnatural, freakish, monstrous,
hideous, ugly, unsightly, misshapen,
deformed, distorted, twisted,
fantastic, fanciful, extravagant,
absurd, surreal, macabre.
≡ normal, graceful.

**ground** *n* 1 BOTTOM, foundation,
surface, land, terrain, dry land, terra
firma, earth, soil, clay, loam, dirt,
dust. 2 *football ground*: field, pitch,
stadium, arena, park.
*v* 1 BASE, found, establish, set, fix,
settle. 2 PREPARE, introduce, initiate,
familiarize with, acquaint with,
inform, instruct, teach, train, drill,
coach, tutor.

**groundless** *adj* baseless,
unfounded, unsubstantiated,

unsupported, empty, imaginary,
false, unjustified, unwarranted,
unprovoked, uncalled-for.
≡ well-founded, reasonable, justified.

**grounds¹** *n* land, terrain, holding,
estate, property, territory, domain,
gardens, park, campus, surroundings,
fields, acres.

**grounds²** *n* base, foundation,
justification, excuse, vindication,
reason, motive, inducement, cause,
occasion, call, score, account,
argument, principle, basis.

**group** *n* band, gang, pack, team,
crew, troop, squad, detachment,
party, faction, set, circle, clique, club,
society, association, organization,
company, gathering, congregation,
crowd, collection, bunch, clump,
cluster, conglomeration,
constellation, batch, lot,
combination, formation, grouping,
class, classification, category, genus,
species.
*v* 1 GATHER, collect, assemble,
congregate, mass, cluster, clump,
bunch. 2 *group them according to size*:
sort, range, arrange, marshal,
organize, order, class, classify,
categorize, band, link, associate.

**grovel** *v* crawl, creep, ingratiate
oneself, toady, suck up (*sl*), flatter,
fawn, cringe, cower, kowtow, defer,
demean oneself.

**grow** *v* 1 INCREASE, rise, expand,
enlarge, swell, spread, extend,
stretch, develop, proliferate,
mushroom. 2 ORIGINATE, arise,
issue, spring, germinate, shoot,
sprout, bud, flower, mature, develop,
progress, thrive, flourish, prosper. 3
CULTIVATE, farm, produce,
propagate, breed, raise. 4 *grow cold*:
become, get, go, turn.
≡ 1 decrease, shrink.

**growl** *v* snarl, snap, yap, rumble,
roar.

**grown-up** *adj* adult, mature, of age,
full-grown, fully-fledged.

**young**, immature.
*n* adult, man, woman.
**F3** child.

**growth** *n* **1** INCREASE, rise, extension, enlargement, expansion, spread, proliferation, development, evolution, progress, advance, improvement, success, prosperity. **2** TUMOUR, lump, swelling, protuberance, outgrowth.
**F3** **1** decrease, decline, failure.

**grub** *v* dig, burrow, delve, probe, root, rummage, forage, ferret, hunt, search, scour, explore.
*n* maggot, worm, larva, pupa, caterpillar, chrysalis.

**grubby** *adj* dirty, soiled, unwashed, mucky, grimy, filthy, squalid, seedy, scruffy.
**F3** clean.

**grudge** *n* resentment, bitterness, envy, jealousy, spite, malice, enmity, antagonism, hate, dislike, animosity, ill-will, hard feelings, grievance.
**F3** favour.
*v* begrudge, resent, envy, covet, dislike, take exception to, object to, mind.

**grudging** *adj* reluctant, unwilling, hesitant, half-hearted, unenthusiastic, resentful, envious, jealous.

**gruelling** *adj* hard, difficult, taxing, demanding, tiring, exhausting, laborious, arduous, strenuous, backbreaking, harsh, severe, tough, punishing.
**F3** easy.

**gruesome** *adj* horrible, disgusting, repellent, repugnant, repulsive, hideous, grisly, macabre, grim, ghastly, awful, terrible, horrific, shocking, monstrous, abominable.
**F3** pleasant.

**gruff** *adj* **1** CURT, brusque, abrupt, blunt, rude, surly, sullen, grumpy, bad-tempered. **2** *a gruff voice*: rough, harsh, rasping, guttural, throaty, husky, hoarse.
**F3** **1** friendly, courteous.

**grumble** *v* complain, moan, whine, bleat, grouch, gripe, mutter, murmur, carp, find fault.

**grumpy** *adj* bad-tempered, ill-tempered, crotchety, crabbed, cantankerous, cross, irritable, surly, sullen, sulky, grouchy, discontented.
**F3** contented.

**guarantee** *n* warranty, insurance, assurance, promise, word of honour, pledge, oath, bond, security, collateral, surety, endorsement, testimonial.
*v* assure, promise, pledge, swear, vouch for, answer for, warrant, certify, underwrite, endorse, secure, protect, insure, ensure, make sure, make certain.

**guard** *v* protect, safeguard, save, preserve, shield, screen, shelter, cover, defend, patrol, police, escort, supervise, oversee, watch, look out, mind, beware.
*n* **1** PROTECTOR, defender, custodian, warder, escort, bodyguard, minder (*sl*), watchman, lookout, sentry, picket, patrol, security. **2** PROTECTION, safeguard, defence, wall, barrier, screen, shield, bumper, buffer, pad.

**guarded** *adj* cautious, wary, careful, watchful, discreet, non-committal, reticent, reserved, secretive, cagey (*infml*).
**F3** communicative, frank.

**guardian** *n* trustee, curator, custodian, keeper, warden, protector, preserver, defender, champion, guard, warder, escort, attendant.

**guess** *v* speculate, conjecture, predict, estimate, judge, reckon, work out, suppose, assume, surmise, think, believe, imagine, fancy, feel, suspect.
*n* prediction, estimate, speculation, conjecture, supposition, assumption, belief, fancy, idea, notion, theory, hypothesis, opinion, feeling, suspicion, intuition.

**guesswork** n speculation, conjecture, estimation, reckoning, supposition, assumption, surmise, intuition.

**guest** n visitor, caller, boarder, lodger, resident, patron, regular.

**guidance** n leadership, direction, management, control, teaching, instruction, advice, counsel, counselling, help, instructions, directions, guidelines, indications, pointers, recommendations.

**guide** v lead, conduct, direct, navigate, point, steer, pilot, manoeuvre, usher, escort, accompany, attend, control, govern, manage, oversee, supervise, superintend, advise, counsel, influence, educate, teach, instruct, train.

n 1 LEADER, courier, navigator, pilot, helmsman, steersman, usher, escort, chaperon, attendant, companion, adviser, counsellor, mentor, guru, teacher, instructor. 2 MANUAL, handbook, guidebook, catalogue, directory. 3 GUIDELINE, example, model, standard, criterion, indication, pointer, signpost, sign, marker.

**guilt** n 1 he confessed his guilt: culpability, responsibility, blame, disgrace, dishonour. 2 a feeling of guilt: guilty conscience, conscience, shame, self-condemnation, self-reproach, regret, remorse, contrition.
F3 1 innocence, righteousness. 2 shamelessness.

**guilty** adj 1 CULPABLE, responsible, blamable, blameworthy, offending, wrong, sinful, wicked, criminal, convicted. 2 CONSCIENCE-STRICKEN, ashamed, shamefaced, sheepish, sorry, regretful, remorseful, contrite, penitent, repentant.
F3 1 innocent, guiltless, blameless. 2 shameless.

**gulf** n bay, bight, basin, gap, opening, separation, rift, split,
breach, cleft, chasm, gorge, abyss, void.

**gullible** adj credulous, suggestible, impressionable, trusting, unsuspecting, foolish, naïve, green, unsophisticated, innocent.
F3 astute.

**gully** n channel, watercourse, gutter, ditch, ravine.

**gulp** v swallow, swig, swill, knock back (infml), bolt, wolf (infml), gobble, guzzle, devour, stuff.
F3 sip, nibble.
n swallow, swig, draught, mouthful.

**gum** n adhesive, glue, paste, cement.
v stick, glue, paste, fix, cement, seal, clog.

**gun** n firearm, handgun, pistol, revolver, shooter (sl), shooting iron (sl), rifle, shotgun, bazooka, howitzer, cannon.

**gurgle** v bubble, babble, burble, murmur, ripple, lap, splash, crow.
n babble, murmur, ripple.

**gush** v 1 FLOW, run, pour, stream, cascade, flood, rush, burst, spurt, spout, jet. 2 ENTHUSE, chatter, babble, jabber, go on (infml), drivel.
n flow, outflow, stream, torrent, cascade, flood, tide, rush, burst, outburst, spurt, spout, jet.

**gust** n blast, burst, rush, flurry, blow, puff, breeze, wind, gale, squall.

**gusto** n zest, relish, appreciation, enjoyment, pleasure, delight, enthusiasm, exuberance, élan, verve, zeal.
F3 distaste, apathy.

**gut** v 1 gut fish: disembowel, draw, clean (out). 2 STRIP, clear, empty, rifle, ransack, plunder, loot, sack, ravage.

**guts** n 1 INTESTINES, bowels, viscera, entrails, insides, innards (infml), belly, stomach. 2 (infml) COURAGE, bravery, pluck, grit, nerve, mettle.

**gutter** n drain, sluice, ditch, trench, trough, channel, duct, conduit, passage, pipe, tube.

**guy** (infml) n fellow, bloke (infml), chap (infml), man, boy, youth, person, individual.

**gypsy, gipsy** n Romany, traveller, wanderer, nomad, tinker.

**gyrate** v turn, revolve, rotate, twirl, pirouette, spin, whirl, wheel, circle, spiral.

# H

**habit** n custom, usage, practice, routine, rule, second nature, way, manner, mode, wont, inclination, tendency, bent, mannerism, quirk, addiction, dependence, fixation, obsession, weakness.

**habitat** n home, abode, domain, element, environment, surroundings, locality, territory, terrain.

**habitual** adj **1** CUSTOMARY, traditional, wonted, routine, usual, ordinary, common, natural, normal, standard, regular, recurrent, fixed, established, familiar. **2** habitual drinker: confirmed, inveterate, hardened, addicted, dependent, persistent.
**F₃** 1 occasional, infrequent.

**hack¹** v cut, chop, hew, notch, gash, slash, lacerate, mutilate, mangle.

**hack²** n scribbler, journalist, drudge, slave.

**hackneyed** adj stale, overworked, tired, worn-out, time-worn, threadbare, unoriginal, corny (infml), clichéed, stereotyped, stock, banal, trite, commonplace, common, pedestrian, uninspired.
**F₃** original, new, fresh.

**hag** n crone, witch, battle-axe (infml), shrew, termagant, vixen.

**haggard** adj drawn, gaunt, careworn, thin, wasted, shrunken, pinched, pale, wan, ghastly.
**F₃** hale.

**haggle** v bargain, negotiate, barter, wrangle, squabble, bicker, quarrel, dispute.

**hail¹** n barrage, bombardment, volley, torrent, shower, rain, storm.
v pelt, bombard, shower, rain, batter, attack, assail.

**hail²** v greet, address, acknowledge, salute, wave, signal to, flag down, shout, call, acclaim, cheer, applaud, honour, welcome.

**hair** n locks, tresses, shock, mop, mane.

**hairdresser** n hairstylist, stylist, barber, coiffeur, coiffeuse.

**hairless** adj bald, bald-headed, shorn, tonsured, shaven, clean-shaven, beardless.
**F₃** hairy, hirsute.

**hair-raising** adj frightening, scary, terrifying, horrifying, shocking, bloodcurdling, spine-chilling, eerie, alarming, startling, thrilling.

**hairstyle** n style, coiffure, hairdo (infml), cut, haircut, set, perm (infml).

> *Hairstyles include*: Afro, backcombed, bangs, beehive, bob, bouffant, braid, bun, chignon, corn rows, cowlick, crewcut, crimped, crop, curled, dreadlocks, Eton crop, French pleat, fringe, frizette, marcel wave, mohican, pageboy, perm, pigtail, plait, pompadour, ponytail, pouffe, quiff, ringlets, shingle, short back and sides, sideboards, sideburns, skinhead, tonsure, topknot, undercut; hair-piece, toupee, wig.

**hairy** *adj* hirsute, bearded, shaggy, bushy, fuzzy, furry, woolly.
 bald, clean-shaven.

**half** *n* fifty per cent, bisection, hemisphere, semicircle, section, segment, portion, share, fraction.
 *adj* semi-, halved, divided, fractional, part, partial, incomplete, moderate, limited.
 whole.
 *adv* partly, partially, incompletely, moderately, slightly.
 completely.

**half-hearted** *adj* lukewarm, cool, weak, feeble, passive, apathetic, uninterested, indifferent, neutral.
 whole-hearted, enthusiastic.

**halfway** *adv* midway, in the middle, centrally.
 *adj* middle, central, equidistant, mid, midway, intermediate.

**hall** *n* hallway, corridor, passage, passageway, entrance-hall, foyer, vestibule, lobby, concert-hall, auditorium, chamber, assembly room.

**hallmark** *n* stamp, mark, trademark, brand-name, sign, indication, symbol, emblem, device, badge.

**hallucinate** *v* dream, imagine, see things, daydream, fantasize, freak out (*sl*), trip (*sl*).

**hallucination** *n* illusion, mirage, vision, apparition, dream, daydream, fantasy, figment, delusion, freak-out (*sl*), trip (*sl*).

**halt** *v* stop, draw up, pull up, pause, wait, rest, break off, discontinue, cease, desist, quit, end, terminate, check, stem, curb, obstruct, impede.
 start, continue.
 *n* stop, stoppage, arrest, interruption, break, pause, rest, standstill, end, close, termination.
 start, continuation.

**halting** *adj* hesitant, stuttering, stammering, faltering, stumbling, broken, imperfect, laboured, awkward.

 fluent.

**halve** *v* bisect, cut in half, split in two, divide, split, share, cut down, reduce, lessen.

**hammer** *v* hit, strike, beat, drum, bang, bash, pound, batter, knock, drive, shape, form, make.
 *n* mallet, gavel.

**hammer out** settle, sort out, negotiate, thrash out, produce, bring about, accomplish, complete, finish.

**hamper** *v* hinder, impede, obstruct, slow down, hold up, frustrate, thwart, prevent, handicap, hamstring, shackle, cramp, restrict, curb, restrain.
 aid, facilitate.

**hand** *n* **1** FIST, palm, paw (*infml*), mitt (*sl*). **2** *give me a hand*: help, aid, assistance, support, participation, part, influence. **3** WORKER, employee, operative, workman, labourer, farm-hand, hireling.
 *v* give, pass, offer, submit, present, yield, deliver, transmit, conduct, convey.

**at hand** near, close, to hand, handy, accessible, available, ready, imminent.

**hand down** bequeath, will, pass on, transfer, give, grant.

**hand out** distribute, deal out, give out, share out, dish out (*infml*), mete out, dispense.

**hand over** yield, relinquish, surrender, turn over, deliver, release, give, donate, present.
 keep, retain.

**handbook** *n* manual, instruction book, guide, guidebook, companion.

**handful** *n* few, sprinkling, scattering, smattering.
 a lot, many.

**handicap** *n* obstacle, block, barrier, impediment, stumbling-block, hindrance, drawback, disadvantage, restriction, limitation, penalty, disability, impairment, defect, shortcoming.
 assistance, advantage.

*v* impede, hinder, disadvantage, hold back, retard, hamper, burden, encumber, restrict, limit, disable.
F3 help, assist.

**handicraft** *n* craft, art, craftwork, handwork, handiwork.

**handiwork** *n* work, doing, responsibility, achievement, product, result, design, invention, creation, production, skill, workmanship, craftsmanship, artisanship.

**handle** *n* grip, handgrip, knob, stock, shaft, hilt.
*v* 1 TOUCH, finger, feel, fondle, pick up, hold, grasp. 2 *handle a situation*: tackle, treat, deal with, manage, cope with, control, supervise.

**handout** *n* 1 CHARITY, alms, dole, largess(e), share, issue, free sample, freebie (*sl*). 2 LEAFLET, circular, bulletin, statement, press release, literature.

**hands** *n* care, custody, possession, charge, authority, command, power, control, supervision.

**handsome** *adj* 1 GOOD-LOOKING, attractive, fair, personable, elegant. 2 GENEROUS, liberal, large, considerable, ample.
F3 1 ugly, unattractive. 2 mean.

**handwriting** *n* writing, script, hand, fist (*infml*), penmanship, calligraphy.

**handy** *adj* 1 AVAILABLE, to hand, ready, at hand, near, accessible, convenient, practical, useful, helpful. 2 SKILFUL, proficient, expert, skilled, clever, practical.
F3 1 inconvenient. 2 clumsy.

**hang** *v* 1 SUSPEND, dangle, swing, drape, drop, flop, droop, sag, trail. 2 FASTEN, attach, fix, stick. 3 *hang in the air*: float, drift, hover, linger, remain, cling.

**hang about** hang around, linger, loiter, dawdle, waste time, associate with, frequent, haunt.

**hang back** hold back, demur, hesitate, shy away, recoil.

**hang on 1** WAIT, hold on, remain, hold

out, endure, continue, carry on, persevere, persist. 2 GRIP, grasp, hold fast. 3 DEPEND ON, hinge on, turn on.
F3 1 give up.

**hanger-on** *n* follower, minion, lackey, toady, sycophant, parasite, sponger, dependant.

**hang-up** *n* inhibition, difficulty, problem, obsession, preoccupation, thing (*infml*), block, mental block.

**hanker** *v* hanker after, crave, hunger for, thirst for, want, wish for, desire, covet, yearn for, long for, pine for, itch for.

**hankering** *n* craving, hunger, thirst, wish, desire, yearning, longing, itch, urge.

**haphazard** *adj* random, chance, casual, arbitrary, hit-or-miss, unsystematic, disorganized, disorderly, careless, slapdash, slipshod.
F3 methodical, orderly.

**happen** *v* occur, take place, arise, crop up, develop, materialize (*infml*), come about, result, ensue, follow, turn out, transpire.

**happening** *n* occurrence, phenomenon, event, incident, episode, occasion, adventure, experience, accident, chance, circumstance, case, affair.

**happiness** *n* joy, joyfulness, gladness, cheerfulness, contentment, pleasure, delight, glee, elation, bliss, ecstasy, euphoria.
F3 unhappiness, sadness.

**happy** *adj* 1 JOYFUL, jolly, merry, cheerful, glad, pleased, delighted, thrilled, elated, satisfied, content, contented. 2 *a happy coincidence*: lucky, fortunate, felicitous, favourable, appropriate, apt, fitting.
F3 1 unhappy, sad, discontented. 2 unfortunate, inappropriate.

**harangue** *n* diatribe, tirade, lecture, speech, address.
*v* lecture, preach, hold forth, spout, declaim, address.

**harass** v  pester, badger, harry, plague, torment, persecute, exasperate, vex, annoy, irritate, bother, disturb, hassle (*infml*), trouble, worry, stress, tire, wear out, exhaust, fatigue.

**harbour** n  port, dock, quay, wharf, marina, mooring, anchorage, haven, shelter.
v  **1** HIDE, conceal, protect, shelter.
**2** *harbour a feeling*: hold, retain, cling to, entertain, foster, nurse, nurture, cherish, believe, imagine.

**hard** adj  **1** SOLID, firm, unyielding, tough, strong, dense, impenetrable, stiff, rigid, inflexible. **2** DIFFICULT, arduous, strenuous, laborious, tiring, exhausting, backbreaking, complex, complicated, involved, knotty, baffling, puzzling, perplexing.
**3** HARSH, severe, strict, callous, unfeeling, unsympathetic, cruel, pitiless, merciless, ruthless, unrelenting, distressing, painful, unpleasant.
**F3** **1** soft, yielding. **2** easy, simple.
**3** kind, pleasant.
adv  industriously, diligently, assiduously, doggedly, steadily, laboriously, strenuously, earnestly, keenly, intently, strongly, violently, intensely, energetically, vigorously.
**hard up** poor, broke (*infml*), penniless, impoverished, in the red, bankrupt, bust, short, lacking.
**F3** rich.

**harden** v  solidify, set, freeze, bake, stiffen, strengthen, reinforce, fortify, buttress, brace, steel, nerve, toughen, season, accustom, train.
**F3** soften, weaken.

**hard-headed** adj  shrewd, astute, businesslike, level-headed, clear-thinking, sensible, realistic, pragmatic, practical, hard-boiled, tough, unsentimental.
**F3** unrealistic.

**hard-hearted** adj  callous, unfeeling, cold, hard, stony, heartless, unsympathetic, cruel, inhuman, pitiless, merciless.
**F3** soft-hearted, kind, merciful.

**hard-hitting** adj  condemnatory, critical, unsparing, no-holds-barred, vigorous, forceful, tough.
**F3** mild.

**hardly** adv  barely, scarcely, just, only just, not quite, not at all, by no means.

**hardship** n  misfortune, adversity, trouble, difficulty, affliction, distress, suffering, trial, tribulation, want, need, privation, austerity, poverty, destitution, misery.
**F3** ease, comfort, prosperity.

**hard-wearing** adj  durable, lasting, strong, tough, sturdy, stout, rugged, resilient.
**F3** delicate.

**hard-working** adj  industrious, diligent, assiduous, conscientious, zealous, busy, energetic.
**F3** idle, lazy.

**hardy** adj  strong, tough, sturdy, robust, vigorous, fit, sound, healthy.
**F3** weak, unhealthy.

**harm** n  damage, loss, injury, hurt, detriment, ill, misfortune, wrong, abuse.
**F3** benefit.
v  damage, impair, blemish, spoil, mar, ruin, hurt, injure, wound, ill-treat, maltreat, abuse, misuse.
**F3** benefit, improve.

**harmful** adj  damaging, detrimental, pernicious, noxious, unhealthy, unwholesome, injurious, dangerous, hazardous, poisonous, toxic, destructive.
**F3** harmless.

**harmless** adj  safe, innocuous, non-toxic, inoffensive, gentle, innocent.
**F3** harmful, dangerous, destructive.

**harmonious** adj  **1** MELODIOUS, tuneful, musical, sweet-sounding.
**2** MATCHING, co-ordinated, balanced, compatible, like-minded, agreeable, cordial, amicable, friendly,

sympathetic.

**E3 1** discordant.

**harmonize** v match, co-ordinate, balance, fit in, suit, tone, blend, correspond, agree, reconcile, accommodate, adapt, arrange, compose.

**E3** clash.

**harmony** n **1** TUNEFULNESS, tune, melody, euphony. **2** *live in harmony*: agreement, unanimity, accord, concord, unity, compatibility, like-mindedness, peace, goodwill, rapport, sympathy, understanding, amicability, friendliness, co-operation, co-ordination, balance, symmetry, correspondence, conformity.

**E3 1** discord. **2** conflict.

**harness** n tackle, gear, equipment, reins, straps, tack.

v control, channel, use, utilize, exploit, make use of, employ, mobilize, apply.

**harrowing** adj distressing, upsetting, heart-rending, disturbing, alarming, frightening, terrifying, nerve-racking, traumatic, agonizing, excruciating.

**harry** v badger, pester, nag, chivvy, harass, plague, torment, persecute, annoy, vex, worry, trouble, bother, hassle (*infml*), disturb, molest.

**harsh** adj **1** SEVERE, strict, Draconian, unfeeling, cruel, hard, pitiless, austere, Spartan, bleak, grim, comfortless. **2** *a harsh sound*: rough, coarse, rasping, croaking, guttural, grating, jarring, discordant, strident, raucous, sharp, shrill, unpleasant. **3** BRIGHT, dazzling, glaring, gaudy, lurid.

**E3 1** lenient. **2** soft.

**harvest** n **1** HARVEST-TIME, ingathering, reaping, collection. **2** CROP, yield, return, produce, fruits, result, consequence.

v reap, mow, pick, gather, collect, accumulate, amass.

**hash** n mess, botch, muddle, mix-up, jumble, confusion, hotchpotch, mishmash.

**haste** n hurry, rush, hustle, bustle, speed, velocity, rapidity, swiftness, quickness, briskness, urgency, rashness, recklessness, impetuosity.

**E3** slowness.

**hasten** v hurry, rush, make haste, run, sprint, dash, tear, race, fly, bolt, accelerate, speed (up), quicken, expedite, dispatch, precipitate, urge, press, advance, step up.

**E3** dawdle, delay.

**hasty** adj hurried, rushed, impatient, headlong, rash, reckless, heedless, thoughtless, impetuous, impulsive, hot-headed, fast, quick, rapid, swift, speedy, brisk, prompt, short, brief, cursory.

**E3** slow, careful, deliberate.

**hat**

> *Hats include*: trilby, bowler, fedora, top-hat, Homburg, derby (*US*), pork-pie hat, flat-cap, beret, bonnet, Tam O'Shanter, tammy, deerstalker, hunting-cap, stovepipe hat, stetson, ten-gallon hat, boater, sunhat, panama, straw hat, picture-hat, pillbox, cloche, beanie (*US*), poke-bonnet, mob-cap, turban, fez, sombrero, sou'wester, glengarry, bearskin, busby, peaked cap, sailor-hat, baseball cap, balaclava, hood, snood, toque, helmet, mortar-board, skullcap, yarmulka, mitre, biretta.

**hatch** v **1** INCUBATE, brood, breed. **2** CONCOCT, formulate, originate, think up, dream up, conceive, devise, contrive, plot, scheme, design, plan, project.

**hate** v dislike, despise, detest, loathe, abhor, abominate, execrate.

**E3** like, love.

n hatred, aversion, dislike, loathing, abhorrence, abomination.

**E3** liking, love.

**hatred** n hate, aversion, dislike, detestation, loathing, repugnance, revulsion, abhorrence, abomination, execration, animosity, ill-will, antagonism, hostility, enmity, antipathy.
Fa liking, love.

**haughty** adj lofty, imperious, high and mighty, supercilious, cavalier, snooty (infml), contemptuous, disdainful, scornful, superior, snobbish, arrogant, proud, stuck-up (infml), conceited.
Fa humble, modest.

**haul** v pull, heave, tug, draw, tow, drag, trail, move, transport, convey, carry, cart, lug, hump (infml).
Fa push.
n LOOT, booty, plunder, swag (sl), spoils, takings, gain, yield, find.

**haunt** v 1 FREQUENT, patronize, visit. 2 memories haunted her: plague, torment, trouble, disturb, recur, prey on, beset, obsess, possess.
n resort, hangout (infml), stamping-ground, den, meeting-place, rendezvous.

**haunting** adj memorable, unforgettable, persistent, recurrent, evocative, nostalgic, poignant.
Fa unmemorable.

**have** v 1 OWN, possess, get, obtain, gain, acquire, procure, secure, receive, accept, keep, hold. 2 FEEL, experience, enjoy, suffer, undergo, endure, put up with. 3 CONTAIN, include, comprise, incorporate, consist of. 4 have a baby: give birth to, bear.
Fa lack.
**have to** must, be forced, be compelled, be obliged, be required, ought, should.

**haven** n harbour, port, anchorage, shelter, refuge, sanctuary, asylum, retreat.

**havoc** n chaos, confusion, disorder, disruption, damage, destruction, ruin, wreck, rack and ruin, devastation, waste, desolation.

**haywire** (infml) adj wrong, tangled, out of control, crazy, mad, wild, chaotic, confused, disordered, disorganized, topsy-turvy.

**hazard** n risk, danger, peril, jeopardy, threat, death-trap, accident, chance.
Fa safety.
v 1 RISK, endanger, jeopardize, expose. 2 CHANCE, gamble, stake, venture, suggest, speculate.

**hazardous** adj risky, dangerous, unsafe, perilous, precarious, insecure, chancy, difficult, tricky.
Fa safe, secure.

**haze** n mist, fog, cloud, steam, vapour, film, mistiness, smokiness, dimness, obscurity.

**hazy** adj misty, foggy, smoky, clouded, cloudy, milky, fuzzy, blurred, ill-defined, veiled, obscure, dim, faint, unclear, indistinct, vague, indefinite, uncertain.
Fa clear, bright, definite.

**head** n 1 SKULL, cranium, brain, mind, mentality, brains (infml), intellect, intelligence, understanding, thought. 2 TOP, peak, summit, crown, tip, apex, height, climax, front, fore, lead. 3 LEADER, chief, captain, commander, boss, director, manager, superintendent, principal, head teacher, ruler.
Fa 1 foot, tail. 2 base, foot. 3 subordinate.
adj leading, front, foremost, first, chief, main, prime, principal, top, highest, supreme, premier, dominant, pre-eminent.
v lead, rule, govern, command, direct, manage, run, superintend, oversee, supervise, control, guide, steer.

**head for** make for, go towards, direct towards, aim for, point to, turn for, steer for.

**head off** forestall, intercept, intervene, interpose, deflect, divert, fend off, ward off, avert, prevent, stop.

**heading** n title, name, headline, rubric, caption, section, division, category, class.

**headland** n promontory, cape, head, point, foreland.

**headlong** adj hasty, precipitate, impetuous, impulsive, rash, reckless, dangerous, breakneck, head-first. adv head first, hurriedly, hastily, precipitately, rashly, recklessly, heedlessly, thoughtlessly, wildly.

**headquarters** n HQ, base (camp), head office, nerve centre.

**headstrong** adj stubborn, obstinate, intractable, pigheaded, wilful, self-willed, perverse, contrary.
F3 tractable, docile.

**headway** n advance, progress, way, improvement.

**heady** adj intoxicating, strong, stimulating, exhilarating, thrilling, exciting.

**heal** v cure, remedy, mend, restore, treat, soothe, salve, settle, reconcile, patch up.

**health** n fitness, constitution, form, shape, trim, fettle, condition, tone, state, healthiness, good condition, wellbeing, welfare, soundness, robustness, strength, vigour.
F3 illness, infirmity.

**healthy** adj 1 WELL, fit, good, fine, in condition, in good shape, in fine fettle, sound, sturdy, robust, strong, vigorous, hale and hearty, blooming, flourishing, thriving. 2 healthy food: wholesome, nutritious, nourishing, bracing, invigorating, healthful.
F3 1 ill, sick, infirm.

**heap** n pile, stack, mound, mountain, lot, mass, accumulation, collection, hoard, stockpile, store.
v pile, stack, mound, bank, build, amass, accumulate, collect, gather, hoard, stockpile, store, load, burden, shower, lavish.

**hear** v 1 LISTEN, catch, pick up, overhear, eavesdrop, heed, pay attention. 2 LEARN, find out,

discover, ascertain, understand, gather. 3 JUDGE, try, examine, investigate.

**hearing** n 1 EARSHOT, sound, range, reach, ear, perception. 2 TRIAL, inquiry, investigation, inquest, audition, interview, audience.

**hearsay** n rumour, word of mouth, talk, gossip, tittle-tattle, report, buzz (infml).

**heart** n 1 SOUL, mind, character, disposition, nature, temperament, feeling, emotion, sentiment, love, tenderness, compassion, sympathy, pity. 2 lose heart: courage, bravery, boldness, spirit, resolution, determination. 3 CENTRE, middle, core, kernel, nucleus, nub, crux, essence.
F3 2 cowardice. 3 periphery.

**by heart** by rote, parrot-fashion, pat, off pat, word for word, verbatim.

*Parts of the heart include:* aortic valve, ascending aorta, bicuspid valve, carotid artery, descending thoracic aorta, inferior vena cava, left atrium, left pulmonary artery, left pulmonary veins, left ventricle, mitral valve, myocardium, papillary muscle, pulmonary valve, right atrium, right pulmonary artery, right pulmonary veins, right ventricle, superior vena cava, tricuspid valve, ventricular septum.

**heartbreaking** adj distressing, sad, tragic, harrowing, heart-rending, pitiful, agonizing, grievous, bitter, disappointing.
F3 heartwarming, heartening.

**heartbroken** adj broken-hearted, desolate, sad, miserable, dejected, despondent, downcast, crestfallen, disappointed, dispirited, grieved, crushed.
F3 delighted, elated.

**hearten** v comfort, console, reassure, cheer (up), buck up (infml), encourage, boost, inspire, stimulate, rouse, pep up (*infml*).

**F3** dishearten, depress, dismay.

**heartfelt** *adj* deep, profound, sincere, honest, genuine, earnest, ardent, fervent, whole-hearted, warm.

**F3** insincere, false.

**heartless** *adj* unfeeling, uncaring, cold, hard, hard-hearted, callous, unkind, cruel, inhuman, brutal, pitiless, merciless.

**F3** kind, considerate, sympathetic, merciful.

**heart-rending** *adj* harrowing, heartbreaking, agonizing, pitiful, piteous, pathetic, tragic, sad, distressing, moving, affecting, poignant.

**heartwarming** *adj* pleasing, gratifying, satisfying, cheering, heartening, encouraging, touching, moving, affecting.

**F3** heartbreaking.

**hearty** *adj* **1** ENTHUSIASTIC, whole-hearted, unreserved, heartfelt, sincere, genuine, warm, friendly, cordial, jovial, cheerful, ebullient, exuberant, boisterous, energetic, vigorous. **2** *a hearty breakfast*: large, sizable, substantial, filling, ample, generous.

**F3 1** half-hearted, cool, cold.

**heat** *n* **1** HOTNESS, warmth, sultriness, closeness, high temperature, fever. **2** ARDOUR, fervour, fieriness, passion, intensity, vehemence, fury, excitement, impetuosity, earnestness, zeal.

**F3 1** cold(ness). **2** coolness.

*v* warm, boil, toast, cook, bake, roast, reheat, warm up, inflame, excite, animate, rouse, stimulate, flush, glow.

**F3** cool, chill.

**heated** *adj* angry, furious, raging, passionate, fiery, stormy, tempestuous, bitter, fierce, intense, vehement, violent, frenzied.

**F3** calm.

**heave** *v* **1** PULL, haul, drag, tug, raise, lift, hitch, hoist, lever, rise, surge. **2** THROW, fling, hurl, cast, toss, chuck, let fly. **3** RETCH, vomit, throw up (*infml*), spew.

**heaven** *n* sky, firmament, next world, hereafter, after-life, paradise, utopia, ecstasy, rapture, bliss, happiness, joy.

**F3** hell.

**heavenly** *adj* **1** BLISSFUL, wonderful, glorious, beautiful, lovely, delightful, out of this world. **2** CELESTIAL, unearthly, supernatural, spiritual, divine, godlike, angelic, immortal, sublime, blessed.

**F3 1** hellish. **2** infernal.

**heavy** *adj* **1** WEIGHTY, hefty, ponderous, burdensome, massive, large, bulky, solid, dense, stodgy. **2** *heavy work*: hard, difficult, tough, arduous, laborious, strenuous, demanding, taxing, harsh, severe. **3** OPPRESSIVE, intense, serious, dull, tedious.

**F3 1** light. **2** easy.

**heavy-handed** *adj* clumsy, awkward, unsubtle, tactless, insensitive, thoughtless, oppressive, overbearing, domineering, autocratic.

**hectic** *adj* busy, frantic, frenetic, chaotic, fast, feverish, excited, heated, furious, wild.

**F3** leisurely.

**hedge** *n* hedgerow, screen, windbreak, barrier, fence, dike, boundary.

*v* **1** SURROUND, enclose, hem in, confine, restrict, fortify, guard, shield, protect, safeguard, cover. **2** STALL, temporize, equivocate, dodge, sidestep, evade, duck.

**heed** *v* listen, pay attention, mind, note, regard, observe, follow, obey.

**F3** ignore, disregard.

**heedless** *adj* oblivious, unthinking, careless, negligent, rash, reckless,

inattentive, unobservant, thoughtless, unconcerned.
> heedful, mindful, attentive.

**hefty** *adj* heavy, weighty, big, large, burly, hulking, beefy, brawny, strong, powerful, vigorous, robust, strapping, solid, substantial, massive, colossal, bulky, unwieldy.
> slight, small.

**height** *n* **1** HIGHNESS, altitude, elevation, tallness, loftiness, stature. **2** TOP, summit, peak, pinnacle, apex, crest, crown, zenith, apogee, culmination, climax, extremity, maximum, limit, ceiling.
> **1** depth.

**heighten** *v* raise, elevate, increase, add to, magnify, intensify, strengthen, sharpen, improve, enhance.
> lower, decrease, diminish.

**hell** *n* **1** *heaven and hell:* underworld, Hades, inferno, lower regions, nether world, abyss. **2** SUFFERING, anguish, agony, torment, ordeal, nightmare, misery.
> **1** heaven.

**hellish** *adj* INFERNAL, devilish, diabolical, fiendish, accursed, damnable, monstrous, abominable, atrocious, dreadful.
> heavenly.

**helm** *n* tiller, wheel, driving seat, reins, saddle, command, control, leadership, direction.

**help** *v* **1** AID, assist, lend a hand, serve, be of use, collaborate, co-operate, back, stand by, support. **2** IMPROVE, ameliorate, relieve, alleviate, mitigate, ease, facilitate.
> **1** hinder. **2** worsen.

*n* aid, assistance, collaboration, co-operation, support, advice, guidance, service, use, utility, avail, benefit.
> hindrance.

**helper** *n* assistant, deputy, auxiliary, subsidiary, attendant, right-hand man, PA, mate, partner, associate, colleague, collaborator, accomplice,

ally, supporter, second.

**helpful** *adj* **1** USEFUL, practical, constructive, worthwhile, valuable, beneficial, advantageous. **2** *a helpful person:* co-operative, obliging, neighbourly, friendly, caring, considerate, kind, sympathetic, supportive.
> **1** useless, futile.

**helping** *n* serving, portion, share, ration, amount, plateful, piece, dollop (*infml*).

**helpless** *adj* weak, feeble, powerless, dependent, vulnerable, exposed, unprotected, defenceless, abandoned, friendless, destitute, forlorn, incapable, incompetent, infirm, disabled, paralysed.
> strong, independent, competent.

**hem** *n* edge, border, margin, fringe, trimming.

**hem in** surround, enclose, box in, confine, restrict.

**henpecked** *adj* dominated, subjugated, browbeaten, bullied, intimidated, meek, timid.
> dominant.

**herald** *n* messenger, courier, harbinger, forerunner, precursor, omen, token, signal, sign, indication.

*v* announce, proclaim, broadcast, advertise, publicize, trumpet, pave the way, precede, usher in, show, indicate, promise.

**heraldry**

---

*Heraldic terms include:* shield, crest, mantling, helmet, supporters, field, charge, compartment, motto, dexter, centre, sinister, annulet, fleur-de-lis, martlet, mullet, rampant, passant, sejant, caboched, statant, displayed, couchant, dormant, urinant, volant, chevron, pile, pall, saltire, quarter, orle, bordure, gyronny, lozenge, impale, escutcheon, antelope, camelopard, cockatrice, eagle, griffin, lion, phoenix, unicorn, wivern, addorsed, bezant, blazon, canton, cinquefoil, quatrefoil, roundel, semé, tierced, undee, urdé.

## herbs and spices

*Herbs and spices include*: angelica, anise, basil, bay, bergamot, borage, camomile, catmint, chervil, chives, comfrey, cumin, dill, fennel, garlic, hyssop, lavender, lemon balm, lovage, marjoram, mint, oregano, parsley, rosemary, sage, savory, sorrel, tarragon, thyme; allspice, caper, caraway seeds, cardamon, cayenne pepper, chilli, cinnamon, cloves, coriander, curry, ginger, mace, mustard, nutmeg, paprika, pepper, saffron, sesame, turmeric, vanilla.

**herd** *n* drove, flock, swarm, pack, press, crush, mass, horde, throng, multitude, crowd, mob, the masses, rabble.

*v* **1** FLOCK, congregate, gather, collect, assemble, rally. **2** LEAD, guide, shepherd, round up, drive, force.

**hereditary** *adj* inherited, bequeathed, handed down, family, ancestral, inborn, inbred, innate, natural, congenital, genetic.

**heresy** *n* heterodoxy, unorthodoxy, free-thinking, apostasy, dissidence, schism, blasphemy.
 orthodoxy.

**heretic** *n* free-thinker, nonconformist, apostate, dissident, dissenter, revisionist, separatist, schismatic, sectarian, renegade.
 conformist.

**heretical** *adj* heterodox, unorthodox, free-thinking, rationalistic, schismatic, impious, irreverent, iconoclastic, blasphemous.
 orthodox, conventional, conformist.

**heritage** *n* **1** INHERITANCE, legacy, bequest, endowment, lot, portion, share, birthright, due. **2** HISTORY,

past, tradition, culture.

**hermit** *n* recluse, solitary, monk, ascetic, anchorite.

**hero** *n* protagonist, lead, celebrity, star, superstar, idol, paragon, goody (*infml*), champion, conqueror.

**heroic** *adj* brave, courageous, fearless, dauntless, undaunted, lion-hearted, stout-hearted, valiant, bold, daring, intrepid, adventurous, gallant, chivalrous, noble, selfless.
 cowardly, timid.

**heroism** *n* bravery, courage, valour, boldness, daring, intrepidity, gallantry, prowess, selflessness.
 cowardice, timidity.

**hesitant** *adj* hesitating, reluctant, half-hearted, uncertain, unsure, indecisive, irresolute, vacillating, wavering, tentative, wary, shy, timid, halting, stammering, stuttering.
 decisive, resolute, confident, fluent.

**hesitate** *v* pause, delay, wait, be reluctant, be unwilling, think twice, hold back, shrink from, scruple, boggle, demur, vacillate, waver, be uncertain, dither, shilly-shally, falter, stumble, halt, stammer, stutter.
 decide.

**hesitation** *n* pause, delay, reluctance, unwillingness, hesitance, scruple(s), qualm(s), misgivings, doubt, second thoughts, vacillation, uncertainty, indecision, irresolution, faltering, stumbling, stammering, stuttering.
 eagerness, assurance.

**hew** *v* cut, fell, axe, lop, chop, hack, sever, split, carve, sculpt, sculpture, fashion, model, form, shape, make.

**heyday** *n* peak, prime, flush, bloom, flowering, golden age, boom time.

**hidden** *adj* **1** *a hidden door*: concealed, covered, shrouded, veiled, disguised, camouflaged, unseen, secret. **2** OBSCURE, dark, occult, secret, covert, close, cryptic, mysterious, abstruse, mystical, latent, ulterior.

**E3** 1 showing, apparent. 2 obvious.

**hide¹** *v* 1 CONCEAL, cover, cloak, shroud, veil, screen, mask, disguise, camouflage, obscure, shadow, eclipse, bury, stash (*infml*), secrete, withhold, keep dark, suppress.
2 TAKE COVER, shelter, lie low, go to ground, hole up (*infml*).
**E3** 1 reveal, show, display.

**hide²** *n* skin, pelt, fell, fur, leather.

**hidebound** *adj* set, rigid, entrenched, narrow-minded, strait-laced, conventional, ultra-conservative.
**E3** liberal, progressive.

**hideous** *adj* ugly, repulsive, grotesque, monstrous, horrid, ghastly, awful, dreadful, frightful, terrible, grim, gruesome, macabre, terrifying, shocking, appalling, disgusting, revolting, horrible.
**E3** beautiful, attractive.

**hiding¹** *n* beating, flogging, whipping, caning, spanking, thrashing, walloping (*infml*).

**hiding²** *n* concealment, cover, veiling, screening, disguise, camouflage.

**hiding-place** *n* hide-away, hideout, lair, den, hole, hide, cover, refuge, haven, sanctuary, retreat.

**hierarchy** *n* pecking order, ranking, grading, scale, series, ladder, echelons, strata.

**high** *adj* 1 TALL, lofty, elevated, soaring, towering. 2 GREAT, strong, intense, extreme. 3 IMPORTANT, influential, powerful, eminent, distinguished, prominent, chief, leading, senior. 4 HIGH-PITCHED, soprano, treble, sharp, shrill, piercing. 5 *a high price*: expensive, dear, costly, exorbitant, excessive.
**E3** 1 low, short. 3 lowly. 4 deep. 5 cheap.

**high-born** *adj* noble, aristocratic, blue-blooded, thoroughbred.
**E3** low-born.

**highbrow** *n* intellectual, egghead

(*infml*), scholar, academic.
*adj* intellectual, sophisticated, cultured, cultivated, academic, bookish, brainy (*infml*), deep, serious, classical.
**E3** low-brow.

**high-class** *adj* upper-class, posh (*infml*), classy (*infml*), top-class, top-flight, high-quality, quality, de luxe, superior, excellent, first-rate, choice, select, exclusive.
**E3** ordinary, mediocre.

**high-flown** *adj* florid, extravagant, exaggerated, elaborate, flamboyant, ostentatious, pretentious, high-standing, grandiose, pompous, bombastic, turgid, artificial, stilted, affected, lofty, highfalutin, la-di-da (*infml*), supercilious.

**high-handed** *adj* overbearing, domineering, bossy (*infml*), imperious, dictatorial, autocratic, despotic, tyrannical, oppressive, arbitrary.

**highlight** *n* high point, high spot, peak, climax, best, cream.
*v* underline, emphasize, stress, accentuate, play up, point up, spotlight, illuminate, show up, set off, focus on, feature.

**highly** *adv* very, greatly, considerably, decidedly, extremely, immensely, tremendously, exceptionally, extraordinarily, enthusiastically, warmly, well.

**highly-strung** *adj* sensitive, neurotic, nervy, jumpy, edgy, temperamental, excitable, restless, nervous, tense.
**E3** calm.

**high-minded** *adj* lofty, noble, moral, ethical, principled, idealistic, virtuous, upright, righteous, honourable, worthy.
**E3** immoral, unscrupulous.

**high-powered** *adj* powerful, forceful, driving, aggressive, dynamic, go-ahead, enterprising, energetic, vigorous.

**high-spirited** *adj* boisterous, bouncy, exuberant, effervescent, frolicsome, ebullient, sparkling, vibrant, vivacious, lively, energetic, spirited, dashing, bold, daring.
**F3** quiet, sedate.

**hijack** *v* commandeer, expropriate, skyjack, seize, take over.

**hike** *v* ramble, walk, trek, tramp, trudge, plod.
*n* ramble, walk, trek, tramp, march.

**hilarious** *adj* funny, amusing, comical, side-splitting, hysterical (*infml*), uproarious, noisy, rollicking, merry, jolly, jovial.
**F3** serious, grave.

**hilarity** *n* mirth, laughter, fun, amusement, levity, frivolity, merriment, jollity, conviviality, high spirits, boisterousness, exuberance, exhilaration.
**F3** seriousness, gravity.

**hill** *n* **1** HILLOCK, knoll, mound, prominence, eminence, elevation, foothill, down, fell, mountain, height. **2** *a steep hill*: slope, incline, gradient, ramp, rise, ascent, acclivity, drop, descent, declivity.

**hinder** *v* hamper, obstruct, impede, encumber, handicap, hamstring, hold up, delay, retard, slow down, hold back, check, curb, stop, prevent, frustrate, thwart, oppose.
**F3** help, aid, assist.

**hindrance** *n* obstruction, impediment, handicap, encumbrance, obstacle, stumbling-block, barrier, bar, check, restraint, restriction, limitation, difficulty, drag, snag, hitch, drawback, disadvantage, inconvenience, deterrent.
**F3** help, aid, assistance.

**hinge** *v* centre, turn, revolve, pivot, hang, depend, rest.

**hint** *n* **1** TIP, advice, suggestion, help, clue, inkling, suspicion, tip-off, reminder, indication, sign, pointer, mention, allusion, intimation, insinuation, implication, innuendo.

**2** *a hint of garlic*: touch, trace, tinge, taste, dash, soupçon, speck.
*v* suggest, prompt, tip off, indicate, imply, insinuate, intimate, allude, mention.

**hire** *v* rent, let, lease, charter, commission, book, reserve, employ, take on, sign up, engage, appoint, retain.
**F3** dismiss, fire.
*n* rent, rental, fee, charge, cost, price.

**hiss** *v* **1** WHISTLE, shrill, whizz, sizzle. **2** JEER, mock, ridicule, deride, boo, hoot.

**historic** *adj* momentous, consequential, important, significant, epoch-making, notable, remarkable, outstanding, extraordinary, celebrated, renowned, famed, famous.
**F3** unimportant, insignificant, unknown.

**historical** *adj* real, actual, authentic, factual, documented, recorded, attested, verifiable.
**F3** legendary, fictional.

**history** *n* **1** PAST, olden days, days of old, antiquity. **2** CHRONICLE, record, annals, archives, chronology, account, narrative, story, tale, saga, biography, life, autobiography, memoirs.

**hit** *v* **1** STRIKE, knock, tap, smack, slap, thrash, whack (*infml*), bash, thump, clout, punch, belt (*infml*), wallop (*infml*), beat, batter. **2** BUMP, collide with, bang, crash, smash, damage, harm.
*n* **1** STROKE, shot, blow, knock, tap, slap, smack, bash, bump, collision, impact, crash, smash. **2** SUCCESS, triumph, winner (*sl*).
**F3 2** failure.

**hit back** retaliate, reciprocate, counter-attack, strike back.

**hit on** chance on, stumble on, light on, discover, invent, realize, arrive at, guess.

**hit out** lash out, assail, attack, rail,

denounce, condemn, criticize.

**hitch** v 1 FASTEN, attach, tie, harness, yoke, couple, connect, join, unite. 2 PULL, heave, yank (*infml*), tug, jerk, hoist, hike (up) (*infml*).
**F3** 1 unhitch, unfasten.
n delay, hold-up, trouble, problem, difficulty, mishap, setback, hiccup, drawback, snag, catch, impediment, hindrance.

**hoard** n collection, accumulation, mass, heap, pile, fund, reservoir, supply, reserve, store, stockpile, cache, treasure-trove.
v collect, gather, amass, accumulate, save, put by, lay up, store, stash away (*infml*), stockpile, keep, treasure.
**F3** use, spend, squander.

**hoarse** adj husky, croaky, throaty, guttural, gravelly, gruff, growling, rough, harsh, rasping, grating, raucous, discordant.
**F3** clear, smooth.

**hoax** n trick, prank, practical joke, put-on, joke, leg-pull (*infml*), spoof, fake, fraud, deception, bluff, humbug, cheat, swindle, con (*infml*).
v trick, deceive, take in, fool, dupe, gull, delude, have on (*infml*), pull someone's leg (*infml*), con (*infml*), swindle, take for a ride (*infml*), cheat, hoodwink, bamboozle (*infml*), bluff.

**hobble** v limp, stumble, falter, stagger, totter, dodder, shuffle.

**hobby** n pastime, diversion, recreation, relaxation, pursuit, sideline.

**hoist** v lift, elevate, raise, erect, jack up, winch up, heave, rear, uplift.
n jack, winch, crane, tackle, lift, elevator.

**hold** v 1 GRIP, grasp, clutch, clasp, embrace, have, own, possess, keep, retain. 2 *hold a meeting*: conduct, carry on, continue, call, summon, convene, assemble. 3 CONSIDER, regard, deem, judge, reckon, think, believe, maintain. 4 BEAR, support, sustain, carry, comprise, contain,

accommodate. 5 IMPRISON, detain, stop, arrest, check, curb, restrain. 6 CLING, stick, adhere, stay.
**F3** 1 drop. 5 release, free, liberate.
n 1 GRIP, grasp, clasp, embrace. 2 INFLUENCE, power, sway, mastery, dominance, authority, control, leverage.

**hold back** 1 CONTROL, curb, check, restrain, suppress, stifle, retain, withhold, repress, inhibit.
2 HESITATE, delay, desist, refrain, shrink, refuse.
**F3** 1 release.

**hold forth** speak, talk, lecture, discourse, orate, preach, declaim.

**hold off** 1 FEND OFF, ward off, stave off, keep off, repel, rebuff. 2 PUT OFF, postpone, defer, delay, wait.

**hold out** 1 OFFER, give, present, extend. 2 LAST, continue, persist, endure, persevere, stand fast, hang on.
**F3** 2 give in, yield.

**hold up** 1 SUPPORT, sustain, brace, shore up, lift, raise. 2 DELAY, detain, retard, slow, hinder, impede.

**hold with** agree with, go along with, approve of, countenance, support, subscribe to, accept.

**holder** n 1 *holders of British passports*: bearer, owner, possessor, proprietor, keeper, custodian, occupant, incumbent. 2 CONTAINER, receptacle, case, housing, cover, sheath, rest, stand.

**hold-up** n 1 DELAY, wait, hitch, setback, snag, difficulty, trouble, obstruction, stoppage, (traffic) jam, bottle-neck. 2 ROBBERY, heist (*sl*), stick-up (*sl*).

**hole** n aperture, opening, orifice, pore, puncture, perforation, eyelet, tear, split, vent, outlet, shaft, slot, gap, breach, break, crack, fissure, fault, defect, flaw, dent, dimple, depression, hollow, cavity, crater, pit, excavation, cavern, cave, chamber, pocket, niche, recess, burrow, nest, lair, retreat.

**holiday** *n* vacation, recess, leave, time off, day off, break, rest, half-term, bank-holiday, feast-day, festival, celebration, anniversary.

**holiness** *n* sacredness, sanctity, spirituality, divinity, piety, devoutness, godliness, saintliness, virtuousness, righteousness, purity.
**F3** impiety.

**hollow** *adj* **1** CONCAVE, indented, depressed, sunken, deep, cavernous, empty, vacant, unfilled. **2** FALSE, artificial, deceptive, insincere, meaningless, empty, vain, futile, fruitless, worthless.
**F3 1** solid. **2** real.
*n* hole, pit, well, cavity, crater, excavation, cavern, cave, depression, concavity, basin, bowl, cup, dimple, dent, indentation, groove, channel, trough, valley.
*v* dig, excavate, burrow, tunnel, scoop, gouge, channel, groove, furrow, pit, dent, indent.

**holy** *adj* **1** *holy ground*: sacred, hallowed, consecrated, sanctified, dedicated, blessed, venerated, revered, spiritual, divine, evangelical. **2** PIOUS, religious, devout, godly, God-fearing, saintly, virtuous, good, righteous, faithful, pure, perfect.
**F3 1** unsanctified. **2** impious, irreligious.

**homage** *n* recognition, acknowledgement, tribute, honour, praise, adulation, admiration, regard, esteem, respect, deference, reverence, adoration, awe, veneration, worship, devotion.

**home** *n* residence, domicile, dwelling-place, abode, base, house, pied-à-terre, hearth, fireside, birthplace, home town, home ground, territory, habitat, element.
*adj* domestic, household, family, internal, local, national, inland.
**F3** foreign, international.
**at home 1** COMFORTABLE, relaxed, at ease. **2** FAMILIAR, knowledgeable,

experienced, skilled.

**homeland** *n* native land, native country, fatherland, motherland.

**homeless** *adj* itinerant, travelling, nomadic, wandering, vagrant, rootless, unsettled, displaced, dispossessed, evicted, exiled, outcast, abandoned, forsaken, destitute, down-and-out.
*n* travellers, vagabonds, vagrants, tramps, down-and-outs, dossers (*sl*), squatters.

**homely** *adj* homelike, homey, comfortable, cosy, snug, relaxed, informal, friendly, intimate, familiar, everyday, ordinary, domestic, natural, plain, simple, modest, unassuming, unpretentious, unsophisticated, folksy, homespun.
**F3** grand, formal.

**homicide** *n* murder, manslaughter, assassination, killing, bloodshed.

**homogeneous** *adj* uniform, consistent, unvarying, identical, similar, alike, akin, kindred, analogous, comparable, harmonious, compatible.
**F3** different.

**homosexual** *n* gay, queer (*sl*), poof (*sl*), lesbian, dike (*sl*).
**F3** heterosexual, straight (*sl*).
*adj* gay, queer (*sl*), lesbian.

**hone** *v* sharpen, whet, point, edge, grind, file, polish.

**honest** *adj* **1** TRUTHFUL, sincere, frank, candid, blunt, outspoken, direct, straight, outright, forthright, straightforward, plain, simple, open, above-board, legitimate, legal, lawful, on the level (*infml*), fair, just, impartial, objective. **2** LAW-ABIDING, virtuous, upright, ethical, moral, high-minded, scrupulous, honourable, reputable, respectable, reliable, trustworthy, true, genuine, real.
**F3 1** dishonest. **2** dishonourable.

**honestly** *adv* truly, really, truthfully, sincerely, frankly, directly, outright, plainly, openly, legitimately, legally, lawfully, on the level, fairly, justly, objectively, honourably, in good faith.

**F3** dishonestly, dishonourably.

**honesty** n **1** TRUTHFULNESS, sincerity, frankness, candour, bluntness, outspokenness, straightforwardness, plain-speaking, explicitness, openness, legitimacy, legality, equity, fairness, justness, objectivity, even-handedness. **2** VIRTUE, uprightness, honour, integrity, morality, scrupulousness, trustworthiness, genuineness, veracity.

**F3** **1** dishonesty.

**honorary** adj unpaid, unofficial, titular, nominal, in name only, honorific, formal.

**F3** paid.

**honour** n **1** REPUTATION, good name, repute, renown, distinction, esteem, regard, respect, credit, dignity, self-respect, pride, integrity, morality, decency, rectitude, probity. **2** AWARD, accolade, commendation, acknowledgement, recognition, tribute, privilege. **3** PRAISE, acclaim, homage, admiration, reverence, worship, adoration.

**F3** **1** dishonour, disgrace.

v **1** PRAISE, acclaim, exalt, glorify, pay homage to, decorate, crown, celebrate, commemorate, remember, admire, esteem, respect, revere, worship, prize, value. **2** honour a promise: keep, observe, respect, fulfil, carry out, discharge, execute, perform.

**F3** **1** dishonour, disgrace.

**honourable** adj great, eminent, distinguished, renowned, respected, worthy, prestigious, trusty, reputable, respectable, virtuous, upright, upstanding, straight, honest, trustworthy, true, sincere, noble, high-minded, principled, moral, ethical, fair, just, right, proper,

decent.

**F3** dishonourable, unworthy, dishonest.

**hoodwink** v deceive, dupe, fool, take in, delude, bamboozle (infml), have on (infml), mislead, hoax, trick, cheat, con (infml), rook, gull, swindle.

**hook** n crook, sickle, peg, barb, trap, snare, catch, fastener, clasp, hasp.

v **1** BEND, crook, curve, curl. **2** CATCH, capture, bag, grab, trap, snare, ensnare, entangle. **3** FASTEN, clasp, hitch, fix, secure.

**hooligan** n ruffian, rowdy, hoodlum, mobster, bovver boy (sl), thug, tough, lout, yob (sl), vandal, delinquent.

**hoop** n ring, circle, round, loop, wheel, band, girdle, circlet.

**hoot** n, v call, cry, shout, shriek, whoop, toot, beep, whistle, boo, jeer, laugh, howl.

**hop** v jump, leap, spring, bound, vault, skip, dance, prance, frisk, limp, hobble.

n jump, leap, spring, bound, vault, bounce, step, skip, dance.

**hope** n hopefulness, optimism, ambition, aspiration, wish, desire, longing, dream, expectation, anticipation, prospect, promise, belief, confidence, assurance, conviction, faith.

**F3** pessimism, despair.

v aspire, wish, desire, long, expect, await, look forward, anticipate, contemplate, foresee, believe, trust, rely, reckon on, assume.

**F3** despair.

**hopeful** adj **1** OPTIMISTIC, bullish (infml), confident, assured, expectant, sanguine, cheerful, buoyant. **2** a hopeful sign: encouraging, heartening, reassuring, favourable, auspicious, promising, rosy, bright.

**F3** **1** pessimistic, despairing. **2** discouraging.

**hopeless** adj **1** PESSIMISTIC, defeatist, negative, despairing, demoralized, downhearted, dejected, despondent, forlorn, wretched. **2** UNATTAINABLE, unachievable, impracticable, impossible, vain, foolish, futile, useless, pointless, worthless, poor, helpless, lost, irremediable, irreparable, incurable. ⊞ 1 hopeful, optimistic. 2 curable.

**horde** n band, gang, pack, herd, drove, flock, swarm, crowd, mob, throng, multitude, host.

**horizon** n skyline, vista, prospect, compass, range, scope, perspective.

**horrible** adj unpleasant, disagreeable, nasty, unkind, horrid, disgusting, revolting, offensive, repulsive, hideous, grim, ghastly, awful, dreadful, frightful, fearful, terrible, abominable, shocking, appalling, horrific. ⊞ pleasant, agreeable, lovely, attractive.

**horrific** adj horrifying, shocking, appalling, awful, dreadful, ghastly, gruesome, terrifying, frightening, scary, harrowing, bloodcurdling.

**horrify** v shock, outrage, scandalize, appal, disgust, sicken, dismay, alarm, startle, scare, frighten, terrify. ⊞ please, delight.

**horror** n **1** recoil in horror: shock, outrage, disgust, revulsion, repugnance, abhorrence, loathing, dismay, consternation, alarm, fright, fear, terror, panic, dread, apprehension. **2** GHASTLINESS, awfulness, frightfulness, hideousness. ⊞ 1 approval, delight.

**horseman, horsewoman** n equestrian, rider, jockey, cavalryman, hussar.

**horseplay** n clowning, buffoonery, foolery, tomfoolery, skylarking, pranks, capers, high jinks, fun and games, rough-and-tumble.

**hospitable** adj friendly, sociable, welcoming, receptive, cordial, amicable, congenial, convivial, genial, kind, gracious, generous, liberal. ⊞ inhospitable, unfriendly, hostile.

**hospitality** n friendliness, sociability, welcome, accommodation, entertainment, conviviality, warmth, cheer, generosity, open-handedness. ⊞ unfriendliness.

**host¹** n **1** COMPE[GR]RE, master of ceremonies, presenter, announcer, anchorman, anchorwoman, linkman. **2** PUBLICAN, innkeeper, landlord, proprietor. v present, introduce, compère.

**host²** n multitude, myriad, array, army, horde, crowd, throng, swarm, pack, band.

**hostage** n prisoner, captive, pawn, surety, security, pledge.

**hostel** n youth hostel, residence, dosshouse (sl), boarding-house, guest-house, hotel, inn.

**hostile** adj belligerent, warlike, ill-disposed, unsympathetic, unfriendly, inhospitable, inimical, antagonistic, opposed, adverse, unfavourable, contrary, opposite. ⊞ friendly, welcoming, favourable.

**hostilities** n war, warfare, battle, fighting, conflict, strife, bloodshed.

**hostility** n opposition, aggression, belligerence, enmity, estrangement, antagonism, animosity, ill-will, malice, resentment, hate, hatred, dislike, aversion, abhorrence. ⊞ friendliness, friendship.

**hot** adj **1** WARM, heated, fiery, burning, scalding, blistering, scorching, roasting, baking, boiling, steaming, sizzling, sweltering, sultry, torrid, tropical. **2** SPICY, peppery, piquant, sharp, pungent, strong. ⊞ 1 cold, cool. 2 mild.

**hotchpotch** n mishmash, medley, miscellany, collection, mix, mixture, jumble, confusion, mess.

**hotel** n boarding-house, guest-house,

pension, motel, inn, public house, pub (*infml*), hostel.

**hotheaded** *adj* headstrong, impetuous, impulsive, hasty, rash, reckless, fiery, volatile, hot-tempered, quick-tempered.
🖙 cool, calm.

**hothouse** *n* greenhouse, glasshouse, conservatory, orangery, vinery.

**hound** *v* chase, pursue, hunt (down), drive, goad, prod, chivvy, nag, pester, badger, harry, harass, persecute.

**house** *n* **1** BUILDING, dwelling, residence, home. **2** DYNASTY, family, clan, tribe.

> *Types of house include*: semi-detached, semi (*infml*), detached, terraced, town-house, council house, cottage, thatched cottage, prefab (*infml*), pied-à-terre, bungalow, chalet bungalow; flat, bedsit, apartment, studio, maisonette, penthouse, granny flat, duplex (*US*), condominium (*US*); manor, hall, lodge, grange, villa, mansion, rectory, vicarage, parsonage, manse, croft, farmhouse, homestead, ranchhouse, chalet, log cabin, shack, shanty, hut, igloo, hacienda.

*v* **1** LODGE, quarter, billet, board, accommodate, put up, take in, shelter, harbour. **2** HOLD, contain, protect, cover, sheathe, place, keep, store.

**household** *n* family, family circle, house, home, ménage, establishment, set-up.
*adj* domestic, home, family, ordinary, plain, everyday, common, familiar, well-known, established.

**householder** *n* resident, tenant, occupier, occupant, owner, landlady, freeholder, leaseholder, proprietor, landlord, home-owner, head of the household.

**housing** *n* **1** ACCOMMODATION, houses, homes, dwellings, habitation, shelter. **2** CASING, case, container,

holder, covering, cover, sheath, protection.

**hovel** *n* shack, shanty, cabin, hut, shed, dump, hole (*infml*).

**hover** *v* **1** HANG, poise, float, drift, fly, flutter, flap. **2** *he hovered by the door*: pause, linger, hang about, hesitate, waver, fluctuate, seesaw.

**however** *conj* nevertheless, nonetheless, still, yet, even so, notwithstanding, though, anyhow.

**howl** *n, v* wail, cry, shriek, scream, shout, yell, roar, bellow, bay, yelp, hoot, moan, groan.

**hub** *n* centre, middle, focus, focal point, axis, pivot, linchpin, nerve centre, core, heart.

**hubbub** *n* noise, racket, din, clamour, commotion, disturbance, riot, uproar, hullabaloo, rumpus, confusion, disorder, tumult, hurly-burly, chaos, pandemonium.
🖙 peace, quiet.

**huddle** *n* **1** CLUSTER, clump, knot, mass, crowd, muddle, jumble. **2** CONCLAVE, conference, meeting.
*v* cluster, gravitate, converge, meet, gather, congregate, crowd, flock, throng, press, cuddle, snuggle, nestle, curl up, crouch, hunch.
🖙 disperse.

**hue** *n* colour, shade, tint, dye, tinge, nuance, tone, complexion, aspect, light.

**huff** *n* pique, sulks, mood, bad mood, anger, rage, passion.

**hug** *v* embrace, cuddle, squeeze, enfold, hold, clasp, clutch, grip, cling to, enclose.
*n* embrace, cuddle, squeeze, clasp, hold, clinch.

**huge** *adj* immense, vast, enormous, massive, colossal, titanic, giant, gigantic, mammoth, monumental, tremendous, great, big, large, bulky, unwieldy.
🖙 tiny, minute.

**hulking** *adj* massive, heavy, unwieldy, bulky, awkward, ungainly.

**hull** *n* body, frame, framework, structure, casing, covering.

**hullabaloo** *n* fuss, palaver, to-do (*infml*), outcry, furore, hue and cry, uproar, pandemonium, rumpus, disturbance, commotion, hubbub.
✷ calm, peace.

**hum** *v* buzz, whirr, purr, drone, thrum, croon, sing, murmur, mumble, throb, pulse, vibrate.
*n* buzz, whirr, purring, drone, murmur, mumble, throb, pulsation, vibration.

**human** *adj* **1** MORTAL, fallible, susceptible, reasonable, rational.
**2** KIND, considerate, understanding, humane, compassionate.
✷ **2** inhuman.
*n* human being, mortal, homo sapiens, man, woman, child, person, individual, body, soul.

**humane** *adj* kind, compassionate, sympathetic, understanding, kind-hearted, good-natured, gentle, tender, loving, mild, lenient, merciful, forgiving, forbearing, kindly, benevolent, charitable, humanitarian, good.
✷ inhumane, cruel.

**humanitarian** *adj* benevolent, charitable, philanthropic, public-spirited, compassionate, humane, altruistic, unselfish.
✷ selfish, self-seeking.
*n* philanthropist, benefactor, good Samaritan, do-gooder, altruist.
✷ egoist, self-seeker.

**humanity** *n* **1** HUMAN RACE, humankind, mankind, womankind, mortality, people. **2** HUMANENESS, kindness, compassion, fellow-feeling, understanding, tenderness, benevolence, generosity, goodwill.
✷ **2** inhumanity.

**humanize** *v* domesticate, tame, civilize, cultivate, educate, enlighten, edify, improve, better, polish, refine.

**humble** *adj* **1** MEEK, submissive,

unassertive, self-effacing, polite, respectful, deferential, servile, subservient, sycophantic, obsequious.
**2** LOWLY, low, mean, insignificant, unimportant, common, commonplace, ordinary, plain, simple, modest, unassuming, unpretentious, unostentatious.
✷ **1** proud, assertive. **2** important, pretentious.
*v* bring down, lower, bring low, abase, demean, sink, discredit, disgrace, shame, humiliate, mortify, chasten, crush, deflate, subdue.
✷ exalt.

**humbug** *n* **1** DECEPTION, pretence, sham, found, swindle, trick, hoax, deceit, trickery. **2** NONSENSE, rubbish, baloney (*sl*), bunkum (*infml*), claptrap (*infml*), eye-wash (*infml*), bluff, cant, hypocrisy.

**humdrum** *adj* boring, tedious, monotonous, routine, dull, dreary, uninteresting, uneventful, ordinary, mundane, everyday, commonplace.
✷ lively, unusual, exceptional.

**humid** *adj* damp, moist, dank, clammy, sticky, muggy, sultry, steamy.
✷ dry.

**humiliate** *v* mortify, embarrass, confound, crush, break, deflate, chasten, shame, disgrace, discredit, degrade, demean, humble, bring low.
✷ dignify, exalt.

**humiliation** *n* mortification, embarrassment, shame, disgrace, dishonour, ignominy, abasement, deflation, put-down, snub, rebuff, affront.
✷ gratification, triumph.

**humility** *n* meekness, submissiveness, deference, self-abasement, servility, humbleness, lowliness, modesty, unpretentiousness.
✷ pride, arrogance, assertiveness.

**humorist** *n* wit, satirist, comedian, comic, joker, wag, jester, clown.

**humorous** *adj* funny, amusing, comic, entertaining, witty, satirical, jocular, facetious, playful, waggish, droll, whimsical, comical, farcical, zany (*infml*), ludicrous, absurd, hilarious, side-splitting.
**Ｅ‌Ａ** serious, humourless.

**humour** *n* **1** WIT, drollery, jokes, jesting, badinage, repartee, facetiousness, satire, comedy, farce, fun, amusement. **2** *in a bad humour*: mood, temper, frame of mind, spirits, disposition, temperament.
*v* go along with, comply with, accommodate, gratify, indulge, pamper, spoil, favour, please, mollify, flatter.

**humourless** *adj* boring, tedious, dull, dry, solemn, serious, glum, morose.
**Ｅ‌Ａ** humorous, witty.

**hump** *n* hunch, lump, knob, bump, projection, protuberance, bulge, swelling, mound, prominence.

**hunch** *n* premonition, presentiment, intuition, suspicion, feeling, impression, idea, guess.
*v* hump, bend, curve, arch, stoop, crouch, squat, huddle, draw in, curl up.

**hunger** *n* **1** HUNGRINESS, emptiness, starvation, malnutrition, famine, appetite, ravenousness, voracity, greed, greediness. **2** *hunger for power*: desire, craving, longing, yearning, itch, thirst.
*v* starve, want, wish, desire, crave, hanker, long, yearn, pine, ache, itch, thirst.

**hungry** *adj* **1** STARVING, underfed, undernourished, peckish (*infml*), empty, hollow, famished, ravenous, greedy. **2** *hungry for knowledge*: desirous, craving, longing, aching, thirsty, eager, avid.
**Ｅ‌Ａ** **1** satisfied, full.

**hunk** *n* chunk, lump, piece, block, slab, wedge, mass, clod.

**hunt** *v* **1** CHASE, pursue, hound, dog, stalk, track, trail. **2** SEEK, look for, search, scour, rummage, forage, investigate.
*n* chase, pursuit, search, quest, investigation.

**hurdle** *n* jump, fence, wall, hedge, barrier, barricade, obstacle, obstruction, stumbling-block, hindrance, impediment, handicap, problem, snag, difficulty, complication.

**hurl** *v* throw, toss, fling, sling, catapult, project, propel, fire, launch, send.

**hurricane** *n* gale, tornado, typhoon, cyclone, whirlwind, squall, storm, tempest.

**hurried** *adj* rushed, hectic, hasty, precipitate, speedy, quick, swift, rapid, passing, brief, short, cursory, superficial, shallow, careless, slapdash.
**Ｅ‌Ａ** leisurely.

**hurry** *v* rush, dash, fly, get a move on (*infml*), hasten, quicken, speed up, hustle, push.
**Ｅ‌Ａ** slow down, delay.
*n* rush, haste, quickness, speed, urgency, hustle, bustle, flurry, commotion.
**Ｅ‌Ａ** leisureliness, calm.

**hurt** *v* **1** *my leg hurts*: ache, pain, throb, sting. **2** INJURE, wound, maltreat, ill-treat, bruise, cut, burn, torture, maim, disable. **3** DAMAGE, impair, harm, mar, spoil. **4** UPSET, sadden, grieve, distress, afflict, offend, annoy.
*n* pain, soreness, discomfort, suffering, injury, wound, damage, harm, distress, sorrow.
*adj* **1** INJURED, wounded, bruised, grazed, cut, scarred, maimed. **2** UPSET, sad, saddened, distressed, aggrieved, annoyed, offended, affronted.

**hurtful** *adj* **1** UPSETTING, wounding, vicious, cruel, mean, unkind, nasty, malicious, spiteful, catty, derogatory, scathing, cutting. **2** HARMFUL, damaging, injurious, pernicious, destructive.

**₣** 1 kind.

**hurtle** *v* dash, tear, race, fly, shoot, speed, rush, charge, plunge, dive, crash, rattle.

**husband** *n* spouse, partner, mate, better half, hubby (*infml*), groom, married man.

**hush** *v* quieten, silence, still, settle, compose, calm, soothe, subdue.

**₣** disturb, rouse.

*n* quietness, silence, peace, stillness, repose, calm, calmness, tranquillity, serenity.

**₣** noise, clamour.

*interj* quiet, hold your tongue, shut up, not another word.

**hush up** keep dark, suppress, conceal, cover up, stifle, gag.

**₣** publicize.

**hush-hush** *adj* secret, confidential, classified, restricted, under wraps (*infml*), top-secret.

**₣** open, public.

**husk** *n* covering, case, shell, pod, hull, rind, bran, chaff.

**husky** *adj* hoarse, croaky, croaking, low, throaty, guttural, gruff, rasping, rough, harsh.

**hustle** *v* hasten, rush, hurry, bustle, force, push, shove, thrust, bundle, elbow, jostle.

**hut** *n* cabin, shack, shanty, booth, shed, lean-to, shelter, den.

**hybrid** *n* cross, crossbreed, half-breed, mongrel, composite, combination, mixture, amalgam, compound.

*adj* crossbred, mongrel, composite, combined, mixed, heterogeneous, compound.

**₣** pure-bred.

**hygiene** *n* sanitariness, sanitation, sterility, disinfection, cleanliness,

purity, wholesomeness.

**₣** insanitariness.

**hygienic** *adj* sanitary, sterile, aseptic, germ-free, disinfected, clean, pure, salubrious, healthy, wholesome.

**₣** unhygienic, insanitary.

**hyperbole** *n* overstatement, exaggeration, magnification, extravagance.

**₣** understatement.

**hypnotic** *adj* mesmerizing, soporific, sleep-inducing, spellbinding, fascinating, compelling, irresistible, magnetic.

**hypnotism** *n* hypnosis, mesmerism, suggestion.

**hypnotize** *v* mesmerize, spellbind, bewitch, enchant, entrance, fascinate, captivate, magnetize.

**hypocrisy** *n* insincerity, double-talk, double-dealing, falsity, deceit, deception, pretence.

**₣** sincerity.

**hypocritical** *adj* insincere, two-faced, self-righteous, double-dealing, false, hollow, deceptive, spurious, deceitful, dissembling, pharisaic(al).

**₣** sincere, genuine.

**hypothesis** *n* theory, thesis, premise, postulate, proposition, supposition, conjecture, speculation.

**hypothetical** *adj* theoretical, imaginary, supposed, assumed, proposed, conjectural, speculative.

**₣** real, actual.

**hysteria** *n* agitation, frenzy, panic, hysterics, neurosis, mania, madness.

**₣** calm, composure.

**hysterical** *adj* **1** FRANTIC, frenzied, berserk, uncontrollable, mad, raving, crazed, demented, overwrought, neurotic. **2** (*infml*) HILARIOUS, uproarious, side-splitting, priceless (*infml*), rich (*infml*).

**₣** 1 calm, composed, self-possessed.

# I

**ice** *n* frost, rime, icicle, glacier, iciness, frostiness, coldness, chill.
*v* freeze, refrigerate, chill, cool, frost, glaze.

**icon** *n* idol, portrait, image, representation, symbol.

**icy** *adj* **1** ICE-COLD, arctic, polar, glacial, freezing, frozen, raw, bitter, biting, cold, chill, chilly. **2** *icy roads*: frosty, slippery, glassy, frozen, icebound, frostbound. **3** HOSTILE, cold, stony, cool, indifferent, aloof, distant, formal.
**E3** **1** hot. **3** friendly, warm.

**idea** *n* **1** THOUGHT, concept, notion, theory, hypothesis, guess, conjecture, belief, opinion, view, viewpoint, judgement, conception, vision, image, impression, perception, interpretation, understanding, inkling, suspicion, clue. **2** *a good idea*: brainwave, suggestion, proposal, proposition, recommendation, plan, scheme, design. **3** AIM, intention, purpose, reason, point, object.

**ideal** *n* perfection, epitome, acme, paragon, exemplar, example, model, pattern, archetype, prototype, type, image, criterion, standard.
*adj* **1** PERFECT, dream, utopian, best, optimum, optimal, supreme, highest, model, archetypal. **2** UNREAL, imaginary, theoretical, hypothetical, unattainable, impractical, idealistic.

**idealist** *n* perfectionist, romantic, visionary, dreamer, optimist.
**E3** realist, pragmatist.

**idealistic** *adj* perfectionist, utopian, visionary, romantic, quixotic, starry-eyed, optimistic, unrealistic,
impractical, impracticable.
**E3** realistic, pragmatic.

**idealize** *v* utopianize, romanticize, glamorize, glorify, exalt, worship, idolize.
**E3** caricature.

**identical** *adj* same, self-same, indistinguishable, interchangeable, twin, duplicate, like, alike, corresponding, matching, equal, equivalent.
**E3** different.

**identification** *n* **1** RECOGNITION, detection, diagnosis, naming, labelling, classification. **2** EMPATHY, association, involvement, rapport, relationship, sympathy, fellow-feeling. **3** IDENTITY CARD, documents, papers, credentials.

**identify** *v* recognize, know, pick out, single out, distinguish, perceive, make out, discern, notice, detect, diagnose, name, label, tag, specify, pinpoint, place, catalogue, classify.
**identify with** empathize with, relate to, associate with, respond to, sympathize with, feel for.

**identity** *n* **1** INDIVIDUALITY, particularity, singularity, uniqueness, self, personality, character, existence. **2** SAMENESS, likeness.

**ideology** *n* philosophy, world-view, ideas, principles, tenets, doctrine(s), convictions, belief(s), faith, creed, dogma.

**idiocy** *n* folly, stupidity, silliness, senselessness, lunacy.
**E3** wisdom, sanity.

**idiom** *n* phrase, expression, colloquialism, language, turn of phrase, phraseology, style, usage, jargon, vernacular.

**idiosyncrasy** *n* characteristic, peculiarity, singularity, oddity, eccentricity, freak, quirk, habit, mannerism, trait, feature.

**idiosyncratic** *adj* personal, individual, characteristic, distinctive, peculiar, singular, odd, eccentric, quirky.

F∃ general, common.

**idiot** *n* fool, blockhead, ass (*infml*), nitwit (*infml*), dimwit, halfwit, imbecile, moron, cretin, simpleton, dunce, ignoramus.

**idiotic** *adj* foolish, stupid, silly, absurd, senseless, daft (*infml*), lunatic, insane, foolhardy, harebrained, halfwitted, moronic, cretinous, crazy.

F∃ sensible, sane.

**idle** *adj* **1** INACTIVE, inoperative, unused, unoccupied, unemployed, jobless, redundant. **2** LAZY, work-shy, indolent. **3** *idle talk*: empty, trivial, casual, futile, vain, pointless, unproductive.

F∃ **1** active. **2** busy.

*v* do nothing, laze, lounge, take it easy, kill time, potter, loiter, dawdle, fritter, waste, loaf, slack, skive (*infml*).

F∃ work.

**idol** *n* icon, effigy, image, graven image, god, deity, fetish, favourite, darling, hero, heroine, pin-up.

**idolize** *v* hero-worship, lionize, exalt, glorify, worship, venerate, revere, admire, adore, love, dote on.

F∃ despise.

**idyllic** *adj* perfect, idealized, heavenly, delightful, charming, picturesque, pastoral, rustic, unspoiled, peaceful, happy.

F∃ unpleasant.

**ignite** *v* set fire to, set alight, catch fire, flare up, burn, conflagrate, fire, kindle, touch off, spark off.

F∃ quench.

**ignoble** *adj* low, mean, petty, base, vulgar, wretched, contemptible, despicable, vile, heinous, infamous,

disgraceful, dishonourable, shameless.

F∃ noble, worthy, honourable.

**ignominious** *adj* humiliating, mortifying, degrading, undignified, shameful, dishonourable, disreputable, disgraceful, despicable, scandalous.

F∃ triumphant, honourable.

**ignorance** *n* unintelligence, illiteracy, unawareness, unconsciousness, oblivion, unfamiliarity, inexperience, innocence, naïvety.

F∃ knowledge, wisdom.

**ignorant** *adj* uneducated, illiterate, unread, untaught, untrained, inexperienced, stupid, clueless (*infml*), uninitiated, unenlightened, uninformed, ill-informed, unwitting, unaware, unconscious, oblivious.

F∃ educated, knowledgeable, clever, wise.

**ignore** *v* disregard, take no notice of, shut one's eyes to, overlook, pass over, neglect, omit, reject, snub, cold-shoulder.

F∃ notice, observe.

**ill** *adj* **1** SICK, poorly, unwell, indisposed, laid up, ailing, off-colour, out of sorts (*infml*), under the weather (*infml*), seedy, queasy, diseased, unhealthy, infirm, frail. **2** *an ill omen*: bad, evil, damaging, harmful, injurious, detrimental, adverse, unfavourable, inauspicious, unpromising, sinister, ominous, threatening, unlucky, unfortunate, difficult, harsh, severe, unkind, unfriendly, antagonistic.

F∃ **1** well. **2** good, favourable, fortunate.

**ill-advised** *adj* imprudent, injudicious, unwise, foolish, ill-considered, thoughtless, hasty, rash, short-sighted, misguided, inappropriate.

F∃ wise, sensible, well-advised.

**ill-bred** *adj* bad-mannered, ill-

mannered, discourteous, impolite, rude, coarse, indelicate.
**⊟** well-bred, polite.

**illegal** adj unlawful, illicit, criminal, wrong, forbidden, prohibited, banned, outlawed, unauthorized, under-the-counter, black-market, unconstitutional, wrongful.
**⊟** legal, lawful.

**illegible** adj unreadable, indecipherable, scrawled, obscure, faint, indistinct.
**⊟** legible.

**illegitimate** adj 1 an illegitimate child: natural, bastard, born out of wedlock (fml). 2 ILLEGAL, unlawful, illicit, unauthorized, unwarranted, improper, incorrect, inadmissible, spurious, invalid, unsound.
**⊟** 1 legitimate. 2 legal.

**ill-fated** adj doomed, ill-starred, ill-omened, unfortunate, unlucky, luckless, unhappy.
**⊟** lucky.

**illicit** adj illegal, unlawful, criminal, wrong, illegitimate, improper, forbidden, prohibited, unauthorized, unlicensed, black-market, contraband, ill-gotten, under-the-counter, furtive, clandestine.
**⊟** legal, permissible.

**illness** n disease, disorder, complaint, ailment, sickness, ill health, ill-being, indisposition, infirmity, disability, affliction.

**illogical** adj irrational, unreasonable, unscientific, invalid, unsound, faulty, fallacious, specious, sophistical, inconsistent, senseless, meaningless, absurd.
**⊟** logical.

**ill-treat** v maltreat, abuse, injure, harm, damage, neglect, mistreat, mishandle, misuse, wrong, oppress.

**illuminate** v 1 LIGHT, light up, brighten, decorate. 2 ENLIGHTEN, edify, instruct, elucidate, illustrate, explain, clarify, clear up.
**⊟** 1 darken. 2 mystify.

**illumination** n light, lights, lighting, beam, ray, brightness, radiance, decoration, ornamentation.
**⊟** darkness.

**illusion** n apparition, mirage, hallucination, figment, fantasy, fancy, delusion, misapprehension, misconception, error, fallacy.
**⊟** reality, truth.

**illusory** adj illusive, deceptive, misleading, apparent, seeming, deluding, delusive, unreal, unsubstantial, sham, false, fallacious, untrue, mistaken.
**⊟** real.

**illustrate** v draw, sketch, depict, picture, show, exhibit, demonstrate, exemplify, explain, interpret, clarify, elucidate, illuminate, decorate, ornament, adorn.

**illustration** n 1 PICTURE, plate, half-tone, photograph, drawing, sketch, figure, representation, decoration. 2 EXAMPLE, specimen, instance, case, analogy, demonstration, explanation, interpretation.

**illustrious** adj great, noble, eminent, distinguished, celebrated, famous, famed, renowned, noted, prominent, outstanding, remarkable, notable, brilliant, excellent, splendid, magnificent, glorious, exalted.
**⊟** ignoble, inglorious.

**ill-will** n hostility, antagonism, bad blood, enmity, unfriendliness, malevolence, malice, spite, animosity, ill-feeling, resentment, hard feelings, grudge, dislike, aversion, hatred.
**⊟** goodwill, friendship.

**image** n 1 IDEA, notion, concept, impression, perception. 2 REPRESENTATION, likeness, picture, portrait, icon, effigy, figure, statue, idol, replica, reflection.

**imaginable** adj conceivable, thinkable, believable, credible, plausible, likely, possible.

unimaginable.

**imaginary** *adj* imagined, fanciful, illusory, hallucinatory, visionary, pretend, make-believe, unreal, non-existent, fictional, fabulous, legendary, mythological, made-up, invented, fictitious, assumed, supposed, hypothetical.

real.

**imagination** *n* imaginativeness, creativity, inventiveness, originality, inspiration, insight, ingenuity, resourcefulness, enterprise, wit, vision, mind's eye, fancy, illusion.

unimaginativeness, reality.

**imaginative** *adj* creative, inventive, innovative, original, inspired, visionary, ingenious, clever, resourceful, enterprising, fanciful, fantastic, vivid.

unimaginative.

**imagine** *v* 1 PICTURE, visualize, envisage, conceive, fancy, fantasize, pretend, make believe, conjure up, dream up, think up, invent, devise, create, plan, project. 2 *I imagine so*: think, believe, judge, suppose, guess, conjecture, assume, take it, gather.

**imbalance** *n* unevenness, inequality, disparity, disproportion, unfairness, partiality, bias.

balance, parity.

**imbecile** *n* idiot, halfwit, simpleton, moron, cretin, fool, blockhead, bungler.

**imbue** *v* permeate, impregnate, pervade, suffuse, fill, saturate, steep, inculcate, instil, tinge, tint.

**imitate** *v* copy, emulate, follow, ape, mimic, impersonate, take off, caricature, parody, send up, spoof, mock, parrot, repeat, echo, mirror, duplicate, reproduce, simulate, counterfeit, forge.

**imitation** *n* 1 MIMICRY, impersonation, impression, take-off, caricature, parody, send-up, spoof, mockery, travesty. 2 COPY, duplicate, reproduction, replica, simulation, counterfeit, fake, forgery, sham, likeness, resemblance, reflection, dummy.
*adj* artificial, synthetic, man-made, ersatz, fake, phoney (*infml*), mock, pseudo, reproduction, simulated, sham, dummy.

genuine.

**imitative** *adj* copying, mimicking, parrot-like, unoriginal, derivative, plagiarized, second-hand, simulated, mock.

**imitator** *n* mimic, impersonator, impressionist, parrot, copycat (*infml*), copier, emulator, follower.

**immaculate** *adj* perfect, unblemished, flawless, faultless, impeccable, spotless, clean, spick and span, pure, unsullied, undefiled, untainted, stainless, blameless, innocent.

blemished, stained, contaminated.

**immaterial** *adj* irrelevant, insignificant, unimportant, minor, trivial, trifling, inconsequential.

relevant, important.

**immature** *adj* young, under-age, adolescent, juvenile, childish, puerile, infantile, babyish, raw, crude, callow, inexperienced, green, unripe, undeveloped.

mature.

**immeasurable** *adj* vast, immense, infinite, limitless, unlimited, boundless, unbounded, endless, bottomless, inexhaustible, incalculable, inestimable.

limited.

**immediate** *adj* 1 INSTANT, instantaneous, direct, prompt, swift, current, present, existing, urgent, pressing. 2 NEAREST, next, adjacent, near, close, recent.

1 delayed. 2 distant.

**immediately** *adv* now, straight away, right away, at once, instantly, directly, forthwith, without delay, promptly, unhesitatingly.

eventually, never.

**immense** *adj* vast, great, huge, enormous, massive, giant, gigantic, tremendous, monumental.
**F3** tiny, minute.

**immensity** *n* magnitude, bulk, expanse, vastness, greatness, hugeness, enormousness, massiveness.
**F3** minuteness.

**immerse** *v* plunge, submerge, submerse, sink, duck, dip, douse, bathe.

**immigrant** *n* incomer, settler, newcomer, alien.
**F3** emigrant.

**imminent** *adj* impending, forthcoming, in the offing, approaching, coming, near, close, looming, menacing, threatening, brewing, in the air.
**F3** remote, far-off.

**immobile** *adj* stationary, motionless, unmoving, still, stock-still, static, immovable, rooted, fixed, frozen, rigid, stiff.
**F3** mobile, moving.

**immobilize** *v* stop, halt, fix, freeze, transfix, paralyse, cripple, disable.
**F3** mobilize.

**immodest** *adj* indecent, revealing, shameless, forward, improper, immoral, obscene, lewd, coarse, risqué.

**immoral** *adj* unethical, wrong, bad, sinful, evil, wicked, unscrupulous, unprincipled, dishonest, corrupt, depraved, degenerate, dissolute, lewd, indecent, pornographic, obscene, impure.
**F3** moral, right, good.

**immortal** *adj* undying, imperishable, eternal, everlasting, perpetual, endless, ceaseless, lasting, enduring, abiding, timeless, ageless.
**F3** mortal.

**immortalize** *v* celebrate, commemorate, memorialize, perpetuate, enshrine.

**immovable** *adj* fixed, rooted,

immobile, stuck, fast, secure, stable, constant, firm, set, determined, resolute, adamant, unshakable, obstinate, unyielding.
**F3** movable.

**immune** *adj* invulnerable, unsusceptible, resistant, proof, protected, safe, exempt, free, clear.
**F3** susceptible.

**immunity** *n* resistance, protection, exemption, indemnity, impunity, exoneration, freedom, liberty, licence, franchise, privilege, right.
**F3** susceptibility.

**immunize** *v* vaccinate, inoculate, inject, protect, safeguard.

**impact** *n* **1** *the impact of the reforms*: effect, consequences, repercussions, impression, power, influence, significance, meaning. **2** COLLISION, crash, smash, bang, bump, blow, knock, contact, jolt, shock, brunt.

**impair** *v* damage, harm, injure, hinder, mar, spoil, worsen, undermine, weaken, reduce, lessen, diminish, blunt.
**F3** improve, enhance.

**impale** *v* pierce, puncture, perforate, run through, spear, lance, spike, skewer, spit, stick, transfix.

**impart** *v* tell, relate, communicate, make known, disclose, divulge, reveal, convey, pass on, give, grant, confer, offer, contribute, lend.
**F3** withhold.

**impartial** *adj* objective, dispassionate, detached, disinterested, neutral, non-partisan, unbiased, unprejudiced, open-minded, fair, just, equitable, even-handed, equal.
**F3** biased, prejudiced.

**impasse** *n* deadlock, stalemate, dead end, cul-de-sac, blind alley, halt, standstill.

**impassive** *adj* expressionless, calm, composed, unruffled, unconcerned, cool, unfeeling, unemotional, unmoved, imperturbable,

unexcitable, stoical, indifferent, dispassionate.
**⊟** responsive, moved.

**impatience** *n* eagerness, keenness, restlessness, agitation, anxiety, nervousness, irritability, intolerance, shortness, brusqueness, haste, rashness.
**⊟** patience.

**impatient** *adj* eager, keen, restless, fidgety, fretful, edgy, irritable, snappy, hot-tempered, quick-tempered, intolerant, brusque, abrupt, impetuous, hasty, precipitate, headlong.
**⊟** patient.

**impeach** *v* accuse, charge, indict, arraign, denounce, impugn, disparage, criticize, censure, blame.

**impeccable** *adj* perfect, faultless, precise, exact, flawless, unblemished, stainless, immaculate, pure, irreproachable, blameless, innocent.
**⊟** faulty, flawed, corrupt.

**impede** *v* hinder, hamper, obstruct, block, clog, slow, retard, hold up, delay, check, curb, restrain, thwart, disrupt, stop, bar.
**⊟** aid, promote, further.

**impediment** *n* hindrance, obstacle, obstruction, barrier, bar, block, stumbling-block, snag, difficulty, handicap, check, curb, restraint, restriction.
**⊟** aid.

**impel** *v* urge, force, oblige, compel, constrain, drive, propel, push, spur, goad, prompt, stimulate, excite, instigate, motivate, inspire, move.
**⊟** deter, dissuade.

**impending** *adj* imminent, forthcoming, approaching, coming, close, near, looming, menacing, threatening.
**⊟** remote.

**impenetrable** *adj* **1** *impenetrable jungle*: solid, thick, dense, impassable. **2** UNINTELLIGIBLE, incomprehensible, unfathomable,

baffling, mysterious, cryptic, enigmatic, obscure, dark, inscrutable.
**⊟ 2** accessible, understandable.

**imperative** *adj* compulsory, obligatory, essential, vital, crucial, pressing, urgent.
**⊟** optional, unimportant.

**imperceptible** *adj* inappreciable, indiscernible, inaudible, faint, slight, negligible, infinitesimal, microscopic, minute, tiny, small, fine, subtle, gradual.
**⊟** perceptible.

**imperfect** *adj* faulty, flawed, defective, damaged, broken, chipped, deficient, incomplete.
**⊟** perfect.

**imperfection** *n* fault, flaw, defect, blemish, deficiency, shortcoming, weakness, failing.
**⊟** perfection.

**imperial** *adj* sovereign, supreme, royal, regal, majestic, grand, magnificent, great, noble.

**imperil** *v* endanger, jeopardize, risk, hazard, expose, compromise, threaten.

**imperious** *adj* overbearing, domineering, autocratic, despotic, tyrannical, dictatorial, high-handed, commanding, arrogant, haughty.
**⊟** humble.

**impersonal** *adj* formal, official, businesslike, bureaucratic, faceless, aloof, remote, distant, detached, neutral, objective, dispassionate, cold, frosty, glassy.
**⊟** informal, friendly.

**impersonate** *v* imitate, mimic, take off, parody, caricature, mock, masquerade as, pose as, act, portray.

**impertinence** *n* rudeness, impoliteness, disrespect, insolence, impudence, cheek (*infml*), brass (*sl*), effrontery, nerve (*infml*), audacity, boldness, brazenness, forwardness, presumption.
**⊟** politeness, respect.

**impertinent** *adj* rude, impolite, ill-mannered, discourteous, disrespectful, insolent, impudent, cheeky (*infml*), saucy (*infml*), pert, bold, brazen, forward, presumptuous, fresh.

**F3** polite, respectful.

**imperturbable** *adj* unexcitable, unflappable (*infml*), calm, tranquil, composed, collected, self-possessed, cool, unmoved, unruffled.

**impervious** *adj* **1** IMPERMEABLE, waterproof, damp-proof, watertight, hermetic, closed, sealed, impenetrable. **2** *impervious to criticism*: immune, invulnerable, untouched, unaffected, unmoved, resistant.

**F3** **1** porous, pervious. **2** responsive, vulnerable.

**impetuous** *adj* impulsive, spontaneous, unplanned, unpremeditated, hasty, precipitate, rash, reckless, thoughtless, unthinking.

**F3** cautious, wary, circumspect.

**impetus** *n* impulse, momentum, force, energy, power, drive, boost, push, spur, stimulus, incentive, motivation.

**impinge** *v* hit, touch (on), affect, influence, encroach, infringe, intrude, trespass, invade.

**implacable** *adj* inexorable, relentless, remorseless, merciless, pitiless, cruel, ruthless, intransigent, inflexible.

**F3** compassionate.

**implant** *v* graft, engraft, embed, sow, plant, fix, root, insert, instil, inculcate.

**implausible** *adj* improbable, unlikely, far-fetched, dubious, suspect, unconvincing, weak, flimsy, thin, transparent.

**F3** plausible, likely, reasonable.

**implement** *n* tool, instrument, utensil, gadget, device, apparatus, appliance.

*v* enforce, effect, bring about, carry out, execute, discharge, perform, do, fulfil, complete, accomplish, realize.

**implicate** *v* involve, embroil, entangle, incriminate, compromise, include, concern, connect, associate.

**F3** exonerate.

**implication** *n* **1** INFERENCE, insinuation, suggestion, meaning, significance, ramification, repercusssion. **2** INVOLVEMENT, entanglement, incrimination, connection, association.

**implicit** *adj* **1** IMPLIED, inferred, insinuated, indirect, unsaid, unspoken, tacit, understood. **2** *implicit belief*: unquestioning, utter, total, full, complete, absolute, unqualified, unreserved, wholehearted.

**F3** **1** explicit. **2** half-hearted.

**imply** *v* suggest, insinuate, hint, intimate, mean, signify, point to, indicate, involve, require.

**F3** state.

**impolite** *adj* rude, discourteous, bad-mannered, ill-mannered, ill-bred, disrespectful, insolent, rough, coarse, vulgar, abrupt.

**F3** polite, courteous.

**importance** *n* momentousness, significance, consequence, substance, matter, concern, interest, usefulness, value, worth, weight, influence, mark, prominence, eminence, distinction, esteem, prestige, status, standing.

**F3** unimportance.

**important** *adj* **1** MOMENTOUS, noteworthy, significant, meaningful, relevant, material, salient, urgent, vital, essential, key, primary, major, substantial, valuable, seminal, weighty, serious, grave, far-reaching. **2** LEADING, foremost, high-level, high-ranking, influential, powerful, pre-eminent, prominent, outstanding, eminent, noted.

**F3** **1** unimportant, insignificant, trivial.

**impose** v 1 INTRODUCE, institute, enforce, promulgate, exact, levy, set, fix, put, place, lay, inflict, burden, encumber, saddle. 2 INTRUDE, butt in, encroach, trespass, obtrude, force oneself, presume, take liberties.

**imposing** adj impressive, striking, grand, stately, majestic, dignified.
**E3** unimposing, modest.

**imposition** n 1 INTRODUCTION, infliction, exaction, levying. 2 INTRUSION, encroachment, liberty, burden, constraint, charge, duty, task, punishment.

**impossible** adj hopeless, impracticable, unworkable, unattainable, unachievable, unobtainable, insoluble, unreasonable, unacceptable, inconceivable, unthinkable, preposterous, absurd, ludicrous, ridiculous.
**E3** possible.

**impostor** n fraud, fake, phoney (infml), quack, charlatan, impersonator, pretender, con man (infml), swindler, cheat, rogue.

**impotent** adj powerless, helpless, unable, incapable, ineffective, incompetent, inadequate, weak, feeble, frail, infirm, disabled, incapacitated, paralysed.
**E3** potent, strong.

**impoverished** adj poor, needy, impecunious, poverty-stricken, destitute, bankrupt, ruined.
**E3** rich.

**impracticable** adj unworkable, unfeasible, unattainable, unachievable, impossible, unviable, useless, unserviceable, inoperable.
**E3** practicable.

**impractical** adj unrealistic, idealistic, romantic, starry-eyed, impracticable, unworkable, impossible, awkward, inconvenient.
**E3** practical, realistic, sensible.

**imprecise** adj inexact, inaccurate, approximate, estimated, rough,

loose, indefinite, vague, woolly, hazy, ill-defined, sloppy, ambiguous, equivocal.
**E3** precise, exact.

**impregnable** adj impenetrable, unconquerable, invincible, unbeatable, unassailable, indestructible, fortified, strong, solid, secure, safe, invulnerable.
**E3** vulnerable.

**impregnate** v 1 SOAK, steep, saturate, fill, permeate, pervade, suffuse, imbue. 2 INSEMINATE, fertilize.

**impress** v 1 I'm not impressed: strike, move, touch, affect, influence, stir, inspire, excite, grab (sl). 2 STAMP, imprint, mark, indent, instil, inculcate.

**impression** n 1 FEELING, awareness, consciousness, sense, illusion, idea, notion, opinion, belief, conviction, suspicion, hunch, memory, recollection. 2 STAMP, mark, print, dent, outline. 3 IMPERSONATION, imitation, take-off, parody, send-up. 4 make a good impression: effect, impact, influence.

**impressionable** adj naïve, gullible, susceptible, vulnerable, sensitive, responsive, open, receptive.

**impressive** adj striking, imposing, grand, powerful, effective, stirring, exciting, moving, touching.
**E3** unimpressive, uninspiring.

**imprint** n print, mark, stamp, impression, sign, logo.
v print, mark, brand, stamp, impress, engrave, etch.

**imprison** v jail, incarcerate, intern, detain, send down (infml), put away (infml), lock up, cage, confine, shut in.
**E3** release, free.

**imprisonment** n incarceration, internment, detention, custody, confinement.
**E3** freedom, liberty.

**improbable** adj uncertain,

questionable, doubtful, unlikely, dubious, implausible, unconvincing, far-fetched, preposterous, unbelievable, incredible.
**E3** probable, likely, convincing.

**impromptu** *adj* improvised, extempore, ad-lib, off the cuff, unscripted, unrehearsed, unprepared, spontaneous.
**E3** rehearsed.
*adv* extempore, ad lib, off the cuff, off the top of one's head, spontaneously, on the spur of the moment.

**improper** *adj* wrong, incorrect, irregular, unsuitable, inappropriate, inopportune, incongruous, out of place, indecent, rude, vulgar, unseemly, unbecoming, shocking.
**E3** proper, appropriate, decent.

**improve** *v* better, ameliorate, enhance, polish, touch up, mend, rectify, correct, amend, reform, upgrade, increase, rise, pick up, develop, look up, advance, progress, get better, recover, recuperate, rally, perk up, mend one's ways, turn over a new leaf.
**E3** worsen, deteriorate, decline.

**improvement** *n* betterment, amelioration, enhancement, rectification, correction, amendment, reformation, increase, rise, upswing, gain, development, advance, progress, furtherance, recovery, rally.
**E3** deterioration, decline.

**improvise** *v* **1** CONTRIVE, devise, concoct, invent, throw together, make do. **2** EXTEMPORIZE, ad-lib, play by ear, vamp.

**imprudent** *adj* unwise, ill-advised, foolish, short-sighted, rash, reckless, hasty, irresponsible, careless, heedless, impolitic, indiscreet.
**E3** prudent, wise, cautious.

**impudence** *n* impertinence, cheek (*infml*), effrontery, nerve (*infml*), face (*infml*), boldness, insolence, rudeness, presumption.

**E3** politeness.

**impudent** *adj* impertinent, cheeky (*infml*), saucy (*infml*), bold, forward, shameless, cocky, insolent, rude, presumptuous, fresh.
**E3** polite.

**impulse** *n* **1** URGE, wish, desire, inclination, whim, notion, instinct, feeling, passion. **2** IMPETUS, momentum, force, pressure, drive, thrust, push, incitement, stimulus, motive.

**impulsive** *adj* impetuous, rash, reckless, hasty, quick, spontaneous, automatic, instinctive, intuitive.
**E3** cautious, premeditated.

**impure** *adj* **1** UNREFINED, adulterated, diluted, contaminated, polluted, tainted, infected, corrupt, debased, unclean, dirty, foul.
**2** OBSCENE, indecent, immodest.
**E3 1** pure. **2** chaste, decent.

**impurity** *n* adulteration, contamination, pollution, infection, corruption, dirtiness, contaminant, dirt, filth, foreign body, mark, spot.
**E3** purity.

**inability** *n* incapability, incapacity, powerlessness, impotence, inadequacy, weakness, handicap, disability.
**E3** ability.

**inaccessible** *adj* isolated, remote, unfrequented, unapproachable, unreachable, unget-at-able (*infml*), unattainable.
**E3** accessible.

**inaccuracy** *n* mistake, error, miscalculation, slip, blunder, fault, defect, imprecision, inexactness, unreliability.
**E3** accuracy, precision.

**inaccurate** *adj* incorrect, wrong, erroneous, mistaken, faulty, flawed, defective, imprecise, inexact, loose, unreliable, unfaithful, untrue.
**E3** accurate, correct.

**inaction** *n* inactivity, immobility, inertia, rest, idleness, lethargy, torpor, stagnation.

**F3** action.

**inactive** *adj* immobile, inert, idle, unused, inoperative, dormant, passive, sedentary, lazy, lethargic, sluggish, torpid, sleepy.

**F3** active, working, busy.

**inadequacy** *n* **1** INSUFFICIENCY, lack, shortage, dearth, want, deficiency, scantiness, meagreness, defectiveness, ineffectiveness, inability, incompetence. **2** *the inadequacies of the system*: fault, defect, imperfection, weakness, failing, shortcoming.

**F3** 1 adequacy.

**inadequate** *adj* **1** INSUFFICIENT, short, wanting, deficient, scanty, sparse, meagre, niggardly. **2** INCOMPETENT, incapable, unequal, unqualified, ineffective, faulty, defective, imperfect, unsatisfactory.

**F3** 1 adequate. 2 satisfactory.

**inadmissible** *adj* unacceptable, irrelevant, immaterial, inappropriate, disallowed, prohibited.

**F3** admissible.

**inadvertent** *adj* accidental, chance, unintentional, unintended, unplanned, unpremeditated, careless.

**F3** deliberate, conscious, careful.

**inadvisable** *adj* unwise, imprudent, injudicious, foolish, silly, ill-advised, misguided, indiscreet.

**F3** advisable, wise.

**inane** *adj* senseless, foolish, stupid, unintelligent, silly, idiotic, fatuous, frivolous, trifling, puerile, mindless, vapid, empty, vacuous, vain, worthless, futile.

**F3** sensible.

**inanimate** *adj* lifeless, dead, defunct, extinct, unconscious, inactive, inert, dormant, immobile, stagnant, spiritless, dull.

**F3** animate, living, alive.

**inappropriate** *adj* unsuitable, inapt, ill-suited, ill-fitted, irrelevant,

incongruous, out of place, untimely, ill-timed, tactless, improper, unseemly, unbecoming, unfitting.

**F3** appropriate, suitable.

**inarticulate** *adj* incoherent, unintelligible, incomprehensible, unclear, indistinct, hesitant, faltering, halting, tongue-tied, speechless, dumb, mute.

**F3** articulate.

**inattention** *n* carelessness, negligence, disregard, absent-mindedness, forgetfulness, daydreaming, preoccupation.

**inattentive** *adj* distracted, dreamy, daydreaming, preoccupied, absent-minded, unmindful, heedless, regardless, careless, negligent.

**F3** attentive.

**inaudible** *adj* silent, noiseless, imperceptible, faint, indistinct, muffled, muted, low, mumbled.

**F3** audible, loud.

**inaugural** *adj* opening, introductory, first, initial.

**inaugurate** *v* institute, originate, begin, commence, start, set up, open, launch, introduce, usher in, initiate, induct, ordain, invest, install, commission, dedicate, consecrate.

**inauspicious** *adj* unfavourable, bad, unlucky, unfortunate, unpromising, discouraging, threatening, ominous, black.

**F3** auspicious, promising.

**inborn** *adj* innate, inherent, natural, native, congenital, inbred, hereditary, inherited, ingrained, instinctive, intuitive.

**F3** learned.

**incalculable** *adj* countless, untold, inestimable, limitless, unlimited, immense, vast.

**F3** limited, restricted.

**incapable** *adj* unable, powerless, impotent, helpless, weak, feeble, unfit, unsuited, unqualified, incompetent, inept, inadequate, ineffective.

capable.

**incapacitate** v disable, cripple, paralyse, immobilize, disqualify, put out of action, lay up, scupper (*infml*).

**incapacity** n incapability, inability, disability, powerlessness, impotence, ineffectiveness, weakness, feebleness, inadequacy, incompetency.
capability.

**incarnation** n personification, embodiment, manifestation, impersonation.

**incautious** adj careless, imprudent, injudicious, ill-judged, unthinking, thoughtless, inconsiderate, rash, reckless, hasty, impulsive.
cautious, careful.

**incense** v anger, enrage, infuriate, madden, exasperate, irritate, rile, provoke, excite.
calm.

**incentive** n bait, lure, enticement, carrot (*infml*), sweetener (*sl*), reward, encouragement, inducement, reason, motive, impetus, spur, stimulus, motivation.
disincentive, discouragement, deterrent.

**incessant** adj ceaseless, unceasing, endless, never-ending, interminable, continual, persistent, constant, perpetual, eternal, everlasting, continuous, unbroken, unremitting, non-stop.
intermittent, sporadic, periodic, temporary.

**incidence** n frequency, commonness, prevalence, extent, range, amount, degree, rate, occurrence.

**incident** n 1 OCCURRENCE, happening, event, episode, adventure, affair, occasion, instance. 2 CONFRONTATION, clash, fight, skirmish, commotion, disturbance, scene, upset, mishap.

**incidental** adj accidental, chance, random, minor, non-essential, secondary, subordinate, subsidiary, ancillary, supplementary, accompanying, attendant, related, contributory.
important, essential.

**incinerate** v burn, cremate, reduce to ashes.

**incision** n cut, opening, slit, gash, notch.

**incisive** adj cutting, keen, sharp, acute, trenchant, piercing, penetrating, biting, caustic, acid, astute, perceptive.
vague.

**incite** v prompt, instigate, rouse, foment, stir up, whip up, work up, excite, animate, provoke, stimulate, spur, goad, impel, drive, urge, encourage, egg on (*infml*).
restrain.

**incitement** n prompting, instigation, agitation, provocation, spur, goad, impetus, stimulus, motivation, encouragement, inducement, incentive.
discouragement.

**inclement** adj intemperate, harsh, severe, stormy, tempestuous, rough.
fine.

**inclination** n 1 LIKING, fondness, taste, predilection, preference, partiality, bias, tendency, trend, disposition, propensity, leaning. 2 *an inclination of 45 degrees:* angle, slope, gradient, incline, pitch, slant, tilt, bend, bow, nod.
1 disinclination, dislike.

**incline** v 1 DISPOSE, influence, persuade, affect, bias, prejudice. 2 LEAN, slope, slant, tilt, tip, bend, bow, tend, veer.
n slope, gradient, ramp, hill, rise, ascent, acclivity, dip, descent, declivity.

**inclined** adj liable, likely, given, apt, disposed of, a mind, willing.

**include** v comprise, incorporate, embody, comprehend, contain, enclose, embrace, encompass, cover, subsume, take in, add, allow for, take into account, involve, rope in.

☒ exclude, omit, eliminate.

**inclusion** *n* incorporation, involvement, addition, insertion.
☒ exclusion.

**inclusive** *adj* comprehensive, full, all-in, all-inclusive, all-embracing, blanket, across-the-board, general, catch-all, overall, sweeping.
☒ exclusive, narrow.

**incognito** *adj* in disguise, disguised, masked, veiled, unmarked, unidentified, unrecognizable, unknown.
☒ undisguised.

**incoherent** *adj* unintelligible, incomprehensible, inarticulate, rambling, stammering, stuttering, unconnected, disconnected, broken, garbled, scrambled, confused, muddled, jumbled, disordered.
☒ coherent, intelligible.

**income** *n* revenue, returns, proceeds, gains, profits, interest, takings, receipts, earnings, pay, salary, wages, means.
☒ expenditure, expenses.

**incoming** *adj* arriving, entering, approaching, coming, homeward, returning, ensuing, succeeding, next, new.
☒ outgoing.

**incomparable** *adj* matchless, unmatched, unequalled, unparalleled, unrivalled, peerless, supreme, superlative, superb, brilliant.
☒ ordinary, run-of-the-mill, poor.

**incompatible** *adj* irreconcilable, contradictory, conflicting, at variance, inconsistent, clashing, mismatched, unsuited.
☒ compatible.

**incompetent** *adj* incapable, unable, unfit, inefficient, inexpert, unskilful, bungling, stupid, useless, ineffective.
☒ competent, able.

**incomplete** *adj* deficient, lacking, short, unfinished, abridged, partial, part, fragmentary, broken, imperfect, defective.

☒ complete, exhaustive.

**incomprehensible** *adj* unintelligible, impenetrable, unfathomable, above one's head, puzzling, perplexing, baffling, mysterious, inscrutable, obscure, opaque.
☒ comprehensible, intelligible.

**inconceivable** *adj* unthinkable, unimaginable, mind-boggling (*infml*), staggering, unheard-of, unbelievable, incredible, implausible.
☒ conceivable.

**inconclusive** *adj* unsettled, undecided, open, uncertain, indecisive, ambiguous, vague, unconvincing, unsatisfying.
☒ conclusive.

**incongruous** *adj* inappropriate, unsuitable, out of place, out of keeping, inconsistent, conflicting, incompatible, irreconcilable, contradictory, contrary.
☒ consistent, compatible.

**inconsequential** *adj* minor, trivial, trifling, unimportant, insignificant, immaterial.
☒ important.

**inconsiderable** *adj* small, slight, negligible, trivial, petty, minor, unimportant, insignificant.
☒ considerable, large.

**inconsiderate** *adj* unkind, uncaring, unconcerned, selfish, self-centred, intolerant, insensitive, tactless, rude, thoughtless, unthinking, careless, heedless.
☒ considerate.

**inconsistent** *adj* **1** CONFLICTING, at variance, at odds, incompatible, contradictory, contrary, incongruous, discordant. **2** CHANGEABLE, variable, irregular, unpredictable, varying, unstable, unsteady, inconstant, fickle.
☒ **2** constant.

**inconsolable** *adj* heartbroken, brokenhearted, devastated, desolate, despairing, wretched.

**inconspicuous** adj hidden, concealed, camouflaged, plain, ordinary, unobtrusive, discreet, low-key, modest, unassuming, quiet, retiring, insignificant.
F3 conspicuous, noticeable, obtrusive.

**incontrovertible** adj indisputable, unquestionable, irrefutable, undeniable, certain, clear, self-evident.
F3 questionable, uncertain.

**inconvenience** n awkwardness, difficulty, annoyance, nuisance, hindrance, drawback, bother, trouble, fuss, upset, disturbance, disruption.
F3 convenience.
v bother, disturb, disrupt, put out, trouble, upset, irk.
F3 convenience.

**inconvenient** adj awkward, ill-timed, untimely, inopportune, unsuitable, difficult, embarrassing, annoying, troublesome, unwieldy, unmanageable.
F3 convenient.

**incorporate** v include, embody, contain, subsume, take in, absorb, assimilate, integrate, combine, unite, merge, blend, mix, fuse, coalesce, consolidate.
F3 separate.

**incorrect** adj wrong, mistaken, erroneous, inaccurate, imprecise, inexact, false, untrue, faulty, ungrammatical, improper, illegitimate, inappropriate, unsuitable.
F3 correct.

**incorrigible** adj irredeemable, incurable, inveterate, hardened, hopeless.

**incorruptible** adj honest, straight, upright, moral, honourable, trustworthy, unbribable, just.
F3 corruptible.

**increase** v raise, boost, add to, improve, enhance, advance, step up, intensify, strengthen, heighten, grow,

develop, build up, wax, enlarge, extend, prolong, expand, spread, swell, magnify, multiply, proliferate, rise, mount, soar, escalate.
F3 decrease, reduce, decline.
n rise, surge, upsurge, upturn, gain, boost, addition, increment, advance, step-up, intensification, growth, development, enlargement, extension, expansion, spread, proliferation, escalation.
F3 decrease, reduction, decline.

**incredible** adj unbelievable, improbable, implausible, far-fetched, preposterous, absurd, impossible, inconceivable, unthinkable, unimaginable, extraordinary, amazing, astonishing, astounding.
F3 credible, believable.

**incredulity** n unbelief, disbelief, scepticism, doubt, distrust, mistrust.
F3 credulity.

**incredulous** adj unbelieving, disbelieving, unconvinced, sceptical, doubting, distrustful, suspicious, dubious, doubtful, uncertain.
F3 credulous.

**incriminate** v inculpate, implicate, involve, accuse, charge, impeach, indict, point the finger at, blame.
F3 exonerate.

**incur** v suffer, sustain, provoke, arouse, bring upon oneself, expose oneself to, meet with, run up, gain, earn.

**incurable** adj **1** an incurable disease: terminal, fatal, untreatable, inoperable, hopeless. **2** INCORRIGIBLE, inveterate, hardened, dyed-in-the-wool.
F3 **1** curable.

**indebted** adj obliged, grateful, thankful.

**indecency** n immodesty, indecorum, impurity, obscenity, pornography, lewdness, vulgarity, coarseness, crudity, foulness, grossness.
F3 decency, modesty.

**indecent** adj improper, immodest,

impure, indelicate, offensive, obscene, pornographic, lewd, licentious, vulgar, coarse, crude, dirty, filthy, foul, gross, outrageous, shocking.
**Fa** decent, modest.

**indecision** *n* indecisiveness, irresolution, vacillation, wavering, hesitation, hesitancy, ambivalence, uncertainty, doubt.
**Fa** decisiveness, resolution.

**indecisive** *adj* undecided, irresolute, undetermined, vacillating, wavering, in two minds, hesitating, faltering, tentative, uncertain, unsure, doubtful, inconclusive, indefinite, indeterminate, unclear.
**Fa** decisive.

**indeed** *adv* really, actually, in fact, certainly, positively, truly, undeniably, undoubtedly, to be sure.

**indefensible** *adj* unjustifiable, inexcusable, unforgivable, unpardonable, insupportable, untenable, wrong, faulty.
**Fa** defensible, excusable.

**indefinite** *adj* unknown, uncertain, unsettled, unresolved, undecided, undetermined, undefined, unspecified, unlimited, ill-defined, vague, indistinct, unclear, obscure, ambiguous, imprecise, inexact, loose, general.
**Fa** definite, limited, clear.

**indefinitely** *adv* for ever, eternally, endlessly, continually, ad infinitum.

**indelible** *adj* lasting, enduring, permanent, fast, ineffaceable, ingrained, indestructible.
**Fa** erasable.

**indemnity** *n* compensation, reimbursement, remuneration, reparation, insurance, guarantee, security, protection, immunity, amnesty.

**indentation** *n* notch, nick, cut, serration, dent, groove, furrow, depression, dip, hollow, pit, dimple.

**independence** *n* autonomy, self-

government, self-determination, self-rule, home rule, sovereignty, freedom, liberty, individualism, separation.
**Fa** dependence.

**independent** *adj* **1** AUTONOMOUS, self-governing, self-determining, sovereign, absolute, non-aligned, neutral, impartial, unbiased. **2** FREE, liberated, unconstrained, individualistic, unconventional, self-sufficient, self-supporting, self-reliant, unaided. **3** INDIVIDUAL, self-contained, separate, unconnected, unrelated.
**Fa** **1** dependent.

**indescribable** *adj* indefinable, inexpressible, unutterable, unspeakable.
**Fa** describable.

**indestructible** *adj* unbreakable, durable, tough, strong, lasting, enduring, abiding, permanent, eternal, everlasting, immortal, imperishable.
**Fa** breakable, mortal.

**indeterminate** *adj* unspecified, unstated, undefined, unfixed, imprecise, inexact, indefinite, vague, open-ended, undecided, undetermined, uncertain.
**Fa** known, specified, fixed.

**index** *n* **1** *index of names*: table, key, list, catalogue, directory, guide. **2** INDICATOR, pointer, needle, hand, sign, token, mark, indication, clue.

**indicate** *v* register, record, show, reveal, display, manifest, point to, designate, specify, point out, mark, signify, mean, denote, express, suggest, imply.

**indication** *n* mark, sign, manifestation, evidence, symptom, signal, warning, omen, intimation, suggestion, hint, clue, note, explanation.

**indicator** *n* pointer, needle, marker, sign, symbol, token, signal, display, dial, gauge, meter, index, guide, signpost.

**indict** v charge, accuse, arraign, impeach, summon, summons, prosecute, incriminate.
☒ exonerate.

**indifference** n apathy, unconcern, coldness, coolness, inattention, disregard, negligence, neutrality, disinterestedness.
☒ interest, concern.

**indifferent** adj **1** UNINTERESTED, unenthusiastic, unexcited, apathetic, unconcerned, unmoved, uncaring, unsympathetic, cold, cool, distant, aloof, detached, uninvolved, neutral, disinterested. **2** MEDIOCRE, average, middling, passable, moderate, fair, ordinary.
☒ **1** interested, caring. **2** excellent.

**indigenous** adj native, aboriginal, original, local, home-grown.
☒ foreign.

**indignant** adj annoyed, angry, irate, heated, fuming, livid, furious, incensed, infuriated, exasperated, outraged.
☒ pleased, delighted.

**indignation** n annoyance, anger, ire, wrath, rage, fury, exasperation, outrage, scorn, contempt.
☒ pleasure, delight.

**indirect** adj **1** ROUNDABOUT, circuitous, wandering, rambling, winding, meandering, zigzag, tortuous. **2** an indirect effect: secondary, incidental, unintended, subsidiary, ancillary.
☒ **1** direct. **2** primary.

**indiscreet** adj tactless, undiplomatic, impolitic, injudicious, imprudent, unwise, foolish, rash, reckless, hasty, careless, heedless, unthinking.
☒ discreet, cautious.

**indiscretion** n mistake, error, slip, boob (infml), faux pas, gaffe, tactlessness, rashness, recklessness, foolishness, folly.

**indiscriminate** adj general,

sweeping, wholesale, random, haphazard, hit or miss, aimless, unsystematic, unmethodical, mixed, motley, miscellaneous.
☒ selective, specific, precise.

**indispensable** adj vital, essential, basic, key, crucial, imperative, required, requisite, needed, necessary.
☒ dispensable, unnecessary.

**indisposed** adj ill, sick, unwell, poorly, ailing, laid up.
☒ well.

**indisputable** adj incontrovertible, unquestionable, irrefutable, undeniable, absolute, undisputed, definite, positive, certain, sure.
☒ doubtful.

**indistinct** adj unclear, ill-defined, blurred, fuzzy, misty, hazy, shadowy, obscure, dim, faint, muffled, confused, unintelligible, vague, woolly, ambiguous, indefinite.
☒ distinct, clear.

**individual** n person, being, creature, party, body, soul, character, fellow. adj distinctive, characteristic, idiosyncratic, peculiar, singular, unique, exclusive, special, personal, own, proper, respective, several, separate, distinct, specific, personalized, particular, single.
☒ collective, shared, general.

**individuality** n character, personality, distinctiveness, peculiarity, singularity, uniqueness, separateness, distinction.
☒ sameness.

**indoctrinate** v brainwash, teach, instruct, school, ground, train, drill.

**induce** v **1** CAUSE, effect, bring about, occasion, give rise to, lead to, incite, instigate, prompt, provoke, produce, generate. **2** COAX, prevail upon, encourage, press, persuade, talk into, move, influence, draw, tempt.
☒ **2** discourage, deter.

**inducement** n lure, bait, attraction,

enticement, encouragement, incentive, reward, spur, stimulus, motive, reason.
**F3** disincentive.

**indulge** v gratify, satisfy, humour, pander to, go along with, give in to, yield to, favour, pet, cosset, mollycoddle, pamper, spoil, treat, regale.

**indulgence** n extravagance, luxury, excess, immoderation, intemperance, favour, tolerance.

**indulgent** adj tolerant, easy-going (*infml*), lenient, permissive, generous, liberal, kind, fond, tender, understanding, patient.
**F3** strict, harsh.

**industrialist** n manufacturer, producer, magnate, tycoon, baron, captain of industry, capitalist, financier.

**industrious** adj busy, productive, hard-working, diligent, assiduous, conscientious, zealous, active, energetic, tireless, persistent, persevering.
**F3** lazy, idle.

**industry** n **1** *the steel industry*: business, trade, commerce, manufacturing, production.
**2** INDUSTRIOUSNESS, diligence, application, effort, labour, toil, persistence, perseverance, determination.

**inebriated** adj drunk, intoxicated, tipsy, merry.
**F3** sober.

**inedible** adj uneatable, unpalatable, indigestible, harmful, noxious, poisonous, deadly.
**F3** edible.

**ineffective** adj useless, worthless, vain, idle, futile, unavailing, fruitless, unproductive, unsuccessful, powerless, impotent, ineffectual, inadequate, weak, feeble, inept, incompetent.
**F3** effective, effectual.

**inefficient** adj uneconomic,

wasteful, money-wasting, time-wasting, incompetent, inexpert, unworkmanlike, slipshod, sloppy, careless, negligent.
**F3** efficient.

**inelegant** adj graceless, ungraceful, clumsy, awkward, laboured, ugly, unrefined, crude, unpolished, rough, unsophisticated, uncultivated, uncouth.
**F3** elegant.

**ineligible** adj disqualified, ruled out, unacceptable, undesirable, unworthy, unsuitable, unfit, unqualified, unequipped.
**F3** eligible.

**inept** adj awkward, clumsy, bungling, incompetent, unskilful, inexpert, foolish, stupid.
**F3** competent, skilful.

**inequality** n unequalness, difference, diversity, dissimilarity, disparity, unevenness, disproportion, bias, prejudice.
**F3** equality.

**inert** adj immobile, motionless, unmoving, still, inactive, inanimate, lifeless, dead, passive, unresponsive, apathetic, dormant, idle, lazy, lethargic, sluggish, torpid, sleepy.
**F3** lively, animated.

**inertia** n immobility, stillness, inactivity, passivity, unresponsiveness, apathy, idleness, laziness, lethargy, torpor.
**F3** activity, liveliness.

**inescapable** adj inevitable, unavoidable, destined, fated, certain, sure, irrevocable, unalterable.
**F3** escapable.

**inevitable** adj unavoidable, inescapable, necessary, definite, certain, sure, decreed, ordained, destined, fated, automatic, assured, fixed, unalterable, irrevocable, inexorable.
**F3** avoidable, uncertain, alterable.

**inexcusable** adj indefensible, unforgivable, unpardonable,

intolerable, unacceptable, outrageous, shameful, blameworthy, reprehensible.
**Ea** excusable, justifiable.

**inexhaustible** adj **1** an inexhaustible supply: unlimited, limitless, boundless, unbounded, infinite, endless, never-ending, abundant. **2** INDEFATIGABLE, tireless, untiring, unflagging, unwearied, unwearying.
**Ea** 1 limited.

**inexpensive** adj cheap, low-priced, reasonable, modest, bargain, budget, low-cost, economical.
**Ea** expensive, dear.

**inexperience** n inexpertness, ignorance, unfamiliarity, strangeness, newness, rawness, naïveness, innocence.
**Ea** experience.

**inexperienced** adj inexpert, untrained, unskilled, amateur, probationary, apprentice, unacquainted, unfamiliar, unaccustomed, new, fresh, raw, callow, young, immature, naïve, unsophisticated, innocent.
**Ea** experienced, mature.

**inexplicable** adj unexplainable, unaccountable, strange, mystifying, puzzling, baffling, mysterious, enigmatic, unfathomable, incomprehensible, incredible, unbelievable, miraculous.
**Ea** explicable.

**inexpressive** adj unexpressive, expressionless, deadpan, inscrutable, blank, vacant, empty, emotionless, impassive.
**Ea** expressive.

**infallible** adj accurate, unerring, unfailing, foolproof, fail-safe, sure-fire (infml), certain, sure, reliable, dependable, trustworthy, sound, perfect, faultless, impeccable.
**Ea** fallible.

**infamous** adj notorious, ill-famed, disreputable, disgraceful, shameful,

shocking, outrageous, scandalous, wicked, iniquitous.
**Ea** illustrious, glorious.

**infamy** n notoriety, disrepute, disgrace, shame, dishonour, discredit, ignominy, wickedness.
**Ea** glory.

**infancy** n **1** BABYHOOD, childhood, youth. **2** BEGINNING, start, commencement, inception, outset, birth, dawn, genesis, emergence, origins, early stages.
**Ea** 1 adulthood.

**infant** n baby, toddler, tot (infml), child, babe (fml), babe in arms (fml).
**Ea** adult.
adj newborn, baby, young, youthful, juvenile, immature, growing, developing, rudimentary, early, initial, new.
**Ea** adult, mature.

**infantile** adj babyish, childish, puerile, juvenile, young, youthful, adolescent, immature.
**Ea** adult, mature.

**infatuated** adj besotted, obsessed, enamoured, smitten (infml), crazy (infml), spellbound, mesmerized, captivated, fascinated, enraptured, ravished.
**Ea** indifferent, disenchanted.

**infatuation** n besottedness, obsession, fixation, passion, crush (sl), love, fondness, fascination.
**Ea** indifference, disenchantment.

**infect** v contaminate, pollute, defile, taint, blight, poison, corrupt, pervert, influence, affect, touch, inspire.

**infection** n illness, disease, virus, epidemic, contagion, pestilence, contamination, pollution, defilement, taint, blight, poison, corruption, influence.

**infectious** adj contagious, communicable, transmissible, infective, catching, spreading, epidemic, virulent, deadly, contaminating, polluting, defiling, corrupting.

**infer** v derive, extrapolate, deduce, conclude, assume, presume, surmise, gather, understand.

**inference** n deduction, conclusion, corollary, consequence, assumption, presumption, surmise, conjecture, extrapolation, construction, interpretation, reading.

**inferior** adj **1** LOWER, lesser, minor, secondary, junior, subordinate, subsidiary, second-class, low, humble, menial. **2** inferior work: substandard, second-rate, mediocre, bad, poor, unsatisfactory, slipshod, shoddy.
**Ea 1** superior. **2** excellent.
n subordinate, junior, underling (infml), minion, vassal, menial.
**Ea** superior.

**inferiority** n **1** SUBORDINATION, subservience, humbleness, lowliness, meanness, insignificance.
**2** MEDIOCRITY, imperfection, inadequacy, slovenliness, shoddiness.
**Ea 1** superiority. **2** excellence.

**infernal** adj hellish, satanic, devilish, diabolical, fiendish, accursed, damned.
**Ea** heavenly.

**infertile** adj barren, sterile, childless, unproductive, unfruitful, arid, parched, dried-up.
**Ea** fertile, fruitful.

**infest** v swarm, teem, throng, flood, overrun, invade, infiltrate, penetrate, permeate, pervade, ravage.

**infidelity** n adultery, unfaithfulness, faithlessness, disloyalty, duplicity, treachery, betrayal, cheating, falseness.
**Ea** fidelity, faithfulness.

**infiltrate** v penetrate, enter, creep into, insinuate, intrude, pervade, permeate, filter, percolate.

**infinite** adj limitless, unlimited, boundless, unbounded, endless, never-ending, inexhaustible, bottomless, innumerable, numberless, uncountable, countless, untold, incalculable, inestimable, immeasurable, unfathomable, vast, immense, enormous, huge, absolute, total.
**Ea** finite, limited.

**infinitesimal** adj tiny, minute, microscopic, minuscule, inconsiderable, insignificant, negligible, inappreciable, imperceptible.
**Ea** great, large, enormous.

**infinity** n eternity, perpetuity, limitlessness, boundlessness, endlessness, inexhaustibility, countlessness, immeasurableness, vastness, immensity.
**Ea** finiteness, limitation.

**infirm** adj weak, feeble, frail, ill, unwell, poorly, sickly, failing, faltering, unsteady, shaky, wobbly, doddery, lame.
**Ea** healthy, strong.

**inflame** v anger, enrage, infuriate, incense, exasperate, madden, provoke, stimulate, excite, rouse, arouse, agitate, foment, kindle, ignite, fire, heat, fan, increase, intensify, worsen, aggravate.
**Ea** cool, quench.

**inflamed** adj sore, swollen, septic, infected, poisoned, red, hot, heated, fevered, feverish.

**inflammable** adj flammable, combustible, burnable.
**Ea** non-flammable, incombustible, flameproof.

**inflammation** n soreness, painfulness, tenderness, swelling, abscess, infection, redness, heat, rash, sore, irritation.

**inflate** v blow up, pump up, blow out, puff out, swell, distend, bloat, expand, enlarge, increase, boost, exaggerate.
**Ea** deflate.

**inflation** n expansion, increase, rise, escalation, hyperinflation.
**Ea** deflation.

**inflexible** adj rigid, stiff, hard, solid,

set, fixed, fast, immovable, firm, strict, stringent, unbending, unyielding, adamant, resolute, relentless, implacable, uncompromising, stubborn, obstinate, intransigent, entrenched, dyed-in-the-wool.

**F3** flexible, yielding, adaptable.

**inflict** *v* impose, enforce, perpetrate, wreak, administer, apply, deliver, deal, mete out, lay, burden, exact, levy.

**influence** *n* power, sway, rule, authority, domination, mastery, hold, control, direction, guidance, bias, prejudice, pull, pressure, effect, impact, weight, importance, prestige, standing.

*v* dominate, control, manipulate, direct, guide, manoeuvre, change, alter, modify, affect, impress, move, stir, arouse, rouse, sway, persuade, induce, incite, instigate, prompt, motivate, dispose, incline, bias, prejudice, predispose.

**influential** *adj* dominant, controlling, leading, authoritative, charismatic, persuasive, convincing, compelling, inspiring, moving, powerful, potent, effective, telling, strong, weighty, momentous, important, significant, instrumental, guiding.

**F3** ineffective, unimportant.

**influx** *n* inflow, inrush, invasion, arrival, stream, flow, rush, flood, inundation.

**inform** *v* tell, advise, notify, communicate, impart, leak, tip off, acquaint, fill in (*infml*), brief, instruct, enlighten, illuminate.

**inform on** betray, incriminate, shop (*sl*), tell on (*infml*), squeal (*sl*), blab, grass (*sl*), denounce.

**informal** *adj* unofficial, unceremonious, casual, relaxed, easy, free, natural, simple, unpretentious, familiar, colloquial.

**F3** formal, solemn.

**information** *n* facts, data, input, gen (*infml*), bumf (*sl*), intelligence, news, report, bulletin, communiqué, message, word, advice, notice, briefing, instruction, knowledge, dossier, database, databank, clues, evidence.

**informative** *adj* educational, instructive, edifying, enlightening, illuminating, revealing, forthcoming, communicative, chatty, gossipy, newsy, helpful, useful, constructive.

**F3** uninformative.

**informed** *adj* **1** *we'll keep you informed*: familiar, conversant, acquainted, enlightened, briefed, primed, posted, up to date, abreast, au fait, in the know (*infml*). **2** *an informed opinion*: well-informed, authoritative, expert, versed, well-read, erudite, learned, knowledgeable, well-researched.

**F3** **1** ignorant, unaware.

**informer** *n* informant, grass (*sl*), supergrass (*sl*), betrayer, traitor, Judas, tell-tale, sneak, spy, mole (*infml*).

**infringe** *v* **1** BREAK, violate, contravene, transgress, overstep, disobey, defy, flout, ignore. **2** INTRUDE, encroach, trespass, invade.

**infuriate** *v* anger, vex, enrage, incense, exasperate, madden, provoke, rouse, annoy, irritate, rile, antagonize.

**F3** calm, pacify.

**ingenious** *adj* clever, shrewd, cunning, crafty, skilful, masterly, imaginative, creative, inventive, resourceful, original, innovative.

**F3** unimaginative.

**ingenuous** *adj* artless, guileless, innocent, honest, sincere, frank, open, plain, simple, unsophisticated, naïve, trusting.

**F3** artful, sly.

**ingrained** *adj* fixed, rooted, deep-rooted, deep-seated, entrenched, immovable, ineradicable, permanent, inbuilt, inborn, inbred.

**ingratiate** v curry favour, flatter, creep, crawl, grovel, fawn, get in with.

**ingratitude** n ungratefulness, thanklessness, unappreciativeness, ungraciousness.
Ⓔ gratitude, thankfulness.

**ingredient** n constituent, element, factor, component, part.

**inhabit** v live, dwell, reside, occupy, possess, colonize, settle, people, populate, stay.

**inhabitant** n resident, dweller, citizen, native, occupier, occupant, inmate, tenant, lodger.

**inherent** adj inborn, inbred, innate, inherited, hereditary, native, natural, inbuilt, built-in, intrinsic, ingrained, essential, fundamental, basic.

**inherit** v succeed to, accede to, assume, come into, be left, receive.

**inheritance** n legacy, bequest, heritage, birthright, heredity, descent, succession.

**inheritor** n heir, heiress, successor, beneficiary, recipient.

**inhibit** v discourage, repress, hold back, suppress, curb, check, restrain, hinder, impede, obstruct, interfere with, frustrate, thwart, prevent, stop, stanch, stem.
Ⓔ encourage, assist.

**inhibited** adj repressed, self-conscious, shy, reticent, withdrawn, reserved, guarded, subdued.
Ⓔ uninhibited, open, relaxed.

**inhibition** n repression, hang-up (sl), self-consciousness, shyness, reticence, reserve, restraint, curb, check, hindrance, impediment, obstruction, bar.
Ⓔ freedom.

**inhuman** adj barbaric, barbarous, animal, bestial, vicious, savage, sadistic, cold-blooded, brutal, cruel, inhumane.
Ⓔ human.

**inhumane** adj unkind, insensitive, callous, unfeeling, heartless, cold-hearted, hard-hearted, pitiless, ruthless, cruel, brutal, inhuman.
Ⓔ humane, kind, compassionate.

**initial** adj first, beginning, opening, introductory, inaugural, original, primary, early, formative.
Ⓔ final, last.

**initially** adv at first, at the beginning, to begin with, to start with, originally, first, firstly, first of all.
Ⓔ finally, in the end.

**initiate** v begin, start, commence, originate, pioneer, institute, set up, introduce, launch, open, inaugurate, instigate, activate, trigger, prompt, stimulate, cause.

**initiation** n admission, reception, entrance, entry, debut, introduction, enrolment, induction, investiture, installation, inauguration, inception.

**initiative** n 1 ENERGY, drive, dynamism, get-up-and-go (infml), ambition, enterprise, resourcefulness, inventiveness, originality, innovativeness. 2 SUGGESTION, recommendation, action, lead, first move, first step.

**inject** v 1 inject drugs: inoculate, vaccinate, shoot (sl). 2 INTRODUCE, insert, add, bring, infuse, instil.

**injection** n inoculation, vaccination, jab (infml), shot (infml), fix (sl), dose, insertion, introduction.

**injunction** n command, order, directive, ruling, mandate, direction, instruction, precept.

**injure** v hurt, harm, damage, impair, spoil, mar, ruin, disfigure, deface, mutilate, wound, cut, break, fracture, maim, disable, cripple, lame, ill-treat, maltreat, abuse, offend, wrong, upset, put out.

**injury** n wound, cut, lesion, fracture, trauma, hurt, mischief, ill, harm, damage, impairment, ruin, disfigurement, mutilation, ill-treatment, abuse, insult, offence, wrong, injustice.

**injustice** n unfairness, inequality, disparity, discrimination, oppression, bias, prejudice, one-sidedness, partisanship, partiality, favouritism, wrong, iniquity.
**F3** justice, fairness.

**inkling** n suspicion, idea, notion, faintest (*infml*), glimmering, clue, hint, intimation, suggestion, allusion, indication, sign, pointer.

**inlet** n bay, cove, creek, fiord, opening, entrance, passage.

**inn** n public house, pub (*infml*), local (*infml*), tavern, hostelry, hotel.

**innate** adj inborn, inbred, inherent, intrinsic, native, natural, instinctive, intuitive.
**F3** acquired, learnt.

**inner** adj internal, interior, inside, inward, innermost, central, middle, concealed, hidden, secret, private, personal, intimate, mental, psychological, spiritual, emotional.
**F3** outer, outward.

**innocence** n **1** GUILTLESSNESS, blamelessness, honesty, virtue, righteousness, purity, chastity, virginity, incorruptibility, harmlessness, innocuousness.
**2** ARTLESSNESS, guilelessness, naïveness, inexperience, ignorance, naturalness, simplicity, unsophistication, unworldliness, credulity, gullibility, trustfulness.
**F3 1** guilt. **2** experience.

**innocent** adj **1** *innocent of the crime*: guiltless, blameless, irreproachable, unimpeachable, honest, upright, virtuous, righteous, sinless, faultless, impeccable, stainless, spotless, immaculate, unsullied, untainted, uncontaminated, pure, chaste, virginal, incorrupt, inoffensive, harmless, innocuous. **2** ARTLESS, guileless, ingenuous, naïve, green, inexperienced, fresh, natural, simple, unsophisticated, unworldly, childlike,

credulous, gullible, trusting.
**F3 1** guilty. **2** experienced.

**innocuous** adj harmless, safe, inoffensive, unobjectionable, innocent.
**F3** harmful.

**innovation** n newness, novelty, neologism, modernization, progress, reform, change, alteration, variation, departure.

**innovative** adj new, fresh, original, creative, imaginative, inventive, resourceful, enterprising, go-ahead, progressive, reforming, bold, daring, adventurous.
**F3** conservative, unimaginative.

**innuendo** n insinuation, aspersion, slur, whisper, hint, intimation, suggestion, implication.

**innumerable** adj numberless, unnumbered, countless, uncountable, untold, incalculable, infinite, numerous, many.

**inoculation** n vaccination, immunization, protection, injection, shot (*infml*), jab (*infml*).

**inoffensive** adj harmless, innocuous, innocent, peaceable, mild, unobtrusive, unassertive, quiet, retiring.
**F3** offensive, harmful, provocative.

**inordinate** adj excessive, immoderate, unwarranted, undue, unreasonable, disproportionate, great.
**F3** moderate, reasonable.

**inquire, enquire** v ASK, question, quiz, query, investigate, look into, probe, examine, inspect, scrutinize, search, explore.

**inquiry, enquiry** n question, query, investigation, inquest, hearing, inquisition, examination, inspection, scrutiny, study, survey, poll, search, probe, exploration.

**inquisitive** adj curious, questioning, probing, searching, prying, peeping, snooping, nosey, interfering, meddlesome, intrusive.

**insane** adj **1** MAD, crazy, mentally ill, lunatic, mental (sl), demented, deranged, unhinged, disturbed. **2** FOOLISH, stupid, senseless, impractical.

F3 **1** sane. **2** sensible.

**insanity** n madness, craziness, lunacy, mental illness, neurosis, psychosis, mania, dementia, derangement, folly, stupidity, senselessness, irresponsibility.

F3 sanity.

**insatiable** adj unquenchable, unsatisfiable, ravenous, voracious, immoderate, inordinate.

**inscribe** v engrave, etch, carve, cut, incise, imprint, impress, stamp, print, write, sign, autograph, dedicate.

**inscription** n engraving, epitaph, caption, legend, lettering, words, writing, signature, autograph, dedication.

**inscrutable** adj incomprehensible, unfathomable, impenetrable, deep, inexplicable, unexplainable, baffling, mysterious, enigmatic, cryptic, hidden.

F3 comprehensible, expressive.

**insect**

> *Insects include*: fly, gnat, midge, mosquito, tsetse-fly, locust, dragonfly, cranefly, daddy longlegs (*infml*), horsefly, mayfly, butterfly, red admiral, cabbage-white, moth, tiger moth, bee, bumblebee, wasp, hornet, aphid, blackfly, greenfly, whitefly, froghopper, ladybird, water boatman, lacewing, beetle, cockroach, roach (*US*), earwig, stick insect, grasshopper, cricket, cicada, flea, louse, nit, leatherjacket, termite, glowworm, woodworm, weevil, woodlouse.
> *Arachnids include*: spider, black widow, tarantula, scorpion, mite, tick.

> *Parts of an insect*: abdomen, antenna, cercus, compound eye,

> forewing, head, hindwing, legs, mandible, mouthpart, ocellus, ovipositor, segment, spiracle, thorax.

**insecure** adj **1** ANXIOUS, worried, nervous, uncertain, unsure, afraid. **2** UNSAFE, dangerous, hazardous; perilous, precarious, unsteady, shaky, loose, unprotected, defenceless, exposed, vulnerable.

F3 **1** confident, self-assured. **2** secure, safe.

**insensible** adj numb, anaesthetized, dead, cold, insensitive, unresponsive, blind, deaf, unconscious, unaware, oblivious, unmindful.

F3 conscious.

**insensitive** adj hardened, tough, resistant, impenetrable, impervious, immune, unsusceptible, thick-skinned, unfeeling, impassive, indifferent, unaffected, unmoved, untouched, uncaring, unconcerned, callous, thoughtless, tactless, crass.

F3 sensitive.

**inseparable** adj indivisible, indissoluble, inextricable, close, intimate, bosom, devoted.

F3 separable.

**insert** v put, place, put in, stick in, push in, introduce, implant, embed, engraft, set, inset, let in, interleave, intercalate, interpolate, interpose. n insertion, enclosure, inset, notice, advertisement, supplement, addition.

**inside** n interior, content, contents, middle, centre, heart, core.

F3 outside.

adv within, indoors, internally, inwardly, secretly, privately.

F3 outside.

adj interior, internal, inner, innermost, inward, secret, classified, confidential, private.

**insides** n entrails, guts, intestines, bowels, innards (*infml*), organs, viscera, belly, stomach.

**insidious** adj subtle, sly, crafty, cunning, wily, deceptive, devious, stealthy, surreptitious, furtive, sneaking, treacherous.

**F3** direct, straightforward.

**insight** n awareness, knowledge, comprehension, understanding, grasp, apprehension, perception, intuition, sensitivity, discernment, judgement, acumen, penetration, observation, vision, wisdom, intelligence.

**insignificant** adj unimportant, irrelevant, meaningless, inconsequential, minor, trivial, trifling, petty, paltry, small, tiny, insubstantial, inconsiderable, negligible, non-essential.

**F3** significant, important.

**insincere** adj hypocritical, two-faced, double-dealing, lying, untruthful, dishonest, deceitful, devious, unfaithful, faithless, untrue, false, feigned, pretended, phoney (*infml*), hollow.

**F3** sincere.

**insinuate** v imply, suggest, allude, hint, intimate, get at (*infml*), indicate.

**insipid** adj tasteless, flavourless, unsavoury, unappetizing, watery, weak, bland, wishy-washy (*infml*), colourless, drab, dull, monotonous, boring, uninteresting, tame, flat, lifeless, spiritless, characterless, trite, unimaginative, dry.

**F3** tasty, spicy, piquant, appetizing.

**insist** v demand, require, urge, stress, emphasize, repeat, reiterate, dwell on, harp on, assert, maintain, claim, contend, hold, vow, swear, persist, stand firm.

**insistence** n demand, entreaty, exhortation, urging, stress, emphasis, repetition, reiteration, assertion, claim, contention, persistence, determination, resolution, firmness.

**insistent** adj demanding, importunate, emphatic, forceful, pressing, urgent, dogged, tenacious, persistent, persevering, relentless, unrelenting, unremitting, incessant.

**insolent** adj rude, abusive, insulting, disrespectful, cheeky (*infml*), impertinent, impudent, saucy (*infml*), bold, forward, fresh, presumptuous, arrogant, defiant, insubordinate.

**F3** polite, respectful.

**insoluble** adj unsolvable, unexplainable, inexplicable, incomprehensible, unfathomable, impenetrable, obscure, mystifying, puzzling, perplexing, baffling.

**F3** explicable.

**insolvent** adj bankrupt, bust, failed, ruined, broke (*infml*), penniless, destitute.

**F3** solvent.

**inspect** v check, vet, look over, examine, search, investigate, scrutinize, study, scan, survey, superintend, supervise, oversee, visit.

**inspection** n check, check-up, examination, scrutiny, scan, study, survey, review, search, investigation, supervision, visit.

**inspector** n supervisor, superintendent, overseer, surveyor, controller, scrutineer, checker, tester, examiner, investigator, reviewer, critic.

**inspiration** n 1 CREATIVITY, imagination, genius, muse, influence, encouragement, stimulation, motivation, spur, stimulus. 2 IDEA, brainwave, insight, illumination, revelation, awakening.

**inspire** v encourage, hearten, influence, impress, animate, enliven, quicken, galvanize, fire, kindle, stir, arouse, trigger, spark off, prompt, spur, motivate, provoke, stimulate, excite, exhilarate, thrill, enthral, enthuse, imbue, infuse.

**inspiring** adj encouraging, heartening, uplifting, invigorating, stirring, rousing, stimulating, exciting, exhilarating, thrilling, enthralling, moving, affecting, memorable, impressive.

**F3** uninspiring, dull.

**instability** n unsteadiness, shakiness, vacillation, wavering, irresolution, uncertainty, unpredictability, changeableness, variability, fluctuation, volatility, capriciousness, fickleness, inconstancy, unreliability, insecurity, unsafeness, unsoundness.
**F3** stability.

**install** v fix, fit, lay, put, place, position, locate, site, situate, station, plant, settle, establish, set up, introduce, institute, inaugurate, invest, induct, ordain.

**instalment** n **1** *pay in instalments*: payment, repayment, portion. **2** EPISODE, chapter, part, section, division.

**instant** n flash, twinkling, trice, moment, tick (*infml*), split second, second, minute, time, occasion. *adj* instantaneous, immediate, on-the-spot, direct, prompt, urgent, unhesitating, quick, fast, rapid, swift.
**F3** slow.

**instead** adv alternatively, preferably, rather.
**instead of** in place of, in lieu of, on behalf of, in preference to, rather than.

**instigate** v initiate, set on, start, begin, cause, generate, inspire, move, influence, encourage, urge, spur, prompt, provoke, stimulate, incite, stir up, whip up, foment, rouse, excite.

**instil** v infuse, imbue, insinuate, introduce, inject, implant, inculcate, impress, din into (*infml*).

**instinct** n intuition, sixth sense, gut reaction (*infml*), impulse, urge, feeling, hunch, flair, knack, gift, talent, feel, faculty, ability, aptitude, predisposition, tendency.

**instinctive** adj natural, native, inborn, innate, inherent, intuitive, impulsive, involuntary, automatic, mechanical, reflex, spontaneous, immediate, unthinking, unpremeditated, gut (*infml*), visceral.

**F3** conscious, voluntary, deliberate.

**institute** v originate, initiate, introduce, enact, begin, start, commence, create, establish, set up, organize, found, inaugurate, open, launch, appoint, install, invest, induct, ordain.
**F3** cancel, discontinue, abolish. n school, college, academy, conservatory, foundation, institution.

**institution** n **1** CUSTOM, tradition, usage, practice, ritual, convention, rule, law. **2** ORGANIZATION, association, society, guild, concern, corporation, foundation, establishment, institute, hospital, home. **3** INITIATION, introduction, enactment, inception, creation, establishment, formation, founding, foundation, installation.

**instruct** v **1** TEACH, educate, tutor, coach, train, drill, ground, school, discipline. **2** ORDER, command, direct, mandate, tell, inform, notify, advise, counsel, guide.

**instruction** n **1** *follow the instructions*: direction, recommendation, advice, guidance, information, order, command, injunction, mandate, directive, ruling. **2** EDUCATION, schooling, lesson(s), tuition, teaching, training, coaching, drilling, grounding, preparation.

**instructive** adj informative, educational, edifying, enlightening, illuminating, helpful, useful.
**F3** unenlightening.

**instructor** n teacher, master, mistress, tutor, coach, trainer, demonstrator, exponent, adviser, mentor, guide, guru.

**instrument** n **1** TOOL, implement, utensil, appliance, gadget, contraption, device, contrivance, apparatus, mechanism. **2** AGENT, agency, vehicle, organ, medium, factor, channel, way, means.

**instrumental** adj active, involved,

contributory, conducive, influential, useful, helpful, auxiliary, subsidiary.
**F3** obstructive, unhelpful.

**insufferable** *adj* intolerable, unbearable, detestable, loathsome, dreadful, impossible.
**F3** pleasant, tolerable.

**insufficiency** *n* inadequacy, shortage, deficiency, lack, scarcity, dearth, want, need, poverty.
**F3** sufficiency, excess.

**insufficient** *adj* inadequate, short, deficient, lacking, sparse, scanty, scarce.
**F3** sufficient, excessive.

**insular** *adj* parochial, provincial, cut off, detached, isolated, remote, withdrawn, inward-looking, blinkered, closed, narrow-minded, narrow, limited, petty.

**insulate** *v* cushion, pad, lag, cocoon, protect, shield, shelter, isolate, separate, cut off.

**insult** *v* abuse, call names, disparage, revile, libel, slander, slight, snub, injure, affront, offend, outrage.
**F3** compliment, praise.
*n* abuse, rudeness, insolence, defamation, libel, slander, slight, snub, affront, indignity, offence, outrage.
**F3** compliment, praise.

**insurance** *n* cover, protection, safeguard, security, provision, assurance, indemnity, guarantee, warranty, policy, premium.

**insure** *v* cover, protect, assure, underwrite, indemnify, guarantee, warrant.

**insurmountable** *adj* insuperable, unconquerable, invincible, overwhelming, hopeless, impossible.
**F3** surmountable.

**insurrection** *n* rising, uprising, insurgence, riot, rebellion, mutiny, revolt, revolution, coup, putsch.

**intact** *adj* unbroken, all in one piece, whole, complete, integral, entire, perfect, sound, undamaged, unhurt,
uninjured.
**F3** broken, incomplete, damaged.

**intangible** *adj* insubstantial, imponderable, elusive, fleeting, airy, shadowy, vague, indefinite, abstract, unreal, invisible.
**F3** tangible, real.

**integral** *adj* **1** *an integral part*: intrinsic, constituent, elemental, basic, fundamental, necessary, essential, indispensable.
**2** COMPLETE, entire, full, whole, undivided.
**F3 1** extra, additional, unnecessary.

**integrate** *v* assimilate, merge, join, unite, combine, amalgamate, incorporate, coalesce, fuse, knit, mesh, mix, blend, harmonize.
**F3** divide, separate.

**integrity** *n* **1** HONESTY, uprightness, probity, incorruptibility, purity, morality, principle, honour, virtue, goodness, righteousness.
**2** COMPLETENESS, wholeness, unity, coherence, cohesion.
**F3 1** dishonesty. **2** incompleteness.

**intellect** *n* mind, brain(s), brainpower, intelligence, genius, reason, understanding, sense, wisdom, judgement.
**F3** stupidity.

**intellectual** *adj* academic, scholarly, intelligent, studious, thoughtful, cerebral, mental, highbrow, cultural.
**F3** low-brow.
*n* thinker, academic, highbrow, egghead, mastermind, genius.
**F3** low-brow.

**intelligence** *n* **1** INTELLECT, reason, wit(s), brain(s) (*infml*), brainpower, cleverness, brightness, aptitude, quickness, alertness, discernment, perception, understanding, comprehension.
**2** INFORMATION, facts, data, low-down (*sl*), knowledge, findings, news, report, warning, tip-off.
**F3 1** stupidity, foolishness.

**intelligent** *adj* clever, bright, smart,

brainy (*infml*), quick, alert, quick-witted, sharp, acute, knowledgeable, well-informed, thinking, rational, sensible.
**F3** unintelligent, stupid, foolish.

**intend** *v* aim, have a mind, contemplate, mean, propose, plan, project, scheme, plot, design, purpose, resolve, determine, destine, mark out, earmark, set apart.

**intense** *adj* great, deep, profound, strong, powerful, forceful, fierce, harsh, severe, acute, sharp, keen, eager, earnest, ardent, fervent, fervid, passionate, vehement, energetic, violent, intensive, concentrated, heightened.
**F3** moderate, mild, weak.

**intensify** *v* increase, step up, escalate, heighten, hot up (*infml*), fire, boost, fuel, aggravate, add to, strengthen, reinforce, sharpen, whet, quicken, deepen, concentrate, emphasize, enhance.
**F3** reduce, weaken.

**intensive** *adj* concentrated, thorough, exhaustive, comprehensive, detailed, in-depth, thoroughgoing, all-out, intense.
**F3** superficial.

**intent** *adj* determined, resolved, resolute, set, bent, concentrated, eager, earnest, committed, steadfast, fixed, alert, attentive, concentrating, preoccupied, engrossed, wrapped up, absorbed, occupied.
**F3** absent-minded, distracted.

**intention** *n* aim, purpose, object, end, point, target, goal, objective, idea, plan, design, view, intent, meaning.

**intentional** *adj* designed, wilful, conscious, planned, deliberate, prearranged, premeditated, calculated, studied, intended, meant.
**F3** unintentional, accidental.

**intercede** *v* mediate, arbitrate, intervene, plead, entreat, beseech, speak.

**intercept** *v* head off, ambush, interrupt, cut off, stop, arrest, catch, take, seize, check, block, obstruct, delay, frustrate, thwart.

**interchangeable** *adj* reciprocal, equivalent, similar, identical, the same, synonymous, standard.
**F3** different.

**interest** *n* **1** IMPORTANCE, significance, note, concern, care, attention, notice, curiosity, involvement, participation. **2** *leisure interests*: activity, pursuit, pastime, hobby, diversion, amusement. **3** ADVANTAGE, benefit, profit, gain.
**F3 1** boredom.
*v* concern, involve, touch, move, attract, appeal to, divert, amuse, occupy, engage, absorb, engross, fascinate, intrigue.
**F3** bore.

**interested** *adj* **1** ATTENTIVE, curious, absorbed, engrossed, fascinated, enthusiastic, keen, attracted. **2** CONCERNED, involved, affected.
**F3 1** uninterested, indifferent, apathetic. **2** disinterested, unaffected.

**interesting** *adj* attractive, appealing, entertaining, engaging, absorbing, engrossing, fascinating, intriguing, compelling, gripping, stimulating, thought-provoking, curious, unusual.
**F3** uninteresting, boring, monotonous, tedious.

**interfere** *v* **1** INTRUDE, poke one's nose in, pry, butt in, interrupt, intervene, meddle, tamper. **2** HINDER, hamper, obstruct, block, impede, handicap, cramp, inhibit, conflict, clash.
**F3 2** assist.

**interference** *n* **1** INTRUSION, prying, interruption, intervention, meddling. **2** OBSTRUCTION, opposition, conflict, clashing.
**F3 2** assistance.

**interim** *adj* temporary, provisional,

stopgap, makeshift, improvised, stand-in, acting, caretaker.

*n* meantime, meanwhile, interval.

**interior** *adj* **1** INTERNAL, inside, inner, central, inward, mental, spiritual, private, secret, hidden. **2** HOME, domestic, inland, up-country, remote.

**E3** **1** exterior, external.

*n* inside, centre, middle, core, heart, depths.

**E3** exterior, outside.

**interjection** *n* exclamation, ejaculation, cry, shout, call, interpolation.

**intermediary** *n* mediator, go-between, middleman, broker, agent.

**intermediate** *adj* midway, halfway, in-between, middle, mid, median, mean, intermediary, intervening, transitional.

**E3** extreme.

**interminable** *adj* endless, never-ending, ceaseless, perpetual, limitless, unlimited, long, long-winded, long-drawn-out, dragging, wearisome.

**E3** limited, brief.

**intermission** *n* interval, entr'acte, interlude, break, recess, rest, respite, breather (*infml*), breathing-space, pause, lull, let-up (*infml*), remission, suspension, interruption, halt, stop, stoppage, cessation.

**intermittent** *adj* occasional, periodic, sporadic, spasmodic, fitful, erratic, irregular, broken.

**E3** continuous, constant.

**internal** *adj* inside, inner, interior, inward, intimate, private, personal, domestic, in-house.

**E3** external.

**international** *adj* global, worldwide, intercontinental, cosmopolitan, universal, general.

**E3** national, local, parochial.

**interplay** *n* exchange, interchange, interaction, reciprocation, give-and-take.

**interpose** *v* insert, introduce,

interject, interpolate, put in, thrust in, interrupt, intrude, interfere, come between, intervene, step in, mediate.

**interpret** *v* explain, expound, elucidate, clarify, throw light on, define, paraphrase, translate, render, decode, decipher, solve, make sense of, understand, construe, read, take.

**interpretation** *n* explanation, clarification, analysis, translation, rendering, version, performance, reading, understanding, sense, meaning.

**interrogate** *v* question, quiz, examine, cross-examine, grill, give the third degree, pump, debrief.

**interrogation** *n* questioning, cross-questioning, examination, cross-examination, grilling, third degree, inquisition, inquiry, inquest.

**interrupt** *v* intrude, barge in (*infml*), butt in, interject, break in, heckle, disturb, disrupt, interfere, obstruct, check, hinder, hold up, stop, halt, suspend, discontinue, cut off, disconnect, punctuate, separate, divide, cut, break.

**interruption** *n* intrusion, interjection, disturbance, disruption, obstruction, impediment, obstacle, hitch, pause, break, halt, stop, stoppage, suspension, discontinuance, disconnection, separation, division.

**intersect** *v* cross, criss-cross, cut across, bisect, divide, meet, converge.

**intersection** *n* junction, interchange, crossroads, crossing.

**intertwine** *v* entwine, interweave, interlace, interlink, twist, twine, cross, weave.

**interval** *n* interlude, intermission, break, rest, pause, delay, wait, interim, meantime, meanwhile, gap, opening, space, distance, period, spell, time, season.

**intervene** *v* **1** STEP IN, mediate, arbitrate, interfere, interrupt, intrude. **2** OCCUR, happen, elapse, pass.

**intervention** *n* involvement, interference, intrusion, mediation, agency, intercession.

**interview** *n* audience, consultation, talk, dialogue, meeting, conference, press conference, oral examination, viva.

*v* question, interrogate, examine, vet.

**intestines** *n* bowels, guts, entrails, insides, innards (*infml*), offal, viscera, vitals.

**intimacy** *n* friendship, closeness, familiarity, confidence, confidentiality, privacy.

**F3** distance.

**intimate**[1] *v* hint, insinuate, imply, suggest, indicate, communicate, impart, tell, state, declare, announce.

**intimate**[2] *adj* friendly, informal, familiar, cosy, warm, affectionate, dear, bosom, close, near, confidential, secret, private, personal, internal, innermost, deep, penetrating, detailed, exhaustive.

**F3** unfriendly, cold, distant.

*n* friend, bosom friend, confidant(e), associate.

**F3** stranger.

**intimidate** *v* daunt, cow, overawe, appal, dismay, alarm, scare, frighten, terrify, threaten, menace, terrorize, bully, browbeat, bulldoze, coerce, pressure, pressurize, lean on (*sl*).

**intolerable** *adj* unbearable, unendurable, insupportable, unacceptable, insufferable, impossible.

**F3** tolerable.

**intolerant** *adj* impatient, prejudiced, bigoted, narrow-minded, small-minded, opinionated, dogmatic, illiberal, uncharitable.

**F3** tolerant.

**intonation** *n* modulation, tone, accentuation, inflection.

**intoxicated** *adj* **1** DRUNK, drunken, inebriated, tipsy. **2** EXCITED, elated, exhilarated, thrilled.

**F3** **1** sober.

**intoxicating** *adj* **1** *intoxicating liquor*: alcoholic, strong.

**2** EXCITING, stimulating, heady, exhilarating, thrilling.

**F3** **1** sobering.

**intoxication** *n* **1** DRUNKENNESS, inebriation, tipsiness.

**2** EXCITEMENT, elation, exhilaration, euphoria.

**F3** **1** sobriety.

**intrepid** *adj* bold, daring, brave, courageous, plucky, valiant, lion-hearted, fearless, dauntless, undaunted, stout-hearted, stalwart, gallant, heroic.

**F3** cowardly, timid.

**intricate** *adj* elaborate, fancy, ornate, rococo, complicated, complex, sophisticated, involved, convoluted, tortuous, tangled, entangled, knotty, perplexing, difficult.

**F3** simple, plain, straightforward.

**intrigue** *n* **1** PLOT, scheme, conspiracy, collusion, machination, manoeuvre, stratagem, ruse, wile, trickery, double-dealing, sharp practice. **2** ROMANCE, liaison, affair, amour, intimacy.

*v* **1** FASCINATE, rivet, puzzle, tantalize, attract, charm, captivate.

**2** PLOT, scheme, conspire, connive, machinate, manoeuvre.

**F3** **1** bore.

**introduce** *v* **1** INSTITUTE, begin, start, commence, establish, found, inaugurate, launch, open, bring in, announce, present, acquaint, familiarize, initiate. **2** PUT FORWARD, advance, submit, offer, propose, suggest.

**F3** **1** end, conclude. **2** remove, take away.

**introduction** *n* **1** INSTITUTION, beginning, start, commencement, establishment, inauguration, launch, presentation, debut, initiation.

**2** FOREWORD, preface, preamble,

prologue, preliminaries, overture,
prelude, lead-in, opening.
**F3** 1 removal, withdrawal. 2 appendix,
conclusion.

**introductory** *adj* preliminary,
preparatory, opening, inaugural,
first, initial, early, elementary, basic.

**introspective** *adj* inward-looking,
contemplative, meditative, pensive,
thoughtful, brooding, introverted,
self-centred, reserved, withdrawn.
**F3** outward-looking.

**introverted** *adj* introspective,
inward-looking, self-centred,
withdrawn, shy, reserved, quiet.
**F3** extroverted.

**intrude** *v* interrupt, butt in, meddle,
interfere, violate, infringe, encroach,
trespass.
**F3** withdraw, stand back.

**intruder** *n* trespasser, prowler,
burglar, raider, invader, infiltrator,
interloper, gatecrasher.

**intrusion** *n* interruption,
interference, violation, infringement,
encroachment, trespass, invasion,
incursion.
**F3** withdrawal.

**intuition** *n* instinct, sixth sense,
perception, discernment, insight,
hunch, feeling, gut feeling (*infml*).
**F3** reasoning.

**intuitive** *adj* instinctive,
spontaneous, involuntary, innate,
untaught.
**F3** reasoned.

**inundate** *v* flood, deluge, swamp,
engulf, submerge, immerse, drown,
bury, overwhelm, overrun.

**invade** *v* enter, penetrate, infiltrate,
burst in, descend on, attack, raid,
seize, occupy, overrun, swarm over,
infest, pervade, encroach, infringe,
violate.
**F3** withdraw, evacuate.

**invalid**[1] *adj* sick, ill, poorly, ailing,
sickly, weak, feeble, frail, infirm,
disabled, bedridden.
**F3** healthy.

*n* patient, convalescent.

**invalid**[2] *adj* 1 FALSE, fallacious,
unsound, ill-founded, unfounded,
baseless, illogical, irrational,
unscientific, wrong, incorrect.
2 ILLEGAL, null, void, worthless.
**F3** 1 valid. 2 legal.

**invaluable** *adj* priceless,
inestimable, incalculable, precious,
valuable, useful.
**F3** worthless, cheap.

**invariable** *adj* fixed, set, unvarying,
unchanging, unchangeable,
permanent, constant, steady,
unwavering, uniform, rigid,
inflexible, habitual, regular.
**F3** variable.

**invariably** *adv* always, without
exception, without fail, unfailingly,
consistently, regularly, habitually.
**F3** never.

**invasion** *n* attack, offensive,
onslaught, raid, incursion, foray,
breach, penetration, infiltration,
intrusion, encroachment,
infringement, violation.
**F3** withdrawal, evacuation.

**invent** *v* conceive, think up, design,
discover, create, originate, formulate,
frame, devise, contrive, improvise,
fabricate, make up, concoct, cook up,
trump up, imagine, dream up.

**invention** *n* 1 *her latest invention*:
design, creation, brainchild,
discovery, development, device,
gadget. 2 LIE, falsehood, deceit,
fabrication, fiction, tall story,
fantasy, figment. 3 INVENTIVENESS,
imagination, creativity, innovation,
originality, ingenuity, inspiration,
genius.
**F3** 2 truth.

**inventive** *adj* imaginative, creative,
innovative, original, ingenious,
resourceful, fertile, inspired, gifted,
clever.

**inventor** *n* designer, discoverer,
creator, originator, author, architect,
maker, scientist, engineer.

**inverse** *adj* inverted, upside down, transposed, reversed, opposite, contrary, reverse, converse.

**invert** *v* upturn, turn upside down, overturn, capsize, upset, transpose, reverse.

 right.

**invertebrate**

> *Invertebrates include: sponges:* calcareous, glass, horny; *jellyfish, corals and sea anemones:* Portuguese man-of-war, box jellyfish, sea wasp, dead-men's fingers, sea pansy, sea gooseberry, Venus's girdle; *echinoderms:* sea lily, feather star, starfish, crown-of-thorns, brittle star, sea urchin, sand dollar, sea cucumber; *worms:* annelid worm, arrow worm, blood fluke, bristle worm, earthworm, eelworm, flatworm, fluke, hookworm, leech, liver fluke, lugworm, peanut worm, pinworm, ragworm, ribbonworm, roundworm, sea mouse, tapeworm, threadworm; *crustaceans:* acorn barnacle, barnacle, brine shrimp, crayfish, daphnia, fairy shrimp, fiddler crab, fish louse, goose barnacle, hermit crab, krill, lobster, mantis shrimp, mussel shrimp, pill bug, prawn, sand hopper, seed shrimp, spider crab, spiny lobster, tadpole shrimp, water flea, whale louse, woodlouse; centipede, millipede, velvet worm.

**invest** *v* **1** SPEND, lay out, put in, sink. **2** PROVIDE, supply, endow, vest, empower, authorize, sanction.

**investigate** *v* inquire into, look into, consider, examine, study, inspect, scrutinize, analyse, go into, probe, explore, search, sift.

**investigation** *n* inquiry, inquest, hearing, examination, study, research, survey, review, inspection, scrutiny, analysis, probe, exploration, search.

**investigator** *n* examiner, researcher, detective, sleuth (*infml*), private detective, private eye (*infml*).

**investment** *n* asset, speculation, venture, stake, contribution, outlay, expenditure, transaction.

**invigorate** *v* vitalize, energize, animate, enliven, liven up, quicken, strengthen, fortify, brace, stimulate, inspire, exhilarate, perk up, refresh, freshen, revitalize, rejuvenate.

 tire, weary, dishearten.

**invincible** *adj* unbeatable, unconquerable, insuperable, unsurmountable, indomitable, unassailable, impregnable, impenetrable, invulnerable, indestructible.

 beatable.

**invisible** *adj* unseen, out of sight, hidden, concealed, disguised, inconspicuous, indiscernible, imperceptible, infinitesimal, microscopic, imaginary, non-existent.

 visible.

**invitation** *n* request, solicitation, call, summons, temptation, enticement, allurement, come-on (*infml*), encouragement, inducement, provocation, incitement, challenge.

**invite** *v* ask, call, summon, welcome, encourage, lead, draw, attract, tempt, entice, allure, bring on, provoke, ask for, request, solicit, seek.

**inviting** *adj* welcoming, appealing, attractive, tempting, seductive, enticing, alluring, pleasing, delightful, captivating, fascinating, intriguing, tantalizing.

 uninviting, unappealing.

**invoke** *v* call upon, conjure, appeal to, petition, solicit, implore, entreat, beg, beseech, supplicate, pray.

**involuntary** *adj* spontaneous, unconscious, automatic, mechanical, reflex, instinctive, conditioned, impulsive, unthinking, blind, uncontrolled, unintentional.

 deliberate, intentional.

**involve** v **1** REQUIRE, necessitate, mean, imply, entail, include, incorporate, embrace, cover, take in, affect, concern. **2** IMPLICATE, incriminate, inculpate, draw in, mix up, embroil, associate. **3** ENGAGE, occupy, absorb, engross, preoccupy, hold, grip, rivet.
**F3** 1 exclude.

**involved** adj **1** CONCERNED, implicated, mixed up, caught up, in on (sl), participating. **2** an involved explanation: complicated, complex, intricate, elaborate, tangled, knotty, tortuous, confusing.
**F3** 1 uninvolved. 2 simple.

**involvement** n concern, interest, responsibility, association, connection, participation, implication, entanglement.

**invulnerable** adj safe, secure, unassailable, impenetrable, invincible, indestructible.
**F3** vulnerable.

**inward** adj incoming, entering, inside, interior, internal, inner, innermost, inmost, personal, private, secret, confidential.
**F3** outward, external.

**iota** n scrap, bit, mite, jot, speck, trace, hint, grain, particle, atom.

**irate** adj annoyed, irritated, indignant, up in arms, angry, enraged, mad (infml), furious, infuriated, incensed, worked up, fuming, livid, exasperated.
**F3** calm, composed.

**iron** adj rigid, inflexible, adamant, determined, hard, steely, tough, strong.
**F3** pliable, weak.
v press, smooth, flatten.

**iron out** resolve, settle, sort out, straighten out, clear up, put right, reconcile, deal with, get rid of, eradicate, eliminate.

**ironic** adj ironical, sarcastic, sardonic, scornful, contemptuous, derisive, sneering, scoffing, mocking, satirical, wry, paradoxical.

**irony** n sarcasm, mockery, satire, paradox, contrariness, incongruity.

**irrational** adj unreasonable, unsound, illogical, absurd, crazy, wild, foolish, silly, senseless, unwise.
**F3** rational.

**irreconcilable** adj incompatible, opposed, conflicting, clashing, contradictory, inconsistent.
**F3** reconcilable.

**irrefutable** adj undeniable, incontrovertible, indisputable, incontestable, unquestionable, unanswerable, certain, sure.

**irregular** adj **1** ROUGH, bumpy, uneven, crooked. **2** VARIABLE, fluctuating, wavering, erratic, fitful, intermittent, sporadic, spasmodic, occasional, random, haphazard, disorderly, unsystematic.
**3** ABNORMAL, unconventional, unorthodox, improper, unusual, exceptional, anomalous.
**F3** 1 smooth, level. 2 regular. 3 conventional.

**irrelevant** adj immaterial, beside the point, inapplicable, inappropriate, unrelated, unconnected, inconsequent, peripheral, tangential.
**F3** relevant.

**irreplaceable** adj indispensable, essential, vital, unique, priceless, peerless, matchless, unmatched.
**F3** replaceable.

**irrepressible** adj ebullient, bubbly, uninhibited, buoyant, resilient, boisterous, uncontrollable, ungovernable, unstoppable.

**irreproachable** adj irreprehensible, blameless, unimpeachable, faultless, impeccable, perfect, unblemished, immaculate, stainless, spotless, pure.
**F3** blameworthy, culpable.

**irresistible** adj overwhelming, overpowering, unavoidable, inevitable, inescapable, uncontrollable, potent, compelling,

**imperative**, pressing, urgent, tempting, seductive, ravishing, enchanting, charming, fascinating.
🔁 resistible, avoidable.

**irresponsible** adj **unreliable**, untrustworthy, careless, negligent, thoughtless, heedless, ill-considered, rash, reckless, wild, carefree, light-hearted, immature.
🔁 responsible, cautious.

**irreverent** adj **1** IMPIOUS, godless, irreligious, profane, sacrilegious, blasphemous. **2** DISRESPECTFUL, discourteous, rude, impudent, impertinent, mocking, flippant.
🔁 **1** reverent. **2** respectful.

**irreversible** adj **irrevocable**, unalterable, final, permanent, lasting, irreparable, irremediable, irretrievable, incurable, hopeless.
🔁 reversible, remediable, curable.

**irrevocable** adj **unalterable**, unchangeable, changeless, invariable, immutable, final, fixed, settled, predetermined, irreversible, irretrievable.
🔁 alterable, flexible, reversible.

**irrigate** v **water**, flood, inundate, wet, moisten, dampen.

**irritable** adj **cross**, bad-tempered, ill-tempered, crotchety, crusty, cantankerous, crabby, testy, short-tempered, snappish, snappy, short, impatient, touchy, edgy, thin-skinned, hypersensitive, prickly, peevish, fretful, fractious.
🔁 good-tempered, cheerful.

**irritate** v **1** ANNOY, get on one's nerves, aggravate (infml), bother, harass, rouse, provoke, rile, anger, enrage, infuriate, incense, exasperate, peeve, put out. **2** INFLAME, chafe, rub, tickle, itch.
🔁 **1** please, gratify.

**irritation** n **displeasure**, dissatisfaction, annoyance, aggravation, provocation, anger, vexation, indignation, fury, exasperation, irritability, crossness, testiness, snappiness, impatience.
🔁 pleasure, satisfaction, delight.

**isolate** v **set apart**, sequester, seclude, keep apart, segregate, quarantine, insulate, cut off, detach, remove, disconnect, separate, divorce, alienate, shut out, ostracize, exclude.
🔁 assimilate, incorporate.

**isolated** adj **1** REMOTE, out-of-the-way, outlying, god-forsaken, deserted, unfrequented, secluded, detached, cut off, lonely, solitary, single. **2** an isolated occurrence: unique, special, exceptional, atypical, unusual, freak, abnormal, anomalous.
🔁 **1** populous. **2** typical.

**isolation** n **quarantine**, solitude, solitariness, loneliness, remoteness, seclusion, retirement, withdrawal, exile, segregation, insulation, separation, detachment, disconnection, dissociation, alienation.

**issue** n **1** MATTER, affair, concern, problem, point, subject, topic, question, debate, argument, dispute, controversy. **2** PUBLICATION, release, distribution, supply, delivery, circulation, promulgation, broadcast, announcement. **3** last week's issue: copy, number, instalment, edition, impression, printing.
v **1** PUBLISH, release, distribute, supply, deliver, give out, deal out, circulate, promulgate, broadcast, announce, put out, emit, produce. **2** ORIGINATE, stem, spring, rise, emerge, burst forth, gush, flow, proceed, emanate, arise.

**itch** v **tickle**, irritate, tingle, prickle, crawl.
n **1** ITCHINESS, tickle, irritation, prickling. **2** EAGERNESS, keenness, desire, longing, yearning, hankering, craving.

**item** n **1** OBJECT, article, thing, piece, component, ingredient, element, factor, point, detail, particular, aspect, feature, consideration, matter. **2** *an item in the local paper*: article, piece, report, account, notice, entry, paragraph.

**itinerant** *adj* travelling, peripatetic, roving, roaming, wandering,

rambling, nomadic, migratory, rootless, unsettled.
**Ea** stationary, settled.

**itinerary** *n* route, course, journey, tour, circuit, plan, programme, schedule.

# J

**jab** *v* poke, prod, dig, nudge, stab, push, elbow, lunge, punch, tap, thrust.

**jackpot** *n* prize, winnings, kitty, pool, pot, reward, award, big time (*infml*), bonanza, stakes.

**jaded** *adj* fatigued, exhausted, dulled, played-out, tired, tired out, weary, spent, bored, fagged (*infml*).
**Ea** fresh, refreshed.

**jagged** *adj* uneven, irregular, notched, indented, rough, serrated, saw-edged, toothed, ragged, pointed, ridged, craggy, barbed, broken.
**Ea** even, smooth.

**jail, gaol** *n* prison, jailhouse, custody, lock-up, penitentiary, guardhouse, inside (*infml*), nick (*sl*), clink (*sl*).
*v* imprison, incarcerate, lock up, put away, send down, confine, detain, intern, impound, immure.

**jailer, gaoler** *n* prison officer, warden, warder, guard, screw (*sl*), keeper, captor.

**jam¹** *v* **1** CRAM, pack, wedge, squash, squeeze, press, crush, crowd, congest, ram, stuff, confine, force. **2** BLOCK, clog, obstruct, stall, stick.
*n* **1** CRUSH, crowd, press, congestion, pack, mob, throng, bottle-neck, traffic jam. **2** PREDICAMENT, trouble, quandary, plight, fix (*infml*).

**jam²** *n* conserve, preserve, jelly, spread, marmalade.

**jangle** *v* clank, clash, jar, clatter,

jingle, chime, rattle, vibrate.
*n* clang, clash, rattle, jar, cacophony, dissonance, din, discord, racket, reverberation.
**Ea** euphony.

**jar¹** *n* pot, container, vessel, receptacle, crock, pitcher, urn, vase, flagon, jug, mug.

**jar²** *v* **1** JOLT, agitate, rattle, shake, vibrate, jangle, rock, disturb, discompose. **2** ANNOY, irritate, grate, nettle (*infml*), offend, upset, irk. **3** BICKER, quarrel, clash, disagree.

**jargon** *n* **1** PARLANCE, cant, argot, vernacular, idiom. **2** NONSENSE, gobbledegook (*infml*), mumbo-jumbo (*infml*), gibberish.

**jarring** *adj* discordant, jangling, harsh, grating, irritating, cacophonous, rasping, strident, upsetting, disturbing, jolting.

**jaundiced** *adj* **1** BITTER, cynical, pessimistic, sceptical, distrustful, disbelieving, envious, jealous, hostile, jaded, suspicious, resentful. **2** DISTORTED, biased, prejudiced, preconceived.

**jaunty** *adj* sprightly, lively, perky, breezy, buoyant, high-spirited, self-confident, carefree, airy, cheeky, debonair, dapper, smart, showy, spruce.
**Ea** depressed, dowdy.

**jaw** (*infml*) *v* chat, chatter, gossip, natter (*infml*), talk, rabbit (on) (*infml*), gabble, babble.

*n* talk, gossip, chat, conversation, discussion, chinwag, natter (*infml*).

**jealous** *adj* **1** ENVIOUS, covetous, grudging, resentful, green (*infml*), green-eyed (*infml*). **2** SUSPICIOUS, wary, distrustful, anxious, possessive, protective.
**Ea** **1** contented, satisfied.

**jealousy** *n* **1** ENVY, covetousness, grudge, resentment, spite, ill-will. **2** SUSPICION, distrust, mistrust, possessiveness.

**jeer** *v* mock, scoff, taunt, jibe, ridicule, sneer, deride, make fun of, chaff, barrack, twit, knock (*infml*), heckle, banter.
*n* mockery, derision, ridicule, taunt, jibe, sneer, scoff, abuse, catcall, dig (*infml*), hiss, hoot.

**jell** *see* **gel**.

**jeopardize** *v* endanger, imperil, risk, hazard, venture, gamble, chance, threaten, menace, expose, stake.
**Ea** protect, safeguard.

**jeopardy** *n* danger, peril, risk, hazard, endangerment, venture, vulnerability, precariousness, insecurity, exposure, liability.
**Ea** safety, security.

**jerk** *n* jolt, tug, twitch, jar, jog, yank, wrench, pull, pluck, lurch, throw, thrust, shrug.
*v* jolt, tug, twitch, jog, yank, wrench, pull, jiggle, lurch, pluck, thrust, shrug, throw, bounce.

**jerky** *adj* fitful, twitchy, spasmodic, jumpy, jolting, convulsive, disconnected, bumpy, bouncy, shaky, rough, unco-ordinated, uncontrolled, incoherent.
**Ea** smooth.

**jest** *n* joke, quip, wisecrack (*infml*), witticism, crack (*infml*), banter, fooling, gag (*infml*), prank, kidding (*infml*), leg-pull (*infml*), trick, hoax.
*v* joke, quip, fool, kid (*infml*), tease, mock, jeer.

**jet**[1] *n* gush, spurt, spout, spray,

spring, sprinkler, sprayer, fountain, flow, stream, squirt.

**jet**[2] *adj* black, pitch-black, ebony, sable, sooty.

**jetty** *n* breakwater, pier, dock, groyne, wharf.

**jewel** *n* **1** GEM, precious stone, gemstone, ornament, rock (*sl*). **2** TREASURE, find, prize, rarity, paragon, pearl.

**jewellery**

*Types of jewellery include*: bangle, bracelet, charm bracelet, anklet, cufflink, tiepin, hatpin, brooch, cameo, earring, nose-ring, ring, signet-ring, solitaire ring, necklace, necklet, choker, pendant, locket, chain, beads, amulet, torque, tiara, coronet, diadem.

**Jewish calendar**

*The Jewish calendar and its Gregorian equivalents*: Tishri (September-October), Hesshvan (October-November), Kislev (November-December), Tevet (December-January), Shevat (January-February), Adar (February-March), Adar Sheni (leap years only), Nisan (March-April), Iyar (April-May), Sivan (May-June), Tammuz (June-July), Av (July-August), Elul (August-September).

**jibe** *see* **gibe**.

**jig** *v* jerk, prance, caper, hop, jump, twitch, skip, bounce, bob, wiggle, shake, wobble.

**jilt** *v* abandon, reject, desert, discard, brush off, ditch (*infml*), drop, spurn, betray.

**jingle** *v* clink, tinkle, ring, chime, chink, jangle, clatter, rattle.
*n* **1** CLINK, tinkle, ringing, clang, rattle, clangour. **2** RHYME, verse, song, tune, ditty, doggerel, melody, poem, chant, chorus.

**ingoism** *n* chauvinism, flag-waving, patriotism, nationalism, imperialism, warmongering, insularity.

**inx** (*infml*) *n* spell, curse, evil eye, hex, voodoo, hoodoo, black magic, gremlin (*infml*), charm, plague.
*v* curse, bewitch, bedevil, doom, plague.

**ob** *n* **1** *she has a good job*: work, employment, occupation, position, post, situation, profession, career, calling, vocation, trade, métier, capacity, business, livelihood. **2** *it's a difficult job*: task, chore, duty, responsibility, charge, commission, mission, activity, affair, concern, proceeding, project, enterprise, office, pursuit, role, undertaking, venture, province, part, place, share, errand, function, contribution, stint, assignment, consignment.

**obless** *adj* unemployed, out of work, laid off, on the dole, inactive, redundant.
**Ⅎ** employed.

**ocular** *adj* joking, jesting, funny, jocose (*fml*), humorous, jovial, amusing, comical, entertaining, facetious, droll, whimsical, teasing, witty.
**Ⅎ** serious.

**og** *v* **1** JOLT, jar, bump, jostle, jerk, joggle, nudge, poke, prod, bounce, push, rock. **2** PROMPT, remind, stir, arouse, activate, stimulate. **3** RUN, trot.
*n* **1** JOLT, bump, jerk, nudge, shove, push, poke, prod, shake. **2** RUN, trot.

**oin** *v* **1** UNITE, connect, combine, conjoin, attach, link, amalgamate, fasten, merge, marry, couple, yoke, tie, splice, knit, cement, add, adhere, annex. **2** ABUT, adjoin, border (on), verge on, touch, meet, coincide, march with. **3** ASSOCIATE, affiliate, accompany, ally, enlist, enrol, enter, sign up, team.
**Ⅎ** **1** divide, separate. **3** leave.

**oint** *n* junction, connection, union, juncture, intersection, hinge, knot, articulation, seam.
*adj* combined, common, communal, joined, shared, united, collective, amalgamated, mutual, co-operative, co-ordinated, consolidated, concerted.

**joke** *n* **1** JEST, quip, crack (*infml*), gag (*infml*), witticism, wisecrack (*infml*), one-liner (*infml*), pun, hoot, whimsy, yarn. **2** TRICK, jape, lark, prank, spoof, fun.
*v* jest, quip, clown, fool, pun, wisecrack (*infml*), kid (*infml*), tease, banter, mock, laugh, frolic, gambol.

**joker** *n* comedian, comic, wit, humorist, jester, trickster, wag, clown, buffoon, kidder, droll, card (*infml*), character, sport.

**jolly** *adj* jovial, merry, cheerful, playful, hearty, happy, exuberant.
**Ⅎ** sad.

**jolt** *v* **1** JAR, jerk, jog, bump, jostle, knock, bounce, shake, push. **2** UPSET, startle, shock, surprise, stun, discompose, disconcert, disturb.
*n* **1** JAR, jerk, jog, bump, blow, impact, lurch, shake. **2** SHOCK, surprise, reversal, setback, start.

**jostle** *v* push, shove, jog, bump, elbow, hustle, jolt, crowd, shoulder, joggle, shake, squeeze, throng.

**jot down** write down, take down, note, list, record, scribble, register, enter.

**journal** *n* newspaper, periodical, magazine, paper, publication, review, weekly, monthly, register, chronicle, diary, gazette, daybook, log, record.

**journalist** *n* reporter, news-writer, hack, correspondent, editor, columnist, feature-writer, commentator, broadcaster, contributor.

**journey** *n* voyage, trip, travel, expedition, passage, trek, tour, ramble, outing, wanderings, safari, progress.
*v* travel, voyage, go, trek, tour, roam,

rove, proceed, wander, tramp, ramble, range, gallivant.

**jovial** *adj* jolly, cheery, merry, affable, cordial, genial.
🔁 gloomy.

**joy** *n* happiness, gladness, delight, pleasure, bliss, ecstasy, elation, joyfulness, exultation, gratification, rapture.
🔁 despair, grief.

**joyful** *adj* happy, pleased, delighted, glad, elated, ecstatic, triumphant.
🔁 sorrowful.

**jubilant** *adj* joyful, rejoicing, overjoyed, delighted, elated, triumphant, exuberant, excited, euphoric, thrilled.

**jubilee** *n* celebration, commemoration, anniversary, festival, festivity, gala, fête, carnival.

**judge** *n* 1 JUSTICE, Law Lord, magistrate, arbiter, adjudicator, arbitrator, mediator, moderator, referee, umpire, beak (*sl*).
2 CONNOISSEUR, authority, expert, evaluator, assessor, critic.
*v* 1 ADJUDICATE, arbitrate, try, referee, umpire, decree, mediate, examine, sentence, review, rule, find.
2 ASCERTAIN, determine, decide, assess, appraise, evaluate, estimate, value, distinguish, discern, reckon, believe, think, consider, conclude, rate. 3 CONDEMN, criticize, doom.

**judgement** *n* 1 VERDICT, sentence, ruling, decree, conclusion, decision, arbitration, finding, result, mediation, order. 2 DISCERNMENT, discrimination, understanding, wisdom, prudence, common sense, sense, intelligence, taste, shrewdness, penetration, enlightenment.
3 ASSESSMENT, evaluation, appraisal, estimate, opinion, view, belief, diagnosis. 4 CONVICTION, damnation, punishment, retribution, doom, fate, misfortune.

**judicial** *adj* legal, judiciary, magistral, forensic, official,

discriminating, critical, impartial.

**judicious** *adj* wise, prudent, careful, cautious, astute, discerning, informed, shrewd, thoughtful, reasonable, sensible, sound, well-judged, well-advised, considered.
🔁 injudicious.

**jug** *n* pitcher, carafe, ewer, flagon, urn, jar, vessel, container.

**juggle** *v* alter, change, manipulate, falsify, rearrange, rig, doctor (*infml*), cook (*infml*), disguise.

**juice** *n* liquid, fluid, extract, essence, sap, secretion, nectar, liquor.

**juicy** *adj* 1 SUCCULENT, moist, lush, watery. 2 (*infml*) INTERESTING, colourful, sensational, racy, risqué, suggestive, lurid.
🔁 1 dry.

**jumble** *v* disarrange, confuse, disorganize, mix (up), muddle, shuffle, tangle.
🔁 order.
*n* disorder, disarray, confusion, mess, chaos, mix-up, muddle, clutter, mixture, hotch-potch, mishmash (*infml*), medley.

**jump** *v* 1 LEAP, spring, bound, vault, clear, bounce, skip, hop, prance, frolic, gambol. 2 START, flinch, jerk, recoil, jump out of one's skin (*infml*), wince, quail. 3 OMIT, leave out, miss, skip, pass over, bypass, disregard, ignore, avoid, digress.
4 RISE, increase, gain, appreciate, ascend, escalate, mount, advance, surge, spiral.
*n* 1 LEAP, spring, bound, vault, hop, skip, bounce, prance, frisk, frolic, pounce. 2 START, jerk, jolt, jar, lurch, shock, spasm, quiver, shiver, twitch.
3 BREAK, gap, interruption, lapse, omission, interval, breach, switch. 4 RISE, increase, escalation, boost, advance, increment, upsurge, upturn, mounting. 5 HURDLE, fence, gate, hedge, barricade, obstacle.

**jumpy** *adj* nervous, anxious, agitated, apprehensive, jittery, tense,

edgy, fidgety, shaky.
**F3** calm, composed.

**junction** n joint, join, joining,
connection, juncture, union,
intersection, linking, coupling,
meeting-point, confluence.

**junior** adj younger, minor, lesser,
lower, subordinate, secondary,
subsidiary, inferior.
**F3** senior.

**junk** n rubbish, refuse, trash, debris,
garbage, waste, scrap, litter, clutter,
oddments, rummage, dregs,
wreckage.

**jurisdiction** n power, authority,
control, influence, dominion,
province, sovereignty, command,
domination, rule, prerogative (fml),
sway, orbit, bounds, area, field,
scope, range, reach, sphere, zone.

**just** adj **1** a just ruler: fair, equitable,
impartial, unbiased, unprejudiced,
fair-minded, even-handed, objective,
righteous, upright, virtuous,
honourable, good, honest,
irreproachable. **2** a just punishment:
deserved, merited, fitting, well-
deserved, appropriate, suitable, due,
proper, reasonable, rightful, lawful,
legitimate.
**F3 1** unjust. **2** undeserved.

**justice** n **1** FAIRNESS, equity,
impartiality, objectivity,
equitableness, justness, legitimacy,
honesty, right, rightfulness, rightness,
justifiableness, reasonableness,

rectitude. **2** LEGALITY, law, penalty,
recompense, reparation, satisfaction.
**3** JUDGE, Justice of the Peace, JP,
magistrate.
**F3** injustice, unfairness.

**justifiable** adj defensible, excusable,
warranted, reasonable, justified,
lawful, legitimate, acceptable,
explainable, forgivable, pardonable,
understandable, valid, well-founded,
right, proper, explicable, fit, tenable.
**F3** unjustifiable.

**justification** n defence, plea,
mitigation, apology, explanation,
excuse, vindication, warrant,
rationalization, reason, grounds.

**justify** v vindicate, exonerate,
warrant, substantiate, defend, acquit,
absolve, excuse, forgive, explain,
pardon, validate, uphold, sustain,
support, maintain, establish.

**jut (out)** v project, protrude, stick
out, overhang, extend.
**F3** recede.

**juvenile** n child, youth, minor,
young person, youngster, adolescent,
teenager, boy, girl, kid (infml),
infant.
adj young, youthful, immature,
childish, puerile, infantile, adolescent,
babyish, unsophisticated.
**F3** mature.

**juxtaposition** n contiguity,
proximity, nearness, closeness,
contact, vicinity, immediacy.

# K

**karate**

*Karate belts include: junior grades
(Kyu): red belt (beginner), white belt
(8th Kyu), yellow belt (7th Kyu),
orange belt (6th Kyu), green belt (5th
Kyu), brown belt (4th-1st Kyu),*

*black belt (1st Dan); senior grades
(Dans): black belts (1st-8th Dan).*

**keel over 1** OVERTURN, capsize,
founder, collapse, upset. **2** FAINT,
pass out, swoon, fall, drop, stagger,
topple over.

**keen** adj **1** EAGER, avid, fervent, enthusiastic, earnest, devoted, diligent, industrious. **2** ASTUTE, shrewd, clever, perceptive, wise, discerning, quick, deep, sensitive. **3** SHARP, piercing, penetrating, incisive, acute, pointed, intense, pungent, trenchant.

**F3 1** apathetic. **2** superficial. **3** dull.

**keep** v **1** RETAIN, hold, preserve, hold on to, hang on to, store, stock, possess, amass, accumulate, collect, stack, conserve, deposit, heap, pile, place, maintain, furnish. **2** CARRY ON, keep on, continue, persist, remain. **3** LOOK AFTER, tend, care for, have charge of, have custody of, maintain, provide for, subsidize, support, sustain, be responsible for, foster, mind, protect, shelter, guard, defend, watch (over), shield, safeguard, feed, nurture, manage. **4** DETAIN, delay, retard, check, hinder, hold (up), impede, obstruct, prevent, block, curb, interfere with, restrain, limit, inhibit, deter, hamper, keep back, control, constrain, arrest, withhold. **5** OBSERVE, comply with, respect, obey, fulfil, adhere to, recognize, keep up, keep faith with, commemorate, celebrate, hold, maintain, perform, perpetuate, mark, honour.

n **1** SUBSISTENCE, board, livelihood, living, maintenance, support, upkeep, means, food, nourishment, nurture. **2** FORT, fortress, tower, castle, citadel, stronghold, dungeon.

**keep back 1** RESTRAIN, check, constrain, curb, impede, limit, prohibit, retard, stop, control, delay. **2** HOLD BACK, restrict, suppress, withhold, conceal, censor, hide, hush up, stifle, reserve, retain.

**keep in 1** REPRESS, keep back, inhibit, bottle up, conceal, stifle, suppress, hide, control, restrain, quell, stop up. **2** CONFINE, detain, shut in, coop up.

**F3 1** declare. **2** release.

**keep on** continue, carry on, endure, persevere, persist, keep at it, last, remain, stay, stay the course, soldier on (infml), hold on, retain, maintain.

**keep up** keep pace, equal, contend, compete, vie, rival, match, emulate, continue, maintain, persevere, support, sustain, preserve.

**keeper** n guard, custodian, curator, caretaker, attendant, guardian, overseer, steward, warder, jailer, gaoler, warden, supervisor, minder (infml), inspector, conservator (fml), defender, governor, superintendent, surveyor.

**keepsake** n memento, souvenir, remembrance, relic, reminder, token, pledge, emblem.

**kernel** n core, grain, seed, nucleus, heart, nub, essence, germ, marrow, substance, nitty-gritty (infml), gist.

**key** n **1** CLUE, cue, indicator, pointer, explanation, sign, answer, solution, interpretation, means, secret. **2** GUIDE, glossary, translation, legend, code, table, index.

adj important, essential, vital, crucial, necessary, principal, decisive, central, chief, main, major, leading, basic, fundamental.

**keynote** n core, centre, heart, substance, theme, gist, essence, emphasis, accent, stress.

**keystone** n cornerstone, core, crux, base, basis, foundation, ground, linchpin, principle, root, mainspring, source, spring, motive.

**kick** v **1** BOOT, hit, strike, jolt. **2** (infml) GIVE UP, quit, stop, leave off, abandon, desist from, break.

n **1** BLOW, recoil, jolt, striking. **2** (infml) STIMULATION, thrill, excitement.

**kick off** begin, commence, start, open, get under way, open the proceedings, set the ball rolling, introduce, inaugurate, initiate.

**kick out** eject, evict, expel, oust,

remove, chuck out (*infml*), discharge, dismiss, get rid of, sack (*infml*), throw out, reject.

**kid**[1] *n* child, youngster, youth, juvenile, infant, girl, boy, teenager, lad, nipper (*infml*), tot (*infml*).

**kid**[2] *v* tease, joke, have on (*infml*), hoax, fool, pull someone's leg (*infml*), pretend, trick, delude, dupe, con (*infml*), jest, hoodwink, humbug, bamboozle.

**kidnap** *v* abduct, capture, seize, hold to ransom, snatch, hijack, steal.

**kill** *v* 1 SLAUGHTER, murder, slay, put to death, exterminate, assassinate, do to death, do in (*infml*), bump off (*infml*), finish off, massacre, smite (*fml*), execute, eliminate (*sl*), destroy, dispatch (*infml*), do away with, butcher, annihilate, liquidate (*sl*), knock off (*infml*), rub out (*sl*). 2 STIFLE, deaden, smother, quash, quell, suppress.

**killer** *n* murderer, assassin, executioner, destroyer, slaughterer, exterminator, butcher (*infml*), cut-throat, gunman, hatchet man (*sl*), hit-man (*sl*).

**killing** *n* 1 SLAUGHTER, murder, massacre, homicide, assassination, execution, slaying, manslaughter, extermination, carnage, bloodshed, elimination, fatality, liquidation. 2 (*infml*) GAIN, fortune, windfall, profit, lucky break, coup, clean-up (*infml*), success, stroke of luck, bonanza (*infml*), hit, big hit.
*adj* (*infml*) 1 FUNNY, hilarious, comical, amusing, side-splitting (*infml*), ludicrous. 2 EXHAUSTING, hard, taxing, arduous.

**kind** *n* sort, type, class, category, set, variety, character, genus, genre, style, brand, family, breed, race, nature, persuasion, description, species, stamp, temperament, manner.
*adj* benevolent, kind-hearted, kindly,

good-hearted, good-natured, helpful, obliging, humane, generous, compassionate, charitable, amiable, friendly, congenial, soft-hearted, thoughtful, warm, warm-hearted, considerate, courteous, sympathetic, tender-hearted, understanding, lenient, mild, hospitable, gentle, indulgent, neighbourly, tactful, giving, good, loving, gracious.
**Fa** cruel, inconsiderate, unhelpful.

**kindle** *v* 1 IGNITE, light, set alight, set on fire. 2 INFLAME, fire, stir, thrill, stimulate, rouse, arouse, awaken, excite, fan, incite, inspire, induce, provoke.

**kindly** *adj* benevolent, kind, compassionate, charitable, good-natured, helpful, warm, generous, cordial, favourable, giving, indulgent, pleasant, sympathetic, tender, gentle, mild, patient, polite.
**Fa** cruel, uncharitable.

**kindness** *n* 1 BENEVOLENCE, kindliness, charity, magnanimity, compassion, generosity, hospitality, humanity, loving-kindness (*fml*), courtesy, friendliness, good will, goodness, grace, indulgence, tolerance, understanding, gentleness. 2 FAVOUR, good turn, assistance, help, service.
**Fa** 1 cruelty, inhumanity. 2 disservice.

**king** *n* monarch, ruler, sovereign, majesty, emperor, chief, chieftain, prince, supremo, leading light (*infml*).

**kingdom** *n* monarchy, sovereignty, reign, realm, empire, dominion, commonwealth, nation, principality, state, country, domain, dynasty, province, sphere, territory, land, division.

**kink** *n* 1 CURL, twist, bend, dent, indentation, knot, loop, crimp, coil, tangle, wrinkle. 2 QUIRK, eccentricity, idiosyncrasy, foible, perversion.

**kinship** *n* 1 KIN, blood, relation. 2

AFFINITY, similarity, association, alliance, connection, correspondence, relationship, tie, community, conformity.

**kiosk** n booth, stall, stand, news-stand, bookstall, cabin, box, counter.

**kiss** v **1** CARESS, peck (*infml*), smooch, neck (*infml*), snog (*sl*). **2** TOUCH, graze, glance, brush, lick, scrape, fan.
    n peck (*infml*), smack (*infml*), smacker (*sl*).

**kit** n equipment, gear, apparatus, supplies, tackle, provisions, outfit, implements, set, tools, trappings, rig, instruments, paraphernalia, utensils, effects, luggage, baggage.

**kit out** equip, fit out, outfit, supply, fix up, furnish, prepare, arm, deck out, dress.

**knack** n flair, faculty, facility, hang (*infml*), bent, skill, talent, genius, gift, trick, propensity, ability, expertise, skilfulness, forte, capacity, handiness, dexterity, quickness, turn.

**knapsack** n bag, pack, haversack, rucksack, backpack.

**knead** v manipulate, press, massage, work, ply, squeeze, shape, rub, form, mould, knuckle.

**knell** n toll, ringing, chime, peel, knoll.

**knick-knack** n trinket, trifle, bauble, gewgaw, gimcrack, bric-à-brac, plaything.

**knife** n blade, cutter, carver, dagger, pen-knife, pocket-knife, switchblade, jack-knife, flick-knife, machete.
    v cut, rip, slash, stab, pierce, wound.

**knit** v **1** JOIN, unite, secure, connect, tie, fasten, link, mend, interlace, intertwine. **2** KNOT, loop, crotchet, weave. **3** WRINKLE, furrow.

**knock** v hit, strike, rap, thump, pound, slap, smack.
    n blow, box, rap, thump, cuff, clip, pounding, hammering, slap, smack.

**knock about 1** WANDER, travel, roam, rove, saunter, traipse, ramble, range.

**2** ASSOCIATE, go around. **3** BEAT UP, batter, abuse, mistreat, hurt, hit, bash, damage, maltreat, manhandle, bruise, buffet.

**knock down** demolish, destroy, fell, floor, level, wreck, raze, pound, batter, clout, smash, wallop.

**knock off 1** (*infml*) FINISH, cease, stop, pack (it) in, clock off, clock out, terminate. **2** (*infml*) STEAL, rob, pilfer, pinch (*infml*), nick (*infml*), filch. **3** DEDUCT, take away. **4** (*sl*) KILL, murder, slay, assassinate, do away with, bump off (*infml*), do in (*infml*), waste (*sl*).

**knockout** (*infml*) n success, triumph, sensation, hit, smash (*infml*), smash-hit (*infml*), winner, stunner (*infml*). **E3** flop, loser.

**knot** v tie, secure, bind, entangle, tangle, knit, entwine, ravel, weave.
    n **1** TIE, bond, joint, fastening, loop, splice, hitch. **2** BUNCH, cluster, clump, group.

> *Types of knot include*: bend, Blackwall hitch, blood knot, bow, bowline, running bowline, carrick bend, clove hitch, common whipping, double-overhang, Englishman's tie (or knot), figure of eight, fisherman's bend, fisherman's knot, flat knot, granny knot, half hitch, highwayman's hitch, hitch, Hunter's bend, loop knot, overhand knot or thumb knot, reef knot or square knot, rolling hitch, round turn and two half hitches, seizing, sheepshank, sheet bend or common bend or swab hitch, slipknot, spade-end knot, surgeon's knot, tie, timber hitch, Turk's head, turle knot, wall knot, weaver's knot, Windsor knot.

**know** v **1** *know French*: understand, comprehend, apprehend, perceive, notice, be aware, fathom, experience, realize, see, undergo. **2** *I know George*: be acquainted with, be

familiar with, recognize, identify.
**3** *know a good wine*: distinguish, discriminate, discern, differentiate, make out, tell.

**knowledge** *n* **1** LEARNING, scholarship, erudition, education, schooling, instruction, tuition, information, enlightenment, know-how. **2** ACQUAINTANCE, familiarity, awareness, cognizance, intimacy, consciousness. **3** UNDERSTANDING, comprehension, cognition, apprehension, recognition, judgement, discernment, ability, grasp, wisdom, intelligence.
**E3 1** ignorance. **2** unawareness.

**knowledgeable** *adj* **1** EDUCATED, scholarly, learned, well-informed, lettered, intelligent. **2** AWARE, acquainted, conscious, familiar, au fait, in the know (*infml*), conversant, experienced.
**E3 1** ignorant.

**known** *adj* acknowledged, recognized, well-known, noted, obvious, patent, plain, admitted, familiar, avowed, commonplace, published, confessed, celebrated, famous.

**kowtow** *v* defer, cringe, fawn, grovel, pander, suck up (*infml*), toady (*infml*), flatter, kneel.

# L

**label** *n* **1** TAG, ticket, docket, mark, marker, sticker, trademark. **2** DESCRIPTION, categorization, identification, characterization, classification, badge, brand.
*v* **1** TAG, mark, stamp. **2** DEFINE, describe, classify, categorize, characterize, identify, class, designate, brand, call, dub, name.

**laborious** *adj* **1** HARD, arduous, difficult, strenuous, tough, backbreaking, wearisome, tiresome, uphill, onerous, heavy, toilsome. **2** HARD-WORKING, industrious, painstaking, indefatigable, diligent.
**E3 1** easy, effortless. **2** lazy.

**labour** *n* **1** WORK, task, job, chore, toil, effort, exertion, drudgery, grind (*infml*), slog (*infml*), sweat (*infml*). **2** WORKERS, employees, workforce, labourers. **3** CHILDBIRTH, birth, delivery, labour pains, contractions.
**E3 1** ease, leisure. **2** management.
*v* **1** WORK, toil, drudge, slave, strive, endeavour, struggle, grind (*infml*), sweat (*infml*), plod, travail (*fml*). **2** TOSS, pitch, roll. **3** OVERDO,

overemphasize, dwell on, elaborate, overstress, strain.
**E3 1** laze, idle, lounge.

**labourer** *n* manual worker, blue-collar worker, navvy, hand, worker, drudge, hireling.

**labyrinth** *n* maze, complexity, intricacy, complication, puzzle, riddle, windings, tangle, jungle.

**lace** *n* **1** NETTING, mesh-work, open-work, tatting, crochet. **2** STRING, cord, thong, tie, shoelace, bootlace.
*v* **1** TIE, do up, fasten, thread, close, bind, attach, string, intertwine, interweave. **2** ADD TO, mix in, spike (*infml*), fortify.

**lacerate** *v* tear, rip, rend, cut, gash, slash, wound, claw, mangle, maim, torture, torment, distress, afflict.

**lack** *n* need, want, scarcity, shortage, insufficiency, dearth, deficiency, absence, scantiness, vacancy, void, privation, deprivation, destitution, emptiness.
**E3** abundance, profusion.
*v* need, want, require, miss.

**lacking** adj needing, wanting, without, short of, missing, minus, inadequate, deficient, defective, flawed.

**lacklustre** adj drab, dull, flat, boring, leaden, lifeless, unimaginative, dim.
**F3** brilliant, inspired.

**laconic** adj terse, succinct, pithy, concise, crisp, taciturn, short, curt, brief.
**F3** verbose, wordy.

**lad** n boy, youth, youngster, kid (*infml*), schoolboy, chap, guy (*infml*), fellow.

**lag** v dawdle, loiter, hang back, linger, straggle, trail, saunter, delay, shuffle, tarry, idle.
**F3** hurry, lead.

**lair** n den, burrow, hole, nest, earth, form, roost, retreat, hideout, refuge, sanctuary, stronghold.

**lake** n lagoon, reservoir, loch, mere, tarn.

**lame** adj 1 DISABLED, handicapped, crippled, limping, hobbling. 2 WEAK, feeble, flimsy, inadequate, unsatisfactory, poor.
**F3** 1 able-bodied. 2 convincing.

**lament** v mourn, bewail, bemoan, grieve, sorrow, weep, wail, complain, deplore, regret.
**F3** rejoice, celebrate.
n lamentation, dirge, elegy, requiem, threnody (*fml*), complaint, moan, wail.

**lamentable** adj 1 DEPLORABLE, regrettable, mournful, distressing, tragic, unfortunate, sorrowful. 2 MEAGRE, low, inadequate, insufficient, mean, unsatisfactory, pitiful, miserable, poor, disappointing.

**lampoon** n satire, skit, caricature, parody, send-up (*infml*), spoof, take-off (*infml*), burlesque.
v satirize, caricature, parody, send up, take off (*infml*), spoof, make fun of, ridicule, mock, burlesque.

**land** n 1 EARTH, ground, soil, terra firma. 2 PROPERTY, grounds, estate, real estate, country, countryside, farmland, tract. 3 COUNTRY, nation, region, territory, province.
v 1 ALIGHT, disembark, dock, berth, touch down, come to rest, arrive, deposit, wind up, end up, drop, settle, turn up. 2 OBTAIN, secure, gain, get, acquire, net, capture, achieve, win.

**landlord** n owner, proprietor, host, publican, innkeeper, hotelier, restaurateur, hotel-keeper, freeholder.
**F3** tenant.

**landmark** n feature, monument, signpost, turning-point, watershed, milestone, beacon, cairn.

**landscape** n scene, scenery, view, panorama, outlook, vista, prospect, countryside, aspect.

**landslide** n landslip, earthfall, rock-fall, avalanche.
adj overwhelming, decisive, emphatic, runaway.

**language** n 1 SPEECH, vocabulary, terminology, parlance. 2 TALK, conversation, discourse. 3 WORDING, style, phraseology, phrasing, expression, utterance, diction.

---

*Language terms include*: brogue, dialect, idiom, patois, tongue, pidgin, creole, lingua franca, vernacular, argot, cant, jargon, doublespeak, gobbledegook, buzzword, journalese, lingo (*infml*), patter, slang, cockney rhyming slang; etymology, lexicography, linguistics, phonetics, semantics, syntax, usage, grammar, orthography, sociolinguistics.

---

**languages**

---

*Languages of the world include*: Aborigine, Afghan, Afrikaans, Arabic, Balinese, Bantu, Basque, Bengali, Burmese, Belorussian, Catalan, Celtic,

Chinese, Cornish, Czech, Danish, Dutch, English, Esperanto, Estonian, Ethiopian, Farsi, Finnish, Flemish, French, Gaelic, German, Greek, Haitian, Hawaiian, Hebrew, Hindi, Hindustani, Hottentot, Hungarian, Icelandic, Indonesian, Inuit, Irish, Iranian, Iraqi, Italian, Japanese, Kurdish, Lapp, Latin, Latvian, Lithuanian, Magyar, Malay, Maltese, Mandarin, Manx, Maori, Nahuatl, Navajo, Norwegian, Persian, Polish, Portuguese, Punjabi, Quechua, Romany, Romanian, Russian, Sanskrit, Scots, Serbo-Croat, Siamese, Sinhalese, Slavonic, Slovak, Slovenian, Somali, Spanish, Swahili, Swedish, Swiss, Tamil, Thai, Tibetan, Tupí, Turkish, Ukrainian, Urdu, Vietnamese, Volapük, Welsh, Yiddish, Zulu.

**languish** v **1** WILT, droop, fade, fail, flag, wither, waste away, weaken, sink, faint, decline, mope, waste, grieve, sorrow, sigh, sicken. **2** PINE, yearn, want, long, desire, hanker, hunger.
**F3 1** flourish.

**lanky** adj gaunt, gangling, scrawny, tall, thin, scraggy, weedy.
**F3** short, squat.

**lap¹** v drink, sip, sup, lick.

**lap²** n circuit, round, orbit, tour, loop, course, circle, distance.
v wrap, fold, envelop, enfold, swathe, surround, cover, swaddle, overlap.

**lapse** n **1** ERROR, slip, mistake, negligence, omission, oversight, fault, failing, indiscretion, aberration, backsliding, relapse. **2** FALL, descent, decline, drop, deterioration. **3** BREAK, gap, interval, lull, interruption, intermission, pause.
v **1** DECLINE, fall, sink, drop, deteriorate, slide, slip, fail, worsen, degenerate, backslide. **2** EXPIRE, run out, end, stop, terminate.

**large** adj **1** BIG, huge, immense, massive, vast, sizable, great, giant, gigantic, bulky, enormous, king-sized, broad, considerable, monumental, substantial. **2** FULL, extensive, generous, liberal, roomy, plentiful, spacious, grand, sweeping, grandiose.
**F3 1** small, tiny.
**at large** free, at liberty, on the loose, on the run, independent.

**largely** adv mainly, principally, chiefly, generally, primarily, predominantly, mostly, considerably, by and large, widely, extensively, greatly.

**lark** n escapade, antic, fling, prank, romp, skylark (infml), revel, mischief, frolic, caper, game.

**lash¹** n blow, whip, stroke, swipe, hit.
v **1** WHIP, flog, beat, hit, thrash, strike, scourge. **2** ATTACK, criticize, lay into, scold.

**lash²** v tie, bind, fasten, secure, make fast, join, affix, rope, tether, strap.

**last¹** adj final, ultimate, closing, latest, rearmost, terminal, furthest, concluding, remotest, utmost, extreme, conclusive, definitive.
**F3** first, initial.
adv finally, ultimately, behind, after.
**F3** first, firstly.
**at last** eventually, finally, in the end, in due course, at length.

**last²** v continue, endure, remain, persist, keep (on), survive, hold out, carry on, wear, stay, hold on, stand up, abide (fml).
**F3** cease, stop, fade.

**lasting** adj enduring, unchanging, unceasing, unending, continuing, permanent, perpetual, lifelong, long-standing, long-term.
**F3** brief, fleeting, short-lived.

**latch** n fastening, catch, bar, bolt, lock, hook, hasp.

**late** adj **1** OVERDUE, behind, behindhand, slow, unpunctual, delayed, last-minute. **2** FORMER, previous,

departed, dead, deceased, past,
preceding, old. **3** RECENT, up-to-
date, current, fresh, new.
**E3 1** early, punctual.

**lately** *adv* recently, of late, latterly.

**latent** *adj* potential, dormant,
undeveloped, unrealized, lurking,
unexpressed, unseen, secret,
concealed, hidden, invisible,
underlying, veiled.
**E3** active, conspicuous.

**later** *adv* next, afterwards,
subsequently, after, successively.
**E3** earlier.

**lateral** *adj* sideways, side, oblique,
sideward, edgeways, marginal,
flanking.

**lather** *n* **1** FOAM, suds, soap-suds,
froth, bubbles, soap, shampoo.
**2** AGITATION, fluster, fuss, dither,
state (*infml*), flutter, flap (*infml*),
fever.
*v* foam, froth, soap, shampoo, whip
up.

**latitude** *n* **1** SCOPE, range, room,
space, play, clearance, breadth,
width, spread, sweep, reach, span,
field, extent. **2** FREEDOM, liberty,
licence, leeway, indulgence.

**latter** *adj* last-mentioned, last, later,
closing, concluding, ensuing,
succeeding, successive, second.
**E3** former.

**laugh** *v* chuckle, giggle, guffaw,
snigger, titter, chortle, split one's
sides, fall about (*infml*), crease up
(*infml*).
*n* giggle, chuckle, snigger, titter,
guffaw, chortle, lark, scream (*infml*),
hoot (*infml*), joke.

**laugh at** mock, ridicule, deride, jeer,
make fun of, scoff at, scorn, taunt.

**laughable** *adj* **1** FUNNY, amusing,
comical, humorous, hilarious, droll,
farcical, diverting. **2** RIDICULOUS,
absurd, ludicrous, preposterous,
nonsensical, derisory, derisive.
**E3 1** serious.

**laughing-stock** *n* figure of fun,

butt, victim, target, fair game.

**laughter** *n* laughing, giggling,
chuckling, chortling, guffawing,
tittering, hilarity, amusement,
merriment, mirth, glee, convulsions.

**launch** *v* **1** PROPEL, dispatch,
discharge, send off, project, float, set
in motion, throw, fire. **2** BEGIN,
commence, start, embark on,
establish, found, open, initiate,
inaugurate, introduce, instigate.

**lavatory** *n* toilet, loo (*infml*), WC,
bathroom, cloakroom, washroom,
water-closet, public convenience,
Ladies (*infml*), Gents (*infml*), bog
(*sl*), urinal, powder-room.

**lavish** *adj* **1** ABUNDANT, lush,
luxuriant, plentiful, profuse,
unlimited, prolific. **2** GENEROUS,
liberal, open-handed, extravagant,
thriftless, prodigal, immoderate,
intemperate, unstinting.
**E3 1** scant. **2** frugal, thrifty.

**law** *n* **1** RULE, act, decree, edict,
order, statute, regulation, command,
ordinance, charter, constitution,
enactment. **2** PRINCIPLE, axiom,
criterion, standard, precept, formula,
code, canon. **3** JURISPRUDENCE,
legislation, litigation.

**law-abiding** *adj* obedient, upright,
orderly, lawful, honest, honourable,
decent, good.
**E3** lawless.

**lawful** *adj* legal, legitimate,
permissible, legalized, authorized,
allowable, warranted, valid, proper,
rightful.
**E3** illegal, unlawful, illicit.

**lawless** *adj* disorderly, rebellious,
anarchic(al), unruly, riotous,
mutinous, unrestrained, chaotic,
wild, reckless.
**E3** law-abiding.

**lawsuit** *n* litigation, suit, action,
proceedings, case, prosecution,
dispute, process, trial, argument,
contest, cause.

**lawyer** *n* solicitor, barrister,

advocate, attorney, counsel, QC.

**lax** *adj* **1** CASUAL, careless, easy-going, slack, lenient, negligent, remiss. **2** IMPRECISE, inexact, indefinite, loose.
**F3 1** strict. **2** exact.

**lay¹** *v* **1** PUT, place, deposit, set down, settle, lodge, plant, set, establish, leave. **2** ARRANGE, position, set out, locate, work out, devise, prepare, present, submit. **3** ATTRIBUTE, ascribe, assign, charge.

**lay in** store (up), stock up, amass, accumulate, hoard, stockpile, gather, collect, build up, glean.

**lay into** (*infml*) attack, assail, pitch into, set about, tear into, let fly at.

**lay off 1** DISMISS, discharge, make redundant, sack (*infml*), pay off, let go. **2** (*infml*) GIVE UP, drop, stop, quit, cease, desist, leave off, leave alone, let up.

**lay on** provide, supply, cater, furnish, give, set up.

**lay out 1** DISPLAY, set out, spread out, exhibit, arrange, plan, design. **2** (*infml*) KNOCK OUT, fell, flatten, demolish. **3** (*infml*) SPEND, pay, shell out (*infml*), fork out (*infml*), give, invest.

**lay up** store up, hoard, accumulate, amass, keep, save, put away.

**lay²** *adj* **1** LAIC, secular. **2** AMATEUR, non-professional, non-specialist.
**F3 1** clergy. **2** expert.

**layer** *n* **1** COVER, coating, coat, covering, film, blanket, mantle, sheet, lamina. **2** STRATUM, seam, thickness, tier, bed, plate, row, ply.

**layman** *n* **1** LAYPERSON, parishioner. **2** AMATEUR, outsider.
**F3 1** clergyman. **2** expert.

**layout** *n* arrangement, design, outline, plan, sketch, draft, map.

**laze** *v* idle, loaf (*infml*), lounge, sit around, lie around, loll.

**lazy** *adj* idle, slothful, slack, work-shy, inactive, lethargic.

**F3** industrious.

**lead** *v* **1** GUIDE, conduct, escort, steer, pilot, usher. **2** RULE, govern, head, preside over, direct, supervise. **3** INFLUENCE, persuade, incline. **4** SURPASS, outdo, excel, outstrip, transcend. **5** PASS, spend, live, undergo.
**F3 1** follow.
*n* **1** PRIORITY, precedence, first place, start, van, vanguard, advantage, edge, margin. **2** LEADERSHIP, guidance, direction, example, model. **3** CLUE, hint, indication, guide, tip, suggestion. **4** TITLE ROLE, starring part, principal.

**lead off** begin, commence, open, get going, start (off), inaugurate, initiate, kick off (*infml*), start the ball rolling.

**lead on** entice, lure, seduce, tempt, draw on, beguile, persuade, string along, deceive, trick.

**lead to** cause, result in, produce, bring about, bring on, contribute to, tend towards.

**lead up to** prepare (the way) for, approach, introduce, make overtures, pave the way.

**leader** *n* head, chief, director, ruler, principal, commander, captain, boss (*infml*), superior, chieftain, ringleader, guide, conductor.
**F3** follower.

**leadership** *n* direction, control, command, management, authority, guidance, domination, pre-eminence, premiership, administration, sway, directorship.

**leading** *adj* main, principal, chief, primary, first, supreme, outstanding, foremost, dominant, ruling, superior, greatest, highest, governing, pre-eminent, number one.
**F3** subordinate.

**leaflet** *n* pamphlet, booklet, brochure, circular, handout.

**league** *n* **1** ASSOCIATION, confederation, alliance, union, federation, confederacy, coalition, combination, band, syndicate, guild, consortium, cartel, combine, partnership, fellowship, compact. **2** CATEGORY, class, level, group. **in league** allied, collaborating, conspiring.

**leak** *n* **1** CRACK, hole, opening, puncture, crevice, chink. **2** LEAKAGE, leaking, seepage, drip, oozing, percolation. **3** DISCLOSURE, divulgence.
*v* **1** SEEP, drip, ooze, escape, spill, trickle, percolate, exude, discharge. **2** DIVULGE, disclose, reveal, let slip, make known, make public, tell, give away, pass on.

**leaky** *adj* leaking, holey, perforated, punctured, split, cracked, porous, permeable.

**lean**[1] *v* **1** SLANT, slope, bend, tilt, list, tend. **2** RECLINE, prop, rest. **3** INCLINE, favour, prefer.

**lean**[2] *adj* **1** THIN, skinny, bony, gaunt, lank, angular, slim, scraggy, scrawny, emaciated. **2** SCANTY, inadequate, bare, barren.
Ea **1** fat.

**leaning** *n* tendency, inclination, propensity, partiality, liking, bent, bias, disposition, aptitude.

**leap** *v* **1** JUMP (OVER), bound, spring, vault, clear, skip, hop, bounce, caper, gambol. **2** SOAR, surge, increase, rocket, escalate, rise.
Ea **2** drop, fall.
*n* **1** JUMP, bound, spring, vault, hop, skip, caper. **2** INCREASE, upsurge, upswing, surge, rise, escalation.

**learn** *v* **1** GRASP, comprehend, understand, master, acquire, pick up, gather, assimilate, discern. **2** MEMORIZE, learn by heart. **3** DISCOVER, find out, ascertain, hear, detect, determine.

**learned** *adj* scholarly, erudite, well-informed, well-read, cultured, academic, lettered, literate, intellectual, versed.
Ea uneducated, illiterate.

**learner** *n* novice, beginner, student, trainee, pupil, scholar, apprentice.

**learning** *n* scholarship, erudition, education, schooling, knowledge, information, letters, study, wisdom, tuition, culture, edification, research.

**lease** *v* let, loan, rent, hire, sublet, charter.

**least** *adj* smallest, lowest, minimum, fewest, slightest, poorest.
Ea most.

**leave**[1] *v* **1** DEPART, go, go away, set out, take off, decamp, exit, move, quit, retire, withdraw, disappear, do a bunk (*infml*). **2** ABANDON, desert, forsake, give up, drop, relinquish, renounce, pull out, surrender, desist, cease. **3** ASSIGN, commit, entrust, consign, bequeath, will, hand down, leave behind, give over, transmit.
Ea **1** arrive. **3** receive.
**leave off** stop, cease, discontinue, desist, abstain, refrain, lay off, quit, terminate, break off, end, halt, give over.
**leave out** omit, exclude, overlook, ignore, except, disregard, pass over, count out, cut (out), eliminate, neglect, reject, cast aside, bar.

**leave**[2] *n* **1** PERMISSION, authorization, consent, allowance, sanction, concession, dispensation, indulgence, liberty, freedom. **2** HOLIDAY, time off, vacation, sabbatical, furlough.
Ea **1** refusal, rejection.

**lecture** *n* **1** DISCOURSE, address, lesson, speech, talk, instruction. **2** REPRIMAND, rebuke, reproof, scolding, harangue, censure, chiding, telling-off (*infml*), talking-to (*infml*), dressing-down (*infml*).
*v* **1** TALK, teach, hold forth, speak, expound, address. **2** REPRIMAND, reprove, scold, admonish, harangue, chide, censure, tell off (*infml*).

**ledge** *n* shelf, sill, mantle, ridge, projection, step.

**leeway** *n* space, room, latitude,

elbow-room, play, scope.

**left** *adj* **1** LEFT-HAND, port, sinistral.
**2** LEFT-WING, socialist, radical,
progressive, revolutionary, liberal,
communist, red (*infml*).
**E3 1** right. **2** right-wing.

**left-overs** *n* leavings, remainder,
remains, remnants, residue, surplus,
scraps, sweepings, refuse, dregs,
excess.

**leg** *n* **1** LIMB, member, shank, pin
(*infml*), stump (*infml*). **2** SUPPORT,
prop, upright, brace. **3** STAGE, part,
section, portion, stretch, segment,
lap.

**legacy** *n* bequest, endowment, gift,
heritage, heritance, inheritance,
birthright, estate, heirloom.

**legal** *adj* **1** LAWFUL, legitimate,
permissible, sanctioned, allowed,
authorized, allowable, legalized,
constitutional, valid, warranted,
above-board, proper, rightful.
**2** JUDICIAL, forensic. **3** judiciary.
**E3 1** illegal.

---

*Legal terms include*: *courts*: county
court, courthouse, courtroom, Court
of Appeal, Court of Protection,
Court of Session, Crown Court,
European Court of Human Rights,
European Court of Justice, High
Court of Justice, House of Lords,
International Court of Justice,
juvenile court, magistrates' court,
Old Bailey, small claims court,
Supreme Court (*North Amer.*);
*criminal law*: acquittal, age of
consent, alibi, arrest, bail, caution,
charge, confession, contempt of
court, dock, fine, guilty, indictment,
innocent, malice aforethought,
pardon, parole, plead guilty, plead
not guilty, prisoner, probation,
remand, reprieve, sentence; *marriage
and divorce*: adultery, alimony,
annulment, bigamy, decree absolute,
decree nisi, divorce, maintenance,
settlement; *people*: accessory,

---

accomplice, accused, advocate,
Attorney General, barrister, brief
(*infml*), clerk of the court, client,
commissioner for oaths, convict,
coroner, criminal, defendant,
Director of Public Prosecutions,
DPP, executor, felon, judge, jury,
justice of the peace, JP, juvenile, Law
Lord, lawyer, Lord Advocate, Lord
Chancellor, Lord Chief Justice,
liquidator, magistrate, notary public,
offender, plaintiff, procurator fiscal,
receiver, Queen's Counsel, QC,
sheriff, solicitor, witness, young
offender; *property or ownership*:
asset, conveyance, copyright, deed,
easement, endowment, estate,
exchange of contracts, fee simple,
foreclosure, freehold, inheritance,
intestacy, lease, leasehold, legacy,
local search, mortgage, patent,
tenancy, title, trademark, will;
*miscellaneous*: act of God, Act of
Parliament, adjournment, affidavit,
agreement, allegation, amnesty,
appeal, arbitration, bar, Bill of
Rights, bench, brief, by-law, charter,
civil law, claim, codicil, common law,
constitution, contract covenant,
cross-examine, courtcase, court
martial, custody, damages, defence,
demand, equity, eviction, evidence,
extradition, grant, hearing, hung
jury, indemnity, injunction, inquest,
inquiry, judgment, judiciary, lawsuit,
legal aid, liability, mandate,
misadventure, miscarriage of justice,
oath, party, penalty, power of
attorney, precedent, probate,
proceedings, proof, proxy, public
inquiry, repeal, sanction, settlement,
statute, subpoena, sue, summons,
testimony, trial, tribunal, verdict,
waiver, ward of court, warrant, will,
writ. *see also* **crime**.

---

**legalize** *v* legitimize, license, permit,
sanction, allow, authorize, warrant,
validate, approve.

**legend** *n* **1** MYTH, story, tale, folk-tale, fable, fiction, narrative. **2** INSCRIPTION, caption, key, motto.

**legendary** *adj* **1** MYTHICAL, fabulous, story-book, fictitious, traditional. **2** FAMOUS, celebrated, renowned, well-known, illustrious.

**legible** *adj* readable, intelligible, decipherable, clear, distinct, neat.
**F3** illegible.

**legislate** *v* enact, ordain, authorize, codify, constitutionalize, prescribe, establish.

**legislation** *n* **1** LAW, statute, regulation, bill, act, charter, authorization, ruling, measure. **2** LAW-MAKING, enactment, codification.

**legislative** *adj* law-making, law-giving, judicial, parliamentary, congressional, senatorial.

**legislator** *n* law-maker, law-giver, member of parliament, parliamentarian.

**legislature** *n* assembly, chamber, house, parliament, congress, senate.

**legitimate** *adj* **1** LEGAL, lawful, authorized, statutory, rightful, proper, correct, real, acknowledged. **2** REASONABLE, sensible, admissible, acceptable, justifiable, warranted, well-founded, valid, true.
**F3** **1** illegal. **2** invalid.

**leisure** *n* relaxation, rest, spare time, time off, ease, freedom, liberty, recreation, retirement, holiday, vacation.
**F3** work.

**leisurely** *adj* unhurried, slow, relaxed, comfortable, easy, unhasty, tranquil, restful, gentle, carefree, laid-back (*infml*), lazy, loose.
**F3** rushed, hectic.

**lend** *v* **1** LOAN, advance. **2** GIVE, grant, bestow, provide, furnish, confer, supply, impart, contribute.
**F3** **1** borrow.

**length** *n* **1** EXTENT, distance, measure, reach, piece, portion,
section, segment. **2** DURATION, period, term, stretch, space, span.

**lengthen** *v* stretch, extend, elongate, draw out, prolong, protract, spin out, eke (out), pad out, increase, expand, continue.
**F3** reduce, shorten.

**lengthy** *adj* long, prolonged, protracted, extended, lengthened, overlong, long-drawn-out, long-winded, rambling, diffuse, verbose, drawn-out, interminable.
**F3** brief, concise.

**lenient** *adj* tolerant, forbearing, sparing, indulgent, merciful, forgiving, soft-hearted, kind, mild, gentle, compassionate.
**F3** strict, severe.

**lessen** *v* decrease, reduce, diminish, lower, ease, abate, contract, die down, dwindle, lighten, slow down, weaken, shrink, abridge, de-escalate, erode, minimize, narrow, moderate, slack, flag, fail, deaden, impair.
**F3** grow, increase.

**lesser** *adj* lower, secondary, inferior, smaller, subordinate, slighter, minor.
**F3** greater.

**lesson** *n* **1** CLASS, period, instruction, lecture, tutorial, teaching, coaching. **2** ASSIGNMENT, exercise, homework, practice, task, drill. **3** EXAMPLE, model, warning, deterrent.

**let** *v* **1** PERMIT, allow, give leave, give permission, authorize, consent to, agree to, sanction, grant, OK, enable, tolerate. **2** LEASE, hire, rent.
**F3** **1** prohibit, forbid.

**let in** admit, accept, receive, take in, include, incorporate, welcome.
**F3** prohibit, bar, forbid.

**let off 1** EXCUSE, absolve, pardon, exempt, forgive, acquit, exonerate, spare, ignore, liberate, release. **2** DISCHARGE, detonate, fire, explode, emit.
**F3** **1** punish.

**let out 1** FREE, release, let go, discharge, leak (*infml*). **2** REVEAL, disclose, make known, utter, betray, let slip.
**E3 1** keep in.

**let up** abate, subside, ease (up), moderate, slacken, diminish, decrease, stop, end, cease, halt.
**E3** continue.

**let-down** *n* anticlimax, disappointment, disillusionment, set-back, betrayal, desertion, wash-out (*infml*).

**lethal** *adj* fatal, deadly, deathly, mortal, dangerous, poisonous, noxious, destructive, devastating.
**E3** harmless, safe.

**lethargy** *n* lassitude, listlessness, sluggishness, torpor, dullness, inertia, slowness, apathy, inaction, indifference, sleepiness, drowsiness, stupor.
**E3** liveliness.

**letter** *n* **1** NOTE, message, line, missive, epistle (*fml*), dispatch, communication, chit, acknowledgement. **2** CHARACTER, symbol, sign, grapheme.

**level** *adj* **1** FLAT, smooth, even, flush, horizontal, aligned, plane.
**2** EQUAL, balanced, even, on a par, neck and neck, matching, uniform.
**E3 1** uneven. **2** unequal.
*v* **1** DEMOLISH, destroy, devastate, flatten, knock down, raze, pull down, bulldoze, tear down, lay low. **2** EVEN OUT, flush, plane, smooth, equalize. **3** DIRECT, point.
*n* **1** HEIGHT, elevation, altitude. **2** POSITION, rank, status, class, degree, grade, standard, standing, plane, echelon, layer, stratum, storey, stage, zone.

**level-headed** *adj* calm, balanced, even-tempered, sensible, steady, reasonable, composed, cool, unflappable, sane, self-possessed, dependable.

**lever** *n* bar, crowbar, jemmy, joy-stick, handle.
*v* force, prise, pry, raise, dislodge, jemmy, shift, move, heave.

**levity** *n* light-heartedness, frivolity, facetiousness, flippancy, irreverence, triviality, silliness.
**E3** seriousness.

**levy** *v* tax, impose, exact, demand, charge.
*n* tax, toll, subscription, contribution, duty, fee, tariff, collection.

**lewd** *adj* obscene, smutty, indecent, bawdy, pornographic, salacious, licentious, lascivious, impure, vulgar, unchaste, lustful.
**E3** decent, chaste.

**liability** *n* **1** ACCOUNTABILITY, duty, obligation, responsibility, onus.
**2** DEBT, arrears, indebtedness.
**3** DRAWBACK, disadvantage, hindrance, impediment, drag (*infml*).

**liable** *adj* **1** INCLINED, likely, apt, disposed, prone, tending, susceptible.
**2** RESPONSIBLE, answerable, accountable, amenable.

**liaison** *n* **1** CONTACT, connection, go-between, link. **2** LOVE AFFAIR, affair, romance, intrigue, amour, entanglement.

**liar** *n* falsifier, perjurer, deceiver, fibber (*infml*).

**libel** *n* defamation, slur, smear, slander, vilification, aspersion, calumny.
*v* defame, slur, smear, slander, vilify, malign.

**libellous** *adj* defamatory, vilifying, slanderous, derogatory, maligning, injurious, scurrilous, untrue.

**liberal** *adj* **1** BROAD-MINDED, open-minded, tolerant, lenient.
**2** PROGRESSIVE, reformist, moderate. **3** GENEROUS, ample, bountiful, lavish, plentiful, handsome.
**E3 1** narrow-minded. **2** conservative.
**3** mean, miserly.

**liberate** *v* free, emancipate, release,

let loose, let go, let out, set free,
deliver, unchain, discharge, rescue,
ransom.

**Ea** imprison, enslave.

**liberty** n **1** FREEDOM, emancipation,
release, independence, autonomy.
**2** LICENCE, permission, sanction,
right, authorization, dispensation,
franchise. **3** FAMILIARITY,
disrespect, overfamiliarity,
presumption, impertinence,
impudence.

**Ea 1** imprisonment. **3** respect.

**at liberty** free, unconstrained,
unrestricted, not confined.

**licence** n **1** PERMISSION, permit,
leave, warrant, authorization,
authority, certificate, charter, right,
imprimatur, entitlement, privilege,
dispensation, carte blanche, freedom,
liberty, exemption, independence.
**2** ABANDON, dissipation, excess,
immoderation, indulgence,
lawlessness, unruliness, anarchy,
disorder, debauchery, dissoluteness,
impropriety, irresponsibility.

**Ea 1** prohibition, restriction.
**2** decorum, moderation.

**license** v permit, allow, authorize,
certify, warrant, entitle, empower,
sanction, commission, accredit.

**Ea** ban, prohibit.

**licentious** adj debauched, dissolute,
profligate, lascivious, immoral,
abandoned, lewd, promiscuous,
libertine, impure, lax, lustful,
disorderly, wanton, unchaste.

**Ea** modest, chaste.

**lick** v tongue, touch, wash, lap, taste,
dart, flick, flicker, play over, smear,
brush.

**lie**[1] v perjure, misrepresent,
fabricate, falsify, fib (infml), invent,
equivocate, prevaricate, forswear
oneself (fml).
n falsehood, untruth, falsification,
fabrication, invention, fiction, deceit,
fib (infml), falsity, white lie,
prevarication, whopper (infml).

**Ea** truth.

**lie**[2] v be, exist, dwell, belong, extend,
remain.

**lie down** repose, rest, recline, stretch
out, lounge, couch, laze.

**life** n **1** BEING, existence, animation,
breath, viability, entity, soul.
**2** DURATION, course, span, career.
**3** LIVELINESS, vigour, vitality,
vivacity, verve, zest, energy, élan,
spirit, sparkle, activity.

**lifeless** adj **1** DEAD, deceased,
defunct, cold, unconscious,
inanimate, insensible, stiff.
**2** LETHARGIC, listless, sluggish, dull,
apathetic, passive, insipid, colourless,
slow. **3** BARREN, bare, empty,
desolate, arid.

**Ea 1** alive. **2** lively.

**lifelike** adj realistic, true-to-life,
real, true, vivid, natural, authentic,
faithful, exact, graphic.

**Ea** unrealistic, unnatural.

**lifelong** adj lifetime, long-lasting,
long-standing, persistent, lasting,
enduring, abiding, permanent,
constant.

**Ea** impermanent, temporary.

**lift** v **1** she lifted the chair: raise,
elevate, hoist, upraise. **2** he lifted
their spirits: uplift, exalt, buoy up,
boost. **3** the ban has been lifted:
revoke, cancel, relax.

**Ea 1** drop. **2** lower.

**light**[1] n **1** ILLUMINATION,
brightness, brilliance, luminescence,
radiance, glow, ray, shine, glare,
gleam, glint, lustre, flash, blaze.
**2** LAMP, lantern, lighter, match,
torch, candle, bulb, beacon. **3** DAY,
daybreak, daylight, daytime, dawn,
sunrise. **4** ENLIGHTENMENT,
explanation, elucidation,
understanding.

**Ea 1** darkness. **3** night.
v **1** IGNITE, fire, set alight, set fire to,
kindle. **2** ILLUMINATE, light up,
lighten, brighten, animate, cheer,
switch on, turn on, put on.

⛏ 1 extinguish. 2 darken.

*adj* 1 ILLUMINATED, bright, brilliant, luminous, glowing, shining, well-lit, sunny. 2 PALE, pastel, fair, blond, blonde, bleached, faded, faint.

⛏ 1 dark. 2 black.

**light²** *adj* 1 WEIGHTLESS, insubstantial, delicate, airy, buoyant, flimsy, feathery, slight. 2 TRIVIAL, inconsiderable, trifling, inconsequential, worthless. 3 CHEERFUL, cheery, carefree, lively, merry, blithe. 4 ENTERTAINING, amusing, funny, humorous, frivolous, witty, pleasing.

⛏ 1 heavy, weighty. 2 important, serious. 3 solemn. 4 serious.

**lighten¹** *v* illuminate, illumine, brighten, light up, shine.

⛏ darken.

**lighten²** *v* 1 EASE, lessen, unload, lift, relieve, reduce, mitigate, alleviate. 2 BRIGHTEN, cheer, encourage, hearten, uplift, gladden, revive, elate, buoy up, inspire.

⛏ 1 burden. 2 depress.

**light-headed** *adj* 1 FAINT, giddy, dizzy, woozy (*infml*), delirious. 2 FLIGHTY, scatter-brained (*infml*), foolish, frivolous, silly, superficial, shallow, feather-brained (*infml*), flippant, vacuous, trifling.

⛏ 2 level-headed, solemn.

**light-hearted** *adj* cheerful, joyful, jolly, happy-go-lucky, bright, carefree, untroubled, merry, sunny, glad, elated, jovial, playful.

⛏ sad, unhappy, serious.

**likable** *adj* loveable, pleasing, appealing, agreeable, charming, engaging, winsome, pleasant, amiable, congenial, attractive, sympathetic.

⛏ unpleasant, disagreeable.

**like¹** *adj* similar, resembling, alike, same, identical, equivalent, akin, corresponding, related, relating, parallel, allied, analogous,

approximating.

⛏ unlike, dissimilar.

**like²** *v* 1 ENJOY, delight in, care for, admire, appreciate, love, adore, hold dear, esteem, cherish, prize, relish, revel in, approve, take (kindly) to. 2 PREFER, choose, select, feel inclined, go for (*infml*), desire, want, wish.

⛏ 1 dislike. 2 reject.

**likelihood** *n* likeliness, probability, possibility, chance, prospect, liability.

⛏ improbability, unlikeliness.

**likely** *adj* 1 PROBABLE, possible, anticipated, expected, liable, prone, tending, predictable, odds-on (*infml*), inclined, foreseeable. 2 CREDIBLE, believable, plausible, feasible, reasonable. 3 PROMISING, hopeful, pleasing, appropriate, proper, suitable.

⛏ 1 unlikely. 3 unsuitable.

*adv* probably, presumably, like as not, in all probability, no doubt, doubtlessly.

**liken** *v* compare, equate, match, parallel, relate, juxtapose, associate, set beside.

**likeness** *n* 1 SIMILARITY, resemblance, affinity, correspondence. 2 REPRESENTATION, image, copy, reproduction, replica, facsimile, effigy, picture, portrait, photograph, counterpart. 3 SEMBLANCE, guise, appearance, form.

⛏ 1 dissimilarity, unlikeness.

**likewise** *adv* moreover, furthermore, in addition, similarly, also, further, besides, by the same token, too.

**liking** *n* fondness, love, affection, preference, partiality, affinity, predilection, penchant, taste, attraction, appreciation, proneness, propensity, inclination, tendency, bias, desire, weakness, fancy, soft spot.

**E3** dislike, aversion, hatred.

**limb** *n* arm, leg, member, appendage, branch, projection, offshoot, wing, fork, extension, part, spur, extremity, bough.

**limber up** *v* loosen up, warm up, work out, exercise, prepare.

**limelight** *n* fame, celebrity, spotlight, stardom, recognition, renown, attention, prominence, publicity, public eye.

**limit** *n* **1** BOUNDARY, bound, border, frontier, confines, edge, brink, threshold, verge, brim, end, perimeter, rim, compass, termination, ultimate, utmost, terminus, extent. **2** CHECK, curb, restraint, restriction, limitation, ceiling, maximum, cut-off point, saturation point, deadline.
*v* check, curb, restrict, restrain, constrain, confine, demarcate, delimit, bound, hem in, ration, specify, hinder.

**limitation** *n* **1** CHECK, restriction, curb, control, constraint, restraint, delimitation, demarcation, block.
**2** INADEQUACY, shortcoming, disadvantage, drawback, condition, qualification, reservation.
**E3 1** extension.

**limited** *adj* restricted, circumscribed, constrained, controlled, confined, checked, defined, finite, fixed, minimal, narrow, inadequate, insufficient.
**E3** limitless.

**limitless** *adj* unlimited, unbounded, boundless, illimited, undefined, immeasurable, incalculable, infinite, countless, endless, never-ending, unending, inexhaustible, untold, vast.
**E3** limited.

**limp¹** *v* hobble, falter, stumble, hop, shuffle, shamble.

**limp²** *adj* **1** FLABBY, drooping, flaccid, floppy, loose, slack, relaxed, lax, soft, flexible, pliable, limber.
**2** TIRED, weary, exhausted, spent,

weak, worn out, lethargic, debilitated, enervated.
**E3 1** stiff. **2** vigorous.

**line¹** *n* **1** STROKE, band, bar, stripe, mark, strip, rule, dash, strand, streak, underline, score, scratch. **2** ROW, rank, queue, file, column, sequence, series, procession, chain, trail. **3** LIMIT, boundary, border, borderline, edge, frontier, demarcation. **4** STRING, rope, cord, cable, thread, filament, wire.
**5** PROFILE, contour, outline, silhouette, figure, formation, configuration. **6** CREASE, wrinkle, furrow, groove, corrugation.
**7** COURSE, path, direction, track, route, axis. **8** APPROACH, avenue, course (of action), belief, ideology, policy, system, position, practice, procedure, method, scheme.
**9** OCCUPATION, business, trade, profession, vocation, job, activity, interest, employment, department, calling, field, province, forte, area, pursuit, specialization, specialty, specialism, speciality. **10** ANCESTRY, family, descent, extraction, lineage, pedigree, stock, race, breed.

**line up 1** ALIGN, range, straighten, marshal, order, regiment, queue up, form ranks, fall in, array, assemble. **2** ORGANIZE, lay on, arrange, prepare, produce, procure, secure, obtain.

**line²** *v* encase, cover, fill, pad, stuff, reinforce.

**lineage** *n* (*fml*) ancestry, descent, extraction, genealogy, family, line, pedigree, race, stock, birth, breed, house, heredity, ancestors, forebears, descendants, offspring, succession.

**lined** *adj* **1** RULED, feint. **2** WRINKLED, furrowed, wizened, worn.
**E3 1** unlined. **2** smooth.

**line-up** *n* array, arrangement, queue, row, selection, cast, team, bill.

**linger** *v* loiter, delay, dally, tarry, wait, remain, stay, hang on, lag,

procrastinate, dawdle, dilly-dally (*infml*), idle, stop, endure, hold out, last, persist, survive.
**F3** leave, rush.

**lining** *n* inlay, interfacing, padding, backing, encasement, stiffening.

**link** *n* **1** CONNECTION, bond, tie, association, joint, relationship, tie-up, union, knot, liaison, attachment, communication. **2** PART, piece, element, member, constituent, component, division.
*v* connect, join, couple, tie, fasten, unite, bind, amalgamate, merge, associate, ally, bracket, identify, relate, yoke, attach, hook up, join forces, team up.
**F3** separate, unfasten.

**lip** *n* edge, brim, border, brink, rim, margin, verge.

**liquid** *n* liquor, fluid, juice, drink, sap, solution, lotion.
*adj* fluid, flowing, liquefied, watery, wet, runny, melted, molten, thawed, clear, smooth.
**F3** solid.

**liquidate** *v* **1** ANNIHILATE, terminate, do away with, dissolve, kill, murder, massacre, assassinate, destroy, dispatch, abolish, eliminate, exterminate, remove, finish off, rub out (*infml*). **2** PAY (OFF), close down, clear, discharge, wind up, sell.

**liquor** *n* alcohol, intoxicant, strong drink, spirits, drink, hard stuff (*infml*), booze (*infml*).

**list¹** *n* catalogue, roll, inventory, register, enumeration, schedule, index, listing, record, file, directory, table, tabulation, tally, series, syllabus, invoice.
*v* enumerate, register, itemize, catalogue, index, tabulate, record, file, enrol, enter, note, bill, book, set down, write down.

**list²** *v* lean, incline, tilt, slope, heel (over), tip.

**listen** *v* hark, attend, pay attention, hear, heed, hearken, hang on (someone's) words, prick up one's ears, take notice, lend an ear, eavesdrop, overhear, give ear.

**listless** *adj* sluggish, lethargic, languid, torpid, enervated, spiritless, limp, lifeless, inert, inactive, impassive, indifferent, uninterested, vacant, apathetic, indolent, depressed, bored, heavy.
**F3** energetic, enthusiastic.

**literal** *adj* **1** VERBATIM, word-for-word, strict, close, actual, precise, faithful, exact, accurate, factual, true, genuine, unexaggerated. **2** PROSAIC, unimaginative, uninspired, matter-of-fact, down-to-earth, humdrum.
**F3** **1** imprecise, loose. **2** imaginative.

**literary** *adj* educated, well-read, bookish, learned, erudite, scholarly, lettered, literate, cultured, cultivated, refined, formal.
**F3** ignorant, illiterate.

**literature** *n* **1** WRITINGS, letters, paper(s). **2** INFORMATION, leaflet(s), pamphlet(s), circular(s), brochure(s), hand-out(s), bumf (*infml*).

> *Types of literature include:*
> allegory, anti-novel, autobiography, belles-lettres (*fml*), biography, classic novel, criticism, drama, epic, epistle, essay, fiction, Gothic novel, lampoon, libretto, magnum opus, non-fiction, novel, novella, parody, pastiche, penny dreadful (*infml*), picaresque novel, poetry, polemic, postil, prose, roman novel, saga, satire, thesis, tragedy, treatise, triad, trilogy, verse. *see also* **poem**; **story**.

**litigation** *n* lawsuit, action, suit, case, prosecution, process, contention.

**litter** *n* **1** RUBBISH, debris, refuse, waste, mess, disorder, clutter, confusion, disarray, untidiness, junk (*infml*), muck, jumble, fragments, shreds. **2** OFFSPRING, young, progeny (*fml*), brood, family.

*v* strew, scatter, mess up, disorder, clutter.

**F3** tidy.

**little** *adj* **1** SMALL, short, tiny, wee (*infml*), minute, teeny (*infml*), diminutive, miniature, infinitesimal, mini, microscopic, petite, pint-size(d) (*infml*), slender. **2** SHORT-LIVED, brief, fleeting, passing, transient. **3** INSUFFICIENT, sparse, scant, meagre, paltry, skimpy. **4** INSIGNIFICANT, inconsiderable, negligible, trivial, petty, trifling, unimportant.

**F3** **1** big. **2** lengthy. **3** ample. **4** considerable.

*adv* barely, hardly, scarcely, rarely, seldom, infrequently, not much.

**F3** frequently.

*n* bit, dash, pinch, spot, trace, drop, dab, speck, touch, taste, particle, hint, fragment, modicum, trifle.

**F3** lot.

**live**[1] *v* **1** BE, exist, breathe, draw breath. **2** LAST, endure, continue, remain, persist, survive. **3** DWELL, inhabit, reside, lodge, abide. **4** PASS, spend, lead.

**F3** **1** die. **2** cease.

**live**[2] *adj* **1** ALIVE, living, existent. **2** LIVELY, vital, active, energetic, dynamic, alert, vigorous. **3** BURNING, glowing, blazing, ignited. **4** RELEVANT, current, topical, pertinent, controversial.

**F3** **1** dead. **2** apathetic.

**livelihood** *n* occupation, employment, job, living, means, income, maintenance, work, support, subsistence, sustenance.

**lively** *adj* **1** ANIMATED, alert, active, energetic, spirited, vivacious, vigorous, sprightly, spry, agile, nimble, quick, keen. **2** CHEERFUL, blithe, merry, frisky, perky, breezy, chirpy (*infml*), frolicsome. **3** BUSY, bustling, brisk, crowded, eventful,

exciting, buzzing. **4** VIVID, bright, colourful, stimulating, stirring, invigorating, racy, refreshing, sparkling.

**F3** **1** moribund, apathetic. **3** inactive.

**liven (up)** enliven, vitalize, put life into, rouse, invigorate, animate, energize, brighten, stir (up), buck up (*infml*), pep up (*infml*), perk up (*infml*), hot up (*infml*).

**F3** dishearten.

**livery** *n* uniform, costume, regalia, dress, clothes, clothing, apparel (*fml*), attire, vestments, suit, garb, habit.

**livid** *adj* **1** LEADEN, black-and-blue, bruised, discoloured, greyish, purple. **2** PALE, pallid, ashen, blanched, bloodless, wan, waxy, pasty. **3** (*infml*) ANGRY, furious, infuriated, irate, outraged, enraged, raging, fuming, indignant, incensed, exasperated, mad (*infml*).

**F3** **3** calm.

**living** *adj* alive, breathing, existing, live, current, extant, operative, strong, vigorous, active, lively, vital, animated.

**F3** dead, sluggish.

*n* **1** BEING, life, animation, existence. **2** LIVELIHOOD, maintenance, support, income, subsistence, sustenance, work, job, occupation, profession, benefice, way of life.

**load** *n* **1** BURDEN, onus, encumbrance, weight, pressure, oppression, millstone. **2** CARGO, consignment, shipment, goods, lading, freight.

*v* **1** BURDEN, weigh down, encumber, overburden, oppress, trouble, weight, saddle with. **2** PACK, pile, heap, freight, fill, stack.

**loaded** *adj* burdened, charged, laden, full, weighted.

**loafer** *n* (*infml*) idler, layabout (*infml*), shirker, skiver (*infml*), sluggard, wastrel, lounger, ne'er-do-well, lazybones (*infml*).

**loan** *n* advance, credit, mortgage,

allowance.

*v* lend, advance, credit, allow.

**loathe** *v* hate, detest, abominate, abhor, despise, dislike.

☒ adore, love.

**loathing** *n* hatred, detestation, abhorrence, abomination, repugnance, revulsion, repulsion, dislike, disgust, aversion, horror.

☒ affection, love.

**loathsome** *adj* detestable, abhorrent, odious, repulsive, abominable, hateful, repugnant, repellent, offensive, horrible, disgusting, vile, revolting, nasty.

**lobby** *v* campaign for, press for, demand, persuade, call for, urge, push for, influence, solicit, pressure, promote.

*n* 1 VESTIBULE, foyer, porch, anteroom, hall, hallway, waiting-room, entrance hall, corridor, passage. 2 PRESSURE GROUP, campaign, ginger group.

**local** *adj* regional, provincial, community, district, neighbourhood, parochial, vernacular, small-town, limited, narrow, restricted, parish(-pump).

☒ national.

*n* 1 INHABITANT, citizen, resident, native. 2 (*infml*) PUB.

**locality** *n* neighbourhood, vicinity, district, area, locale, region, position, place, site, spot, scene, setting.

**locate** *v* 1 FIND, discover, unearth, run to earth (*infml*), track down, detect, lay one's hands on (*infml*), pin-point, identify. 2 SITUATE, settle, fix, establish, place, put, set, seat.

**location** *n* position, situation, place, locus, whereabouts, venue, site, locale, bearings, spot, point.

**lock** *n* fastening, bolt, clasp, padlock.

*v* 1 FASTEN, secure, bolt, latch, seal, shut. 2 JOIN, unite, engage, link, mesh, entangle, entwine, clench.

3 CLASP, hug, embrace, grasp, encircle, enclose, clutch, grapple.

☒ unlock.

**lock out** shut out, refuse admittance to, keep out, exclude, bar, debar.

**lock up** imprison, jail, confine, shut in, shut up, incarcerate, secure, cage, pen, detain, close up.

☒ free.

**lodge** *n* hut, cabin, cottage, chalet, shelter, retreat, den, gatehouse, house, hunting-lodge, meeting-place, club, haunt.

*v* 1 ACCOMMODATE, put up (*infml*), quarter, board, billet, shelter. 2 LIVE, stray, reside. 3 FIX, imbed, implant, get stuck. 4 DEPOSIT, place, put, submit, register.

**lodger** *n* boarder, paying guest, resident, tenant, roomer, inmate, guest.

**lodgings** *n* accommodation, digs (*infml*), dwelling, quarters, billet, abode, boarding-house, rooms, pad (*infml*), residence.

**log** *n* 1 TIMBER, trunk, block, chunk. 2 RECORD, diary, journal, logbook, daybook, account, tally.

*v* record, register, write up, note, book, chart, tally.

**logic** *n* reasoning, reason, sense, deduction, rationale, argumentation.

**logical** *adj* reasonable, rational, reasoned, coherent, consistent, valid, sound, well-founded, clear, sensible, deducible, methodical, well-organized.

☒ illogical, irrational.

**loiter** *v* dawdle, hang about, idle, linger, dally, dilly-dally (*infml*), delay, mooch, lag, saunter.

**lone** *adj* single, sole, one, only, isolated, solitary, separate, separated, unattached, unaccompanied, unattended.

☒ accompanied.

**loneliness** *n* aloneness, isolation, lonesomeness, solitariness, solitude, seclusion, desolation.

**lonely** adj **1** ALONE, friendless, lonesome, solitary, abandoned, forsaken, companionless, unaccompanied, destitute.
**2** ISOLATED, uninhabited, remote, out-of-the-way, unfrequented, secluded, abandoned, deserted, forsaken, desolate.
**1** popular. **2** crowded, populous.

**long** adj lengthy, extensive, extended, expanded, prolonged, protracted, stretched, spread out, sustained, expansive, far-reaching, long-drawn-out, interminable, slow.
**E3** brief, short, fleeting, abbreviated.
**long for** yearn for, crave, want, wish, desire, dream of, hanker for, pine, thirst for, lust after, covet, itch for, yen for (infml).

**longing** n craving, desire, yearning, hungering, hankering, yen, thirst, wish, urge, coveting, aspiration, ambition.

**long-lasting** adj permanent, imperishable, enduring, unchanging, unfading, continuing, abiding, long-standing, prolonged, protracted.
**E3** short-lived, ephemeral, transient.

**long-standing** adj established, long-established, long-lived, long-lasting, enduring, abiding, time-honoured, traditional.

**long-suffering** adj uncomplaining, forbearing, forgiving, tolerant, easy-going, patient, stoical.

**long-winded** adj lengthy, overlong, prolonged, diffuse, verbose, wordy, voluble, long-drawn-out, discursive, repetitious, rambling, tedious.
**E3** brief, terse.

**look** v **1** WATCH, see, observe, view, survey, regard, gaze, study, stare, examine, inspect, scrutinize, glance, contemplate, scan, peep, gawp (infml). **2** SEEM, appear, show, exhibit, display.
n **1** VIEW, survey, inspection, examination, observation, sight, review, once-over (infml), glance,

glimpse, gaze, peek. **2** APPEARANCE, aspect, manner, semblance, mien, expression, bearing, face, complexion.
**look after** take care of, mind, care for, attend to, take charge of, tend, keep an eye on, watch over, protect, supervise, guard.
**E3** neglect.

**look down on** despise, scorn, sneer at, hold in contempt, disdain, look down one's nose at (infml), turn one's nose up at (infml).
**E3** esteem, approve.

**look forward to** anticipate, await, expect, hope for, long for, envisage, envision, count on, wait for, look for.

**look into** investigate, probe, research, study, go into, examine, enquire about, explore, check out, inspect, scrutinize, look over, plumb, fathom.

**look out** pay attention, watch out, beware, be careful, keep an eye out.

**look over** inspect, examine, check, give a once-over (infml), cast an eye over, look through, scan, view.

**look up 1** SEARCH FOR, research, hunt for, find, track down. **2** VISIT, call on, drop in on, look in on, pay a visit to, stop by, drop by. **3** IMPROVE, get better, pick up, progress, come on.

**look up to** admire, esteem, respect, revere, honour, have a high opinion of.

**look-alike** n double, replica, twin, spitting image (infml), living image, clone, spit (infml), ringer (infml), doppelgänger.

**look-out** n **1** GUARD, sentry, watch, watch-tower, watchman, sentinal, tower, post. **2** (infml) CONCERN, responsibility, worry, affair, business, problem.

**loom** v appear, emerge, take shape, menace, threaten, impend, hang over, dominate, tower, overhang, rise, soar, overshadow, overtop.

**loop** n hoop, ring, circle, noose, coil, eyelet, loophole, spiral, curve, curl, kink, twist, whorl, twirl, turn, bend.
v coil, encircle, roll, bend, circle,

curve round, turn, twist, spiral, connect, join, knot, fold, braid.

**loophole** n let-out, escape, evasion, excuse, pretext, plea, pretence.

**loose** adj **1** FREE, unfastened, untied, movable, unattached, insecure, wobbly. **2** SLACK, lax, baggy, hanging. **3** IMPRECISE, vague, inexact, ill-defined, indefinite, inaccurate, indistinct.
▣ **1** firm, secure. **2** tight. **3** precise.

**loosen** v **1** EASE, relax, loose, slacken, undo, unbind, untie, unfasten. **2** FREE, set free, release, let go, let out, deliver.
▣ **1** tighten.

**loot** n spoils, booty, plunder, haul, swag (*infml*), prize.
v plunder, pillage, rob, sack, rifle, raid, maraud, ransack, ravage.

**lop-sided** adj asymmetrical, unbalanced, askew, off balance, uneven.
▣ balanced, symmetrical.

**lord** n **1** PEER, noble, earl, duke, count, baron. **2** MASTER, ruler, superior, overlord, leader, commander, governor, king.

**lordly** adj **1** NOBLE, dignified, aristocratic. **2** PROUD, arrogant, disdainful, haughty, imperious, condescending, high-handed, domineering, overbearing.
▣ **1** low(ly). **2** humble.

**lore** n knowledge, wisdom, learning, erudition, scholarship, traditions, teaching, beliefs, sayings.

**lose** v **1** MISLAY, misplace, forget, miss, forfeit. **2** WASTE, squander, dissipate, use up, exhaust, expend, drain. **3** FAIL, fall short, suffer defeat.
▣ **1** gain. **2** make. **3** win.

**loser** n failure, also-ran, runner-up, flop (*infml*), no-hoper.
▣ winner.

**loss** n **1** DEPRIVATION, disadvantage, defeat, failure, losing, bereavement, damage, destruction,

ruin, hurt. **2** WASTE, depletion, disappearance, deficiency, deficit.
▣ **1** gain.

**lost** adj **1** MISLAID, missing, vanished, disappeared, misplaced, astray. **2** CONFUSED, disoriented, bewildered, puzzled, baffled, perplexed, preoccupied. **3** WASTED, squandered, ruined, destroyed.
▣ **1** found.

**lot** n **1** COLLECTION, batch, assortment, quantity, group, set, crowd. **2** SHARE, portion, allowance, ration, quota, part, piece, parcel.

**lotion** n ointment, balm, cream, salve.

**lottery** n **1** DRAW, raffle, sweepstake. **2** SPECULATION, venture, risk, gamble.

**loud** adj **1** NOISY, deafening, booming, resounding, ear-piercing, ear-splitting, piercing, thundering, blaring, clamorous, vociferous.
**2** GARISH, gaudy, glaring, flashy, brash, showy, ostentatious, tasteless.
▣ **1** quiet. **2** subdued.

**lounge** v relax, loll, idle, laze, waste time, kill time, lie about, take it easy, sprawl, recline, lie back, slump.
n sitting-room, living-room, drawing-room, day-room, parlour.

**lovable** adj adorable, endearing, winsome, captivating, charming, engaging, attractive, fetching, sweet, lovely, pleasing, delightful.
▣ detestable, hateful.

**love** v **1** *he loves his wife*: adore, cherish, dote on, treasure, hold dear, idolize, worship. **2** *I love macaroons*: like, take pleasure in, enjoy, delight in, appreciate, desire, fancy.
▣ detest, hate.
n adoration, affection, fondness, attachment, regard, liking, amorousness, ardour, devotion, adulation, passion, rapture, tenderness, warmth, inclination, infatuation, delight, enjoyment, soft spot (*infml*), weakness, taste,

friendship.

**Ⓔ** detestation, hate, loathing.

**love affair** *n* affair, romance, liaison, relationship, love, passion.

**lovely** *adj* beautiful, charming, delightful, attractive, enchanting, pleasing, pleasant, pretty, adorable, agreeable, enjoyable, sweet, winning, exquisite.

**Ⓔ** ugly, hideous.

**lover** *n* beloved, admirer, boyfriend, girlfriend, sweetheart, suitor, mistress, fiancé(e), flame (*infml*).

**loving** *adj* amorous, affectionate, devoted, doting, fond, ardent, passionate, warm, warm-hearted, tender.

**low** *adj* **1** SHORT, small, squat, stunted, little, shallow, deep, depressed, sunken. **2** INADEQUATE, deficient, poor, sparse, meagre, paltry, scant, insignificant.
**3** UNHAPPY, depressed, downcast, gloomy. **4** BASE, coarse, vulgar, mean, contemptible. **5** CHEAP, inexpensive, reasonable. **6** subdued, muted, soft.

**Ⓔ** **1** high. **2** high. **3** cheerful.
**4** honourable. **5** exorbitant. **6** loud.

**lower** *adj* inferior, lesser, subordinate, secondary, minor, second-class, low-level, lowly, junior.

**Ⓔ** higher.

*v* **1** DROP, depress, sink, descend, let down. **2** REDUCE, decrease, cut, lessen, diminish.

**Ⓔ** **1** raise. **2** increase.

**lowly** *adj* humble, low-born, obscure, poor, plebeian, plain, simple, modest, ordinary, inferior, meek, mild, mean, submissive, subordinate.

**Ⓔ** lofty, noble.

**low-spirited** *adj* depressed, gloomy, heavy-hearted, low, down, down-hearted, despondent, fed up (*infml*), sad, unhappy, miserable, moody.

**Ⓔ** high-spirited, cheerful.

**loyal** *adj* true, faithful, steadfast,

staunch, devoted, trustworthy, sincere, patriotic.

**Ⓔ** disloyal, treacherous.

**loyalty** *n* allegiance, faithfulness, fidelity, devotion, steadfastness, constancy, trustworthiness, reliability, patriotism.

**Ⓔ** disloyalty, treachery.

**lubricate** *v* oil, grease, smear, wax, lard.

**luck** *n* **1** CHANCE, fortune, accident, fate, fortuity (*fml*), fluke (*infml*), destiny. **2** GOOD FORTUNE, success, break (*infml*), godsend.

**Ⓔ** **1** design. **2** misfortune.

**luckily** *adv* fortunately, happily, providentially.

**Ⓔ** unfortunately.

**lucky** *adj* fortunate, favoured, auspicious, successful, prosperous, timely.

**Ⓔ** unlucky.

**lucrative** *adj* profitable, well-paid, remunerative, advantageous.

**Ⓔ** unprofitable.

**ludicrous** *adj* absurd, ridiculous, preposterous, nonsensical, laughable, farcical, silly, comical, funny, outlandish, crazy (*infml*).

**Ⓔ** serious.

**lug** *v* pull, drag, haul, carry, tow, heave, hump.

**luggage**

*Types of luggage include*: case, suitcase, vanity-case, bag, holdall, portmanteau, valise, overnight-bag, kit-bag, flight bag, hand-luggage, travel bag, Gladstone bag, grip, rucksack, knapsack, haversack, backpack, briefcase, attaché case, portfolio, satchel, basket, hamper, trunk, chest, box.

**lukewarm** *adj* cool, half-hearted, apathetic, tepid, indifferent, unenthusiastic, uninterested, unresponsive, unconcerned.

**lull** *v* soothe, subdue, calm, hush,

pacify, quieten down, quiet, quell, compose.

**⊟** agitate.

*n* calm, peace, quiet, tranquillity, stillness, let-up, pause, hush, silence.

**⊟** agitation.

**lumber**[1] *n* clutter, jumble, rubbish, bits and pieces, odds and ends, junk.

**lumber**[2] *v* clump, shamble, plod, shuffle, stump, trundle.

**luminous** *adj* glowing, illuminated, lit, lighted, radiant, shining, fluorescent, brilliant, lustrous, bright.

**lump** *n* 1 MASS, cluster, clump, clod, ball, bunch, piece, chunk, cake, hunk, nugget, wedge. 2 SWELLING, growth, bulge, bump, protuberance, protrusion, tumour.

*v* collect, mass, gather, cluster, combine, coalesce, group, consolidate, unite.

**lunacy** *n* madness, insanity, aberration, derangement, mania, craziness (*infml*), idiocy, imbecility, folly, absurdity, stupidity.

**⊟** sanity.

**lunatic** *n* psychotic, psychopath, madman, maniac, loony (*infml*), nutcase (*infml*), nutter (*infml*), fruitcake (*infml*).

*adj* mad, insane, deranged, psychotic, irrational, crazy (*infml*), bonkers (*infml*).

**⊟** sane.

**lunge** *v* thrust, jab, stab, pounce, plunge, pitch into, charge, dart, dash, dive, poke, strike (at), fall upon, grab (at), hit (at), leap.

*n* thrust, stab, pounce, charge, jab, pass, cut, spring.

**lurch** *v* roll, rock, pitch, sway, stagger, reel, list.

**lure** *v* tempt, entice, draw, attract, allure, seduce, ensnare, lead on.

*n* temptation, enticement, attraction, bait, inducement.

**lurid** *adj* 1 SENSATIONAL, shocking, startling, graphic, exaggerated.

2 MACABRE, gruesome, gory, ghastly, grisly. 3 BRIGHTLY COLOURED, garish, glaring, loud, vivid.

**lurk** *v* skulk, prowl, lie in wait, crouch, lie low, hide, snoop.

**luscious** *adj* delicious, juicy, succulent, appetizing, mouth-watering, sweet, tasty, savoury, desirable.

**lush** *adj* 1 FLOURISHING, luxuriant, abundant, prolific, overgrown, green, verdant. 2 SUMPTUOUS, opulent, ornate, plush, rich.

**lust** *n* 1 SENSUALITY, libido, lechery, licentiousness, lewdness. 2 CRAVING, desire, appetite, longing, passion, greed, covetousness.

**lust after** desire, crave, yearn for, want, need, hunger for, thirst for.

**lustre** *n* 1 SHINE, gloss, sheen, gleam, glow, brilliance, brightness, radiance, sparkle, resplendence, burnish, glitter, glint. 2 GLORY, honour, prestige, illustriousness.

**lusty** *adj* robust, strong, sturdy, vigorous, hale, hearty, healthy, gutsy (*infml*), energetic, strapping, rugged, powerful.

**luxurious** *adj* sumptuous, opulent, lavish, de luxe, plush, magnificent, splendid, expensive, costly, self-indulgent, pampered.

**⊟** austere, spartan.

**luxury** *n* sumptuousness, opulence, hedonism, splendour, affluence, richness, magnificence, pleasure, indulgence, gratification, comfort, extravagance, satisfaction.

**⊟** austerity.

**lying** *adj* deceitful, dishonest, false, untruthful, double-dealing, two-faced (*infml*).

**⊟** honest, truthful.

*n* dishonesty, untruthfulness, deceit, falsity, fibbing (*infml*), perjury, duplicity, fabrication, double-dealing.

**⊟** honesty, truthfulness.

# M

**macabre** *adj* gruesome, grisly, grim, horrible, frightful, dreadful, ghostly, eerie.

**machine** *n* **1** INSTRUMENT, device, contrivance, tool, mechanism, engine, apparatus, appliance. **2** AGENCY, organization, structure, system.

**machinery** *n* **1** INSTRUMENTS, mechanism, tools, apparatus, equipment, tackle, gear. **2** ORGANIZATION, channels, structure, system, procedure.

**mad** *adj* **1** INSANE, lunatic, unbalanced, psychotic, deranged, demented, out of one's mind, crazy (*infml*), nuts (*infml*), barmy (*infml*), bonkers (*infml*). **2** (*infml*) ANGRY, furious, enraged, infuriated, incensed. **3** IRRATIONAL, illogical, unreasonable, absurd, preposterous, foolish. **4** FANATICAL, enthusiastic, infatuated, ardent.
**Ε3 1** sane. **2** calm. **3** sensible. **4** apathetic.

**madden** *v* anger, enrage, infuriate, incense, exasperate, provoke, annoy, irritate.
**Ε3** calm, pacify.

**madly** *adv* **1** *he rolled his eyes madly*: insanely, dementedly, hysterically, wildly. **2** *madly cleaning up*: excitedly, frantically, furiously, recklessly, violently, energetically, rapidly, hastily, hurriedly. **3** *madly in love*: intensely, extremely, exceedingly, fervently, devotedly.

**madman, madwoman** *n* lunatic, psychotic, psychopath, maniac, loony (*infml*), nutcase (*infml*), fruitcake (*infml*).

**magazine** *n* **1** JOURNAL, periodical, paper, weekly, monthly, quarterly. **2** ARSENAL, storehouse, ammunition dump, depot, ordnance.

**magic** *n* **1** SORCERY, enchantment, occultism, black art, witchcraft, spell. **2** CONJURING, illusion, sleight of hand, trickery. **3** CHARM, fascination, glamour, allure.
*adj* charming, enchanting, bewitching, fascinating, spellbinding.

**magician** *n* sorcerer, miracle-worker, conjuror, enchanter, wizard, witch, warlock, spellbinder, wonder-worker.

**magnanimous** *adj* generous, liberal, open-handed, benevolent, selfless, charitable, big-hearted, kind, noble, unselfish, ungrudging.
**Ε3** mean.

**magnate** *n* tycoon, captain of industry, industrialist, mogul, entrepreneur, plutocrat, baron, personage, notable.

**magnetic** *adj* attractive, alluring, fascinating, charming, mesmerizing, seductive, irresistible, entrancing, captivating, gripping, absorbing, charismatic.
**Ε3** repellent, repulsive.

**magnetism** *n* attraction, allure, fascination, charm, lure, appeal, drawing power, draw, pull, hypnotism, mesmerism, charisma, grip, magic, power, spell.

**magnificent** *adj* splendid, grand, imposing, impressive, glorious, gorgeous, brilliant, excellent, majestic, superb, sumptuous, noble, elegant, fine, rich.
**Ε3** modest, humble, poor.

**magnify** *v* enlarge, amplify, increase, expand, intensify, boost, enhance,

greaten, heighten, deepen, build up, exaggerate, dramatize, overemphasize, overplay, overstate, overdo, blow up (*infml*).
🠪 belittle, play down.

**magnitude** *n* 1 SIZE, extent, measure, amount, expanse, dimensions, mass, proportions, quantity, volume, bulk, largeness, space, strength, amplitude.
2 IMPORTANCE, consequence, significance, weight, greatness, moment, intensity.

**maiden** *n* girl, virgin, lass, lassie, damsel (*fml*), miss.

**mail** *n* post, letters, correspondence, packages, parcels, delivery.
*v* post, send, dispatch, forward.

**maim** *v* mutilate, wound, incapacitate, injure, disable, hurt, impair, cripple, lame.

**main** *adj* principal, chief, leading, first, foremost, predominant, pre-eminent, primary, supreme, paramount, central, cardinal, outstanding, essential, critical, crucial, necessary, vital.
🠪 minor, unimportant, insignificant.
*n* pipe, duct, conduit, channel, cable, line.

**mainly** *adv* primarily, principally, chiefly, in the main, mostly, on the whole, for the most part, generally, in general, especially, as a rule, above all, largely, overall.

**mainstay** *n* support, buttress, bulwark, linchpin, prop, pillar, backbone, foundation.

**maintain** *v* 1 CARRY ON, continue, keep (up), sustain, retain. 2 CARE FOR, conserve, look after, take care of, preserve, support, finance, supply. 3 ASSERT, affirm, claim, contend, declare, hold, state, insist, believe, fight for.
🠪 2 neglect. 3 deny.

**maintenance** *n* 1 CONTINUATION, continuance, perpetuation. 2 CARE, conservation, preservation, support,

repairs, protection, upkeep, running. 3 KEEP, subsistence, living, livelihood, allowance, alimony.
🠪 2 neglect.

**majestic** *adj* magnificent, grand, dignified, noble, royal, stately, splendid, imperial, impressive, exalted, imposing, regal, sublime, superb, lofty, monumental, pompous.
🠪 lowly, unimpressive, unimposing.

**majesty** *n* grandeur, glory, dignity, magnificence, nobility, royalty, resplendence, splendour, stateliness, pomp, exaltedness, impressiveness, loftiness.

**major** *adj* greater, chief, main, larger, bigger, higher, leading, outstanding, notable, supreme, uppermost, significant, crucial, important, key, keynote, great, senior, older, superior, pre-eminent, vital, weighty.
🠪 minor, unimportant, trivial.

**majority** *n* 1 BULK, mass, preponderance, most, greater part. 2 ADULTHOOD, maturity, manhood, womanhood, years of discretion.
🠪 1 minority.

**make** *v* 1 CREATE, manufacture, fabricate, construct, build, produce, put together, originate, compose, form, shape. 2 CAUSE, bring about, effect, accomplish, occasion, give rise to, generate, render, perform. 3 COERCE, force, oblige, constrain, compel, prevail upon, pressurize, press, require. 4 APPOINT, elect, designate, nominate, ordain, install. 5 EARN, gain, net, obtain, acquire. 6 CONSTITUTE, compose, comprise, add up to, amount to.
🠪 1 dismantle. 5 spend.
*n* brand, sort, type, style, variety, manufacture, model, mark, kind, form, structure.

**make off** run off, run away, depart, bolt, leave, fly, cut and run (*infml*), beat a hasty retreat (*infml*), clear off (*infml*).

**make out 1** DISCERN, perceive,

decipher, distinguish, recognize, see, detect, discover, understand, work out, grasp, follow, fathom. **2 DRAW UP**, complete, fill in, write out. **3 MAINTAIN**, imply, claim, assert, describe, demonstrate, prove. **4 MANAGE**, get on, progress, succeed, fare (*fml*).

**make up 1 CREATE**, invent, devise, fabricate, construct, originate, formulate, dream up, compose. **2 COMPLETE**, fill, supply, meet, supplement. **3 COMPRISE**, constitute, compose, form. **4 BE RECONCILED**, make peace, settle differences, bury the hatchet (*infml*), forgive and forget, call it quits (*infml*).

**make up for** compensate for, make good, make amends for, redress, recompense, redeem, atone for.

**make-believe** *n* pretence, imagination, fantasy, unreality, play-acting, role-play, dream, charade.
**Ea** reality.

**maker** *n* creator, manufacturer, constructor, builder, producer, director, architect, author.

**makeshift** *adj* temporary, improvised, rough and ready, provisional, substitute, stop-gap, expedient, make-do.
**Ea** permanent.

**make-up** *n* **1 COSMETICS**, paint, powder, maquillage, war paint (*infml*). **2 CONSTITUTION**, nature, composition, character, construction, form, format, formation, arrangement, organization, style, structure, assembly.

**maladjusted** *adj* disturbed, unstable, confused, alienated, neurotic, estranged.
**Ea** well-adjusted.

**male** *adj* masculine, manly, virile, boyish, he-.
**Ea** female.

*Male terms include*: boy, lad, youth, man, gentleman, gent (*infml*), bachelor, chap (*infml*), bloke (*infml*), guy (*infml*), son, brother, boyfriend, beau, toy boy (*sl*), fiancé, bridegroom, husband, father, uncle, nephew, grandfather, patriarch, godfather, widower, sugar daddy (*sl*), hunk (*sl*), gigolo, homosexual, gay, rent boy, male chauvinist pig (MCP) (*sl*); bull, dog, buck, tup, cock, cockerel, stallion, billy-goat, boar, dog fox, stag, ram, tom cat, drake, gander.

**malevolent** *adj* malicious, malign, spiteful, vindictive, ill-natured, hostile, vicious, venomous, evil-minded.
**Ea** benevolent, kind.

**malformation** *n* irregularity, deformity, distortion, warp.

**malformed** *adj* misshapen, irregular, deformed, distorted, twisted, warped, crooked, bent.
**Ea** perfect.

**malfunction** *n* fault, defect, failure, breakdown.
*v* break down, go wrong, fail.

**malice** *n* malevolence, enmity, animosity, ill-will, hatred, hate, spite, vindictiveness, bitterness.
**Ea** love.

**malicious** *adj* malevolent, ill-natured, malign, spiteful, venomous, vicious, vengeful, evil-minded, bitter, resentful.
**Ea** kind, friendly.

**malign** *adj* malignant, malevolent, bad, evil, harmful, hurtful, injurious, destructive, hostile.
**Ea** benign.
*v* defame, slander, libel, disparage, abuse, run down (*infml*), harm, injure.
**Ea** praise.

**malignant** *adj* **1 MALEVOLENT**, malicious, spiteful, evil, hostile, vicious, venomous, destructive, harmful, hurtful, pernicious. **2 FATAL**, deadly, incurable, dangerous, cancerous, uncontrollable, virulent.

☒ 1 kind. 2 benign.

**malpractice** n misconduct, mismanagement, negligence, impropriety, dereliction of duty (fml), abuse, misdeed.

**maltreat** v ill-treat, mistreat, misuse, abuse, injure, harm, damage, hurt.
☒ care for.

**mammal**

> *Mammals include*: aardvark, African black rhinoceros, African elephant, anteater, antelope, armadillo, baboon, Bactrian camel, badger, bat, bear, beaver, bushbaby, cat, chimpanzee, chipmunk, cow, deer, dog, dolphin, duck-billed platypus, dugong, echidna, flying lemur, fox, gerbil, gibbon, giraffe, goat, gorilla, guinea pig, hamster, hare, hedgehog, hippopotamus, horse, human being, hyena, Indian elephant, kangaroo, koala, lemming, leopard, lion, manatee, marmoset, marmot, marsupial mouse, mole, mouse, opossum, orang utan, otter, pig, porcupine, porpoise, rabbit, raccoon, rat, sea cow, sea lion, seal, sheep, shrew, sloth, squirrel, tamarin, tapir, tiger, vole, wallaby, walrus, weasel, whale, wolf, zebra. *see also* **cat**; **cattle**; **dog**; **marsupial**; **monkey**; **rodent**.

**mammoth** adj enormous, huge, vast, colossal, gigantic, giant, massive, immense, monumental, mighty.
☒ tiny, minute.

**man** n 1 MALE, gentleman, fellow, bloke (infml), chap (infml), guy (infml). 2 HUMAN BEING, person, individual, adult, human. 3 HUMANITY, humankind, mankind, human race, people, Homo sapiens, mortals. 4 MANSERVANT, servant, worker, employee, hand, soldier, valet, houseman, houseboy.
v staff, crew, take charge of, operate, occupy.

**manacle** v handcuff, shackle, restrain, fetter, chain, put in chains, bind, curb, check, hamper, inhibit.
☒ free, unshackle.

**manage** v 1 ACCOMPLISH, succeed, bring about, bring off, effect. 2 ADMINISTER, direct, run, command, govern, preside over, rule, superintend, supervise, oversee, conduct. 3 CONTROL, influence, deal with, handle, operate, manipulate, guide. 4 COPE, fare, survive, get by, get along, get on, make do.
☒ 1 fail. 2 mismanage.

**manageable** adj tractable, governable, controllable, amenable, submissive, docile.
☒ unmanageable.

**management** n 1 ADMINISTRATION, direction, control, government, command, running, superintendence, supervision, charge, care, handling. 2 MANAGERS, directors, directorate, executive, executives, governors, board, bosses (infml), supervisors.
☒ 1 mismanagement. 2 workers.

**manager** n director, executive, administrator, controller, superintendent, supervisor, overseer, governor, organizer, head, boss (infml).

**mandate** n order, command, decree, edict, injunction, charge, directive, warrant, authorization, authority, instruction, commission, sanction.

**mandatory** adj obligatory, compulsory, binding, required, necessary, requisite, essential.
☒ optional.

**mangle** v mutilate, disfigure, mar, maim, spoil, butcher, destroy, deform, wreck, twist, maul, distort, crush, cut, hack, tear, rend.

**mangy** adj seedy, shabby, scruffy, scabby, tatty (infml), shoddy, moth-eaten, dirty, mean.

**manhandle** v 1 *the porters*

*manhandled the baggage*: haul, heave, hump, pull, push, shove, tug. **2** *the police manhandled the demonstrators*: maul, mistreat, maltreat, misuse, abuse, knock about (*infml*), rough up (*infml*).

**manhood** *n* **1** ADULTHOOD, maturity. **2** MASCULINITY, virility, manliness, manfulness, machismo (*infml*).

**mania** *n* **1** MADNESS, insanity, lunacy, psychosis, derangement, disorder, aberration, craziness (*infml*), frenzy. **2** PASSION, craze, rage, obsession, compulsion, enthusiasm, fad (*infml*), infatuation, fixation, craving.

*Manias (by name of disorder) include*: dipsomania (*alcohol*), bibliomania (*books*), ailuromania (*cats*), demomania (*crowds*), necromania (*dead bodies*), thanatomania (*death*), cynomania (*dogs*), narcomania (*drugs*), pyromania (*fire-raising*), anthomania (*flowers*), hippomania (*horses*), mythomania (*lying and exaggerating*), egomania (*oneself*), ablutomania (*personal cleanliness*), hedonomania (*pleasure*), megalomania (*power*), theomania (*religion*), nymphomania (*sex*), monomania (*single idea or thing*), kleptomania (*stealing*), tomomania (*surgery*), logomania (*talking*), ergomania (*work*). *see also* **phobia**.

**maniac** *n* **1** LUNATIC, madman, madwoman, psychotic, psychopath, loony (*infml*). **2** ENTHUSIAST, fan (*infml*), fanatic, fiend (*infml*), freak (*infml*).

**manifest** *adj* obvious, evident, clear, apparent, plain, open, patent, noticeable, conspicuous, unmistakable, visible, unconcealed.
**F3** unclear.
*v* show, exhibit, display, demonstrate,

reveal, set forth, expose, prove, illustrate, establish.
**F3** conceal.

**manifestation** *n* display, exhibition, demonstration, show, revelation, exposure, disclosure, appearance, expression, sign, indication.

**manifesto** *n* statement, declaration, policies, platform.

**manifold** *adj* (*fml*) many, numerous, varied, various, diverse, multiple, kaleidoscopic, abundant, copious.

**manipulate** *v* **1** HANDLE, control, wield, operate, use, manoeuvre, influence, engineer, guide, direct, steer, negotiate, work. **2** FALSIFY, rig, juggle with, doctor (*infml*), cook (*infml*), fiddle (*infml*).

**mankind** *n* humankind, humanity, human race, man, Homo sapiens, people.

**manly** *adj* masculine, male, virile, manful, macho (*infml*), robust.

**man-made** *adj* synthetic, manufactured, simulated, imitation, artificial.
**F3** natural.

**manner** *n* **1** WAY, method, means, fashion, style, procedure, process, form. **2** BEHAVIOUR, conduct, bearing, demeanour, air, appearance, look, character.

**mannerism** *n* idiosyncrasy, peculiarity, characteristic, quirk, trait, feature, foible, habit.

**manners** *n* behaviour, conduct, demeanour, etiquette, politeness, bearing, courtesy, formalities, social graces, p's and q's.

**manoeuvre** *n* move, movement, operation, action, exercise, plan, ploy, plot, ruse, strategem, machination, gambit, tactic, trick, scheme, dodge (*infml*).
*v* **1** MOVE, manipulate, handle, guide, pilot, steer, navigate, jockey, direct, drive, exercise. **2** CONTRIVE, engineer, plot, scheme, wangle (*infml*), pull strings (*infml*), manipulate,

manage, plan, devise, negotiate.

**mantle** *n* cloak, cover, covering, cape, hood, blanket, shawl, veil, wrap, shroud, screen.

**manual** *n* handbook, guide, guidebook, instructions, Bible, vade mecum, directions.
*adj* hand-operated, by hand, physical, human.

**manufacture** *v* **1** MAKE, produce, construct, build, fabricate, create, assemble, mass-produce, turn out, process, forge, form. **2** INVENT, make up, concoct, fabricate, think up.
*n* production, making, construction, fabrication, mass-production, assembly, creation, formation.

**manufacturer** *n* maker, producer, industrialist, constructor, factory-owner, builder, creator.

**manure** *n* fertilizer, compost, muck, dung.

**many** *adj* numerous, countless, lots of (*infml*), manifold (*fml*), various, varied, sundry, diverse, umpteen (*infml*).
**E3** few.

**map** *n* chart, plan, street plan, atlas, graph, plot.

**mar** *v* spoil, impair, harm, hurt, damage, deface, disfigure, mutilate, injure, maim, scar, detract from, mangle, ruin, wreck, tarnish.
**E3** enhance.

**marauder** *n* bandit, brigand, robber, raider, plunderer, pillager, pirate, buccaneer, outlaw, ravager, predator.

**march** *v* walk, stride, parade, pace, file, tread, stalk.
*n* **1** STEP, pace, stride. **2** WALK, trek, hike, footslog (*infml*). **3** PROCESSION, parade, demonstration, demo (*infml*). **4** ADVANCE, development, progress, evolution, passage.

**margin** *n* **1** BORDER, edge, boundary, bound, periphery, perimeter, rim, brink, limit, confine,

verge, side, skirt. **2** ALLOWANCE, play, leeway, latitude, scope, room, space, surplus, extra.

**marginal** *adj* borderline, peripheral, negligible, minimal, insignificant, minor, slight, doubtful, low, small.
**E3** central, core.

**marine** *adj* sea, maritime, naval, nautical, seafaring, sea-going, ocean-going, salt-water.

**mariner** *n* sailor, seaman, seafarer, deckhand, navigator, tar (*infml*), sea-dog (*infml*), salt (*infml*).

**marital** *adj* conjugal, matrimonial, married, wedded, nuptial (*fml*), connubial (*fml*).

**maritime** *adj* marine, nautical, naval, seafaring, sea, seaside, oceanic, coastal.

**mark** *n* **1** SPOT, stain, blemish, blot, blotch, smudge, dent, impression, scar, scratch, bruise, line. **2** SYMBOL, sign, indication, emblem, brand, stamp, token, characteristic, feature, proof, evidence, badge. **3** TARGET, goal, aim, objective, purpose.
*v* **1** STAIN, blemish, blot, smudge, dent, scar, scratch, bruise. **2** BRAND, label, stamp, characterize, identify, distinguish. **3** EVALUATE, assess, correct, grade. **4** HEED, listen, mind, note, observe, regard, notice, take to heart.

**marked** *adj* **1** NOTICEABLE, obvious, conspicuous, evident, pronounced, distinct, decided, emphatic, considerable, remarkable, apparent, glaring. **2** SUSPECTED, watched, doomed.
**E3** **1** unnoticeable, slight.

**market** *n* mart, marketplace, bazaar, fair, exchange, outlet.
*v* sell, retail, hawk, peddle.
**E3** buy.

**maroon** *v* abandon, cast away, desert, put ashore, strand, leave, isolate.

**marriage** *n* **1** MATRIMONY,

wedlock, wedding, nuptials (*fml*).
**2** UNION, alliance, merger, coupling,
amalgamation, link, association,
confederation.
**⊟ 1** divorce. **2** separation.

**marrow** *n* essence, heart, nub,
kernel, core, soul, spirit, substance,
quick, stuff, gist.

**marry** *v* **1** WED, join in matrimony,
tie the knot (*infml*), get hitched
(*infml*), get spliced (*infml*). **2** UNITE,
ally, join, merge, match, link, knit.
**⊟ 1** divorce. **2** separate.

**marsh** *n* marshland, bog, swamp,
fen, morass, quagmire, slough.

**marshal** *v* **1** ARRANGE, dispose,
order, line up, align, array, rank,
organize, assemble, gather, muster,
group, collect, draw up, deploy.
**2** GUIDE, lead, escort, conduct,
usher.

**marsupial**

> *Marsupials include*: bandicoot,
> cuscus, kangaroo, rat kangaroo, tree
> kangaroo, wallaroo, koala, marsupial
> anteater, marsupial mouse, marsupial
> mole, marsupial rat, opossum,
> pademelon, phalanger, Tasmanian
> Devil, Tasmanian wolf, wallaby, rock
> wallaby, wombat.

**martial** *adj* warlike, military,
belligerent, soldierly, militant, heroic,
brave.

**marvel** *n* wonder, miracle,
phenomenon, prodigy, spectacle,
sensation, genius.
*v* wonder, gape, gaze, be amazed at.

**marvellous** *adj* **1** WONDERFUL,
excellent, splendid, superb,
magnificent, terrific (*infml*), super,
fantastic (*infml*).
**2** EXTRAORDINARY, amazing,
astonishing, astounding, miraculous,
remarkable, surprising, unbelievable,
incredible, glorious.
**⊟ 1** terrible, awful. **2** ordinary, run-of-
the-mill.

**masculine** *adj* **1** MALE, manlike,
manly, mannish, virile, macho.
**2** VIGOROUS, strong, strapping,
robust, powerful, muscular, red-
blooded, bold, brave, gallant,
resolute, stout-hearted.
**⊟ 1** feminine.

**mash** *v* crush, pulp, beat, pound,
pulverize, pummel, grind, smash.

**mask** *n* disguise, camouflage, façade,
front, concealment, cover-up, cover,
guise, pretence, semblance, cloak,
veil, blind, show, veneer, visor.
*v* disguise, camouflage, cover,
conceal, cloak, veil, hide, obscure,
screen, shield.
**⊟** expose, uncover.

**masquerade** *n* **1** MASQUE, masked
ball, costume ball, fancy dress party.
**2** DISGUISE, counterfeit, cover-up,
cover, deception, front, pose,
pretence, guise, cloak.
*v* disguise, impersonate, pose, pass
oneself off, mask, play, pretend,
profess, dissimulate.

**mass** *n* **1** HEAP, pile, load,
accumulation, aggregate, collection,
conglomeration, combination,
entirety, whole, totality, sum, lot,
group, batch, bunch. **2** QUANTITY,
multitude, throng, troop, crowd,
band, horde, mob. **3** MAJORITY,
body, bulk. **4** SIZE, dimension,
magnitude, immensity. **5** LUMP,
piece, chunk, block, hunk.
*adj* widespread, large-scale,
extensive, comprehensive, general,
indiscriminate, popular, across-the-
board, sweeping, wholesale, blanket.
**⊟** limited, small-scale.
*v* collect, gather, assemble,
congregate, crowd, rally, cluster,
muster, swarm, throng.
**⊟** separate.

**massacre** *n* slaughter, murder,
extermination, carnage, butchery,
holocaust, blood bath, annihilation,
killing.
*v* slaughter, butcher, murder, mow

down, wipe out, exterminate,
annihilate, kill, decimate.

**massage** n manipulation, kneading,
rubbing, rub-down.

v manipulate, knead, rub (down).

**massive** adj huge, immense,
enormous, vast, colossal, gigantic,
big, bulky, monumental, solid,
substantial, heavy, large-scale,
extensive.

Ea tiny, small.

**master** n 1 RULER, chief, governor,
head, lord, captain, boss (infml),
employer, commander, controller,
director, manager, superintendent,
overseer, principal, overlord, owner.
2 EXPERT, genius, virtuoso, past
master, maestro, dab hand (infml),
ace (infml), pro (infml). 3 TEACHER,
tutor, instructor, schoolmaster,
guide, guru, preceptor (fml).

Ea 1 servant, underling. 2 amateur.
3 learner, pupil.

adj 1 CHIEF, principal, main,
leading, foremost, prime,
predominant, controlling, great,
grand. 2 EXPERT, masterly, skilled,
skilful, proficient.

Ea 1 subordinate. 2 inept.

v 1 CONQUER, defeat, subdue,
subjugate, vanquish, triumph over,
overcome, quell, rule, control.
2 LEARN, grasp, acquire, get the hang
of (infml), manage.

**masterful** adj 1 ARROGANT,
authoritative, domineering,
overbearing, high-handed, despotic,
dictatorial, autocratic, bossy (infml),
tyrannical, powerful. 2 EXPERT,
masterly, skilful, skilled, dexterous,
first-rate, professional.

Ea 1 humble. 2 inept, unskilful.

**masterly** adj expert, skilled, skilful,
dexterous, adept, adroit, first-rate,
ace (infml), excellent, superb,
superior, supreme.

Ea inept, clumsy.

**masterpiece** n master-work,
magnum opus, pièce de résistance,

chef d'oeuvre, jewel.

**mastery** n 1 PROFICIENCY, skill,
ability, command, expertise,
virtuosity, knowledge, know-how,
dexterity, familiarity, grasp.
2 CONTROL, command, domination,
supremacy, upper hand, dominion,
authority.

Ea 1 incompetence. 2 subjugation.

**match** n 1 CONTEST, competition,
bout, game, test, trial. 2 EQUAL,
equivalent, peer, counterpart, fellow,
mate, rival, copy, double, replica,
look-alike, twin, duplicate.
3 MARRIAGE, alliance, union,
partnership, affiliation.

v 1 EQUAL, compare, measure up to,
rival, compete, oppose, contend, vie,
pit against. 2 FIT, go with, accord,
agree, suit, correspond, harmonize,
tally, co-ordinate, blend, adapt, go
together, relate, tone with, accompany.
3 JOIN, marry, unite, mate, link,
couple, combine, ally, pair, yoke,
team.

Ea 2 clash. 3 separate.

**matching** adj corresponding,
comparable, equivalent, like,
identical, co-ordinating, similar,
duplicate, same, twin.

Ea clashing.

**matchless** adj unequalled, peerless,
incomparable, unmatched,
unparalleled, unsurpassed,
unrivalled, inimitable, unique.

**mate** n 1 FRIEND, companion,
comrade, pal (infml), colleague,
partner, fellow-worker, co-worker,
associate. 2 SPOUSE, husband, wife.
3 ASSISTANT, helper, subordinate.
4 MATCH, fellow, twin.

v 1 COUPLE, pair, breed, copulate. 2
JOIN, match, marry, wed.

**material** n 1 STUFF, substance,
body, matter. 2 FABRIC, textile,
cloth. 3 INFORMATION, facts, data,
evidence, constituents, work, notes.

adj 1 PHYSICAL, concrete, tangible,
substantial. 2 RELEVANT, significant,

important, meaningful, pertinent,
essential, vital, indispensable, serious.
**F3 1** abstract. **2** irrelevant.
**materialize** v appear, arise, take
shape, turn up, happen, occur.
**F3** disappear.

**mathematical terms**

*Mathematical terms include*: acute
angle, addition, algebra, algorithm,
analysis, angle, apex, approximate,
arc, area, argument, arithmetic,
arithmetic progression, asymmetrical,
average, axis, axis of symmetry, bar
chart, bar graph, base, bearing,
binary, binomial, breadth, calculus,
capacity, cardinal number, Cartesian
coordinates, chance, chord,
circumference, coefficient,
combination, commutative operation,
complement, complementary angle,
complex number, concave, concentric
circles, congruent, conjugate angles,
constant, continuous distribution,
converse, convex, coordinate,
correlation, cosine, covariance, cross
section, cube, cube root, curve,
decimal, degree, denominator, depth,
derivative, determinant, diagonal,
diameter, differentiation, directed
number, distribution, dividend,
division, divisor, edge, equal,
equation, equidistant, even number,
exponent, exponential, face, factor,
factorial, Fibonacci sequence,
formula, fraction, function,
geometric progression, geometry,
gradient, graph, greater than, group,
harmonic progression, height, helix,
histogram, horizontal, hyperbola,
hypotenuse, identity, infinity, integer,
integration, irrational number,
latitude, length, less than, linear, line,
locus, logarithm, longitude, magic
square, matrix, maximum, mean,
measure, median, minimum, minus,
mirror image, mirror symmetry,
Möbius strip, mode, modulus,
multiple, multiplication, natural

logarithm, natural number, negative
number, number, numerator, oblique,
obtuse angle, odd number, operation,
ordinal number, origin, parabola,
parallel lines, parallel planes,
parameter, percentage, percentile,
perimeter, permutation,
perpendicular, pi, pie chart, place
value, plane figure, plus, point,
positive number, prime number,
probability, product, proportion,
protractor, Pythagoras's theorem,
quadrant, quadratic equation,
quadrilateral, quartile, quotient,
radian, radius, random sample, ratio,
rational number, real numbers,
reciprocal, recurring decimal,
reflection, reflex angle, regression,
remainder, right-angle, right-angled
triangle, root, rotation, rotational
symmetry, sample, scalar segment,
secant, sector, set, side, simultaneous
equation, sine, speed, spiral, square,
square root, standard deviation,
straight line, subset, subtractor,
supplementary angles, symmetry,
tangent, three-dimensional, total,
transcendental number, triangulation,
trigonometry, unit, universal set,
variable, variance, vector, velocity,
Venn diagram, vertex, vertical,
volume, whole number, width, zero.

**matrimonial** adj marital, nuptial,
marriage, wedding, married, wedded,
conjugal.
**matter** n **1** SUBJECT, issue, topic,
question, affair, business, concern,
event, episode, incident. **2**
IMPORTANCE, significance,
consequence, note. **3** TROUBLE,
problem, difficulty, worry.
**4** SUBSTANCE, stuff, material, body,
content.
v count, be important, make a
difference, mean something.
**matter-of-fact** adj unemotional,
prosaic, emotionless,
straightforward, sober,

unimaginative, flat, deadpan (*infml*). **F3** emotional.

**mature** *adj* **1** ADULT, grown-up, grown, full-grown, fully fledged, complete, perfect, perfected, well-thought-out. **2** RIPE, ripened, seasoned, mellow, ready.
**F3 1** childish. **2** immature.
*v* grow up, come of age, develop, mellow, ripen, perfect, age, bloom, fall due.

**maturity** *n* **1** ADULTHOOD, majority, womanhood, manhood, wisdom, experience. **2** RIPENESS, readiness, mellowness, perfection.
**F3 1** childishness. **2** immaturity.

**maul** *v* abuse, ill-treat, manhandle, maltreat, molest, paw, beat (up), knock about, rough up, claw, lacerate, batter.

**maxim** *n* saying, proverb, adage, axiom, aphorism, epigram, motto, byword, precept, rule.

**maximum** *adj* greatest, highest, largest, biggest, most, utmost, supreme.
**F3** minimum.
*n* most, top (point), utmost, upper limit, peak, pinnacle, summit, height, ceiling, extremity, zenith (*fml*).
**F3** mimimum.

**maybe** *adv* perhaps, possibly, perchance (*fml*).
**F3** definitely.

**maze** *n* labyrinth, network, tangle, web, complex, confusion, puzzle, intricacy.

**meadow** *n* field, grassland, pasture, lea.

**meagre** *adj* **1** SCANTY, sparse, inadequate, deficient, skimpy, paltry, negligible, poor. **2** THIN, puny, insubstantial, bony, emaciated, scrawny, slight.
**F3 1** ample. **2** fat.

**meal**

*Meals include*: breakfast, wedding breakfast, elevenses (*infml*), brunch, lunch, luncheon, tea, tea-break, tea-party, tiffin, afternoon tea, cream-tea, high-tea, evening meal, dinner, TV dinner, supper, harvest supper, fork supper, banquet, feast, blow-out (*sl*), barbecue, buffet, spread, picnic, snack, take-away.

**mean¹** *adj* **1** MISERLY, niggardly, parsimonious, selfish, tight (*infml*), tight-fisted, stingy (*infml*), penny-pinching (*infml*). **2** UNKIND, unpleasant, nasty, bad-tempered, cruel. **3** LOWLY, base, poor, humble, wretched.
**F3 1** generous. **2** kind. **3** splendid.

**mean²** *v* **1** SIGNIFY, represent, denote, stand for, symbolize, suggest, indicate, imply. **2** INTEND, aim, propose, design. **3** CAUSE, give rise to, involve, entail.

**mean³** *adj* average, intermediate, middle, halfway, median, normal.
**F3** extreme.
*n* average, middle, mid-point, norm, median, compromise, middle course, middle way, happy medium, golden mean.
**F3** extreme.

**meander** *v* **1** WIND, zigzag, turn, twist, snake, curve. **2** WANDER, stray, amble, ramble, stroll.

**meaning** *n* **1** SIGNIFICANCE, sense, import, implication, gist, trend, explanation, interpretation. **2** AIM, intention, purpose, object, idea. **3** VALUE, worth, point.

**meaningful** *adj* **1** IMPORTANT, significant, relevant, valid, useful, worthwhile, material, purposeful, serious. **2** EXPRESSIVE, speaking, suggestive, warning, pointed.
**F3 1** unimportant, worthless.

**meaningless** *adj* **1** SENSELESS, pointless, purposeless, useless, insignificant, aimless, futile, insubstantial, trifling, trivial. **2** EMPTY, hollow, vacuous, vain, worthless, nonsensical, absurd.

**E3** 1 important, meaningful.
2 worthwhile.

**means** *n* 1 METHOD, mode, way, medium, course, agency, process, instrument, channel, vehicle.
2 RESOURCES, funds, money, income, wealth, riches, substance, wherewithal, fortune, affluence.

**measure** *n* 1 PORTION, ration, share, allocation, quota. 2 SIZE, quantity, magnitude, amount, degree, extent, range, scope, proportion.
3 RULE, gauge, scale, standard, criterion, norm, touchstone, yardstick, test, meter. 4 STEP, course, action, deed, procedure, method, act, bill, statute.
*v* quantify, evaluate, assess, weigh, value, gauge, judge, sound, fathom, determine, calculate, estimate, plumb, survey, compute, measure out, measure off.

**measure up to** equal, meet, match, compare with, touch, rival, make the grade.

**measured** *adj* deliberate, planned, reasoned, slow, unhurried, steady, studied, well-thought-out, calculated, careful, considered, precise.

**measurement** *n* 1 DIMENSION, size, extent, amount, magnitude, area, capacity, height, depth, length, width, weight, volume.
2 ASSESSMENT, evaluation, estimation, computation, calculation, calibration, gauging, judgement, appraisal, appreciation, survey.

*SI (Système International d'Unités) base units include:* ampere, candela, kelvin, kilogram, metre, mole, second.
*SI derivatives and other measurements include:* acre, angstrom, atmosphere, bar, barrel, becquerel, bushel, cable, calorie, centimetre, century, chain, coulomb, cubic centimetre, cubic foot, cubic inch, cubic metre, cubic yard, day, decade, decibel, degree, dyne, erg, farad, fathom, fluid ounce, fresnel, foot, foot-pound, furlong, gallon, gill, gram, hand, hectare, hertz, horsepower, hour, hundredweight, inch, joule, kilometre, knot, league, litre, lumen, micrometre, mile, millennium, millibar, millilitre, minute, month, nautical mile, newton, ohm, ounce, pascal, peak, pint, pound, pound per square inch, radian, rod, siemens, span, square centimetre, square foot, square inch, square kilometre, square metre, square yard, steradian, stone, therm, ton, tonne, volt, watt, week, yard, year.

**meat** *n* 1 FLESH. 2 (*infml*) FOOD, rations, provisions, nourishment, sustenance, subsistence, eats (*infml*).

*Kinds of meat include:* beef, pork, lamb, mutton, ham, bacon, gammon, chicken, turkey, goose, duck, rabbit, hare, venison, pheasant, grouse, partridge, pigeon, quail; offal, liver, heart, tongue, kidney, brains, brawn, pig's knuckle, trotters, oxtail, sweetbread, tripe; steak, minced beef, sausage, rissole, faggot, beefburger, hamburger, black pudding, paté.

*Cuts of meat include:* shoulder, collar, hand, loin, hock, leg, chop, shin, knuckle, rib, spare-rib, breast, brisket, chine, cutlet, fillet, rump, scrag, silverside, topside, sirloin, flank, escalope, neck, saddle.

**mechanical** *adj* automatic, involuntary, instinctive, routine, habitual, impersonal, emotionless, cold, matter-of-fact, unfeeling, lifeless, dead, dull.
**E3** conscious.

**mechanism** *n* 1 MACHINE, machinery, engine, appliance,

instrument, tool, motor, works,
workings, gadget, device, apparatus,
contrivance, gears, components.
**2** MEANS, method, agency, process,
procedure, system, technique,
medium, structure, operation,
functioning, performance.

**meddle** v interfere, intervene, pry,
snoop (infml), intrude, butt in,
tamper.

**meddlesome** adj interfering,
meddling, prying, intrusive,
intruding, mischievous.

**mediate** v arbitrate, conciliate,
intervene, referee, umpire, intercede,
moderate, reconcile, negotiate,
resolve, settle, step in.

**mediator** n arbitrator, referee,
umpire, intermediary, negotiator, go-
between, interceder, judge,
moderator, intercessor, conciliator,
peacemaker, Ombudsman.

**medical terms**

*Medical terms include:* abortion,
allergy, amputation, analgesic,
antibiotics, antiseptic, bandage,
barium meal, biopsy, blood bank,
blood count, blood donor, blood
group, blood pressure, blood test,
caesarean, cardiopulmonary
resuscitation (CPR), case history,
casualty, cauterization, cervical
smear, check-up, childbirth,
circulation, circumcision, clinic,
complication, compress, consultant,
consultation, contraception,
convulsion, cure, diagnosis, dialysis,
dislocate, dissection, doctor, donor,
dressings, enema, examination, gene,
health screening, home visit,
hormone replacement therapy
(HRT), hospice, hospital,
immunization, implantation,
incubation, infection, inflammation,
injection, injury, inoculation,
intensive care, labour, miscarriage,
mouth-to-mouth, nurse, ointment,
operation, paraplegia, post-mortem,

pregnancy, prescription, prognosis,
prosthesis, psychosomatic,
quarantine, radiotherapy, recovery,
rehabilitation, relapse, remission,
respiration, resuscitation, scan, side
effect, sling, smear test, specimen,
splint, sterilization, steroid, surgery,
suture, symptom, syndrome, therapy,
tourniquet, tranquillizer, transfusion,
transplant, trauma, treatment,
tumour, ultrasound scanning,
vaccination, vaccine, virus, x-ray.

**medicinal** adj therapeutic, healing,
remedial, curative, restorative,
medical.

**medicine** n medication, drug, cure,
remedy, medicament, prescription,
pharmaceutical, panacea.

*Types of medicine include:* tablet,
capsule, pill, painkiller, lozenge,
pastille, gargle, linctus, tonic, laxative,
suppository, antacid, ointment, arnica,
eye drops, ear drops, nasal spray,
inhaler, Ventolin, antibiotic, penicillin,
emetic, gripe-water, paregoric. *see
also* **drug**.

*Forms of alternative medicine
include:* acupuncture, aromatherapy,
chiropractic, herbal remedies,
homeopathy, naturopathy, osteopathy,
reflexology.

**mediocre** adj ordinary, average,
middling, medium, indifferent,
unexceptional, undistinguished, so-so
(infml), run-of-the-mill,
commonplace, insignificant, second-
rate, inferior, uninspired.
F3 exceptional, extraordinary,
distinctive.

**mediocrity** n **1** ORDINARINESS,
unimportance, insignificance,
poorness, inferiority, indifference. **2**
NONENTITY, nobody.

**meditate** v **1** REFLECT, ponder,

ruminate, contemplate, muse, brood, think. **2** THINK OVER, consider, deliberate, mull over, study, speculate, scheme, plan, devise, intend.

**medium** *adj* average, middle, median, mean, medial, intermediate, middling, midway, standard, fair.
*n* **1** AVERAGE, middle, mid-point, middle ground, compromise, centre, happy medium, golden mean.
**2** MEANS, agency, channel, vehicle, instrument, way, mode, form, avenue, organ. **3** PSYCHIC, spiritualist, spiritist, clairvoyant.

**medley** *n* assortment, mixture, miscellany, pot-pourri, hotchpotch, hodge-podge, collection, jumble.

**meek** *adj* modest, long-suffering, forbearing, humble, docile, patient, unassuming, unpretentious, resigned, gentle, peaceful, tame, timid, submissive, spiritless.
Ⓕ arrogant, assertive, rebellious.

**meet** *v* **1** ENCOUNTER, come across, run across, run into, chance on, bump into (*infml*). **2** EXPERIENCE, encounter, face, go through, undergo, endure. **3** GATHER, collect, assemble, congregate, convene.
**4** FULFIL, satisfy, match, answer, measure up to, equal, discharge, perform. **5** JOIN, converge, come together, connect, cross, intersect, touch, abut, unite.
Ⓕ **3** scatter. **5** diverge.

**meeting** *n* **1** ENCOUNTER, confrontation, rendezvous, engagement, assignation, introduction, tryst (*fml*).
**2** ASSEMBLY, gathering, congregation, conference, convention, rally, get-together, forum, conclave, session.
**3** CONVERGENCE, confluence, junction, intersection, union.

**melancholy** *adj* depressed, dejected, downcast, down, down-hearted, gloomy, low, low-spirited, heavy-hearted, sad, unhappy, despondent, dispirited, miserable, mournful, dismal, sorrowful, moody.
Ⓕ cheerful, elated, joyful.
*n* depression, dejection, gloom, despondency, low spirits, blues (*infml*), sadness, unhappiness, sorrow.
Ⓕ elation, joy.

**mellow** *adj* **1** MATURE, ripe, juicy, full-flavoured, sweet, tender, mild.
**2** GENIAL, cordial, affable, pleasant, relaxed, placid, serene, tranquil, cheerful, happy, jolly. **3** SMOOTH, melodious, rich, rounded, soft.
Ⓕ **1** unripe. **2** cold. **3** harsh.
*v* mature, ripen, improve, sweeten, soften, temper, season, perfect.

**melodious** *adj* tuneful, musical, melodic, harmonious, dulcet, sweet-sounding, euphonious (*fml*), silvery.
Ⓕ discordant, grating, harsh.

**melodramatic** *adj* histrionic, theatrical, overdramatic, exaggerated, overemotional, sensational, hammy (*infml*).

**melody** *n* tune, music, song, refrain, harmony, theme, air, strain.

**melt** *v* liquefy, dissolve, thaw, fuse, deliquesce (*fml*).
Ⓕ freeze, solidify.
**melt away** disappear, vanish, fade, evaporate, dissolve, disperse.

**member** *n* adherent, associate, subscriber, representative, comrade, fellow.

**memento** *n* souvenir, keepsake, remembrance, reminder, token, memorial, record, relic.

**memoirs** *n* reminiscences, recollections, autobiography, life story, diary, chronicles, annals, journals, records, confessions, experiences.

**memorable** *adj* unforgettable, remarkable, significant, impressive, notable, noteworthy, extraordinary, important, outstanding, momentous.
Ⓕ forgettable, trivial, unimportant.

**memorial** *n* remembrance,

monument, souvenir, memento,
record, stone, plaque, mausoleum.
*adj* commemorative, celebratory.

**memorize** *v* learn, learn by heart,
commit to memory, remember.
🖙 forget.

**memory** *n* recall, retention,
recollection, remembrance,
reminiscence, commemoration.
🖙 forgetfulness.

**menace** *v* threaten, frighten, alarm,
intimidate, terrorize, loom.
*n* 1 INTIMIDATION, threat,
terrorism, warning. 2 DANGER, peril,
hazard, jeopardy, risk. 3 NUISANCE,
annoyance, pest.

**mend** *v* 1 REPAIR, renovate, restore,
refit, fix, patch, cobble, darn, heal.
2 RECOVER, get better, improve.
3 REMEDY, correct, rectify, reform,
revise.
🖙 1 break. 2 deteriorate. 3 destroy.

**menial** *adj* low, lowly, humble, base,
dull, humdrum, routine, degrading,
demeaning, ignominious, unskilled,
subservient, servile, slavish.
*n* servant, domestic, labourer,
minion, attendant, drudge, slave,
underling, skivvy (*infml*), dog's-body
(*infml*).

**mental** *adj* 1 INTELLECTUAL,
abstract, conceptual, cognitive,
cerebral, theoretical, rational.
2 (*infml*) MAD, insane, lunatic, crazy,
unbalanced, deranged, psychotic,
disturbed, loony (*infml*).
🖙 1 physical. 2 sane.

**mentality** *n* 1 INTELLECT, brains,
understanding, faculty, rationality.
2 FRAME OF MIND, character,
disposition, personality, psychology,
outlook.

**mention** *v* refer to, speak of, allude
to, touch on, name, cite,
acknowledge, bring up, report, make
known, impart, declare,
communicate, broach, divulge,
disclose, intimate, point out, reveal,
state, hint at, quote.

*n* reference, allusion, citation,
observation, recognition, remark,
acknowledgement, announcement,
notification, tribute, indication.

**mercenary** *adj* 1 GREEDY,
avaricious, covetous, grasping,
acquisitive, materialistic. 2 HIRED,
paid, venal.

**merchandise** *n* goods,
commodities, stock, produce,
products, wares, cargo, freight,
shipment.

**merchant** *n* trader, dealer, broker,
trafficker, wholesaler, retailer, seller,
shopkeeper, vendor.

**merciful** *adj* compassionate,
forgiving, forbearing, humane,
lenient, sparing, tender-hearted,
pitying, gracious, humanitarian,
kind, liberal, sympathetic, generous,
mild.
🖙 hard-hearted, merciless.

**merciless** *adj* pitiless, relentless,
unmerciful, ruthless, hard-hearted,
hard, heartless, implacable,
inhumane, unforgiving, remorseless,
unpitying, unsparing, severe, cruel,
callous, inhuman.
🖙 compassionate, merciful.

**mercy** *n* 1 COMPASSION, clemency,
forgiveness, forbearance, leniency,
pity, humanitarianism, kindness,
grace. 2 BLESSING, godsend, good
luck, relief.
🖙 1 cruelty, harshness.

**mere** *adj* sheer, plain, simple, bare,
utter, pure, absolute, complete, stark,
unadulterated, common, paltry,
petty.

**merge** *v* join, unite, combine,
converge, amalgamate, blend,
coalesce, mix, intermix, mingle, melt
into, fuse, meet, meld, incorporate,
consolidate.

**merger** *n* amalgamation, union,
fusion, combination, coalition,
consolidation, confederation,
incorporation.

**merit** *n* worth, excellence, value,

quality, good, goodness, virtue, asset, credit, advantage, strong point, talent, justification, due, claim.
**F3** fault.
*v* deserve, be worthy of, earn, justify, warrant.

**merriment** *n* fun, jollity, mirth, hilarity, laughter, conviviality, festivity, amusement, revelry, frolic, liveliness, joviality.
**F3** gloom, seriousness.

**merry** *adj* jolly, light-hearted, mirthful, joyful, happy, convivial, festive, cheerful, glad.
**F3** gloomy, melancholy, sober.

**mesh** *n* net, network, netting, lattice, web, tangle, entanglement, snare, trap.
*v* engage, interlock, dovetail, fit, connect, harmonize, co-ordinate, combine, come together.

**mess** *n* 1 CHAOS, untidiness, disorder, disarray, confusion, muddle, jumble, clutter, disorganization, mix-up, shambles (*infml*). 2 DIFFICULTY, trouble, predicament, fix (*infml*).
**F3** 1 order, tidiness.

**mess about** mess around, fool around, play, play around, play about, muck about (*infml*), interfere, tamper, trifle.

**mess up** 1 DISARRANGE, jumble, muddle, tangle, dishevel, disrupt. 2 BOTCH, bungle, spoil, muck up (*infml*).

**message** *n* 1 COMMUNICATION, bulletin, dispatch, communiqué, report, missive (*fml*), errand, letter, memorandum, note, notice, cable. 2 MEANING, idea, point, theme, moral.

**messenger** *n* courier, emissary (*fml*), envoy, go-between, herald, runner, carrier, bearer, harbinger, agent, ambassador.

**messy** *adj* untidy, unkempt, dishevelled, disorganized, chaotic, sloppy, slovenly, confused, dirty, grubby, muddled, cluttered.
**F3** neat, ordered, tidy.

**metamorphosis** *n* change, alteration, transformation, rebirth, regeneration, transfiguration, conversion, modification, change-over.

**metaphor** *n* figure of speech, allegory, analogy, symbol, picture, image.

**metaphorical** *adj* figurative, allegorical, symbolic.

**mete out** allot, apportion, deal out, dole out, hand out, measure out, share out, ration out, portion, distribute, dispense, divide out, assign, administer.

**meteoric** *adj* rapid, speedy, swift, sudden, overnight, instantaneous, momentary, brief, spectacular, brilliant, dazzling.

**method** *n* 1 WAY, approach, means, course, manner, mode, fashion, process, procedure, route, technique, style, plan, scheme, programme. 2 ORGANIZATION, order, structure, system, pattern, form, planning, regularity, routine.

**methodical** *adj* systematic, structured, organized, ordered, orderly, tidy, regular, planned, efficient, disciplined, businesslike, deliberate, neat, scrupulous, precise, meticulous, painstaking.
**F3** chaotic, irregular, confused.

**meticulous** *adj* precise, scrupulous, exact, punctilious, fussy, detailed, accurate, thorough, fastidious, painstaking, strict.
**F3** careless, slapdash.

**metropolis** *n* capital, city, municipality, megalopolis.

**mettle** *n* 1 CHARACTER, temperament, disposition. 2 SPIRIT, courage, vigour, nerve, boldness, daring, indomitability, pluck, resolve, valour, bravery, fortitude.

**microbe** *n* micro-organism, bacterium, bacillus, germ, virus, pathogen, bug (*infml*).

**microscopic** *adj* minute, tiny, minuscule, infinitesimal, indiscernible, imperceptible, negligible.
**Ea** huge, enormous.

**middle** *adj* central, halfway, mean, median, intermediate, inner, inside, intervening.
*n* centre, halfway point, midpoint, mean, heart, core, midst, inside, bull's eye.
**Ea** extreme, end, edge, beginning, border.

**middling** *adj* mediocre, medium, ordinary, moderate, average, unexceptional, unremarkable, run-of-the-mill, indifferent, modest, passable, tolerable, so-so (*infml*), OK (*infml*).

**midget** *n* person of restricted growth, pygmy, dwarf, Tom Thumb, gnome.
**Ea** giant.
*adj* tiny, small, miniature, little, pocket, pocket-sized.
**Ea** giant.

**midst** *n* middle, centre, mid-point, heart, hub, interior.

**migrant** *n* traveller, wanderer, itinerant, emigrant, immigrant, rover, nomad, globe-trotter, drifter, gypsy, tinker, vagrant.

**migrate** *v* move, resettle, relocate, wander, roam, rove, journey, emigrate, travel, voyage, trek, drift.

**mild** *adj* **1** *mild manners*: gentle, calm, peaceable, placid, tender, soft, good-natured, kind, amiable, lenient, compassionate. **2** *mild weather*: calm, temperate, warm, balmy, clement, fair, pleasant. **3** *mild coffee*: bland, mellow, smooth, subtle, soothing.
**Ea 1** harsh, fierce. **2** stormy. **3** strong.

**militant** *adj* aggressive, belligerent, vigorous, fighting, warring.
**Ea** pacifist, peaceful.
*n* activist, combatant, fighter, struggler, warrior, aggressor, belligerent.

**military** *adj* martial, armed, soldierly, warlike, service.
*n* army, armed forces, soldiers, forces, services.

**militate against** oppose, counter, counteract, count against, tell against, weigh against, contend, resist.

**milk** *v* drain, bleed, tap, extract, draw off, exploit, use, express, press, pump, siphon, squeeze, wring.

**milky** *adj* white, milk-white, chalky, opaque, clouded, cloudy.

**mill** *n* **1** FACTORY, plant, works, workshop, foundry. **2** GRINDER, crusher, quern, roller.
*v* grind, pulverize, powder, pound, crush, roll, press, grate.

**mime** *n* dumb show, pantomime, gesture, mimicry.
*v* gesture, signal, act out, represent, simulate, impersonate, mimic.

**mimic** *v* imitate, parody, caricature, take off (*infml*), ape, parrot, impersonate, echo, mirror, simulate, look like.
*n* imitator, impersonator, impressionist, caricaturist, copy-cat (*infml*), copy.

**mimicry** *n* imitation, imitating, impersonation, copying, parody, impression, caricature, take-off (*infml*), burlesque.

**mince** *v* **1** CHOP, cut, hash, dice, grind, crumble. **2** DIMINISH, suppress, play down, tone down, hold back, moderate, weaken, soften, spare.

**mind** *n* **1** INTELLIGENCE, intellect, brains, reason, sense, understanding, wits, mentality, thinking, thoughts, grey matter (*infml*), head, genius, concentration, attention, spirit, psyche. **2** MEMORY, remembrance, recollection. **3** OPINION, view, point of view, belief, attitude, judgement, feeling, sentiment. **4** INCLINATION, disposition, tendency, will, wish, intention, desire.

*v* **1** CARE, object, take offence, resent, disapprove, dislike. **2** REGARD, heed, pay attention, pay heed to, note, obey, listen to, comply with, follow, observe, be careful, watch. **3** LOOK AFTER, take care of, watch over, guard, have charge of, keep an eye on (*infml*).

**bear in mind** consider, remember, note.

**make up one's mind** decide, choose, determine, settle, resolve.

**mindful** *adj* aware, conscious, alive (to), alert, attentive, careful, watchful, wary.

**F3** heedless, inattentive.

**mindless** *adj* **1** THOUGHTLESS, senseless, illogical, irrational, stupid, foolish, gratuitous, negligent. **2** MECHANICAL, automatic, tedious.

**F3** **1** thoughtful, intelligent.

**mine** *n* **1** PIT, colliery, coalfield, excavation, vein, seam, shaft, trench, deposit. **2** SUPPLY, source, stock, store, reserve, fund, hoard, treasury, wealth.

*v* excavate, dig for, dig up, delve, quarry, extract, unearth, tunnel, remove, undermine.

**minerals**

*Minerals include:* alabaster, albite, anhydrite, asbestos, aventurine, azurite, bentonite, blacklead, bloodstone, blue john, borax, cairngorm, calamine, calcite, calcspar, cassiterite, chalcedony, chlorite, chrysoberyl, cinnabar, corundum, dolomite, emery, feldspar, fluorite, fluorspar, fool's gold, French chalk, galena, graphite, gypsum, haematite, halite, haüyne, hornblende, hyacinth, idocrase, jacinth, jargoon, jet, kandite, kaolinite, lapis lazuli, lazurite, magnetite, malachite, meerschaum, mica, microcline, montmorillonite, orthoclase, plumbago, pyrites, quartz, rock salt, rutile, saltpetre, sanidine, silica, smithsonite, sodalite, spar, sphalerite, spinel, talc, uralite, uranite, vesuvianite, wurtzite, zircon.

**mingle** *v* **1** MIX, intermingle, intermix, combine, blend, merge, unite, alloy, coalesce, join, compound. **2** ASSOCIATE, socialize, circulate, hobnob (*infml*), rub shoulders (*infml*).

**miniature** *adj* tiny, small, scaled-down, minute, diminutive, baby, pocket-sized, pint-size(d) (*infml*), little, mini (*infml*).

**F3** giant.

**minimal** *adj* least, smallest, minimum, slightest, littlest, negligible, minute, token.

**minimize** *v* **1** REDUCE, decrease, diminish. **2** BELITTLE, make light of, make little of, disparage, deprecate, discount, play down, underestimate, underrate.

**F3** **1** maximize.

**minimum** *n* least, lowest point, slightest, bottom.

**F3** maximum.

*adj* minimal, least, lowest, slightest, smallest, littlest, tiniest.

**F3** maximum.

**minion** *n* **1** ATTENDANT, follower, underling, lackey, hireling. **2** DEPENDANT, hanger-on, favourite, darling, sycophant, yes-man (*infml*), bootlicker (*infml*).

**minister** *n* **1** OFFICIAL, office-holder, politician, dignitary, diplomat, ambassador, delegate, envoy, consul, cabinet minister, agent, aide, administrator, executive. **2** CLERGYMAN, churchman, cleric, parson, priest, pastor, vicar, preacher, ecclesiastic (*fml*), divine.

*v* attend, serve, tend, take care of, wait on, cater to, accommodate, nurse.

**ministry** *n* **1** GOVERNMENT, cabinet, department, office, bureau, administration. **2** THE CHURCH, holy orders, the priesthood.

**minor** *adj* lesser, secondary, smaller, inferior, subordinate, subsidiary, junior, younger, insignificant, inconsiderable, negligible, petty, trivial, trifling, second-class, unclassified, slight, light.
**F3** major, significant, important.

**mint** *v* coin, stamp, strike, cast, forge, punch, make, manufacture, produce, construct, devise, fashion, invent, make up.
*adj* perfect, brand-new, fresh, immaculate, unblemished, excellent, first-class.

**minute**[1] *n* moment, second, instant, flash, jiffy (*infml*), tick (*infml*).

**minute**[2] *adj* **1** TINY, infinitesimal, minuscule, microscopic, miniature, inconsiderable, negligible, small. **2** DETAILED, precise, meticulous, painstaking, close, critical, exhaustive.
**F3 1** gigantic, huge. **2** cursory, superficial.

**minutes** *n* proceedings, record(s), notes, memorandum, transcript, transactions, details, tapes.

**miracle** *n* wonder, marvel, prodigy, phenomenon.

**miraculous** *adj* wonderful, marvellous, phenomenal, extraordinary, amazing, astounding, astonishing, unbelievable, supernatural, incredible, inexplicable, unaccountable, superhuman.
**F3** natural, normal.

**mirage** *n* illusion, optical illusion, hallucination, fantasy, phantasm.

**mirror** *n* **1** GLASS, looking-glass, reflector. **2** REFLECTION, likeness, image, double, copy.
*v* reflect, echo, imitate, copy, represent, show, depict, mimic.

**mirth** *n* merriment, hilarity, gaiety, fun, laughter, jollity, jocularity, amusement, revelry, glee, cheerfulness.
**F3** gloom, melancholy.

**misapprehension** *n*

misunderstanding, misconception, misinterpretation, misreading, error, mistake, fallacy, delusion.

**misappropriate** *v* steal, embezzle, peculate, pocket, swindle (*infml*), misspend, misuse, misapply, abuse, pervert.

**misbehave** *v* offend, transgress, trespass, get up to mischief, mess about, muck about (*infml*), play up, act up (*infml*).

**misbehaviour** *n* misconduct, misdemeanour, impropriety, disobedience, naughtiness, insubordination.

**miscalculate** *v* misjudge, get wrong, slip up, blunder, boob (*infml*), miscount, overestimate, underestimate.

**miscarriage** *n* failure, breakdown, abortion, mishap, mismanagement, error, disappointment.
**F3** success.

**miscarry** *v* fail, abort, come to nothing, fall through, misfire, founder, come to grief.
**F3** succeed.

**miscellaneous** *adj* mixed, varied, various, assorted, diverse, diversified, sundry, motley, jumbled, indiscriminate.

**miscellany** *n* mixture, variety, assortment, collection, anthology, medley, mixed bag, pot-pourri, hotch-potch, jumble, diversity.

**mischief** *n* **1** TROUBLE, harm, evil, damage, injury, disruption. **2** MISBEHAVIOUR, naughtiness, impishness, pranks.

**mischievous** *adj* **1** MALICIOUS, evil, spiteful, vicious, wicked, pernicious, destructive, injurious. **2** NAUGHTY, impish, rascally, roguish, playful, teasing.
**F3 1** kind. **2** well-behaved, good.

**misconception** *n* misapprehension, misunderstanding, misreading, error, fallacy, delusion, the wrong end of the stick (*infml*).

**misconduct** n misbehaviour, impropriety, misdemeanour, malpractice, mismanagement, wrong-doing.

**miser** n niggard, skinflint, penny-pincher (*infml*), Scrooge.
**Ea** spendthrift.

**miserable** adj 1 UNHAPPY, sad, dejected, despondent, downcast, heartbroken, wretched, distressed, crushed. 2 CHEERLESS, depressing, dreary, impoverished, shabby, gloomy, dismal, forlorn, joyless, squalid. 3 CONTEMPTIBLE, despicable, ignominious, detestable, disgraceful, deplorable, shameful. 4 MEAGRE, paltry, niggardly, worthless, pathetic, pitiful.
**Ea** 1 cheerful, happy. 2 pleasant. 4 generous.

**miserly** adj mean, niggardly, tight, stingy (*infml*), sparing, parsimonious, cheese-paring, beggarly, penny-pinching (*infml*), mingy (*infml*).
**Ea** generous, spendthrift.

**misery** n 1 UNHAPPINESS, sadness, suffering, distress, depression, despair, gloom, grief, wretchedness, affliction. 2 PRIVATION, hardship, deprivation, poverty, want, oppression, destitution. 3 (*infml*) SPOILSPORT, pessimist, killjoy, wet blanket (*infml*).
**Ea** 1 contentment. 2 comfort.

**misfire** v miscarry, go wrong, abort, fail, fall through, flop (*infml*), founder, fizzle out, come to grief.
**Ea** succeed.

**misfit** n individualist, nonconformist, eccentric, maverick, drop-out, loner, lone wolf.
**Ea** conformist.

**misfortune** n bad luck, mischance, mishap, ill-luck, setback, reverse, calamity, catastrophe, disaster, blow, accident, tragedy, trouble, hardship, trial, tribulation.
**Ea** luck, success.

**misgiving** n doubt, uncertainty,

hesitation, qualm, reservation, apprehension, scruple, suspicion, second thoughts, niggle, anxiety, worry, fear.
**Ea** confidence.

**misguided** adj misled, misconceived, ill-considered, ill-advised, ill-judged, imprudent, rash, misplaced, deluded, foolish, erroneous.
**Ea** sensible, wise.

**mishap** n misfortune, ill-fortune, misadventure, accident, setback, calamity, disaster, adversity.

**misinterpret** v misconstrue, misread, misunderstand, mistake, distort, garble.

**misjudge** v miscalculate, mistake, misinterpret, misconstrue, misunderstand, overestimate, underestimate.

**mislay** v lose, misplace, miss, lose sight of.

**mislead** v misinform, misdirect, deceive, delude, lead astray, fool.

**misleading** adj deceptive, confusing, unreliable, ambiguous, biased, loaded, evasive, tricky (*infml*).
**Ea** unequivocal, authoritative, informative.

**mismanage** v mishandle, botch, bungle, make a mess of, mess up, misrule, misspend, misjudge, foul up, mar, waste.

**misprint** n mistake, error, erratum, literal, typo (*infml*).

**misrepresent** v distort, falsify, slant, pervert, twist, garble, misquote, exaggerate, minimize, misconstrue, misinterpret.

**miss** v 1 FAIL, miscarry, lose, let slip, let go, omit, overlook, pass over, slip, leave out, mistake, trip, misunderstand, err. 2 AVOID, escape, evade, dodge, forego, skip, bypass, circumvent. 3 PINE FOR, long for, yearn for, regret, grieve for, mourn, sorrow for, want, wish, need, lament.

*n* failure, error, blunder, mistake, omission, oversight, fault, flop (*infml*), fiasco.

**misshapen** *adj* deformed, distorted, twisted, malformed, warped, contorted, crooked, crippled, grotesque, ugly, monstrous.
**E3** regular, shapely.

**missile** *n* projectile, shot, guided missile, arrow, shaft, dart, rocket, bomb, shell, flying bomb, grenade, torpedo, weapon.

**missing** *adj* absent, lost, lacking, gone, mislaid, unaccounted-for, wanting, disappeared, astray, strayed, misplaced.
**E3** found, present.

**mission** *n* **1** TASK, undertaking, assignment, operation, campaign, crusade, business, errand.
**2** CALLING, duty, purpose, vocation, raison d'être, aim, charge, office, job, work. **3** COMMISSION, ministry, delegation, deputation, legation, embassy.

**missionary** *n* evangelist, campaigner, preacher, proselytizer, apostle, crusader, propagandist, champion, promoter, emissary, envoy, ambassador.

**mist** *n* haze, fog, vapour, smog, cloud, condensation, film, spray, drizzle, dew, steam, veil, dimness.
**mist over** cloud over, fog, dim, blur, steam up, obscure, veil.
**E3** clear.

**mistake** *n* error, inaccuracy, slip, slip-up, oversight, lapse, blunder, Ilanger (*infml*), boob (*infml*), gaffe, fault, faux pas, solecism (*fml*), indiscretion, misjudgment, miscalculation, misunderstanding, misprint, misspelling, misreading, mispronunciation, howler (*infml*).
*v* misunderstand, misapprehend, misconstrue, misjudge, misread, miscalculate, confound, confuse, slip up, blunder, err, boob (*infml*).

**mistaken** *adj* wrong, incorrect,

erroneous, inaccurate, inexact, untrue, inappropriate, ill-judged, inauthentic, false, deceived, deluded, misinformed, misled, faulty.
**E3** correct, right.

**mistreat** *v* abuse, ill-treat, ill-use, maltreat, harm, hurt, batter, injure, knock about, molest.

**mistress** *n* **1** LOVER, live-in lover, kept woman, concubine, courtesan, girlfriend, paramour, woman, lady-love. **2** TEACHER, governess, tutor.

**mistrust** *v* distrust, doubt, suspicion, wariness, misgiving, reservations, qualm, hesitancy, chariness, caution, uncertainty, scepticism, apprehension.
**E3** trust.
*v* distrust, doubt, suspect, be wary of, beware, have reservations, fear.
**E3** trust.

**misty** *adj* hazy, foggy, cloudy, blurred, fuzzy, murky, smoky, unclear, dim, indistinct, obscure, opaque, vague, veiled.
**E3** clear.

**misunderstand** *v* misapprehend, misconstrue, misinterpret, misjudge, mistake, get wrong, miss the point, mishear, get hold of the wrong end of the stick (*infml*).
**E3** understand.

**misunderstanding** *n* **1** MISTAKE, error, misapprehension, misconception, misjudgement, misinterpretation, misreading, mix-up. **2** DISAGREEMENT, argument, dispute, conflict, clash, difference, breach, quarrel, discord, rift.
**E3 1** understanding. **2** agreement.

**misuse** *n* mistreatment, maltreatment, abuse, harm, ill-treatment, misapplication, misappropriation, waste, perversion, corruption, exploitation.
*v* abuse, misapply, misemploy, ill-use, ill-treat, harm, mistreat, wrong, distort, injure, corrupt, pervert, waste, squander, misappropriate, exploit,

dissipate.

**mitigating** adj extenuating, justifying, vindicating, modifying, qualifying.

**mix** v 1 COMBINE, blend, mingle, intermingle, intermix, amalgamate, compound, homogenize, synthesize, merge, join, unite, coalesce, fuse, incorporate, fold in. 2 ASSOCIATE, consort, fraternize, socialize, mingle, join, hobnob (infml).
**E3** 1 divide, separate.
n mixture, blend, amalgam, assortment, combination, conglomerate, compound, fusion, synthesis, medley, composite, mishmash (infml).

**mix up** confuse, bewilder, muddle, perplex, puzzle, confound, mix, jumble, complicate, garble, involve, implicate, disturb, upset, snarl up.

**mixed** adj 1 mixed race: combined, hybrid, mingled, crossbred, mongrel, blended, composite, compound, incorporated, united, alloyed, amalgamated, fused. 2 mixed biscuits: assorted, varied, miscellaneous, diverse, diversified, motley. 3 mixed feelings: ambivalent, equivocal, conflicting, contradicting, uncertain.

**mixture** n mix, blend, combination, amalgamation, amalgam, compound, conglomeration, composite, coalescence, alloy, brew, synthesis, union, fusion, concoction, cross, hybrid, assortment, variety, miscellany, medley, mélange, mixed bag, pot-pourri, jumble, hotchpotch.

**moan** n lament, lamentation, sob, wail, howl, whimper, whine, grumble, complaint, grievance, groan.
v 1 LAMENT, wail, sob, weep, howl, groan, whimper, mourn, grieve. 2 (infml) COMPLAIN, grumble, whine, whinge (infml), gripe (infml), carp.
**E3** 1 rejoice.

**mob** n 1 CROWD, mass, throng, multitude, horde, host, swarm, gathering, group, collection, flock, herd, pack, set, tribe, troop, company, crew, gang. 2 POPULACE, rabble, masses, hoi polloi, plebs (infml), riff-raff (infml).
v crowd, crowd round, surround, swarm round, jostle, overrun, set upon, besiege, descend on, throng, pack, pester, charge.

**mobile** adj 1 MOVING, movable, portable, peripatetic, travelling, roaming, roving, itinerant, wandering, migrant. 2 FLEXIBLE, agile, active, energetic, nimble. 3 CHANGING, changeable, ever-changing, expressive, lively.
**E3** 1 immobile.

**mobilize** v assemble, marshal, rally, conscript, muster, call up, enlist, activate, galvanize, organize, prepare, ready, summon, animate.

**mock** v 1 RIDICULE, jeer, make fun of, laugh at, disparage, deride, scoff, sneer, taunt, scorn, tease. 2 IMITATE, simulate, mimic, ape, caricature, satirize.
adj imitation, counterfeit, artificial, sham, simulated, synthetic, false, fake, forged, fraudulent, bogus, phoney (infml), pseudo, spurious, feigned, faked, pretended, dummy.

**mockery** n 1 RIDICULE, jeering, scoffing, scorn, derision, contempt, disdain, disrespect, sarcasm. 2 PARODY, satire, sham, travesty.

**mocking** adj scornful, derisive, contemptuous, sarcastic, satirical, taunting, scoffing, sardonic, snide (infml), insulting, irreverent, impudent, disrespectful, disdainful, cynical.

**model** n 1 COPY, replica, representation, facsimile, imitation, mock-up. 2 EXAMPLE, exemplar, pattern, standard, ideal, mould, prototype, template. 3 DESIGN, style, type, version, mark. 4 MANNEQUIN, dummy, sitter, subject, poser.

*adj* exemplary, perfect, typical, ideal.
*v* 1 MAKE, form, fashion, mould, sculpt, carve, cast, shape, work, create, design, plan. 2 DISPLAY, wear, show off.

**moderate** *adj* 1 MEDIOCRE, medium, ordinary, fair, indifferent, average, middle-of-the-road. 2 REASONABLE, restrained, sensible, calm, controlled, cool, mild, well-regulated.
■ 1 exceptional. 2 immoderate.
*v* control, regulate, decrease, lessen, soften, restrain, tone down, play down, diminish, ease, curb, calm, check, modulate, repress, subdue, soft-pedal, tame, subside, pacify, mitigate, allay, alleviate, abate, dwindle.

**moderately** *adv* somewhat, quite, rather, fairly, slightly, reasonably, passably, to some extent.
■ extremely.

**moderation** *n* 1 DECREASE, reduction. 2 RESTRAINT, self-control, caution, control, composure, sobriety, abstemiousness, temperance, reasonableness.

**modern** *adj* current, contemporary, up-to-date, new, fresh, latest, late, novel, present, present-day, recent, up-to-the-minute, newfangled (*infml*), advanced, avant-garde, progressive, modernistic, innovative, inventive, state-of-the-art, go-ahead, fashionable, stylish, in vogue, in style, modish, trendy (*infml*).
■ old-fashioned, old, out-of-date, antiquated.

**modernize** *v* renovate, refurbish, rejuvenate, regenerate, streamline, revamp, renew, update, improve, do up, redesign, reform, remake, remodel, refresh, transform, modify, progress.
■ regress.

**modest** *adj* 1 UNASSUMING, humble, self-effacing, quiet, reserved, retiring, unpretentious, discreet,

bashful, shy. 2 MODERATE, ordinary, unexceptional, fair, reasonable, limited, small.
■ 1 immodest, conceited. 2 exceptional, excessive.

**modesty** *n* humility, humbleness, self-effacement, reticence, reserve, quietness, decency, propriety, demureness, shyness, bashfulness, coyness.
■ immodesty, vanity, conceit.

**modify** *v* 1 CHANGE, alter, redesign, revise, vary, adapt, adjust, transform, reform, convert, improve, reorganize. 2 MODERATE, reduce, temper, tone down, limit, soften, qualify.

**modulate** *v* modify, adjust, balance, alter, soften, lower, regulate, vary, harmonize, inflect, tune.

**moist** *adj* damp, clammy, humid, wet, dewy, rainy, muggy, marshy, drizzly, watery, soggy.
■ dry, arid.

**moisten** *v* moisturize, dampen, damp, wet, water, lick, irrigate.
■ dry.

**moisture** *n* water, liquid, wetness, wateriness, damp, dampness, dankness, humidity, vapour, dew, mugginess, condensation, steam, spray.
■ dryness.

**molest** *v* 1 ANNOY, disturb, bother, harass, irritate, persecute, pester, plague, tease, torment, hound, upset, worry, trouble, badger. 2 ATTACK, accost, assail, hurt, ill-treat, maltreat, mistreat, abuse, harm, injure.

**mollusc**

*Molluscs include*: abalone, conch, cowrie, cuttlefish, clam, cockle, limpet, mussel, nautilus, nudibranch, octopus, oyster, periwinkle, scallop, sea slug, slug, freshwater snail, land snail, marine snail, squid, tusk shell, whelk.

**moment** *n* second, instant, minute, split second, trice, jiffy (*infml*), tick (*infml*).

*v* check, watch, keep track of, keep under surveillance, keep an eye on, follow, track, supervise, observe, note, survey, trace, scan, record, plot, detect.

**momentary** *adj* brief, short, short-lived, temporary, transient, transitory, fleeting, ephemeral, hasty, quick, passing.
**Ⅎ** lasting, permanent.

**momentous** *adj* significant, important, critical, crucial, decisive, weighty, grave, serious, vital, fateful, historic, earth-shaking, epoch-making, eventful, major.
**Ⅎ** insignificant, unimportant, trivial.

**momentum** *n* impetus, force, energy, impulse, drive, power, thrust, speed, velocity, impact, incentive, stimulus, urge, strength, push.

**monarch** *n* sovereign, crowned head, ruler, king, queen, emperor, empress, prince, princess, tsar, potentate.

**monarchy** *n* 1 KINGDOM, empire, principality, realm, domain, dominion. 2 ROYALISM, sovereignty, autocracy, monocracy, absolutism, despotism, tyranny.

**monastery** *n* friary, priory, abbey, cloister, charterhouse.

**monastic** *adj* reclusive, withdrawn, secluded, cloistered, austere, ascetic, celibate, contemplative.
**Ⅎ** secular, worldly.

**monetary** *adj* financial, fiscal, pecuniary (*fml*), budgetary, economic, capital, cash.

**money** *n* currency, cash, legal tender, banknotes, coin, funds, capital, dough (*infml*), dosh (*infml*), riches, wealth.

**mongrel** *n* cross, crossbreed, hybrid, half-breed.
*adj* crossbred, hybrid, half-breed, bastard, mixed, ill-defined.
**Ⅎ** pure-bred, pedigree.

**monitor** *n* 1 SCREEN, display, VDU, recorder, scanner. 2 SUPERVISOR, watchdog, overseer, invigilator, adviser, prefect.

**monkey** *n* 1 PRIMATE, simian, ape. 2 (*infml*) SCAMP, imp, urchin, brat, rogue, scallywag (*infml*), rascal.

> *Monkeys include:* ape, baboon, capuchin, colobus monkey, drill and mandrill, guenon, guereza, howler monkey, langur, leaf monkey, macaque, mangabey, marmoset, night monkey (or douroucouli), proboscis monkey, rhesus monkey, saki, spider monkey, squirrel money, tamarin, titi, toque, uakari (or cacajou), woolly monkey.

**monopolize** *v* dominate, take over, appropriate, corner, control, hog (*infml*), engross, occupy, preoccupy, take up, tie up.
**Ⅎ** share.

**monotonous** *adj* boring, dull, tedious, uninteresting, tiresome, wearisome, unchanging, uneventful, unvaried, uniform, toneless, flat, colourless, repetitive, routine, plodding, humdrum, soul-destroying.
**Ⅎ** lively, varied, colourful.

**monotony** *n* tedium, dullness, boredom, sameness, tiresomeness, uneventfulness, flatness, wearisomeness, uniformity, routine, repetitiveness.
**Ⅎ** liveliness, colour.

**monster** *n* 1 BEAST, fiend, brute, barbarian, savage, villain, giant, ogre, ogress, troll, mammoth. 2 FREAK, monstrosity, mutant.
*adj* huge, gigantic, giant, colossal, enormous, immense, massive, monstrous, jumbo, mammoth, vast, tremendous.
**Ⅎ** tiny, minute.

**monstrous** *adj* 1 WICKED, evil, vicious, cruel, criminal, heinous, outrageous, scandalous, disgraceful, atrocious, abhorrent, dreadful, frightful, horrible, horrifying, terrible. **2** UNNATURAL, inhuman, freakish, grotesque, hideous, deformed, malformed, misshapen. **3** HUGE, enormous, colossal, gigantic, vast, immense, massive, mammoth.

**monument** n memorial, cenotaph, headstone, gravestone, tombstone, shrine, mausoleum, cairn, barrow, cross, marker, obelisk, pillar, statue, relic, remembrance, commemoration, testament, reminder, record, memento, evidence, token.

**monumental** adj **1** IMPRESSIVE, imposing, awe-inspiring, awesome, overwhelming, significant, important, epoch-making, historic, magnificent, majestic, memorable, notable, outstanding, abiding, immortal, lasting, classic. **2** HUGE, immense, enormous, colossal, vast, tremendous, massive, great.

**3** COMMEMORATIVE, memorial.
**F3** insignificant, unimportant.

**mood** n **1** DISPOSITION, frame of mind, state of mind, temper, humour, spirit, tenor, whim. **2** BAD TEMPER, sulk, the sulks, pique, melancholy, depression, blues (infml), doldrums, dumps (infml).

**moody** adj changeable, temperamental, unpredictable, capricious, irritable, short-tempered, crabby (infml), crotchety, crusty (infml), testy, touchy, morose, angry, broody, mopy, sulky, sullen, gloomy, melancholy, miserable, downcast, doleful, glum, impulsive, fickle, flighty.
**F3** equable, cheerful.

**moon** v idle, loaf, mooch, languish, pine, mope, brood, daydream, dream, fantasize.

**moor**[1] v fasten, secure, tie up, drop anchor, anchor, berth, dock, make fast, fix, hitch, bind.

**F3** loose.

**moor**[2] n moorland, heath, fell, upland.

**mop** n head of hair, shock, mane, tangle, thatch, mass.
v swab, sponge, wipe, clean, wash, absorb, soak.

**mope** v brood, fret, sulk, pine, languish, droop, despair, grieve, idle.

**moral** adj ethical, virtuous, good, right, principled, honourable, decent, upright, upstanding, straight, righteous, high-minded, honest, incorruptible, proper, blameless, chaste, clean-living, pure, just, noble.
**F3** immoral.
n lesson, message, teaching, dictum, meaning, maxim, adage, precept, saying, proverb, aphorism, epigram.

**morale** n confidence, spirits, esprit de corps, self-esteem, state of mind, heart, mood.

**morality** n ethics, morals, ideals, principles, standards, virtue, rectitude, righteousness, decency, goodness, honesty, integrity, justice, uprightness, propriety, conduct, manners.
**F3** immorality.

**morals** n morality, ethics, principles, standards, ideals, integrity, scruples, behaviour, conduct, habits, manners.

**morbid** adj **1** GHOULISH, ghastly, gruesome, macabre, hideous, horrid, grim. **2** GLOOMY, pessimistic, melancholy, sombre. **3** SICK, unhealthy, unwholesome, insalubrious.

**more** adj further, extra, additional, added, new, fresh, increased, other, supplementary, repeated, alternative, spare.
**F3** less.
adv further, longer, again, besides, moreover, better.
**F3** less.

**moreover** adv furthermore, further, besides, in addition, as well, also, additionally, what is more.

**morning** n daybreak, daylight, dawn, sunrise, break of day, before noon.

**morose** adj ill-tempered, bad-tempered, moody, sullen, sulky, surly, gloomy, grim, gruff, sour, taciturn, glum, grouchy (*infml*), crabby (*infml*), saturnine.
**F3** cheerful, communicative.

**morsel** n bit, scrap, piece, fragment, crumb, bite, mouthful, nibble, taste, soupçon, titbit, slice, fraction, modicum, grain, atom, part.

**mortal** adj 1 WORLDLY, earthly, bodily, human, perishable, temporal. 2 FATAL, lethal, deadly. 3 EXTREME, great, severe, intense, grave, awful.
**F3** 1 immortal.
n human being, human, individual, person, being, body, creature.
**F3** immortal, god.

**mortality** n 1 HUMANITY, death, impermanence, perishability. 2 FATALITY, death rate.
**F3** 1 immortality.

**mortified** adj humiliated, shamed, ashamed, humbled, embarrassed, crushed.

**mostly** adv mainly, on the whole, principally, chiefly, generally, usually, largely, for the most part, as a rule.

**mother** n 1 PARENT, procreator (*fml*), progenitress (*fml*), dam, mamma, mummy (*infml*), mummy (*infml*), matriarch, ancestor, matron, old woman (*infml*). 2 ORIGIN, source.
v 1 BEAR, produce, nurture, raise, rear, nurse, care for, cherish. 2 PAMPER, spoil, baby, indulge, overprotect, fuss over.

**motherly** adj maternal, caring, comforting, affectionate, kind, loving, protective, warm, tender, gentle, fond.
**F3** neglectful, uncaring.

**motif** n theme, idea, topic, concept, pattern, design, figure, form, logo, shape, device, ornament, decoration.

**motion** n 1 MOVEMENT, action, mobility, moving, activity, locomotion, travel, transit, passage, passing, progress, change, flow, inclination. 2 GESTURE, gesticulation, signal, sign, wave, nod. 3 PROPOSAL, suggestion, recommendation, proposition.
v signal, gesture, gesticulate, sign, wave, nod, beckon, direct, usher.

**motionless** adj unmoving, still, stationary, static, immobile, at a standstill, fixed, halted, at rest, resting, standing, paralysed, inanimate, lifeless, frozen, rigid, stagnant.
**F3** active, moving.

**motivate** v prompt, incite, impel, spur, provoke, stimulate, drive, lead, stir, urge, push, propel, persuade, move, inspire, encourage, cause, trigger, induce, kindle, draw, arouse, bring.
**F3** deter, discourage.

**motive** n ground(s), cause, reason, purpose, motivation, object, intention, influence, rationale, thinking, incentive, impulse, stimulus, inspiration, incitement, urge, encouragement, design, desire, consideration.
**F3** deterrent, disincentive.

**mottled** adj speckled, dappled, blotchy, flecked, piebald, stippled, streaked, tabby, spotted, freckled, variegated.
**F3** monochrome, uniform.

**motto** n saying, slogan, maxim, watchword, catchword, byword, precept, proverb, adage, formula, rule, golden rule, dictum.

**mould**¹ n 1 CAST, form, die, template, pattern, matrix. 2 SHAPE, form, format, pattern, structure, style, type, build, construction, cut, design, kind, model, sort, stamp, arrangement, brand, frame, character, nature, quality, line, make.

*v* 1 FORGE, cast, shape, stamp, make, form, create, design, construct, sculpt, model, work. 2 INFLUENCE, direct, control.

**mould²** *n* mildew, fungus, mouldiness, mustiness, blight.

**mouldy** *adj* mildewed, blighted, musty, decaying, corrupt, rotten, fusty, putrid, bad, spoiled, stale.
**Ea** fresh, wholesome.

**mound** *n* 1 HILL, hillock, hummock, rise, knoll, bank, dune, elevation, ridge, embankment, earthwork. 2 HEAP, pile, stack.

**mount** *v* 1 PRODUCE, put on, set up, prepare, stage, exhibit, display, launch. 2 INCREASE, grow, accumulate, multiply, rise, intensify, soar, swell. 3 CLIMB, ascend, get up, go up, get on, clamber up, scale, get astride.
**Ea** 2 decrease, descend. 3 descend, dismount, go down.

*n* horse, steed, support, mounting.

**mountain** *n* 1 HEIGHT, elevation, mount, peak, mound, alp, tor, massif. 2 HEAP, pile, stack, mass, abundance, backlog.

**mountainous** *adj* 1 CRAGGY, rocky, hilly, high, highland, upland, alpine, soaring, steep. 2 HUGE, towering, enormous, immense.
**Ea** 1 flat. 2 tiny.

**mourn** *v* grieve, lament, sorrow, bemoan, miss, regret, deplore, weep, wail.
**Ea** rejoice.

**mournful** *adj* sorrowful, sad, unhappy, desolate, grief-stricken, heavy-hearted, heartbroken, broken-hearted, cast-down, downcast, miserable, tragic, woeful, melancholy, sombre, depressed, dejected, gloomy, dismal.
**Ea** joyful.

**mourning** *n* bereavement, grief, grieving, lamentation, sadness, sorrow, desolation, weeping.

**Ea** rejoicing.

**mouth** *n* 1 LIPS, jaws, trap (*infml*), gob (*sl*). 2 OPENING, aperture, orifice, cavity, entrance, gateway, inlet, estuary.

*v* enunciate, articulate, utter, pronounce, whisper, form.

> *Parts of the mouth and types of teeth include:* cleft palate, gum, hard palate, hare lip, inferior dental arch, isthmus of fauces, labial commissure, lower lip, palatoglossal arch, palatopharyngeal arch, softpalate, superior dental arch, tongue, tonsil, upper lip, uvula.

**movable** *adj* mobile, portable, transportable, changeable, alterable, adjustable, flexible, transferable.
**Ea** fixed, immovable.

**move** *v* 1 STIR, go, advance, budge, change, proceed, progress, make strides. 2 TRANSPORT, carry, transfer. 3 DEPART, go away, leave, decamp, migrate, remove, move house, relocate. 4 PROMPT, stimulate, urge, impel, drive, propel, motivate, incite, persuade, induce, inspire. 5 AFFECT, touch, agitate, stir, impress, excite.

*n* 1 MOVEMENT, motion, step, manoeuvre, action, device, stratagem. 2 REMOVAL, relocation, migration, transfer.

**movement** *n* 1 REPOSITIONING, move, moving, relocation, activity, act, action, agitation, stirring, transfer, passage. 2 CHANGE, development, advance, evolution, current, drift, flow, shift, progress, progression, trend, tendency. 3 CAMPAIGN, crusade, drive, group, organization, party, faction.

**moving** *adj* 1 MOBILE, active, in motion. 2 TOUCHING, affecting, poignant, impressive, emotive, arousing, stirring, inspiring, inspirational, exciting, thrilling, persuasive, stimulating.

**F3 1** immobile. **2** unemotional.

**mow** *v* cut, trim, crop, clip, shear, scythe.

**much** *adv* greatly, considerably, a lot, frequently, often.

*adj* copious, plentiful, ample, considerable, a lot, abundant, great, substantial.

*n* plenty, a lot, lots (*infml*), loads (*infml*), heaps (*infml*), lashings (*infml*).

**F3** little.

**muck** *n* dirt, dung, manure, mire, filth, mud, sewage, slime, gunge (*infml*), ordure, scum, sludge.

**muck up** ruin, wreck, spoil, mess up, make a mess of, botch, bungle, cock up (*sl*).

**mud** *n* clay, mire, ooze, dirt, sludge, silt.

**muddle** *v* **1** DISORGANIZE, disorder, mix up, mess up, jumble, scramble, tangle. **2** CONFUSE, bewilder, bemuse, perplex.

*n* chaos, confusion, disorder, mess, mix-up, jumble, clutter, tangle.

**muddy** *adj* **1** DIRTY, foul, miry, mucky, marshy, boggy, swampy, quaggy, grimy. **2** CLOUDY, indistinct, obscure, opaque, murky, hazy, blurred, fuzzy, dull.

**F3 1** clean. **2** clear.

**muffle** *v* **1** WRAP, envelop, cloak, swathe, cover. **2** DEADEN, dull, quieten, silence, stifle, dampen, muzzle, suppress.

**F3 2** amplify.

**mug**[1] *n* cup, beaker, pot, tankard.

**mug**[2] *v* set upon, attack, assault, waylay, steal from, rob, beat up, jump (on).

**muggy** *adj* humid, sticky, stuffy, sultry, close, clammy, oppressive, sweltering, moist, damp.

**F3** dry.

**mull over** *v* reflect on, ponder, contemplate, think over, think about, ruminate, consider, weigh up, chew over, meditate, study, examine,

deliberate.

**multiple** *adj* many, numerous, manifold, various, several, sundry, collective.

**multiply** *v* increase, proliferate, expand, spread, reproduce, propagate, breed, accumulate, intensify, extend, build up, augment, boost.

**F3** decrease, lessen.

**multitude** *n* crowd, throng, horde, swarm, mob, mass, herd, congregation, host, lot, lots, legion, public, people, populace.

**F3** few, scattering.

**munch** *v* eat, chew, crunch, masticate (*fml*).

**mundane** *adj* banal, ordinary, everyday, commonplace, prosaic, humdrum, workaday, routine.

**F3** extraordinary.

**municipal** *adj* civic, city, town, urban, borough, community, public.

**murder** *n* homicide, killing, manslaughter, slaying, assassination, massacre, bloodshed.

*v* kill, slaughter, slay, assassinate, butcher, massacre.

**murderer** *n* killer, homicide, slayer, slaughterer, assassin, butcher, cut-throat.

**murderous** *adj* **1** HOMICIDAL, brutal, barbarous, bloodthirsty, bloody, cut-throat, killing, lethal, cruel, savage, ferocious, deadly.

**2** (*infml*) DIFFICULT, exhausting, strenuous, unpleasant, dangerous.

**murky** *adj* dark, dismal, gloomy, dull, overcast, misty, foggy, dim, cloudy, obscure, veiled, grey.

**F3** bright, clear.

**murmur** *n* mumble, muttering, whisper, undertone, humming, rumble, drone, grumble.

*v* mutter, mumble, whisper, buzz, hum, rumble, purr, burble.

**muscular** *adj* brawny, beefy (*infml*), sinewy, athletic, powerfully built, strapping, hefty, powerful, husky,

robust, stalwart, vigorous, strong.
**F3** puny, flabby, weak.

## mushrooms and toadstools

*Types of mushroom and toadstool include: edible:* beefsteak fungus, blewits, boletus, chestnut boletus, button mushroom, cep, champignon, chanterelle, clouded agaric, common morel, cultivated mushroom, dingy agaric, fairy ring, the goat's lip, gypsy mushroom, honey fungus, horn of plenty, horse mushroom, lawyer's wig, man on horseback, march mushroom, oyster mushroom, parasol mushroom, penny bun, saffron milk cap, shaggy parasol, slippery jack, sweetbread mushroom, truffle, trumpet agaric, velvet shank, winter mushroom, wood hedgehog; *inedible/poisonous:* amanita, common ink cap, copper trumpet, death cap, destroying angel, devil's boletus, earth ball, false morel, fly agaric, mower's mushroom, panther cap, purple boletus, satan's mushroom, shaggy milk cap, stinking parasol, sulphur tuft, verdigris agaric, woolly milk cap, yellow-staining mushroom.

## music

*Types of music include:* acid house, ambient, ballet, ballroom, bluegrass, blues, boogie-woogie, chamber, choral, classical, country-and-western, dance, disco, Dixieland, doo-wop, drum and bass, electronic, folk, folk rock, funk, gangsta, garage, gospel, grunge, hardcore, hard rock, heavy metal, hip-hop, honky-tonk, house, incidental, instrumental, jazz, jazz-funk, jazz-pop, jazz-rock, jive, jungle, karaoke, operatic, orchestral, pop, punk rock, ragtime, rap, reggae, rhythm and blues (R & B), rock and roll, rock, sacred, ska, skiffle, soft rock, soul, swing, techno, thrash metal, trance, trip-hop.

**musical** *adj* tuneful, melodious, melodic, harmonious, dulcet, sweet-sounding, lyrical.
**F3** discordant, unmusical.

## musical instruments

*Musical instruments include:* balalaika, banjo, cello, double-bass, guitar, harp, hurdy-gurdy, lute, lyre, mandolin, sitar, spinet, ukulele, viola, violin, fiddle (*infml*); zither; accordion, concertina, squeeze-box (*infml*), clavichord, harmonium, harpsichord, keyboard, melodeon, organ, Wurlitzer®, piano, grand piano, Pianola®, player-piano, synthesizer, virginals; bagpipes, bassoon, bugle, clarinet, cor anglais, cornet, didgeridoo, euphonium, fife, flugelhorn, flute, French horn, harmonica, horn, kazoo, mouth-organ, oboe, Pan-pipes, piccolo, recorder, saxophone, sousaphone, trombone, trumpet, tuba; castanets, cymbal, glockenspiel, maracas, marimba, tambourine, triangle, tubular bells, xylophone; bass-drum, bongo, kettle-drum, snare-drum, tenor-drum, timpani, tom-tom.

## musical terms

*Musical terms include:* accelerando, acciaccatura, accidental, accompaniment, acoustic, adagio, ad lib, a due, affettuoso, agitato, al fine, al segno, alla breve, alla cappella, allargando, allegretto, allegro, al segno, alto, amoroso, andante, animato, appoggiatura, arco, arpeggio, arrangement, a tempo, attacca, bar, bar line, double bar line, baritone, bass, beat, bis, breve, buffo, cadence, cantabile, cantilena, chord, chromatic, clef, alto clef, bass clef, tenor clef, treble clef, coda, col canto, con brio, concert, con fuoco, con moto, consonance, contralto, counterpoint, crescendo, crotchet, cross-fingering, cue, da capo, decrescendo, demisemiquaver, descant, diatonic, diminuendo, dissonance, dolce, doloroso, dominant, dotted note, dotted rest, downbeat, drone, duplet, triplet, quadruplet, quintuplet, sextuplet, encore, ensemble, expression, finale, fine, fingerboard, flat, double flat, forte, fortissimo, fret, glissando, grave, harmonics, harmony, hemidemisemiquaver, hold, imitation, improvisation, interval, augmented interval, diminished interval, second interval, third interval, fourth interval, fifth interval, sixth interval, seventh interval, major interval, minor interval, perfect interval, intonation, key, key signature, langsam, larghetto, largo, leading note, ledger line, legato, lento, lyric, maestoso, major, manual, marcato, mediant, medley, melody, metre, mezza voce, mezzo forte, microtone, middle C, minim, minor, moderato, mode, modulation, molto, mordent, movement, mute, natural, non troppo, note, obbligato, octave, orchestra, ostinato, part, pause, pedal point, pentatonic, perdendo, phrase, pianissimo, piano, piece, pitch, pizzicato, presto, quarter tone, quaver, rallentando, recital, refrain, resolution, rest, rhythm, ritenuto, root, scale, score, semibreve, semiquaver, semitone, semplice, sempre, senza, sequence, sforzando, shake, sharp, double sharp, slur, smorzando, solo, soprano, sostenuto, sotto voce, spiritoso, staccato, staff, stave, subdominant, subito, submediant, sul ponticello, supertonic, swell, syncopation, tablature, tacet, tanto, tempo, tenor, tenuto, theme, tie, timbre, time signature, compound time, simple

time, two-two time, three-four time, four-four time, six-eight time, tone, tonic sol-fa, transposition, treble, tremolo, triad, trill, double trill, tune, tuning, turn, tutti, upbeat, unison, vibrato, vigoroso, virtuoso, vivace.

## musician

*Musicians include*: instrumentalist, accompanist, performer, player; bugler, busker, cellist, clarinettist, drummer, flautist, fiddler, guitarist, harpist, oboist, organist, pianist, piper, soloist, trombonist, trumpeter, violinist; singer, vocalist, balladeer, diva, prima donna; conductor, maestro; band, orchestra, group, backing group, ensemble, chamber orchestra, choir, duo, duet, trio, quartet, quintet, sextet, octet, nonet.

**muster** *v* assemble, convene, gather, call together, mobilize, round up, marshal, come together, congregate, collect, group, meet, rally, mass, throng, call up, summon, enrol.

**musty** *adj* mouldy, mildewy, stale, stuffy, fusty, dank, airless, decayed, smelly.

**mutation** *n* change, alteration, variation, modification, transformation, deviation, anomaly, evolution.

**mute** *adj* silent, dumb, voiceless, wordless, speechless, mum (*infml*), unspoken, noiseless, unexpressed, unpronounced.

**E3** vocal, talkative.

*v* tone down, subdue, muffle, lower, moderate, dampen, deaden, soften, silence.

**mutilate** *v* **1** MAIM, injure, dismember, disable, disfigure, lame, mangle, cut to pieces, cut up, butcher. **2** SPOIL, mar, damage, cut, censor.

**mutinous** *adj* rebellious, insurgent, insubordinate, disobedient, seditious,

revolutionary, riotous, subversive, bolshie (*infml*), unruly.
‡ obedient, compliant.

**mutiny** *n* rebellion, insurrection, revolt, revolution, rising, uprising, insubordination, disobedience, defiance, resistance, riot, strike.
*v* rebel, revolt, rise up, resist, protest, disobey, strike.

**mutter** *v* 1 MUMBLE, murmur, rumble. 2 COMPLAIN, grumble, grouse (*infml*).

**mutual** *adj* reciprocal, shared, common, joint, interchangeable, interchanged, exchanged, complementary.

**muzzle** *v* restrain, stifle, suppress, gag, mute, silence, censor, choke.

**mysterious** *adj* enigmatic, cryptic, mystifying, inexplicable, incomprehensible, puzzling, perplexing, obscure, strange, unfathomable, unsearchable, mystical, baffling, curious, hidden, insoluble, secret, weird, secretive, veiled, dark, furtive.
‡ straightforward, comprehensible.

**mystery** *n* 1 ENIGMA, puzzle, secret, riddle, conundrum, question.
2 OBSCURITY, secrecy, ambiguity.

**mystical** *adj* occult, arcane, mystic, esoteric, supernatural, paranormal, transcendental, metaphysical, hidden, mysterious.

**mystify** *v* puzzle, bewilder, baffle,

perplex, confound, confuse.

**myth** *n* legend, fable, fairytale, allegory, parable, saga, story, fiction, tradition, fancy, fantasy, superstition.

**mythical** *adj* 1 MYTHOLOGICAL, legendary, fabled, fairytale.
2 FICTITIOUS, imaginary, made-up, invented, make-believe, non-existent, unreal, pretended, fanciful.
‡ 1 historical. 2 actual, real.

**mythology** *n* legend, myths, lore, tradition(s), folklore, folk-tales, tales.

> *Mythological creatures and spirits include:* abominable snowman (or yeti), afrit, basilisk, bunyip, Cecrops, centaur, Cerberus, Chimera, cockatrice, Cyclops, dragon, dryad, Echidna, elf, Erinyes (or Furies), Fafnir, fairy, faun, Frankenstein's monster, genie, Geryon, Gigantes, gnome, goblin, golem, Gorgon, griffin, Harpies, hippocampus, hippogriff, hobgoblin, imp, kelpie, kraken, lamia, leprechaun, Lilith, Loch Ness monster, mermaid, merman, Minotaur, naiad, nereid, nymph, ogre, ogress, orc, oread, Pegasus, phoenix, pixie, roc, salamander, sasquatch, satyr, sea serpent, Siren, Sphinx, sylph, troll, Typhoeus, unicorn, werewolf, wivern.

# N

**nag** *v* scold, berate, irritate, annoy, pester, badger, plague, torment, harass, henpeck (*infml*), harry, vex, upbraid, goad.

**nail** *v* fasten, attach, secure, pin, tack, fix, join.
*n* 1 FASTENER, pin, tack, spike, skewer. 2 TALON, claw.

**naïve** *adj* unsophisticated, ingenuous, innocent, unaffected, artless, guileless, simple, natural, childlike, open, trusting, unsuspecting, gullible, credulous, wide-eyed.
‡ experienced, sophisticated.

**naïvety** *n* ingenuousness, innocence,

inexperience, naturalness, simplicity, openness, frankness, gullibility, credulity.
**E3** experience, sophistication.
**naked** adj **1** NUDE, bare, undressed, unclothed, uncovered, stripped, stark-naked, disrobed, denuded, in the altogether (*infml*). **2** OPEN, unadorned, undisguised, unqualified, plain, stark, overt, blatant, exposed.
**E3 1** clothed, covered. **2** concealed.
**name** n **1** TITLE, appellation (*fml*), designation, label, term, epithet, handle (*infml*). **2** REPUTATION, character, repute, renown, esteem, eminence, fame, honour, distinction, note.
v **1** CALL, christen, baptize, term, title, entitle, dub, label, style.
**2** DESIGNATE, nominate, cite, choose, select, specify, classify, commission, appoint.
**nameless** adj **1** UNNAMED, anonymous, unidentified, unknown, obscure. **2** INEXPRESSIBLE, indescribable, unutterable, unspeakable, unmentionable, unheard-of.
**E3 1** named.
**namely** adv that is, ie, specifically, viz, that is to say.
**nap** v doze, sleep, snooze (*infml*), nod (off), drop off, rest, kip (*infml*).
n rest, sleep, siesta, catnap, forty winks (*infml*), kip (*infml*).
**narcotic** n drug, opiate, sedative, tranquillizer, pain-killer.
adj soporific, hypnotic, sedative, analgesic, pain-killing, numbing, dulling, calming, stupefying.
**narrate** v tell, relate, report, recount, describe, unfold, recite, state, detail.
**narrative** n story, tale, chronicle, account, history, report, detail, statement.
**narrator** n storyteller, chronicler, reporter, raconteur, commentator, writer.

**narrow** adj **1** TIGHT, confined, constricted, cramped, slim, slender, thin, fine, tapering, close. **2** LIMITED, restricted, circumscribed. **3** NARROW-MINDED, biased, bigoted, exclusive, dogmatic.
**E3 1** wide. **2** broad. **3** broad-minded, tolerant.
v constrict, limit, tighten, reduce, diminish, simplify.
**E3** broaden, widen, increase.
**narrow-minded** adj illiberal, biased, bigoted, prejudiced, reactionary, small-minded, conservative, intolerant, insular, petty.
**E3** broad-minded.
**nasty** adj **1** UNPLEASANT, repellent, repugnant, repulsive, objectionable, offensive, disgusting, sickening, horrible, filthy, foul, polluted, obscene. **2** MALICIOUS, mean, spiteful, vicious, malevolent.
**E3 1** agreeable, pleasant, decent.
**2** benevolent, kind.
**nation** n country, people, race, state, realm, population, community, society.
**national** adj countrywide, civil, domestic, nationwide, state, internal, general, governmental, public, widespread, social.
n citizen, native, subject, inhabitant, resident.
**nationalism** n patriotism, allegiance, loyalty, chauvinism, xenophobia, jingoism.
**nationality** n race, nation, ethnic group, birth, tribe, clan.
**native** adj **1** LOCAL, indigenous, domestic, vernacular, home, aboriginal, autochthonous (*fml*), mother, original. **2** INBORN, inherent, innate, inbred, hereditary, inherited, congenital, instinctive, natural, intrinsic, natal.
n inhabitant, resident, national, citizen, dweller, aborigine, autochthon (*fml*).

**F3** foreigner, outsider, stranger.

**natural** adj **1** ORDINARY, normal, common, regular, standard, usual, typical. **2** INNATE, inborn, instinctive, intuitive, inherent, congenital, native, indigenous. **3** GENUINE, pure, authentic, unrefined, unprocessed, unmixed, real. **4** SINCERE, unaffected, genuine, artless, ingenuous, guileless, simple, unsophisticated, open, candid, spontaneous.
**F3 1** unnatural. **2** acquired. **3** artificial. **4** affected, disingenuous.

**naturalistic** adj natural, realistic, true-to-life, representational, lifelike, graphic, real-life, photographic.

**naturally** adj **1** OF COURSE, as a matter of course, simply, obviously, logically, typically, certainly, absolutely. **2** NORMALLY, genuinely, instinctively, spontaneously.

**nature** n **1** ESSENCE, quality, character, features, disposition, attributes, personality, make-up, constitution, temperament, mood, outlook, temper. **2** KIND, sort, type, description, category, variety, style, species. **3** UNIVERSE, world, creation, earth, environment. **4** COUNTRYSIDE, country, landscape, scenery, natural history.

**naughty** adj **1** BAD, badly behaved, mischievous, disobedient, wayward, exasperating, playful, roguish. **2** INDECENT, obscene, bawdy, risqué, smutty.
**F3 1** good, well-behaved. **2** decent.

**nausea** n **1** VOMITING, sickness, retching, queasiness, biliousness. **2** DISGUST, revulsion, loathing, repugnance.

**nauseate** v sicken, disgust, revolt, repel, offend, turn one's stomach (*infml*).

**nautical** adj naval, marine, maritime, sea-going, seafaring, sailing, oceanic, boating.

**navigate** v steer, drive, direct, pilot, guide, handle, manoeuvre, cruise, sail, skipper, voyage, journey, cross, helm, plot, plan.

**navigation** n sailing, steering, cruising, voyaging, seamanship, helmsmanship.

**navy** n fleet, ships, flotilla, armada, warships.

**near** adj **1** NEARBY, close, bordering, adjacent, adjoining, alongside, neighbouring. **2** IMMINENT, impending, forthcoming, coming, approaching. **3** DEAR, familiar, close, related, intimate, akin.
**F3 1** far. **2** distant. **3** remote.

**nearby** adj near, neighbouring, adjoining, adjacent, accessible, convenient, handy.
**F3** faraway.
adv near, within reach, at close quarters, close at hand, not far away.

**nearly** adv almost, practically, virtually, closely, approximately, more or less, as good as, just about, roughly, well-nigh.
**F3** completely, totally.

**neat** adj **1** TIDY, orderly, smart, spruce, trim, clean, spick-and-span (*infml*), shipshape. **2** DEFT, clever, adroit, skilful, expert. **3** UNDILUTED, unmixed, unadulterated, straight, pure.
**F3 1** untidy. **2** clumsy. **3** diluted.

**nebulous** adj vague, hazy, imprecise, indefinite, indistinct, cloudy, misty, obscure, uncertain, unclear, dim, ambiguous, confused, fuzzy, shapeless, amorphous.
**F3** clear.

**necessary** adj needed, required, essential, compulsory, indispensable, vital, imperative, mandatory, obligatory, needful, unavoidable, inevitable, inescapable, inexorable, certain.
**F3** unnecessary, inessential, unimportant.

**necessitate** v require, involve,

entail, call for, demand, oblige, force, constrain, compel.

**necessity** n **1** REQUIREMENT, obligation, prerequisite, essential, fundamental, need, want, compulsion, demand. **2** INDISPENSABILITY, inevitability, needfulness. **3** POVERTY, destitution, hardship.

**need** v miss, lack, want, require, demand, call for, necessitate, have need of, have to, crave.
n **1** *a need for caution*: call, demand, obligation, requirement. **2** *the country's needs*: essential, necessity, requisite, prerequisite, desideratum. **3** *a need for equipment*: want, lack, insufficiency, inadequacy, neediness, shortage.

**needless** adj unnecessary, gratuitous, uncalled-for, unwanted, redundant, superfluous, useless, pointless, purposeless.
F3 necessary, essential.

**needy** adj poor, destitute, impoverished, penniless, disadvantaged, deprived, poverty-stricken, underprivileged.
F3 affluent, wealthy, well-off.

**negate** v **1** NULLIFY, annul, cancel, invalidate, undo, countermand, abrogate (*fml*), neutralize, quash, retract, reverse, revoke, rescind, wipe out, void, repeal. **2** DENY, contradict, oppose, disprove, refute, repudiate.
F3 **2** affirm.

**negative** adj **1** CONTRADICTORY, contrary, denying, opposing, invalidating, neutralizing, nullifying, annulling. **2** UNCO-OPERATIVE, cynical, pessimistic, unenthusiastic, uninterested, unwilling.
F3 **1** affirmative, positive.
**2** constructive, positive.
n contradiction, denial, opposite, refusal.

**neglect** v **1** DISREGARD, ignore, leave alone, abandon, pass by, rebuff, scorn, disdain, slight, spurn.

**2** FORGET, fail (in), omit, overlook, let slide, shirk, skimp.
F3 **1** cherish, appreciate. **2** remember.
n negligence, disregard, carelessness, failure, inattention, indifference, slackness, dereliction of duty, forgetfulness, heedlessness, oversight, slight, disrespect.
F3 care, attention, concern.

**negligence** n inattentiveness, carelessness, laxity, neglect, slackness, thoughtlessness, forgetfulness, indifference, omission, oversight, disregard, failure, default.
F3 attentiveness, care, regard.

**negligent** adj neglectful, inattentive, remiss, thoughtless, casual, lax, careless, indifferent, offhand, nonchalant, slack, uncaring, forgetful.
F3 attentive, careful, scrupulous.

**negligible** adj unimportant, insignificant, small, imperceptible, trifling, trivial, minor, minute.
F3 significant.

**negotiate** v **1** CONFER, deal, mediate, arbitrate, bargain, arrange, transact, work out, manage, settle, consult, contract. **2** GET ROUND, cross, surmount, traverse, pass.

**negotiation** n mediation, arbitration, debate, discussion, diplomacy, bargaining, transaction.

**negotiator** n arbitrator, go-between, mediator, intermediary, moderator, intercessor, adjudicator, broker, ambassador, diplomat.

**neighbourhood** n district, locality, vicinity, community, locale, environs, confines, surroundings, region, proximity.

**neighbouring** adj adjacent, bordering, near, nearby, adjoining, connecting, next, surrounding.
F3 distant, remote.

**neighbourly** adj sociable, friendly, amiable, kind, helpful, genial, hospitable, obliging, considerate, companionable.

**nerve** n **1** COURAGE, bravery, mettle, pluck, guts (*infml*), spunk (*infml*), spirit, vigour, intrepidity, daring, fearlessness, firmness, resolution, fortitude, steadfastness, will, determination, endurance, force. **2** (*infml*) AUDACITY, impudence, cheek (*infml*), effrontery, brazenness, boldness, chutzpah (*infml*), impertinence, insolence.
**E3 1** weakness. **2** timidity.

**nerve-racking** adj harrowing, distressing, trying, stressful, tense, maddening, worrying, difficult, frightening.

**nerves** n nervousness, tension, stress, anxiety, worry, strain, fretfulness.

**nervous** adj highly-strung, excitable, anxious, agitated, nervy (*infml*), on edge, edgy, jumpy (*infml*), jittery (*infml*), tense, fidgety, apprehensive, neurotic, shaky, uneasy, worried, flustered, fearful.
**E3** calm, relaxed.

**nest** n **1** BREEDING-GROUND, den, roost, eyrie, lair. **2** RETREAT, refuge, haunt, hideaway.

**nestle** v snuggle, huddle, cuddle, curl up.

**net**[1] n mesh, web, network, netting, open-work, lattice, lace.
v catch, trap, capture, bag, ensnare, entangle, nab (*infml*).

**net**[2] adj nett, clear, after tax, final, lowest.
v bring in, clear, earn, make, realize, receive, gain, obtain, accumulate.

**network** n system, organization, arrangement, structure, interconnections, complex, grid, net, maze, mesh, labyrinth, channels, circuitry, convolution, grill, tracks.

**neurosis** n disorder, affliction, abnormality, disturbance, derangement, deviation, obsession, phobia.

**neurotic** adj disturbed, maladjusted, anxious, nervous, overwrought, unstable, unhealthy, deviant, abnormal, compulsive, obsessive.

**neuter** v castrate, emasculate, doctor, geld, spay.

**neutral** adj **1** IMPARTIAL, uncommitted, unbia(s)sed, non-aligned, disinterested, unprejudiced, undecided, non-partisan, non-committal, objective, indifferent, dispassionate, even-handed. **2** DULL, nondescript, colourless, drab, expressionless, indistinct.
**E3 1** biased, partisan. **2** colourful.

**neutralize** v counteract, counterbalance, offset, negate, cancel, nullify, invalidate, undo, frustrate.

**never-ending** adj everlasting, eternal, non-stop, perpetual, unceasing, uninterrupted, unremitting, interminable, incessant, unbroken, permanent, persistent, unchanging, relentless.
**E3** fleeting, transitory.

**nevertheless** adv nonetheless, notwithstanding, still, anyway, even so, yet, however, anyhow, but, regardless.

**new** adj **1** NOVEL, original, fresh, different, unfamiliar, unusual, brand-new, mint, unknown, unused, virgin, newborn. **2** MODERN, contemporary, current, latest, recent, up-to-date, up-to-the-minute, topical, trendy (*infml*), ultra-modern, advanced, newfangled (*infml*). **3** CHANGED, altered, modernized, improved, renewed, restored, redesigned. **4** ADDED, additional, extra, more, supplementary.
**E3 1** usual. **2** outdated, out-of-date. **3** old.

**newcomer** n immigrant, alien, foreigner, incomer, colonist, settler, arrival, outsider, stranger, novice, beginner.

**news** n report, account, information, intelligence, dispatch, communiqué, bulletin, gossip, hearsay, rumour, statement, story, word, tidings, latest, release, scandal, revelation, lowdown (*infml*), exposé, disclosure, gen (*infml*), advice.

**next** *adj* **1** ADJACENT, adjoining, neighbouring, nearest, closest. **2** FOLLOWING, subsequent, succeeding, ensuing, later.

Ea **2** previous, preceding.

*adv* afterwards, subsequently, later, then.

**nibble** *n* bite, morsel, taste, titbit, bit, crumb, snack, piece.

*v* bite, eat, peck, pick at, nosh (*sl*), munch, gnaw.

**nice** *adj* **1** PLEASANT, agreeable, delightful, charming, likable, attractive, good, kind, friendly, well-mannered, polite, respectable. **2** SUBTLE, delicate, fine, fastidious, discriminating, scrupulous, precise, exact, accurate, careful, strict.

Ea **1** nasty, disagreeable, unpleasant. **2** careless.

**nicety** *n* **1** DELICACY, refinement, subtlety, distinction, nuance. **2** PRECISION, accuracy, meticulousness, scrupulousness, minuteness, finesse.

**niche** *n* **1** RECESS, alcove, hollow, nook, cubby-hole, corner, opening. **2** POSITION, place, vocation, calling, métier, slot.

**nick** *n* **1** NOTCH, indentation, chip, cut, groove, dent, scar, scratch, mark. **2** (*sl*) PRISON, jail, police station.

*v* **1** NOTCH, cut, dent, indent, chip, score, scratch, scar, mark, damage, snick. **2** (*sl*) STEAL, pilfer, knock off (*infml*), pinch (*infml*).

**nickname** *n* pet name, sobriquet, epithet, diminutive.

**night** *n* night-time, darkness, dark, dead of night.

Ea day, daytime.

**nightfall** *n* sunset, dusk, twilight, evening, gloaming.

Ea dawn, sunrise.

**nightmare** *n* **1** BAD DREAM, hallucination. **2** ORDEAL, horror, torment, trial.

**nil** *n* nothing, zero, none, nought, naught, love, duck, zilch (*sl*).

**nimble** *adj* agile, active, lively, sprightly, spry, smart, quick, brisk, nippy (*infml*), deft, alert, light-footed, prompt, ready, swift, quick-witted.

Ea clumsy, slow.

**nip**[1] *v* bite, pinch, squeeze, snip, clip, tweak, catch, grip, nibble.

**nip**[2] *n* dram, draught, shot, swallow, mouthful, drop, sip, taste, portion.

**nobility** *n* **1** NOBLENESS, dignity, grandeur, illustriousness, stateliness, majesty, magnificence, eminence, excellence, superiority, uprightness, honour, virtue, worthiness. **2** ARISTOCRACY, peerage, nobles, gentry, élite, lords, high society.

Ea **1** baseness. **2** proletariat.

> *Titles of the nobility include*:
> aristocrat, baron, baroness, baronet, count, countess, dame, dowager, duchess, duke, earl, grand duke, governor, knight, lady, laird, liege, liege lord, life peer, lord, marchioness, marquess, marquis, noble, nobleman, noblewoman, peer, peeress, ruler, seigneur, squire, thane, viscount, viscountess.

**noble** *n* aristocrat, peer, lord, lady, nobleman, noblewoman.

Ea commoner.

*adj* **1** ARISTOCRATIC, high-born, titled, high-ranking, patrician, blue-blooded (*infml*). **2** MAGNIFICENT, magnanimous, splendid, stately, generous, dignified, distinguished, eminent, grand, great, honoured, honourable, imposing, impressive, majestic, virtuous, worthy, excellent, elevated, fine, gentle.

Ea **1** low-born. **2** ignoble, base, contemptible.

**nobody** n no-one, nothing, nonentity, menial, cipher.
F3 somebody.

**nod** v 1 GESTURE, indicate, sign, signal, salute, acknowledge. 2 AGREE, assent. 3 SLEEP, doze, drowse, nap.
n gesture, indication, sign, signal, salute, greeting, beck, acknowledgement.

**noise** n sound, din, racket, row, clamour, clash, clatter, commotion, outcry, hubbub, uproar, cry, blare, talk, pandemonium, tumult, babble.
F3 quiet, silence.
v report, rumour, publicize, announce, circulate.

**noiseless** adj silent, inaudible, soundless, quiet, mute, still, hushed.
F3 loud, noisy.

**noisy** adj loud, deafening, ear-splitting, clamorous, piercing, vocal, vociferous, tumultuous, boisterous, obstreperous.
F3 quiet, silent, peaceful.

**nomad** n traveller, wanderer, itinerant, rambler, roamer, rover, migrant.

**nominal** adj 1 TITULAR, supposed, purported, professed, ostensible, so-called, theoretical, self-styled, puppet, symbolic. 2 TOKEN, minimal, trifling, trivial, insignificant, small.
F3 1 actual, genuine, real.

**nominate** v propose, choose, select, name, designate, submit, suggest, recommend, put up, present, elect, appoint, assign, commission, elevate, term.

**nomination** n proposal, choice, selection, submission, suggestion, recommendation, designation, election, appointment.

**nominee** n candidate, entrant, contestant, appointee, runner, assignee.

**nonchalant** adj unconcerned, detached, dispassionate, offhand, blasé, indifferent, casual, cool, collected, apathetic, careless, insouciant.
F3 concerned, careful.

**non-committal** adj guarded, unrevealing, cautious, wary, reserved, ambiguous, discreet, equivocal, evasive, circumspect, careful, neutral, indefinite, politic, tactful, tentative, vague.

**nonconformist** n dissenter, rebel, individualist, dissident, radical, protester, heretic, iconoclast, eccentric, maverick, secessionist.
F3 conformist.

**nondescript** adj featureless, indeterminate, undistinctive, undistinguished, unexceptional, ordinary, commonplace, plain, dull, uninspiring, uninteresting, unclassified.
F3 distinctive, remarkable.

**none** pron no-one, not any, not one, nobody, nil, zero.

**nonplussed** adj disconcerted, confounded, taken aback, stunned, bewildered, astonished, astounded, dumbfounded, perplexed, stumped, flabbergasted, flummoxed, puzzled, baffled, dismayed, embarrassed.

**nonsense** n rubbish, trash, drivel, balderdash, gibberish, gobbledygook, senselessness, stupidity, silliness, foolishness, folly, rot (infml), blather, twaddle, ridiculousness, claptrap (infml), cobblers (sl).
F3 sense, wisdom.

**nonsensical** adj ridiculous, meaningless, senseless, foolish, inane, irrational, silly, incomprehensible, ludicrous, absurd, fatuous, crazy (infml).
F3 reasonable, sensible, logical.

**non-stop** adj never-ending, uninterrupted, continuous, incessant, constant, endless, interminable, unending, unbroken, round-the-clock, on-going.
F3 intermittent, occasional.

**nook** n recess, alcove, corner, cranny, niche, cubby-hole, hide-out, retreat, shelter, cavity.

**norm** n average, mean, standard, rule, pattern, criterion, model, yardstick, benchmark, measure, reference.

**normal** adj usual, standard, general, common, ordinary, conventional, average, regular, routine, typical, mainstream, natural, accustomed, well-adjusted, straight, rational, reasonable.
**Ea** abnormal, irregular, peculiar.

**normality** n usualness, commonness, ordinariness, regularity, routine, conventionality, balance, adjustment, typicality, naturalness, reason, rationality.
**Ea** abnormality, irregularity, peculiarity.

**normally** adv ordinarily, usually, as a rule, typically, commonly, characteristically.
**Ea** abnormally, exceptionally.

**nosegay** n bouquet, posy, spray, bunch.

**nosey** (*infml*) adj inquisitive, meddlesome, prying, interfering, snooping, curious, eavesdropping.

**nostalgia** n yearning, longing, regretfulness, remembrance, reminiscence, homesickness, pining.

**nostalgic** adj yearning, longing, wistful, emotional, regretful, sentimental, homesick.

**notable** adj noteworthy, remarkable, noticeable, striking, extraordinary, impressive, outstanding, marked, unusual, celebrated, distinguished, famous, eminent, well-known, notorious, renowned, rare.
**Ea** ordinary, commonplace, usual.
n celebrity, notability, VIP, personage, somebody, dignitary, luminary, worthy.
**Ea** nobody, nonentity.

**notably** adv markedly, noticeably,

particularly, remarkably, strikingly, conspicuously, distinctly, especially, impressively, outstandingly, eminently.

**notation** n symbols, characters, code, signs, alphabet, system, script, noting, record, shorthand.

**notch** n cut, nick, indentation, incision, score, groove, cleft, mark, snip, degree, grade, step.
v cut, nick, score, scratch, indent, mark.

**note** n **1** COMMUNICATION, letter, message, memorandum, reminder, memo (*infml*), line, jotting, record. **2** ANNOTATION, comment, gloss, remark. **3** INDICATION, signal, token, mark, symbol. **4** EMINENCE, distinction, consequence, fame, renown, reputation. **5** HEED, attention, regard, notice, observation.
v **1** NOTICE, observe, perceive, heed, detect, mark, remark, mention, see, witness. **2** RECORD, register, write down, enter.

**noted** adj famous, well-known, renowned, notable, celebrated, eminent, prominent, great, acclaimed, illustrious, distinguished, respected, recognized.
**Ea** obscure, unknown.

**notes** n jottings, record, impressions, report, sketch, outline, synopsis, draft.

**noteworthy** adj remarkable, significant, important, notable, memorable, exceptional, extraordinary, unusual, outstanding.
**Ea** commonplace, unexceptional, ordinary.

**nothing** n nought, zero, nothingness, zilch (*sl*), nullity, non-existence, emptiness, void, nobody, nonentity.
**Ea** something.

**notice** v note, remark, perceive, observe, mind, see, discern, distinguish, mark, detect, heed, spot.
**Ea** ignore, overlook.

*n* **1** NOTIFICATION, announcement, information, declaration, communication, intelligence, news, warning, instruction. **2** ADVERTISEMENT, poster, sign, bill. **3** REVIEW, comment, criticism. **4** ATTENTION, observation, awareness, note, regard, consideration, heed.

**noticeable** *adj* perceptible, observable, appreciable, unmistakable, conspicuous, evident, manifest, clear, distinct, significant, striking, plain, obvious, measurable.
**F3** inconspicuous, unnoticeable.

**notification** *n* announcement, information, notice, declaration, advice, warning, intelligence, message, publication, statement, communication.

**notify** *v* inform, tell, advise, announce, declare, warn, acquaint, alert, publish, disclose, reveal.

**notion** *n* **1** IDEA, thought, concept, conception, belief, impression, view, opinion, understanding, apprehension. **2** INCLINATION, wish, whim, fancy, caprice.

**notoriety** *n* infamy, disrepute, dishonour, disgrace, scandal.

**notorious** *adj* infamous, disreputable, scandalous, dishonourable, disgraceful, ignominious, flagrant, well-known.

**nought** *n* zero, nil, zilch, naught, nothing, nothingness.

**nourish** *v* **1** NURTURE, feed, foster, care for, provide for, sustain, support, tend, nurse, maintain, cherish. **2** STRENGTHEN, encourage, promote, cultivate, stimulate.

**nourishment** *n* nutrition, food, sustenance, diet.

**novel** *adj* new, original, fresh, innovative, unfamiliar, unusual, uncommon, different, imaginative, unconventional, strange.
**F3** hackneyed, familiar, ordinary.
*n* fiction, story, tale, narrative,
romance.

**novelty** *n* **1** NEWNESS, originality, freshness, innovation, unfamiliarity, uniqueness, difference, strangeness. **2** GIMMICK, gadget, trifle, memento, knick-knack, curiosity, souvenir, trinket, bauble, gimcrack.

**novice** *n* beginner, tiro, learner, pupil, trainee, probationer, apprentice, neophyte (*fml*), amateur, newcomer.
**F3** expert.

**now** *adv* **1** IMMEDIATELY, at once, directly, instantly, straight away, promptly, next. **2** AT PRESENT, nowadays, these days.

**noxious** *adj* harmful, poisonous, pernicious, toxic, injurious, unhealthy, deadly, destructive, noisome, foul.
**F3** innocuous, wholesome.

**nuance** *n* subtlety, suggestion, shade, hint, suspicion, gradation, distinction, overtone, refinement, touch, trace, tinge, degree, nicety.

**nub** *n* centre, heart, core, nucleus, kernel, crux, gist, pith, point, essence.

**nucleus** *n* centre, heart, nub, core, focus, kernel, pivot, basis, crux.

**nude** *adj* naked, bare, undressed, unclothed, stripped, stark-naked, uncovered, starkers (*infml*), in one's birthday suit (*infml*).
**F3** clothed, dressed.

**nudge** *v*, *n* poke, prod, shove, dig, jog, prompt, push, elbow, bump.

**nuisance** *n* annoyance, inconvenience, bother, irritation, pest, pain (*infml*), drag (*infml*), bore, problem, trial, trouble, drawback.

**null** *adj* void, invalid, ineffectual, useless, vain, worthless, powerless, inoperative.
**F3** valid.

**nullify** *v* annul, revoke, cancel, invalidate, abrogate, abolish, negate, rescind, quash, repeal, counteract.
**F3** validate.

**numb** *adj* benumbed, insensible,

unfeeling, deadened, insensitive, frozen, immobilized.
🔁 sensitive.
*v* deaden, anaesthetize, freeze, immobilize, paralyse, dull, stun.
🔁 sensitize.

**number** *n* **1** FIGURE, numeral, digit, integer, unit. **2** TOTAL, sum, aggregate, collection, amount, quantity, several, many, company, crowd, multitude, throng, horde. **3** COPY, issue, edition, impression, volume, printing.
*v* count, calculate, enumerate, reckon, total, add, compute, include.

**numerous** *adj* many, abundant, several, plentiful, copious, profuse, sundry.
🔁 few.

**nurse** *v* **1** TEND, care for, look after, treat. **2** BREAST-FEED, feed, suckle, nurture, nourish. **3** PRESERVE, sustain, support, cherish, encourage, keep, foster, promote.
*n* sister, matron, nursemaid, nanny.

**nurture** *n* **1** FOOD, nourishment. **2** REARING, upbringing, training, care, cultivation, development, education, discipline.
*v* **1** FEED, nourish, nurse, tend, care for, foster, support, sustain. **2** BRING UP, rear, cultivate, develop, educate, instruct, train, school, discipline.

**nut**

> *Varieties of nut include*: almond, beech nut, brazil nut, cashew, chestnut, cobnut, coconut, filbert, hazelnut, macadamia, monkey nut, peanut, pecan, pistachio, walnut.

**nutrition** *n* food, nourishment, sustenance.

**nutritious** *adj* nourishing, nutritive, wholesome, healthful, health-giving, good, beneficial, strengthening, substantial, invigorating.
🔁 bad, unwholesome.

# O

**oasis** *n* **1** SPRING, watering-hole. **2** REFUGE, haven, island, sanctuary, retreat.

**oath** *n* **1** VOW, pledge, promise, word, affirmation, assurance, word of honour. **2** CURSE, imprecation, swear-word, profanity, expletive, blasphemy.

**obedient** *adj* compliant, docile, acquiescent, submissive, tractable, yielding, dutiful, law-abiding, deferential, respectful, subservient, observant.
🔁 disobedient, rebellious, wilful.

**obesity** *n* fatness, overweight, corpulence, stoutness, grossness, plumpness, portliness, bulk.
🔁 thinness, slenderness, skinniness.

**obey** *v* **1** COMPLY, submit, surrender, yield, be ruled by, bow to, take orders from, defer (to), give way, follow, observe, abide by, adhere to, conform, heed, keep, mind, respond. **2** CARRY OUT, discharge, execute, act upon, fulfil, perform.
🔁 **1** disobey.

**object**[1] *n* **1** THING, entity, article, body. **2** AIM, objective, purpose, goal, target, intention, motive, end, reason, point, design. **3** TARGET, recipient, butt, victim.

**object**[2] *v* protest, oppose, demur, take exception, disapprove, refuse, complain, rebut, repudiate.
🔁 agree, acquiesce.

**objection** *n* protest, dissent, disapproval, opposition, demur, complaint, challenge, scruple.
**F3** agreement, assent.

**objectionable** *adj* unacceptable, unpleasant, offensive, obnoxious, repugnant, disagreeable, abhorrent, detestable, deplorable, despicable.
**F3** acceptable.

**objective** *adj* impartial, unbiased, detached, unprejudiced, open-minded, equitable, dispassionate, even-handed, neutral, disinterested, just, fair.
**F3** subjective.
*n* object, aim, goal, end, purpose, ambition, mark, target, intention, design.

**obligation** *n* duty, responsibility, onus, charge, commitment, liability, requirement, bond, contract, debt, burden, trust.

**obligatory** *adj* compulsory, mandatory, statutory, required, binding, essential, necessary, enforced.
**F3** optional.

**oblige** *v* 1 COMPEL, constrain, coerce, require, make, necessitate, force, bind. 2 HELP, assist, accommodate, do a favour, serve, gratify, please.

**obliging** *adj* accommodating, co-operative, helpful, considerate, agreeable, friendly, kind, civil.
**F3** unhelpful.

**oblique** *adj* slanting, sloping, inclined, angled, tilted.

**obliterate** *v* eradicate, destroy, annihilate, delete, blot out, wipe out, erase.

**oblivion** *n* obscurity, nothingness, unconsciousness, void, limbo.
**F3** awareness.

**oblivious** *adj* unaware, unconscious, inattentive, careless, heedless, blind, insensible, negligent.
**F3** aware.

**obnoxious** *adj* unpleasant,

disagreeable, disgusting, loathsome, nasty, horrid, odious, repulsive, revolting, repugnant, sickening, nauseating.
**F3** pleasant.

**obscene** *adj* indecent, improper, immoral, impure, filthy, dirty, bawdy, lewd, licentious, pornographic, scurrilous, suggestive, disgusting, foul, shocking, shameless, offensive.
**F3** decent, wholesome.

**obscenity** *n* 1 INDECENCY, immodesty, impurity, impropriety, lewdness, licentiousness, suggestiveness, pornography, dirtiness, filthiness, foulness, grossness, indelicacy, coarseness.
2 ATROCITY, evil, outrage, offence.
3 PROFANITY, expletive, swear-word, four-letter word.

**obscure** *adj* 1 UNKNOWN, unimportant, little-known, unheard-of, undistinguished, nameless, inconspicuous, humble, minor.
2 INCOMPREHENSIBLE, enigmatic, cryptic, recondite, esoteric, accrue, mysterious, deep, abstruse, confusing. 3 INDISTINCT, unclear, indefinite, shadowy, blurred, cloudy, faint, hazy, dim, misty, shady, vague, murky, gloomy, dusky.
**F3** 1 famous, renowned. 2 intelligible, straightforward. 3 clear, definite.
*v* conceal, cloud, obfuscate, hide, cover, blur, disguise, mask, overshadow, shadow, shade, cloak, veil, shroud, darken, dim, eclipse, screen, block out.
**F3** clarify, illuminate.

**obsequious** *adj* servile, ingratiating, grovelling, fawning, sycophantic, cringing, deferential, flattering, smarmy (*infml*), unctuous, oily, submissive, subservient, slavish.

**observance** *n* 1 ADHERENCE, compliance, observation, performance, obedience, fulfilment, honouring, notice, attention.

**2** RITUAL, custom, ceremony, practice, celebration.

**observant** *adj* attentive, alert, vigilant, watchful, perceptive, eagle-eyed, wide-awake, heedful.
**F3** unobservant.

**observation** *n* **1** ATTENTION, notice, examination, inspection, scrutiny, monitoring, study, watching, consideration, discernment. **2** REMARK, comment, utterance, thought, statement, pronouncement, reflection, opinion, finding, note.

**observe** *v* **1** WATCH, see, study, notice, contemplate, keep an eye on, perceive. **2** REMARK, comment, say, mention. **3** ABIDE BY, comply with, honour, keep, fulfil, celebrate, perform.
**F3 1** miss. **3** break, violate.

**observer** *n* watcher, spectator, viewer, witness, looker-on, onlooker, eyewitness, commentator, bystander, beholder.

**obsess** *v* preoccupy, dominate, rule, monopolize, haunt, grip, plague, prey on, possess.

**obsession** *n* preoccupation, fixation, idée fixe, ruling passion, compulsion, fetish, hang-up (*infml*), infatuation, mania, enthusiasm.

**obsessive** *adj* consuming, compulsive, gripping, fixed, haunting, tormenting, maddening.

**obsolete** *adj* outmoded, disused, out of date, old-fashioned, passé, dated, outworn, old, antiquated, antique, dead, extinct.
**F3** modern, current, up-to-date.

**obstacle** *n* barrier, bar, obstruction, impediment, hurdle, hindrance, check, snag, stumbling-block, drawback, difficulty, hitch, catch, stop, interference, interruption.
**F3** advantage, help.

**obstinate** *adj* stubborn, inflexible, immovable, intractable, pig-headed (*infml*), unyielding, intransigent,

persistent, dogged, headstrong, bloody-minded (*sl*), strong-minded, self-willed, steadfast, firm, determined, wilful.
**F3** flexible, tractable.

**obstruct** *v* block, impede, hinder, prevent, check, frustrate, hamper, clog, choke, bar, barricade, stop, stall, retard, restrict, thwart, inhibit, hold up, curb, arrest, slow down, interrupt, interfere with, shut off, cut off, obscure.
**F3** assist, further.

**obstruction** *n* barrier, blockage, bar, barricade, hindrance, impediment, check, stop, stoppage, difficulty.
**F3** help.

**obstructive** *adj* hindering, delaying, blocking, stalling, unhelpful, awkward, difficult, restrictive, inhibiting.
**F3** co-operative, helpful.

**obtain** *v* **1** ACQUIRE, get, gain, come by, attain, procure, secure, earn, achieve. **2** PREVAIL, exist, hold, be in force, be the case, stand, reign, rule, be prevalent.

**obtrusive** *adj* **1** PROMINENT, protruding, noticeable, obvious, blatant, forward. **2** INTRUSIVE, interfering, prying, meddling, nosey (*infml*), pushy (*infml*).
**F3 1** unobtrusive.

**obtuse** *adj* slow, stupid, thick (*infml*), dull, dense, crass, dumb (*infml*), stolid, dull-witted, thick-skinned.
**F3** bright, sharp.

**obvious** *adj* evident, self-evident, manifest, patent, clear, plain, distinct, transparent, undeniable, unmistakable, conspicuous, glaring, apparent, open, unconcealed, visible, noticeable, perceptible, pronounced, recognizable, self-explanatory, straightforward, prominent.
**F3** unclear, indistinct, obscure.

**obviously** *adv* plainly, clearly,

evidently, manifestly, undeniably, unmistakably, without doubt, certainly, distinctly, of course.

**occasion** n **1** EVENT, occurrence, incident, time, instance, chance, case, opportunity. **2** REASON, cause, excuse, justification, ground(s). **3** CELEBRATION, function, affair, party.

**occasional** adj periodic, intermittent, irregular, sporadic, infrequent, uncommon, incidental, odd, rare, casual.
**E3** frequent, regular, constant.

**occasionally** adv sometimes, on occasion, from time to time, at times, at intervals, now and then, now and again, irregularly, periodically, every so often, once in a while, off and on, infrequently.
**E3** frequently, often, always.

**occult** adj mystical, supernatural, magical, esoteric, mysterious, concealed, arcane, recondite, obscure, secret, hidden, veiled.

**occupant** n occupier, holder, inhabitant, resident, householder, tenant, user, lessee, squatter, inmate.

**occupation** n **1** JOB, profession, work, vocation, employment, trade, post, calling, business, line, pursuit, craft, walk of life, activity. **2** INVASION, seizure, conquest, control, takeover. **3** OCCUPANCY, possession, holding, tenancy, tenure, residence, habitation, use.

**occupy** v **1** INHABIT, live in, possess, reside in, stay in, take possession of, own. **2** ABSORB, take up, engross, engage, hold, involve, preoccupy, amuse, busy, interest. **3** INVADE, seize, capture, overrun, take over. **4** FILL, take up, use.

**occur** v happen, come about, take place, transpire, chance, come to pass, materialize, befall, develop, crop up, arise, appear, turn up, obtain, result, exist, be present, be found.

**occurrence** n **1** INCIDENT, event, happening, affair, circumstance, episode, instance, case, development, action. **2** INCIDENCE, existence, appearance, manifestation.

**odd** adj **1** UNUSUAL, strange, uncommon, peculiar, abnormal, exceptional, curious, atypical, different, queer, bizarre, eccentric, remarkable, unconventional, weird, irregular, extraordinary, outlandish, rare. **2** OCCASIONAL, incidental, irregular, random, casual. **3** UNMATCHED, unpaired, single, spare, surplus, left-over, remaining, sundry, various, miscellaneous.
**E3** **1** normal, usual. **2** regular.

**oddity** n **1** ABNORMALITY, peculiarity, rarity, eccentricity, idiosyncrasy, phenomenon, quirk. **2** CURIOSITY, character, freak, misfit.

**oddment** n bit, scrap, left-over, fragment, offcut, end, remnant, shred, snippet, patch.

**odds** n **1** LIKELIHOOD, probability, chances. **2** ADVANTAGE, edge, lead, superiority.

**odious** adj offensive, loathsome, unpleasant, obnoxious, disgusting, hateful, repulsive, revolting, repugnant, foul, execrable, detestable, abhorrent, horrible, horrid, abominable.
**E3** pleasant.

**odour** n smell, scent, fragrance, aroma, perfume, redolence, stench, stink (infml).

**off** adj **1** ROTTEN, bad, sour, turned, rancid, mouldy, decomposed. **2** CANCELLED, postponed. **3** AWAY, absent, gone. **4** SUBSTANDARD, below par, disappointing, unsatisfactory, slack.
adv away, elsewhere, out, at a distance, apart, aside.

**off-colour** adj indisposed, off form, under the weather, unwell, sick, out of sorts, ill, poorly.

**offence** *n* **1** MISDEMEANOUR, transgression, violation, wrong, wrong-doing, infringement, crime, misdeed, sin, trespass. **2** AFFRONT, insult, injury. **3** RESENTMENT, indignation, pique, umbrage, outrage, hurt, hard feelings.

**offend** *v* **1** HURT, insult, injure, affront, wrong, wound, displease, snub, upset, annoy, outrage. **2** DISGUST, repel, sicken. **3** TRANSGRESS, sin, violate, err.
**F3 1** please.

**offender** *n* transgressor, wrong-doer, culprit, criminal, miscreant, guilty party, law-breaker, delinquent.

**offensive** *adj* **1** DISAGREEABLE, unpleasant, objectionable, displeasing, disgusting, odious, obnoxious, repellent, repugnant, revolting, loathsome, vile, nauseating, nasty, detestable, abominable. **2** INSOLENT, abusive, rude, insulting, impertinent.
**F3 1** pleasant. **2** polite.
*n* attack, assault, onslaught, invasion, raid, sortie.

**offer** *v* **1** PRESENT, make available, advance, extend, put forward, submit, suggest, hold out, provide, sell. **2** PROFFER, propose, bid, tender. **3** VOLUNTEER, come forward, show willing (*infml*).
*n* proposal, bid, submission, tender, suggestion, proposition, overture, approach, attempt, presentation.

**offering** *n* present, gift, donation, contribution, subscription.

**offhand** *adj* casual, unconcerned, uninterested, take-it-or-leave-it (*infml*), brusque, abrupt, perfunctory, informal, cavalier, careless.
*adv* impromptu, off the cuff, extempore (*fml*), off the top of one's head, immediately.
**F3** calculated, planned.

**office** *n* **1** RESPONSIBILITY, duty, obligation, charge, commission, occupation, situation, post, employment, function, appointment, business, role, service. **2** WORKPLACE, workroom, bureau.

**officer** *n* official, office-holder, public servant, functionary, dignitary, bureaucrat, administrator, representative, executive, agent, appointee.

**official** *adj* authorized, authoritative, legitimate, formal, licensed, accredited, certified, approved, authenticated, authentic, bona fide, proper.
**F3** unofficial.
*n* office-bearer, officer, functionary, bureaucrat, executive, representative, agent.

*Officials include*: agent, ambassador, bailiff, bureaucrat, captain, chairman, chairwoman, chairperson, chancellor, chief, clerk, commander, commissar, commissioner, congressman, congresswoman, consul, coroner, councillor, delegate, diplomat, director, elder, envoy, equerry, Eurocrat, executive, Euro-MP, gauleiter, governor, hakim, inspector, justice of the peace (JP), magistrate, manager, mandarin, marshal, mayor, mayoress, member of parliament, minister, monitor, notary, ombudsman, overseer, prefect, president, principal, proctor, proprietor, public prosecutor, registrar, senator (*North Amer.*), sheriff, steward, superintendent, supervisor, usher.

**officiate** *v* preside, superintend, conduct, chair, manage, oversee, run.

**officious** *adj* obtrusive, dictatorial, intrusive, bossy (*infml*), interfering, meddlesome, over-zealous, self-important, pushy (*infml*), forward, bustling, importunate (*fml*).

**offload** *v* unburden, unload, jettison, dump, drop, deposit, get rid of, discharge.

**off-putting** adj intimidating, daunting, disconcerting, discouraging, disheartening, formidable, unnerving, unsettling, demoralizing, disturbing.

**offset** v counterbalance, compensate for, cancel out, counteract, make up for, balance out, neutralize.

**offshoot** n branch, outgrowth, limb, arm, development, spin-off, by-product, appendage.

**offspring** n child, children, young, issue, progeny (*fml*), brood, heirs, successors, descendants.
**E3** parent(s).

**often** adv frequently, repeatedly, regularly, generally, again and again, time after time, time and again, much.
**E3** rarely, seldom, never.

**ogre** n giant, monster, fiend, bogeyman, demon, devil, troll.

**oil** v grease, lubricate, anoint.

**oily** adj **1** GREASY, fatty. **2** UNCTUOUS, smooth, obsequious, ingratiating, smarmy (*infml*), glib, flattering.

**ointment** n salve, balm, cream, lotion, liniment, embrocation.

**OK** (*infml*) adj acceptable, all right, fine, permitted, in order, fair, satisfactory, reasonable, tolerable, passable, not bad, good, adequate, convenient, correct, accurate.
n authorization, approval, endorsement, go-ahead, permission, green light, consent, agreement.
v approve, authorize, pass, give the go-ahead to, give the green light to (*infml*), rubber-stamp, agree to.
interj all right, fine, very well, agreed, right, yes.

**old** adj **1** AGED, elderly, advanced in years, grey, senile. **2** ANCIENT, original, primitive, antiquated, mature. **3** LONG-STANDING, long-established, time-honoured, traditional. **4** OBSOLETE, old-fashioned, out of date, worn-out, decayed, decrepit. **5** FORMER, previous, earlier, one-time, ex-.
**E3** **1** young. **2** new. **4** modern. **5** current.

**old-fashioned** adj outmoded, out of date, outdated, dated, unfashionable, obsolete, behind the times, antiquated, archaic, passé, obsolescent.
**E3** modern, up-to-date.

**omen** n portent, sign, warning, premonition, foreboding, augury, indication.

**ominous** adj portentous, inauspicious, foreboding, menacing, sinister, fateful, unpromising, threatening.
**E3** auspicious, favourable.

**omission** n exclusion, gap, oversight, failure, lack, neglect, default, avoidance.

**omit** v leave out, exclude, miss out, pass over, overlook, drop, skip, eliminate, forget, neglect, leave undone, fail, disregard, edit out.
**E3** include.

**once** adv formerly, previously, in the past, at one time, long ago, in times past, once upon a time, in the old days.
**at once 1** IMMEDIATELY, instantly, directly, right away, straightaway, without delay, now, promptly, forthwith. **2** SIMULTANEOUSLY, together, at the same time.

**oncoming** adj approaching, advancing, upcoming, looming, onrushing, gathering.

**one** adj **1** SINGLE, solitary, lone, individual, only. **2** UNITED, harmonious, like-minded, whole, entire, complete, equal, identical, alike.

**onerous** (*fml*) adj oppressive, burdensome, demanding, laborious, hard, taxing, difficult, troublesome, exacting, exhausting, heavy, weighty.
**E3** easy, light.

**one-sided** *adj* **1** UNBALANCED, unequal, lopsided. **2** UNFAIR, unjust, prejudiced, biased, partial, partisan. **3** UNILATERAL, independent.
**Ea 1** balanced. **2** impartial. **3** bilateral, multilateral.

**ongoing** *adj* **1** CONTINUING, continuous, unbroken, uninterrupted, constant. **2** DEVELOPING, evolving, progressing, growing, in progress, unfinished, unfolding.

**onlooker** *n* bystander, observer, spectator, looker-on, eye-witness, witness, watcher, viewer.

**only** *adv* just, at most, merely, simply, purely, barely, exclusively, solely.
*adj* sole, single, solitary, lone, unique, exclusive, individual.

**onset** *n* **1** BEGINNING, start, commencement, inception, outset, outbreak. **2** ASSAULT, attack, onslaught, onrush.
**Ea 1** end, finish.

**onslaught** *n* attack, assault, offensive, charge, bombardment, blitz.

**onus** *n* burden, responsibility, load, obligation, duty, liability, task.

**onward(s)** *adv* forward, on, ahead, in front, beyond, forth.
**Ea** backward(s).

**ooze** *v* seep, exude, leak, percolate, escape, dribble, drip, drop, discharge, bleed, secrete, emit, overflow with, filter, drain.

**opaque** *adj* **1** CLOUDY, clouded, murky, dull, dim, hazy, muddied, muddy, turbid. **2** OBSCURE, unclear, impenetrable, incomprehensible, unintelligible, enigmatic, difficult.
**Ea 1** transparent. **2** clear, obvious.

**open** *adj* **1** UNCLOSED, ajar, gaping, uncovered, unfastened, unlocked, unsealed, yawning, lidless. **2** UNRESTRICTED, free, unobstructed, clear, accessible, exposed, unprotected, unsheltered, vacant, wide, available. **3** OVERT, obvious,

plain, evident, manifest, noticeable, flagrant, conspicuous. **4** UNDECIDED, unresolved, unsettled, debatable, problematic, moot. **5** FRANK, candid, honest, guileless, natural, ingenuous, unreserved.
**Ea 1** shut. **2** restricted. **3** hidden. **4** decided. **5** reserved.
*v* **1** UNFASTEN, undo, unlock, uncover, unseal, unblock, uncork, clear, expose. **2** EXPLAIN, divulge, disclose, lay bare. **3** EXTEND, spread (out), unfold, separate, split. **4** BEGIN, start, commence, inaugurate, initiate, set in motion, launch.
**Ea 1** close, shut. **2** hide. **4** end, finish.

**open-air** *adj* outdoor, alfresco.
**Ea** indoor.

**opening** *n* **1** APERTURE, breach, gap, orifice, break, chink, crack, fissure, cleft, chasm, hole, split, vent, rupture. **2** START, onset, beginning, inauguration, inception, birth, dawn, launch. **3** OPPORTUNITY, chance, occasion, break (*infml*), place, vacancy.
**Ea 2** close, end.
*adj* beginning, commencing, starting, first, inaugural, introductory, initial, early, primary.
**Ea** closing.

**openly** *adv* overtly, frankly, candidly, blatantly, flagrantly, plainly, unashamedly, unreservedly, glaringly, in public, in full view, shamelessly.
**Ea** secretly, slyly.

**operate** *v* **1** *it operates on batteries*: function, act, perform, run, work, go. **2** *she can operate that machine*: control, handle, manage, use, utilize, manoeuvre.

**operation** *n* **1** FUNCTIONING, action, running, motion, movement, performance, working. **2** INFLUENCE, manipulation, handling, management, use, utilization. **3** UNDERTAKING, enterprise, affair, procedure, proceeding, process, business, deal, transaction, effort. **4** CAMPAIGN, action, task, manoeuvre, exercise.

**operational** *adj* working, in working order, usable, functional, going, viable, workable, ready, prepared, in service.
**F3** out of order.

**operative** *adj* **1** OPERATIONAL, in operation, in force, functioning, active, effective, efficient, in action, workable, viable, serviceable, functional. **2** KEY, crucial, important, relevant, significant.
**F3 1** inoperative, out of service.

**opinion** *n* belief, judgement, view, point of view, idea, perception, stance, theory, impression, feeling, sentiment, estimation, assessment, conception, mind, notion, way of thinking, persuasion, attitute.

**opinionated** *adj* dogmatic, doctrinaire, dictatorial, arrogant, inflexible, obstinate, stubborn, uncompromising, single-minded, prejudiced, biased, bigoted.
**F3** open-minded.

**opponent** *n* adversary, enemy, antagonist, foe, competitor, contestant, challenger, opposer, opposition, rival, objector, dissident.
**F3** ally.

**opportunity** *n* chance, opening, break (*infml*), occasion, possibility, hour, moment.

**oppose** *v* **1** RESIST, withstand, counter, attack, combat, contest, stand up to, take a stand against, take issue with, confront, defy, face, fight, fly in the face of, hinder, obstruct, bar, check, prevent, thwart. **2** COMPARE, contrast, match, offset, counterbalance, play off.
**F3 1** defend, support.

**opposed** *adj* in opposition, against, hostile, conflicting, opposing, opposite, antagonistic, clashing, contrary, incompatible, anti.
**F3** in favour.

**opposite** *adj* **1** FACING, fronting, corresponding. **2** OPPOSED, antagonistic, conflicting, contrary, hostile, adverse, contradictory, antithetical, irreconcilable, unlike, reverse, inconsistent, different, contrasted, differing.
**F3 2** same.
*n* reverse, converse, contrary, antithesis, contradiction, inverse.
**F3** same.

**opposition** *n* **1** ANTAGONISM, hostility, resistance, obstructiveness, unfriendliness, disapproval. **2** OPPONENT, antagonist, rival, foe, other side.
**F3 1** co-operation, support. **2** ally, supporter.

**oppress** *v* **1** BURDEN, afflict, lie heavy on, harass, depress, sadden, torment, vex. **2** SUBJUGATE, suppress, subdue, overpower, overwhelm, crush, trample, tyrannize, persecute, maltreat, abuse.

**oppression** *n* tyranny, subjugation, subjection, repression, despotism, suppression, injustice, cruelty, brutality, abuse, persecution, maltreatment, harshness, hardship.

**oppressive** *adj* **1** AIRLESS, stuffy, close, stifling, suffocating, sultry, muggy, heavy. **2** TYRANNICAL, despotic, overbearing, overwhelming, repressive, harsh, unjust, inhuman, cruel, brutal, burdensome, onerous, intolerable.
**F3 1** airy. **2** just, gentle.

**oppressor** *n* tyrant, bully, taskmaster, slave-driver, despot, dictator, persecutor, tormentor, intimidator, autocrat.

**optimistic** *adj* confident, assured, sanguine, hopeful, positive, cheerful, buoyant, bright, idealistic, expectant.
**F3** pessimistic.

**optimum** *adj* best, ideal, perfect, optimal, superlative, top, choice.
**F3** worst.

**option** *n* choice, alternative, preference, possibility, selection.

**optional** *adj* voluntary, discretionary, elective, free, unforced. **F3** compulsory.

**oral** *adj* verbal, spoken, unwritten, vocal. **F3** written.

**orbit** *n* 1 CIRCUIT, cycle, circle, course, path, trajectory, track, revolution, rotation. 2 RANGE, scope, domain, influence, sphere of influence, compass.
*v* revolve, circle, encircle, circumnavigate.

**ordeal** *n* trial, test, tribulation(s), affliction, trouble(s), suffering, anguish, agony, pain, persecution, torture, nightmare.

**order** *n* 1 COMMAND, directive, decree, injunction, instruction, direction, edict, ordinance, mandate, regulation, rule, precept, law. 2 REQUISITION, request, booking, commission, reservation, application, demand. 3 ARRANGEMENT, organization, grouping, disposition, sequence, categorization, classification, method, pattern, plan, system, array, layout, line-up, structure. 4 PEACE, quiet, calm, tranquillity, harmony, law and order, discipline. 5 ASSOCIATION, society, community, fraternity, brotherhood, sisterhood, lodge, guild, company, organization, denomination, sect, union. 6 CLASS, kind, sort, type, rank, species, hierarchy, family. **F3** 3 confusion, disorder. 4 anarchy.
*v* 1 COMMAND, instruct, direct, bid, decree, require, authorize. 2 REQUEST, reserve, book, apply for, requisition. 3 ARRANGE, organize, dispose, classify, group, marshal, sort out, lay out, manage, control, catalogue.

**out of order** 1 BROKEN, broken down, not working, inoperative. 2 DISORDERED, disorganized, out of sequence. 3 UNSEEMLY, improper, un-called-for, incorrect, wrong.

**orderly** *adj* 1 ORDERED, systematic, neat, tidy, regular, methodical, in order, well-organized, well-regulated. 2 WELL-BEHAVED, controlled, disciplined, law-abiding. **F3** 1 chaotic. 2 disorderly.

**ordinary** *adj* common, commonplace, regular, routine, standard, average, everyday, run-of-the-mill, usual, unexceptional, unremarkable, typical, normal, customary, common-or-garden, plain, familiar, habitual, simple, conventional, modest, mediocre, indifferent, pedestrian, prosaic, undistinguished. **F3** extraordinary, unusual.

**organ** *n* 1 DEVICE, instrument, implement, tool, element, process, structure, unit, member. 2 MEDIUM, agency, forum, vehicle, voice, mouthpiece, publication, newspaper, periodical, journal.

**organic** *adj* natural, biological, living, animate.

**organization** *n* 1 ASSOCIATION, institution, society, company, firm, corporation, federation, group, league, club, confederation, consortium. 2 ARRANGEMENT, system, classification, methodology, order, formation, grouping, method, plan, structure, pattern, composition, configuration, design.

**organize** *v* 1 STRUCTURE, co-ordinate, arrange, order, group, marshal, classify, systematize, tabulate, catalogue. 2 ESTABLISH, found, set up, develop, form, frame, construct, shape, run. **F3** 1 disorganize.

**orgy** *n* debauch, carousal, revelry, bout, bacchanalia, indulgence, excess, spree.

**orientation** *n* 1 SITUATION, bearings, location, direction, position, alignment, placement, attitude. **2** INITIATION, training, acclimatization, familiarization, adaptation, adjustment, settling in.

**origin** n **1** SOURCE, spring, fount, foundation, base, cause, derivation, provenance, roots, well-spring. **2** BEGINNING, commencement, start, inauguration, launch, dawning, creation, emergence. **3** ANCESTRY, descent, extraction, heritage, family, lineage, parentage, pedigree, birth, paternity, stock.

**F3** **2** end, termination.

**original** adj **1** FIRST, early, earliest, initial, primary, archetypal, rudimentary, embryonic, starting, opening, commencing, first-hand. **2** NOVEL, innovative, new, creative, fresh, imaginative, inventive, unconventional, unusual, unique.

**F3** **1** latest. **2** hackneyed, unoriginal. n prototype, master, paradigm, model, pattern, archetype, standard, type.

**originate** v **1** RISE, arise, spring, stem, issue, flow, proceed, derive, come, evolve, emerge, be born. **2** CREATE, invent, inaugurate, introduce, give birth to, develop, discover, establish, begin, commence, start, set up, launch, pioneer, conceive, form, produce, generate.

**F3** **1** end, terminate.

**ornament** n decoration, adornment, embellishment, garnish, trimming, accessory, frill, trinket, bauble, jewel. v decorate, adorn, embellish, garnish, trim, beautify, brighten, dress up, deck, gild.

**ornamental** adj decorative, embellishing, adorning, attractive, showy.

**ornate** adj elaborate, ornamented, fancy, decorated, baroque, rococo, florid, flowery, fussy, busy, sumptuous.

**F3** plain.

**orthodox** adj conformist, conventional, accepted, official, traditional, usual, well-established, established, received, customary, conservative, recognized, authoritative.

**F3** nonconformist, unorthodox.

**ostensible** adj alleged, apparent, presumed, seeming, supposed, so-called, professed, outward, pretended, superficial.

**F3** real.

**ostentatious** adj showy, flashy, pretentious, vulgar, loud, garish, gaudy, flamboyant, conspicuous, extravagant.

**F3** restrained.

**ostracize** v exclude, banish, exile, expel, excommunicate, reject, segregate, send to Coventry, shun, snub, boycott, avoid, cold-shoulder (infml), cut.

**F3** accept, welcome.

**other** adj **1** DIFFERENT, dissimilar, unlike, separate, distinct, contrasting. **2** MORE, further, extra, additional, supplementary, spare, alternative.

**oust** v expel, eject, depose, displace, turn out, throw out, overthrow, evict, drive out, unseat, dispossess, disinherit, replace, topple.

**F3** install, settle.

**out** adj **1** AWAY, absent, elsewhere, not at home, gone, outside, abroad. **2** REVEALED, exposed, disclosed, public, evident, manifest. **3** FORBIDDEN, unacceptable, impossible, disallowed, excluded. **4** OUT OF DATE, unfashionable, old-fashioned, dated, passé, antiquated. **5** EXTINGUISHED, finished, expired, dead, used up.

**F3** **1** in. **2** concealed. **3** allowed. **4** up to date.

**outbreak** n eruption, outburst, explosion, flare-up, upsurge, flash, rash, burst, epidemic.

**outburst** n outbreak, eruption, explosion, flare-up, outpouring, burst, fit, gush, surge, storm, spasm, seizure, gale, attack, fit of temper.

**outcast** n castaway, exile, pariah, outsider, untouchable, refugee, reject, persona non grata.

**outcome** n result, consequence, upshot, conclusion, effect, end result.

**outcry** n protest, complaint, protestation, objection, dissent, indignation, uproar, cry, exclamation, clamour, row, commotion, noise, hue and cry, hullabaloo (*infml*), outburst.

**outdated** adj out of date, old-fashioned, dated, unfashionable, outmoded, behind the times, obsolete, obsolescent, antiquated, archaic.

Ⓔ fashionable, modern.

**outdo** v surpass, exceed, beat, excel, outstrip, outshine, get the better of, overcome, outclass, outdistance.

**outdoor** adj out-of-door(s), outside, open-air.

Ⓔ indoor.

**outer** adj 1 EXTERNAL, exterior, outside, outward, surface, superficial, peripheral. 2 OUTLYING, distant, remote, further.

Ⓔ 1 internal. 2 inner.

**outfit** n 1 CLOTHES, costume, ensemble, get-up (*infml*), togs (*infml*), garb. 2 EQUIPMENT, gear (*infml*), kit, rig, trappings, paraphernalia. 3 (*infml*) ORGANIZATION, firm, business, corporation, company, group, team, unit, set, set-up, crew, gang, squad.

**outgoing** adj 1 SOCIABLE, friendly, unreserved, amiable, warm, approachable, expansive, open, extrovert, cordial, easy-going, communicative, demonstrative, sympathetic. 2 DEPARTING, retiring, former, last, past, ex-.

Ⓔ 1 reserved. 2 incoming.

**outing** n excursion, expedition, jaunt, pleasure trip, trip, spin, picnic.

**outlandish** adj unconventional, unfamiliar, bizarre, strange, odd, weird, eccentric, alien, exotic, barbarous, foreign, extraordinary.

Ⓔ familiar, ordinary.

**outlaw** n bandit, brigand, robber, desperado, highwayman, criminal, marauder, pirate, fugitive.

v ban, disallow, forbid, prohibit, exclude, embargo, bar, debar, banish, condemn.

Ⓔ allow, legalize.

**outlay** n expenditure, expenses, outgoings, disbursement (*fml*), cost, spending.

Ⓔ income.

**outlet** n 1 EXIT, way out, vent, egress, escape, opening, release, safety valve, channel. 2 RETAILER, shop, store, market.

Ⓔ 1 entry, inlet.

**outline** n 1 SUMMARY, synopsis, précis, bare facts, sketch, thumbnail sketch, abstract. 2 PROFILE, form, contour, silhouette, shape.

v sketch, summarize, draft, trace, rough out.

**outlook** n 1 VIEW, viewpoint, point of view, attitude, perspective, frame of mind, angle, slant, standpoint, opinion. 2 EXPECTATIONS, future, forecast, prospect, prognosis.

**outlying** adj distant, remote, far-off, far-away, far-flung, outer, provincial.

Ⓔ inner.

**out-of-the-way** adj remote, isolated, far-flung, far-off, far-away, distant, inaccessible, little-known, obscure, unfrequented.

**output** n production, productivity, product, yield, manufacture, achievement.

**outrage** n 1 ANGER, fury, rage, indignation, shock, affront, horror. 2 ATROCITY, offence, injury, enormity, barbarism, crime, violation, evil, scandal.

v anger, infuriate, affront, incense, enrage, madden, disgust, injure, offend, shock, scandalize.

**outrageous** adj 1 ATROCIOUS, abominable, shocking, scandalous, offensive, disgraceful, monstrous, heinous, unspeakable, horrible. **2** EXCESSIVE, exorbitant, immoderate, unreasonable, extortionate, inordinate, preposterous.

F3 **2** acceptable, reasonable.

**outright** *adj* total, utter, absolute, complete, downright, out-and-out, unqualified, unconditional, perfect, pure, thorough, direct, definite, categorical, straightforward.

F3 ambiguous, indefinite.

*adv* **1** TOTALLY, absolutely, completely, utterly, thoroughly, openly, without restraint, straightforwardly, positively, directly, explicitly. **2** *killed outright*: instantaneously, at once, there and then, instantly, immediately.

**outset** *n* start, beginning, opening, inception, commencement, inauguration, kick-off (*infml*).

F3 end, conclusion.

**outside** *adj* **1** EXTERNAL, exterior, outer, surface, superficial, outward, extraneous, outdoor, outermost, extreme. **2** *an outside chance*: remote, marginal, distant, faint, slight, slim, negligible.

F3 **1** inside.

*n* exterior, façade, front, surface, face, appearance, cover.

F3 inside.

**outsider** *n* stranger, intruder, alien, non-member, non-resident, foreigner, newcomer, visitor, intruder, interloper, misfit, odd man out.

**outskirts** *n* suburbs, vicinity, periphery, fringes, borders, boundary, edge, margin.

F3 centre.

**outspoken** *adj* candid, frank, forthright, blunt, unreserved, plain-spoken, direct, explicit.

F3 diplomatic, reserved.

**outstanding** *adj* **1** EXCELLENT, distinguished, eminent, pre-eminent, celebrated, exceptional, superior, remarkable, prominent, superb,

great, notable, impressive, striking, superlative, important, noteworthy, memorable, special, extraordinary. **2** OWING, unpaid, due, unsettled, unresolved, uncollected, pending, payable, remaining, ongoing, leftover.

F3 **1** ordinary, unexceptional. **2** paid, settled.

**outstrip** *v* surpass, exceed, better, outdo, beat, top, transcend, outshine, pass, gain on, leave behind, leave standing, outrun, outdistance, overtake, eclipse.

**outward** *adj* external, exterior, outer, outside, surface, superficial, visible, apparent, observable, evident, supposed, professed, public, obvious, ostensible.

F3 inner, private.

**outwardly** *adv* apparently, externally, to all appearances, visibly, superficially, supposedly, seemingly, on the surface, at first sight.

**outweigh** *v* override, prevail over, overcome, take precedence over, cancel out, make up for, compensate for, predominate.

**outwit** *v* outsmart, outthink, get the better of, trick, better, beat, dupe, cheat, deceive, defraud, swindle.

**outworn** *adj* outdated, out of date, outmoded, stale, discredited, defunct, old-fashioned, hackneyed, rejected, obsolete, disused, exhausted.

F3 fresh, new.

**oval** *adj* egg-shaped, elliptical, ovoid, ovate.

**ovation** *n* applause, acclaim, acclamation, praises, plaudits (*fml*), tribute, clapping, cheering, bravos.

F3 abuse, catcalls.

**over** *adj* finished, ended, done with, concluded, past, gone, completed, closed, in the past, settled, up, forgotten, accomplished.

*adv* **1** ABOVE, beyond, overhead, on high. **2** EXTRA, remaining, surplus, superfluous, left, unclaimed, unused, unwanted, in excess, in addition.

*prep* **1** ABOVE, on, on top of, upon, in charge of, in command of.

**2** EXCEEDING, more than, in excess of.

**overact** *v* overplay, exaggerate, overdo, ham (*infml*).
■ underact, underplay.

**overall** *adj* total, all-inclusive, all-embracing, comprehensive, inclusive, general, universal, global, broad, blanket, complete, all-over.
■ narrow, specific.
*adv* in general, on the whole, by and large, broadly, generally speaking.

**overbearing** *adj* imperious, domineering, arrogant, dictatorial, tyrannical, high-handed, haughty, bossy (*infml*), cavalier, autocratic, oppressive.
■ meek, unassertive.

**overcast** *adj* cloudy, grey, dull, dark, sombre, sunless, hazy, lowering.
■ bright, clear.

**overcharge** *v* surcharge, short-change, cheat, extort, rip off (*infml*), sting (*infml*), do (*infml*), diddle (*infml*).
■ undercharge.

**overcome** *v* conquer, defeat, beat, surmount, triumph over, vanquish, rise above, master, overpower, overwhelm, overthrow, subdue.

**overcrowded** *adj* congested, packed (out), jam-packed, crammed full, chock-full, overpopulated, overloaded, swarming.
■ deserted, empty.

**overdo** *v* exaggerate, go too far, carry to excess, go overboard (*infml*), lay it on thick (*infml*), overindulge, overstate, overact, overplay, overwork.

**overdue** *adj* late, behindhand, behind schedule, delayed, owing, unpunctual, slow.
■ early.

**overeat** *v* gorge, binge, overindulge,

guzzle, stuff oneself, make a pig of oneself, pig out (*infml*), gormandize.
■ abstain, starve.

**overflow** *v* spill, overrun, run over, pour over, well over, brim over, bubble over, surge, flood, inundate, deluge, shower, submerge, soak, swamp, teem.
*n* overspill, spill, inundation, flood, overabundance, surplus.

**overhang** *v* jut, project, bulge, protrude, stick out, extend.

**overhaul** *v* **1** RENOVATE, repair, service, recondition, mend, examine, inspect, check, survey, re-examine, fix. **2** OVERTAKE, pull ahead of, outpace, outstrip, gain on, pass.
*n* reconditioning, repair, renovation, check, service, examination, inspection, going-over (*infml*).

**overhead** *adv* above, up above, on high, upward.
■ below, underfoot.
*adj* elevated, aerial, overhanging, raised.

**overjoyed** *adj* delighted, elated, euphoric, ecstatic, in raptures, enraptured, thrilled, jubilant, over the moon (*infml*).
■ sad, disappointed.

**overload** *v* burden, oppress, strain, tax, weigh down, overcharge, encumber.

**overlook** *v* **1** FRONT ON TO, face, look on to, look over, command a view of. **2** MISS, disregard, ignore, omit, neglect, pass over, let pass, let ride, slight. **3** EXCUSE, forgive, pardon, condone, wink at, turn a blind eye to.
■ **2** notice. **3** penalize.

**overpower** *v* overcome, conquer, overwhelm, vanquish, defeat, beat, subdue, overthrow, quell, master, crush, immobilize, floor.

**overpowering** *adj* overwhelming, powerful, strong, forceful, irresistible, uncontrollable, compelling, extreme, oppressive, suffocating, unbearable, nauseating, sickening.

**overrate** v overestimate, overvalue, overpraise, magnify, blow up, make too much of.

Ⓔ underrate.

**overrule** v overturn, override, countermand, revoke, reject, rescind, reverse, invalidate, cancel, vote down.

**overrun** v 1 INVADE, occupy, infest, overwhelm, inundate, run riot, spread over, swamp, swarm over, surge over, ravage, overgrow. 2 EXCEED, overshoot, overstep, overreach.

**overseer** n supervisor, boss (*infml*), chief, foreman, forewoman, manager, superintendent.

**overshadow** v 1 OBSCURE, cloud, darken, dim, spoil, veil. 2 OUTSHINE, eclipse, excel, surpass, dominate, dwarf, put in the shade, rise above, tower above.

**oversight** n 1 LAPSE, omission, fault, error, slip-up, mistake, blunder, carelessness, neglect. 2 SUPERVISION, responsibility, care, charge, control, custody, keeping, administration, management, direction.

**overt** adj open, manifest, plain, evident, observable, obvious, apparent, public, professed, unconcealed.

Ⓔ covert, secret.

**overtake** v 1 PASS, catch up with, outdistance, outstrip, draw level with, pull ahead of, overhaul. 2 COME UPON, befall, happen, strike, engulf.

**overthrow** v depose, oust, bring down, topple, unseat, displace, dethrone, conquer, vanquish, beat, defeat, crush, overcome, overpower, overturn, overwhelm, subdue, master, abolish, upset.

Ⓔ install, protect, reinstate, restore.

n ousting, unseating, defeat,

deposition, dethronement, fall, rout, undoing, suppression, downfall, end, humiliation, destruction, ruin.

**overtone** n suggestion, intimation, nuance, hint, undercurrent, insinuation, connotation, association, feeling, implication, sense, flavour.

**overture** n 1 APPROACH, advance, offer, invitation, proposal, proposition, suggestion, signal, move, motion. 2 PRELUDE, opening, introduction, opening move, (opening) gambit.

**overturn** v 1 CAPSIZE, upset, upturn, tip over, topple, overbalance, keel over, knock over, spill. 2 OVERTHROW, repeal, rescind, reverse, annul, abolish, destroy, quash, set aside.

**overwhelm** v 1 OVERCOME, overpower, destroy, defeat, crush, rout, devastate. 2 OVERRUN, inundate, snow under, submerge, swamp, engulf. 3 CONFUSE, bowl over, stagger, floor.

**overwork** v overstrain, overload, exploit, exhaust, overuse, overtax, strain, wear out, oppress, burden, weary.

**overwrought** adj tense, agitated, keyed up, on edge, worked up, wound up, frantic, overcharged, overexcited, excited, beside oneself, uptight (*infml*).

Ⓔ calm.

**owing** adj unpaid, due, owed, in arrears, outstanding, payable, unsettled, overdue.

**owing to** because of, as a result of, on account of, thanks to.

**own** adj personal, individual, private, particular, idiosyncratic.

v possess, have, hold, retain, keep, enjoy.

**own up** admit, confess, come clean (*infml*), tell the truth, acknowledge.

**owner** n possessor, holder, landlord, landlady, proprietor, proprietress, master, mistress, freeholder.

# P

**pace** *n* step, stride, walk, gait, tread, movement, motion, progress, rate, speed, velocity, celerity, quickness, rapidity, tempo, measure.

*v* step, stride, walk, march, tramp, pound, patrol, mark out, measure.

**pacifist** *n* peace-lover, pacificist, conscientious objector, peacemaker, peace-monger, dove.

‡ warmonger, hawk.

**pacify** *v* appease, conciliate, placate, mollify, calm, compose, soothe, assuage, allay, moderate, soften, lull, still, quiet, silence, quell, crush, put down, tame, subdue.

‡ anger.

**pack** *n* 1 PACKET, box, carton, parcel, package, bundle, burden, load, backpack, rucksack, haversack, knapsack, kitbag. 2 GROUP, company, troop, herd, flock, band, crowd, gang, mob.

*v* 1 WRAP, parcel, package, bundle, stow, store. 2 FILL, load, charge, cram, stuff, crowd, throng, press, ram, wedge, compact, compress.

**package** *n* parcel, pack, packet, box, carton, bale, consignment.

*v* parcel (up), wrap (up), pack (up), box, batch.

**packed** *adj* filled, full, jam-packed, chock-a-block, crammed, crowded, congested.

‡ empty, deserted.

**packet** *n* pack, carton, box, bag, package, parcel, case, container, wrapper, wrapping, packing.

**pact** *n* treaty, convention, covenant, bond, alliance, cartel, contract, deal, bargain, compact, agreement, arrangement, understanding.

‡ disagreement, quarrel.

**pad** *n* 1 CUSHION, pillow, wad, buffer, padding, protection.
2 WRITING-PAD, note-pad, jotter, block.

*v* fill, stuff, wad, pack, wrap, line, cushion, protect.

**pad out** expand, inflate, fill out, augment, amplify, elaborate, flesh out, lengthen, stretch, protract, spin out.

**padding** *n* 1 FILLING, stuffing, wadding, packing, protection.
2 VERBIAGE, verbosity, wordiness, waffle (*infml*), bombast, hot air.

**paddle**¹ *n* oar, scull.

*v* row, oar, scull, propel, steer.

**paddle**² *v* wade, splash, slop, dabble.

**pagan** *n* heathen, atheist, unbeliever, infidel, idolater.

‡ believer.

*adj* heathen, irreligious, atheistic, godless, infidel, idolatrous.

**page**¹ *n* LEAF, sheet, folio, side.

**page**² *n* page-boy, attendant, messenger, bell-boy, footman, servant.

*v* call, send for, summon, bid, announce.

**pageant** *n* procession, parade, show, display, tableau, scene, play, spectacle, extravaganza.

**pageantry** *n* pomp, ceremony, grandeur, magnificence, splendour, glamour, glitter, spectacle, parade, display, show, extravagance, theatricality, drama, melodrama.

**pain** *n* 1 HURT, ache, throb, cramp, spasm, twinge, pang, stab, sting, smart, soreness, tenderness, discomfort, distress, suffering, affliction, trouble, anguish, agony, torment, torture. 2 (*infml*)

NUISANCE, bother, bore (*infml*), annoyance, vexation, burden, headache (*infml*).

*v* hurt, afflict, torment, torture, agonize, distress, upset, sadden, grieve.

☒ please, delight, gratify.

**pained** *adj* hurt, injured, wounded, stung, offended, aggrieved, reproachful, distressed, upset, saddened, grieved.

☒ pleased, gratified.

**painful** *adj* **1** SORE, tender, aching, throbbing, smarting, stabbing, agonizing, excruciating. **2** *a painful experience*: unpleasant, disagreeable, distressing, upsetting, saddening, harrowing, traumatic. **3** HARD, difficult, laborious, tedious.

☒ **1** painless, soothing. **2** pleasant, agreeable. **3** easy.

**pain-killer** *n* analgesic, anodyne, anaesthetic, palliative, sedative, drug, remedy.

**painless** *adj* pain-free, trouble-free, effortless, easy, simple, undemanding.

☒ painful, difficult.

**pains** *n* trouble, bother, effort, labour, care, diligence.

**painstaking** *adj* careful, meticulous, scrupulous, thorough, conscientious, diligent, assiduous, industrious, hardworking, dedicated, devoted, persevering.

☒ careless, negligent.

**paint** *n* colour, colouring, pigment, dye, tint, stain.

---

*Paints include*: acrylic paint, colourwash, distemper, eggshell, emulsion, enamel, gloss paint, gouache, glaze, lacquer, masonry paint, matt paint, oil paint, oils, pastel, poster paint, primer, undercoat, varnish, watercolour, whitewash.

---

*v* **1** COLOUR, dye, tint, stain, lacquer, varnish, glaze, apply, daub, coat, cover, decorate. **2** PORTRAY, depict, describe, recount, picture, represent.

**painting** *n* oil painting, oil, watercolour, picture, portrait, landscape, still life, miniature, illustration, fresco, mural.

**pair** *n* couple, brace, twosome, duo, twins, two of a kind.

*v* match (up), twin, team, mate, marry, wed, splice, join, couple, link, bracket, put together.

☒ separate, part.

**palace** *n* castle, château, mansion, stately home, basilica, dome.

**palatable** *adj* tasty, appetizing, eatable, edible, acceptable, satisfactory, pleasant, agreeable, enjoyable, attractive.

☒ unpalatable, unacceptable, unpleasant, disagreeable.

**palate** *n* taste, appreciation, liking, relish, enjoyment, appetite, stomach, heart.

**palatial** *adj* grand, magnificent, splendid, majestic, regal, stately, grandiose, imposing, luxurious, de luxe, sumptuous, opulent, plush, spacious.

**pale** *adj* **1** PALLID, livid, ashen, ashy, white, chalky, pasty, pasty-faced, waxen, waxy, wan, sallow, anaemic. **2** *pale blue*: light, pastel, faded, washed-out, bleached, colourless, insipid, vapid, weak, feeble, faint, dim.

☒ **1** ruddy. **2** dark.

*v* whiten, blanch, bleach, fade, dim.

☒ colour, blush.

**pall**[1] *n* shroud, veil, mantle, cloak, cloud, shadow, gloom, damper.

**pall**[2] *v* tire, weary, jade, sate, satiate, cloy, sicken.

**palm** *n* hand, paw (*infml*), mitt (*sl*).

*v* take, grab, snatch, appropriate.

**palm off** foist, impose, fob off, offload, unload, pass off.

**palpable** *adj* solid, substantial, material, real, touchable, tangible,

visible, apparent, clear, plain, obvious, evident, manifest, conspicuous, blatant, unmistakable.
**F3** impalpable, imperceptible, intangible, elusive.

**palpitate** v flutter, quiver, tremble, shiver, vibrate, beat, pulsate, pound, thump, throb.

**paltry** adj meagre, derisory, contemptible, mean, low, miserable, wretched, poor, sorry, small, slight, trifling, inconsiderable, negligible, trivial, minor, petty, unimportant, insignificant, worthless.
**F3** substantial, significant, valuable.

**pamper** v cosset, coddle, mollycoddle, humour, gratify, indulge, overindulge, spoil, pet, fondle.
**F3** neglect, ill-treat.

**pamphlet** n leaflet, brochure, booklet, folder, circular, handout, notice.

**pan** n saucepan, frying-pan, pot, casserole, container, vessel.

**panache** n flourish, flamboyance, ostentation, style, flair, élan, dash, spirit, enthusiasm, zest, energy, vigour, verve.

**pandemonium** n chaos, disorder, confusion, commotion, rumpus, turmoil, turbulence, tumult, uproar, din, bedlam, hubbub, hullabaloo, hue and cry, to-do (infml).
**F3** order, calm, peace.

**pander to** humour, indulge, pamper, please, gratify, satisfy, fulfil, provide, cater to.

**panel** n board, committee, jury, team.

**pang** n pain, ache, twinge, stab, sting, prick, gripe, spasm, throe, agony, anguish, discomfort, distress.

**panic** n agitation, flap (infml), alarm, dismay, consternation, fright, fear, horror, terror, frenzy, hysteria.
**F3** calmness, confidence.

v lose one's nerve, lose one's head, go

to pieces, flap (infml), overreact.
**F3** relax.

**panic-stricken** adj alarmed, frightened, horrified, terrified, petrified, scared stiff, in a cold sweat, panicky, frantic, frenzied, hysterical.
**F3** relaxed, confident.

**panorama** n view, vista, prospect, scenery, landscape, scene, spectacle, perspective, overview, survey.

**panoramic** adj scenic, wide, sweeping, extensive, far-reaching, widespread, overall, general, universal.
**F3** narrow, restricted, limited.

**pant** v puff, blow, gasp, wheeze, breathe, sigh, heave, throb, palpitate.

**pants** n 1 UNDERPANTS, drawers, panties, briefs, knickers (infml), Y-fronts, boxer shorts, trunks, shorts. 2 TROUSERS, slacks, jeans.

**paper** n 1 NEWSPAPER, daily, broadsheet, tabloid, rag (sl), journal, organ. 2 DOCUMENT, credential, authorization, identification, certificate, deed. 3 a paper on alternative medicine: essay, composition, dissertation, thesis, treatise, article, report.

---

*Types of paper include*: art paper, bank, blotting paper, bond, carbon paper, cartridge paper, crêpe paper, greaseproof paper, graph paper, manila, notepaper, parchment, rice paper, silver paper, sugar paper, tissue paper, toilet paper, tracing paper, vellum, wallpaper, wrapping paper, writing-paper; card, cardboard, pasteboard; A4, foolscap, quarto, atlas, crown.

---

**parable** n fable, allegory, lesson, moral tale, story.

**parade** n procession, cavalcade, motorcade, march, column, file, train, review, ceremony, spectacle, pageant, show, display, exhibition.

v 1 MARCH, process, file past.

**2** SHOW, display, exhibit, show off, vaunt, flaunt, brandish.

**paradise** *n* heaven, Utopia, Shangri-La, Elysium, Eden, bliss, delight.
**E3** hell, Hades.

**paradox** *n* contradiction, inconsistency, incongruity, absurdity, oddity, anomaly, mystery, enigma, riddle, puzzle.

**paradoxical** *adj* self-contradictory, contradictory, conflicting, inconsistent, incongruous, absurd, illogical, improbable, impossible, mysterious, enigmatic, puzzling, baffling.

**paragon** *n* ideal, exemplar, epitome, quintessence, model, pattern, archetype, prototype, standard, criterion.

**paragraph** *n* passage, section, part, portion, subsection, subdivision, clause, item.

**parallel** *adj* equidistant, aligned, coextensive, alongside, analogous, equivalent, corresponding, matching, like, similar, resembling.
**E3** divergent, different.
*n* **1** MATCH, equal, twin, duplicate, analogue, equivalent, counterpart.
**2** SIMILARITY, resemblance, likeness, correspondence, correlation, equivalence, analogy, comparison.
*v* match, echo, conform, agree, correspond, correlate, compare, liken.
**E3** diverge, differ.

**paralyse** *v* cripple, lame, disable, incapacitate, immobilize, anaesthetize, numb, deaden, freeze, transfix, halt, stop.

**paralysed** *adj* paralytic, paraplegic, quadriplegic, crippled, lame, disabled, incapacitated, immobilized, numb.
**E3** able-bodied.

**paralysis** *n* paraplegia, quadriplegia, palsy, numbness, deadness, immobility, halt, standstill, stoppage, shutdown.

**parameter** *n* variable, guideline, indication, criterion, specification, limitation, restriction, limit, boundary.

**paramount** *adj* supreme, highest, topmost, predominant, pre-eminent, prime, principal, main, chief, cardinal, primary, first, foremost.
**E3** lowest, last.

**paraphernalia** *n* equipment, gear, tackle, apparatus, accessories, trappings, bits and pieces, odds and ends, belongings, effects, stuff, things, baggage.

**paraphrase** *n* rewording, rephrasing, restatement, version, interpretation, rendering, translation.
*v* reword, rephrase, restate, interpret, render, translate.

**parasite** *n* sponger, scrounger, cadger, hanger-on, leech, bloodsucker.

**parcel** *n* package, packet, pack, box, carton, bundle.
*v* package, pack, wrap, bundle, tie up.

**parcel out** divide, carve up, apportion, allocate, allot, share out, distribute, dispense, dole out, deal out, mete out.

**parch** *v* dry (up), desiccate, dehydrate, bake, burn, scorch, sear, blister, wither, shrivel.

**parched** *adj* **1** ARID, waterless, dry, dried up, dehydrated, scorched, withered, shrivelled. **2** (*infml*) THIRSTY, gasping (*infml*).

**pardon** *v* forgive, condone, overlook, excuse, vindicate, acquit, absolve, remit, let off, reprieve, free, liberate, release.
**E3** punish, discipline.
*n* forgiveness, mercy, clemency, indulgence, amnesty, excuse, acquittal, absolution, reprieve, release, discharge.
**E3** punishment, condemnation.

**pardonable** *adj* forgivable, excusable, justifiable, warrantable, understandable, allowable,

permissible, minor, venial.
**F3** inexcusable.

**pare** v peel, skin, shear, clip, trim, crop, cut, dock, lop, prune, cut back, reduce, decrease.

**parent** n father, mother, dam, sire, progenitor, begetter, procreator, guardian.

**parish** n district, community, parishioners, church, churchgoers, congregation, flock, fold.

**park** n grounds, estate, parkland, gardens, woodland, reserve, pleasure-ground.
v put, position, deposit, leave.

**parliament** n legislature, senate, congress, house, assembly, convocation, council, diet.

**parliaments and political assemblies**

*Names of parliaments and political assemblies include*: House of Representatives, Senate (Australia); Nationalrat, Bundesrat (Austria); Narodno Sobraniye (Bulgaria); House of Commons, Senate (Canada); National People's Congress (China); Folketing (Denmark); People's Assembly (Egypt); Eduskunta (Finland); National Assembly, Senate (France); Bundesrat, Bundestag, Landtag (Germany); Althing (Iceland); Lok Sabha, Rajya Sabha (India); Majlis (Iran); Dáil, Seanad (Ireland); Knesset (Israel); Camera dei Deputati, Senato (Italy); Diet (Japan); Staten-Generaal (Netherlands); House of Representatives (New Zealand); Storting (Norway); Sejm (Poland); Cortes (Portugal); State Duma, Federation Council (Russia); House of Assembly (South Africa); Cortes (Spain); Riksdag (Sweden); Nationalrat, Ständerat, Bundesrat (Switzerland); Porte (Turkey); House of Commons, House of Lords (UK); House of Representatives, Senate

(US); National Assembly (Vietnam).

**parliamentary** adj governmental, senatorial, congressional, legislative, law-making.

**parochial** adj insular, provincial, parish-pump, petty, small-minded, narrow-minded, inward-looking, blinkered, limited, restricted, confined.
**F3** national, international.

**parody** n caricature, lampoon, burlesque, satire, send-up, spoof, skit, mimicry, imitation, take-off, travesty, distortion.
v caricature, lampoon, burlesque, satirize, send up, spoof, mimic, imitate, ape, take off.

**paroxysm** n fit, seizure, spasm, convulsion, attack, outburst, outbreak, explosion.

**parry** v ward off, fend off, repel, repulse, field, deflect, block, avert, avoid, evade, duck, dodge, sidestep, shun.

**parson** n vicar, rector, priest, minister, pastor, preacher, clergyman, reverend, cleric, churchman.

**part** n **1** COMPONENT, constituent, element, factor, piece, bit, particle, fragment, scrap, segment, fraction, portion, share, section, division, department, branch, sector, district, region, territory. **2** ROLE, character, duty, task, responsibility, office, function, capacity.
**F3** 1 whole, totality.
v separate, detach, disconnect, sever, split, tear, break, break up, take apart, dismantle, come apart, split up, divide, disunite, part company, disband, disperse, scatter, leave, depart, withdraw, go away.

**part with** relinquish, let go of, give up, yield, surrender, renounce, forgo, abandon, discard, jettison.

**partial** adj **1** *a partial victory*: incomplete, limited, restricted,

**party**

imperfect, fragmentary, unfinished.
**2** BIASED, prejudiced, partisan, one-sided, discriminatory, unfair, unjust, predisposed, coloured, affected.
**F3 1** complete, total. **2** impartial, disinterested, unbiased, fair.
**partial to** fond of, keen on, crazy about (*infml*), mad about (*infml*).

**partiality** *n* liking, fondness, predilection (*fml*), proclivity, inclination, preference, predisposition.

**participant** *n* entrant, contributor, participator, member, party, co-operator, helper, worker.

**participate** *v* take part, join in, contribute, engage, be involved, enter, share, partake, co-operate, help, assist.

**participation** *n* involvement, sharing, partnership, co-operation, contribution, assistance.

**particle** *n* bit, piece, fragment, scrap, shred, sliver, speck, morsel, crumb, iota, whit, jot, tittle, atom, grain, drop.

**particular** *adj* **1** *on that particular day*: specific, precise, exact, distinct, special, peculiar. **2** EXCEPTIONAL, remarkable, notable, marked, thorough, unusual, uncommon.
**3** FUSSY, discriminating, choosy (*infml*), finicky, fastidious.
**F3 1** general.
*n* detail, specific, point, feature, item, fact, circumstance.

**particularly** *adv* especially, exceptionally, remarkably, notably, extraordinarily, unusually, uncommonly, surprisingly, in particular, specifically, explicitly, distinctly.

**parting** *n* **1** DEPARTURE, going, leave-taking, farewell, goodbye, adieu. **2** DIVERGENCE, separation, division, partition, rift, split, rupture, breaking.
**F3 1** meeting. **2** convergence.
*adj* departing, farewell, last, dying,

final, closing, concluding.
**F3** first.

**partisan** *n* devotee, adherent, follower, disciple, backer, supporter, champion, stalwart, guerrilla, irregular.
*adj* biased, prejudiced, partial, predisposed, discriminatory, one-sided, factional, sectarian.
**F3** impartial.

**partition** *n* **1** DIVIDER, barrier, wall, panel, screen, room-divider.
**2** DIVISION, break-up, splitting, separation, parting, severance.
*v* **1** SEPARATE, divide, subdivide, wall off, fence off, screen. **2** SHARE, divide, split up, parcel out.

**partly** *adv* somewhat, to some extent, to a certain extent, up to a point, slightly, fractionally, moderately, relatively, in part, partially, incompletely.
**F3** completely, totally.

**partner** *n* associate, ally, confederate, colleague, team-mate, collaborator, accomplice, helper, mate, sidekick (*infml*), oppo (*infml*), companion, comrade, consort, spouse, husband, wife.

**partnership** *n* **1** ALLIANCE, confederation, affiliation, combination, union, syndicate, co-operative, association, society, corporation, company, firm, fellowship, fraternity, brotherhood.
**2** COLLABORATION, co-operation, participation, sharing.

**party** *n* **1** CELEBRATION, festivity, social, do (*infml*), knees-up (*sl*), rave-up (*sl*), get-together, gathering, reunion, function, reception, at-home, housewarming. **2** *a search party*: team, squad, crew, gang, band, group, company, detachment.
**3** *a political party*: faction, side, league, cabal, alliance, association, grouping, combination. **4** PERSON, individual, litigant, plaintiff, defendant.

*Types of party include*: acid-house party, barbecue, bash (*sl*), beanfeast (*infml*), beano (*infml*), birthday party, bunfight (*infml*), ceilidh, dinner party, disco, discotheque, do (*infml*), flatwarming, garden party, gathering of the clan (*infml*), Hallowe'en party, hen party, hooley, hootnanny (*North Amer. infml*), housewarming, orgy, picnic, pyjama party, rave, rave-up (*sl*), social, soirée, stag party, stag night, supper party, tea party, thrash (*infml*), welcoming party.

**pass**[1] *v* **1** SURPASS, exceed, go beyond, outdo, outstrip, overtake, leave behind. **2** *pass time*: spend, while away, fill, occupy. **3** GO PAST, go by, elapse, lapse, proceed, roll, flow, run, move, go, disappear, vanish. **4** GIVE, hand, transfer, transmit. **5** ENACT, ratify, validate, adopt, authorize, sanction, approve. **6** *pass an exam*: succeed, get through, qualify, graduate.
*n* **1** THROW, kick, move, lunge, swing. **2** PERMIT, passport, identification, ticket, licence, authorization, warrant, permission.
**pass away** die, pass on, expire, decease, give up the ghost.
**pass off 1** FEIGN, counterfeit, fake, palm off. **2** HAPPEN, occur, take place, go off.
**pass out 1** FAINT, lose consciousness, black out, collapse, flake out, keel over (*infml*), drop. **2** GIVE OUT, hand out, dole out, distribute, deal out, share out.
**pass over** disregard, ignore, overlook, miss, omit, leave, neglect.

**pass**[2] *n* col, defile, gorge, ravine, canyon, gap, passage.

**passable** *adj* **1** SATISFACTORY, acceptable, allowable, tolerable, average, ordinary, unexceptional, moderate, fair, adequate, all right, OK (*infml*), mediocre. **2** CLEAR,

unobstructed, unblocked, open, navigable.
**F3 1** unacceptable, excellent.
**2** obstructed, blocked, impassable.

**passage** *n* **1** PASSAGEWAY, aisle, corridor, hall, hallway, lobby, vestibule, doorway, opening, entrance, exit. **2** THOROUGHFARE, way, route, road, avenue, path, lane, alley. **3** EXTRACT, excerpt, quotation, text, paragraph, section, piece, clause, verse. **4** JOURNEY, voyage, trip, crossing.

**passenger** *n* traveller, voyager, commuter, rider, fare, hitch-hiker.

**passer-by** *n* bystander, witness, looker-on, onlooker, spectator.

**passing** *adj* ephemeral, transient, short-lived, temporary, momentary, fleeting, brief, short, cursory, hasty, quick, slight, superficial, shallow, casual, incidental.
**F3** lasting, permanent.

**passion** *n* feeling, emotion, love, adoration, infatuation, fondness, affection, lust, itch, desire, craving, fancy, mania, obsession, craze, eagerness, keenness, avidity, zest, enthusiasm, fanaticism, zeal, ardour, fervour, warmth, heat, fire, spirit, intensity, vehemence, anger, indignation, fury, rage, outburst.
**F3** coolness, indifference, self-possession.

**passionate** *adj* **1** ARDENT, fervent, eager, keen, avid, enthusiastic, fanatical, zealous, warm, hot, fiery, inflamed, aroused, excited, impassioned, intense, strong, fierce, vehement, violent, stormy, tempestuous, wild, frenzied.
**2** EMOTIONAL, excitable, hot-headed, impetuous, impulsive, quick-tempered, irritable. **3** LOVING, affectionate, lustful, erotic, sexy, sensual, sultry.
**F3** phlegmatic, laid back (*infml*).
**3** frigid.

**passive** *adj* receptive, unassertive,

submissive, docile, unresisting, non-violent, patient, resigned, long-suffering, indifferent, apathetic, lifeless, inert, inactive, non-participating.

**E3** active, lively, responsive, involved.

**past** *adj* **1** OVER, ended, finished, completed, done, over and done with. **2** FORMER, previous, preceding, foregoing, late, recent. **3** ANCIENT, bygone, olden, early, gone, no more, extinct, defunct, forgotten.

**E3** 2 future.

*n* **1** *in the past*: history, former times, olden days, antiquity. **2** LIFE, background, experience, track record.

**E3** 1 future.

**pasta**

*Forms and shapes of pasta include*: agnolotti, anelli, angel's hair, bombolotti, bucatini, cannelloni, capelletti, casarecci, conchiglie, crescioni, ditali, elbow macaroni, farfalline, fedelini, fettuccine, fiochetti, fusilli, gnocchi, lasagne, lasagne verde, linguini, lumache, macaroni, mafalde, manicotti, maruzze, mezzani, noodle, noodle farfel, penne, pennine, ravioli, rigatoni, ruoti, spaghetti, spaghetti bolognese, stelline, tagliatelle, tortellini, trofie, vermicelli, ziti.

**paste** *n* adhesive, glue, gum, mastic, putty, cement.

*v* stick, glue, gum, cement, fix.

**pastel** *adj* delicate, soft, soft-hued, light, pale, subdued, faint.

**pastime** *n* hobby, activity, game, sport, recreation, play, fun, amusement, entertainment, diversion, distraction, relaxation.

**E3** work, employment.

**pastoral** *adj* **1** RURAL, country, rustic, bucolic, agricultural, agrarian, idyllic. **2** ECCLESIASTICAL, clerical, priestly, ministerial.

**E3** 1 urban.

**pastry**

*Types of pastry include*: American crust pastry, biscuit-crumb pastry, cheese pastry, choux, Danish pastry, filo pastry, flaky pastry, flan pastry, hot-water crust pastry, one-stage pastry, pâte à savarin, pâte brisée, pâte frolle, pâte sablée, pâte sucrée, plain pastry, pork-pie pastry, puff pastry, rich shortcrust pastry, rough-puff pastry, short pastry, shortcrust pastry, suetcrust pastry, sweet pastry.

**pasture** *n* grass, grassland, meadow, field, paddock, pasturage, grazing.

**pasty** *adj* pale, pallid, wan, anaemic, pasty-faced, sickly, unhealthy.

**E3** ruddy, healthy.

**pat** *v* tap, dab, slap, touch, stroke, caress, fondle, pet.

*n* tap, dab, slap, touch, stroke, caress.

*adv* precisely, exactly, perfectly, flawlessly, faultlessly, fluently.

**E3** imprecisely, inaccurately, wrongly.

*adj* glib, fluent, smooth, slick, ready, easy, facile, simplistic.

**patch** *n* piece, bit, scrap, spot, area, stretch, tract, plot, lot, parcel.

*v* mend, repair, fix, cover, reinforce.

**patchy** *adj* uneven, irregular, inconsistent, variable, random, fitful, erratic, sketchy, bitty, spotty, blotchy.

**E3** even, uniform, regular, consistent.

**patent** *adj* obvious, evident, conspicuous, manifest, clear, transparent, apparent, visible, palpable, unequivocal, open, overt, blatant, flagrant, glaring.

**E3** hidden, opaque.

**path** *n* route, course, direction, way, passage, road, avenue, lane, footpath, bridleway, trail, track, walk.

**pathetic** *adj* **1** PITIABLE, poor, sorry, lamentable, miserable, sad, distressing, moving, touching, poignant, plaintive, heart-rending,

heartbreaking. **2** (*infml*)
CONTEMPTIBLE, derisory,
deplorable, useless, worthless,
inadequate, meagre, feeble.
**F3** 1 cheerful. **2** admirable, excellent,
valuable.

**patience** *n* calmness, composure,
self-control, restraint, tolerance,
forbearance, endurance, fortitude,
long-suffering, submission,
resignation, stoicism, persistence,
perseverance, diligence.
**F3** impatience, intolerance,
exasperation.

**patient** *adj* calm, composed, self-
possessed, self-controlled, restrained,
even-tempered, mild, lenient,
indulgent, understanding, forgiving,
tolerant, accommodating, forbearing,
long-suffering, uncomplaining,
submissive, resigned, philosophical,
stoical, persistent, persevering.
**F3** impatient, restless, intolerant,
exasperated.
*n* invalid, sufferer, case, client.

**patriotic** *adj* nationalistic,
chauvinistic, jingoistic, loyal, flag-
waving.

**patrol** *n* **1** GUARD, sentry, sentinel,
watchman. **2** *on patrol*: watch,
surveillance, policing, protection,
defence.
*v* police, guard, protect, defend, go
the rounds, tour, inspect.

**patron** *n* **1** BENEFACTOR,
philanthropist, sponsor, backer,
supporter, sympathizer, advocate,
champion, defender, protector,
guardian, helper. **2** CUSTOMER,
client, frequenter, regular, shopper,
buyer, purchaser, subscriber.

**patronage** *n* custom, business,
trade, sponsorship, backing, support.

**patronize** *v* **1** SPONSOR, fund, back,
support, maintain, help, assist,
promote, foster, encourage. **2**
FREQUENT, shop at, buy from, deal
with.

**patronizing** *adj* condescending,

stooping, overbearing, high-handed,
haughty, superior, snobbish,
supercilious, disdainful.
**F3** humble, lowly.

**patter** *v* tap, pat, pitter-patter, beat,
pelt, scuttle, scurry.
*n* **1** PATTERING, tapping, pitter-
patter, beating. **2** *a salesman's patter*:
chatter, gabble, jabber, line, pitch,
spiel (*sl*), jargon, lingo (*infml*).

**pattern** *n* **1** SYSTEM, method, order,
plan. **2** DECORATION,
ornamentation, ornament, figure,
motif, design, style. **3** MODEL,
template, stencil, guide, original,
prototype, standard, norm.

**patterned** *adj* decorated,
ornamented, figured, printed.
**F3** plain.

**paunch** *n* abdomen, belly, pot-belly,
beer-belly, corporation (*infml*).

**pause** *v* halt, stop, cease,
discontinue, break off, interrupt, take
a break, rest, wait, delay, hesitate.
*n* halt, stoppage, interruption, break,
rest, breather (*infml*), lull, let-up
(*infml*), respite, gap, interval, interlude,
intermission, wait, delay, hesitation.

**pave** *v* flag, tile, floor, surface,
cover, asphalt, tarmac, concrete.

**paw** *v* maul, manhandle, mishandle,
molest.
*n* foot, pad, forefoot, hand.

**pawn**[1] *n* dupe, puppet, tool,
instrument, toy, plaything.

**pawn**[2] *v* deposit, pledge, stake,
mortgage, hock (*sl*), pop (*sl*).

**pay** *v* **1** REMIT, settle, discharge,
reward, remunerate, recompense,
reimburse, repay, refund, spend, pay
out. **2** BENEFIT, profit, pay off, bring
in, yield, return. **3** ATONE, make
amends, compensate, answer, suffer.
*n* remuneration, wages, salary,
earnings, income, fee, stipend,
honorarium, emoluments, payment,
reward, recompense, compensation,
reimbursement.

**pay back 1** REPAY, refund, reimburse,

recompense, settle, square.

**2** RETALIATE, get one's own back, take revenge, get even with, reciprocate, counter-attack.

**pay off 1** DISCHARGE, settle, square, clear. **2** DISMISS, fire, sack (*infml*), lay off. **3** *the preparations paid off*: succeed, work.

**pay out** spend, disburse, hand over, fork out (*infml*), shell out (*infml*), lay out.

**payable** adj owed, owing, unpaid, outstanding, in arrears, due, mature.

**payment** n remittance, settlement, discharge, premium, outlay, advance, deposit, instalment, contribution, donation, allowance, reward, remuneration, pay, fee, hire, fare, toll.

**peace** n **1** SILENCE, quiet, hush, stillness, rest, relaxation, tranquillity, calm, calmness, composure, contentment. **2** ARMISTICE, truce, cease-fire, conciliation, concord, harmony, agreement, treaty.

**F3** 1 noise, disturbance. **2** war, disagreement.

**peaceable** adj pacific, peace-loving, unwarlike, non-violent, conciliatory, friendly, amicable, inoffensive, gentle, placid, easy-going (*infml*), mild.

**F3** belligerent, aggressive.

**peaceful** adj quiet, still, restful, relaxing, tranquil, serene, calm, placid, unruffled, undisturbed, untroubled, friendly, amicable, peaceable, pacific, gentle.

**F3** noisy, disturbed, troubled, violent.

**peacemaker** n appeaser, conciliator, mediator, arbitrator, intercessor, peace-monger, pacifist.

**peak** n top, summit, pinnacle, crest, crown, zenith, height, maximum, climax, culmination, apex, tip, point.

**F3** nadir, trough.

v climax, culminate, come to a head.

**peal** n chime, carillon, toll, knell, ring, clang, ringing, reverberation,

rumble, roar, crash, clap.

v chime, toll, ring, clang, resonate, reverberate, resound, rumble, roll, roar, crash.

**peasant** n rustic, provincial, yokel, bumpkin, oaf, boor, lout.

**peculiar** adj **1** *a peculiar sound*: strange, odd, curious, funny, weird, bizarre, extraordinary, unusual, abnormal, exceptional, unconventional, offbeat, eccentric, way-out (*sl*), outlandish, exotic.

**2** CHARACTERISTIC, distinctive, specific, particular, special, individual, personal, idiosyncratic, unique, singular.

**F3** 1 ordinary, normal. **2** general.

**peculiarity** n oddity, bizarreness, abnormality, exception, eccentricity, quirk, mannerism, feature, trait, mark, quality, attribute, characteristic, distinctiveness, particularity, idiosyncrasy.

**pedantic** adj stilted, fussy, particular, precise, exact, punctilious, hair-splitting, nit-picking, finical, academic, bookish, erudite.

**F3** imprecise, informal, casual.

**peddle** v sell, vend, flog (*infml*), hawk, tout, push, trade, traffic, market.

**pedestal** n plinth, stand, support, mounting, foot, base, foundation, platform, podium.

**pedestrian** n walker, foot-traveller.

adj dull, boring, flat, uninspired, banal, mundane, run-of-the-mill, commonplace, ordinary, mediocre, indifferent, prosaic, stodgy, plodding.

**F3** exciting, imaginative.

**pedigree** n genealogy, family tree, lineage, ancestry, descent, line, family, parentage, derivation, extraction, race, breed, stock, blood.

**peel** v pare, skin, strip, scale, flake (off).

n skin, rind, zest, peeling.

**peep** v look, peek, glimpse, spy, squint, peer, emerge, issue, appear.

*n* look, peek, glimpse, glance, squint.

**peephole** *n* spyhole, keyhole, pinhole, hole, opening, aperture, slit, chink, crack, fissure, cleft, crevice.

**peer**[1] *v* look, gaze, scan, scrutinize, examine, inspect, spy, snoop, peep, squint.

**peer**[2] *n* 1 ARISTOCRAT, noble, nobleman, lord, duke, marquess, marquis, earl, count, viscount, baron. 2 EQUAL, counterpart, equivalent, match, fellow.

**peerage** *n* aristocracy, nobility, upper crust.

**peeress** *n* aristocrat, noble, noblewoman, lady, dame, duchess, marchioness, countess, viscountess, baroness.

**peevish** *adj* petulant, querulous, fractious, fretful, touchy, irritable, cross, grumpy, ratty (*infml*), crotchety, ill-tempered, crabbed, cantankerous, crusty, snappy, short-tempered, surly, sullen, sulky.
**F3** good-tempered.

**peg** *v* 1 FASTEN, secure, fix, attach, join, mark. 2 *peg prices*: control, stabilize, limit, freeze, fix, set.
*n* pin, dowel, hook, knob, marker, post, stake.

**pejorative** *adj* derogatory, disparaging, belittling, slighting, unflattering, uncomplimentary, unpleasant, bad, negative.
**F3** complimentary.

**pelt** *v* 1 THROW, hurl, bombard, shower, assail, batter, beat, hit, strike. 2 POUR, teem, rain cats and dogs (*infml*). 3 RUSH, hurry, charge, belt (*infml*), tear, dash, speed, career.

**pen**[1] *n* fountain-pen, ballpoint, Biro®, felt-tip pen.
*v* write, compose, draft, scribble, jot down.

**pen**[2] *n* enclosure, fold, stall, sty, coop, cage, hutch.
*v* enclose, fence, hedge, hem in, confine, cage, coop, shut up.

**penalize** *v* punish, discipline,

correct, fine, handicap.
**F3** reward.

**penalty** *n* punishment, retribution, fine, forfeit, handicap, disadvantage.
**F3** reward.

**penance** *n* atonement, reparation, punishment, penalty, mortification.

**pendant** *n* medallion, locket, necklace.

**pending** *adj* impending, in the offing, forthcoming, imminent, undecided, in the balance.
**F3** finished, settled.

**penetrate** *v* pierce, stab, prick, puncture, probe, sink, bore, enter, infiltrate, permeate, seep, pervade, suffuse.

**penetrating** *adj* piercing, stinging, biting, incisive, sharp, keen, acute, shrewd, discerning, perceptive, observant, profound, deep, searching, probing.
**F3** blunt.

**penitence** *n* repentance, contrition, remorse, regret, shame, self-reproach.

**penitent** *adj* repentant, contrite, sorry, apologetic, remorseful, regretful, conscience-stricken, shamefaced, humble.
**F3** unrepentant, hard-hearted, callous.

**penniless** *adj* poor, poverty-stricken, impoverished, destitute, bankrupt, ruined, bust, broke (*infml*), stony-broke (*sl*).
**F3** rich, wealthy, affluent.

**pension** *n* annuity, superannuation, allowance, benefit.

**pensive** *adj* thoughtful, reflective, contemplative, meditative, ruminative, absorbed, preoccupied, absent-minded, wistful, solemn, serious, sober.
**F3** carefree.

**pent-up** *adj* repressed, inhibited, restrained, bottled-up, suppressed, stifled.

**people** *n* persons, individuals, humans, human beings, mankind,

humanity, folk, public, general public, populace, rank and file, population, inhabitants, citizens, community, society, race, nation.
*v* populate, inhabit, occupy, settle, colonize.

**pep** (*infml*) *n* energy, vigour, verve, spirit, vitality, liveliness, get-up-and-go (*infml*), exuberance, high spirits.

**pep up** (*infml*) invigorate, vitalize, liven up, quicken, stimulate, excite, exhilarate, inspire.
**Ea** tone down.

**perceive** *v* **1** SEE, discern, make out, detect, discover, spot, catch sight of, notice, observe, view, remark, note, distinguish, recognize. **2** SENSE, feel, apprehend, learn, realize, appreciate, be aware of, know, grasp, understand, gather, deduce, conclude.

**perceptible** *adj* perceivable, discernible, detectable, appreciable, distinguishable, observable, noticeable, obvious, evident, conspicuous, clear, plain, apparent, visible.
**Ea** imperceptible, inconspicuous.

**perception** *n* sense, feeling, impression, idea, conception, apprehension, awareness, consciousness, observation, recognition, grasp, understanding, insight, discernment, taste.

**perceptive** *adj* discerning, observant, sensitive, responsive, aware, alert, quick, sharp, astute, shrewd.
**Ea** unobservant.

**perch** *v* land, alight, settle, sit, roost, balance, rest.

**percolate** *v* filter, strain, seep, ooze, leak, drip, penetrate, permeate, pervade.

**peremptory** *adj* imperious, commanding, dictatorial, autocratic, authoritative, assertive, high-handed, overbearing, domineering, bossy (*infml*), abrupt, curt, summary,

arbitrary.

**perennial** *adj* lasting, enduring, everlasting, eternal, immortal, undying, imperishable, unceasing, incessant, never-ending, constant, continual, uninterrupted, perpetual, persistent, unfailing.

**perfect** *adj* **1** FAULTLESS, impeccable, flawless, immaculate, spotless, blameless, pure, superb, excellent, matchless, incomparable. **2** EXACT, precise, accurate, right, correct, true. **3** IDEAL, model, exemplary, ultimate, consummate, expert, accomplished, experienced, skilful. **4** *perfect strangers*: utter, absolute, sheer, complete, entire, total.
**Ea 1** imperfect, flawed, blemished. **2** inaccurate, wrong. **3** inexperienced, unskilled.
*v* fulfil, consummate, complete, finish, polish, refine, elaborate.
**Ea** spoil, mar.

**perfection** *n* faultlessness, flawlessness, excellence, superiority, ideal, model, paragon, crown, pinnacle, acme, consummation, completion.
**Ea** imperfection, flaw.

**perfectionist** *n* idealist, purist, pedant, stickler.

**perfectly** *adv* **1** UTTERLY, absolutely, quite, thoroughly, completely, entirely, wholly, totally, fully. **2** FAULTLESSLY, flawlessly, impeccably, ideally, exactly, correctly.
**Ea 1** partially. **2** imperfectly, badly.

**perforate** *v* hole, punch, drill, bore, pierce, prick, stab, puncture, penetrate.

**perforation** *n* hole, bore, prick, puncture, dotted line.

**perform** *v* **1** DO, carry out, execute, discharge, fulfil, satisfy, complete, achieve, accomplish, bring off, pull off, effect, bring about. **2** *perform a play*: stage, put on, present, enact,

represent, act, play, appear as.
**3** FUNCTION, work, operate, behave,
produce.

**performance** *n* **1** SHOW, act, play,
appearance, gig (*sl*), presentation,
production, interpretation, rendition,
representation, portrayal, acting.
**2** ACTION, deed, doing, carrying out,
execution, implementation,
discharge, fulfilment, completion,
achievement, accomplishment.
**3** FUNCTIONING, operation,
behaviour, conduct.

---

*Types of performance include*: act,
audition, benefit, box-office hit,
bomb (*North Amer. colloq.*), charity
concert, commandperformance,
concert, début, dress rehearsal, dry
run, encore, entertainment,
exhibition, farewell performance, first
house, firstnight, flop (*colloq.*), full
house, gala night, gig, last night, last
night at the Proms, matinée, one-
night stand, opening night, play, pop
concert, première, preview,
production, readthrough, recital,
rehearsal, rendition, runthrough,
second house, sell-out, shortrun,
show, sketch, smash hit (*colloq.*),
sneak preview, theatre, turn. *see also*
**theatrical**.

---

**performer** *n* actor, actress, player,
artiste, entertainer.
**perfume** *n* scent, fragrance, smell,
odour, aroma, bouquet, sweetness,
balm, essence, cologne, toilet water,
incense.
**perhaps** *adv* maybe, possibly,
conceivably, feasibly.
**peril** *n* danger, hazard, risk,
jeopardy, uncertainty, insecurity,
threat, menace.
**E3** safety, security.
**perilous** *adj* dangerous, unsafe,
hazardous, risky, chancy, precarious,
insecure, unsure, vulnerable,
exposed, menacing, threatening, dire.

**E3** safe, secure.
**perimeter** *n* circumference, edge,
border, boundary, frontier, limit,
bounds, confines, fringe, margin,
periphery.
**E3** middle, centre, heart.
**period** *n* era, epoch, age, generation,
date, years, time, term, season, stage,
phase, stretch, turn, session, interval,
space, span, spell, cycle.
**periodic** *adj* occasional, infrequent,
sporadic, intermittent, recurrent,
repeated, regular, periodical,
seasonal.
**periodical** *n* magazine, journal,
publication, weekly, monthly,
quarterly.
**peripheral** *adj* **1** MINOR, secondary,
incidental, unimportant, irrelevant,
unnecessary, marginal, borderline,
surface, superficial. **2** OUTLYING,
outer, outermost.
**E3** **1** major, crucial. **2** central.
**perish** *v* rot, decay, decompose,
disintegrate, crumble, collapse, fall,
die, expire, pass away.
**perishable** *adj* destructible,
biodegradable, decomposable, short-
lived.
**E3** imperishable, durable.
**perk** (*infml*) *n* perquisite, fringe
benefit, benefit, bonus, dividend,
gratuity, tip, extra, plus (*infml*).
**perk up** (*infml*) brighten, cheer up,
buck up (*infml*), revive, liven up, pep up
(*infml*), rally, recover, improve, look
up.
**permanence** *n* fixedness, stability,
imperishability, perpetuity,
constancy, endurance, durability.
**E3** impermanence, transience.
**permanent** *adj* fixed, stable,
unchanging, imperishable,
indestructible, unfading, eternal,
everlasting, lifelong, perpetual,
constant, steadfast, perennial, long-
lasting, lasting, enduring, durable.
**E3** temporary, ephemeral, fleeting.
**permeable** *adj* porous, absorbent,

absorptive, penetrable.
🔄 impermeable, watertight.

**permeate** v pass through, soak through, filter through, seep through, penetrate, infiltrate, pervade, imbue, saturate, impregnate, fill.

**permissible** adj permitted, allowable, allowed, admissible, all right, acceptable, proper, authorized, sanctioned, lawful, legal, legitimate.
🔄 prohibited, banned, forbidden.

**permission** n consent, assent, agreement, approval, go-ahead, green light (infml), authorization, sanction, leave, warrant, permit, licence, dispensation, freedom, liberty.
🔄 prohibition.

**permissive** adj liberal, broad-minded, tolerant, forbearing, lenient, easy-going (infml), indulgent, overindulgent, lax, free.
🔄 strict, rigid.

**permit** v allow, let, consent, agree, admit, grant, authorize, sanction, warrant, license.
🔄 prohibit, forbid.
n pass, passport, visa, licence, warrant, authorization, sanction, permission.
🔄 prohibition.

**perpendicular** adj vertical, upright, erect, straight, sheer, plumb.
🔄 horizontal.

**perpetrate** v commit, carry out, execute, do, perform, inflict, wreak.

**perpetual** adj eternal, everlasting, infinite, endless, unending, never-ending, interminable, ceaseless, unceasing, incessant, continuous, uninterrupted, constant, persistent, continual, repeated, recurrent, perennial, permanent, lasting, enduring, abiding, unchanging.
🔄 intermittent, temporary, ephemeral, transient.

**perpetuate** v continue, keep up, maintain, preserve, keep alive, immortalize, commemorate.

**perplex** v puzzle, baffle, mystify, stump, confuse, muddle, confound, bewilder, dumbfound.

**persecute** v hound, pursue, hunt, bother, worry, annoy, pester, harass, molest, abuse, ill-treat, maltreat, oppress, tyrannize, victimize, martyr, distress, afflict, torment, torture, crucify.
🔄 pamper, spoil.

**persecution** n harassment, molestation, abuse, maltreatment, discrimination, oppression, subjugation, suppression, tyranny, punishment, torture, martyrdom.

**perseverance** n persistence, determination, resolution, doggedness, tenacity, diligence, assiduity, dedication, commitment, constancy, steadfastness, stamina, endurance, indefatigability.

**persevere** v continue, carry on, stick at it (infml), keep going, soldier on, persist, plug away (infml), remain, stand firm, stand fast, hold on, hang on.
🔄 give up, stop, discontinue.

**persist** v remain, linger, last, endure, abide, continue, carry on, keep at it, persevere, insist.
🔄 desist, stop.

**persistent** adj **1** INCESSANT, endless, never-ending, interminable, continuous, unrelenting, relentless, unremitting, constant, steady, continual, repeated, perpetual, lasting, enduring. **2** persistent effort: persevering, determined, resolute, dogged, tenacious, stubborn, obstinate, steadfast, zealous, tireless, unflagging, indefatigable.

**person** n individual, being, human being, human, man, woman, body, soul, character, type.

**personal** adj own, private, confidential, intimate, special, particular, individual, exclusive, idiosyncratic, distinctive.
🔄 public, general, universal.

**personality** n **1** CHARACTER, nature, disposition, temperament, individuality, psyche, traits, make-up, charm, charisma, magnetism. **2** CELEBRITY, notable, personage, public figure, VIP (infml), star.

**personify** v embody, epitomize, typify, exemplify, symbolize, represent, mirror.

**personnel** n staff, workforce, workers, employees, crew, human resources, manpower, people, members.

**perspective** n aspect, angle, slant, attitude, standpoint, viewpoint, point of view, view, vista, scene, prospect, outlook, proportion, relation.

**perspiration** n sweat, secretion, moisture, wetness.

**perspire** v sweat, exude, secrete, swelter, drip.

**persuade** v coax, prevail upon, lean on, cajole, wheedle, inveigle, talk into, induce, bring round, win over, convince, convert, sway, influence, lead on, incite, prompt, urge.
**E3** dissuade, deter, discourage.

**persuasion** n **1** COAXING, cajolery, wheedling, inducement, enticement, pull, power, influence, conviction, conversion. **2** OPINION, school (of thought), party, faction, side, conviction, faith, belief, denomination, sect.

**persuasive** adj convincing, plausible, cogent, sound, valid, influential, forceful, weighty, effective, telling, potent, compelling, moving, touching.
**E3** unconvincing.

**pertinent** adj appropriate, suitable, fitting, apt, apposite, relevant, to the point, material, applicable.
**E3** inappropriate, unsuitable, irrelevant.

**perturb** v disturb, bother, trouble, upset, worry, alarm, disconcert, unsettle, discompose, ruffle, fluster, agitate, vex.

**E3** reassure, compose.

**peruse** v study, pore over, read, browse, look through, scan, scrutinize, examine, inspect, check.

**pervade** v affect, penetrate, permeate, percolate, charge, fill, imbue, infuse, suffuse, saturate, impregnate.

**pervasive** adj prevalent, common, extensive, widespread, general, universal, inescapable, omnipresent, ubiquitous.

**perverse** adj contrary, wayward, wrong-headed, wilful, headstrong, stubborn, obstinate, unyielding, intransigent, disobedient, rebellious, troublesome, unmanageable, ill-tempered, cantankerous, unreasonable, incorrect, improper.
**E3** obliging, co-operative, reasonable.

**perversion** n **1** CORRUPTION, depravity, debauchery, immorality, vice, wickedness, deviance, kinkiness (infml), abnormality. **2** TWISTING, distortion, misrepresentation, travesty, misinterpretation, aberration, deviation, misuse, misapplication.

**pervert** v **1** pervert the truth: twist, warp, distort, misrepresent, falsify, garble, misinterpret. **2** CORRUPT, lead astray, deprave, debauch, debase, degrade, abuse, misuse, misapply.
n deviant, debauchee, degenerate, weirdo (infml).

**perverted** adj twisted, warped, distorted, deviant, kinky (infml), unnatural, abnormal, unhealthy, corrupt, depraved, debauched, debased, immoral, evil, wicked.
**E3** natural, normal.

**pessimistic** adj negative, cynical, fatalistic, defeatist, resigned, hopeless, despairing, despondent, dejected, downhearted, glum, morose, melancholy, depressed, dismal, gloomy, bleak.
**E3** optimistic.

**pest** n nuisance, bother, annoyance, irritation, vexation, trial, curse, scourge, bane, blight, bug.

**pester** v nag, badger, hound, hassle (*infml*), harass, plague, torment, provoke, worry, bother, disturb, annoy, irritate, pick on, get at (*infml*).

**pet** n favourite, darling, idol, treasure, jewel.
adj favourite, favoured, preferred, dearest, cherished, special, particular, personal.
v stroke, caress, fondle, cuddle, kiss, neck (*sl*), snog (*sl*).

**peter out** dwindle, taper off, fade, wane, ebb, fail, cease, stop.

**petition** n appeal, round robin, application, request, solicitation, plea, entreaty, prayer, supplication, invocation.
v appeal, call upon, ask, crave, solicit, bid, urge, press, implore, beg, plead, entreat, beseech, supplicate, pray.

**petrify** v terrify, horrify, appal, paralyse, numb, stun, dumbfound.

**petty** adj 1 MINOR, unimportant, insignificant, trivial, secondary, lesser, small, little, slight, trifling, paltry, inconsiderable, negligible. 2 SMALL-MINDED, mean, ungenerous, grudging, spiteful.
**Ea** 1 important, significant. 2 generous.

**petulant** adj fretful, peevish, cross, irritable, snappish, bad-tempered, ill-humoured, moody, sullen, sulky, sour, ungracious.

**phantom** n ghost, spectre, spirit, apparition, vision, hallucination, illusion, figment.

**phase** n stage, step, time, period, spell, season, chapter, position, point, aspect, state, condition.
**phase out** wind down, run down, ease off, taper off, eliminate, dispose of, get rid of, remove, withdraw, close, terminate.

**phenomenal** adj marvellous, sensational, stupendous, amazing, remarkable, extraordinary, exceptional, unusual, unbelievable, incredible.

**phenomenon** n 1 OCCURRENCE, happening, event, incident, episode, fact, appearance, sight. 2 WONDER, marvel, miracle, prodigy, rarity, curiosity, spectacle, sensation.

**philanthropic** adj humanitarian, public-spirited, altruistic, unselfish, benevolent, kind, charitable, alms-giving, generous, liberal, open-handed.
**Ea** misanthropic.

**philanthropist** n humanitarian, benefactor, patron, sponsor, giver, donor, contributor, altruist.
**Ea** misanthrope.

**philanthropy** n humanitarianism, public-spiritedness, altruism, unselfishness, benevolence, kind-heartedness, charity, alms-giving, patronage, generosity, liberality, open-handedness.
**Ea** misanthropy.

**philosophical** adj 1 *a philosophical discussion*: metaphysical, abstract, theoretical, analytical, rational, logical, erudite, learned, wise, thoughtful. 2 RESIGNED, patient, stoical, unruffled, calm, composed.

**philosophy** n metaphysics, rationalism, reason, logic, thought, thinking, wisdom, knowledge, ideology, world-view, doctrine, beliefs, convictions, values, principles, attitude, viewpoint.

*Philosophical terms include*: absolutism, aesthetics, agnosticism, altruism, antinomianism, a posteriori, a priori, asceticism, atheism, atomism, behaviourism, deduction, deism, deontology, determinism, dialectical materialism, dogmatism, dualism, egoism, empiricism, entailment, Epicureanism, epistemology, ethics, existentialism, fatalism, hedonism, historicism, humanism, idealism, identity, induction, instrumentalism, interactionism, intuition, jurisprudence, libertarianism, logic, logical positivism, materialism, metaphysics, monism, naturalism, nihilism, nominalism, objectivism, ontology, pantheism, phenomenalism, phenomenology, positivism, pragmatism, prescriptivism, rationalism, realism, reductionism, relativism, scepticism, scholasticism, sensationalism, sense data, solipsism, stoicism, structuralism, subjectivism, substance, syllogism, teleology, theism, transcendentalism, utilitarianism.

**phlegmatic** *adj* placid, stolid, impassive, unemotional, unconcerned, indifferent, matter-of-fact, stoical.
**≠** emotional, passionate.

**phobia** *n* fear, terror, dread, anxiety, neurosis, obsession, hang-up (*infml*), thing (*infml*), aversion, dislike, hatred, horror, loathing, revulsion, repulsion.
**≠** love, liking.

*Phobias (by name of fear) include:*
zoophobia (*animals*), apiphobia (*bees*), ailurophobia (*cats*), necrophobia (*corpses*), scotophobia (*darkness*), cynophobia (*dogs*), claustrophobia (*enclosed places*), panphobia (*everything*), pyrophobia (*fire*), xenophobia (*foreigners*), phasmophobia (*ghosts*), acrophobia (*high places*), hippophobia (*horses*), entomophobia (*insects*), astraphobia (*lightning*), autophobia (*loneliness*), agoraphobia (*open spaces*), toxiphobia (*poison*), herpetophobia (*reptiles*), ophiophobia (*snakes*), tachophobia (*speed*), arachnophobia (*spiders*), triskaidekaphobia (*thirteen*), brontophobia (*thunder*), hydrophobia (*water*).

**phone** *v* telephone, ring (up), call (up), dial, contact, get in touch, give a buzz (*infml*), give a tinkle (*infml*).

**phoney** (*infml*) *adj* fake, counterfeit, forged, bogus, trick, false, spurious, assumed, affected, put-on, sham, pseudo, imitation.
**≠** real, genuine.

**photocopy** *v* copy, duplicate, Photostat®, Xerox®, print, run off.
*n* copy, duplicate, Photostat®, Xerox®.

**photograph** *n* photo, snap, snapshot, print, shot, slide, transparency, picture, image, likeness.
*v* snap, take, film, shoot, video, record.

*Photographic accessories include:* air-shutter release, battery, cable release, camera bag, eye-cup, eyepiece magnifier, film, cartridge film, cassette film, disc film, film pack, filter, colour filter, heat filter, polarizing filter, skylight filter, flashbulb, flashcube, flashgun, flash unit, hot shoe, lens, afocal lens, auxiliary lens, close-up lens, fish-eye lens, macro lens, supplementary lens, telephoto lens, teleconverter, wide-angle lens, zoom lens, lens cap, lens hood, lens shield, light meter, exposure meter, spot meter, diffuser, barn doors, honeycomb diffuser, parabolic reflector, snoot, slide mount, viewfinder, right-angle finder, camcorder battery discharger/charger/tester, cassette adaptor, remote control, tele-cine converter, video editor, video light, video mixer. *see also* **camera**.

*Photographic equipment includes:*

camera, stand, tripod, flash umbrella, boom arm; developer bath, developing tank, dry mounting press, easel, enlarger, enlarger timer, film-drying cabinet, fixing bath, focus magnifier, light-box, negative carrier, print washer, contact printer, print-drying rack, paper drier, safelight, stop bath, Vertoscope®, viewer; slide viewer, slide projector, film projector, screen.

**phrase** *n* construction, clause, idiom, expression, saying, utterance, remark.

*v* word, formulate, frame, couch, present, put, express, say, utter, pronounce.

**physical** *adj* bodily, corporeal, fleshy, incarnate, mortal, earthly, material, concrete, solid, substantial, tangible, visible, real, actual.

🖙 mental, spiritual.

**physics**

*Terms used in physics include*: absolute zero, acceleration, acoustics, alpha particles, analogue signal, applied physics, Archimedes principle, area, atom, beta particles, Big Bang theory, boiling point, bubble-chamber, capillary action, centre of gravity, centre of mass, centrifugal force, chain reaction, charge, charged particle, circuit, circuit-breaker, couple, critical mass, cryogenics, density, diffraction, digital, dynamics, efficiency, elasticity, electric current, electric discharge, electricity, electrodynamics, electromagnetic spectrum, electromagnetic waves, electron, energy, engine, entropy, equation, equilibrium, evaporation, field, flash point, force, formula, freezing point, frequency, friction, fundamental constant, gamma ray, gas, gate, grand united theory (GUT), gravity, half-life, heat, heavy water, hydraulics, hydrodynamics, hydrostatics, incandescence, indeterminacy principle, inertia, infrared, interference, ion, kinetic energy, kinetic theory, Kelvin effect, laser (light amplification by stimulated emission of radiation), latent heat, law, laws of motion, laws of reflection, laws of refraction, laws of thermodynamics, lens, lever, light, light emission, light intensity, light source, liquid, longitudinal wave, luminescence, Mach number, magnetic field, magnetism, mass, mechanics, microwaves, mirror, Mohs scale, molecule, moment, momentum, motion, neutron, nuclear, nuclear fission, nuclear fusion, nuclear physics, nucleus, optical centre, optics, oscillation, parallel motion, particle, periodic law, perpetual motion, phonon, photon, photosensitivity, polarity, potential energy, power, pressure, principle, process, proton, quantum chromodynamics (QCD), quantum electrodynamics (QED), quantum mechanics, quantum theory, quark, radiation, radioactive element, radioactivity, radioisotope, radio wave, ratio, reflection, refraction, relativity, resistance, resonance, rule, semiconductor, sensitivity, separation, SI unit, sound, sound wave, specific gravity, specific heat capacity, spectroscopy, spectrum, speed, states of matter, statics, substance, superstring theory, supersymmetry, surface tension, temperature, tension, theory, theory of relativity, thermodynamics, Thomson effect, transverse wave, ultrasound, ultraviolet, uncertainty principle, velocity, visible spectrum, viscosity, volume, wave, wave property, weight, white heat, work, X-ray. *see also* **atom**.

**physician** *n* doctor, medical

practitioner, medic (*infml*), general practitioner, GP, houseman, intern, registrar, consultant, specialist, healer.

**physique** *n* body, figure, shape, form, build, frame, structure, constitution, make-up.

**pick** *v* 1 SELECT, choose, opt for, decide on, settle on, single out. 2 GATHER, collect, pluck, harvest, cull.
*n* 1 CHOICE, selection, option, decision, preference. 2 BEST, cream, flower, élite, elect.

**pick on** bully, torment, persecute, nag, get at (*infml*), needle (*infml*), bait.

**pick out** notice, perceive, recognize, distinguish, tell apart, separate, single out, hand-pick, choose, select.

**pick up** 1 LIFT, raise, hoist. 2 *I'll pick you up at eight*: call for, fetch, collect. 3 LEARN, master, grasp, gather. 4 IMPROVE, rally, recover, perk up (*infml*). 5 BUY, purchase. 6 OBTAIN, acquire, gain. 7 *pick up an infection*: catch, contract, get.

**picket** *n* picketer, protester, demonstrator, striker.
*v* protest, demonstrate, boycott, blockade, enclose, surround.

**pickle** *v* preserve, conserve, souse, marinade, steep, cure, salt.

**pictorial** *adj* graphic, diagrammatic, schematic, representational, vivid, striking, expressive, illustrated, picturesque, scenic.

**picture** *n* 1 PAINTING, portrait, landscape, drawing, sketch, illustration, engraving, photograph, print, representation, likeness, image, effigy. 2 DEPICTION, portrayal, description, account, report, impression. 3 *the picture of health*: embodiment, personification, epitome, archetype, essence. 4 FILM, movie (*infml*), motion picture.
*v* 1 IMAGINE, envisage, envision, conceive, visualize, see. 2 DEPICT,

describe, represent, show, portray, draw, sketch, paint, photograph, illustrate.

**picturesque** *adj* 1 ATTRACTIVE, beautiful, pretty, charming, quaint, idyllic, scenic. 2 DESCRIPTIVE, graphic, vivid, colourful, striking.
**E∃** 1 unattractive. 2 dull.

**piece** *n* 1 FRAGMENT, bit, scrap, morsel, mouthful, bite, lump, chunk, slice, sliver, snippet, shred, offcut, sample, component, constituent, element, part, segment, section, division, fraction, share, portion, quantity. 2 ARTICLE, item, study, work, composition, creation, specimen, example.

**pier** *n* 1 JETTY, breakwater, landing-stage, quay, wharf. 2 SUPPORT, upright, pillar, post.

**pierce** *v* penetrate, enter, stick into, puncture, drill, bore, probe, perforate, punch, prick, stab, lance, bayonet, run through, spear, skewer, spike, impale, transfix.

**piercing** *adj* 1 *a piercing cry*: shrill, high-pitched, loud, ear-splitting, sharp. 2 PENETRATING, probing, searching. 3 COLD, bitter, raw, biting, keen, fierce, severe, wintry, frosty, freezing. 4 PAINFUL, agonizing, excruciating, stabbing, lacerating.

**piety** *n* piousness, devoutness, godliness, saintliness, holiness, sanctity, religion, faith, devotion, reverence.
**E∃** impiety, irreligion.

**pig** *n* swine, hog, sow, boar, animal, beast, brute, glutton, gourmand.

**pigeonhole** *n* compartment, niche, slot, cubby-hole, cubicle, locker, box, place, section, class, category, classification.
*v* compartmentalize, label, classify, sort, file, catalogue, alphabetize, shelve, defer.

**pigment** *n* colour, hue, tint, dye, stain, paint, colouring, tincture.

**pile**[1] n  stack, heap, mound, mountain, mass, accumulation, collection, assortment, hoard, stockpile.
v  stack, heap, mass, amass, accumulate, build up, gather, assemble, collect, hoard, stockpile, store, load, pack, jam, crush, crowd, flock, flood, stream, rush, charge.

**pile**[2] n  post, column, upright, support, bar, beam, foundation.

**pile**[3] n  nap, shag, plush, fur, hair, fuzz, down.

**pilfer** v  steal, pinch (infml), nick (infml), knock off (sl), filch, lift, shoplift, rob, thieve.

**pilgrim** n  crusader, traveller, wanderer.

**pilgrimage** n  crusade, mission, expedition, journey, trip, tour.

**pill** n  tablet, capsule, pellet.

**pillar** n  column, shaft, post, mast, pier, upright, pile, support, prop, mainstay, bastion, tower of strength.

**pilot** n  1 FLYER, aviator, airman. 2 NAVIGATOR, steersman, helmsman, coxswain, captain, leader, director, guide.
v  fly, drive, steer, direct, control, handle, manage, operate, run, conduct, lead, guide, navigate.
adj  experimental, trial, test, model.

**pimple** n  spot, zit (sl), blackhead, boil, swelling.

**pin** v  tack, nail, fix, affix, attach, join, staple, clip, fasten, secure, hold down, restrain, immobilize.
n  tack, nail, screw, spike, rivet, bolt, peg, fastener, clip, staple, brooch.
**pin down** 1 PINPOINT, identify, determine, specify. 2 FORCE, make, press, pressurize.

**pinch** v  1 SQUEEZE, compress, crush, press, tweak, nip, hurt, grip, grasp. 2 (infml) STEAL, nick, pilfer, filch, snatch.
n  1 SQUEEZE, tweak, nip. 2 DASH, soupçon, taste, bit, speck, jot, mite. 3 EMERGENCY, crisis, predicament,

difficulty, hardship, pressure, stress.

**pine** v  long, yearn, ache, sigh, grieve, mourn, wish, desire, crave, hanker, hunger, thirst.

**pinnacle** n  1 PEAK, summit, top, cap, crown, crest, apex, vertex, acme, zenith, height, eminence. 2 SPIRE, steeple, turret, pyramid, cone, obelisk, needle.

**pinpoint** v  identify, spot, distinguish, locate, place, home in on, zero in on (infml), pin down, determine, specify, define.

**pioneer** n  colonist, settler, frontiersman, frontierswoman, explorer, developer, pathfinder, trailblazer, leader, innovator, inventor, discoverer, founder.
v  invent, discover, originate, create, initiate, instigate, begin, start, launch, institute, found, establish, set up, develop, open up.

**pious** adj  1 DEVOUT, godly, saintly, holy, spiritual, religious, reverent, good, virtuous, righteous, moral. 2 SANCTIMONIOUS, holier-than-thou, self-righteous, goody-goody (infml), hypocritical.
**F3** 1 impious, irreligious, irreverent.

**pipe** n  tube, hose, piping, tubing, pipeline, line, main, flue, duct, conduit, channel, passage, conveyor.
v  1 CHANNEL, funnel, siphon, carry, convey, conduct, transmit, supply, deliver. 2 WHISTLE, chirp, tweet, cheep, peep, twitter, sing, warble, trill, play, sound.

**piquant** adj  1 piquant sauce: spicy, tangy, savoury, salty, peppery, pungent, sharp, biting, stinging. 2 LIVELY, spirited, stimulating, provocative, interesting, sparkling.
**F3** 1 bland, insipid. 2 dull, banal.

**pique** n  annoyance, irritation, vexation, displeasure, offence, huff (infml), resentment, grudge.

**piqued** adj  annoyed, irritated, vexed, riled, angry, displeased, offended, miffed (infml), peeved (*infml*), put out, resentful.

**pit** *n* mine, coalmine, excavation, trench, ditch, hollow, depression, indentation, dent, hole, cavity, crater, pothole, gulf, chasm, abyss.

**pitch** *v* **1** THROW, fling, toss, chuck (*infml*), lob, bowl, hurl, heave, sling, fire, launch, aim, direct. **2** PLUNGE, dive, plummet, drop, fall headlong, tumble, lurch, roll, wallow. **3** *pitch camp*: erect, put up, set up, place, station, settle, plant, fix.
*n* **1** *cricket pitch*: ground, field, playing-field, arena, stadium.
**2** SOUND, tone, timbre, modulation, frequency, level. **3** GRADIENT, incline, slope, tilt, angle, degree, steepness.

**piteous** *adj* poignant, moving, touching, distressing, heart-rending, plaintive, mournful, sad, sorrowful, woeful, wretched, pitiful, pitiable, pathetic.

**pitfall** *n* danger, peril, hazard, trap, snare, stumbling-block, catch, snag, drawback, difficulty.

**pith** *n* importance, significance, moment, weight, value, consequence, substance, matter, marrow, meat, gist, essence, crux, nub, heart, core, kernel.

**pithy** *adj* succinct, concise, compact, terse, short, brief, pointed, trenchant, forceful, cogent, telling.
**E3** wordy, verbose.

**pitiful** *adj* **1** CONTEMPTIBLE, despicable, low, mean, vile, shabby, deplorable, lamentable, woeful, inadequate, hopeless, pathetic (*infml*), insignificant, paltry, worthless. **2** PITEOUS, doleful, mournful, distressing, heart-rending, pathetic, pitiable, sad, miserable, wretched, poor, sorry.

**pitiless** *adj* merciless, cold-hearted, unsympathetic, unfeeling, uncaring, hard-hearted, callous, cruel, inhuman, brutal, cold-blooded, ruthless, relentless, unremitting, inexorable, harsh.
**E3** merciful, compassionate, kind, gentle.

**pittance** *n* modicum, crumb, drop (in the ocean), chicken-feed (*infml*), peanuts (*sl*), trifle.

**pitted** *adj* dented, holey, potholed, pockmarked, blemished, scarred, marked, notched, indented, rough.

**pity** *n* **1** SYMPATHY, commiseration, regret, understanding, fellow-feeling, compassion, kindness, tenderness, mercy, forbearance. **2** *what a pity!*: shame, misfortune, bad luck.
**E3** **1** cruelty, anger, scorn.
*v* feel sorry for, feel for, sympathize with, commiserate with, grieve for, weep for.

**pivot** *n* axis, hinge, axle, spindle, kingpin, linchpin, swivel, hub, focal point, centre, heart.
*v* **1** SWIVEL, turn, spin, revolve, rotate, swing. **2** DEPEND, rely, hinge, hang, lie.

**placard** *n* poster, bill, notice, sign, advertisement.

**placate** *v* appease, pacify, conciliate, mollify, calm, assuage, soothe, lull, quiet.
**E3** anger, enrage, incense, infuriate.

**place** *n* **1** SITE, locale, venue, location, situation, spot, point, position, seat, space, room. **2** CITY, town, village, locality, neighbourhood, district, area, region. **3** BUILDING, property, dwelling, residence, house, flat, apartment, home.
*v* put, set, plant, fix, position, locate, situate, rest, settle, lay, stand, deposit, leave.

**in place of** instead of, in lieu of, as a replacement for, as a substitute for, as an alternative to.

**out of place** inappropriate, unsuitable, unfitting, unbecoming, unseemly.

**take place** happen, occur, come about.

**placid** *adj* calm, composed, unruffled, untroubled, cool, self-

possessed, level-headed,
imperturbable, mild, gentle, equable,
even-tempered, serene, tranquil, still,
quiet, peaceful, restful.
**Ea** excitable, agitated, disturbed.

**plagiarize** v crib, copy, reproduce,
imitate, counterfeit, pirate, infringe
copyright, poach, steal, lift,
appropriate, borrow.

**plague** n **1** PESTILENCE, epidemic,
disease, infection, contagion,
infestation. **2** NUISANCE, annoyance,
curse, scourge, trial, affliction,
torment, calamity.
v annoy, vex, bother, disturb, trouble,
distress, upset, pester, harass, hound,
haunt, bedevil, afflict, torment,
torture, persecute.

**plain** adj **1** plain cookery: ordinary,
basic, simple, unpretentious, modest,
unadorned, unelaborate, restrained.
**2** OBVIOUS, evident, patent, clear,
understandable, apparent, visible,
unmistakable. **3** FRANK, candid,
blunt, outspoken, direct, forthright,
straightforward, unambiguous, plain-
spoken, open, honest, truthful.
**4** UNATTRACTIVE, ugly,
unprepossessing, unlovely. **5** plain
fabric: unpatterned, unvariegated,
uncoloured, self-coloured.
**Ea 1** fancy, elaborate. **2** unclear,
obscure. **3** devious, deceitful.
**4** attractive, good-looking.
**5** patterned.
n grassland, prairie, steppe, lowland,
flat, plateau, tableland.

**plaintive** adj doleful, mournful,
melancholy, wistful, sad, sorrowful,
grief-stricken, piteous, heart-rending,
high-pitched.

**plan** n **1** BLUEPRINT, layout,
diagram, chart, map, drawing,
sketch, representation, design.
**2** IDEA, suggestion, proposal,
proposition, project, scheme, plot,
system, method, procedure, strategy,
programme, schedule, scenario.
v **1** PLOT, scheme, design, invent,

devise, contrive, formulate, frame,
draft, outline, prepare, organize,
arrange. **2** AIM, intend, propose,
contemplate, envisage, foresee.

**planet**

> *Planets within the Earth's solar
> system (nearest the sun shown first)
> are:* Mercury, Venus, Earth, Mars,
> Jupiter, Saturn, Uranus, Neptune,
> Pluto.

**plant**

> *Plants include:* annual, biennial,
> perennial, herbaceous plant,
> evergreen, succulent, cultivar, hybrid,
> house plant, pot plant; flower, herb,
> shrub, bush, tree, vegetable, grass,
> vine, weed, cereal, wild flower, air-
> plant, water-plant, cactus, fern, moss,
> algae, lichen, fungus; bulb, corm,
> seedling, sapling, bush, climber. *see
> also* **flower**; **shrub**.

n factory, works, foundry, mill, shop,
yard, workshop, machinery,
apparatus, equipment, gear.
v **1** SOW, seed, bury, transplant. **2**
INSERT, put, place, set, fix, lodge,
root, settle, found, establish.

**plaster** n sticking-plaster, dressing,
bandage, plaster of Paris, mortar,
stucco.
v daub, smear, coat, cover, spread.

**plastic** adj soft, pliable, flexible,
supple, malleable, mouldable,
ductile, receptive, impressionable,
manageable.
**Ea** rigid, inflexible.

> *Types of plastic include:* Bakelite®,
> Biopol®, celluloid®, epoxy resin,
> Perspex®, phenolic resin, plexiglass,
> polyester, polyethylene, polymethyl
> methacrylate, polynorbornene,
> polypropylene, polystyrene,
> polythene, polyurethane, PTFE
> (polytetrafluoroethylene), PVC

**plate** 400

(polyvinyl chloride), uPVC, silicone, Teflon®, transpolyisoprene, urea formaldehyde, vinyl.

**plate** n 1 DISH, platter, salver, helping, serving, portion. 2 ILLUSTRATION, picture, print, lithograph.
v coat, cover, overlay, veneer, laminate, electroplate, anodize, galvanize, platinize, gild, silver, tin.

**platform** n 1 STAGE, podium, dais, rostrum, stand. 2 POLICY, party line, principles, tenets, manifesto, programme, objectives.

**platitude** n banality, commonplace, truism, cliché, chestnut.

**plausible** adj credible, believable, reasonable, logical, likely, possible, probable, convincing, persuasive, smooth-talking, glib.
Ea implausible, unlikely, improbable.

**play** v 1 AMUSE ONESELF, have fun, enjoy oneself, revel, sport, romp, frolic, caper. 2 PARTICIPATE, take part, join in, compete. 3 *France played Italy*: oppose, vie with, challenge, take on. 4 ACT, perform, portray, represent, impersonate.
Ea 1 work.
n 1 FUN, amusement, entertainment, diversion, recreation, sport, game, hobby, pastime. 2 DRAMA, tragedy, comedy, farce, show, performance. 3 MOVEMENT, action, flexibility, give, leeway, latitude, margin, scope, range, room, space.
Ea 1 work.

**play down** minimize, make light of, gloss over, underplay, understate, undervalue, underestimate.
Ea exaggerate.

**play on** exploit, take advantage of, turn to account, profit by, trade on, capitalize on.

**play up** 1 EXAGGERATE, highlight, spotlight, accentuate, emphasize, stress. 2 MISBEHAVE, malfunction, trouble, bother, annoy, hurt.

**playboy** n philanderer, womanizer, ladies' man, rake, libertine.

**player** n 1 CONTESTANT, competitor, participant, sportsman, sportswoman. 2 PERFORMER, entertainer, artiste, actor, actress, musician, instrumentalist.

**playful** adj sportive, frolicsome, lively, spirited, mischievous, roguish, impish, puckish, kittenish, good-natured, jesting, teasing, humorous, tongue-in-cheek.
Ea serious.

**playwright** n dramatist, scriptwriter, screenwriter.

**plea** n 1 APPEAL, petition, request, entreaty, supplication, prayer, invocation. 2 DEFENCE, justification, excuse, explanation, claim.

**plead** v 1 BEG, implore, beseech, entreat, appeal, petition, ask, request. 2 *plead ignorance*: assert, maintain, claim, allege.

**pleasant** adj agreeable, nice, fine, lovely, delightful, charming, likable, amiable, friendly, affable, good-humoured, cheerful, congenial, enjoyable, amusing, pleasing, gratifying, satisfying, acceptable, welcome, refreshing.
Ea unpleasant, nasty, unfriendly.

**please** v 1 DELIGHT, charm, captivate, entertain, amuse, cheer, gladden, humour, indulge, gratify, satisfy, content, suit. 2 WANT, will, wish, desire, like, prefer, choose, think fit.
Ea 1 displease, annoy, anger, sadden.

**pleased** adj contented, satisfied, gratified, glad, happy, delighted, thrilled, euphoric.
Ea displeased, annoyed.

**pleasing** adj gratifying, satisfying, acceptable, good, pleasant, agreeable, nice, delightful, charming, attractive, engaging, winning.
Ea unpleasant, disagreeable.

**pleasure** n amusement, entertainment, recreation, fun,

**plunder**

enjoyment, gratification, satisfaction, contentment, happiness, joy, delight, comfort, solace.

Fa sorrow, pain, trouble, displeasure.

**pleat** *v* tuck, fold, crease, flute, crimp, gather, pucker.

**pledge** *n* **1** PROMISE, vow, word of honour, oath, bond, covenant, guarantee, warrant, assurance, undertaking. **2** DEPOSIT, security, surety, bail.

*v* promise, vow, swear, contract, engage, undertake, vouch, guarantee, secure.

**plentiful** *adj* ample, abundant, profuse, copious, overflowing, lavish, generous, liberal, bountiful, fruitful, productive.

Fa scarce, scanty, rare.

**plenty** *n* abundance, profusion, plethora, lots (*infml*), loads (*infml*), masses (*infml*), heaps (*infml*), piles (*infml*), stacks (*infml*), enough, sufficiency, quantity, mass, volume, fund, mine, store.

Fa scarcity, lack, want, need.

**pliable** *adj* pliant, flexible, bendable, bendy (*infml*), supple, lithe, malleable, plastic, yielding, adaptable, accommodating, manageable, tractable, docile, compliant, biddable, persuadable, responsive, receptive, impressionable, susceptible.

Fa rigid, inflexible, headstrong.

**plight** *n* predicament, quandary, dilemma, extremity, trouble, difficulty, straits, state, condition, situation, circumstances, case.

**plod** *v* **1** TRUDGE, tramp, stump, lumber, plough through. **2** DRUDGE, labour, toil, grind, slog, persevere, soldier on.

**plot** *n* **1** CONSPIRACY, intrigue, machination, scheme, plan, stratagem. **2** STORY, narrative, subject, theme, storyline, thread, outline, scenario. **3** *plot of land*: patch, tract, area, allotment, lot,

parcel.

*v* **1** CONSPIRE, intrigue, machinate, scheme, hatch, lay, cook up, devise, contrive, plan, project, design, draft. **2** CHART, map, mark, locate, draw, calculate.

**plotter** *n* conspirator, intriguer, machinator, schemer.

**ploy** *n* manoeuvre, stratagem, tactic, move, device, contrivance, scheme, game, trick, artifice, dodge, wile, ruse, subterfuge.

**pluck** *n* courage, bravery, spirit, mettle, nerve (*infml*), guts (*infml*), grit, backbone, fortitude, resolution, determination.

Fa cowardice.

*v* **1** PULL, draw, tug, snatch, pull off, remove, pick, collect, gather, harvest. **2** *pluck a guitar*: pick, twang, strum.

**plucky** *adj* brave, courageous, bold, daring, intrepid, heroic, valiant, spirited.

Fa cowardly, weak, feeble.

**plug** *n* **1** STOPPER, bung, cork, spigot. **2** (*infml*) ADVERTISEMENT, publicity, mention, puff.

*v* **1** STOP (UP), bung, cork, block, choke, close, seal, fill, pack, stuff. **2** (*infml*) ADVERTISE, publicize, promote, push, mention.

**plumb** *adv* **1** VERTICALLY, perpendicularly. **2** PRECISELY, exactly, dead, slap (*infml*), bang (*infml*).

*v* sound, fathom, measure, gauge, penetrate, probe, search, explore.

**plummet** *v* plunge, dive, nose-dive, descend, drop, fall, tumble.

Fa soar.

**plump** *adj* fat, obese, dumpy, tubby, stout, round, rotund, portly, chubby, podgy, fleshy, full, ample, buxom.

Fa thin, skinny.

**plump for** opt for, choose, select, favour, back, support.

**plunder** *v* loot, pillage, ravage, devastate, sack, raid, ransack, rifle, steal, rob, strip.

*n* loot, pillage, booty, swag (*sl*), spoils, pickings, ill-gotten gains, prize.

**plunge** *v* **1** DIVE, jump, nose-dive, swoop, dive-bomb, plummet, descend, go down, sink, drop, fall, pitch, tumble, hurtle, career, charge, dash, rush, tear. **2** IMMERSE, submerge, dip.

*n* dive, jump, swoop, descent, drop, fall, tumble, immersion, submersion.

**ply** *n* layer, fold, thickness, strand, sheet, leaf.

**poach** *v* steal, pilfer, appropriate, trespass, encroach, infringe.

**pocket** *n* pouch, bag, envelope, receptacle, compartment, hollow, cavity.

*adj* small, little, mini (*infml*), concise, compact, portable, miniature.

*v* take, appropriate, help oneself to, lift, pilfer, filch, steal, nick (*infml*), pinch (*infml*).

**pod** *n* shell, husk, case, hull.

**poem**

> *Types of poem include*: ballad, elegy, epic, haiku, idyll, lay, limerick, lyric, madrigal, nursery-rhyme, ode, pastoral, roundelay, sonnet, tanka.

**poet** *n* versifier, rhymer, rhymester, lyricist, bard, minstrel.

**poetic** *adj* poetical, lyrical, moving, artistic, graceful, flowing, metrical, rhythmical, rhyming.
**Ⅎ** prosaic.

**poignant** *adj* moving, touching, affecting, tender, distressing, upsetting, heartbreaking, heart-rending, piteous, pathetic, sad, painful, agonizing.

**point** *n* **1** FEATURE, attribute, aspect, facet, detail, particular, item, subject, topic. **2** *what's the point?*: use, purpose, motive, reason, object, intention, aim, end, goal, objective. **3** ESSENCE, crux, core, pith, gist, thrust, meaning, drift, burden. **4** PLACE, position, situation, location, site, spot. **5** MOMENT, instant, juncture, stage, time, period. **6** DOT, spot, mark, speck, full stop.

*v* **1** *point a gun*: aim, direct, train, level. **2** INDICATE, signal, show, signify, denote, designate.

**point of view** opinion, view, belief, judgement, attitude, position, standpoint, viewpoint, outlook, perspective, approach, angle, slant.

**point out** show, indicate, draw attention to, point to, reveal, identify, specify, mention, bring up, allude to, remind.

**point-blank** *adj* direct, forthright, straightforward, plain, explicit, open, unreserved, blunt, frank, candid.
*adv* directly, forthrightly, straightforwardly, plainly, explicitly, openly, bluntly, frankly, candidly.

**pointed** *adj* sharp, keen, edged, barbed, cutting, incisive, trenchant, biting, penetrating, telling.

**pointer** *n* **1** ARROW, indicator, needle, hand. **2** TIP, recommendation, suggestion, hint, guide, indication, advice, warning, caution.

**pointless** *adj* useless, futile, vain, fruitless, unproductive, unprofitable, worthless, senseless, absurd, meaningless, aimless.
**Ⅎ** useful, profitable, meaningful.

**poise** *n* calmness, composure, self-possession, presence of mind, coolness, equanimity, aplomb, assurance, dignity, elegance, grace, balance, equilibrium.
*v* balance, position, hover, hang, suspend.

**poised** *adj* **1** DIGNIFIED, graceful, calm, composed, unruffled, collected, self-possessed, cool, self-confident, assured. **2** *poised for action*: prepared, ready, set, waiting, expectant.

**poison** *n* toxin, venom, bane, blight, cancer, malignancy, contagion, contamination, corruption.

*v* infect, contaminate, pollute, taint, adulterate, corrupt, deprave, pervert, warp.

**poisonous** *adj* toxic, venomous, lethal, deadly, fatal, mortal, noxious, pernicious, malicious.

**poke** *v* prod, stab, jab, stick, thrust, push, shove, nudge, elbow, dig, butt, hit, punch.

*n* prod, jab, thrust, shove, nudge, dig, butt, punch.

**pole**[1] *n* bar, rod, stick, shaft, spar, upright, post, stake, mast, staff.

**pole**[2] *n* antipode, extremity, extreme, limit.

  **poles apart** irreconcilable, worlds apart, incompatible, like chalk and cheese.

**police** *n* police force, constabulary, the Law (*infml*), the Bill (*sl*), the fuzz (*sl*).

*v* check, control, regulate, monitor, watch, observe, supervise, oversee, patrol, guard, protect, defend, keep the peace.

**policeman, policewoman** *n* officer, constable, PC, cop (*sl*), copper (*infml*), bobby (*infml*).

**policy** *n* **1** CODE OF PRACTICE, rules, guidelines, procedure, method, practice, custom, protocol. **2** COURSE OF ACTION, line, course, plan, programme, scheme, stance, position.

**polish** *v* **1** SHINE, brighten, smooth, rub, buff, burnish, clean, wax. **2** IMPROVE, enhance, brush up, touch up, finish, perfect, refine, cultivate.
  **Ea 1** tarnish, dull.

*n* **1** *a tin of polish*: wax, varnish. **2** SHINE, gloss, sheen, lustre, brightness, brilliance, sparkle, smoothness, finish, glaze, veneer. **3** REFINEMENT, cultivation, class, breeding, sophistication, finesse, style, elegance, grace, poise.
  **Ea 2** dullness. **3** clumsiness.

**polished** *adj* **1** SHINING, shiny,

glossy, lustrous, gleaming, burnished, smooth, glassy, slippery. **2** FAULTLESS, flawless, impeccable, perfect, outstanding, superlative, masterly, expert, professional, skilful, accomplished, perfected. **3** REFINED, cultivated, genteel, well-bred, polite, sophisticated, urbane, suave, elegant, graceful.
  **Ea 1** tarnished. **2** inexpert. **3** gauche.

**polite** *adj* courteous, well-mannered, respectful, civil, well-bred, refined, cultured, gentlemanly, ladylike, gracious, obliging, thoughtful, considerate, tactful, diplomatic.
  **Ea** impolite, discourteous, rude.

**political ideologies**

> *Political ideologies include*:
> absolutism, anarchism,
> authoritarianism, Bolshevism,
> Christian democracy, collectivism,
> communism, conservatism,
> democracy, egalitarianism, fascism,
> federalism, holism, imperialism,
> individualism, liberalism, Maoism,
> Marxism, nationalism, Nazism,
> neocolonialism, neo-fascism, neo-
> nazism, pluralism, republicanism,
> social democracy, socialism,
> syndicalism, Thatcherism, theocracy,
> totalitarianism, unilateralism,
> Trotskyism, Whiggism.

**politician** *n* Member of Parliament, MP, minister, statesman, stateswoman, legislator.

**politics** *n* public affairs, civics, affairs of state, statecraft, government, diplomacy, statesmanship, political science.

> *Terms used in politics include*:
> alliance, apartheid, ballot, bill,
> blockade, cabinet, campaign, civil
> service, coalition, constitution,
> council, coup d'état, détente,
> election, electoral register, ethnic
> cleansing, general election, glasnost,

go to the country, government, green paper, Hansard, judiciary, left wing, lobby, local government, majority, mandate, manifesto, nationalization, parliament, party, party line, perestroika, prime minister's question time, privatization, propaganda, proportional representation, rainbow coalition, referendum, right wing, sanction, shadow cabinet, sovereignty, state, summit, summit conference, term of office, trade union, veto, vote, welfare state, whip, three-line whip, white paper.

*People in politics include*: activist, ambassador, Black Rod, capitalist, Communist, commie (*infml*), comrade, Conservative, Democrat, Deputy Speaker, dictator, dissident, dry (*infml*), extremist, Green, high commissioner, independent, lefty (*infml*), Liberal, Liberal Democrat, loyalist, Marxist, Marxist-Leninist, member of parliament, minister, moderate, MP, party chairman, party member, party worker, pinko (*infml*), politician, premier, president, prime minister, radical, red (*infml*), Republican, revolutionary, secretary of state, Social Democrat, Socialist, speaker, Tory, Trotskyite, true-blue, wet (*infml*), Whig.

*Political parties include*: Alliance, Co-operative, Communist, Conservative and Unionist, Democratic, Democratic Left, Democratic Unionist, Fianna Fáil, Fine Gael, Green, Labour, Liberal, Liberal Democratic, Militant Labour, National Front, Parliamentary, Parliamentary Labour, Plaid Cymru, Progressive Democrats, Republican, Scottish Conservative and Unionist, Scottish Liberal Democratic, Scottish National, Sinn Féin, Social and Liberal Democratic, Social Democratic and Labour, Ulster Democratic Unionist, Ulster Popular Unionist, Ulster Unionist, Welsh

Liberal Democratic. *see also* **government systems**; **parliaments and assemblies**; **political ideologies**.

**poll** *n* ballot, vote, voting, plebiscite, referendum, straw-poll, sampling, canvass, opinion poll, survey, census, count, tally.

**pollute** *v* contaminate, infect, poison, taint, adulterate, debase, corrupt, dirty, foul, soil, defile, sully, stain, mar, spoil.

**pollution** *n* impurity, contamination, infection, taint, adulteration, corruption, dirtiness, foulness, defilement.

**F3** purification, purity, cleanness.

**pomp** *n* ceremony, ceremonial, ritual, solemnity, formality, ceremoniousness, state, grandeur, splendour, magnificence, pageantry, show, display, parade, ostentation, flourish.

**F3** austerity, simplicity.

**pompous** *adj* self-important, arrogant, grandiose, supercilious, overbearing, imperious, magisterial, bombastic, high-flown, overblown, windy, affected, pretentious, ostentatious.

**F3** unassuming, modest, simple, unaffected.

**pool**[1] *n* puddle, pond, lake, mere, tarn, watering-hole, paddling-pool, swimming-pool.

**pool**[2] *n* **1** FUND, reserve, accumulation, bank, kitty, purse, pot, jackpot. **2** SYNDICATE, cartel, ring, combine, consortium, collective, group, team.

*v* contribute, chip in (*infml*), combine, amalgamate, merge, share, muck in (*infml*).

**poor** *adj* **1** IMPOVERISHED, poverty-stricken, badly off, hard-up, broke (*infml*), stony-broke (*sl*), skint (*sl*), bankrupt, penniless, destitute, miserable, wretched, distressed,

straitened, needy, lacking, deficient, insufficient, scanty, skimpy, meagre, sparse, depleted, exhausted. **2** BAD, substandard, unsatisfactory, inferior, mediocre, below par, low-grade, second-rate, third-rate, shoddy, imperfect, faulty, weak, feeble, pathetic (*infml*), sorry, worthless, fruitless. **3** UNFORTUNATE, unlucky, luckless, ill-fated, unhappy, miserable, pathetic, pitiable, pitiful.
**F3 1** rich, wealthy, affluent. **2** superior, impressive. **3** fortunate, lucky.

**poorly** *adj* ill, sick, unwell, indisposed, ailing, sickly, off colour, below par, out of sorts (*infml*), under the weather (*infml*), seedy, groggy, rotten (*infml*).
**F3** well, healthy.

**pop** *v* burst, explode, go off, bang, crack, snap.
*n* bang, crack, snap, burst, explosion.

**popular** *adj* well-liked, favourite, liked, favoured, approved, in demand, sought-after, fashionable, modish, trendy (*infml*), prevailing, current, accepted, conventional, standard, stock, common, prevalent, widespread, universal, general, household, famous, well-known, celebrated, idolized.
**F3** unpopular.

**popularise** *v* spread, propagate, universalize, democratize, simplify.

**popularly** *adv* commonly, widely, universally, generally, usually, customarily, conventionally, traditionally.

**populate** *v* people, occupy, settle, colonize, inhabit, live in, overrun.

**population** *n* inhabitants, natives, residents, citizens, occupants, community, society, people, folk.

**populous** *n* crowded, packed, swarming, teeming, crawling, overpopulated.
**F3** deserted.

**pornographic** *adj* obscene, indecent, dirty, filthy, blue, risqué,
bawdy, coarse, gross, lewd, erotic, titillating.

**porous** *adj* permeable, pervious, penetrable, absorbent, spongy, honeycombed, pitted.
**F3** impermeable, impervious.

**portable** *adj* movable, transportable, compact, lightweight, manageable, handy, convenient.
**F3** fixed, immovable.

**porter**[1] *n* bearer, carrier, baggage-attendant, baggage-handler.

**porter**[2] *n* doorman, commissionaire, door-keeper, gatekeeper, janitor, caretaker, concierge.

**portion** *n* share, allocation, allotment, parcel, allowance, ration, quota, measure, part, section, division, fraction, percentage, bit, fragment, morsel, piece, segment, slice, serving, helping.

**portly** *adj* stout, corpulent, rotund, round, fat, plump, obese, overweight, heavy, large.
**F3** slim, thin, slight.

**portrait** *n* picture, painting, drawing, sketch, caricature, miniature, icon, photograph, likeness, image, representation, vignette, profile, characterization, description, depiction, portrayal.

**portray** *v* draw, sketch, paint, illustrate, picture, represent, depict, describe, evoke, play, impersonate, characterize, personify.

**portrayal** *n* representation, characterization, depiction, description, evocation, presentation, performance, interpretation, rendering.

**pose** *v* **1** MODEL, sit, position. **2** PRETEND, feign, affect, put on an act, masquerade, pass oneself off, impersonate. **3** *pose a question*: set, put forward, submit, present.
*n* **1** POSITION, stance, air, bearing, posture, attitude. **2** PRETENCE, sham, affectation, façade, front, masquerade, role, act.

**poser**[1] *n* puzzle, riddle, conundrum, brain-teaser, mystery, enigma, problem, vexed question.

**poser**[2] *n* poseur, poseuse, posturer, attitudinizer, exhibitionist, show-off, pseud (*infml*), phoney (*infml*).

**posh** (*infml*) *adj* smart, stylish, fashionable, high-class, upper-class, la-di-da (*sl*), grand, luxurious, lavish, swanky (*infml*), luxury, deluxe, up-market, exclusive, select, classy (*infml*), swish (*infml*).
**Ea** inferior, cheap.

**position** *n* 1 PLACE, situation, location, site, spot, point.
2 POSTURE, stance, pose, arrangement, disposition. 3 JOB, post, occupation, employment, office, duty, function, role. 4 RANK, grade, level, status, standing. 5 OPINION, point of view, belief, view, outlook, viewpoint, standpoint, stand.
*v* put, place, set, fix, stand, arrange, dispose, lay out, deploy, station, locate, situate, site.

**positive** *adj* 1 SURE, certain, convinced, confident, assured.
2 *positive criticism*: helpful, constructive, practical, useful, optimistic, hopeful, promising.
3 DEFINITE, decisive, conclusive, clear, unmistakable, explicit, unequivocal, express, firm, emphatic, categorical, undeniable, irrefutable, indisputable, incontrovertible.
4 ABSOLUTE, utter, sheer, complete, perfect.
**Ea** 1 uncertain. 2 negative.
3 indefinite, vague.

**possess** *v* 1 OWN, have, hold, enjoy, be endowed with. 2 SEIZE, take, obtain, acquire, take over, occupy, control, dominate, bewitch, haunt.

**possession** *n* ownership, title, tenure, occupation, custody, control, hold, grip.

**possessions** *n* belongings,

property, things, paraphernalia, effects, goods, chattels, movables, assets, estate, wealth, riches.

**possessive** *adj* selfish, clinging, overprotective, domineering, dominating, jealous, covetous, acquisitive, grasping.
**Ea** unselfish, sharing.

**possibility** *n* likelihood, probability, odds, chance, risk, danger, hope, prospect, potentiality, conceivability, practicability, feasibility.
**Ea** impossibility, impracticability.

**possible** *adj* potential, promising, likely, probable, imaginable, conceivable, practicable, feasible, viable, tenable, workable, achievable, attainable, accomplishable, realizable.
**Ea** impossible, unthinkable, impracticable, unattainable.

**possibly** *adv* perhaps, maybe, hopefully (*infml*), by any means, at all, by any chance.

**post**[1] *n* pole, stake, picket, pale, pillar, column, shaft, support, baluster, upright, stanchion, strut, leg.
*v* display, stick up, pin up, advertise, publicize, announce, make known, report, publish.

**post**[2] *n* office, job, employment, position, situation, place, vacancy, appointment, assignment, station, beat.
*v* station, locate, situate, position, place, put, appoint, assign, second, transfer, move, send.

**post**[3] *n* mail, letters, dispatch, collection, delivery.
*v* mail, send, dispatch, transmit.

**poster** *n* notice, bill, sign, placard, sticker, advertisement, announcement.

**posterity** *n* descendants, successors, progeny, issue, offspring, children.

**postpone** *v* put off, defer, put back, hold over, delay, adjourn, suspend, shelve, pigeonhole, freeze, put on ice.

advance, forward.

**postscript** n PS (*infml*), addition, supplement, afterthought, addendum, codicil, appendix, afterword, epilogue.
 introduction, prologue.

**postulate** v theorize, hypothesize, suppose, assume, propose, advance, lay down, stipulate.

**posture** n position, stance, pose, attitude, disposition, bearing, carriage, deportment.

**posy** n bouquet, spray, buttonhole, corsage.

**pot** n receptacle, vessel, teapot, coffee pot, urn, jar, vase, bowl, basin, pan, cauldron, crucible.

**potent** adj powerful, mighty, strong, intoxicating, pungent, effective, impressive, cogent, convincing, persuasive, compelling, forceful, dynamic, vigorous, authoritative, commanding, dominant, influential, overpowering.
 impotent, weak.

**potential** adj possible, likely, probable, prospective, future, aspiring, would-be, promising, budding, embryonic, undeveloped, dormant, latent, hidden, concealed, unrealized.
 n possibility, ability, capability, capacity, aptitude, talent, powers, resources.

**potion** n mixture, concoction, brew, beverage, drink, draught, dose, medicine, tonic, elixir.

**potpourri** n medley, mixture, jumble, hotchpotch, miscellany, collection.

**potter** v tinker, fiddle, mess about (*infml*), dabble, loiter, fritter.

**pottery** n earthenware, stoneware, terracotta, ceramics, crockery, china, porcelain.

*Terms used in pottery include*: armorial, art pottery, basalt, blanc-de-chine, bronzing, celadon, ceramic, china clay, cloisonné, crackleware, crazing, creamware, delft, earthenware, enamel, faïence, fairing, figure, firing, flambé, flatback, glaze, grotesque, ground, ironstone, jasper, kiln, lustre, maiolica, majolica, maker's mark, mandarin palette, model, monogram, overglaze, porcelain, sagger, scratch blue, sgraffito, slip, slip-cast, spongeware, Staffordshire, stoneware, terracotta, tin-glazed earthenware, transfer printing, underglaze, Willow pattern.

**pounce** v fall on, dive on, swoop, drop, attack, strike, ambush, spring, jump, leap, snatch, grab.

**pound**[1] v **1** STRIKE, thump, beat, drum, pelt, hammer, batter, bang, bash, smash. **2** PULVERIZE, powder, grind, mash, crush. **3** *his heart was pounding*: throb, pulsate, palpitate, thump, thud.

**pound**[2] n enclosure, compound, corral, yard, pen, fold.

**pour** v **1** *pour a drink*: serve, decant, tip. **2** SPILL, issue, discharge, flow, stream, run, rush, spout, spew, gush, cascade, crowd, throng, swarm.

**pout** v scowl, glower, grimace, pull a face, sulk, mope.
 grin, smile.
 n scowl, glower, grimace, long face.
 grin, smile.

**poverty** n poorness, impoverishment, insolvency, bankruptcy, pennilessness, penury, destitution, distress, hardship, privation, need, necessity, want, lack, deficiency, shortage, inadequacy, insufficiency, depletion, scarcity, meagreness, paucity, dearth.
 wealth, richness, affluence, plenty.

**powdery** adj dusty, sandy, grainy, granular, powdered, pulverized, ground, fine, loose, dry, crumbly, friable, chalky.

**power** n **1** COMMAND, authority, sovereignty, rule, dominion, control, influence. **2** RIGHT, privilege, prerogative, authorization, warrant. **3** POTENCY, strength, intensity, force, vigour, energy. **4** ABILITY, capability, capacity, potential, faculty, competence.

**F3** **1** subjection. **3** weakness. **4** inability.

**powerful** *adj* dominant, prevailing, leading, influential, high-powered, authoritative, commanding, potent, effective, strong, mighty, robust, muscular, energetic, forceful, telling, impressive, convincing, persuasive, compelling, winning, overwhelming.

**F3** impotent, ineffective, weak.

**powerless** *adj* impotent, incapable, ineffective, weak, feeble, frail, infirm, incapacitated, disabled, paralysed, helpless, vulnerable, defenceless, unarmed.

**F3** powerful, potent, able.

**practicable** *adj* possible, feasible, performable, achievable, attainable, viable, workable, practical, realistic.

**F3** impracticable.

**practical** *adj* **1** REALISTIC, sensible, commonsense, practicable, workable, feasible, down-to-earth, matter-of-fact, pragmatic, hardnosed (*infml*), hard-headed, businesslike, experienced, trained, qualified, skilled, accomplished, proficient, hands on, applied. **2** USEFUL, handy, serviceable, utilitarian, functional, working, everyday, ordinary.

**F3** **1** impractical, unskilled, theoretical.

**practically** *adv* **1** ALMOST, nearly, well-nigh, virtually, pretty well, all but, just about, in principle, in effect, essentially, fundamentally, to all intents and purposes. **2** REALISTICALLY, sensibly, reasonably, rationally, pragmatically.

**practice** *n* **1** CUSTOM, tradition, convention, usage, habit, routine, way, method, system, procedure, policy. **2** REHEARSAL, run-through,

dry run, dummy run, try-out, training, drill, exercise, work-out, study, experience. **3** *in practice*: effect, reality, actuality, action, operation, performance, use, application.

**F3** **3** theory, principle.

**practise** *v* **1** DO, perform, execute, implement, carry out, apply, put into practice, follow, pursue, engage in, undertake. **2** REHEARSE, run through, repeat, drill, exercise, train, study, perfect.

**practised** *adj* experienced, seasoned, veteran, trained, qualified, accomplished, skilled, versed, knowledgeable, able, proficient, expert, masterly, consummate, finished.

**F3** unpractised, inexperienced, inexpert.

**pragmatic** *adj* practical, realistic, sensible, matter-of-fact, businesslike, efficient, hard-headed, hardnosed (*infml*), unsentimental.

**F3** unrealistic, idealistic, romantic.

**praise** *n* approval, admiration, commendation, congratulation, compliment, flattery, adulation, eulogy, applause, ovation, cheering, acclaim, recognition, testimonial, tribute, accolade, homage, honour, glory, worship, adoration, devotion, thanksgiving.

**F3** criticism, revilement.

*v* commend, congratulate, admire, compliment, flatter, eulogize, wax lyrical, rave over (*infml*), extol, promote, applaud, cheer, acclaim, hail, recognize, acknowledge, pay tribute to, honour, laud, glorify, magnify, exalt, worship, adore, bless.

**F3** criticize, revile.

**praiseworthy** *adj* commendable, fine, excellent, admirable, worthy, deserving, honourable, reputable, estimable, sterling.

**F3** blameworthy, dishonourable, ignoble.

**prank** *n* trick, practical joke, joke, stunt, caper, frolic, lark, antic, escapade.

**pray** *v* invoke, call on, supplicate, entreat, implore, plead, beg, beseech, petition, ask, request, crave, solicit.

**prayer** *n* collect, litany, devotion, communion, invocation, supplication, entreaty, plea, appeal, petition, request.

**preach** *v* address, lecture, harangue, pontificate, sermonize, evangelize, moralize, exhort, urge, advocate.

**precarious** *adj* unsafe, dangerous, treacherous, risky, hazardous, chancy, uncertain, unsure, dubious, doubtful, unpredictable, unreliable, unsteady, unstable, shaky, wobbly, insecure, vulnerable.
**F3** safe, certain, stable, secure.

**precaution** *n* safeguard, security, protection, insurance, providence, forethought, caution, prudence, foresight, anticipation, preparation, provision.

**precautionary** *adj* safety, protective, preventive, provident, cautious, prudent, judicious, preparatory, preliminary.

**precede** *v* come before, lead, come first, go before, take precedence, introduce, herald, usher in.
**F3** follow, succeed.

**precedence** *n* priority, preference, pride of place, superiority, supremacy, pre-eminence, lead, first place, seniority, rank.

**precedent** *n* example, instance, pattern, model, standard, criterion.

**precinct** *n* **1** ZONE, area, district, quarter, sector, division, section. **2** BOUNDARY, limit, bound, confine.

**precious** *adj* **1** VALUED, treasured, prized, cherished, beloved, dearest, darling, favourite, loved, adored, idolized. **2** VALUABLE, expensive, costly, dear, priceless, inestimable, rare, choice, fine.

**precipitate** *v* hasten, hurry, speed,

accelerate, quicken, expedite, advance, further, bring on, induce, trigger, cause, occasion.
*adj* sudden, unexpected, abrupt, quick, swift, rapid, brief, hasty, hurried, headlong, breakneck, frantic, violent, impatient, hot-headed, impetuous, impulsive, rash, reckless, heedless, indiscreet.
**F3** cautious, careful.

**precipitous** *adj* steep, sheer, perpendicular, vertical, high.
**F3** gradual.

**precise** *adj* exact, accurate, right, punctilious, correct, factual, faithful, authentic, literal, word-for-word, express, definite, explicit, unequivocal, unambiguous, clear-cut, distinct, detailed, blow-by-blow, minute, nice, particular, specific, fixed, rigid, strict, careful, meticulous, scrupulous, fastidious.
**F3** imprecise, inexact, ambiguous, careless.

**precisely** *adv* exactly, absolutely, just so, accurately, correctly, literally, verbatim, word for word, strictly, minutely, clearly, distinctly.

**precision** *n* exactness, accuracy, correctness, faithfulness, explicitness, distinctness, detail, particularity, rigour, care, meticulousness, scrupulousness, neatness.
**F3** imprecision, inaccuracy.

**precocious** *adj* forward, ahead, advanced, early, premature, mature, developed, gifted, clever, bright, smart, quick, fast.
**F3** backward.

**preconceive** *v* presuppose, presume, assume, anticipate, project, imagine, conceive, envisage, expect, visualize, picture.

**preconception** *n* presupposition, presumption, assumption, conjecture, anticipation, expectation, prejudgement, bias, prejudice.

**precondition** *n* condition, stipulation, requirement,

prerequisite, essential, necessity, must.

**precursor** n antecedent, forerunner, sign, indication, herald, harbinger, messenger, usher, pioneer, trail-blazer.

**F3** follower, successor.

**predecessor** n ancestor, forefather, forebear, antecedent, forerunner, precursor.

**F3** successor, descendant.

**predestination** n destiny, fate, lot, doom, predetermination, foreordination.

**predetermined** adj 1 PREDESTINED, destined, fated, doomed, ordained, foreordained. 2 PREARRANGED, arranged, agreed, fixed, set.

**predicament** n situation, plight, trouble, mess, fix, spot (infml), quandary, dilemma, impasse, crisis, emergency.

**predict** v foretell, prophesy, foresee, forecast, prognosticate, project.

**predictable** adj foreseeable, expected, anticipated, likely, probable, imaginable, foreseen, foregone, certain, sure, reliable, dependable.

**F3** unpredictable, uncertain.

**prediction** n prophecy, forecast, prognosis, augury, divination, fortune-telling, soothsaying.

**predispose** v dispose, incline, prompt, induce, make, sway, influence, affect, bias, prejudice.

**predominant** adj dominant, prevailing, preponderant, chief, main, principal, primary, capital, paramount, supreme, sovereign, ruling, controlling, leading, powerful, potent, prime, important, influential, forceful, strong.

**F3** minor, lesser, weak.

**pre-eminent** adj supreme, unsurpassed, unrivalled, unequalled, unmatched, matchless, incomparable, inimitable, chief, foremost, leading,

eminent, distinguished, renowned, famous, prominent, outstanding, exceptional, excellent, superlative, transcendent, superior.

**F3** inferior, unknown.

**preface** n foreword, introduction, preamble, prologue, prelude, preliminaries.

**F3** epilogue, postscript.

v precede, prefix, lead up to, introduce, launch, open, begin, start.

**F3** end, finish, complete.

**prefer** v favour, like better, would rather, would sooner, want, wish, desire, choose, select, pick, opt for, go for, plump for, single out, advocate, recommend, back, support, fancy, elect, adopt.

**F3** reject.

**preferable** adj better, superior, nicer, preferred, favoured, chosen, desirable, advantageous, advisable, recommended.

**F3** inferior, undesirable.

**preference** n 1 FAVOURITE, first choice, choice, pick, selection, option, wish, desire. 2 LIKING, fancy, inclination, predilection, partiality, favouritism, preferential treatment.

**preferential** adj better, superior, favoured, privileged, special, favourable, advantageous.

**F3** equal.

**pregnant** adj 1 a pregnant woman: expectant, expecting, with child (fml). 2 a pregnant pause: meaningful, significant, eloquent, expressive, suggestive, charged, loaded, full.

**prejudice** n 1 BIAS, partiality, partisanship, discrimination, unfairness, injustice, intolerance, narrow-mindedness, bigotry, chauvinism, racism, sexism. 2 HARM, damage, impairment, hurt, injury, detriment, disadvantage, loss, ruin.

**F3** 1 fairness, tolerance. 2 benefit, advantage.

*v* **1** BIAS, predispose, incline, sway, influence, condition, colour, slant, distort, load, weight. **2** HARM, damage, impair, hinder, undermine, hurt, injure, mar, spoil, ruin, wreck.
**F3** benefit, help, advance.

**prejudiced** *adj* biased, partial, predisposed, subjective, partisan, one-sided, discriminatory, unfair, unjust, loaded, weighted, intolerant, narrow-minded, bigoted, chauvinist, racist, sexist, jaundiced, distorted, warped, influenced, conditioned.
**F3** impartial, fair, tolerant.

**prejudicial** *adj* harmful, damaging, hurtful, injurious, detrimental, disadvantageous, unfavourable, inimical.
**F3** beneficial, advantageous.

**preliminaries** *n* preparation, groundwork, foundations, basics, rudiments, formalities, introduction, preface, prelude, opening, beginning, start.

**preliminary** *adj* preparatory, prior, advance, exploratory, experimental, trial, test, pilot, early, earliest, first, initial, primary, qualifying, inaugural, introductory, opening.
**F3** final, closing.

**prelude** *n* overture, introduction, preface, foreword, preamble, prologue, opening, opener, preliminary, preparation, beginning, start, commencement, precursor, curtain raiser.
**F3** finale, epilogue.

**premature** *adj* early, immature, green, unripe, embryonic, half-formed, incomplete, undeveloped, abortive, hasty, ill-considered, rash, untimely, inopportune, ill-timed.
**F3** late, tardy.

**premeditated** *adj* planned, intended, intentional, deliberate, wilful, conscious, cold-blooded, calculated, considered, contrived, preplanned, prearranged, predetermined.

**F3** unpremeditated, spontaneous.

**première** *n* first performance, opening, opening night, first night, début.

**premise** *n* proposition, statement, assertion, postulate, thesis, argument, basis, supposition, hypothesis, presupposition, assumption.

**premises** *n* building, property, establishment, office, grounds, estate, site, place.

**premonition** *n* presentiment, feeling, intuition, hunch, idea, suspicion, foreboding, misgiving, fear, apprehension, anxiety, worry, warning, omen, sign.

**preoccupation** *n* **1** OBSESSION, fixation, hang-up (*infml*), concern, interest, enthusiasm, hobby-horse. **2** DISTRACTION, absent-mindedness, reverie, obliviousness, oblivion.

**preoccupied** *adj* **1** OBSESSED, intent, immersed, engrossed, engaged, taken up, wrapped up, involved. **2** DISTRACTED, abstracted, absent-minded, daydreaming, absorbed, faraway, heedless, oblivious, pensive.

**preparation** *n* **1** READINESS, provision, precaution, safeguard, foundation, groundwork, spadework, basics, rudiments, preliminaries, plans, arrangements. **2** MIXTURE, compound, concoction, potion, medicine, lotion, application.

**preparatory** *adj* preliminary, introductory, opening, initial, primary, basic, fundamental, rudimentary, elementary.

**prepare** *v* **1** GET READY, warm up, train, coach, study, make ready, adapt, adjust, plan, organize, arrange, pave the way. **2** *prepare a meal*: make, produce, construct, assemble, concoct, contrive, devise, draft, draw up, compose.
**3** PROVIDE, supply, equip, fit out, rig out.

**prepare oneself** brace oneself, steel oneself, gird oneself, fortify oneself.

**prepared** *adj* ready, waiting, set, fit, inclined, disposed, willing, planned, organized, arranged.
**E3** unprepared, unready.

**preponderant** *adj* greater, larger, superior, predominant, prevailing, overriding, overruling, controlling, foremost, important, significant.

**preposterous** *adj* incredible, unbelievable, absurd, ridiculous, ludicrous, foolish, crazy, nonsensical, unreasonable, monstrous, shocking, outrageous, intolerable, unthinkable, impossible.
**E3** sensible, reasonable, acceptable.

**prerequisite** *n* precondition, condition, proviso, qualification, requisite, requirement, imperative, necessity, essential, must.
**E3** extra.

**prescribe** *v* ordain, decree, dictate, rule, command, order, require, direct, assign, specify, stipulate, lay down, set, appoint, impose, fix, define, limit.

**prescription** *n* 1 INSTRUCTION, direction, formula. 2 MEDICINE, drug, preparation, mixture, remedy, treatment.

**presence** *n* 1 ATTENDANCE, company, occupancy, residence, existence. 2 AURA, air, demeanour, bearing, carriage, appearance, poise, self-assurance, personality, charisma. 3 NEARNESS, closeness, proximity, vicinity.
**E3** absence. 2 remoteness.

**present**[1] *adj* 1 ATTENDING, here, there, near, at hand, to hand, available, ready. 2 *at the present time*: current, contemporary, present-day, immediate, instant, existent, existing.
**E3** 1 absent. 2 past, out-of-date.

**present**[2] *v* 1 SHOW, display, exhibit, demonstrate, mount, stage, put on, introduce, announce. 2 AWARD,

confer, bestow, grant, give, donate, hand over, entrust, extend, hold out, offer, tender, submit.

**present**[3] *n* gift, prezzie (*infml*), offering, donation, grant, endowment, benefaction, bounty, largess, gratuity, tip, favour.

**presentable** *adj* neat, tidy, clean, respectable, decent, proper, suitable, acceptable, satisfactory, tolerable.
**E3** unpresentable, untidy, shabby.

**presentation** *n* 1 SHOW, performance, production, staging, representation, display, exhibition, demonstration, talk, delivery, appearance, arrangement. 2 AWARD, conferral, bestowal, investiture.

**present-day** *adj* current, present, existing, living, contemporary, modern, up-to-date, fashionable.
**E3** past, future.

**presently** *adv* 1 SOON, shortly, in a minute, before long, by and by. 2 CURRENTLY, at present, now.

**preserve** *v* 1 PROTECT, safeguard, guard, defend, shield, shelter, care for, maintain, uphold, sustain, continue, perpetuate, keep, retain, conserve, save, store. 2 *preserve food*: bottle, tin, can, pickle, salt, cure, dry.
**E3** 1 destroy, ruin.
*n* 1 *home-made preserves*: conserve, jam, marmalade, jelly, pickle. 2 DOMAIN, realm, sphere, area, field, speciality. 3 RESERVATION, sanctuary, game reserve, safari park.

**preside** *v* chair, officiate, conduct, direct, manage, administer, control, run, head, lead, govern, rule.

**press** *v* 1 CRUSH, squash, squeeze, compress, stuff, cram, crowd, push, depress. 2 *press clothes*: iron, smooth, flatten. 3 HUG, embrace, clasp, squeeze. 4 URGE, plead, petition, campaign, demand, insist on, compel, constrain, force, pressure, pressurize, harass.
*n* 1 CROWD, throng, multitude, mob, horde, swarm, pack, crush, push.

**2** JOURNALISTS, reporters, correspondents, the media, newspapers, papers, Fleet Street, fourth estate.

**pressing** *adj* urgent, high-priority, burning, crucial, vital, essential, imperative, serious, important.
**☒** unimportant, trivial.

**pressure** *n* **1** FORCE, power, load, burden, weight, heaviness, compression, squeezing, stress, strain. **2** DIFFICULTY, problem, demand, constraint, obligation, urgency.

**pressurize** *v* force, compel, constrain, oblige, drive, bulldoze, coerce, press, pressure, lean on (*infml*), browbeat, bully.

**prestige** *n* status, reputation, standing, stature, eminence, distinction, esteem, regard, importance, authority, influence, fame, renown, kudos, credit, honour.
**☒** humbleness, unimportance.

**prestigious** *adj* esteemed, respected, reputable, important, influential, great, eminent, prominent, illustrious, renowned, celebrated, exalted, imposing, impressive, up-market.
**☒** humble, modest.

**presume** *v* **1** ASSUME, take it, think, believe, suppose, surmise, infer, presuppose, take for granted, count on, rely on, depend on, bank on, trust. **2** *presume to criticize*: dare, make so bold, go so far, venture, undertake.

**presumption** *n* **1** ASSUMPTION, belief, opinion, hypothesis, presupposition, supposition, surmise, conjecture, guess, likelihood, probability. **2** PRESUMPTUOUSNESS, boldness, audacity, impertinence, cheek (*infml*), nerve (*infml*), impudence, insolence, forwardness, assurance.
**☒** **2** humility.

**presumptuous** *adj* bold, audacious,

impertinent, impudent, insolent, over-familiar, forward, pushy, arrogant, over-confident, conceited.
**☒** humble, modest.

**pretence** *n* show, display, appearance, cover, front, façade, veneer, cloak, veil, mask, guise, sham, feigning, faking, simulation, deception, trickery, wile, ruse, excuse, pretext, bluff, falsehood, deceit, fabrication, invention, make-believe, charade, acting, play-acting, posturing, posing, affectation, pretension, pretentiousness.
**☒** honesty, openness.

**pretend** *v* **1** AFFECT, put on, assume, feign, sham, counterfeit, fake, simulate, bluff, impersonate, pass oneself off, act, play-act, mime, go through the motions. **2** CLAIM, allege, profess, purport. **3** IMAGINE, make believe, suppose.

**pretender** *n* claimant, aspirant, candidate.

**pretension** *n* **1** PRETENTIOUSNESS, pomposity, self-importance, airs, conceit, vanity, snobbishness, affectation, pretence, show, showiness, ostentation. **2** CLAIM, profession, demand, aspiration, ambition.
**☒** **1** modesty, humility, simplicity.

**pretentious** *adj* pompous, self-important, conceited, immodest, snobbish, affected, mannered, showy, ostentatious, extravagant, over-the-top, exaggerated, magniloquent, high-sounding, inflated, grandiose, ambitious, overambitious.
**☒** modest, humble, simple, straightforward.

**pretext** *n* excuse, ploy, ruse, cover, cloak, mask, guise, semblance, appearance, pretence, show.

**pretty** *adj* attractive, good-looking, beautiful, fair, lovely, bonny, cute, winsome, appealing, charming, dainty, graceful, elegant, fine, delicate, nice.

**☲** plain, unattractive, ugly.
*adv* fairly, somewhat, rather, quite, reasonably, moderately, tolerably.

**prevail** *v* **1** PREDOMINATE, preponderate, abound. **2** WIN, triumph, succeed, overcome, overrule, reign, rule.
**☲ 2** lose.

**prevail upon** persuade, talk into, prompt, induce, incline, sway, influence, convince, win over.

**prevailing** *adj* predominant, preponderant, main, principal, dominant, controlling, powerful, compelling, influential, reigning, ruling, current, fashionable, popular, mainstream, accepted, established, set, usual, customary, common, prevalent, widespread.
**☲** minor, subordinate.

**prevalent** *adj* widespread, extensive, rampant, rife, frequent, general, customary, usual, universal, ubiquitous, common, everyday, popular, current, prevailing.
**☲** uncommon, rare.

**prevaricate** *v* hedge, equivocate, quibble, cavil, dodge, evade, shift, shuffle, lie, deceive.

**prevent** *v* stop, avert, avoid, head off, ward off, stave off, intercept, forestall, anticipate, frustrate, thwart, check, restrain, inhibit, hinder, hamper, impede, obstruct, block, bar.
**☲** cause, help, foster, encourage, allow.

**prevention** *n* avoidance, frustration, check, hindrance, impediment, obstruction, obstacle, bar, elimination, precaution, safeguard, deterrence.
**☲** cause, help.

**preventive** *adj* preventative, anticipatory, pre-emptive, inhibitory, obstructive, precautionary, protective, counteractive, deterrent.
**☲** causative.

**previous** *adj* preceding, foregoing,

earlier, prior, past, former, ex-, one-time, sometime, erstwhile.
**☲** following, subsequent, later.

**previously** *adv* formerly, once, earlier, before, beforehand.
**☲** later.

**prey** *n* quarry, victim, game, kill.

**prey on 1** HUNT, kill, devour, feed on, live off, exploit. **2** *prey on one's mind*: haunt, trouble, distress, worry, burden, weigh down, oppress.

**price** *n* value, worth, cost, expense, outlay, expenditure, fee, charge, levy, toll, rate, bill, assessment, valuation, estimate, quotation, figure, amount, sum, payment, reward, penalty, forfeit, sacrifice, consequences.
*v* value, rate, cost, evaluate, assess, estimate.

**priceless** *adj* **1** INVALUABLE, inestimable, incalculable, expensive, costly, dear, precious, valuable, prized, treasured, irreplaceable. **2** (*infml*) FUNNY, amusing, comic, hilarious, riotous, side-splitting, killing (*infml*), rich (*infml*).
**☲ 1** cheap, run-of-the-mill.

**prick** *v* pierce, puncture, perforate, punch, jab, stab, sting, bite, prickle, itch, tingle.
*n* puncture, perforation, pinhole, stab, pang, twinge, sting, bite.

**prickle** *n* thorn, spine, barb, spur, point, spike, needle.
*v* tingle, itch, smart, sting, prick.

**prickly** *adj* **1** THORNY, brambly, spiny, barbed, spiky, bristly, rough, scratchy. **2** IRRITABLE, edgy, touchy, grumpy, short-tempered.
**☲ 1** smooth. **2** relaxed, easy-going (*infml*).

**pride** *n* **1** CONCEIT, vanity, egotism, bigheadedness, boastfulness, smugness, arrogance, self-importance, presumption, haughtiness, superciliousness, snobbery, pretentiousness. **2** DIGNITY, self-respect, self-esteem, honour. **3** SATISFACTION,

gratification, pleasure, delight.
⊟ **1** humility, modesty. **2** shame.

**priest** *n* minister, vicar, padre, father, man of God, man of the cloth, clergyman, churchman.

**priggish** *adj* smug, self-righteous, goody-goody (*infml*), sanctimonious, holier-than-thou, puritanical, prim, prudish, narrow-minded.
⊟ broadminded.

**prim** *adj* prudish, strait-laced, formal, demure, proper, priggish, prissy, fussy, particular, precise, fastidious.
⊟ informed, relaxed, easy-going (*infml*).

**primarily** *adv* chiefly, principally, mainly, mostly, basically, fundamentally, especially, particularly, essentially.

**primary** *adj* **1** FIRST, earliest, original, initial, introductory, beginning, basic, fundamental, essential, radical, rudimentary, elementary, simple. **2** CHIEF, principal, main, dominant, leading, foremost, supreme, cardinal, capital, paramount, greatest, highest, ultimate.
⊟ **2** secondary, subsidiary, minor.

**prime** *adj* best, choice, select, quality, first-class, first-rate, excellent, top, supreme, pre-eminent, superior, senior, leading, ruling, chief, principal, main, predominant, primary.
⊟ second-rate, secondary.
*n* height, peak, zenith, heyday, flower, bloom, maturity, perfection.

**primeval** *adj* earliest, first, original, primordial, early, old, ancient, prehistoric, primitive, instinctive.
⊟ modern.

**primitive** *adj* **1** CRUDE, rough, unsophisticated, uncivilized, barbarian, savage. **2** EARLY, elementary, rudimentary, primary, first, original, earliest.
⊟ **1** advanced, sophisticated,

civilized.

**princely** *adj* **1** SOVEREIGN, imperial, royal, regal, majestic, stately, grand, noble. **2** *princely sum*: generous, liberal, lavish, sumptuous, magnificent, handsome.

**principal** *adj* main, chief, key, essential, cardinal, primary, first, foremost, leading, dominant, prime, paramount, pre-eminent, supreme, highest.
⊟ minor, subsidiary, lesser, least.
*n* head, head teacher, headmaster, headmistress, chief, leader, boss, director, manager, superintendent.

**principally** *adv* mainly, mostly, chiefly, primarily, predominantly, above all, particularly, especially.

**principle** *n* **1** RULE, formula, law, canon, axiom, dictum, precept, maxim, truth, tenet, doctrine, creed, dogma, code, standard, criterion, proposition, fundamental, essential. **2** *a man of principle*: HONOUR, integrity, rectitude, uprightness, virtue, decency, morality, morals, ethics, standards, scruples, conscience.

**print** *v* mark, stamp, imprint, impress, engrave, copy, reproduce, run off, publish, issue.
*n* **1** LETTERS, characters, lettering, type, typescript, typeface, fount. **2** MARK, impression, fingerprint, footprint. **3** COPY, reproduction, picture, engraving, lithograph, photograph, photo.

**prior** *adj* earlier, preceding, foregoing, previous, former.
⊟ later.

**prior to** before, preceding, earlier than.
⊟ after, following.

**priority** *n* right of way, precedence, seniority, rank, superiority, pre-eminence, supremacy, the lead, first place, urgency.
⊟ inferiority.

**prison** *n* jail, nick (*sl*), clink (*sl*), cooler (*sl*), penitentiary, cell, lock-up, cage, dungeon, imprisonment, confinement, detention, custody.

**prisoner** n captive, hostage, convict, jail-bird (infml), inmate, internee, detainee.

**privacy** n secrecy, confidentiality, independence, solitude, isolation, seclusion, concealment, retirement, retreat.

**private** adj secret, classified, hush-hush (infml), off the record, unofficial, confidential, intimate, personal, individual, own, exclusive, particular, special, separate, independent, solitary, isolated, secluded, hidden, concealed, reserved, withdrawn.
**F3** public, open.

**in private** privately, in confidence, secretly, in secret, behind closed doors, in camera.
**F3** publicly, openly.

**privilege** n advantage, benefit, concession, birthright, title, due, right, prerogative, entitlement, freedom, liberty, franchise, licence, sanction, authority, immunity, exemption.
**F3** disadvantage.

**privileged** adj advantaged, favoured, special, sanctioned, authorized, immune, exempt, élite, honoured, ruling, powerful.
**F3** disadvantaged, under-privileged.

**prize** n reward, trophy, medal, award, winnings, jackpot, purse, premium, stake(s), honour, accolade.
adj best, top, first-rate, excellent, outstanding, champion, winning, prize-winning, award-winning.
**F3** second-rate.
v treasure, value, appreciate, esteem, revere, cherish, hold dear.
**F3** despise.

**probability** n likelihood, odds, chances, expectation, prospect, chance, possibility.
**F3** improbability.

**probable** adj likely, odds-on,

expected, credible, believable, plausible, feasible, possible, apparent, seeming.
**F3** improbable, unlikely.

**probation** n apprenticeship, trial period, trial, test.

**probe** v prod, poke, pierce, penetrate, sound, plumb, explore, examine, scrutinize, investigate, go into, look into, search, sift, test.
n 1 BORE, drill. 2 INQUIRY, inquest, investigation, exploration, examination, test, scrutiny, study, research.

**problem** n 1 TROUBLE, worry, predicament, quandary, dilemma, difficulty, complication, snag.
2 QUESTION, poser, puzzle, brain-teaser, conundrum, riddle, enigma.
adj difficult, unmanageable, uncontrollable, unruly, delinquent.
**F3** well-behaved, manageable.

**procedure** n routine, process, method, system, technique, custom, practice, policy, formula, course, scheme, strategy, plan of action, move, step, action, conduct, operation, performance.

**proceed** v 1 the permission to proceed: advance, go ahead, move on, progress, continue, carry on, press on. 2 ORIGINATE, derive, flow, start, stem, spring, arise, issue, result, ensue, follow, come.
**F3** 1 stop, retreat.

**proceedings** n 1 MATTERS, affairs, business, dealings, transactions, report, account, minutes, records, archives, annals. 2 EVENTS, happenings, deeds, doings, moves, steps, measures, action, course of action.

**proceeds** n revenue, income, returns, receipts, takings, earnings, gain, profit, yield, produce.
**F3** expenditure, outlay.

**process** n 1 PROCEDURE, operation, practice, method, system, technique, means, manner, mode,

way, stage, step. **2** COURSE,
progression, advance, progress,
development, evolution, formation,
growth, movement, action,
proceeding.
v  deal with, handle, treat, prepare,
refine, transform, convert, change,
alter.

**procession** n  march, parade,
cavalcade, motorcade, cortège, file,
column, train, succession, series,
sequence, course, run.

**proclaim** v  announce, declare,
pronounce, affirm, give out, publish,
advertise, make known, profess,
testify, show, indicate.

**proclamation** n  announcement,
declaration, pronouncement,
affirmation, publication,
promulgation, notice, notification,
manifesto, decree, edict.

**procrastinate** v  defer, put off,
postpone, delay, retard, stall,
temporize, play for time, dally, dilly-
dally (infml), drag one's feet,
prolong, protract.
**F3** advance, proceed.

**procure** v  acquire, buy, purchase,
get, obtain, find, come by, pick up,
lay hands on, earn, gain, win, secure,
appropriate, requisition.
**F3** lose.

**prod** v  poke, jab, dig, elbow, nudge,
push, shove, goad, spur, urge, egg on
(infml), prompt, stimulate, motivate.
n  poke, jab, dig, elbow, nudge, push,
shove, prompt, reminder, stimulus,
motivation.

**prodigy** n  genius, virtuoso, wonder,
marvel, miracle, phenomenon,
sensation, freak, curiosity, rarity,
child genius, wonder child, whizz kid
(infml).

**produce** v  **1** CAUSE, occasion, give
rise to, provoke, bring about, result
in, effect, create, originate, invent,
make, manufacture, fabricate,
construct, compose, generate, yield,
bear, deliver. **2** ADVANCE, put

forward, present, offer, give, supply,
provide, furnish, bring out, bring
forth, show, exhibit, demonstrate.
**3** produce a play: direct, stage,
mount, put on.
n  crop, harvest, yield, output,
product.

**product** n  **1** COMMODITY,
merchandise, goods, end-product,
artefact, work, creation, invention,
production, output, yield, produce,
fruit, return. **2** RESULT, consequence,
outcome, issue, upshot, offshoot,
spin-off, by-product, legacy.
**F3** 2 cause.

**production** n  **1** MAKING,
manufacture, fabrication,
construction, assembly, creation,
origination, preparation, formation.
**2** an amateur production: staging,
presentation, direction, management.
**F3** 1 consumption.

**productive** adj  fruitful, profitable,
rewarding, valuable, worthwhile,
useful, constructive, creative,
inventive, fertile, rich, teeming, busy,
energetic, vigorous, efficient,
effective.
**F3** unproductive, fruitless, useless.

**productivity** n  productiveness,
yield, output, work rate, efficiency.

**profane** adj  secular, temporal, lay,
unconsecrated, unhallowed,
unsanctified, unholy, irreligious,
impious, sacrilegious, blasphemous,
ungodly, irreverent, disrespectful,
abusive, crude, coarse, foul, filthy,
unclean.
**F3** sacred, religious, respectful.
v  desecrate, pollute, contaminate,
defile, debase, pervert, abuse, misuse.
**F3** revere, honour.

**profess** v  admit, confess,
acknowledge, own, confirm, certify,
declare, announce, proclaim, state,
assert, affirm, maintain, claim,
allege, make out, pretend.

**profession** n  **1** CAREER, job,
occupation, employment, business,

line (of work), trade, vocation, calling, métier, craft, office, position. **2** ADMISSION, confession, acknowledgement, declaration, announcement, statement, testimony, assertion, affirmation, claim.

**professional** *adj* qualified, licensed, trained, experienced, practised, skilled, expert, masterly, proficient, competent, businesslike, efficient.
₣₃ amateur, unprofessional.
*n* expert, authority, specialist, pro (*infml*), master, virtuoso, dab hand (*infml*).
₣₃ amateur.

**proficiency** *n* skill, skilfulness, expertise, mastery, talent, knack, dexterity, finesse, aptitude, ability, competence.
₣₃ incompetence.

**proficient** *adj* able, capable, skilled, qualified, trained, experienced, accomplished, expert, masterly, gifted, talented, clever, skilful, competent, efficient.
₣₃ unskilled, incompetent.

**profile** *n* **1** SIDE VIEW, outline, contour, silhouette, shape, form, figure, sketch, drawing, diagram, chart, graph. **2** BIOGRAPHY, curriculum vitae, thumbnail sketch, vignette, portrait, study, analysis, examination, survey, review.

**profit** *n* gain, surplus, excess, bottom line, revenue, return, yield, proceeds, receipts, takings, earnings, winnings, interest, advantage, benefit, use, avail, value, worth.
₣₃ loss.
*v* gain, make money, pay, serve, avail, benefit.
₣₃ lose.

**profit by, profit from** exploit, take advantage of, use, utilize, turn to advantage, capitalize on, cash in on, reap the benefit of.

**profitable** *adj* cost-effective, economic, commercial, money-making, lucrative, remunerative,

paying, rewarding, successful, fruitful, productive, advantageous, beneficial, useful, valuable, worthwhile.
₣₃ unprofitable, loss-making, non-profit-making.

**profound** *adj* **1** DEEP, great, intense, extreme, heartfelt, marked, far-reaching, extensive, exhaustive. **2** *a profound remark*: serious, weighty, penetrating, thoughtful, philosophical, wise, learned, erudite, abstruse.
₣₃ **1** shallow, slight, mild.

**profuse** *adj* ample, abundant, plentiful, copious, generous, liberal, lavish, rich, luxuriant, excessive, immoderate, extravagant, overabundant, superabundant, overflowing.
₣₃ inadequate, sparse.

**profusion** *n* abundance, plenty, wealth, multitude, plethora, glut, excess, surplus, superfluity, extravagance.
₣₃ inadequacy, scarcity.

**programme** *n* **1** SCHEDULE, timetable, agenda, calendar, order of events, listing, line-up, plan, scheme, project, syllabus, curriculum. **2** *radio programme*: broadcast, transmission, show, performance, production, presentation.

**progress** *n* movement, progression, passage, journey, way, advance, headway, step forward, breakthrough, development, evolution, growth, increase, improvement, betterment, promotion.
₣₃ recession, deterioration, decline.
*v* proceed, advance, go forward, forge ahead, make progress, make headway, come on, develop, grow, mature, blossom, improve, better, prosper, increase.
₣₃ deteriorate, decline.

**progression** *n* cycle, chain, string, succession, series, sequence, order, course, advance, headway, progress, development.

**progressive** *adj* **1** MODERN, avant-garde, advanced, forward-looking, enlightened, liberal, radical, revolutionary, reformist, dynamic, enterprising, go-ahead, up-and-coming. **2** ADVANCING, continuing, developing, growing, increasing, intensifying.
F3 **1** regressive.

**prohibit** *v* forbid, ban, bar, veto, proscribe, outlaw, rule out, preclude, prevent, stop, hinder, hamper, impede, obstruct, restrict.
F3 permit, allow, authorize.

**project** *n* assignment, contract, task, job, work, occupation, activity, enterprise, undertaking, venture, plan, scheme, programme, design, proposal, idea, conception.
*v* **1** PREDICT, forecast, extrapolate, estimate, reckon, calculate. **2** THROW, fling, hurl, launch, propel. **3** PROTRUDE, stick out, bulge, jut out, overhang.

**projection** *n* **1** PROTUBERANCE, bulge, overhang, ledge, sill, shelf, ridge. **2** PREDICTION, forecast, extrapolation, estimate, reckoning, calculation, computation.

**proliferate** *v* multiply, reproduce, breed, increase, build up, intensify, escalate, mushroom, snowball, spread, expand, flourish, thrive.
F3 dwindle.

**prolific** *adj* productive, fruitful, fertile, profuse, copious, abundant.
F3 unproductive.

**prolong** *v* lengthen, extend, stretch, protract, draw out, spin out, drag out, delay, continue, perpetuate.
F3 shorten.

**prominence** *n* **1** FAME, celebrity, renown, eminence, distinction, greatness, importance, reputation, name, standing, rank, prestige.
**2** BULGE, protuberance, bump, hump, lump, mound, rise, elevation,

projection, process, headland, promontory, cliff, crag.
F3 **1** unimportance, insignificance.

**prominent** *adj* **1** NOTICEABLE, conspicuous, obvious, unmistakable, striking, eye-catching. **2** BULGING, protuberant, projecting, jutting, protruding, obtrusive. **3** *a prominent writer*: famous, well-known, celebrated, renowned, noted, eminent, distinguished, respected, leading, foremost, chief, main, important, popular, outstanding.
F3 **1** inconspicuous. **3** unknown, unimportant, insignificant.

**promiscuity** *n* looseness, laxity, permissiveness, wantonness, immorality, licentiousness, debauchery, depravity.
F3 chastity, morality.

**promiscuous** *adj* loose, immoral, licentious, dissolute, casual, random, haphazard, indiscriminate.
F3 chaste, moral.

**promise** *v* **1** VOW, pledge, swear, take an oath, contract, undertake, give one's word, vouch, warrant, guarantee, assure. **2** AUGUR, presage, indicate, suggest, hint at.
*n* **1** VOW, pledge, oath, word of honour, bond, compact, covenant, guarantee, assurance, undertaking, engagement, commitment.
**2** POTENTIAL, ability, capability, aptitude, talent.

**promising** *adj* auspicious, propitious, favourable, rosy, bright, encouraging, hopeful, talented, gifted, budding, up-and-coming.
F3 unpromising, inauspicious, discouraging.

**promote** *v* **1** ADVERTISE, plug (*infml*), publicize, hype (*sl*), popularize, market, sell, push, recommend, advocate, champion, endorse, sponsor, support, back, help, aid, assist, foster, nurture, further, forward, encourage, boost, stimulate, urge. **2** UPGRADE,

advance, move up, raise, elevate,
exalt, honour.
**Ɛӡ 1** disparage, hinder. **2** demote.
**promotion** *n* **1** ADVANCEMENT,
upgrading, rise, preferment,
elevation, exaltation.
**2** ADVERTISING, plugging (*infml*),
publicity, hype (*sl*), campaign,
propaganda, marketing, pushing,
support, backing, furtherance,
development, encouragement,
boosting.
**Ɛӡ 1** demotion. **2** disparagement,
obstruction.
**prompt¹** *adj* punctual, on time,
immediate, instantaneous, instant,
direct, quick, swift, rapid, speedy,
unhesitating, willing, ready, alert,
responsive, timely, early.
**Ɛӡ** slow, hesitant, late.
*adv* promptly, punctually, exactly, on
the dot, to the minute, sharp.
**prompt²** *v* cause, give rise to, result
in, occasion, produce, instigate, call
forth, elicit, provoke, incite, urge,
encourage, inspire, move, stimulate,
motivate, spur, prod, remind.
**Ɛӡ** deter, dissuade.
*n* reminder, cue, hint, help, jolt,
prod, spur, stimulus.
**prone** *adj* **1** LIKELY, given, inclined,
disposed, predisposed, bent, apt,
liable, subject, susceptible,
vulnerable. **2** *she lay prone*: face
down, prostrate, flat, horizontal, full-
length, stretched, recumbent.
**Ɛӡ 1** unlikely, immune. **2** upright,
supine.
**pronounce** *v* **1** SAY, utter, speak,
express, voice, vocalize, sound,
enunciate, articulate, stress.
**2** DECLARE, announce, proclaim,
decree, judge, affirm, assert.
**pronounced** *adj* clear, distinct,
definite, positive, decided, marked,
noticeable, conspicuous, evident,
obvious, striking, unmistakable,
strong, broad.
**Ɛӡ** faint, vague.

**pronunciation** *n* speech, diction,
elocution, enunciation, articulation,
delivery, accent, stress, inflection,
intonation, modulation.
**proof** *n* evidence, documentation,
demonstration, verification,
confirmation, corroboration,
substantiation.
**prop** *v* **1** SUPPORT, sustain, uphold,
maintain, shore, stay, buttress,
bolster, underpin, set. **2** *propped
against the wall*: lean, rest, stand.
*n* support, stay, mainstay, strut,
buttress, brace, truss.
**propaganda** *n* advertising,
publicity, hype (*sl*), indoctrination,
brainwashing, disinformation.
**propagate** *v* **1** SPREAD, transmit,
broadcast, diffuse, disseminate,
circulate, publish, promulgate,
publicize, promote. **2** INCREASE,
multiply, proliferate, generate,
produce, breed, beget, spawn,
procreate, reproduce.
**propel** *v* move, drive, impel, force,
thrust, push, shove, launch, shoot,
send.
**Ɛӡ** stop.
**proper** *adj* **1** RIGHT, correct,
accurate, exact, precise, true,
genuine, real, actual. **2** ACCEPTED,
correct, suitable, appropriate, fitting,
decent, respectable, polite, formal.
**Ɛӡ 1** wrong. **2** improper, indecent.
**property** *n* **1** ESTATE, land, real
estate, acres, premises, buildings,
house(s), wealth, riches, resources,
means, capital, assets, holding(s),
belongings, possessions, effects,
goods, chattels. **2** FEATURE, trait,
quality, attribute, characteristic,
idiosyncrasy, peculiarity, mark.
**prophecy** *n* prediction, augury,
forecast, prognosis.
**prophesy** *v* predict, foresee, augur,
foretell, forewarn, forecast.
**prophet** *n* seer, soothsayer,
foreteller, forecaster, oracle,
clairvoyant, fortune-teller.

**proportion** *n* **1** PERCENTAGE, fraction, part, division, share, quota, amount. **2** RATIO, relationship, correspondence, symmetry, balance, distribution.
▪ **2** disproportion, imbalance.

**proportional** *adj* proportionate, relative, commensurate, consistent, corresponding, analogous, comparable, equitable, even.
▪ disproportionate.

**proportions** *n* dimensions, measurements, size, magnitude, volume, capacity.

**proposal** *n* proposition, suggestion, recommendation, motion, plan, scheme, project, design, programme, manifesto, presentation, bid, offer, tender, terms.

**propose** *v* **1** SUGGEST, recommend, move, advance, put forward, introduce, bring up, table, submit, present, offer, tender. **2** INTEND, mean, aim, purpose, plan, design. **3** NOMINATE, put up.
▪ **1** withdraw.

**proprietor, proprietress** *n* landlord, landlady, title-holder, freeholder, leaseholder, landowner, owner, possessor.

**prosecute** *v* accuse, indict, sue, prefer charges, take to court, litigate, summon, put on trial, try.
▪ defend.

**prosody**

> *Forms of prosody include*: abstract verse, Alcaic verse, alexandrine, alliteration, amphibrach, amphimacer, Anacreontic verse, anacrusis, analysed rhyme, anapaest, antibacchius, antispast, Archilochian verse, asclepiad, assonance, asynartete, ballade, blank verse, broken rhyme, bouts rimés, caesura, canto, catalexis, choliamb, choree, choriamb, cinquain, couplet, dactyl, decastich, dipody, dispondee, distich, ditrochee, dizain, dochmius, elision,

enjambment, envoy, epitrite, epode, eye rhyme, false quantity, feminine caesura, feminine ending, feminine rhyme, foot, free verse, galliambic, glyconic, heptameter, heptapody, heroic couplet, hexameter, hexastich, hypermetrical, iamb, ictus, Ionic, kyrielle, laisse, Leonine rhyme, linked verse, long-measure, macaronic, masculine ending, masculine rhyme, metre, miurus, monometer, monorhyme, paeon, pantoum, pentameter, pentastich, Petrarchan sonnet, Pherecratean, Pindaric, poulters' measure, pyrrhic, Pythian verse, quatorzain, quatrain, reported verses, rhopalic, rhyme royal, rime riche, rime suffisante, rondeau, rondel, rove-over, Sapphic, senarius, septenarius, sonnet, Spencerian stanza, spondee, sprung rhythm, strophe, substituion, synaphea, tetrameter, tetrapody, tetrastich, tribrach, trimeter, triolet, tripody, triseme, trochee, villanelle, virelay.

**prospect** *n* chance, odds, probability, likelihood, possibility, hope, expectation, anticipation, outlook, future.
▪ unlikelihood.

**prospective** *adj* future, -to-be, intended, designate, destined, forthcoming, approaching, coming, imminent, awaited, expected, anticipated, likely, possible, probable, potential, aspiring, would-be.
▪ current.

**prospectus** *n* plan, scheme, programme, syllabus, manifesto, outline, synopsis, pamphlet, leaflet, brochure, catalogue, list.

**prosper** *v* boom, thrive, flourish, flower, bloom, succeed, get on, advance, progress, grow rich.
▪ fail.

**prosperity** *n* boom, plenty, affluence, wealth, riches, fortune,

well-being, luxury, the good life, success, good fortune.
**E3** adversity, poverty.

**prosperous** *adj* booming, thriving, flourishing, blooming, successful, fortunate, lucky, rich, wealthy, affluent, well-off, well-to-do.
**E3** unfortunate, poor.

**prostrate** *adj* flat, horizontal, prone, fallen, overcome, overwhelmed, crushed, paralysed, powerless, helpless, defenceless.
**E3** triumphant.
*v* lay low, overcome, overwhelm, crush, overthrow, tire, wear out, fatigue, exhaust, drain, ruin.
**E3** strengthen.

**prostrate oneself** bow down, kneel, kowtow, submit, grovel, cringe, abase oneself.

**protagonist** *n* hero, heroine, lead, principal, leader, prime mover, champion, advocate, supporter, proponent, exponent.

**protect** *v* safeguard, defend, guard, escort, cover, screen, shield, secure, watch over, look after, care for, support, shelter, harbour, keep, conserve, preserve, save.
**E3** attack, neglect.

**protection** *n* **1** *protection of the environment*: care, custody, charge, guardianship, safekeeping, conservation, preservation, safety, safeguard. **2** BARRIER, buffer, bulwark, defence, guard, shield, armour, screen, cover, shelter, refuge, security, insurance.
**E3** neglect, attack.

**protective** *adj* **1** POSSESSIVE, defensive, motherly, maternal, fatherly, paternal, watchful, vigilant, careful. **2** *protective clothing*: waterproof, fireproof, insulating.
**E3** aggressive, threatening.

**protest** *n* objection, disapproval, opposition, dissent, complaint, protestation, outcry, appeal, demonstration.

**E3** acceptance.
*v* **1** OBJECT, take exception, complain, appeal, demonstrate, oppose, disapprove, disagree, argue. **2** *protest one's innocence*: assert, maintain, contend, insist, profess.
**E3** **1** accept.

**protester** *n* demonstrator, agitator, rebel, dissident, dissenter.

**protocol** *n* procedure, formalities, convention, custom, etiquette, manners, good form, propriety.

**protracted** *adj* long, lengthy, prolonged, extended, drawn-out, long-drawn-out, overlong, interminable.
**E3** brief, shortened.

**protrude** *v* stick out, poke out, come through, bulge, jut out, project, extend, stand out, obtrude.

**proud** *adj* **1** CONCEITED, vain, egotistical, bigheaded, boastful, smug, complacent, arrogant, self-important, cocky, presumptuous, haughty, high and mighty, overbearing, supercilious, snooty (*infml*), snobbish, toffee-nosed (*infml*), stuck-up (*infml*). **2** SATISFIED, contented, gratified, pleased, delighted, honoured. **3** DIGNIFIED, noble, honourable, worthy, self-respecting.
**E3** **1** humble, modest, unassuming. **2** ashamed. **3** deferential, ignoble.

**prove** *v* show, demonstrate, attest, verify, confirm, corroborate, substantiate, bear out, document, certify, authenticate, validate, justify, establish, determine, ascertain, try, test, check, examine, analyse.
**E3** disprove, discredit, falsify.

**proverb** *n* saying, adage, aphorism, maxim, byword, dictum, precept.

**proverbial** *adj* axiomatic, accepted, conventional, traditional, customary, time-honoured, famous, well-known, legendary, notorious, typical, archetypal.

**provide** *v* **1** SUPPLY, furnish, stock,

equip, outfit, prepare for, cater, serve, present, give, contribute, yield, lend, add, bring. **2** PLAN FOR, allow, make provision, accommodate, arrange for, take precautions. **3** STATE, specify, stipulate, lay down, require.

**F3** 1 take, remove.

**providence** n **1** FATE, destiny, divine intervention, God's will, fortune, luck. **2** PRUDENCE, far-sightedness, foresight, caution, care, thrift.

**F3** 2 improvidence.

**provident** adj prudent, far-sighted, judicious, cautious, careful, thrifty, economical, frugal.

**F3** improvident.

**providential** adj timely, opportune, convenient, fortunate, lucky, happy, welcome, heaven-sent.

**F3** untimely.

**providing** conj provided, with the proviso, given, as long as, on condition, on the understanding.

**province** n **1** REGION, area, district, zone, county, shire, department, territory, colony, dependency. **2** RESPONSIBILITY, concern, duty, office, role, function, field, sphere, domain, department, line.

**provincial** adj regional, local, rural, rustic, country, home-grown, small-town, parish-pump, parochial, insular, inward-looking, limited, narrow, narrow-minded, small-minded.

**F3** national, cosmopolitan, urban, sophisticated.

**provision** n **1** PLAN, arrangement, preparation, measure, precaution. **2** STIPULATION, specification, proviso, condition, term, requirement.

**provisional** adj temporary, interim, transitional, stopgap, makeshift, conditional, tentative.

**F3** permanent, fixed, definite.

**provisions** n food, foodstuff, groceries, eatables (infml), sustenance, rations, supplies, stocks, stores.

**proviso** n condition, term, requirement, stipulation, qualification, reservation, restriction, limitation, provision, clause, rider.

**provocation** n cause, grounds, justification, reason, motive, stimulus, motivation, incitement, instigation, annoyance, aggravation (infml), vexation, grievance, offence, insult, affront, injury, taunt, challenge, dare.

**provocative** adj **1** ANNOYING, aggravating (infml), galling, outrageous, offensive, insulting, abusive. **2** STIMULATING, exciting, challenging. **3** EROTIC, titillating, arousing, sexy, seductive, alluring, tempting, inviting, tantalizing, teasing, suggestive.

**F3** 1 conciliatory.

**provoke** v **1** ANNOY, irritate, rile, aggravate (infml), offend, insult, anger, enrage, infuriate, incense, madden, exasperate, tease, taunt. **2** CAUSE, occasion, give rise to, produce, generate, induce, elicit, evoke, excite, inspire, move, stir, prompt, stimulate, motivate, incite, instigate.

**F3** 1 please, pacify. **2** result.

**prowess** n accomplishment, attainment, ability, aptitude, skill, expertise, mastery, command, talent, genius.

**proximity** n closeness, nearness, vicinity, neighbourhood, adjacency, juxtaposition.

**F3** remoteness.

**proxy** n agent, factor, deputy, stand-in, substitute, representative, delegate, attorney.

**prudent** adj wise, sensible, politic, judicious, shrewd, discerning, careful, cautious, wary, vigilant, circumspect, discreet, provident, far-sighted, thrifty.

**pry** *v* meddle, interfere, poke one's nose in, intrude, peep, peer, snoop, nose, ferret, dig, delve.

**F3** mind one's own business.

**pseudonym** *n* false name, assumed name, alias, incognito, pen name, nom de plume, stage name.

**psychic** *adj* spiritual, supernatural, occult, mystic(al), clairvoyant, extra-sensory, telepathic, mental, psychological, intellectual, cognitive.

**psychological** *adj* mental, cerebral, intellectual, cognitive, emotional, subjective, subconscious, unconscious, psychosomatic, irrational, unreal.

**F3** physical, real.

**puberty** *n* pubescence, adolescence, teens, youth, growing up, maturity.

**F3** childhood, immaturity, old age.

**public** *adj* 1 *public buildings*: state, national, civil, community, social, collective, communal, common, general, universal, open, unrestricted. 2 KNOWN, well-known, recognized, acknowledged, overt, open, exposed, published.

**F3** 1 private, personal. 2 secret.

*n* people, nation, country, population, populace, masses, citizens, society, community, voters, electorate, followers, supporters, fans, audience, patrons, clientèle, customers, buyers, consumers.

**public house** pub (*infml*), local (*infml*), bar, saloon, inn, tavern.

**publication** *n* 1 BOOK, newspaper, magazine, periodical, booklet, leaflet, pamphlet, handbill. 2 ANNOUNCEMENT, declaration, notification, disclosure, release, issue, printing, publishing.

**publicity** *n* advertising, plug (*infml*), hype (*sl*), promotion, build-up, boost, attention, limelight, splash.

**publicize** *v* advertise, plug (*infml*), hype (*sl*), promote, push, spotlight, broadcast, make known, blaze.

**publish** *v* 1 ANNOUNCE, declare, communicate, make known, divulge, disclose, reveal, release, publicize, advertise. 2 *publish a book*: produce, print, issue, bring out, distribute, circulate, spread, diffuse.

**pucker** *v* gather, ruffle, wrinkle, shrivel, crinkle, crumple, crease, furrow, purse, screw up, contract, compress.

**puerile** *adj* childish, babyish, infantile, juvenile, immature, irresponsible, silly, foolish, inane, trivial.

**F3** mature.

**puff** *n* 1 BREATH, waft, whiff, draught, flurry, gust, blast. 2 *a puff on a cigarette*: pull, drag.

*v* 1 BREATHE, pant, gasp, gulp, wheeze, blow, waft, inflate, expand, swell. 2 *puff a cigarette*: smoke, pull, drag, draw, suck.

**puffy** *adj* puffed up, inflated, swollen, bloated, distended, enlarged.

**pugnacious** *adj* hostile, aggressive, belligerent, contentious, disputatious, argumentative, quarrelsome, hot-tempered.

**F3** peaceable.

**pull** *v* 1 TOW, drag, haul, draw, tug, jerk, yank (*infml*). 2 REMOVE, take out, extract, pull out, pluck, uproot, pull up, rip, tear. 3 ATTRACT, draw, lure, allure, entice, tempt, magnetize. 4 DISLOCATE, sprain, wrench, strain.

**F3** 1 push, press. 3 repel, deter, discourage.

*n* 1 TOW, drag, tug, jerk, yank (*infml*). 2 ATTRACTION, lure, allurement, drawing power, magnetism, influence, weight.

**pull apart** separate, part, dismember, dismantle, take to pieces.

**F3** join.

**pull down** destroy, demolish, knock down, bulldoze.

**F3** build, erect, put up.

**pull off** 1 ACCOMPLISH, achieve, bring off, succeed, manage, carry out.

2 DETACH, remove.

**F3** 1 fail. 2 attach.

**pull out** retreat, withdraw, leave, depart, quit, move out, evacuate, desert, abandon.

**F3** join, arrive.

**pull through** recover, rally, recuperate, survive, weather.

**pull together** co-operate, work together, collaborate, team up.

**F3** fight.

**pull up** 1 STOP, halt, park, draw up, pull in, pull over, brake.

2 REPRIMAND, tell off (*infml*), tick off (*infml*), take to task, rebuke, criticize.

**pulp** *n* flesh, marrow, paste, purée, mash, mush, pap.

*v* crush, squash, pulverize, mash, purée, liquidize.

**pulsate** *v* pulse, beat, throb, pound, hammer, drum, thud, thump, vibrate, oscillate, quiver.

**pulse** *n* beat, stroke, rhythm, throb, pulsation, beating, pounding, drumming, vibration, oscillation.

**pulverize** *v* 1 CRUSH, pound, grind, mill, powder. 2 DEFEAT, destroy, demolish, annihilate.

**pump** *v* push, drive, force, inject, siphon, draw, drain.

**pump up** blow up, inflate, puff up, fill.

**pun** *n* play on words, double entendre, witticism, quip.

**punch**[1] *v* hit, strike, pummel, jab, bash, clout, cuff, box, thump, sock (*sl*), wallop (*infml*).

*n* 1 BLOW, jab, bash, clout, thump, wallop (*infml*). 2 FORCE, impact, effectiveness, drive, vigour, verve, panache.

**punch**[2] *v* perforate, pierce, puncture, prick, bore, drill, stamp, cut.

**punctilious** *adj* scrupulous, conscientious, meticulous, careful, exact, precise, strict, formal, proper, particular, finicky, fussy.

**F3** lax, informal.

**punctual** *adj* prompt, on time, on the dot, exact, precise, early, in good time.

**F3** unpunctual, late.

**punctuation**

> *Punctuation marks include*: comma, full stop, period, colon, semicolon, brackets, parentheses, square brackets, inverted commas, speech marks, quotation marks, quotes (*infml*), exclamation mark, question mark, apostrophe, asterisk, star, hyphen, dash, oblique stroke, solidus, backslash.

**puncture** *n* 1 FLAT TYRE, flat (*infml*), blow-out. 2 LEAK, hole, perforation, cut, nick.

*v* prick, pierce, penetrate, perforate, hole, cut, nick, burst, rupture, flatten, deflate.

**pungent** *adj* strong, hot, peppery, spicy, aromatic, tangy, piquant, sharp, keen, acute, sour, bitter, acrid, caustic, stinging, biting, cutting, incisive, pointed, piercing, penetrating, sarcastic, scathing.

**F3** mild, bland, tasteless.

**punish** *v* penalize, discipline, correct, chastise, castigate, scold, beat, flog, lash, cane, spank, fine, imprison.

**F3** reward.

**punishment** *n* discipline, correction, chastisement, beating, flogging, penalty, fine, imprisonment, sentence, deserts, retribution, revenge.

**F3** reward.

**punitive** *adj* penal, disciplinary, retributive, retaliatory, vindictive, punishing.

**puny** *adj* weak, feeble, frail, sickly, undeveloped, underdeveloped, stunted, undersized, diminutive, little, tiny, insignificant.

**F3** strong, sturdy, large, important.

**pupil** *n* student, scholar, schoolboy, schoolgirl, learner, apprentice, beginner, novice, disciple, protégé(e).

teacher.

**purchase** v buy, pay for, invest in (*infml*), procure, acquire, obtain, get, secure, gain, earn, win.

sell.

n acquisition, buy (*infml*), investment, asset, possession, property.

sale.

**purchaser** n buyer, consumer, shopper, customer, client.

seller, vendor.

**pure** adj 1 *pure gold*: unadulterated, unalloyed, unmixed, undiluted, neat, solid, simple, natural, real, authentic, genuine, true. 2 STERILE, uncontaminated, unpolluted, germ-free, aseptic, antiseptic, disinfected, sterilized, hygienic, sanitary, clean, immaculate, spotless, clear. 3 SHEER, utter, complete, total, thorough, absolute, perfect, unqualified. 4 CHASTE, virginal, undefiled, unsullied, moral, upright, virtuous, blameless, innocent. 5 *pure mathematics*: theoretical, abstract, conjectural, speculative, academic.

1 impure, adulterated. 2 contaminated, polluted. 4 immoral. 5 applied.

**purely** adv 1 UTTERLY, completely, totally, entirely, wholly, thoroughly, absolutely. 2 ONLY, simply, merely, just, solely, exclusively.

**purge** v 1 PURIFY, cleanse, clean out, scour, clear, absolve. 2 OUST, remove, get rid of, eject, expel, root out, eradicate, exterminate, wipe out, kill.

n removal, ejection, expulsion, witch hunt, eradication, extermination.

**purify** v refine, filter, clarify, clean, cleanse, decontaminate, sanitize, disinfect, sterilize, fumigate, deodorize.

contaminate, pollute, defile.

**purist** n pedant, literalist, formalist, stickler, quibbler, nit-picker.

**puritanical** adj puritan, moralistic,

disciplinarian, ascetic, abstemious, austere, severe, stern, strict, strait-laced, prim, proper, prudish, disapproving, stuffy, stiff, rigid, narrow-minded, bigoted, fanatical, zealous.

hedonistic, liberal, indulgent, broad-minded.

**purity** n 1 CLEARNESS, clarity, cleanness, cleanliness, untaintedness, wholesomeness. 2 SIMPLICITY, authenticity, genuineness, truth. 3 CHASTITY, decency, morality, integrity, rectitude, uprightness, virtue, innocence, blamelessness.

1 impurity. 3 immorality.

**purpose** n 1 INTENTION, aim, objective, end, goal, target, plan, design, vision, idea, point, object, reason, motive, rationale, principle, result, outcome. 2 DETERMINATION, resolve, resolution, drive, single-mindedness, dedication, devotion, constancy, steadfastness, persistence, tenacity, zeal. 3 USE, function, application, good, advantage, benefit, value.

**on purpose** purposely, deliberately, intentionally, consciously, knowingly, wittingly, wilfully.

accidentally, impulsively, spontaneously.

**purposeful** adj determined, decided, resolved, resolute, single-minded, constant, steadfast, persistent, persevering, tenacious, strong-willed, positive, firm, deliberate.

purposeless, aimless.

**purse** n 1 MONEY-BAG, wallet, pouch. 2 MONEY, means, resources, finances, funds, coffers, treasury, exchequer. 3 REWARD, award, prize.

v pucker, wrinkle, draw together, close, tighten, contract, compress.

**pursue** v 1 *pursue an activity*: perform, engage in, practise, conduct, carry on, continue, keep on, keep up, maintain, persevere in, persist in, hold to, aspire to, aim for, strive for, try for. **2** CHASE, go after, follow, track, trail, shadow, tail, dog, harass, harry, hound, hunt, seek, search for, investigate, inquire into.

**pursuit** n **1** CHASE, hue and cry, tracking, stalking, trail, hunt, quest, search, investigation. **2** ACTIVITY, interest, hobby, pastime, occupation, trade, craft, line, speciality, vocation.

**push** v **1** PROPEL, thrust, ram, shove, jostle, elbow, prod, poke, press, depress, squeeze, squash, drive, force, constrain. **2** PROMOTE, advertise, publicize, boost, encourage, urge, egg on (*infml*), incite, spur, influence, persuade, pressurize, bully.

F3 **1** pull. **2** discourage, dissuade.
n **1** KNOCK, shove, nudge, jolt, prod, poke, thrust. **2** ENERGY, vigour, vitality, go (*infml*), drive, effort, dynamism, enterprise, initiative, ambition, determination.

**pushy** adj assertive, self-assertive, ambitious, forceful, aggressive, over-confident, forward, bold, brash, arrogant, presumptuous, assuming, bossy (*infml*).

F3 unassertive, unassuming.

**put** v **1** PLACE, lay, deposit, plonk (*infml*), set, fix, settle, establish, stand, position, dispose, situate, station, post. **2** APPLY, impose, inflict, levy, assign, subject. **3** WORD, phrase, formulate, frame, couch, express, voice, utter, state. **4** *put a suggestion*: submit, present, offer, suggest, propose.

**put across** put over, communicate, convey, express, explain, spell out, bring home to, get through to.

**put aside** put by, set aside, keep, retain, save, reserve, store, stow, stockpile, stash (*infml*), hoard, salt away.

**put away** (*infml*) **1** CONSUME, devour, eat, drink. **2** IMPRISON, jail, lock up, commit, certify.

**put back 1** DELAY, defer, postpone,
reschedule. **2** REPLACE, return.

F3 **1** bring forward.

**put down 1** WRITE DOWN, transcribe, enter, log, register, record, note. **2** CRUSH, quash, suppress, defeat, quell, silence, snub, slight, squash, deflate, humble, take down a peg, shame, humiliate, mortify. **3** *put down a sick dog*: kill, put to sleep. **4** ASCRIBE, attribute, blame, charge.

**put forward** advance, suggest, recommend, nominate, propose, move, table, introduce, present, submit, offer, tender.

**put in** insert, enter, input, submit, install, fit.

**put off 1** DELAY, defer, postpone, reschedule. **2** DETER, dissuade, discourage, dishearten, demoralize, daunt, dismay, intimidate, disconcert, confuse, distract.

F3 **2** encourage.

**put on 1** ATTACH, affix, apply, place, add, impose. **2** PRETEND, feign, sham, fake, simulate, affect, assume. **3** STAGE, mount, produce, present, do, perform.

**put out 1** PUBLISH, announce, broadcast, circulate. **2** EXTINGUISH, quench, douse, smother, switch off, turn off. **3** INCONVENIENCE, impose on, bother, disturb, trouble, upset, hurt, offend, annoy, irritate, irk, anger, exasperate.

F3 **2** light.

**put through** accomplish, achieve, complete, conclude, finalize, execute, manage, bring off.

**put up 1** ERECT, build, construct, assemble. **2** ACCOMMODATE, house, lodge, shelter. **3** *put up prices*: raise, increase. **4** PAY, invest, give, advance, float, provide, supply, pledge, offer.

**put up to** prompt, incite, encourage, egg on (*infml*), urge, goad.

F3 discourage, dissuade.

**put up with** stand, bear, abide, stomach, endure, suffer, tolerate, allow, accept, stand for, take, take

lying down.
**F3** object to, reject.

**putrid** adj rotten, decayed, decomposed, mouldy, off, bad, rancid, addled, corrupt, contaminated, tainted, polluted, foul, rank, fetid, stinking.
**F3** fresh, wholesome.

**put-upon** adj imposed on, taken advantage of, exploited, used, abused, maltreated, persecuted.

**puzzle** v 1 BAFFLE, mystify, perplex, confound, stump (infml), floor (infml), confuse, bewilder, flummox (infml). 2 THINK, ponder, meditate, consider, mull over, deliberate, figure, rack one's brains.

n question, poser, brain-teaser, mind-bender, crossword, rebus, anagram, riddle, conundrum, mystery, enigma, paradox.

**puzzle out** solve, work out, figure out, decipher, decode, crack, unravel, untangle, sort out, resolve, clear up.

**puzzled** adj baffled, mystified, perplexed, confounded, at a loss, beaten, stumped (infml), confused, bewildered, nonplussed, lost, at sea, flummoxed (infml).
**F3** clear.

**pyromaniac** n arsonist, incendiary, fire-raiser, firebug (infml).

# Q

**quagmire** n bog, marsh, quag, fen, swamp, morass, mire, quicksand.

**quail** v recoil, back away, shy away, shrink, flinch, cringe, cower, tremble, quake, shudder, falter.

**quaint** adj picturesque, charming, twee (infml), old-fashioned, antiquated, old-world, olde-worlde (infml), unusual, strange, odd, curious, bizarre, fanciful, whimsical.
**F3** modern.

**quake** v shake, tremble, shudder, quiver, shiver, quail, vibrate, wobble, rock, sway, move, convulse, heave.

**qualification** n 1 CERTIFICATE, diploma, training, skill, competence, ability, capability, capacity, aptitude, suitability, fitness, eligibility. 2 RESTRICTION, limitation, reservation, exception, exemption, condition, caveat, provision, proviso, stipulation, modification.

**qualified** adj 1 CERTIFIED, chartered, licensed, professional, trained, experienced, practised, skilled, accomplished, expert,

knowledgeable, skilful, talented, proficient, competent, efficient, able, capable, fit, eligible. 2 qualified praise: reserved, guarded, cautious, restricted, limited, bounded, contingent, conditional, provisional, equivocal.
**F3** 1 unqualified. 2 unconditional, whole-hearted.

**qualify** v 1 TRAIN, prepare, equip, fit, pass, graduate, certify, empower, entitle, authorize, sanction, permit. 2 MODERATE, reduce, lessen, diminish, temper, soften, weaken, mitigate, ease, adjust, modify, restrain, restrict, limit, delimit, define, classify.
**F3** 1 disqualify.

**quality** n 1 PROPERTY, characteristic, peculiarity, attribute, aspect, feature, trait, mark. 2 of poor quality: standard, grade, class, kind, sort, nature, character, calibre, status, rank, value, worth, merit, condition. 3 EXCELLENCE, superiority, pre-eminence, distinction, refinement.

**qualm** n misgiving, apprehension, fear, anxiety, worry, disquiet, uneasiness, scruple, hesitation, reluctance, uncertainty, doubt.

**quandary** n dilemma, predicament, impasse, perplexity, bewilderment, confusion, mess, fix, hole (*infml*), problem, difficulty.

**quantity** n amount, number, sum, total, aggregate, mass, lot, share, portion, quota, allotment, measure, dose, proportion, part, content, capacity, volume, weight, bulk, size, magnitude, expanse, extent, length, breadth.

**quarrel** n row, argument, slanging match (*infml*), wrangle, squabble, tiff, misunderstanding, disagreement, dispute, dissension, controversy, difference, conflict, clash, contention, strife, fight, scrap, brawl, feud, vendetta, schism.

**F3** agreement, harmony.

v row, argue, bicker, squabble, wrangle, be at loggerheads, fall out, disagree, dispute, dissent, differ, be at variance, clash, contend, fight, scrap, feud.

**F3** agree.

**quarrelsome** adj argumentative, disputatious, contentious, belligerent, ill-tempered, irritable.

**F3** peaceable, placid.

**quarry** n prey, victim, object, goal, target, game, kill, prize.

**quarter** n district, sector, zone, neighbourhood, locality, vicinity, area, region, province, territory, division, section, part, place, spot, point, direction, side.

v station, post, billet, accommodate, put up, lodge, board, house, shelter.

**quarters** n accommodation, lodgings, billet, digs (*infml*), residence, dwelling, habitation, domicile, rooms, barracks, station, post.

**quash** v annul, revoke, rescind,

overrule, cancel, nullify, void, invalidate, reverse, set aside, squash, crush, quell, suppress, subdue, defeat, overthrow.

**F3** confirm, vindicate, reinstate.

**quaver** v shake, tremble, quake, shudder, quiver, vibrate, pulsate, oscillate, flutter, flicker, trill, warble.

**quay** n wharf, pier, jetty, dock, harbour.

**queasy** adj sick, ill, unwell, queer, groggy, green, nauseated, sickened, bilious, squeamish, faint, dizzy, giddy.

**queen** n 1 monarch, sovereign, ruler, majesty, princess, empress, consort. 2 beauty, belle.

**queer** adj 1 ODD, mysterious, strange, unusual, uncommon, weird, unnatural, bizarre, eccentric, peculiar, funny, puzzling, curious, remarkable. 2 *I feel queer*: unwell, ill, sick, queasy, light-headed, faint, giddy, dizzy. 3 SUSPECT, suspicious, shifty, dubious, shady (*infml*). 4 (*sl*) HOMOSEXUAL, gay, lesbian.

**F3** 1 ordinary, usual, common. 2 well.

**quell** v subdue, quash, crush, squash, suppress, put down, overcome, conquer, defeat, overpower, moderate, mitigate, allay, alleviate, soothe, calm, pacify, hush, quiet, silence, stifle, extinguish.

**quench** v 1 *quench one's thirst*: slake, satisfy, sate, cool.

2 EXTINGUISH, douse, put out, snuff out.

**querulous** adj peevish, fretful, fractious, cantankerous, cross, irritable, complaining, grumbling, discontented, dissatisfied, critical, carping, captious, fault-finding, fussy.

**F3** placid, uncomplaining, contented.

**query** v ask, inquire, question, challenge, dispute, quarrel with, doubt, suspect, distrust, mistrust, disbelieve.

**F3** accept.

n question, inquiry, problem,
uncertainty, doubt, suspicion,
scepticism, reservation, hesitation.

**quest** n search, hunt, pursuit,
investigation, inquiry, mission,
crusade, enterprise, undertaking,
venture, journey, voyage, expedition,
exploration, adventure.

**question** v interrogate, quiz, grill,
pump, interview, examine, cross-
examine, debrief, ask, inquire,
investigate, probe, query, challenge,
dispute, doubt, disbelieve.
n 1 QUERY, inquiry, poser, problem,
difficulty. 2 ISSUE, matter, subject,
topic, point, proposal, proposition,
motion, debate, dispute, controversy.

**questionable** adj debatable,
disputable, unsettled, undetermined,
unproven, uncertain, arguable,
controversial, vexed, doubtful,
dubious, suspicious, suspect, shady
(infml), fishy (infml), iffy (sl).
⧉ unquestionable, indisputable,
certain.

**questionnaire** n quiz, test, survey,
opinion poll.

**queue** n line, tailback, file,
crocodile, procession, train, string,
succession, series, sequence, order.

**quibble** v carp, cavil, split hairs, nit-
pick, equivocate, prevaricate.
n complaint, objection, criticism,
query.

**quick** adj 1 FAST, swift, rapid,
speedy, express, hurried, hasty,
cursory, fleeting, brief, prompt,
ready, immediate, instant,
instantaneous, sudden, brisk, nimble,
sprightly, agile. 2 CLEVER,
intelligent, quick-witted, smart,
sharp, keen, shrewd, astute,
discerning, perceptive, responsive,
receptive.
⧉ 1 slow, sluggish, lethargic.
2 unintelligent, dull.

**quicken** v 1 ACCELERATE, speed,
hurry, hasten, precipitate, expedite,
dispatch, advance. 2 ANIMATE,

enliven, invigorate, energize,
galvanize, activate, rouse, arouse,
stimulate, excite, inspire, revive,
refresh, reinvigorate, reactivate.
⧉ 1 slow, retard. 2 dull.

**quiet** adj 1 SILENT, noiseless,
inaudible, hushed, soft, low.
2 PEACEFUL, still, tranquil, serene,
calm, composed, undisturbed,
untroubled, placid. 3 SHY, reserved,
reticent, uncommunicative, taciturn,
unforthcoming, retiring, withdrawn,
thoughtful, subdued, meek. 4 a quiet
spot: isolated, unfrequented, lonely,
secluded, private.
⧉ 1 noisy, loud. 2 excitable.
3 extrovert.
n quietness, silence, hush, peace, lull,
stillness, tranquillity, serenity, calm,
rest, repose.
⧉ noise, loudness, disturbance,
bustle.

**quieten** v 1 SILENCE, hush, mute,
soften, lower, diminish, reduce, stifle,
muffle, deaden, dull. 2 SUBDUE,
pacify, quell, quiet, still, smooth,
calm, soothe, compose, sober.
⧉ 2 disturb, agitate.

**quilt** n bedcover, coverlet,
bedspread, counterpane, eiderdown,
duvet.

**quip** n joke, jest, crack, gag (infml),
witticism, riposte, retort, gibe.

**quirk** n freak, eccentricity, curiosity,
oddity, peculiarity, idiosyncrasy,
mannerism, habit, trait, foible, whim,
caprice, turn, twist.

**quit** v 1 LEAVE, depart, go, exit,
decamp, desert, forsake, abandon,
renounce, relinquish, surrender, give
up, resign, retire, withdraw. 2 quit
smoking: stop, cease, end,
discontinue, desist, drop, give up,
pack in (sl).

**quite** adv 1 MODERATELY, rather,
somewhat, fairly, relatively,
comparatively. 2 UTTERLY,
absolutely, totally, completely,
entirely, wholly, fully, perfectly,

exactly, precisely.

**quiver** v shake, tremble, shudder, shiver, quake, quaver, vibrate, palpitate, flutter, flicker, oscillate, wobble.

n shake, tremble, shudder, shiver, tremor, vibration, palpitation, flutter, flicker, oscillation, wobble.

**quiz** n questionnaire, test, examination, competition.

v question, interrogate, grill, pump, examine, cross-examine.

**quizzical** adj questioning, inquiring, curious, amused, humorous, teasing,

mocking, satirical, sardonic, sceptical.

**quota** n ration, allowance, allocation, assignment, share, portion, part, slice, cut (infml), percentage, proportion.

**quotation** n 1 CITATION, quote (infml), extract, excerpt, passage, piece, cutting, reference. 2 ESTIMATE, quote (infml), tender, figure, price, cost, charge, rate.

**quote** v cite, refer to, mention, name, reproduce, echo, repeat, recite, recall, recollect.

# R

**rabble** n crowd, throng, horde, herd, mob, masses, populace, riff-raff.

**rabble-rouser** n agitator, troublemaker, incendiary, demagogue, ringleader.

**race**[1] n sprint, steeplechase, marathon, scramble, regatta, competition, contest, contention, rivalry, chase, pursuit, quest.

v run, sprint, dash, tear, fly, gallop, speed, career, dart, zoom, rush, hurry, hasten.

*Types of race and famous races include:* cycle race, cyclo-cross, road race, time trial, Milk Race, Tour de France; greyhound race, Greyhound Derby; horserace, Cheltenham Gold Cup, the Classics (Derby, Oaks, One Thousand Guineas, St. Leger, Two Thousand Guineas), Grand National, Kentucky Derby, Melbourne Cup, Prix de l'Arc de Triomphe, steeplechase, trotting race, harness race; motorcycle race, motocross, scramble, speedway, Isle of Man Tourist Trophy (TT); motor-race, GrandPrix, Indianapolis 500, Le Mans, Monte Carlo rally, RAC

Rally, stock car race; rowing, regatta, Boat Race; running, cross-country, dash (NorthAmer.), hurdles, marathon, London Marathon, relay, sprint, steeplechase, track event; ski race, downhill, slalom; swimming race; walking race, walkathon; yacht race, Admiral's Cup, America's Cup; egg-and-spoon race, pancake race, sack race, wheelbarrow race.

**race**[2] n nation, people, tribe, clan, house, dynasty, family, kindred, ancestry, line, blood, stock, genus, species, breed.

**race-course** n racetrack, course, track, circuit, lap, turf, speedway.

**racial** adj national, tribal, ethnic, folk, genealogical, ancestral, inherited, genetic.

**racism** n racialism, xenophobia, chauvinism, jingoism, discrimination, prejudice, bias.

**rack** n shelf, stand, support, structure, frame, framework.

**racket** n 1 NOISE, din, uproar, row, fuss, outcry, clamour, commotion, disturbance, pandemonium, hurly-burly, hubbub. 2 SWINDLE, con (*infml*), fraud, fiddle, deception, trick, dodge, scheme, business, game.

**racy** *adj* **1** RIBALD, bawdy, risqué, naughty, indecent, indelicate, suggestive. **2** LIVELY, animated, spirited, energetic, dynamic, buoyant, boisterous.

**radiance** *n* light, luminosity, incandescence, radiation, brightness, brilliance, shine, lustre, gleam, glow, glitter, resplendence, splendour, happiness, joy, pleasure, delight, rapture.

**radiant** *adj* bright, luminous, shining, gleaming, glowing, beaming, glittering, sparkling, brilliant, resplendent, splendid, glorious, happy, joyful, delighted, ecstatic.
F∃ dull, miserable.

**radiate** *v* shine, gleam, glow, beam, shed, pour, give off, emit, emanate, diffuse, issue, disseminate, scatter, spread (out), diverge, branch.

**radical** *adj* **1** BASIC, fundamental, primary, essential, natural, native, innate, intrinsic, deep-seated, profound. **2** *radical changes*: drastic, comprehensive, thorough, sweeping, far-reaching, thoroughgoing, complete, total, entire. **3** FANATICAL, militant, extreme, extremist, revolutionary.
F∃ **1** superficial. **3** moderate.
*n* fanatic, militant, extremist, revolutionary, reformer, reformist, fundamentalist.

**raffle** *n* draw, lottery, sweepstake, sweep, tombola.

**rage** *n* **1** ANGER, wrath, fury, frenzy, tantrum, temper. **2** (*infml*) *all the rage*: craze, fad, thing (*infml*), fashion, vogue, style, passion, enthusiasm, obsession.
*v* fume, seethe, rant, rave, storm, thunder, explode, rampage.

**ragged** *adj* **1** *ragged clothes*: frayed, torn, ripped, tattered, worn-out, threadbare, tatty, shabby, scruffy, unkempt, down-at-heel. **2** JAGGED,

serrated, indented, notched, rough, uneven, irregular, fragmented, erratic, disorganized.

**raid** *n* attack, onset, onslaught, invasion, inroad, incursion, foray, sortie, strike, blitz, swoop, bust (*sl*), robbery, break-in, hold-up.
*v* loot, pillage, plunder, ransack, rifle, maraud, attack, descend on, invade, storm.

**raider** *n* attacker, invader, looter, plunderer, ransacker, marauder, robber, thief, brigand, pirate.

**railing** *n* fence, paling, barrier, parapet, rail, balustrade.

**railway** *n* track, line, rails, underground, tube (*infml*), subway, metro.

**rain** *n* rainfall, precipitation, raindrops, drizzle, shower, cloudburst, downpour, deluge, torrent, storm, thunderstorm, squall.
*v* spit, drizzle, shower, pour, teem, pelt, bucket (*infml*), deluge.

**rainy** *adj* wet, damp, showery, drizzly.
F∃ dry.

**raise** *v* **1** LIFT, elevate, hoist, jack up, erect, build, construct.
**2** INCREASE, augment, escalate, magnify, heighten, strengthen, intensify, amplify, boost, enhance.
**3** *raise funds*: get, obtain, collect, gather, assemble, rally, muster, recruit. **4** BRING UP, rear, breed, propagate, grow, cultivate, develop.
**5** *raise a subject*: bring up, broach, introduce, present, put forward, moot, suggest.
F∃ **1** lower. **2** decrease, reduce.
**5** suppress.

**rake** *v* hoe, scratch, scrape, graze, comb, scour, search, hunt, ransack, gather, collect, amass, accumulate.

**rally** *v* **1** GATHER, collect, assemble, congregate, convene, muster, summon, round up, unite, marshal, organize, mobilize, reassemble, regroup, reorganize. **2** RECOVER,

recuperate, revive, improve, pick up.
*n* **1** GATHERING, assembly,
convention, convocation, conference,
meeting, jamboree, reunion, march,
demonstration. **2** RECOVERY,
recuperation, revival, comeback,
improvement, resurgence, renewal.

**ram** *v* **1** HIT, strike, butt, hammer,
pound, drum, crash, smash, slam.
**2** FORCE, drive, thrust, cram, stuff,
pack, crowd, jam, wedge.

**ramble** *v* **1** WALK, hike, trek, tramp,
traipse, stroll, amble, saunter,
straggle, wander, roam, rove,
meander, wind, zigzag. **2** CHATTER,
babble, rabbit (on) (*infml*), witter
(on) (*infml*), expatiate, digress, drift.
*n* walk, hike, trek, tramp, stroll,
saunter, tour, trip, excursion.

**rambler** *n* hiker, walker, stroller,
rover, roamer, wanderer, wayfarer.

**rambling** *adj* **1** SPREADING,
sprawling, straggling, trailing.
**2** CIRCUITOUS, roundabout,
digressive, wordy, long-winded, long-
drawn-out, disconnected, incoherent.
◼ **2** direct.

**ramification** *n* branch, offshoot,
development, complication, result,
consequence, upshot, implication.

**ramp** *n* slope, incline, gradient, rise.

**rampage** *v* run wild, run amok, run
riot, rush, tear, storm, rage, rant,
rave.
*n* rage, fury, frenzy, storm, uproar,
violence, destruction.
**on the rampage** wild, amok, berserk,
violent, out of control.

**rampant** *adj* unrestrained,
uncontrolled, unbridled, unchecked,
wanton, excessive, fierce, violent,
raging, wild, riotous, rank, profuse,
rife, widespread, prevalent.

**ramshackle** *adj* dilapidated,
tumbledown, broken-down,
crumbling, ruined, derelict, jerry-
built, unsafe, rickety, shaky,
unsteady, tottering, decrepit.
◼ solid, stable.

**rancid** *adj* sour, off, bad, musty,
stale, rank, foul, fetid, putrid, rotten.
◼ sweet.

**random** *adj* arbitrary, chance,
fortuitous, casual, incidental,
haphazard, irregular, unsystematic,
unplanned, accidental, aimless,
purposeless, indiscriminate, stray.
◼ systematic, deliberate.

**range** *n* **1** SCOPE, compass, scale,
gamut, spectrum, sweep, spread,
extent, distance, reach, span, limits,
bounds, parameters, area, field,
domain, province, sphere, orbit. **2** *a*
*range of fittings*: variety, diversity,
assortment, selection, sort, kind,
class, order, series, string, chain.
*v* **1** EXTEND, stretch, reach, spread,
vary, fluctuate. **2** ALIGN, arrange,
order, rank, classify, catalogue.

**rank**[1] *n* **1** GRADE, degree, class,
caste, status, standing, position,
station, condition, estate, echelon,
level, stratum, tier, classification,
sort, type, group, division. **2** ROW,
line, range, column, file, series, order,
formation.

---

*Ranks in the armed services include*:
*air force*: aircraftsman,
aircraftswoman, corporal, sergeant,
warrant officer, pilot officer, flying
officer, flight lieutenant, squadron-
leader, wing commander, group-
captain, air-commodore, air-vice-
marshal, air-marshal, air-chief-
marshal, marshal of the Royal Air
Force; *army*: private, lance-corporal,
corporal, sergeant, warrant officer,
lieutenant, captain, major, lieutenant-
colonel, colonel, brigadier, major
general, lieutenant-general, general,
field marshal; *navy*: able seaman,
rating, petty officer, chief petty officer,
sublieutenant, lieutenant, lieutenant-
commander, commander, captain,
commodore, rear admiral, vice-
admiral, admiral, admiral of the fleet.
*see also* **soldier**.

*v* grade, class, rate, place, position, range, sort, classify, categorize, order, arrange, organize, marshal.

**rank²** *adj* **1** UTTER, total, complete, absolute, unmitigated, thorough, sheer, downright, out-and-out, arrant, gross, flagrant, glaring, outrageous. **2** FOUL, repulsive, disgusting, revolting, stinking, putrid, rancid, stale.

**rankle** *v* annoy, irritate, rile, nettle, gall, irk, anger.

**ransack** *v* search, scour, comb, rummage, rifle, raid, sack, strip, despoil, ravage, loot, plunder, pillage.

**ransom** *n* price, money, payment, pay-off, redemption, deliverance, rescue, liberation, release.

*v* buy off, redeem, deliver, rescue, liberate, free, release.

**rant** *v* shout, cry, yell, roar, bellow, declaim, bluster, rave.

**rap** *v* **1** KNOCK, hit, strike, tap, thump. **2** (*sl*) REPROVE, reprimand, criticize, censure.

*n* **1** KNOCK, blow, tap, thump. **2** (*sl*) REBUKE, reprimand, censure, blame, punishment.

**rape** *n* violation, assault, abuse, maltreatment.

*v* violate, assault, abuse, maltreat.

**rapid** *adj* swift, speedy, quick, fast, express, lightning, prompt, brisk, hurried, hasty, precipitate, headlong. ◲ slow, leisurely, sluggish.

**rapport** *n* bond, link, affinity, relationship, empathy, sympathy, understanding, harmony.

**rapt** *adj* engrossed, absorbed, preoccupied, intent, gripped, spellbound, enthralled, captivated, fascinated, entranced, charmed, enchanted, delighted, ravished, enraptured, transported.

**rapture** *n* delight, happiness, joy, bliss, ecstasy, euphoria, exaltation.

**rare** *adj* **1** UNCOMMON, unusual, scarce, sparse, sporadic, infrequent.

**2** EXQUISITE, superb, excellent, superlative, incomparable, exceptional, remarkable, precious. ◲ **1** common, abundant, frequent.

**rarefied** *adj* exclusive, select, private, esoteric, refined, high, noble, sublime.

**rarely** *adv* seldom, hardly ever, infrequently, little. ◲ often, frequently.

**raring** *adj* eager, keen, enthusiastic, ready, willing, impatient, longing, itching, desperate.

**rarity** *n* **1** CURIOSITY, curio, gem, pearl, treasure, find. **2** UNCOMMONNESS, unusualness, strangeness, scarcity, shortage, sparseness, infrequency. ◲ **2** commonness, frequency.

**rascal** *n* rogue, scoundrel, scamp, scallywag, imp, devil, villain, good-for-nothing, wastrel.

**rash¹** *adj* reckless, ill-considered, foolhardy, ill-advised, madcap, hare-brained, hot-headed, headstrong, impulsive, impetuous, hasty, headlong, unguarded, unwary, indiscreet, imprudent, careless, heedless, unthinking. ◲ cautious, wary, careful.

**rash²** *n* eruption, outbreak, epidemic, plague.

**rasp** *n* grating, scrape, grinding, scratch, harshness, hoarseness, croak.

*v* grate, scrape, grind, file, sand, scour, abrade, rub.

**rate** *n* **1** SPEED, velocity, tempo, time, ratio, proportion, relation, degree, grade, rank, rating, standard, basis, measure, scale. **2** CHARGE, fee, hire, toll, tariff, price, cost, value, worth, tax, duty, amount, figure, percentage.

*v* **1** JUDGE, regard, consider, deem, count, reckon, figure, estimate, evaluate, assess, weigh, measure, grade, rank, class, classify. **2** ADMIRE, respect, esteem, value, prize. **3**

DESERVE, merit.

**rather** adv **1** MODERATELY, relatively, slightly, a bit, somewhat, fairly, quite, pretty, noticeably, significantly, very. **2** PREFERABLY, sooner, instead.

**ratify** v approve, uphold, endorse, sign, legalize, sanction, authorize, establish, affirm, confirm, certify, validate, authenticate.
**Ea** repudiate, reject.

**rating** n class, rank, degree, status, standing, position, placing, order, grade, mark, evaluation, assessment, classification, category.

**ratio** n percentage, fraction, proportion, relation, relationship, correspondence, correlation.

**ration** n quota, allowance, allocation, allotment, share, portion, helping, part, measure, amount. v apportion, allot, allocate, share, deal out, distribute, dole out, dispense, supply, issue, control, restrict, limit, conserve, save.

**rational** adj logical, reasonable, sound, well-founded, realistic, sensible, clear-headed, judicious, wise, sane, normal, balanced, lucid, reasoning, thinking, intelligent, enlightened.
**Ea** irrational, illogical, insane, crazy.

**rationale** n logic, reasoning, philosophy, principle, basis, grounds, explanation, reason, motive, motivation, theory.

**rationalize** v **1** JUSTIFY, excuse, vindicate, explain, account for. **2** REORGANIZE, streamline.

**rations** n food, provisions, supplies, stores.

**rattle** v clatter, jingle, jangle, clank, shake, vibrate, jolt, jar, bounce, bump.
**rattle off** reel off, list, run through, recite, repeat.

**raucous** adj harsh, rough, hoarse, husky, rasping, grating, jarring, strident, noisy, loud.

**ravage** v destroy, devastate, lay waste, demolish, raze, wreck, ruin, spoil, damage, loot, pillage, plunder, sack, despoil.
n destruction, devastation, havoc, damage, ruin, desolation, wreckage, pillage, plunder.

**rave** v rage, storm, thunder, roar, rant, ramble, babble, splutter.
adj (infml) enthusiastic, rapturous, favourable, excellent, wonderful.

**ravenous** adj hungry, starving, starved, famished, greedy, voracious, insatiable.

**ravine** n canyon, gorge, gully, pass.

**raving** adj mad, insane, crazy, hysterical, delirious, wild, frenzied, furious, berserk.

**ravish** v enrapture, delight, overjoy, enchant, charm, captivate, entrance, fascinate, spellbind.

**ravishing** adj delightful, enchanting, charming, lovely, beautiful, gorgeous, stunning, radiant, dazzling, alluring, seductive.

**raw** adj **1** raw vegetables: uncooked, fresh. **2** UNPROCESSED, unrefined, untreated, crude, natural. **3** PLAIN, bare, naked, basic, harsh, brutal, realistic. **4** SCRATCHED, grazed, scraped, open, bloody, sore, tender, sensitive. **5** COLD, chilly, bitter, biting, piercing, freezing, bleak. **6** a raw recruit: new, green, immature, callow, inexperienced, untrained, unskilled.
**Ea 1** cooked, done. **2** processed, refined. **5** warm. **6** experienced, skilled.

**ray** n beam, shaft, flash, gleam, flicker, glimmer, glint, spark, trace, hint, indication.

**raze** v demolish, pull down, tear down, bulldoze, flatten, level, destroy.

**re** prep about, concerning, regarding, with regard to, with reference to.

**reach** v arrive at, get to, attain, achieve, make, amount to, hit, strike,

touch, contact, stretch, extend, grasp.
*n* range, scope, compass, distance,
spread, extent, stretch, grasp,
jurisdiction, command, power,
influence.

**react** *v* respond, retaliate,
reciprocate, reply, answer,
acknowledge, act, behave.

**reaction** *n* response, effect, reply,
answer, acknowledgement, feedback,
counteraction, reflex, recoil,
reciprocation, retaliation.

**reactionary** *adj* conservative, right-
wing, rightist, die-hard, counter-
revolutionary.
**F3** progressive, revolutionary.
*n* conservative, right-winger, rightist,
die-hard, counter-revolutionary.
**F3** progressive, revolutionary.

**read** *v* **1** STUDY, peruse, pore over,
scan, skim, decipher, decode,
interpret, construe, understand,
comprehend. **2** RECITE, declaim,
deliver, speak, utter. **3** *the gauge
read zero*: indicate, show, display,
register, record.

**readable** *adj* **1** LEGIBLE,
decipherable, intelligible, clear,
understandable, comprehensible. **2**
INTERESTING, enjoyable,
entertaining, gripping,
unputdownable (*infml*).
**F3 1** illegible. **2** unreadable.

**readily** *adv* willingly, unhesitatingly,
gladly, eagerly, promptly, quickly,
freely, smoothly, easily, effortlessly.
**F3** unwillingly, reluctantly.

**reading** *n* **1** STUDY, perusal,
scrutiny, examination, inspection,
interpretation, understanding,
rendering, version, rendition, recital.
**2** *a reading from the Bible*: passage,
lesson.

**ready** *adj* **1** *ready to go*: prepared,
waiting, set, fit, arranged, organized,
completed, finished. **2** WILLING,
inclined, disposed, happy, game
(*infml*), eager, keen. **3** AVAILABLE,
to hand, present, near, accessible,

convenient, handy. **4** PROMPT,
immediate, quick, sharp, astute,
perceptive, alert.
**F3 1** unprepared. **2** unwilling,
reluctant, disinclined. **3** unavailable,
inaccessible. **4** slow.

**real** *adj* actual, existing, physical,
material, substantial, tangible,
genuine, authentic, bona fide,
official, rightful, legitimate, valid,
true, factual, certain, sure, positive,
veritable, honest, sincere, heartfelt,
unfeigned, unaffected.
**F3** unreal, imaginary, false.

**realistic** *adj* **1** PRACTICAL, down-
to-earth, commonsense, sensible,
level-headed, clear-sighted,
businesslike, hard-headed, pragmatic,
matter-of-fact, rational, logical,
objective, detached, unsentimental,
unromantic. **2** LIFELIKE, faithful,
truthful, true, genuine, authentic,
natural, real, real-life, graphic,
representational.
**F3 1** unrealistic, impractical,
irrational, idealistic.

**reality** *n* truth, fact, certainty,
realism, actuality, existence,
materiality, tangibility, genuineness,
authenticity, validity.

**realize** *v* **1** UNDERSTAND,
comprehend, grasp, catch on, cotton
on (*infml*), recognize, accept,
appreciate. **2** ACHIEVE, accomplish,
fulfil, complete, implement, perform.
**3** SELL FOR, fetch, make, earn,
produce, net, clear.

**really** *adv* actually, truly, honestly,
sincerely, genuinely, positively,
certainly, absolutely, categorically,
very, indeed.

**realm** *n* kingdom, monarchy,
principality, empire, country, state,
land, territory, area, region,
province, domain, sphere, orbit,
field, department.

**rear** *n* back, stern, end, tail, rump,
buttocks, posterior, behind, bottom,
backside (*infml*).

**E** front.

*adj* back, hind, hindmost, rearmost, last.

**E** front.

*v* **1** *rear a child*: bring up, raise, breed, grow, cultivate, foster, nurse, nurture, train, educate. **2** RISE, tower, soar, raise, lift.

**reason** *n* **1** CAUSE, motive, incentive, rationale, explanation, excuse, justification, defence, warrant, ground, basis, case, argument, aim, intention, purpose, object, end, goal. **2** SENSE, logic, reasoning, rationality, sanity, mind, wit, brain, intellect, understanding, wisdom, judgement, common sense, gumption.

*v* work out, solve, resolve, conclude, deduce, infer, think.

**reason with** urge, persuade, move, remonstrate with, argue with, debate with, discuss with.

**reasonable** *adj* **1** SENSIBLE, wise, well-advised, sane, intelligent, rational, logical, practical, sound, reasoned, well-thought-out, plausible, credible, possible, viable. **2** *a reasonable price*: acceptable, satisfactory, tolerable, moderate, average, fair, just, modest, inexpensive.

**E** **1** irrational. **2** exorbitant.

**reasoning** *n* logic, thinking, thought, analysis, interpretation, deduction, supposition, hypothesis, argument, case, proof.

**reassure** *v* comfort, cheer, encourage, hearten, inspirit, brace, bolster.

**E** alarm.

**rebate** *n* refund, repayment, reduction, discount, deduction, allowance.

**rebel** *v* revolt, mutiny, rise up, run riot, dissent, disobey, defy, resist, recoil, shrink.

**E** conform.

*n* revolutionary, insurrectionary,

mutineer, dissenter, nonconformist, schismatic, heretic.

**rebellion** *n* revolt, revolution, rising, uprising, insurrection, insurgence, mutiny, resistance, opposition, defiance, disobedience, insubordination, dissent, heresy.

**rebellious** *adj* revolutionary, insurrectionary, insurgent, seditious, mutinous, resistant, defiant, disobedient, insubordinate, unruly, disorderly, ungovernable, unmanageable, intractable, obstinate.

**E** obedient, submissive.

**rebirth** *n* reincarnation, resurrection, renaissance, regeneration, renewal, restoration, revival, revitalization, rejuvenation.

**rebound** *v* recoil, backfire, return, bounce, ricochet, boomerang.

**rebuff** *v* spurn, reject, refuse, decline, turn down, repulse, discourage, snub, slight, cut, cold-shoulder.

*n* rejection, refusal, repulse, check, discouragement, snub, brush-off (*infml*), slight, put-down, cold shoulder.

**rebuke** *v* reprove, castigate, chide, scold, tell off (*infml*), admonish, tick off (*infml*), reprimand, upbraid, rate, censure, blame, reproach.

**E** praise, compliment.

*n* reproach, reproof, reprimand, lecture, dressing-down (*infml*), telling-off (*infml*), ticking-off (*infml*), admonition, censure, blame.

**E** praise, commendation.

**recall** *v* remember, recollect, cast one's mind back, evoke, bring back.

**recapitulate** *v* recap, summarize, review, repeat, reiterate, restate, recount.

**recede** *v* go back, return, retire, withdraw, retreat, ebb, wane, sink, decline, diminish, dwindle, decrease, lessen, shrink, slacken, subside, abate.

**E** advance.

**receipt** *n* **1** VOUCHER, ticket, slip,

counterfoil, stub, acknowledgement.
**2** RECEIVING, reception, acceptance, delivery.

**receipts** *n* takings, income, proceeds, profits, gains, return.

**receive** *v* **1** TAKE, accept, get, obtain, derive, acquire, pick up, collect, inherit. **2** *receive guests*: admit, let in, greet, welcome, entertain, accommodate.
**3** EXPERIENCE, undergo, suffer, sustain, meet with, encounter.
**4** REACT TO, respond to, hear, perceive, apprehend.
**1** give, donate.

**recent** *adj* late, latest, current, present-day, contemporary, modern, up-to-date, new, novel, fresh, young.
**old, out-of-date.

**recently** *adv* lately, newly, freshly.

**receptacle** *n* container, vessel, holder.

**reception** *n* **1** ACCEPTANCE, admission, greeting, recognition, welcome, treatment, response, reaction, acknowledgement, receipt.
**2** PARTY, function, do (*infml*), entertainment.

**receptive** *adj* open-minded, amenable, accommodating, suggestible, susceptible, sensitive, responsive, open, accessible, approachable, friendly, hospitable, welcoming, sympathetic, favourable, interested.
** narrow-minded, resistant, unresponsive.

**recess** *n* **1** BREAK, interval, intermission, rest, respite, holiday, vacation. **2** ALCOVE, niche, nook, corner, bay, cavity, hollow, depression, indentation.

**recession** *n* slump, depression, downturn, decline.
** boom, upturn.

**recipe** *n* formula, prescription, ingredients, instructions, directions, method, system, procedure, technique.

**reciprocal** *adj* mutual, joint, shared, give-and-take, complementary, alternating, corresponding, equivalent, interchangeable.

**reciprocate** *v* respond, reply, requite, return, exchange, swap, trade, match, equal, correspond, interchange, alternate.

**recital** *n* performance, concert, recitation, reading, narration, account, rendition, interpretation, repetition.

**recitation** *n* passage, piece, party piece, poem, monologue, narration, story, tale, recital, telling.

**recite** *v* repeat, tell, narrate, relate, recount, speak, deliver, articulate, declaim, perform, reel off, itemize, enumerate.

**reckless** *adj* heedless, thoughtless, mindless, careless, negligent, irresponsible, imprudent, ill-advised, indiscreet, rash, hasty, foolhardy, daredevil, wild.
** cautious, wary, careful, prudent.

**reckon** *v* **1** CALCULATE, compute, figure out, work out, add up, total, tally, count, number, enumerate. **2** DEEM, regard, consider, esteem, value, rate, judge, evaluate, assess, estimate, gauge.
**3** THINK, believe, imagine, fancy, suppose, surmise, assume, guess, conjecture.
**reckon on** rely on, depend on, bank on, count on, trust in, hope for, expect, anticipate, foresee, plan for, bargain for, figure on, take into account, face.

**reckoning** *n* **1** *by my reckoning*: calculation, computation, estimate.
**2** BILL, account, charge, due, score, settlement. **3** JUDGEMENT, retribution, doom.

**reclaim** *v* recover, regain, recapture, retrieve, salvage, rescue, redeem, restore, reinstate, regenerate.

**recline** *v* rest, repose, lean back, lie, lounge, loll, sprawl, stretch out.

**recognition** *n* **1** IDENTIFICATION, detection, discovery, recollection, recall, remembrance, awareness, perception, realization, understanding. **2** CONFESSION, admission, acceptance, acknowledgement, gratitude, appreciation, honour, respect, greeting, salute.

**recognize** v **1** IDENTIFY, know, remember, recollect, recall, place, see, notice, spot, perceive. **2** CONFESS, own, acknowledge, accept, admit, grant, concede, allow, appreciate, understand, realize.

**recollect** v recall, remember, cast one's mind back, reminisce.

**recollection** n recall, remembrance, memory, souvenir, reminiscence, impression.

**recommend** v advocate, urge, exhort, advise, counsel, suggest, propose, put forward, advance, praise, commend, plug (infml), endorse, approve, vouch for.
F3 disapprove.

**recommendation** n advice, counsel, suggestion, proposal, advocacy, endorsement, approval, sanction, blessing, praise, commendation, plug (infml), reference, testimonial.
F3 disapproval.

**recompense** n compensation, indemnification, damages, reparation, restitution, amends, requital, repayment, reward, payment, remuneration, pay, wages.

**reconcile** v reunite, conciliate, pacify, appease, placate, propitiate, accord, harmonize, accommodate, adjust, resolve, settle, square.
F3 estrange, alienate.

**reconciliation** n reunion, conciliation, pacification, appeasement, propitiation, rapprochement, détente, settlement, agreement, harmony, accommodation, adjustment, compromise.
F3 estrangement, separation.

**reconnoitre** v explore, survey, scan, spy out, recce (sl), inspect, examine, scrutinize, investigate, patrol.

**reconstruct** v remake, rebuild, reassemble, re-establish, refashion, remodel, reform, reorganize, recreate, restore, renovate, regenerate.

**record** n **1** REGISTER, log, report, account, minutes, memorandum, note, entry, document, file, dossier, diary, journal, memoir, history, annals, archives, documentation, evidence, testimony, trace.
**2** RECORDING, disc, single, CD, compact disc, album, release, LP.
**3** break the record: fastest time, best performance, personal best, world record. **4** BACKGROUND, track record, curriculum vitae, career.
v **1** NOTE, enter, inscribe, write down, transcribe, register, log, put down, enrol, report, minute, chronicle, document, keep, preserve. **2** TAPE-RECORD, tape, videotape, video, cut.

**recording** n release, performance, record, disc, CD, cassette, tape, video.

> *Types of recording include*: album, audiotape, cassette, CD, compact disc, digital recording, disc, EP (extended play), 45, gramophone record, long-playing record, LP, magnetic tape, mono recording, record, 78, single, stereo recording, tape, tape-recording, tele-recording, video, videocassette, video disc, videotape, vinyl (infml).

**recount** v tell, relate, impart, communicate, report, narrate, describe, depict, portray, detail, repeat, rehearse, recite.

**recoup** v recover, retrieve, regain, get back, make good, repay, refund, reimburse, compensate.

**recover** v **1** recover from illness: get

better, improve, pick up, rally, mend, heal, pull through, get over, recuperate, revive, convalesce, come round. **2** REGAIN, get back, recoup, retrieve, retake, recapture, repossess, reclaim, restore.

**F3 1** worsen. **2** lose, forfeit.

**recovery** n **1** RECUPERATION, convalescence, rehabilitation, mending, healing, improvement, upturn, rally, revival, restoration. **2** RETRIEVAL, salvage, reclamation, repossession, recapture.

**F3 1** worsening. **2** loss, forfeit.

**recreation** n fun, enjoyment, pleasure, amusement, diversion, distraction, entertainment, hobby, pastime, game, sport, play, leisure, relaxation, refreshment.

**recrimination** n countercharge, accusation, counter-attack, retaliation, reprisal, retort, quarrel, bickering.

**recruit** v enlist, draft, conscript, enrol, sign up, engage, take on, mobilize, raise, gather, obtain, procure.
n beginner, novice, initiate, learner, trainee, apprentice, conscript, convert.

**rectify** v correct, put right, right, remedy, cure, repair, fix, mend, improve, amend, adjust, reform.

**recuperate** v recover, get better, improve, pick up, rally, revive, mend, convalesce.

**F3** worsen.

**recur** v repeat, persist, return, reappear.

**recurrent** adj recurring, chronic, persistent, repeated, repetitive, regular, periodic, frequent, intermittent.

**recycle** v reuse, reprocess, reclaim, recover, salvage, save.

**red** adj **1** SCARLET, vermilion, cherry, ruby, crimson, maroon, pink, reddish, bloodshot, inflamed. **2** RUDDY, florid, glowing, rosy, flushed, blushing, embarrassed,

shamefaced. **3** red hair: ginger, carroty, auburn, chestnut, Titian.

**redden** v blush, flush, colour, go red, crimson.

**redeem** v **1** BUY BACK, repurchase, cash (in), exchange, change, trade, ransom, reclaim, regain, repossess, recoup, recover, recuperate, retrieve, salvage. **2** COMPENSATE FOR, make up for, offset, outweigh, atone for, expiate, absolve, acquit, discharge, release, liberate, emancipate, free, deliver, rescue, save.

**reduce** v **1** LESSEN, decrease, contract, shrink, slim, shorten, curtail, trim, cut, slash, discount, rebate, lower, moderate, weaken, diminish, impair. **2** DRIVE, force, degrade, downgrade, demote, humble, humiliate, impoverish, subdue, overpower, master, vanquish.

**F3 1** increase, raise, boost.

**reduction** n decrease, drop, fall, decline, lessening, moderation, weakening, diminution, contraction, compression, shrinkage, narrowing, shortening, curtailment, restriction, limitation, cutback, cut, discount, rebate, devaluation, depreciation, deduction, subtraction, loss.

**F3** increase, rise, enlargement.

**redundant** adj **1** UNEMPLOYED, out of work, laid off, dismissed. **2** SUPERFLUOUS, surplus, excess, extra, supernumerary, unneeded, unnecessary, unwanted. **3** WORDY, verbose, repetitious, tautological.

**F3 1** necessary, essential. **3** concise.

**reel** v stagger, totter, wobble, rock, sway, waver, falter, stumble, lurch, pitch, roll, revolve, gyrate, spin, wheel, twirl, whirl, swirl.

**refer** v **1** SEND, direct, point, guide, pass on, transfer, commit, deliver. **2** refer to a catalogue: consult, look up, turn to, resort to. **3** ALLUDE, mention, touch on, speak of, bring up, recommend, cite, quote.

**4** APPLY, concern, relate, belong, pertain.

**referee** *n* umpire, judge, adjudicator, arbitrator, mediator, ref (*infml*).
*v* umpire, judge, adjudicate, arbitrate.

**reference** *n* **1** ALLUSION, remark, mention, citation, quotation, illustration, instance, note. **2** TESTIMONIAL, recommendation, endorsement, character. **3** RELATION, regard, respect, connection, bearing.

**refine** *v* process, treat, purify, clarify, filter, distil, polish, hone, improve, perfect, elevate, exalt.

**refined** *adj* civilized, cultured, cultivated, polished, sophisticated, urbane, genteel, gentlemanly, ladylike, well-bred, well-mannered, polite, civil, elegant, fine, delicate, subtle, precise, exact, sensitive, discriminating.
**F3** coarse, vulgar, rude.

**refinement** *n* **1** MODIFICATION, alteration, amendment, improvement. **2** CULTIVATION, sophistication, urbanity, gentility, breeding, style, elegance, taste, discrimination, subtlety, finesse.
**F3 1** deterioration. **2** coarseness, vulgarity.

**reflect** *v* **1** MIRROR, echo, imitate, reproduce, portray, depict, show, reveal, display, exhibit, manifest, demonstrate, indicate, express, communicate. **2** THINK, ponder, consider, mull (over), deliberate, contemplate, meditate, muse.

**reflection** *n* **1** IMAGE, likeness, echo, impression, indication, manifestation, observation, view, opinion. **2** THINKING, thought, study, consideration, deliberation, contemplation, meditation, musing.

**reform** *v* change, amend, improve, ameliorate, better, rectify, correct, mend, repair, rehabilitate, rebuild, reconstruct, remodel, revamp, renovate, restore, regenerate, reconstitute, reorganize, shake up (*infml*), revolutionize, purge.
*n* change, amendment, improvement, rectification, correction, rehabilitation, renovation, reorganization, shake-up (*infml*), purge.

**refrain** *v* stop, cease, quit, leave off, renounce, desist, abstain, forbear, avoid.

**refresh** *v* **1** COOL, freshen, enliven, invigorate, fortify, revive, restore, renew, rejuvenate, revitalize, reinvigorate. **2** *refresh one's memory*: jog, stimulate, prompt, prod.
**F3 1** tire, exhaust.

**refreshing** *adj* cool, thirst-quenching, bracing, invigorating, energizing, stimulating, inspiring, fresh, new, novel, original.

**refreshment** *n* sustenance, food, drink, snack, revival, restoration, renewal, reanimation, reinvigoration, revitalization.

**refuge** *n* sanctuary, asylum, shelter, protection, security, retreat, hideout, hide-away, resort, harbour, haven.

**refugee** *n* exile, émigré, displaced person, fugitive, runaway, escapee.

**refund** *v* repay, reimburse, rebate, return, restore.
*n* repayment, reimbursement, rebate, return.

**refusal** *n* rejection, no, rebuff, repudiation, denial, negation.
**F3** acceptance.

**refuse¹** *v* reject, turn down, decline, spurn, repudiate, rebuff, repel, deny, withhold.
**F3** accept, allow, permit.

**refuse²** *n* rubbish, waste, trash, garbage, junk, litter.

**refute** *v* disprove, rebut, confute, give the lie to, discredit, counter, negate.

**regain** *v* recover, get back, recoup, reclaim, repossess, retake, recapture, retrieve, return to.

**regal** adj majestic, kingly, queenly, princely, imperial, royal, sovereign, stately, magnificent, noble, lordly.

**regard** v consider, deem, judge, rate, value, think, believe, suppose, imagine, look upon, view, observe, watch.
n care, concern, consideration, attention, notice, heed, respect, deference, honour, esteem, admiration, affection, love, sympathy.
F∃ disregard, contempt.

**regarding** prep with regard to, as regards, concerning, with reference to, re, about, as to.

**regardless** adj disregarding, heedless, unmindful, neglectful, inattentive, unconcerned, indifferent.
F∃ heedful, mindful, attentive.
adv anyway, nevertheless, nonetheless, despite everything, come what may.

**regime** n government, rule, administration, management, leadership, command, control, establishment, system.

**regimented** adj strict, disciplined, controlled, regulated, standardized, ordered, methodical, systematic, organized.
F∃ free, lax, disorganized.

**region** n land, terrain, territory, country, province, area, district, zone, sector, neighbourhood, range, scope, expanse, domain, realm, sphere, field, division, section, part, place.

*Types of geographical region and community include*: antarctic, arctic, area, bailiwick, banana republic, basin, belt, Black Country, borough, built-up area, burgh, capital city, catchment area, city, coast, colony, commune, continent, country, countryside, county, county town, desert, development area, diocese, district, dockland, domain, dominion, duchy, East End, emirate, empire, estate, The Fens, forest, free state, ghetto, ghost town, grassland, green belt, hamlet, health resort, heartland, heath, hemisphere, home-town, hundred, industrial park, inner city, interior, jungle, kibbutz, kingdom, lowlands, manor, market town, marshland, metropolis, The Midlands, mission, municipality, nation, new town, no-man's land, old country, orient, outback, outpost, outskirts, pampas, parish, plain, port, postal district, prairie, principality, protectorate, province, quarter, realm, red-light district, region, republic, reservation, resort, riding, riviera, rural district, satellite town, savannah, scrubland, seaside, settlement, shanty town, shire, spa, state, steppe, subcontinent, suburb, territory, Third World, time zone, town, township, tract, tropics, tundra, urban district, veld, village, wasteland, West Country, West End, wilderness, woodland, zone.

**register** n roll, roster, list, index, catalogue, directory, log, record, chronicle, annals, archives, file, ledger, schedule, diary, almanac.
v 1 RECORD, note, log, enter, inscribe, mark, list, catalogue, chronicle, enrol, enlist, sign on, check in. 2 SHOW, reveal, betray, display, exhibit, manifest, express, say, read, indicate.

**regret** v rue, repent, lament, mourn, grieve, deplore.
n remorse, contrition, compunction, self-reproach, shame, sorrow, grief, disappointment, bitterness.

**regretful** adj remorseful, rueful, repentant, contrite, penitent, conscience-stricken, ashamed, sorry, apologetic, sad, sorrowful, disappointed.
F∃ impenitent, unashamed.

**regrettable** adj unfortunate, unlucky, unhappy, sad,

disappointing, upsetting, distressing, lamentable, deplorable, shameful, wrong, ill-advised.

**F3** fortunate, happy.

**regular** adj **1** ROUTINE, habitual, typical, usual, customary, time-honoured, conventional, orthodox, correct, official, standard, normal, ordinary, common, commonplace, everyday. **2** PERIODIC, rhythmic, steady, constant, fixed, set, unvarying, uniform, even, level, smooth, balanced, symmetrical, orderly, systematic, methodical.

**F3 1** unusual, unconventional. **2** irregular.

**regulate** v control, direct, guide, govern, rule, administer, manage, handle, conduct, run, organize, order, arrange, settle, square, monitor, set, adjust, tune, moderate, balance.

**regulation** n rule, statute, law, ordinance, edict, decree, order, commandment, precept, dictate, requirement, procedure.

adj standard, official, statutory, prescribed, required, orthodox, accepted, customary, usual, normal.

**rehearsal** n practice, drill, exercise, dry run, run-through, preparation, reading, recital, narration, account, enumeration, list.

**rehearse** v practise, drill, train, go over, prepare, try out, repeat, recite, recount, relate.

**reign** n rule, sway, monarchy, empire, sovereignty, supremacy, power, command, dominion, control, influence.

v rule, govern, command, prevail, predominate, influence.

**reimburse** v refund, repay, return, restore, recompense, compensate, indemnify, remunerate.

**reinforce** v strengthen, fortify, toughen, harden, stiffen, steel, brace, support, buttress, shore, prop, stay, supplement, augment, increase,

emphasize, stress, underline.

**F3** weaken, undermine.

**reinforcements** n auxiliaries, reserves, back-up, support, help.

**reinstate** v restore, return, replace, recall, reappoint, reinstall, re-establish.

**reject** v refuse, deny, decline, turn down, veto, disallow, condemn, despise, spurn, rebuff, jilt, exclude, repudiate, repel, renounce, eliminate, scrap, discard, jettison, cast off.

**F3** accept, choose, select.

n failure, second, discard, cast-off.

**rejection** n refusal, denial, veto, dismissal, rebuff, brush-off, exclusion, repudiation, renunciation, elimination.

**F3** acceptance, choice, selection.

**rejoice** v celebrate, revel, delight, glory, exult, triumph.

**rejoicing** n celebration, revelry, merrymaking, festivity, happiness, gladness, joy, delight, elation, jubilation, exultation, triumph.

**relapse** v worsen, deteriorate, degenerate, weaken, sink, fail, lapse, revert, regress, backslide.

n worsening, deterioration, setback, recurrence, weakening, lapse, reversion, regression, backsliding.

**relate** v **1** LINK, connect, join, couple, ally, associate, correlate. **2** REFER, apply, concern, pertain, appertain. **3** relate an anecdote: tell, recount, narrate, report, describe, recite. **4** IDENTIFY, sympathize, empathize, understand, feel for.

**related** adj kindred, akin, affiliated, allied, associated, connected, linked, interrelated, interconnected, accompanying, concomitant, joint, mutual.

**F3** unrelated, unconnected.

**relation** n **1** LINK, connection, bond, relationship, correlation, comparison, similarity, affiliation, interrelation, interconnection, interdependence, regard, reference.

2 RELATIVE, family, kin, kindred.

**relations** n 1 RELATIVES, family, kin, kindred. 2 RELATIONSHIP, terms, rapport, liaison, intercourse, affairs, dealings, interaction, communications, contact, associations, connections.

**relationship** n bond, link, connection, association, liaison, rapport, affinity, closeness, similarity, parallel, correlation, ratio, proportion.

**relative** adj comparative, proportional, proportionate, commensurate, corresponding, respective, appropriate, relevant, applicable, related, connected, interrelated, reciprocal, dependent. n relation, family, kin.

**relax** v slacken, loosen, lessen, reduce, diminish, weaken, lower, soften, moderate, abate, remit, relieve, ease, rest, unwind, calm, tranquillize, sedate.
**F3** tighten, intensify.

**relaxation** n 1 REST, repose, refreshment, leisure, recreation, fun, amusement, entertainment, enjoyment, pleasure. 2 SLACKENING, lessening, reduction, moderation, abatement, let-up (*infml*), détente, easing.
**F3** 2 tension, intensification.

**relaxed** adj informal, casual, laid-back (*infml*), easy-going (*infml*), carefree, happy-go-lucky, cool, calm, composed, collected, unhurried, leisurely.
**F3** tense, nervous, formal.

**relay** n 1 BROADCAST, transmission, programme, communication, message, dispatch. 2 *work in relays*: shift, turn.
v broadcast, transmit, communicate, send, spread, carry, supply.

**release** v loose, unloose, unleash, unfasten, extricate, free, liberate, deliver, emancipate, acquit, absolve, exonerate, excuse, exempt, discharge,

issue, publish, circulate, distribute, present, launch, unveil.
**F3** imprison, detain, check.
n freedom, liberty, liberation, deliverance, emancipation, acquittal, absolution, exoneration, exemption, discharge, issue, publication, announcement, proclamation.
**F3** imprisonment, detention.

**relent** v give in, give way, yield, capitulate, unbend, relax, slacken, soften, weaken.

**relentless** adj unrelenting, unremitting, incessant, persistent, unflagging, ruthless, remorseless, implacable, merciless, pitiless, unforgiving, cruel, harsh, fierce, grim, hard, punishing, uncompromising, inflexible, unyielding, inexorable.
**F3** merciful, yielding.

**relevant** adj pertinent, material, significant, germane, related, applicable, apposite, apt, appropriate, suitable, fitting, proper, admissible.
**F3** irrelevant, inapplicable, inappropriate, unsuitable.

**reliable** adj unfailing, certain, sure, dependable, responsible, trusty, trustworthy, honest, true, faithful, constant, staunch, solid, safe, sound, stable, predictable, regular.
**F3** unreliable, doubtful, untrustworthy.

**reliance** n dependence, trust, faith, belief, credit, confidence, assurance.

**relic** n memento, souvenir, keepsake, token, survival, remains, remnant, scrap, fragment, vestige, trace.

**relief** n reassurance, consolation, comfort, ease, alleviation, cure, remedy, release, deliverance, help, aid, assistance, support, sustenance, refreshment, diversion, relaxation, rest, respite, break, breather (*infml*), remission, let-up (*infml*), abatement.

**relieve** v reassure, console, comfort, ease, soothe, alleviate, mitigate, cure, release, deliver, free, unburden,

lighten, soften, slacken, relax, calm, help, aid, assist, support, sustain.
Ⓕ aggravate, intensify.

**religion**

---
*Religions include*: Christianity, Church of England (C of E), Church of Scotland, Baptists, Catholicism, Methodism, Protestantism, Presbyterianism, Anglicanism, Congregationalism, Calvinism, evangelicalism, Free Church, Jehovah's Witnesses, Mormonism, Quakerism, Amish; Baha'ism, Buddhism, Confucianism, Hinduism, Islam, Jainism, Judaism, Sikhism, Taoism, Shintoism, Zen, Zoroastrianism, voodoo, druidism.
---

**religious** *adj* **1** SACRED, holy, divine, spiritual, devotional, scriptural, theological, doctrinal. **2** *a religious person*: devout, godly, pious, God-fearing, church-going, reverent, righteous.
Ⓕ **1** secular. **2** irreligious, ungodly.

**religious officer**

---
*Religious officers include*: abbess, abbot, archbishop, archdeacon, bishop, canon, cardinal, chancellor, chaplain, clergy, clergyman, clergywoman, curate, deacon, deaconess, dean, elder, father, friar, minister, monk, Monsignor, mother superior, nun, padre, parson, pastor, pope, prelate, priest, prior, proctor, rector, vicar; ayatollah, Dalai Lama, guru, imam, rabbi.
---

**relinquish** *n* let go, release, hand over, surrender, yield, cede, give up, resign, renounce, repudiate, waive, forgo, abandon, desert, forsake, drop, discard.
Ⓕ keep, retain.

**relish** *v* like, enjoy, savour, appreciate, revel in.
*n* **1** SEASONING, condiment, sauce, pickle, spice, piquancy, tang.
**2** ENJOYMENT, pleasure, delight, gusto, zest.

**reluctant** *adj* unwilling, disinclined, indisposed, hesitant, slow, backward, loth, averse, unenthusiastic, grudging.
Ⓕ willing, ready, eager.

**rely** *v* depend, lean, count, bank, reckon, trust, swear by.

**remain** *v* stay, rest, stand, dwell, abide, last, endure, survive, prevail, persist, continue, linger, wait.
Ⓕ go, leave, depart.

**remainder** *n* rest, balance, surplus, excess, remnant, remains.

**remaining** *adj* left, unused, unspent, unfinished, residual, outstanding, surviving, persisting, lingering, lasting, abiding.

**remains** *n* rest, remainder, residue, dregs, leavings, leftovers, scraps, crumbs, fragments, remnants, oddments, traces, vestiges, relics, body, corpse, carcase, ashes, debris.

**remark** *v* comment, observe, note, mention, say, state, declare.
*n* comment, observation, opinion, reflection, mention, utterance, statement, assertion, declaration.

**remarkable** *adj* striking, impressive, noteworthy, surprising, amazing, strange, odd, unusual, uncommon, extraordinary, phenomenal, exceptional, outstanding, notable, conspicuous, prominent, distinguished.
Ⓕ average, ordinary, commonplace, usual.

**remedy** *n* cure, antidote, countermeasure, corrective, restorative, medicine, treatment, therapy, relief, solution, answer, panacea.
*v* correct, rectify, put right, redress, counteract, cure, heal, restore, treat, help, relieve, soothe, ease, mitigate, mend, repair, fix, solve.

**remember** *v* **1** RECALL, recollect,

summon up, think back, reminisce, recognize, place. **2** MEMORIZE, learn, retain.
**F∃ 1** forget.

**remind** v prompt, nudge, hint, jog one's memory, refresh one's memory, bring to mind, call to mind, call up.

**reminder** n prompt, nudge, hint, suggestion, memorandum, memo, souvenir, memento.

**reminiscence** n memory, remembrance, memoir, anecdote, recollection, recall, retrospection, review, reflection.

**reminiscent** adj suggestive, evocative, nostalgic.

**remit** v send, transmit, dispatch, post, mail, forward, pay, settle. n brief, orders, instructions, guidelines, terms of reference, scope, authorization, responsibility.

**remittance** n sending, dispatch, payment, fee, allowance, consideration.

**remnant** n scrap, piece, bit, fragment, end, off cut, leftover, remainder, balance, residue, shred, trace, vestige.

**remorse** n regret, compunction, ruefulness, repentance, penitence, contrition, self-reproach, shame, guilt, bad conscience, sorrow, grief.

**remote** adj **1** DISTANT, far, faraway, far-off, outlying, out-of-the-way, inaccessible, god-forsaken, isolated, secluded, lonely.
**2** DETACHED, aloof, standoffish, uninvolved, reserved, withdrawn. **3** a remote possibility: slight, small, slim, slender, faint, negligible, unlikely, improbable.
**F∃ 1** close, nearby, accessible.
**2** friendly.

**remove** v detach, pull off, amputate, cut off, extract, pull out, withdraw, take away, take off, strip, shed, doff, expunge, efface, erase, delete, strike out, get rid of, abolish, purge, eliminate, dismiss, discharge, eject,

throw out, oust, depose, displace, dislodge, shift, move, transport, transfer, relocate.

**remuneration** n pay, wages, salary, emolument, stipend, fee, retainer, earnings, income, profit, reward, recompense, payment, remittance, repayment, reimbursement, compensation, indemnity.

**render** v **1** they rendered it harmless: make, cause to be, leave. **2** GIVE, provide, supply, tender, present, submit, hand over, deliver.
**3** TRANSLATE, transcribe, interpret, explain, clarify, represent, perform, play, sing.

**renew** v **1** RENOVATE, modernize, refurbish, refit, recondition, mend, repair, overhaul, remodel, reform, transform, recreate, reconstitute, re-establish, regenerate, revive, resuscitate, refresh, rejuvenate, reinvigorate, revitalize, restore, replace, replenish, restock.
**2** REPEAT, restate, reaffirm, extend, prolong, continue, recommence, restart, resume.

**renounce** v abandon, forsake, give up, resign, relinquish, surrender, discard, reject, spurn, disown, repudiate, disclaim, deny, recant, abjure.

**renovate** v restore, renew, recondition, repair, overhaul, modernize, refurbish, refit, redecorate, do up, remodel, reform, revamp, improve.

**renown** n fame, celebrity, stardom, acclaim, glory, eminence, illustriousness, distinction, note, mark, esteem, reputation, honour.
**F∃** obscurity, anonymity.

**renowned** adj famous, well-known, celebrated, acclaimed, famed, noted, eminent, distinguished, illustrious, notable.
**F∃** unknown, obscure.

**rent** n rental, lease, hire, payment, fee.

*v* let, sublet, lease, hire, charter.

**repair** *v* mend, fix, patch up, overhaul, service, rectify, redress, restore, renovate, renew.
*n* mend, patch, darn, overhaul, service, maintenance, restoration, adjustment, improvement.

**repartee** *n* banter, badinage, jesting, wit, riposte, retort.

**repay** *v* refund, reimburse, compensate, recompense, reward, remunerate, pay, settle, square, get even with, retaliate, reciprocate, revenge, avenge.

**repeal** *v* revoke, rescind, abrogate, quash, annul, nullify, void, invalidate, cancel, countermand, reverse, abolish.
**Ⅎ** enact.

**repeat** *v* restate, reiterate, recapitulate, echo, quote, recite, relate, retell, reproduce, duplicate, renew, rebroadcast, reshow, replay, rerun, redo.
*n* repetition, echo, reproduction, duplicate, rebroadcast, reshowing, replay, rerun.

**repeatedly** *adv* time after time, time and (time) again, again and again, over and over, frequently, often.

**repel** *v* **1** DRIVE BACK, repulse, check, hold off, ward off, parry, resist, oppose, fight, refuse, decline, reject, rebuff. **2** DISGUST, revolt, nauseate, sicken, offend.
**Ⅎ** **1** attract. **2** delight.

**repent** *n* regret, rue, sorrow, lament, deplore, atone.

**repentance** *n* penitence, contrition, remorse, compunction, regret, sorrow, grief, guilt, shame.

**repentant** *adj* penitent, contrite, sorry, apologetic, remorseful, regretful, rueful, chastened, ashamed.
**Ⅎ** unrepentant.

**repercussion** *n* result, consequence, backlash, reverberation, echo, rebound, recoil.

**repetition** *n* restatement,

reiteration, recapitulation, echo, return, reappearance, recurrence, duplication, tautology.

**repetitive** *adj* recurrent, monotonous, tedious, boring, dull, mechanical, unchanging, unvaried.

**replace** *v* **1** *replace the lid*: put back, return, restore, make good, reinstate, re-establish. **2** SUPERSEDE, succeed, follow, supplant, oust, deputize, substitute.

**replacement** *n* substitute, stand-in, understudy, fill-in, supply, proxy, surrogate, successor.

**replenish** *v* refill, restock, reload, recharge, replace, restore, renew, supply, provide, furnish, stock, fill, top up.

**replica** *n* model, imitation, reproduction, facsimile, copy, duplicate, clone.

**reply** *v* answer, respond, retort, rejoin, react, acknowledge, return, echo, reciprocate, counter, retaliate.
*n* answer, response, retort, rejoinder, riposte, repartee, reaction, comeback, acknowledgement, return, echo, retaliation.

**report** *n* article, piece, write-up, record, account, relation, narrative, description, story, tale, gossip, hearsay, rumour, talk, statement, communiqué, declaration, announcement, communication, information, news, word, message, note.
*v* state, announce, declare, proclaim, air, broadcast, relay, publish, circulate, communicate, notify, tell, recount, relate, narrate, describe, detail, cover, document, record, note.

**reporter** *n* journalist, correspondent, columnist, newspaperman, newspaperwoman, hack, newscaster, commentator, announcer.

**represent** *v* stand for, symbolize, designate, denote, mean, express, evoke, depict, portray, describe, picture, draw, sketch, illustrate, exemplify, typify, epitomize, embody, personify, appear as, act as, enact, perform, show, exhibit, be, amount to, constitute.

**representation** n **1** LIKENESS, image, icon, picture, portrait, illustration, sketch, model, statue, bust, depiction, portrayal, description, account, explanation. **2** PERFORMANCE, production, play, show, spectacle.

**representative** n delegate, deputy, proxy, stand-in, spokesperson, spokesman, spokeswoman, ambassador, commissioner, agent, salesman, saleswoman, rep (*infml*), traveller.
adj typical, illustrative, exemplary, archetypal, characteristic, usual, normal, symbolic.
**Ⓕ** unrepresentative, atypical.

**repress** v inhibit, check, control, curb, restrain, suppress, bottle up, hold back, stifle, smother, muffle, silence, quell, crush, quash, subdue, overpower, overcome, master, subjugate, oppress.

**repression** n inhibition, restraint, suppression, suffocation, gagging, censorship, authoritarianism, despotism, tyranny, oppression, domination, control, constraint, coercion.

**repressive** adj oppressive, authoritarian, despotic, tyrannical, dictatorial, autocratic, totalitarian, absolute, harsh, severe, tough, coercive.

**reprieve** v pardon, let off, spare, rescue, redeem, relieve, respite.
n pardon, amnesty, suspension, abeyance, postponement, deferment, remission, respite, relief, let-up (*infml*), abatement.

**reprimand** n rebuke, reproof, reproach, admonition, telling-off (*infml*), ticking-off (*infml*), lecture, talking-to (*infml*), dressing-down

(*infml*), censure, blame.
v rebuke, reprove, reproach, admonish, scold, chide, tell off (*infml*), tick off (*infml*), lecture, criticize, slate (*infml*), censure, blame.

**reprisal** n retaliation, counter-attack, retribution, requital, revenge, vengeance.

**reproach** v rebuke, reprove, reprimand, upbraid, scold, chide, reprehend, blame, censure, condemn, criticize, disparage, defame.
n rebuke, reproof, reprimand, scolding, blame, censure, condemnation, criticism, disapproval, scorn, contempt, shame, disgrace.

**reproachful** adj reproving, upbraiding, scolding, censorious, critical, fault-finding, disapproving, scornful.
**Ⓕ** complimentary.

**reproduce** v **1** COPY, transcribe, print, duplicate, mirror, echo, repeat, imitate, emulate, match, simulate, recreate, reconstruct. **2** BREED, spawn, procreate, generate, propagate, multiply.

**reproduction** n **1** COPY, print, picture, duplicate, facsimile, replica, clone, imitation. **2** BREEDING, procreation, generation, propagation, multiplication.
**Ⓕ** **1** original.

**reproductive** adj procreative, generative, sexual, sex, genital.

**reproof** n rebuke, reproach, reprimand, admonition, upbraiding, dressing-down (*infml*), scolding, telling-off (*infml*), ticking-off (*infml*), censure, condemnation, criticism.
**Ⓕ** praise.

**reprove** v rebuke, reproach, reprimand, upbraid, scold, chide, tell off (*infml*), reprehend, admonish, censure, condemn, criticize.
**Ⓕ** praise.

**reptile**

*Reptiles include*: adder, puff adder,

grass snake, tree snake, asp, viper, rattlesnake, sidewinder, anaconda, boa constrictor, cobra, king cobra, mamba, python; lizard, frilled lizard, chameleon, gecko, iguana, skink, slow-worm; turtle, green turtle, hawksbill turtle, terrapin, tortoise, giant tortoise; alligator, crocodile.

**repugnance** n reluctance, distaste, dislike, aversion, hatred, loathing, abhorrence, horror, repulsion, revulsion, disgust.
**F3** liking, pleasure, delight.

**repulsive** adj repellent, repugnant, revolting, disgusting, nauseating, sickening, offensive, distasteful, objectionable, obnoxious, foul, vile, loathsome, abominable, abhorrent, hateful, horrid, unpleasant, disagreeable, ugly, hideous, forbidding.
**F3** attractive, pleasant, delightful.

**reputable** adj respectable, reliable, dependable, trustworthy, upright, honourable, creditable, worthy, good, excellent, irreproachable.
**F3** disreputable, infamous.

**reputation** n honour, character, standing, stature, esteem, opinion, credit, repute, fame, renown, celebrity, distinction, name, good name, bad name, infamy, notoriety.

**reputed** adj alleged, supposed, said, rumoured, believed, thought, considered, regarded, estimated, reckoned, held, seeming, apparent, ostensible.
**F3** actual, true.

**request** v ask for, solicit, demand, require, seek, desire, beg, entreat, supplicate, petition, appeal.
n appeal, call, demand, requisition, desire, application, solicitation, suit, petition, entreaty, supplication, prayer.

**require** v 1 NEED, want, wish, desire, lack, miss. 2 *you are required to attend*: oblige, force, compel, constrain, make, ask, request,

instruct, direct, order, demand, necessitate, take, involve.

**requirement** n need, necessity, essential, must, requisite, prerequisite, demand, stipulation, condition, term, specification, proviso, qualification, provision.

**requisite** adj required, needed, necessary, essential, obligatory, compulsory, set, prescribed.

**requisition** v request, put in for, demand, commandeer, appropriate, take, confiscate, seize, occupy.

**rescue** v save, recover, salvage, deliver, free, liberate, release, redeem, ransom.
**F3** capture, imprison.
n saving, recovery, salvage, deliverance, liberation, release, redemption, salvation.
**F3** capture.

**research** n investigation, inquiry, fact-finding, groundwork, examination, analysis, scrutiny, study, search, probe, exploration, experimentation.
v investigate, examine, analyse, scrutinize, study, search, probe, explore, experiment.

**resemblance** n likeness, similarity, sameness, parity, conformity, closeness, affinity, parallel, comparison, analogy, correspondence, image, facsimile.
**F3** dissimilarity.

**resemble** v be like, look like, take after, favour, mirror, echo, duplicate, parallel, approach.
**F3** differ from.

**resent** v grudge, begrudge, envy, take offence at, take umbrage at, take amiss, object to, grumble at, take exception to, dislike.
**F3** accept, like.

**resentful** adj grudging, envious, jealous, bitter, embittered, hurt, wounded, offended, aggrieved, put out, miffed (*infml*), peeved (*infml*), indignant, angry, vindictive.

 ◨ satisfied, contented.

**resentment** n grudge, envy, jealousy, bitterness, spite, malice, ill-will, ill-feeling, animosity, hurt, umbrage, pique, displeasure, irritation, indignation, vexation, anger, vindictiveness.
◨ contentment, happiness.

**reservation** n 1 DOUBT, scepticism, misgiving, qualm, scruple, hesitation, second thought. 2 PROVISO, stipulation, qualification. 3 RESERVE, preserve, park, sanctuary, homeland, enclave. 4 BOOKING, engagement, appointment.

**reserve** v 1 SET APART, earmark, keep, retain, hold back, save, store, stockpile. 2 *reserve a seat*: book, engage, order, secure.
◨ 1 use up.
n 1 STORE, stock, supply, fund, stockpile, cache, hoard, savings. 2 SHYNESS, reticence, secretiveness, coolness, aloofness, modesty, restraint. 3 RESERVATION, preserve, park, sanctuary. 4 REPLACEMENT, substitute, stand-in.
◨ 2 friendliness, openness.

**reserved** adj 1 BOOKED, engaged, taken, spoken for, set aside, earmarked, meant, intended, designated, destined, saved, held, kept, retained. 2 SHY, retiring, reticent, unforthcoming, uncommunicative, secretive, silent, taciturn, unsociable, cool, aloof, standoffish, unapproachable, modest, restrained, cautious.
◨ 1 unreserved, free, available. 2 friendly, open.

**reside** v live, inhabit, dwell, lodge, stay, sojourn, settle, remain.

**residence** n dwelling, habitation, domicile, abode, seat, place, home, house, lodgings, quarters, hall, manor, mansion, palace, villa, country-house, country-seat.

**resident** n inhabitant, citizen, local, householder, occupier, tenant, lodger, guest.
◨ non-resident.

**residual** adj remaining, leftover, unused, unconsumed, net.

**resign** v stand down, leave, quit, abdicate, vacate, renounce, relinquish, forgo, waive, surrender, yield, abandon, forsake.
◨ join.

**resign oneself** reconcile oneself, accept, bow, submit, yield, comply, acquiesce.
◨ resist.

**resignation** n 1 STANDING-DOWN, abdication, retirement, departure, notice, renunciation, relinquishment, surrender. 2 ACCEPTANCE, acquiescence, submission, non-resistance, passivity, patience, stoicism, defeatism.
◨ 2 resistance.

**resigned** adj reconciled, philosophical, stoical, patient, unprotesting, unresisting, submissive, defeatist.
◨ resistant.

**resilient** adj 1 *resilient material*: flexible, pliable, supple, plastic, elastic, springy, bouncy. 2 STRONG, tough, hardy, adaptable, buoyant.
◨ 1 rigid, brittle.

**resist** v oppose, defy, confront, fight, combat, weather, withstand, repel, counteract, check, avoid, refuse.
◨ submit, accept.

**resistant** adj 1 OPPOSED, antagonistic, defiant, unyielding, intransigent, unwilling. 2 PROOF, impervious, immune, invulnerable, tough, strong.
◨ 1 compliant, yielding.

**resolute** adj determined, resolved, set, fixed, unwavering, staunch, firm, steadfast, relentless, single-minded, persevering, dogged, tenacious, stubborn, obstinate, strong-willed, undaunted, unflinching, bold.
◨ irresolute, weak-willed, half-

hearted.

**resolution** *n* **1** DETERMINATION, resolve, willpower, commitment, dedication, devotion, firmness, steadfastness, persistence, perseverance, doggedness, tenacity, zeal, courage, boldness. **2** DECISION, judgement, finding, declaration, proposition, motion.
**F3** **1** half-heartedness, uncertainty, indecision.

**resolve** *v* decide, make up one's mind, determine, fix, settle, conclude, sort out, work out, solve.

**resort** *v* go, visit, frequent, patronize, haunt.
*n* recourse, refuge, course (of action), alternative, option, chance, possibility.
**resort to** turn to, use, utilize, employ, exercise.

**resound** *v* resonate, reverberate, echo, re-echo, ring, boom, thunder.

**resounding** *adj* **1** RESONANT, reverberating, echoing, ringing, sonorous, booming, thunderous, full, rich, vibrant. **2** *a resounding victory*: decisive, conclusive, crushing, thorough.
**F3** **1** faint.

**resource** *n* **1** SUPPLY, reserve, stockpile, source, expedient, contrivance, device.
**2** RESOURCEFULNESS, initiative, ingenuity, inventiveness, talent, ability, capability.

**resourceful** *adj* ingenious, imaginative, creative, inventive, innovative, original, clever, bright, sharp, quick-witted, able, capable, talented.

**resources** *n* materials, supplies, reserves, holdings, funds, money, wealth, riches, capital, assets, property, means.

**respect** *n* **1** ADMIRATION, esteem, appreciation, recognition, honour, deference, reverence, veneration, politeness, courtesy. **2** *in every respect*: point, aspect, facet, feature,

characteristic, particular, detail, sense, way, regard, reference, relation, connection.
**F3** **1** disrespect.
*v* **1** ADMIRE, esteem, regard, appreciate, value. **2** OBEY, observe, heed, follow, honour, fulfil.
**F3** **1** despise, scorn. **2** ignore, disobey.

**respectable** *adj* **1** HONOURABLE, worthy, respected, dignified, upright, honest, decent, clean-living. **2** ACCEPTABLE, tolerable, passable, adequate, fair, reasonable, appreciable, considerable.
**F3** **1** dishonourable, disreputable. **2** inadequate, paltry.

**respectful** *adj* deferential, reverential, humble, polite, well-mannered, courteous, civil.
**F3** disrespectful.

**respective** *adj* corresponding, relevant, various, several, separate, individual, personal, own, particular, special.

**respond** *v* answer, reply, retort, acknowledge, react, return, reciprocate.

**response** *n* answer, reply, retort, comeback, acknowledgement, reaction, feedback.
**F3** query.

**responsibility** *n* fault, blame, guilt, culpability, answerability, accountability, duty, obligation, burden, onus, charge, care, trust, authority, power.

**responsible** *adj* **1** *a responsible citizen*: GUILTY, culpable, at fault, to blame, liable, answerable, accountable. **2** dependable, reliable, conscientious, trustworthy, honest, sound, steady, sober, mature, sensible, rational. **3** IMPORTANT, authoritative, executive, decision-making.
**F3** **2** irresponsible, unreliable, untrustworthy.

**rest¹** *n* **1** LEISURE, relaxation, repose, lie-down, sleep, snooze, nap, siesta, idleness, inactivity, motionlessness, standstill, stillness, tranquillity, calm. **2** BREAK, pause, breathing-space, breather (*infml*), intermission, interlude, interval, recess, holiday, vacation, halt, cessation, lull, respite. **3** SUPPORT, prop, stand, base.

**E3 1** action, activity. **2** work.

*v* **1** PAUSE, halt, stop, cease.
**2** RELAX, repose, sit, recline, lounge, laze, lie down, sleep, snooze, doze.
**3** DEPEND, rely, hinge, hang, lie.
**4** LEAN, prop, support, stand.

**E3 1** continue. **2** work.

**rest²** *n* remainder, others, balance, surplus, excess, residue, remains, leftovers, remnants.

**restaurant** *n* eating-house, bistro, steakhouse, grill room, dining-room, snack-bar, buffet, cafeteria, café.

**restful** *adj* relaxing, soothing, calm, tranquil, serene, peaceful, quiet, undisturbed, relaxed, comfortable, leisurely, unhurried.

**E3** tiring, restless.

**restless** *adj* fidgety, unsettled, disturbed, troubled, agitated, nervous, anxious, worried, uneasy, fretful, edgy, jumpy, restive, unruly, turbulent, sleepless.

**E3** calm, relaxed, comfortable.

**restore** *v* **1** REPLACE, return, reinstate, rehabilitate, re-establish, reintroduce, re-enforce. **2** *restore a building*: renovate, renew, rebuild, reconstruct, refurbish, retouch, recondition, repair, mend, fix.
**3** REVIVE, refresh, rejuvenate, revitalize, strengthen.

**E3 1** remove. **2** damage. **3** weaken.

**restrain** *v* hold back, keep back, suppress, subdue, repress, inhibit, check, curb, bridle, stop, arrest, prevent, bind, tie, chain, fetter, manacle, imprison, jail, confine, restrict, regulate, control, govern.

**E3** encourage, liberate.

**restrained** *adj* moderate, temperate,

mild, subdued, muted, quiet, soft, low-key, unobtrusive, discreet, tasteful, calm, controlled, steady, self-controlled.

**E3** unrestrained.

**restraint** *n* moderation, inhibition, self-control, self-discipline, hold, grip, check, curb, rein, bridle, suppression, bondage, captivity, confinement, imprisonment, bonds, chains, fetters, straitjacket, restriction, control, constraint, limitation, tie, hindrance, prevention.

**E3** liberty.

**restrict** *v* limit, bound, demarcate, control, regulate, confine, contain, cramp, constrain, impede, hinder, hamper, handicap, tie, restrain, curtail.

**E3** broaden, free.

**restriction** *n* limit, bound, confine, limitation, constraint, handicap, check, curb, restraint, ban, embargo, control, regulation, rule, stipulation, condition, proviso.

**E3** freedom.

**result** *n* effect, consequence, sequel, repercussion, reaction, outcome, upshot, issue, end-product, fruit, score, answer, verdict, judgement, decision, conclusion.

**E3** cause.

*v* follow, ensue, happen, occur, issue, emerge, arise, spring, derive, stem, flow, proceed, develop, end, finish, terminate, culminate.

**E3** cause.

**resume** *v* restart, recommence, reopen, reconvene, continue, carry on, go on, proceed.

**E3** cease.

**resumption** *n* restart, recommencement, reopening, renewal, resurgence, continuation.

**E3** cessation.

**resurrect** *v* restore, revive, resuscitate, reactivate, bring back, reintroduce, renew.

**E3** kill, bury.

**resurrection** n restoration, revival, resuscitation, renaissance, rebirth, renewal, resurgence, reappearance, return, comeback.

**resuscitate** v revive, resurrect, save, rescue, reanimate, quicken, reinvigorate, revitalize, restore, renew.

**retain** v 1 KEEP, hold, reserve, hold back, save, preserve. 2 *retain information*: remember, memorize. 3 EMPLOY, engage, hire, commission.
≠ 1 release. 2 forget. 3 dismiss.

**retaliate** v reciprocate, counter-attack, hit back, strike back, fight back, get one's own back, get even with, take revenge.

**retaliation** n reprisal, counter-attack, revenge, vengeance, retribution.

**reticent** adj reserved, shy, uncommunicative, unforthcoming, tight-lipped, secretive, taciturn, silent, quiet.
≠ communicative, forward, frank.

**retire** v leave, depart, withdraw, retreat, recede.
≠ join, enter, advance.

**retirement** n withdrawal, retreat, solitude, loneliness, seclusion, privacy, obscurity.

**retiring** adj shy, bashful, timid, shrinking, quiet, reticent, reserved, self-effacing, unassertive, modest, unassuming, humble.
≠ bold, forward, assertive.

**retort** v answer, reply, respond, rejoin, return, counter, retaliate.
n answer, reply, response, rejoinder, riposte, repartee, quip.

**retract** v take back, withdraw, recant, reverse, revoke, rescind, cancel, repeal, repudiate, disown, disclaim, deny.
≠ assert, maintain.

**retreat** v draw back, recoil, shrink, turn tail (*infml*), withdraw, retire, leave, depart, quit.
≠ advance.

n 1 WITHDRAWAL, departure, evacuation, flight. 2 SECLUSION, privacy, hideaway, den, refuge, asylum, sanctuary, shelter, haven.
≠ 1 advance, charge.

**retrieve** v fetch, bring back, regain, get back, recapture, repossess, recoup, recover, salvage, save, rescue, redeem, restore, return.
≠ lose.

**retrograde** adj retrogressive, backward, reverse, negative, downward, declining, deteriorating.
≠ progressive.

**retrospect** n hindsight, afterthought, re-examination, review, recollection, remembrance.
≠ prospect.

**return** v 1 COME BACK, reappear, recur, go back, backtrack, regress, revert. 2 GIVE BACK, hand back, send back, deliver, put back, replace, restore. 3 *return a favour*: reciprocate, requite, repay, refund, reimburse, recompense.
≠ 1 leave, depart. 2 take.
n 1 REAPPEARANCE, recurrence, comeback, home-coming.
2 REPAYMENT, recompense, replacement, restoration, reinstatement, reciprocation.
3 REVENUE, income, proceeds, takings, yield, gain, profit, reward, advantage, benefit.
≠ 1 departure, disappearance.
2 removal. 3 payment, expense, loss.

**reveal** v expose, uncover, unveil, unmask, show, display, exhibit, manifest, disclose, divulge, betray, leak, tell, impart, communicate, broadcast, publish, announce, proclaim.
≠ hide, conceal, mask.

**revel in** enjoy, relish, savour, delight in, thrive on, bask in, glory in, lap up, indulge in, wallow in, luxuriate in.

**revelation** n uncovering, unveiling, exposure, unmasking, show, display, exhibition, manifestation, disclosure, confession, admission, betrayed, giveaway, leak, news, information, communication, broadcasting, publication, announcement, proclamation.

**revelry** n celebration, festivity, party, merrymaking, jollity, fun, carousal, debauchery.

F3 sobriety.

**revenge** n vengeance, satisfaction, reprisal, retaliation, requital, retribution.

v avenge, repay, retaliate, get one's own back.

**revenue** n income, return, yield, interest, profit, gain, proceeds, receipts, takings.

F3 expenditure.

**reverberate** v echo, re-echo, resound, resonate, ring, boom, vibrate.

**revere** v respect, esteem, honour, pay homage to, venerate, worship, adore, exalt.

F3 despise, scorn.

**reverence** n respect, deference, honour, homage, admiration, awe, veneration, worship, adoration, devotion.

F3 contempt, scorn.

**reverent** adj reverential, respectful, deferential, humble, dutiful, awed, solemn, pious, devout, adoring, loving.

F3 irreverent, disrespectful.

**reversal** n negation, cancellation, annulment, nullification, countermanding, revocation, rescinding, repeal, reverse, turnabout, turnaround, U-turn, volte-face, upset.

F3 advancement, progress.

**reverse** v 1 BACK, retreat, backtrack, undo, negate, cancel, annul, invalidate, countermand, overrule, revoke, rescind, repeal, retract, quash, overthrow.

2 TRANSPOSE, turn round, invert,

up-end, overturn, upset, change, alter.

F3 1 advance, enforce.

n 1 UNDERSIDE, back, rear, inverse, converse, contrary, opposite, antithesis. 2 MISFORTUNE, mishap, misadventure, adversity, affliction, hardship, trial, blow, disappointment, setback, check, delay, problem, difficulty, failure, defeat.

adj opposite, contrary, converse, inverse, inverted, backward, back, rear.

**revert** v return, go back, resume, lapse, relapse, regress.

**review** v 1 CRITICIZE, assess, evaluate, judge, weigh, discuss, examine, inspect, scrutinize, study, survey, recapitulate. 2 review the situation: reassess, re-evaluate, re-examine, reconsider, rethink, revise.

n 1 CRITICISM, critique, assessment, evaluation, judgement, report, commentary, examination, scrutiny, analysis, study, survey, recapitulation, reassessment, re-evaluation, re-examination, revision. 2 MAGAZINE, periodical, journal.

**revise** v 1 revise one's opinion: change, alter, modify, amend, correct, update, edit, rewrite, reword, recast, revamp, reconsider, re-examine, review. 2 STUDY, learn, swot up (infml), cram (infml).

**revival** n resuscitation, revitalization, restoration, renewal, renaissance, rebirth, reawakening, resurgence, upsurge.

**revive** v resuscitate, reanimate, revitalize, restore, renew, refresh, animate, invigorate, quicken, rouse, awaken, recover, rally, reawaken, rekindle, reactivate.

F3 weary.

**revoke** v repeal, rescind, quash, abrogate, annul, nullify, invalidate, negate, cancel, countermand, reverse, retract, withdraw.

F3 enforce.

**revolt** n   revolution, rebellion, mutiny, rising, uprising, insurrection, putsch, coup (d'état), secession, defection.
   v   1 REBEL, mutiny, rise, riot, resist, dissent, defect. 2 DISGUST, sicken, nauseate, repel, offend, shock, outrage, scandalize.
   🖃 1 submit. 2 please, delight.

**revolting** adj   disgusting, sickening, nauseating, repulsive, repellent, obnoxious, nasty, horrible, foul, loathsome, abhorrent, distasteful, offensive, shocking, appalling.
   🖃 pleasant, delightful, attractive, palatable.

**revolution** n   1 REVOLT, rebellion, mutiny, rising, uprising, insurrection, putsch, coup (d'état), reformation, change, transformation, innovation, upheaval, cataclysm. 2 ROTATION, turn, spin, cycle, circuit, round, circle, orbit, gyration.

**revolutionary** n   rebel, mutineer, insurgent, anarchist, revolutionist.
   adj   1 REBEL, rebellious, mutinous, insurgent, subversive, seditious, anarchistic. 2 revolutionary ideas: new, innovative, avant-garde, different, drastic, radical, thoroughgoing.
   🖃 1 conservative.

**revolve** v   rotate, turn, pivot, swivel, spin, wheel, whirl, gyrate, circle, orbit.

**revulsion** n   repugnance, disgust, distaste, dislike, aversion, hatred, loathing, abhorrence, abomination.
   🖃 delight, pleasure, approval.

**reward** n   prize, honour, medal, decoration, bounty, pay-off, bonus, premium, payment, remuneration, recompense, repayment, requital, compensation, gain, profit, return, benefit, merit, desert, retribution.
   🖃 punishment.
   v   pay, remunerate, recompense, repay, requite, compensate, honour, decorate.
   🖃 punish.

**rewarding** adj   profitable, remunerative, lucrative, productive, fruitful, worthwhile, valuable, advantageous, beneficial, satisfying, gratifying, pleasing, fulfilling, enriching.
   🖃 unrewarding.

**rhetoric** n   eloquence, oratory, grandiloquence, magniloquence, bombast, pomposity, hyperbole, verbosity, wordiness.

> *Rhetorical devices include:*
> abscission, alliteration, amplification, anacoluthon, anadiplosis, anaphora, anastrophe, anticlimax, antimetabole, antimetathesis, antiphrasis, antithesis, antonomasia, aporia, apostrophe, asyndeton, auxesis, bathos, catachresis, chiasmus, climax, diallage, diegesis, dissimile, double entendre, dramatic irony, dysphemism, ellipsis, enantiosis, enumeration, epanadiplosis, epanalepsis, epanaphora, epanodos, epanorthosis, epigram, epiphonema, epistrophe, epizeuxis, erotema, erotetic, euphemism, figure of speech, hendiadys, hypallage, hyperbole, hypostrophe, hypotyposis, hysteron-proteron, increment, innuendo, irony, litotes, meiosis, metalepsis, metaphor, mixed metaphor, metonymy, onomatopoeia, oxymoron, parabole, paradox, paraleipsis, parenthesis, pathetic fallacy, personification, prolepsis, pun, rhetorical question, simile, syllepsis, symploce, synchoresis, synchrysis, synecdoche, synoeciosis, tautology, transferred epithet, trope, vicious circle, zeugma.

**rhetorical** adj   oratorical, grandiloquent, magniloquent, bombastic, declamatory, pompous, high-sounding, grand, high-flown, flowery, florid, flamboyant, showy, pretentious, artificial, insincere.

**rhyme** *n* poetry, verse, poem, ode, limerick, jingle, song, ditty.

**rhythm** *n* beat, pulse, time, tempo, metre, measure, movement, flow, lilt, swing, accent, cadence, pattern.

**rhythmic** *adj* rhythmical, metric, metrical, pulsating, throbbing, flowing, lilting, periodic, regular, steady.

**rich** *adj* **1** WEALTHY, affluent, moneyed, prosperous, well-to-do, well-off, loaded (*sl*). **2** PLENTIFUL, abundant, copious, profuse, prolific, ample, full. **3** FERTILE, fruitful, productive, lush. **4** *rich food*: creamy, fatty, full-bodied, heavy, full-flavoured, strong, spicy, savoury, tasty, delicious, luscious, juicy, sweet. **5** *rich colours*: deep, intense, vivid, bright, vibrant, warm. **6** EXPENSIVE, precious, valuable, lavish, sumptuous, opulent, luxurious, splendid, gorgeous, fine, elaborate, ornate.

**Fa** **1** poor, impoverished. **3** barren. **4** plain, bland. **5** dull, soft. **6** plain.

**riches** *n* wealth, affluence, money, gold, treasure, fortune, assets, property, substance, resources, means.

**Fa** poverty.

**rickety** *adj* unsteady, wobbly, shaky, unstable, insecure, flimsy, jerry-built, decrepit, ramshackle, broken-down, dilapidated, derelict.

**Fa** stable, strong.

**rid** *v* clear, purge, free, deliver, relieve, unburden.

**riddle**[1] *n* enigma, mystery, conundrum, brain-teaser, puzzle, poser, problem.

**riddle**[2] *v* **1** PERFORATE, pierce, puncture, pepper, fill, permeate, pervade, infest. **2** SIFT, sieve, strain, filter, mar, winnow.

**ride** *v* sit, move, progress, travel, journey, gallop, trot, pedal, drive, steer, control, handle, manage.

*n* journey, trip, outing, jaunt, spin, drive, lift.

**ridicule** *n* satire, irony, sarcasm, mockery, jeering, scorn, derision, taunting, teasing, chaff, banter, badinage, laughter.

**Fa** praise.

*v* satirize, send up, caricature, lampoon, burlesque, parody, mock, make fun of, jeer, scoff, deride, sneer, tease, rib (*infml*), humiliate, taunt.

**Fa** praise.

**ridiculous** *adj* ludicrous, absurd, nonsensical, silly, foolish, stupid, contemptible, derisory, laughable, farcical, comical, funny, hilarious, outrageous, preposterous, incredible, unbelievable.

**Fa** sensible.

**rife** *adj* abundant, rampant, teeming, raging, epidemic, prevalent, widespread, general, common, frequent.

**Fa** scarce.

**rift** *n* **1** SPLIT, breach, break, fracture, crack, fault, chink, cleft, cranny, crevice, gap, space, opening. **2** DISAGREEMENT, difference, separation, division, schism, alienation.

**Fa** **2** unity.

**rig** *n* equipment, kit, outfit, gear, tackle, apparatus, machinery, fittings, fixtures.

**rig out** equip, kit out, outfit, fit (out), supply, furnish, clothe, dress (up).

**right** *adj* **1** *the right answer*: correct, accurate, exact, precise, true, factual, actual, real. **2** PROPER, fitting, seemly, becoming, appropriate, suitable, fit, admissible, satisfactory, reasonable, desirable, favourable, advantageous. **3** FAIR, just, equitable, lawful, honest, upright, good, virtuous, righteous, moral, ethical, honourable. **4** RIGHT-WING, conservative, Tory.

**Fa** **1** wrong, incorrect. **2** improper, unsuitable. **3** unfair, wrong. **4** left-wing.

*adv* **1** CORRECTLY, accurately, exactly, precisely, factually, properly, satisfactorily, well, fairly. **2** *right to the bottom*: straight, directly, completely, utterly.

**F3** **1** wrongly, incorrectly, unfairly.

*n* **1** PRIVILEGE, prerogative, due, claim, business, authority, power. **2** JUSTICE, legality, good, virtue, righteousness, morality, honour, integrity, uprightness.

**F3** **2** wrong.

*v* rectify, correct, put right, fix, repair, redress, vindicate, avenge, settle, straighten, stand up.

**right away** straight away, immediately, at once, now, instantly, directly, forthwith, without delay, promptly.

**F3** later, eventually.

**rightful** *adj* legitimate, lawful, legal, just, bona fide, true, real, genuine, valid, authorized, correct, proper, suitable, due.

**F3** wrongful, unlawful.

**rigid** *adj* stiff, inflexible, unbending, cast-iron, hard, firm, set, fixed, unalterable, invariable, austere, harsh, severe, unrelenting, strict, rigorous, stringent, stern, uncompromising, unyielding.

**F3** flexible, elastic.

**rigorous** *adj* strict, stringent, rigid, firm, exact, precise, accurate, meticulous, painstaking, scrupulous, conscientious, thorough.

**F3** lax, superficial.

**rile** *v* annoy, irritate, nettle, pique, peeve (*infml*), put out, upset, irk, vex, anger, exasperate.

**F3** calm, soothe.

**rim** *n* lip, edge, brim, brink, verge, margin, border, circumference.

**F3** centre, middle.

**rind** *n* peel, skin, husk, crust.

**ring¹** *n* **1** CIRCLE, round, loop, hoop, halo, band, girdle, collar, circuit, arena, enclosure. **2** GROUP,

cartel, syndicate, association, organization, gang, crew, mob, band, cell, clique, coterie.

*v* surround, encircle, gird, circumscribe, encompass, enclose.

**ring²** *v* **1** CHIME, peal, toll, tinkle, clink, jingle, clang, sound, resound, resonate, reverberate, buzz. **2** TELEPHONE, phone, call, ring up.

*n* **1** CHIME, peal, toll, tinkle, clink, jingle, clang. **2** PHONE CALL, call, buzz (*infml*), tinkle (*infml*).

**rinse** *v* swill, bathe, wash, clean, cleanse, flush, wet, dip.

**riot** *n* insurrection, rising, uprising, revolt, rebellion, anarchy, lawlessness, affray, disturbance, turbulence, disorder, confusion, commotion, tumult, turmoil, uproar, row, quarrel, strife.

**F3** order, calm.

*v* revolt, rebel, rise up, run riot, run wild, rampage.

**rip** *v* tear, rend, split, separate, rupture, burst, cut, slit, slash, gash, lacerate, hack.

*n* tear, rent, split, cleavage, rupture, cut, slit, slash, gash, hole.

**rip off** (*sl*) overcharge, swindle, defraud, cheat, diddle, do (*infml*), fleece, sting (*sl*), con (*infml*), trick, dupe, exploit.

**ripe** *adj* **1** RIPENED, mature, mellow, seasoned, grown, developed, complete, finished, perfect. **2** READY, suitable, right, favourable, auspicious, propitious, timely, opportune.

**F3** **2** untimely, inopportune.

**ripen** *v* develop, mature, mellow, season, age.

**rise** *v* **1** GO UP, ascend, climb, mount, slope (up), soar, tower, grow, increase, escalate, intensify. **2** STAND UP, get up, arise, jump up, spring up. **3** ADVANCE, progress, improve, prosper. **4** ORIGINATE, spring, flow, issue, emerge, appear.

**F3** **1** fall, descend. **2** sit down.

3 declare.

**n 1** ASCENT, climb, slope, incline, hill, elevation. **2** INCREASE, increment, upsurge, upturn, advance, progress, improvement, advancement, promotion.

**F3 1** descent, valley **2** fall.

**risk** n danger, peril, jeopardy, hazard, chance, possibility, uncertainty, gamble, speculation, venture, adventure.

**F3** safety, certainty.

v endanger, imperil, jeopardize, hazard, chance, gamble, venture, dare.

**risky** adj dangerous, unsafe, perilous, hazardous, chancy, uncertain, touch-and-go, dicey (infml), tricky, precarious.

**F3** safe.

**risqué** adj indecent, improper, indelicate, suggestive, coarse, crude, earthy, bawdy, racy, naughty, blue.

**F3** decent, proper.

**ritual** n custom, tradition, convention, usage, practice, habit, wont, routine, procedure, ordinance, prescription, form, formality, ceremony, ceremonial, solemnity, rite, sacrament, service, liturgy, observance, act.

adj customary, traditional, conventional, habitual, routine, procedural, prescribed, set, formal, ceremonial.

**F3** informal.

**rival** n competitor, contestant, contender, challenger, opponent, adversary, antagonist, match, equal, peer.

**F3** colleague, associate.

adj competitive, competing, opposed, opposing, conflicting.

**F3** associate.

v compete with, contend with, vie with, oppose, emulate, match, equal.

**F3** co-operate.

**rivalry** n competitiveness, competition, contest, contention, conflict, struggle, strife, opposition,

antagonism.

**F3** co-operation.

**river** n waterway, watercourse, tributary, stream, brook, beck, creek, estuary.

**road** n roadway, motorway, bypass, highway, thoroughfare, street, avenue, boulevard, crescent, drive, lane, track, route, course, way, direction.

**roam** v wander, rove, range, travel, walk, ramble, stroll, amble, prowl, drift, stray.

**F3** stay.

**roar** v, n bellow, yell, shout, cry, bawl, howl, hoot, guffaw, thunder, crash, blare, rumble.

**F3** whisper.

**rob** v steal from, hold up, raid, burgle, loot, pillage, plunder, sack, rifle, ransack, swindle, rip off (sl), do (infml), cheat, defraud, deprive.

**robbery** n theft, stealing, larceny, hold-up, stick-up (sl), heist (sl), raid, burglary, pillage, plunder, fraud, embezzlement, swindle, rip-off (sl).

**robot** n automaton, machine, android, zombie.

**robust** adj strong, sturdy, tough, hardy, vigorous, powerful, muscular, athletic, fit, healthy, well.

**F3** weak, feeble, unhealthy.

**rock**¹ n boulder, stone, pebble, crag, outcrop.

*Rocks include: basalt, breccia, chalk, coal, conglomerate, flint, gabbro, gneiss, granite, gravel, lava, limestone, marble, marl, obsidian, ore, porphyry, pumice stone, sandstone, schist, serpentine, shale, slate.*

**rock**² v **1** SWAY, swing, tilt, tip, shake, wobble, roll, pitch, toss, lurch, reel, stagger, totter. **2** news that rocked the nation: shock, stun, daze, dumbfound, astound, astonish, surprise, startle.

**rocky**¹ adj stony, pebbly, craggy,

rugged, rough, hard, flinty.
**F3** smooth, soft.

**rocky²** *adj* unsteady, shaky, wobbly, staggering, tottering, unstable, unreliable, uncertain, weak.
**F3** steady, stable, dependable, strong.

**rod** *n* bar, shaft, strut, pole, stick, baton, wand, cane, switch, staff, mace, sceptre.

**rodent**

Rodents include: agouti, bandicoot, beaver, black rat, brown rat, cane rat, capybara, cavy, chinchilla, chipmunk, cony, coypu, dormouse, fieldmouse, ferret, gerbil, gopher, grey squirrel, groundhog, guinea pig, hamster, hare, harvest mouse, hedgehog, jerboa, kangaroo rat, lemming, marmot, meerkat, mouse, muskrat, musquash, pika, porcupine, prairie dog, rabbit, rat, red squirrel, sewer-rat, squirrel, vole, water rat, water vole, woodchuck.

**rogue** *n* scoundrel, rascal, scamp, villain, miscreant, crook (*infml*), swindler, fraud, cheat, con man (*infml*), reprobate, wastrel, ne'er-do-well.

**role** *n* part, character, representation, portrayal, impersonation, function, capacity, task, duty, job, post, position.

**roll** *v* **1** ROTATE, revolve, turn, spin, wheel, twirl, whirl, gyrate, move, run, pass. **2** WIND, coil, furl, twist, curl, wrap, envelop, enfold, bind. **3** *the ship rolled*: rock, sway, swing, pitch, toss, lurch, reel, wallow, undulate. **4** PRESS, flatten, smooth, level. **5** RUMBLE, roar, thunder, boom, resound, reverberate.
*n* **1** ROLLER, cylinder, drum, reel, spool, bobbin, scroll. **2** REGISTER, roster, census, list, inventory, index, catalogue, directory, schedule, record, chronicle, annals. **3** ROTATION, revolution, cycle, turn, spin, wheel,

twirl, whirl, gyration, undulation.
**4** RUMBLE, roar, thunder, boom, resonance, reverberation.

**roll up** (*infml*) arrive, assemble, gather, congregate, convene.
**F3** leave.

**romance** *n* **1** LOVE AFFAIR, affair, relationship, liaison, intrigue, passion. **2** LOVE STORY, novel, story, tale, fairytale, legend, idyll, fiction, fantasy. **3** ADVENTURE, excitement, melodrama, mystery, charm, fascination, glamour, sentiment.
*v* lie, fantasize, exaggerate, overstate.

**romantic** *adj* **1** IMAGINARY, fictitious, fanciful, fantastic, legendary, fairy-tale, idyllic, utopian, idealistic, quixotic, visionary, starry-eyed, dreamy, unrealistic, impractical, improbable, wild, extravagant, exciting, fascinating.
**2** SENTIMENTAL, loving, amorous, passionate, tender, fond, lovey-dovey (*infml*), soppy, mushy, sloppy.
**F3** **1** real, practical. **2** unromantic, unsentimental.
*n* sentimentalist, dreamer, visionary, idealist, utopian.
**F3** realist.

**room**

Types of room include: attic, loft, box-room, bedroom, boudoir, spare room, dressing-room, guest room, nursery, playroom, sitting-room, lounge, front room, living-room, drawing-room, salon, reception room, chamber, lounge-diner, dining-room, study, den (*infml*), library, kitchen, kitchen-diner, kitchenette, breakfast room, larder, pantry, scullery, bathroom, en suite bathroom, toilet, lavatory, WC, loo (*infml*), cloakroom, laundry, utility room, porch, hall, landing, conservatory, sun lounge, cellar, basement; classroom, music-room, laboratory, office, sick-room, dormitory, workroom, studio, workshop, storeroom, waiting-room, anteroom, foyer, mezzanine, family room, games room.

*n* space, volume, capacity, headroom, legroom, elbow-room, scope, range, extent, leeway, latitude, margin, allowance, chance, opportunity.

**roomy** *adj* spacious, capacious, large, sizable, broad, wide, extensive, ample, generous.

**F3** cramped, small, tiny.

**root**¹ *n* **1** TUBER, rhizome, stem. **2** ORIGIN, source, derivation, cause, starting point, fount, fountainhead, seed, germ, nucleus, heart, core, nub, essence, seat, base, bottom, basis, foundation.

*v* anchor, moor, fasten, fix, set, stick, implant, embed, entrench, establish, ground, base.

**root out** unearth, dig out, uncover, discover, uproot, eradicate, extirpate, eliminate, exterminate, destroy, abolish, clear away, remove.

**root**² *v* dig, delve, burrow, forage, hunt, rummage, ferret, poke, pry, nose.

**roots** *n* beginning(s), origins, family, heritage, background, birthplace, home.

**rope** *n* line, cable, cord, string, strand.

*v* tie, bind, lash, fasten, hitch, moor, tether.

**rope in** enlist, engage, involve, persuade, inveigle.

**roster** *n* rota, schedule, register, roll, list.

**rostrum** *n* platform, stage, dais, podium.

**rot** *v* decay, decompose, putrefy, fester, perish, corrode, spoil, go bad, go off, degenerate, deteriorate, crumble, disintegrate, taint, corrupt.

*n* **1** DECAY, decomposition, putrefaction, corrosion, rust, mould. **2** (*infml*) NONSENSE, rubbish, poppycock (*infml*), drivel, claptrap.

**rotary** *adj* rotating, revolving,

turning, spinning, whirling, gyrating.

**F3** fixed.

**rotate** *v* revolve, turn, spin, gyrate, pivot, swivel, roll.

**rotation** *n* revolution, turn, spin, gyration, orbit, cycle, sequence, succession, turning, spinning.

**rotten** *adj* **1** DECAYED, decomposed, putrid, addled, bad, off, mouldy, fetid, stinking, rank, foul, rotting, decaying, disintegrating.

**2** INFERIOR, bad, poor, inadequate, low-grade, lousy, crummy (*sl*), ropy (*sl*), mean, nasty, beastly, dirty, despicable, contemptible, dishonourable, wicked. **3** (*infml*) ILL, sick, unwell, poorly, grotty (*sl*), rough (*infml*).

**F3 1** fresh. **2** good. **3** well.

**rough** *adj* **1** UNEVEN, bumpy, lumpy, rugged, craggy, jagged, irregular, coarse, bristly, scratchy. **2** HARSH, severe, tough, hard, cruel, brutal, drastic, extreme, brusque, curt, sharp. **3** APPROXIMATE, estimated, imprecise, inexact, vague, general, cursory, hasty, incomplete, unfinished, crude, rudimentary. **4** *rough sea*: choppy, agitated, turbulent, stormy, tempestuous, violent, wild. **5** (*infml*) ILL, sick, unwell, poorly, off colour, rotten (*infml*).

**F3 1** smooth. **2** mild. **3** accurate. **4** calm. **5** well.

**round** *adj* **1** SPHERICAL, globular, ball-shaped, circular, ring-shaped, disc-shaped, cylindrical, rounded, curved. **2** ROTUND, plump, stout, portly.

*n* **1** CIRCLE, ring, band, disc, sphere, ball, orb. **2** CYCLE, series, sequence, succession, period, bout, session. **3** BEAT, circuit, lap, course, routine. *v* circle, skirt, flank, bypass.

**round off** finish (off), complete, end, close, conclude, cap, crown.

**F3** begin.

**round on** turn on, attack, lay into,

abuse.

**round up** herd, marshal, assemble, gather, rally, collect, group.
☒ disperse, scatter.

**roundabout** *adj* circuitous, tortuous, twisting, winding, indirect, oblique, devious, evasive.
☒ straight, direct.

**rouse** *v* wake (up), awaken, arouse, call, stir, move, start, disturb, agitate, anger, provoke, stimulate, instigate, incite, inflame, excite, galvanize, whip up.
☒ calm.

**rout** *n* defeat, conquest, overthrow, beating, thrashing, flight, stampede.
☒ win.
*v* defeat, conquer, overthrow, crush, beat, hammer (*infml*), thrash, lick, put to flight, chase, dispel, scatter.

**route** *n* course, run, path, road, avenue, way, direction, itinerary, journey, passage, circuit, round, beat.

**routine** *n* 1 PROCEDURE, way, method, system, order, pattern, formula, practice, usage, custom, habit. 2 *comedy routine*: act, piece, programme, performance.
*adj* customary, habitual, usual, typical, ordinary, run-of-the-mill, normal, standard, conventional, unoriginal, predictable, familiar, everyday, banal, humdrum, dull, boring, monotonous, tedious.
☒ unusual, different, exciting.

**row¹** *n* line, tier, bank, rank, range, column, file, queue, string, series, sequence.

**row²** *n* 1 ARGUMENT, quarrel, dispute, controversy, squabble, tiff, slanging match (*infml*), fight, brawl. 2 NOISE, racket, din, uproar, commotion, disturbance, rumpus, fracas.
☒ 2 calm.
*v* argue, quarrel, wrangle, bicker, squabble, fight, scrap.

**rowdy** *adj* noisy, loud, rough, boisterous, disorderly, unruly,

riotous, wild.
☒ quiet, peaceful.

**royal** *adj* regal, majestic, kingly, queenly, princely, imperial, monarchical, sovereign, august, grand, stately, magnificent, splendid, superb.

**rub** *v* apply, spread, smear, stroke, caress, massage, knead, chafe, grate, scrape, abrade, scour, scrub, clean, wipe, smooth, polish, buff, shine.

**rub out** erase, efface, obliterate, delete, cancel.

**rubbish** *n* 1 REFUSE, garbage, trash, junk, litter, waste, dross, debris, flotsam and jetsam. 2 NONSENSE, drivel, claptrap, twaddle, gibberish, gobbledegook, balderdash, poppycock (*infml*), rot (*infml*), cobblers (*sl*).
☒ 2 sense.

**ruddy** *adj* red, scarlet, crimson, blushing, flushed, rosy, glowing, healthy, blooming, florid, sunburnt.
☒ pale.

**rude** *adj* 1 IMPOLITE, discourteous, disrespectful, impertinent, impudent, cheeky (*infml*), insolent, offensive, insulting, abusive, ill-mannered, ill-bred, uncouth, uncivilized, unrefined, unpolished, uneducated, untutored, uncivil, curt, brusque, abrupt, sharp, short. 2 *a rude joke*: obscene, vulgar, coarse, dirty, naughty, gross.
☒ 1 polite, courteous, civil. 2 clean, decent.

**rudimentary** *adj* primary, initial, introductory, elementary, basic, fundamental, primitive, undeveloped, embryonic.
☒ advanced, developed.

**rudiments** *n* basics, fundamentals, essentials, principles, elements, ABC, beginnings, foundations.

**rugged** *adj* 1 ROUGH, bumpy, uneven, irregular, jagged, rocky, craggy, stark. 2 STRONG, robust, hardy, tough, muscular, weather-beaten.

**⟨≡⟩ 1** smooth.

**ruin** n destruction, devastation, wreckage, havoc, damage, disrepair, decay, disintegration, breakdown, collapse, fall, downfall, failure, defeat, overthrow, ruination, undoing, insolvency, bankruptcy, crash.

**⟨≡⟩** development, reconstruction.

v spoil, mar, botch, mess up (*infml*), damage, break, smash, shatter, wreck, destroy, demolish, raze, devastate, overwhelm, overthrow, defeat, crush, impoverish, bankrupt.

**⟨≡⟩** develop, restore.

**rule** n **1** REGULATION, law, statute, ordinance, decree, order, direction, guide, precept, tenet, canon, maxim, axiom, principle, formula, guideline, standard, criterion. **2** REIGN, sovereignty, supremacy, dominion, mastery, power, authority, command, control, influence, regime, government, leadership. **3** CUSTOM, convention, practice, routine, habit, wont.

v **1** *rule a country*: reign, govern, command, lead, administer, manage, direct, guide, control, regulate, prevail, dominate. **2** JUDGE, adjudicate, decide, find, determine, resolve, establish, decree, pronounce.

**as a rule** usually, normally, ordinarily, generally.

**rule out** exclude, eliminate, reject, dismiss, preclude, prevent, ban, prohibit, forbid, disallow.

**ruler**

Titles of rulers include: Aga, begum, caesar, caliph, consul, duce, emir, emperor, empress, Führer, governor, governor-general, head of state, kaiser, khan, king, maharajah, maharani, mikado, monarch, nawab, nizam, pharaoh, president, prince, princess, queen, rajah, rani, regent, shah, sheikh, shogun, sovereign, sultan, sultana, suzerain, tsar, viceroy.

**ruling** n judgement, adjudication, verdict, decision, finding, resolution, decree, pronouncement.

adj reigning, sovereign, supreme, governing, commanding, leading, main, chief, principal, dominant, predominant, controlling.

**rumour** n hearsay, gossip, talk, whisper, word, news, report, story, grapevine, bush telegraph.

**run** v **1** SPRINT, jog, race, career, tear, dash, hurry, rush, speed, bolt, dart, scoot, scuttle. **2** GO, pass, move, proceed, issue. **3** FUNCTION, work, operate, perform. **4** *run a company*: head, lead, administer, direct, manage, superintend, supervise, oversee, control, regulate.

**5** COMPETE, contend, stand, challenge. **6** LAST, continue, extend, reach, stretch, spread, range.

**7** FLOW, stream, pour, gush.

n **1** JOG, gallop, race, sprint, spurt, dash, rush. **2** DRIVE, ride, spin, jaunt, excursion, outing, trip, journey. **3** SEQUENCE, series, string, chain, course.

**run after** chase, pursue, follow, tail.

**⟨≡⟩** flee.

**run away** escape, flee, abscond, bolt, scarper (*sl*), beat it (*infml*), run off, make off, clear off (*infml*).

**⟨≡⟩** stay.

**run down 1** CRITICIZE, belittle, disparage, denigrate, defame. **2** RUN OVER, knock over, hit, strike. **3** TIRE, weary, exhaust, weaken. **4** *run down production*: reduce, decrease, drop, cut, trim, curtail.

**⟨≡⟩ 1** praise. **4** increase.

**run into** meet, encounter, run across, bump into, hit, strike, collide with.

**⟨≡⟩** miss.

**run out** expire, terminate, end, cease, close, finish, dry up, fail.

**runaway** n escaper, escapee, fugitive, absconder, deserter, refugee. adj escaped, fugitive, loose, uncontrolled.

**rundown** n 1 REDUCTION, decrease, decline, drop, cut. 2 SUMMARY, résumé, synopsis, outline, review, recap, run-through.

**runner** n jogger, sprinter, athlete, competitor, participant, courier, messenger.

**running** adj successive, consecutive, unbroken, uninterrupted, continuous, constant, perpetual, incessant, unceasing, moving, flowing. ◆ broken, occasional.
n 1 ADMINISTRATION, direction, management, organization, co-ordination, superintendency, supervision, leadership, charge, control, regulation, functioning, working, operation, performance, conduct. 2 out of the running: contention, contest, competition.

**runny** adj flowing, fluid, liquid, liquefied, melted, molten, watery, diluted. ◆ solid.

**run-of-the-mill** adj ordinary, common, everyday, average, unexceptional, unremarkable, undistinguished, unimpressive, mediocre. ◆ exceptional.

**rupture** n split, tear, burst, puncture, break, breach, fracture, crack, separation, division, estrangement, schism, rift, disagreement, quarrel, falling-out, bust-up (infml).
v split, tear, burst, puncture, break, fracture, crack, sever, separate, divide.

**rural** adj country, rustic, pastoral, agricultural, agrarian. ◆ urban.

**rush** v hurry, hasten, quicken, accelerate, speed (up), press, push, dispatch, bolt, dart, shoot, fly, tear, career, dash, race, run, sprint, scramble, stampede, charge.
n hurry, haste, urgency, speed, swiftness, dash, race, scramble, stampede, charge, flow, surge.

**rust** n corrosion, oxidation.
v corrode, decay, rot, oxidize, tarnish, deteriorate, decline.

**rustic** adj 1 PASTORAL, sylvan, bucolic, countrified, country, rural. 2 PLAIN, simple, rough, crude, coarse, rude, clumsy, awkward, artless, unsophisticated, unrefined, uncultured, provincial, uncouth, boorish, oafish. ◆ 1 urban. 2 urbane, sophisticated, cultivated, polished.

**rustle** v, n crackle, whoosh, swish, whisper.

**rusty** adj 1 CORRODED, rusted, rust-covered, oxidized, tarnished, discoloured, dull. 2 UNPRACTISED, weak, poor, deficient, dated, old-fashioned, outmoded, antiquated, stale, stiff, creaking.

**ruthless** adj merciless, pitiless, hard-hearted, hard, heartless, unfeeling, callous, cruel, inhuman, brutal, savage, cut-throat, fierce, ferocious, relentless, unrelenting, inexorable, implacable, harsh, severe. ◆ merciful, compassionate.

# S

**sabotage** v damage, spoil, mar, disrupt, vandalize, wreck, destroy, thwart, scupper, cripple, incapacitate, disable, undermine, weaken.
n vandalism, damage, impairment, disruption, wrecking, destruction.

**sack** (infml) v dismiss, fire, discharge, axe (infml), lay off, make redundant.

*n* dismissal, discharge, one's cards, notice, the boot (*infml*), the push (*infml*), the elbow (*infml*), the axe (*infml*), the chop (*infml*).

**sacred** *adj* holy, divine, heavenly, blessed, hallowed, sanctified, consecrated, dedicated, religious, devotional, ecclesiastical, priestly, saintly, godly, venerable, revered, sacrosanct, inviolable.
**E꒓** temporal, profane.

**sacred writing**

> *Sacred writings include*: Holy Bible, the Gospel, Old Testament, New Testament, Epistle, Torah, Pentateuch, Talmud, Koran, Bhagavad-Gita, Veda, Granth, Zend-Avesta.

**sacrifice** *v* surrender, forfeit, relinquish, let go, abandon, renounce, give up, forgo, offer, slaughter.
*n* offering, immolation, slaughter, destruction, surrender, renunciation, loss.

**sacrilege** *n* blasphemy, profanity, heresy, desecration, profanation, violation, outrage, irreverence, disrespect, mockery.
**E꒓** piety, reverence, respect.

**sacrosanct** *adj* sacred, hallowed, untouchable, inviolable, impregnable, protected, secure.

**sad** *adj* **1** UNHAPPY, sorrowful, tearful, grief-stricken, heavy-hearted, upset, distressed, miserable, low-spirited, downcast, glum, long-faced, crestfallen, dejected, down-hearted, despondent, melancholy, depressed, low, gloomy, dismal. **2** *sad news*: upsetting, distressing, painful, depressing, touching, poignant, heart-rending, tragic, grievous, lamentable, regrettable, sorry, unfortunate, serious, grave, disastrous.
**E꒓** **1** happy, cheerful. **2** fortunate, lucky.

**sadden** *v* upset, distress, grieve, depress, dismay, discourage, dishearten.
**E꒓** cheer, please, gratify, delight.

**saddle** *v* burden, encumber, lumber, impose, tax, charge, load (*infml*).

**sadistic** *adj* cruel, inhuman, brutal, savage, vicious, merciless, pitiless, barbarous, bestial, unnatural, perverted.

**safe** *adj* **1** HARMLESS, innocuous, non-toxic, non-poisonous, uncontaminated. **2** UNHARMED, undamaged, unscathed, uninjured, unhurt, intact, secure, protected, guarded, impregnable, invulnerable, immune. **3** UNADVENTUROUS, cautious, prudent, conservative, sure, proven, tried, tested, sound, dependable, reliable, trustworthy.
**E꒓** **1** dangerous, harmful. **2** vulnerable, exposed. **3** risky.

**safeguard** *v* protect, preserve, defend, guard, shield, screen, shelter, secure.
**E꒓** endanger, jeopardize.
*n* protection, defence, shield, security, surety, guarantee, assurance, insurance, cover, precaution.

**safe-keeping** *n* protection, care, custody, keeping, charge, trust, guardianship, surveillance, supervision.

**safety** *n* protection, refuge, sanctuary, shelter, cover, security, safeguard, immunity, impregnability, safeness, harmlessness, reliability, dependability.
**E꒓** danger, jeopardy, risk.

**sag** *v* bend, give, bag, droop, hang, fall, drop, sink, dip, decline, slump, flop, fail, flag, weaken, wilt.
**E꒓** bulge, rise.

**sail** *v* **1** *sail for France*: embark, set sail, weigh anchor, put to sea, cruise, voyage. **2** CAPTAIN, skipper, pilot, navigate, steer. **3** GLIDE, plane, sweep, float, skim, scud, fly.

**sailor** *n* seafarer, mariner, seaman,

marine, rating, yachtsman, yachtswoman.

**saintly** *adj* godly, pious, devout, God-fearing, holy, religious, blessed, angelic, pure, spotless, innocent, blameless, sinless, virtuous, upright, worthy, righteous.
**F3** godless, unholy, wicked.

**sake** *n* benefit, advantage, good, welfare, wellbeing, gain, profit, behalf, interest, account, regard, respect, cause, reason.

**salary** *n* pay, remuneration, emolument, stipend, wages, earnings, income.

**sale** *n* selling, marketing, vending, disposal, trade, traffic, transaction, deal, auction.

*Types of sale include*: auction, autumn sale, bargain offer, bazaar, bazumble, boot-sale, bring-and-buy, car-boot sale, charity sale, church bazaar, clearance sale, closing-down sale, cold-call, end-of-line sale, end-of-season sale, exhibition, exposition, fair, fleamarket, forced sale, garage sale, grand opening sale, introductory offer, January sale, jumble sale, mail order, market, mid-season sale, on-promotion, open market, private sale, public sale, pyramid selling, remainder sale, rummage sale, sale of bankrupt stock, sale of the century, sale of work, second-hand sale, special offer, spring sale, stocktaking sale, summer sale, tabletop sale, telesales, trade show, trash and treasure sale, winter sale.

**salesperson** *n* salesman, saleswoman, sales assistant, shop assistant, shop-boy, shop-girl, shopkeeper, representative, rep (*infml*).

**salient** *adj* important, significant, chief, main, principal, striking, conspicuous, noticeable, obvious, prominent, outstanding, remarkable.

**sallow** *adj* yellowish, pale, pallid, wan, pasty, sickly, unhealthy, anaemic, colourless.
**F3** rosy, healthy.

**salt** *n* seasoning, taste, flavour, savour, relish, piquancy.

**salty** *adj* salt, salted, saline, briny, brackish, savoury, spicy, piquant, tangy.
**F3** fresh, sweet.

**salubrious** *adj* sanitary, hygienic, health-giving, healthy, wholesome, pleasant.

**salutary** *adj* good, beneficial, advantageous, profitable, valuable, helpful, useful, practical, timely.

**salute** *v* greet, acknowledge, recognize, wave, hail, address, nod, bow, honour.
*n* greeting, acknowledgement, recognition, wave, gesture, hail, address, handshake, nod, bow, tribute, reverence.

**salvage** *v* save, preserve, conserve, rescue, recover, recuperate, retrieve, reclaim, redeem, repair, restore.
**F3** waste, abandon.

**salvation** *n* deliverance, liberation, rescue, saving, preservation, redemption, reclamation.
**F3** loss, damnation.

**salve** *n* ointment, lotion, cream, balm, liniment, embrocation, medication, preparation, application.

**same** *adj* identical, twin, duplicate, indistinguishable, equal, selfsame, very, alike, like, similar, comparable, equivalent, matching, corresponding, mutual, reciprocal, interchangeable, substitutable, synonymous, consistent, uniform, unvarying, changeless, unchanged.
**F3** different, inconsistent, variable, changeable.

**sample** *n* specimen, example, cross-section, model, pattern, swatch, piece, demonstration, illustration, instance, sign, indication, foretaste.
*v* try, test, taste, sip, inspect,

experience.

*adj* representative, specimen, demonstrative, illustrative, dummy, trial, test, pilot.

**sanctify** *v* hallow, consecrate, bless, anoint, dedicate, cleanse, purify, exalt, canonize.

**Ea** desecrate, defile.

**sanctimonious** *adj* self-righteous, holier-than-thou, pious, moralizing, smug, superior, hypocritical, pharisaical.

**Ea** humble.

**sanction** *n* authorization, permission, agreement, OK (*infml*), approval, go-ahead, ratification, confirmation, support, backing, endorsement, licence, authority.

**Ea** veto, disapproval.

*v* authorize, allow, permit, approve, ratify, confirm, support, back, endorse, underwrite, accredit, license, warrant.

**Ea** veto, forbid, disapprove.

**sanctions** *n* restrictions, boycott, embargo, ban, prohibition, penalty.

**sanctity** *n* holiness, sacredness, inviolability, piety, godliness, religiousness, devotion, grace, spirituality, purity, goodness, righteousness.

**Ea** unholiness, secularity, worldliness, godlessness, impurity.

**sanctuary** *n* **1** CHURCH, temple, tabernacle, shrine, altar. **2** ASYLUM, refuge, protection, shelter, haven, retreat.

**sand** *n* beach, shore, strand, sands, grit.

**sane** *adj* normal, rational, right-minded, all there (*infml*), balanced, stable, sound, sober, level-headed, sensible, judicious, reasonable, moderate.

**Ea** insane, mad, crazy, foolish.

**sanitary** *adj* clean, pure, uncontaminated, unpolluted, aseptic, germ-free, disinfected, hygienic, salubrious, healthy, wholesome.

**Ea** insanitary, unwholesome.

**sanity** *n* normality, rationality, reason, sense, common sense, balance of mind, stability, soundness, level-headedness, judiciousness.

**Ea** insanity, madness.

**sap** *v* bleed, drain, exhaust, weaken, undermine, deplete, reduce, diminish, impair.

**Ea** strengthen, build up, increase.

**sarcasm** *n* irony, satire, mockery, sneering, derision, scorn, contempt, cynicism, bitterness.

**sarcastic** *adj* ironical, satirical, mocking, taunting, sneering, derisive, scathing, disparaging, cynical, incisive, cutting, biting, caustic.

**sardonic** *adj* mocking, jeering, sneering, derisive, scornful, sarcastic, biting, cruel, heartless, malicious, cynical, bitter.

**sash** *n* belt, girdle, cummerbund, waistband.

**satanic** *adj* satanical, diabolical, devilish, demonic, fiendish, hellish, infernal, inhuman, malevolent, wicked, evil, black.

**Ea** holy, divine, godly, saintly, benevolent.

**satire** *n* ridicule, irony, sarcasm, wit, burlesque, skit, send-up, spoof, take-off, parody, caricature, travesty.

**satirical** *adj* ironical, sarcastic, mocking, irreverent, taunting, derisive, sardonic, incisive, cutting, biting, caustic, cynical, bitter.

**satirize** *v* ridicule, mock, make fun of, burlesque, lampoon, send up, take off, parody, caricature, criticize, deride.

**Ea** acclaim, honour.

**satisfaction** *n* **1** GRATIFICATION, contentment, happiness, pleasure, enjoyment, comfort, ease, well-being, fulfilment, self-satisfaction, pride. **2** SETTLEMENT, compensation, reimbursement, indemnification, damages, reparation, amends, redress, recompense, requital, vindication.

**≠** dissatisfaction, displeasure.

**satisfactory** adj acceptable, passable, up to the mark, all right, OK (infml), fair, average, competent, adequate, sufficient, suitable, proper.

**≠** unsatisfactory, unacceptable, inadequate.

**satisfy** v 1 GRATIFY, indulge, content, please, delight, quench, slake, sate, satiate, surfeit. 2 satisfy requirements: meet, fulfil, discharge, settle, answer, fill, suffice, serve, qualify. 3 ASSURE, convince, persuade.

**≠** 1 dissatisfy. 2 fail.

**saturate** v soak, steep, souse, drench, waterlog, impregnate, permeate, imbue, suffuse, fill.

**saucy** (infml) adj cheeky (infml), impertinent, impudent, insolent, disrespectful, pert, forward, presumptuous, flippant.

**≠** polite, respectful.

**saunter** v stroll, amble, mosey (infml), mooch (infml), wander, ramble (sl), meander.

n stroll, walk, constitutional, ramble.

**savage** adj wild, untamed, undomesticated, uncivilized, primitive, barbaric, barbarous, fierce, ferocious, vicious, beastly, cruel, inhuman, brutal, sadistic, bloodthirsty, bloody, murderous, pitiless, merciless, ruthless, harsh.

**≠** tame, civilized, humane, mild.

n brute, beast, barbarian.

v attack, bite, claw, tear, maul, mangle.

**save** v 1 ECONOMIZE, cut back, conserve, preserve, keep, retain, hold, reserve, store, lay up, set aside, put by, hoard, stash (infml), collect, gather. 2 RESCUE, deliver, liberate, free, salvage, recover, reclaim. 3 PROTECT, guard, screen, shield, safeguard, spare, prevent, hinder.

**≠** 1 spend, squander, waste, discard.

n economy, thrift, discount,

reduction, bargain, cut, conservation, preservation.

**≠** expense, waste, loss.

**savings** n capital, investments, nest egg, fund, store, reserves, resources.

**saviour** n rescuer, deliverer, redeemer, liberator, emancipator, guardian, protector, defender, champion.

**≠** destroyer.

**savour** n taste, flavour, smack, smell, tang, piquancy, salt, spice, relish, zest.

v relish, enjoy, delight in, revel in, like, appreciate.

**≠** shrink from.

**savoury** adj 1 TASTY, appetizing, delicious, mouthwatering, luscious, palatable. 2 savoury pancakes: salty, spicy, aromatic, piquant, tangy.

**≠** 1 unappetizing, tasteless, insipid. 2 sweet.

**say** v 1 EXPRESS, phrase, put, render, utter, voice, articulate, enunciate, pronounce, deliver, speak, orate, recite, repeat, read, indicate. 2 ANSWER, reply, respond, rejoin, retort, exclaim, ejaculate, comment, remark, observe, mention, add, drawl, mutter, grunt. 3 TELL, instruct, order, communicate, convey, intimate, report, announce, declare, state, assert, affirm, maintain, claim, allege, rumour, suggest, imply, signify, reveal, disclose, divulge. 4 GUESS, estimate, reckon, judge, imagine, suppose, assume, presume, surmise.

*Other words for say include:* accuse, acknowledge, add, admit, admonish, advise, affirm, agree, allege, announce, answer, argue, ask, assert, assume, babble, banter, bark, bawl, beg, begin, bellow, blare, blaspheme, blurt, boast, brag, call, chant, chatter, claim, coax, command, comment, complain, conclude, confide, continue, contradict, correct, counter, croak, cry, curse, declare, demand, deny, describe, detail, disclose, dispute, divulge, echo, elaborate, elucidate, emphasize, enjoin, enquire, estimate, exclaim, expostulate, express, falter, finish, flounder, gasp, greet, groan, growl, grumble, grunt, guess, hint, howl, imagine, implore, imply, indicate, infer, inform, insinuate, instruct, interrogate, interrupt, intervene, intimate, jeer, jest, joke, laugh, lecture, lie, mention, mimic, moan, mock, mouth, mumble, murmur, mutter, nag, observe, offer, orate, order, persist, persuade, phrase, pipe, plead, point out, predict, press, presume, proclaim, profess, proffer, prompt, pronounce, propose, protest, query, question, quote, rage, rail, rant, read, reassure, rebuke, recite, recommend, reckon, rehearse, reiterate, rejoice, relate, remark, remonstrate, renounce, repeat, reply, report, respond, request, resolve, respond, retaliate, retort, retract, reveal, roar, scoff, scold, scream, screech, shout, shriek, snap, snarl, speak, specify, squeak, stammer, state, storm, stutter, submit, suggest, surmise, swear, sympathize, taunt, tease, tell, testify, thunder, urge, utter, venture, voice, volunteer, vow, whine, whisper, wonder, yell.

**saying** n adage, proverb, dictum, precept, axiom, aphorism, maxim, motto, slogan, phrase, expression, quotation, statement, remark.

**scale**¹ n ratio, proportion, measure, degree, extent, spread, reach, range, scope, compass, spectrum, gamut, sequence, series, progression, order, hierarchy, ranking, ladder, steps, gradation, graduation, calibration, register.
v climb, ascend, mount, clamber, scramble, shin up, conquer, surmount.

**scale**² n encrustation, deposit, crust, layer, film, lamina, plate, flake, scurf.

**scamp** n rogue, rascal, scallywag, monkey, imp, devil.

**scamper** v scuttle, scurry, scoot, dart, dash, run, sprint, rush, hurry, hasten, fly, romp, frolic, gambol.

**scan** v 1 EXAMINE, scrutinize, study, search, survey, sweep, investigate, check. 2 SKIM, glance at, flick through, thumb through.
n screening, examination, scrutiny, search, probe, check, investigation, survey, review.

**scandal** n outrage, offence, outcry, uproar, furore, gossip, rumours, smear, dirt, discredit, dishonour, disgrace, shame, embarrassment, ignominy.

**scandalize** v shock, horrify, appal, dismay, disgust, repel, revolt, offend, affront, outrage.

**scandalous** adj shocking, appalling, atrocious, abominable, monstrous, unspeakable, outrageous, disgraceful, shameful, disreputable, infamous, improper, unseemly, defamatory, scurrilous, slanderous, libellous, untrue.

**scanty** adj deficient, short, inadequate, insufficient, scant, little, limited, restricted, narrow, poor, meagre, insubstantial, thin, skimpy, sparse, bare.
🔁 adequate, sufficient, ample, plentiful, substantial.

**scar** n mark, lesion, wound, injury, blemish, stigma.
v mark, disfigure, spoil, damage, brand, stigmatize.

**scarce** adj few, rare, infrequent, uncommon, unusual, sparse, scanty, insufficient, deficient, lacking.
🔁 plentiful, common.

**scarcely** adv hardly, barely, only just.

**scarcity** n lack, shortage, dearth, deficiency, insufficiency, paucity, rareness, rarity, infrequency, uncommonness, sparseness, scantiness.

☒ glut, plenty, abundance, sufficiency, enough.

**scare** v frighten, startle, alarm, dismay, daunt, intimidate, unnerve, threaten, menace, terrorize, shock, appal, panic, terrify.

☒ reassure, calm.

n fright, start, shock, alarm, panic, hysteria, terror.

☒ reassurance, comfort.

**scared** adj frightened, fearful, nervous, anxious, worried, startled, shaken, panic-stricken, terrified.

☒ confident, reassured.

**scary** adj frightening, alarming, daunting, intimidating, disturbing, shocking, horrifying, terrifying, hair-raising, bloodcurdling, spine-chilling, chilling, creepy, eerie, spooky (infml).

**scathing** adj sarcastic, scornful, critical, trenchant, cutting, biting, caustic, acid, vitriolic, bitter, harsh, brutal, savage, unsparing.

☒ complimentary.

**scatter** v disperse, dispel, dissipate, disband, disunite, separate, divide, break up, disintegrate, diffuse, broadcast, disseminate, spread, sprinkle, sow, strew, fling, shower.

☒ gather, collect.

**scatterbrained** adj forgetful, absent-minded, empty-headed, feather-brained, scatty (infml), careless, inattentive, thoughtless, unreliable, irresponsible, frivolous.

☒ sensible, sober, efficient, careful.

**scattering** n sprinkling, few, handful, smattering.

☒ mass, abundance.

**scavenge** v forage, rummage, rake, search, scrounge.

**scenario** n outline, synopsis, summary, résumé, storyline, plot, scheme, plan, programme, projection, sequence, situation, scene.

**scene** n 1 PLACE, area, spot, locale, site, situation, position, whereabouts,

location, locality, environment, milieu, setting, contact, background, backdrop, set, stage. 2 LANDSCAPE, panorama, view, vista, prospect, sight, spectacle, picture, tableau, pageant. 3 EPISODE, incident, part, division, act, clip. 4 *don't make a scene*: fuss, commotion, to-do (infml), performance, drama, exhibition, display, show.

**scenery** n landscape, terrain, panorama, view, vista, outlook, scene, background, setting, surroundings, backdrop, set.

**scenic** adj panoramic, picturesque, attractive, pretty, beautiful, grand, striking, impressive, spectacular, breathtaking, awe-inspiring.

☒ dull, dreary.

**scent** n 1 PERFUME, fragrance, aroma, bouquet, smell, odour. 2 *follow the scent*: track, trail.

☒ 1 stink.

v smell, sniff (out), nose (out), sense, perceive, detect, discern, recognize.

**scented** adj perfumed, fragrant, sweet-smelling, aromatic.

☒ malodorous, stinking.

**sceptic** n doubter, unbeliever, disbeliever, agnostic, atheist, rationalist, questioner, scoffer, cynic.

☒ believer.

**sceptical** adj doubting, doubtful, unconvinced, unbelieving, disbelieving, questioning, distrustful, mistrustful, hesitating, dubious, suspicious, scoffing, cynical, pessimistic.

☒ convinced, confident, trusting.

**scepticism** n doubt, unbelief, disbelief, agnosticism, atheism, rationalism, distrust, suspicion, cynicism, pessimism.

☒ belief, faith.

**schedule** n timetable, programme, agenda, diary, calendar, itinerary, plan, scheme, list, inventory, catalogue, table, form.

v timetable, time, table, programme,

plan, organize, arrange, appoint,
assign, book, list.

**schematic** *adj* diagrammatic,
representational, symbolic,
illustrative, graphic.

**scheme** *n* **1** PROGRAMME, schedule,
plan, project, idea, proposal,
proposition, suggestion, draft,
outline, blueprint, schema, diagram,
chart, layout, pattern, design, shape,
configuration, arrangement.
**2** INTRIGUE, plot, conspiracy,
device, stratagem, ruse, ploy, shift,
manoeuvre, tactic(s), strategy,
procedure, system, method.
  *v* plot, conspire, connive, collude,
intrigue, machinate, manoeuvre,
manipulate, pull strings, mastermind,
plan, project, contrive, devise, frame,
work out.

**schism** *n* **1** DIVISION, split, rift,
rupture, break, breach, disunion,
separation, severance, estrangement,
discord. **2** SPLINTER GROUP,
faction, sect.

**scholar** *n* pupil, student, academic,
intellectual, egghead (*infml*),
authority, expert.
  ⊟ dunce, ignoramus.

**scholarly** *adj* learned, erudite,
lettered, academic, scholastic, school,
intellectual, highbrow, bookish,
studious, knowledgeable, well-read,
analytical, scientific.
  ⊟ uneducated, illiterate.

**scholarship** *n* **1** ERUDITION,
learnedness, learning, knowledge,
wisdom, education, schooling. **2** *a
scholarship to a public school*: grant,
award, bursary, endowment,
fellowship, exhibition.

**school** *n* college, academy, institute,
institution, seminary, faculty,
department, discipline, class, group,
pupils, students.
  *v* educate, teach, instruct, tutor,
coach, train, discipline, drill, verse,
prime, prepare, indoctrinate.

**schooling** *n* education, book-

learning, teaching, instruction,
tuition, coaching, training, drill,
preparation, grounding, guidance,
indoctrination.

**science** *n* technology, discipline,
specialization, knowledge, skill,
proficiency, technique, art.

*Sciences include*: acoustics,
aerodynamics, aeronautics,
agricultural science, anatomy,
anthropology, archaeology,
astronomy, astrophysics, behavioural
science, biochemistry, biology,
biophysics, botany, chemistry,
chemurgy, climatology, computer
science, cybernetics, diagnostics,
dietetics, domestic science, dynamics,
earth science, ecology, economics,
electrodynamics, electronics,
engineering, entomology,
environmental science, food science,
genetics, geochemistry, geographical
science, geology, geophysics,
graphology, hydraulics, information
technology, inorganic chemistry, life
science, linguistics, macrobiotics,
materials science, mathematics,
mechanical engineering, mechanics,
medical science, metallurgy,
meteorology, microbiology,
mineralogy, morphology, natural
science, nuclear physics, organic
chemistry, ornithology, pathology,
pharmacology, physics, physiology,
political science, psychology,
radiochemistry, robotics, sociology,
space technology,
telecommunications,
thermodynamics, toxicology,
ultrasonics, veterinary science,
zoology.

**scientific** *adj* methodical,
systematic, controlled, regulated,
analytical, mathematical, exact,
precise, accurate, scholarly,
thorough.

**scintillating** *adj* sparkling,

glittering, flashing, bright, shining, brilliant, dazzling, exciting, stimulating, lively, animated, vivacious, ebullient, witty.

**F3** dull.

**scoff**[1] v mock, ridicule, poke fun, taunt, tease, rib (sl), jeer, sneer, pooh-pooh, scorn, despise, revile, deride, belittle, disparage, knock (infml).

**F3** praise, compliment, flatter.

**scoff**[2] v eat, consume, devour, put away (infml), gobble, guzzle, wolf (infml), bolt, gulp.

**F3** fast, abstain.

**scold** v chide, tell off (infml), tick off (infml), reprimand, reprove, rebuke, take to task, admonish, upbraid, reproach, blame, censure, lecture, nag.

**F3** praise, commend.

**scolding** n castigation, telling-off, ticking-off (infml), dressing-down, reprimand, reproof, rebuke, lecture, talking-to, earful (infml).

**F3** praise, commendation.

**scoop** n 1 LADLE, spoon, dipper, bailer, bucket, shovel. 2 EXCLUSIVE, coup, inside story, revelation, exposé, sensation, latest (infml).

v gouge, scrape, hollow, empty, excavate, dig, shovel, ladle, spoon, dip, bail.

**scope** n 1 RANGE, compass, field, area, sphere, ambit, terms of reference, confines, reach, extent, span, breadth, coverage. 2 scope for improvement: room, space, capacity, elbow-room, latitude, leeway, freedom, liberty, opportunity.

**scorch** v burn, singe, char, blacken, scald, roast, sear, parch, shrivel, wither.

**scorching** adj burning, boiling, baking, roasting, sizzling, blistering, sweltering, torrid, tropical, searing, red-hot.

**score** n 1 RESULT, total, sum, tally, points, marks. 2 SCRATCH, line,

groove, mark, nick, notch.

v 1 RECORD, register, chalk up, notch up, count, total, make, earn, gain, achieve, attain, win, have the advantage, have the edge, be one up. 2 SCRATCH, scrape, graze, mark, groove, gouge, cut, incise, engrave, indent, nick, slash.

**scorn** n contempt, scornfulness, disdain, sneering, derision, mockery, ridicule, sarcasm, disparagement, disgust.

**F3** admiration, respect.

v despise, look down on, disdain, sneer at, scoff at, deride, mock, laugh at, slight, spurn, refuse, reject, dismiss.

**F3** admire, respect.

**scornful** adj contemptuous, disdainful, supercilious, haughty, arrogant, sneering, scoffing, derisive, mocking, jeering, sarcastic, scathing, disparaging, insulting, slighting, dismissive.

**F3** admiring, respectful.

**scour**[1] v scrape, abrade, rub, polish, burnish, scrub, clean, wash, cleanse, purge, flush.

**scour**[2] v search, hunt, comb, drag, ransack, rummage, forage, rake.

**scourge** n 1 AFFLICTION, misfortune, torment, terror, bane, evil, curse, plague, penalty, punishment. 2 WHIP, lash.

**F3** 1 blessing, godsend, boon.

v 1 AFFLICT, torment, curse, plague, devastate, punish, chastise, discipline. 2 WHIP, flog, beat, lash, cane, flail, thrash.

**scout** v spy out, reconnoitre, explore, investigate, check out, survey, case (sl), spy, snoop, search, seek, hunt, probe, look, watch, observe.

n spy, reconnoitre, vanguard, outrider, escort, lookout, recruiter, spotter.

**scowl** v, n frown, glower, glare, grimace, pout.

**◻** smile, grin, beam.

**scraggy** adj scrawny, skinny, thin, lean, lanky, bony, angular, gaunt, undernourished, emaciated, wasted.
**◻** plump, sleek.

**scramble** v **1** CLIMB, scale, clamber, crawl, shuffle, scrabble, grope. **2** RUSH, hurry, hasten, run, push, jostle, struggle, strive, vie, contend.
n rush, hurry, race, dash, hustle, bustle, commotion, confusion, muddle, struggle, free-for-all, mêlée.

**scrap¹** n bit, piece, fragment, part, fraction, crumb, morsel, bite, mouthful, sliver, shred, snippet, atom, iota, grain, particle, mite, trace, vestige, remnant, leftover, waste, junk.
v discard, throw away, jettison, shed, abandon, drop, dump, ditch (sl), cancel, axe, demolish, break up, write off.
**◻** recover, restore.

**scrap²** n fight, scuffle, brawl, dust-up (infml), quarrel, row, argument, squabble, wrangle, dispute, disagreement.
**◻** peace, agreement.
v fight, brawl, quarrel, argue, fall out, squabble, bicker, wrangle, disagree.
**◻** agree.

**scrape** v grate, grind, rasp, file, abrade, scour, rub, clean, remove, erase, scrabble, claw, scratch, graze, skin, bark, scuff.

**scrappy** adj bitty, disjointed, piecemeal, fragmentary, incomplete, sketchy, superficial, slapdash, slipshod.
**◻** complete, finished.

**scratch** v claw, gouge, score, mark, cut, incise, etch, engrave, scrape, rub, scuff, graze, gash, lacerate.
n mark, line, scrape, scuff, abrasion, graze, gash, laceration.

**scrawny** adj scraggy, skinny, thin, lean, lanky, angular, bony, underfed, undernourished, emaciated.

**◻** fat, plump.

**scream** v, n shriek, screech, cry, shout, yell, bawl, roar, howl, wail, squeal, yelp.

**screen** v **1** screen a film: show, present, broadcast. **2** SHIELD, protect, safeguard, defend, guard, cover, mask, veil, cloak, shroud, hide, conceal, shelter, shade. **3** SORT, grade, sift, sieve, filter, process, evaluate, gauge, examine, scan, vet.
**◻** **2** uncover, expose.
n partition, divider, shield, guard, cover, mask, veil, cloak, shroud, concealment, shelter, shade, awning, canopy, net, mesh.

**screw** v fasten, adjust, tighten, contract, compress, squeeze, extract, extort, force, constrain, pressurize, turn, wind, twist, wring, distort, wrinkle.

**scribble** v write, pen, jot, dash off, scrawl, doodle.

**scribe** n writer, copyist, amanuensis, secretary, clerk.

**script** n **1** a film script: text, lines, words, dialogue, screenplay, libretto, book. **2** WRITING, handwriting, hand, longhand, calligraphy, letters, manuscript, copy.

**scrounge** v cadge, beg, sponge.

**scrounger** n cadger, sponger, parasite.

**scrub** v **1** scrub the floor: rub, brush, clean, wash, cleanse, scour. **2** (infml) ABOLISH, cancel, delete, abandon, give up, drop, discontinue.

**scruffy** adj untidy, messy, unkempt, dishevelled, bedraggled, run-down, tattered, shabby, disreputable, worn-out, ragged, seedy, squalid, slovenly.
**◻** tidy, well-dressed.

**scruple** n reluctance, hesitation, doubt, qualm, misgiving, uneasiness, difficulty, perplexity.
v hesitate, think twice, hold back, shrink.

**scruples** n standards, principles,

morals, ethics.

**scrupulous** adj **1** PAINSTAKING, meticulous, conscientious, careful, rigorous, strict, exact, precise, minute, nice. **2** PRINCIPLED, moral, ethical, honourable, upright.
Ea **1** superficial, careless, reckless.
**2** unscrupulous, unprincipled.

**scrutinize** v examine, inspect, study, scan, analyse, sift, investigate, probe, search, explore.

**scrutiny** n examination, inspection, study, analysis, investigation, inquiry, search, exploration.

**scuff** v scrape, scratch, graze, abrade, rub, brush, drag.

**scuffle** v fight, scrap, tussle, brawl, grapple, struggle, contend, clash.
n fight, scrap, tussle, brawl, fray, set-to, rumpus, commotion, disturbance, affray.

**sculpt** v sculpture, carve, chisel, hew, cut, model, mould, cast, form, shape, fashion.

**scum** n froth, foam, film, impurities, dross, dregs, rubbish, trash.

**scurrilous** adj rude, vulgar, coarse, foul, obscene, indecent, salacious, offensive, abusive, insulting, disparaging, defamatory, slanderous, libellous, scandalous.
Ea polite, courteous, complimentary.

**scurry** v dash, rush, hurry, hasten, bustle, scramble, scuttle, scamper, scoot, dart, run, sprint, trot, race, fly, skim, scud.

**sea** n **1** OCEAN, main, deep, briny (infml). **2** a sea of faces: multitude, abundance, profusion, mass.
adj marine, maritime, ocean, oceanic, salt, saltwater, aquatic, seafaring.
Ea land, air.
**at sea** adrift, lost, confused, bewildered, baffled, puzzled, perplexed, mystified.

**seafaring** adj sea-going, ocean-going, sailing, nautical, naval, marine, maritime.

**seal** v **1** seal a jar: close, shut, stop, plug, cork, stopper, waterproof, fasten, secure. **2** SETTLE, conclude, finalize, stamp.
Ea **1** unseal.
n stamp, signet, insignia, imprimatur, authentication, assurance, attestation, confirmation, ratification.

**seal off** block up, close off, shut off, fence off, cut off, segregate, isolate, quarantine.
Ea open up.

**seam** n **1** JOIN, joint, weld, closure, line. **2** coal seam: layer, stratum, vein, lode.

**seamy** adj disreputable, sleazy, sordid, squalid, unsavoury, rough, dark, low, nasty, unpleasant.
Ea respectable, wholesome, pleasant.

**sear** v burn, scorch, brown, fry, sizzle, seal, cauterize, brand, parch, shrivel, wither.

**search** v seek, look, hunt, rummage, rifle, ransack, scour, comb, sift, probe, explore, frisk (sl), examine, scrutinize, inspect, check, investigate, inquire, pry.
n hunt, quest, pursuit, rummage, probe, exploration, examination, scrutiny, inspection, investigation, inquiry, research, survey.

**searching** adj penetrating, piercing, keen, sharp, close, intent, probing, thorough, minute.
Ea vague, superficial.

**seaside** n coast, shore, beach, sands.

**season** n period, spell, phase, term, time, span, interval.
v **1** season food: flavour, spice, salt. **2** AGE, mature, ripen, harden, toughen, train, prepare, condition, treat, temper.

**seasonable** adj timely, well-timed, welcome, opportune, convenient, suitable, appropriate, fitting.
Ea unseasonable, inopportune.

**seasoned** adj mature, experienced,

practised, well-versed, veteran, old,
hardened, toughened, conditioned,
acclimatized, weathered.
**F3** inexperienced, novice.

**seasoning** n flavouring, spice,
condiment, salt, pepper, relish, sauce,
dressing.

**seat** n **1** CHAIR, bench, pew, stool,
throne. **2** *country seat*: residence,
abode, house, mansion. **3** PLACE,
site, situation, location,
headquarters, centre, heart, hub,
axis, source, cause, bottom, base,
foundation, footing, ground.
v sit, place, set, locate, install, fit, fix,
settle, accommodate, hold, contain,
take.

**seating** n seats, chairs, places,
room, accommodation.

**secluded** adj private, cloistered,
sequestered, shut away, cut off,
isolated, lonely, solitary, remote, out-
of-the-way, sheltered, hidden,
concealed.
**F3** public, accessible.

**seclusion** n privacy, retirement,
retreat, isolation, solitude,
remoteness, shelter, hiding,
concealment.

**second**[1] adj duplicate, twin, double,
repeated, additional, further, extra,
supplementary, alternative, other,
alternate, next, following,
subsequent, succeeding, secondary,
subordinate, lower, inferior, lesser,
supporting.
n helper, assistant, backer, supporter.
v approve, agree with, endorse, back,
support, help, assist, aid, further,
advance, forward, promote,
encourage.

**second**[2] n minute, tick (*infml*),
moment, instant, flash, jiffy (*infml*).

**secondary** adj subsidiary,
subordinate, lower, inferior, lesser,
minor, unimportant, ancillary,
auxiliary, supporting, relief, back-up,
reserve, spare, extra, second,
alternative, indirect, derived,

resulting.
**F3** primary, main, major.

**second-hand** adj used, old, worn,
hand-me-down, borrowed,
derivative, secondary, indirect,
vicarious.
**F3** new.

**second-rate** adj inferior,
substandard, second-class, second-
best, poor, low-grade, shoddy, cheap,
tawdry, mediocre, undistinguished,
uninspired, uninspiring.
**F3** first-rate.

**secrecy** n privacy, seclusion,
confidentiality, confidence,
covertness, concealment, disguise,
camouflage, furtiveness,
surreptitiousness, stealthiness,
stealth, mystery.
**F3** openness.

**secret** adj **1** PRIVATE, discreet,
covert, hidden, concealed, unseen,
shrouded, covered, disguised,
camouflaged, undercover, furtive,
surreptitious, stealthy, sly,
underhand, under-the-counter, hole-
and-corner, cloak-and-dagger,
clandestine, underground, backstairs,
back-door. **2** CLASSIFIED,
confidential, hush-hush (*infml*),
unpublished, undisclosed,
unrevealed, unknown. **3** CRYPTIC,
mysterious, occult, arcane, recondite,
deep. **4** SECRETIVE, close, retired,
secluded, out-of-the-way.
**F3 1** public, open. **2** well-known.
n confidence, mystery, enigma, code,
key, formula, recipe.

**secretary** n personal assistant, PA,
typist, stenographer, clerk.

**secrete**[1] v hide, conceal, stash away
(*infml*), bury, cover, screen, shroud,
veil, disguise, take, appropriate.
**F3** uncover, reveal, disclose.

**secrete**[2] v exude, discharge, release,
give off, emit, emanate, produce.

**secretion** n exudation, discharge,
release, emission.

**secretive** adj tight-lipped, close,

cagey (*infml*), uncommunicative, unforthcoming, reticent, reserved, withdrawn, quiet, deep, cryptic, enigmatic.

🔁 open, communicative, forthcoming.

**sect** *n* denomination, cult, division, subdivision, group, splinter group, faction, camp, wing, party, school.

**sectarian** *adj* factional, partisan, cliquish, exclusive, narrow, limited, parochial, insular, narrow-minded, bigoted, fanatical, doctrinaire, dogmatic, rigid.

🔁 non-sectarian, cosmopolitan, broad-minded.

**section** *n* division, subdivision, chapter, paragraph, passage, instalment, part, component, fraction, fragment, bit, piece, slice, portion, segment, sector, zone, district, area, region, department, branch, wing.

🔁 whole.

**sector** *n* zone, district, quarter, area, region, section, division, subdivision, part.

🔁 whole.

**secular** *adj* lay, temporal, worldly, earthly, civil, state, non-religious, profane.

🔁 religious.

**secure** *adj* 1 SAFE, unharmed, undamaged, protected, sheltered, shielded, immune, impregnable, fortified, fast, tight, fastened, locked, fixed, immovable, stable, steady, solid, firm, well-founded, reliable, dependable, steadfast, certain, sure, conclusive, definite. 2 CONFIDENT, assured, reassured.

🔁 1 insecure, vulnerable. 2 uneasy, ill at ease.

*v* 1 OBTAIN, acquire, gain, get. 2 FASTEN, attach, fix, make fast, tie, moor, lash, chain, lock (up), padlock, bolt, batten down, nail, rivet.

🔁 1 lose. 2 unfasten.

**security** *n* 1 SAFETY, immunity,

asylum, sanctuary, refuge, cover, protection, defence, surveillance, safe-keeping, preservation, care, custody. 2 *security for a loan*: collateral, surety, pledge, guarantee, warranty, assurance, insurance, precautions, safeguards.

3 CONFIDENCE, conviction, certainty, positiveness.

🔁 1 insecurity.

**sedate** *adj* staid, dignified, solemn, grave, serious, sober, decorous, proper, seemly, demure, composed, unruffled, serene, tranquil, calm, quiet, cool, collected, imperturbable, unflappable (*infml*), deliberate, slow-moving.

🔁 undignified, lively, agitated.

**sedative** *adj* calming, soothing, anodyne, lenitive, tranquillizing, relaxing, soporific, depressant.

🔁 rousing.

*n* tranquillizer, sleeping-pill, narcotic, barbiturate.

**sedentary** *adj* sitting, seated, desk-bound, inactive, still, stationary, immobile, unmoving.

🔁 active.

**sediment** *n* deposit, residue, grounds, lees, dregs.

**sedition** *n* agitation, rabble-rousing, subversion, disloyalty, treachery, treason, insubordination, mutiny, rebellion, revolt.

🔁 calm, loyalty.

**seduce** *v* entice, lure, allure, attract, tempt, charm, beguile, ensnare, lead astray, mislead, deceive, corrupt, dishonour, ruin.

🔁 repel.

**seduction** *n* enticement, lure, attraction, temptation, come-on (*infml*), corruption, ruin.

**seductive** *adj* enticing, alluring, attractive, tempting, tantalizing, inviting, come-hither (*infml*), flirtatious, sexy, provocative, beguiling, captivating, bewitching, irresistible.

**E3** unattractive, repulsive.

**see** v **1** PERCEIVE, glimpse, discern, spot, make out, distinguish, identify, sight, notice, observe, watch, view, look at, mark, note. **2** IMAGINE, picture, visualize, envisage, foresee, anticipate. **3** *I see your point*: understand, comprehend, grasp, fathom, follow, realize, recognize, appreciate, regard, consider, deem. **4** DISCOVER, find out, learn, ascertain, determine, decide. **5** LEAD, usher, accompany, escort, court, go out with, date. **6** VISIT, consult, interview, meet.

**see to** attend to, deal with, take care of, look after, arrange, organize, manage, do, fix, repair, sort out.

**seed** n pip, stone, kernel, nucleus, grain, germ, sperm, ovum, egg, ovule, spawn, embryo, source, start, beginning.

**seedy** adj **1** SHABBY, scruffy, tatty, mangy, sleazy, squalid, grotty (*infml*), crummy (*sl*), run-down, dilapidated, decaying. **2** UNWELL, ill, sick, poorly, ailing, off-colour.

**E3 2** well.

**seek** v look for, search for, hunt, pursue, follow, inquire, ask, invite, request, solicit, petition, entreat, want, desire, aim, aspire, try, attempt, endeavour, strive.

**seem** v appear, look, feel, sound, pretend to be.

**seeming** adj apparent, ostensible, outward, superficial, surface, quasi-, pseudo, specious.

**E3** real.

**seep** v ooze, leak, exude, well, trickle, dribble, percolate, permeate, soak.

**seethe** v **1** BOIL, simmer, bubble, effervesce, fizz, foam, froth, ferment, rise, swell, surge, teem, swarm. **2** RAGE, fume, smoulder, storm.

**see-through** adj transparent, translucent, sheer, filmy, gauzy, gossamer(y), flimsy.

**E3** opaque.

**segment** n section, division, compartment, part, bit, piece, slice, portion, wedge.

**E3** whole.

**segregate** v separate, keep apart, cut off, isolate, quarantine, set apart, exclude.

**E3** unite, join.

**segregation** n separation, isolation, quarantine, apartheid, discrimination.

**E3** unification.

**seize** v grab, snatch, grasp, clutch, grip, hold, take, confiscate, impound, appropriate, commandeer, hijack, annex, abduct, catch, capture, arrest, apprehend, nab (*infml*), collar (*infml*).

**E3** let go, release, hand back.

**seizure** n **1** FIT, attack, convulsion, paroxysm, spasm. **2** TAKING, confiscation, appropriation, hijack, annexation, abduction, capture, arrest, apprehension.

**E3** release, liberation.

**seldom** adv rarely, infrequently, occasionally, hardly ever.

**E3** often, usually.

**select** v choose, pick, single out, decide on, appoint, elect, prefer, opt for.

*adj* selected, choice, top, prime, first-class, first-rate, hand-picked, élite, exclusive, limited, privileged, special, excellent, superior, posh (*infml*).

**E3** second-rate, ordinary, general.

**selection** n choice, pick, option, preference, assortment, variety, range, line-up, miscellany, medley, potpourri, collection, anthology.

**selective** adj particular, choosy (*infml*), careful, discerning, discriminating.

**E3** indiscriminate.

**self** n ego, personality, identity, person.

**self-centred** adj selfish, self-seeking, self-serving, self-interested,

egotistic(al), narcissistic, self-absorbed, egocentric.
**F3** altruistic.

**self-confident** adj confident, self-reliant, self-assured, assured, self-possessed, cool, fearless.
**F3** unsure, self-conscious.

**self-conscious** adj uncomfortable, ill at ease, awkward, embarrassed, shamefaced, sheepish, shy, bashful, coy, retiring, shrinking, self-effacing, nervous, insecure.
**F3** natural, unaffected, confident.

**self-control** n calmness, composure, cool, patience, self-restraint, restraint, self-denial, temperance, self-discipline, self-mastery, will-power.

**self-denial** n moderation, temperance, abstemiousness, asceticism, self-sacrifice, unselfishness, selflessness.
**F3** self-indulgence.

**self-evident** adj obvious, manifest, clear, undeniable, axiomatic, unquestionable, incontrovertible, inescapable.

**self-government** n autonomy, independence, home rule, democracy.
**F3** subjection.

**self-indulgent** adj hedonistic, dissolute, dissipated, profligate, extravagant, intemperate, immoderate.
**F3** abstemious.

**selfish** adj self-interested, self-seeking, mean, miserly, mercenary, greedy, covetous, self-centred, egocentric, egotistic(al).
**F3** unselfish, selfless, generous, considerate.

**selfless** adj unselfish, altruistic, self-denying, self-sacrificing, generous, philanthropic.
**F3** selfish, self-centred.

**self-respect** n pride, dignity, self-esteem, self-assurance, self-confidence.

**self-righteous** adj smug,

complacent, superior, goody-goody (infml), pious, sanctimonious, holier-than-thou, pietistic, hypocritical, pharisaical.

**self-sacrifice** n self-denial, self-renunciation, selflessness, altruism, unselfishness, generosity.
**F3** selfishness.

**self-satisfied** adj smug, complacent, self-congratulatory, self-righteous.
**F3** humble.

**self-styled** adj self-appointed, professed, so-called, would-be.

**self-supporting** adj self-sufficient, self-financing, independent, self-reliant.
**F3** dependent.

**sell** v barter, exchange, trade, auction, vend, retail, stock, handle, deal in, trade in, traffic in, merchandise, hawk, peddle, push, advertise, promote, market.
**F3** buy.

**seller** n vendor, merchant, trader, dealer, supplier, stockist, retailer, shopkeeper, salesman, saleswoman, agent, representative, rep (infml), traveller.
**F3** buyer, purchaser.

**semblance** n appearance, air, show, pretence, guise, mask, front, façade, veneer, apparition, image, resemblance, likeness, similarity.

**send** v 1 POST, mail, dispatch, consign, remit, forward, convey, deliver. 2 TRANSMIT, broadcast, communicate. 3 PROPEL, drive, move, throw, fling, hurl, launch, fire, shoot, discharge, emit, direct.

**send for** summon, call for, request, order, command.
**F3** dismiss.

**send up** satirize, mock, ridicule, parody, take off, mimic, imitate.

**send-off** n farewell, leave-taking, departure, start, goodbye.
**F3** arrival.

**senile** adj old, aged, doddering,

decrepit, failing, confused.

**senior** adj older, elder, higher, superior, high-ranking, major, chief.
**F3** junior.

**seniority** n priority, precedence, rank, standing, status, age, superiority, importance.

**sensation** n 1 FEELING, sense, impression, perception, awareness, consciousness, emotion. 2 *the report caused a sensation*: commotion, stir, agitation, excitement, thrill, furore, outrage, scandal.

**sensational** adj 1 EXCITING, thrilling, electrifying, breathtaking, startling, amazing, astounding, staggering, dramatic, spectacular, impressive, exceptional, excellent, wonderful, marvellous, smashing (*infml*). 2 SCANDALOUS, shocking, horrifying, revealing, melodramatic, lurid.
**F3** ordinary, run-of-the-mill.

**sense** n 1 FEELING, sensation, impression, perception, awareness, consciousness, appreciation, faculty. 2 REASON, logic, mind, brain(s), wit(s), wisdom, intelligence, cleverness, understanding, discernment, judgement, intuition. 3 MEANING, significance, definition, interpretation, implication, point, purpose, substance.
**F3** 2 foolishness. 3 nonsense.
v feel, suspect, intuit, perceive, detect, notice, observe, realize, appreciate, understand, comprehend, grasp.

**senseless** adj 1 FOOLISH, stupid, unwise, silly, idiotic, mad, crazy, daft (*infml*), ridiculous, ludicrous, absurd, meaningless, nonsensical, fatuous, irrational, illogical, unreasonable, pointless, purposeless, futile.
2 UNCONSCIOUS, out, stunned, anaesthetized, deadened, numb, unfeeling.
**F3** 1 sensible, meaningful. 2 conscious.

**sensible** adj wise, prudent,

judicious, well-advised, shrewd, far-sighted, intelligent, level-headed, down-to-earth, commonsense, sober, sane, rational, logical, reasonable, realistic, practical, functional, sound.
**F3** senseless, foolish, unwise.

**sensitive** adj 1 SUSCEPTIBLE, vulnerable, impressionable, tender, emotional, thin-skinned, temperamental, touchy, irritable, sensitized, responsive, aware, perceptive, discerning, appreciative.
2 DELICATE, fine, exact, precise.
**F3** 1 insensitive, thick-skinned.
2 imprecise, approximate.

**sensual** adj self-indulgent, voluptuous, worldly, physical, animal, carnal, fleshly, bodily, sexual, erotic, sexy, lustful, randy (*infml*), lecherous, lewd, licentious.
**F3** ascetic.

**sensuous** adj pleasurable, gratifying, voluptuous, rich, lush, luxurious, sumptuous.
**F3** ascetic, plain, simple.

**sentence** n judgement, decision, verdict, condemnation, pronouncement, ruling, decree, order.
v judge, pass judgement on, condemn, doom, punish, penalize.

**sentiment** n 1 THOUGHT, idea, feeling, opinion, view, judgement, belief, persuasion, attitude.
2 EMOTION, sensibility, tenderness, soft-heartedness, romanticism, sentimentality, mawkishness.

**sentimental** adj tender, soft-hearted, emotional, gushing, touching, pathetic, tear-jerking, weepy (*infml*), maudlin, mawkish, nostalgic, romantic, lovey-dovey (*infml*), slushy, mushy, sloppy, schmaltzy, soppy, corny (*infml*).
**F3** unsentimental, realistic, cynical.

**sentry** n sentinel, guard, picket, watchman, watch, look-out.

**separable** adj divisible, detachable, removable, distinguishable, distinct.

inseparable.

**separate** *v* divide, sever, part, split (up), divorce, part company, diverge, disconnect, uncouple, disunite, disaffiliate, disentangle, segregate, isolate, cut off, abstract, remove, detach, withdraw, secede.
join, unite, combine.
*adj* single, individual, particular, independent, alone, solitary, segregated, isolated, apart, divorced, divided, disunited, disconnected, disjointed, detached, unattached, unconnected, unrelated, different, disparate, distinct, discrete, several, sundry.
together, attached.

**separation** *n* division, severance, parting, leave-taking, farewell, split-up, break-up, divorce, split, rift, gap, divergence, disconnection, disengagement, dissociation, estrangement, segregation, isolation, detachment.
unification.

**septic** *adj* infected, poisoned, festering, putrefying, putrid.

**sequel** *n* follow-up, continuation, development, result, consequence, outcome, issue, upshot, pay-off, end, conclusion.

**sequence** *n* succession, series, run, progression, chain, string, train, line, procession, order, arrangement, course, track, cycle, set.

**serene** *adj* calm, tranquil, cool, composed, placid, untroubled, undisturbed, still, quiet, peaceful.
troubled, disturbed.

**series** *n* set, cycle, succession, sequence, run, progression, chain, string, line, train, order, arrangement, course.

**serious** *adj* **1** IMPORTANT, significant, weighty, momentous, crucial, critical, urgent, pressing, acute, grave, worrying, difficult, dangerous, grim, severe, deep, far-reaching. **2** UNSMILING, long-faced,

humourless, solemn, sober, stern, thoughtful, pensive, earnest, sincere.
**1** trivial, slight. **2** smiling, facetious, frivolous.

**sermon** *n* address, discourse, lecture, harangue, homily, talking-to (*infml*).

**serrated** *adj* toothed, notched, indented, jagged.
smooth.

**servant** *n* domestic, maid, valet, steward, attendant, retainer, hireling, lackey, menial, skivvy (*infml*), slave, help, helper, assistant, ancillary.
master, mistress.

**serve** *v* **1** WAIT ON, attend, minister to, work for, help, aid, assist, benefit, further. **2** *serve a purpose*: fulfil, complete, answer, satisfy, discharge, perform, act, function. **3** DISTRIBUTE, dole out, present, deliver, provide, supply.

**service** *n* **1** EMPLOYMENT, work, labour, business, duty, function, performance. **2** USE, usefulness, utility, advantage, benefit, help, assistance. **3** SERVICING, maintenance, overhaul, check. **4** *church service*: worship, observance, ceremony, rite.
*v* maintain, overhaul, check, repair, recondition, tune.

**serviceable** *adj* usable, useful, helpful, profitable, advantageous, beneficial, utilitarian, simple, plain, unadorned, strong, tough, durable, hard-wearing, dependable, efficient, functional, practical, convenient.
unserviceable, unusable.

**servile** *adj* obsequious, sycophantic, toadying, cringing, fawning, grovelling, bootlicking, slavish, subservient, subject, submissive, humble, abject, low, mean, base, menial.
assertive, aggressive.

**session** *n* sitting, hearing, meeting, assembly, conference, discussion, period, time, term, semester, year.

**set** v **1** PUT, place, locate, situate, position, arrange, prepare, lodge, fix, stick, park, deposit. **2** SCHEDULE, appoint, designate, specify, name, prescribe, ordain, assign, allocate, impose, fix, establish, determine, decide, conclude, settle, resolve. **3** ADJUST, regulate, synchronize, co-ordinate. **4** *the sun sets*: go down, sink, dip, subside, disappear, vanish. **5** CONGEAL, thicken, gel, gel, stiffen, solidify, harden, crystallize.

**F3** **4** rise.

n batch, series, sequence, kit, outfit, compendium, assortment, collection, class, category, group, band, gang, crowd, circle, clique, faction.

adj scheduled, appointed, arranged, prepared, prearranged, fixed, established, decided, decided, agreed, settled, firm, strict, rigid, inflexible, prescribed, formal, conventional, traditional, customary, usual, routine, regular, standard, stock, stereotyped, hackneyed.

**F3** movable, free, spontaneous, undecided.

**set about** begin, start, embark on, undertake, tackle, attack.

**set aside 1** PUT ASIDE, lay aside, keep (back), save, reserve, set apart, separate, select, earmark. **2** ANNUL, abrogate, cancel, revoke, reverse, overturn, overrule, reject, discard.

**set back** delay, hold up, slow, retard, hinder, impede.

**set off 1** LEAVE, depart, set out, start (out), begin. **2** DETONATE, light, ignite, touch off, trigger off, explode. **3** DISPLAY, show off, enhance, contrast.

**set on** set upon, attack, turn on, go for, fall upon, lay into, beat up (*infml*).

**set out 1** LEAVE, depart, set off, start (out), begin. **2** LAY OUT, arrange, display, exhibit, present, describe, explain.

**set up** raise, elevate, erect, build, construct, assemble, compose, form,

create, establish, institute, found, inaugurate, initiate, begin, start, introduce, organize, arrange, prepare.

**setback** n delay, hold-up, problem, snag, hitch, hiccup, reverse, misfortune, upset, disappointment, defeat.

**F3** boost, advance, help, advantage.

**setting** n mounting, frame, surroundings, milieu, environment, background, context, perspective, period, position, location, locale, site, scene, scenery.

**settle** v **1** ARRANGE, order, adjust, reconcile, resolve, complete, conclude. **2** SINK, subside, drop, fall, descend, land, alight. **3** CHOOSE, appoint, fix, establish, determine, decide, agree, confirm. **4** COLONIZE, occupy, populate, people, inhabit, live, reside. **5** *settle a bill*: pay, clear, discharge.

**settlement** n **1** RESOLUTION, agreement, arrangement, decision, conclusion, termination, satisfaction. **2** PAYMENT, clearance, clearing, discharge. **3** COLONY, outpost, community, kibbutz, camp, encampment, hamlet, village.

**settler** n colonist, colonizer, pioneer, frontiersman, frontierswoman, planter, immigrant, incomer, newcomer, squatter.

**F3** native.

**set-up** n system, structure, organization, arrangement, business, conditions, circumstances.

**sever** v cut, cleave, split, rend, part, separate, divide, cut off, amputate, detach, disconnect, disjoin, disunite, dissociate, estrange, alienate, break off, dissolve, end, terminate.

**F3** join, unite, combine, attach.

**several** adj some, many, various, assorted, sundry, diverse, different, distinct, separate, particular, individual.

**severe** adj **1** STERN, disapproving, sober, strait-laced, strict, rigid, unbending, harsh, tough, hard, difficult, demanding, arduous, punishing, rigorous, grim, forbidding, cruel, biting, cutting, scathing, pitiless, merciless, oppressive, relentless, inexorable, acute, bitter, intense, extreme, fierce, violent, distressing, serious, grave, critical, dangerous. **2** PLAIN, simple, unadorned, unembellished, functional, restrained, austere, ascetic.

**F3** **1** kind, compassionate, sympathetic, lenient, mild. **2** decorated, ornate.

**sew** v stitch, tack, baste, hem, darn, embroider.

**sex** n **1** GENDER, sexuality. **2** SEXUAL INTERCOURSE, intercourse, sexual relations, copulation, coitus, lovemaking, fornication, reproduction, union, intimacy.

**sexual** adj sex, reproductive, procreative, genital, coital, venereal, carnal, sensual, erotic.

> *Sexual orientations include*:
> bisexual, AC/DC (sl),
> hermaphrodite, unisexual,
> heterosexual, homosexual, gay, queer
> (sl), cissy (sl), pretty boy (sl), nancy
> (sl), nancy boy (sl), pansy (sl), faggot
> (sl), rent boy, lesbian, lez (sl), dyke
> (sl), butch (sl), transsexual,
> transvestite, cross-dresser.

**sexy** adj sensual, voluptuous, nubile, beddable (infml), seductive, inviting, flirtatious, arousing, provoking, provocative, titillating, pornographic, erotic, salacious, suggestive.

**F3** sexless.

**shabby** adj **1** RAGGED, tattered, frayed, worn, worn-out, mangy, moth-eaten, scruffy, tatty, disreputable, dilapidated, run-down, seedy, dirty, dingy, poky. **2** *a shabby*

*trick*: contemptible, despicable, rotten, mean, low, cheap, shoddy, shameful, dishonourable.

**F3** **1** smart. **2** honourable, fair.

**shack** n hut, cabin, shanty, hovel, shed, lean-to.

**shade** n **1** SHADINESS, shadow, darkness, obscurity, semi-darkness, dimness, gloom, gloominess, twilight, dusk, gloaming. **2** AWNING, canopy, cover, shelter, screen, blind, curtain, shield, visor, umbrella, parasol. **3** COLOUR, hue, tint, tone, tinge. **4** TRACE, dash, hint, suggestion, suspicion, nuance, gradation, degree, amount, variety. **5** GHOST, spectre, phantom, spirit, apparition, semblance.

v shield, screen, protect, cover, shroud, veil, hide, conceal, obscure, cloud, dim, darken, shadow, overshadow.

**shadow** n **1** SHADE, darkness, obscurity, semi-darkness, dimness, gloom, twilight, dusk, gloaming, cloud, cover, protection. **2** SILHOUETTE, shape, image, representation. **3** TRACE, hint, suggestion, suspicion, vestige, remnant.

v **1** OVERSHADOW, overhang, shade, shield, screen, obscure, darken. **2** FOLLOW, tail, dog, stalk, trail, watch.

**shadowy** adj dark, gloomy, murky, obscure, dim, faint, indistinct, ill-defined, vague, hazy, nebulous, intangible, unsubstantial, ghostly, spectral, illusory, dreamlike, imaginary, unreal.

**shady** adj **1** SHADED, shadowy, dim, dark, cool, leafy. **2** (infml) DUBIOUS, questionable, suspect, suspicious, fishy (infml), dishonest, crooked, unreliable, untrustworthy, disreputable, unscrupulous, unethical, underhand.

**F3** **1** sunny, sunlit, bright. **2** honest, trustworthy, honourable.

**shaft** n   handle, shank, stem, upright, pillar, pole, rod, bar, stick, arrow, dart, beam, ray, duct, passage.

**shaggy** adj   hairy, long-haired, hirsute, bushy, woolly, unshorn, dishevelled, unkempt.
**F3** bald, shorn, close-cropped.

**shake** v   **1** WAVE, flourish, brandish, wag, waggle, agitate, rattle, joggle, jolt, jerk, twitch, convulse, heave, throb, vibrate, oscillate, fluctuate, waver, wobble, totter, sway, rock, tremble, quiver, quake, shiver, shudder. **2** *the news shook her*: upset, distress, shock, frighten, unnerve, intimidate, disturb, discompose, unsettle, agitate, stir, rouse.
**shake off**   get rid of, dislodge, lose, elude, give the slip, leave behind, outdistance, outstrip.

**shake-up** (*infml*) n   reorganization, rearrangement, reshuffle, disturbance, upheaval.

**shaky** adj   **1** TREMBLING, quivering, faltering, tentative, uncertain. **2** UNSTABLE, unsteady, insecure, precarious, wobbly, rocky, tottery, rickety, weak. **3** DUBIOUS, questionable, suspect, unreliable, unsound, unsupported.
**F3 2** firm, strong.

**shallow** adj   superficial, surface, skin-deep, slight, flimsy, trivial, frivolous, foolish, idle, empty, meaningless, unscholarly, ignorant, simple.
**F3** deep, profound.

**sham** n   pretence, fraud, counterfeit, forgery, fake, imitation, simulation, hoax, humbug.
*adj*   false, fake, counterfeit, spurious, bogus, phoney (*infml*), pretended, feigned, put-on, simulated, artificial, mock, imitation, synthetic.
**F3** genuine, authentic, real.
*v*   pretend, feign, affect, put on, simulate, imitate, fake, counterfeit.

**shame** n   disgrace, dishonour, discredit, stain, stigma, disrepute, infamy, scandal, ignominy, humiliation, degradation, shamefacedness, remorse, guilt, embarrassment, mortification.
**F3** honour, credit, distinction, pride.
*v*   embarrass, mortify, abash, confound, humiliate, ridicule, humble, put to shame, show up, disgrace, dishonour, discredit, debase, degrade, sully, taint, stain.

**shamefaced** adj   ashamed, conscience-stricken, remorseful, contrite, apologetic, sorry, sheepish, red-faced, blushing, embarrassed, mortified, abashed, humiliated, uncomfortable.
**F3** unashamed, proud.

**shameful** adj   **1** *a shameful waste of money*: disgraceful, outrageous, scandalous, indecent, abominable, atrocious, wicked, mean, low, vile, reprehensible, contemptible, unworthy, ignoble. **2** EMBARRASSING, mortifying, humiliating, ignominious.
**F3 1** honourable, creditable, worthy.

**shameless** adj   **1** UNASHAMED, unabashed, unrepentant, impenitent, barefaced, flagrant, blatant, brazen, brash, audacious, insolent, defiant, hardened, incorrigible. **2** IMMODEST, indecent, improper, unprincipled, wanton, dissolute, corrupt, depraved.
**F3 1** ashamed, shamefaced, contrite. **2** modest.

**shape** n   **1** FORM, outline, silhouette, profile, model, mould, pattern, cut, lines, contours, figure, physique, build, frame, format, configuration. **2** APPEARANCE, guise, likeness, semblance. **3** *in good shape*: condition, state, form, health, trim, fettle.

*Geometrical shapes include*: polygon, circle, semicircle, quadrant, oval, ellipse, crescent, triangle, equilateral triangle, isosceles triangle, scalene triangle, quadrilateral, square, rectangle, oblong, rhombus, diamond, kite, trapezium, parallelogram, pentagon, hexagon, heptagon, octagon, nonagon, decagon; polyhedron, cube, cuboid, prism, pyramid, tetrahedron, pentahedron, octahedron, cylinder, cone, sphere, hemisphere.

*v* form, fashion, model, mould, cast, forge, sculpt, carve, whittle, make, produce, construct, create, devise, frame, plan, prepare, adapt, adjust, regulate, accommodate, modify, remodel.

**shapeless** *adj* formless, amorphous, unformed, nebulous, unstructured, irregular, misshapen, deformed, dumpy.

**share** *v* divide, split, go halves, partake, participate, share out, distribute, dole out, give out, deal out, apportion, allot, allocate, assign. *n* portion, ration, quota, allowance, allocation, allotment, lot, part, division, proportion, percentage, cut (*infml*), dividend, due, contribution, whack (*infml*).

**sharp** *adj* **1** *a sharp needle*: pointed, keen, edged, knife-edged, razor-sharp, cutting, serrated, jagged, barbed, spiky. **2** CLEAR, clear-cut, well-defined, distinct, marked, crisp. **3** QUICK-WITTED, alert, shrewd, astute, perceptive, observant, discerning, penetrating, clever, crafty, cunning, artful, sly. **4** SUDDEN, abrupt, violent, fierce, intense, extreme, severe, acute, piercing, stabbing. **5** PUNGENT, piquant, sour, tart, vinegary, bitter, acerbic, acid. **6** TRENCHANT, incisive, cutting, biting, caustic, sarcastic, sardonic, scathing, vitriolic, acrimonious.
**F3 1** blunt. **2** blurred. **3** slow, stupid. **4** gentle. **5** bland. **6** mild.
*adv* punctually, promptly, on the dot, exactly, precisely, abruptly, suddenly, unexpectedly.
**F3** approximately, roughly.

**sharpen** *v* edge, whet, hone, grind, file.
**F3** blunt.

**shatter** *v* break, smash, splinter, shiver, crack, split, burst, explode, blast, crush, demolish, destroy, devastate, wreck, ruin, overturn, upset.

**sheath** *n* **1** SCABBARD, case, sleeve, envelope, shell, casing, covering. **2** CONDOM, rubber (*sl*), French letter (*sl*).

**shed**[1] *v* cast (off), moult, slough, discard, drop, spill, pour, shower, scatter, diffuse, emit, radiate, shine, throw.

**shed**[2] *n* outhouse, lean-to, hut, shack.

**sheen** *n* lustre, gloss, shine, shimmer, brightness, brilliance, shininess, polish, burnish.
**F3** dullness, tarnish.

**sheepish** *adj* ashamed, shamefaced, embarrassed, mortified, chastened, abashed, uncomfortable, self-conscious, silly, foolish.
**F3** unabashed, brazen, bold.

**sheer** *adj* **1** UTTER, complete, total, absolute, thorough, mere, pure, unadulterated, downright, out-and-out, rank, thoroughgoing, unqualified, unmitigated. **2** *a sheer drop*: vertical, perpendicular, precipitous, abrupt, steep. **3** THIN, fine, flimsy, gauzy, gossamer, translucent, transparent, see-through.
**F3 2** gentle, gradual. **3** thick, heavy.

**sheet** *n* cover, blanket, covering, coating, coat, film, layer, stratum, skin, membrane, lamina, veneer, overlay, plate, leaf, page, folio, piece, panel, slab, pane, expanse, surface.

**shelf** *n* ledge, mantelpiece, sill, step, bench, counter, bar, bank, sandbank, reef, terrace.

**shell** *n* covering, hull, husk, pod, rind, crust, case, casing, body, chassis, frame, framework, structure, skeleton.

*v* **1** *shell nuts*: hull, husk, pod. **2** BOMB, bombard, barrage, blitz, attack.

**shelter** *v* cover, shroud, screen, shade, shadow, protect, safeguard, defend, guard, shield, harbour, hide, accommodate, put up.

🖃 expose.

*n* cover, roof, shade, shadow, protection, defence, guard, security, safety, sanctuary, asylum, haven, refuge, retreat, accommodation, lodging.

🖃 exposure.

**sheltered** *adj* covered, shaded, shielded, protected, cosy, snug, warm, quiet, secluded, isolated, retired, withdrawn, reclusive, cloistered, unworldly.

🖃 exposed.

**shelve** *v* postpone, defer, put off, suspend, halt, put aside, pigeonhole, put on ice, mothball.

🖃 expedite, implement.

**shield** *n* buckler, escutcheon, defence, bulwark, rampart, screen, guard, cover, shelter, protection, safeguard.

*v* defend, guard, protect, safeguard, screen, shade, shadow, cover, shelter.

🖃 expose.

**shift** *v* change, vary, fluctuate, alter, adjust, move, budge, remove, dislodge, displace, relocate, reposition, rearrange, transpose, transfer, switch, swerve, veer.

*n* change, fluctuation, alteration, modification, move, removal, displacement, rearrangement, transposition, transfer, switch.

**shifty** *adj* untrustworthy, dishonest, deceitful, scheming, contriving, tricky, wily, crafty, cunning, devious, evasive, slippery, furtive, underhand, dubious, shady (*infml*).

🖃 dependable, honest, open.

**shimmer** *v* glisten, gleam, glimmer, glitter, scintillate, twinkle.

*n* lustre, gleam, glimmer, glitter, glow.

**shine** *v* **1** BEAM, radiate, glow, flash, glare, gleam, glint, glitter, sparkle, twinkle, shimmer, glisten, glimmer. **2** POLISH, burnish, buff, brush, rub. **3** *shine at athletics*: excel, stand out.

*n* **1** LIGHT, radiance, glow, brightness, glare, gleam, sparkle, shimmer. **2** GLOSS, polish, burnish, sheen, lustre, glaze.

**shining** *adj* **1** BRIGHT, radiant, glowing, beaming, flashing, gleaming, glittering, glistening, shimmering, twinkling, sparkling, brilliant, resplendent, splendid, glorious. **2** *a shining example*: conspicuous, outstanding, leading, eminent, celebrated, distinguished, illustrious.

🖃 **1** dark.

**shiny** *adj* polished, burnished, sheeny, lustrous, glossy, sleek, bright, gleaming, glistening.

🖃 dull, matt.

**ship** *n* vessel, craft, liner, steamer, tanker, trawler, ferry, boat, yacht.

**shirk** *v* dodge, evade, avoid, duck (*infml*), shun, slack, skive (*infml*).

**shiver** *v* shudder, tremble, quiver, quake, shake, vibrate, palpitate, flutter.

*n* shudder, quiver, shake, tremor, twitch, start, vibration, flutter.

**shock** *v* disgust, revolt, sicken, offend, appal, outrage, scandalize, horrify, astound, stagger, stun, stupefy, numb, paralyse, traumatize, jolt, jar, shake, agitate, unsettle, disquiet, unnerve, confound, dismay.

🖃 delight, please, gratify, reassure.

*n* fright, start, jolt, impact, collision, surprise, bombshell, thunderbolt, blow, trauma, upset, distress, dismay, consternation, disgust, outrage.

🖃 delight, pleasure, reassurance.

**shocking** *adj* appalling, outrageous, scandalous, horrifying, disgraceful, deplorable, intolerable, unbearable,

atrocious, abominable, monstrous, unspeakable, detestable, abhorrent, dreadful, awful, terrible, frightful, ghastly, hideous, horrible, disgusting, revolting, repulsive, sickening, nauseating, offensive, distressing.
**E₃** acceptable, satisfactory, pleasant, delightful.

**shoddy** *adj* inferior, second-rate, cheap, tawdry, tatty, trashy, rubbishy, poor, careless, slipshod, slapdash.
**E₃** superior, well-made.

**shoot** *v* **1** FIRE, discharge, launch, propel, hurl, fling, project. **2** DART, bolt, dash, tear, rush, race, sprint, speed, charge, hurtle. **3** HIT, kill, blast, bombard, gun down, snipe at, pick off.
*n* sprout, bud, offshoot, branch, twig, sprig, slip, scion.

**shop**

> *Types of shop include:* bazaar, market, indoor market, mini-market, corner shop, shopping mall, department store, supermarket, superstore, hypermarket, cash-and-carry; butcher, baker, grocer, greengrocer, fishmonger, dairy, delicatessen, health-food shop, farm shop, fish and chip shop, take-away, off-licence, tobacconist, sweet shop, confectioner, tuck shop; bookshop, newsagent, stationer, chemist, pharmacy, tailor, outfitter, dress shop, boutique, milliner, shoe shop, haberdasher, draper, florist, jeweller, toy shop, hardware shop, ironmonger, saddler, radio and TV shop, video shop; launderette, hairdresser, barber, betting shop, bookmaker, bookie (*infml*), pawnbroker, post office.

**shore¹** *n* seashore, beach, sand(s), shingle, strand, waterfront, front, promenade, coast, seaboard, lakeside, bank.

**shore²** *v* support, hold, prop, stay,

underpin, buttress, brace, strengthen, reinforce.

**short** *adj* **1** BRIEF, cursory, fleeting, momentary, transitory, ephemeral, concise, succinct, terse, pithy, compact, compressed, shortened, curtailed, abbreviated, abridged, summarized. **2** BRUSQUE, curt, gruff, snappy, sharp, abrupt, blunt, direct, rude, impolite, discourteous, uncivil. **3** SMALL, little, low, petite, diminutive, squat, dumpy.
**4** INADEQUATE, insufficient, deficient, lacking, wanting, low, poor, meagre, scant, sparse.
**E₃ 1** long, lasting. **2** polite. **3** tall. **4** adequate, ample.

**shortage** *n* inadequacy, insufficiency, deficiency, shortfall, deficit, lack, want, need, scarcity, paucity, poverty, dearth, absence.
**E₃** sufficiency, abundance, surplus.

**shortcoming** *n* defect, imperfection, fault, flaw, drawback, failing, weakness, foible.

**shorten** *v* cut, trim, prune, crop, dock, curtail, truncate, abbreviate, abridge, reduce, lessen, decrease, diminish, take up.
**E₃** lengthen, enlarge, amplify.

**shortly** *adv* soon, before long, presently, by and by.

**short-sighted** *adj* **1** MYOPIC, near-sighted. **2** IMPROVIDENT, imprudent, injudicious, unwise, impolitic, ill-advised, careless, hasty, ill-considered.
**E₃** long-sighted, far-sighted.

**shot** *n* **1** BULLET, missile, projectile, ball, pellet, slug (*infml*), discharge, blast. **2** (*infml*) ATTEMPT, try, effort, endeavour, go (*infml*), bash (*infml*), crack (*infml*), stab (*infml*), guess, turn.

**shoulder** *v* **1** PUSH, shove, jostle, thrust, press. **2** ACCEPT, assume, take on, bear, carry, sustain.

**shout** *n, v* call, cry, scream, shriek, yell, roar, bellow, bawl, howl, bay, cheer.

**shove** v push, thrust, drive, propel, force, barge, jostle, elbow, shoulder, press, crowd.

**shovel** n spade, scoop, bucket.
v dig, scoop, dredge, clear, move, shift, heap.

**show** v 1 REVEAL, expose, uncover, disclose, divulge, present, offer, exhibit, manifest, display, indicate, register, demonstrate, prove, illustrate, exemplify, explain, instruct, teach, clarify, elucidate.
2 *show him out*: lead, guide, conduct, usher, escort, accompany, attend.
**⊟** 1 hide, cover.
n 1 OSTENTATION, parade, display, flamboyance, panache, pizzazz (*infml*), showiness, exhibitionism, affectation, pose, pretence, illusion, semblance, façade, impression, appearance, air. 2 DEMONSTRATION, presentation, exhibition, exposition, fair, display, parade, pageant, extravaganza, spectacle, entertainment, performance, production, staging, showing, representation.

**show off** parade, strut, swagger, brag, boast, swank (*infml*), flaunt, brandish, display, exhibit, demonstrate, advertise, set off, enhance.

**show up 1** (*infml*) ARRIVE, come, turn up, appear, materialize (*infml*).
2 HUMILIATE, embarrass, mortify, shame, disgrace, let down. 3 REVEAL, show, expose, unmask, lay bare, highlight, pinpoint.

**showdown** n confrontation, clash, crisis, climax, culmination.

**shower** n rain, stream, torrent, deluge, hail, volley, barrage.
v spray, sprinkle, rain, pour, deluge, inundate, overwhelm, load, heap, lavish.

**show-off** n swaggerer, braggart, boaster, swanker (*infml*), exhibitionist, peacock, poser, poseur, egotist.

**showy** adj flashy, flamboyant, ostentatious, gaudy, garish, loud, tawdry, fancy, ornate, pretentious, pompous, swanky (*infml*), flash (*infml*).
**⊟** quiet, restrained.

**shred** n ribbon, tatter, rag, scrap, snippet, sliver, bit, piece, fragment, jot, iota, atom, grain, mite, whit, trace.

**shrewd** adj astute, judicious, well-advised, calculated, far-sighted, smart, clever, intelligent, sharp, keen, acute, alert, perceptive, observant, discerning, discriminating, knowing, calculating, cunning, crafty, artful, sly.
**⊟** unwise, obtuse, naïve, unsophisticated.

**shriek** v, n scream, screech, squawk, squeal, cry, shout, yell, wail, howl.

**shrill** adj high, high-pitched, treble, sharp, acute, piercing, penetrating, screaming, screeching, strident, ear-splitting.
**⊟** deep, low, soft, gentle.

**shrink** v 1 CONTRACT, shorten, narrow, decrease, lessen, diminish, dwindle, shrivel, wrinkle, wither.
2 RECOIL, back away, shy away, withdraw, retire, balk, quail, cower, cringe, wince, flinch, shun.
**⊟** 1 expand, stretch. 2 accept, embrace.

**shrivel** v wrinkle, pucker, wither, wilt, shrink, dwindle, parch, dehydrate, desiccate, scorch, sear, burn, frizzle.

**shroud** v wrap, envelop, swathe, cloak, veil, screen, hide, conceal, blanket, cover.
**⊟** uncover, expose.
n winding-sheet, pall, mantle, cloak, veil, screen, blanket, covering.

**shrub**

*Shrubs* include: azalea, berberis, broom, buddleia, camellia, clematis, cotoneaster, daphne, dogwood, euonymus, firethorn, flowering currant, forsythia, fuchsia, heather, hebe, holly, honeysuckle, hydrangea, ivy, japonica, jasmine, laburnum, laurel, lavender, lilac, magnolia, mallow, mimosa, mock orange, peony, privet, musk rose, rhododendron, rose, spiraea, viburnum, weigela, witch hazel, wistaria. *see also* **flower**; **plant**.

**shudder** v  shiver, shake, tremble, quiver, quake, heave, convulse.
n  shiver, quiver, tremor, spasm, convulsion.

**shuffle** v  **1** MIX (UP), intermix, jumble, confuse, disorder, rearrange, reorganize, shift around, switch.
**2** *shuffle across the room*: shamble, scuffle, scrape, drag, limp, hobble.

**shun** v  avoid, evade, elude, steer clear of, shy away from, spurn, ignore, cold-shoulder, ostracize.
F3 accept, embrace.

**shut** v  close, slam, seal, fasten, secure, lock, latch, bolt, bar.
F3 open.

**shut down** close, stop, cease, terminate, halt, discontinue, suspend, switch off, inactivate.

**shut in** enclose, box in, hem in, fence in, immure, confine, imprison, cage.

**shut off** seclude, isolate, cut off, separate, segregate.

**shut out** **1** EXCLUDE, bar, debar, lock out, ostracize, banish. **2** HIDE, conceal, cover, mask, screen, veil.

**shut up** **1** SILENCE, gag, quiet, hush up, pipe down (*infml*), hold one's tongue, clam up (*infml*). **2** CONFINE, coop up, imprison, incarcerate, jail, intern.

**shy** adj  timid, bashful, reticent, reserved, retiring, diffident, coy, self-conscious, inhibited, modest, self-effacing, shrinking, hesitant, cautious, chary, suspicious, nervous.
F3 bold, assertive, confident.

**sick** adj  **1** ILL, unwell, indisposed, laid up, poorly, ailing, sickly, under

the weather, weak, feeble. **2** VOMITING, queasy, bilious, seasick, airsick. **3** *sick of waiting*: bored, fed up (*infml*), tired, weary, disgusted, nauseated.
F3 **1** well, healthy.

**sicken** v  nauseate, revolt, disgust, repel, put off, turn off (*sl*).
F3 delight, attract.

**sickening** adj  nauseating, revolting, disgusting, offensive, distasteful, foul, vile, loathsome, repulsive.
F3 delightful, pleasing, attractive.

**sickly** adj  **1** UNHEALTHY, infirm, delicate, weak, feeble, frail, wan, pallid, ailing, indisposed, sick, bilious, faint, languid.
**2** NAUSEATING, revolting, sweet, syrupy, cloying, mawkish.
F3 **1** healthy, robust, sturdy, strong.

**sickness** n  **1** ILLNESS, disease, malady, ailment, complaint, affliction, ill-health, indisposition, infirmity. **2** VOMITING, nausea, queasiness, biliousness.
F3 health.

**side** n  **1** EDGE, margin, fringe, periphery, border, boundary, limit, verge, brink, bank, shore, quarter, region, flank, hand, face, facet, surface. **2** STANDPOINT, viewpoint, view, aspect, angle, slant. **3** TEAM, party, faction, camp, cause, interest.
adj  lateral, flanking, marginal, secondary, subsidiary, subordinate, lesser, minor, incidental, indirect, oblique.

**side with** agree with, team up with, support, vote for, favour, prefer.

**sidestep** v  avoid, dodge, duck, evade, elude, skirt, bypass.
F3 tackle, deal with.

**sidetrack** v  deflect, head off, divert, distract.

**sideways** adv  sidewards, edgeways, laterally, obliquely.
adj  sideward, side, lateral, slanted, oblique, indirect, sidelong.

**sidle** v  slink, edge, inch, creep,

sneak.

**sieve** v sift, strain, separate, remove.
n colander, strainer, sifter, riddle,
screen.

**sift** v 1 SIEVE, strain, filter, riddle,
screen, winnow, separate, sort.
2 EXAMINE, scrutinize, investigate,
analyse, probe, review.

**sigh** v breathe, exhale, moan,
complain, lament, grieve.

**sight** n 1 VISION, eyesight, seeing,
observation, perception. 2 VIEW,
look, glance, glimpse, range, field of
vision, visibility. 3 APPEARANCE,
spectacle, show, display, exhibition,
scene, eyesore, monstrosity, fright
(*infml*).
v see, observe, spot, glimpse,
perceive, discern, distinguish, make
out.

**sightseer** n tourist, visitor,
holidaymaker, tripper, excursionist.

**sign** n 1 SYMBOL, token, character,
figure, representation, emblem,
badge, insignia, logo. 2 INDICATION,
mark, signal, gesture, evidence,
manifestation, clue, pointer, hint,
suggestion, trace. 3 NOTICE, poster,
board, placard. 4 PORTENT, omen,
forewarning, foreboding.
v autograph, initial, endorse, write.

**sign up** enlist, enrol, join (up),
volunteer, register, sign on, recruit,
take on, hire, engage, employ.

**signal** n sign, indication, mark,
gesture, cue, go-ahead, password,
light, indicator, beacon, flare, rocket,
alarm, alert, warning, tip-off.
v wave, gesticulate, gesture, beckon,
motion, nod, sign, indicate,
communicate.

**signature** n autograph, initials,
mark, endorsement, inscription.

**significance** n importance,
relevance, consequence, matter,
interest, consideration, weight, force,
meaning, implication, sense, point,
message.
**E3** insignificance, unimportance,

pettiness.

**significant** adj 1 IMPORTANT,
relevant, consequential, momentous,
weighty, serious, noteworthy, critical,
vital, marked, considerable,
appreciable. 2 MEANINGFUL,
symbolic, expressive, suggestive,
indicative, symptomatic.
**E3** 1 insignificant, unimportant,
trivial. 2 meaningless.

**signify** v 1 MEAN, denote,
symbolize, represent, stand for,
indicate, show, express, convey,
transmit, communicate, intimate,
imply, suggest. 2 MATTER, count.

**silence** n quiet, quietness, hush,
peace, stillness, calm, lull,
noiselessness, soundlessness,
muteness, dumbness, speechlessness,
taciturnity, uncommunicativeness,
reticence, reserve.
**E3** noise, sound, din, uproar.
v quiet, quieten, hush, mute, deaden,
muffle, stifle, gag, muzzle, suppress,
subdue, quell, still, dumbfound.

**silent** adj inaudible, noiseless,
soundless, quiet, peaceful, still,
hushed, muted, mute, dumb,
speechless, tongue-tied, taciturn,
mum, reticent, reserved, tacit,
unspoken, unexpressed, understood,
voiceless, wordless.
**E3** noisy, loud, talkative.

**silhouette** n outline, contour,
delineation, shape, form,
configuration, profile, shadow.

**silky** adj silken, fine, sleek, lustrous,
glossy, satiny, smooth, soft, velvety.

**silly** adj foolish, stupid, imprudent,
senseless, pointless, idiotic, daft
(*infml*), ridiculous, ludicrous,
preposterous, absurd, meaningless,
irrational, illogical, childish, puerile,
immature, irresponsible,
scatterbrained.
**E3** wise, sensible, sane, mature, clever,
intelligent.

**silt** n sediment, deposit, alluvium,
sludge, mud, ooze.

**silt up** block, clog, choke.

**similar** *adj* like, alike, close, related, akin, corresponding, equivalent, analogous, comparable, uniform, homogeneous.
 dissimilar, different.

**similarity** *n* likeness, resemblance, similitude, closeness, relation, correspondence, congruence, equivalence, analogy, comparability, compatibility, agreement, affinity, homogeneity, uniformity.
 dissimilarity, difference.

**simmer** *v* boil, bubble, seethe, stew, burn, smoulder, fume, rage.

**simmer down** calm down, cool down, control oneself, collect oneself.

**simple** *adj* **1** *a simple question*: easy, elementary, straightforward, uncomplicated, uninvolved, clear, lucid, plain, understandable, comprehensible.
 **2** UNSOPHISTICATED, natural, innocent, artless, guileless, ingenuous, naïve, green, foolish, stupid, silly, idiotic, half-witted, simple-minded, feeble-minded, backward.
 **1** difficult, hard, complicated, intricate. **2** sophisticated, worldly, artful, clever.

**simplicity** *n* simpleness, ease, straightforwardness, uncomplicatedness, clarity, purity, plainness, restraint, naturalness, innocence, artlessness, candour, openness, sincerity, directness.
 difficulty, complexity, intricacy, sophistication.

**simplify** *v* disentangle, untangle, decipher, clarify, paraphrase, abridge, reduce, streamline.
 complicate, elaborate.

**simplistic** *adj* oversimplified, superficial, shallow, sweeping, facile, simple, naïve.
 analytical, detailed.

**simply** *adv* **1** MERELY, just, only, solely, purely, utterly, completely,

totally, wholly, absolutely, quite, really, undeniably, unquestionably, clearly, plainly, obviously. **2** EASILY, straightforwardly, directly, intelligibly.

**simulate** *v* pretend, affect, assume, put on, act, feign, sham, fake, counterfeit, reproduce, duplicate, copy, imitate, mimic, parrot, echo, reflect.

**simultaneous** *adj* synchronous, synchronic, concurrent, contemporaneous, coinciding, parallel.
 asynchronous.

**sin** *n* wrong, offence, transgression, trespass, misdeed, lapse, fault, error, crime, wrongdoing, sinfulness, wickedness, iniquity, evil, impiety, ungodliness, unrighteousness, guilt.
 *v* offend, transgress, trespass, lapse, err, misbehave, stray, go astray, fall, fall from grace.

**sincere** *adj* honest, truthful, candid, frank, open, direct, straightforward, plain-spoken, serious, earnest, heartfelt, wholehearted, real, true, genuine, pure, unadulterated, unmixed, natural, unaffected, artless, guileless, simple.
 insincere, hypocritical, affected.

**sincerity** *n* honour, integrity, probity, uprightness, honesty, truthfulness, candour, frankness, openness, directness, straightforwardness, seriousness, earnestness, wholeheartedness, genuineness.
 **1, 3** insincerity.

**sinewy** *adj* muscular, brawny, strong, sturdy, robust, vigorous, athletic, wiry, stringy.

**sinful** *adj* wrong, wrongful, criminal, bad, wicked, iniquitous, erring, fallen, immoral, corrupt, depraved, impious, ungodly, unholy, irreligious, guilty.
 sinless, righteous, godly.

**sing** *v* chant, intone, vocalize, croon,

serenade, yodel, trill, warble, chirp, pipe, whistle, hum.

**singe** v scorch, char, blacken, burn, sear.

**singer**

> *Singers include:* balladeer, minstrel, troubadour, opera singer, diva, prima donna, soloist, precentor, choirboy, choirgirl, chorister, chorus, folk-singer, pop star, crooner, carol-singer; soprano, coloratura soprano, castrato, tenor, treble, contralto, alto, baritone, bass; songster, vocalist.

**single** adj one, unique, singular, individual, particular, exclusive, sole, only, lone, solitary, separate, distinct, free, unattached, unmarried, celibate, unshared, undivided, unbroken, simple, one-to-one, man-to-man.
**F3** multiple.

**single out** choose, select, pick, hand-pick, distinguish, identify, separate, set apart, isolate, highlight, pinpoint.

**single-handed** adj, adv solo, alone, unaccompanied, unaided, unassisted, independent(ly).

**single-minded** adj determined, resolute, dogged, persevering, tireless, unwavering, fixed, unswerving, undeviating, steadfast, dedicated, devoted.

**sinister** adj ominous, menacing, threatening, disturbing, disquieting, unlucky, inauspicious, malevolent, evil.
**F3** auspicious, harmless, innocent.

**sink** v 1 DESCEND, slip, fall, drop, slump, lower, stoop, succumb, lapse, droop, sag, dip, set, disappear, vanish. 2 DECREASE, lessen, subside, abate, dwindle, diminish, ebb, fade, flag, weaken, fail, decline, worsen, degenerate, degrade, decay, collapse. 3 FOUNDER, dive, plunge, plummet, submerge, immerse, engulf, drown. 4 *sink a well*: bore, drill, penetrate, dig, excavate, lay, conceal.

**F3** 1 rise. 2 increase. 3 float.

**sinner** n wrong-doer, miscreant, offender, transgressor, trespasser, backslider, reprobate, evil-doer, malefactor.

**sinuous** adj lithe, slinky, curved, wavy, undulating, tortuous, twisting, winding, meandering, serpentine, coiling.
**F3** straight.

**sip** v taste, sample, drink, sup.
n taste, drop, spoonful, mouthful.

**sit** v 1 SETTLE, rest, perch, roost, brood, pose. 2 SEAT, accommodate, hold, contain. 3 MEET, assemble, gather, convene, deliberate.

**site** n location, place, spot, position, situation, station, setting, scene, plot, lot, ground, area.
v locate, place, position, situate, station, set, install.

**sitting** n session, period, spell, meeting, assembly, hearing, consultation.

**situation** n 1 SITE, location, position, place, spot, seat, locality, locale, setting, scenario. 2 STATE OF AFFAIRS, case, circumstances, predicament, state, condition, status, rank, station, post, office, job, employment.

**sizable** adj large, substantial, considerable, respectable, goodly, largish, biggish, decent, generous.
**F3** small, tiny.

**size** n magnitude, measurement(s), dimensions, proportions, volume, bulk, mass, height, length, extent, range, scale, amount, greatness, largeness, bigness, vastness, immensity.

**size up** gauge, assess, evaluate, weigh up, measure.

**sizzle** v hiss, crackle, spit, sputter, fry, frizzle.

**skeleton** n bones, frame, structure, framework, bare bones, outline, draft, sketch.

**sketch** v draw, depict, portray,

represent, pencil, paint, outline, delineate, draft, rough out, block out.

*n* drawing, vignette, design, plan, diagram, outline, delineation, skeleton, draft.

**sketchy** *adj* rough, vague, incomplete, unfinished, scrappy, bitty, imperfect, inadequate, insufficient, slight, superficial, cursory, hasty.

⊟ full, complete.

**skilful** *adj* able, capable, adept, competent, proficient, deft, adroit, handy, expert, masterly, accomplished, skilled, practised, experienced, professional, clever, tactical, cunning.

⊟ inept, clumsy, awkward.

**skill** *n* skilfulness, ability, aptitude, facility, handiness, talent, knack, art, technique, training, experience, expertise, expertness, mastery, proficiency, competence, accomplishment, cleverness, intelligence.

**skilled** *adj* trained, schooled, qualified, professional, experienced, practised, accomplished, expert, masterly, proficient, able, skilful.

⊟ unskilled, inexperienced.

**skim** *v* 1 BRUSH, touch, skate, plane, float, sail, glide, fly. 2 SCAN, look through, skip. 3 CREAM, separate.

**skimp** *v* economize, scrimp, pinch, cut corners, stint, withhold.

⊟ squander, waste.

**skin** *n* hide, pelt, membrane, film, coating, surface, outside, peel, rind, husk, casing, crust.

*v* flay, fleece, strip, peel, scrape, graze.

**skinny** *adj* thin, lean, scrawny, scraggy, skeletal, skin-and-bone, emaciated, underfed, undernourished.

⊟ fat, plump.

**skip** *v* 1 HOP, jump, leap, dance, gambol, frisk, caper, prance. 2 *skip a*

*page*: miss, omit, leave out, cut.

**skirmish** *n* fight, combat, battle, engagement, encounter, conflict, clash, brush, scrap, tussle, set-to, dust-up (*infml*).

**skirt** *v* circle, circumnavigate, border, edge, flank, bypass, avoid, evade, circumvent.

**skit** *n* satire, parody, caricature, spoof, take-off, sketch.

**skulk** *v* lurk, hide, prowl, sneak, creep, slink.

**sky** *n* space, atmosphere, air, heavens, blue.

**slab** *n* piece, block, lump, chunk, hunk, wodge (*infml*), wedge, slice, portion.

**slack** *adj* 1 LOOSE, limp, sagging, baggy. 2 LAZY, sluggish, slow, quiet, idle, inactive. 3 NEGLECTFUL, negligent, careless, inattentive, remiss, permissive, lax, relaxed, easy-going (*infml*).

⊟ 1 tight, taut, stiff, rigid. 2 busy. 3 diligent.

*n* looseness, give, play, room, leeway, excess.

*v* idle, shirk, skive (*infml*), neglect.

**slacken off** loosen, release, relax, ease, moderate, reduce, lessen, decrease, diminish, abate, slow (down).

⊟ tighten, increase, intensify, quicken.

**slacker** *n* idler, shirker, skiver (*infml*), dawdler, clock-watcher, good-for-nothing, layabout.

**slam** *v* 1 BANG, crash, dash, smash, throw, hurl, fling. 2 (*infml*) CRITICIZE, slate (*infml*), pan (*infml*).

**slander** *n* defamation, calumny, misrepresentation, libel, scandal, smear, slur, aspersion, backbiting.

*v* defame, vilify, malign, denigrate, disparage, libel, smear, slur, backbite.

⊟ praise, compliment.

**slanderous** *adj* defamatory, false, untrue, libellous, damaging, malicious, abusive, insulting.

**slant** *v* 1 TILT, slope, incline, lean,

# slanting

492

warp, bend, weight, bias, colour.

*n* **1** SLOPE, incline, gradient, ramp,
camber, pitch, tilt, angle, diagonal.
**2** BIAS, emphasis, attitude, viewpoint.

**slanting** *adj* sloping, tilted, oblique,
diagonal.

**slap** *n* smack, spank, cuff, blow,
bang, clap.

*v* **1** SMACK, spank, hit, strike, cuff,
clout, bang, clap. **2** DAUB, plaster,
spread, apply.

**slash** *v* cut, slit, gash, lacerate, rip,
tear, rend.

*n* cut, incision, slit, gash, laceration,
rip, tear, rent.

**slate** *v* scold, rebuke, reprimand,
berate, censure, blame, criticize, slam
(*infml*).

**F3** praise.

**slaughter** *n* killing, murder,
massacre, extermination, butchery,
carnage, blood-bath, bloodshed.

*v* kill, slay, murder, massacre,
exterminate, liquidate, butcher.

**slave** *n* servant, drudge, vassal, serf,
villein, captive.

*v* toil, labour, drudge, sweat, grind,
slog.

**slaver** *v* dribble, drivel, slobber,
drool, salivate.

**slavery** *n* servitude, bondage,
captivity, enslavement, serfdom,
thraldom, subjugation.

**F3** freedom, liberty.

**slavish** *adj* **1** UNORIGINAL,
imitative, unimaginative, uninspired,
literal, strict. **2** SERVILE, abject,
submissive, sycophantic, grovelling,
cringing, fawning, menial, low, mean.

**F3 1** original, imaginative.
**2** independent, assertive.

**sleek** *adj* shiny, glossy, lustrous,
smooth, silky, well-groomed.

**F3** rough, unkempt.

**sleep** *v* doze, snooze, slumber, kip
(*sl*), doss (down) (*sl*), hibernate, drop
off, nod off, rest, repose.

*n* doze, snooze, nap, forty winks,

shut-eye (*infml*), kip (*sl*), slumber,
hibernation, rest, repose, siesta.

**sleepless** *adj* unsleeping, awake,
wide-awake, alert, vigilant, watchful,
wakeful, restless, disturbed,
insomniac.

**sleepy** *adj* drowsy, somnolent, tired,
weary, heavy, slow, sluggish, torpid,
lethargic, inactive, quiet, dull,
soporific, hypnotic.

**F3** awake, alert, wakeful, restless.

**slender** *adj* **1** SLIM, thin, lean,
slight, svelte, graceful. **2** *a slender
chance*: faint, remote, slight,
inconsiderable, tenuous, flimsy,
feeble, inadequate, insufficient,
meagre, scanty.

**F3 1** fat. **2** appreciable, considerable,
ample.

**slice** *n* piece, sliver, wafer, rasher,
tranche, slab, wedge, segment,
section, share, portion, helping, cut
(*infml*), whack (*infml*).

*v* carve, cut, chop, divide, segment.

**slick** *adj* **1** GLIB, plausible, deft,
adroit, dexterous, skilful,
professional. **2** SMOOTH, sleek,
glossy, shiny, polished.

**slide** *v* slip, slither, skid, skate, ski,
toboggan, glide, plane, coast, skim.

**slight** *adj* **1** MINOR, unimportant,
insignificant, negligible, trivial,
paltry, modest, small, little,
inconsiderable, insubstantial.
**2** SLENDER, slim, diminutive, petite,
delicate.

**F3 1** major, significant, noticeable,
considerable. **2** large, muscular.

*v* scorn, despise, disdain, disparage,
insult, affront, offend, snub, cut, cold-
shoulder, ignore, disregard, neglect.

**F3** respect, praise, compliment, flatter.

*n* insult, affront, slur, snub, rebuff,
rudeness, discourtesy, disrespect,
contempt, disdain, indifference,
disregard, neglect.

**slim** *adj* **1** SLENDER, thin, lean,
svelte, trim. **2** SLIGHT, remote, faint,
poor.

**⊞ 1** fat, chubby. **2** strong, considerable.

*v* lose weight, diet, reduce.

**slimy** *adj* **1** MUDDY, miry, mucous, viscous, oily, greasy, slippery. **2** SERVILE, obsequious, sycophantic, toadying, smarmy, oily, unctuous.

**sling** *v* **1** THROW, hurl, fling, catapult, heave, pitch, lob, toss, chuck (*infml*). **2** HANG, suspend, dangle, swing.

**slink** *v* sneak, steal, creep, sidle, slip, prowl, skulk.

**slinky** *adj* close-fitting, figure-hugging, clinging, skin-tight, sleek, sinuous.

**slip**¹ *v* slide, glide, skate, skid, stumble, trip, fall, slither, slink, sneak, steal, creep.

*n* mistake, error, slip-up (*infml*), bloomer (*infml*), blunder, fault, indiscretion, boob (*infml*), omission, oversight, failure.

**slip**² *n* piece, strip, voucher, chit, coupon, certificate.

**slippery** *adj* **1** SLIPPY, icy, greasy, glassy, smooth, dangerous, treacherous, perilous. **2** *a slippery character*: dishonest, untrustworthy, false, duplicitous, two-faced, crafty, cunning, devious, evasive, smooth, smarmy.

**⊞ 1** rough. **2** trustworthy, reliable.

**slipshod** *adj* careless, slap-dash, sloppy, slovenly, untidy, negligent, lax, casual.

**⊞** careful, fastidious, neat, tidy.

**slit** *v* cut, gash, slash, slice, split, rip, tear.

*n* opening, aperture, vent, cut, incision, gash, slash, split, tear, rent.

**slither** *v* slide, slip, glide, slink, creep, snake, worm.

**sliver** *n* flake, shaving, paring, slice, wafer, shred, fragment, chip, splinter, shiver, shard.

**slobber** *v* dribble, drivel, slaver, drool, salivate.

**slogan** *n* jingle, motto, catch-phrase,

catchword, watchword, battle-cry, war cry.

**slop** *v* spill, overflow, slosh, splash, splatter, spatter.

**slope** *v* slant, lean, tilt, tip, pitch, incline, rise, fall.

*n* incline, gradient, ramp, hill, ascent, descent, slant, tilt, pitch, inclination.

**sloppy** *adj* **1** WATERY, wet, liquid, runny, mushy, slushy. **2** *sloppy work*: careless, hit-or-miss, slap-dash, slipshod, slovenly, untidy, messy, clumsy, amateurish. **3** SOPPY, sentimental, schmaltzy, slushy, mushy.

**⊞ 1** solid. **2** careful, exact, precise.

**slot** *n* hole, opening, aperture, slit, vent, groove, channel, gap, space, time, vacancy, place, spot, position, niche.

*v* insert, fit, place, position, assign, pigeonhole.

**slouch** *v* stoop, hunch, droop, slump, lounge, loll, shuffle, shamble.

**slovenly** *adj* sloppy, careless, slipshod, untidy, scruffy, slatternly, sluttish.

**⊞** neat, smart.

**slow** *adj* **1** LEISURELY, unhurried, lingering, loitering, dawdling, lazy, sluggish, slow-moving, creeping, gradual, deliberate, measured, plodding, delayed, late, unpunctual. **2** STUPID, slow-witted, dim, thick (*infml*). **3** PROLONGED, protracted, long-drawn-out, tedious, boring, dull, uninteresting, uneventful.

**⊞ 1** quick, fast, swift, rapid, speedy. **2** clever, intelligent. **3** brisk, lively, exciting.

*v* brake, decelerate, delay, hold up, retard, handicap, check, curb, restrict.

**⊞** speed, accelerate.

**sluggish** *adj* lethargic, listless, torpid, heavy, dull, slow, slow-moving, slothful, lazy, idle, inactive, lifeless, unresponsive.

**⊞** brisk, vigorous, lively, dynamic.

**slump** v **1** COLLAPSE, fall, drop, plunge, plummet, sink, decline, deteriorate, worsen, crash, fail. **2** DROOP, sag, bend, stoop, slouch, loll, lounge, flop.
n recession, depression, stagnation, downturn, low, trough, decline, deterioration, worsening, fall, drop, collapse, crash, failure.
**F3** boom.

**sly** adj wily, foxy, crafty, cunning, artful, guileful, clever, canny, shrewd, astute, knowing, subtle, devious, shifty, tricky, furtive, stealthy, surreptitious, underhand, covert, secretive, scheming, conniving, mischievous, roguish.
**F3** honest, frank, candid, open.

**smack** v hit, strike, slap, spank, whack (infml), thwack (infml), clap, box, cuff, pat, tap.
n blow, slap, spank, whack (infml), thwack (infml), box, cuff, pat, tap.
adv bang, slap-bang, right, plumb, straight, directly, exactly, precisely.

**small** adj **1** LITTLE, tiny, minute, minuscule, short, slight, puny, petite, diminutive, pint-size(d) (infml), miniature, mini, pocket, pocket-sized, young. **2** PETTY, trifling, trivial, unimportant, insignificant, minor, inconsiderable, negligible. **3** INADEQUATE, insufficient, scanty, meagre, paltry, mean, limited.
**F3 1** large, big, huge. **2** great, considerable. **3** ample.

**small-minded** adj petty, mean, ungenerous, illiberal, intolerant, bigoted, narrow-minded, parochial, insular, rigid, hidebound.
**F3** liberal, tolerant, broad-minded.

**smarmy** adj smooth, oily, unctuous, servile, obsequious, sycophantic, toadying, ingratiating, crawling, fawning.

**smart** adj **1** smart clothes: elegant, stylish, chic, fashionable, modish, neat, tidy, spruce, trim, well-groomed. **2** CLEVER, intelligent,

bright, sharp, acute, shrewd, astute.
**F3 1** dowdy, unfashionable, untidy, scruffy. **2** stupid, slow.
v sting, hurt, prick, burn, tingle, twinge, throb.

**smarten** v neaten, tidy, spruce up, groom, clean, polish, beautify.

**smash** v **1** smash a window: break, shatter, shiver, ruin, wreck, demolish, destroy, defeat, crush. **2** CRASH, collide, strike, bang, bash, thump.
n accident, crash, collision, pile-up.

**smattering** n bit, modicum, dash, sprinkling, basics, rudiments, elements.

**smear** v **1** DAUB, plaster, spread, cover, coat, rub, smudge, streak. **2** DEFAME, malign, vilify, blacken, sully, stain, tarnish.
n **1** STREAK, smudge, blot, blotch, splodge, daub. **2** DEFAMATION, slander, libel, mudslinging, muck-raking.

**smell** n odour, whiff, scent, perfume, fragrance, bouquet, aroma, stench, stink, pong (infml).
v sniff, nose, scent, stink, reek, pong (infml).

---

*Ways of describing smells include:*
*pleasant*: aroma, bouquet, fragrance, incense, nose, odour, pot pourri, perfume, redolence, scent;
*unpleasant*: b.o. (body odour), fetor, funk (North Amer.), hum, malodour, mephitis, miasma, niff (slang), pong (colloq.), pungency, reek, sniff, stench, stink, whiff.

---

**smelly** adj malodorous, pongy (infml), stinking, reeking, foul, bad, off, fetid, putrid, high, strong.

**smile** n, v grin, beam, simper, smirk, leer, laugh.

**smoke** n fumes, exhaust, gas, vapour, mist, fog, smog.
v fume, smoulder, cure, dry.

**smoky** adj sooty, black, grey, grimy, murky, cloudy, hazy, foggy.

**smooth** adj 1 LEVEL, plane, even, flat, horizontal, flush. 2 STEADY, unbroken, flowing, regular, uniform, rhythmic, easy, effortless. 3 SHINY, polished, glossy, silky, glassy, calm, undisturbed, serene, tranquil, peaceful. 4 SUAVE, agreeable, smooth-talking, glib, plausible, persuasive, slick, smarmy, unctuous, ingratiating.
**E3** 1 rough, lumpy. 2 irregular, erratic, unsteady. 3 rough, choppy.
v 1 IRON, press, roll, flatten, level, plane, file, sand, polish. 2 EASE, alleviate, assuage, allay, mitigate, calm, mollify.
**E3** 1 roughen, wrinkle, crease.

**smother** v suffocate, asphyxiate, strangle, throttle, choke, stifle, extinguish, snuff, muffle, suppress, repress, hide, conceal, cover, shroud, envelop, wrap.

**smoulder** v burn, smoke, fume, rage, seethe, simmer.

**smudge** v blur, smear, daub, mark, spot, stain, dirty, soil.
n blot, stain, spot, blemish, blur, smear, streak.

**smug** adj complement, self-satisfied, superior, holier-than-thou, self-righteous, priggish, conceited.
**E3** humble, modest.

**snack** n refreshment(s), bite, nibble, titbit, elevenses (infml).

**snag** n disadvantage, inconvenience, drawback, catch, problem, difficulty, complication, setback, hitch, obstacle, stumbling-block.
v catch, rip, tear, hole, ladder.

**snap** v 1 the twig snapped: break, crack, split, separate. 2 BITE, nip, bark, growl, snarl, retort, crackle, pop. 3 SNATCH, seize, catch, grasp, grip.
n break, crack, bite, nip, flick, fillip, crackle, pop.
adj immediate, instant, on-the-spot, abrupt, sudden.

**snappy** adj 1 SMART, stylish, chic,

fashionable, modish, trendy (infml). 2 QUICK, hasty, brisk, lively, energetic. 3 CROSS, irritable, edgy, touchy, brusque, quick-tempered, ill-natured, crabbed, testy.
**E3** 1 dowdy. 2 slow.

**snare** v trap, ensnare, entrap, catch, net.
n trap, wire, net, noose, catch, pitfall.

**snarl**¹ v growl, grumble, complain.

**snarl**² v tangle, knot, ravel, entangle, enmesh, embroil, confuse, muddle, complicate.

**snatch** v grab, seize, kidnap, take, nab (infml), pluck, pull, wrench, wrest, gain, win, clutch, grasp, grip.

**sneak** v 1 CREEP, steal, slip, slink, sidle, skulk, lurk, prowl, smuggle, spirit. 2 TELL TALES, split (sl), inform on, grass on (sl).
n tell-tale, informer, grass (sl).

**sneaking** adj private, secret, furtive, surreptitious, hidden, lurking, suppressed, grudging, nagging, niggling, persistent, worrying, uncomfortable, intuitive.

**sneer** v scorn, disdain, look down on, deride, scoff, jeer, mock, ridicule, gibe, laugh, snigger.
n scorn, disdain, derision, jeer, mockery, ridicule, gibe, snigger.

**snide** adj derogatory, disparaging, sarcastic, cynical, scornful, sneering, hurtful, unkind, nasty, mean, spiteful, malicious, ill-natured.
**E3** complimentary.

**sniff** v breathe, inhale, snuff, snuffle, smell, nose, scent.

**snigger** v, n laugh, giggle, titter, chuckle, sneer.

**snip** v cut, clip, trim, crop, dock, slit, nick, notch.

**snippet** n piece, scrap, cutting, clipping, fragment, particle, shred, snatch, part, portion, segment, section.

**snobbery** n snobbishness, superciliousness, snootiness (infml), airs, loftiness, arrogance, pride, pretension, condescension.

**snobbish** adj supercilious, disdainful, snooty (infml), stuck-up (infml), toffee-nosed (infml), superior, lofty, high and mighty, arrogant, pretentious, affected, condescending, patronizing.

**snoop** v spy, sneak, pry, nose, interfere, meddle.

**snooze** v nap, doze, sleep, kip (sl). n nap, catnap, forty winks, doze, siesta, sleep, kip (sl).

**snub** v rebuff, brush off, cut, cold-shoulder, slight, rebuke, put down, squash, humble, shame, humiliate, mortify.
n rebuff, brush-off, slight, affront, insult, rebuke, put-down, humiliation.

**snug** adj cosy, warm, comfortable, homely, friendly, intimate, sheltered, secure, tight, close-fitting.

**soak** v wet, drench, saturate, penetrate, permeate, infuse, bathe, marinate, souse, steep, submerge, immerse.

**soaking** adj soaked, drenched, sodden, waterlogged, saturated, sopping, wringing, dripping, streaming.
**₣** dry.

**soar** v fly, wing, glide, plane, tower, rise, ascend, climb, mount, escalate, rocket.
**₣** fall, plummet.

**sob** v cry, weep, bawl, howl, blubber, snivel.

**sober** adj 1 TEETOTAL, temperate, moderate, abstinent, abstemious. 2 SOLEMN, dignified, serious, staid, steady, sedate, quiet, serene, calm, composed, unruffled, unexcited, cool, dispassionate, level-headed, practical, realistic, reasonable, rational, clear-headed. 3 sober dress: sombre, drab, dull, plain, subdued, restrained.
**₣** 1 drunk, intemperate. 2 frivolous, excited, unrealistic, irrational. 3 flashy, garish.

**so-called** adj alleged, supposed, purported, ostensible, nominal, self-styled, professed, would-be, pretended.

**sociable** adj outgoing, gregarious, friendly, affable, companionable, genial, convivial, cordial, warm, hospitable, neighbourly, approachable, accessible, familiar.
**₣** unsociable, withdrawn, unfriendly, hostile.

**social** adj communal, public, community, common, general, collective, group, organized.
n party, do (infml), get-together, gathering.

**socialize** v mix, mingle, fraternize, get together, go out, entertain.

**society** n 1 COMMUNITY, population, culture, civilization, nation, people, mankind, humanity. 2 CLUB, circle, group, association, organization, company, corporation, league, union, guild, fellowship, fraternity, brotherhood, sisterhood, sorority. 3 FRIENDSHIP, companionship, camaraderie, fellowship, company. 4 UPPER CLASSES, aristocracy, gentry, nobility, elite.

**soft** adj 1 YIELDING, pliable, flexible, elastic, plastic, malleable, spongy, squashy, pulpy. 2 soft colours: pale, light, pastel, delicate, subdued, muted, quiet, low, dim, faint, diffuse, mild, bland, gentle, soothing, sweet, mellow, melodious, dulcet, pleasant. 3 FURRY, downy, velvety, silky, smooth. 4 LENIENT, lax, permissive, indulgent, tolerant, easy-going (infml), kind, generous, gentle, merciful, soft-hearted, tender, sensitive, weak, spineless.
**₣** 1 hard. 2 harsh. 3 rough. 4 strict, severe.

**soften** v 1 MODERATE, temper, mitigate, lessen, diminish, abate, alleviate, ease, soothe, palliate, quell, assuage, subdue, mollify, appease, calm, still, relax. 2 MELT, liquefy, dissolve, reduce. **3** CUSHION, pad, muffle, quicken, lower, lighten.

**soft-hearted** *adj* sympathetic, compassionate, kind, benevolent, charitable, generous, warm-hearted, tender, sentimental.
 F3 hard-hearted, callous.

**soggy** *adj* wet, damp, moist, soaked, drenched, sodden, waterlogged, saturated, sopping, dripping, heavy, boggy, spongy, pulpy.

**soil**¹ *n* earth, clay, loam, humus, dirt, dust, ground, land, region, country.

**soil**² *v* dirty, begrime, stain, spot, smudge, smear, foul, muddy, pollute, defile, besmirch, sully, tarnish.

**solace** *n* comfort, consolation, relief, alleviation, support, cheer.

**soldier** *n*

*Types of soldier include*: cadet, private, sapper, NCO, orderly, officer, gunner, infantryman, trooper, fusilier, rifleman, paratrooper, sentry, guardsman, marine, commando, tommy, dragoon, cavalryman, lancer, hussar, conscript, recruit, regular, Territorial, GI (*US*), warrior, mercenary, legionnaire, guerrilla, partisan, centurion; troops; serviceman, servicewoman, fighter. *see also* **rank**.

**sole** *adj* only, unique, exclusive, individual, single, singular, one, lone, solitary, alone.
 F3 shared, multiple.

**solemn** *adj* **1** *a solemn expression*: serious, grave, sober, sedate, sombre, glum, thoughtful, earnest, awed, reverential. **2** GRAND, stately, majestic, ceremonial, ritual, formal, ceremonious, pompous, dignified, august, venerable, awe-inspiring, impressive, imposing, momentous.
 F3 **1** light-hearted. **2** frivolous.

**solicit** *v* ask, request, seek, crave, beg, beseech, entreat, implore, pray,

supplicate, sue, petition, canvass, importune.

**solicitor** *n* lawyer, advocate, attorney, barrister, QC.

**solicitous** *adj* caring, attentive, considerate, concerned, anxious, worried.

**solid** *adj* **1** HARD, firm, dense, compact, strong, sturdy, substantial, sound, unshakable. **2** *a solid white line*: unbroken, continuous, uninterrupted. **3** RELIABLE, dependable, trusty, worthy, decent, upright, sensible, level-headed, stable, serious, sober. **4** REAL, genuine, pure, concrete, tangible.
 F3 **1** liquid, gaseous, hollow. **2** broken, dotted. **3** unreliable, unstable. **4** unreal.

**solidarity** *n* unity, agreement, accord, unanimity, consensus, harmony, concord, cohesion, like-mindedness, camaraderie, team spirit, soundness, stability.
 F3 discord, division, schism.

**solidify** *v* harden, set, jell, congeal, coagulate, clot, cake, crystallize.
 F3 soften, liquefy, dissolve.

**solitary** *adj* sole, single, lone, alone, lonely, lonesome, friendless, unsociable, reclusive, withdrawn, retired, sequestered, cloistered, secluded, separate, isolated, remote, out-of-the-way, inaccessible, unfrequented, unvisited, untrodden.
 F3 accompanied, gregarious, busy.

**solitude** *n* aloneness, loneliness, reclusiveness, retirement, privacy, seclusion, isolation, remoteness.
 F3 companionship.

**solution** *n* **1** ANSWER, result, explanation, resolution, key, remedy. **2** MIXTURE, blend, compound, suspension, emulsion, liquid.

**solve** *v* work out, figure out, puzzle out, decipher, crack, disentangle, unravel, answer, resolve, settle, clear up, clarify, explain, interpret.

**sombre** *adj* dark, funereal, drab,

dull, dim, obscure, shady, shadowy, gloomy, dismal, melancholy, mournful, sad, joyless, sober, serious, grave.
🔁 bright, cheerful, happy.

**someday** adv  sometime, one day, eventually, ultimately.
🔁 never.

**sometimes** adv  occasionally, now and again, now and then, once in a while, from time to time.
🔁 always, never.

**song** n  ballad, madrigal, lullaby, shanty, anthem, hymn, carol, chant, chorus, air, tune, melody, lyric, number, ditty.

*Types of song include:* air, anthem, aria, ballad, barcarole, bird call, bird song, blues, calypso, cantata, canticle, cantilena, canzone, canzonet, carol, chanson, chansonette, chant, chorus, descant, dirge, ditty, elegy, epinikion, epithalamium, folk-song, gospel song, hymn, jingle, love-song, lied, lilt, lullaby, madrigal, nursery rhyme, ode, plainchant, plainsong, pop song, psalm, recitative, requiem, rock and roll, roundelay, serenade, shanty, spiritual, Negro spiritual, war song, wassail, yodel.

**soon** adv  shortly, presently, in a minute, before long, in the near future.

**soothe** v  alleviate, relieve, ease, salve, comfort, allay, calm, compose, tranquillize, settle, still, quiet, hush, lull, pacify, appease, mollify, assuage, mitigate, soften.
🔁 aggravate, irritate, annoy, vex.

**sophisticated** adj  **1** URBANE, cosmopolitan, worldly, worldly-wise, cultured, cultivated, refined, polished. **2** *sophisticated technology*: advanced, highly-developed, complicated, complex, intricate, elaborate, delicate, subtle.

🔁 **1** unsophisticated, naïve.
**2** primitive, simple.

**soporific** adj  sleep-inducing, hypnotic, sedative, tranquillizing, sleepy, somnolent.
🔁 stimulating, invigorating.

**soppy** adj  sentimental, lovey-dovey (*infml*), weepy (*infml*), sloppy, slushy, mushy, corny (*infml*), mawkish, cloying, soft, silly, daft (*infml*).

**sorcery** n  magic, black magic, witchcraft, wizardry, necromancy, voodoo, spell, incantation, charm, enchantment.

**sordid** adj  dirty, filthy, unclean, foul, vile, squalid, sleazy, seamy, seedy, disreputable, shabby, tawdry, corrupt, degraded, degenerate, debauched, low, base, despicable, shameful, wretched, mean, miserly, niggardly, grasping, mercenary, selfish, self-seeking.
🔁 pure, honourable, upright.

**sore** adj  **1** PAINFUL, hurting, aching, smarting, stinging, tender, sensitive, inflamed, red, raw.
**2** ANNOYED, irritated, vexed, angry, upset, hurt, wounded, afflicted, aggrieved, resentful.
🔁 **2** pleased, happy.
n  wound, lesion, swelling, inflammation, boil, abscess, ulcer.

**sorrow** n  sadness, unhappiness, grief, mourning, misery, woe, distress, affliction, anguish, heartache, heartbreak, misfortune, hardship, trouble, worry, trial, tribulation, regret, remorse.
🔁 happiness, joy.

**sorry** adj  **1** APOLOGETIC, regretful, remorseful, contrite, penitent, repentant, conscience-stricken, guilt-ridden, shamefaced. **2** *in a sorry state*: pathetic, pitiful, poor, wretched, miserable, sad, unhappy, dismal. **3** SYMPATHETIC, compassionate, understanding, pitying, concerned, moved.
🔁 **1** impenitent, unashamed. **2** happy,

cheerful. **3** uncaring.

**sort** *n* kind, type, genre, ilk, family, race, breed, species, genus, variety, order, class, category, group, denomination, style, make, brand, stamp, quality, nature, character, description.

*v* class, group, categorize, distribute, divide, separate, segregate, sift, screen, grade, rank, order, classify, catalogue, arrange, organize, systematize.

**sort out** resolve, clear up, clarify, tidy up, neaten, choose, select.

**soul** *n* **1** SPIRIT, psyche, mind, reason, intellect, character, inner being, essence, life, vital force. **2** INDIVIDUAL, person, man, creature. **3** woman.

**sound**$^1$ *n* noise, din, report, resonance, reverberation, tone, timbre, tenor, description.

*v* **1** RING, toll, chime, peal, resound, resonate, reverberate, echo. **2** ARTICULATE, enunciate, pronounce, voice, express, utter, say, declare, announce.

**sound**$^2$ *adj* **1** FIT, well, healthy, vigorous, robust, sturdy, firm, solid, whole, complete, intact, perfect, unbroken, undamaged, unimpaired, unhurt, uninjured. **2** VALID, well-founded, reasonable, rational, logical, orthodox, right, true, proven, reliable, trustworthy, secure, substantial, thorough, good.
**E3** **1** unfit, ill, shaky. **2** unsound, unreliable, poor.

**sound**$^3$ *v* measure, plumb, fathom, probe, examine, test, inspect, investigate.

**sour** *adj* **1** TART, sharp, acid, pungent, vinegary, bitter, rancid. **2** EMBITTERED, acrimonious, ill-tempered, peevish, crabbed, crusty, disagreeable.
**E3** **1** sweet, sugary. **2** good-natured, generous.

**source** *n* origin, derivation, beginning, start, commencement,

cause, root, rise, spring, fountainhead, wellhead, supply, mine, originator, authority, informant.

**souvenir** *n* memento, reminder, remembrance, keepsake, relic, token.

**sovereign** *n* ruler, monarch, king, queen, emperor, empress, potentate, chief.

*adj* ruling, royal, imperial, absolute, unlimited, supreme, paramount, predominant, principal, chief, dominant, independent, autonomous.

**sow** *v* plant, seed, scatter, strew, spread, disseminate, lodge, implant.

**space** *n* **1** ROOM, place, seat, accommodation, capacity, volume, extent, expansion, scope, range, play, elbow-room, leeway, margin. **2** BLANK, omission, gap, opening, lacuna, interval, intermission, chasm.

**spacious** *adj* roomy, capacious, ample, big, large, sizable, broad, wide, huge, vast, extensive, open, uncrowded.
**E3** small, narrow, cramped, confined.

**span** *n* spread, stretch, reach, range, scope, compass, extent, length, distance, duration, term, period, spell.

*v* arch, vault, bridge, link, cross, traverse, extend, cover.

**spank** *v* smack, slap, wallop (*infml*), whack (*infml*), thrash, slipper, cane.

**spare** *adj* reserve, emergency, extra, additional, leftover, remaining, unused, over, surplus, superfluous, supernumerary, unwanted, free, unoccupied.
**E3** necessary, vital, used.

*v* **1** PARDON, let off, reprieve, release, free. **2** GRANT, allow, afford, part with.

**sparing** *adj* economical, thrifty, careful, prudent, frugal, meagre, miserly.
**E3** unsparing, liberal, lavish.

**spark** *n* flash, flare, gleam, glint, flicker, hint, trace, vestige, scrap, atom, jot.

*v* kindle, set off, trigger, start, cause, occasion, prompt, provoke, stimulate, stir, excite, inspire.

**sparkle** *v* 1 TWINKLE, glitter, scintillate, flash, gleam, glint, glisten, shimmer, coruscate, shine, beam.

2 EFFERVESCE, fizz, bubble.

*n* twinkle, glitter, flash, gleam, glint, flicker, spark, radiance, brilliance, dazzle, spirit, vitality, life, animation.

**sparse** *adj* scarce, scanty, meagre, scattered, infrequent, sporadic.

**F3** plentiful, thick, dense.

**spartan** *adj* austere, harsh, severe, rigorous, strict, disciplined, ascetic, abstemious, temperate, frugal, plain, simple, bleak, joyless.

**F3** luxurious, self-indulgent.

**spasm** *n* burst, eruption, outburst, frenzy, fit, convulsion, seizure, attack, contraction, jerk, twitch, tic.

**spasmodic** *adj* sporadic, occasional, intermittent, erratic, irregular, fitful, jerky.

**F3** continuous, uninterrupted.

**spate** *n* flood, deluge, torrent, rush, outpouring, flow.

**speak** *v* talk, converse, say, state, declare, express, utter, voice, articulate, enunciate, pronounce, tell, communicate, address, lecture, harangue, hold forth, declaim, argue, discuss.

**speaker** *n* lecturer, orator, spokesperson, spokesman, spokeswoman.

**special** *adj* 1 *a special occasion*: important, significant, momentous, major, noteworthy, distinguished, memorable, remarkable, extraordinary, exceptional.

2 DIFFERENT, distinctive, characteristic, peculiar, singular, individual, unique, exclusive, select, choice, particular, specific, unusual, precise, detailed.

**F3** 1 normal, ordinary, usual.

2 general, common.

**specialist** *n* consultant, authority, expert, master, professional, connoisseur.

**speciality** *n* strength, forte, talent, field, specialty, pièce de résistance.

**specific** *adj* precise, exact, fixed, limited, particular, special, definite, unequivocal, clear-cut, explicit, express, unambiguous.

**F3** vague, approximate.

**specification** *n* requirement, condition, qualification, description, listing, item, particular, detail.

**specify** *v* stipulate, spell out, define, particularize, detail, itemize, enumerate, list, mention, cite, name, designate, indicate, describe, delineate.

**specimen** *n* sample, example, instance, illustration, model, pattern, paradigm, exemplar, representative, copy, exhibit.

**spectacle** *n* show, performance, display, exhibition, parade, pageant, extravaganza, scene, sight, curiosity, wonder, marvel, phenomenon.

**spectacular** *adj* grand, splendid, magnificent, sensational, impressive, striking, stunning, staggering, amazing, remarkable, dramatic, daring, breathtaking, dazzling, eye-catching, colourful.

**F3** unimpressive, ordinary.

**spectator** *n* watcher, viewer, onlooker, looker-on, bystander, passer-by, witness, eye-witness, observer.

**F3** player, participant.

**spectre** *n* ghost, phantom, spirit, wraith, apparition, vision, presence.

**speculate** *v* wonder, contemplate, meditate, muse, reflect, consider, deliberate, theorize, suppose, guess, conjecture, surmise, gamble, risk, hazard, venture.

**speculative** *adj* conjectural, hypothetical, theoretical, notional, abstract, academic, tentative, risky, hazardous, uncertain, unpredictable.

**speech** n **1** DICTION, articulation, enunciation, elocution, delivery, utterance, voice, language, tongue, parlance, dialect, jargon. **2** *make a speech*: oration, address, discourse, talk, lecture, harangue, spiel (*sl*), conversation, dialogue, monologue, soliloquy.

**speechless** adj dumbfounded, thunderstruck, amazed, aghast, tongue-tied, inarticulate, mute, dumb, silent, mum.

**E3** talkative.

**speed** n velocity, rate, pace, tempo, quickness, swiftness, rapidity, celerity, alacrity, haste, hurry, dispatch, rush, acceleration.

**E3** slowness, delay.

*v* race, tear, belt (*infml*), zoom, career, bowl along, sprint, gallop, hurry, rush, hasten, accelerate, quicken, put one's foot down (*infml*), step on it (*infml*).

**E3** slow, delay.

**speedy** adj fast, quick, swift, rapid, nimble, express, prompt, immediate, hurried, hasty, precipitate, cursory.

**E3** slow, leisurely.

**spell**¹ n period, time, bout, session, term, season, interval, stretch, patch, turn, stint.

**spell**² n charm, incantation, magic, sorcery, witchery, bewitchment, enchantment, fascination, glamour.

**spellbound** adj transfixed, hypnotized, mesmerized, fascinated, enthralled, gripped, entranced, captivated, bewitched, enchanted, charmed.

**spend** v **1** *spend money*: disburse, pay out, fork out (*infml*), shell out (*infml*), invest, lay out, splash out (*infml*), waste, squander, fritter, expend, consume, use up, exhaust. **2** PASS, fill, occupy, use, employ, apply, devote.

**E3 1** save, hoard.

**spendthrift** n squanderer, prodigal, profligate, wastrel.

**E3** miser.

*adj* improvident, extravagant, prodigal, wasteful.

**sphere** n **1** BALL, globe, orb, round. **2** DOMAIN, realm, province, department, territory, field, range, scope, compass, rank, function, capacity.

**spherical** adj round, rotund, ball-shaped, globe-shaped.

**spicy** adj **1** PIQUANT, hot, pungent, tangy, seasoned, aromatic, fragrant. **2** RACY, risqué, ribald, suggestive, indelicate, improper, indecorous, unseemly, scandalous, sensational.

**E3 1** bland, insipid. **2** decent.

**spike** n point, prong, tine, spine, barb, nail, stake.

*v* impale, stick, spear, skewer, spit.

**spill** v overturn, upset, slop, overflow, disgorge, pour, tip, discharge, shed, scatter.

**spin** v turn, revolve, rotate, twist, gyrate, twirl, pirouette, wheel, whirl, swirl, reel.

n **1** TURN, revolution, twist, gyration, twirl, pirouette, whirl, swirl. **2** COMMOTION, agitation, panic, flap (*infml*), state (*infml*), tizzy (*infml*). **3** DRIVE, ride, run.

**spin out** prolong, protract, extend, lengthen, amplify, pad out.

**spindle** n axis, pivot, pin, rod, axle.

**spine** n **1** BACKBONE, spinal column, vertebral column, vertebrae. **2** THORN, barb, prickle, bristle, quill.

**spineless** adj weak, feeble, irresolute, ineffective, cowardly, faint-hearted, lily-livered, yellow (*sl*), soft, wet, submissive, weak-kneed.

**E3** strong, brave.

**spiral** adj winding, coiled, corkscrew, helical, whorled, scrolled, circular.

n coil, helix, corkscrew, screw, whorl, convolution.

**spire** n steeple, pinnacle, peak, summit, top, tip, point, spike.

**spirit** n **1** SOUL, psyche, mind,

breath, life. **2** GHOST, spectre, phantom, apparition, angel, demon, fairy, sprite. **3** LIVELINESS, vivacity, animation, sparkle, vigour, energy, zest, fire, ardour, motivation, enthusiasm, zeal, enterprise, resolution, willpower, courage, backbone, mettle. **4** *the spirit of the law*: meaning, sense, substance, essence, gist, tenor, character, quality. **5** MOOD, humour, temper, disposition, temperament, feeling, morale, attitude, outlook.

**spirited** *adj* lively, vivacious, animated, sparkling, high-spirited, vigorous, energetic, active, ardent, zealous, bold, courageous, mettlesome, plucky.
**Ea** spiritless, lethargic, cowardly.

**spiritual** *adj* unworldly, incorporeal, immaterial, otherwordly, heavenly, divine, holy, sacred, religious, ecclesiastical.
**Ea** physical, material.

**spit** *v* expectorate, eject, discharge, splutter, hiss.
*n* spittle, saliva, slaver, drool, dribble, sputum, phlegm, expectoration.

**spite** *n* spitefulness, malice, venom, gall, bitterness, rancour, animosity, ill feeling, grudge, malevolence, malignity, ill nature, hate, hatred.
**Ea** goodwill, compassion, affection.
*v* annoy, irritate, irk, vex, provoke, gall, hurt, injure, offend, put out.

**spiteful** *adj* malicious, venomous, catty, bitchy, snide, barbed, cruel, vindictive, vengeful, malevolent, malignant, ill-natured, ill-disposed, nasty.
**Ea** charitable, affectionate.

**splash** *v* **1** BATHE, wallow, paddle, wade, dabble, plunge, wet, wash, shower, spray, squirt, sprinkle, spatter, splatter, splodge, spread, daub, plaster, slop, slosh, plop, surge, break, dash, strike, buffet, smack. **2** PUBLICIZE, flaunt, blazon, trumpet.

*n* **1** SPOT, patch, splatter, splodge, burst, touch, dash. **2** PUBLICITY, display, ostentation, effect, impact, stir, excitement, sensation.

**splendid** *adj* brilliant, dazzling, glittering, lustrous, bright, radiant, glowing, glorious, magnificent, gorgeous, resplendent, sumptuous, luxurious, lavish, rich, fine, grand, stately, imposing, impressive, great, outstanding, remarkable, exceptional, sublime, supreme, superb, excellent, first-class, wonderful, marvellous, admirable.
**Ea** drab, ordinary, run-of-the-mill.

**splendour** *n* brightness, radiance, brilliance, dazzle, lustre, glory, resplendence, magnificence, richness, grandeur, majesty, solemnity, pomp, ceremony, display, show, spectacle.
**Ea** drabness, squalor.

**splice** *v* join, unite, wed, marry, bind, tie, plait, braid, interweave, interlace, intertwine, entwine, mesh, knit, graft.

**splinter** *n* sliver, shiver, chip, shard, fragment, flake, shaving, paring.
*v* split, fracture, smash, shatter, shiver, fragment, disintegrate.

**split** *v* divide, separate, partition, part, disunite, disband, open, gape, fork, diverge, break, splinter, shiver, snap, crack, burst, rupture, tear, rend, rip, slit, slash, cleave, halve, slice up, share, distribute, parcel out.
*n* **1** DIVISION, separation, partition, break, breach, gap, cleft, crevice, crack, fissure, rupture, tear, rent, rip, rift, slit, slash. **2** SCHISM, disunion, dissension, discord, difference, divergence, break-up.
*adj* divided, cleft, cloven, bisected, dual, twofold, broken, fractured, cracked, ruptured.

**split up** part, part company, disband, break up, separate, divorce.

**spoil** *v* **1** MAR, upset, wreck, ruin, destroy, damage, impair, harm, hurt, injure, deface, disfigure, blemish.

**2** *spoil a child*: indulge, pamper, cosset, coddle, mollycoddle, baby, spoon-feed. **3** DETERIORATE, go bad, go off, sour, turn, curdle, decay, decompose.

**spoils** *n* plunder, loot, booty, haul, swag (*sl*), pickings, gain, acquisitions, prizes, winnings.

**sponge** *v* **1** WIPE, mop, clean, wash. **2** CADGE, scrounge.

**sponger** *n* cadger, scrounger, parasite, hanger-on.

**spongy** *adj* soft, cushioned, yielding, elastic, springy, porous, absorbent, light.

**sponsor** *n* patron, backer, angel (*infml*), promoter, underwriter, guarantor, surety.
*v* finance, fund, bankroll, subsidize, patronize, back, promote, underwrite, guarantee.

**spontaneous** *adj* natural, unforced, untaught, instinctive, impulsive, unpremeditated, free, willing, unhesitating, voluntary, unprompted, impromptu, extempore.
**F3** forced, studied, planned, deliberate.

**sporadic** *adj* occasional, intermittent, infrequent, isolated, spasmodic, erratic, irregular, uneven, random, scattered.
**F3** frequent, regular.

**sport** *n* **1** GAME, exercise, activity, pastime, amusement, entertainment, diversion, recreation, play. **2** FUN, mirth, humour, joking, jesting, banter, teasing, mockery, ridicule.

*Sports include*: badminton, fives, lacrosse, squash, table-tennis, ping-pong (*infml*); tennis; American football, baseball, basketball, billiards, boules, bowls, cricket, croquet, football, golf, handball, hockey, netball, pétanque, pitch and putt, polo, pool, putting, rounders, Rugby, snooker, soccer, tenpin bowling, volleyball; athletics, cross-country,

decathlon, discus, high-jump, hurdling, javelin, long-jump, marathon, pentathlon, pole vault, running, shot put, triple-jump; angling, canoeing, diving, fishing, rowing, sailing, skin-diving, surfing, swimming, synchronized swimming, water polo, water-skiing, windsurfing, yachting; bobsleigh, curling, ice-hockey, ice-skating, skiing, speed skating, tobogganing (luging); aerobics, fencing, gymnastics, jogging, keep-fit, roller-skating, trampolining; archery, darts, quoits; boxing, judo, jujitsu, karate, tae kwon do, weightlifting, wrestling; climbing, mountaineering, rock-climbing, walking, orienteering, pot-holing; cycle racing, drag-racing, go-karting, motor racing, speedway racing, stock-car racing, greyhound-racing, horse-racing, show-jumping, trotting, hunting, shooting, clay-pigeon shooting; gliding, sky-diving.

*Types of sports equipment include*: ball, basketball, boule, bowl, jack, wood, football, netball, rugby ball, tenpin bowling ball, volleyball; fishing-rod, fly rod, spinning rod, fishing-line, paternoster, reel, fly reel, hook, gaff, gang-hook, jig, trace, lure, bait, fly, float, net, keep-net, priest, disgorger; bow, arrow, crossbow, bolt; badminton racket, shuttlecock, net; baseball bat, baseball, mitt, catcher's glove; boxing glove, gum shield, punch-bag, punch-ball; cricket bat, cricket ball, wicket, stump, bail, nets; épée, foil, sabre, face-guard, mask; discus, hammer, javelin, shot; golf club, golf ball, tee, golfing glove; asymmetrical bars, horizontal bar, isometric bar, parallel-bars, beam, balance-beam, mat, pommel horse, vaulting horse, rings, rope, springboard, trampoline; hockey stick, hockey ball, ice-hockey

stick, puck, hockey skate; curling
stone; ice-skate, roller-skate,
rollerblade, roller boot, speed skate,
skateboard; ski, ski stick, snow
board, toboggan; snooker ball,
billiard ball, cue ball, table, cue, rest,
bridge, rack, chalk; squash racket,
squash ball; table-tennis bat, table-
tennis ball, net; tennis racket, tennis
ball, net, racket press; oar, aqualung,
snorkel, water-ski, sailboard,
surfboard.

*v* wear, display, exhibit, show off.

**sporting** *adj* sportsmanlike,
gentlemanly, decent, considerate,
fair.

**F3** unsporting, ungentlemanly, unfair.

**sporty** *adj* **1** ATHLETIC, fit,
energetic, outdoor. **2** STYLISH,
trendy (*infml*), jaunty, natty (*infml*),
snazzy (*infml*), showy, loud, flashy,
casual, informal.

**spot** *n* **1** DOT, speckle, fleck, mark,
speck, blotch, blot, smudge, daub,
splash, stain, discoloration, blemish,
flaw, pimple. **2** PLACE, point,
position, situation, location, site,
scene, locality. **3** (*infml*) PLIGHT,
predicament, quandary, difficulty,
trouble, mess.

*v* see, notice, observe, detect,
discern, identify, recognize.

**spotless** *adj* immaculate, clean,
white, gleaming, spick and span,
unmarked, unstained, unblemished,
unsullied, pure, chaste, virgin,
untouched, innocent, blameless,
faultless, irreproachable.

**F3** dirty, impure.

**spotted** *adj* dotted, speckled,
flecked, mottled, dappled, pied.

**spotty** *adj* pimply, pimpled, blotchy,
spotted.

**spouse** *n* husband, wife, partner,
mate, better half (*infml*).

**spout** *v* jet, spurt, squirt, spray,
shoot, gush, stream, surge, erupt,
emit, discharge.

*n* jet, fountain, geyser, gargoyle,
outlet, nozzle, rose, spray.

**sprawl** *v* spread, straggle, trail,
ramble, flop, slump, slouch, loll,
lounge, recline, repose.

**spray**[1] *v* shower, spatter, sprinkle,
scatter, diffuse, wet, drench.

*n* **1** MOISTURE, drizzle, mist, foam,
froth. **2** AEROSOL, atomizer,
sprinkler.

**spray**[2] *n* sprig, branch, corsage,
posy, bouquet, garland, wreath.

**spread** *v* **1** STRETCH, extend,
sprawl, broaden, widen, dilate,
expand, swell, mushroom,
proliferate, escalate, open, unroll,
unfurl, unfold, fan out, cover, lay
out, arrange. **2** SCATTER, strew,
diffuse, radiate, disseminate,
broadcast, transmit, communicate,
promulgate, propagate, publicize,
advertise, publish, circulate,
distribute.

**F3** **1** close, fold. **2** suppress.

*n* **1** STRETCH, reach, span, extent,
expanse, sweep, compass. **2** *the spread
of disease*: advance, development,
expansion, increase, proliferation,
escalation, diffusion, dissemination,
dispersion.

**spree** *n* bout, fling, binge, splurge,
orgy, revel.

**sprightly** *adj* agile, nimble, spry,
active, energetic, lively, spirited,
vivacious, hearty, brisk, jaunty,
cheerful, blithe, airy.

**F3** doddering, inactive, lifeless.

**spring**[1] *v* **1** JUMP, leap, vault,
bound, hop, bounce, rebound, recoil.
**2** ORIGINATE, derive, come, stem,
arise, start, proceed, issue, emerge,
emanate, appear, sprout, grow,
develop.

*n* **1** JUMP, leap, vault, bound,
bounce. **2** SPRINGINESS, resilience,
give, flexibility, elasticity, buoyancy.

**spring**[2] *n* source, origin, beginning,
cause, root, fountainhead, wellhead,
wellspring, well, geyser, spa.

**springy** adj bouncy, resilient, flexible, elastic, stretchy, rubbery, spongy, buoyant.
₣₃ hard, stiff.

**sprinkle** v shower, spray, spatter, scatter, strew, dot, pepper, dust, powder.

**sprint** v run, race, dash, tear, belt (infml), dart, shoot.

**sprout** v shoot, bud, germinate, grow, develop, come up, spring up.

**spruce** adj smart, elegant, neat, trim, dapper, well-dressed, well-turned-out, well-groomed, sleek.
₣₃ scruffy, untidy.

**spruce up** neaten, tidy, smarten up, groom.

**spur** v goad, prod, poke, prick, stimulate, prompt, incite, drive, propel, impel, urge, encourage, motivate.
₣₃ curb, discourage.
n incentive, encouragement, inducement, motive, stimulus, incitement, impetus, fillip.
₣₃ curb, disincentive.

**spurious** adj false, fake, counterfeit, forged, bogus, phoney (infml), mock, sham, feigned, pretended, simulated, imitation, artificial.
₣₃ genuine, authentic, real.

**spurn** v reject, turn down, scorn, despise, disdain, rebuff, repulse, slight, snub, cold-shoulder, ignore, disregard.
₣₃ accept, embrace.

**spurt** v gush, squirt, jet, shoot, burst, erupt, surge.
n burst, rush, surge, spate, fit, access.

**spy** n secret agent, undercover agent, double agent, mole (infml), fifth columnist, scout, snooper.
v spot, glimpse, notice, observe, discover.

**squabble** v bicker, wrangle, quarrel, row, argue, dispute, clash, brawl, scrap, fight.

**squad** n crew, team, gang, band, group, company, brigade, troop, force, outfit.

**squalid** adj dirty, filthy, unclean, foul, disgusting, repulsive, sordid, seedy, dingy, untidy, slovenly, unkempt, broken-down, run-down, neglected, uncared-for, low, mean, nasty.
₣₃ clean, pleasant, attractive.

**squander** v waste, misspend, misuse, lavish, blow (sl), fritter away, throw away, dissipate, scatter, spend, expend, consume.

**square** v settle, reconcile, tally, agree, accord, harmonize, correspond, match, balance, straighten, level, align, adjust, regulate, adapt, tailor, fit, suit.
adj 1 QUADRILATERAL, rectangular, right-angled, perpendicular, straight, true, even, level. 2 FAIR, equitable, just, ethical, honourable, honest, genuine, above-board, on the level (infml).

**squash** v 1 CRUSH, flatten, press, squeeze, compress, crowd, trample, stamp, pound, pulp, smash, distort. 2 SUPPRESS, silence, quell, quash, annihilate, put down, snub, humiliate.
₣₃ 1 stretch, expand.

**squat** adj short, stocky, thickset, dumpy, chunky, stubby.
₣₃ slim, lanky.
v crouch, stoop, bend, sit.

**squawk** v, n screech, shriek, cry, croak, cackle, crow, hoot.

**squeak** v, n squeal, whine, creak, peep, cheep.

**squeal** v, n cry, shout, yell, yelp, wail, scream, screech, shriek, squawk.

**squeamish** adj queasy, nauseated, sick, delicate, fastidious, particular, prudish.

**squeeze** v 1 PRESS, squash, crush, pinch, nip, compress, grip, clasp, clutch, hug, embrace, enfold, cuddle. 2 squeeze into a corner: cram, stuff, pack, crowd, wedge, jam, force, ram, push, thrust, shove, jostle. **3** WRING, wrest, extort, milk, bleed, force, lean on (*infml*).

*n* **1** PRESS, squash, crush, crowd, congestion, jam. **2** HUG, embrace, hold, grasp, clasp.

**squirt** *v* spray, spurt, jet, shoot, spout, gush, ejaculate, discharge, emit, eject, expel.

*n* spray, spurt, jet.

**stab** *v* pierce, puncture, cut, wound, injure, gore, knife, spear, stick, jab, thrust.

*n* **1** ACHE, pang, twinge, prick, puncture, cut, incision, gash, wound, jab. **2** (*infml*) TRY, attempt, endeavour, bash (*infml*).

**stability** *n* steadiness, firmness, soundness, constancy, steadfastness, strength, sturdiness, solidity, durability, permanence.

E3 instability, unsteadiness, insecurity, weakness.

**stable** *adj* steady, firm, secure, fast, sound, sure, constant, steadfast, reliable, established, well-founded, deep-rooted, strong, sturdy, durable, lasting, enduring, abiding, permanent, unchangeable, unalterable, invariable, immutable, fixed, static, balanced.

E3 unstable, wobbly, shaky, weak.

**stack** *n* heap, pile, mound, mass, load, accumulation, hoard, stockpile.

*v* heap, pile, load, amass, accumulate, assemble, gather, save, hoard, stockpile.

**staff** *n* **1** *member of staff*: personnel, workforce, employees, workers, crew, team, teachers, officers. **2** STICK, cane, rod, baton, wand, pole, prop.

**stage** *n* point, juncture, step, phase, period, division, lap, leg, length, level, floor.

*v* mount, put on, present, produce, give, do, perform, arrange, organize, stage-manage, orchestrate, engineer.

**stagger** *v* **1** LURCH, totter, teeter, wobble, sway, rock, reel, falter,

hesitate, waver. **2** SURPRISE, amaze, astound, astonish, stun, stupefy, dumbfound, flabbergast (*infml*), shake, shock, confound, overwhelm.

**stagnant** *adj* still, motionless, standing, brackish, stale, sluggish, torpid, lethargic.

E3 fresh, moving.

**stagnate** *v* vegetate, idle, languish, decline, deteriorate, degenerate, decay, rot, rust.

**staid** *adj* sedate, calm, composed, sober, demure, solemn, serious, grave, quiet, steady.

E3 jaunty, debonair, frivolous, adventurous.

**stain** *v* **1** MARK, spot, blemish, blot, smudge, discolour, dirty, soil, taint, contaminate, sully, tarnish, blacken, disgrace. **2** DYE, tint, tinge, colour, paint, varnish.

*n* mark, spot, blemish, blot, smudge, discoloration, smear, slur, disgrace, shame, dishonour.

**stake**[1] *n* post, pole, standard, picket, pale, paling, spike, stick.

**stake**[2] *n* bet, wager, pledge, interest, concern, involvement, share, investment, claim.

*v* gamble, bet, wager, pledge, risk, chance, hazard, venture.

**stale** *adj* **1** *stale bread*: dry, hard, old, musty, fusty, flat, insipid, tasteless. **2** OVERUSED, hackneyed, clichéed, stereotyped, jaded, worn-out, unoriginal, trite, banal, commonplace.

E3 **1** crisp. **2** new.

**stalemate** *n* draw, tie, deadlock, impasse, standstill, halt.

E3 progress.

**stalk**[1] *v* track, trail, hunt, follow, pursue, shadow, tail, haunt.

**stalk**[2] *n* stem, twig, branch, trunk.

**stall** *v* temporize, play for time, delay, hedge, equivocate, obstruct, stonewall.

**stalwart** *adj* strong, sturdy, robust, rugged, stout, strapping, muscular,

athletic, vigorous, valiant, daring,
intrepid, indomitable, determined,
resolute, staunch, steadfast, reliable,
dependable.
**F3** weak, feeble, timid.

**stamina** n energy, vigour, strength,
power, force, grit, resilience,
resistance, endurance,
indefatigability, staying power.
**F3** weakness.

**stammer** v stutter, stumble, falter,
hesitate, splutter.

**stamp** v 1 TRAMPLE, crush, beat,
pound. 2 IMPRINT, impress, print,
inscribe, engrave, emboss, mark,
brand, label, categorize, identify,
characterize.
n print, imprint, impression, seal,
signature, authorization, mark,
hallmark, attestation, brand, cast,
mould, cut, form, fashion, sort, kind,
type, breed, character, description.

**stampede** n charge, rush, dash,
sprint, flight, rout.
v charge, rush, dash, tear, run,
sprint, gallop, shoot, fly, flee, scatter.

**stance** n posture, deportment,
carriage, bearing, position,
standpoint, viewpoint, angle, point of
view, attitude.

**stand** v 1 PUT, place, set, erect, up-
end, position, station. 2 *I can't stand
it*: bear, tolerate, abide, endure,
suffer, experience, undergo,
withstand, weather. 3 RISE, get up,
stand up.
n base, pedestal, support, frame,
rack, table, stage, platform, place,
stall, booth.

**stand by** support, back, champion,
defend, stick up for, uphold, adhere to,
hold to, stick by.
**F3** let down.

**stand down** step down, resign,
abdicate, quit, give up, retire,
withdraw.
**F3** join.

**stand for** represent, symbolize, mean,
signify, denote, indicate.

**stand in for** deputize for, cover for,
understudy, replace, substitute for.

**stand out** show, catch the eye, stick
out, jut out, project.

**stand up for** defend, stick up for, side
with, fight for, support, protect,
champion, uphold.
**F3** attack.

**stand up to** defy, oppose, resist,
withstand, endure, face, confront,
brave.
**F3** give in to.

**standard** n 1 NORM, average, type,
model, pattern, example, sample,
guideline, benchmark, touchstone,
yardstick, rule, measure, gauge, level,
criterion, requirement, specification,
grade, quality. 2 FLAG, ensign,
pennant, pennon, colours, banner.
adj normal, average, typical, stock,
classic, basic, staple, usual,
customary, popular, prevailing,
regular, approved, accepted,
recognized, official, orthodox, set,
established, definitive.
**F3** abnormal, unusual, irregular.

**standardize** v normalize, equalize,
homogenize, stereotype, mass-
produce.
**F3** differentiate.

**standards** n principles, ideals,
morals, ethics.

**standoffish** adj aloof, remote,
distant, unapproachable, unsociable,
uncommunicative, reserved, cold.
**F3** friendly.

**standpoint** n position, station,
vantagepoint, stance, viewpoint,
angle, point of view.

**standstill** n stop, halt, pause, lull,
rest, stoppage, jam, log-jam, hold-up,
impasse, deadlock, stalemate.
**F3** advance, progress.

**staple** adj basic, fundamental,
primary, key, main, chief, major,
principal, essential, necessary,
standard.
**F3** minor.

**star** n celebrity, personage,

luminary, idol, lead, leading man, leading lady, superstar.

*Types of star include*: nova, supernova, pulsar, falling-star, shooting-star, meteor, comet, Halley's comet, red giant, supergiant, white dwarf, red dwarf, brown dwarf, neutron star, Pole Star, Polaris, North Star.

**stare** v gaze, look, watch, gape, gawp, gawk, goggle, glare.
n gaze, look, glare.

**stark** adj 1 *stark landscape*: bare, barren, bleak, bald, plain, simple, austere, harsh, severe, grim, dreary, gloomy, depressing. 2 UTTER, unmitigated, total, consummate, absolute, sheer, downright, out-and-out, flagrant, arrant.

**start** v 1 BEGIN, commence, originate, initiate, introduce, pioneer, create, found, establish, set up, institute, inaugurate, launch, open, kick off (*infml*), instigate, activate, trigger, set off, set out, leave, depart, appear, arise, issue. 2 JUMP, jerk, twitch, flinch, recoil.
F3 1 stop, finish, end.
n 1 BEGINNING, commencement, outset, inception, dawn, birth, break, outburst, onset, origin, initiation, introduction, foundation, inauguration, launch, opening, kick-off (*infml*). 2 JUMP, jerk, twitch, spasm, convulsion, fit.
F3 1 stop, finish, end.

**startle** v surprise, amaze, astonish, astound, shock, scare, frighten, alarm, agitate, upset, disturb.
F3 calm.

**starvation** n hunger, undernourishment, malnutrition, famine.
F3 plenty, excess.

**starve** v hunger, fast, diet, deprive, refuse, deny, die, perish.
F3 feed, gorge.

**starving** adj hungry, underfed, undernourished, ravenous, famished.

**state** v say, declare, announce, report, communicate, assert, aver, affirm, specify, present, express, put, formulate, articulate, voice.
n 1 CONDITION, shape, situation, position, circumstances, case. 2 NATION, country, land, territory, kingdom, republic, government. 3 (*infml*) PANIC, flap (*infml*), tizzy (*infml*), bother, plight, predicament. 4 POMP, ceremony, dignity, majesty, grandeur, glory, splendour.
adj national, governmental, public, official, formal, ceremonial, pompous, stately.

**stately** adj grand, imposing, impressive, elegant, majestic, regal, royal, imperial, noble, august, lofty, pompous, dignified, measured, deliberate, solemn, ceremonious.
F3 informal, unimpressive.

**statement** n account, report, bulletin, communiqué, announcement, declaration, proclamation, communication, utterance, testimony.

**static** adj stationary, motionless, immobile, unmoving, still, inert, resting, fixed, constant, changeless, unvarying, stable.
F3 dynamic, mobile, varying.

**station** n place, location, position, post, headquarters, base, depot.
v locate, set, establish, install, garrison, post, send, appoint, assign.

**stationary** adj motionless, immobile, unmoving, still, static, inert, standing, resting, parked, moored, fixed.
F3 mobile, moving, active.

**statue** n figure, head, bust, effigy, idol, statuette, carving, bronze.

**status** n rank, grade, degree, level, class, station, standing, position, state, condition, prestige, eminence, distinction, importance, consequence, weight.

**F3** unimportance, insignificance.

**staunch** *adj* loyal, faithful, hearty, strong, stout, firm, sound, sure, true, trusty, reliable, dependable, steadfast.
**F3** unfaithful, weak, unreliable.

**stay** *v* 1 LAST, continue, endure, abide, remain, linger, persist.
2 RESIDE, dwell, live, settle, sojourn, stop, halt, pause, wait.
**F3** 1 go, leave.
*n* visit, holiday, stopover, sojourn.

**steady** *adj* stable, balanced, poised, fixed, immovable, firm, poised, settled, still, calm, imperturbable, equable, even, uniform, consistent, unvarying, unchanging, constant, persistent, unremitting, incessant, uninterrupted, unbroken, regular, rhythmic, steadfast, unwavering.
**F3** unsteady, unstable, variable, wavering.
*v* balance, stabilize, fix, secure, brace, support.

**steal** *v* 1 *steal a car*: thieve, pilfer, filch, pinch (*infml*), nick (*infml*), take, appropriate, snatch, swipe, shoplift, poach, embezzle, lift, plagiarize. 2 CREEP, tiptoe, slip, slink, sneak.
**F3** 1 return, give back.

**stealthy** *adj* surreptitious, clandestine, covert, secret, unobtrusive, secretive, quiet, furtive, sly, cunning, sneaky, underhand.
**F3** open.

**steam** *n* vapour, mist, haze, condensation, moisture, dampness.

**steep** *adj* 1 *a steep slope*: sheer, precipitous, headlong, abrupt, sudden, sharp. 2 (*infml*) EXCESSIVE, extreme, stiff, unreasonable, high, exorbitant, extortionate, overpriced.
**F3** 1 gentle, gradual. 2 moderate, low.

**steer** *v* pilot, guide, direct, control, govern, conduct.

**stem**[1] *n* stalk, shoot, stock, branch, trunk.

**stem**[2] *v* stop, halt, arrest, stanch,

staunch, block, dam, check, curb, restrain, contain, resist, oppose.
**F3** encourage.

**stench** *n* stink, reek, pong (*infml*), smell, odour.

**step** *n* 1 PACE, stride, footstep, tread, footprint, print, trace, track.
2 MOVE, act, action, deed, measure, procedure, process, proceeding, progression, movement, stage, phase, degree. 3 RUNG, stair, level, rank, point.
*v* pace, stride, tread, stamp, walk, move.

**step down** stand down, resign, abdicate, quit, leave, retire, withdraw.
**F3** join.

**step up** increase, raise, augment, boost, build up, intensify, escalate, accelerate, speed up.
**F3** decrease.

**stereotype** *n* formula, convention, mould, pattern, model.
*v* categorize, pigeonhole, typecast, standardize, formalize, conventionalize, mass-produce.
**F3** differentiate.

**sterile** *adj* 1 GERM-FREE, aseptic, sterilized, disinfected, antiseptic, uncontaminated. 2 INFERTILE, barren, arid, bare, unproductive, fruitless, pointless, useless, abortive.
**F3** 1 septic. 2 fertile, fruitful.

**sterilize** *v* disinfect, fumigate, purify, clean, cleanse.
**F3** contaminate, infect.

**stern** *adj* strict, severe, authoritarian, rigid, inflexible, unyielding, hard, tough, rigorous, stringent, harsh, cruel, unsparing, relentless, unrelenting, grim, forbidding, stark, austere.
**F3** kind, gentle, mild, lenient.

**stew** *v* boil, simmer, braise, casserole.

**stick**[1] *v* 1 THRUST, poke, stab, jab, pierce, penetrate, puncture, spear, transfix. 2 GLUE, gum, paste, cement, bond, fuse, weld, solder,

adhere, cling, hold. **3** ATTACH, affix, fasten, secure, fix, pin, join, bind.
**4** put, place, position, set, install, deposit, drop.

**stick at** persevere, plug away (*infml*), persist, continue.

**Ea** give up.

**stick out** protrude, jut out, project, extend.

**stick up for** stand up for, speak up for, defend, champion, support, uphold.

**Ea** attack.

**stick²** *n* branch, twig, wand, baton, staff, sceptre, cane, birch, rod, pole, stake.

**sticky** *adj* **1** ADHESIVE, gummed, tacky, gluey, gummy, viscous, glutinous, gooey (*infml*). **2** (*infml*) a *sticky situation*: difficult, tricky, thorny, unpleasant, awkward, embarrassing, delicate. **3** HUMID, clammy, muggy, close, oppressive, sultry.

**Ea 1** dry. **2** easy. **3** fresh, cool.

**stiff** *adj* **1** RIGID, inflexible, unbending, unyielding, hard, solid, hardened, solidified, firm, tight, taut, tense. **2** FORMAL, ceremonious, pompous, stand-offish, cold, prim, priggish, austere, strict, severe, harsh. **3** DIFFICULT, hard, tough, arduous, laborious, awkward, exacting, rigorous.

**Ea 1** flexible. **2** informal. **3** easy.

**stiffen** *v* harden, solidify, tighten, tense, brace, reinforce, starch, thicken, congeal, coagulate, jell, set.

**stifle** *v* smother, suffocate, asphyxiate, strangle, choke, extinguish, muffle, dampen, deaden, silence, hush, suppress, quell, check, curb, restrain, repress.

**Ea** encourage.

**stigma** *n* brand, mark, stain, blot, spot, blemish, disgrace, shame, dishonour.

**Ea** credit, honour.

**still** *adj* stationary, motionless, lifeless, stagnant, smooth,

undisturbed, unruffled, calm, tranquil, serene, restful, peaceful, hushed, quiet, silent, noiseless.

**Ea** active, disturbed, agitated, noisy.

*v* calm, soothe, allay, tranquillize, subdue, restrain, hush, quieten, silence, pacify, settle, smooth.

**Ea** agitate, stir up.

*adv* yet, even so, nevertheless, nonetheless, notwithstanding, however.

**stilted** *adj* artificial, unnatural, stiff, wooden, forced, constrained.

**Ea** fluent, flowing.

**stimulate** *v* rouse, arouse, animate, quicken, fire, inflame, inspire, motivate, encourage, induce, urge, impel, spur, prompt, goad, provoke, incite, instigate, trigger off.

**Ea** discourage, hinder, prevent.

**stimulus** *n* incentive, encouragement, inducement, spur, goad, provocation, incitement.

**Ea** discouragement.

**sting** *v* **1** *bees sting*: bite, prick, hurt, injure, wound. **2** SMART, tingle, burn, pain.

*n* bite, nip, prick, smart, tingle.

**stingy** *adj* mean, miserly, niggardly, tight-fisted (*infml*), parsimonious, penny-pinching.

**Ea** generous, liberal.

**stink** *v* smell, reek, pong (*infml*), hum (*sl*).

*n* smell, odour, stench, pong (*infml*), niff (*sl*).

**stint** *n* spell, stretch, period, time, shift, turn, bit, share, quota.

**stipulate** *v* specify, lay down, require, demand, insist on.

**stipulation** *n* specification, requirement, demand, condition, proviso.

**stir** *v* **1** MOVE, budge, touch, affect, inspire, excite, thrill, disturb, agitate, shake, tremble, quiver, flutter, rustle. **2** MIX, blend, beat.

*n* activity, movement, bustle, flurry, commotion, ado, fuss, to-do (*infml*).

uproar, tumult, disturbance, disorder, agitation, excitement, ferment.
**F3** calm.

**stir up** rouse, arouse, awaken, animate, quicken, kindle, fire, inflame, stimulate, spur, prompt, provoke, incite, instigate, agitate.
**F3** calm, discourage.

**stock** n **1** GOODS, merchandise, wares, commodities, capital, assets, inventory, repertoire, range, variety, assortment, source, supply, fund, reservoir, store, reserve, stockpile, hoard. **2** PARENTAGE, ancestry, descent, extraction, family, line, lineage, pedigree, race, breed, species, blood. **3** LIVESTOCK, animals, cattle, horses, sheep, herds, flocks.
adj standard, basic, regular, routine, ordinary, run-of-the-mill, usual, customary, traditional, conventional, set, stereotyped, hackneyed, overused, banal, trite.
**F3** original, unusual.
v keep, carry, sell, trade in, deal in, handle, supply, provide.

**stock up** gather, accumulate, amass, lay in, provision, fill, replenish, store (up), save, hoard, pile up.

**stocky** adj sturdy, solid, thickset, chunky, short, squat, dumpy, stubby.
**F3** tall, skinny.

**stoical** adj patient, long-suffering, uncomplaining, resigned, philosophical, indifferent, impassive, unemotional, phlegmatic, dispassionate, cool, calm, imperturbable.
**F3** excitable, anxious.

**stolid** adj slow, heavy, dull, bovine, wooden, blockish, lumpish, impassive, phlegmatic, unemotional.
**F3** lively, interested.

**stomach** n tummy (infml), gut, inside(s), belly, abdomen, paunch, pot.
v tolerate, bear, stand, abide, endure, suffer, submit to, take.

**stony** adj **1** BLANK, expressionless, hard, cold, frigid, icy, indifferent, unfeeling, heartless, callous, merciless, pitiless, inexorable, hostile. **2** stony beach: pebbly, shingly, rocky.
**F3 1** warm, soft-hearted, friendly.

**stoop** v **1** HUNCH, bow, bend, incline, lean, duck, squat, crouch, kneel. **2** stoop to blackmail: descend, sink, lower oneself, resort, go so far as, condescend, deign.

**stop** v **1** HALT, cease, end, finish, conclude, terminate, discontinue, suspend, interrupt, pause, quit, refrain, desist, pack in (sl).
**2** PREVENT, bar, frustrate, thwart, intercept, hinder, impede, check, restrain. **3** SEAL, close, plug, block, obstruct, arrest, stem, stanch.
**F3 1** start, continue.
n **1** STATION, terminus, destination. **2** REST, break, pause, stage. **3** HALT, standstill, stoppage, cessation, end, finish, conclusion, termination, discontinuation.
**F3 3** start, beginning, continuation.

**stoppage** n stop, halt, standstill, arrest, blockage, obstruction, check, hindrance, interruption, shutdown, closure, strike, walk-out, sit-in.
**F3** start, continuation.

**stopper** n cork, bung, plug.

**store** v save, keep, put aside, lay by, reserve, stock, lay in, deposit, lay down, lay up, accumulate, hoard, salt away, stockpile, stash (infml).
**F3** use.
n **1** STOCK, supply, provision, fund, reserve, mine, reservoir, hoard, cache, stockpile, accumulation, quantity, abundance, plenty, lot.
**2** STOREROOM, storehouse, warehouse, repository, depository.
**F3** scarcity.

**storey** n floor, level, stage, tier, flight, deck.

**storm** n **1** TEMPEST, thunderstorm, squall, blizzard, gale, hurricane, whirlwind, tornado, cyclone.

*Kinds of storm include*: blizzard, buran, cloudburst, cyclone, downpour, dust-devil, dust-storm, electrical storm, gale, haboob, hailstorm, hurricane, monsoon, rainstorm, sand storm, snow storm, squall, tempest, thunderstorm, tornado, typhoon, whirlwind. *see also* **wind**.

**2** OUTBURST, uproar, furore, outcry, row, rumpus, commotion, tumult, disturbance, turmoil, stir, agitation, rage, outbreak, attack, assault.
**F3** 2 calm.

*v* charge, rush, attack, assault, assail, roar, thunder, rage, rant, rave, fume.

**stormy** *adj* tempestuous, squally, rough, choppy, turbulent, wild, raging, windy, gusty, blustery, foul.
**F3** calm.

**story** *n* **1** TALE, fairy-tale, fable, myth, legend, novel, romance, fiction, yarn, anecdote, episode, plot, narrative, history, chronicle, record, account, relation, recital, report, article, feature.

*Types of story include*: adventure story, bedtime story, blockbuster (*infml*), children's story, comedy, black comedy, crime story, detective story, fable, fairy-tale, fantasy, folk tale, ghost story, historical novel, horror story, legend, love story, Mills & Boon®, mystery, myth, parable, romance, saga, science fiction, sci-fi (*infml*), short story, spiel, spine-chiller, spy story, supernatural tale, tall story, thriller, western, whodunit (*infml*).

**2** LIE, falsehood, untruth.

**stout** *adj* **1** FAT, plump, fleshy, portly, corpulent, overweight, heavy, bulky, big, brawny, beefy, hulking, burly, muscular, athletic. **2** *stout packaging*: strong, tough, durable, thick, sturdy, robust, hardy,

vigorous. **3** BRAVE, courageous, valiant, plucky, fearless, bold, intrepid, dauntless, resolute, stalwart.
**F3** 1 thin, lean, slim. 2 weak.
3 cowardly, timid.

**stow** *v* put away, store, load, pack, cram, stuff, stash (*infml*).
**F3** unload.

**straight** *adj* **1** *a straight line*: level, even, flat, horizontal, upright, vertical, aligned, direct, undeviating, unswerving, true, right. **2** TIDY, neat, orderly, shipshape, organized.
**3** HONOURABLE, honest, law-abiding, respectable, upright, trustworthy, reliable, straightforward, fair, just. **4** FRANK, candid, blunt, forthright, direct. **5** *straight whisky*: undiluted, neat, unadulterated, unmixed.
**F3** 1 bent, crooked. 2 untidy.
3 dishonest. 4 evasive. 5 diluted.
*adv* directly, point-blank, honestly, frankly, candidly.

**straight away** at once, immediately, instantly, right away, directly, now, there and then.
**F3** later, eventually.

**straighten** *v* unbend, align, tidy, neaten, order, arrange.
**F3** bend, twist.

**straighten out** clear up, sort out, settle, resolve, correct, rectify, disentangle, regularize.
**F3** confuse, muddle.

**straightforward** *adj* **1** EASY, simple, uncomplicated, clear, elementary.
**2** HONEST, truthful, sincere, genuine, open, frank, candid, direct, forthright.
**F3** 1 complicated. 2 evasive, devious.

**strain**¹ *v* **1** PULL, wrench, twist, sprain, tear, stretch, extend, tighten, tauten. **2** SIEVE, sift, screen, separate, filter, purify, drain, wring, squeeze, compress, express. **3** WEAKEN, tire, tax, overtax, overwork, labour, try, endeavour, struggle, strive, exert, force, drive.

*n* stress, anxiety, burden, pressure, tension, tautness, pull, sprain, wrench, injury, exertion, effort, struggle, force.
**F3** relaxation.

**strain²** *n* **1** STOCK, ancestry, descent, extraction, family, lineage, pedigree, blood, variety, type. **2** TRAIT, streak, vein, tendency, trace, suggestion, suspicion.

**strained** *adj* forced, constrained, laboured, false, artificial, unnatural, stiff, tense, unrelaxed, uneasy, uncomfortable, awkward, embarrassed, self-conscious.
**F3** natural, relaxed.

**strait-laced** *adj* prudish, stuffy, starchy, prim, proper, strict, narrow, narrow-minded, puritanical, moralistic.
**F3** broad-minded.

**strand** *n* fibre, filament, wire, thread, string, piece, length.

**stranded** *adj* marooned, high and dry, abandoned, forsaken, in the lurch, helpless, grounded, beached, shipwrecked, wrecked.

**strange** *adj* **1** ODD, peculiar, funny (*infml*), curious, queer, weird, bizarre, eccentric, abnormal, irregular, uncommon, unusual, exceptional, remarkable, extraordinary, mystifying, perplexing, unexplained. **2** NEW, novel, untried, unknown, unheard-of, unfamiliar, unacquainted, foreign, alien, exotic.
**F3 1** ordinary, common. **2** well-known, familiar.

**stranger** *n* newcomer, visitor, guest, non-member, outsider, foreigner, alien.
**F3** local, native.

**strangle** *n* throttle, choke, asphyxiate, suffocate, stifle, smother, suppress, gag, repress, inhibit.

**strap** *n* thong, tie, band, belt, leash. *v* **1** BEAT, lash, whip, flog, belt. **2** FASTEN, secure, tie, bind.

**stratagem** *n* plan, scheme, plot, intrigue, ruse, ploy, trick, dodge, manoeuvre, device, artifice, wile, subterfuge.

**strategic** *adj* important, key, critical, decisive, crucial, vital, tactical, planned, calculated, deliberate, politic, diplomatic.
**F3** unimportant.

**strategy** *n* tactics, planning, policy, approach, procedure, plan, programme, design, scheme.

**stray** *v* wander (off), get lost, err, ramble, roam, rove, range, meander, straggle, drift, diverge, deviate, digress.
*adj* **1** LOST, abandoned, homeless, wandering, roaming. **2** RANDOM, chance, accidental, freak, odd, erratic.

**streak** *n* line, stroke, smear, band, stripe, strip, layer, vein, trace, dash, touch, element, strain.
*v* **1** BAND, stripe, fleck, striate, smear, daub. **2** SPEED, tear, hurtle, sprint, gallop, fly, dart, flash, whistle, zoom, whizz, sweep.

**stream** *n* **1** RIVER, creek, brook, beck, burn, rivulet, tributary. **2** CURRENT, drift, flow, run, gush, flood, deluge, cascade, torrent.
*v* issue, well, surge, run, flow, course, pour, spout, gush, flood, cascade.

**streamer** *n* ribbon, banner, pennant, pennon, flag, ensign, standard.

**streamlined** *adj* aerodynamic, smooth, sleek, graceful, efficient, well-run, smooth-running, rationalized, time-saving, organized, slick.
**F3** clumsy, inefficient.

**strength** *n* toughness, robustness, sturdiness, lustiness, brawn, muscle, sinew, power, might, force, vigour, energy, stamina, health, fitness, courage, fortitude, spirit, resolution, firmness, effectiveness, potency, concentration, intensity, vehemence.
**F3** weakness, feebleness, impotence.

**strengthen** v reinforce, brace, steel, fortify, buttress, bolster, support, toughen, harden, stiffen, consolidate, substantiate, corroborate, confirm, encourage, hearten, refresh, restore, invigorate, nourish, increase, heighten, intensify.
🔄 weaken, undermine.

**strenuous** adj 1 *strenuous work*: hard, tough, demanding, gruelling, taxing, laborious, uphill, arduous, tiring, exhausting. 2 ACTIVE, energetic, vigorous, eager, earnest, determined, resolute, spirited, tireless, indefatigable.
🔄 1 easy, effortless.

**stress** n 1 PRESSURE, strain, tension, worry, anxiety, weight, burden, trauma, hassle (*infml*). 2 EMPHASIS, accent, accentuation, beat, force, weight, importance, significance.
🔄 1 relaxation.
v emphasize, accentuate, highlight, underline, underscore, repeat.
🔄 understate, downplay.

**stretch** n 1 EXPANSE, spread, sweep, reach, extent, distance, space, area, tract. 2 PERIOD, time, term, spell, stint, run.
v pull, tighten, tauten, strain, tax, extend, lengthen, elongate, expand, spread, unfold, unroll, inflate, swell, reach.
🔄 compress.
**stretch out** extend, relax, hold out, put out, lie down, reach.
🔄 draw back.

**strict** adj 1 *a strict teacher*: stern, authoritarian, no-nonsense, firm, rigid, inflexible, stringent, rigorous, harsh, severe, austere. 2 EXACT, precise, accurate, literal, faithful, true, absolute, utter, total, complete, thoroughgoing, meticulous, scrupulous, particular, religious.
🔄 1 easy-going (*infml*), flexible.
2 loose.

**strident** adj loud, clamorous,

vociferous, harsh, raucous, grating, rasping, shrill, screeching, unmusical, discordant, clashing, jarring, jangling.
🔄 quiet, soft.

**strife** n conflict, discord, dissension, controversy, animosity, friction, rivalry, contention, quarrel, row, wrangling, struggle, fighting, combat, battle, warfare.
🔄 peace.

**strike** n 1 INDUSTRIAL ACTION, work-to-rule, go-slow, stoppage, sit-in, walk-out, mutiny, revolt. 2 HIT, blow, stroke, raid, attack.
v 1 STOP WORK, down tools, work to rule, walk out, protest, mutiny, revolt. 2 HIT, knock, collide with, slap, smack, cuff, clout, thump, wallop (*infml*), beat, pound, hammer, buffet, raid, attack, afflict. 3 IMPRESS, affect, touch, register. 4 FIND, discover, unearth, uncover, encounter, reach.
**strike out** cross out, delete, strike through, cancel, strike off, remove.
🔄 add.

**striking** adj noticeable, conspicuous, salient, outstanding, remarkable, extraordinary, memorable, impressive, dazzling, arresting, astonishing, stunning.
🔄 unimpressive.

**string** n 1 *a piece of string*: twine, cord, rope, cable, line, strand, fibre. 2 SERIES, succession, sequence, chain, line, row, file, queue, procession, train.
v thread, link, connect, tie up, hang, suspend, festoon, loop.

**stringent** adj binding, strict, severe, rigorous, tough, rigid, inflexible, tight.
🔄 lax, flexible.

**strip**[1] v peel, skin, flay, denude, divest, deprive, undress, disrobe, unclothe, uncover, expose, lay bare, bare, empty, clear, gut, ransack, pillage, plunder, loot.
🔄 dress, clothe, cover.

**strip²** n  ribbon, thong, strap, belt, sash, band, stripe, lath, slat, piece, bit, slip, shred.

**stripe** n  band, line, bar, chevron, flash, streak, fleck, strip, belt.

**strive** v  try, attempt, endeavour, struggle, strain, work, toil, labour, fight, contend, compete.

**stroke** n  1 CARESS, pat, rub. 2 BLOW, hit, knock, swipe. 3 SWEEP, flourish, movement, action, move, line.
v  caress, fondle, pet, touch, pat, rub, massage.

**stroll** v  saunter, amble, dawdle, ramble, wander.
n  saunter, amble, walk, constitutional, turn, ramble.

**strong** adj  1 TOUGH, resilient, durable, hard-wearing, heavy-duty, robust, sturdy, firm, sound, lusty, strapping, stout, burly, well-built, beefy, brawny, muscular, sinewy, athletic, fit, healthy, hardy, powerful, mighty, potent. 2 INTENSE, deep, vivid, fierce, violent, vehement, keen, eager, zealous, fervent, ardent, dedicated, staunch, stalwart, determined, resolute, tenacious, strong-minded, strong-willed, self-assertive. 3 HIGHLY-FLAVOURED, piquant, hot, spicy, highly-seasoned, sharp, pungent, undiluted, concentrated. 4 *strong argument*: convincing, persuasive, cogent, effective, telling, forceful, weighty, compelling, urgent.
**E3** 1 weak, feeble. 2 indecisive. 3 mild, bland. 4 unconvincing.

**stronghold** n  citadel, bastion, fort, fortress, castle, keep, refuge.

**structure** n  construction, erection, building, edifice, fabric, framework, form, shape, design, configuration, conformation, make-up, formation, arrangement, organization, set-up.
v  construct, assemble, build, form, shape, design, arrange, organize.

**struggle** v  strive, work, toil, labour, strain, agonize, fight, battle, wrestle, grapple, contend, compete, vie.
**E3** yield, give in.
n  difficulty, problem, effort, exertion, pains, agony, work, labour, toil, clash, conflict, strife, fight, battle, skirmish, encounter, combat, hostilities, contest.
**E3** ease, submission, co-operation.

**stub** n  end, stump, remnant, fag-end (*infml*), dog-end (*infml*), butt, counterfoil.

**stubborn** adj  obstinate, stiff-necked, mulish, pig-headed, obdurate, intransigent, rigid, inflexible, unbending, unyielding, dogged, persistent, tenacious, headstrong, self-willed, wilful, refractory, difficult, unmanageable.
**E3** compliant, flexible, yielding.

**stuck** adj  1 FAST, jammed, firm, fixed, fastened, joined, glued, cemented. 2 BEATEN, stumped (*infml*), baffled.
**E3** 1 loose.

**stuck-up** (*infml*) adj  snobbish, toffee-nosed (*infml*), supercilious, snooty (*infml*), haughty, high and mighty, condescending, proud, arrogant, conceited, bigheaded (*infml*).
**E3** humble, modest.

**student** n  undergraduate, postgraduate, scholar, schoolboy, schoolgirl, pupil, disciple, learner, trainee, apprentice.

**studied** adj  deliberate, conscious, wilful, intentional, premeditated, planned, calculated, contrived, forced, unnatural, over-elaborate.
**E3** unplanned, impulsive, natural.

**studio** n  workshop, workroom.

**studious** adj  scholarly, academic, intellectual, bookish, serious, thoughtful, reflective, diligent, hard-working, industrious, assiduous, careful, attentive, earnest, eager.
**E3** lazy, idle, negligent.

**study** v  read, learn, revise, cram, swot (*infml*), mug up (*infml*), read up, research, investigate, analyse, survey, scan, examine, scrutinize, peruse, pore over, contemplate, meditate, ponder, consider, deliberate.

*n* **1** READING, homework, preparation, learning, revision, cramming, swotting (*infml*), research, investigation, inquiry, analysis, examination, scrutiny, inspection, contemplation, consideration, attention. **2** REPORT, essay, thesis, paper, monograph, survey, review, critique. **3** OFFICE, den (*infml*).

*Subjects of study include*: accountancy, agriculture, anatomy, anthropology, archaeology, architecture, art, astrology, astronomy, biology, botany, building studies, business studies, calligraphy, chemistry, CDT (craft, design and technology), civil engineering, the Classics, commerce, computer studies, cosmology, craft, dance, design, domestic science, drama, dressmaking, driving, ecology, economics, education, electronics, engineering, environmental studies, ethnology, eugenics, fashion, fitness, food technology, forensics, genetics, geography, geology, heraldry, history, home economics, horticulture, information technology (IT), journalism, languages, law, leisure studies, lexicography, linguistics, literature, logistics, management studies, marketing, mathematics, mechanics, media studies, medicine, metallurgy, metaphysics, meteorology, music, mythology, natural history, oceanography, ornithology, pathology, penology, personal and social education (PSE), personal, health and social education (PHSE), pharmacology, philosophy, photography, physics, physiology, politics, pottery, psychology, religious studies, science, shorthand, social sciences, sociology, sport, statistics, surveying, technology, theology, typewriting, visual arts, word processing, writing, zoology.

**stuff** *v* **1** PACK, stow, load, fill, cram, crowd, force, push, shove, ram, wedge, jam, squeeze, compress. **2** GORGE, gormandise, overindulge, guzzle, gobble, sate, satiate.
**F3** **1** unload, empty. **2** nibble.
*n* **1** MATERIAL, fabric, matter, substance, essence. **2** (*infml*) BELONGINGS, possessions, things, objects, articles, goods, luggage, paraphernalia, gear (*infml*), clobber (*infml*), kit, tackle, equipment, materials.

**stuffing** *n* padding, wadding, quilting, filling, force-meat.

**stuffy** *adj* **1** *a stuffy room*: musty, stale, airless, unventilated, suffocating, stifling, oppressive, heavy, close, muggy, sultry. **2** STAID, strait-laced, prim, conventional, old-fashioned, pompous, dull, dreary, uninteresting, stodgy.
**F3** **1** airy, well-ventilated. **2** informal, modern, lively.

**stumble** *v* **1** TRIP, slip, fall, lurch, reel, stagger, flounder, blunder. **2** STAMMER, stutter, hesitate, falter.
**stumble on** come across, chance upon, happen upon, find, discover, encounter.

**stumbling-block** *n* obstacle, hurdle, barrier, bar, obstruction, hindrance, impediment, difficulty, snag.

**stump** *n* end, remnant, trunk, stub.
*v* (*infml*) defeat, outwit, confound, perplex, puzzle, baffle, mystify, confuse, bewilder, flummox (*infml*), bamboozle (*infml*), dumbfound.
**F3** assist.
**stump up** (*infml*) pay, hand over, fork out (*infml*), shell out (*infml*), donate, contribute, cough up (*infml*).
**F3** receive.

**stun** v amaze, astonish, astound, stagger, shock, daze, stupefy, dumbfound, flabbergast (*infml*), overcome, confound, confuse, bewilder.

**stunning** (*infml*) adj beautiful, lovely, gorgeous, ravishing, dazzling, brilliant, striking, impressive, spectacular, remarkable, wonderful, marvellous, great, sensational.
Ɛɜ ugly, awful.

**stunt¹** n feat, exploit, act, deed, enterprise, trick, turn, performance.

**stunt²** v stop, arrest, check, restrict, slow, retard, hinder, impede, dwarf.
Ɛɜ promote, encourage.

**stupefy** v daze, stun, numb, dumbfound, shock, stagger, amaze, astound.

**stupendous** adj huge, enormous, gigantic, colossal, vast, prodigious, phenomenal, tremendous, breathtaking, overwhelming, staggering, stunning, amazing, astounding, fabulous, fantastic, superb, wonderful, marvellous.
Ɛɜ ordinary, unimpressive.

**stupid** adj 1 SILLY, foolish, irresponsible, ill-advised, indiscreet, foolhardy, rash, senseless, mad, lunatic, brainless, half-witted, idiotic, imbecilic, moronic, feeble-minded, simple-minded, slow, dim, dull, dense, thick, dumb, dopey, crass, inane, puerile, mindless, futile, pointless, meaningless, nonsensical, absurd, ludicrous, ridiculous, laughable. 2 DAZED, groggy, stupefied, stunned, sluggish, semiconscious.
Ɛɜ 1 sensible, wise, clever, intelligent. 2 alert.

**stupor** n daze, stupefaction, torpor, lethargy, inertia, trance, coma, numbness, insensibility, unconsciousness.
Ɛɜ alertness, consciousness.

**sturdy** adj strong, robust, durable, well-made, stout, substantial, solid, well-built, powerful, muscular, athletic, hardy, vigorous, flourishing, hearty, staunch, stalwart, steadfast, firm, resolute, determined.
Ɛɜ weak, flimsy, puny.

**stutter** v stammer, hesitate, falter, stumble, mumble.

**style** n 1 APPEARANCE, cut, design, pattern, shape, form, sort, type, kind, genre, variety, category. 2 ELEGANCE, smartness, chic, flair, panache, stylishness, taste, polish, refinement, sophistication, urbanity, fashion, vogue, trend, mode, dressiness, flamboyance, affluence, luxury, grandeur. 3 *style of working*: technique, approach, method, manner, mode, fashion, way, custom. 4 WORDING, phrasing, expression, tone, tenor.
Ɛɜ 2 inelegance, tastelessness.
v 1 DESIGN, cut, tailor, fashion, shape, adapt. 2 DESIGNATE, term, name, call, address, title, dub, label.

**stylish** adj chic, fashionable, á la mode, modish, in vogue, voguish, trendy (*infml*), snappy, natty (*infml*), snazzy (*infml*), dressy, smart, elegant, classy (*infml*), polished, refined, sophisticated, urbane.
Ɛɜ old-fashioned, shabby.

**suave** adj polite, courteous, charming, agreeable, affable, soft-spoken, smooth, unctuous, sophisticated, urbane, worldly.
Ɛɜ rude, unsophisticated.

**subconscious** adj subliminal, unconscious, intuitive, inner, innermost, hidden, latent, repressed, suppressed.
Ɛɜ conscious.

**subdue** v overcome, quell, suppress, repress, overpower, crush, defeat, conquer, vanquish, overrun, subject, subjugate, humble, break, tame, master, discipline, control, check, moderate, reduce, soften, quieten, damp, mellow.
Ɛɜ arouse, awaken.

**subdued** adj **1** SAD, downcast, dejected, crestfallen, quiet, serious, grave, solemn. **2** QUIET, muted, hushed, soft, dim, shaded, sombre, sober, restrained, unobtrusive, low-key, subtle.
**E₃ 1** lively, excited. **2** striking, obtrusive.

**subject** n **1** TOPIC, theme, matter, issue, question, point, case, affair, business, discipline, field. **2** NATIONAL, citizen, participant, client, patient, victim.
**E₃ 2** monarch, ruler, master.
adj **1** LIABLE, disposed, prone, susceptible, vulnerable, open, exposed. **2** SUBJUGATED, captive, bound, obedient, answerable, subordinate, inferior, subservient, submissive. **3** DEPENDENT, contingent, conditional.
**E₃ 1** vulnerable. **2** free, superior. **3** unconditional.
v expose, lay open, submit, subjugate, subdue.

**subjection** n subjugation, defeat, captivity, bondage, chains, shackles, slavery, enslavement, oppression, domination, mastery.

**subjective** adj biased, prejudiced, personal, individual, idiosyncratic, emotional, intuitive, instinctive.
**E₃** objective, unbiased, impartial.

**sublime** adj exalted, elevated, high, lofty, noble, majestic, great, grand, imposing, magnificent, glorious, transcendent, spiritual.
**E₃** lowly, base.

**submerge** v submerse, immerse, plunge, duck, dip, sink, drown, engulf, overwhelm, swamp, flood, inundate, deluge.
**E₃** surface.

**submerged** adj submersed, immersed, underwater, sunk, sunken, drowned, swamped, inundated, hidden, concealed, unseen.

**submission** n **1** SURRENDER, capitulation, resignation, acquiescence, assent, compliance, obedience, deference, submissiveness, meekness, passivity.
**2** PRESENTATION, offering, contribution, entry, suggestion, proposal.
**E₃ 1** intransigence, intractability.

**submissive** adj yielding, unresisting, resigned, patient, uncomplaining, accommodating, biddable, obedient, deferential, ingratiating, subservient, humble, meek, docile, subdued, passive.
**E₃** intransigent, intractable.

**submit** v **1** YIELD, give in, surrender, capitulate, knuckle under, bow, bend, stoop, succumb, agree, comply. **2** PRESENT, tender, offer, put forward, suggest, propose, table, state, claim, argue.
**E₃ 1** resist. **2** withdraw.

**subordinate** adj secondary, auxiliary, ancillary, subsidiary, dependent, inferior, lower, junior, minor, lesser.
**E₃** superior, senior.
n inferior, junior, assistant, attendant, second, aide, dependant, underling (infml).
**E₃** superior, boss.

**subscribe** v **1** subscribe to a theory: support, endorse, back, advocate, approve, agree. **2** GIVE, donate, contribute.

**subscription** n membership fee, dues, payment, donation, contribution, offering, gift.

**subsequent** adj following, later, future, next, succeeding, consequent, resulting, ensuing.
**E₃** previous, earlier.

**subside** v sink, collapse, settle, descend, fall, drop, lower, decrease, lessen, diminish, dwindle, decline, wane, ebb, recede, moderate, abate, die down, quieten, slacken, ease.
**E₃** rise, increase.

**subsidiary** adj auxiliary, supplementary, additional, ancillary, assistant, supporting, contributory, secondary, subordinate, lesser, minor.

Ⓔ primary, chief, major.

n branch, offshoot, division, section, part.

**subsidize** v support, back, underwrite, sponsor, finance, fund, aid, promote.

**subsidy** n grant, allowance, assistance, help, aid, contribution, sponsorship, finance, support, backing.

**subsistence** n living, survival, existence, livelihood, maintenance, support, keep, sustenance, nourishment, food, provisions, rations.

**substance** n 1 MATTER, material, stuff, fabric, essence, pith, entity, body, solidity, concreteness, reality, actuality, ground, foundation.

2 SUBJECT, subject-matter, theme, gist, meaning, significance, force.

**substandard** adj second-rate, inferior, imperfect, damaged, shoddy, poor, inadequate, unacceptable.

Ⓔ first-rate, superior, perfect.

**substantial** adj large, big, sizable, ample, generous, great, considerable, significant, important, worthwhile, massive, bulky, hefty, well-built, stout, sturdy, strong, sound, durable.

Ⓔ small, insignificant, weak.

**substantiate** v prove, verify, confirm, support, corroborate, authenticate, validate.

Ⓔ disprove, refute.

**substitute** v 1 CHANGE, exchange, swap, switch, interchange, replace.

2 STAND IN, fill in (infml), cover, deputize, understudy, relieve.

n reserve, stand-by, temp (infml), supply, locum, understudy, stand-in, replacement, relief, surrogate, proxy, agent, deputy, makeshift, stopgap.

adj reserve, temporary, acting,

surrogate, proxy, replacement, alternative.

**subterfuge** n trick, stratagem, scheme, ploy, ruse, dodge, manoeuvre, machination, deviousness, evasion, deception, artifice, pretence, excuse.

Ⓔ openness, honesty.

**subtle** adj 1 DELICATE, understated, implied, indirect, slight, tenuous, faint, mild, fine, nice, refined, sophisticated, deep, profound.

2 ARTFUL, cunning, crafty, sly, devious, shrewd, astute.

Ⓔ 1 blatant, obvious. 2 artless, open.

**subtract** v deduct, take away, remove, withdraw, debit, detract, diminish.

Ⓔ add.

**suburbs** n suburbia, commuter belt, residential area, outskirts.

Ⓔ centre, heart.

**subversive** adj seditious, treasonous, treacherous, traitorous, inflammatory, incendiary, disruptive, riotous, weakening, undermining, destructive.

Ⓔ loyal.

n seditionist, terrorist, freedom fighter, dissident, traitor, quisling, fifth columnist.

**succeed** v 1 TRIUMPH, make it, get on, thrive, flourish, prosper, make good, manage, work. 2 *winter succeeds autumn*: follow, replace, result, ensue.

Ⓔ 1 fail. 2 precede.

**succeeding** adj following, next, subsequent, ensuing, coming, to come, later, successive.

Ⓔ previous, earlier.

**success** n 1 TRIUMPH, victory, luck, fortune, prosperity, fame, eminence, happiness. 2 CELEBRITY, star, somebody, winner, bestseller, hit, sensation.

Ⓔ 1 failure, disaster.

**successful** adj 1 VICTORIOUS, winning, lucky, fortunate,

prosperous, wealthy, thriving, flourishing, booming, moneymaking, lucrative, profitable, rewarding, satisfying, fruitful, productive. **2** *a successful writer*: famous, well-known, popular, leading, bestselling, top, unbeaten.

**F3** **1** unsuccessful, unprofitable, fruitless. **2** unknown.

**succession** *n* sequence, series, order, progression, run, chain, string, cycle, continuation, flow, course, line, train, procession.

**successive** *adj* consecutive, sequential, following, succeeding.

**succinct** *adj* short, brief, terse, pithy, concise, compact, condensed, summary.

**F3** long, lengthy, wordy, verbose.

**succulent** *adj* fleshy, juicy, moist, luscious, mouthwatering, lush, rich, mellow.

**F3** dry.

**succumb** *v* give way, yield, give in, submit, knuckle under, surrender, capitulate, collapse, fall.

**F3** overcome, master.

**suck** *v* draw in, imbibe, absorb, soak up, extract, drain.

**sudden** *adj* unexpected, unforeseen, surprising, startling, abrupt, sharp, quick, swift, rapid, prompt, hurried, hasty, rash, impetuous, impulsive, snap (*infml*).

**F3** expected, predictable, gradual, slow.

**sue** *v* prosecute, charge, indict, summon, solicit, appeal.

**suffer** *v* **1** HURT, ache, agonize, grieve, sorrow. **2** BEAR, support, tolerate, endure, sustain, experience, undergo, go through, feel.

**suffering** *n* pain, discomfort, agony, anguish, affliction, distress, misery, hardship, ordeal, torment, torture.

**F3** ease, comfort.

**sufficient** *adj* enough, adequate, satisfactory, effective.

**F3** insufficient, inadequate.

**suffocate** *v* asphyxiate, smother, stifle, choke, strangle, throttle.

**suggest** *v* **1** PROPOSE, put forward, advocate, recommend, advise, counsel. **2** IMPLY, insinuate, hint, intimate, evoke, indicate.

**suggestion** *n* **1** PROPOSAL, proposition, motion, recommendation, idea, plan. **2** IMPLICATION, insinuation, innuendo, hint, intimation, suspicion, trace, indication.

**suggestive** *adj* **1** EVOCATIVE, reminiscent, expressive, meaning, indicative. **2** *a suggestive remark*: indecent, immodest, improper, indelicate, off-colour, risqué, bawdy, dirty, smutty, provocative.

**F3** **1** inexpressive. **2** decent, clean.

**suit** *v* **1** SATISFY, gratify, please, answer, match, tally, agree, correspond, harmonize. **2** FIT, befit, become, tailor, adapt, adjust, accommodate, modify.

**F3** **1** displease, clash.

*n* outfit, costume, dress, clothing.

**suitable** *adj* appropriate, fitting, convenient, opportune, suited, due, apt, apposite, relevant, applicable, fit, adequate, satisfactory, acceptable, befitting, becoming, seemly, proper, right.

**F3** unsuitable, inappropriate.

**sulk** *v* mope, brood, pout.

**sulky** *adj* brooding, moody, morose, resentful, grudging, disgruntled, put out, cross, bad-tempered, sullen, aloof, unsociable.

**F3** cheerful, good-tempered, sociable.

**sullen** *adj* **1** SULKY, moody, morose, glum, gloomy, silent, surly, sour, perverse, obstinate, stubborn. **2** DARK, gloomy, sombre, dismal, cheerless, dull, leaden, heavy.

**F3** **1** cheerful, happy. **2** fine, clear.

**sully** *v* dirty, soil, defile, pollute, contaminate, taint, spoil, mar, spot, blemish, besmirch, stain, tarnish, disgrace, dishonour.

**F3** cleanse, honour.

**sultry** *adj* hot, sweltering, stifling, stuffy, oppressive, close, humid, muggy, sticky.
**F3** cool, cold.

**sum** *n* total, sum total, aggregate, whole, entirety, number, quantity, amount, tally, reckoning, score, result.

**sum up** summarize, review, recapitulate, conclude, close.

**summarize** *v* outline, précis, condense, abridge, abbreviate, shorten, sum up, encapsulate, review.
**F3** expand (on).

**summary** *n* synopsis, résumé, outline, abstract, précis, condensation, digest, compendium, abridgement, summing-up, review, recapitulation.
*adj* short, succinct, brief, cursory, hasty, prompt, direct, unceremonious, arbitrary.
**F3** lengthy, careful.

**summit** *n* top, peak, pinnacle, apex, point, crown, head, zenith, acme, culmination, height.
**F3** bottom, foot, nadir.

**summon** *v* call, send for, invite, bid, beckon, gather, assemble, convene, rally, muster, mobilize, rouse, arouse.
**F3** dismiss.

**sumptuous** *adj* luxurious, plush, lavish, extravagant, opulent, rich, costly, expensive, dear, splendid, magnificent, gorgeous, superb, grand.
**F3** plain, poor.

**sunbathe** *v* sun, bask, tan, brown, bake.

**sunburnt** *adj* brown, tanned, bronzed, weather-beaten, burnt, red, blistered, peeling.
**F3** pale.

**sundry** *adj* various, diverse, miscellaneous, assorted, varied, different, several, some, a few.

**sunken** *adj* submerged, buried, recessed, lower, depressed, concave,
hollow, haggard, drawn.

**sunny** *adj* 1 FINE, cloudless, clear, summery, sunshiny, sunlit, bright, brilliant. 2 CHEERFUL, happy, joyful, smiling, beaming, radiant, light-hearted, buoyant, optimistic, pleasant.
**F3** 1 sunless, dull. 2 gloomy.

**sunrise** *n* dawn, crack of dawn, daybreak, daylight.

**sunset** *n* sundown, dusk, twilight, gloaming, evening, nightfall.

**superb** *adj* excellent, first-rate, first-class, superior, choice, fine, exquisite, gorgeous, magnificent, splendid, grand, wonderful, marvellous, admirable, impressive, breathtaking.
**F3** bad, poor, inferior.

**superficial** *adj* surface, external, exterior, outward, apparent, seeming, cosmetic, skin-deep, shallow, slight, trivial, lightweight, frivolous, casual, cursory, sketchy, hasty, hurried, passing.
**F3** internal, deep, thorough.

**superfluous** *adj* extra, spare, excess, surplus, remaining, redundant, supernumerary, unnecessary, needless, unwanted, uncalled-for, excessive.
**F3** necessary, needed, wanted.

**superintend** *v* supervise, oversee, overlook, inspect, run, manage, administer, direct, control, handle.

**superior** *adj* 1 EXCELLENT, first-class, first-rate, top-notch (*infml*), top-flight (*infml*), high-class, exclusive, choice, select, fine, de luxe, admirable, distinguished, exceptional, unrivalled, par excellence. 2 BETTER, preferred, greater, higher, senior. 3 HAUGHTY, lordly, pretentious, snobbish, snooty (*infml*), supercilious, disdainful, condescending, patronizing.
**F3** 1 inferior, average. 2 worse, lower. 3 humble.
*n* senior, elder, better, boss, chief, principal, director, manager, foreman,

supervisor.

**Ea** inferior, junior, assistant.

**superiority** n advantage, lead, edge, supremacy, ascendancy, pre-eminence, predominance.

**Ea** inferiority.

**superlative** adj best, greatest, highest, supreme, transcendent, unbeatable, unrivalled, unparalleled, matchless, peerless, unsurpassed, unbeaten, consummate, excellent, outstanding.

**Ea** poor, average.

**supernatural** adj paranormal, unnatural, abnormal, metaphysical, spiritual, psychic, mystic, occult, hidden, mysterious, miraculous, magical, phantom, ghostly.

**Ea** natural, normal.

**supersede** v succeed, replace, supplant, usurp, oust, displace, remove.

**superstition** n myth, old wives' tale, fallacy, delusion, illusion.

**superstitious** adj mythical, false, fallacious, irrational, groundless, delusive, illusory.

**Ea** rational, logical.

**supervise** v oversee, watch over, look after, superintend, run, manage, administer, direct, conduct, preside over, control, handle.

**supervision** n surveillance, care, charge, superintendence, oversight, running, management, administration, direction, control, guidance, instruction.

**supervisor** n overseer, inspector, superintendent, boss, chief, director, administrator, manager, foreman, forewoman.

**supplant** v replace, supersede, usurp, oust, displace, remove, overthrow, topple, unseat.

**supple** adj flexible, bending, pliant, pliable, plastic, lithe, graceful, loose-limbed, double-jointed, elastic.

**Ea** stiff, rigid, inflexible.

**supplement** n addition, extra,

insert, pull-out, addendum, appendix, codicil, postscript, sequel.

v add to, augment, boost, reinforce, fill up, top up, complement, extend, eke out.

**Ea** deplete, use up.

**supplementary** adj additional, extra, auxiliary, secondary, complementary, accompanying.

**supplier** n dealer, seller, vendor, wholesaler, retailer.

**supplies** n stores, provisions, food, equipment, materials, necessities.

**supply** v provide, furnish, equip, outfit, stock, fill, replenish, give, donate, grant, endow, contribute, yield, produce, sell.

**Ea** take, receive.

n source, amount, quantity, stock, fund, reservoir, store, reserve, stockpile, hoard, cache.

**Ea** lack.

**support** v 1 BACK, second, defend, champion, advocate, promote, foster, help, aid, assist, rally round, finance, fund, subsidize, underwrite. 2 HOLD UP, bear, carry, sustain, brace, reinforce, strengthen, prop, buttress, bolster. 3 MAINTAIN, keep, provide for, feed, nourish. 4 support a statement: endorse, confirm, verify, authenticate, corroborate, substantiate, document.

**Ea** 1 oppose. 3 live off. 4 contradict.

n 1 BACKING, allegiance, loyalty, defence, protection, patronage, sponsorship, approval, encouragement, comfort, relief, help, aid, assistance. 2 PROP, stay, post, pillar, brace, crutch, foundation, underpinning.

**Ea** 1 opposition, hostility.

**supporter** n fan, follower, adherent, advocate, champion, defender, seconder, patron, sponsor, helper, ally, friend.

**Ea** opponent.

**supportive** adj helpful, caring, attentive, sympathetic,

understanding, comforting, reassuring, encouraging.
**≠** discouraging.

**suppose** v assume, presume, expect, infer, conclude, guess, conjecture, surmise, believe, think, consider, judge, imagine, conceive, fancy, pretend, postulate, hypothesize.
**≠** know.

**supposed** adj alleged, reported, rumoured, assumed, presumed, reputed, putative, imagined, hypothetical.
**≠** known, certain.

**supposed to** meant to, intended to, expected to, required to, obliged to.

**supposition** n assumption, presumption, guess, conjecture, speculation, theory, hypothesis, idea, notion.
**≠** knowledge.

**suppress** v crush, stamp out, quash, quell, subdue, stop, silence, censor, stifle, smother, strangle, conceal, withhold, hold back, contain, restrain, check, repress, inhibit.
**≠** encourage, incite.

**supreme** adj best, greatest, highest, top, crowning, culminating, first, leading, foremost, chief, principal, head, sovereign, pre-eminent, predominant, prevailing, world-beating, unsurpassed, second-to-none, incomparable, matchless, consummate, transcendent, superlative, prime, ultimate, extreme, final.
**≠** lowly, poor.

**sure** adj **1** CERTAIN, convinced, assured, confident, decided, positive, definite, unmistakable, clear, accurate, precise, unquestionable, indisputable, undoubted, undeniable, irrevocable, inevitable, bound.
**2** SAFE, secure, fast, solid, firm, steady, stable, guaranteed, reliable, dependable, trustworthy, steadfast, unwavering, unerring, unfailing, infallible, effective.

**≠** **1** unsure, uncertain, doubtful.
**2** unsafe, insecure.

**surface** n outside, exterior, façade, veneer, covering, skin, top, side, face, plane.
**≠** inside, interior.
v rise, arise, come up, emerge, appear, materialise, come to light.
**≠** sink, disappear, vanish.

**surly** adj gruff, brusque, churlish, ungracious, bad-tempered, cross, crabbed, grouchy, crusty, sullen, sulky, morose.
**≠** friendly, polite.

**surpass** v beat, outdo, exceed, outstrip, better, excel, transcend, outshine, eclipse.

**surplus** n excess, residue, remainder, balance, superfluity, glut, surfeit.
**≠** lack, shortage.
adj excess, superfluous, redundant, extra, spare, remaining, unused.

**surprise** v startle, amaze, astonish, astound, stagger, flabbergast (infml), bewilder, confuse, nonplus, disconcert, dismay.
n amazement, astonishment, incredulity, wonder, bewilderment, dismay, shock, start, bombshell, revelation.
**≠** composure.

**surprised** adj startled, amazed, astonished, astounded, staggered, flabbergasted (infml), thunderstruck, dumbfounded, speechless, shocked, nonplussed.
**≠** unsurprised, composed.

**surprising** adj amazing, astonishing, astounding, staggering, stunning, incredible, extraordinary, remarkable, startling, unexpected, unforeseen.
**≠** unsurprising, expected.

**surrender** v capitulate, submit, resign, concede, yield, give in, cede, give up, quit, relinquish, abandon, renounce, forgo, waive.
n capitulation, resignation,

submission, yielding, relinquishment, renunciation.

**surreptitious** *adj* furtive, stealthy, sly, covert, veiled, hidden, secret, clandestine, underhand, unauthorized.

**F3** open, obvious.

**surround** *v* encircle, ring, girdle, encompass, envelop, encase, enclose, hem in, besiege.

**surrounding** *adj* encircling, bordering, adjacent, adjoining, neighbouring, nearby.

**surroundings** *n* neighbourhood, vicinity, locality, setting, environment, background, milieu, ambience.

**survey** *v* view, contemplate, observe, supervise, scan, scrutinize, examine, inspect, study, research, review, consider, estimate, evaluate, assess, measure, plot, plan, map, chart, reconnoitre.
*n* review, overview, scrutiny, examination, inspection, study, pull, appraisal, assessment, measurement.

**survive** *v* outlive, outlast, endure, last, stay, remain, live, exist, withstand, weather.

**F3** succumb, die.

**susceptible** *adj* liable, prone, inclined, disposed, given, subject, receptive, responsive, impressionable, suggestible, weak, vulnerable, open, sensitive, tender.

**F3** resistant, immune.

**suspect** *v* **1** DOUBT, distrust, mistrust, call into question. **2** *I suspect you're right*: believe, fancy, feel, guess, conjecture, speculate, surmise, suppose, consider, conclude, infer.
*adj* suspicious, doubtful, dubious, questionable, debatable, unreliable, iffy (*sl*), dodgy (*infml*), fishy (*infml*).

**F3** acceptable, reliable.

**suspend** *v* **1** HANG, dangle, swing. **2** ADJOURN, interrupt, discontinue, cease, delay, defer, postpone, put off,

shelve. **3** EXPEL, dismiss, exclude, debar.

**F3** **2** continue. **3** restore, reinstate.

**suspense** *n* uncertainty, insecurity, anxiety, tension, apprehension, anticipation, expectation, expectancy, excitement.

**F3** certainty, knowledge.

**suspension** *n* adjournment, interruption, break, intermission, respite, remission, stay, moratorium, delay, deferral, postponement, abeyance.

**F3** continuation.

**suspicion** *n* **1** DOUBT, scepticism, distrust, mistrust, wariness, caution, misgiving, apprehension. **2** TRACE, hint, suggestion, soupçon, touch, tinge, shade, glimmer, shadow. **3** IDEA, notion, hunch.

**F3** **1** trust.

**suspicious** *adj* **1** DOUBTFUL, sceptical, unbelieving, suspecting, distrustful, mistrustful, wary, chary, apprehensive, uneasy. **2** DUBIOUS, questionable, suspect, irregular, shifty, shady (*infml*), dodgy (*infml*), fishy (*infml*).

**F3** **1** trustful, confident. **2** trustworthy, innocent.

**sustain** *v* **1** NOURISH, provide for, nurture, foster, help, aid, assist, comfort, relieve, support, uphold, endorse, bear, carry. **2** MAINTAIN, keep going, keep up, continue, prolong, hold.

**sustained** *adj* prolonged, protracted, long-drawn-out, steady, continuous, constant, perpetual, unremitting.

**F3** broken, interrupted, intermittent, spasmodic.

**sustenance** *n* nourishment, food, provisions, fare, maintenance, subsistence, livelihood.

**swagger** *v* bluster, boast, crow, brag, swank (*infml*), parade, strut.
*n* bluster, show, ostentation, arrogance.

**swallow** v 1 CONSUME, devour, eat, gobble up, guzzle, drink, quaff, knock back (infml), gulp, down (infml). 2 ENGULF, enfold, envelop, swallow up, absorb, assimilate, accept, believe.

**swamp** n bog, marsh, fen, slough, quagmire, quicksand, mire, mud.
v flood, inundate, deluge, engulf, submerge, sink, drench, saturate, waterlog, overload, overwhelm, besiege, beset.

**swap, swop** v exchange, transpose, switch, interchange, barter, trade, traffic.

**swarm** n crowd, throng, mob, mass, multitude, myriad, host, army, horde, herd, flock, drove, shoal.
v 1 flock, flood, stream, mass, congregate, crowd, throng.
2 swarming with tourists: teem, crawl, bristle, abound.

**swarthy** adj dark, dark-skinned, dark-complexioned, dusky, black, brown, tanned.
E3 fair, pale.

**sway** v 1 ROCK, roll, lurch, swing, wave, oscillate, fluctuate, bend, incline, lean, divert, veer, swerve.
2 INFLUENCE, affect, persuade, induce, convince, convert, overrule, dominate, govern.

**swear** v 1 VOW, promise, pledge, avow, attest, asseverate, testify, affirm, assert, declare, insist.
2 CURSE, blaspheme.

**swear-word** n expletive, four-letter word, curse, oath, imprecation, obscenity, profanity, blasphemy, swearing, bad language.

**sweat** n 1 PERSPIRATION, moisture, stickiness. 2 ANXIETY, worry, agitation, panic. 3 TOIL, labour, drudgery, chore.
v perspire, swelter, exude.

**sweaty** adj damp, moist, clammy, sticky, sweating, perspiring.
E3 dry, cool.

**sweep** v 1 sweep the floor: brush, dust, clean, clear, remove. 2 PASS, sail, fly, glide, scud, skim, glance, whisk, tear, hurtle.
n arc, curve, bend, swing, stroke, movement, gesture, compass, scope, range, extent, span, stretch, expanse, vista.

**sweeping** adj general, global, all-inclusive, all-embracing, blanket, across-the-board, broad, wide-ranging, extensive, far-reaching, comprehensive, thoroughgoing, radical, wholesale, indiscriminate, oversimplified, simplistic.
E3 specific, narrow.

**sweet** adj 1 SUGARY, syrupy, sweetened, honeyed, saccharine, luscious, delicious. 2 PLEASANT, delightful, lovely, attractive, beautiful, pretty, winsome, cute, appealing, lovable, charming, agreeable, amiable, affectionate, tender, kind, treasured, precious, dear, darling. 3 FRESH, clean, wholesome, pure, clear, perfumed, fragrant, aromatic, balmy. 4 sweet music: melodious, tuneful, harmonious, euphonious, musical, dulcet, soft, mellow.
E3 1 savoury, salty, sour, bitter.
2 unpleasant, nasty, ugly. 3 foul.
4 discordant.
n dessert, pudding, afters (infml).

**sweets**

> *Sweets include*: barley sugar, bull's eye, butterscotch, caramel, chewing-gum, chocolate, fondant, fruit pastille, fudge, gobstopper, gumdrop, humbug, jelly, jelly bean, liquorice, liquorice allsort, lollipop, Mars®, marshmallow, marzipan, nougat, peppermint, praline, rock, Edinburgh rock, toffee, toffee apple, truffle, Turkish delight.

**sweeten** v sugar, honey, mellow, soften, soothe, appease, temper, cushion.

Ea sour, embitter.

**swell** v expand, dilate, inflate, blow up, puff up, bloat, distend, fatten, bulge, balloon, billow, surge, rise, mount, increase, enlarge, extend, grow, augment, heighten, intensify.

Ea shrink, contract, decrease, dwindle.

n billow, wave, undulation, surge, rise, increase, enlargement.

**swelling** n lump, tumour, bump, bruise, blister, boil, inflammation, bulge, protuberance, puffiness, distension, enlargement.

**sweltering** adj hot, tropical, baking, scorching, stifling, suffocating, airless, oppressive, sultry, steamy, sticky, humid.

Ea cold, cool, fresh, breezy, airy.

**swerve** v turn, bend, incline, veer, swing, shift, deviate, stray, wander, diverge, deflect, sheer.

**swift** adj fast, quick, rapid, speedy, express, flying, hurried, hasty, short, brief, sudden, prompt, ready, agile, nimble, nippy (infml).

Ea slow, sluggish, unhurried.

**swimsuit** n swimming costume, bathing-costume, bathing-suit, bikini, trunks.

**swindle** v cheat, defraud, diddle, do (infml), overcharge, fleece, rip off (sl), trick, deceive, dupe, con (infml), bamboozle (infml).

n fraud, fiddle, racket, sharp practice, double-dealing, trickery, deception, con (infml), rip-off (sl).

**swindler** n cheat, fraud, impostor, con man (infml), trickster, shark, rogue, rascal.

**swing** v hang, suspend, dangle, wave, brandish, sway, rock, oscillate, vibrate, fluctuate, vary, veer, swerve, turn, whirl, twirl, spin, rotate.

n sway, rock, oscillation, vibration, fluctuation, variation, change, shift, movement, motion, rhythm.

**swingeing** adj harsh, severe, stringent, drastic, punishing, devastating, excessive, extortionate, oppressive, heavy.

Ea mild.

**swipe** v **1** HIT, strike, lunge, lash out, slap, whack (infml), wallop (infml), sock (sl). **2** (infml) STEAL, pilfer, lift, pinch (infml).

n stroke, blow, slap, smack, clout, whack (infml), wallop (infml).

**swirl** v churn, agitate, spin, twirl, whirl, wheel, eddy, twist, curl.

**switch** v change, exchange, swap, trade, interchange, transpose, substitute, replace, shift, rearrange, turn, veer, deviate, divert, deflect.

n change, alteration, shift, exchange, swap, interchange, substitution, replacement.

**swivel** v pivot, spin, rotate, revolve, turn, twirl, pirouette, gyrate, wheel.

**swollen** adj bloated, distended, inflated, tumid, puffed up, puffy, inflamed, enlarged, bulbous, bulging.

Ea shrunken, shrivelled.

**swoop** v dive, plunge, drop, fall, descend, stoop, pounce, lunge, rush.

n dive, plunge, drop, descent, pounce, lunge, rush, attack, onslaught.

**swop** see swap.

**sword** n blade, foil, rapier, sabre, scimitar.

**swot** (infml) v study, work, learn, memorize, revise, cram, mug up (infml), bone up (sl).

**syllabus** n curriculum, course, programme, schedule, plan.

**symbol** n sign, token, representation, mark, emblem, badge, logo, character, ideograph, figure, image.

*Symbols include*: badge, brand, cipher, coat of arms, crest, emblem, hieroglyph, icon, ideogram, insignia, logo, logogram, monogram, motif, pictograph, swastika, token, totem, trademark; ampersand, asterisk, caret, dagger, double-dagger, obelus.

**symbolic** *adj* symbolical,
representative, emblematic, token,
figurative, metaphorical, allegorical,
meaningful, significant.

**symbolize** *v* represent, stand for,
denote, mean, signify, typify,
exemplify, epitomize, personify.

**symmetrical** *adj* balanced, even,
regular, parallel, corresponding,
proportional.
E3 asymmetrical, irregular.

**symmetry** *n* balance, evenness,
regularity, parallelism,
correspondence, proportion,
harmony, agreement.
E3 asymmetry, irregularity.

**sympathetic** *adj* understanding,
appreciative, supportive, comforting,
consoling, commiserating, pitying,
interested, concerned, solicitous,
caring, compassionate, tender, kind,
warm-hearted, well-disposed,
affectionate, agreeable, friendly,
congenial, like-minded, compatible.
E3 unsympathetic, indifferent, callous,
antipathetic.

**sympathize** *v* understand, comfort,
commiserate, pity, feel for,
empathize, identify with, respond to.
E3 ignore, disregard.

**sympathy** *n* 1 UNDERSTANDING,
comfort, consolation, condolences,
commiseration, pity, compassion,
tenderness, kindness, warmth,
thoughtfulness, empathy, fellow-
feeling, affinity, rapport.
2 AGREEMENT, accord,
correspondence, harmony.
E3 1 indifference, insensitivity,
callousness. 2 disagreement.

**symptom** *n* sign, indication,
evidence, manifestation, expression,
feature, characteristic, mark, token,
warning.

**symptomatic** *adj* indicative, typical,
characteristic, associated, suggestive.

**synonymous** *adj* interchangeable,
substitutable, the same, identical,
similar, comparable, tantamount,
equivalent, corresponding.
E3 antonymous, opposite.

**synopsis** *n* outline, abstract,
summary, résumé, précis,
condensation, digest, abridgement,
review, recapitulation.

**synthesize** *v* unite, combine,
amalgamate, integrate, merge, blend,
compound, alloy, fuse, weld,
coalesce, unify.
E3 separate, analyse, resolve.

**synthetic** *adj* manufactured, man-
made, simulated, artificial, ersatz,
imitation, fake, bogus, mock, sham,
pseudo.
E3 genuine, real, natural.

**system** *n* 1 METHOD, mode,
technique, procedure, process,
routine, practice, usage, rule.
2 ORGANIZATION, structure, set-up,
systematization, co-ordination,
orderliness, methodology, logic,
classification, arrangement, order,
plan, scheme.

**systematic** *adj* methodical, logical,
ordered, well-ordered, planned, well-
planned, organized, well-organized,
structured, systematized,
standardized, orderly, businesslike,
efficient.
E3 unsystematic, arbitrary, disorderly,
inefficient.

# T

**tab** *n* flap, tag, marker, label, sticker,
ticket.

**table** *n* 1 BOARD, slab, counter,
worktop, desk, bench, stand.

**2** DIAGRAM, chart, graph, timetable, schedule, programme, list, inventory, catalogue, index, register, record.
v propose, suggest, submit, put forward.

**taboo** adj forbidden, prohibited, banned, proscribed, unacceptable, unmentionable, unthinkable.
**F3** permitted, acceptable.
n ban, interdiction, prohibition, restriction, anathema, curse.

**tacit** adj unspoken, unexpressed, unvoiced, silent, understood, implicit, implied, inferred.
**F3** express, explicit.

**taciturn** adj silent, quiet, uncommunicative, unforthcoming, reticent, reserved, withdrawn, aloof, distant, cold.
**F3** talkative, communicative, forthcoming.

**tack** n **1** NAIL, pin, drawing-pin, staple. **2** COURSE, path, bearing, heading, direction, line, approach, method, way, technique, procedure, plan, tactic, attack.
v add, append, attach, affix, fasten, fix, nail, pin, staple, stitch, baste.

**tackle** n **1** a rugby tackle: attack, challenge, interception, intervention, block. **2** EQUIPMENT, tools, implements, apparatus, rig, outfit, gear, trappings, paraphernalia.
v **1** BEGIN, embark on, set about, try, attempt, undertake, take on, challenge, confront, encounter, face up to, grapple with, deal with, attend to, handle, grab, seize, grasp.
**2** INTERCEPT, block, halt, stop.
**F3 1** avoid, sidestep.

**tact** n tactfulness, diplomacy, discretion, prudence, delicacy, sensitivity, perception, discernment, judgement, understanding, thoughtfulness, consideration, skill, adroitness, finesse.
**F3** tactlessness, indiscretion.

**tactful** adj diplomatic, discreet, politic, judicious, prudent, careful,

delicate, subtle, sensitive, perceptive, discerning, understanding, thoughtful, considerate, polite, skilful, adroit.
**F3** tactless, indiscreet, thoughtless, rude.

**tactic** n approach, course, way, means, method, procedure, plan, stratagem, scheme, ruse, ploy, subterfuge, trick, device, shift, move, manoeuvre.

**tactical** adj strategic, planned, calculated, artful, cunning, shrewd, skilful, clever, smart, prudent, politic, judicious.

**tactics** n strategy, campaign, plan, policy, approach, line of attack, moves, manoeuvres.

**tactless** adj undiplomatic, indiscreet, indelicate, inappropriate, impolitic, imprudent, careless, clumsy, blundering, insensitive, unfeeling, hurtful, unkind, thoughtless, inconsiderate, rude, impolite, discourteous.
**F3** tactful, diplomatic, discreet.

**tag** n label, sticker, tab, ticket, mark, identification, note, slip, docket.
v **1** LABEL, mark, identify, designate, term, call, name, christen, nickname, style, dub. **2** ADD, append, annex, adjoin, affix, fasten.

**tag along** follow, shadow, tail, trail, accompany.

**tail** n end, extremity, rear, rear end, rump, behind (infml), posterior (infml), appendage.
v follow, pursue, shadow, dog, stalk, track, trail.

**tail off** decrease, decline, drop, fall away, fade, wane, dwindle, taper off, peter out, die (out).
**F3** increase, grow.

**tailor** n outfitter, dressmaker.
v fit, suit, cut, trim, style, fashion, shape, mould, alter, modify, adapt, adjust, accommodate.

**tailor-made** adj made-to-measure, custom-built, ideal, perfect, right, suited, fitted.

**E3** unsuitable.

**taint** v contaminate, infect, pollute,
adulterate, corrupt, deprave, stain,
blemish, blot, smear, tarnish,
blacken, dirty, soil, muddy, defile,
sully, harm, damage, blight, spoil,
ruin, shame, disgrace, dishonour.
n contamination, infection,
pollution, corruption, stain, blemish,
fault, flaw, defect, spot, blot, smear,
stigma, shame, disgrace, dishonour.

**take** v 1 SEIZE, grab, snatch, grasp,
hold, catch, capture, get, obtain,
acquire, secure, gain, win, derive,
adopt, assume, pick, choose, select,
accept, receive. 2 REMOVE, eliminate,
take away, subtract, deduct, steal,
filch, purloin, nick (*infml*), pinch
(*infml*), appropriate, abduct, carry
off. 3 NEED, necessitate, require,
demand, call for. 4 *take me home*:
convey, carry, bring, transport, ferry,
accompany, escort, lead, guide,
conduct, usher. 5 BEAR, tolerate,
stand, stomach, abide, endure, suffer,
undergo, withstand.

**E3** 1 leave, refuse. 2 replace, put back.

**take aback** surprise, astonish,
astound, stagger, stun, startle,
disconcert, bewilder, dismay, upset.

**take apart** take to pieces, dismantle,
disassemble, analyse.

**take back** reclaim, repossess,
withdraw, retract, recant, repudiate,
deny, eat one's words.

**take down** 1 DISMANTLE,
disassemble, demolish, raze, level,
lower. 2 NOTE, record, write down, put
down, set down, transcribe.

**take in** 1 ABSORB, assimilate, digest,
realize, appreciate, understand,
comprehend, grasp, admit, receive,
shelter, accommodate, contain,
include, comprise, incorporate,
embrace, encompass, cover. 2
DECEIVE, fool, dupe, con (*infml*),
mislead, trick, hoodwink, bamboozle
(*infml*), cheat, swindle.

**take off** 1 REMOVE, doff, divest, shed,
discard, drop. 2 LEAVE, depart, go,
decamp, disappear. 3 IMITATE,
mimic, parody, caricature, satirize,
mock, send up.

**take on** 1 ACCEPT, assume, acquire,
undertake, tackle, face, contend with,
fight, oppose. 2 *take on staff*: employ,
hire, enlist, recruit, engage, retain.

**take up** 1 OCCUPY, fill, engage,
engross, absorb, monopolize, use up.
2 *take up a hobby*: start, begin, embark
on, pursue, carry on, continue.
3 RAISE, lift. 4 ACCEPT, adopt,
assume.

**take-off** n imitation, mimicry,
impersonation, parody, caricature,
spoof, send-up, travesty.

**takeover** n merger, amalgamation,
combination, incorporation, coup.

**takings** n receipts, gate, proceeds,
profits, gain, returns, revenue, yield,
income, earnings, pickings.

**tale** n story, yarn, anecdote, spiel
(*sl*), narrative, account, report,
rumour, tall story, old wives' tale,
superstition, fable, myth, legend,
saga, lie, fib, falsehood, untruth,
fabrication.

**talent** n gift, endowment, genius,
flair, feel, knack, bent, aptitude,
faculty, skill, ability, capacity, power,
strength, forte.

**E3** inability, weakness.

**talented** adj gifted, brilliant, well-
endowed, versatile, accomplished,
able, capable, proficient, adept,
adroit, deft, clever, skilful.

**E3** inept.

**talk** v speak, utter, articulate, say,
communicate, converse, chat, gossip,
natter (*infml*), chatter, discuss,
confer, negotiate.

n 1 CONVERSATION, dialogue,
discussion, conference, meeting,
consultation, negotiation, chat,
chatter, natter (*infml*), gossip, hearsay,
rumour, tittle-tattle. 2 *give a talk*:
lecture, seminar, symposium, speech,

address, discourse, sermon, spiel (*sl*).
**3** LANGUAGE, dialect, slang, jargon,
speech, utterance, words.

**talk into** encourage, coax, sway,
persuade, convince, bring round, win
over.
F3 dissuade.

**talk out of** discourage, deter, put off,
dissuade.
F3 persuade, convince.

**talkative** *adj* garrulous, voluble,
vocal, communicative, forthcoming,
unreserved, expansive, chatty,
gossipy, verbose, wordy.
F3 taciturn, quiet, reserved.

**talking-to** (*infml*) *n* lecture, dressing-
down (*infml*), telling-off (*infml*),
ticking-off (*infml*), scolding,
reprimand, rebuke, reproof,
reproach, criticism.
F3 praise, commendation.

**tall** *adj* high, lofty, elevated, soaring,
towering, big, great, giant, gigantic.
F3 short, low, small.

**tally** *v* **1** AGREE, concur, tie in,
square, accord, harmonize, coincide,
correspond, match, conform, suit, fit.
**2** ADD (UP), total, count, reckon,
figure.
F3 **1** disagree, differ.
*n* record, count, total, score,
reckoning, account.

**tame** *adj* **1** *a tame rabbit*:
domesticated, broken in, trained,
disciplined, manageable, tractable,
amenable, gentle, docile, meek,
submissive, unresisting, obedient,
biddable. **2** DULL, boring, tedious,
uninteresting, humdrum, flat, bland,
insipid, weak, feeble, uninspired,
unadventurous, unenterprising,
lifeless, spiritless.
F3 **1** wild, unmanageable, rebellious.
**2** exciting.
*v* domesticate, house-train, break in,
train, discipline, master, subjugate,
conquer, bridle, curb, repress,
suppress, quell, subdue, temper,
soften, mellow, calm, pacify, humble.

**tamper** *v* interfere, meddle, mess
(*infml*), tinker, fiddle, fix, rig,
manipulate, juggle, alter, damage.

**tang** *n* sharpness, bite, piquancy,
pungency, taste, flavour, savour,
smack, smell, aroma, scent, whiff,
tinge, touch, trace, hint, suggestion,
overtone.

**tangible** *adj* touchable, tactile,
palpable, solid, concrete, material,
substantial, physical, real, actual,
perceptible, discernible, evident,
manifest, definite, positive.
F3 intangible, abstract, unreal.

**tangle** *n* knot, snarl-up, twist, coil,
convolution, mesh, web, maze,
labyrinth, mess, muddle, jumble,
mix-up, confusion, entanglement,
embroilment, complication.
*v* entangle, knot, snarl, ravel, twist,
coil, interweave, interlace, intertwine,
catch, ensnare, entrap, enmesh,
embroil, implicate, involve, muddle,
confuse.
F3 disentangle.

**tangled** *adj* knotty, snarled, matted,
tousled, dishevelled, messy, muddled,
jumbled, confused, twisted,
convoluted, tortuous, involved,
complicated, complex, intricate.

**tangy** *adj* sharp, biting, acid, tart,
spicy, piquant, pungent, strong,
fresh.
F3 tasteless, insipid.

**tank** *n* container, reservoir, cistern,
aquarium, vat, basin.

**tantalize** *v* tease, taunt, torment,
torture, provoke, lead on, titillate,
tempt, entice, bait, balk, frustrate,
thwart.
F3 gratify, satisfy, fulfil.

**tantamount** *adj* as good as,
equivalent, commensurate, equal,
synonymous, the same as.

**tantrum** *n* temper, rage, fury, storm,
outburst, fit, scene, paddy (*infml*).

**tap**[1] *v* hit, strike, knock, rap, beat,
drum, pat, touch.
*n* knock, rap, beat, pat, touch.

**tap²** n **1** STOPCOCK, valve, faucet, spigot, spout. **2** STOPPER, plug, bung.

v use, utilize, exploit, mine, quarry, siphon, bleed, milk, drain.

**tape** n band, strip, binding, ribbon, video, cassette.

v record, video, bind, secure, stick, seal.

**taper** v narrow, attenuate, thin, slim, decrease, reduce, lessen, dwindle, fade, wane, peter out, tail off, die away.

F3 widen, flare, swell, increase.

n spill, candle, wick.

**target** n aim, object, end, purpose, intention, ambition, goal, destination, objective, butt, mark, victim, prey, quarry.

**tariff** n price list, schedule, charges, rate, toll, tax, levy, customs, excise, duty.

**tarnish** v discolour, corrode, rust, dull, dim, darken, blacken, sully, taint, stain, blemish, spot, blot, mar, spoil.

F3 polish, brighten.

**tart¹** n pie, flan, pastry, tartlet, patty.

**tart²** adj sharp, acid, sour, bitter, vinegary, tangy, piquant, pungent, biting, cutting, trenchant, incisive, caustic, astringent, acerbic, scathing, sardonic.

F3 bland, sweet.

**task** n job, chore, duty, charge, imposition, assignment, exercise, mission, errand, undertaking, enterprise, business, occupation, activity, employment, work, labour, toil, burden.

**taste** n **1** FLAVOUR, savour, relish, smack, tang. **2** SAMPLE, bit, piece, morsel, titbit, bite, nibble, mouthful, sip, drop, dash, soupçon. **3** *a taste for adventure*: liking, fondness, partiality, preference, inclination, leaning, desire, appetite.

**4** DISCRIMINATION, discernment, judgement, perception, appreciation, sensitivity, refinement, polish, culture, cultivation, breeding, decorum, finesse, style, elegance, tastefulness.

F3 **1** blandness. **3** distaste.

**4** tastelessness.

v savour, relish, sample, nibble, sip, try, test, differentiate, distinguish, discern, perceive, experience, undergo, feel, encounter, meet, know.

> *Ways of describing taste include*:
> acid, acrid, appetizing, bitter,
> bittersweet, citrus, creamy, delicious,
> flavoursome, fruity, hot, meaty,
> moreish, peppery, piquant, pungent,
> sapid, salty, savoury, scrumptious
> (*infml*), sharp, sour, spicy, sugary,
> sweet, tangy, tart, tasty, yummy
> (*infml*).

**tasteful** adj refined, polished, cultured, cultivated, elegant, smart, stylish, aesthetic, artistic, harmonious, beautiful, exquisite, delicate, graceful, restrained, well-judged, judicious, correct, fastidious, discriminating.

F3 tasteless, garish, tawdry.

**tasteless** adj **1** FLAVOURLESS, insipid, bland, mild, weak, watery, flat, stale, dull, boring, uninteresting, vapid. **2** INELEGANT, graceless, unseemly, improper, indiscreet, crass, rude, crude, vulgar, kitsch, naff (*sl*), cheap, tawdry, flashy, gaudy, garish, loud.

F3 **1** tasty. **2** tasteful, elegant.

**tasty** adj luscious, palatable, appetizing, mouthwatering, delicious, flavoursome, succulent, scrumptious (*infml*), yummy (*sl*), tangy, piquant, savoury, sweet.

F3 tasteless, insipid.

**tattered** adj ragged, frayed, threadbare, ripped, torn, tatty, shabby, scruffy.

F3 smart, neat.

**tatters** n rags, shreds, ribbons,

pieces.

**taunt** v tease, torment, provoke, bait, goad, jeer, mock, ridicule, gibe, rib (*sl*), deride, sneer, insult, revile, reproach.

n jeer, catcall, gibe, dig, sneer, insult, reproach, taunting, teasing, provocation, ridicule, sarcasm, derision, censure.

**taut** adj tight, stretched, contracted, strained, tense, unrelaxed, stiff, rigid.
F3 slack, loose, relaxed.

**tautological** adj repetitive, superfluous, redundant, pleonastic, verbose, wordy.
F3 succinct, economical.

**tautology** n repetition, duplication, superfluity, redundancy, pleonasm.

**tawdry** adj cheap, vulgar, tasteless, fancy, showy, flashy, gaudy, garish, tinselly, glittering.
F3 fine, tasteful.

**tax** n levy, charge, rate, tariff, customs, contribution, imposition, burden, load.

*Taxes include*: airport tax, capital gains tax, capital transfer tax, community charge, corporation tax, council tax, customs, death duty, estate duty, excise, income tax, inheritance tax, PAYE, poll tax, property tax, rates, surtax, tithe, toll, value added tax (VAT).

v levy, charge, demand, exact, assess, impose, burden, load, strain, stretch, try, tire, weary, exhaust, drain, sap, weaken.

**teach** v instruct, train, coach, tutor, lecture, drill, ground, verse, discipline, school, educate, enlighten, edify, inform, impart, inculcate, advise, counsel, guide, direct, show, demonstrate.
F3 learn.

**teacher** n schoolteacher, schoolmaster, master, schoolmistress, mistress, educator, pedagogue, tutor,

lecturer, professor, don, instructor, trainer, coach, adviser, counsellor, mentor, guide, guru.
F3 pupil.

**teaching** n 1 INSTRUCTION, tuition, training, grounding, schooling, education, pedagogy, indoctrination. 2 DOGMA, doctrine, tenet, precept, principle.

**team** n side, line-up, squad, shift, crew, gang, band, group, company, stable.

**team up** join, unite, couple, combine, band together, co-operate, collaborate, work together.

**tear** v 1 RIP, rend, divide, rupture, sever, shred, scratch, claw, gash, lacerate, mutilate, mangle. 2 PULL, snatch, grab, seize, wrest. 3 *tear down the street*: dash, rush, hurry, speed, race, run, sprint, fly, shoot, dart, bolt, belt (*infml*), career, charge.

n rip, rent, slit, hole, split, rupture, scratch, gash, laceration.

**tearful** adj crying, weeping, sobbing, whimpering, blubbering, sad, sorrowful, upset, distressed, emotional, weepy (*infml*).
F3 happy, smiling, laughing.

**tears** n crying, weeping, sobbing, wailing, whimpering, blubbering, sorrow, distress.

**tease** v taunt, provoke, bait, annoy, irritate, aggravate (*infml*), needle (*infml*), badger, worry, pester, plague, torment, tantalize, mock, ridicule, gibe, banter, rag (*sl*), rib (*sl*).

**technical** adj mechanical, scientific, technological, electronic, computerized, specialized, expert, professional.

**technique** n method, system, procedure, manner, fashion, style, mode, way, means, approach, course, performance, execution, delivery, artistry, craftsmanship, skill, facility, proficiency, expertise, know-how (*infml*), art, craft, knack, touch.

**tempestuous**

**tedious** *adj* boring, monotonous, uninteresting, unexciting, dull, dreary, drab, banal, humdrum, tiresome, wearisome, tiring, laborious, long-winded, long-drawn-out.
**F3** lively, interesting, exciting.

**teeming** *adj* swarming, crawling, alive, bristling, seething, full, packed, brimming, overflowing, bursting, replete, abundant, fruitful, thick.
**F3** lacking, sparse, rare.

**teenage** *adj* teenaged, adolescent, young, youthful, juvenile, immature.

**teenager** *n* adolescent, youth, boy, girl, minor, juvenile.

**teetotal** *adj* temperate, abstinent, abstemious, sober, on the wagon (*sl*).

**telepathy** *n* mind-reading, thought transference, sixth sense, ESP, clairvoyance.

**telephone** *n* phone, handset, receiver, blower (*infml*).
*v* phone, ring (up), call (up), dial, buzz (*infml*), contact, get in touch.

**telescope** *v* contract, shrink, compress, condense, abridge, squash, crush, shorten, curtail, truncate, abbreviate, reduce, cut, trim.

**television** *n* TV, receiver, set, telly (*infml*), the box (*infml*), goggle-box (*infml*), idiot box (*infml*), small screen.

**tell** *v* **1** INFORM, notify, let know, acquaint, impart, communicate, speak, utter, say, state, confess, divulge, disclose, reveal. **2** *tell a story*: narrate, recount, relate, report, announce, describe, portray, mention. **3** ORDER, command, direct, instruct, authorize.
**4** DIFFERENTIATE, distinguish, discriminate, discern, recognize, identify, discover, see, understand, comprehend.

**tell off** (*infml*) scold, chide, tick off (*infml*), upbraid, reprimand, rebuke, reprove, lecture, berate, dress down (*infml*), reproach, censure.

**temerity** *n* impudence, impertinence, cheek (*infml*), gall, nerve (*infml*), audacity, boldness, daring, rashness, recklessness, impulsiveness.
**F3** caution, prudence.

**temper** *n* **1** MOOD, humour, nature, temperament, character, disposition, constitution. **2** ANGER, rage, fury, passion, tantrum, paddy (*infml*), annoyance, irritability, ill-humour. **3** CALM, composure, self-control, cool (*sl*).
**F3** 2 calmness, self-control. 3 anger, rage.
*v* **1** MODERATE, lessen, reduce, calm, soothe, allay, assuage, palliate, mitigate, modify, soften. **2** HARDEN, toughen, strengthen.

**temperament** *n* nature, character, personality, disposition, tendency, bent, constitution, make-up, soul, spirit, mood, humour, temper, state of mind, attitude, outlook.

**temperamental** *adj* **1** MOODY, emotional, neurotic, highly-strung, sensitive, touchy, irritable, impatient, passionate, fiery, excitable, explosive, volatile, mercurial, capricious, unpredictable, unreliable.
**2** NATURAL, inborn, innate, inherent, constitutional, ingrained.
**F3** 1 calm, level-headed, steady.

**temperance** *n* teetotalism, prohibition, abstinence, abstemiousness, sobriety, continence, moderation, restraint, self-restraint, self-control, self-discipline, self-denial.
**F3** intemperance, excess.

**temperate** *adj* **1** *temperate climate*: mild, clement, balmy, fair, equable, balanced, stable, gentle, pleasant, agreeable. **2** TEETOTAL, abstinent, abstemious, sober, continent, moderate, restrained, controlled, even-tempered, calm, composed, reasonable, sensible.
**F3** 2 intemperate, extreme, excessive.

**tempestuous** *adj* stormy, windy,

gusty, blustery, squally, turbulent, tumultuous, rough, wild, violent, furious, raging, heated, passionate, intense.

**F3** calm.

**temple** *n* shrine, sanctuary, church, tabernacle, mosque, pagoda.

**tempo** *n* time, rhythm, metre, beat, pulse, speed, velocity, rate, pace.

**temporal** *adj* secular, profane, worldly, earthly, terrestrial, material, carnal, fleshly, mortal.

**F3** spiritual.

**temporary** *adj* impermanent, provisional, interim, makeshift, stopgap, temporal, transient, transitory, passing, ephemeral, evanescent, fleeting, brief, short-lived, momentary.

**F3** permanent, everlasting.

**tempt** *v* entice, coax, persuade, woo, bait, lure, allure, attract, draw, seduce, invite, tantalize, provoke, incite.

**F3** discourage, dissuade, repel.

**temptation** *n* enticement, inducement, coaxing, persuasion, bait, lure, allure, appeal, attraction, draw, pull, seduction, invitation.

**tenable** *adj* credible, defensible, justifiable, reasonable, rational, sound, arguable, believable, defendable, plausible, viable, feasible.

**F3** untenable, indefensible, unjustifiable.

**tenant** *n* renter, lessee, leaseholder, occupier, occupant, resident, inhabitant.

**tend¹** *v* incline, lean, bend, bear, head, aim, lead, go, move, gravitate.

**tend²** *v* look after, care for, cultivate, keep, maintain, manage, handle, guard, protect, watch, mind, nurture, nurse, minister to, serve, attend.

**F3** neglect, ignore.

**tendency** *n* trend, drift, movement, course, direction, bearing, heading, bias, partiality, predisposition, propensity, readiness, liability,

susceptibility, proneness, inclination, leaning, bent, disposition.

**tender¹** *adj* **1** KIND, gentle, caring, humane, considerate, compassionate, sympathetic, warm, fond, affectionate, loving, amorous, romantic, sentimental, emotional, sensitive, tender-hearted, soft-hearted. **2** YOUNG, youthful, immature, green, raw, new, inexperienced, impressionable, vulnerable. **3** SOFT, succulent, fleshy, dainty, delicate, fragile, frail, weak, feeble. **4** SORE, painful, aching, smarting, bruised, inflamed, raw.

**F3 1** hard-hearted, callous. **2** mature. **3** tough, hard.

**tender²** *v* offer, proffer, extend, give, present, submit, propose, suggest, advance, volunteer.

*n* **1** *legal tender*: currency, money. **2** OFFER, bid, estimate, quotation, proposal, proposition, suggestion, submission.

**tense** *adj* **1** TIGHT, taut, stretched, strained, stiff, rigid. **2** NERVOUS, anxious, worried, jittery, uneasy, apprehensive, edgy, fidgety, restless, jumpy, overwrought, keyed up. **3** STRESSFUL, exciting, worrying, fraught.

**F3 1** loose, slack. **2** calm, relaxed.

*v* tighten, contract, brace, stretch, strain.

**F3** loosen, relax.

**tension** *n* **1** TIGHTNESS, tautness, stiffness, strain, stress, pressure. **2** NERVOUSNESS, anxiety, worry, uneasiness, apprehension, edginess, restlessness, suspense.

**F3 1** looseness. **2** calm(ness), relaxation.

**tent** *n* tepee, wigwam, marquee, big top.

**tentative** *adj* experimental, exploratory, speculative, hesitant, faltering, cautious, unsure, uncertain, doubtful, undecided, provisional, indefinite, unconfirmed.

**E3** definite, decisive, conclusive, final.

**tenuous** *adj* thin, slim, slender, fine, slight, insubstantial, flimsy, fragile, delicate, weak, shaky, doubtful, dubious, questionable.
**E3** strong, substantial.

**tepid** *adj* lukewarm, cool, half-hearted, unenthusiastic, apathetic.
**E3** cold, hot, passionate.

**term** *n* **1** WORD, name, designation, appellation, title, epithet, phrase, expression. **2** TIME, period, course, duration, spell, span, stretch, interval, space, semester, session, season.
*v* call, name, dub, style, designate, label, tag, title, entitle.

**terminal** *adj* **1** LAST, final, concluding, ultimate, extreme, utmost. **2** *terminal illness*: FATAL, deadly, lethal, mortal, incurable.
**E3 1** initial.

**terminate** *v* finish, complete, conclude, cease, end, stop, close, discontinue, wind up, cut off, abort, lapse, expire.
**E3** begin, start, initiate.

**terminology** *n* language, jargon, phraseology, vocabulary, words, terms, nomenclature.

**terminus** *n* end, close, termination, extremity, limit, boundary, destination, goal, target, depot, station, garage, terminal.

**terms** *n* **1** *on good terms*: relations, relationship, footing, standing, position. **2** CONDITIONS, specifications, stipulations, provisos, provisions, qualifications, particulars. **3** RATES, charges, fees, prices, tariff.

**terrain** *n* land, ground, territory, country, countryside, landscape, topography.

**terrestrial** *adj* earthly, worldly, global, mundane.
**E3** cosmic, heavenly.

**terrible** *adj* bad, awful, frightful, dreadful, shocking, appalling,

outrageous, disgusting, revolting, repulsive, offensive, abhorrent, hateful, horrid, horrible, unpleasant, obnoxious, foul, vile, hideous, gruesome, horrific, harrowing, distressing, grave, serious, severe, extreme, desperate.
**E3** excellent, wonderful, superb.

**terribly** (*infml*) *adv* very, much, greatly, extremely, exceedingly, awfully, frightfully, decidedly, seriously.

**terrific** (*infml*) *adj* **1** EXCELLENT, wonderful, marvellous, super, smashing (*infml*), outstanding, brilliant, magnificent, superb, fabulous (*infml*), fantastic (*infml*), sensational, amazing, stupendous, breathtaking. **2** HUGE, enormous, gigantic, tremendous, great, intense, extreme, excessive.
**E3 1** awful, terrible, appalling.

**terrify** *v* petrify, horrify, appal, shock, terrorize, intimidate, frighten, scare, alarm, dismay.

**territory** *n* country, land, state, dependency, province, domain, preserve, jurisdiction, sector, region, area, district, zone, tract, terrain.

**terror** *n* fear, panic, dread, trepidation, horror, shock, fright, alarm, dismay, consternation, terrorism, intimidation.

**terrorize** *v* threaten, menace, intimidate, oppress, coerce, bully, browbeat, frighten, scare, alarm, terrify, petrify, horrify, shock.

**terse** *adj* short, brief, succinct, concise, compact, condensed, epigrammatic, pithy, incisive, snappy, curt, brusque, abrupt, laconic.
**E3** long-winded, verbose.

**test** *v* try, experiment, examine, assess, evaluate, check, investigate, analyse, screen, prove, verify.
*n* trial, try-out, experiment, examination, assessment, evaluation, check, investigation, analysis, proof,

probation, ordeal.

**testify** v give evidence, depose, state, declare, assert, swear, avow, attest, vouch, certify, corroborate, affirm, show, bear witness.

**testimonial** n reference, character, credential, certificate, recommendation, endorsement, commendation, tribute.

**testimony** n evidence, statement, affidavit, submission, deposition, declaration, profession, attestation, affirmation, support, proof, verification, confirmation, witness, demonstration, manifestation, indication.

**tether** n chain, rope, cord, line, lead, leash, bond, fetter, shackle, restraint, fastening.

v tie, fasten, secure, restrain, chain, rope, leash, bind, lash, fetter, shackle, manacle.

**text** n words, wording, content, matter, body, subject, topic, theme, reading, passage, paragraph, sentence, book, textbook, source.

**texture** n consistency, feel, surface, grain, weave, tissue, fabric, structure, composition, constitution, character, quality.

**thank** v say thank you, be grateful, appreciate, acknowledge, recognize, credit.

**thankful** adj grateful, appreciative, obliged, indebted, pleased, contented, relieved.
**F3** ungrateful, unappreciative.

**thankless** adj unrecognized, unappreciated, unrequited, unrewarding, unprofitable, fruitless.
**F3** rewarding, worthwhile.

**thanks** n gratitude, gratefulness, appreciation, acknowledgement, recognition, credit, thanksgiving, thank-offering.

**thanks to** because of, owing to, due to, on account of, as a result of, through.

**thaw** v melt, defrost, defreeze, de-ice, soften, liquefy, dissolve, warm, heat

up.
**F3** freeze.

**theatrical** adj 1 DRAMATIC, thespian. 2 MELODRAMATIC, histrionic, mannered, affected, artificial, pompous, ostentatious, showy, extravagant, exaggerated, overdone.

---

*Theatrical forms include:* ballet, burlesque, cabaret, circus, comedy, black comedy, comedy of humours, comedy of manners, comedy of menace, commedia dell'arte, duologue, farce, fringe theatre, Grand Guignol, kabuki, Kensington gore, Kitchen-Sink, legitimate drama, masque, melodrama, mime, miracle play, monologue, morality play, mummery, music hall, musical, musical comedy, mystery play, Noh, opera, operetta, pageant, pantomime, play, Punch and Judy, puppet theatre, revue, street theatre, tableau, theatre-in-the-round, Theatre of the Absurd, Theatre of Cruelty, tragedy. *see also* **performance**.

---

**theft** n robbery, thieving, stealing, pilfering, larceny, shop-lifting, kleptomania, fraud, embezzlement.

**theme** n subject, topic, thread, motif, keynote, idea, gist, essence, burden, argument, thesis, dissertation, composition, essay, text, matter.

**theorem** n formula, principle, rule, statement, deduction, proposition, hypothesis.

**theoretical** adj hypothetical, conjectural, speculative, abstract, academic, doctrinaire, pure, ideal.
**F3** practical, applied, concrete.

**theorize** v hypothesize, suppose, guess, conjecture, speculate, postulate, propound, formulate.

**theory** n hypothesis, supposition, assumption, presumption, surmise, guess, conjecture, speculation, idea,

notion, abstraction, philosophy, thesis, plan, proposal, scheme, system.
☞ certainty, practice.

**therapeutic** *adj* remedial, curative, healing, restorative, tonic, medicinal, corrective, good, beneficial.
☞ harmful, detrimental.

**therapy** *n* treatment, remedy, cure, healing, tonic.

**therefore** *adv* so, then, consequently, as a result.

**thesis** *n* 1 *doctoral thesis*: dissertation, essay, composition, treatise, paper, monograph.
2 SUBJECT, topic, theme, idea, opinion, view, theory, hypothesis, proposal, proposition, premise, statement, argument, contention.

**thick** *adj* 1 WIDE, broad, fat, heavy, solid, dense, impenetrable, close, compact, concentrated, condensed, viscous, coagulated, clotted. 2 FULL, packed, crowded, chock-a-block, swarming, teeming, bristling, brimming, bursting, numerous, abundant. 3 (*infml*) STUPID, foolish, slow, dull, dim-witted, brainless, simple.
☞ 1 thin, slim, slender, slight.
2 sparse. 3 clever, brainy (*infml*).

**thicken** *v* condense, stiffen, congeal, coagulate, clot, cake, gel, jell, set.
☞ thin.

**thicket** *n* wood, copse, coppice, grove, spinney.

**thickness** *n* 1 WIDTH, breadth, diameter, density, viscosity, bulk, body. 2 LAYER, stratum, ply, sheet, coat.
☞ 1 thinness.

**thick-skinned** *adj* insensitive, unfeeling, callous, tough, hardened, hard-boiled.
☞ thin-skinned, sensitive.

**thief** *n* robber, bandit, mugger, pickpocket, shop-lifter, burglar, house-breaker, plunderer, poacher, stealer, pilferer, filcher,

kleptomaniac, swindler, embezzler.

**thin** *adj* 1 LEAN, slim, slender, narrow, attenuated, slight, skinny, bony, skeletal, scraggy, scrawny, lanky, gaunt, spare, underweight, undernourished, emaciated. 2 *thin fabric*: fine, delicate, light, flimsy, filmy, gossamer, sheer, see-through, transparent, translucent. 3 SPARSE, scarce, scattered, scant, meagre, poor, inadequate, deficient, scanty, skimpy. 4 WEAK, feeble, runny, watery, diluted.
☞ 1 fat, broad. 2 thick, dense, solid. 3 plentiful, abundant. 4 strong.
*v* 1 NARROW, attenuate, diminish, reduce, trim, weed out. 2 WEAKEN, dilute, water down, rarefy, refine.

**thing** *n* 1 ARTICLE, object, entity, creature, body, substance, item, detail, particular, feature, factor, element, point, fact, concept, thought. 2 DEVICE, contrivance, gadget, tool, implement, instrument, apparatus, machine, mechanism.
3 ACT, deed, feat, action, task, responsibility, problem. 4 CIRCUMSTANCE, eventuality, happening, occurrence, event, incident, phenomenon, affair, proceeding. 5 (*infml*) OBSESSION, preoccupation, fixation, fetish, phobia, hang-up (*infml*).

**things** *n* belongings, possessions, effects, paraphernalia, stuff (*infml*), goods, luggage, baggage, equipment, gear (*infml*), clobber (*infml*), odds and ends, bits and pieces.

**think** *v* 1 BELIEVE, hold, consider, regard, esteem, deem, judge, estimate, reckon, calculate, determine, conclude, reason.
2 CONCEIVE, imagine, suppose, presume, surmise, expect, foresee, envisage, anticipate. 3 *think it over*: ponder, mull over, chew over, ruminate, meditate, contemplate, muse, cogitate, reflect, deliberate, weigh up, recall, recollect, remember.

**think up** devise, contrive, dream up, imagine, conceive, visualize, invent, design, create, concoct.

**thinker** n philosopher, theorist, ideologist, brain, intellect, mastermind.

**thinking** n reasoning, philosophy, thoughts, conclusions, theory, idea, opinion, view, outlook, position, judgement, assessment.
adj reasoning, rational, intellectual, intelligent, cultured, sophisticated, philosophical, analytical, reflective, contemplative, thoughtful.

**third-rate** adj low-grade, poor, bad, inferior, mediocre, indifferent, shoddy, cheap and nasty.
E3 first-rate.

**thirst** n 1 THIRSTINESS, dryness, drought. 2 DESIRE, longing, yearning, hankering, craving, hunger, appetite, lust, passion, eagerness, keenness.

**thirsty** adj 1 DRY, parched (infml), gasping (infml), dehydrated, arid. 2 thirsty for knowledge: desirous, longing, yearning, hankering, craving, hungry, burning, itching, dying, eager, avid, greedy.

**thorn** n spike, point, barb, prickle, spine, bristle, needle.

**thorough** adj full, complete, total, entire, utter, absolute, perfect, pure, sheer, unqualified, unmitigated, out-and-out, downright, sweeping, all-embracing, comprehensive, all-inclusive, exhaustive, thoroughgoing, intensive, in-depth, conscientious, efficient, painstaking, scrupulous, meticulous, careful.
E3 partial, superficial, careless.

**though** conj although, even if, notwithstanding, while, allowing, granted.
adv however, nevertheless, nonetheless, yet, still, even so, all the same, for all that.

**thought** n 1 THINKING, attention, heed, regard, consideration, study,

scrutiny, introspection, meditation, contemplation, cogitation, reflection, deliberation. 2 IDEA, notion, concept, conception, belief, conviction, opinion, view, judgement, assessment, conclusion, plan, design, intention, purpose, aim, hope, dream, expectation, anticipation.
3 THOUGHTFULNESS, consideration, kindness, care, concern, compassion, sympathy, gesture, touch.

**thoughtful** adj 1 PENSIVE, wistful, dreamy, abstracted, reflective, contemplative, introspective, thinking, absorbed, studious, serious, solemn. 2 CONSIDERATE, kind, unselfish, helpful, caring, attentive, heedful, mindful, careful, prudent, cautious, wary.
E3 2 thoughtless, insensitive, selfish.

**thoughtless** adj 1 INCONSIDERATE, unthinking, insensitive, unfeeling, tactless, undiplomatic, unkind, selfish, uncaring. 2 absent-minded, inattentive, heedless, mindless, foolish, stupid, silly, rash, reckless, ill-considered, imprudent, careless, negligent, remiss.
E3 1 thoughtful, considerate. 2 careful.

**thrash** v 1 PUNISH, beat, whip, lash, flog, scourge, cane, belt, spank, clobber, wallop (infml), lay into. 2 DEFEAT, beat, trounce, hammer (infml), slaughter (infml), crush, overwhelm, rout. 3 THRESH, flail, toss, jerk.
**thrash out** discuss, debate, negotiate, settle, resolve.

**thread** n 1 COTTON, yarn, strand, fibre, filament, string, line.
2 COURSE, direction, drift, tenor, theme, motif, plot, storyline.

**threadbare** adj 1 threadbare clothes: worn, frayed, ragged, moth-eaten, scruffy, shabby.
2 HACKNEYED, overused, old, stale, tired, trite, commonplace, stock, stereotyped.
E3 1 new. 2 fresh.

**threat** *n* menace, warning, omen, portent, presage, foreboding, danger, risk, hazard, peril.

**threaten** *v* menace, intimidate, browbeat, pressurize, bully, terrorize, warn, portend, presage, forebode, foreshadow, endanger, jeopardize, imperil.

**threatening** *adj* menacing, intimidatory, warning, cautionary, ominous, inauspicious, sinister, grim, looming, impending.

**threshold** *n* doorstep, sill, doorway, door, entrance, brink, verge, starting-point, dawn, beginning, start, outset, opening.

**thrift** *n* economy, husbandry, saving, conservation, frugality, prudence, carefulness.
**F∃** extravagance, waste.

**thrifty** *adj* economical, saving, frugal, sparing, prudent, careful.
**F∃** extravagant, profligate, prodigal, wasteful.

**thrill** *n* excitement, adventure, pleasure, stimulation, charge, kick, buzz (*sl*), sensation, glow, tingle, throb, shudder, quiver, tremor.
*v* excite, electrify, galvanize, exhilarate, rouse, arouse, move, stir, stimulate, flush, glow, tingle, throb, shudder, tremble, quiver, shake.
**F∃** bore.

**thrive** *v* flourish, prosper, boom, grow, increase, advance, develop, bloom, blossom, gain, profit, succeed.
**F∃** languish, stagnate, fail, die.

**throb** *v* pulse, pulsate, beat, palpitate, vibrate, pound, thump.
*n* pulse, pulsation, beat, palpitation, vibration, pounding, thumping.

**throttle** *v* strangle, choke, asphyxiate, suffocate, smother, stifle, gag, silence, suppress, inhibit.

**through** *prep* **1** BETWEEN, by, via, by way of, by means of, using. **2** *all through the night*: throughout, during, in. **3** BECAUSE OF, as a result of, thanks to.
*adj* **1** FINISHED, ended, completed, done. **2** *through train*: direct, express, non-stop.

**throw** *v* **1** HURL, heave, lob, pitch, chuck (*infml*), sling, cast, fling, toss, launch, propel, send. **2** *throw light*: shed, cast, project, direct. **3** BRING DOWN, floor, upset, overturn, dislodge, unseat, unsaddle, unhorse. **4** (*infml*) PERPLEX, baffle, confound, confuse, disconcert, astonish, dumbfound.
*n* heave, lob, pitch, sling, fling, toss, cast.

**throw away 1** DISCARD, jettison, dump, ditch (*sl*), scrap, dispose of, throw out. **2** WASTE, squander, fritter away, blow (*sl*).
**F∃** keep, preserve, salvage, rescue.

**throw off** shed, cast off, drop, abandon, shake off, get rid of, elude.

**throw out 1** EVICT, turn out, expel, turf out (*infml*), eject, emit, radiate, give off. **2** REJECT, discard, dismiss, turn down, jettison, dump, ditch (*sl*), throw away, scrap.

**throw up 1** (*infml*) VOMIT, spew, regurgitate, disgorge, retch, heave. **2** abandon, renounce, relinquish, resign, quit, leave. **3** GIVE UP.

**thrust** *v* push, shove, butt, ram, jam, wedge, stick, poke, prod, jab, lunge, pierce, stab, plunge, press, force, impel, drive, propel.
*n* push, shove, poke, prod, lunge, stab, drive, impetus, momentum.

**thud**, *n*, *v* thump, clump, knock, clunk, smack, wallop (*infml*), crash, bang, thunder.

**thug** *n* ruffian, tough, robber, bandit, mugger, killer, murderer, assassin, gangster, hooligan.

**thump** *n* knock, blow, punch, clout, box, cuff, smack, whack (*infml*), wallop (*infml*), crash, bang, thud, beat, throb.
*v* hit, strike, knock, punch, clout, box, cuff, smack, thrash, whack

(*infml*), wallop (*infml*), crash, bang, thud, batter, pound, hammer, beat, throb.

**thunder** *n* boom, reverberation, crash, bang, crack, clap, peal, rumble, roll, roar, blast, explosion.
*v* boom, resound, reverberate, crash, bang, crack, clap, peal, rumble, roll, roar, blast.

**thunderous** *adj* booming, resounding, reverberating, roaring, loud, noisy, deafening, ear-splitting.

**thus** *adv* so, hence, therefore, consequently, then, accordingly, like this, in this way, as follows.

**thwart** *v* frustrate, foil, stymie, defeat, hinder, impede, obstruct, block, check, baffle, stop, prevent, oppose.
**F3** help, assist, aid.

**tick** *n* 1 CLICK, tap, stroke, tick-tock. 2 (*infml*) *wait a tick*: moment, instant, flash, jiffy (*infml*), second, minute.
*v* 1 MARK, indicate, choose, select. 2 CLICK, tap, beat.

**tick off** (*infml*) scold, chide, reprimand, rebuke, reproach, reprove, upbraid, tell off (*infml*).
**F3** praise, compliment.

**ticket** *n* pass, card, certificate, token, voucher, coupon, docket, slip, label, tag, sticker.

**tickle** *v* excite, thrill, delight, please, gratify, amuse, entertain, divert.

**ticklish** *adj* sensitive, touchy, delicate, thorny, awkward, difficult, tricky, critical, risky, hazardous, dodgy (*infml*).
**F3** easy, simple.

**tide** *n* current, ebb, flow, stream, flux, movement, course, direction, drift, trend, tendency.

**tidy** *adj* 1 NEAT, orderly, methodical, systematic, organized, clean, spick-and-span, shipshape, smart, spruce, trim, well-kept, ordered, uncluttered. 2 (*infml*) *a tidy sum*: large, substantial, sizable, considerable,

good, generous, ample.
**F3** 1 untidy, messy, disorganized. 2 small, insignificant.
*v* neaten, straighten, order, arrange, clean, smarten, spruce up, groom.

**tie** *v* knot, fasten, secure, moor, tether, attach, join, connect, link, unite, rope, lash, strap, bind, restrain, restrict, confine, limit, hamper, hinder.
*n* 1 KNOT, fastening, joint, connection, link, liaison, relationship, bond, affiliation, obligation, commitment, duty, restraint, restriction, limitation, hindrance. 2 DRAW, dead heat, stalemate, deadlock.

**tie up** 1 MOOR, tether, attach, secure, rope, lash, bind, truss, wrap up, restrain. 2 CONCLUDE, terminate, wind up, settle. 3 OCCUPY, engage, engross.

**tier** *n* floor, storey, level, stage, stratum, layer, belt, zone, band, echelon, rank, row, line.

**tight** *adj* 1 TAUT, stretched, tense, rigid, stiff, firm, fixed, fast, secure, close, cramped, constricted, compact, snug, close-fitting. 2 SEALED, hermetic, -proof, impervious, airtight, watertight. 3 (*infml*) MEAN, stingy, miserly, niggardly, parsimonious, tight-fisted (*infml*). 4 *tight security*: strict, severe, stringent, rigorous.
**F3** 1 loose, slack. 2 open. 3 generous. 4 lax.

**tighten** *v* tauten, stretch, tense, stiffen, fix, fasten, secure, narrow, close, cramp, constrict, crush, squeeze.
**F3** loosen, relax.

**tight-fisted** (*infml*) *adj* mean, stingy, miserly, mingy (*infml*), niggardly, penny-pinching, sparing, parsimonious, tight (*infml*), grasping.
**F3** generous, charitable.

**till** *v* cultivate, work, plough, dig, farm.

**tilt** *v* slope, incline, slant, pitch, list, tip, lean.
*n* slope, incline, angle, inclination, slant, pitch, list.

**timber** *n* wood, trees, forest, beam, lath, plank, board, log.

**time** *n* **1** SPELL, stretch, period, term, season, session, span, duration, interval, space, while. **2** TEMPO, beat, rhythm, metre, measure. **3** MOMENT, point, juncture, stage, instance, occasion, date, day, hour. **4** AGE, era, epoch, life, lifetime, generation, heyday, peak.

*Periods of time include:* eternity, eon, era, age, generation, epoch, millennium, chiliad, century, lifetime, decade, decennium, quinquennium, year, light-year, yesteryear, quarter, month, fortnight, week, midweek, weekend, long weekend, day, today, tonight, yesterday, tomorrow, morrow, weekday, hour, minute, second, moment, instant, millisecond, microsecond, nanosecond; dawn, sunrise, sun-up, the early hours, wee small hours (*infml*), morning, morn, a.m., daytime, midday, noon, high noon, p.m., afternoon, tea-time, evening, twilight, dusk, sunset, nightfall, bedtime, night, night-time; season, spring, summer, midsummer, autumn, fall, (*North Amer.*) winter.

*v* clock, measure, meter, regulate, control, set, schedule, timetable.

**timeless** *adj* ageless, immortal, everlasting, eternal, endless, permanent, changeless, unchanging.

**timely** *adj* well-timed, seasonable, suitable, appropriate, convenient, opportune, propitious, prompt, punctual.
🔁 ill-timed, unsuitable, inappropriate.

**timetable** *n* schedule, programme, agenda, calendar, diary, rota, roster, list, listing, curriculum.

**timid** *adj* shy, bashful, modest, shrinking, retiring, nervous, apprehensive, afraid, timorous, fearful, cowardly, faint-hearted, spineless, irresolute.
🔁 brave, bold, audacious.

**tinge** *n* tint, dye, colour, shade, touch, trace, suggestion, hint, smack, flavour, pinch, drop, dash, bit, sprinkling, smattering.
*v* tint, dye, stain, colour, shade, suffuse, imbue.

**tingle** *v* sting, prickle, tickle, itch, thrill, throb, quiver, vibrate.
*n* stinging, prickling, pins and needles, tickle, tickling, itch, itching, thrill, throb, quiver, shiver, gooseflesh, goose-pimples.

**tinker** *v* fiddle, play, toy, trifle, potter, dabble, meddle, tamper.

**tint** *n* dye, stain, rinse, wash, colour, hue, shade, tincture, tinge, tone, cast, streak, trace, touch.
*v* dye, colour, tinge, streak, stain, taint, affect.

**tiny** *adj* minute, microscopic, infinitesimal, teeny (*infml*), small, little, slight, negligible, insignificant, diminutive, petite, dwarfish, pint-sized (*infml*), pocket, miniature, mini (*infml*).
🔁 huge, enormous, immense.

**tip**[1] *n* end, extremity, point, nib, apex, peak, pinnacle, summit, acme, top, cap, crown, head.
*v* cap, crown, top, surmount.

**tip**[2] *v* lean, incline, slant, list, tilt, topple over, capsize, upset, overturn, spill, pour out, empty, unload, dump.
*n* dump, rubbish-heap, refuse-heap.

**tip**[3] *n* **1** CLUE, pointer, hint, suggestion, advice, warning, tip-off, information, inside information, forecast. **2** GRATUITY, gift, perquisite.
*v* **1** ADVISE, suggest, warn, caution, forewarn, tip off, inform, tell. **2** *tip the driver:* reward, remunerate.

**tire** *v* weary, fatigue, wear out,

exhaust, drain, enervate.

☒ enliven, invigorate, refresh.

**tired** *adj* **1** WEARY, drowsy, sleepy, flagging, fatigued, worn out, exhausted, dog-tired, drained, jaded, fagged (*sl*), bushed (*infml*), whacked (*infml*), shattered (*infml*), beat (*infml*), dead-beat (*infml*), all in (*infml*), knackered (*infml*). **2** *tired of waiting*: fed up, bored, sick.

☒ **1** lively, energetic, rested, refreshed. **3** new.

**tireless** *adj* untiring, unwearied, unflagging, indefatigable, energetic, vigorous, diligent, industrious, resolute, determined.

☒ weary, lazy.

**tiresome** *adj* troublesome, trying, annoying, irritating, exasperating, wearisome, dull, boring, tedious, monotonous, uninteresting, tiring, fatiguing, laborious.

☒ interesting, stimulating, easy.

**tiring** *adj* wearying, fatiguing, exhausting, draining, demanding, exacting, taxing, arduous, strenuous, laborious.

**tissue** *n* substance, matter, material, fabric, stuff, gauze, web, mesh, network, structure, texture.

**titbit** *n* morsel, scrap, appetizer, snack, delicacy, dainty, treat.

**titillate** *v* stimulate, arouse, turn on (*sl*), excite, thrill, tickle, provoke, tease, tantalize, intrigue, interest.

**title** *n* **1** NAME, appellation, denomination, term, designation, label, epithet, nickname, pseudonym, rank, status, office, position. **2** HEADING, headline, caption, legend, inscription. **3** RIGHT, prerogative, privilege, claim, entitlement, ownership, deeds.

*v* entitle, name, call, dub, style, term, designate, label.

**titter** *v* laugh, chortle, chuckle, giggle, snigger, mock.

**titular** *adj* honorary, formal, official, so-called, nominal, token.

**toast** *v* grill, brown, roast, heat, warm.

*n* drink, pledge, tribute, salute, compliment, health.

**together** *adv* jointly, in concert, side by side, shoulder to shoulder, in unison, as one, simultaneously, at the same time, all at once, collectively, en masse, closely, continuously, consecutively, successively, in succession, in a row, hand in hand.

☒ separately, individually, alone.

**toil** *n* labour, hard work, donkey-work, drudgery, sweat, graft (*infml*), industry, application, effort, exertion, elbow grease.

*v* labour, work, slave, drudge, sweat, grind, slog, graft (*infml*), plug away (*infml*), persevere, strive, struggle.

**toilet** *n* lavatory, WC, loo (*infml*), bog (*sl*), bathroom, cloakroom, washroom, rest room, public convenience, Ladies (*infml*), Gents (*infml*), urinal, convenience, powder room.

**token** *n* **1** SYMBOL, emblem, representation, mark, sign, indication, manifestation, demonstration, expression, evidence, proof, clue, warning, reminder, memorial, memento, souvenir, keepsake. **2** *gift token*: voucher, coupon, counter, disc.

*adj* symbolic, emblematic, nominal, minimal, perfunctory, superficial, cosmetic, hollow, insincere.

**tolerable** *adj* bearable, endurable, sufferable, acceptable, passable, adequate, reasonable, fair, average, all right, OK (*infml*), not bad, mediocre, indifferent, so-so (*infml*), unexceptional, ordinary, run-of-the-mill.

☒ intolerable, unbearable, insufferable.

**tolerance** *n* **1** TOLERATION, patience, forbearance, open-mindedness, broad-mindedness, magnanimity, sympathy, understanding, lenity, indulgence, permissiveness. **2** VARIATION, fluctuation, play, allowance, clearance. **3** RESISTANCE, resilience, toughness, endurance, stamina. **🖃 1** intolerance, prejudice, bigotry, narrow-mindedness.

**tolerant** *adj* patient, forbearing, long-suffering, open-minded, fair, unprejudiced, broad-minded, liberal, charitable, kind-hearted, sympathetic, understanding, forgiving, lenient, indulgent, easy-going (*infml*), permissive, lax, soft. **🖃** intolerant, biased, prejudiced, bigoted, unsympathetic.

**tolerate** *v* endure, suffer, put up with, bear, stand, abide, stomach, swallow, take, receive, accept, admit, allow, permit, condone, countenance, indulge.

**toll¹** *v* ring, peal, chime, knell, sound, strike, announce, call.

**toll²** *n* charge, fee, payment, levy, tax, duty, tariff, rate, cost, penalty, demand, loss.

**tomb** *n* grave, burial-place, vault, crypt, sepulchre, catacomb, mausoleum, cenotaph.

**tone** *n* **1** *tone of voice*: note, timbre, pitch, volume, intonation, modulation, inflection, accent, stress, emphasis, force, strength. **2** TINT, tinge, colour, hue, shade, cast, tonality. **3** AIR, manner, attitude, mood, spirit, humour, temper, character, quality, feel, style, effect, vein, tenor, drift.
*v* match, co-ordinate, blend, harmonize.

**tone down** moderate, temper, subdue, restrain, soften, dim, dampen, play down, reduce, alleviate, assuage, mitigate.

**tongue** *n* language, speech, discourse, talk, utterance, articulation, parlance, vernacular, idiom, dialect, patois.

**tongue-tied** *adj* speechless,

dumbstruck, inarticulate, silent, mute, dumb, voiceless. **🖃** talkative, garrulous, voluble.

**tonic** *n* cordial, pick-me-up, restorative, refresher, bracer, stimulant, shot in the arm (*infml*), boost, fillip.

**too** *adv* **1** ALSO, as well, in addition, besides, moreover, likewise. **2** EXCESSIVELY, inordinately, unduly, over, overly, unreasonably, ridiculously, extremely, very.

**tool** *n* **1** IMPLEMENT, instrument, utensil, gadget, device, contrivance, contraption, apparatus, appliance, machine, means, vehicle, medium, agency, agent, intermediary. **2** PUPPET, pawn, dupe, stooge, minion, hireling.

---

*Types of tool include*: bolster, caulking-iron, crowbar, hod, jackhammer, jointer, mattock, pick, pick-axe, plumb-line, sledgehammer; chaser, clamp, dividers, dolly, drill, hacksaw, jack, pincers, pliers, protractor, punch, rule, sander, scriber, snips, socket-wrench, soldering-iron, spraygun, tommy bar, vice; auger, awl, brace and bit, bradawl, chisel, file, fretsaw, hammer, handsaw, jack-plane, jig-saw, level, mallet, plane, rasp, saw, screwdriver, set-square, spirit level, tenon-saw, T-square; billhook, chainsaw, chopper, dibber, fork, grass-rake, hay fork, hoe, pitchfork, plough, pruning-knife, pruning-shears, rake, scythe, secateurs, shears, shovel, sickle, spade, thresher, trowel; needle, scissors, pinking-shears, bodkin, crochet hook, forceps, scalpel, tweezers, tongs, cleaver, steel, gimlet, mace, mortar, pestle, paper-cutter, paper-knife, stapler, pocket-knife, penknife.

---

**top** *n* **1** HEAD, tip, vertex, apex, crest, crown, peak, pinnacle, summit, acme, zenith, culmination, height. **2**

LID, cap, cover, cork, stopper.
**F3** 1 bottom, base, nadir.
*adj* highest, topmost, upmost, uppermost, upper, superior, head, chief, leading, first, foremost, principal, sovereign, ruling, pre-eminent, dominant, prime, paramount, greatest, maximum, best, finest, supreme, crowning, culminating.
**F3** bottom, lowest, inferior.
*v* 1 TIP, cap, crown, cover, finish (off), decorate, garnish. 2 BEAT, exceed, outstrip, better, excel, best, surpass, eclipse, outshine, outdo, surmount, transcend. 3 HEAD, lead, rule, command.

**topic** *n* subject, theme, issue, question, matter, point, thesis, text.

**topical** *adj* current, contemporary, up-to-date, up-to-the-minute, recent, newsworthy, relevant, popular, familiar.

**topple** *v* totter, overbalance, tumble, fall, collapse, upset, overturn, capsize, overthrow, oust.

**torment** *v* tease, provoke, annoy, vex, trouble, worry, harass, hound, pester, bother, bedevil, plague, afflict, distress, harrow, pain, torture, persecute.
*n* provocation, annoyance, vexation, bane, scourge, trouble, bother, nuisance, harassment, worry, anguish, distress, misery, affliction, suffering, pain, agony, ordeal, torture, persecution.

**torrent** *n* stream, volley, outburst, gush, rush, flood, spate, deluge, cascade, downpour.
**F3** trickle.

**tortuous** *adj* twisting, winding, meandering, serpentine, zigzag, circuitous, roundabout, indirect, convoluted, complicated, involved.
**F3** straight, straightforward.

**torture** *v* pain, agonize, excruciate, crucify, rack, martyr, persecute, torment, afflict, distress.

*n* pain, agony, suffering, affliction, distress, misery, anguish, torment, martyrdom, persecution.

**toss** *v* 1 FLIP, cast, fling, throw, chuck (*infml*), sling, hurl, lob.
2 ROLL, heave, pitch, lurch, jolt, shake, agitate, rock, thrash, squirm, wriggle.
*n* flip, cast, fling, throw, pitch.

**total** *n* sum, whole, entirety, totality, all, lot, mass, aggregate, amount.
*adj* full, complete, entire, whole, integral, all-out, utter, absolute, unconditional, unqualified, outright, undisputed, perfect, consummate, thoroughgoing, sheer, downright, thorough.
**F3** partial, limited, restricted.
*v* add (up), sum (up), tot (up), count (up), reckon, amount to, come to, reach.

**totter** *v* stagger, reel, lurch, stumble, falter, waver, teeter, sway, rock, shake, quiver, tremble.

**touch** *n* 1 FEEL, texture, brush, stroke, caress, pat, tap, contact. 2 *a touch of garlic*: trace, spot, dash, pinch, soupçon, suspicion, hint, suggestion, speck, jot, tinge, smack.
3 SKILL, art, knack, flair, style, method, manner, technique, approach.
*v* 1 FEEL, handle, finger, brush, graze, stroke, caress, fondle, pat, tap, hit, strike, contact, meet, abut, adjoin, border. 2 MOVE, stir, upset, disturb, impress, inspire, influence, affect, concern, regard. 3 REACH, attain, equal, match, rival, better.
**touch on** mention, broach, speak of, remark on, refer to, allude to, cover, deal with.

**touched** *adj* 1 MOVED, stirred, affected, disturbed, impressed.
2 MAD, crazy, deranged, disturbed, eccentric, dotty (*infml*), daft (*infml*), barmy (*infml*).

**touching** *adj* moving, stirring, affecting, poignant, pitiable, pitiful, pathetic, sad, emotional, tender.

**touchy** *adj* irritable, irascible, quick-tempered, bad-tempered, grumpy, grouchy, crabbed, cross, peevish, captious, edgy, over-sensitive.
F3 calm, imperturbable.

**tough** *adj* **1** STRONG, durable, resilient, resistant, hardy, sturdy, solid, rigid, stiff, inflexible, hard, leathery. **2** *tough criminal*: rough, violent, vicious, callous, hardened, obstinate. **3** HARSH, severe, strict, stern, firm, resolute, determined, tenacious. **4** ARDUOUS, laborious, exacting, hard, difficult, puzzling, perplexing, baffling, knotty, thorny, troublesome.
F3 **1** fragile, delicate, weak, tender.
**2** gentle, soft. **3** gentle. **4** easy, simple.
*n* brute, thug, bully, ruffian, hooligan, lout, yob (*sl*).

**tour** *n* circuit, round, visit, expedition, journey, trip, outing, excursion, drive, ride, course.
*v* visit, go round, sightsee, explore, travel, journey, drive, ride.

**tourist** *n* holidaymaker, visitor, sightseer, tripper, excursionist, traveller, voyager, globetrotter.

**tournament** *n* championship, series, competition, contest, match, event, meeting.

**tow** *v* pull, tug, draw, trail, drag, lug, haul, transport.

**towards** *prep* **1** TO, approaching, nearing, close to, nearly, almost.
**2** *his feelings towards her*: regarding, with regard to, with respect to, concerning, about, for.

**tower** *n* steeple, spire, belfry, turret, fortification, bastion, citadel, fort, fortress, castle, keep.
*v* rise, rear, ascend, mount, soar, loom, overlook, dominate, surpass, transcend, exceed, top.

*Types of tower and famous towers include*: barbican, bastille, bastion, belfry, bell tower, belvedere, campanile, castle, church tower, citadel, column, demi-bastion, donjon, Eiffel Tower, fort, fortification, fortress, gate-tower, high-rise building, hill-fort, keep, lookout tower, martello tower, minar, minaret, mirador, pagoda, peel-tower, scaffold tower, skyscraper, smock mill, spire, steeple, tower block, tower mill, Tower of London, Tower of Pisa, turret, watchtower, water tower.

**towering** *adj* soaring, tall, high, lofty, elevated, monumental, colossal, gigantic, great, magnificent, imposing, impressive, sublime, supreme, surpassing, overpowering, extreme, inordinate.
F3 small, tiny, minor, trivial.

**toxic** *adj* poisonous, harmful, noxious, unhealthy, dangerous, deadly, lethal.
F3 harmless, safe.

**toy** *n* plaything, game, doll, knick-knack.
*v* play, tinker, fiddle, sport, trifle, dally.

**trace** *n* trail, track, spoor, footprint, footmark, mark, token, sign, indication, evidence, record, relic, remains, remnant, vestige, shadow, hint, suggestion, suspicion, soupçon, dash, drop, spot, bit, jot, touch, tinge, smack.
*v* **1** COPY, draw, sketch, outline, delineate, depict, mark, record, map, chart. **2** FIND, discover, detect, unearth, track (down), trail, stalk, hunt, seek, follow, pursue, shadow.

**track** *n* footstep, footprint, footmark, scent, spoor, trail, wake, mark, trace, slot, groove, rail, path, way, route, orbit, line, course, drift, sequence.
*v* stalk, trail, hunt, trace, follow, pursue, chase, dog, tail, shadow.
**track down** find, discover, trace, hunt down, run to earth, sniff out, ferret out,

dig up, unearth, expose, catch, capture.

**tract** n stretch, extent, expanse, plot, lot, territory, area, region, zone, district, quarter.

**trade** n 1 COMMERCE, traffic, business, dealing, buying, selling, shopkeeping, barter, exchange, transactions, custom.
2 OCCUPATION, job, business, profession, calling, craft, skill.
v traffic, peddle, do business, deal, transact, buy, sell, barter, exchange, swap, switch, bargain.

**trademark** n brand, label, name, sign, symbol, logo, insignia, crest, emblem, badge, hallmark.

**trader** n merchant, tradesman, broker, dealer, buyer, seller, vendor, supplier, wholesaler, retailer, shopkeeper, trafficker, peddler.

**tradition** n convention, custom, usage, way, habit, routine, ritual, institution, folklore.

**traditional** adj conventional, customary, habitual, usual, accustomed, established, fixed, long-established, time-honoured, old, historic, folk, oral, unwritten.
**Ξ** unconventional, innovative, new, modern, contemporary.

**traffic** n 1 VEHICLES, shipping, transport, transportation, freight, passengers. 2 TRADE, commerce, business, dealing, trafficking, barter, exchange. 3 COMMUNICATION, dealings, relations.
v peddle, buy, sell, trade, do business, deal, bargain, barter, exchange.

**tragedy** n adversity, misfortune, unhappiness, affliction, blow, calamity, disaster, catastrophe.

**tragic** adj sad, sorrowful, miserable, unhappy, unfortunate, unlucky, ill-fated, pitiable, pathetic, heartbreaking, shocking, appalling, dreadful, awful, dire, calamitous, disastrous, catastrophic, deadly, fatal.

**Ξ** happy, comic, successful.

**trail** v 1 DRAG, pull, tow, droop, dangle, extend, stream, straggle, dawdle, lag, loiter, linger. 2 TRACK, stalk, hunt, follow, pursue, chase, shadow, tail.
n track, footprints, footmarks, scent, trace, path, footpath, road, route, way.

**train** v 1 TEACH, instruct, coach, tutor, educate, improve, school, discipline, prepare, drill, exercise, work out, practise, rehearse.
2 POINT, direct, aim, level.
n 1 train of events: sequence, succession, series, progression, order, string, chain, line, file, procession, convoy, cortège, caravan. 2 RETINUE, entourage, attendants, court, household, staff, followers, following.

**trainer** n teacher, instructor, coach, tutor, handler.

**training** n teaching, instruction, coaching, tuition, education, schooling, discipline, preparation, grounding, drill, exercise, working-out, practice, learning, apprenticeship.

**trait** n feature, attribute, quality, characteristic, idiosyncrasy, peculiarity, quirk.

**traitor** n betrayer, informer, deceiver, double-crosser, turncoat, renegade, deserter, defector, quisling, collaborator.
**Ξ** loyalist, supporter, defender.

**tramp** v walk, march, tread, stamp, stomp, stump, plod, trudge, traipse, trail, trek, hike, ramble, roam, rove.
n vagrant, vagabond, hobo, down-and-out, dosser (sl).

**trample** v tread, stamp, crush, squash, flatten.

**trance** n dream, reverie, daze, stupor, unconsciousness, spell, ecstasy, rapture.

**tranquil** adj calm, composed, cool, imperturbable, unexcited, placid, sedate, relaxed, laid-back (infml), serene, peaceful, restful, still,

undisturbed, untroubled, quiet, hushed, silent.
**ᴇᴅ** agitated, disturbed, troubled, noisy.

**tranquillizer** *n* sedative, opiate, narcotic, barbiturate.

**transaction** *n* deal, bargain, agreement, arrangement, negotiation, business, affair, matter, proceeding, enterprise, undertaking, deed, action, execution, discharge.

**transcend** *v* surpass, excel, outshine, eclipse, outdo, outstrip, beat, surmount, exceed, overstep.

**transcribe** *v* write out, copy, reproduce, rewrite, transliterate, translate, render, take down, note, record.

**transcript** *n* transcription, copy, reproduction, duplicate, transliteration, translation, version, note, record, manuscript.

**transfer** *v* change, transpose, move, shift, remove, relocate, transplant, transport, carry, convey, transmit, consign, grant, hand over.
*n* change, changeover, transposition, move, shift, removal, relocation, displacement, transmission, handover, transference.

**transfix** *v* **1** FASCINATE, spellbind, mesmerize, hypnotize, paralyse.
**2** IMPALE, spear, skewer, spike, stick.

**transform** *v* change, alter, adapt, convert, remodel, reconstruct, transfigure, revolutionize.
**ᴇᴅ** preserve, maintain.

**transformation** *n* change, alteration, mutation, conversion, metamorphosis, transfiguration, revolution.
**ᴇᴅ** preservation, conservation.

**transient** *adj* transitory, passing, flying, fleeting, brief, short, momentary, ephemeral, short-lived, temporary, short-term.
**ᴇᴅ** lasting, permanent.

**transit** *n* passage, journey, travel, movement, transfer, transportation, conveyance, carriage, haulage,

shipment.

**transition** *n* passage, passing, progress, progression, development, evolution, flux, change, alteration, conversion, transformation, shift.

**transitional** *adj* provisional, temporary, passing, intermediate, developmental, changing, fluid, unsettled.
**ᴇᴅ** initial, final.

**translate** *v* interpret, render, paraphrase, simplify, decode, decipher, transliterate, transcribe, change, alter, convert, transform, improve.

**translation** *n* rendering, version, interpretation, gloss, crib, rewording, rephrasing, paraphrase, simplification, transliteration, transcription, change, alteration, conversion, transformation.

**transmission** *n* **1** BROADCASTING, diffusion, spread, communication, conveyance, carriage, transport, shipment, sending, dispatch, relaying, transfer. **2** *a live transmission*: broadcast, programme, show, signal.
**ᴇᴅ 1** reception.

**transmit** *v* communicate, impart, convey, carry, bear, transport, send, dispatch, forward, relay, transfer, broadcast, radio, disseminate, network, diffuse, spread.
**ᴇᴅ** receive.

**transparency** *n* slide, photograph, picture.

**transparent** *adj* **1** *transparent plastic*: clear, see-through, translucent, sheer. **2** PLAIN, distinct, clear, lucid, explicit, unambiguous, unequivocal, apparent, visible, obvious, evident, manifest, patent, undisguised, open, candid, straightforward.
**ᴇᴅ 1** opaque. **2** unclear, ambiguous.

**transplant** *v* move, shift, displace, remove, uproot, transfer, relocate, resettle, repot.
**ᴇᴅ** leave.

**transport** v convey, carry, bear, take, fetch, bring, move, shift, transfer, ship, haul, remove, deport.
n conveyance, carriage, transfer, transportation, shipment, shipping, haulage, removal.

**transpose** v swap, exchange, switch, interchange, transfer, shift, rearrange, reorder, change, alter, move, substitute.

**transverse** adj cross, crosswise, transversal, diagonal, oblique.

**trap** n snare, net, noose, springe, gin, booby-trap, pitfall, danger, hazard, ambush, trick, wile, ruse, stratagem, device, trickery, artifice, deception.
v snare, net, entrap, ensnare, enmesh, catch, take, ambush, corner, trick, deceive, dupe.

**trash** n rubbish, garbage, refuse, junk, waste, litter, sweepings, offscourings, scum, dregs.

**trauma** n injury, wound, hurt, damage, pain, suffering, anguish, agony, torture, ordeal, shock, jolt, upset, disturbance, upheaval, strain, stress.
Ea healing.

**traumatic** adj painful, hurtful, injurious, wounding, shocking, upsetting, distressing, disturbing, unpleasant, frightening, stressful.
Ea healing, relaxing.

**travel** v journey, voyage, go, wend, move, proceed, progress, wander, ramble, roam, rove, tour, cross, traverse.
Ea stay, remain.

> *Methods of travel include*: fly, aviate, pilot, shuttle, sail, cruise, punt, paddle, row, steam, ride, cycle, bike (*infml*), freewheel, drive, motor, bus, walk, hike, march, ramble, trek, orienteer, hitch-hike, commute.

n travelling, touring, tourism, globetrotting.

> *Forms of travel include*: flight, cruise, sail, voyage, ride, drive, march, walk, hike, ramble, excursion, holiday, jaunt, outing, tour, trip, visit, expedition, safari, trek, circumnavigation, exploration, journey, migration, mission, pilgrimage.

**traveller** n **1** TOURIST, explorer, voyager, globetrotter, holidaymaker, tripper (*infml*), excursionist, passenger, commuter, wanderer, rambler, hiker, wayfarer, migrant, nomad, gypsy, itinerant, tinker, vagrant. **2** SALESMAN, saleswoman, representative, rep (*infml*), agent.

**travelling** adj touring, wandering, roaming, roving, wayfaring, migrant, migratory, nomadic, itinerant, peripatetic, mobile, moving, vagrant, homeless.
Ea fixed.

**travels** n voyage, expedition, passage, journey, trip, excursion, tour, wanderings.

**travesty** n mockery, parody, take-off, send-up, farce, caricature, distortion, sham, apology.

**treacherous** adj **1** TRAITOROUS, disloyal, unfaithful, faithless, unreliable, untrustworthy, false, untrue, deceitful, double-crossing. **2** *treacherous roads*: dangerous, hazardous, risky, perilous, precarious, icy, slippery.
Ea **1** loyal, faithful, dependable. **2** safe, stable.

**treachery** n treason, betrayal, disloyalty, infidelity, falseness, duplicity, double-dealing.
Ea loyalty, dependability.

**tread** v walk, step, pace, stride, march, tramp, trudge, plod, stamp, trample, walk on, press, crush, squash.
n walk, footfall, footstep, step, pace, stride.

**treason** n treachery, perfidy, disloyalty, duplicity, subversion, sedition, mutiny, rebellion.

F3 loyalty.

**treasonable** *adj* traitorous, perfidious, disloyal, false, subversive, seditious, mutinous.

F3 loyal.

**treasure** *n* fortune, wealth, riches, money, cash, gold, jewels, hoard, cache.

*v* prize, value, esteem, revere, worship, love, adore, idolize, cherish, preserve, guard.

F3 disparage, belittle.

**treat** *n* indulgence, gratification, pleasure, delight, enjoyment, fun, entertainment, excursion, outing, party, celebration, feast, banquet, gift, surprise, thrill.

*v* 1 DEAL WITH, manage, handle, use, regard, consider, discuss, cover. 2 TEND, nurse, minister to, attend to, care for, heal, cure. 3 PAY FOR, buy, stand, give, provide, entertain, regale, feast.

**treatise** *n* essay, dissertation, thesis, monograph, paper, pamphlet, tract, study, exposition.

**treatment** *n* 1 HEALING, cure, remedy, medication, therapy, surgery, care, nursing.

2 MANAGEMENT, handling, use, usage, conduct, discussion, coverage.

**treaty** *n* pact, convention, agreement, covenant, compact, negotiation, contract, bond, alliance.

**tree** *n* bush, shrub, evergreen, conifer.

*Trees include*: acacia, acer, alder, almond, apple, ash, aspen, balsa, bay, beech, birch, blackthorn, blue gum, box, cedar, cherry, chestnut, coconut palm, cottonwood, cypress, date palm, dogwood, Dutch elm, ebony, elder, elm, eucalyptus, fig, fir, gum, hawthorn, hazel, hickory, hornbeam, horse chestnut, Japanese maple, larch, laurel, lime, linden, mahogany, maple, monkey puzzle, mountain ash, oak, palm, pear, pine, plane, plum, poplar, prunus, pussy willow, redwood, rowan, rubber tree, sandalwood, sapele, sequoia, silver birch, silver maple, spruce, sycamore, teak, walnut, weeping willow, whitebeam, willow, witch hazel, yew, yucca; bonsai, conifer, deciduous, evergreen, fruit, hardwood, ornamental, palm, softwood.

**trek** *n* hike, walk, march, tramp, journey, expedition, safari.

*v* hike, walk, march, tramp, trudge, plod, journey, rove, roam.

**tremble** *v* shake, vibrate, quake, shiver, shudder, quiver, wobble, rock.

*n* shake, vibration, quake, shiver, shudder, quiver, tremor, wobble.

F3 steadiness.

**tremendous** *adj* wonderful, marvellous, stupendous, sensational, spectacular, extraordinary, amazing, incredible, terrific, impressive, huge, immense, vast, colossal, gigantic, towering, formidable.

F3 ordinary, unimpressive.

**tremor** *n* shake, quiver, tremble, shiver, quake, quaver, wobble, vibration, agitation, thrill, shock, earthquake.

F3 steadiness.

**trend** *n* course, flow, drift, tendency, inclination, leaning, craze, rage (*infml*), fashion, vogue, mode, style, look.

**trespass** *v* invade, intrude, encroach, poach, infringe, violate, offend, wrong.

F3 obey, keep to.

*n* invasion, intrusion, encroachment, poaching, infringement, violation, contravention, offence, misdemeanour.

**trespasser** *n* intruder, poacher, offender, criminal.

**trial** *n* 1 LITIGATION, lawsuit, hearing, inquiry, tribunal.

**2** EXPERIMENT, test, examination, check, dry run, dummy run, practice, rehearsal, audition, contest. **3** AFFLICTION, suffering, grief, misery, distress, adversity, hardship, ordeal, trouble, nuisance, vexation, tribulation.

**F3** 3 relief, happiness.

*adj* experimental, test, pilot, exploratory, provisional, probationary.

**tribe** *n* race, nation, people, clan, family, house, dynasty, blood, stock, group, caste, class, division, branch.

**tribute** *n* **1** PRAISE, commendation, compliment, accolade, homage, respect, honour, credit, acknowledgement, recognition, gratitude. **2** PAYMENT, levy, charge, tax, duty, gift, offering, contribution.

**trick** *n* fraud, swindle, deception, deceit, artifice, illusion, hoax, practical joke, joke, leg-pull (*infml*), prank, antic, caper, frolic, feat, stunt, ruse, wile, dodge, subterfuge, trap, device, knack, technique, secret.

*adj* false, mock, artificial, imitation, ersatz, fake, forged, counterfeit, feigned, sham, bogus.

**F3** real, genuine.

*v* deceive, delude, dupe, fool, hoodwink, beguile, mislead, bluff, hoax, pull someone's leg (*infml*), cheat, swindle, diddle, defraud, con (*infml*), trap, outwit.

**trickery** *n* deception, illusion, sleight-of-hand, pretence, artifice, guile, deceit, dishonesty, cheating, swindling, fraud, imposture, double-dealing, monkey business, funny business (*sl*), chicanery, skulduggery, hocus-pocus.

**F3** straightforwardness, honesty.

**trickle** *v* dribble, run, leak, seep, ooze, exude, drip, drop, filter, percolate.

**F3** stream, gush.

*n* dribble, drip, drop, leak, seepage.

**F3** stream, gush.

**tricky** *adj* **1** *a tricky problem*:

difficult, awkward, problematic, complicated, knotty, thorny, delicate, ticklish. **2** CRAFTY, artful, cunning, sly, wily, foxy, subtle, devious, slippery, scheming, deceitful.

**F3** 1 easy, simple. **2** honest.

**trifle** *n* **1** LITTLE, bit, spot, drop, dash, touch, trace. **2** TOY, plaything, trinket, bauble, knick-knack, triviality, nothing.

*v* toy, play, sport, flirt, dally, dabble, fiddle, meddle, fool.

**trifling** *adj* small, paltry, slight, negligible, inconsiderable, unimportant, insignificant, minor, trivial, petty, silly, frivolous, idle, empty, worthless.

**F3** important, significant, serious.

**trigger** *v* cause, start, initiate, activate, set off, spark off, provoke, prompt, elicit, generate, produce.

*n* lever, catch, switch, spur, stimulus.

**trim** *adj* **1** NEAT, tidy, orderly, shipshape, spick-and-span, spruce, smart, dapper. **2** SLIM, slender, streamlined, compact.

**F3** 1 untidy, scruffy.

*v* **1** CUT, clip, crop, dock, prune, pare, shave. **2** DECORATE, ornament, embellish, garnish, dress, array, adjust, arrange, order, neaten, tidy.

*n* condition, state, order, form, shape, fitness, health.

**trimmings** *n* **1** GARNISH, decorations, ornaments, frills, extras, accessories. **2** CUTTINGS, clippings, parings, ends.

**trinket** *n* bauble, jewel, ornament, knick-knack.

**trio** *n* threesome, triad, triumvirate, trinity, triplet, trilogy.

**trip** *n* outing, excursion, tour, jaunt, ride, drive, spin, journey, voyage, expedition, foray.

*v* stumble, slip, fall, tumble, stagger, totter, blunder.

**triple** *adj* treble, triplicate, threefold, three-ply, three-way.

*v* treble, triplicate.

**trite** *adj* banal, commonplace, ordinary, run-of-the-mill, stale, tired, worn, threadbare, unoriginal, hackneyed, overused, stock, stereotyped, clichéed, corny (*infml*).
**F∃** original, new, fresh.

**triumph** *n* **1** WIN, victory, conquest, walk-over, success, achievement, accomplishment, feat, coup, masterstroke, hit, sensation. **2** EXULTATION, jubilation, rejoicing, celebration, elation, joy, happiness.
**F∃** **1** failure.
*v* win, succeed, prosper, conquer, vanquish, overcome, overwhelm, prevail, dominate, celebrate, rejoice, glory, gloat.
**F∃** lose, fail.

**triumphant** *adj* winning, victorious, conquering, successful, exultant, jubilant, rejoicing, celebratory, glorious, elated, joyful, proud, boastful, gloating, swaggering.
**F∃** defeated, humble.

**trivial** *adj* unimportant, insignificant, inconsequential, incidental, minor, petty, paltry, trifling, small, little, inconsiderable, negligible, worthless, meaningless, frivolous, banal, trite, commonplace, everyday.
**F∃** important, significant, profound.

**triviality** *n* unimportance, insignificance, pettiness, smallness, worthlessness, meaninglessness, frivolity, trifle, detail, technicality.
**F∃** importance, essential.

**troop** *n* contingent, squadron, unit, division, company, squad, team, crew, gang, band, bunch, group, body, pack, herd, flock, horde, crowd, throng, multitude.
*v* go, march, parade, stream, flock, swarm, throng.

**troops** *n* army, military, soldiers, servicemen, servicewomen.

**trophy** *n* cup, prize, award, souvenir, memento.

**tropical** *adj* hot, torrid, sultry,

sweltering, stifling, steamy, humid.
**F∃** arctic, cold, cool, temperate.

**trot** *v* jog, run, scamper, scuttle, scurry.

**trouble** *n* **1** PROBLEM, difficulty, struggle, annoyance, irritation, bother, nuisance, inconvenience, misfortune, adversity, trial, tribulation, pain, suffering, affliction, distress, grief, woe, heartache, concern, uneasiness, worry, anxiety, agitation. **2** UNREST, strife, tumult, commotion, disturbance, disorder, upheaval. **3** *back trouble*: disorder, complaint, ailment, illness, disease, disability, defect. **4** EFFORT, exertion, pains, care, attention, thought.
**F∃** **1** relief, calm. **2** order. **3** health.
*v* annoy, vex, harass, torment, bother, inconvenience, disturb, upset, distress, sadden, pain, afflict, burden, worry, agitate, disconcert, perplex.
**F∃** reassure, help.

**troublemaker** *n* agitator, rabble-rouser, incendiary, instigator, ringleader, stirrer, mischief-maker.
**F∃** peacemaker.

**troublesome** *adj* **1** ANNOYING, irritating, vexatious, irksome, bothersome, inconvenient, difficult, hard, tricky, thorny, taxing, demanding, laborious, tiresome, wearisome. **2** UNRULY, rowdy, turbulent, trying, unco-operative, insubordinate, rebellious.
**F∃** **1** easy, simple. **2** helpful.

**trough** *n* gutter, conduit, trench, ditch, gully, channel, groove, furrow, hollow, depression.

**trousers** *n* pants, slacks, jeans, denims, Levis®, flannels, bags (*infml*), dungarees, breeches, shorts.

**truancy** *n* absence, absenteeism, shirking, skiving (*infml*).
**F∃** attendance.

**truant** *n* absentee, deserter, runaway, idler, shirker, skiver (*infml*), dodger.
*adj* absent, missing, runaway.

**truce** *n* cease-fire, peace, armistice,

cessation, moratorium, suspension, stay, respite, let-up (*infml*), lull, rest, break, interval, intermission.
**F3** war, hostilities.

**truck** *n* lorry, van, wagon, trailer, float, cart, barrow.

**trudge** *v* tramp, plod, clump, stump, lumber, traipse, slog, labour, trek, hike, walk, march.
*n* tramp, traipse, slog, haul, trek, hike, walk, march.

**true** *adj* **1** REAL, genuine, authentic, actual, veritable, exact, precise, accurate, correct, right, factual, truthful, veracious, sincere, honest, legitimate, valid, rightful, proper. **2** FAITHFUL, loyal, constant, steadfast, staunch, firm, trustworthy, trusty, honourable, dedicated, devoted.
**F3** **1** false, wrong, incorrect, inaccurate. **2** unfaithful, faithless.

**truism** *n* truth, platitude, commonplace, cliché.

**truly** *adv* very, greatly, extremely, really, genuinely, sincerely, honestly, truthfully, undeniably, indubitably, indeed, in fact, in reality, exactly, precisely, correctly, rightly, properly.
**F3** slightly, falsely, incorrectly.

**trumpet** *n* bugle, horn, clarion, blare, blast, roar, bellow, cry, call.
*v* blare, blast, roar, bellow, shout, proclaim, announce, broadcast, advertise.

**truncate** *v* shorten, abbreviate, curtail, cut, lop, dock, prune, pare, clip, trim, crop.
**F3** lengthen, extend.

**trunk** *n* **1** CASE, suitcase, chest, coffer, box, crate. **2** TORSO, body, frame, shaft, stock, stem, stalk.

**truss** *v* tie, strap, bind, pinion, fasten, secure, bundle, pack.
**F3** untie, loosen.
*n* binding, bandage, support, brace, prop, stay, shore, strut, joist.

**trust** *n* **1** FAITH, belief, credence, credit, hope, expectation, reliance,

confidence, assurance, conviction, certainty. **2** CARE, charge, custody, safekeeping, guardianship, protection, responsibility, duty.
**F3** **1** distrust, mistrust, scepticism, doubt.
*v* **1** BELIEVE, imagine, assume, presume, suppose, surmise, hope, expect, rely on, depend on, count on, bank on, swear by. **2** ENTRUST, commit, consign, confide, give, assign, delegate.
**F3** **1** distrust, mistrust, doubt, disbelieve.

**trusting** *adj* trustful, credulous, gullible, naïve, innocent, unquestioning, unsuspecting, unguarded, unwary.
**F3** distrustful, suspicious, cautious.

**trustworthy** *adj* honest, upright, honourable, principled, dependable, reliable, steadfast, true, responsible, sensible.
**F3** untrustworthy, dishonest, unreliable, irresponsible.

**truth** *n* **1** TRUTHFULNESS, veracity, candour, frankness, honesty, sincerity, genuineness, authenticity, realism, exactness, precision, accuracy, validity, legitimacy, honour, integrity, uprightness, faithfulness, fidelity, loyalty, constancy. **2** *tell the truth*: facts, reality, actuality, fact, axiom, maxim, principle, truism.
**F3** **1** deceit, dishonesty, falseness. **2** lie, falsehood.

**truthful** *adj* veracious, frank, candid, straight, honest, sincere, true, veritable, exact, precise, accurate, correct, realistic, faithful, trustworthy, reliable.
**F3** untruthful, deceitful, false, untrue.

**try** *v* **1** ATTEMPT, endeavour, venture, undertake, seek, strive. **2** HEAR, judge. **3** EXPERIMENT, test, sample, taste, inspect, examine, investigate, evaluate, appraise.
*n* **1** ATTEMPT, endeavour, effort, go

**turn**

(*infml*), bash (*infml*), crack (*infml*), shot (*infml*), stab (*infml*). **2** EXPERIMENT, test, trial, ample, taste.

**trying** *adj* annoying, irritating, aggravating (*infml*), vexatious, exasperating, troublesome, tiresome, wearisome, difficult, hard, tough, arduous, taxing, demanding, testing. ⊟ easy.

**tub** *n* bath, basin, vat, tun, butt, cask, barrel, keg.

**tube** *n* hose, pipe, cylinder, duct, conduit, spout, channel.

**tuck** *v* **1** INSERT, push, thrust, stuff, cram. **2** FOLD, pleat, gather, crease. *n* fold, pleat, gather, pucker, crease.

**tuft** *n* crest, beard, tassel, knot, clump, cluster, bunch.

**tug** *v* pull, draw, tow, haul, drag, lug, heave, wrench, jerk, pluck. *n* pull, tow, haul, heave, wrench, jerk, pluck.

**tuition** *n* teaching, instruction, coaching, training, lessons, schooling, education.

**tumble** *v* fall, stumble, trip, topple, overthrow, drop, flop, collapse, plummet, pitch, roll, toss. *n* fall, stumble, trip, drop, plunge, roll, toss.

**tumult** *n* commotion, turmoil, disturbance, upheaval, stir, agitation, unrest, disorder, chaos, pandemonium, noise, clamour, din, racket, hubbub, hullabaloo, row, rumpus, uproar, riot, fracas, brawl, affray, strife. ⊟ peace, calm, composure.

**tumultuous** *adj* turbulent, stormy, raging, fierce, violent, wild, hectic, boisterous, rowdy, noisy, disorderly, unruly, riotous, restless, agitated, troubled, disturbed, excited. ⊟ calm, peaceful, quiet.

**tune** *n* melody, theme, motif, song, air, strain. *v* pitch, harmonize, set, regulate, adjust, adapt, temper, attune, synchronize.

**tuneful** *adj* melodious, melodic, catchy, musical, euphonious, harmonious, pleasant, mellow, sonorous. ⊟ tuneless, discordant.

**tunnel** *n* passage, passageway, gallery, subway, underpass, burrow, hole, mine, shaft, chimney. *v* burrow, dig, excavate, mine, bore, penetrate, undermine, sap.

**turbulent** *adj* rough, choppy, stormy, blustery, tempestuous, raging, furious, violent, wild, tumultuous, unbridled, boisterous, rowdy, disorderly, unruly, undisciplined, obstreperous, rebellious, mutinous, riotous, agitated, unsettled, unstable, confused, disordered. ⊟ calm, composed.

**turmoil** *n* confusion, disorder, tumult, commotion, disturbance, trouble, disquiet, agitation, turbulence, stir, ferment, flurry, bustle, chaos, pandemonium, bedlam, noise, din, hubbub, row, uproar. ⊟ calm, peace, quiet.

**turn** *v* **1** REVOLVE, circle, spin, twirl, whirl, twist, gyrate, pivot, hinge, swivel, rotate, roll, move, shift, invert, reverse, bend, veer, swerve, divert. **2** MAKE, transform, change, alter, modify, convert, adapt, adjust, fit, mould, shape, form, fashion, remodel. **3** *turn cold*: go, become, grow. **4** RESORT, have recourse, apply, appeal. **5** SOUR, curdle, spoil, go off, go bad. *n* **1** REVOLUTION, cycle, round, circle, rotation, spin, twirl, twist, gyration, bend, curve, loop, reversal. **2** CHANGE, alteration, shift, deviation. **3** *it's your turn*: go, chance, opportunity, occasion, stint, period, spell. **4** ACT, performance, performer.

**turn away** reject, avert, deflect, deviate, depart. ⊟ accept, receive.

**turn down 1** *turn down an offer*: reject, decline, refuse, spurn, rebuff, repudiate. **2** LOWER, lessen, quieten, soften, mute, muffle.
◨ **1** accept. **2** turn up.

**turn in 1** GO TO BED, retire. **2** HAND OVER, give up, surrender, deliver, hand in, tender, submit, return, give back.
◨ **1** get up. **2** keep.

**turn off 1** BRANCH OFF, leave, quit, depart from, deviate, divert. **2** SWITCH OFF, turn out, stop, shut down, unplug, disconnect. **3** (*sl*) REPEL, sicken, nauseate, disgust, offend, displease, disenchant, alienate, bore, discourage, put off.
◨ **1** join. **2** turn on. **3** turn on (*sl*).

**turn on 1** SWITCH ON, start (up), activate, connect. **2** (*sl*) AROUSE, stimulate, excite, thrill, please, attract. **3** HINGE ON, depend on, rest on. **4** ATTACK, round on, fall on.
◨ **1** turn off. **2** turn off (*sl*).

**turn out 1** HAPPEN, come about, transpire, ensue, result, end up, become, develop, emerge. **2** SWITCH OFF, turn off, unplug, disconnect. **3** APPEAR, present, dress, clothe. **4** PRODUCE, make, manufacture, fabricate, assemble. **5** EVICT, throw out, expel, deport, banish, dismiss, discharge, drum out, kick out, sack (*infml*). **6** *turn out the attic*: empty, clear, clean out.
◨ **2** turn on. **5** admit. **6** fill.

**turn over 1** THINK OVER, think about, mull over, ponder, deliberate, reflect on, contemplate, consider, examine. **2** HAND OVER, surrender, deliver, transfer. **3** OVERTURN, upset, upend, invert, capsize, keel over.

**turn up 1** ATTEND, come, arrive, appear, show up (*infml*). **2** AMPLIFY, intensify, raise, increase. **3** DISCOVER, find, unearth, dig up, expose, disclose, reveal, show.
◨ **1** stay away. **2** turn down.

**turning** *n* turn-off, junction, crossroads, fork, bend, curve, turn.

**turning-point** *n* crossroads, watershed, crux, crisis.

**turnout** *n* **1** ATTENDANCE, audience, gate, crowd, assembly, congregation. **2** APPEARANCE, outfit, dress, clothes.

**tutor** *n* teacher, instructor, coach, educator, lecturer, supervisor, guide, mentor, guru, guardian.
*v* teach, instruct, train, drill, coach, educate, school, lecture, supervise, direct, guide.

**tweak** *v, n* twist, pinch, squeeze, nip, pull, tug, jerk, twitch.

**twee** (*infml*) *adj* sweet, cute, pretty, dainty, quaint, sentimental, affected, precious.

**twiddle** *v* turn, twirl, swivel, twist, wiggle, adjust, fiddle, finger.

**twilight** *n* dusk, half-light, gloaming, gloom, dimness, sunset, evening.

**twin** *n* double, look-alike, likeness, duplicate, clone, match, counterpart, corollary, fellow, mate.
*adj* identical, matching, corresponding, symmetrical, parallel, matched, paired, double, dual, duplicate, twofold.
*v* match, pair, couple, link, join.

**twine** *n* string, cord, thread, yarn.
*v* wind, coil, spiral, loop, curl, bend, twist, wreathe, wrap, surround, encircle, entwine, plait, braid, knit, weave.

**twinge** *n* pain, pang, throb, spasm, throe, stab, stitch, pinch, prick.

**twinkle** *v* sparkle, glitter, shimmer, glisten, glimmer, flicker, wink, flash, glint, gleam, shine.
*n* sparkle, scintillation, glitter, shimmer, glisten, glimmer, flicker, wink, flash, glint, gleam, light.

**twirl** *v* spin, whirl, pirouette, wheel, rotate, revolve, swivel, pivot, turn, twist, gyrate, wind, coil.
*n* spin, whirl, pirouette, rotation, revolution, turn, twist, gyration, convlution, spiral, coil.

**twist** *v* **1** TURN, screw, wring, spin,

swivel, wind, zigzag, bend, coil, spiral, curl, wreathe, twine, entwine, intertwine, weave, entangle, wriggle, squirm, writhe. **2** *twist one's ankle*: wrench, rick, sprain, strain. **3** CHANGE, alter, garble, misquote, misrepresent, distort, contort, warp, pervert.
*n* **1** TURN, screw, spin, roll, bend, curve, arc, curl, loop, zigzag, coil, spiral, convolution, squiggle, tangle. **2** CHANGE, variation, break.
**3** PERVERSION, distortion, contortion. **4** SURPRISE, quirk, oddity, peculiarity.

**twisted** *adj* warped, perverted, deviant, unnatural.
**E3** straight.

**twitch** *v* jerk, jump, start, blink, tremble, shake, pull, tug, tweak, snatch, pluck.
*n* spasm, convulsion, tic, tremor, jerk, jump, start.

**twitter** *v* chirp, chirrup, tweet, cheep, sing, warble, whistle, chatter.

**two-faced** *adj* hypocritical, insincere, false, lying, deceitful, treacherous, double-dealing, devious, untrustworthy.
**E3** honest, candid, frank.

**tycoon** *n* industrialist, entrepreneur, captain of industry, magnate, mogul, baron, supremo, capitalist, financier.

**type** *n* **1** SORT, kind, form, genre, variety, strain, species, breed, group, class, category, subdivision, classification, description, designation, stamp, mark, order, standard. **2** ARCHETYPE, embodiment, prototype, original, model, pattern, specimen, example. **3** PRINT, printing, characters, letters, lettering, face, fount, font.

**typhoon** *n* whirlwind, cyclone, tornado, twister (*infml*), hurricane, tempest, storm, squall.

**typical** *adj* standard, normal, usual, average, conventional, orthodox, stock, model, representative, illustrative, indicative, characteristic, distinctive.
**E3** atypical, unusual.

**typify** *v* embody, epitomize, encapsulate, personify, characterize, exemplify, symbolize, represent, illustrate.

**tyrannical** *adj* dictatorial, despotic, autocratic, absolute, arbitrary, authoritarian, domineering, overbearing, high-handed, imperious, magisterial, ruthless, harsh, severe, oppressive, overpowering, unjust, unreasonable.
**E3** liberal, tolerant.

**tyranny** *n* dictatorship, despotism, autocracy, absolutism, authoritarianism, imperiousness, ruthlessness, harshness, severity, oppression, injustice.
**E3** democracy, freedom.

**tyrant** *n* dictator, despot, autocrat, absolutist, authoritarian, bully, oppressor, slave-driver, taskmaster.

# U

**ubiquitous** *adj* omnipresent, ever-present, everywhere, universal, global, pervasive, common, frequent.
**E3** rare, scarce.

**ugly** *adj* **1** UNATTRACTIVE, unsightly, plain, unprepossessing, ill-favoured, hideous, monstrous, misshapen, deformed.
**2** UNPLEASANT, disagreeable, nasty, horrid, objectionable, offensive, disgusting, revolting, repulsive, vile, frightful, terrible.

**E3 1** attractive, beautiful, handsome, pretty. **2** pleasant.

**ulterior** *adj* secondary, hidden, concealed, undisclosed, unexpressed, covert, secret, private, personal, selfish.
**E3** overt.

**ultimate** *adj* final, last, closing, concluding, eventual, terminal, furthest, remotest, extreme, utmost, greatest, highest, supreme, superlative, perfect, radical, fundamental, primary.

**ultimately** *adv* finally, eventually, at last, in the end, after all.

**umpire** *n* referee, linesman, judge, adjudicator, arbiter, arbitrator, mediator, moderator.
*v* referee, judge, adjudicate, arbitrate, mediate, moderate, control.

**umpteen** (*infml*) *adj* a good many, numerous, plenty, millions, countless, innumerable.
**E3** few.

**unabashed** *adj* unashamed, unembarrassed, brazen, blatant, bold, confident, undaunted, unconcerned, undismayed.
**E3** abashed, sheepish.

**unable** *adj* incapable, powerless, impotent, unequipped, unqualified, unfit, incompetent, inadequate.
**E3** able, capable.

**unacceptable** *adj* intolerable, inadmissible, unsatisfactory, undesirable, unwelcome, objectionable, offensive, unpleasant.
**E3** acceptable, satisfactory.

**unaccompanied** *adj* alone, unescorted, unattended, lone, solo, single-handed.
**E3** accompanied.

**unaccountable** *adj* inexplicable, unexplainable, unfathomable, impenetrable, incomprehensible, baffling, puzzling, mysterious, astonishing, extraordinary, strange, odd, peculiar, singular, unusual, uncommon, unheard-of.

**E3** explicable, explainable.

**unaccustomed** *adj* **1** *unaccustomed to such luxury*: unused, unacquainted, unfamiliar, unpractised, inexperienced. **2** STRANGE, unusual, uncommon, different, new, unexpected, surprising, uncharacteristic, unprecedented.
**E3 1** accustomed, familiar. **2** customary.

**unaffected** *adj* **1** UNMOVED, unconcerned, indifferent, impervious, untouched, unchanged, unaltered. **2** UNSOPHISTICATED, artless, naïve, ingenuous, unspoilt, plain, simple, straightforward, unpretentious, unassuming, sincere, honest, genuine.
**E3 1** moved, influenced. **2** affected, pretentious, insincere.

**unalterable** *adj* unchangeable, invariable, unchanging, immutable, final, inflexible, unyielding, rigid, fixed, permanent.
**E3** alterable, flexible.

**unanimity** *n* consensus, unity, agreement, concurrence, accord, like-mindedness, concord, harmony, unison, concert.
**E3** disagreement, disunity.

**unanimous** *adj* united, concerted, joint, common, as one, in agreement, in accord, harmonious.
**E3** disunited, divided.

**unapproachable** *adj* inaccessible, remote, distant, aloof, standoffish, withdrawn, reserved, unsociable, unfriendly, forbidding.
**E3** approachable, friendly.

**unarmed** *adj* defenceless, unprotected, exposed, open, vulnerable, weak, helpless.
**E3** armed, protected.

**unashamed** *adj* shameless, unabashed, impenitent, unrepentant, unconcealed, undisguised, open, blatant.

**unasked** *adj* uninvited, unbidden,

unrequested, unsought, unsolicited, unwanted, voluntary, spontaneous.
**F3** invited, wanted.

**unassuming** *adj* unassertive, self-effacing, retiring, modest, humble, meek, unobtrusive, unpretentious, simple, restrained.
**F3** presumptuous, assertive, pretentious.

**unattached** *adj* unmarried, single, free, available, footloose, fancy-free, independent, unaffiliated.
**F3** engaged, committed.

**unattended** *adj* ignored, disregarded, unguarded, unwatched, unsupervised, unaccompanied, unescorted, alone.
**F3** attended, escorted.

**unauthorized** *adj* unofficial, unlawful, illegal, illicit, illegitimate, irregular, unsanctioned.
**F3** authorized, legal.

**unavoidable** *adj* inevitable, inescapable, inexorable, certain, sure, fated, destined, obligatory, compulsory, mandatory, necessary.
**F3** avoidable.

**unaware** *adj* oblivious, unconscious, ignorant, uninformed, unknowing, unsuspecting, unmindful, heedless, blind, deaf.
**F3** aware, conscious.

**unbalanced** *adj* **1** INSANE, mad, crazy, lunatic, deranged, disturbed, demented, irrational, unsound. **2** *an unbalanced report*: biased, prejudiced, one-sided, partisan, unfair, unjust, unequal, uneven, asymmetrical, lopsided, unsteady, unstable.
**F3** **1** sane. **2** unbiased.

**unbearable** *adj* intolerable, unacceptable, insupportable, insufferable, unendurable, excruciating.
**F3** bearable, acceptable.

**unbeatable** *adj* invincible, unconquerable, unstoppable, unsurpassable, matchless, supreme,

excellent.

**unbecoming** *adj* unseemly, improper, unsuitable, inappropriate, unbefitting, ungentlemanly, unladylike, unattractive, unsightly.
**F3** suitable, attractive.

**unbelief** *n* atheism, agnosticism, scepticism, doubt, incredulity, disbelief.
**F3** belief, faith.

**unbelievable** *adj* incredible, inconceivable, unthinkable, unimaginable, astonishing, staggering, extraordinary, impossible, improbable, unlikely, implausible, unconvincing, far-fetched, preposterous.
**F3** believable, credible.

**unborn** *adj* embryonic, expected, awaited, coming, future.

**unbounded** *adj* boundless, limitless, unlimited, unrestricted, unrestrained, unchecked, unbridled, infinite, endless, immeasurable, vast.
**F3** limited, restrained.

**unbreakable** *adj* indestructible, shatterproof, toughened, resistant, proof, durable, strong, tough, rugged, solid.
**F3** breakable, fragile.

**unbridled** *adj* immoderate, excessive, uncontrolled, unrestrained, unchecked.

**unbroken** *adj* **1** INTACT, whole, entire, complete, solid, undivided. **2** UNINTERRUPTED, continuous, endless, ceaseless, incessant, unceasing, constant, perpetual, progressive, successive. **3** *unbroken record*: unbeaten, unsurpassed, unequalled, unmatched.
**F3** **1** broken. **2** intermittent, fitful.

**uncalled-for** *adj* gratuitous, unprovoked, unjustified, unwarranted, undeserved, unnecessary, needless.
**F3** timely.

**uncanny** *adj* weird, strange, queer, bizarre, mysterious, unaccountable,

incredible, remarkable,
extraordinary, fantastic, unnatural,
unearthly, supernatural, eerie,
creepy, spooky (*infml*).

**uncaring** *adj* unconcerned,
unmoved, unsympathetic,
inconsiderate, unfeeling, cold,
callous, indifferent, uninterested.
**F3** caring, concerned.

**unceasing** *adj* ceaseless, incessant,
unending, endless, never-ending, non-
stop, continuous, unbroken,
constant, perpetual, continual,
persistent, relentless, unrelenting,
unremitting.
**F3** intermittent, spasmodic.

**uncertain** *adj* **1** UNSURE,
unconvinced, doubtful, dubious,
undecided, ambivalent, hesitant,
wavering, vacillating.
**2** INCONSTANT, changeable,
variable, erratic, irregular, shaky,
unsteady, unreliable.
**3** UNPREDICTABLE, unforeseeable,
undetermined, unsettled, unresolved,
unconfirmed, indefinite, vague,
insecure, risky, iffy (*sl*).
**F3 1** certain, sure. **2** steady.
**3** predictable.

**uncertainty** *n* doubt, scepticism,
irresolution, dilemma, hesitation,
misgiving, confusion, bewilderment,
perplexity, puzzlement, unreliability,
unpredictability, insecurity.
**F3** certainty.

**unchanging** *adj* unvarying,
changeless, steady, steadfast,
constant, perpetual, lasting,
enduring, abiding, eternal,
permanent.
**F3** changing, changeable.

**uncharitable** *adj* unkind, cruel,
hard-hearted, callous, unfeeling,
insensitive, unsympathetic,
unfriendly, mean, ungenerous.
**F3** kind, sensitive, charitable,
generous.

**uncharted** *adj* unexplored,
undiscovered, unplumbed, foreign,
alien, strange, unfamiliar, new,
virgin.
**F3** familiar.

**uncivilized** *adj* primitive, barbaric,
savage, wild, untamed, uncultured,
unsophisticated, unenlightened,
uneducated, illiterate, uncouth,
antisocial.
**F3** civilized, cultured.

**unclean** *adj* dirty, soiled, filthy,
foul, polluted, contaminated, tainted,
impure, unhygienic, unwholesome,
corrupt, defiled, sullied.
**F3** clean, hygienic.

**unclear** *adj* indistinct, hazy, dim,
obscure, vague, indefinite,
ambiguous, equivocal, uncertain,
unsure, doubtful, dubious.
**F3** clear, evident.

**uncomfortable** *adj* **1** CRAMPED,
hard, cold, ill-fitting, irritating,
painful, disagreeable. **2** AWKWARD,
embarrassed, self-conscious, uneasy,
troubled, worried, disturbed,
distressed, disquieted, conscience-
stricken.
**F3 1** comfortable. **2** relaxed.

**uncommon** *adj* rare, scarce,
infrequent, unusual, abnormal,
atypical, unfamiliar, strange, odd,
curious, bizarre, extraordinary,
remarkable, notable, outstanding,
exceptional, distinctive, special.
**F3** common, usual, normal.

**uncommunicative** *adj* silent,
taciturn, tight-lipped, close, secretive,
unforthcoming, unresponsive, curt,
brief, reticent, reserved, shy, retiring,
withdrawn, unsociable.
**F3** communicative, forthcoming.

**uncompromising** *adj* unyielding,
unbending, inflexible,
unaccommodating, rigid, firm, strict,
tough, hard-line, inexorable,
intransigent, stubborn, obstinate, die-
hard.
**F3** flexible.

**unconcealed** *adj* open, patent,
obvious, evident, manifest, blatant,

conspicuous, noticeable, visible, apparent.

**F3** hidden, secret.

**unconcerned** *adj* indifferent, apathetic, uninterested, nonchalant, carefree, relaxed, complacent, cool, composed, untroubled, unworried, unruffled, unmoved, uncaring, unsympathetic, callous, aloof, remote, distant, detached, dispassionate, uninvolved, oblivious.

**F3** concerned, worried, interested.

**unconditional** *adj* unqualified, unreserved, unrestricted, unlimited, absolute, utter, full, total, complete, entire, whole-hearted, thoroughgoing, downright, outright, positive, categorical, unequivocal.

**F3** conditional, qualified, limited.

**unconnected** *adj* **1** IRRELEVANT, unrelated, unattached, detached, separate, independent.
**2** DISCONNECTED, incoherent, irrational, illogical.

**F3 1** connected, relevant.

**unconscious** *adj* **1** STUNNED, knocked out, out, out cold, out for the count, concussed, comatose, senseless, insensible. **2** UNAWARE, oblivious, blind, deaf, heedless, unmindful, ignorant. **3** *an unconscious reaction*: involuntary, automatic, reflex, instinctive, impulsive, innate, subconscious, subliminal, repressed, suppressed, latent, unwitting, inadvertent, accidental, unintentional.

**F3 1** conscious. **2** aware. **3** intentional.

**uncontrollable** *adj* ungovernable, unmanageable, unruly, wild, mad, furious, violent, strong, irrepressible.

**F3** controllable, manageable.

**uncontrolled** *adj* unrestrained, unbridled, unchecked, rampant, wild, unruly, undisciplined.

**F3** controlled, restrained.

**unconventional** *adj* unorthodox, alternative, different, offbeat, eccentric, idiosyncratic, individual,

original, odd, unusual, irregular, abnormal, bizarre, way-out (*sl*).

**F3** conventional, orthodox.

**unconvincing** *adj* implausible, unlikely, improbable, questionable, doubtful, dubious, suspect, weak, feeble, flimsy, lame.

**F3** convincing, plausible.

**unco-ordinated** *adj* clumsy, awkward, ungainly, ungraceful, inept, disjointed.

**F3** graceful.

**uncouth** *adj* coarse, crude, vulgar, rude, ill-mannered, unseemly, improper, clumsy, awkward, gauche, graceless, unrefined, uncultivated, uncultured, uncivilized, rough.

**F3** polite, refined, urbane.

**uncover** *v* unveil, unmask, unwrap, strip, bare, open, expose, reveal, show, disclose, divulge, leak, unearth, exhume, discover, detect.

**F3** cover, conceal, suppress.

**uncritical** *adj* undiscerning, undiscriminating, unselective, unquestioning, credulous, accepting, trusting, gullible, naive.

**F3** discerning, discriminating, sceptical.

**uncultivated** *adj* fallow, wild, rough, natural.

**F3** cultivated.

**uncultured** *adj* unsophisticated, unrefined, uncultivated, uncivilized, rough, uncouth, boorish, rustic, coarse, crude, ill-bred.

**F3** cultured, sophisticated.

**undaunted** *adj* undeterred, undiscouraged, undismayed, unbowed, resolute, steadfast, brave, courageous, fearless, bold, intrepid, dauntless, indomitable.

**F3** discouraged, timorous.

**undecided** *adj* uncertain, unsure, in two minds, ambivalent, doubtful, hesitant, wavering, irresolute, uncommitted, indefinite, vague, dubious, debatable, moot, unsettled, open.

decided, certain, definite.

**undemonstrative** *adj* aloof,
distant, remote, withdrawn, reserved,
reticent, uncommunicative, stiff,
formal, cool, cold, unemotional,
restrained, impassive, phlegmatic.
demonstrative, communicative.

**undeniable** *adj* irrefutable,
unquestionable, incontrovertible,
sure, certain, undoubted, proven,
clear, obvious, patent, evident,
manifest, unmistakable.
questionable.

**under** *prep* below, underneath,
beneath, lower than, less than,
inferior to, subordinate to.
over, above.

**under way** moving, in motion, going,
in operation, started, begun, in
progress, afoot.

**undercover** *adj* secret, hush-hush
(*infml*), private, confidential, spy,
intelligence, underground,
clandestine, surreptitious, furtive,
covert, hidden, concealed.
open, unconcealed.

**undercurrent** *n* undertone,
overtone, hint, suggestion, tinge,
flavour, aura, atmosphere, feeling,
sense, movement, tendency, trend,
drift.

**underestimate** *v* underrate,
undervalue, misjudge, miscalculate,
minimize, belittle, disparage, dismiss.
overestimate, exaggerate.

**undergo** *v* experience, suffer,
sustain, submit to, bear, stand,
endure, weather, withstand.

**underground** *adj* **1** *an underground
passage*: subterranean, buried,
sunken, covered, hidden, concealed.
**2** SECRET, covert, undercover,
revolutionary, subversive, radical,
experimental, avant-garde,
alternative, unorthodox, unofficial.

**undergrowth** *n* brush, scrub,
vegetation, ground cover, bracken,
bushes, brambles, briars.

**underhand** *adj* unscrupulous,

unethical, immoral, improper, sly,
crafty, sneaky, stealthy,
surreptitious, furtive, clandestine,
devious, dishonest, deceitful,
deceptive, fraudulent, crooked
(*infml*), shady (*infml*).
honest, open, above board.

**underline** *v* mark, underscore,
stress, emphasize, accentuate,
italicize, highlight, point up.
play down, soft-pedal.

**underlying** *adj* basic, fundamental,
essential, primary, elementary, root,
intrinsic, latent, hidden, lurking,
veiled.

**undermine** *v* mine, tunnel,
excavate, erode, wear away, weaken,
sap, sabotage, subvert, vitiate, mar,
impair.
strengthen, fortify.

**underprivileged** *adj*
disadvantaged, deprived, poor,
needy, impoverished, destitute,
oppressed.
privileged, fortunate, affluent.

**underrate** *v* underestimate,
undervalue, belittle, disparage,
depreciate, dismiss.
overrate, exaggerate.

**undersized** *adj* small, tiny, minute,
miniature, pygmy, dwarf, stunted,
underdeveloped, underweight, puny.
oversized, big, overweight.

**understand** *v* **1** *I don't understand*:
grasp, comprehend, take in, follow,
get (*infml*), cotton on (*infml*),
fathom, penetrate, make out, discern,
perceive, see, realize, recognize,
appreciate, accept. **2** SYMPATHIZE,
empathize, commiserate. **3** BELIEVE,
think, know, hear, learn, gather,
assume, presume, suppose, conclude.
**1** misunderstand.

**understanding** *n* **1** GRASP,
comprehension, knowledge, wisdom,
intelligence, intellect, sense,
judgement, discernment, insight,
appreciation, awareness, impression,
perception, belief, idea, notion,

opinion, interpretation.
**2** AGREEMENT, arrangement, pact, accord, harmony. **3** SYMPATHY, empathy.
*adj* sympathetic, compassionate, kind, considerate, sensitive, tender, loving, patient, tolerant, forbearing, forgiving.
**E3** unsympathetic, insensitive, impatient, intolerant.

**understate** *v* underplay, play down, soft-pedal, minimize, make light of, belittle, dismiss.
**E3** exaggerate.

**understood** *adj* accepted, assumed, presumed, implied, implicit, inferred, tacit, unstated, unspoken, unwritten.

**understudy** *n* stand-in, double, substitute, replacement, reserve, deputy.

**undertake** *v* **1** PLEDGE, promise, guarantee, agree, contract, covenant. **2** BEGIN, commence, embark on, tackle, try, attempt, endeavour, take on, accept, assume.

**undertaking** *n* **1** ENTERPRISE, venture, business, affair, task, project, operation, attempt, endeavour, effort. **2** PLEDGE, commitment, promise, vow, word, assurance.

**undertone** *n* hint, suggestion, whisper, murmur, trace, tinge, touch, flavour, feeling, atmosphere, undercurrent.

**undervalue** *v* underrate, underestimate, misjudge, minimize, depreciate, disparage, dismiss.
**E3** overrate, exaggerate.

**underwater** *adj* subaquatic, undersea, submarine, submerged, sunken.

**underwear** *n* underclothes, undergarments, lingerie, undies (*infml*), smalls (*infml*).

**underweight** *adj* thin, undersized, underfed, undernourished, half-starved.
**E3** overweight.

**underwrite** *v* endorse, authorize, sanction, approve, back, guarantee, insure, sponsor, fund, finance, subsidize, subscribe, sign, initial, countersign.

**undesirable** *adj* unwanted, unwelcome, unacceptable, unsuitable, unpleasant, disagreeable, distasteful, repugnant, offensive, objectionable, obnoxious.
**E3** desirable, pleasant.

**undignified** *adj* inelegant, ungainly, clumsy, foolish, unseemly, improper, unsuitable, inappropriate.
**E3** dignified, elegant.

**undisguised** *adj* unconcealed, open, overt, explicit, frank, genuine, apparent, patent, obvious, evident, manifest, blatant, naked, unadorned, stark, utter, outright, thoroughgoing.
**E3** secret, concealed, hidden.

**undisputed** *adj* uncontested, unchallenged, unquestioned, undoubted, indisputable, incontrovertible, undeniable, irrefutable, accepted, acknowledged, recognized, sure, certain, conclusive.
**E3** debatable, uncertain.

**undistinguished** *adj* unexceptional, unremarkable, unimpressive, ordinary, run-of-the-mill, everyday, banal, indifferent, mediocre, inferior.
**E3** distinguished, exceptional.

**undivided** *adj* solid, unbroken, intact, whole, entire, full, complete, combined, united, unanimous, concentrated, exclusive, whole-hearted.

**undo** *v* **1** UNFASTEN, untie, unbuckle, unbutton, unzip, unlock, unwrap, unwind, open, loose, loosen, separate. **2** ANNUL, nullify, invalidate, cancel, offset, neutralize, reverse, overturn, upset, quash, defeat, undermine, subvert, mar, spoil, ruin, wreck, shatter, destroy.
**E3 1** fasten, do up.

**undoing** *n* downfall, ruin, ruination, collapse, destruction, defeat, overthrow, reversal, weakness, shame, disgrace.

**undone** *adj* **1** UNACCOMPLISHED, unfulfilled, unfinished, uncompleted, incomplete, outstanding, left, omitted, neglected, forgotten. **2** UNFASTENED, untied, unlaced, unbuttoned, unlocked, open, loose.
**F3** **1** done, accomplished, complete. **2** fastened.

**undoubted** *adj* unchallenged, undisputed, acknowledged, unquestionable, indisputable, incontrovertible, undesirable, indubitable, sure, certain, definite, obvious, patent.

**undress** *v* strip, peel off (*infml*), disrobe, take off, divest, remove, shed.

**undressed** *adj* unclothed, disrobed, stripped, naked, stark naked, nude.
**F3** clothed.

**undue** *adj* unnecessary, needless, uncalled-for, unwarranted, undeserved, unreasonable, disproportionate, excessive, immoderate, inordinate, extreme, extravagant, improper.
**F3** reasonable, moderate, proper.

**unduly** *adv* too, over, excessively, immoderately, inordinately, disproportionately, unreasonably, unjustifiably, unnecessarily.
**F3** moderately, reasonably.

**unearth** *v* dig up, exhume, disinter, excavate, uncover, expose, reveal, find, discover, detect.
**F3** bury.

**unearthly** *adj* **1** SUPERNATURAL, ghostly, eerie, uncanny, weird, strange, spine-chilling. **2** *at this unearthly hour*: unreasonable, outrageous, ungodly.
**F3** **2** reasonable.

**uneasy** *adj* uncomfortable, anxious, worried, apprehensive, tense, strained, nervous, agitated, shaky, jittery, edgy, upset, troubled, disturbed, unsettled, restless,

impatient, unsure, insecure.
**F3** calm, composed.

**uneducated** *adj* unschooled, untaught, unread, ignorant, illiterate, uncultivated, uncultured, philistine, benighted.
**F3** educated.

**unemotional** *adj* cool, cold, unfeeling, impassive, indifferent, apathetic, unresponsive, undemonstrative, unexcitable, phlegmatic, objective, dispassionate.
**F3** emotional, excitable.

**unemployed** *adj* jobless, out of work, laid off, redundant, unwaged, on the dole (*infml*), idle, unoccupied.
**F3** employed, occupied.

**unending** *adj* endless, never-ending, unceasing, ceaseless, incessant, interminable, constant, continual, perpetual, everlasting, eternal, undying.
**F3** transient, intermittent.

**unenviable** *adj* undesirable, unpleasant, disagreeable, uncongenial, uncomfortable, thankless, difficult.
**F3** enviable, desirable.

**unequal** *adj* different, varying, dissimilar, unlike, unmatched, uneven, unbalanced, disproportionate, asymmetrical, irregular, unfair, unjust, biased, discriminatory.
**F3** equal.

**unequivocal** *adj* unambiguous, explicit, clear, plain, evident, distinct, unmistakable, express, direct, straight, definite, positive, categorical, incontrovertible, absolute, unqualified, unreserved.
**F3** ambiguous, vague, qualified.

**unethical** *adj* unprofessional, immoral, improper, wrong, unscrupulous, unprincipled, dishonourable, disreputable, illegal, illicit, dishonest, underhand, shady (*infml*).
**F3** ethical.

**uneven** adj 1 *uneven ground*: rough, bumpy. 2 ODD, unequal, inequitable, unfair, unbalanced, one-sided, asymmetrical, lopsided, crooked. 3 IRREGULAR, intermittent, spasmodic, fitful, jerky, unsteady, variable, changeable, fluctuating, erratic, inconsistent, patchy.
**Ea** 1 flat, level. 2 even, equal. 3 regular.

**uneventful** adj uninteresting, unexciting, quiet, unvaried, boring, monotonous, tedious, dull, routine, humdrum, ordinary, commonplace, unremarkable, unexceptional, unmemorable.
**Ea** eventful, memorable.

**unexceptional** adj unremarkable, unmemorable, typical, average, normal, usual, ordinary, indifferent, mediocre, unimpressive.
**Ea** exceptional, impressive.

**unexpected** adj unforeseen, unanticipated, unpredictable, chance, accidental, fortuitous, sudden, abrupt, surprising, startling, amazing, astonishing, unusual.
**Ea** expected, predictable.

**unfair** adj unjust, inequitable, partial, biased, prejudiced, bigoted, discriminatory, unbalanced, one-sided, partisan, arbitrary, undeserved, unmerited, unwarranted, uncalled-for, unethical, unscrupulous, unprincipled, wrongful, dishonest.
**Ea** fair, just, unbiased, deserved.

**unfaithful** adj disloyal, treacherous, false, untrue, deceitful, dishonest, untrustworthy, unreliable, fickle, inconstant, adulterous, two-timing, duplicitous, double-dealing, faithless, unbelieving, godless.
**Ea** faithful, loyal, reliable.

**unfamiliar** adj strange, unusual, uncommon, curious, alien, foreign, uncharted, unexplored, unknown, different, new, novel, unaccustomed, unacquainted, inexperienced,

unpractised, unskilled, unversed.
**Ea** familiar, customary, conversant.

**unfashionable** adj outmoded, dated, out of date, out, passé, old-fashioned, antiquated, obsolete.
**Ea** fashionable.

**unfasten** v undo, untie, loosen, unlock, open, uncouple, disconnect, separate, detach.
**Ea** fasten.

**unfavourable** adj inauspicious, unpromising, ominous, threatening, discouraging, inopportune, untimely, unseasonable, ill-suited, unfortunate, unlucky, disadvantageous, bad, poor, adverse, contrary, negative, hostile, unfriendly, uncomplimentary.
**Ea** favourable, auspicious, promising.

**unfeeling** adj insensitive, cold, hard, stony, callous, heartless, hard-hearted, cruel, inhuman, pitiless, uncaring, unsympathetic, apathetic.
**Ea** sensitive, sympathetic.

**unfinished** adj incomplete, uncompleted, half-done, sketchy, rough, crude, imperfect, lacking, wanting, deficient, undone, unaccomplished, unfulfilled.
**Ea** finished, perfect.

**unfit** adj 1 UNSUITABLE, inappropriate, unsuited, ill-equipped, unqualified, ineligible, untrained, unprepared, unequal, incapable, incompetent, inadequate, ineffective, useless. 2 UNHEALTHY, out of condition, flabby, feeble, decrepit.
**Ea** 1 fit, suitable, competent. 2 healthy.

**unfold** v 1 DEVELOP, evolve. 2 REVEAL, disclose, show, present, describe, explain, clarify, elaborate. 3 *unfold a map*: open, spread, flatten, straighten, stretch out, undo, unfurl, unroll, uncoil, unwrap, uncover.
**Ea** 2 withhold, suppress. 3 fold, wrap.

**unforeseen** adj unpredicted, unexpected, unanticipated, surprising, startling, sudden, unavoidable.
**Ea** expected, predictable.

**unforgettable** *adj* memorable, momentous, historic, noteworthy, notable, impressive, remarkable, exceptional, extraordinary.
**F3** unmemorable, unexceptional.

**unforgivable** *adj* unpardonable, inexcusable, unjustifiable, indefensible, reprehensible, shameful, disgraceful, deplorable.
**F3** forgivable, venial.

**unfortunate** *adj* 1 UNLUCKY, luckless, hapless, unsuccessful, poor, wretched, unhappy, doomed, ill-fated, hopeless, calamitous, disastrous, ruinous.
2 REGRETTABLE, lamentable, deplorable, adverse, unfavourable, unsuitable, inappropriate, inopportune, untimely, ill-timed.
**F3** 1 fortunate, happy. 2 favourable, appropriate.

**unfounded** *adj* baseless, groundless, unsupported, unsubstantiated, unproven, unjustified, idle, false, spurious, trumped-up, fabricated.
**F3** substantiated, justified.

**unfriendly** *adj* unsociable, standoffish, aloof, distant, unapproachable, inhospitable, uncongenial, unneighbourly, unwelcoming, cold, chilly, hostile, aggressive, quarrelsome, inimical, antagonistic, ill-disposed, disagreeable, surly, sour.
**F3** friendly, amiable, agreeable.

**ungainly** *adj* clumsy, awkward, gauche, inelegant, gawky, unco-ordinated, lumbering, unwieldy.
**F3** graceful, elegant.

**ungodly** *adj* 1 UNREASONABLE, outrageous, intolerable, unearthly, unsocial. 2 IMPIOUS, irreligious, godless, blasphemous, profane, immoral, corrupt, depraved, sinful, wicked.

**ungrateful** *adj* unthankful, unappreciative, ill-mannered, ungracious, selfish, heedless.
**F3** grateful, thankful.

**unguarded** *adj* 1 *in an unguarded moment*: unwary, careless, incautious, imprudent, impolitic, indiscreet, undiplomatic, thoughtless, unthinking, heedless, foolish, foolhardy, rash, ill-considered.
2 UNDEFENDED, unprotected, exposed, vulnerable, defenceless.
**F3** 1 guarded, cautious. 2 defended, protected.

**unhappy** *adj* 1 SAD, sorrowful, miserable, melancholy, depressed, dispirited, despondent, dejected, downcast, crestfallen, long-faced, gloomy. 2 UNFORTUNATE, unlucky, ill-fated, unsuitable, inappropriate, inapt, ill-chosen, tactless, awkward, clumsy.
**F3** 1 happy. 2 fortunate, suitable.

**unharmed** *adj* undamaged, unhurt, uninjured, unscathed, whole, intact, safe, sound.
**F3** harmed, damaged.

**unhealthy** *adj* 1 UNWELL, sick, ill, poorly, ailing, sickly, infirm, invalid, weak, feeble, frail, unsound.
2 UNWHOLESOME, insanitary, unhygienic, harmful, detrimental, morbid, unnatural.
**F3** 1 healthy, fit. 2 wholesome, hygienic, natural.

**unheard-of** *adj* 1 UNTHINKABLE, inconceivable, unimaginable, undreamed-of, unprecedented, unacceptable, offensive, shocking, outrageous, preposterous.
2 UNKNOWN, unfamiliar, new, unusual, obscure.
**F3** 1 normal, acceptable. 2 famous.

**unheeded** *adj* ignored, disregarded, disobeyed, unnoticed, unobserved, unremarked, overlooked, neglected, forgotten.
**F3** noted, observed.

**unhesitating** *adj* immediate, instant, instantaneous, prompt, ready, automatic, spontaneous, unquestioning, unwavering, unfaltering, whole-hearted, implicit,

**E3** hesitant, tentative.

**unholy** *adj* **1** IMPIOUS, irreligious, sinful, iniquitous, immoral, corrupt, depraved, wicked, evil. **2** (*infml*) *an unholy mess*: unreasonable, shocking, outrageous, ungodly, unearthly.
**E3 1** holy, pious, godly. **2** reasonable.

**unhurried** *adj* slow, leisurely, deliberate, easy, relaxed, calm, easy-going (*infml*), laid-back (*sl*).
**E3** hurried, hasty, rushed.

**unidentified** *adj* unknown, unrecognized, unmarked, unnamed, nameless, anonymous, incognito, unfamiliar, strange, mysterious.
**E3** identified, known, named.

**uniform** *n* outfit, costume, livery, insignia, regalia, robes, dress, suit.
*adj* same, identical, like, alike, similar, homogeneous, consistent, regular, equal, smooth, even, flat, monotonous, unvarying, unchanging, constant, unbroken.
**E3** different, varied, changing.

**unify** *v* unite, join, bind, combine, integrate, merge, amalgamate, consolidate, coalesce, fuse, weld.
**E3** separate, divide, split.

**unimaginable** *adj* inconceivable, mind-boggling (*infml*), unbelievable, incredible, impossible, fantastic, undreamed-of, unthinkable, unheard-of.

**unimaginative** *adj* uninspired, unoriginal, predictable, hackneyed, banal, ordinary, dull, boring, routine, matter-of-fact, dry, barren, lifeless, unexciting, tame.
**E3** imaginative, creative, original.

**unimportant** *adj* insignificant, inconsequential, irrelevant, immaterial, minor, trivial, trifling, petty, slight, negligible, worthless.
**E3** important, significant, relevant, vital.

**unimpressive** *adj* unspectacular, undistinguished, unexceptional, unremarkable, uninteresting, dull, average, commonplace, indifferent,

mediocre.
**E3** impressive, memorable, notable.

**uninhabited** *adj* unoccupied, vacant, empty, deserted, abandoned, unpeopled, unpopulated.

**uninhibited** *adj* unconstrained, unreserved, unselfconscious, liberated, free, unrestricted, uncontrolled, unrestrained, abandoned, natural, spontaneous, frank, candid, open, relaxed, informal.
**E3** inhibited, repressed, constrained, restrained.

**unintelligible** *adj* incomprehensible, incoherent, inarticulate, double Dutch, garbled, scrambled, jumbled, muddled, indecipherable, illegible.
**E3** intelligible, comprehensible, clear.

**unintentional** *adj* unintended, accidental, fortuitous, inadvertent, unplanned, unpremeditated, involuntary, unconscious, unwitting.
**E3** intentional, deliberate.

**uninterested** *adj* indifferent, unconcerned, uninvolved, bored, listless, apathetic, unenthusiastic, blasé, impassive, unresponsive.
**E3** interested, concerned, enthusiastic, responsive.

**uninteresting** *adj* boring, tedious, monotonous, humdrum, dull, drab, dreary, dry, flat, tame, uneventful, unexciting, uninspiring, unimpressive.
**E3** interesting, exciting.

**uninterrupted** *adj* unbroken, continuous, non-stop, unending, constant, continual, steady, sustained, undisturbed, peaceful.
**E3** broken, intermittent.

**uninvited** *adj* unasked, unsought, unsolicited, unwanted, unwelcome.
**E3** invited.

**union** *n* alliance, coalition, league, association, federation, confederation, confederacy, merger, combination, amalgamation, blend,

mixture, synthesis, fusion, unification, unity.
**F3** separation, alienation, estrangement.

**unique** *adj* single, one-off, sole, only, lone, solitary, unmatched, matchless, peerless, unequalled, unparalleled, unrivalled, incomparable, inimitable.
**F3** common.

**unison** *n* concert, co-operation, unanimity, unity.

**unit** *n* item, part, element, constituent, piece, component, module, section, segment, portion, entity, whole, one, system, assembly.

**unite** *v* join, link, couple, marry, ally, co-operate, band, associate, federate, confederate, combine, pool, amalgamate, merge, blend, unify, consolidate, coalesce, fuse.
**F3** separate, sever.

**united** *adj* allied, affiliated, corporate, unified, combined, pooled, collective, concerted, one, unanimous, agreed, in agreement, in accord, like-minded.
**F3** disunited.

**unity** *n* agreement, accord, concord, harmony, peace, consensus, unanimity, solidarity, integrity, oneness, wholeness, union, unification.
**F3** disunity, disagreement, discord, strife.

**universal** *adj* worldwide, global, all-embracing, all-inclusive, general, common, across-the-board, total, whole, entire, all-round, unlimited.

**unjust** *adj* unfair, inequitable, wrong, partial, biased, prejudiced, one-sided, partisan, unreasonable, unjustified, undeserved.
**F3** just, fair, reasonable.

**unjustifiable** *adj* indefensible, inexcusable, unforgivable, unreasonable, unwarranted, immoderate, excessive, unacceptable, outrageous.

**F3** justifiable, acceptable.

**unkempt** *adj* dishevelled, tousled, rumpled, uncombed, ungroomed, untidy, messy, scruffy, shabby, slovenly.
**F3** well-groomed, tidy.

**unkind** *adj* cruel, inhuman, inhumane, callous, hard-hearted, unfeeling, insensitive, thoughtless, inconsiderate, uncharitable, nasty, malicious, spiteful, mean, malevolent, unfriendly, uncaring, unsympathetic.
**F3** kind, considerate.

**unknown** *adj* unfamiliar, unheard-of, strange, alien, foreign, mysterious, dark, obscure, hidden, concealed, undisclosed, secret, untold, new, uncharted, unexplored, undiscovered, unidentified, unnamed, nameless, anonymous, incognito.
**F3** known, familiar.

**unlawful** *adj* illegal, criminal, illicit, illegitimate, unconstitutional, outlawed, banned, prohibited, forbidden, unauthorized.
**F3** lawful, legal.

**unlikely** *adj* **1** IMPROBABLE, implausible, far-fetched, unconvincing, unbelievable, incredible, unimaginable, unexpected, doubtful, dubious, questionable, suspect, suspicious. **2** SLIGHT, faint, remote, distant.
**F3 1** likely, plausible.

**unlimited** *adj* limitless, unrestricted, unbounded, boundless, infinite, endless, countless, incalculable, immeasurable, vast, immense, extensive, great, indefinite, absolute, unconditional, unqualified, all-encompassing, total, complete, full, unconstrained, unhampered.
**F3** limited.

**unload** *v* unpack, empty, discharge, dump, offload, unburden, relieve.
**F3** load.

**unlock** *v* unbolt, unlatch, unfasten, undo, open, free, release.

🔒 lock, fasten.

**unloved** *adj* unpopular, disliked, hated, detested, unwanted, rejected, spurned, loveless, uncared-for, neglected.
🔁 loved.

**unlucky** *adj* unfortunate, luckless, unhappy, miserable, wretched, ill-fated, ill-starred, jinxed, doomed, cursed, unfavourable, inauspicious, ominous, unsuccessful, disastrous.
🔁 lucky.

**unmanageable** *adj* **1** UNWIELDY, bulky, cumbersome, awkward, inconvenient, unhandy.
**2** UNCONTROLLABLE, wild, unruly, disorderly, difficult.
🔁 **1** manageable. **2** controllable.

**unmarried** *adj* single, unwed, celibate, unattached, available.
🔁 married.

**unmask** *v* unveil, uncloak, uncover, bare, expose, reveal, show, disclose, discover, detect.
🔁 mask, conceal.

**unmentionable** *adj* unspeakable, unutterable, taboo, immodest, indecent, shocking, scandalous, shameful, disgraceful, abominable.

**unmistakable** *adj* clear, plain, distinct, pronounced, obvious, evident, manifest, patent, glaring, explicit, unambiguous, unequivocal, positive, definite, sure, certain, unquestionable, indisputable, undeniable.
🔁 unclear, ambiguous.

**unmoved** *adj* unaffected, untouched, unshaken, dry-eyed, unfeeling, cold, dispassionate, indifferent, impassive, unresponsive, unimpressed, firm, adamant, inflexible, unbending, undeviating, unwavering, steady, unchanged, resolute, resolved, determined.
🔁 moved, affected, shaken.

**unnatural** *adj* **1** ABNORMAL, anomalous, freakish, irregular, unusual, strange, odd, peculiar, queer, bizarre, extraordinary, uncanny, supernatural, inhuman, perverted. **2** AFFECTED, feigned, artificial, false, insincere, unspontaneous, contrived, laboured, stilted, forced, strained, self-conscious, stiff.
🔁 **1** natural, normal. **2** sincere, fluent.

**unnecessary** *adj* unneeded, needless, uncalled-for, unwanted, non-essential, dispensable, expendable, superfluous, redundant, tautological.
🔁 necessary, essential, indispensable.

**unnerve** *v* daunt, intimidate, frighten, scare, discourage, demoralize, dismay, disconcert, upset, worry, shake, rattle (*infml*), confound, fluster.
🔁 nerve, brace, steel.

**unnoticed** *adj* unobserved, unremarked, unseen, unrecognized, undiscovered, overlooked, ignored, disregarded, neglected, unheeded.
🔁 noticed, noted.

**unobtrusive** *adj* inconspicuous, unnoticeable, unassertive, self-effacing, humble, modest, unostentatious, unpretentious, restrained, low-key, subdued, quiet, retiring.
🔁 obtrusive, ostentatious.

**unoccupied** *adj* uninhabited, vacant, empty, free, idle, inactive, workless, jobless, unemployed.
🔁 occupied, busy.

**unofficial** *adj* unauthorized, illegal, informal, off-the-record, personal, private, confidential, undeclared, unconfirmed.
🔁 official.

**unorthodox** *adj* unconventional, nonconformist, heterodox, alternative, fringe, irregular, abnormal, unusual.
🔁 orthodox, conventional.

**unpaid** *adj* **1** *unpaid bills*: outstanding, overdue, unsettled, owing, due, payable. **2** *unpaid work*:

voluntary, honorary, unsalaried, unwaged, unremunerative, free.
F3 1 paid.

**unpalatable** *adj* **1** UNAPPETIZING, distasteful, insipid, bitter, uneatable, inedible. **2** UNPLEASANT, disagreeable, unattractive, offensive, repugnant.
F3 **1** palatable. **2** pleasant.

**unparalleled** *adj* unequalled, unmatched, matchless, peerless, incomparable, unrivalled, unsurpassed, supreme, superlative, rare, exceptional, unprecedented.

**unpleasant** *adj* disagreeable, ill-natured, nasty, objectionable, offensive, distasteful, unpalatable, unattractive, repulsive, bad, troublesome.
F3 pleasant, agreeable, nice.

**unpopular** *adj* disliked, hated, detested, unloved, unsought-after, unfashionable, undesirable, unwelcome, unwanted, rejected, shunned, avoided, neglected.
F3 popular, fashionable.

**unprecedented** *adj* new, original, revolutionary, unknown, unheard-of, exceptional, remarkable, extraordinary, abnormal, unusual, freakish, unparalleled, unrivalled.
F3 usual.

**unpredictable** *adj* unforeseeable, unexpected, changeable, variable, inconstant, unreliable, fickle, unstable, erratic, random, chance.
F3 predictable, foreseeable, constant.

**unprepared** *adj* unready, surprised, unsuspecting, ill-equipped, unfinished, incomplete, half-baked, unplanned, unrehearsed, spontaneous, improvised, ad-lib, off-the-cuff.
F3 prepared, ready.

**unpretentious** *adj* unaffected, natural, plain, simple, unobtrusive, honest, straightforward, humble, modest, unassuming, unostentatious.
F3 pretentious.

**unproductive** *adj* infertile, sterile, barren, dry, arid, unfruitful, fruitless, futile, vain, idle, useless, ineffective, unprofitable, unremunerative, unrewarding.
F3 productive, fertile.

**unprofessional** *adj* amateurish, inexpert, unskilled, sloppy, incompetent, inefficient, casual, negligent, lax, unethical, unprincipled, improper, unseemly, unacceptable, inadmissible.
F3 professional, skilful.

**unprotected** *adj* unguarded, unattended, undefended, unfortified, unarmed, unshielded, unsheltered, uncovered, exposed, open, naked, vulnerable, defenceless, helpless.
F3 protected, safe, immune.

**unqualified** *adj* **1** UNTRAINED, inexperienced, amateur, ineligible, unfit, incompetent, incapable, unprepared, ill-equipped.
**2** ABSOLUTE, categorical, utter, total, complete, thorough, consummate, downright, unmitigated, unreserved, whole-hearted, outright, unconditional, unrestricted.
F3 **1** qualified, professional.
**2** conditional, tentative.

**unravel** *v* unwind, undo, untangle, disentangle, free, extricate, separate, resolve, sort out, solve, work out, figure out, puzzle out, penetrate, interpret, explain.
F3 tangle, complicate.

**unreal** *adj* false, artificial, synthetic, mock, fake, sham, imaginary, visionary, fanciful, make-believe, pretend (*infml*), fictitious, made-up, fairy-tale, legendary, mythical, fantastic, illusory, immaterial, insubstantial, hypothetical.
F3 real, genuine.

**unrealistic** *adj* impractical, idealistic, romantic, quixotic, impracticable, unworkable, unreasonable, impossible.

◫ realistic, pragmatic.

**unreasonable** adj **1** UNFAIR, unjust, biased, unjustifiable, unjustified, unwarranted, undue, uncalled-for. **2** IRRATIONAL, illogical, inconsistent, arbitrary, absurd, nonsensical, far-fetched, preposterous, mad, senseless, silly, foolish, stupid, headstrong, opinionated, perverse. **3** *unreasonable prices*: excessive, immoderate, extravagant, exorbitant, extortionate.
◫ **1** reasonable, fair. **2** rational, sensible. **3** moderate.

**unrecognizable** adj unidentifiable, disguised, incognito, changed, altered.

**unrefined** adj raw, untreated, unprocessed, unfinished, unpolished, crude, coarse, vulgar, unsophisticated, uncultivated, uncultured.
◫ refined, finished.

**unrelated** adj unconnected, unassociated, irrelevant, extraneous, different, dissimilar, unlike, disparate, distinct, separate, independent.
◫ related, similar.

**unrelenting** adj relentless, unremitting, uncompromising, inexorable, incessant, unceasing, ceaseless, endless, unbroken, continuous, constant, continual, perpetual, steady, unabated, remorseless, unmerciful, merciless, pitiless, unsparing.
◫ spasmodic, intermittent.

**unreliable** adj unsound, fallible, deceptive, false, mistaken, erroneous, inaccurate, unconvincing, implausible, uncertain, undependable, untrustworthy, unstable, fickle, irresponsible.
◫ reliable, dependable, trustworthy.

**unrepentant** adj impenitent, unapologetic, unabashed, unashamed, shameless, incorrigible,

confirmed, hardened, obdurate.
◫ repentant, penitent, ashamed.

**unrest** n protest, rebellion, turmoil, agitation, restlessness, dissatisfaction, dissension, disaffection, worry.
◫ peace, calm.

**unrestricted** adj unlimited, unbounded, unopposed, unhindered, unimpeded, unobstructed, clear, free, open, public, unconditional, absolute.
◫ restricted, limited.

**unripe** adj unripened, green, immature, undeveloped, unready.
◫ ripe, mature.

**unrivalled** adj unequalled, unparalleled, unmatched, matchless, peerless, incomparable, inimitable, unsurpassed, supreme, superlative.

**unruffled** adj undisturbed, untroubled, imperturbable, collected, composed, cool, calm, tranquil, serene, peaceful, smooth, level, even.
◫ troubled, anxious.

**unruly** adj uncontrollable, unmanageable, ungovernable, intractable, disorderly, wild, rowdy, riotous, rebellious, mutinous, lawless, insubordinate, disobedient, wayward, wilful, headstrong, obstreperous.
◫ manageable, orderly.

**unsafe** adj dangerous, perilous, risky, hazardous, treacherous, unreliable, uncertain, unsound, unstable, precarious, insecure, vulnerable, exposed.
◫ safe, secure.

**unsatisfactory** adj unacceptable, imperfect, defective, faulty, inferior, poor, weak, inadequate, insufficient, deficient, unsuitable, displeasing, dissatisfying, unsatisfying, frustrating, disappointing.
◫ satisfactory, pleasing.

**unscathed** adj unhurt, uninjured, unharmed, undamaged, untouched, whole, intact, safe, sound.
◫ hurt, injured.

**unscrupulous** *adj* unprincipled, ruthless, shameless, dishonourable, dishonest, crooked (*infml*), corrupt, immoral, unethical, improper.
**F3** scrupulous, ethical, proper.

**unseemly** *adj* improper, indelicate, indecorous, unbecoming, undignified, unrefined, disreputable, discreditable, undue, inappropriate, unsuitable.
**F3** seemly, decorous.

**unseen** *adj* unnoticed, unobserved, undetected, invisible, hidden, concealed, veiled, obscure.
**F3** visible.

**unselfish** *adj* selfless, altruistic, self-denying, self-sacrificing, disinterested, noble, magnanimous, generous, liberal, charitable, philanthropic, public-spirited, humanitarian, kind.
**F3** selfish.

**unsentimental** *adj* realistic, practical, pragmatic, hard-headed, tough, unromantic, level-headed.
**F3** sentimental, idealistic.

**unsettle** *v* disturb, upset, trouble, bother, discompose, ruffle, fluster, unbalance, shake, agitate, rattle (*infml*), disconcert, confuse, throw.

**unsettled** *adj* **1** DISTURBED, upset, troubled, agitated, anxious, uneasy, tense, edgy, flustered, shaken, unnerved, disoriented, confused. **2** UNRESOLVED, undetermined, undecided, open, uncertain, doubtful. **3** *unsettled weather*: changeable, variable, unpredictable, inconstant, unstable, insecure, unsteady, shaky. **4** UNPAID, outstanding, owing, payable, overdue.
**F3** **1** composed. **2** certain. **3** settled. **4** paid.

**unshakable** *adj* firm, well-founded, fixed, stable, immovable, unassailable, unwavering, constant, steadfast, staunch, sure, resolute, determined.
**F3** insecure.

**unsightly** *adj* ugly, unattractive,

unprepossessing, hideous, repulsive, repugnant, off-putting, unpleasant, disagreeable.
**F3** attractive.

**unskilled** *adj* untrained, unqualified, inexperienced, unpractised, inexpert, unprofessional, amateurish, incompetent.
**F3** skilled.

**unsociable** *adj* unfriendly, aloof, distant, standoffish, withdrawn, introverted, reclusive, retiring, reserved, taciturn, unforthcoming, uncommunicative, cold, chilly, uncongenial, unneighbourly, inhospitable, hostile.
**F3** sociable, friendly.

**unsolicited** *adj* unrequested, unsought, uninvited, unasked, unwanted, unwelcome, uncalled-for, gratuitous, voluntary, spontaneous.
**F3** requested, invited.

**unsophisticated** *adj* artless, guileless, innocent, ingenuous, naïve, inexperienced, unworldly, childlike, natural, unaffected, unpretentious, unrefined, plain, simple, straightforward, uncomplicated, uninvolved.
**F3** sophisticated, worldly, complex.

**unsound** *adj* **1** *unsound reasoning*: faulty, flawed, defective, ill-founded, fallacious, false, erroneous, invalid, illogical. **2** UNHEALTHY, unwell, ill, diseased, weak, frail, unbalanced, deranged, unhinged. **3** UNSTABLE, unsteady, wobbly, shaky, insecure, unsafe.
**F3** **1** sound. **2** well. **3** stable.

**unspeakable** *adj* unutterable, inexpressible, indescribable, awful, dreadful, frightful, terrible, horrible, shocking, appalling, monstrous, inconceivable, unbelievable.

**unspoilt** *adj* preserved, unchanged, untouched, natural, unaffected, unsophisticated, unharmed, undamaged, unimpaired, unblemished, perfect.

**unspoken** *adj* unstated, undeclared, unuttered, unexpressed, unsaid, voiceless, wordless, silent, tacit, implicit, implied, inferred, understood, assumed.
**F₃** stated, explicit.

**unstable** *adj* **1** CHANGEABLE, variable, fluctuating, vacillating, wavering, fitful, erratic, inconsistent, volatile, capricious, inconstant, unpredictable, unreliable, untrustworthy. **2** UNSTEADY, wobbly, shaky, rickety, insecure, unsafe, risky, precarious, tottering, unbalanced.
**F₃** **1** stable. **2** steady.

**unsteady** *adj* unstable, wobbly, shaky, rickety, insecure, unsafe, treacherous, precarious, tottering, unreliable, inconstant, irregular, flickering.
**F₃** steady, firm.

**unsuccessful** *adj* failed, abortive, vain, futile, useless, ineffective, unavailing, fruitless, unproductive, sterile, luckless, unlucky, unfortunate, losing, beaten, defeated, frustrated, thwarted.
**F₃** successful, effective, fortunate, winning.

**unsuitable** *adj* inappropriate, inapt, unsuited, unfit, unacceptable, improper, unseemly, unbecoming, incompatible, incongruous.
**F₃** suitable, appropriate.

**unsung** *adj* unhonoured, unpraised, unacknowledged, unrecognized, overlooked, disregarded, neglected, forgotten, unknown, obscure.
**F₃** honoured, famous, renowned.

**unsure** *adj* uncertain, doubtful, dubious, suspicious, sceptical, unconvinced, unpersuaded, undecided, hesitant, tentative.
**F₃** sure, certain, confident.

**unsurpassed** *adj* surpassing, supreme, transcendent, unbeaten, unexcelled, unequalled, unparalleled,

unrivalled, incomparable, matchless, superlative, exceptional.

**unsuspecting** *adj* unwary, unaware, unconscious, trusting, trustful, unsuspicious, credulous, gullible, ingenuous, naïve, innocent.
**F₃** suspicious, knowing.

**unsympathetic** *adj* unpitying, unconcerned, unmoved, unresponsive, indifferent, insensitive, unfeeling, cold, heartless, soulless, hard-hearted, callous, cruel, inhuman, unkind, hard, stony, hostile, antagonistic.
**F₃** sympathetic, compassionate.

**untangle** *v* disentangle, extricate, unravel, undo, resolve, solve.
**F₃** tangle, complicate.

**unthinkable** *adj* inconceivable, unimaginable, unheard-of, unbelievable, incredible, impossible, improbable, unlikely, implausible, unreasonable, illogical, absurd, preposterous, outrageous, shocking.

**unthinking** *adj* thoughtless, inconsiderate, insensitive, tactless, indiscreet, rude, heedless, careless, negligent, rash, impulsive, instinctive, unconscious, automatic, mechanical.
**F₃** considerate, conscious.

**untidy** *adj* messy, cluttered, disorderly, muddled, jumbled, unsystematic, chaotic, topsy-turvy, scruffy, dishevelled, unkempt, slovenly, sloppy, slipshod.
**F₃** tidy, neat.

**untie** *v* undo, unfasten, unknot, unbind, free, release, loose, loosen.
**F₃** tie, fasten.

**untimely** *adj* early, premature, unseasonable, ill-timed, inopportune, inconvenient, awkward, unsuitable, inappropriate, unfortunate, inauspicious.
**F₃** timely, opportune.

**untiring** *adj* unflagging, tireless, indefatigable, dogged, persevering, persistent, tenacious, determined, resolute, devoted, dedicated,

constant, incessant, unremitting, steady, staunch, unfailing.
**F3** inconstant, wavering.

**untold** *adj* uncounted, unnumbered, unreckoned, incalculable, innumerable, uncountable, countless, infinite, measureless, boundless, inexhaustible, undreamed-of, unimaginable.

**untouched** *adj* unharmed, undamaged, unimpaired, unhurt, uninjured, unscathed, safe, intact, unchanged, unaltered, unaffected.
**F3** damaged, affected.

**untrained** *adj* unskilled, untaught, unschooled, uneducated, inexperienced, unqualified, amateur, unprofessional, inexpert.
**F3** trained, expert.

**untried** *adj* untested, unproved, experimental, exploratory, new, novel, innovative, innovatory.
**F3** tried, tested, proven.

**untrue** *adj* **1** FALSE, fallacious, deceptive, misleading, wrong, incorrect, inaccurate, mistaken, erroneous. **2** UNFAITHFUL, disloyal, untrustworthy, dishonest, deceitful, untruthful.
**F3** **1** true, correct. **2** faithful, honest.

**untrustworthy** *adj* dishonest, deceitful, untruthful, disloyal, unfaithful, faithless, treacherous, false, untrue, capricious, fickle, fly-by-night, unreliable, untrusty.
**F3** trustworthy, reliable.

**untruth** *n* lie, fib, whopper (*infml*), story, tale, fiction, invention, fabrication, falsehood, lying, untruthfulness, deceit, perjury.
**F3** truth.

**untruthful** *adj* lying, deceitful, dishonest, crooked (*infml*), hypocritical, two-faced, insincere, false, untrue.
**F3** truthful, honest.

**unused** *adj* leftover, remaining, surplus, extra, spare, available, new, fresh, blank, clean, untouched,

unexploited, unemployed, idle.
**F3** used.

**unusual** *adj* uncommon, rare, unfamiliar, strange, odd, curious, queer, bizarre, unconventional, irregular, abnormal, extraordinary, remarkable, exceptional, different, surprising, unexpected.
**F3** usual, normal, ordinary.

**unveil** *v* uncover, expose, bare, reveal, disclose, divulge, discover.
**F3** cover, hide.

**unwanted** *adj* undesired, unsolicited, uninvited, unwelcome, outcast, rejected, unrequired, unneeded, unnecessary, surplus, extra, superfluous, redundant.
**F3** wanted, needed, necessary.

**unwarranted** *adj* unjustified, undeserved, unprovoked, uncalled-for, groundless, unreasonable, unjust, wrong.
**F3** warranted, justifiable, deserved.

**unwary** *adj* unguarded, incautious, careless, imprudent, indiscreet, thoughtless, unthinking, heedless, reckless, rash, hasty.
**F3** wary, cautious.

**unwelcome** *adj* **1** UNWANTED, undesirable, unpopular, uninvited, excluded, rejected. **2** *unwelcome news*: unpleasant, disagreeable, upsetting, worrying, distasteful, unpalatable, unacceptable.
**F3** **1** welcome, desirable. **2** pleasant.

**unwell** *adj* ill, sick, poorly, indisposed, off-colour, ailing, sickly, unhealthy.
**F3** well, healthy.

**unwieldy** *adj* unmanageable, inconvenient, awkward, clumsy, ungainly, bulky, massive, hefty, weighty, ponderous, cumbersome.
**F3** handy, dainty.

**unwilling** *adj* reluctant, disinclined, indisposed, resistant, opposed, averse, loath, slow, unenthusiastic, grudging.
**F3** willing, enthusiastic.

**unwind** *v* 1 UNROLL, unreel, unwrap, undo, uncoil, untwist, unravel, disentangle. 2 (*infml*) RELAX, wind down, calm down.
☒ 1 wind, roll.

**unwitting** *adj* unaware, unknowing, unsuspecting, unthinking, unconscious, involuntary, accidental, chance, inadvertent, unintentional, unintended, unplanned.
☒ 1 knowing, conscious, deliberate.

**unworldly** *adj* spiritual, transcendental, metaphysical, otherworldly, visionary, idealistic, impractical, unsophisticated, inexperienced, innocent, naïve.
☒ worldly, materialistic, sophisticated.

**unworthy** *adj* undeserving, inferior, ineligible, unsuitable, inappropriate, unfitting, unbecoming, unseemly, improper, unprofessional, shameful, disgraceful, dishonourable, discreditable, ignoble, base, contemptible, despicable.
☒ worthy, commendable.

**unwritten** *adj* verbal, oral, word-of-mouth, unrecorded, tacit, implicit, understood, accepted, recognized, traditional, customary, conventional.
☒ written, recorded.

**upbraid** *v* reprimand, admonish, rebuke, reprove, reproach, scold, chide, castigate, berate, criticize, censure.
☒ praise, commend.

**upbringing** *n* bringing-up, raising, rearing, breeding, parenting, care, nurture, cultivation, education, training, instruction, teaching.

**update** *v* modernize, revise, amend, correct, renew, renovate, revamp.

**upgrade** *v* promote, advance, elevate, raise, improve, enhance.
☒ downgrade, demote.

**upheaval** *n* disruption, disturbance, upset, chaos, confusion, disorder, turmoil, shake-up (*infml*), revolution, overthrow.

**uphill** *adj* hard, difficult, arduous, tough, taxing, strenuous, laborious, tiring, wearisome, exhausting, gruelling, punishing.
☒ easy.

**uphold** *v* support, maintain, hold to, stand by, defend, champion, advocate, promote, back, endorse, sustain, fortify, strengthen, justify, vindicate.
☒ abandon, reject.

**upkeep** *n* maintenance, preservation, conservation, care, running, repair, support, sustenance, subsistence, keep.
☒ neglect.

**upper** *adj* higher, loftier, superior, senior, top, topmost, uppermost, high, elevated, exalted, eminent, important.
☒ lower, inferior, junior.

**uppermost** *adj* highest, loftiest, top, topmost, greatest, supreme, first, primary, foremost, leading, principal, main, chief, dominant, predominant, paramount, pre-eminent.
☒ lowest.

**upright** *adj* 1 VERTICAL, perpendicular, erect, straight. 2 RIGHTEOUS, good, virtuous, upstanding, noble, honourable, ethical, principled, incorruptible, honest, trustworthy.
☒ 1 horizontal, flat. 2 dishonest.

**uprising** *n* rebellion, revolt, mutiny, rising, insurgence, insurrection, revolution.

**uproar** *n* noise, din, racket, hubbub, hullabaloo, pandemonium, tumult, turmoil, turbulence, commotion, confusion, disorder, clamour, outcry, furore, riot, rumpus.

**uproot** *v* pull up, rip up, root out, weed out, remove, displace, eradicate, destroy, wipe out.

**upset** *v* 1 DISTRESS, grieve, dismay, trouble, worry, agitate, disturb, bother, fluster, ruffle, discompose, shake, unnerve, disconcert, confuse, disorganize. **2** TIP, spill, overturn, capsize, topple, overthrow, destabilize, unsteady.

*n* **1** TROUBLE, worry, agitation, disturbance, bother, disruption, upheaval, shake-up (*infml*), reverse, surprise, shock. **2** *stomach upset*: disorder, complaint, bug (*infml*), illness, sickness.

*adj* distressed, grieved, hurt, annoyed, dismayed, troubled, worried, agitated, disturbed, bothered, shaken, disconcerted, confused.

**upshot** *n* result, consequence, outcome, issue, end, conclusion, finish, culmination.

**upside down** inverted, upturned, wrong way up, upset, overturned, disordered, muddled, jumbled, confused, topsy-turvy, chaotic.

**up-to-date** *adj* current, contemporary, modern, fashionable, trendy (*infml*), latest, recent, new.
**E3** out-of-date, old-fashioned.

**upturn** *n* revival, recovery, upsurge, upswing, rise, increase, boost, improvement.
**E3** downturn, drop.

**urban** *adj* town, city, inner-city, metropolitan, municipal, civic, built-up.
**E3** country, rural.

**urge** *v* advise, counsel, recommend, advocate, encourage, exhort, implore, beg, beseech, entreat, plead, press, constrain, compel, force, push, drive, impel, goad, spur, hasten, induce, incite, instigate.
**E3** discourage, dissuade, deter, hinder.
*n* desire, wish, inclination, fancy, longing, yearning, itch, impulse, compulsion, impetus, drive, eagerness.
**E3** disinclination.

**urgency** *n* hurry, haste, pressure, stress, importance, seriousness, gravity, imperativeness, need, necessity.

**urgent** *adj* immediate, instant, top-priority, important, critical, crucial, imperative, exigent, pressing, compelling, persuasive, earnest, eager, insistent, persistent.
**E3** unimportant.

**usable** *adj* working, operational, serviceable, functional, practical, exploitable, available, current, valid.
**E3** unusable, useless.

**usage** *n* **1** TREATMENT, handling, management, control, running, operation, employment, application, use. **2** TRADITION, custom, practice, habit, convention, etiquette, rule, regulation, form, routine, procedure, method.

**use** *v* utilize, employ, exercise, practise, operate, work, apply, wield, handle, treat, manipulate, exploit, enjoy, consume, exhaust, expend, spend.
*n* utility, usefulness, value, worth, profit, advantage, benefit, good, avail, help, service, point, object, end, purpose, reason, cause, occasion, need, necessity, usage, application, employment, operation, exercise.

**use up** finish, exhaust, drain, sap, deplete, consume, devour, absorb, waste, squander, fritter.

**used** *adj* second-hand, cast-off, hand-me-down, nearly new, worn, dog-eared, soiled.
**E3** unused, new, fresh.

**useful** *adj* handy, convenient, all-purpose, practical, effective, productive, fruitful, profitable, valuable, worthwhile, advantageous, beneficial, helpful.
**E3** useless, ineffective, worthless.

**useless** *adj* futile, fruitless, unproductive, vain, idle, unavailing, hopeless, pointless, worthless, unusable, broken-down, clapped-out (*sl*), unworkable, impractical, ineffective, inefficient, incompetent, weak.
**E3** useful, helpful, effective.

**usher** *n* usherette, doorkeeper, attendant, escort, guide.
*v* escort, accompany, conduct, lead, direct, guide, show, pilot, steer.

**usual** *adj* normal, typical, stock, standard, regular, routine, habitual, customary, conventional, accepted, recognized, accustomed, familiar, common, everyday, general, ordinary, unexceptional, expected, predictable.
F3 unusual, strange, rare.

**usually** *adv* normally, generally, as a rule, ordinarily, typically, traditionally, regularly, commonly, by and large, on the whole, mainly, chiefly, mostly.
F3 exceptionally.

**usurp** *v* take over, assume, arrogate, seize, take, annex, appropriate, commandeer, steal.

**utensil** *n* tool, implement, instrument, device, contrivance, gadget, apparatus, appliance.

**utility** *n* usefulness, use, value, profit, advantage, benefit, avail, service, convenience, practicality, efficacy, efficiency, fitness, serviceableness.

**utmost** *adj* **1** *with the utmost care*: extreme, maximum, greatest, highest, supreme, paramount. **2** FARTHEST, furthermost, remotest, outermost, ultimate, final, last.
*n* best, hardest, most, maximum.

**utter**[1] *adj* absolute, complete, total, entire, thoroughgoing, out-and-out, downright, sheer, stark, arrant, unmitigated, unqualified, perfect, consummate.

**utter**[2] *v* speak, say, voice, vocalize, verbalize, express, articulate, enunciate, sound, pronounce, deliver, state, declare, announce, proclaim, tell, reveal, divulge.

**utterance** *n* statement, remark, comment, expression, articulation, delivery, speech, declaration, announcement, proclamation, pronouncement.

**utterly** *adv* absolutely, completely, totally, fully, entirely, wholly, thoroughly, downright, perfectly.

**U-turn** *n* about-turn, volte-face, reversal, backtrack.

# V

**vacancy** *n* opportunity, opening, position, post, job, place, room, situation.

**vacant** *adj* **1** EMPTY, unoccupied, unfilled, free, available, void, not in use, unused, uninhabited. **2** BLANK, expressionless, vacuous, inane, inattentive, absent, absent-minded, unthinking, dreamy.
F3 **1** occupied, engaged.

**vacate** *v* leave, depart, evacuate, abandon, withdraw, quit.

**vacuum** *n* emptiness, void, nothingness, vacuity, space, chasm, gap.

**vague** *adj* **1** ILL-DEFINED, blurred, indistinct, hazy, dim, shadowy, misty, fuzzy, nebulous, obscure. **2** INDEFINITE, imprecise, unclear, uncertain, undefined, undetermined, unspecific, generalized, inexact, ambiguous, evasive, loose, woolly.
F3 **1** clear. **2** definite.

**vain** *adj* **1** *a vain attempt*: useless, worthless, futile, abortive, fruitless, pointless, unproductive, unprofitable, unavailing, hollow, groundless, empty, trivial, unimportant. **2** CONCEITED, proud, self-satisfied, arrogant, self-important, egotistical, bigheaded (*infml*), swollen-headed (*infml*), stuck-up (*infml*), affected, pretentious, ostentatious, swaggering.

**E3** 1 fruitful, successful. 2 modest, self-effacing.

**valiant** *adj* brave, courageous, gallant, fearless, intrepid, bold, dauntless, heroic, plucky, indomitable, staunch.

**E3** cowardly, fearful.

**valid** *adj* 1 LOGICAL, well-founded, well-grounded, sound, good, cogent, convincing, telling, conclusive, reliable, substantial, weighty, powerful, just. 2 OFFICIAL, legal, lawful, legitimate, authentic, bona fide, genuine, binding, proper.

**E3** 1 false, weak. 2 unofficial, invalid.

**valley** *n* dale, vale, dell, glen, hollow, cwm, depression, gulch.

**valuable** *adj* 1 *valuable necklace*: precious, prized, valued, costly, expensive, dear, high-priced, treasured, cherished, estimable. 2 *valuable suggestions*: helpful, worthwhile, useful, beneficial, invaluable, constructive, fruitful, profitable, important, serviceable, worthy, handy.

**E3** 1 worthless. 2 useless.

**value** *n* 1 COST, price, rate, worth. 2 WORTH, use, usefulness, utility, merit, importance, desirability, benefit, advantage, significance, good, profit.

*v* 1 PRIZE, appreciate, treasure, esteem, hold dear, respect, cherish. 2 EVALUATE, assess, estimate, price, appraise, survey, rate.

**E3** 1 disregard, neglect. 2 undervalue.

**vanish** *v* disappear, fade, dissolve, evaporate, disperse, melt, die out, depart, exit, fizzle out, peter out.

**E3** appear, materialize.

**vanity** *n* 1 CONCEIT, conceitedness, pride, arrogance, self-conceit, self-love, self-satisfaction, narcissism, egotism, pretension, ostentation,

affectation, airs, bigheadedness (*infml*), swollen-headedness (*infml*). 2 WORTHLESSNESS, uselessness, emptiness, futility, pointlessness, unreality, hollowness, fruitlessness, triviality.

**E3** 1 modesty, worth.

**vapour** *n* steam, mist, fog, smoke, breath, fumes, haze, damp, dampness, exhalation.

**variable** *adj* changeable, inconstant, varying, shifting, mutable, unpredictable, fluctuating, fitful, unstable, unsteady, wavering, vacillating, temperamental, fickle, flexible.

**E3** fixed, invariable, stable.

**variance** *n* 1 VARIATION, difference, discrepancy, divergence, inconsistency, disagreement. 2 DISAGREEMENT, disharmony, conflict, discord, division, dissent, dissension, quarrelling, strife.

**E3** 1 agreement. 2 harmony.

**variation** *n* diversity, variety, deviation, discrepancy, diversification, alteration, change, difference, departure, modification, modulation, inflection, novelty, innovation.

**E3** monotony, uniformity.

**varied** *adj* assorted, diverse, miscellaneous, mixed, various, sundry, heterogeneous (*fml*), different, wide-ranging.

**E3** standardized, uniform.

**variegated** *adj* multicoloured, many-coloured, parti-coloured, varicoloured, speckled, mottled, dappled, pied, streaked, motley.

**E3** monochrome, plain.

**variety** *n* 1 ASSORTMENT, miscellany, mixture, collection, medley, pot-pourri, range. 2 DIFFERENCE, diversity, dissimilarity, discrepancy, variation, multiplicity. 3 SORT, kind, class, category, species, type, breed, brand, make, strain.

**E3** 2 uniformity, similitude.

**various** *adj* different, differing, diverse, varied, varying, assorted, miscellaneous, heterogeneous (*fml*), distinct, diversified, mixed, many, several.

**varnish** *n* lacquer, glaze, resin, polish, gloss, coating.

**vary** *v* **1** CHANGE, alter, modify, modulate, diversify, reorder, transform, alternate, inflect, permutate. **2** DIVERGE, differ, disagree, depart, fluctuate.

**vast** *adj* huge, immense, massive, gigantic, enormous, great, colossal, extensive, tremendous, sweeping, unlimited, fathomless, immeasurable, never-ending, monumental, monstrous, far-flung.

**vault¹** *v* leap, spring, bound, clear, jump, hurdle, leap-frog.

**vault²** *n* **1** CELLAR, crypt, strongroom, repository, cavern, depository, wine-cellar, tomb, mausoleum. **2** ARCH, roof, span, concave.

**vaunt** (*fml*) *v* boast, brag, exult in, flaunt, show off, parade, trumpet, crow.

**E3** belittle, minimize.

**veer** *v* swerve, swing, change, shift, diverge, deviate, wheel, turn, sheer, tack.

**vegetable**

> *Vegetables include*: artichoke, aubergine, bean, beetroot, broad bean, broccoli, Brussel's sprout, butter bean, cabbage, calabrese, capsicum, carrot, cauliflower, celeriac, celery, chicory, courgette, cress, cucumber, eggplant (*US*), endive, fennel, French bean, garlic, kale, leek, lentil, lettuce, mange tout, marrow, mushroom, okra, onion, parsnip, pea, pepper, petit pois, potato, spud (*infml*), pumpkin, radish, runner bean, shallot, soya bean, spinach, spring onion, swede, sweetcorn, sweet potato, turnip,

watercress, yam, zucchini (*US*).

> *Vegetable dishes include*: aubergine roll, baba ganoush, bhaji, onion bhaji, bubble and squeak, cauliflower cheese, champ, chillada, colcannon, coleslaw, couscous, crudités, dal, dolma, duchesse potatoes, fasolia, felafel, fondue, gado-gado, gnocchi, guacamole, gumbo, hummus, imam bayildi, latke, macaroni cheese, macédoine, mushy peas, nut cutlet, paella, pakora, pease pudding, peperonata, pilau, pissaladière, polenta, ratatouille, raita, risotto, rösti, salad, caesar salad, green salad, warm salad, mixed salad, salade niçoise, Waldorf salad, winter salad, sauerkraut, stovies, stuffed marrow, stuffed mushroom, succotash, tabbouleh, tahina, tsatsiki, vegetable chilli, vegetable curry, vegetable soup, vegetarian goulash, vichyssoise.

**vegetate** *v* stagnate, degenerate, deteriorate, rusticate, go to seed, idle, rust, languish.

**vehement** *adj* impassioned, passionate, ardent, fervent, intense, forceful, emphatic, heated, strong, powerful, urgent, enthusiastic, animated, eager, earnest, forcible, fierce, violent, zealous.

**E3** apathetic, indifferent.

**vehicle** *n* **1** CONVEYANCE, transport. **2** MEANS, agency, channel, medium, mechanism, organ.

> *Vehicles include*: plane, boat, ship, car, taxi, hackney-carriage, bicycle, bike (*infml*), cycle, tandem, tricycle, boneshaker (*infml*), penny-farthing, motor-cyclemotor-bike, scooter, bus, omnibus, minibus, double-decker (*infml*), coach, charabanc, caravan, caravanette, camper, train, Pullman, sleeper, wagon-lit, tube, tram, monorail, maglev, trolleybus; van;

Transit®, lorry, truck, juggernaut, pantechnicon, trailer, tractor, fork-lift truck, steam-roller, tank, wagon; bobsleigh, sled, sledge, sleigh, toboggan, troika; barouche, brougham, dog-cart, dray, four-in-hand, gig, hansom, landau, phaeton, post-chaise, stagecoach, sulky, surrey, trap; rickshaw, sedan-chair, litter. *see also* **aircraft; boats and ships; car.**

**veil** v screen, cloak, cover, mask, shadow, shield, obscure, conceal, hide, disguise, shade.
**E3** expose, uncover.
n cover, cloak, curtain, mask, screen, disguise, film, blind, shade, shroud.

**vein** n **1** STREAK, stripe, stratum, seam, lode, blood vessel. **2** MOOD, tendency, bent, strain, temper, tenor, tone, frame of mind, mode, style.

*Veins and arteries include*: aorta, axillary, brachial, carotid, femoral, frontal, gastric, hepatic, iliac, jugular, portal, pulmonary, radial, renal, saphena, subclavian, superior, temporal, tibial.

**vendetta** n feud, blood-feud, enmity, rivalry, quarrel, bad blood, bitterness.

**veneer** n front, façade, appearance, coating, surface, show, mask, gloss, pretence, guise, finish.

**venerable** adj respected, revered, esteemed, honoured, venerated, dignified, grave, wise, august, aged, worshipped.

**venerate** v revere, respect, honour, esteem, worship, hallow (*fml*), adore.
**E3** despise, anathematize.

**vengeance** n retribution, revenge, retaliation, reprisal, requital, tit for tat.
**E3** forgiveness.

**venom** n **1** POISON, toxin. **2** RANCOUR, ill-will, malice, malevolence, spite, bitterness,

acrimony, hate, virulence.

**venomous** adj **1** POISONOUS, toxic, virulent, harmful, noxious.
**2** MALICIOUS, spiteful, vicious, vindictive, baleful, hostile, malignant, rancorous, baneful.
**E3 1** harmless.

**vent** n opening, hole, aperture, outlet, passage, orifice, duct.
v air, express, voice, utter, release, discharge, emit.

**ventilate** v **1** *ventilate a room*: air, aerate, freshen. **2** *ventilate one's feelings*: air, broadcast, debate, discuss.

**venture** v **1** DARE, advance, make bold, put forward, presume, suggest, volunteer. **2** RISK, hazard, endanger, imperil, jeopardize, speculate, wager, stake.
n risk, chance, hazard, speculation, gamble, undertaking, project, adventure, endeavour, enterprise, operation, fling.

**verbal** adj spoken, oral, verbatim, unwritten, word-of-mouth.

**verbatim** adv word for word, exactly, literally, to the letter, precisely.

**verbose** adj long-winded, wordy, prolix, loquacious, diffuse, circumlocutory.
**E3** succinct, brief.

**verdict** n decision, judgement, conclusion, finding, adjudication, assessment, opinion, sentence.

**verge** n border, edge, margin, limit, rim, brim, brink, boundary, threshold, extreme, edging.
**verge on** approach, border on, come close to, near.

**verify** v confirm, corroborate, substantiate, authenticate, bear out, prove, support, validate, testify, attest.
**E3** invalidate, discredit.

**vernacular** adj indigenous, local, native, popular, vulgar, informal, colloquial, common.

*n* language, speech, tongue, parlance, dialect, idiom, jargon.

**versatile** *adj* adaptable, flexible, all-round, multipurpose, multifaceted, adjustable, many-sided, general-purpose, functional, resourceful, handy, variable.

**F3** inflexible.

**verse** *n* poetry, rhyme, stanza, metre, doggerel, jingle.

**versed** *adj* skilled, proficient, practised, experienced, familiar, acquainted, learned, knowledgeable, conversant, seasoned, qualified, competent, accomplished.

**version** *n* **1** RENDERING, reading, interpretation, account, translation, paraphrase, adaptation, portrayal. **2** TYPE, kind, variant, form, model, style, design.

**vertical** *adj* upright, perpendicular, upstanding, erect, on end.

**F3** horizontal.

**vertigo** *n* dizziness, giddiness, light-headedness.

**verve** *n* vitality, vivacity, animation, energy, dash, élan, liveliness, sparkle, vigour, enthusiasm, gusto, life, relish, spirit, force.

**F3** apathy, lethargy.

**very** *adv* extremely, greatly, highly, deeply, truly, terribly (*infml*), remarkably, excessively, exceeding(ly), acutely, particularly, really, absolutely, noticeably, unusually.

**F3** slightly, scarcely.

*adj* actual, real, same, selfsame, identical, true, genuine, simple, utter, sheer, pure, perfect, plain, mere, bare, exact, appropriate.

**vestige** *n* trace, suspicion, indication, sign, hint, evidence, whiff, inkling, glimmer, token, scrap, remains, remainder, remnant, residue.

**vet** *v* investigate, examine, check, scrutinize, scan, inspect, survey, review, appraise, audit.

**veteran** *n* master, pastmaster, old hand, old stager, old-timer, pro (*infml*), war-horse.

**F3** novice, recruit.

*adj* experienced, practised, seasoned, long-serving, expert, adept, proficient, old.

**F3** inexperienced.

**veto** *v* reject, turn down, forbid, disallow, ban, prohibit, rule out, block.

**F3** approve, sanction.

*n* rejection, ban, embargo, prohibition, thumbs down (*infml*).

**F3** approval, assent.

**vex** *v* irritate, annoy, provoke, pester, trouble, upset, worry, bother, put out (*infml*), harass, hassle (*infml*), aggravate (*infml*), needle (*infml*), disturb, distress, agitate, exasperate, torment, fret.

**F3** calm, soothe.

**vexed** *adj* **1** IRRITATED, annoyed, provoked, upset, troubled, worried, nettled, put out, exasperated, bothered, confused, perplexed, aggravated (*infml*), harassed, hassled (*infml*), ruffled, riled, disturbed, distressed, displeased, agitated. **2** *a vexed question*: difficult, controversial, contested, disputed.

**viable** *adj* feasible, practicable, possible, workable, usable, operable, achievable, sustainable.

**F3** impossible, unworkable.

**vibrant** *adj* **1** ANIMATED, vivacious, vivid, bright, brilliant, colourful, lively, responsive, sparkling, spirited, sensitive. **2** THRILLING, dynamic, electrifying, electric.

**vibrate** *v* quiver, pulsate, shudder, shiver, resonate, reverberate, throb, oscillate, tremble, undulate, sway, swing, shake.

**vice** *n* **1** EVIL, evil-doing, depravity, immorality, wickedness, sin, corruption, iniquity (*fml*), profligacy (*fml*), degeneracy. **2** FAULT, failing, defect, shortcoming, weakness, imperfection, blemish, bad habit, besetting sin.

**F3** 1 virtue, morality.

**vicinity** *n* neighbourhood, area, locality, district, precincts, environs, proximity.

**vicious** *adj* **1** WICKED, bad, wrong, immoral, depraved, unprincipled, diabolical, corrupt, debased, perverted, profligate (*fml*), vile, heinous. **2** MALICIOUS, spiteful, vindictive, virulent, cruel, mean, nasty, slanderous, venomous, defamatory. **3** SAVAGE, wild, violent, barbarous, brutal, dangerous.

**F3** 1 virtuous. 2 kind.

**victim** *n* sufferer, casualty, prey, scapegoat, martyr, sacrifice, fatality.

**F3** offender, attacker.

**victimize** *v* **1** OPPRESS, persecute, discriminate against, pick on, prey on, bully, exploit. **2** CHEAT, deceive, defraud, swindle (*infml*), dupe, hoodwink, fool.

**victorious** *adj* conquering, champion, triumphant, winning, unbeaten, successful, prize-winning, top, first.

**F3** defeated, unsuccessful.

**victory** *n* conquest, win, triumph, success, superiority, mastery, vanquishment, subjugation, overcoming.

**F3** defeat, loss.

**vie** *v* strive, compete, contend, struggle, contest, fight, rival.

**view** *n* **1** OPINION, attitude, belief, judgement, estimation, feeling, sentiment, impression, notion. **2** SIGHT, scene, vision, vista, outlook, prospect, perspective, panorama, landscape. **3** SURVEY, inspection, examination, observation, scrutiny, scan. **4** GLIMPSE, look, sight, perception.

*v* **1** CONSIDER, regard, contemplate, judge, think about, speculate.
**2** OBSERVE, watch, see, examine, inspect, look at, scan, survey, witness,

perceive.

**viewer** *n* spectator, watcher, observer, onlooker.

**viewpoint** *n* attitude, position, perspective, slant, standpoint, stance, opinion, angle, feeling.

**vigilant** *adj* watchful, alert, attentive, observant, on one's guard, on the lookout, cautious, wide-awake, sleepless, unsleeping.

**F3** careless.

**vigorous** *adj* energetic, active, lively, healthy, strong, strenuous, robust, lusty, sound, vital, brisk, dynamic, forceful, forcible, powerful, stout, spirited, full-blooded, effective, efficient, enterprising, flourishing, intense.

**F3** weak, feeble.

**vigour** *n* energy, vitality, liveliness, health, robustness, stamina, strength, resilience, soundness, spirit, verve, gusto, activity, animation, power, potency, force, forcefulness, might, dash, dynamism.

**F3** weakness.

**vile** *adj* **1** *a vile sinner*: base, contemptible, debased, depraved, degenerate, bad, wicked, wretched, worthless, sinful, miserable, mean, evil, impure, corrupt, despicable, disgraceful, degrading, vicious, appalling. **2** *a vile meal*: disgusting, foul, nauseating, sickening, repulsive, repugnant, revolting, noxious, offensive, nasty, loathsome, horrid.

**F3** 1 pure, worthy. 2 pleasant, lovely.

**villain** *n* evil-doer, miscreant (*fml*), scoundrel, rogue, malefactor (*fml*), criminal, reprobate, rascal.

**villainous** *adj* wicked, bad, criminal, evil, sinful, vicious, notorious, cruel, inhuman, vile, depraved, disgraceful, terrible.

**F3** good.

**vindicate** (*fml*) *v* **1** CLEAR, acquit, excuse, exonerate, absolve, rehabilitate. **2** JUSTIFY, uphold, support, maintain, defend, establish, advocate, assert, verify.

**vindictive** adj spiteful, unforgiving, implacable, vengeful, relentless, unrelenting, revengeful, resentful, punitive, venomous, malevolent, malicious.

F3 forgiving.

**vintage** n year, period, era, epoch, generation, origin, harvest, crop. adj choice, best, fine, prime, select, superior, rare, mature, old, ripe, classic, venerable, veteran.

**violate** v 1 CONTRAVENE, disobey, disregard, transgress, break, flout, infringe. 2 OUTRAGE, debauch, defile, rape, ravish, dishonour, desecrate, profane, invade.

F3 1 observe.

**violence** n 1 FORCE, strength, power, vehemence, might, intensity, ferocity, fierceness, severity, tumult, turbulence, wildness. 2 BRUTALITY, destructiveness, cruelty, bloodshed, murderousness, savagery, passion, fighting, frenzy, fury, hostilities.

**violent** adj 1 INTENSE, strong, severe, sharp, acute, extreme, harmful, destructive, devastating, injurious, powerful, painful, agonizing, forceful, forcible, harsh, ruinous, rough, vehement, tumultuous, turbulent. 2 CRUEL, brutal, aggressive, bloodthirsty, impetuous, hot-headed, headstrong, murderous, savage, wild, vicious, unrestrained, uncontrollable, ungovernable, passionate, furious, intemperate, maddened, outrageous, riotous, fiery.

F3 1 calm, moderate. 2 peaceful, gentle.

**virgin** n girl, maiden, celibate, vestal. adj virginal, chaste, intact, immaculate, maidenly, pure, modest, new, fresh, spotless, stainless, undefiled, untouched, unsullied.

**virile** adj man-like, masculine, male, manly, macho (infml), robust,

vigorous, potent, lusty, red-blooded, forceful, strong, rugged.

F3 effeminate, impotent.

**virtual** adj effective, essential, practical, implied, implicit, potential.

**virtually** adv practically, in effect, almost, nearly, as good as, in essence.

**virtue** n 1 GOODNESS, morality, rectitude, uprightness, worthiness, righteousness, probity (fml), integrity, honour, incorruptibility, justice, high-mindedness, excellence. 2 QUALITY, worth, merit, advantage, asset, credit, strength.

F3 1 vice.

**virtuoso** n expert, master, maestro, prodigy, genius.

**virtuous** adj good, moral, righteous, upright, worthy, honourable, irreproachable, incorruptible, exemplary, unimpeachable, high-principled, blameless, clean-living, excellent, innocent.

F3 immoral, vicious.

**virulent** adj 1 POISONOUS, toxic, venomous, deadly, lethal, malignant, injurious, pernicious, intense. 2 HOSTILE, resentful, spiteful, acrimonious, bitter, vicious, vindictive, malevolent, malicious.

F3 1 harmless.

**visible** adj perceptible, discernible, detectable, apparent, noticeable, observable, distinguishable, discoverable, evident, unconcealed, undisguised, unmistakable, conspicuous, clear, obvious, manifest, open, palpable, plain, patent.

F3 invisible, indiscernible, hidden.

**vision** n 1 APPARITION, hallucination, illusion, delusion, mirage, phantom, ghost, chimera, spectre, wraith. 2 IDEA, ideal, conception, insight, view, picture, image, fantasy, dream, daydream. 3 SIGHT, seeing, eyesight, perception, discernment, far-sightedness, foresight, penetration.

**visionary** *adj* idealistic, impractical, romantic, dreamy, unrealistic, utopian, unreal, fanciful, prophetic, speculative, unworkable, illusory, imaginary.
*n* idealist, romantic, dreamer, daydreamer, fantasist, prophet, mystic, seer, utopian, rainbow-chaser, theorist.
**E₃** pragmatist.

**visit** *v* call on, call in, stay with, stay at, drop in on (*infml*), stop by (*infml*), look in, look up, pop in (*infml*), see.
*n* call, stay, stop, excursion, sojourn (*fml*).

**visitor** *n* caller, guest, company, tourist, holidaymaker.

**vista** *n* view, prospect, panorama, perspective, outlook, scene.

**visualize** *v* picture, envisage, imagine, conceive.

**vital** *adj* 1 CRITICAL, crucial, important, imperative, key, significant, basic, fundamental, essential, necessary, requisite, indispensable, urgent, life-or-death, decisive, forceful. 2 LIVING, alive, lively, life-giving, invigorating, spirited, vivacious, vibrant, vigorous, dynamic, animated, energetic, quickening (*fml*).
**E₃** 1 inessential, peripheral. 2 dead.

**vitality** *n* life, liveliness, animation, vigour, energy, vivacity, spirit, sparkle, exuberance, go (*infml*), strength, stamina.

**vitamin**

*Vitamins include*: aneurin (thiamine), ascorbic acid, bioflavonoid/citrin, biotin, calciferol, cholecalciferol, cyanocobalamin, ergocalciferol, folic acid, linoleic acid, linolenic acid, menadione, nicotinic acid (niacin), pantothenic acid, phylloquinone, pteroic acid, pyridoxine (adermin), retinol,

riboflavin, tocopherol.

**vitriolic** *adj* bitter, abusive, virulent, vicious, venomous, malicious, caustic, biting, sardonic, scathing, destructive.

**vivacious** *adj* lively, animated, spirited, high-spirited, effervescent, ebullient, cheerful, sparkling, bubbly, light-hearted.

**vivid** *adj* 1 BRIGHT, colourful, intense, strong, rich, vibrant, brilliant, glowing, dazzling, vigorous, expressive, dramatic, flamboyant, animated, lively, lifelike, spirited. 2 MEMORABLE, powerful, graphic, clear, distinct, striking, sharp, realistic.
**E₃** 1 colourless, dull. 2 vague.

**vocabulary** *n* language, words, glossary, lexicon, dictionary, word-book, thesaurus, idiom.

**vocal** *adj* 1 SPOKEN, said, oral, uttered, voiced. 2 ARTICULATE, eloquent, expressive, noisy, clamorous, shrill, strident, outspoken, frank, forthright, plain-spoken.
**E₃** 1 unspoken. 2 inarticulate.

**vocation** *n* calling, pursuit, career, métier, mission, profession, trade, employment, work, role, post, job, business, office.

**vociferous** *adj* noisy, vocal, clamorous, loud, obstreperous, strident, vehement, thundering, shouting.
**E₃** quiet.

**vogue** *n* fashion, mode, style, craze, popularity, trend, prevalence, acceptance, custom, fad (*infml*), the latest (*infml*), the rage (*infml*), the thing (*infml*).

**voice** *n* 1 SPEECH, utterance, articulation, language, words, sound, tone, intonation, inflection, expression, mouthpiece, medium, instrument, organ. 2 SAY, vote, opinion, view, decision, option, will.

*v* express, say, utter, air, articulate, speak of, verbalize, assert, convey, disclose, divulge, declare, enunciate.

**void** *adj* **1** EMPTY, emptied, free, unfilled, unoccupied, vacant, clear, bare, blank, drained. **2** ANNULLED, inoperative, invalid, cancelled, ineffective, futile, useless, vain, worthless.

**F3** **1** full. **2** valid.

*n* emptiness, vacuity, vacuum, chasm, blank, blankness, space, lack, want, cavity, gap, hollow, opening.

**volatile** *adj* changeable, inconstant, unstable, variable, erratic, temperamental, unsteady, unsettled, fickle, mercurial, unpredictable, capricious, restless, giddy, flighty, up and down (*infml*), lively.

**F3** constant, steady.

**volley** *n* barrage, bombardment, hail, shower, burst, blast, discharge, explosion.

**voluble** *adj* fluent, glib, articulate, loquacious (*fml*), talkative, forthcoming, garrulous.

**volume** *n* **1** BULK, size, capacity, dimensions, amount, mass, quantity, aggregate, amplitude, body. **2** BOOK, tome, publication.

**voluminous** *adj* roomy, capacious, ample, spacious, billowing, vast, bulky, huge, large.

**voluntary** *adj* **1** FREE, gratuitous, optional, spontaneous, unforced, willing, unpaid, honorary. **2** CONSCIOUS, deliberate, purposeful, intended, intentional, wilful.

**F3** **1** compulsory. **2** involuntary.

**volunteer** *v* offer, propose, put forward, present, suggest, step forward, advance.

**voluptuous** *adj* **1** SENSUAL, licentious, luxurious. **2** EROTIC, shapely, sexy (*infml*), seductive, provocative, enticing.

**vomit** *v* be sick, bring up, heave, retch, throw up (*infml*), puke (*infml*).

**vote** *n* ballot, poll, election, franchise, referendum.

*v* elect, ballot, choose, opt, plump for, declare, return.

**vouch for** guarantee, support, back, endorse, confirm, certify, affirm, assert, attest to, speak for, swear to, uphold.

**vow** *v* promise, pledge, swear, dedicate, devote, profess, consecrate, affirm.

*n* promise, oath, pledge.

**voyage** *n* journey, trip, passage, expedition, crossing.

**vulgar** *adj* **1** TASTELESS, flashy, gaudy, tawdry, cheap and nasty (*infml*). **2** UNREFINED, uncouth, coarse, common, crude, ill-bred, impolite, indecorous. **3** INDECENT, suggestive, risqué, rude, indelicate. **4** ORDINARY, general, popular, vernacular.

**F3** **1** tasteful. **2** correct. **3** decent.

**vulnerable** *adj* unprotected, exposed, defenceless, susceptible, weak, sensitive, wide open.

**F3** protected, strong.

# W

**wad** *n* chunk, plug, roll, ball, wodge (*infml*), lump, hunk, mass, block.

**waddle** *v* toddle, totter, wobble, sway, rock, shuffle.

**waffle** *v* jabber, prattle, blather, rabbit on (*infml*), witter on (*infml*).

*n* blather, prattle, wordiness, padding, nonsense, gobbledegook (*infml*), hot air (*infml*).

**waft** *v* drift, float, blow, transport,

transmit.

*n* breath, puff, draught, current, breeze, scent, whiff.

**wag** *v* shake, waggle, wave, sway, swing, bob, nod, wiggle, oscillate, flutter, vibrate, quiver, rock.

**wage** *n* pay, fee, earnings, salary, wage-packet, payment, stipend, remuneration, emolument (*fml*), allowance, reward, hire, compensation, recompense.

*v* carry on, conduct, engage in, undertake, practise, pursue.

**waif** *n* orphan, stray, foundling.

**wail** *v* moan, cry, howl, lament, weep, complain, yowl (*infml*).

*n* moan, cry, howl, lament, complaint, weeping.

**wait** *v* delay, linger, hold back, hesitate, pause, hang around, hang fire, remain, rest, stay.

**F3** proceed, go ahead.

*n* hold-up, hesitation, delay, interval, pause, halt.

**waive** *v* renounce, relinquish, forgo, resign, surrender, yield.

**wake¹** *v* **1** RISE, get up, arise, rouse, came to, bring round. **2** STIMULATE, stir, activate, arouse, animate, excite, fire, galvanize.

**F3** 1 sleep.

*n* funeral, death-watch, vigil, watch.

**wake²** *n* trail, track, path, aftermath, backwash, wash, rear, train, waves.

**walk** *v* step, stride, pace, proceed, advance, march, plod, tramp, traipse, trek, trudge, saunter, amble, stroll, tread, hike, promenade, move, hoof it, accompany, escort.

*n* **1** *he has an odd walk*: carriage, gait, step, pace, stride. **2** *go for a walk*: stroll, amble, ramble, saunter, march, hike, tramp, trek, traipse, trudge, trail. **3** *a tree-lined walk*: footpath, path, walkway, avenue, pathway, promenade, alley, esplanade, lane, pavement, sidewalk.

**walk of life** field, area, sphere, line, activity, arena, course, pursuit, calling, métier, career, vocation, profession, trade.

**walker** *n* pedestrian, rambler, hiker.

**walk-out** *n* strike, stoppage, industrial action, protest, rebellion, revolt.

**walk-over** *n* pushover (*infml*), doddle (*infml*), child's play, piece of cake (*infml*), cinch (*infml*).

**wall** *n* **1** PARTITION, screen, panel, divider, fence, hedge, enclosure, membrane, bulk-head.

**2** FORTIFICATION, barricade, rampart, parapet, stockade, embankment, bulwark, palisade.

**3** OBSTACLE, obstruction, barrier, block, impediment.

**wallow** *v* **1** *wallow in mud*: loll, lie, roll, wade, welter, lurch, flounder, splash. **2** *wallow in nostalgia*: indulge, luxuriate, relish, revel, bask, enjoy, glory, delight.

**wand** *n* rod, baton, staff, stick, sprig, mace, sceptre, twig.

**wander** *v* **1** ROAM, rove, ramble, meander, saunter, stroll, prowl, drift, range, stray, straggle. **2** DIGRESS, diverge, deviate, depart, go astray, swerve, veer, err. **3** RAMBLE, rave, babble, gibber.

*n* excursion, ramble, stroll, saunter, meander, prowl, cruise.

**wanderer** *n* itinerant, traveller, voyager, drifter, rover, rambler, stroller, stray, straggler, ranger, nomad, gypsy, vagrant, vagabond, rolling stone (*infml*).

**wane** *v* diminish, decrease, decline, weaken, subside, fade, dwindle, ebb, lessen, abate, sink, drop, taper off, dim, droop, contract, shrink, fail, wither.

**F3** increase, wax.

**wangle** (*infml*) *v* manipulate, arrange, contrive, engineer, fix, scheme, manoeuvre, work, pull off, manage, fiddle (*infml*).

**want** *v* **1** DESIRE, wish, crave, covet, fancy, long for, pine for, yearn for,

hunger for, thirst for. **2** NEED, require, demand, lack, miss, call for.
*n* **1** DESIRE, demand, longing, requirement, wish, need, appetite.
**2** LACK, dearth, insufficiency, deficiency, shortage, inadequacy.
**3** POVERTY, privation, destitution.

**wanting** *adj* **1** ABSENT, missing, lacking, short, insufficient.
**2** INADEQUATE, imperfect, faulty, defective, substandard, poor, deficient, unsatisfactory.
**1** sufficient. **2** adequate.

**wanton** *adj* malicious, immoral, shameless, arbitrary, unprovoked, unjustifiable, unrestrained, rash, reckless, wild.

**war** *n* warfare, hostilities, fighting, battle, combat, conflict, strife, struggle, bloodshed, contest, contention, enmity.
peace, cease-fire.

*Types of war include*: ambush, armed conflict, assault, attack, battle, biological warfare, blitz, blitzkrieg, bombardment, chemical warfare, civil war, Cod wars, cold war, counter-attack, engagement, germ warfare, guerrilla warfare, holy war, hot war, invasion, jihad, jungle warfare, limited war, manoeuvres, nuclear war, Opium Wars, private war, resistance, skirmish, state of siege, struggle, total war, trade war, war of attrition, war of nerves, world war.
*Famous wars include*: American Civil War (Second American Revolution), American Revolution (War of Independence), Boer War, Crimean War, Crusades, English Civil War, Falklands War, Franco-Prussian War, Gulf War, Hundred Years War, Indian Wars, Iran-Iraq War, Korean War, Mexican War, Napoleonic War, Peasants' War, Russo-Finnish War (Winter War), Russo-Japanese War, Russo-Turkish Wars, Seven Years War, Six-Day War, Spanish-American War, Spanish-American Wars of Independence, Spanish Civil War, Suez Crisis, Thirty Years War, Vietnam War, War of 1812, War of the Pacific, Wars of the Roses, World War I (the Great War), World War II.

*v* wage war, fight, take up arms, battle, clash, combat, strive, skirmish, struggle, contest, contend.

**ward** *n* **1** ROOM, apartment, unit. **2** DIVISION, area, district, quarter, precinct, zone. **3** CHARGE, dependant, protégé(e), minor.

**ward off** avert, fend off, deflect, parry, repel, stave off, thwart, beat off, forestall, evade, turn away, block, avoid.

**warden** *n* keeper, custodian, guardian, warder, caretaker, curator, ranger, steward, watchman, superintendent, administrator, janitor.

**warder** *n* jailer, keeper, prison officer, guard, wardress, custodian.

**wardrobe** *n* **1** CUPBOARD, closet. **2** CLOTHES, outfit, attire.

**warehouse** *n* store, storehouse, depot, depository, repository, stockroom, entrepot.

**wares** *n* goods, merchandise, commodities, stock, products, produce, stuff.

**warfare** *n* war, fighting, hostilities, battle, arms, combat, strife, struggle, passage of arms, contest, conflict, contention, discord, blows.
peace.

**warlike** *adj* belligerent, aggressive, bellicose, pugnacious, combative, bloodthirsty, war-mongering, militaristic, hostile, antagonistic, unfriendly.
friendly, peaceable.

**warm** *adj* **1** HEATED, tepid, lukewarm. **2** ARDENT, passionate, fervent, vehement, earnest, zealous. **3** *warm colours*: rich, intense, mellow, cheerful. **4** FRIENDLY, amiable, cordial, affable, kindly, genial, hearty, hospitable, sympathetic, affectionate, tender. **5** FINE, sunny, balmy, temperate, close.

F3 **1** cool. **2** indifferent. **3** cold. **4** unfriendly. **5** cool.

*v* **1** HEAT (UP), reheat, melt, thaw. **2** ANIMATE, interest, please, delight, stimulate, stir, rouse, excite.

F3 **1** cool.

**warmth** *n* **1** WARMNESS, heat. **2** FRIENDLINESS, affection, cordiality, tenderness. **3** ARDOUR, enthusiasm, passion, fervour, zeal, eagerness.

F3 **1** coldness. **2** unfriendliness. **3** indifference.

**warn** *v* caution, alert, admonish, advise, notify, counsel, put on one's guard, inform, tip off (*infml*).

**warning** *n* **1** CAUTION, alert, admonition, advice, notification, notice, advance notice, counsel, hint, lesson, alarm, threat, tip-off (*infml*). **2** OMEN, augury, premonition, presage, sign, signal, portent.

**warp** *v* twist, bend, contort, deform, distort, kink, misshape, pervert, corrupt, deviate.

F3 straighten.

*n* twist, bend, contortion, deformation, distortion, bias, kink, irregularity, turn, bent, defect, deviation, quirk, perversion.

**warrant** *n* authorization, authority, sanction, permit, permission, licence, guarantee, warranty, security, pledge, commission, voucher.

*v* **1** GUARANTEE, pledge, certify, assure, declare, affirm, vouch for, answer for, underwrite, uphold, endorse. **2** AUTHORIZE, entitle, empower, sanction, permit, allow, license, justify, excuse, approve, call for, commission, necessitate, require.

**wary** *adj* cautious, guarded, careful,

chary, on one's guard, on the lookout, prudent, distrustful, suspicious, heedful, attentive, alert, watchful, vigilant, wide-awake.

F3 unwary, careless, heedless.

**wash** *v* **1** CLEAN, cleanse, launder, scrub, swab down, rinse, swill. **2** BATHE, bath, shower, douche, shampoo.

*n* **1** CLEANING, cleansing, bath, bathe, laundry, laundering, scrub, shower, shampoo, washing, rinse. **2** FLOW, sweep, wave, swell.

**wash-out** (*infml*) *n* failure, disaster, disappointment, fiasco, flop (*infml*), debacle.

F3 success, triumph.

**waste** *v* **1** SQUANDER, misspend, misuse, fritter away, dissipate, lavish, spend, throw away, blow (*infml*). **2** CONSUME, erode, exhaust, drain, destroy, spoil.

F3 **1** economize. **2** preserve.

*n* **1** SQUANDERING, dissipation, prodigality, wastefulness, extravagance, loss.

**2** MISAPPLICATION, misuse, abuse, neglect. **3** RUBBISH, refuse, trash, garbage, leftovers, debris, dregs, effluent, litter, scrap, slops, offscouring(s), dross.

*adj* **1** USELESS, worthless, unwanted, unused, left-over, superfluous, supernumerary, extra. **2** BARREN, desolate, empty, uninhabited, bare, devastated, uncultivated, unprofitable, wild, dismal, dreary.

**wasted** *adj* **1** UNNECESSARY, needless, useless. **2** EMACIATED, withered, shrivelled, shrunken, gaunt, washed-out, spent.

F3 **1** necessary. **2** robust.

**wasteful** *adj* extravagant, spendthrift, prodigal, profligate, uneconomical, thriftless, unthrifty, ruinous, lavish, improvident.

F3 economical, thrifty.

**wasteland** *n* wilderness, desert, barrenness, waste, wild(s), void.

**watch** v 1 OBSERVE, see, look at, regard, note, notice, mark, stare at, peer at, gaze at, view. 2 GUARD, look after, keep an eye on, mind, protect, superintend, take care of, keep. 3 PAY ATTENTION, be careful, take heed, look out.

n 1 TIMEPIECE, wristwatch, clock, chronometer. 2 VIGILANCE, watchfulness, vigil, observation, surveillance, notice, lookout, attention, heed, alertness, inspection, supervision.

**watch out** notice, be vigilant, look out, keep one's eyes open.

**watch over** guard, protect, stand guard over, keep an eye on, look after, mind, shield, defend, shelter, preserve.

**watchdog** n 1 GUARD DOG, house-dog. 2 MONITOR, inspector, scrutineer, vigilante, ombudsman, guardian, custodian, protector.

**watcher** n spectator, observer, onlooker, looker-on, viewer, lookout, spy, witness.

**watchful** adj vigilant, attentive, heedful, observant, alert, guarded, on one's guard, wide awake, suspicious, wary, chary, cautious.

Ea unobservant, inattentive.

**watchman** n guard, security guard, caretaker, custodian.

**water** n rain, sea, ocean, lake, river, stream.

v wet, moisten, dampen, soak, spray, sprinkle, irrigate, drench, flood, hose.

Ea dry out, parch.

**water down** dilute, thin, water, weaken, adulterate, mix, tone down, soften, qualify.

**waterfall** n fall, cascade, chute, cataract, torrent.

**watertight** adj 1 WATERPROOF, sound, hermetic. 2 IMPREGNABLE, unassailable, airtight, flawless, foolproof, firm, incontrovertible.

Ea 1 leaky.

**watery** adj 1 LIQUID, fluid, moist, wet, damp. 2 WEAK, watered-down,

diluted, insipid, tasteless, thin, runny, soggy, flavourless, washy, wishy-washy (infml).

Ea 1 dry.

**wave** v 1 BECKON, gesture, gesticulate, indicate, sign, signal, direct. 2 BRANDISH, flourish, flap, flutter, shake, sway, swing, waft, quiver, ripple.

n 1 BREAKER, roller, billow, ripple, tidal wave, wavelet, undulation, white horse (infml). 2 SURGE, sweep, swell, upsurge, ground swell, current, drift, movement, rush, tendency, trend, stream, flood, outbreak, rash.

**waver** v 1 VACILLATE, falter, hesitate, dither, fluctuate, vary, seesaw. 2 OSCILLATE, shake, sway, wobble, tremble, totter, rock.

Ea 1 decide.

**wavy** adj undulating, rippled, curly, curvy, ridged, sinuous, winding, zigzag.

**wax** v grow, increase, rise, swell, develop, enlarge, expand, magnify, mount, fill out, become.

Ea decrease, wane.

**way** n 1 METHOD, approach, manner, technique, procedure, means, mode, system, fashion. 2 CUSTOM, practice, habit, usage, characteristic, idiosyncrasy, trait, style, conduct, nature. 3 DIRECTION, course, route, path, road, channel, access, avenue, track, passage, highway, street, thoroughfare, lane.

**by the way** incidentally, in passing.

**wayward** adj wilful, capricious, perverse, contrary, changeable, fickle, unpredictable, stubborn, self-willed, unmanageable, headstrong, obstinate, disobedient, rebellious, insubordinate, intractable, unruly, incorrigible.

Ea tractable, good-natured.

**weak** adj 1 FEEBLE, frail, infirm, unhealthy, sickly, delicate, debilitated, exhausted, fragile, flimsy. 2 VULNERABLE, unprotected,

unguarded, defenceless, exposed.
**3** POWERLESS, impotent, spineless,
cowardly, indecisive, ineffectual,
irresolute, poor, lacking, lame,
inadequate, defective, deficient,
inconclusive, unconvincing,
untenable. **4** FAINT, slight, low, soft,
muffled, dull, imperceptible.
**5** INSIPID, tasteless, watery, thin,
diluted, runny.
**E3 1** strong. **2** secure. **3** powerful.
**4** strong. **5** strong.

**weaken** v **1** ENFEEBLE, exhaust,
debilitate, sap, undermine, dilute,
diminish, lower, lessen, reduce,
moderate, mitigate, temper, soften
(up), thin, water down. **2** TIRE, flag,
fail, give way, droop, fade, abate,
ease up, dwindle.
**E3 1** strengthen.

**weakness** n **1** FEEBLENESS,
debility, infirmity, impotence, frailty,
powerlessness, vulnerability.
**2** FAULT, failing, flaw, shortcoming,
blemish, defect, deficiency, foible. **3**
LIKING, inclination, fondness,
penchant, passion, soft spot (*infml*).
**E3 1** strength. **2** strength. **3** dislike.

**wealth** n **1** MONEY, cash, riches,
assets, affluence, prosperity, funds,
mammon, fortune, capital, opulence,
means, substance, resources, goods,
possessions, property, estate. **2**
ABUNDANCE, plenty, bounty,
fullness, profusion, store.
**E3 1** poverty.

**wealthy** adj rich, prosperous,
affluent, well-off, moneyed, opulent,
comfortable, well-heeled, well-to-do,
flush (*infml*), loaded (*sl*), rolling in it
(*infml*).
**E3** poor, impoverished.

**weapon**

*Weapons include*: gun, airgun, pistol,
revolver, automatic, Colt®, Luger®,
magnum, Mauser, six-gun, six-
shooter, rifle, air rifle, Winchester®
rifle, carbine, shotgun, blunderbuss,
musket, elephant gun, machine-gun,
kalashnikov, submachine-gun, Uzi,
tommy-gun, sten gun, Bren gun,
cannon, field gun, gatling-gun,
howitzer, mortar, turret-gun; knife,
bowie knife, flick-knife, stiletto,
dagger, dirk, poniard, sword, épée,
foil, rapier, sabre, scimitar, bayonet,
broadsword, claymore, lance, spear,
pike, machete; bomb, atom bomb, H-
bomb, cluster-bomb, depth-charge,
incendiary bomb, Mills bomb, mine,
land-mine, napalm bomb, time-bomb;
bow and arrow, longbow, crossbow,
blowpipe, catapult, boomerang, sling,
harpoon, bolas, rocket, bazooka,
ballistic missile, Cruise missile,
Exocet®, Scud (*infml*), torpedo, hand
grenade, flame-thrower; battleaxe,
pole-axe, halberd, tomahawk, cosh,
cudgel, knuckleduster, shillelagh,
truncheon; gas, CS gas, mustard gas,
tear-gas.

**wear** v **1** DRESS IN, have on, put on,
don, sport, carry, bear, display,
show. **2** DETERIORATE, erode,
corrode, consume, fray, rub, abrade,
waste, grind.
n **1** CLOTHES, clothing, dress,
garments, outfit, costume, attire.
**2** DETERIORATION, erosion,
corrosion, wear and tear, friction,
abrasion.

**wear off** decrease, abate, dwindle,
diminish, subside, wane, weaken, fade,
lessen, ebb, peter out, disappear.
**E3** increase.

**wear out** **1** EXHAUST, fatigue, tire
(out), enervate, sap. **2** DETERIORATE,
wear through, erode, impair, consume,
fray.

**wearing** adj exhausting, fatiguing,
tiresome, tiring, wearisome, trying,
taxing, oppressive, irksome,
exasperating.
**E3** refreshing.

**weary** adj tired, exhausted, fatigued,
sleepy, worn out, drained, drowsy,

jaded, all in (*infml*), done in (*infml*), fagged out (*infml*), knackered (*infml*), dead beat (*infml*), dog-tired (*infml*), whacked (*infml*).
**F3** refreshed.

**wearying** *adj* tiring, fatiguing, exhausting, wearisome, wearing, taxing, trying.
**F3** refreshing.

**weather** *n* climate, conditions, temperature.

*Types of weather include*: breeze, wind, squall, gale, hurricane, tornado, typhoon, monsoon, cyclone, whirlwind, chinook, mistral, cloud, mist, dew, fog, smog, rain, drizzle, shower, deluge, downpour, rainbow, sunshine, heatwave, haze, drought, storm, tempest, thunder, lightning, frost, hoar frost, hail, sleet, snow, snowstorm, ice, black ice, thaw, slush.

*v* 1 ENDURE, survive, live through, come through, ride out, rise above, stick out, withstand, surmount, stand, brave, overcome, resist, pull through, suffer. 2 EXPOSE, toughen, season, harden.
**F3** 1 succumb.

**weave** *v* 1 INTERLACE, lace, plait, braid, intertwine, spin, knit, entwine, intercross, fuse, merge, unite. 2 CREATE, compose, construct, contrive, put together, fabricate. 3 WIND, twist, zigzag, criss-cross.

**web** *n* network, net, netting, lattice, mesh, webbing, interlacing, weft, snare, tangle, trap.

**wedding** *n* marriage, matrimony, nuptials (*fml*), wedlock, bridal.
**F3** divorce.

**wedge** *n* lump, block, chunk, wodge, chock.
*v* jam, cram, pack, ram, squeeze, stuff, push, lodge, block, thrust, crowd, force.

**weedy** (*infml*) *adj* thin, skinny, puny, scrawny, undersized, weak,

feeble, frail, weak-kneed, insipid, wet (*infml*), wimpish (*infml*).
**F3** strong.

**weep** *v* cry, sob, moan, lament, wail, mourn, grieve, bawl, blubber, snivel, whimper, blub (*infml*).
**F3** rejoice.

**weigh** *v* 1 BEAR DOWN, oppress. 2 CONSIDER, contemplate, evaluate, meditate on, mull over, ponder, think over, examine, reflect on, deliberate.

**weigh down** oppress, overload, load, burden, bear down, weigh upon, press down, get down (*infml*), depress, afflict, trouble, worry.
**F3** lighten, hearten.

**weigh up** assess, examine, size up, balance, consider, contemplate, deliberate, mull over, ponder, think over, discuss, chew over (*infml*).

**weight** *n* 1 HEAVINESS, gravity, burden, load, pressure, mass, force, ballast, tonnage, poundage. 2 IMPORTANCE, significance, substance, consequence, impact, moment, influence, value, authority, clout (*infml*), power, preponderance, consideration.
**F3** 1 lightness.
*v* 1 LOAD, weigh down, oppress, handicap. 2 BIAS, unbalance, slant, prejudice.

**weighty** *adj* 1 HEAVY, burdensome, substantial, bulky. 2 IMPORTANT, significant, consequential, crucial, critical, momentous, serious, grave, solemn. 3 DEMANDING, difficult, exacting, taxing.
**F3** 1 light. 2 unimportant.

**weird** *adj* strange, uncanny, bizarre, eerie, creepy, supernatural, unnatural, ghostly, freakish, mysterious, queer, grotesque, spooky (*infml*), far-out (*infml*), way-out (*infml*).
**F3** normal, usual.

**welcome** *adj* acceptable, desirable, pleasing, pleasant, agreeable, gratifying, appreciated, delightful, refreshing.

☒ unwelcome.

*n* reception, greeting, salutation (*infml*), acceptance, hospitality, red carpet (*infml*).

*v* greet, hail, receive, salute, meet, accept, approve of, embrace.

☒ reject, snub.

**weld** *v* fuse, unite, bond, join, solder, bind, connect, seal, link, cement.

☒ separate.

**welfare** *n* well-being, health, prosperity, happiness, benefit, good, advantage, interest, profit, success.

**well¹** *n* spring, well-spring, fountain, fount, source, reservoir, well-head, waterhole.

*v* flow, spring, surge, gush, stream, brim over, jet, spout, spurt, swell, pour, flood, ooze, run, trickle, rise, seep.

**well²** *adv* rightly, correctly, properly, skilfully, ably, expertly, successfully, adequately, sufficiently, suitably, easily, satisfactorily, thoroughly, greatly, fully, considerably, completely, agreeably, pleasantly, happily, kindly, favourably, splendidly, substantially, comfortably, readily, carefully, clearly, highly, deeply, justly.

☒ badly, inadequately, incompetently, wrongly.

*adj* 1 HEALTHY, in good health, fit, able-bodied, sound, robust, strong, thriving, flourishing.

2 SATISFACTORY, right, all right, good, pleasing, proper, agreeable, fine, lucky, fortunate.

☒ 1 ill. 2 bad.

**well-balanced** *adj* 1 RATIONAL, reasonable, level-headed, well-adjusted, stable, sensible, sane, sound, sober, together (*sl*).

2 SYMMETRICAL, even, harmonious.

☒ 1 unbalanced. 2 asymmetrical.

**well-being** *n* welfare, happiness, comfort, good.

**well-bred** *adj* well-mannered, polite,

well-brought-up, mannerly, courteous, civil, refined, cultivated, cultured, genteel.

☒ ill-bred.

**well-dressed** *adj* smart, well-groomed, elegant, fashionable, chic, stylish, neat, trim, spruce, tidy.

☒ badly dressed, scruffy.

**well-known** *adj* famous, renowned, celebrated, famed, eminent, notable, noted, illustrious, familiar.

☒ unknown.

**well-off** *adj* rich, wealthy, affluent, prosperous, well-to-do, moneyed, thriving, successful, comfortable, fortunate.

☒ poor, badly-off.

**well-thought-of** *adj* respected, highly regarded, esteemed, admired, honoured, revered.

☒ despised.

**well-worn** *adj* timeworn, stale, tired, trite, overused, unoriginal, hackneyed, commonplace, stereotyped, threadbare, corny (*infml*).

☒ original.

**wet** *adj* 1 DAMP, moist, soaked, soaking, sodden, saturated, soggy, sopping, watery, waterlogged, drenched, dripping, spongy, dank, clammy. 2 RAINING, rainy, showery, teeming, pouring, drizzling, humid. 3 (*infml*) WEAK, feeble, weedy, wimpish (*infml*), spineless, soft, ineffectual, namby-pamby, irresolute, timorous.

☒ 1 dry. 2 dry. 3 strong.

*n* wetness, moisture, damp, dampness, liquid, water, clamminess, condensation, humidity, rain, drizzle.

☒ dryness.

*v* moisten, damp, dampen, soak, saturate, drench, steep, water, irrigate, spray, splash, sprinkle, imbue, dip.

☒ dry.

**whack** *v* hit, strike, smack, thrash, slap, beat, bash (*infml*), bang, cuff, thump, box, buffet, rap, wallop (*infml*), belt (*infml*), clobber (*infml*), clout (*infml*), sock (*infml*).

*n* smack, slap, blow, hit, rap, stroke, thump, cuff, box, bang, clout (*infml*), bash (*infml*), wallop (*infml*).

**wharf** *n* dock, quay, quayside, jetty, landing-stage, dockyard, marina, pier.

**wheedle** *v* cajole, coax, persuade, inveigle, charm, flatter, entice, court, draw.

**E3** force.

**wheel** *n* turn, revolution, circle, rotation, gyration, pivot, roll, spin, twirl, whirl.

*v* turn, rotate, circle, gyrate, orbit, spin, twirl, whirl, swing, roll, revolve, swivel.

**wheeze** *v* pant, gasp, cough, hiss, rasp, whistle.

**whereabouts** *n* location, position, place, situation, site, vicinity.

**whet** *v* **1** SHARPEN, hone, file, grind. **2** STIMULATE, stir, rouse, arouse, provoke, kindle, quicken, incite, awaken, increase.

**E3 1** blunt. **2** dampen.

**whiff** *n* breath, puff, hint, trace, blast, draught, odour, smell, aroma, sniff, scent, reek, stink, stench.

**whim** *n* fancy, caprice, notion, quirk, freak, humour, conceit, fad, vagary, urge.

**whimper** *v* cry, sob, weep, snivel, whine, grizzle, mewl, moan, whinge (*infml*).

*n* sob, snivel, whine, moan.

**whimsical** *adj* fanciful, capricious, playful, impulsive, eccentric, funny, droll, curious, queer, unusual, weird, odd, peculiar, quaint, dotty (*infml*).

**whine** *n* **1** CRY, sob, whimper, moan, wail. **2** COMPLAINT, grumble, grouse, gripe (*infml*), grouch (*infml*).

*v* **1** CRY, sob, whimper, grizzle, moan, wail. **2** COMPLAIN, carp, grumble, whinge (*infml*), gripe (*infml*), grouch (*infml*).

**whip** *v* **1** BEAT, flog, lash, flagellate,

scourge, birch, cane, strap, thrash, punish, chastise, discipline, castigate (*fml*). **2** PULL, jerk, snatch, whisk, dash, dart, rush, tear, flit, flash, fly. **3** GOAD, drive, spur, push, urge, stir, rouse, agitate, incite, provoke, instigate.

*n* lash, scourge, switch, birch, cane, horsewhip, riding-crop, cat-o'-nine-tails.

**whirl** *v* swirl, spin, turn, twist, twirl, pivot, pirouette, swivel, wheel, rotate, revolve, reel, roll, gyrate, circle.

*n* **1** SPIN, twirl, twist, gyration, revolution, pirouette, swirl, turn, wheel, rotation, circle, reel, roll. **2** CONFUSION, daze, flurry, commotion, agitation, bustle, hubbub, hurly-burly, giddiness, tumult, uproar.

**whirlwind** *n* tornado, cyclone, vortex.

*adj* hasty, impulsive, quick, rapid, speedy, swift, lightning, headlong, impetuous, rash.

**E3** deliberate, slow.

**whisk** *v* **1** WHIP, beat. **2** DART, dash, rush, hurry, speed, hasten, race. **3** BRUSH, sweep, flick, wipe, twitch.

**whisper** *v* **1** MURMUR, mutter, mumble, breathe, hiss, rustle, sigh. **2** HINT, intimate, insinuate, gossip, divulge.

**E3 1** shout.

*n* **1** MURMUR, undertone, sigh, hiss, rustle. **2** HINT, suggestion, suspicion, breath, whiff, rumour, report, innuendo, insinuation, trace, tinge, soupçon, buzz.

**white** *adj* **1** PALE, pallid, wan, ashen, colourless, anaemic, pasty. **2** LIGHT, snowy, milky, creamy, ivory, hoary, silver, grey. **3** PURE, immaculate, spotless, stainless, undefiled.

**E3 1** ruddy. **2** dark. **3** defiled.

**whiten** *v* bleach, blanch, whitewash, pale, fade.

◨ blacken, darken.

**whittle** *v* **1** CARVE, cut, scrape,
shave, trim, pare, hew, shape.
**2** ERODE, eat away, wear away,
diminish, consume, reduce,
undermine.

**whole** *adj* **1** COMPLETE, entire,
integral, full, total, unabridged,
uncut, undivided, unedited.
**2** INTACT, unharmed, undamaged,
unbroken, inviolate, perfect, in one
piece, mint, unhurt. **3** WELL, healthy,
fit, sound, strong.
◨ **1** partial. **2** damaged. **3** ill.
*n* total, aggregate, sum total, entirety,
all, fullness, totality, ensemble, entity,
unit, lot, piece, everything.
◨ part.

**on the whole** generally, mostly, in
general, generally speaking, as a rule,
for the most part, all in all, all things
considered, by and large.

**whole-hearted** *adj* unreserved,
unstinting, unqualified, passionate,
enthusiastic, earnest, committed,
dedicated, devoted, heartfelt,
emphatic, warm, sincere, unfeigned,
genuine, complete, true, real, zealous.
◨ half-hearted.

**wholesale** *adj* comprehensive, far-
reaching, extensive, sweeping, wide-
ranging, mass, broad, outright, total,
massive, indiscriminate.
◨ partial.

**wholesome** *adj* **1** *wholesome food*:
healthy, hygienic, salubrious,
sanitary, nutritious, nourishing,
beneficial, salutary, invigorating,
bracing. **2** *wholesome entertainment*:
moral, decent, clean, proper,
improving, edifying, uplifting, pure,
virtuous, righteous, honourable,
respectable.
◨ **1** unhealthy. **2** unwholesome.

**wholly** *adv* completely, entirely,
fully, purely, absolutely, totally,
utterly, comprehensively, altogether,
perfectly, thoroughly, all, exclusively,
only.

◨ partly.

**wicked** *adj* **1** EVIL, sinful, immoral,
depraved, corrupt, vicious,
unprincipled, iniquitous, heinous,
debased, abominable, ungodly,
unrighteous, shameful. **2** BAD,
unpleasant, harmful, offensive, vile,
worthless, difficult, dreadful,
distressing, awful, atrocious, severe,
intense, nasty, injurious,
troublesome, terrible, foul, fierce.
**3** NAUGHTY, mischievous, roguish.
◨ **1** good, upright. **2** harmless.

**wide** *adj* **1** BROAD, roomy, spacious,
vast, immense. **2** DILATED,
expanded, full. **3** EXTENSIVE, wide-
ranging, comprehensive, far-
reaching, general. **4** LOOSE, baggy.
**5** OFF-TARGET, distant, remote.
◨ **1** narrow. **3** restricted. **5** near.
*adv* **1** ASTRAY, off course, sweeping,
off the mark. **2** FULLY, completely, all
the way.
◨ **1** on target.

**widen** *v* distend, dilate, expand,
extend, spread, stretch, enlarge,
broaden.
◨ narrow.

**widespread** *adj* extensive,
prevalent, rife, general, sweeping,
universal, wholesale, far-reaching,
unlimited, broad, common,
pervasive, far-flung.
◨ limited.

**width** *n* breadth, diameter, wideness,
compass, thickness, span, scope,
range, measure, girth, beam,
amplitude, extent, reach.

**wield** *v* **1** *wield a weapon*: brandish,
flourish, swing, wave, handle, ply,
manage, manipulate. **2** *wield power*:
have, hold, possess, employ, exert,
exercise, use, utilize, maintain,
command.

**wife** *n* partner, spouse, mate, better
half, bride.

**wild** *adj* **1** UNTAMED,
undomesticated, feral, savage,
barbarous, primitive, uncivilized,

natural, ferocious, fierce.
**2** UNCULTIVATED, desolate, waste,
uninhabited. **3** unrestrained, unruly,
unmanageable, violent, turbulent,
rowdy, lawless, disorderly, riotous,
boisterous. **4** STORMY, tempestuous,
rough, blustery, choppy. **5** UNTIDY,
unkempt, messy, dishevelled, tousled.
**6** RECKLESS, rash, imprudent,
foolish, foolhardy, impracticable,
irrational, outrageous, preposterous,
wayward, extravagant. **7** MAD, crazy
(*infml*), frenzied, distraught,
demented.
**E3 1** civilized, tame. **2** cultivated.
**3** restrained. **4** calm. **5** tidy. **6** sensible.
**7** sane.

**wilderness** *n* desert, wasteland,
waste, wilds, jungle.

**wiles** *n* trick, stratagem, ruse, ploy,
device, contrivance, guile,
manoeuvre, subterfuge, cunning,
dodge (*infml*), deceit, cheating,
trickery, fraud, craftiness, chicanery.
**E3** guilelessness.

**wilful** *adj* **1** DELIBERATE, conscious,
intentional, voluntary, premeditated.
**2** SELF-WILLED, obstinate,
stubborn, pig-headed, obdurate,
intransigent, inflexible, perverse,
wayward, contrary.
**E3 1** unintentional. **2** good-natured.

**will** *n* **1** VOLITION, choice, option,
preference, decision, discretion.
**2** WISH, desire, inclination, feeling,
fancy, disposition, mind. **3** PURPOSE,
resolve, resolution, determination,
will-power, aim, intention,
command.
*v* **1** WANT, desire, choose, compel,
command, decree, order, ordain.
**2** BEQUEATH, leave, hand down, pass
on, transfer, confer, dispose of.

**willing** *adj* disposed, inclined,
agreeable, compliant, ready,
prepared, consenting, content,
amenable, biddable, pleased, well-
disposed, favourable, happy, eager,
enthusiastic.

**E3** unwilling, disinclined, reluctant.

**wilt** *v* droop, sag, wither, shrivel,
flop, flag, dwindle, weaken, diminish,
fail, fade, languish, ebb, sink, wane.
**E3** perk up.

**wily** *adj* shrewd, cunning, scheming,
artful, crafty, foxy, intriguing, tricky,
underhand, shifty, deceitful,
deceptive, astute, sly, guileful,
designing, crooked, fly (*infml*).
**E3** guileless.

**win** *v* **1** BE VICTORIOUS, triumph,
succeed, prevail, overcome, conquer,
come first, carry off, finish first. **2**
GAIN, acquire, achieve, attain,
accomplish, receive, procure, secure,
obtain, get, earn, catch, net.
**E3** fail, lose.
*n* victory, triumph, conquest,
success, mastery.
**E3** defeat.

**win over** persuade, prevail upon,
convince, influence, convert, sway,
talk round, charm, allure, attract.

**wind**[1] *n* air, breeze, draught, gust,
puff, breath, air-current, blast,
current, bluster, gale, hurricane,
tornado, cyclone.

> *Types of wind include:* anticyclone,
> austral wind, berg wind, bise, bora,
> Cape doctor, chinook, cyclone,
> doctor, east wind, El Niño, etesian,
> Favonian wind, föhn, gregale,
> harmattan, helm wind, khamsin,
> levant, libeccio, meltemi, mistral,
> monsoon, north wind, nor'wester,
> pampero, prevailing wind, samiel,
> simoom, sirocco, snoweater,
> southerly, southerly buster, trade
> wind, tramontana, westerly, wet
> chinook, williwaw, willy-willy,
> zephyr, zonda. *see also* **storm**.

**wind**[2] *v* coil, twist, turn, curl, curve,
bend, loop, spiral, zigzag, twine,
encircle, furl, deviate, meander,
ramble, wreath, roll, reel.
**wind down 1** SLOW (DOWN), slacken

off, lessen, reduce, subside, diminish, dwindle, decline. **2** RELAX, unwind, quieten down, ease up, calm down.
**F3 1** increase.

**wind up 1** CLOSE (DOWN), end, conclude, terminate, finalize, finish, liquidate. **2** END UP, finish up, find oneself, settle. **3** (*infml*) ANNOY, irritate, disconcert, fool, trick, kid (*infml*).
**F3 1** begin.

**windfall** *n* bonanza, godsend, jackpot, treasure-trove, stroke of luck, find.

**window** *n* pane, light, opening, skylight, rose-window, casement, oriel, dormer.

**windy** *adj* breezy, blowy, blustery, squally, windswept, stormy, tempestuous, gusty.
**F3** calm.

**wine**

> *Types of wine include*: alcohol-free, dry, brut, sec, demi-sec, sweet, sparkling, table wine, house wine; red wine, house red (*infml*), white wine, house white (*infml*), rosé, blush wine, fortified wine, mulled wine, tonic wine, vintage wine, plonk (*infml*); sherry, dry sherry, fino, medium sherry, amontillado, sweet sherry, oloroso; port, ruby, tawny, white port, vintage port.

> *Varieties of wine include*: Alsace, Asti, Auslese, Beaujolais, Beaujolais Nouveau, Beaune, Bordeaux, Burgundy, cabernet sauvignon, Chablis, Chambertin, champagne, Chardonnay, Chianti, claret, Côtes du Rhône, Dão, Douro, Frascati, Graves, hock, Lambrusco, Liebfraumilch, Mâcon, Madeira, Malaga, Marsala, Mateus Rosé, Médoc, Merlot, moselle, Muscadet, muscatel, Niersteiner, retsina, Riesling, Rioja, Sauterne, Sekt,

> Soave, Spätlese, Tarragona, Valpolicella, vinho verde.

**wing** *n* branch, arm, section, faction, group, grouping, flank, circle, coterie, set, segment, side, annexe, adjunct, extension.

**wink** *v* blink, flutter, glimmer, glint, twinkle, gleam, sparkle, flicker, flash. *n* **1** BLINK, flutter, sparkle, twinkle, glimmering, gleam, glint. **2** INSTANT, second, split second, flash.

**winner** *n* champion, victor, prizewinner, medallist, title-holder, world-beater, conqueror.
**F3** loser.

**winning** *adj* **1** CONQUERING, triumphant, unbeaten, undefeated, victorious, successful. **2** WINSOME, charming, attractive, captivating, engaging, fetching, enchanting, endearing, delightful, amiable, alluring, lovely, pleasing, sweet.
**F3 1** losing. **2** unappealing.

**winnow** *v* sift, separate, screen, divide, cull, select, part, fan.

**wintry** *adj* cold, chilly, bleak, cheerless, desolate, dismal, harsh, snowy, frosty, freezing, frozen, icy.

**wipe** *v* **1** RUB, clean, dry, dust, brush, mop, swab, sponge, clear. **2** REMOVE, erase, take away, take off.
**wipe out** eradicate, obliterate, destroy, massacre, exterminate, annihilate, erase, expunge, raze, abolish, blot out, efface.

**wiry** *adj* muscular, sinewy, lean, tough, strong.
**F3** puny.

**wisdom** *n* discernment, penetration, sagacity, reason, sense, astuteness, comprehension, enlightenment, judgement, judiciousness, understanding, knowledge, learning, intelligence, erudition, foresight, prudence.
**F3** folly, stupidity.

**wise** *adj* **1** DISCERNING, sagacious,

perceptive, rational, informed, well-informed, understanding, erudite, enlightened, knowing, intelligent, clever, aware, experienced. **2** WELL-ADVISED, judicious, prudent, reasonable, sensible, sound, long-sighted, shrewd.

**Ea 1** foolish, stupid. **2** ill-advised.

**wish** *v* **1** DESIRE, want, yearn, long, hanker, covet, crave, aspire, hope, hunger, thirst, prefer, need. **2** ASK, bid, require, order, instruct, direct, command.

*n* **1** DESIRE, want, hankering, aspiration, inclination, hunger, thirst, liking, preference, yearning, urge, whim, hope. **2** REQUEST, bidding, order, command, will.

**wisp** *n* shred, strand, thread, twist, piece, lock.

**wispy** *adj* thin, straggly, frail, fine, attenuated, insubstantial, light, flimsy, fragile, delicate, ethereal, gossamer, faint.

**Ea** substantial.

**wistful** *adj* **1** THOUGHTFUL, pensive, musing, reflective, wishful, contemplative, dreamy, dreaming, meditative. **2** MELANCHOLY, sad, forlorn, disconsolate, longing, mournful.

**wit** *n* **1** HUMOUR, repartee, facetiousness, drollery, banter, jocularity, levity. **2** INTELLIGENCE, cleverness, brains, sense, reason, common sense, wisdom, understanding, judgement, insight, intellect. **3** HUMORIST, comedian, comic, satirist, joker, wag.

**Ea 1** seriousness. **2** stupidity.

**witch** *n* sorceress, enchantress, occultist, magician, hag.

**witchcraft** *n* sorcery, magic, wizardry, occultism, the occult, the black art, black magic, enchantment, necromancy, voodoo, spell, incantation, divination, conjuration.

**withdraw** *v* **1** RECOIL, shrink back, draw back, pull back. **2** RECANT,

disclaim, take back, revoke, rescind, retract, cancel, abjure, recall, take away. **3** DEPART, go (away), absent oneself, retire, remove, leave, back out, fall back, drop out, retreat, secede. **4** DRAW OUT, extract, pull out.

**withdrawal** *n* **1** REPUDIATION, recantation, disclaimer, disavowal, revocation, recall, secession, abjuration. **2** DEPARTURE, exit, exodus, retirement, retreat. **3** EXTRACTION, removal.

**withdrawn** *adj* **1** RESERVED, unsociable, shy, introvert, quiet, retiring, aloof, detached, shrinking, uncommunicative, unforthcoming, taciturn, silent. **2** REMOTE, isolated, distant, secluded, out-of-the-way, private, hidden, solitary.

**Ea 1** extrovert, outgoing.

**wither** *v* shrink, shrivel, dry, wilt, droop, decay, disintegrate, wane, perish, fade, languish, decline, waste.

**Ea** flourish, thrive.

**withering** *adj* **1** DESTRUCTIVE, deadly, death-dealing, devastating. **2** SCORNFUL, contemptuous, scathing, snubbing, humiliating, mortifying, wounding.

**Ea 2** encouraging, supportive.

**withhold** *v* keep back, retain, hold back, suppress, restrain, repress, control, check, reserve, deduct, refuse, hide, conceal.

**Ea** give, accord.

**withstand** *v* resist, oppose, stand fast, stand one's ground, stand, stand up to, confront, brave, face, cope with, take on, thwart, defy, hold one's ground, hold out, last out, hold off, endure, bear, tolerate, put up with, survive, weather.

**Ea** give in, yield.

**witness** *n* **1** TESTIFIER, attestant, deponent (*fml*). **2** ONLOOKER, eye-witness, looker-on, observer, spectator, viewer, watcher, bystander.

*v* **1** SEE, observe, notice, note, view, watch, look on, mark, perceive. **2** TESTIFY, attest, bear witness, depose (*fml*), confirm, bear out, corroborate. **3** ENDORSE, sign, countersign.

**witty** *adj* humorous, amusing, comic, sharp-witted, droll, whimsical, original, brilliant, clever, ingenious, lively, sparkling, funny, facetious, fanciful, jocular.

🔁 dull, unamusing.

**wizard** *n* **1** SORCERER, magician, warlock, enchanter, necromancer, occultist, witch, conjurer. **2** (*infml*) EXPERT, adept, virtuoso, ace, master, maestro, prodigy, genius, star (*infml*), whiz (*infml*), hotshot (*infml*).

**wizened** *adj* shrivelled, shrunken, dried up, withered, wrinkled, gnarled, thin, worn, lined.

**wobble** *v* shake, oscillate, tremble, quake, sway, teeter, totter, rock, seesaw, vibrate, waver, dodder, fluctuate, hesitate, dither, vacillate, shilly-shally.

**wobbly** *adj* unstable, shaky, rickety, unsteady, wonky (*infml*), teetering, tottering, doddering, doddery, uneven, unbalanced, unsafe.

🔁 stable, steady.

**woman** *n* female, lady, girl, matriarch, maiden, maid.

**womanly** *adj* feminine, female, ladylike, womanish.

**wonder** *n* **1** MARVEL, phenomenon, miracle, prodigy, sight, spectacle, rarity, curiosity. **2** AWE, amazement, astonishment, admiration, wonderment, fascination, surprise, bewilderment.

*v* **1** MEDITATE, speculate, ponder, ask oneself, question, conjecture, puzzle, enquire, query, doubt, think. **2** MARVEL, gape, be amazed, be surprised.

**wonderful** *adj* **1** MARVELLOUS, magnificent, oustanding, excellent,

superb, admirable, delightful, phenomenal, sensational, stupendous, tremendous, super (*infml*), terrific (*infml*), brilliant (*infml*), great (*infml*), fabulous (*infml*), fantastic (*infml*). **2** AMAZING, astonishing, astounding, startling, surprising, extraordinary, incredible, remarkable, staggering, strange.

🔁 **1** appalling, dreadful. **2** ordinary.

**woo** *v* **1** (*fml*) *woo a lover*: court, chase, pursue. **2** *woo custom*: encourage, cultivate, attract, look for, seek.

**wood** *n* **1** TIMBER, lumber, planks. **2** FOREST, woods, woodland, trees, plantation, thicket, grove, coppice, copse, spinney.

---

*Types of wood include*: timber, lumber (*North Amer.*), hardwood, softwood, heartwood, sapwood, seasoned wood, green wood, bitterwood, brushwood, cordwood, firewood, kindling, matchwood, plywood, pulpwood, whitewood, chipboard, hardboard, wood veneer, afrormosia, ash, balsa, beech, cedar, cherry, chestnut, cottonwood, deal, ebony, elm, mahogany, African mahogany, maple, oak, pine, redwood, rosewood, sandalwood, sapele, satinwood, teak, walnut, willow. *see also* **tree**.

---

**wooded** *adj* forested, timbered, woody, tree-covered, sylvan (*fml*).

**wooden** *adj* **1** TIMBER, woody. **2** EMOTIONLESS, expressionless, awkward, clumsy, stilted, lifeless, spiritless, unemotional, stiff, rigid, leaden, deadpan, blank, empty, slow.

🔁 **2** lively.

**wool** *n* fleece, down, yarn.

**woolly** *adj* **1** WOOLLEN, fleecy, woolly-haired, downy, shaggy, fuzzy, frizzy. **2** UNCLEAR, ill-defined, hazy, blurred, confused, muddled, vague, indefinite, nebulous.

**F3** 2 clear, distinct.

*n* jumper, sweater, jersey, pullover, cardigan.

**word** *n* 1 NAME, term, expression, designation, utterance, vocable (*fml*). 2 CONVERSATION, chat, talk, discussion, consultation. 3 INFORMATION, news, report, communication, notice, message, bulletin, communiqué, statement, dispatch, declaration, comment, assertion, account, remark, advice, warning. 4 PROMISE, pledge, oath, assurance, vow, guarantee. 5 COMMAND, order, decree, commandment, go-ahead (*infml*), green light (*infml*).

*v* phrase, express, couch, put, say, explain, write.

**words** *n* 1 ARGUMENT, dispute, quarrel, disagreement, altercation, bickering, row, squabble. 2 LYRICS, libretto, text, book.

**wordy** *adj* verbose, long-winded, loquacious (*fml*), garrulous, prolix, rambling, diffuse, discursive.

**F3** concise.

**work** *n* 1 OCCUPATION, job, employment, profession, trade, business, career, calling, vocation, line, métier, livelihood, craft, skill. 2 TASK, assignment, undertaking, job, chore, responsibility, duty, commission. 3 TOIL, labour, drudgery, effort, exertion, industry, slog (*infml*), graft (*infml*), elbow grease (*infml*). 4 CREATION, production, achievement, composition, opus.

**F3** 1 play, rest, hobby.

*v* 1 BE EMPLOYED, have a job, earn one's living. 2 LABOUR, toil, drudge, slave. 3 FUNCTION, go, operate, perform, run, handle, manage, use, control. 4 BRING ABOUT, accomplish, achieve, create, cause, pull off (*infml*). 5 CULTIVATE, farm, dig, till. 6 MANIPULATE, knead,

mould, shape, form, fashion, make, process.

**F3** 1 be unemployed. 2 play, rest. 3 fail.

**work out** 1 SOLVE, resolve, calculate, figure out, puzzle out, sort out, understand, clear up. 2 DEVELOP, evolve, go well, succeed, prosper, turn out, pan out (*infml*). 3 PLAN, devise, arrange, contrive, invent, construct, put together. 4 ADD UP TO, amount to, total, come out.

**work up** incite, stir up, rouse, arouse, animate, excite, move, stimulate, inflame, spur, instigate, agitate, generate.

**worker** *n* employee, labourer, working man, working woman, artisan, craftsman, tradesman, hand, operative, wage-earner, breadwinner, proletarian.

**workforce** *n* workers, employees, personnel, labour force, staff, labour, work-people, shop-floor.

**working** *n* functioning, operation, running, routine, manner, method, action.

*adj* 1 FUNCTIONING, operational, running, operative, going. 2 EMPLOYED, active.

**F3** 1 inoperative. 2 idle.

**workmanship** *n* skill, craft, craftsmanship, expertise, art, handicraft, handiwork, technique, execution, manufacture, work, finish.

**works** *n* 1 FACTORY, plant, workshop, mill, foundry, shop. 2 ACTIONS, acts, doings. 3 PRODUCTIONS, output, oeuvre, writings, books. 4 MACHINERY, mechanism, workings, action, movement, parts, installations.

**workshop** *n* 1 WORKS, workroom, atelier, studio, factory, plant, mill, shop. 2 STUDY GROUP, seminar, symposium, discussion group, class.

**world** *n* 1 EARTH, globe, planet, star, universe, cosmos, creation, nature. 2 EVERYBODY, everyone,

people, human race, humankind,
humanity. **3** SPHERE, realm, field,
area, domain, division, system,
society, province, kingdom. **4** TIMES,
epoch, era, period, age, days, life.

**worldly** adj **1** TEMPORAL, earthly,
mundane, terrestrial, physical,
secular, unspiritual, profane. **2**
WORLDLY-WISE, sophisticated,
urbane, cosmopolitan, experienced,
knowing, streetwise (infml).
**3** MATERIALISTIC, selfish,
ambitious, grasping, greedy,
covetous, avaricious.
**Ⅎ** **1** spiritual, eternal.
**2** unsophisticated.

**worn** adj **1** SHABBY, threadbare,
worn-out, tatty, tattered, frayed,
ragged. **2** EXHAUSTED, tired, weary,
spent, fatigued, careworn, drawn,
haggard, jaded.
**Ⅎ** **1** new, unused. **2** fresh.

**worn out 1** SHABBY, threadbare,
useless, used, tatty, tattered, on its last
legs, ragged, moth-eaten, frayed,
decrepit. **2** TIRED OUT, exhausted,
weary, done in (infml), all in (infml),
dog-tired (infml), knackered (infml).
**Ⅎ** **1** new, unused. **2** fresh.

**worried** adj anxious, troubled,
uneasy, ill at ease, apprehensive,
concerned, bothered, upset, fearful,
afraid, frightened, on edge,
overwrought, tense, strained,
nervous, disturbed, distraught,
distracted, fretful, distressed,
agonized.
**Ⅎ** calm, unworried, unconcerned.

**worry** v **1** BE ANXIOUS, be troubled,
be distressed, agonize, fret.
**2** IRRITATE, plague, pester, torment,
upset, unsettle, annoy, bother,
disturb, vex, tease, nag, harass,
harry, perturb, hassle (infml).
**3** ATTACK, go for, savage.
**Ⅎ** **1** be unconcerned. **2** comfort.
n **1** PROBLEM, trouble, responsibility,
burden, concern, care, trial,
annoyance, irritation, vexation.

**2** ANXIETY, apprehension, unease,
misgiving, fear, disturbance, agitation,
torment, misery, perplexity.
**Ⅎ** **2** comfort, reassurance.

**worsen** v **1** EXACERBATE,
aggravate, intensify, heighten. **2** GET
WORSE, weaken, deteriorate,
degenerate, decline, sink, go downhill
(infml).
**Ⅎ** improve.

**worship** v venerate, revere,
reverence, adore, exalt, glorify,
honour, praise, idolize, adulate, love,
respect, pray to, deify.
**Ⅎ** despise, hate.
n veneration, reverence, adoration,
devotion(s), homage, honour, glory,
glorification, exaltation, praise,
prayer(s), respect, regard, love,
adulation, deification, idolatry.

**worth** n worthiness, merit, value,
benefit, advantage, importance,
significance, use, usefulness, utility,
quality, good, virtue, excellence,
credit, desert(s), cost, rate, price,
help, assistance, avail.
**Ⅎ** worthlessness.

**worthless** adj **1** VALUELESS,
useless, pointless, meaningless, futile,
unavailing, unimportant, insignificant,
trivial, unusable, cheap, poor,
rubbishy, trashy, trifling, paltry. **2**
CONTEMPTIBLE, despicable, good-
for-nothing, vile.
**Ⅎ** **1** valuable. **2** worthy.

**worthwhile** adj profitable, useful,
valuable, worthy, good, helpful,
beneficial, constructive, gainful,
justifiable, productive.
**Ⅎ** worthless.

**worthy** adj praiseworthy, laudable,
creditable, commendable, valuable,
worthwhile, admirable, fit, deserving,
appropriate, respectable, reputable,
good, honest, honourable, excellent,
decent, upright, righteous.
**Ⅎ** unworthy, disreputable.

**wound** n **1** INJURY, trauma, hurt,
cut, gash, lesion, laceration, scar.

**2** HURT, distress, trauma, torment, heartbreak, harm, damage, anguish, grief, shock.

*v* **1** DAMAGE, harm, hurt, injure, hit, cut, gash, lacerate, slash, pierce.

**2** DISTRESS, offend, insult, pain, mortify, upset, slight, grieve.

**wrangle** *n* argument, quarrel, dispute, controversy, squabble, tiff, row (*infml*), bickering, disagreement, clash, altercation, contest, slanging match (*infml*), set-to (*infml*).

**F∃** agreement.

*v* argue, quarrel, disagree, dispute, bicker, altercate, contend, fall out (*infml*), row (*infml*), squabble, scrap, fight, spar.

**F∃** agree.

**wrap** *v* envelop, fold, enclose, cover, pack, shroud, wind, surround, package, muffle, cocoon, cloak, roll up, bind, bundle up, immerse.

**F∃** unwrap.

**wrap up 1** WRAP, pack up, package, parcel. **2** (*infml*) CONCLUDE, finish off, end, bring to a close, terminate, wind up, complete, round off.

**wrapper** *n* wrapping, packaging, envelope, cover, jacket, dust jacket, sheath, sleeve, paper.

**wreak** *v* inflict, exercise, create, cause, bring about, perpetrate, vent, unleash, express, execute, carry out, bestow.

**wreath** *n* garland, coronet, chaplet, festoon, crown, band, ring.

**wreck** *v* destroy, ruin, demolish, devastate, shatter, smash, break, spoil, play havoc with, ravage, write off.

**F∃** conserve, repair.

*n* ruin, destruction, devastation, mess, demolition, ruination, write-off, disaster, loss, disruption.

**wreckage** *n* debris, remains, rubble, ruin, fragments, flotsam, pieces.

**wrench** *v* yank, wrest, jerk, pull, tug, force, sprain, strain, rick, tear, twist, wring, rip, distort.

*v* struggle, strive, fight, scuffle, grapple, tussle, combat, contend, contest, vie, battle.

**wretch** *n* scoundrel, rogue, villain, good-for-nothing, ruffian, rascal, vagabond, miscreant, outcast.

**wretched** *adj* **1** ATROCIOUS, awful, deplorable, appalling. **2** UNHAPPY, sad, miserable, melancholy, depressed, dejected, disconsolate, downcast, forlorn, gloomy, doleful, distressed, broken-hearted, crestfallen.

**3** PATHETIC, pitiable, pitiful, unfortunate, sorry, hopeless, poor.

**4** CONTEMPTIBLE, despicable, vile, worthless, shameful, inferior, low, mean, paltry.

**F∃ 1** excellent. **2** happy. **3** enviable. **4** worthy.

**wriggle** *v* squirm, writhe, wiggle, worm, twist, snake, slink, crawl, edge, sidle, manoeuvre, squiggle, dodge, extricate, zigzag, waggle, turn.

*n* wiggle, twist, squirm, jiggle, jerk, turn, twitch.

**wring** *v* **1** SQUEEZE, twist, wrench, wrest, extract, mangle, screw.

**2** EXACT, extort, coerce, force.

**3** DISTRESS, pain, hurt, rack, rend, pierce, torture, wound, stab, tear.

**wrinkle** *n* furrow, crease, corrugation, line, fold, gather, pucker, crumple.

*v* crease, corrugate, furrow, fold, crinkle, crumple, shrivel, gather, pucker.

**write** *v* pen, inscribe, record, jot down, set down, take down, transcribe, scribble, scrawl, correspond, communicate, draft, draw up, copy, compose, create.

**write off 1** DELETE, cancel, cross out, disregard. **2** WRECK, destroy, crash, smash up.

**writer** *n* author, scribe, wordsmith, novelist, dramatist, essayist, playwright, columnist, diarist, hack, penpusher, scribbler, secretary, copyist, clerk.

*Writers include*: annalist, author, autobiographer, bard, biographer, calligraphist, chronicler, clerk, columnist, composer, contributor, copyist, copywriter, correspondent, court reporter, diarist, dramatist, editor, essayist, fabler, fiction writer, ghost writer, hack, historian, journalist, leader-writer, lexicographer, librettist, lyricist, novelist, pen-friend, penman, pen-pal, penpusher (*infml*), penwoman, playwright, poet, poet laureate, reporter, rhymer, satirist, scribbler, scribe, scriptwriter, short-story writer, sonneteer, stenographer, storyteller (*infml*).

**writhe** *v* squirm, wriggle, thresh, thrash, twist, wiggle, toss, coil, contort, struggle.

**writing** *n* 1 HANDWRITING, calligraphy, script, penmanship, scrawl, scribble, hand, print. 2 DOCUMENT, letter, book, composition, letters, literature, work, publication.

**wrong** *adj* 1 INACCURATE, incorrect, mistaken, erroneous, false, fallacious, in error, imprecise. 2 INAPPROPRIATE, unsuitable, unseemly, improper, indecorous, unconventional, unfitting, incongruous, inapt. 3 UNJUST, unethical, unfair, unlawful, immoral, illegal, illicit, dishonest, criminal, crooked (*infml*), reprehensible, blameworthy, guilty, to blame, bad, wicked, sinful, iniquitous, evil. 4 DEFECTIVE, faulty, out of order, amiss, awry.

**E₃** 1 correct, right. 2 suitable, right. 3 good, moral.

*adv* amiss, astray, awry, inaccurately, incorrectly, wrongly, mistakenly, faultily, badly, erroneously, improperly.

**E₃** right.

*n* sin, misdeed, offence, crime, immorality, sinfulness, transgression, wickedness, wrong-doing, trespass (*fml*), injury, grievance, abuse, injustice, iniquity, inequity, infringement, unfairness, error.

**E₃** right.

*v* abuse, ill-treat, mistreat, maltreat, injure, ill-use, hurt, harm, discredit, dishonour, misrepresent, malign, oppress, cheat.

**wrongdoer** *n* offender, law-breaker, transgressor, criminal, delinquent, felon, miscreant, evil-doer, sinner, trespasser, culprit.

**wrongful** *adj* immoral, improper, unfair, unethical, unjust, unlawful, illegal, illegitimate, illicit, dishonest, criminal, blameworthy, dishonourable, wrong, reprehensible, wicked, evil.

**E₃** rightful.

**wry** *adj* 1 *wry humour*: ironic, sardonic, dry, sarcastic, mocking, droll. 2 TWISTED, distorted, deformed, contorted, warped, uneven, crooked.

**E₃** 2 straight.

# Y

**yank** *v, n* jerk, tug, pull, wrench, snatch, haul, heave.

**yap** *v* 1 BARK, yelp. 2 (*infml*) CHATTER, jabber, babble, prattle, yatter, jaw (*infml*).

**yardstick** *n* measure, gauge, criterion, standard, benchmark, touchstone, comparison.

**yarn** n 1 THREAD, fibre, strand. 2 STORY, tale, anecdote, fable, fabrication, tall story, cock-and-bull story (infml).

**yawning** adj gaping, wide, wide-open, huge, vast, cavernous.

**yearly** adj annual, per year, per annum, perennial.
adv annually, every year, once a year, perennially.

**yearn for** long for, pine for, desire, want, wish for, crave, covet, hunger for, hanker for, ache for, languish for, itch for.

**yell** v shout, scream, bellow, roar, bawl, shriek, squeal, howl, holler (infml), screech, squall, yelp, yowl, whoop.
≠ whisper.
n shout, scream, cry, roar, bellow, shriek, howl, screech, squall, whoop.
≠ whisper.

**yelp** v yap, bark, squeal, cry, yell, howl, bay.
n yap, bark, yip, squeal, cry, yell, howl.

**yield** v 1 SURRENDER, renounce, abandon, abdicate, cede, part with, relinquish. 2 GIVE WAY, capitulate, concede, submit, succumb, give (in), admit defeat, bow, cave in, knuckle under, resign oneself, go along with, permit, allow, acquiesce, accede, agree, comply, consent. 3 PRODUCE, bear, supply, provide, generate, bring

in, bring forth, furnish, return, earn, pay.
≠ 1 hold. 2 resist, withstand.
n return, product, earnings, harvest, crop, produce, output, profit, revenue, takings, proceeds, income.

**yoke** n 1 HARNESS, bond, link. 2 BURDEN, bondage, enslavement, slavery, oppression, subjugation, servility.
v couple, link, join, tie, harness, hitch, bracket, connect, unite.

**young** adj 1 YOUTHFUL, juvenile, baby, infant, junior, adolescent. 2 IMMATURE, early, new, recent, green, growing, fledgling, unfledged, inexperienced.
≠ 1 adult, old. 2 mature, old.
n offspring, babies, issue, litter, progeny, brood, children, family.

**youngster** n child, boy, girl, toddler, youth, teenager, kid (infml).

**youth** n 1 ADOLESCENT, youngster, juvenile, teenager, kid (infml), boy, young man. 2 YOUNG PEOPLE, the young, younger generation. 3 ADOLESCENCE, childhood, immaturity, boyhood, girlhood.
≠ 3 adulthood.

**youthful** adj young, boyish, girlish, childish, immature, juvenile, inexperienced, fresh, active, lively, well-preserved.
≠ aged.

# Z

...ny (...nfml) adj comical, funny, ...ng, eccentric, droll, crazy ..., clownish, loony (infml), ...cky..., (infml).
...seri...ous.

n ...ardour, fervour, passion, ...mth..., fire, enthusiasm, devotion, ...it, k...eenness, zest, eagerness,

earnestness, dedication, fanaticism, gusto, verve.
≠ apathy, indifference.

**zealot** n fanatic, extremist, bigot, militant, partisan.

**zealous** adj ardent, fervent, impassioned, passionate, devoted, burning, enthusiastic, intense,

fanatical, militant, keen, eager, earnest, spirited.
**⊟** apathetic, indifferent.

**zenith** *n* summit, peak, height, pinnacle, apex, high point, top, optimum, climax, culmination, acme, meridian, vertex.
**⊟** nadir.

**zero** *n* nothing, nought, nil, nadir, bottom, cipher, zilch (*infml*), duck, love.

**zest** *n* **1** GUSTO, appetite, enthusiasm, enjoyment, keenness, zeal, exuberance, interest.
**2** FLAVOUR, taste, relish, savour, spice, tang, piquancy.
**⊟ 1** apathy.

**zigzag** *v* meander, snake, wind, twist, curve.

*adj* meandering, crooked, serpentine, sinuous, twisting, winding.
**⊟** straight.

**zodiac**

---

*The signs of the zodiac (with their symbols) are:* Aries (Ram), Taurus (Bull), Gemini (Twins), Cancer (Crab), Leo (Lion), Virgo (Virgin), Libra (Balance), Scorpio (Scorpion), Sagittarius (Archer), Capricorn (Goat), Aquarius (Water-bearer), Pisces (Fishes).

---

**zone** *n* region, area, district, territory, section, sector, belt, sphere, tract, stratum.

**zoom** *v* race, rush, tear, dash, speed, fly, hurtle, streak, flash, shoot, whirl, dive, buzz, zip.